Environmental Law Reports

Environmental Law Reports

Volume 31

2023

SWEET & MAXWELL

 THOMSON REUTERS

This volume should be cited as [2023] Env. L.R.

Published in 2023 by Thomson Reuters, trading as Sweet & Maxwell. Thomson Reuters is registered in England & Wales, Company No.1679046. Registered Office and address for service: 5 Canada Square, Canary Wharf, London, E14 5AQ. For further information on our products and services, visit *http://www.sweetandmaxwell.co.uk*.

Computerset by Sweet & Maxwell. Printed and bound in Great Britain by Hobbs the Printers Ltd, Totton, Hampshire.
A CIP catalogue record for this book is available from the British Library.

ISBN: 978-0-414-11323-7

LEGAL TAXONOMY
FROM SWEET & MAXWELL

Each case report in this volume has been allocated keywords from the Legal Taxonomy utilised by Sweet & Maxwell to provide a standardised way of describing legal concepts. These keywords are identical to those used in Westlaw UK and have been used for many years in other publications such as Legal Journals Index. The keywords provide a means of identifying similar concepts in other Sweet & Maxwell publications and online services to which keywords from the Legal Taxonomy have been applied. Keywords follow the Taxonomy Logo at the beginning of each item. Please send any suggestions to sweetandmaxwell.taxonomy@tr.com. A separate Index is no longer included in this publication. Please refer to the cover/Table of Contents of the publication to assist with your location of particular topics covered by this issue.

For orders and enquiries, go to: *http://www.tr.com/uki-legal-contact*; Tel: 0345 600 9355.

EU materials in this publication is acknowledged as © European Union, 1998–2023. Only EU legislation published in the electronic version of the Official Journal of the European Union is deemed authentic.

Crown copyright material is reproduced with the permission of the Controller of HMSO and the King's Printer for Scotland.

FSC
www.fsc.org
MIX
Paper from
responsible sources
FSC® C020438

Table of Cases

Table of International and European Legislation

DECISIONS

Table of Statutes

xxx

Table of Statutory Instruments

NAMUR-EST ENVIRONNEMENT ASBL v REGION WALLONNE

European Court of Justice (Third Chamber)

(C-463/20)

A. Prechal, President of the Second Chamber, acting as President of the Third Chamber, J. Passer (Rapporteur), F. Biltgen, L.S. Rossi and N. Wahl, Judges, J. Kokott, AG: 24 February 2022

[2023] Env. L.R. 1

☞ Derogations; Development consent; Environmental impact assessments; EU law; Habitats; Protected species; Public participation

H1 *Nature conservation—Habitats Directive—Environmental assessment—concept of 'development consent'—derogation from species protection requirements—whether derogation under art.16 of Directive 92/43 formed part of 'development consent' procedure within meaning of art.1(2) of Directive 201/92—whether preliminary derogation decision required prior public participation*

H2   A request for a preliminary ruling was made in proceedings concerning a decision granting a derogation from the animal and plant species protection measures, with a view to the working of a limestone aggregate quarry. The derogation decision authorised disturbance of a certain number of protected plant and animal species and the deterioration or destruction of certain areas of their respective natural habitats, in connection with the project, provided that a series of mitigation measures were implemented. An action for annulment of the derogation decision was brought, where it was argued that the decision was part of the development consent procedure, within the meaning of Directive 2011/92 art.1(2), but was not preceded by a procedure meeting the requirements of that Directive. In particular, it was argued that, in order to meet those requirements and to enable effective public participation, the assessment of the environmental impact of such a project and the accompanying public consultation had to take place before the adoption of a measure such as the derogation decision, not afterwards, as had been the case. Questions were referred to the CJEU asking, essentially, whether Directive 2011/92 meant that:

   (i) such a derogation decision adopted under art.16(1) of the Habitats Directive formed part of the development consent procedure where (a) the project could not be carried out without the developer having first obtained that decision, and (b) the competent authority retained the ability to assess the project's environmental impact more strictly than was done in the derogation decision; and

   (ii) if so, such a preliminary decision authorising derogation need not necessarily be preceded by public participation, provided that such participation was ensured before the adoption of the development consent decision for the project.

H3   **Held:**

H4   (1) Article 1(2) of Directive 2011/92 defined the concept of "development consent" by referring to a decision different in nature from the derogation decision and excluded that latter decision from being regarded, in isolation, as amounting to a "development consent". However, those elements did not preclude such a decision, when taken together with the subsequent decision on the developer's entitlement to proceed with the project, as forming part of the development consent for that project. The grant of development consent was the end point of a decision-making process which began with the developer submitting an application and which, from a procedural perspective, included each and every step required in order to process that application. Directive 2011/92 meant that derogation decisions such as that at issue did form part of the development consent procedure, within the meaning of art.1(2)(c), where (i) the project could not be carried out without the developer having first obtained that decision, and (ii) the authority competent for granting development consent retained the ability to assess the project's environmental impact more strictly than was done in that decision.

H5   (2) Articles 6 and 8 of Directive 2011/92 required Member States to take the necessary measures to ensure that public participation took place in accordance with a set of requirements. It may be more difficult to reconcile those various requirements in the context of a multi-stage decision-making process, depending on the different stages of the process and the distribution of competences among the various authorities called upon to take part in it. In particular, that was the case where a given authority was called upon to assess, at a preliminary or intermediate stage of such a decision-making process, only some of the environmental effects of the project concerned. In such a case, public participation may be confined to the part of the environmental effects of the project which fell within that authority's competence, to the exclusion not only of those which did not, but also of the interaction or interrelationship between them.

H6   (3) The requirement for public participation under Directive 2011/92 was intimately linked with the obligation to assess environmental impacts. In view of that, the requirement of early participation of the public in the decision-making process provided for in art.6 did not necessarily mean that the adoption of a preliminary decision relating to some of the project's effects on the environment had to be preceded by public participation, provided that such participation was effective. That requirement implied, first, that it took place before the adoption of the development consent decision, secondly, that it enabled the public to express its views in a useful and comprehensive manner on all the environmental effects of that project and thirdly, that the competent authority for granting consent for the project could take full account of that participation. It was for the national court to verify that those conditions had been met.

H7 **Cases referred to:**

AB v Krajowa Rada Sadownictwa (C-824/18) EU:C:2021:153; [2022] 4 W.L.R. 36; [2021] 3 C.M.L.R. 5

Abraham v Region Wallonne (C-2/07) EU:C:2008:133; [2008] Env. L.R. 32

Ambulanz Glockner v Landkreis Sudwestpfalz (C-475/99) EU:C:2001:577; [2002] 4 C.M.L.R. 21

Asociatia Forumul Judecatorilor Din Romania v Inspectia Judiciara (C-83/19) EU:C:2021:393; [2021] 3 C.M.L.R. 27

Auroux v Commune de Roanne (C-220/05) EU:C:2007:31

Brussels Hoofdstedelijk Gewest v Vlaams Gewest (C-275/09) EU:C:2011:154; [2011] Env. L.R. 26; [2011] P.T.S.R. D37

Bund fur Umwelt und Naturschutz Deutschland, Landesverband Nordrhein-Westfalen eV v Bezirksregierung Arnsberg (C-115/09) EU:C:2011:289; [2011] Env. L.R. 29; [2011] 3 C.M.L.R. 15

Compagnie d'entreprises CFE SA v Region de Bruxelles-Capitale (C-43/18) EU:C:2019:483; [2020] Env. L.R. 11

Commission v Spain (C-404/09) EU:C:2011:768

Commission v Germany (C-137/14) EU:C:2015:683

Commission of the European Communities v Ireland (C-392/96) EU:C:1999:431; [2000] Q.B. 636; [2000] 2 W.L.R. 958

Commission v Ireland (Derrybrien Wind Farm) (C-261/18) EU:C:2019:955

Commission v Poland (C-526/16) EU:C:2018:356

Commission of the European Communities v United Kingdom (C-508/03) EU:C:2006:287; [2007] Env. L.R. 1; [2006] 3 W.L.R. 492

Criminal Proceedings against AZ (C-510/19) EU:C:2020:953; [2021] 2 C.M.L.R. 6; [2021] C.E.C. 1059

Criminal Proceedings against dos Santos Palhota (C-515/08) EU:C:2010:589; [2011] 1 C.M.L.R. 34

European Commission v Ireland (C-50/09) EU:C:2011:109; [2011] Env. L.R. 25; [2011] P.T.S.R. 1122

Fussl Modestrasse Mayr GmbH v SevenOne Media GmbH (C-555/19) EU:C:2021:89; [2021] 2 C.M.L.R. 29

Germany v Esso Raffinage (C-471/18 P) EU:C:2021:48

HA v Belgium (C-194/19) EU:C:2021:270; [2021] 3 C.M.L.R. 15

Holohan v An Bord Pleanala (C-461/17) EU:C:2018:883; [2019] Env. L.R. 16; [2019] P.T.S.R. 1054

Inter-Environnement Wallonie ASBL v Conseil des Ministres (C-411/17) EU:C:2019:622; [2020] Env. L.R. 9

Junqueras Vies (C-502/19) EU:C:2019:1115

Land Nordrhein-Westfalen (C-535/18) EU:C:2020:391

Lesoochranárske zoskupenie VLK (C-243/15) EU:C:2016:838

Leth v Austria (C-420/11) EU:C:2013:166; [2013] Env. L.R. 26; [2013] 3 C.M.L.R. 2

Minister Sprawiedliwości (C-55/20) EU:C:2022:6

One Voice and Ligue pour la protection des oiseaux (C-900/19) EU:C:2021:211

Proceedings Brought by Luonnonsuojeluyhdistys Tapiola Pohjois-Savo—Kainuu ry (C-674/17) EU:C:2019:851; [2020] Env. L.R. 17; [2020] 2 C.M.L.R. 1

R. (on the application of Barker) v Bromley LBC (C-290/03) EU:C:2006:286; [2007] Env. L.R. 2; [2006] Q.B. 764

R. (on the application of Wells) v Secretary of State for Transport, Local Government and the Regions (C-201/02) EU:C:2004:12; [2004] Env. L.R. 27; [2004] 1 C.M.L.R. 31

Sappi Austria Produktions-GmbH & Co KG v Landeshauptmann von Steiermark (C-629/19) EU:C:2020:824; [2021] Env. L.R. 17; [2020] P.T.S.R. 2114

Stichting Natuur en Milieu v College van Gedeputeerde Staten van Groningen (C-165/09)–(C-167/09) EU:C:2011:348; [2012] Env. L.R. 2; [2011] 3 C.M.L.R. 21

Texdata Software GmbH (C-418/11) EU:C:2013:588; [2014] 1 C.M.L.R. 52

Vereniging voor Energie Milieu en Water v Directeur van de Dienst Uitvoering en Toezicht Energie (C-17/03) EU:C:2005:362; [2005] 5 C.M.L.R. 8

Wightman v Secretary of State for Exiting the European Union (C-621/18) EU:C:2018:999; [2019] Q.B. 199; [2018] 3 W.L.R. 1965

H8 Legislation referred to:

TFEU art.267

Directive 92/43 (Habitats) arts 12, 13 and 16 and Annex IV

Convention on access to information, public participation in decision-making and access to justice in environmental matters 1998 (Aarhus Convention)

Directive 2000/60 (Water Framework) art.4

Directive 2003/35 (Public Participation) art.3

Decision 2005/370

Directive 2008/1 (IPPC)

Directive 2009/147 (Birds) arts 5 and 9

Directive 2010/75 (Industrial Emissions)

Directive 2011/92 (EIA) arts 1, 2, 3, 4, 5, 6, 7, 8 and 11 and Annexes I and IV

Directive 2014/52 (Amending EIA)

H9 *J. Sambon*, avocat, appeared on behalf of Namur-Est Environnement ASBL.

L. de Meeûs and *C. H. Born*, avocats, appeared on behalf of Cimenteries CBR SA.

C. Pochet, M. Van Regemorter and *S. Baeyens*, acting as Agents, and *P. Moërynck*, avocat, appeared on behalf of the Belgian Government.

M. Smolek, J. Vláčil and *L. Dvořáková*, acting as Agents, appeared on behalf of the Czech Government.

C. Hermes, M. Noll–Ehlers and *F. Thiran*, acting as Agents, appeared on behalf of the European Commission.

OPINION[1]

I. Introduction

AG1   Under the EIA Directive,[2] certain projects require development consent and, prior to that, an environmental impact assessment – that is to say, a report on any significant effects that they may have on the environment – and public participation.

---

[1] Original language: German.

[2] Directive 2011/92 of the European Parliament and of the Council of 13 December 2011 on the assessment of the effects of certain public and private projects on the environment ([2011] OJ L26/1) 'the EIA Directive'.

If the project may affect strictly protected species under the Habitats Directive[3] or the Birds Directive,[4] such effects must be taken into account in the environmental impact assessment.

AG2   In the context of the reopening of a quarry in the Belgian region of Wallonia, the present proceedings raise the question as to whether the competent authorities may nevertheless authorise derogations from the protection of strictly protected species even before the environmental impact assessment is carried out. Neither the Habitats Directive nor the Birds Directive nor the applicable Belgian or Walloon law provides for an environmental impact assessment or public participation in respect of decisions on derogations from species protection. However, the referring court takes the view that the development consent under species protection law at issue is a practically necessary precondition for the realisation of a project within the meaning of the EIA Directive, with the result that the latter might preclude such a preliminary decision.

II. Legal framework

A. The EIA Directive

AG3   Recital 2 of the EIA Directive specifies the objective of the environmental impact assessment:

> '… Effects on the environment should be taken into account at the earliest possible stage in all the technical planning and decision-making processes.'

AG4   Article 1(2)(c) of the EIA Directive defines the term 'development consent' as 'the decision of the competent authority or authorities which entitles the developer to proceed with the project'.

AG5   Article 2(1) to (3) of the EIA Directive governs the status of the environmental impact assessment in the development consent procedure:

> '1. Member States shall adopt all measures necessary to ensure that, before consent is given, projects likely to have significant effects on the environment by virtue, inter alia, of their nature, size or location are made subject to a requirement for development consent and an assessment with regard to their effects. Those projects are defined in Article 4.
>
> 2. The environmental impact assessment may be integrated into the existing procedures for development consent to projects in the Member States, or, failing this, into other procedures or into procedures to be established to comply with the aims of this Directive.
>
> 3. Member States may provide for a single procedure in order to fulfil the requirements of this Directive and the requirements of [the IPPC Directive[5]].'

---

[3] Council Directive 92/43 of 21 May 1992 on the conservation of natural habitats and of wild fauna and flora ([1992] OJ L206/7), as amended by Council Directive 2013/17 of 13 May 2013 ([2013] OJ L158/193) ('the Habitats Directive').
[4] Directive 2009/147 of the European Parliament and of the Council of 30 November 2009 on the conservation of wild birds ([2010] OJ L20/7), last amended by Council Directive 2013/17 of 13 May 2013 adapting certain directives in the field of environment, by reason of the accession of the Republic of Croatia ([2013] OJ L158/193) ('the Birds Directive').
[5] Directive 2008/1 of the European Parliament and of the Council of 15 January 2008 concerning integrated pollution prevention and control ([2008] OJ L24/8); 'the IPPC Directive'.

AG6   The environmental impact assessment is described in greater detail in Article 3 of the EIA Directive:

> 'The environmental impact assessment shall identify, describe and assess in an appropriate manner, in the light of each individual case and in accordance with Articles 4 to 12, the direct and indirect effects of a project on the following factors:
> (a) human beings, fauna and flora;
> (b) soil, water, air, climate and the landscape;
> (c) material assets and the cultural heritage;
> (d) the interaction between the factors referred to in points (a), (b) and (c).'

AG7   Pursuant to Article 4(1) of, and point 19 of Annex I to, the EIA Directive, quarries where the surface of the site exceeds 25 hectares are always to be regarded as projects likely to have significant effects on the environment. Therefore, their effects on the environment must be assessed in accordance with the directive.

AG8   Article 5(1) of, and point 3 of Annex IV to, the EIA Directive require the developer to supply in an appropriate form a description of the aspects of the environment likely to be significantly affected by the proposed project, including, in particular, fauna and flora.

AG9   Article 6 of the EIA Directive contains the fundamental provisions concerning public participation:

> '1. Member States shall take the measures necessary to ensure that the authorities likely to be concerned by the project by reason of their specific environmental responsibilities are given an opportunity to express their opinion on the information supplied by the developer and on the request for development consent. …
> 2. The public shall be informed … of the following matters early … and, at the latest, as soon as information can reasonably be provided:
> (a) the request for development consent;
> (b) the fact that the project is subject to an environmental impact assessment procedure and, where relevant, the fact that Article 7 applies;
> (c) details of the competent authorities responsible for taking the decision, those from which relevant information can be obtained, those to which comments or questions can be submitted, and details of the time schedule for transmitting comments or questions;
> (d) the nature of possible decisions or, where there is one, the draft decision;
> (e) an indication of the availability of the information gathered pursuant to Article 5;
> (f) an indication of the times and places at which, and the means by which, the relevant information will be made available;
> (g) details of the arrangements for public participation made pursuant to paragraph 5 of this Article.
> 3. Member States shall ensure that, within reasonable time-frames, the following is made available to the public concerned:

    (a) any information gathered pursuant to Article 5;
    (b) in accordance with national legislation, the main reports and
         advice issued to the competent authority or authorities at the
         time when the public concerned is informed in accordance with
         paragraph 2 of this Article;
    (c) in accordance with the provisions of [Directive 2003/4/EC⁶],
         information other than that referred to in paragraph 2 of this
         Article which is relevant for the decision in accordance with
         Article 8 of this Directive and which only becomes available
         after the time the public concerned was informed in accordance
         with paragraph 2 of this Article.
  4. The public concerned shall be given early and effective opportunities
      to participate in the environmental decision-making procedures referred
      to in Article 2(2) and shall, for that purpose, be entitled to express
      comments and opinions when all options are open to the competent
      authority or authorities before the decision on the request for
      development consent is taken.
  5. … .'

AG10   The importance of the environmental impact assessment for the development
consent procedure is laid down in Article 8 of the EIA Directive:

   'The results of consultations and the information gathered pursuant to Articles
   5, 6 and 7 must be taken into consideration in the development consent
   procedure.'

AG11   Article 11 of the EIA Directive lays down rules on actions brought against
decisions which are subject to public participation under the EIA Directive:

   '1. Member States shall ensure that, in accordance with the relevant
        national legal system, members of the public concerned:
        (a) having a sufficient interest, or alternatively;
        (b) maintaining the impairment of a right, where administrative
             procedural law of a Member State requires this as a
             precondition;
        have access to a review procedure before a court of law or another
        independent and impartial body established by law to challenge the
        substantive or procedural legality of decisions, acts or omissions subject
        to the public participation provisions of this Directive.
   2. Member States shall determine at what stage the decisions, acts or
       omissions may be challenged.
   3. What constitutes a sufficient interest and impairment of a right shall
       be determined by the Member States, consistently with the objective
       of giving the public concerned wide access to justice. …'

---

⁶ Directive of the European Parliament and of the Council of 28 January 2003 on public access to environmental
information and repealing Council Directive 90/313 ([2003] OJ L41/26).

B. Directive 2014/52/EU

AG12   The new version of Article 2(3) of the EIA Directive, introduced by Directive 2014/52,[7] which is not yet applicable in the present proceedings, is also of interest:

> '3. In the case of projects for which the obligation to carry out assessments of the effects on the environment arises simultaneously from this Directive and from [the Habitats Directive] and/or [the Birds Directive], Member States shall, where appropriate, ensure that coordinated and/or joint procedures fulfilling the requirements of that Union legislation are provided for.
>
> In the case of projects for which the obligation to carry out assessments of the effects on the environment arises simultaneously from this Directive and Union legislation other than the Directives listed in the first subparagraph, Member States may provide for coordinated and/or joint procedures.
>
> Under the coordinated procedure referred to in the first and second subparagraphs, Member States shall endeavour to coordinate the various individual assessments of the environmental impact of a particular project, required by the relevant Union legislation, by designating an authority for this purpose, without prejudice to any provisions to the contrary contained in other relevant Union legislation. Under the joint procedure referred to in the first and second subparagraphs, Member States shall endeavour to provide for a single assessment of the environmental impact of a particular project required by the relevant Union legislation, without prejudice to any provisions to the contrary contained in other relevant Union legislation.
>
> The Commission shall provide guidance regarding the setting up of any coordinated or joint procedures for projects that are simultaneously subject to assessments under this Directive and [the Habitats Directive, the Water Framework Directive,[8] the Birds Directive and Directive 2010/75[9]].'

C. Protection of species

AG13   Articles 12 and 13 of, and Annex IV to, the Habitats Directive require the establishment of a system of strict protection for certain species of flora and fauna, prohibiting many forms of detriment caused to those species. Article 16 allows derogation from those protective provisions under certain conditions.

AG14   Articles 5 and 9 of the Birds Directive provide similar rules for all European bird species.

---

[7] Directive of the European Parliament and of the Council of 16 April 2014 amending the EIA Directive ([2014] OJ L124/1).

[8] Directive 2000/60 of the European Parliament and of the Council of 23 October 2000 establishing a framework for Community action in the field of water policy ([2000] OJ L327/1); 'the Water Framework Directive'.

[9] Directive of the European Parliament and of the Council of 24 November 2010 on industrial emissions (integrated pollution prevention and control) ([2010] OJ L334/17).

III. Facts and request for a preliminary ruling

AG15   On 4 November 2008, the public limited company Sagrex applied for a single permit to resume working of the Bossimé quarry, to dig a tunnel between the Bossimé and Lives-sur-Meuse quarries, to install a conveyor belt in the Lives-sur-Meuse quarry and to develop a riverside loading quay for barges on the Meuse in the Walloon Region of Belgium. The project covers an area of over 50 hectares.

AG16   On 12 May 2010, the Département de la nature and des forêts (Department of Nature and Forests) of the Walloon Region issued an unfavourable opinion, on the ground that the project did not take into account the obligations of species protection.

AG17   On 15 April 2016, Sagrex made an application for a derogation from the species protection measures, to which it attached a study entitled 'Destruction of environments and relocation of plant species in order to work the Bossimé quarry'. On 27 June 2016, the Inspector General of the Department of Nature and Forests granted the derogation sought, and it accordingly authorised Sagrex to cause detriment to various plant and animal species, on the condition that it applies certain mitigating measures. This is the contested measure.

AG18   On 30 September 2016, Sagrex filed amended plans and a corresponding supplementary impact study in support of its application for a single permit.

AG19   A public inquiry into the amended project was held from 21 November to 21 December 2016 and generated a large number of objections.

AG20   On 21 December 2016, the Department of Nature and Forests issued a favourable opinion on the application for a single permit, subject to conditions. That opinion was based on the following reasons, among others:

> 'Whereas by means of the recommendations set out in the application file, the obligations arising from the derogation of 27 June 2016 and the conditions set out below, the significant nature conservation impacts of this project can be reduced to an acceptable level, in particular in the light of the compensatory measures; …'

AG21   On 25 September 2017, the competent minister of the Walloon Region nevertheless refused the single permit. Sagrex's parent company, Cimenteries CBR SA, brought an action for annulment against that decision, which, however, was dismissed by judgment of 14 May 2020.

AG22   Nevertheless, by application lodged on 18 January 2017, the non-profit association Namur-Est Environnement had already applied to the Conseil d'État (Council of State, Belgium) for annulment of the decision of 27 June 2016 granting the derogations from the measures to protect plant and animal species laid down in the loi sur la conservation de la nature (Law on nature conservation, Belgium). Cimenteries CBR intervened in those proceedings.

AG23   In the request for a preliminary ruling, the Conseil d'État (Council of State) submits that the sole purpose of the decision on derogation is to authorise the disturbance of animals and degradation of the areas of habitat of those species. By contrast, the principal decision entitling the developer to proceed with its project is the single permit which may, following a public inquiry, be refused or made subject to stricter conditions than those laid down by the contested measure. The authority responsible for issuing single permits must examine all the planning and environmental aspects of the project for working the quarry. Accordingly, the authority may assess the effects of that working more strictly in the light of the parameters set by the body that issued the contested measure. Indeed, in the present case, the authority refused to grant the single permit to work the quarry.

AG24   Therefore, the Conseil d'État (Council of State) addresses the following questions to the Court:

> '(1) Do a decision "authorising the disturbance of animals and degradation of the areas of habitat of those species for the working of a quarry" and the decision authorising or refusing that working (single permit) form a single development consent (within the meaning of Article 1(2)(c) of the EIA Directive) relating to a single project (within the meaning of Article 1(2)(a) of that directive) where, first, that working cannot take place without the first of those decisions and, second, the authority responsible for issuing single permits retains the ability to determine the environmental effects of that working more strictly having regard to the parameters set by the body that issued the first decision?
>
> (2) If the answer to that first question is in the affirmative, are the requirements laid down by that directive, specifically in Articles 2, 5, 6, 7 and 8, sufficiently met where the public participation phase takes place after adoption of the decision "authorising the disturbance of animals and degradation of the areas of habitat of those species for the working of a quarry" but before adoption of the principal decision entitling the developer to proceed to work the quarry?'

AG25   Written observations have been submitted by Namur-Est Environnement, Cimenteries CBR, the Kingdom of Belgium, the Czech Republic and the European Commission. With the exception of the Czech Republic, they also took part in the hearing held on 9 September 2021.

IV. Legal assessment

AG26   The request for a preliminary ruling seeks to clarify the relationship between two authorisations that relate to the same project. The authorisations concerned are, on the one hand, the permit initially granted to derogate from the rules on the protection of certain animal and plant species in the implementation of the project (permit under species protection law) and, on the other hand, the 'global authorisation' for the project as a whole, which was the subject of an environmental impact assessment after the development consent under species protection law had been granted, but that permit was ultimately refused.

AG27   In that context, the starting point for the request for a preliminary ruling is an action brought against the permit under species protection law. The applicant NGO, Namur-Est Environnement, takes the view that the EIA Directive precludes provisional authorisation for derogations from the rules on species protection granted independently of the environmental impact assessment.

AG28   The first question seeks to ascertain whether the two authorisations together constitute a development consent within the meaning of the EIA Directive. If that is the case, the issue to be discussed in relation to the second question is whether it is compatible with that directive for the permit under species protection law to be granted before the environmental impact assessment has been carried out.

AG29   Article 2(1) of the EIA Directive provides that Member States are to adopt all measures necessary to ensure that, before consent is given, projects likely to have significant effects on the environment by virtue, inter alia, of their nature, size or location are made subject to a requirement for development consent and an assessment with regard to their effects. Development consent is defined in Article 1(2)(c) as the decision which entitles the developer to proceed with the project.

AG30   This means that, first, the projects referred to must be made subject to a requirement for development consent and, second, the effects of the projects on the environment must be assessed before such development consent is granted.

AG31   It is common ground that the quarry project at issue is subject to those requirements. Pursuant to Article 4(1) of, and point 19 of Annex I to, the EIA Directive, quarries where the surface of the site exceeds 25 hectares are always to be regarded as projects likely to have significant effects on the environment. The project in question covers an area of over 50 hectares, with the result that an environmental impact assessment is necessary.

AG32   However, it needs to be clarified whether the authorisation for the project must include the permit under species protection law and – if so – whether it is permissible for the permit under species protection law to be granted even before the environmental impact assessment has been carried out.

A. Admissibility of the first question

AG33   The Kingdom of Belgium submits that the first question is inadmissible because it is based on the incorrect assumption that the permit under species protection law is a precondition for the granting of the global authorisation. If that objection is well founded, there would be no need to answer the second question because it is asked only in the event that the first question is answered in the affirmative.

AG34   It is true that the Court may refuse to rule on a question referred for a preliminary ruling by a national court where it is quite obvious that the interpretation of EU law that is sought bears no relation to the actual facts of the main action or its purpose,[10] as claimed by the Kingdom of Belgium in relation to the first question.

AG35   However, in proceedings under Article 267 TFEU, which are based on a clear separation of functions between the national courts and the Court of Justice, the national court alone has jurisdiction to find and assess the facts in the case before it and to interpret and apply national law.[11] Therefore, it is not for the Court to rule on the interpretation of provisions of national law or to decide whether the referring court's interpretation of them is correct.[12] Therefore, the Court must take account of the factual and legal context of requests for preliminary rulings, as described in the order for reference.[13]

AG36   Although, in what follows, the relationship between the permit under species protection law and the global authorisation must be examined from the perspective of EU law, the starting point is a question of national law. It is therefore necessary

[10] Judgments of 10 December 2018, *Wightman* (C-621/18) EU:C:2018:999 at [27] and of 14 October 2020, *Sappi Austria Produktion and Wasserverband 'Region Gratkorn-Gratwein'* (C-629/19) EU:C:2020:824 at [26].

[11] Judgments of 26 May 2011, *Stichting Natuur en Milieu* (C-165/09)–(C-167/09) EU:C:2011:348 at [47] and of 3 February 2021, *Fussl Modestrasse Mayr* (C-555/19) EU:C:2021:89 at [29].

[12] Judgments of 18 January 2007, *Auroux* (C-220/05) EU:C:2007:31 at [25]; of 7 October 2010, *Santos Palhota* (C-515/08) EU:C:2010:589 at [18]; and of 26 September 2013, *Texdata Software* (C-418/11) EU:C:2013:588 at [28].

[13] Judgments of 25 October 2001, *Ambulanz Glöckner* (C-475/99) EU:C:2001:577 at [10]; of 26 September 2013, *Texdata Software* (C-418/11) EU:C:2013:588 at [29]; and of 15 April 2021, *État belge (Circumstances subsequent to the transfer decision)* (C-194/19) EU:C:2021:270 at [26].

in that respect to proceed on the basis of the view taken by the Conseil d'État (Council of State), as set forth in the request for a preliminary ruling and on which the question referred to the Court is predicated.

AG37   Moreover, the Kingdom of Belgium's submission is also not convincing in terms of content, since the permit under species protection law was expressly applied for in relation to the implementation of the quarry project. According to the observations submitted in the hearing, detriment caused to protected species is accordingly permissible only within the framework of the project, and therefore requires, at least in practice, the approval of the project as a whole. A further reason why such a link with the project appears to be necessary under EU law is that only the objectives of the measure concerned, in this case the project, can justify a derogation from the obligations of species protection in accordance with Article 16 of the Habitats Directive[14] and Article 9 of the Birds Directive.[15]

AG38   Therefore, the Kingdom of Belgium's objections regarding the admissibility of the first question and thus of the request for a preliminary ruling as a whole are unfounded.

B. The response to the reference for a preliminary ruling

AG39   In my view, however, the two questions asked by the Conseil d'État (Council of State) must be answered *together*. Ultimately, the issue cannot be whether the two authorisations together formally constitute development consent under the EIA Directive, but only whether that directive allows certain environmental effects of a project to be decided on before the environmental impact assessment is carried out.

AG40   However, the rules of the EIA Directive and the relevant case-law on the integration of decisions on certain environmental aspects of a project into the environmental impact assessment seem to provide contradictory guidance for answering that question.

AG41   The starting point is the objective of a comprehensive assessment of all environmental effects in the environmental impact assessment (see section 1).

AG42   However, the EIA Directive contains provisions on the coordination of authorisation procedures, which suggest that it is not necessary to decide on all the environmental effects of a project in a single procedure (see section 2). Furthermore, the Court has recognised the possibility of consent procedures comprising several stages which require an environmental impact assessment only at certain stages (see section 3). It might be inferred from this that the permit under species protection law can be granted independently of and prior to the environmental impact assessment.

AG43   However, final decisions on certain environmental effects taken before the environmental impact assessment has been carried out ultimately run counter to important fundamental principles of environmental impact assessment. This is because, first, public participation must take place at an early stage, when all options are open; second, the findings of the environmental impact assessment must be taken into account in the decision on the project; and, third, comprehensive legal protection against that decision must be available (see section 4).

---

[14] See judgment of 10 October 2019, *Luonnonsuojeluyhdistys Tapiola* (C-674/17) EU:C:2019:851 at [41] et seq.
[15] See judgment of 17 March 2021, *One Voice and Ligue pour la protection des oiseaux* (C-900/19) EU:C:2021:211 at [37] et seq. and [61].

1. Protection of species in the environmental impact assessment

AG44   The environmental impact assessment covers all significant environmental effects, including, where relevant, significant effects on protected species.[16] According to Article 3(a) of the EIA Directive, it is to identify, describe and assess in an appropriate manner, in the light of each individual case, the direct and indirect effects of a project on, inter alia, fauna and flora. In accordance with Article 5(1) and point 3 of Annex IV, such effects must therefore be described by the developer. No exceptions are provided for certain environmental effects.

AG45   It is not always easy in practice to delineate the effects that could be significant and must therefore be the subject of the environmental impact assessment. However, the assessment must cover at least the information necessary to assess the compatibility of the project with the applicable environmental law.

AG46   In that respect, the Court has ruled that the information to be provided must contain the data that are necessary in order to assess the effects of a project on the status of the bodies of water concerned in the light of the criteria and requirements laid down in, inter alia, Article 4(1) of the Water Framework Directive,[17] the so-called ban on deterioration.[18]

AG47   Accordingly, as submitted by Cimenteries CBR, derogations from the rules of EU law on the protection of species, that is to say, from the prohibitions under Articles 12 and 13 of the Habitats Directive and Article 5 of the Birds Directive, must also be described. This is because such derogations from the requirements of EU environmental law are significant by their very nature, irrespective of whether they should ultimately be justified under Article 16 of the Habitats Directive or Article 9 of the Birds Directive. However, derogations from purely national rules on species protection can also be significant.

AG48   Such information must be made available to the public under Article 6(3)(a) of the EIA Directive[19] and is therefore the subject of public participation. Moreover, in accordance with Article 6(1), the authorities responsible for species protection must also be involved.

AG49   Therefore, Member States may not exclude certain environmental effects and, in particular, adverse effects on species protected under EU law from the environmental impact assessment.

2. Coordination of different procedures

AG50   In the light of the comprehensive environmental impact assessment, the definition of development consent in Article 1(2)(c) of the EIA Directive suggests, at first glance, that that consent must also include all environmental effects of the project. This is because, according to that provision, such development consent is a single decision of the competent authority or authorities which entitles the developer to proceed with the project. This could mean that not only must the authorities responsible for various environmental effects be involved in the environmental impact assessment in accordance with Article 6(1), but the development consent must also comprehensively regulate those effects.

---

[16] See, to that effect, judgments of 24 November 2011, *Commission v Spain (Alto Sil)* (C-404/09) EU:C:2011:768 at [86]; and of 7 November 2018, *Holohan* (C-461/17) EU:C:2018:883 at [57]–[59]; and my Opinion in the latter case (EU:C:2018:649) AG84–87.

[17] Cited in fn.8.

[18] Judgment of 28 May 2020, *Land Nordrhein-Westfalen* (C-535/18) EU:C:2020:391 at [81].

[19] See, to that effect, judgment of 28 May 2020, *Land Nordrhein-Westfalen* (C-535/18) EU:C:2020:391 at [83].

AG51   However, it follows in particular from Article 2(3) of the EIA Directive that the procedure for the environmental impact assessment and the consent granted on that basis does not have to combine all authorisations related to the project, or even all authorisations under environmental law. Rather, that provision *allows* Member States to provide for a single procedure in order to fulfil the requirements of the EIA Directive and the IPPC Directive[20] (now Directive 2010/75 on industrial emissions[21]). It follows *a contrario* that it is equally permissible under that provision to apply *different* procedures for the implementation of the two directives and to grant *separate* authorisations.

AG52   This is confirmed by Article 2(2) of the EIA Directive, which provides that the environmental impact assessment may be integrated into the existing procedures for consent to projects or, failing this, into other procedures or into procedures to be established to comply with the aims of the directive.

AG53   It should also be noted that the new version of Article 2(3) of the EIA Directive, which was created by Directive 2014/52 and is not yet applicable in the present proceedings, does not change this at all, but only requires coordination with regard to impact assessments in connection with protected areas under the Habitats Directive and the Birds Directive, which are not relevant in the present case.

AG54   The Member States therefore have a certain margin of discretion.[22] In particular, they do not have to provide for a single procedure in which all the environmental effects of a project are decided upon by means of a single authorisation.

AG55   Therefore, the EIA Directive does not preclude, in principle, the granting of specific authorisations in respect of certain environmental effects, such as species protection, in relation to projects requiring an environmental impact assessment.

3. Temporal coordination of different proceedings

AG56   However, it is still not clear whether it is permissible for certain environmental effects of a project to be finally decided upon *before* the environmental impact assessment is carried out.

AG57   In that context, various parties have discussed the case-law on authorisation procedures comprising several stages. With that case-law, the Court seeks to optimise the two objectives of an environmental impact assessment which is both comprehensive and early, while respecting the procedural autonomy of the Member States.

AG58   In accordance with that case-law, national law may provide that the procedure is to be carried out in several stages, one involving a principal decision and the other involving an implementing decision which cannot extend beyond the parameters set by the principal decision. In such a case, the effects which the project may have on the environment must (as a rule) be identified and assessed at the time of the procedure relating to the principal decision.[23]

AG59   However, a comprehensive assessment would not be possible at that stage if the environmental effects can be identified only in the procedure relating to the

---

[20] Cited in fn.5.
[21] Cited in fn.9.
[22] Judgment of 3 March 2011, *Commission v Ireland* (C-50/09) EU:C:2011:109 at [75].
[23] Judgments of 7 January 2004, *Wells* (C-201/02) EU:C:2004:12 at [52]; of 4 May 2006, *Barker* (C-290/03) EU:C:2006:286 at [47]; of 28 February 2008, *Abraham* (C-2/07) EU:C:2008:133 at [26]; and of 29 July 2019, *Inter-Environnement Wallonie and Bond Beter Leefmilieu Vlaanderen* (C-411/17) EU:C:2019:622 at [86].

implementing decision. In such a case, the assessment must be carried out only in the procedure relating to that second decision, that is to say, at a later stage.[24]

AG60   The Court has even held that a rule under which an environmental impact assessment can be carried out only at the initial stage, and not at the later stage relating to authorisation for matters not yet dealt with, is contrary to the EIA Directive.[25] This is in line with the objective of a comprehensive environmental impact assessment, which would be undermined if the assessment had to be carried out at a time when it is not yet possible to establish all the effects of the project.

AG61   As submitted by the Kingdom of Belgium and the Czech Republic, it is doubtful that the permit under species protection law is a principal decision on the project within the meaning of that case-law, as it concerns only one aspect of the project. It rather appears, on the face of it, to be an attempt to remove a specific obstacle before making further onerous efforts towards obtaining the global authorisation, or to ascertain whether this is possible at all. The reason for this is that development consent for the project was still precluded by species protection in 2010. Cimenteries CBR nevertheless categorises the permit under species protection law in that capacity as one stage of a consent procedure comprising several stages.

AG62   However, the main point of interest for the present case is the fact that, in accordance with that case-law, the EIA Directive allows certain issues to be decided upon before the environmental impact assessment has been carried out. However, if 'principal decisions', which by their nature may relate to many environmental effects of the project, are permissible without an environmental impact assessment, provisional decisions on specific aspects with limited environmental effects should a fortiori be permissible.

4. Importance of the results of the environmental impact assessment for the development consent and legal protection

AG63   However, the case-law on authorisation procedures comprising several stages is based on the original version of the EIA Directive and does not yet take into account the changes[26] brought about by the Aarhus Convention.[27] In that respect, attention should be drawn, in particular, to Article 6(4) of the EIA Directive. Accordingly, the public should be able to make its views known at an early stage and in an effective manner when all options are open and before the decision on the request for development consent is taken.

AG64   Those requirements prohibit the taking of final decisions on certain environmental effects of a project before the public has had the opportunity to express its view on those effects in the environmental impact assessment. This is because all options would no longer be open in that case.

AG65   Furthermore, Article 8 of the EIA Directive provides that the results of consultations and the information gathered pursuant to Articles 5, 6 and 7 are to be taken into account in the development consent procedure. In accordance with recital 2 and settled case-law, this means that the competent authority is to take

---

[24] See the references in fn.22.
[25] Judgment of 4 May 2006, *Commission v United Kingdom* (C-508/03) EU:C:2006:287 at [105].
[26] Article 3 of Directive 2003/35 of the European Parliament and of the Council of 26 May 2003 providing for public participation in respect of the drawing up of certain plans and programmes relating to the environment and amending with regard to public participation and access to justice Council Directives 85/337 and 96/61 ([2003] OJ L156/17).
[27] Convention on access to information, public participation in decision-making and access to justice in environmental matters of 1998 ([2005] OJ L124/4), approved by Council Decision 2005/370 of 17 February 2005 ([2005] OJ L124/1).

account of the effects on the environment at the earliest possible stage in all the technical planning and decision-making processes, the objective being to prevent the creation of pollution or nuisances at source rather than subsequently trying to counteract their effects.[28]

AG66   However, if the authorities decide on certain environmental effects before the environmental impact assessment has been carried out, they obviously cannot yet take into account the results of the consultations and the information gathered.[29]

AG67   Finally, the legal protection to be guaranteed under Article 11 of the EIA Directive, a provision that also implements the Aarhus Convention, must also be taken into account in that context. In accordance with that provision, the substantive or procedural legality of decisions, acts or omissions subject to the public participation provisions of the EIA Directive may be challenged under certain conditions.

AG68   The development consent for a project under Article 2(1) of the EIA Directive is a decision that may be challenged under Article 11 thereof.

AG69   It is true that the EIA Directive does not specify what the consequences of certain findings of the environmental impact assessment are for that consent.[30] Rather, those consequences are laid down in other legislation, for instance, in the case of species protection, in the Habitats Directive or the Birds Directive, and in the relevant laws transposing such legislation into national law.

AG70   Therefore, the legality of the development consent under Article 2(1) of the EIA Directive, which is granted on the basis of the environmental impact assessment, depends on whether the project at issue respects those other provisions of environmental law. If it has become apparent in the context of the environmental impact assessment that the project is incompatible with environmental requirements of other legislation, the granting of such consent is excluded.[31]

AG71   Therefore, judicial review under Article 11 of the EIA Directive includes at least the rules of national law implementing EU environmental law and the rules of EU environmental law having direct effect.[32]

AG72   Moreover, since the right of action under Article 11 of the EIA Directive is linked to the comprehensive environmental impact assessment, it is to be exercised on the basis of the findings made in that assessment. This is because those findings make it possible to identify environmental objections that can support such an action, or they can show that there are no grounds for an action.

AG73   It would be incompatible with this to take *final* decisions on certain environmental effects before the environmental impact assessment has even been carried out. Even if it were possible for such a decision on certain aspects to be challenged separately, such an action would generally have to be brought without the findings of the environmental impact assessment.

AG74   Therefore, a preliminary decision on certain environmental effects of a project which is subject to environmental impact assessment can be only *provisional* in

---

[28] Judgments of 7 January 2004, *Wells* (C-201/02) EU:C:2004:12 at [51]; of 12 November 2019, *Commission v Ireland (Derrybrien Wind Farm)* (C-261/18) EU:C:2019:955 at [73]; and of 28 May 2020, *Land Nordrhein-Westfalen* (C-535/18) EU:C:2020:391 at [78].

[29] See judgment of 3 March 2011, *Commission v Ireland* (C-50/09) EU:C:2011:109 at [81], [84] and [85].

[30] See my Opinion in *Leth* (C-420/11) EU:C:2012:701, AG48.

[31] See, to that effect, judgment of 28 May 2020, *Land Nordrhein-Westfalen* (C-535/18) EU:C:2020:391 at [75] and [76], concerning the Water Framework Directive.

[32] Judgments of 12 May 2011, *Bund für Umwelt und Naturschutz Deutschland, Landesverband Nordrhein-Westfalen* (C-115/09) EU:C:2011:289 at [48]; of 15 October 2015, *Commission v Germany* (C-137/14) EU:C:2015:683 at [92]; and of 8 November 2016, *Lesoochranárske zoskupenie VLK* (C-243/15) EU:C:2016:838 at [59].

nature. Final decisions may be taken only on the basis of that assessment and therefore necessarily after it. Furthermore, it must be possible for them to be challenged in full, and independently of the provisional decision, in accordance with Article 11 of the EIA Directive.

AG75   Therefore, the provisional decision cannot establish full legal certainty for the developer with regard to its subject matter and outcome, but it may provide guidance as to whether, on the basis of the information available, certain environmental effects may stand in the way of the project.

AG76   According to the information in the request for a preliminary ruling and the submissions of Cimenteries CBR, it cannot be ruled out that Belgian law satisfies those requirements. Under that law, the authority responsible for issuing single permits retains the ability to determine the environmental effects of the working of a quarry more strictly having regard to the parameters set by the body that issued the first decision. If that is the case, when granting the development consent under Article 2(1) of the EIA Directive, that authority would be able to give due consideration to any conflicts with species protection which became apparent only in the course of the environmental impact assessment. However, various parties argued at the hearing that the permit under species protection law can nevertheless become final independently of the environmental impact assessment, thereby calling the comprehensive legal protection under Article 11 into question.

V. Conclusion

AG77   I therefore propose that the Court give the following answer to the request for a preliminary ruling:

> It is compatible with Directive 2011/92/EU of the European Parliament and of the Council of 13 December 2011 on the assessment of the effects of certain public and private projects on the environment to take a provisional decision to authorise adverse effects on protected species in a project even before the adoption of the principal decision entitling the developer to proceed with its project and before public participation in the environmental impact assessment of that project.
>
> However, the environmental impact assessment must include the effects of the project on protected species in accordance with Articles 3, 5, 6 and 7 of Directive 2011/92, even if a provisional decision has already been taken on those effects. Furthermore, irrespective of the decision taken in advance, the competent authorities must refuse the development consent provided for in Article 2(1) of the directive in so far as the assessment shows that the project is incompatible with the provisions of EU law on species protection. Lastly, the authorisation to derogate from the requirements of species protection in relation to the project must be challengeable on the basis of the environmental impact assessment in accordance with Article 11 of the directive.

JUDGMENT[33]

1   This request for a preliminary ruling concerns the interpretation of Articles 1, 2 and 5 to 8 of Directive 2011/92/EU of the European Parliament and of the Council of 13 December 2011 on the assessment of the effects of certain public and private projects on the environment (OJ 2012 L 26, p. 1, corrigendum OJ 2015 L 174, p. 44).

2   The request has been made in the context of a dispute between Namur-Est Environnement ASBL and the Région wallonne (Walloon Region, Belgium) concerning the decision by which the latter granted Sagrex SA a derogation from the animal and plant species protection measures provided for in the applicable legislation, with a view to the working of a limestone aggregate quarry ('the derogation decision').

Legal context

European Union law

Directive 92/43/EEC

3   Council Directive 92/43/EEC of 21 May 1992 on the conservation of natural habitats and of wild fauna and flora (OJ 1992 L 206, p. 7) provides, in Articles 12 and 13 thereof, that the Member States are to take the requisite measures to establish a system of strict protection for the animal and plant species listed in Annexes IV(a) and IV(b) to that directive.

4   Article 16 of Directive 92/43 states, in paragraph 1 thereof, that, provided that there is no satisfactory alternative and the derogation is not detrimental to the maintenance of the species concerned at a favourable conservation status in their natural range, Member States may derogate, inter alia, from Articles 12 and 13 of the same directive for one or more of the reasons set out in points (a) to (e) of that paragraph 1.

Directive 2011/92

5   Article 1(2) of Directive 2011/92 contains inter alia the following definitions:

> '(a) "project" means:
>   – the execution of construction works or of other installations or schemes,
>   – other interventions in the natural surroundings and landscape including those involving the extraction of mineral resources;
>   …
> (c) "development consent" means the decision of the competent authority or authorities which entitles the developer to proceed with the project;
>   …'

6   Article 2 of that directive provides, in paragraphs 1 and 2 thereof:

---

[33] Language of the case: French.

'1. Member States shall adopt all measures necessary to ensure that, before consent is given, projects likely to have significant effects on the environment by virtue, inter alia, of their nature, size or location are made subject to a requirement for development consent and an assessment with regard to their effects. Those projects are defined in Article 4.

2. The environmental impact assessment may be integrated into the existing procedures for consent to projects in the Member States ...'

7   Article 3 of the said directive states:

'The environmental impact assessment shall identify, describe and assess in an appropriate manner, in the light of each individual case ..., the direct and indirect effects of a project on the following factors:
   (a) human beings, fauna and flora;
   (b) soil, water, air, climate and the landscape;
   (c) material assets and the cultural heritage;
   (d) the interaction between the factors referred to in points (a), (b) and (c).'

8   Article 5 of the same directive provides, in paragraph 1 thereof, that, 'in the case of projects which, pursuant to Article 4, are to be made subject to an environmental impact assessment in accordance with this article and Articles 6 to 10, Member States shall adopt the necessary measures to ensure that the developer supplies in an appropriate form the information specified in Annex IV', in so far as that information is considered relevant in any given case and the developer may reasonably be required to compile it. By virtue of that annex, the information to be provided must include, in particular, 'a description of the aspects of the environment likely to be significantly affected by the proposed project, including, in particular, ... fauna, flora ... and the interrelationship between the above factors'.

9   Article 6 of Directive 2011/92 is worded as follows:

'1. Member States shall take the measures necessary to ensure that the authorities likely to be concerned by the project by reason of their specific environmental responsibilities are given an opportunity to express their opinion on the information supplied by the developer and on the request for development consent. ...

2. The public shall be informed ... of the following matters early in the environmental decision-making procedures referred to in Article 2(2) and, at the latest, as soon as information can reasonably be provided:
   (a) the request for development consent;
   (b) the fact that the project is subject to an environmental impact assessment procedure and, where relevant, the fact that Article 7 applies;
   ...
   (d) the nature of possible decisions or, where there is one, the draft decision;
   (e) an indication of the availability of the information gathered pursuant to Article 5;
   (f) an indication of the times and places at which, and the means by which, the relevant information will be made available;

(g) details of the arrangements for public participation made pursuant to paragraph 5 of this article.

3. Member States shall ensure that, within reasonable time-frames, the following is made available to the public concerned:

(a) any information gathered pursuant to Article 5;

(b) in accordance with national legislation, the main reports and advice issued to the competent authority or authorities at the time when the public concerned is informed in accordance with paragraph 2 of this article;

(c) in accordance with the provisions of Directive 2003/4/EC of the European Parliament and of the Council of 28 January 2003 on public access to environmental information, information other than that referred to in paragraph 2 of this article which is relevant for the decision in accordance with Article 8 of this directive and which only becomes available after the time the public concerned was informed in accordance with paragraph 2 of this article.

4. The public concerned shall be given early and effective opportunities to participate in the environmental decision-making procedures referred to in Article 2(2) and shall, for that purpose, be entitled to express comments and opinions when all options are open to the competent authority or authorities before the decision on the request for development consent is taken.

…'

10   Article 7 of Directive 2011/92 lays down specific procedures for the environmental impact assessment in cases where a project is likely to have significant effects on the environment in several Member States.

11   Article 8 of that directive states that 'the results of consultations and the information gathered pursuant to Articles 5, 6 and 7 shall be taken into consideration in the development consent procedure'.

12   Annex I to Directive 2011/92 lists the projects that must be made subject, by virtue of Article 4(1) of that directive, to an assessment in accordance with Articles 5 to 10 thereof. Point 19 of that annex mentions 'quarries and open-cast mining where the surface of the site exceeds 25 hectares'.

Belgian law

13   Directive 92/43 was transposed into Belgian law by the Loi du 12 juillet 1973 sur la conservation de la nature (Law of 12 July 1973 on nature conservation) (*Moniteur belge*, 11 September 1973, p. 10306), as amended by the Décret de la Région wallonne du 6 décembre 2001 relatif à la conservation des sites Natura 2000 ainsi que de la faune et de la flore sauvages (Decree of the Walloon Region of 6 December 2001 on the conservation of Natura 2000 sites and of wild fauna and flora) (*Moniteur belge*, 22 January 2002, p. 2017) ('the Law on nature conservation').

14   Articles 2a, 3 and 3a of the Law on nature conservation establish a regime for the protection of a range of species of birds, mammals and plants which are either protected under Directive 92/43 or threatened in Wallonia. That regime is based on measures such as the prohibition of the trapping, capturing and killing, or the

collecting, cutting and uprooting of the species concerned, the prohibition on disturbing those species intentionally, the prohibition of the keeping, transporting, exchanging, buying or selling or giving of those species and the prohibition on destroying or damaging their natural habitats.

15   Article 5 of that law states that the government of the Walloon Region may grant derogations from those measures, subject to certain conditions and for certain reasons.

16   Article 5a of the same law provides for the possibility of making an application for a derogation from those measures, while assigning to the government of the Walloon Region the responsibility for defining the form and content of that application, as well as the conditions and procedures for the grant of the derogation sought.

17   It is common ground that neither the Law on nature conservation nor the decision adopted by the government of the Walloon Region for its application provides, first, that an environmental impact assessment of the derogation sought must be conducted and, second, that the public concerned must be consulted before the derogation is granted.

The dispute in the main proceedings and the questions referred for a preliminary ruling

18   On 4 November 2008, Sagrex submitted to the competent authority of the Walloon Region an application for a single permit for a project to resume working a quarry covering an area of over 50 hectares situated at Bossimé (Belgium), to construct installations and related developments, in particular on the banks of the Meuse.

19   On 12 May 2010, the Namur external management of the Département de la nature et des forêts (Department of Nature and Forests) of the Walloon Region issued an unfavourable opinion on that application, in which it stated, first, that the project at issue in the main proceedings adjoined a Natura 2000 site and covered two sites of significant biological interest and would lead to the total or partial destruction of the latter two sites and to the complete or partial disappearance of the natural habitats of various protected species of birds, insects, reptiles and plants found there. Second, it found that, despite that situation, the dossier accompanying the project made no mention of the existence of any authorisation to derogate from the measures for the conservation of protected species prescribed in the applicable legislation. Third and last, it expressed the view that the alterations which the developer planned to carry out before, during and after the construction works for with the project were not likely, given the nature and scale of the project, to mitigate or compensate for the impact on the natural habitats concerned.

20   On 1 September 2010, the competent authority of the Walloon Region invited Sagrex to submit to it amended plans and a supplementary environmental impact assessment for the project at issue in the main proceedings.

21   On 15 April 2016, Sagrex submitted to the Inspector General of the Department of Nature and Forests of the Walloon Region an application for derogation from the plant and animal species protection measures prescribed by the Law on nature conservation in connection with that project.

22   On 27 June 2016, the Inspector General adopted the derogation decision referred to in paragraph 2 above. That decision authorises Sagrex to disturb a certain number

of protected plant and animal species and to cause the deterioration or destruction of certain areas of their respective natural habitats, in connection with the project at issue in the main proceedings, provided that it implements a series of mitigation measures.

23   On 30 September 2016, Sagrex submitted to the competent authority of the Walloon Region the amended plans and supplementary assessment for the project that had been requested of it on 1 September 2010.

24   A public inquiry into the project, as amended and supplemented, was held from 21 November to 21 December 2016 and generated numerous objections relating to the impact of the project at issue on protected species and on their habitats.

25   On 21 December 2016, the Namur external management of the Department of Nature and Forests issued a favourable opinion, subject to conditions, on Sagrex's application for a single permit, in which it noted, in the first place, that the project at issue in the main proceedings partly adjoined a Natura 2000 site, but that there was no risk of any significant impact on that site. As regards, in the second place, the two sites of significant biological interest adjacent to the project, that management, first of all, considered that, absent special precautionary measures, the project was likely to have a significant impact on protected plant and animal species found there and on their respective habitats. Next, it expressed the view that, by implementing the mitigation and compensatory measures proposed by Sagrex and specified by the derogation decision, the project would not harm those species and would bring about only a progressive destruction of their respective habitats, which would moreover be offset by the development of new natural habitats. Last, it concluded that, taking all those factors into account, it could reasonably be assumed that, at the end of the 30-year operating period planned by Sagrex, the sites affected by the quarry would still be of significant biological interest, such that the environmental impact of the project at issue in the main proceedings could be regarded as having been reduced to an acceptable level.

26   By a decree of 25 September 2017, the Walloon Region's Minister for the Environment and Town and Country Planning nevertheless refused to grant the single permit for which Sagrex had applied. The action for annulment of that decree brought by Sagrex's parent company, Cimenteries CBR SA, was subsequently dismissed by a judgment of the Conseil d'État (Council of State, Belgium) of 14 May 2020.

27   In the interim, Namur-Est Environnement brought before the Council of State an application for annulment of the derogation decision, in which it argues, inter alia, that that decision is part of the development consent procedure, within the meaning of Article 1(2) of Directive 2011/92, but was not preceded by a procedure meeting the requirements referred to in Articles 2 *et seq.* of that directive. In particular, that association maintains, in essence, that, in order to meet those requirements and to enable both the public concerned to participate effectively in the procedure and the competent authority to take account of that participation, the assessment of the environmental impact of a project such as that at issue in the main proceedings and the accompanying public consultation must take place before the adoption of a measure such as the derogation decision, not afterwards, as in this case.

28   The Walloon Region counters, in substance, that the derogation decision cannot be regarded as part of the development consent procedure, as defined in Directive 2011/92, since the Inspector General of the Department of Nature and Forests of

the Walloon Region did no more than authorise Sagrex, not only in a targeted manner and prior to the assessment of the project at issue in the main proceedings by another authority but also without prejudging that assessment in any way, to derogate from the plant and animal species protective measures prescribed by the applicable legislation, in response to the interested party's application to that effect. More generally, it argues that the application for derogation and the application for a single permit also submitted by Sagrex fall under two different, albeit related, legal regimes and decision-making processes, and not the same legal regime or decision-making process.

29   Cimenteries CBR maintains also that the derogation decision is merely an ancillary measure that cannot, in itself, be regarded as amounting to development consent for the project at issue. In addition, that company considers that the assessment prescribed by Directive 2011/92 and the public consultation which must accompany it can – and indeed must – take place only after the derogation decision, in order that the public may participate usefully in the procedure and express its views on the project as fully as possible, so that the competent authority can then take full account of that participation.

30   Having weighed those various arguments, the referring court observes, first of all, in its request for a preliminary ruling, that projects such as that at issue in the main proceedings cannot receive development consent in the form of a single permit without the developer having first obtained a derogation such as that granted in the derogation decision. Consequently, the derogation decision may be regarded as a necessary prerequisite but not in itself sufficient for development consent to be granted. The referring court also states that the principal decision entitling the developer to proceed with its project is the single permit, which may, following a public inquiry, be refused or granted on conditions stricter than those contained in the derogation decision, the authority responsible for issuing that permit being required to examine all of the environmental aspects of the project and as such being in a position to assess more strictly its impact against the parameters determined by the author of the derogation decision.

31   Next, the referring court questions whether, in that legal and factual context, measures such as the derogation decision and the subsequent decision by which a developer is granted a single permit are to be regarded, taken together, as forming part of a multi-stage decision-making process the end result of which is either the grant or the refusal of development consent for a project, as defined in Directive 2011/92. Lastly, it questions whether, in the affirmative, the participation of the public concerned in that multi-stage decision-making process must be ensured before a measure such as the derogation decision is adopted or whether it may take place between that adoption and the point at which the competent authority decides on the single permit sought by the developer.

32   Regarding those latter two aspects, the referring court indicates that the legal and factual context characterising the dispute in the main proceedings appears different from the situations involving multi-stage consent procedures that have been brought before the Court until now, from the judgment of 7 January 2004, *Wells* (C-201/02) EU:C:2004:12.

33   It is in those circumstances that the Conseil d'État (Council of State, Belgium) decided to stay the proceedings and refer the following questions to the Court of Justice for a preliminary ruling:

'(1) Do a decision "authorising the disturbance of animals and degradation of the areas of habitat of those species for the working of a quarry" and the decision authorising or refusing that working (single permit) form a single development consent (within the meaning of [Article 1(2)(c)] of … [Directive 2011/92]) relating to a single project (within the meaning of [Article 1(2)(a)] of that directive) where, first, that working cannot take place without the first of those decisions and, second, the authority responsible for issuing single permits retains the ability to determine the environmental effects of that working more strictly having regard to the parameters set by the body that issued the first decision?

(2) If the answer to that first question is in the affirmative, are the requirements laid down by that directive, specifically in Articles 2, 5, 6, 7 and 8, sufficiently met where the public participation phase takes place after adoption of the decision "authorising the disturbance of animals and degradation of the areas of habitat of those species for the working of a quarry" but before adoption of the principal decision entitling the developer to proceed to work the quarry?'

The questions referred for a preliminary ruling

The first question

34   By its first question, the referring court asks, in essence, whether Directive 2011/92 must be interpreted as meaning that a decision adopted under Article 16(1) of Directive 92/43 and which authorises a developer to derogate from the applicable species protection measures in order to carry out a project within the meaning of Article 1(2)(a) of Directive 2011/92 forms part of the development consent procedure, within the meaning of Article 1(2)(c) of that directive, where, first, the project cannot be carried out without the developer having first obtained that decision and, second, the authority competent for granting development consent for such a project retains the ability to assess the project's environmental impact more strictly than was done in that decision.

Admissibility

35   In its written and oral observations, the Belgian Government has argued, in essence, that the first question should be dismissed as inadmissible on the ground that it is based on two incorrect legal premises and because the correct interpretation of the provisions of EU law and of national law which the referring court mentions leads to the conclusion that that question is manifestly unrelated to the actual facts of the main action or its purpose. It alleges that the grant of a derogation from the species protection measures prescribed by the provisions of national law transposing Directive 92/43 may be requested, under those provisions, either before or after obtaining the single permit which realises that consent, with the result that the derogation decision is not a prerequisite for obtaining a single permit, but a legally independent act. That interpretation is consistent with EU law since no provision of that law requires that a decision like the derogation decision, which grants a derogation from those measures, must necessarily precede the grant of development consent for a project such as that at issue in the main proceedings, within the meaning of Directive 2011/92.

36   In that regard, it follows from the Court's case-law, in the first place, that arguments relating to the substance of a question referred by a national court cannot, by their very nature, lead to the inadmissibility of the question (judgments of 2 March 2021, *AB (Appointment of judges to the Supreme Court—Actions)* (C-824/18) EU:C:2021:153, paragraph 80 and of 13 January 2022, *Minister Sprawiedliwości* (C-55/20) EU:C:2022:6, paragraph 83.

37   In the present case, it must be observed that a part of the Belgian Government's line of argument, summarised in paragraph 35 above, rests on an interpretation of the provisions of EU law mentioned by the referring court in its first question and that it therefore concerns the substance of that question.

38   In the second place, it is solely for the national court before which the dispute has been brought, and which must assume responsibility for the subsequent judicial decision, to determine, in the light of the particular circumstances of the case, both the need for a preliminary ruling in order to enable it to deliver judgment and the relevance of the questions which it submits to the Court (judgments of 10 December 2018, *Wightman* (C-621/18) EU:C:2018:999, paragraph 26 and of 19 December 2019, *Junqueras Vies* (C-502/19) EU:C:2019:1115, paragraph 55). Consequently, where the questions submitted concern the interpretation of EU law, the Court is in principle required to give a ruling (judgments of 24 November 2020, *Openbaar Ministerie (Forgery of documents)* (C-510/19) EU:C:2020:953, paragraph 25 and of 18 May 2021, *Asociaţia 'Forumul Judecătorilor din România'* (C-83/19), (C-127/19), (C-195/19), (C-291/19), (C-355/19) and (C-397/19) EU:C:2021:393, paragraph 115).

39   It follows that questions relating to EU law referred by the national courts enjoy a presumption of relevance and that the Court may refuse to rule on such questions only where it is quite obvious that the interpretation that is sought bears no relation to the actual facts of the main action or its purpose, where the problem is hypothetical, or where the Court does not have before it the factual or legal material necessary to give a useful answer to those questions (judgments of 10 December 2018, *Wightman* (C-621/18) EU:C:2018:999, paragraph 27 and of 19 December 2019, *Junqueras Vies* (C-502/19) EU:C:2019:1115, paragraph 56).

40   Moreover, the procedure laid down in Article 267 TFEU is based on a clear separation of functions between national courts and tribunals and the Court, the latter being empowered to rule on the interpretation or the validity of the acts of EU law referred to in that provision, taking account of the factual and legal context of the questions referred for a preliminary ruling, as described by the referring court, and not to decide whether the referring court's interpretation of provisions of national law is correct. Accordingly, a reference for a preliminary ruling cannot be examined in the light of the interpretation of national law relied on by the government of a Member State (see, to that effect, judgments of 26 September 2013, *Texdata Software* (C-418/11) EU:C:2013:588, paragraphs 28 and 29, and of 15 April 2021, *État belge (Circumstances subsequent to the transfer decision)* (C-194/19) EU:C:2021:270, paragraph 26).

41   In the present case, the first question concerns, quite clearly, the interpretation of EU law, as mentioned in paragraph 37 above. Moreover, the considerations underlying that question, summarised in paragraphs 30 to 32 above, attest both to the relevance of that question, in the specific factual context which characterises the dispute in the main proceedings, and to the need, in the referring court's opinion, for an answer from the Court.

42   Having regard to all those matters, the first question is not manifestly unrelated to the actual facts of the dispute in the main action or its purpose. Consequently, it must be held to be admissible.

Substance

43   In the first place, Article 1(2)(a) of Directive 2011/92 and Article 1(2)(c) thereof define respectively the terms 'project' and 'development consent', for the purposes of that directive, the first referring to the execution of construction works or of other installations or schemes and other interventions in the natural surroundings and landscape, the second referring to the decision of the competent authority or authorities entitling the developer to proceed with the project.

44   However, those textual elements do not in themselves enable an answer to be given to the first question, by which the referring court seeks to establish, in essence, whether a decision such as the derogation decision must – even though it does not constitute a 'decision of the competent authority or authorities which entitles the developer to proceed with the project' to which it relates – be regarded as forming part of the development consent for the project given the links it has with that decision. Admittedly, the said elements define the concept of 'development consent' by referring to a decision different in nature from the derogation decision and they exclude, consequently, that latter decision from being regarded, in isolation and as such, as amounting to a 'development consent', within the meaning of Article 1(2)(c) of Directive 2011/92, for the project to which it relates. Nevertheless, those elements do not preclude such a decision from being regarded, when taken together with the subsequent decision on the developer's entitlement to proceed with the project, as forming part of the development consent for that project or, as the case may be, of the refusal of development consent for it.

45   In those conditions, in accordance with the settled case-law of the Court, in interpreting Directive 2011/92, it is appropriate to consider not only the wording of the provisions mentioned in the two preceding paragraphs, but also the context in which they occur and the objectives pursued by the rules of which they are a part (judgments of 7 June 2005, *VEMW* (C-17/03) EU:C:2005:362, paragraph 41 and of 21 January 2021, *Germany v Esso Raffinage* (C-471/18 P) EU:C:2021:48, paragraph 81).

46   As regards, in the second place, the context in which the definitions given in points (a) and (c) of Article 1(2) of the directive occur, it must be observed, first of all, that, as is apparent from the directive as a whole, the development consent decision is meant to be taken upon the conclusion of the entire process for the assessment of projects likely to have significant effects on the environment, which are referred to in Article 2(1) of the same directive.

47   Those provisions thus make it clear that the grant of development consent for a project is the end point of a decision-making process which begins with the developer submitting an application and which, from a procedural perspective, includes each and every step that is required in order to process that application.

48   Next, those provisions show that, from a substantive rather than procedural perspective, that decision-making process must lead the competent authority to take full account of the effects that projects subject to the dual requirement for assessment and development consent laid down in Article 2(1) of Directive 2011/92

are likely to have on the environment, as the Advocate General observed in point 44 of her Opinion.

49   Thus, Article 2(1) of Directive 2011/92 refers generally to the 'significant effects on the environment' that such projects are likely to have, without referring specifically to any one type of significant effect or excluding any other type of significant effect from its scope. Similarly, Article 3 of the directive refers generally to the 'direct and indirect effects' of those projects on the environment.

50   It follows that the decision-making process instituted by Directive 2011/92 must address, in particular, the significant effects that a project subject to the directive is likely to have on the fauna and flora present in the various areas that may be affected by the project, such as the construction zone and the areas adjacent to it, as indeed has already been made clear in the Court's case-law (see, to that effect, judgment of 24 November 2011, *Commission v Spain* (C-404/09) EU:C:2011:768, paragraphs 84 to 87).

51   It is, moreover, for that reason that Article 5 of Directive 2011/92 requires the developer to supply specific information on that subject to the competent authority.

52   It follows that, in the specific case where the execution of a project subject to the dual requirement for assessment and development consent laid down in Article 2(1) of Directive 2011/92 involves the developer applying for and obtaining a derogation from the plant and animal species protection measures prescribed by the provisions of national law transposing Articles 12 and 13 of Directive 92/43 and where, consequently, the project is likely to have an impact on those species, the assessment of the project must address, in particular, that impact.

53   It is therefore irrelevant that Directive 92/43 does not itself lay down any obligation to assess the impact that that a derogation is likely to have on the species concerned, that directive being independent in scope from Directive 2011/92 and applying without prejudice to the environmental impact assessment obligation introduced by the latter directive, the scope of which is general, as is apparent from the Court's case-law (see, to that effect, judgments of 21 September 1999, *Commission v Ireland* (C-392/96) EU:C:1999:431, paragraph 71; of 31 May 2018, *Commission v Poland* (C-526/16) EU:C:2018:356, paragraph 72; and of 12 June 2019, *CFE* (C-43/18) EU:C:2019:483, paragraph 52).

54   Lastly, it becomes clear on considering the context of the provisions mentioned by the referring court in its first question that the assessment of the environmental impact of a given project may take place not only in the course of the procedure leading to the development consent decision referred to in Article 1(2)(c) of Directive 2011/92, but also in the course of a procedure leading to a decision prior to that development consent decision, in which case those various decisions may be regarded as forming part of a complex decision-making process in that it is carried out in several stages (see, by analogy, judgments of 7 January 2004, *Wells* (C-201/02) EU:C:2004:12, paragraphs 47, 52 and 53, and of 17 March 2011, *Brussels Hoofdstedelijk Gewest* (C-275/09) EU:C:2011:154, paragraph 32).

55   Article 2(2) of Directive 2011/92 expressly provides that that environmental impact assessment may be integrated into existing national consent procedures, which implies, first, that that assessment need not necessarily be conducted in the context of a procedure specially created for that purpose and, second, that it need not necessarily be conducted in the course of single procedure.

56   The Member States therefore have a discretion enabling them to determine the procedural conditions under which that assessment is to be conducted and to

apportion the various competences relating to that assessment among several different authorities, in particular by conferring on each of them decision-making powers in the matter, as the Court has already observed (see, to that effect, judgment of 3 March 2011, *Commission v Ireland* (C-50/09) EU:C:2011:109, paragraphs 72 to 74).

57   Nevertheless, that discretion must be exercised in accordance with the requirements laid down by Directive 2011/92 and in full compliance with the directive's aims (judgment of 3 March 2011, *Commission v Ireland* (C-50/09) EU:C:2011:109, paragraph 75).

58   It is important to note in this connection, first, that the environmental impact assessment of a project must, in any event, be a full assessment and must take place before a development consent decision is taken with regard to the project (see, to that effect, judgment of 3 March 2011, *Commission v Ireland* (C-50/09) EU:C:2011:109, paragraphs 76 and 77).

59   It follows that, where a Member State confers power to assess some of the environmental effects of a project and to take a decision upon the conclusion of that partial assessment on an authority other than the one on which it confers power to give development consent for the project, that decision must necessarily be adopted before development consent is given. If it were otherwise, the development consent would be given on an incomplete basis and would not, therefore, meet the applicable requirements (see, to that effect, judgment of 3 March 2011, *Commission v Ireland* (C-50/09) EU:C:2011:109, paragraphs 81 and 84).

60   Second, it follows expressly from Article 3 of Directive 2011/92 that the obligation to carry out a full assessment of the environmental effects of a project, mentioned in paragraphs 48 and 58 above, means that account must be taken not only of each of those effects taken individually, but also of the interaction between them, and thus of the project's overall impact on the environment. Similarly, Annex IV to Directive 2011/92 requires the developer to provide information, inter alia, on the interrelationship between the effects that a project may simultaneously have on various aspects of the environment, such as fauna and flora.

61   That overall assessment may lead the competent authority to conclude that, having regard to the interaction or interrelationship between the various environmental effects of a project, those effects must be assessed more strictly or, as the case may be, less strictly than one or other effect, considered in isolation, has been assessed beforehand.

62   It follows that, where a Member State confers the power to assess some of the environmental effects of a project and to take a decision upon the conclusion of that partial assessment on an authority other than the one on which it confers the power to give development consent for the project, that partial assessment must not prejudge the overall assessment that the authority competent for granting development consent must in any event carry out and that preliminary decision must not prejudge the decision adopted on the conclusion of the overall assessment, as the Advocate General essentially observed in points 73 and 74 of her Opinion.

63   In the present case, the information given in the order for reference, and in particular that summarised in paragraph 30 above, and the wording of the first question indicate that those requirements have been observed, subject to the checks to be carried out by the referring court. Indeed, they make it apparent, first, that development consent for a project such as that at issue in the main action cannot be given without the project developer having obtained a decision authorising it

to derogate from the applicable species protection measures, which means that decision must necessarily be adopted prior to that development consent. Second, the authority competent for granting development consent retains the ability to assess the environmental impact of the project more strictly than was done in the derogation decision.

64   Lastly, in the third place, as regards the objectives pursued by Directive 2011/92, and in particular its essential objective of ensuring a high level of protection of the environment and of human health by laying down minimum requirements for the assessment of the environmental impact of projects, the interpretation which emerges from the contextual elements considered in paragraphs 46 to 63 above contributes to the attainment of such an objective, by enabling the Member States to entrust a given authority with the responsibility for adopting a preliminary, focussed decision on certain environmental effects of projects subject to assessment, while reserving to the authority competent for granting development consent the task of conducting a full and final assessment of the project.

65   Indeed, if the outcome of that partial assessment is negative, the developer may then either abandon its project, without having to continue with the complex assessment and consent procedure instituted by Directive 2011/92, or modify the project in such a way as to remedy the negative effects highlighted by the partial assessment, leaving it to the competent authority to take the final decision on the modified project. Conversely, if the outcome is positive, the authority will be free to take account of the decision previously taken, even though it does not bind it in its final assessment or with regard to the legal consequences to be drawn from that final assessment. The existence of a partial assessment giving rise to a preliminary decision is thus liable to constitute, in all cases, a factor of quality, effectiveness and increased consistency of the assessment and consent procedure.

66   In the light of all the foregoing considerations, the answer to the first question is that Directive 2011/92 must be interpreted as meaning that a decision adopted under Article 16(1) of Directive 92/43 and which authorises a developer to derogate from the applicable species protection measures in order to carry out a project within the meaning of Article 1(2)(a) of Directive 2011/92 forms part of the development consent procedure, within the meaning of Article 1(2)(c) of that directive, where, first, the project cannot be carried out without the developer having first obtained that decision and, secondly, the authority competent for granting development consent for such a project retains the ability to assess the project's environmental impact more strictly than was done in that decision.

The second question

67   By its second question, which is asked should its first question be answered in the affirmative, the referring court asks, in essence, whether Directive 2011/92 must be interpreted, having regard in particular to Articles 6 and 8 thereof, as meaning that the adoption of a preliminary decision authorising a developer to derogate from the applicable species protection measures in order to carry out a project, within the meaning of Article 1(2)(a) of that directive, need not necessarily be preceded by public participation, provided that such participation is ensured before the adoption of the decision to be taken by the competent authority for the possible development consent for the project.

68   In this connection, Article 6 of Directive 2011/92 provides, in paragraphs 2 and 3 thereof, that a set of information relating to projects subject to the dual requirement for assessment and development consent introduced by that directive must be communicated to the public or made available to it, depending on the case, 'early in the … decision-making procedures … and, at the latest, as soon as information can reasonably be provided'. That article also states, in paragraph 4 thereof, that 'the public concerned shall be given early and effective opportunities to participate in the … decision-making procedures … and shall, for that purpose, be entitled to express comments and opinions when all options are open to the competent authority or authorities before the decision on the request for development consent is taken'.

69   For its part, Article 8 of that directive states that the results of consultations and the information gathered, inter alia, as a result of public participation, are to be taken into account by the competent authority when deciding whether or not to grant development consent for the project concerned.

70   As follows from those provisions, they require the Member States to take the necessary measures to ensure that, in the course of the procedure for assessing and granting consent for projects subject to Directive 2011/92, public participation takes place in accordance with a set of requirements.

71   First of all, both the communication to the public or the making available to the public of the information which is to serve as a basis for that participation and the opportunity for the public to express comments and opinions on that information and, more generally, on the project concerned and its environmental impact, must occur at an early stage and, in any event, before a decision is taken on whether to grant development consent for the project.

72   Secondly, that participation must be effective, which means that the public should be able to express views on the project concerned and its environmental impact not only in a useful and comprehensive manner, but also at a juncture when all options are open.

73   Third, the results of that public participation must be taken into account by the competent authority when deciding whether or not to grant development consent for the project concerned.

74   It may, however, prove more difficult to reconcile those various requirements in the context of a multi-stage decision-making process, depending on the different stages of the process and the distribution of competences among the various authorities called upon to take part in it.

75   Such is the case, in particular, where a given authority is called upon to assess, at a preliminary or intermediate stage of such a decision-making process, only some of the environmental effects of the project concerned. In such a case, public participation may be confined to the part of the environmental effects of the project which fall within that authority's competence, to the exclusion not only of those which do not, but also of the interaction or interrelationship between them.

76   In such a situation, it should be considered that the requirement of early public participation in the decision-making process must be interpreted and applied in a manner which accommodates the equally important requirement of effective public participation in the process.

77   On this point, it follows from the Court's settled case-law that, where a project is the subject of a decision-making process that is carried out in several stages and involves the adoption of, first, a principal decision and, subsequently, an implementing decision, the obligation imposed by Directive 2011/92 to assess the

environmental impact of the project must, in principle, be discharged before the principal decision is adopted, except where it is impossible to identify and assess all of the effects on the environment at that stage, in which case a global impact assessment must be carried out before the implementing decision is adopted (judgments of 7 January 2004, *Wells* (C-201/02) EU:C:2004:12, paragraphs 52 and 53, of 28 February 2008, *Abraham* (C-2/07) EU:C:2008:133, paragraph 26, and of 29 July 2019, *Inter-Environnement Wallonie and Bond Beter Leefmilieu Vlaanderen* (C-411/17) EU:C:2019:622, paragraphs 85 and 86).

78   The requirement for public participation set out by that directive is intimately linked with that obligation to conduct an assessment, as follows from paragraphs 47 and 68 above.

79   In view of that link, it must be considered, by analogy, that, in the situation described in paragraph 75 above, the requirement of early participation of the public in the decision-making process provided for in Article 6 of Directive 2011/92 does not mean that the adoption of a preliminary decision relating to some of the project's effects on the environment must be preceded by public participation, provided that that participation is effective, a requirement which implies, first, that it takes place before the adoption of the decision to be taken by the competent authority on development consent for that project, secondly, that it enables the public to express its views in a useful and comprehensive manner on all the environmental effects of that project and, third, that the authority competent for granting consent for the project may take full account of that participation.

80   It is for the national court alone to verify that those conditions have been met in this instance and thus that the public was able to express its views, in a useful and comprehensive manner, on all the environmental effects of the project at issue in the main proceedings between the date of adoption of the preliminary decision that authorised the developer to derogate from the applicable species protection measures, with a view to carrying out that project, and the date at which the authority competent for granting development consent for the project announced its decision.

81   In the light of all the foregoing considerations, the answer to the second question is that Directive 2011/92 must be interpreted, having regard in particular to Articles 6 and 8 thereof, as meaning that the adoption of a preliminary decision authorising a developer to derogate from the applicable species protection measures in order to carry out a project, within the meaning of Article 1(2)(a) of that directive, need not necessarily be preceded by public participation, provided that such participation is effectively ensured before the adoption of the decision to be taken by the competent authority for the possible development consent for the project.

Costs

82   Since these proceedings are, for the parties to the main proceedings, a step in the action pending before the national court, the decision on costs is a matter for that court. Costs incurred in submitting observations to the Court, other than the costs of those parties, are not recoverable.

On those grounds, the Court (Third Chamber) hereby rules:

1. Directive 2011/92/EU of the European Parliament and of the Council of 13 December 2011 on the assessment of the effects of certain public and private

projects on the environment must be interpreted as meaning that a decision adopted under Article 16(1) of Council Directive 92/43/EEC of 21 May 1992 on the conservation of natural habitats and of wild fauna and flora and which authorises a developer to derogate from the applicable species protection measures in order to carry out a project within the meaning of Article 1(2)(a) of Directive 2011/92 forms part of the development consent procedure, within the meaning of Article 1(2)(c) of that directive, where, first, the project cannot be carried out without the developer having first obtained that decision and, second, the authority competent for granting development consent for such a project retains the ability to assess the project's environmental impact more strictly than was done in that decision.

2. Directive 2011/92 must be interpreted, having regard in particular to Articles 6 and 8 thereof, as meaning that the adoption of a preliminary decision authorising a developer to derogate from the applicable species protection measures in order to carry out a project, within the meaning of Article 1(2)(a) of that directive, need not necessarily be preceded by public participation, provided that such participation is effectively ensured before the adoption of the decision to be taken by the competent authority for the possible development consent for the project.

R. (ON THE APPLICATION OF TARIAN HAFREN SEVERN SHIELD CYF) v MARINE MANAGEMENT ORGANISATION

QUEEN'S BENCH DIVISION (ADMINISTRATIVE COURT)

Holgate J: 24 March 2022

[2022] EWHC 683 (Admin); [2023] Env. L.R. 2

⊂ Dredging; Licence conditions; Marine licences; Nationally significant infrastructure projects; Nuclear installations; Reasons; Ultra vires; Variation; Waste disposal; Water pollution

H1   *Marine conservation—marine licensing—Marine and Coastal Access Act 2009 s.72—variations to marine licensesdredging—re-disposal of contaminated sediment—varying licence to include activities not included within original licence— whether power to vary licence to include new activities—whether duty to provide reasons for variation—waste hierarchy—'good surface water' status—whether variations of marine licence had taken into account requirement to meet waste hierarchy and good surface water status*

H2   The Interested Party, HPC, was the developer and promoter of the Hinkley Point C nuclear power station project. In October 2011, HPC applied for a development consent order under the Planning Act 2008, to authorise the construction of the power station. The Order was approved and came into force in April 2013. The project involved various activities which required licensing from the Defendant MMO as the appropriate licensing authority. In June 2013, MMO granted a licence authorising (amongst other things) the dredging of waste materials from one area to be deposited at a waste disposal site lying within the Severn estuary. The MMO granted a series of four variations to the original licence between 2014–19. In December 2019, MMO granted a fifth variation to the original licence to cover three activities which had not been authorised previously.

H3   The Claimant THSS was a company formed by a group of concerned individuals to oppose the dumping of dredged materials from the Hinkley Point C project back into the Severn. The primary concern was that the dredged material contained fine radioactive particles which raised a risk of low levels of radiation.

H4   In December 2020, HPC applied for a sixth variation of the original licence. The proposals sought to carry forward activities authorised by the original licence alongside further activities which had not been authorised previously, but which were considered necessary because of an evolving design of the project. In August 2021, MMO issued a notice approving the variation to the original licence. THSS sought to challenge that approval. THSS argued:

(1) That the power to vary a licence 'for any other reason that appears to the authority to be relevant' under s.72 of the Marine and Coastal Access Act 2009 (the 2009 Act) could not be used to authorise a wholly different activity which had not been previously authorised by that licence. The addition of a new activity was a wholly different or new activity which could only be authorised by a fresh licence.

(2) If the power to vary under s.72 of the 2009 Act covered previously unauthorised activities, such a power could only be exercised if the MMO considered that they had a relevant reason for doing so. Where such a reason existed, the MMO were under a legal obligation to identify that reason. The MMO did not have, or failed to identify a reason for their use of the power to vary the original licence.

(3) In varying the original licence, the MMO failed to apply the waste hierarchy set out in the Waste Framework Directive, art.4(1) and Waste (England and Wales) Regulations 2011.

(4) In varying the licence, the MMO failed to consider whether the proposals jeopardised the attainment of 'good surface water status' under the Water Framework Directive 2006/60, art.4(1).

H5 **Held,** in refusing the application:

H6 (1) The changes to the marine licence in the instant case fell well within the legal concept of a variation under the 2009 Act. As a matter of ordinary English, a variation could widen the scope of a marine licence, and there was nothing in the language of the 2009 Act to indicate that the power to vary under s.72 could not be used to enlarge the scope of a marine licence. The Act explicitly recognised the need for the content and engineering of a project, particularly one of a complex nature, to continue to evolve after the MMO first granted a licence for marine activities. Ultimately, the language used by Parliament did not exclude the authorisation under s.72 of a marine activity which had not previously been authorised under the licence in question, so long as that activity could properly be said to represent a variation of that licence. What might qualify as a variation would be affected by the terms of the original licence (including its conditions); the nature and extent of the activities already authorised and any previous variations; and the nature and extent of the proposed addition to the licence. It would also be relevant to consider the nature of the project to which the marine licence related, or any other relevant statutory authorisation, for example an authorisation referred to in the marine licence or which formed part of the context for the licence. Those considerations might involve matters of judgement which Parliament had entrusted to the MMO and which it was well-qualified to assess.

H7 (2) Section 72 of the 2009 Act did not impose an obligation to give reasons where the ground for exercising the power to vary fell within the terms of s.72(a)–(c) itself and the position was no different under the broad principles found in s.72(3)(d). In the instant case, it was plain that the MMO lawfully considered that the licence should be varied for reasons that appeared relevant. Parliament had identified the matters set out in s.72(3)(a)–(c) as being sufficient to be the basis for the exercise of the power to vary, suspend or revoke a licence, but had not considered it appropriate to set down an exhaustive list of such matters. The MMO was instead allowed to have regard to additional matters it considered relevant. If the MMO did not have what it considered to be a relevant reason, the power in s.72(3)(d) would not be engaged. The language of that provision guarded against any attempt to exercise the power in an arbitrary manner for no reason at all. That should not, however, be treated as giving rise to a duty to provide reasons for the decision.

H8   (3) The relevant section of the DCO and the relevant policy document, the South West Marine Plan (SWMP) dealt with 'preparing for re-use' of the dredged sediment—as required under the second tier of the waste hierarchy. The documents stated that proposals for the sustainable relocation of dredged material involved relocating the dredged material back into the system that it was removed from to maintain the sediment budget of the system. This could be carried out if the relevant material was in an appropriate condition and it was the best option for the system. The MMO had determined that the material was in an 'appropriate condition'. Thus, what was required fell within the second tier of the waste hierarchy, 'preparing for re-use', because the disposal was necessary to maintain sediment budget of the system. The dredging was already authorised by the marine licence and that had not been challenged. Given that the disposal (or rather relocation back into the system) was for a purpose falling within the second tier of the waste hierarchy, there was no need for the MMO to make any further assessment against lower tiers in the hierarchy.

H9   (4) The 'good status' objective was properly taken into account in the assessment by HPC and the MMO. There was nothing in art.4(1) of the Water Framework Directive or in related case law to suggest that a regulatory approval must be refused unless the project would contribute (e.g. positively) towards the attainment of a good surface water status or good chemical status. There was no indication that, for example, a proposal must contribute to that objective by reducing existing chemical levels which caused the current status of the water body to be less than 'good'.

H10 **Cases referred to:**
Cusack v Harrow LBC [2013] UKSC 40; [2013] 1 W.L.R. 2022; [2013] R.T.R. 26
DB Symmetry Ltd v Swindon BC [2020] EWCA Civ 1331; [2021] P.T.S.R. 432; [2021] J.P.L. 683
Dover DC v Campaign to Protect Rural England (Kent) [2017] UKSC 79; [2018] 1 W.L.R. 108; [2018] Env. L.R. 17
Edinburgh City Council v Secretary of State for Scotland [1997] 1 W.L.R. 1447; [1998] J.P.L. 224; 1998 S.C. (H.L.) 33 HL(SC)
Jones v Mordue [2015] EWCA Civ 1243; [2016] 1 W.L.R. 2682; [2016] J.P.L. 476
Lambeth LBC v Secretary of State for Housing, Communities and Local Government [2019] UKSC 33; [2019] 1 W.L.R. 4317; [2019] P.T.S.R. 1388
Leeds City Council v RG [2007] EWHC 1612 (Admin); [2007] 1 W.L.R. 3025; (2008) 172 J.P.N. 55
Owners of the SS Magnhild v MacIntyre Bros & Co [1920] 3 K.B. 321; (1920) 4 Ll. L. Rep. 130 KBD
R. (on the application of Keir) v Natural England [2021] EWHC 1059 (Admin); [2022] Env. L.R. 3
R. (on the application of Langley) v Preston Crown Court [2008] EWHC 2623 (Admin); [2009] 1 W.L.R. 1612; [2009] C.P. Rep. 11

R. (on the application of Mott) v Environment Agency [2016] EWCA Civ 564; [2016] 1 W.L.R. 4338; [2017] Env. L.R. 1

R. (on the application of Plan B Earth) v Secretary of State for Transport [2020] EWCA Civ 214; [2020] P.T.S.R. 1446; [2020] J.P.L. 1005

R. (on the application of Powell) v Marine Management Organisation [2017] EWHC 1491 (Admin); [2017] L.L.R. 808

R. (on the application of Spurrier) v Secretary of State for Transport [2019] EWHC 1070 (Admin); [2020] P.T.S.R. 240; [2019] J.P.L. 1163

R. (on the application of Swire) v Canterbury City Council [2022] EWHC 390 (Admin); [2022] J.P.L. 1026

Sharp v North Essex Magistrates' Court [2017] EWCA Civ 1143; [2017] 1 W.L.R. 3789; [2018] Env. L.R. 4

UBB Waste Essex Ltd v Essex CC [2019] EWHC 1924 (Admin)

H11 **Legislation referred to:**

Interpretation Act 1978 s.6

Directive 2000/60 (Water Framework)

Planning and Compulsory Purchase Act 2004 ss.38 and 73

Hinckley and Bosworth (Parish Electoral Arrangements) Order 2007 (SI 2007/151)

Marine Works (Environmental Impact Assessment) Regulations 2007 (SI 2007/1518) regs 2(1), 4(c), 12, 16, 21A and 22

Planning Act 2008 ss.98, 118 and 120

Directive 2008/98 (Waste Framework) art.4(1)

Directive 2008/105 (Water Quality Standards)

Marine and Coastal Access Act 2009 ss.2(2)(3), 49, 65(1), 66(1), 67, 68(1)(3)(4), 69(1)(3), 70, 71(1)(2)(3), 72(1)(3)(7), 72A, 72A(2)(9), 73(3), 78 and 85(1), Pt 4

Marine Licensing (Delegation of Functions) Order 2011 (SI 2011/627) art.5

Marine Licensing (Licence Application Appeals) Regulations 2011 (SI 2011/934) regs 4, 5, 12, 15 and 22, Pt 5

Marine Licensing (Notices Appeals) Regulations 2011 (SI 2011/936) regs 3(1)(2) and 5(1)(2)

Waste (England and Wales) Regulations 2011 (SI 2011/988) reg.22

Hinkley Point C (Nuclear Generating Station) Order 2013 (SI 2013/648)

Environment (Wales) Act 2016

Water Environment (Water Framework Directive) (England and Wales) Regulations 2017 (SI 2017/407) reg.3(1)

Conservation of Habitats and Species Regulations 2017 (SI 2017/1012)

H12 *D. Wolfe QC* and *G. Thomas* (instructed by Leigh Day) appeared on behalf of the Claimant.

S. Blackmore and *M. Dale-Harris* (instructed by Browne Jacobson) appeared on behalf of the Defendant.

J. Strachan QC and *V. Hutton* (instructed by Eversheds Sutherland) appeared on behalf of the Interested Party.

JUDGMENT

MR. JUSTICE HOLGATE:

Introduction

1   The main issue in this claim is whether the power to vary a marine licence under the Marine and Coastal Act 2009 ("MCAA 2009") cannot be used to license a "marine licensable activity" which has not already been included in the licence being varied. The claimant says that the power of variation cannot be used to license what it describes as a "new activity". That may only properly be authorised by the grant of a new marine licence. The claimant's challenge is to the variation approved by the defendant, the Marine Management Organisation ("MMO") on 2 August 2021.

2   The claimant is a company incorporated on 7 October 2021 by a group of scientists, organisations and individuals to oppose the disposal of material dredged from the Severn Estuary as part of the Hinkley Point C project back into the Severn. A number of the people involved in the company have opposed works of the same type going back to the grant of a marine licence in 2014. The claimant is concerned that the material dredged contains fine radioactive particles, involving a risk of low levels of radiation.

3   NNB Generation Company (HPC) Limited ("HPC"), the Interested Party, is the promoter of the Hinkley Point C nuclear power station project. In October 2011 it made an application for a development consent order ("DCO") under the Planning Act 2008 ("PA 2008") to authorise the construction of the station as a "nationally significant infrastructure project". The Panel conducted a statutory examination into that application between March and September 2012. They submitted their report to the Secretary of State for Energy and Climate Change on 19 December 2012. The Secretary of State issued his decision letter granting development consent on 18 March 2013. The order was made as SI 2013 No. 648 and came into force on 9 April 2013. There was an opportunity to challenge the order under s.118 of the PA 2008, subject to a 6 week time limit.

4   The project involves a number of activities or works which are required to be licensed by a marine licence granted under the MCAA 2009. The Secretary of State for Environment, Food and Rural Affairs is the "appropriate licensing authority" for the purposes of marine licensing under Part 4 of the MCAA 2009. However, by The Marine Licensing (Delegation of Functions) Order 2011 (SI 2011 No. 627) ("the 2011 Order") the Secretary of State has delegated to the MMO certain functions under Part 4, including the determination of applications for a marine licence and the variation of such licences. The MMO exercises those functions as a delegate acting on behalf of the Secretary of State (see s.98(1)(b) of the MCAA 2009 and articles 3 and 4 of the 2011 Order).

5   In June 2012 HPC applied to the MMO for the grant of a marine licence for marine works related to the project. On 7 June 2013 the MMO granted that licence ("the original licence"). The licence recorded the proposal for the material it authorised to be dredged at Bridgwater Bay (about 5km north of Bridgwater, Somerset) to be disposed of at the Cardiff Grounds licensed disposal site, also lying within the Severn Estuary, but located about 3km off the South Wales coast. That disposal fell outside the territorial jurisdiction of the MMO, but inside that of the

Welsh Ministers. On 11 July 2014 a separate marine licence was granted by Natural Resource Wales ("NRW") on behalf of the Welsh Ministers for disposal of the dredged material at the Cardiff Grounds site ("the NRW licence").

6   The MMO granted a series of four variations to the original licence in 2014, 2016, 2017 and 2019.

7   On 20 December 2019 the MMO granted a fifth variation of the original licence ("version 6"). This licence included three types of activity at Combwich Wharf within the River Parrett which had not been authorised by the original licence or earlier variations (e.g. capital dredging, maintenance dredging and desilting).

8   Neither the original licence, nor any of the first to fifth variations thereof, were the subject of judicial review.

9   In April 2020 HPC entered into discussions with the MMO regarding an application they intended to make for a further variation of the marine licence. In August 2020 HPC raised the possibility of using the already designated disposal site at Portishead, in the Bristol Channel, not far from the Somerset coast. The site has an area of about 200 ha. In August 2020 the MMO identified the nature of the additional information they would require and said that the proposed variation would have to be the subject of environmental impact assessment under the Marine Works (Environmental Impact Assessment) Regulations 2007 (SI 2007 No.1518) ("the EIA Regulations 2007").

10   On 20 August 2020 HPC submitted a scoping request to the MMO in respect of the further EIA work. On 17 September 2020 the MMO issued its scoping opinion.

11   On 21 December 2020 HPC submitted its application for a sixth variation of the marine licence granted in 2013. The proposal sought to carry forward activities authorised by the original licence or earlier revisions thereof (with or without updates resulting from detailed design work). It also proposed further activities, that is activities not previously authorised in earlier iterations of the licence, but now considered necessary because of the evolution of the detailed design. By way of example, the application proposed updated dredging details for the cooling water intakes and outfalls and, as a new matter, disposal of the dredged material at Portishead. It is that disposal which the claimant seeks to challenge in these proceedings.

12   The application was supported by *inter alia* the following documents issued in February 2021: -

> • a Report to support the variation of the licence;
> • an Environmental Statement on the disposal of dredged material at the Portishead disposal site;
> • a Water Framework Directive Assessment for the disposal of dredged material at the Portishead site.

HPC also submitted a Habitats Regulations Assessment ("HRA") for the purposes of the Conservation of Habitats and Species Regulations (SI 2017 No.1012) ("the Habitats Regulations") in relation to effects of the proposal on *inter alia* the Severn Estuary Special Area of Conservation ("SAC").

13   On 12 February 2021 the MMO sent the application and supporting reports to public authority consultees, notably NRW, Natural England ("NE"), the Environment Agency ("EA"), Devon and Severn Inshore Fisheries and Conservation Authority ("D&S IFCA"), North Somerset Council ("NSC") and Portishead Town

Council ("PTC"). In addition, because the proposal was an EIA application, it had to be publicised in two local newspapers, allowing a public consultation period of 6 weeks from 19 February 2021 (regulation 16 of the EIA Regulations 2007).

14   The MMO also sent the application documents to their independent consultants ABPmer for review. The consultants responded on 9 March 2021. They stated that they had not found "any significant marine water or sediment quality, marine ecology or navigation issues" with the proposed use of the Portishead site. But they provided a number of detailed criticisms of and comments upon the application documents.

15   In April 2021 HPC issued a Supplemental Environmental Information Report and an Addendum to the Environmental Statement responding to comments which had been made.

16   NE, the EA and NRW raised no objections to the proposal. NE and NRW agreed with the HRA carried out by the MMO.

17   On 31 July 2021 the MMO issued a decision granting EIA consent for the proposal in accordance with regulations 4(c), 21A and 22 of the EIA Regulations 2007.

18   On 2 August 2021 the MMO issued its notice pursuant to s.72(3)(d) of the MCAA 2009, approving the variation of the licence sought by HPC. This is the decision challenged by the claimant in these proceedings.

The Project Works

19   Mr. Guy Buckenham is the Head of Strategic and Emerging Markets Policy and Regulation Limited for HPC's parent company, EDF Energy Limited. He explains that the project forms an essential part of the UK's strategy for low-carbon energy infrastructure. Existing nuclear power stations produce 20% of the country's electricity, but by 2030 all but one of those will be closed. Hinkley Point C will make the UK less reliant on energy imports and more resilient to shortages caused by low wind conditions. Compared to a gas generation alternative, the project would avoid 9 million tonnes of carbon dioxide emissions for each year of full operation over a 60-year life span.

20   Hinkley Point C will have the capacity to produce 1.6 GW per reactor unit, or 3.2 GW in total. The dates for commercial operation are currently scheduled as 26 June 2026 for Unit 1 and 26 June 2027 for Unit 2.

21   Mr. Jonathan Smith is the Balance Plant Area Delivery Director for the scheme. He explains that it is one of the largest and most technologically complex construction projects in the UK, involving more than £20bn of contracts and 6000 people employed across the country. Construction began in 2016.

22   When in operation, the heat produced in the two pressurised water reactors will be used to convert water in separate circuits into pressurised steam to turn the turbines and generate electricity. Large volumes of water will need to be taken from the Bristol Channel via further separate circuits to cool and condense the steam for reuse. There will be two intake tunnels, one for each reactor unit and a combined outfall tunnel to return water to the Estuary after it has been used to cool the steam. The two intake tunnels will extend 3.3km into the Bristol Channel and be located 33m under the seabed. Each will be 6m wide. They are designed to be capable of bringing in water from the Severn at a rate of 132,000 litres of water a

second. The outfall tunnel is 7m in diameter and extends 2km into the Bristol Channel.

23   Areas of the seabed have been dredged to create pits so that gravel beds maybe laid to accommodate substantial head structures, four intake heads and two outfall heads. Six vertical shafts will be drilled down through the seabed to connect each of these head structures with the respective intake and outfall tunnels. The intake heads are each 44m long, 8m high and weigh about 5,000 tonnes. The outfall heads are each 16m long, 8m high and weigh about 2,500 tonnes.

24   Two types of dredging are involved. "Capital" dredging refers to the removal of sediment for the carrying out of project works, in this instance the creation of the six pits for the heads. "Maintenance" dredging refers to the removal of sediment or silt that accumulates over a period of time, for example between the carrying out of two stages of the project.

25   This case is solely concerned with the disposal of sediment dredged in the six pit areas at the locations of the six head structures. It is necessary to relate this work to the relevant activities authorised by the marine licences.

26   The original marine licence granted in 2013 authorised a number of licensable activities. Activity 1.1 authorised dredging at six locations to prepare for the construction works, including placement of the intake and outfall head structures. This comprised capital dredging and any maintenance dredging needed before the installation of the heads. Activity 1.1 specifically stated that the dredged material would be disposed of at Cardiff Grounds, subject to obtaining a marine licence from NRW.

27   Activity 1.2 authorised the drilling of the six vertical shafts and the installation of liners. Activity 1.3 authorised the deposition, or disposal, of the drill arisings from the six shafts on the seabed. Activity 1.4 authorised disposal below the sea bed of the three machines used to bore the intake and outfall tunnels.

28   Activity 1.5 authorised the preparation of the site for, and the installation of, the four intake heads and two outfall heads above the vertical shafts, together with any maintenance dredging necessary to remove any build-up of silt following the initial dredging under activity 1.1.

29   In 2018 initial capital dredging works were carried out for the four intake and two outfall pits. This involved the removal of 57,000m³ of material which was disposed of at the Cardiff Grounds pursuant to a further licence granted by NRW in 2018.

30   The fifth licence variation was granted by the MMO in 2019. This sub-divided the dredging originally labelled as activity 1.1. Now activity 1.1 refers to capital dredging and increases the amount of material involved. Activity 1.2 refers to maintenance dredging and states that "the maintenance dredge material" will be disposed of at "the Cardiff Grounds licensed disposal site, *unless otherwise agreed by the MMO*" (emphasis added). This implies that that disposal may take place within the territorial area covered by the MMO.

31   The sixth variation approved by the MMO on 2 August 2021, the decision the subject of this challenge, contains more details on the capital and maintenance dredging under activities 1.1. and 1.2. The maximum volumes were increased. Mr. Smith explains that the design had evolved from that used for the initial dredging works in 2018. For example, the pits had been reshaped and enlarged. The intake pits had been widened, the outfall pits joined and the profiles altered. Activities 1.1 and 1.2 were also varied so as to refer to disposal entirely at the Portishead site

or at the Cardiff Grounds site. Disposal would be to one or other of the two locations, but not to both.

32   Condition 5.2.30 of the sixth variation of the licence prohibits capital dredging and related disposal outside the period July to November 2021 without the agreement of the MMO. Condition 5.2.34 prohibits maintenance dredging and related disposal outside the period July to November 2021 and April to September 2022. These are referred to as "weather windows". They also protect "sensitive mobile receptors" within the Estuary.

33   Activity 4.1 refers for the first time to use of the Portishead disposal site. It authorises disposal of both capital and maintenance dredged material during the weather windows set out in the conditions.

34   HPC had planned that during the 2021 window not only the dredging but also the laying of the gravel beds and the installation of the heads would be completed. However, because of a delay in obtaining approval of the variation, the work could not begin until 7 August 2021. It was only possible to complete the dredging works during that window. A total of 242,000m^3 of material was dredged, comprising 209,000m^3 of capital dredging and 33,000m^3 of maintenance dredging. Of this material only 132,387m^3 needed to be disposed of at Portishead because of overflow losses, propeller wash and re-suspension (para.17 of Mr. Smith's witness statement).

35   Over the last winter some silt has built up in the pits which have been dredged. Mr. Smith estimates that there remains less than 150,000m^3 of such material to be removed as maintenance dredging. It must be removed before the gravel beds can be laid and the heads installed in each of the six pits. He explains that this work needs to start in April 2022 and be completed in the 2022 window. The boring and lining of the intake and outfall tunnels is expected to be completed by the second quarter of 2022. The heads are to be connected to those tunnels by the vertical shafts which will be drilled in 2023. It is anticipated that each generating unit's cooling water pumping station and open forebay receiving the intake tunnels will be completed by July 2024. That is said to be key to the commissioning of the power station.

36   The MMO and HPC describe the Portishead site as an established, "highly dispersive" disposal site. That has not been disputed by the claimant in these proceedings. Mr. Chris Fayers, the Head of Environment in the Safety and Regulation Department of HPC, explains in paragraphs 10 and 14 of his witness statement that: -

   (i)   Bristol Ports Company has a marine licence authorising disposal of up to 1.2m wet tonnes of dredged material a year at Portishead. Between 2014 and 2016 their average disposal was 936,000 wet tonnes a year. But this has reduced to between 2,500 and 180,000 wet tonnes a year between 2017 and 2019;

   (ii)   There is capacity for additional disposal of dredged material at Portishead;

   (iii)   The capital dredging for the works on the intake and outfall pits and the disposal of that material at Portishead has concluded, "resulting in its dispersal with the Severn Estuary SAC. That is irreversible".

These matters have not been challenged by the claimant.

37   There is no challenge to the authorisation of the maintenance dredging of the silt which has recently built up in the pits already created and which now needs to

be removed. In practice the only currently licensed activity which would be affected by this judicial review is the disposal of that silt.

The Grounds of Challenge

38   The claimant has refined its grounds of challenge over time. I summarise the grounds as presented at the hearing: -

> **Ground 1**
> The decision on 2 August 2021 to vary the marine licence was ultra vires the MCAA 2009 and, in particular s.72. The power to vary may not be used to add a wholly different activity which was not previously authorised by that licence. Here the licence being varied had not authorised disposal of dredged material. The addition of that disposal was a wholly different or new activity which could not be authorised by a variation of the existing licence. Instead, that activity could only lawfully be authorised by a fresh licence granted under s.71. The MMO's power in s.72(3)(d) to vary a licence "for any other reason that appears to the authority to be relevant" may not be relied upon to authorise a new or wholly different activity.
>
> **Ground 2**
> However, if ground 1 should fail, and the power to vary under s.72(3)(d) may be used to authorise an activity not previously authorised by the licence being varied, that power may only be exercised if the MMO considers that they have a relevant reason for doing so. The MMO are under a legal obligation to identify that reason. In this case the MMO did not have, or they failed to identify, a reason for their use of the power under s.72(3)(d). Neither a proposal made by a licensee in an application to the MMO, nor the content of such a proposal, can constitute a legally adequate reason for the exercise of that power.
>
> **Ground 4**
> In deciding to vary the licence, the MMO failed to comply with regulation 22 of the Waste (England and Wales) Regulations 2011 (SI 2011 No.988) ("the 2011 Regulations"). In particular, the MMO failed to apply the waste hierarchy set out in Article 4(1) of the Waste Framework Directive (Directive 2008/98/EC as amended).
>
> **Ground 5**
> In deciding to vary the licence, the MMO failed to comply with the Water Framework Directive (Directive 2000/60/EC as amended), to which effect has been given by The Water Environment (Water Framework Directive) (England and Wales) Regulations (SI 2017 No.407) ("the 2017 Regulations"). In particular, the MMO failed to consider whether the proposed disposal would jeopardise the attainment of "good surface water status" under Article 4(1) of the Directive. This ground is solely aimed at the chemical status of the Lower Severn water body. It is alleged that because the proposal would maintain the pre-existing "poor quality" of the water body, it would be bound to jeopardise the attainment of the "good" status and so, as a matter of law, the MMO was required to refuse the application to vary the marine licence.

39   The claimant had also obtained permission to pursue ground 3. This was an extensive attack on the lawfulness of the HRA carried out by the MMO for the

purposes of the Habitats Regulations. The MMO provided a detailed response to that challenge, which was supported by Natural England. In its skeleton argument dated 18 February 2022 the claimant announced that it no longer pursued ground 3.

40   Ms. Sasha Blackmore, who together with Mr. Matthew Dale-Harris appeared for the defendant, identified points taken by the claimant in, for example, its pleadings, which no longer appeared to be pursued. At the hearing it was understood and accepted by all parties that the court would only address those legal challenges which the claimant advanced in its oral submissions.

41   The claim for judicial review was filed on 8 October 2021, the day after the claimant was incorporated. By that stage the material from the capital and maintenance dredging carried out in the summer of 2021 had been disposed of at Portishead. As HPC says, and the claimant does not dispute, that position is, in practical terms, irreversible.

42   Initially, in paragraph 90 of the Statement of Facts the claimant sought wide-ranging relief, which included the quashing of the whole of the decision issued on 2 August 2021, declaratory relief and "a mandatory order requiring appropriate remedial steps to be taken by the Defendant and the IP".

43   However, in an email sent on 7 March 2022 the claimant's solicitors limited the quashing order sought to just activity 4.1 in the sixth licence variation (i.e. the disposal of dredged material at Portishead) and declaratory relief. The claimant no longer asked for the whole of the variation decision to be quashed and abandoned the hopeless request for mandatory relief to compel the taking of "remedial" steps.

44   I have already referred to the claimant's opposition to the disposal in the Severn of dredged materials with, it is said, a risk of low levels of radioactivity. During the consultation exercise such concerns were also raised by NSC. Section 5.3 of the MMO's Report on the EIA Consent Decision (dated 31 July 2021) referred to the Convention on the Prevention of Marine Pollution by Dumping of Waste and Other Matter ("the London Convention" 1972). Only materials within levels of radioactivity recognised as *de minimis*, which may effectively be regarded as non-radioactive, may be considered for disposal at sea. The MMO's consultants, ABPmer, were satisfied that the test results presented showed that the material to be dredged would be non-radioactive. Section 5.3.3 of the Report summarised in some detail points which had been raised by NSC, the responses of the HPC and the MMO's views. In section 5.3.4 the MMO explained why the methodology laid down by the International Atomic Energy Agency was appropriate, the test results satisfactory and the proposed disposal compliant with the London Convention. Paragraph 25 of the witness statement of Mr. Rowan Smith, the claimant's solicitor, referred to the compliant test results obtained by the Centre for Environment, Fisheries and Aquaculture Science. It should be recorded that none of the grounds of challenge in this judicial review raise any issues about the way in which the MMO has dealt with the subject of radioactivity.

45   The Court's role in judicial review is limited to determining issues of law. The Court is not permitted to go into the forbidden territory of resolving issues of expert or technical opinion which have arisen in the consultation process or in the exchange of pleadings and evidence in these proceedings (see e.g. *R. (Plan B Earth) v Secretary of State for Transport* [2020] P.T.S.R. 1446 at [180] and *R. (Keir) v Natural England* [2022] Env. L.R. 3).

The Marine and Coastal Access Act 2009

46   The background to this legislation was summarised in *Powell v Marine Management Organisation* [2017] EWHC 1491 (Admin) at [42] to [47]. The object was to introduce an integrated, stream-lined marine licensing system, based upon marine plans. The legislation was to be "targeted on things that need to be controlled", flexible, proportionate and risk-based. Only those activities posing a significant risk to *inter alia* the environment would be regulated. The statutory framework was summarised in [48] to [67]. Those passages were not contentious in the present litigation.

47   Section 2 is entitled "general objective". Subsections (1) to (3) provide:

> "(1) It is the duty of the MMO to secure that the MMO functions are so exercised that the carrying on of activities by persons in the MMO's area is managed, regulated or controlled—
>
>> (a) with the objective of making a contribution to the achievement of sustainable development (see subsections (2) and (4) to (11)),
>> (b) taking account of all relevant facts and matters (see subsection (3)), and
>> (c) in a manner which is consistent and co-ordinated (see subsection (12)).
>
> Any reference in this Act to the MMO's "general objective" is a reference to the duty imposed on the MMO by this subsection.
>
> (2) In pursuit of its general objective, the MMO may take any action which it considers necessary or expedient for the purpose of furthering any social, economic or environmental purposes.
>
> (3) For the purposes of subsection (1)(b), the facts and matters that may be taken into account include each of the following—
>
>> (a) scientific evidence, whether available to, or reasonably obtainable by, the MMO;
>> (b) other evidence so available or obtainable relating to the social, economic or environmental elements of sustainable development;
>> (c) such facts or matters not falling within paragraph (a) or (b) as the MMO may consider appropriate."

48   Section 2(3)(c) indicates the broad and flexible nature of the judgment which the MMO may exercise in pursuit of its statutory objectives.

49   Sections 49 to 57 deal with the adoption of marine plans containing policies for specific parts of the UK marine area. Sections 58 and 59 require public authorities to reach decisions on "authorisations", which include the determination of applications for a marine licence and the variation of any such licence, in accordance with the relevant marine plan, "unless relevant considerations indicate otherwise".

50   Part 4 of the MCAA 2009 deals with various forms of marine licensing, including enforcement action. Chapter 1 specifically deals with marine licences.

51   Section 65(1) prohibits anyone from carrying on or causing or permitting any other person to carry on, a "licensable marine activity" "except in accordance with a marine licence granted by the appropriate licensing authority". Thus, it is insufficient just to obtain a marine licence. The licensed activity must be carried on so as to comply with the terms of the licence. A person who contravenes s.65(1),

or who fails to comply with any condition of a marine licence commits an offence (s.85(1)).

52   Section 66 defines what are licensable marine activities. The list includes: -

> "1. To deposit any substance or object within the UK marine licensing area, either in the sea or on or under the seabed, from—
>   (a) any vehicle, vessel, aircraft or marine structure,
>   (b) any container floating in the sea, or
> …
> 7. To construct, alter or improve any works within the UK marine licensing area either—
>   (a) in or over the sea, or
>   (b) on or under the seabed.
> …
> 9. To carry out any form of dredging within the UK marine licensing area (whether or not involving the removal of any material from the sea or seabed)."

53   Thus, dredging from, and the deposition of dredged materials in, the sea are activities which must be authorised by a marine licence. Item 7 in the list relates to the common example of construction, improvement of alteration of works in or over the sea or the seabed. Those works would include jetties, piers, wharves, pontoons, piles, platforms, pipes and tunnels. They would also include the construction and operation of complex projects such as harbour and marina developments and windfarms.

54   Section 67 provides for the making of an application to, in this case, the MMO.

55   Section 68(1) requires the making of an application for a marine licence to be published. Section 68(3) requires notice to be given to a local authority in whose area an activity is proposed to be carried out. The licensing authority may not proceed with the application until these requirements are satisfied. (s.68(4)).

56   Section 69 deals with the determination of applications. Subsection (1) provides: -

> "(1) In determining an application for a marine licence (including the terms on which it is to be granted and what conditions, if any, are to be attached to it), the appropriate licensing authority must have regard to—
>   (a) the need to protect the environment,
>   (b) the need to protect human health,
>   (c) the need to prevent interference with legitimate uses of the sea,
>   and such other matters as the authority thinks relevant"

Like s.2(3)(c), s.69(1)(c) gives the MMO a broad and flexible discretion to take into account such matters as it considers relevant.

57   By s.69(3) the MMO must take into account any representations it receives from any person having an interest in the outcome of the application.

58   Where an application is made for a licence to authorise "works" (item 7 in s.66(1)), the MMO must have regard to the effects of any intended use of those works.

59   Section 70 gives the MMO a discretion to cause an inquiry to be held in connection with the determination of an application for a marine licence.

60   Section 71 deals with the grant of a marine licence. Section 71(1) and (2) provides: -

"(1) The appropriate licensing authority, having considered an application for a marine licence, must—

(a) grant the licence unconditionally,

(b) grant the licence subject to such conditions as the authority thinks fit, or

(c) refuse the application.

(2) The conditions that may be attached to a licence under subsection (1)(b) may relate to—

(a) the activities authorised by the licence;

(b) precautions to be taken or works to be carried out (whether before, during or after the carrying out of the authorised activities) in connection with or in consequence of those activities."

61   Without prejudice to the generality of s.71(1) and (2), subsection (3) sets out particular types of condition which may be imposed. Under sub-paragraph (a), a condition may provide that: -

"that no activity authorised by the licence be carried out until the authority or some other specified person has given such further approval of the activity as may be specified;"

Under sub-paragraph (f) a condition may require that any activity authorised by the licence must take place at a specified site.

62   Section 73 required the Secretary of State to make regulations to enable any person who applies for a marine licence to appeal against a decision under s.71. He has made The Marine Licensing (Licence Application Appeals) Regulations 2011 (SI 2011 No.934). Regulation 4 confers a right of appeal against a decision to refuse to grant a licence or against the imposition of conditions. The appeal is determined by an Inspector (regulation 5). The Secretary of State determines whether the appeal is to be dealt with by way of written representations, a hearing or an inquiry (regulation 8). Where the MMO is the decision-maker, it must give notice of the appeal to any person who had made representations on the application and to any other person it considers likely to have an interest, so that they may send written representations to the Secretary of State (regulation 9). Part 5 lays down the procedure for hearings and inquiries. Notice of the date of the hearing or inquiry must be given to persons who have made representations or are likely to be interested in the appeal (regulation 12). A person who has made representations is entitled to appear at the hearing or inquiry and to give evidence (regulations 15 and 16). If the appeal is allowed the Inspector may direct the MMO to grant a licence on such terms and conditions as he may direct (regulation 22).

63   Section 72, which lies at the heart of grounds 1 and 2, deals with the variation, suspension, revocation and transfer of a licence. Section 72 (1) to (3) and (7) to (8) provide: -

"(1) A licensing authority may by notice vary, suspend or revoke a licence granted by it if it appears to the authority that there has been a breach of any of its provisions.

(2) A licensing authority may by notice vary, suspend or revoke a licence granted by it if it appears to the authority that—

(a) in the course of the application for the licence, any person either supplied information to the authority that was false or misleading or failed to supply information, and

(b) if the correct information had been supplied the authority would have, or it is likely that the authority would have, refused the application or granted the licence in different terms.

(3) A licensing authority may by notice vary, suspend or revoke a licence granted by it if it appears to the authority that the licence ought to be varied, suspended or revoked—

(a) because of a change in circumstances relating to the environment or human health;

(b) because of increased scientific knowledge relating to either of those matters;

(c) in the interests of safety of navigation;

(d) for any other reason that appears to the authority to be relevant.

....

(7) On an application made by a licensee, the licensing authority which granted the licence—

(a) may transfer the licence from the licensee to another person, and

(b) if it does so, must vary the licence accordingly.

(8) A licence may not be transferred except in accordance with subsection (7).

...."

64   Section 108(1) required the Secretary of State to make regulations providing for appeals against notices issued under *inter alia* s. 72. He has made The Marine Licensing (Notices Appeals) Regulations 2011 (SI 2011 No. 936). By regulation 3(1) a person to whom a notice under s.72 varying, suspending or revoking a licence has been issued, may appeal to the First-Tier Tribunal against the notice. Such appeals are dealt with by the General Regulatory Chamber. Where a licensee appeals against a notice varying a licence, that notice is suspended in relation to the subject-matter of the appeal until the appeal is determined (regulation 3(2)). In any appeal the burden of proof lies on the licensing authority (regulation 5(1)). In making its decision, the Tribunal may withdraw, confirm or vary the notice or remit the matter to the authority (regulation 5(2)).

65   The Environment (Wales) Act 2016 inserted s.72A into the MCAA 2009 for cases where the Welsh Ministers are the appropriate licensing authority "in relation to a marine licence granted under this Part". The authority may require the licensee to pay a fee for "dealing with an application by the licensee for a variation, suspension, revocation or transfer of the licence under s.72" (s.72A(2)(c)). Where a licensee who has applied for a variation, suspension, revocation of a transfer of a licence under s.72 fails to pay the requisite fee, the licensing authority may refuse to proceed with the application (s.72A(9)).

Ground 1

A summary of the Claimant's submissions

66   Mr. David Wolfe QC, who together with Mr. Gethin Thomas, appeared on behalf of the claimant, submitted that the issue of *vires* depends upon the true construction

of the legislation. That is to be understood by reference to the language used by Parliament, according to its natural and ordinary meaning, read in its statutory context. The statute should be read as a whole.

67   The claimant contends that a licensable marine activity must be authorised by the grant of a marine licence under s.71, following the procedure prescribed by sections 65 to 71.

68   The effect of s.65 is that no person may carry on a "licensable marine activity" as defined in s.66 without a marine licence. Mr. Wolfe QC submits that a marine activity may only be licensed where an application made under s.67 results in the grant of a marine licence under s.71. The conditions which may be imposed on a licence may relate to the activities it authorises or to precautions to be taken, or works to be carried out, in connection with or in consequence of those activities (s.71(2)). Likewise, certain types of condition specified in s.71(3) relate to the activity or "any activity" authorised by the licence.

69   Mr. Wolfe submits that a marine licence can only authorise the activities it specifies and cannot amount to a generalised permission "which can roam around and bring in new activities by variation". Thus, the requirement in s.68(3) for notifying a local authority of an application depends upon the activity to which it relates being in a specific location. The special procedure in s.78 allows applications for both a marine licence and a harbour order to be considered together if the latter concerns the activity for which the licence is required (or other works to be undertaken in connection therewith). So, it is submitted, a marine licence cannot authorise dredging in general or deposition in general.

70   The claimant submits that the original marine licence, and the variations up to and including the fifth variation, did not authorise deposition of dredged material. They simply authorised dredging. The power under s.72 to vary a licence cannot be used to add a new activity not previously authorised by the licence being varied. That would not fall within the notion of "varying" a licence or represent a "variation" of that licence.

71   Next, Mr. Wolfe submitted that s.72(1) to (3) is concerned with action taken by the licensing authority against the licensee, where the authority acts of its own motion. Section 72 does not allow for an application to be made by the licensee to the authority seeking, for example, a variation of a licence.

72   He also pointed to the procedural implications of the parties' competing interpretations of the legislation. If a new activity has to be the subject of a fresh marine licence under s.71, the application procedure provides for publicity and for participation by interested parties making representations. Article 5 of the 2011 Order (as amended) enables a local planning authority (such as NSC) or an Inshore Fisheries and Conservation Authority (such as D&S IFCA) to state that in their opinion an activity in a licence application meets the criteria in article 5(7)(a), so that the Secretary of State must consider whether to determine the application himself, instead of the MMO. If the Secretary of State decides to "call in" the application, a public inquiry would be expected to be held. In the event of an appeal against a refusal of a marine licence, interested parties who had made representations on the licence application would be able to participate in the appeal process, whether by way of written representations, or at a hearing or public inquiry. By contrast, where the MMO is considering whether to vary a licence there is no statutory procedure to enable interested parties and the public to participate (unless, as in the present case, the proposal was subject to EIA under the EIA Regulations 2007).

Furthermore, the MMO does not have a power to hold a public inquiry (contrast s.70) and the power in Article 5 of the 2011 Order for the Secretary of State to call in the matter for his own determination do not apply. Any appeal by the licensee against the decision of the MMO is heard by the First Tier Tribunal without public participation.

73   So far as the present case is concerned, Mr. Wolfe accepted that because the EIA Regulations 2007 had applied to the handling of HPC's application to vary under s.72, no complaint is made about any inability (or reduced ability) of interested parties and the public to participate in the process leading to the decision made on 2 August 2021. Instead, the only procedural difference which arose in the circumstances of this case was that the Secretary of State had no power to consider, on the representations made by NSC and D&S IFCA, whether he would call in the application for his own decision.

74   Mr. Wolfe submitted that the construction of s.72 for which the Secretary of State and HPC contend would undermine the statutory scheme. For example, an application could be made, and a licence granted under s.71, for a single marine activity, perhaps something of a modest nature, and then might be altered by a series of variations to add any number of other activities without following the procedures applicable to an application for a licence, so as to "morph" into something "beyond recognition".

Discussion

75   A number of matters became common ground during the hearing.

76   First, a single licence can cover more than one activity. That is clear from the reference to "activities" in the plural in s.71(2)(a). But in addition, s.6(c) of the Interpretation Act 1978 applies so that any reference to an "activity" in the singular (see e.g. s.65(1)(a)) includes the plural.

77   Second, the MMO's power to vary, suspend or revoke a licence can be exercised upon an application made by the licensee. This is clear from the MCAA 2009 itself (see s.72A(2)(c) and (9)). It is also apparent that Parliament has proceeded on that basis when enacting the EIA Regulations 2007. This can be seen in, for example, the definitions in regulation 2(1) of "application", "EIA consent decision", "regulated activity", "regulatory approval" (which includes a variation of a marine licence) and "regulatory decision" and also in regulation 12 (dealing with applications) and regulation 22 (dealing with the making of the EIA consent decision). Indeed, in the present case the carrying out of the EIA process in relation to the decision to vary the marine licence proceeded on the basis that s.72 of the MCAA 2009 does permit the making of an application for such a variation.

78   In my judgment, the express reference in s.72(7) to an "application" by a licensee to transfer a licence cannot be taken to imply that a licensee cannot otherwise make an application under s.72. The effect of s.72(8) is that a licence can only be transferred on an application made by the licensee under s.72(7). Not surprisingly, Parliament has decided that the MMO should not have the power to direct a transfer of a licence without the licensee's consent. Hence transfer of a licence, exclusively upon an application made by the licensee, is dealt with separately in s.72.

79   Section 72(1), (2) and (3) operate differently. They enable the MMO to give a notice varying, suspending or revoking a licence. Thus, under those provisions the MMO may act of its own motion (in the absence of any application), or it may

issue such a notice as its determination of an application by a licensee. It is possible to conceive of circumstances in which a licensee might wish to have his licence suspended or revoked, for example in order to bring to an end ongoing responsibilities for and the costs of maintaining a structure and of complying with the terms of the related licence.

80   The key point to emerge from this second point of common ground is that Mr. Wolfe's submission that s.72(3) is only concerned with actions which may be "done to" or steps taken against, a licensee is untenable.

81   Third, it is now common ground that s.72 can be used to vary an activity authorised by a licence under s.71. It is therefore incorrect to say that a marine licensable activity can only be authorised by a marine licence. Where the power of variation under s.72 is properly used, for example, to extend the geographical area of an activity or to extend a work such as a pier, the activity in question is authorised by the original licence and by the notice of variation. Where such an extension is duly authorised by a s.72 variation, there is no need for the licensee to obtain a fresh marine licence.

82   All this goes to show that the real question under ground 1 is what is meant by "vary" in s.72. Ms. Blackmore, together with Mr. James Strachan QC and Ms. Victoria Hutton who appeared on behalf of HPC, submitted that determining or defining the outermost reach of the power to vary might raise some difficult questions in other cases. They suggested that it is unnecessary to address that subject in the present case, because the disposal of dredged material, authorised by the sixth variation of the licence, fell well within the ambit of s.72.

83   The powers in s.72 to suspend or to revoke a marine licence, by definition, do not involve any extension to the ambit of the activities authorised by a licensee. But it does not follow that the word "vary" must be construed as if it only enables the scope of a licence to be cut down rather than enlarged. As a matter of ordinary English a variation can widen the scope of a marine licence, just as an anti-social behaviour order may be extended in relation to its duration or the geographical area within which restrictions apply (see e.g. *Leeds City Council v RG* [2007] 1 W.L.R. 3025; *R. (Langley) v Preston Crown Court* [2009] 1 W.L.R. 1612). There is nothing in the language of the MCAA 2009 to indicate that the power to vary under s.72 cannot be used to enlarge the scope of a marine licence. So, Mr. Wolfe rightly accepted that where an activity is authorised by a licence, for example, the deposition of dredged material, its geographical area may be extended by a variation under s.72. Likewise, a physical extension of licensed works such as a pier may be authorised under the power to vary the original licence for the pier. On the other hand, Mr. Wolfe would draw the line at a proposal to move the location of a proposed pier already authorised under a marine licence by any distance which is more than *de minimis*. For example, moving the whole of the proposed structure by say 25m would, he submits, require a fresh licence and could not be the subject of a s.72 variation.

84   The main issue between the parties is this: whereas the claimant submits that the power to vary a licence cannot authorise a new activity not previously authorised by the licence, the MMO and HPC say that the language of the legislation does not exclude this possibility, so long as the new activity can properly be said to represent a variation of the existing licence in its current form.

85   In her first witness statement, Ms. Lindsey Mullan, a Marine Licensing Senior Case Manager with the MMO, explains that it is common for multiple variations

to be made to the marine licence for a major infrastructure project (see paragraph 49 *et seq*). In practice, these have included the addition of new marine activities. She says that the marine environment is dynamic and complex. Self-evidently, the carrying out of development in coastal waters can be challenging and the licensee may have to cope with aggressive conditions. The design requirements, mitigation and safety measures of a project may need to change over time, during both the development and operational phases. Some projects evolve over a long time from an initial design or concept to the construction stage. A scheme may be undertaken in several phases.

86   Ms. Mullan refers to two major projects as examples where new activities were introduced as licence variations: Terminal 2 and the new marina at the Western Docks, Dover and the Dogger Bank, Teeside B Sofia Offshore Windfarm. In the latter case, the deemed marine licence was varied so as to permit an increase in the number of fibre-optic cables laid with the high voltage direct current cables. But it was also varied so as to authorise the laying of cables between the wind turbine generators and the offshore converter platform, something which had not previously been included in the licence at all.

87   The MCAA 2009 explicitly recognises the need for the content and engineering of a project, particularly one of a complex nature, to continue to evolve after the MMO first grants a licence for marine activities. Section 71(3)(a) authorises the imposition of a licence condition prohibiting the carrying out of an activity authorised by that licence until the MMO (or another authority) has given "such further approval of the activity as may be specified". This provision may be used where relatively little detail is available for a particular "work" at the stage when a marine licence is first granted authorising that activity in principle. Further details may be reserved for subsequent approval. I acknowledge that such a condition may only allow details to be reserved in relation to the same activity. But in practice the difference between what is first authorised by the licence and what is authorised under the condition, without needing to rely upon the power of variation in s.72, may be very considerable. The licence may describe the activity authorised in broad, generic terms, whereas an approval given under a condition may relate to a very detailed design and specification, setting out, for example, the number and size of structures and/or equipment and the extent of the area involved. Where such matters are dealt with under condition there will be no need to obtain a new marine licence.

88   Ms Mullan also identifies a practical advantage of the MMO's approach to s.72. Where the power of variation can properly be used, all the activities authorised and the licensing conditions are contained in a single document, rather than being split between several licences. Both the activities and the licensing conditions may be interrelated. The understanding of those relationships, whether by the licensee, an enforcing authority or the public, is likely to be improved by having them expressed in a single document.

89   Ultimately, Mr. Wolfe accepted that differing procedural consequences, according to whether a proposal is dealt with under s.71 or under s.72, provide no real help to the court in choosing between the competing interpretations of s.72 or to determine the ambit of the power to vary. This includes, for example, the requirement which can arise under s.68(3) that a local authority be notified of an application for a marine licence. Even when a licence is granted the MMO may

impose a condition restricting an activity to a particular location, but is not obliged
to do so.

90   In any event, I accept the submissions for MMO and HPC that, in the light of
R. (Sharp) v North Essex Magistrates' Court [2017] 1 W.L.R. 3789 at [38(v)], a
constraint on the ability of interested parties to challenge a proposal on its merits
does not affect the proper construction of the language used by Parliament to confer
the powers in issue. In this case that principle applies *a fortiori* because of the
absence of any rigid demarcation between s.71 and s.72. On a true reading of those
provisions, some matters are capable of being dealt with under either section.

91   Although it is not necessary for my conclusions, I would add that in the event
of the MMO refusing to approve an application by a licensee to vary a licence,
there is no right of appeal. Regulation 3 of SI 2011 No 936 only allows an appeal
to be brought against a *notice* varying, suspending or revoking a licence. So where
an application to vary is refused by the MMO, or the MMO refuses to act under
s.72(3), there is no appeal process from which interested parties are excluded.

92   In my judgment, the risk of "morphing" or "licensing creep" to which Mr. Wolfe
referred, does not help the court to decide between the two competing constructions
of s.72 or otherwise to determine the correct interpretation of that provision. Even
on the claimant's construction there would be the possibility of a licensee seeking
to enlarge an activity already authorised in the licence very considerably and so
"morphing" into something of a radically different nature from that originally
licensed. By contrast, a licensee's proposal may be for a new activity involving
only a modest, unobjectionable addition to the authorised activities. The new
activity may be entirely incidental. As Mr. Strachan submitted, the claimant's
analysis lacks coherence.

93   In my judgment the real control in s.72 to address Mr. Wolfe's concern about
"morphing" is that a proposal must not exceed what can properly be regarded as
a variation of the licence.

94   Ultimately it is the language used by Parliament in the MCAA 2009 which
defines the ambit of s.72(3). Putting to one side revocation or suspension, the MMO
is only empowered to vary a licence. It is that concept of variation which limits
the exercise of that particular power. The claimant's argument depends upon reading
additional words into, or putting a gloss upon, s.72, for which there is no
justification. The language used by Parliament does not exclude the authorisation
under s.72 of a marine activity which has not previously been authorised under the
licence in question, so long as that activity can properly be said to represent a
variation of that licence. There is no legal requirement to distinguish between
proposals to extend an authorised activity or to add a new activity. The relevant
question is whether either would go beyond varying the marine licence.

95   It would not be appropriate in this case for the court to seek to define exhaustively
what may or may not constitute a variation of a marine licence, or to define the
outermost reach of the power to vary. It is sufficient for me to say that what may
qualify as a variation will be affected by the terms of the original licence (including
its conditions), the nature and extent of the activities already authorised by that
document and any previous variations, and the nature and extent of the proposed
addition to the licence. It is also relevant to consider the nature of the project to
which the marine licence relates, or any other relevant statutory authorisation, for
example an authorisation referred to in the marine licence or which forms part of
the context for the licence. The relationship between all these factors is plainly

relevant. These considerations may to some extent involve matters of judgment, which Parliament has entrusted to the MMO, and which it is well qualified to assess, as Ms Mullan's witness statement demonstrates.

96   There was a difference between the parties as to how certain conditions of the DCO and of the marine licences should be read. But there was agreement that the general principles which are now well-established for the interpretation of planning permissions should be applied. Many of the leading authorities and some of the key principles were identified in *Swire v Canterbury City Council* [2022] EWHC 390 (Admin) at [30] to [34] and do not need to be rehearsed in detail here. I would, however, also refer to the judgment of Lieven J in *UBB Waste Essex Ltd v Essex CC* [2019] EWHC 1924 (Admin), in particular at [26] to [35].

97   For the purposes of the present case the following points are particularly pertinent: -

(i)   The question is what would a reasonable reader understand the words used in the DCO or the marine licences to mean, in the context of each consent and its conditions, read as a whole;

(ii)   In the case of the DCO, it is relevant to have regard to the decision letter of the Secretary of State which decided to grant the application for the DCO. That is a public document;

(iii)   The Court should have regard to the natural and ordinary meaning of the words used and the purpose of the consent and relevant conditions;

(iv)   The reasons given for the imposition of a condition are relevant to its meaning. The MMO's guidance on making an application for a marine licence states that they will give reasons for the imposition of a condition on a licence;

(v)   The context in which the DCO and the marine licences must be interpreted includes the legal framework within which each consent was granted. The reasonable reader must be treated as being equipped with some knowledge of the relevant law and practice relating to DCOs and marine licences;

(vi)   The words of the consent are to be interpreted using common sense (*Lambeth LBC v Secretary of State for Housing, Communities and Local Government* [2019] 1 W.L.R. 4317 at [19]; *DB Symmetry Ltd v Swindon BC* [2021] P.T.S.R. 432 at [60]).

98   During the examination of HPC's application for the DCO, NE initially said that they were not satisfied that the project would not be likely to have a significant effect upon the Severn Estuary SAC and Ramsar site (Report of the Panel para. 5.71). One of the main concerns was the possibility of material dredged from the Severn being disposed of outside the estuary. That "would undermine the sediment budget and affect the estuary habitat feature of the Severn Estuary SAC and Ramsar site" (para. 5.73).

99   The MMO also expressed concerns about dredging and disposal. They understood that dredged materially was to be disposed of locally or otherwise at the Cardiff Grounds disposal site. Initially they thought that disposal elsewhere would require the "designation" of a new disposal site and said alternatives to disposal at sea should be considered under the Waste Framework Directive, presumably referring to the waste hierarchy in Article 4(1) (para. 5.90). Subsequently, the MMO withdrew its concerns on the basis that "the issue" would be addressed through the marine

licensing process (para. 5.91). Mr. Wolfe sought to persuade the court that that issue related to the application of the waste hierarchy.

100   However, at page 27 of its EIA Consent Decision Report dated 31 July 2021 the MMO explained why it changed its position during the examination of the DCO. The sediment budget of the Severn Estuary SAC is protected under the Habitats Regulations and therefore dredged material must be disposed of within the SAC. The Decision Report refers to the "requirement" that was included in the DCO (see below) with the agreement of all the statutory marine stakeholders, that is EA, NE, the MMO and the Countryside Council for Wales (subsequently merged into NRW). The MMO stated: -

> "The proposed disposal options that retain marine sediment within the water body align with the WaFD requirements under the waste hierarchy"

It is clear, therefore, that by the end of the examination the MMO's position on the handling of dredged material had changed from that set out in para. 5.90 of the Panel's Report so as to align with that of NE. They told the Panel that they were content with the requirements proposed for the DCO. All this is summarised in paragraphs 5.91 and 5.92 of the Report.

101   The Panel's conclusions on the subject are clear. At paragraph 5.125 they expressly acknowledged the concerns that removal of dredged material from the Severn Estuary could undermine the sediment budget and affect the estuary habitat features of the SAC, Ramsar site and also the Bridgwater Bay Site of Special Scientific Interest. Because of the absence of any guarantee that dredged material would not be removed from the Estuary, the Panel recommended the imposition of a "requirement" (or condition) in the DCO pursuant to s.120(2) of the PA 2008, then referred to as "PW35", "to ensure that sediment is retained in the estuary". PW 35 was expressed in these terms: -

> "Dredged material arising from the authorised project shall not be disposed of except within the Severn Estuary SAC."

102   Likewise, at paragraph 57 of Appendix C to their Report, the Panel said: -

> "Natural England are concerned that the supply of sediment in the Severn Estuary Special Area of Conservation (SAC) should be maintained, in order to replenish intertidal habitats following the erosion of material. Accordingly, they consider that a requirement should be imposed to prevent the disposal of dredged material outside the Severn Estuary SAC."

In paragraph 58 the Panel identified three parts of the project for which HPC planned to carry out dredging. Given that marine licences had yet to be issued for two parts, including the installation of the cooling water infrastructure, the Panel said that a "project-wide" requirement in the form of PW35 should be included in the DCO (para. 59).

103   The Secretary of State accepted the Panel's reasoning and recommendation on this matter and decided that the requirement should be included in the DCO. The text remained the same but the reference changed to PW23.

104   Mr. Wolfe submitted that PW23 only bites in relation to dredged material which is disposed of. Accordingly, PW23 does not exclude the possibility of dredged materials being re-used, for example, as part of a landscaping scheme on the main construction site. That reading of PW23 is untenable. Having regard to the clearly

stated reasons for the imposition of the requirement, and applying common sense, PW23 is to be read as requiring all material dredged from the Severn to be disposed of within the SAC. That reading is necessary in order to give effect to the very reason for the imposition of the requirement, namely to maintain the sediment budget within the SAC. There is nothing in the language of PW23 which requires it to be read as allowing (or not excluding) the dredged material being dealt with other than by disposal within the Estuary, for example by re-use or recycling. That would conflict with the stated purpose of the requirement.

105   For these reasons, I reject Mr. Wolfe's submission that in its EIA Consent Decision Report (and elsewhere) the MMO misinterpreted PW23 of the DCO. It is plain that the DCO was granted on the basis that any dredging undertaken for the project must maintain the sediment balance of the SAC by returning the material dredged to the SAC. The fact that a marine licence would subsequently be needed for that dredging and disposal does not detract from this legal requirement imposed by the Secretary of State in the DCO.

106   Section 32 of the original marine licence provided a description of the project and treated the DCO as forming part of the context for that licence. The reasonable reader of the licence would be expected to be aware of relevant provisions of the DCO. The original marine licence did not authorise any disposal of dredged materials. But the methodology for the dredging authorised as activity 1.1 had regard to the HPC's proposal that the dredged material would be disposed of at the Cardiff Grounds site within the SAC.

107   Given NE's concern regarding sediment budgeting in the SAC, and its position as the statutory national conservation body for the purposes of the Habitats Regulations, the MMO would have been expected to address the issue of what would happen to dredged material when considering whether to authorise dredging. Condition 5.2.24 of the original marine licence stated: -

> "Dredged material shall not be disposed of except within the Severn Estuary Special Area of Conservation"

The reason for the condition was said to be "to maintain the sediment budget of the area". This condition replicated requirement PW23 of the DCO. They both have the same meaning. This is reinforced by condition 5.2.25 which required the licensee to notify to the MMO the volume of dredged material and the location in which it was disposed of within a time limit of six weeks so that the MMO would be informed of "activities happening *in the marine area*" (emphasis added).

108   I also note that activity 1.3, the deposition of drill arisings, was programmed to take place over the same period as activity 1.1. There would appear to be no reason why the original marine licence did not also authorise the disposal of the dredged material within the SAC, other than the fact that the disposal site then proposed fell within the jurisdiction of NRW and not the MMO. Indeed, the NRW licence was granted on 11 July 2014.

109   As we have seen, the fifth variation of the original marine licence granted by the MMO, divided the dredging authorised into activity 1.1 (capital dredging) and activity 1.2 (maintenance dredging). Activity 1.1 stated that the dredged material would be disposed of at the Cardiff Grounds site in reliance upon the NRW licence. Activity 1.2 stated that the maintenance dredged material would be disposed at the same location "unless otherwise agreed by the MMO". Thus, so far as maintenance

dredging was concerned, the fifth variation envisaged that the material dredged
might be disposed of in the MMO's territory.

110   Conditions 5.2.22 and 5.2.23 (in relation to activity 1.1) and conditions 5.2.26
and 5.2.27 (in relation to activity 1.2) were to the same effect, and were imposed
for the same reasons, as the conditions in the original licence referred to above.
For example, condition 5.2.22 now reads: -

> "All material from activity 1.1 of this licence must only be disposed to a
> licensed disposal site within the Severn Estuary Special Area of Conservation"

111   I can see the force of Mr. Strachan's submission that by the fifth variation of
the original licence, the MMO had included in the licence a statement that they
would consider agreeing to a disposal site in the Severn and so, in relation at least
to maintenance dredged material (which is the only type of dredging which remained
to be carried out by the time of this judicial review), it can be said that disposal at
the Portishead site is not an entirely new activity which was not previously
comprehended in the licence. The difference is one of location and therefore a
permissible variation of the licence, even on the approach for which the claimant
contends.

112   But I have explained why I consider the claimant's approach to involve an
impermissible gloss on the legislation. In my judgment, the resolution of ground
1 should be based on the approach in [94] to [95] above.

113   The marine licence and the variations of that licence have been granted in the
context of the DCO for the power station. That project includes the following
essential features: -

(i)   The intake and outfall tunnels for the cooling water system;
(ii)   The vertical shafts at the ends of the tunnels;
(iii) The head structures;
(iv)   The dredging needed to create pits for the gravel beds and head structures;
(v)   The disposal of that dredged material in a location within the Severn Estuary
SAC.

114   Features (ii) to (iv) have previously been authorised by the marine licence (with
its variations). Feature (v) is an inevitable consequence of features (ii) to (iv). The
disposal of the dredged material in the Severn Estuary SAC is necessary in order
to comply with the Habitats Regulations and conditions imposed on the original
marine licence (with its previous variations). It is an ancillary or incidental aspect
of the activities previously licensed by the MMO. The disposal is limited to the
material which the licensee is already authorised to dredge. The licence envisaged
that disposal would be to a designated disposal site. The MMO had been unable
to authorise the use of the Cardiff Grounds site merely because it fell outside its
territorial jurisdiction. The application for the sixth variation sought approval for
disposal at one designated site in the SAC instead of another which had been
proposed. It was a change of location.

115   In the light of these factors, the nature of the change to the marine licence made
by the introduction of activity 4.1 fell well within the legal concept of a variation
of that licence. Accordingly, there was nothing unlawful in the MMO's decision
that it was appropriate for HPC's proposal to be dealt with as a variation of the
licence under s.73(2). In so far as this may be a matter to be decided by the court
itself, I unhesitatingly reach the same conclusion.

116   For these reasons ground 1 must be rejected. The alteration proposed did not go beyond the ambit of that which could lawfully be considered and approved under s.72(3)(d) of the MCAA 2009.

Ground 2

The Claimant's submissions

117   Mr. Wolfe submitted that the MMO's power under s.72(3)(d) cannot lawfully be exercised unless: -

(i)   There is a reason for the exercise of that power;
(ii) Which appears to the MMO to be relevant;

By "relevant" the claimant suggests that the reason must fall within the scope of s.72(3).

118   It is incorrect to treat s.72(3)(d) as an open-ended discretion to vary a marine licence, because that would render s.72(3)(a) to (c) unnecessary. Section 72(3)(d) should be read *ejusdem generis* with s.72(3)(a) to (c). The "genus" here was said to comprise triggers and characteristics external to the licensed activity or activities. Accordingly, mere desire on the part of the licensee to change the scope of a licence would not suffice as a "relevant reason" under s.72(3)(d).

119   In oral submissions, Mr. Wolfe altered his definition of the "genus" in s.72(3) so as to refer to matters which are done by the MMO to the licensee. On this basis he submitted that the mere content of a proposal by a licensee to vary a licence could not constitute a reason for the exercise of the power under s.72(3)(d).

120   The claimant also submits that the MMO failed to identify or state any reason for the exercise of the power under s.72(3)(d) here. This complaint is said to be based on an implied obligation on the part of the MMO, not only to have what appears to them to be a relevant reason, but to express that reason. The claimant also relies upon a common law obligation to give reasons arising from the duty to act fairly (*R. (CPRE Kent) v Dover DC* [2018] 1 W.L.R. 108).

121   At the outset, Mr. Wolfe submitted that jurisdiction is not conferred on the MMO by s.72(3)(d) unless firstly, there is a reason for the power to be exercised and secondly, the MMO consider that reason to be relevant. He suggested that this requires two stages which should not be "collapsed" into one. In reply Mr. Wolfe defined the two questions differently: (1) is there a relevant reason and (2) on the merits should the power to vary, suspend or revoke be exercised? He went on to add that although these are two separate questions, in some (undefined) circumstances they may be answered compendiously.

Discussion

122   According to their ordinary and natural meaning, the words in s.72(3)(d) "for any other reason that appears to the authority to be relevant" give the MMO a broad discretion to vary, suspend or revoke a licence. The flexibility conferred by that language is in line with s.2(1) to (3) of the MCAA 2009. The MMO is under a general duty to exercise its functions so that the carrying out of activities in the MMO's area is managed and regulated *inter alia* taking into account "all relevant facts and matters". Those matters include such facts and matters not falling within the specific categories set out in s.2(3)(a) and (b) "as the MMO may consider

appropriate" (s.2(3)(c)). By s.2(2) the MMO is empowered to take "any action which it considers necessary or expedient for the purpose of furthering any social, economic or environmental purpose". Parliament has conferred a very broad discretion as to the steps the MMO may take, or the matters which it may take into account, alongside the more specific functions set out in the body of the legislation.

123   Mr. Wolfe is seeking to read down the ordinary meaning of the broad language in s.72(3)(d), by recourse to two canons of construction. First, meaning should be given to all the language used by Parliament, so that provisions are not treated as otiose or redundant (*Bennion, Bailey and Northbury on Statutory Interpretation (8th ed)* at section 21.2). Second, as I have said, he relies on the *ejusdem generis* ("of the same kind") principle to limit the wide language of s.72(3)(d) to matters falling within the same class as that to which s.72(3)(a) to (c) belong.

124   *Bennion* points out that canons of constructions are not to be rigidly applied. Instead, they provide useful tools for analysing the language used (section 20.1). In *Cusack v Harrow LBC* [2013] 1 W.L.R. 2022 Lord Neuberger PSC said that canons of constructions have a valuable part to play but "as guidelines rather than railway lines". Although they embody logic or common sense, they exist to illuminate and help, but not to constrain or inhibit ([57] to [60]).

125   There may be a reason why Parliament has enacted specific provisions followed by a broad provision, so that giving effect to that broad language does not render the specific language otiose. This may depend upon the nature of that broad text and its context. Here the broad language used in s.72(3)(d) refers to a reason that the MMO *considers to be relevant.* But in s.72(3)(a) to (c) we see Parliament laying down matters which it considered to provide a relevant basis for the exercise of the power in s.72(3) *in any event.* As *Bennion* indicates in section 17.4, sometimes Parliament provides a list of examples, or specific instances, in which a power may be used, together with a general provision. Here Parliament was able to identify the matters set out in s.72(3)(a) to (c) as being sufficient to found the exercise of the power to vary, suspend or revoke a licence, but did not consider it appropriate to set down an exhaustive list of such matters. Given the nature of the regulatory regime and the widely ranging circumstances in which it has to be applied, it is wholly unsurprising that Parliament did not seek to envisage all the situations or factors which might arise. Instead, it allowed the regulatory body responsible for operating the licensing regime to have regard to additional matters it considers to be relevant. That legislative approach does not in any way involve treating s.72(3)(a) to (c) as redundant or superfluous.

126   For the *ejusdem generis* principle to apply there must be a sufficient indication in the legislation of a category that can properly be described as a *genus,* or what McCardie J described in *Magnhild (Owners) v MacIntyre Bros and Co* [1920] 3 K.B. 321 at 330 as a common and dominant feature. Neither of the approaches put forward by Mr. Wolfe properly identify a *genus*.

127   First, s.72(3) (a) to (c) cannot be explained as being limited to matters external to an activity authorised by a licence. For example, s.72(3)(b) could apply to a change in scientific understanding about the impacts of a licensed activity on the environment or human health. It would be absurd to read s.72(3) as not allowing the MMO to vary, suspend or revoke a licence in such circumstances. Likewise, s.72(3)(c) allows reconsideration of the impact of a licensed activity on the safety of navigation. There is no reason why safety of navigation must be external to a licensed activity.

128   Second, Mr. Wolfe's alternative formulation of a *genus* is also untenable. For reasons already given, s.72(3) is not limited to matters done to, or steps taken against, the licensee or the licensed activities. Section 72(3) enables the MMO to vary, suspend or revoke a licence both of its own motion and in response to an application by the licensee. The *ejusdem generis* principle therefore cannot be used to exclude the content of a proposal by the licensee to vary a licence from the ambit of s.72(3)(d).

129   Third, and in any event, the attempt to apply the *ejusdem generis* principle here must give way to the explicit language which Parliament has chosen to use: "*any other* reason that *appears to the authority* to be relevant" (emphasis added). Read in the context of the statutory scheme as a whole, the words mean exactly what they say.

130   The MMO is entitled to treat the contents of a licensee's proposal and the MMO's views on the merits of that proposal as a relevant reason for varying a licence.

131   Reduced to its bare essentials, s.73(3) gives a power to revoke a licence if the MMO considers that it ought to be varied for at least one of the four types of reason listed. The reason may come from the MMO acting of its own motion or on an application made by the licensee. There is no legal requirement for a two stage approach to s.72(3)(d) to be applied by the MMO, any more than, for example, in the application of s.38(6) of the Planning and Compulsory Purchase Act 2004 (see *Edinburgh City Council v Secretary of State for Scotland* [1997] 1 W.L.R. 1447 at 1459H to 1460C). The MMO may apply each of the alternative bases for making a variation in sub-paragraphs (a) to (d) as a composite expression. For example, they may decide that the licence should be varied to deal with a change in environmental circumstances or to address the safety of navigation. Likewise, they may consider that it is appropriate to allow an unobjectionable variation to a licence proposed by a licensee. A proposed variation and its merits may straightforwardly provide the reason why the MMO accept that a licence should be varied under s.72(3)(d).

132   I accept that if the MMO did not have what it considers to be a relevant reason, then the power in s.72(3)(d) would not be engaged. The language of that provision guards against any attempt to exercise the power in an arbitrary manner for no reason at all. But that should not be treated as giving rise to a duty to provide reasons for the decision. The two concepts should not be elided or confused. Section 72(3) does not impose an obligation to give reasons where the ground for exercising the power to vary falls within sub-paragraphs (a), (b) or (c) and the position is no different where (d) applies. The decision in *Dover* is not in point. In that case fairness required the giving of reasons in the interests of transparency to explain why a decision had been taken against the recommendation of the authority's officer, and where the reasons for taking that course could not otherwise be inferred. Here the legal issue is simply whether the MMO had a reason they considered to be relevant for exercising the power in s.73(2)(d).

133   The MMO's internal consideration of an application goes through a series of "gateways". Gateway 2 involves a review of the application prior to the carrying out of formal consultation. It includes consideration of whether a matter should be treated as a variation and impacts for a range of statutory controls. Gateway 3 involves an assessment of the overall application documentation together with consultation responses to see whether the proposal is acceptable for the purposes of making a determination.

134   The MMO's rubric for the Gateway 2 stage stated that consideration should be
given to the nature and scale of the change proposed compared to the initial licence,
whether the proposed variation would represent a separate and discrete "project",
and the need to advertise and consult. That language broadly accords with the
approach I have set out above. How far it would need to be applied in any particular
case would depend upon an officer's judgment in the circumstances of that case.
Here, the officer stated that the proposed variation concerned updates of the
construction methodology and the inclusion of the disposal of dredged material.
After having reviewed the application and supporting information she considered
that the matter could be dealt with by a variation. In my judgment that demonstrates
that the officer approached the matter lawfully. Of course, at that stage she was
not considering the merits of the matter.

135   The substance of the proposal and the merits of the different aspects of the
application to vary were considered at the determination stage. The EIA Consent
Decision Report contains a detailed assessment of the impacts of the different
components of the proposal. For example, the document assessed the merits of the
proposed disposal at the Portishead site. That site had been selected because of its
depth and the strength of the water flows there. The site is highly dispersive and
had already been designated for disposal of dredged material. There was sufficient
capacity to accommodate the disposal requirements of both Bristol Ports Company
and HPC, the latter's deposit being relatively small (pp.22-23). Portishead would
be acceptable for disposal by HPC, subject to a robust assessment of environmental
impacts (p.25). That assessment was summarised in the decision document. At
paragraphs 5.4.5 and 5.24 the MMO concluded that the Portishead site is an
acceptable location for the disposal of the dredged material.

136   On 2 August 2021 the MMO gave notice of its decision to vary the marine
licence, following "careful consideration of all the evidence submitted to the MMO".
The issuing of this decision as a "regulatory approval" was linked to the
consideration of the EIA Consent Decision Report (see regulations 22 to 24 of the
EIA Regulations 2007). That assessment of the impact and merits of the proposal
forms part of the reasons for the decision to vary under s.73(2)(d).

137   Ms. Mullan has fairly summarised what happened in this case (see paras. 75, 78
and 79 of first witness statement). It was not a difficult decision for the MMO to
treat HPC's application as a variation of the licence. Essentially the works were
in line with the works consented under the original marine licence and its variations
to date. The activities proposed were "intrinsically linked" to that licence, the
dredged material needed to be disposed of, and it had always been envisaged that
that would take place within the estuary. The principle of a disposal to an external
disposal site was well understood and was considered routine. The matter was the
subject of full consultation by virtue of the EIA Regulations 2007.

138   It is plain from the material before the court that the MMO did lawfully consider
that the licence ought to be varied for reasons that appeared to the authority to be
relevant. For all these reasons, ground 2 must be rejected.

Ground 4

139   Regulation 22 of the 2011 Regulations requires the MMO, acting on behalf of
the Secretary of State, to discharge his functions under Part 4 of the MCAA 2009
inter alia for the purpose of ensuring that the waste hierarchy in article 4 of the

Waste Framework Directive is applied to the generation of waste. Those functions include the exercise of the power to vary a marine licence in s.72 of the MCAA 2009.

140   The waste hierarchy in article 4(1) of the Directive sets out the following order of priority for *inter alia* waste management legislation: -

> "(a) prevention;
> (b) preparing for re-use;
> (c) recycling;
> (d) other recovery e.g. energy recovery; and
> (e) disposal"

141   I note that Article 4(2) requires Member States to take into account "environmental impacts" in accordance with Article 13. That article requires Member States to ensure that waste management is carried out without harming the environment. Regulation 22 of the 2011 Regulations also requires the MMO to exercise its functions under Part 4 of the MCAA 2009 for the purposes of implementing Article 13.

A summary of the claimant's submissions

142   Mr. Wolfe submits that the claimant failed to apply the waste hierarchy in its determination of the application to vary HPC's marine licence. He says that the MMO misdirected itself by (a) interpreting PW23 of the DCO as requiring disposal of dredged material into the Severn Estuary SAC, and (b) regarding the DCO as having determined the issue of disposal to the sea. Mr. Wolfe also criticises the MMO for failing to have regard to the South West Marine Plan which requires proposals for the disposal of dredged material to be assessed against the waste hierarchy and treats "direct disposal" as a last resort. D&S IFCA said in their consultation response that HPC had failed to consider the terrestrial use of the dredged material, for example in landscaping schemes. Despite the exhortation in the rubric for the MMO's Gateways to assess the handling of dredge material against each tier in the waste hierarchy, the defendant simply accepted HPC's assessment which relied upon PW23 in the DCO.

Discussion

143   I have already rejected the claimant's argument on the interpretation of PW23 of the DCO (and the conditions of the marine licence to the same effect) under ground 1.

144   It is convenient to look next at the South West Marine Plan. Policy SW-DD-3 does indeed state that it must be demonstrated that proposals for disposal of dredged material have been assessed against the waste hierarchy. However, the claimant's argument completely overlooks paragraph 282 of the Plan which deals with the second tier in the hierarchy, "preparing for re-use". Paragraph 282 states: -

> "Preparing for re-use relates to the re-use of dredged material as sediments, which are commonly referred to as beneficial use projects. Alternative use therefore encompasses beneficial use projects. Examples include:
>
> • engineering uses, such as for construction materials, flood defence, land reclamation, and beach nourishment

> • environmental enhancement, including habitat creation and
> enhancement, and recreation
> • sustainable relocation involves relocating the dredged material back
> into the system that it was removed from to maintain the sediment budget
> of a system, which can be done if the material is in an appropriate
> condition and it is the best option for the system"

145   The return of the dredged material to the SAC falls within the last bullet point
of paragraph 282. The MMO has determined that the material is in an "appropriate
condition" and that is not the subject of legal challenge. Thus, what is required by
PW23 of the DCO, and also by the conditions in the marine licence to the same
effect, falls within the second tier of the waste hierarchy, "preparing for re-use",
because the disposal within the SAC is necessary to maintain its sediment budget.
This is not a method of "last resort" at the bottom of the hierarchy.

146   Unsurprisingly, the claimant does not suggest that tier (a), "prevention", should
have been assessed. That tier is concerned with avoiding the dredging in the first
place. But here the dredging is already authorised by the marine licence and that
has not been challenged. Given that the disposal (or rather relocation back into the
system) is for a purpose falling within the second tier, there was no need for the
MMO to make any further assessment against lower tiers in the hierarchy.

147   It also follows that the allegation that the MMO wrongly fettered its consideration
of the application by its reliance upon PW23 of the DCO is misconceived. Both
PW 23 and conditions of the marine licence tot eh same effect were directly relevant
to the correct application of the waste hierarchy in accordance with the South West
Marine Plan (see also p. 27 of the EIA Consent Decision Report).

148   It is also incorrect for the claimant to assert that the MMO failed to have regard
to the South West Marine Plan. The defendant expressly stated that its decision
had been taken in accordance with the Plan in its notice of Variation dated 2 August
2021. The MMO also addressed the Plan in the EIA Consent Decision Report.

149   HPC's Environmental Statement is consistent with the above analysis. Paragraph
2.1.2 correctly relied upon PW23 of the DCO. Although it was unnecessary to do
so, the Statement recorded the assessment that had been made of other alternatives
involving re-use or recycling, before returning at paragraph 2.2.6 to the key point
that the views of the nature conservation bodies had resulted in the requirement to
return the dredged material to the Severn Estuary SAC. Mr. Barry Phillips, a Lead
Advisor with NE, confirms that his body's stance remains that the dredged material
must be returned to the SAC to maintain the natural balance of sediment in the
Estuary and ensure that there will be no likely significant effects upon qualifying
features of the SAC and Ramsar site (paragraph 12.4 of his witness statement).

150   There is no merit in Mr. Wolfe's criticism of the MMO's responses in the
Gateway documents that they had simply expressed agreement with paragraph
2.1.2 of the Environmental Statement and its reliance upon PW23 of the DCO. For
the reasons given above, when that paragraph is read properly in context, which
includes the South West Marine Plan, the conditions imposed on previous versions
of the marine licence and the views of the statutory nature conservation bodies,
there was no failure by HPC or by the MMO to apply article 4 of the Waste
Framework Directive. But in any event in its Gateway 2 record the MMO did take
into account HPC's assessments of alternatives involving re-use.

151   The claimant rightly decided not to pursue ground 3, its challenge to the HRA carried out under the Habitats Regulations. Given the detailed responses from the MMO and from HPC to ground 4, it is most surprising that the claimant persisted with ground 4. The legal complaints were hopeless. Ground 4 is rejected.

Ground 5

152   Regulation 3(1) of the 2017 Regulations requires *inter alia* the Secretary of State to exercise his "relevant functions" so as to secure compliance with the requirements of the Water Framework Directive. By regulation 2(1) "relevant functions" includes Part 4 of the MCAA 2009 (see schedule 2). The suggestion by HPC that regulation 3(1) of the 2017 Regulations does not apply to the MMO is wholly untenable. The MMO exercises functions under Part 4 of the MCAA 2009 acting as a delegate on behalf of the Secretary of State. Plainly therefore, and as the MMO rightly accepted, the MMO is subject to regulation 3(1) and article 4 of the Water Framework Directive.

153   Certain provisions of the Directive are complex, but I need only summarise parts of the Directive relevant to this ground of challenge.

154   The definition in Article 2 of "surface water" includes certain inland waters, transitional waters and coastal waters. "Transitional waters" are bodies of surface water in the vicinity of river mouths which are partly saline in character as a result of proximity to coastal waters, but which are substantially influenced by freshwater flows. It is common ground that the relevant water body, the Lower Severn, qualifies as a transitional water.

155   Article 4 is entitled "Environmental objectives". Article 4(1)(a)(i) requires Member States to implement the measures necessary "to prevent deterioration of the status of all bodies of surface water", subject to certain provisions which are agreed not to be relevant here (the "first objective"). So far as is relevant, article 4(1)(a)(ii) requires Member States to protect, enhance and restore all bodies of surface water with the aim of achieving "good surface water status" in accordance with Annex V, within a specified timescale ("the second objective"). That timescale is not relevant for the resolution of ground 5.

156   Article 2 defines "good surface water status" as "the status achieved by a surface water body when both its ecological status and its chemical status are at least 'good'". "Good ecological status" is defined by the complex provisions in Annex V. However, this challenge is not concerned with that aspect but solely with the limb concerned with "good surface water chemical status". That expression is defined to mean "the chemical status required to meet the environmental objectives for surface waters established in Article 4(1)(a), that is the chemical status achieved by a body of surface water in which concentration of pollutants do not exceed the environmental quality standards established in Annex IX and under Article 16(7), and under other relevant Community legislation setting environmental quality standards at Community level". The superficial nature of the claimant's challenge under ground 5 meant that the claimant made no submissions on the implications of this definition or the complexities of the other provisions referred to there.

157   The Court should have in mind that the application of these provisions involves the use of expert judgment by a regulatory authority on technical, scientific subjects. Accordingly, in so far as is appropriate, the court affords an enhanced margin of appreciation to a decision based on matters of technical, evaluative judgment (see

e.g. *R. (Mott) v Environment Agency* [2016] 1 W.L.R. 4338; *R. (Spurrier) v Secretary of State for Transport* [2020] P.T.S.R. 240 at [170] to [179] and *R. (Plan B Earth) v Secretary of State for Transport* [2020] P.T.S.R. 1446 at [177]).

158   In addition, the principles summarised in *Keir* at [46] and [78] are relevant. The decision makers in the MMO should be treated as familiar with the statutory framework, the relevant legal and policy principles applicable and to have taken them into account and applied the relevant tests, unless there is a sufficient, positive contra-indication in the evidence before the court (see also *Jones v Mordue* [2016] 1 W.L.R. 2682). Furthermore, the internal records of the decision-making process and the formal decision documents should be read fairly and with an appropriate degree of benevolence when seeking to understand how a decision was reached. They must be read as a whole and in the context of the material and issues with which they, and the parties involved, are taken to be familiar. They must not be read in an overly forensic or legalistic way.

A summary of the claimant's submissions

159   Mr. Wolfe relied upon the decision of the Grand Chamber of the CJEU in *Bund fur Umwelt und Naturschultz Deutschland eV v Bundesrepublik Deutschland* (C-461/13) EU:C:2015:433. At [29] to [51] the Court held firstly, that article 4(1)(a) applies to the authorisation of individual projects as well as to water management planning. Secondly, a Member State is required to refuse authorisation for an individual project (unless a derogation under Article 4(7) is granted) where either (i) it may cause a deterioration in the status of a surface water body or (ii) "it jeopardises the attainment of good surface water status or of good ecological potential and good surface water chemical status" by the relevant date. In other words, a regulatory authority must be satisfied that neither the first nor the second objective of article 4(1)(a) would be harmed before granting a project approval.

160   The claimant does not challenge the MMO's handling of the first objective. The MMO was satisfied that there would not be a deterioration in surface water status through the disposal of dredged material at the designated Portishead site. The claimant sole submission is that the MMO did not address the requirement that that deposition should not jeopardise the attainment of "good surface water *chemical* status".

161   Essentially, the claimant makes two specific criticisms. First, HPC's material showed that the current status of the Lower Severn water body is only "moderate" (the category below "good") because it fails the relevant standards for two chemicals, mercury and brominated diphenyl ethers. The MMO's conclusion that the disposal at Portishead would not have an adverse effect on water quality would result in the maintenance of that existing "poor quality" (as the claimant puts it) in relation to chemical status. Thus, the MMO failed to determine whether the disposal would jeopardise the attainment of "good" water quality status.

162   Second, this criticism is reinforced by the fact that ultimately in its Gateway 3 decision the MMO merely concluded that the "risks would be within acceptable limits".

Discussion

163   There is nothing in the language of Article 4(1)(a) or in the decision in *Bund fur Umwelt* to suggest that a regulatory approval must be refused unless the project

would itself contribute (e.g. positively) towards the attainment of a good surface water status, or good chemical status. Those legal sources do not indicate that, for example, a proposal must contribute to that objective by reducing existing chemical levels which cause the current status of the water body to be less than "good", *a fortiori* where there is no evidence to indicate that either the proposal, or the project of which it forms a part, would contribute to those chemical levels.

164   The legal issues in the *Bund fur Umwelt* case were concerned with very different matters, in particular whether article 4(1)(a) applies to decision-making on regulatory project approvals as well as water management planning, and whether Article 4(1)(a) is infringed where a proposal would cause the quality of a water body to deteriorate without reducing its "status class". The requirement laid down by the CJEU in relation to the second objective of Article 4(1)(a) is that a project should not *jeopardise* the attainment of good surface water status. "Jeopardise" means endanger or put at risk.

165   Mr. Wolfe did not explain how this proposal, which would not cause any harm to the chemical quality of the water body (including the two chemicals for which it is currently failing), could itself jeopardise, let alone "would be bound to jeopardise", its enhancement from a moderate to a good status. For that reason alone ground 5 should fail.

166   But I am also grateful to Ms. Blackmore for taking the court carefully through the relevant documents in some detail to show that there is no foundation in the evidence for the claimant's criticisms. Those criticisms looked selectively at only a few passages in the material and out of context.

167   Paragraph 5.1 of HPC's report to accompany its application to vary the licence introduced the WFD assessment they had carried out referring to relevant requirements of the Directive and 2017 Regulations.

168   Paragraph 5.2.1 of the Environmental Statement referred to "the fundamental requirement" of the WFD to attain "good overall water body status". Paragraph 5.2.12 correctly stated that a licensed project must demonstrate that "it will not cause or contribute to deterioration in the water body or jeopardise the water body achieving good status". Table 9.5 on p.155 acknowledged that the Lower Severn currently fails in relation to chemical status as regards mercury and brominated diphenyl ethers and therefore has a "moderate" status. Paragraph 9.5.4 stated that because of the short-term nature of the works, taking place over a period of only 6 months, it was not expected that there would be any changes to the baseline environmental conditions. Analysis had shown that the dredged material would be of an acceptable quality for disposal at sea (paras. 9.6.2 and 9.9.4 to 9.9.6). The proposal would not affect the water body's capacity to reach "good environmental potential".

169   Paragraph 2.1.5 of HPC's WFD Assessment stated that the aim of the impact assessment was to determine whether the proposal would have a "non-temporary" effect on the status of one or more of the WFD water quality elements at the scale of the water body. "The process requires the assessment to consider whether the activity is likely to cause the parameter to fail to achieve good chemical status". Paragraph 2.1.16 expressly stated that if during the impact assessment stage it were to be shown that the proposal would be likely to affect water status at water body level, for example, by preventing achievement of a WFD objective, potential measures would have to be investigated. Paragraphs 2.1.7 to 2.1.8 summarised the provisions in Article 4(1)(a) for derogating from the requirements of Article 4(1)(a).

HPC's documents showed that they had the relevant legislative provisions well in mind.

170   Table 3.7 of the WFD Assessment showed that the proposed disposal would not release any chemicals on the Environmental Quality Standards Directive ("EQSD") list (see Directive 2008/105/EC reflected also in the 2017 Regulations). Further details were contained in chapter 9 of the Environmental Statement. Table 3.10 of the WFD assessment report summarised the impact assessment in relation to the risk of "WFD deterioration". It was concluded that there would be no deterioration and no mitigation was required. Sections 3.4 and 3.5 of the assessment said that there was no need for any measures to be taken to manage any WFD compliance risk or to seek a derogation under Article 4(7) of the Directive. The conclusion in Section 4.1.1 was that the disposal would not compromise the objectives of the Directive.

171   The MMO's Gateway 2 record gave a short summary of the assessment by HPC.

172   The MMO then commissioned a review of HPC's work by its independent, specialist consultants ABPmer. They provided a detailed report dated 9 March 2021. They made one criticism of the WFD assessment which they described as a "minor omission" which could be "readily addressed". In relation to table 3.10, it was said that there was a lack of further consideration of contaminants that would be released, noting that the Lower Severn was currently failing standards for two chemicals. The consultant did not criticise, for example, paragraphs 3.4.1, 3.5.1 or 4.1.1 of the WFD assessment. I also note that at page 4 of their review, the independent consultants said: -

> "We have not identified any significant marine water or sediment quality, marine ecology or navigation issues with the use of the Portishead disposal site"

173   Mr. Wolfe referred to the chemical contamination issues raised by D&S IFCA and by NSC.

174   HPC provided a Supplementary Environmental Information Report dated 14 April 2021 which added to the information previously supplied in order to address the comments which had been made. This included an addition to table 3.10.

175   The MMO's Gateway 3 document recorded that EA and NE raised no concerns on these matters. The MMO referred to issues raised by ABPmer and others and the further information supplied by HPC in response. Following a further review of that material, ABPmer had confirmed to the MMO that they were satisfied with the information provided by HPC. It was against that overall background that the MMO stated that it considered the "risks to be within acceptable limits". An expert body such as the MMO was entitled to summarise its views in an internal document in this way. Gateway 3 does not amount to a decision letter. Given also that jeopardising the attainment of good quality status is a risk-based concept, there is no basis for the court to infer from the language used that the MMO did not take into account the second objective of article 4(1) of the Directive (see also *Keir*).

176   Section 5.2 of the EIA Consent Decision Report also considered chemical contamination. There is no need for me to refer to the details of the assessment. However, I note that in relation to polycyclic aromatic hydrocarbons (PAHs), which had been raised by D&S IFCA, the MMO stated that the levels of PAH contamination are typical for industrialised estuaries such as the Severn. They occur widely within the estuary because of the dynamic nature of the movement

of sediment. The amount of sediment remobilised by the disposal of the material dredged by HPC would be a fraction of the sediment remobilised on each tide in the estuary. The disposal would not exacerbate the existing failure of the Severn in relation to two chemical contaminants.

177   Page 32 of the EIA Consent Decision Report noted that, according to HPC's assessment, the disposal would not compromise the objectives of the Water Framework Directive. Page 34 of the Report noted that following the submission of supplemental information by HPC on 14 April 2021 the EA responded with no objections. Ms. Blackmore is right to emphasise the EA's particular status as the "appropriate agency" responsible for many of the key functions under the 2017 Regulations.

178   There is no merit in ground 5. The "good status" objective was properly taken into account in the assessment by HPC, ABPmer and by the MMO. As in the case of ground 4, it is most surprising that the claimant chose to pursue this matter as a legal ground of challenge, given the detailed responses provided by the MMO and HPC and, in this instance, the lack of support from the *Bund fur Umwelt* decision for the claimant's legal argument.

Conclusion

179   Each of the grounds of challenge has been rejected. The claim for judicial review is dismissed.

R. (ON THE APPLICATION OF JAMES) v DOVER DC

QUEEN'S BENCH DIVISION (ADMINISTRATIVE COURT)

Lang J. DBE: 28 April 2022

[2022] EWHC 961 (Admin); [2023] Env. L.R. 3

⚖ Areas of Outstanding Natural Beauty; Duty to provide reasons; Fallback position; Motor sports; Noise; Planning permission; Right to respect for home; Right to respect for private and family life; Statutory nuisance

H1 *Town & Country Planning—statutory nuisance—judicial review—noise and other nuisance from motor racing circuit—relationship between pollution control and planning regimes—whether 'fallback position' unlawfully assessed as existing noise levels constituting a statutory nuisance—whether failure to properly assess impact on AONB—whether failure to give adequate reasons and to have regard to art.8 of ECHR*

H2   The claimant (J) sought judicial review of the grant of planning permission by the defendant council (D) for development at a Motor Racing Circuit in an Area of Outstanding Natural Beauty (AONB). The Circuit had been in operation for over 50 years, with a long history of planning permissions and concerns about noise. D served an abatement notice on the Circuit, on the basis that it was satisfied that a statutory nuisance under the Environmental Protection Act 1990 s.79(1)(g) "exists and is likely to recur" from "the emissions from noise from motor vehicle activities, motorsports events and associated activities on site". A revised abatement notice restricted the recurrence of the noise nuisance by requiring that specified noise limits were not exceeded for the 52 events which were allowed each calendar year. This was expressed by allowing two event days per year with unrestricted noise levels and noise limits for the remaining events. In 2019, the application was made for permission to develop the Circuit and to increase the days of operation. The Officer's Report recommended that permission be granted, subject to conditions, for reasons including that:

> "Whilst the use of the circuit would be significantly expanded, it is considered that this would be balanced against the improved management of the circuit and more stringent monitoring (which would be secured by condition). Overall, the development would not exacerbate the impacts of noise and, therefore, no additional planning harm would be caused."

H3   J submitted that she and other local residents were adversely affected by noise from the Circuit. She argued that D erred in law in reaching its decision; (i) in regarding the existing level of noise, which was a statutory nuisance and/or causing noise at a Significant Observed Adverse Effect Level (SOAEL), as a fallback position against which to judge the application for development; (ii) in its approach to the effect of the proposed development on the AONB; (iii) failing to give adequate reasons for the Decision; and (iv) failing to have regard to ECHR art.8 and/or a breach of art.8, contrary to the Human Rights Act 1998.

H4   **Held,** in dismissing the claim:

H5   (1) Whether or not there had been any proceedings under the pollution control regime, the planning decision-maker should assume that the regime would operate effectively in the future, to avoid needless duplication. However, where there had been such proceedings, they would be a material consideration which the planning decision-maker must consider and take into account. In the present case, D had correctly taken the view that the statutory nuisance proceedings and notices were a material planning consideration which it had to consider. The Officer gave a detailed and balanced account of the issues on noise which Members had to consider and gave appropriate advice. The Officer had been correct to identify the fallback position as that which currently existed, under the existing planning permission and the existing revised abatement notice. D was not required to have considered what was required in order to control the nuisance, whether by way of a further abatement notice or otherwise and take that into account as the correct fallback position. That would not be a fallback position, as defined. Nor would it be consistent with the NPPF. It followed that the Officer had not been required to consider or advise Members as to what further abatement notices might be served in the future. It was not their responsibility to make any decision on such matters, and speculation would not have been appropriate.

H6   (2) At the heart of the objection to the fallback position was that the current level of noise amounted to a statutory nuisance and/or a SOAEL, and therefore it could not properly be relied upon. There was no legal basis for this submission. In the view of the Officers, the revised abatement notice restricted, but did not eliminate, the nuisance. Once satisfied that a statutory nuisance existed, D complied with its duty under s.80(2A) and served an abatement notice which required the nuisance to be restricted in accordance with its schedule. It was a matter for D's discretion whether it chose to impose all or any of the requirements available in s.80(1). There was no duty to serve a notice that required the statutory nuisance to be abated. The revised notice was lawful and could be relied upon as part of the fallback position. For those reasons, it was not irrational to treat the revised abatement notice as part of the fallback position.

H7   (3) Although the objectors alleged that the Circuit was being operated in breach of the revised abatement notice, the Officer advised Members no breaches had been identified on visits made. Members were correctly advised in to consider whether the proposed planning permission would be more effective in controlling noise levels, because it would include more stringent and more effective conditions than the existing planning permission and revised abatement notice. Planning conditions were more flexible and could include a wider range of requirements than an abatement notice, which had to be capable of forming the basis of a criminal charge. It was a matter for the Officer's discretion to determine how much of the history of the abatement notices needed to be relayed to Members. There had been sufficient evidence upon which the Officer and Members could rationally come to the conclusion that the increased number of days upon which activities were permitted would not increase the impact on local residents. The Officer had also given Members detailed and appropriate advice on the AONB.

H8   (4) The statement made under the Town and Country Planning (Environmental Impact Assessment) Regulations 2017 (SI 2017/571) reg.30, read together with the detailed Officer's Report, the Minutes and the Decision Notice, met the standard of reasons required for the statement under the EIA Regulations. Aside from that duty, a planning authority was generally not required to give reasons for the grant of planning permission.

H9   (5) Both the Officer and Members had art.8 well in mind. Alternatively, even if art.8 was not adequately considered in the Officer's Report, it was highly likely that the decision would not have been substantially different if it had specifically addressed art.8 in the report.

H10 **Cases referred to:**

Botta v Italy (21439/93) (1998) 26 E.H.R.R. 241; 4 B.H.R.C. 81; (1999) 2 C.C.L. Rep. 53 ECtHR

Coventry (t/a RDC Promotions) v Lawrence [2014] UKSC 13; [2014] A.C. 822; [2014] Env. L.R. 25

Dover DC v Campaign to Protect Rural England (Kent) [2017] UKSC 79; [2018] 1 W.L.R. 108; [2018] Env. L.R. 17

Gateshead MBC v Secretary of State for the Environment [1995] Env. L.R. 37; (1996) 71 P. & C.R. 350; [1994] 1 P.L.R. 85 CA (Civ Div)

Lough v First Secretary of State [2004] EWCA Civ 905; [2004] 1 W.L.R. 2557; [2005] 1 P. & C.R. 5

Mansell v Tonbridge and Malling BC [2017] EWCA Civ 1314; [2019] P.T.S.R. 1452; [2018] J.P.L. 176

Monkhill Ltd v Secretary of State for Housing, Communities and Local Government [2021] EWCA Civ 74; [2021] P.T.S.R. 1432; [2021] J.P.L. 1178

Moore v Secretary of State for Communities and Local Government [2013] EWCA Civ 1194; [2014] J.P.L. 362

Norman v Secretary of State for Housing, Communities and Local Government [2018] EWHC 2910 (Admin); [2019] Env. L.R. 14

R. (on the application of Newsmith Stainless Ltd) v Secretary of State for the Environment, Transport and the Regions [2001] EWHC 74 (Admin); [2017] P.T.S.R. 1126

R. (on the application of Frack Free Balcombe Residents Association) v West Sussex CC [2014] EWHC 4108 (Admin)

R. (on the application of Palmer) v Herefordshire Council [2016] EWCA Civ 1061; [2017] 1 W.L.R. 411

R. (on the application of RLT Built Environment Ltd) v Cornwall Council [2016] EWHC 2817 (Admin); [2017] J.P.L. 378; [2017] A.C.D. 16

Seddon Properties Ltd v Secretary of State for the Environment (1981) 42 P. & C.R. 26; (1978) 248 E.G. 951; [1978] J.P.L. 835 QBD

South Buckinghamshire DC v Porter [2004] UKHL 33; [2004] 1 W.L.R. 1953; [2005] 1 P. & C.R. 6

Tatar v Romania (App. No.67021/01) unreported 27 January 2009 ECtHR

H11 **Legislation referred to:**

ECHR art.8

TFEU art.191
Rio Declaration on Environment and Development,
Senior Courts Act 1981 s.31
Environmental Protection Act 1990 ss.79, 80 and 82
Town and Country Planning Act 1990 s.70
Human Rights Act 1998 s.6
Countryside and Rights of Way Act 2000 s.85
Planning and Compulsory Purchase Act 2004 s.38
Town and Country Planning (Environmental Impact Assessment) Regulations
2017 (SI 2017/571) regs 29 and 30

H12 *E. Dehon* (instructed by Richard Buxton Solicitors) appeared on behalf of the
claimant.
R. Banwell (instructed by Legal Services) appeared on behalf of the defendant.
K. Leigh (instructed by Direct Access) appeared on behalf of the interested party.

JUDGMENT

MRS JUSTICE LANG:
1   The Claimant seeks judicial review of the Decision by the Defendant ("the
Council"), dated 29 May 2020, to grant planning permission for development at
Lydden Hill Race Circuit, Wootton, Kent CT4 6ET ("the Race Circuit").

2   The Race Circuit is a motor sports venue, operated by the Interested Party ("IP").
It is located approximately one kilometre north-east of Wootton Village, in the
Kent Downs Area of Outstanding Natural Beauty ("AONB"). The Claimant resides
in Wootton Village, and she and other local residents are adversely affected by
noise from the Race Circuit. The Council is the local planning authority for the
area.

3   The Claimant submits that the Council erred in law in reaching its Decision on
the following grounds:

 i)   Error of law in regarding the existing level of noise, which was a statutory
nuisance and/or causing noise at a Significant Observed Adverse Effect
Level ("SOAEL"), as a fallback position against which to judge the IP's
application for planning permission to develop the Race Circuit;

 ii) Error of law in its approach to the effect of the proposed development on
the Kent Downs AONB;

 iii) Failure to give adequate reasons for the decision;

 iv) Failure to have regard to Article 8 of the European Convention on Human
Rights ("ECHR"), and/or a breach of Article 8, contrary to the Human Rights
Act 1998 ("HRA 1998").

4   Permission was initially refused on the papers, but subsequently granted by
Timothy Corner QC, sitting as a Deputy Judge of the High Court, at an oral renewal
hearing on 19 November 2020.

History

5   The Race Circuit has been in operation for over 50 years. There is a lengthy
history of planning permissions at the site, and concerns about noise.

6   The AONB Management Plan provides that the Race Circuit and the surrounding area has a tranquillity index rating of medium to medium/low.

7   Permanent planning permission was first granted in 1986. Prior to the Decision, the Race Circuit operated under the limitations and conditions of planning permission DOV/14/00415, dated 11 July 2014. It maintained conditions which had previously been included in planning permission DOV/12/00589, but varied the earlier permission so as to allow several one-off events to take place in 2014.

8   The relevant conditions of planning permission DOV/14/00415 were as follows:

> "1. Notwithstanding the provisions of the Town and Country Planning (General Permitted Development) Order 1995 (or any order revoking and re-enacting that Order with or without modification), the site shall not be used for any purpose other than motor car, motor cycle and kart racing (including practice for those purposes).
> Reason: To prevent an over-intensive development and in the interests of visual and residential amenity and preserving the character of the AONB.
> 2. The following one-off events are permitted to be carried out on the land in 2014:
>
>> * One additional hour of racing on Sunday 25th May 2014, between 4pm and 5pm (for the World Rallycross Championships);
>> * Three consecutive weekends of two-day racing events in May 2014 (10th-11th May, 17th-18th May and 24th-25th May);
>> * Three consecutive weekends of two-day racing events in June-July 2014 (21st-22nd June, 28th-29th June and 5th-6th July 2014).
>
> Reason: To ensure that the event days comply with those permitted under this application and in the interests of sustainability and residential amenity.
> 3. Except for those events specifically set out in condition 2, the permitted uses shall not be carried out on the land on:
>> (a) More than 52 days in any calendar year;
>> (b) Consecutive days in excess of 12 occasions in any calendar year;
>> (c) More than 2 consecutive days;
>> (d) Two consecutive days at intervals of less than 10 clear days;
>> (e) Except between the hours of 9am and 6pm on weekdays and 10.30am and 4pm on Sundays.
>
> For the purposes of this condition and condition 3, the term 'calendar year' means a period commencing on 1 April in one year and ending on 31 March in the succeeding year....
> Reason: In the interests of residential and visual amenity.
> 4. A schedule of the days in which the use of the track is anticipated in the succeeding calendar year shall be submitted to the Local Planning Authority no later than 31st March each year. The Local Planning Authority shall be notified of any change in the submitted schedule prior to any change to the agreed schedule.
> Reason: In the interests of residential amenity and to ensure that the track is being used in accordance with approved details.
> 5. The public shall not be admitted to the site other than on days when public race meetings take place.

Reason: In the interests of visual and residential amenity and preserving the character of the AONB.

6. Noise emitted from public address system on the site shall not exceed 40dB LAeq (5 minutes) at any time as measured at map grid reference points 230.465, 232.468, 240.464 and 245.466.The public address system shall, on request, be available for measuring and testing purposes by the Local Planning Authority at any reasonable time.

Reason: In the interest of residential amenity.

7. The public address system shall be used only on days on which spectators are admitted to the site, between the hours of 9am and 6pm on weekdays and 10.30am and 4pm on Sundays. Its use, except in the event of an emergency, shall be limited to the purposes of commentary on racing and race practising. The public address system may be additionally used on the aforementioned days between the hours of 8am to 9am on weekdays and 9.30am to 10.30am on Sundays for the purpose of pre-race testing and the making of announcements to competitors.

Reason: In the interest of residential amenity and preserving the character of the AONB.

8. All vehicles operating on the track shall be fitted with noise emission control equipment in accordance with the current Technical Regulations of the RAC Motor Sports Association or, as may be appropriate, the Auto Cycle Union. For track events regulated by the RAC, MSA vehicles shall not be admitted to the track if they exceed the maximum noise limit for that class of vehicles, as set out by that organisation. Vehicles not complying with those regulations shall not be admitted to the track without the prior written consent of the Local Planning Authority. Reason: In the interest of residential amenity and preserving the character of the AONB."

9   There is a history of the Council addressing noise complaints concerning the Race Circuit from 1982. From 2011 onwards, the Council's Environmental Protection Team ("EPT") investigated whether noise from the Race Circuit was causing a statutory noise nuisance. Following a number of visits to three different residential properties, carried out in 2014, and analysis of noise recorded at those properties, the Council's Environmental Protection Officers recommended that a noise abatement notice be served under the Environmental Protection Act 1990, because noise levels from the track constituted a statutory nuisance at residential properties.

10   On 29 April 2015, the Council served an abatement notice on the Race Circuit, on the basis that it was satisfied that a statutory nuisance under section 79(1)(g) of the Environmental Protection Act 1990 "exists and is likely to recur". The cause of the nuisance was "the emissions from noise from motor vehicle activities, motorsports events and associated activities on site".

11   The abatement notice required the noise to be restricted by controlling the number of days on which events were allowed to take place, and stipulating a decibel level (measured at specific points) which should not be exceeded, apart from when certain exemptions applied. The Council's Head of Legal Services later described these in an email to the IP's legal representative as "the minimum that would provide the community with some relief".

12   On 19 May 2015, the Race Circuit appealed against the abatement notice. At the same time, it sought to regularise the position by making a planning application to develop the Race Circuit and increase the number of days upon which it could operate.

13   Twenty one residents affected by the noise, including the Claimant, provided witness statements for the appeal in support of the Council. As part of the appeal process, the Council obtained an independent expert report from an acoustician and former environmental health officer, of MAS Environmental Ltd ("MAS"), dated 23 November 2015. This considered both the abatement notice appeal, and the proposed planning application and Noise Management Plan. As to the latter, the expert criticised the proposed increase in the number of days of impact from 52 to 156, stating that whilst "the maximum static noise emission level of vehicles on these extra days is lower than proposed for 52 of the days it does not equate to any meaningful known reduction in community levels as there are too many variables." (paragraph 2.25).

14   The expert concluded that the Race Circuit caused substantial adverse noise, amounting to a statutory nuisance. He supported the approach adopted in the abatement notice of restricting the noise, but observed that "it may allow an excessive number of highly noisy days" and that, as "the noise intrusion is substantial, adverse impact on the use of dwellings will remain during event days even with the decibel limits set" by the abatement notice (paragraphs 2.35-2.36). The expert concluded:

> "In my experience a community facing 52 days of disruption of motor sport noise at these levels around their home in any one year and with limited periods of respite will continue to experience material interference arguably higher than should be tolerated" (paragraph 5.67).

15   In November and December 2015, the Council and the Race Circuit came to an agreement, as a result of which the Race Circuit undertook to withdraw the appeal and the Council undertook to withdraw the abatement notice and serve a revised abatement notice.

16   The Council also undertook to withdraw the revised abatement notice once planning application DOV/15/00827 (or any amended or resubmitted application for similar development) had been determined and any appeal concluded.

17   On 3 December 2015 the Council withdrew the first abatement notice and served the revised abatement notice on the Race Circuit. The revised abatement notice stated that the Council was satisfied that a statutory nuisance under section 79(1)(g) of the Environmental Protection Act 1990 "exists and is likely to recur". The cause of the nuisance was "the emissions from noise from motor vehicle activities, motorsports events and associated activities on site".

18   The revised abatement notice restricted the recurrence of the noise nuisance by requiring that specified noise limits were not exceeded for the 52 events which were allowed each calendar year. This was expressed by allowing two event days per calendar year with unrestricted noise levels and noise limits for the remaining events being restricted to 24 events no greater than 55 dB LAeq 1hour and 26 events no greater than 50 dB LAeq 1hour as measured at specified locations. Compliance with the revised abatement notice is monitored in accordance with the Council's monitoring Guidance Note.

19   The Council commissioned a further report from MAS in 2017 on the IP's application for planning permission. The application was refused by the Council, for non noise-related reasons, on 6 June 2018.

20   On 25 May 2019, the IP again applied for planning permission to develop the Race Circuit and to increase the days of operation.

21   The Non-Technical Summary of the IP's Environmental Statement in support of the application described the increase in days of operation as follows:

> **"Operational Phase**
> 8.4.5 In relation to additional activity, the proposed development would allow for 52 days where noise levels would be limited to 45 dB LAeq (Category 4) and 52 days where noise levels would be limited to 40 dB LAeq (Category 5), with the remaining days of "other activity" not expected to produce noise of any note. These sound levels are all below the LOAEL threshold, such that impacts are assessed to be Negligible or None.
>
> 8.4.6 At present permitted track operating hours on Sundays are 10.30am - 4pm. The proposed track operating hours for two Sundays per year are 9am - 5pm (i.e. a total of 2.5 additional operating hours on no more than 2 Sundays per year). These impacts are to be offset by the removal of one operating day from Category 1, 2 or 3, i.e. removing an entire day of minor, moderate or major adverse impact from the annual calendar to offset 2.5 hours of additional activity on a Sunday. The impact of the proposed additional hours on 2 Sundays per year is therefore assessed as Negligible at worst.
>
> …
>
> **Conclusions**
> 8.4.10 In conclusion, the proposals will result in impacts of Negligible significance."

22   Data from Three Spires Acoustics, in a report commissioned by concerned residents, was provided to the Council indicating numerous breaches of the revised abatement notice. These were included as appendices to representations objecting to the application for planning permission.

23   The Officer's Report ("OR") recommended that permission be granted, subject to conditions, for the reasons summarised in the "Overall Conclusions" which were as follows (so far as material):

> **"3. Overall Conclusions**
> 3.1 In June 2018 planning permission was refused for a comparable application for two reasons. The first reason related to the proposed erection of engineering units (Use Classes B1 and B2). In the absence of evidence to justify a functional need for the units to be located at the site or an overriding public benefit, the units were considered to be unsustainable. The second reason for refusal related to harm caused to the scenic beauty of the AONB, by virtue of the location, scale, height, design and use of materials of the buildings on site and the location and scale of the camping area. Following the refusal, the applicant has significantly amended the scheme in response to these reasons for refusal, omitting the engineering units (therefore addressing the first reason for refusal) and omitting the camping area which was cited in the second reason for refusal. The second reason for refusal also relied upon the visual impact caused by the buildings on site. These buildings have been rationalized

into one building which is significantly smaller than the previously proposed building and would be positioned in a relatively concealed location. The previous application was considered acceptable in all other material respects (including noise and transportation), subject to conditions. This decision is material to the assessment of the current application.

3.2 Whilst the development accords with most relevant policies in the development plan, the location of the site conflicts with the blanket presumption against development which would generate travel outside of the settlement confines found within policy DM11. The increased use of the site is also contrary to Policy AS13, which states that proposals to expand the use of Lydden Circuit for motor sports or intensify its frequency will be refused, albeit many of the proposed additional uses are not motor sports. Notwithstanding the judgement that these policies carry reduced weight, it is therefore necessary to consider whether there are material considerations which indicate that permission should be granted.

3.3 The site lies within the Kent Downs Area of Outstanding Natural Beauty for which there is statutory protection and, as such, the development is considered to be in a sensitive location. The proposed Pavilion has been substantially reduced in size since the 2015 application was refused and would be located in a relatively discreet position on the site, where its visual impact would be limited. Where views would be possible, the building would be seen within the context of the existing features of the race circuit which already give the site an appearance which is distinct from the surrounding countryside. A landscaping scheme has also been proposed to provide further mitigation. Given the scale of the development and its location in the AONB, members may wish to undertake a Site Visit, to enable them to reach their own views on the landscape impacts of the development; however, this report concludes that the impact on the character of the landscape would be minor (albeit the sites location within the AONB requires that great weight be given to this harm).

3.4 Noise is an important consideration in the assessment of the development, with the existing site causing a managed (through a Noise Abatement Notice) nuisance to neighbouring properties and the majority of objections raising noise as a concern. Regard has been had for the Noise Policy Statement for England and advice has been received from the Councils Environmental Health team. Whilst the use of the circuit would be significantly expanded, it is considered that this would be balanced against the improved management of the circuit and more stringent monitoring (which would be secured by condition). Overall, the development would not exacerbate the impacts of noise and, therefore, no additional planning harm would be caused. The development would not harm the living conditions of neighbours in any other respect, subject to conditions.

…

3.10 The development would draw significant investment into the District and provide significant employment benefits, gaining the support of the Councils Strategic Tourism Manager, Tourism Manager Head of Inward Investment. Given the demography of the District and the unemployment rate, this benefit must be attributed substantial weight in the planning balance.

3.11 As the development is contrary to the development plan, it is necessary to considered whether the material considerations indicate that the development plan should be set aside and permission be granted. The National Planning Policy Framework has been assessed, being and important material consideration. It is acknowledged that this is a balanced case, which largely turns on whether the economic benefits are sufficient to provide an exceptional circumstance, and public interest, to set aside the conflict with parts of the development and to warrant major development within the AONB. Whilst the development would cause some harm to the character of the area, it is concluded that the economic benefits of this application, when weighed against the level of harm caused, are compelling.

3.12 Overall, it is considered that the application has overcome the concerns which led to the 2015 application being refused for two reasons (the principle of the engineering units and visual harm). The proposed development would cause a minor adverse impact on the character and beauty of the area, albeit within the context of the site which is already visually distinct from the agrarian countryside beyond. However, the development would provide significant benefits, most notably in terms of its potential contribution to the local economy. The application will also provide a more appropriate access onto the A2 and greater controls of noise. Whilst it is acknowledged that the application conflicts with policies DM11 and AS13, it is considered that the benefits of the application, in particular the economic benefit, indicate that these conflicts should be set aside and planning permission be granted."

24   At a meeting of the Planning Committee on 30 January 2020, the application for planning permission was approved, subject to conditions. On 29 May 2020, planning permission was granted.

Legal principles and policy/guidance

Judicial review

25   In a claim for judicial review, the Claimant must establish a public law error on the part of the decision-maker. The exercise of planning judgment and the weighing of the various issues are matters for the decision-maker and not for the Court: *Seddon Properties Ltd v Secretary of State for the Environment* (1981) 42 P. & C.R. 26. A legal challenge is not an opportunity for a review of the planning merits: *Newsmith v Secretary of State for the Environment, Transport and the Regions* [2001] EWHC 74 (Admin).

The development plan and material considerations

26   Section 70(2) of the Town and Country Planning Act 1990 ("TCPA 1990") provides that the decision-maker shall have regard to the provisions of the development plan, so far as material to the application. Section 38(6) of the Planning and Compulsory Purchase Act ("PCPA 2004") provides:

"If regard is to be had to the development plan for the purpose of any determination to be made under the planning Acts, the determination must be made in accordance with the plan unless material considerations indicate otherwise."

Planning officers' reports

27   The principles to be applied when considering a challenge to a planning officer's report were summarised by the Court of Appeal in *Mansell v Tonbridge and Malling BC* [2019] P.T.S.R. 1452, per Lindblom LJ, at [42]:

> "42. The principles on which the court will act when criticism is made of a planning officer's report to committee are well settled. To summarise the law as it stands:
>
> (1) The essential principles are as stated by the Court of Appeal in *R. v Selby DC Ex p. Oxton Farms* [1997] E.G. 60 (C.S.) (see, in particular, the judgment of Judge L.J., as he then was). They have since been confirmed several times by this court, notably by Sullivan L.J. in *R. (on the application of Siraj) v Kirklees MC* [2010] EWCA Civ 1286, at paragraph 19, and applied in many cases at first instance (see, for example, the judgment of Hickinbottom J., as he then was, in *R. (on the application of Zurich Assurance Ltd (t/a Threadneedle Property Investments)) v North Lincolnshire Council* [2012] EWHC 3708 (Admin), at paragraph 15).
>
> (2) The principles are not complicated. Planning officers' reports to committee are not to be read with undue rigour, but with reasonable benevolence, and bearing in mind that they are written for councillors with local knowledge (see the judgment of Baroness Hale of Richmond in *R. (on the application of Morge) v Hampshire CC* [2011] UKSC 2, at paragraph 36, and the judgment of Sullivan J., as he then was, in *R. v Mendip DC Ex p. Fabre* (2000) 80 P. & C.R. 500, at p.509). Unless there is evidence to suggest otherwise, it may reasonably be assumed that, if the members followed the officer's recommendation, they did so on the basis of the advice that he or she gave (see the judgment of Lewison L.J. in *Palmer v Herefordshire Council* [2016] EWCA Civ 1061, at paragraph 7). The question for the court will always be whether, on a fair reading of the report as a whole, the officer has materially misled the members on a matter bearing upon their decision, and the error has gone uncorrected before the decision was made. Minor or inconsequential errors may be excused. It is only if the advice in the officer's report is such as to misdirect the members in a material way — so that, but for the flawed advice it was given, the committee's decision would or might have been different — that the court will be able to conclude that the decision itself was rendered unlawful by that advice.
>
> (3) Where the line is drawn between an officer's advice that is significantly or seriously misleading — misleading in a material way — and advice that is misleading but not significantly so will always depend on the context and circumstances in which the advice was given, and on the possible consequences of it. There will be cases in which a planning officer has inadvertently led a committee astray by making some significant error of fact (see, for example *R. (on the application of Loader) v Rother DC* [2016] EWCA Civ 795), or has plainly misdirected the members as to the meaning of a relevant policy (see, for example, *Watermead Parish Council v Aylesbury Vale DC* [2017] EWCA Civ 152). There will be others where the officer has simply failed to deal with a matter on which the committee ought to receive explicit advice if the local planning authority is to be seen

to have performed its decision-making duties in accordance with the law (see, for example, *R. (on the application of Williams) v Powys CC* [2017] EWCA Civ 427). But unless there is some distinct and material defect in the officer's advice, the court will not interfere."

Noise and nuisance

28   Sections 79 to 82 of the Environmental Protection Act 1990 ("EPA 1990") deal with control of statutory nuisances.

29   Section 80 makes provision for the service of an abatement notice by a local authority, as follows:

"80.

(1) Subject to subsection (2A) where a local authority is satisfied that a statutory nuisance exists, or is likely to occur or recur, in the area of the authority, the local authority shall serve a notice ("an abatement notice") imposing all or any of the following requirements—

(a) requiring the abatement of the nuisance or prohibiting or restricting its occurrence or recurrence;

(b) requiring the execution of such works, and the taking of such other steps, as may be necessary for any of those purposes, and the notice shall specify the time or times within which the requirements of the notice are to be complied with.....

(2A) Where a local authority is satisfied that a statutory nuisance falling within paragraph (g) of section 79(1) above exists, or is likely to occur or recur, in the area of the authority, the authority shall—

(a) serve an abatement notice in respect of the nuisance in accordance with subsections (1) and (2) above; or

(b) take such other steps as it thinks appropriate for the purpose of persuading the appropriate person to abate the nuisance or prohibit or restrict its occurrence or recurrence.

(2B) If a local authority has taken steps under subsection (2A)(b) above and either of the conditions in subsection (2C) below is satisfied, the authority shall serve an abatement notice in respect of the nuisance.

(2C) The conditions are—

(a) that the authority is satisfied at any time before the end of the relevant period that the steps taken will not be successful in persuading the appropriate person to abate the nuisance or prohibit or restrict its occurrence or recurrence;

(b) that the authority is satisfied at the end of the relevant period that the nuisance continues to exist, or continues to be likely to occur or recur, in the area of the authority."

30   Section 82 makes provision for summary proceedings in the Magistrates Court by persons aggrieved by statutory nuisances.

"82.

(1) A magistrates' court may act under this section on a complaint ... made by any person on the ground that he is aggrieved by the existence of a statutory nuisance.

(2) If the magistrates' court ... is satisfied that the alleged nuisance exists, or that although abated it is likely to recur on the same premises ..., the court shall make an order for either or both of the following purposes—
    (a) requiring the defendant ... to abate the nuisance, within a time specified in the order, and to execute any works necessary for that purpose;
    (b) prohibiting a recurrence of the nuisance, and requiring the defendant ..., within a time specified in the order, to execute any works necessary to prevent the recurrence."

31   Paragraph 183 of the National Planning Policy Framework ("the Framework") provides:

"183. The focus of planning policies and decisions should be on whether proposed development is an acceptable use of land, rather than the control of processes or emissions (where these are subject to separate pollution control regimes). Planning decisions should assume that these regimes will operate effectively. Equally, where a planning decision has been made on a particular development, the planning issues should not be revisited through the permitting regimes operated by pollution control authorities."

32   The existence of other pollution control regimes, such as under the EPA 1990, are material planning considerations and planning decision makers should take those regimes into account in their decision-making and assume that they will operate effectively: *Gateshead MBC v Secretary of State for the Environment* [1995] Env. L.R. 37 (CA), per Glidewell LJ, at [44]; *R. (Frack Free Balcombe Residents Association) v West Sussex CC* [2014] EWHC 4108 (Admin), per Gilbart J., at [26]–[28]. The Court has emphasised that planning decision-makers "must not simply rely on the earlier grant of the environmental permit and abdicate responsibility for [their] decision making": *Norman v Secretary of State for Housing, Communities and Local Government* [2018] EWHC 2910 (Admin), per Justine Thornton QC, sitting as a Deputy High Court Judge, at [52].

33   The Planning Practice Guidance provides material guidance on noise, as follows:

"How can noise impacts be determined?
Plan-making and decision making need to take account of the acoustic environment and in doing so consider:

    • whether or not a significant adverse effect is occurring or likely to occur;
    • whether or not an adverse effect is occurring or likely to occur; and
    • whether or not a good standard of amenity can be achieved.

In line with the Explanatory note of the noise policy statement for England, this would include identifying whether the overall effect of the noise exposure (including the impact during the construction phase wherever applicable) is, or would be, above or below the significant observed adverse effect level and the lowest observed adverse effect level for the given situation. As noise is a complex technical issue, it may be appropriate to seek experienced specialist assistance when applying this policy.
Paragraph: 003 Reference ID: 30-003-20190722
Revision date: 22 07 2019

What are the observed effect levels?

> • Significant observed adverse effect level: This is the level of noise exposure above which significant adverse effects on health and quality of life occur.
> • Lowest observed adverse effect level: this is the level of noise exposure above which adverse effects on health and quality of life can be detected.
> • No observed effect level: this is the level of noise exposure below which no effect at all on health or quality of life can be detected.

Although the word 'level' is used here, this does not mean that the effects can only be defined in terms of a single value of noise exposure. In some circumstances adverse effects are defined in terms of a combination of more than one factor such as noise exposure, the number of occurrences of the noise in a given time period, the duration of the noise and the time of day the noise occurs.

See the noise policy statement for England for further information.

Paragraph: 004 Reference ID: 30-004-20190722

Revision date: 22 07 2019

How can it be established whether noise is likely to be a concern?

At the lowest extreme, when noise is not perceived to be present, there is by definition no effect. As the noise exposure increases, it will cross the 'no observed effect' level. However, the noise has no adverse effect so long as the exposure does not cause any change in behaviour, attitude or other physiological responses of those affected by it. The noise may slightly affect the acoustic character of an area but not to the extent there is a change in quality of life. If the noise exposure is at this level no specific measures are required to manage the acoustic environment.

As the exposure increases further, it crosses the 'lowest observed adverse effect' level boundary above which the noise starts to cause small changes in behaviour and attitude, for example, having to turn up the volume on the television or needing to speak more loudly to be heard. The noise therefore starts to have an adverse effect and consideration needs to be given to mitigating and minimising those effects (taking account of the economic and social benefits being derived from the activity causing the noise).

Increasing noise exposure will at some point cause the 'significant observed adverse effect' level boundary to be crossed. Above this level the noise causes a material change in behaviour such as keeping windows closed for most of the time or avoiding certain activities during periods when the noise is present. If the exposure is predicted to be above this level the planning process should be used to avoid this effect occurring, for example through the choice of sites at the plan-making stage, or by use of appropriate mitigation such as by altering the design and layout. While such decisions must be made taking account of the economic and social benefit of the activity causing or affected by the noise, it is undesirable for such exposure to be caused.

At the highest extreme, noise exposure would cause extensive and sustained adverse changes in behaviour and / or health without an ability to mitigate the effect of the noise. The impacts on health and quality of life are such that regardless of the benefits of the activity causing the noise, this situation should be avoided.

This table summarises the noise exposure hierarchy, based on the likely average response of those affected. [*The PPG provides a link to the Noise Exposure Hierarchy Table*]
Paragraph: 005 Reference ID: 30-0055-20190722
Revision date: 22 27 2019"

Local Policies

34   The relevant policies in the Core Strategy were set out in the OR, at internal pages 3 to 4. Policy AS13 is a site-specific policy for the Race Circuit, saved in the Dover District Local Plan, which provides:

"AS13 - Proposals to expand the use of Lydden Circuit for motor sports or intensify its frequency will be refused. Only development ancillary to its existing use will be permitted."

Areas of Outstanding Natural Beauty

35   Section 85 of the Countryside and Rights of Way Act 2000 provides that public bodies have a general duty "in exercising or performing any functions in relation to, or so as to affect, land in an area of outstanding natural beauty" to "have regard to the purpose of conserving and enhancing the natural beauty of the area of outstanding natural beauty".

36   Paragraph 172 of the Framework affords protection to AONBs as follows:

"172. Great weight should be given to conserving and enhancing landscape and scenic beauty in National Parks, the Broads and Areas of Outstanding Natural Beauty, which have the highest status of protection in relation to these issues. The conservation and enhancement of wildlife and cultural heritage are also important considerations in these areas, and should be given great weight in National Parks and the Broads. The scale and extent of development within these designated areas should be limited. Planning permission should be refused for major development [FN55 For the purposes of paragraphs 172 and 173, whether a proposal is 'major development' is a matter for the decision maker, taking into account its nature, scale and setting, and whether it could have a significant adverse impact on the purposes for which the area has been designated or defined.] other than in exceptional circumstances, and where it can be demonstrated that the development is in the public interest. Consideration of such applications should include an assessment of:

a) the need for the development, including in terms of any national considerations, and the impact of permitting it, or refusing it, upon the local economy;
b) the cost of, and scope for, developing outside the designated area, or meeting the need for it in some other way; and
c) any detrimental effect on the environment, the landscape and recreational opportunities, and the extent to which that could be moderated."

37   Paragraph 180 of the Framework provides:

"180. Planning policies and decisions should also ensure that new development is appropriate for its location taking into account the likely effects (including cumulative effects) of pollution on health, living conditions and the natural environment, as well as the potential sensitivity of the site or the wider area to impacts that could arise from the development. In doing so they should:

> a) mitigate and reduce to a minimum potential adverse impacts resulting from noise from new development — and avoid noise giving rise to significant adverse impacts on health and the quality of life [FN60 See Explanatory Note to the *Noise Policy Statement for England* (Department for Environment, Food & Rural Affairs, 2010).];
> b) identify and protect tranquil areas which have remained relatively undisturbed by noise and are prized for their recreational and amenity value for this reason; and
> c) limit the impact of light pollution from artificial light on local amenity, intrinsically dark landscapes and nature conservation."

38   These policies were considered by the Court of Appeal in *Monkhill Ltd v Secretary of State for Housing, Communities and Local Government* [2021] EWCA Civ 74, per Sir Keith Lindblom SPT, at [32]–[34]:

"32. I agree. The most important point here, however, as Holgate J. recognised (in paragraph 53 of his judgment), is that the requirement in the policy in the first part of paragraph 172 for "great weight" be given to the conservation and enhancement of landscape and scenic beauty in an AONB does not prevent its application providing a clear reason for the refusal of planning permission.
33. That it can be so applied is plain from the policy's context and purpose. Its context is a chapter of the NPPF whose objectives, as stated in the chapter heading, are "Conserving and enhancing the natural environment". The central aim of the policies in that chapter, stated in paragraph 170, is "protecting and enhancing valued landscapes", including those in AONBs. This is consistent with the statutory obligation in section 85(1) of the Countryside and Rights of Way Act to "have regard to the purpose of conserving and enhancing the natural beauty of the [AONB]". Paragraph 172 itself is in terms that stress the imperative of protection. Emphasis is placed on "conserving", as well as "enhancing", an AONB's landscape and scenic beauty. AONBs are described there as having "the highest status of protection in relation to these issues", and the "scale and extent of development" within them and the other designated areas, the policy says, "should be limited".
34. I accept Mr Moules' submission that the language of the first part of paragraph 172, read in that context and in the light of that purpose, can perfectly well found a "clear reason for [refusal]", in accordance with paragraph 11d)i. It embodies the principle that decisions on applications for planning permission, as well as policies in development plans, should work to "[conserve and enhance] landscape and scenic beauty" in AONBs, so that in a relevant case, when the policy is applied, a balance will be struck in which appropriate weight is given to any conflict with that objective, and in striking the balance the decision-maker will have in mind the need to protect the AONB and to limit the scale and extent of development within it. In doing this, the decision-maker will have to exercise planning judgment. The

application of the policy necessarily involves a balancing exercise in which any harmful effects of the proposed development on the AONB are given due weight, having regard to what the policy says, and any benefits of the proposal are set against them, leading to a conclusion, as a matter of planning judgment, on whether there is a "clear reason for refusing the development proposed". If there are no benefits to set against the harm to the AONB, or if there are benefits but they are insufficient to outweigh the harm, the decision-maker might properly conclude that the "application" of the policy does indeed provide "a clear reason for refusing the development proposed"."

39   A number of Local Plan policies reflect the Framework policies, as do the specific policies of the Kent Downs AONB Management Plan (2014-2019).

Ground 1

Submissions

40   The Claimant submitted that the Defendant erred in regarding the existing level of noise, which was a statutory nuisance and/or causing noise at a SOAEL, as a fallback position against which to judge the application for planning permission to develop the Race Circuit.

41   The proceedings under the EPA 1990 and the abatement notices were a material planning consideration. Applying paragraph 183 of the Framework, the Council should have assumed that the pollution control regime would operate properly to control the nuisance, and if the current revised abatement notice was not doing so, that a further abatement notice would be served (see *Frack Free Balcombe Residents Association* at [100]–[101]; *Norman* at [52]-[53]). On that assumption, the Council should have considered what was required in order to control the nuisance, whether by way of a further abatement notice or otherwise, and take that into account as the correct fallback position. The OR should have advised Members accordingly. Instead the Council erroneously adopted the approach of regarding the fallback position as the existing planning permission and the existing revised abatement notice, although the Council was aware that they did not adequately control the noise or abate the nuisance.

42   Further, the OR failed to inform Members of important matters, in particular, the history of the abatement notices (including the undertaking to withdraw the revised abatement notice once the planning application was concluded); the views of MAS, acting as an independent expert engaged by the Council; and that the revised abatement notice represented what the Council viewed as the "minimum that would provide the community with some relief" (referred to in paragraph 11 above).

43   In the alternative, the Claimant submitted that it was irrational for the Council to regard the maintenance of a nuisance to be a fallback position. The Claimant further submitted that it was irrational for the Council to consent to an intensification of the use, leading to noise on more days in the year, when it knew that the current use was giving rise to a SOAEL.

44   In response, the Defendant submitted that the OR correctly identified the fallback position as the existing planning permission and revised abatement notice. This could not be characterised as irrational. There was no requirement to consider or advise Members as to what further abatement notices might be served in the future.

45   The Defendant submitted that the OR was a detailed and accurate document which provided sufficient information to Members to enable them to decide the relevant issues. The planning officer was not required to provide Members with the further material listed by the Claimant, or advise them upon it.

46   The OR and the Planning Committee were entitled to come to the conclusion that, although the Race Circuit would be in use on more days of the year, the quieter nature of the activities on those days, combined with the noise limits imposed, and improved controls, meant that there would not be any increase in impact on local residents.

Conclusions

47   In my judgment, the purpose of paragraph 183 of the Framework is to avoid needless duplication between the two schemes of statutory control where the pollution control regimes operate parallel to the planning regime. Whether or not there have been any proceedings under the pollution control regime, the planning decision-maker should assume that the regime will operate effectively in the future. However, where there have been such proceedings, they will be a material consideration which the planning decision-maker must consider and take into account.

48   In this case, the Council correctly took the view that the proceedings under the EPA 1990 and the abatement notices were a material planning consideration which the Council had to consider.

49   In my judgment, the OR gave a detailed and balanced account of the issues on noise which Members had to consider, and gave appropriate advice.

50   First, the OR recorded the comments of the EPT, as follows:

> "DDC Environmental Health — It has already been established, through the service of a noise abatement notice (NAB) under the Environmental Protection Act 1990 on Lydden Circuit on 03rd December 2015 that noise levels from the circuit have an adverse impact on residents. Whilst it is accepted that the areas of planning and nuisance cover separate strands of law, reference to the abatement notice is pertinent when assessing residential amenity via planning applications.
>
> The abatement notice accepts nuisance exists and seeks to restrict it by limiting noise levels and how often the circuit is used. It may therefore be argued that any increase in noise levels would represent a Significant Observed Adverse Effect Level (SOAEL) and therefore be detrimental to the residential amenity of those living around the circuit. SOAEL is described under 2014 planning guidance as triggered when the impact of noise can be described as causing:
>
>> 'material change in behaviour and/or attitude, e.g. avoiding certain activities during periods of intrusion … having to keep windows closed most of the time because of the noise. Quality of life diminished due to change in acoustic character of the area'
>
> On that basis, it may be considered there are no grounds for increased activity. This need not be the case. Activity increase does not necessarily equate to impact increase. Activity that is inaudible or not discernible from the ambient sound environment would not add adverse impact from noise and can be

permitted. It is also the case that sound which is infrequently heard, benign in character and occurs at times of reduced amenity value is unlikely to add to intrusion and thus there are clearly forms of activity that can be permitted. Changes have been made in the Noise Management Plan (NMP) that address concerns previously raised regarding the potential of adverse impact from the development. In particular it is noted that tests were conducted to establish trackside drive-by LAmax decibel limit levels. This is, in part, intended to address tyre squeal, backfire, etc. There is also a clause whereby track officials have discretion to remove vehicles generating excessive levels of noise from e.g. turbo-chatter, tyre squeal etc. The NMP, and hence the noise limits specified within it, will form part of the operating procedures that will be submitted for approval by the Local Planning Authority prior to use under this application, should permission be granted.

The NMP also provides detail on the category of events proposed to be held on the site. This breaks events down into 5 categories with varying noise levels and permitted uses. The abatement notice referred to above requires certain noise limits measured over the period of an hour to be met. Under the current [NMP] there are in effect 3 categories:

- 2 event days with unrestricted noise levels
- 24 event days where the noise level must not exceed 55db LAeq (1hr) at specified monitoring points
- 26 event days where the noise level must not exceed 50db LAeq (1hr) at specified monitoring points

The application seeks to add an additional 313 (314 on a leap year) days, 104 of which fall into a fourth and fifth category as detailed below:

- Category 1 - 2 event days with unrestricted noise levels
- Category 2 - 24 event days where the noise level must not exceed 55db LAeq (30mins) at specified monitoring points
- Category 3 - 26 event days where the noise level must not exceed 50db LAeq (30mins) at specified monitoring points.

The reduced measurement period from 1 hour to 30 minutes for Category 2 and 3 events provides an increased level of control regarding noise emission from the site. The noise levels for Category 4 and 5 events are further reduced and the measurement period drops to 15 minutes. Noise surveys at nearby noise sensitive properties, taken when there was no activity from the circuit, indicate residual levels are around 45dB LAeq(t).

These controls along with those in the draft NMP, whilst not guaranteeing inaudibility, will aid in preventing adverse impact for the additional 104 days proposed under categories 4 and 5.

The proposal also seeks an additional 2.5 hours on two Sundays. This amounts to an additional 5 hours per year. It is felt that increased activity on a Sunday will have a negative effect on the community. Accordingly, any additional Sunday hours would be above the SOAEL thereby creating a limited adverse impact. However, we note the circuit propose that if a period of additional 2.5 hours of time takes place on a Sunday in association with an event falling within Categories 1 and 2 the number of days permitted to be used by a Category 2 event within that same calendar period will be reduced by 1 day.

If the additional 2.5 hours were to take place within Categories 3, 4 or 5 the number of days permitted to be used by a Category 3 event within that same calendar period will be reduced by 1 day. We therefore suggest this is conditioned.

The NMP also refers to 'Other Activity' and states the site and circuit may be used on other days for activities not falling into Category 1 to 5. We note media activities are included in both Category 5 and 'other activities'. We feel media activities should come under Category 5. There is no limit specified on the amount of other activities or potential noise levels and controls. It is therefore possible the site could be in continuous use without any respite to the surrounding area. We therefore feel other activities should have a limit on the number of days and should only cover events where vehicle use is ancillary to the event e.g. back up vehicles for non-motorised bicycle racing events. The only situations where this would not apply is in emergencies or for road driving lessons by an instructor approved by the DVLA.

Regarding respite to the surrounding area, we feel it is important to have days where no motor vehicles use the site. This could be achieved by taking a similar approach to Goodwood Motor Circuit where a total of 49 silent days are specified. These days include Good Friday, Xmas Day, Boxing Day and New Years Day. We also suggest this includes Armistice Day.

The Goodwood silent days mean that no motor vehicles may use the site....

We suggest that these 49 days include 10 weekends, and this is a requirement under condition.

....

The NMP should be reviewed every 6 months for the first two years after approval and then annually thereafter. The review will be conducted between Lydden Hill Race Circuit, Dover District Council and those living and working in the area. This would necessitate the setting up of a consultative committee. The setup of such a committee should be a requirement under the NMP and be required by condition. The Local Planning Authority would subsequently decide if changes are needed.

.....

To Conclude, whilst the current use of the circuit does impact on the locality through the current 52-day use, it is felt the altered NMP addresses some of the issues previously raised and sets out greater controls on the proposed increased use of the site. In order to ensure these controls are implemented we suggest conditions be included should permission be granted.

A series of 14 conditions are recommended which include: submission and approval of a final Noise Management Plan; limiting the use of the circuit to the activities proposed, defining the activities and confirming which activities fall into each category; submission and approval of details for the noise monitoring system and its maintenance, including details for the retention of noise data; limiting the number of days usage and hours of operation, including breaking the use down into categories; allowing additional use of Sundays, subject to the loss of a full days use as compensation; limiting noise from the circuit in accordance with the categories and setting out how monitoring shall take place; limiting noise from loudspeakers; restricting use of the circuit on two consecutive days more than 12 times a year, restricting use on more than two consecutive days; and requiring intervals between pairs of consecutive days use, in respect of Category 1-3 days; publication of a calendar of events and requiring advance notice of any changes; submission and approval of a Construction Management Plan; requiring recording of any breaches in maximum noise levels and the action taken to remedy it; provision of a publicly accessible website as a source of information on the circuit and its activities; and reporting of any contamination which has not previously been identified."

51   The OR went on to summarise the objections from members of the public, including local residents. Objectors also sent their representations directly to members of the Planning Committee.

52   The OR addressed the issue of noise at length, in paragraphs 2.51 to 2.82, covering relevant policy on noise, the current planning permission, the revised abatement notice and the application.

53   At OR 2.64, the planning officer summarised the current position, which he treated as the fallback position:

"2.64 Regard must be had for the current use of the site, which is lawful and can continue without requiring further permissions (subject to adherence with the planning permission and, under separate legislation, the Noise Abatement Notice). Under its current restrictions, it is acknowledged that the circuit has the potential to create significant level of noise for 52 days per year.
Environmental Health, who have been monitoring the circuit for several years (and who served the Noise Abatement Notice), consider that the circuit is causing a statutory nuisance and that, whilst this nuisance is limited by the Noise Abatement Notice, the noise remains at a level considered to represent a Significant Observed Adverse Effect (SOAEL) causing:

'material change in behaviour and/or attitude, e.g. avoiding certain activities during periods of intrusion; where there is no alternative ventilation, having to keep windows closed most of the time because of the noise. Potential for sleep disturbance resulting in difficulty in getting to sleep, premature awakening and difficulty in getting back to sleep. Quality of life diminished due to change in acoustic character of the area'.

Having visited the circuit on numerous occasions over a period of almost five years (both on race days and non-race days), and having regard for third party representations, I concur with this view, although it must be noted that the changed behaviour is less likely to affect sleep due to the time limits applied to the circuit for its events (some disturbance may still occur, for example due to the noise from camping or to those who sleep during the day such as shift workers). Having reached this conclusion, it is considered that this existing level of harm forms the fallback position, against which the current proposals should be assessed."

54   The OR summarised the proposed changes at paragraph 2.65:

"2.65 At present, having regard for the planning permission for the circuit, together with the restrictions of the Noise Abatement Notice, the circuit can operate for:

• 2 days of unlimited noise ('Category 1')

• 24 days where noise cannot exceed 55dB LAeq 1 hour 'Category 2') at specified monitoring points
• 26 days where noise cannot exceed 50dB LAeq 1 hour 'Category 3') at specified monitoring points

The current application seeks to continue operating on these days and increase the current usage through the addition of the following uses:

• 52 days (for demonstration/corporate events, car testing, river experience days, quiet vehicle festivals and shows, use of the site or road speed driving of vehicles at no more than 70mph and ancillary noise) where noise cannot exceed 45dB LAeq 15 minutes. ('Category 4')
• 52 days (for car testing, driver training, driver experience days, slow speed cavalcades, demonstrations, photo shoots and media activities, and use of the site for road speed driving of motor vehicles at no more than 70mph and ancillary noise) where noise cannot exceed 40dB LAeq 15 minutes. ('Category 5')
• An option to extending operating hours by up to two and a half hours on up to two Sundays per year, with one category 2 or 3 day being lost in compensation for each extended Sunday. If a period of up to an additional 2.5 hours of time takes place on a Sunday in association with an event falling within Categories 1 and 2 the number of days permitted to be used by a Category 2 event within that same calendar period will be reduced by 1 day. If the additional 2.5 hours were to take place within Categories 3, 4 or 5 the number of days permitted to be used by a Category 3 event within that same calendar period will be reduced by 1 day.
• Up to 209 (210 in a leap year) for 'other activity', not falling within the above categories. This may include use by conventional road vehicles ancillary to charitable or other events, road driving lessons, emergency incident training, photo shoots, media activities and use by non-motorised bicycles for training during daylight hours, including non-motorised bicycle events. ('Other Activity')."

55   At paragraph 2.67, the OR set out the advice given by the EPT, and correctly advised:

"Whilst the additional activities could exacerbate the existing SOAEL of noise, it is necessary to consider whether the additional activities would exacerbate the existing SOAEL and if so whether this additional harm can be mitigated."

56   At paragraph 2.69, the OR described how the Noise Management Plan would be "an extra layer of control to detail how the circuit will manage noise so that the noise limits are not exceeded".

57   At paragraph 2.70, the OR set out the proposed categories of activity, their designated noise limits, and the more stringent methods of measuring noise which were proposed. These matters were considered in more detail at paragraphs 2.73 — 2.74. At paragraph 2.71, the OR also reminded Members that the EPT had recommended "silent days" on which no motor vehicles would be permitted to use

the site. Noise from the public address system was to be restricted (paragraph 2.75). The calendar of events was to be subject to increased controls (paragraph 2.76).

58   At paragraph 2.77, the OR correctly advised Members on the criteria to be satisfied before conditions could be imposed (paragraph 2.77) and concurred with the EPT's recommendations as to the conditions to be imposed which would "provide significant benefits (reducing the impacts from the existing uses of the site) to off-set the limited impacts from the additional uses of the site".

59   The OR concluded, at paragraph 3.4:

> "3.4 Noise is an important consideration in the assessment of the development, with the existing site causing a managed (through a Noise Abatement Notice) nuisance to neighbouring properties and the majority of objections raising noise as a concern. Regard has been had for the Noise Policy Statement for England and advice has been received from the Councils Environmental Health team. Whilst the use of the circuit would be significantly expanded, it is considered that this would be balanced against the improved management of the circuit and more stringent monitoring (which would be secured by condition). Overall, the development would not exacerbate the impacts of noise and, therefore, no additional planning harm would be caused. The development would not harm the living conditions of neighbours in any other respect, subject to conditions."

60   The minutes of the Planning Committee meeting on 30 January 2020 recorded as follows:

> "Using a map reproduced from the AONB Management Plan, the site currently had a medium to medium-low level of tranquillity. Subject to conditions, and as set out in the report, Members were advised that it was not considered that the level of tranquillity would be significantly diminished as a result of the proposals.
>
> Third parties had raised numerous objections relating to the current levels of noise and the potential for increased levels should the application be granted. Noise levels were currently controlled by conditions attached to planning permission DOV/14/00415. These conditions, which limited the circuit to 52 days' use per year and required the submission of a calendar of events each year, amongst other things, were not considered to be robust and made the identification of breaches difficult. Under separate (non-planning) legislation, the Council's Environmental Health team had served a noise abatement notice which had established that noise from the circuit was causing a statutory nuisance and sought to limit that nuisance. Environmental Health officers visited the site around 12 times a year and had identified no breaches. The current application sought to retain current uses, as specified within the noise abatement notice, but reduced the period over which noise was averaged from one hour to thirty minutes in respect of the 55 decibel and 50 decibel events. This reduction in the time period over which noise would be averaged reduced the ability to dilute periods of louder noise with quieter periods, thus reducing the impact of these days on the aural environment. Residents would also be invited to join a new consultative committee.
>
> The application also sought to increase the use of the site for quieter, non-racing events. A full description of the proposed uses was set out at

paragraph 2.65 of the report. There would also be 49 silent days with no activities. Whilst the circuit's use would increase significantly, this was considered to be mitigated by the enhanced control of the circuit, including a noise management plan, the provision of a permanent noise monitoring system (with access to readings by the Local Planning Authority and their publication on the circuit's website), a calendar of events, and the reduction from one hour to 30 minutes over which noise would be averaged for category 2 and 3 events. Members had been provided with the draft wording of the proposed noise conditions that would be attached to any permission granted."

61   In my judgment, the planning officer was correct to identify the fallback position as that which currently existed, under the existing planning permission and the existing revised abatement notice. The term fallback has acquired a specific meaning in planning law. The *Encyclopedia of Planning Law and Practice* states at paragraph 1.002.29:

"Sometimes an applicant can demonstrate that the grant of a permission will be less harmful than a use or development which has previously been permitted; this is known, unsurprisingly, as fall-back"

In *Mansell v Tonbridge and Malling BC* [2017] EWCA Civ 1314, Lindblom LJ considered the status of a fallback development as a material consideration at [27], confirming that there must be a "real prospect" that it would be reverted to.

62   I do not accept the Claimant's submission that the Council should have considered what was required in order to control the nuisance, whether by way of a further abatement notice or otherwise, and take that into account as the correct fallback position. That would not be a fallback position, as defined above. Nor would it be consistent with the Framework policy in paragraph 183. It follows that the OR was not required to consider or advise Members as to what further abatement notices might be served in the future. It was not their responsibility to make any decision on such matters, and speculation would not have been appropriate. In my view, there is no support for the Claimant's submission in paragraph 183 of the Framework, nor the authorities cited on paragraph 183.

63   At the heart of the Claimant's objection to the fallback position adopted in the OR is that the current level of noise amounts to a statutory nuisance and/or a SOAEL, and therefore it cannot properly be relied upon. There is no legal basis for this submission. The Claimant relies on *Lawrence v Fen Tigers Ltd* [2014] 2 W.L.R. 433, but the issues in that case were quite different and the judgment does not provide any support for the Claimant's submissions.

64   In my view, the Claimant has simply misunderstood the Council's approach. In the view of the OR and the EPT, the revised abatement notice restricted, but did not eliminate, the nuisance. Once satisfied that a statutory nuisance existed, the Council complied with its duty under section 80(2A) EPA 1990 and served an abatement notice which required the nuisance to be restricted in accordance with the schedule to the notice. It was a matter for the Council's discretion whether it chose to impose all or any of the requirements available in section 80(1) EPA 1990. There was no duty to serve a notice that required the statutory nuisance to be abated. The revised abatement notice was lawful and could be relied upon by the Council and the IP as part of the fallback position. For these reasons, it was not irrational for the Council to treat the revised abatement notice as part of the fallback position.

65   Although the objectors alleged that the IP was operating the Race Circuit in breach of the revised abatement notice, the EPT and the OR did not accept this. The OR advised Members that Environmental Health officers visited the site around 12 times per year and had identified no breaches of the revised abatement notice. It is reasonable to infer that Members accepted the evidence from the EPT, as endorsed by the planning officer, and recorded in the minutes of their meeting on 30 January 2020.

66   In my judgment, Members were correctly advised in the OR to consider whether the proposed planning permission would be more effective in controlling noise levels, because it would include more stringent and more effective conditions than the existing planning permission and revised abatement notice.

67   In my view, it was a matter for the planning officer's discretion to determine how much of the history of the abatement notices — in particular, the Magistrates Courts proceedings, the evidence of the MAS consultants in 2015 and 2017, and the undertaking to withdraw the revised abatement notice — needed to be relayed to Members. I consider that it was background information which was not directly relevant to the issues that Members had to decide. Applying the test in *Mansell*, it cannot be said that Members were seriously misled.

68   The Council submitted at the hearing that it was reasonable for it to decide to address the noise issues at the Race Circuit by way of detailed planning conditions rather than by way of a further abatement notice. Planning conditions are more flexible and can include a wider range of requirements than an abatement notice, which have to be capable of forming the basis of a criminal charge in the Magistrates Court. In my view, that was an exercise of discretionary judgment on the part of the Council.

69   The Claimant's alternative submission was that it was irrational for the Council to consent to an intensification of the use, leading to noise on more days in the year, when it knew that the current use was giving rise to a SOAEL.

70   In my judgment, this issue turned on the evidence. The EPT and the OR advised that, although the Race Circuit would be in use on more days of the year, the quieter nature of the activities on those days, combined with the noise limits imposed, and improved controls and monitoring, meant that there would not be any increase in impact on local residents. The OR set out the basis for this advice in considerable detail.

71   I accept the Council's submission that, in assessing acceptable noise levels in the community, it formed the view that an assessment based solely on BS4142: 2014 or the World Health Organisation ("WHO") Community Noise Guidelines, would not be suitable.

72   At paragraph 2.66, the OR summarised the evidence in regard to the noise level in the area when no events are taking place:

> "Surveys were carried out in 2013 and 2015 as part of the previous application. These were carried out over a three-week period in the summer which indicated that, at the most noise sensitive noise monitoring point, the modal noise level when no events are taking place at the circuit is 51dB LAeq, 1 hour. During visits to the site, it is noted that noise from traffic on the A2 is audible a significant distant away, albeit this noise has a relatively constant, benign

character. It is also noted that the areas around the A2, and around the circuit are shown on the Tranquillity Map within the Kent Downs AONB Management Plan as having a medium to medium/low level of tranquillity."

The research surveys referred to here were carried out by Three Spires Acoustics, consultants commissioned by local residents, as part of the Noise Abatement Notice Compliance Survey in 2017.

73   Following receipt of further written submissions by the parties, made at my request, I accepted the Council's submission that the relevant baseline level in the community was 51dB LAeq representing the ambient noise level. That level had first been agreed with the community as the relevant baseline measurement in the context of assessing compliance with the revised abatement notice. 51dB LAeq was a long standing, accepted position. Following misgivings by local residents about how the revised abatement notice was being enforced, a Guidance Note on monitoring noise under its terms was prepared in consultation with local residents and their acoustic consultants. It set out that:

"After selecting the noisiest monitoring site (of the four shown on the Revised Notice map), an initial 30 minute reading is to be taken and if readings are at or below 51dB LAeq then no further readings would take place that day (para 7). At that level, a statutory nuisance would not be experienced in the community;
If readings are over 51dB LAeq during the first 30 minutes then officers should continue to monitor until at least 2 hours of data is gathered (paras 8 and 9); and
Audio readings should be taken throughout when readings are in excess of 51dB LAeq (para 10)."

74   In my judgment, there was sufficient evidence upon which the planning officer and Members could rationally come to the conclusion that the increased number of days upon which activities were permitted would not increase the impact on local residents.

75   For the reasons set out above, Ground 1 does not succeed.

Ground 2

Submissions

76   The Claimant submitted that the Council erred in law, in two respects, in its approach to the effect of the proposed development on the Kent Downs AONB.

77   First, it was irrational for the OR to conclude, at paragraph 2.82, that the additional use of the site "would not significantly diminish its tranquillity beyond the application site", given that there would be a change from 313 days per year without noise, to 316 days per year with noise (see *Moore v Secretary of State for Communities and Local Government* [2013] EWCA Civ 1194, at [21]–[29]).

78   Second, the OR's starting point was unlawful when it undertook the assessment required by paragraph 172 of the Framework, as it condoned a level of noise which it accepted was a statutory nuisance and/or SOAEL. The current lack of tranquillity was capable of improvement under the statutory nuisance regime and its application should have been assessed in that context.

79   In response, the Council submitted that it was rational to conclude that the additional use of the site would not significantly diminish the tranquillity of the AONB, because of the quieter type of activities that would be permitted on the additional days, and the more effective noise control conditions in place overall.

80   The approach set out in paragraph 172 of the Framework does not require permission to be granted only for development that reduces noise impacts to levels that are not a statutory nuisance, or below SOAELs, still less to zero.

Conclusions

81   In my judgment, the OR gave Members detailed and appropriate advice on the AONB.

82   The OR set out section 85 of the Countryside and Rights of Way Act 2000, the relevant policies from the Framework, and the Kent Downs AONB Management Plan. It summarised the objections from the Kent Downs AONB Unit, dated 7 August 2019, though not the paragraph on tranquillity which stated:

> **"Tranquillity**
> In addition to the landscape and visual impacts of the proposal, impacts on tranquillity are also relevant. Tranquillity is identified as one of the special characteristics of the AONB and policy SD7 of the AONB Management Plan advises that new development which impact on tranquillity will be opposed unless they can be satisfactorily mitigated. The AONB Unit has concerns that the proposal will introduce a significant intensification of use of the site, increased from the current 52 days per year to potential year round daily activity, both in terms of overall visitor numbers as well as in respect of new daily activity, with 104 days to be used for activities including car testing, driver experience days and driver training in addition to 52 days per year for motorsport activities, with the remainder of the year the site permitted to be used for activities including emergency incident training, cycle racing and driving lessons. This extensive increase in intensification of use of the site would result in a deterioration of tranquillity at the site."

I am satisfied that the issues on tranquillity raised here were duly considered in the OR.

83   The OR advised at paragraph 2.82:

> "2.82 Notwithstanding the above, it is also necessary to consider the noise impacts on the tranquillity of this area of countryside, being within the AONB. Paragraph 180 of the NPPF states that planning decisions should "identify and protect tranquil areas which have remained relatively undisturbed by noise and are prized for their recreational and amenity value for this reason". It is acknowledged that the presence of the A2 and the circuit has already diminished the tranquillity of this part of the AONB, as confirmed by Tranquillity Map included within the Kent Downs AONB Management Plan 2014-2019, which shows the areas around the circuit to have medium or medium to low tranquillity. The assessment of noise above, focuses on noise impacts to residential properties. Whilst distinct from impacts on tranquillity, it is accepted that, without mitigation, the noise impacts of the development

would undoubtedly diminish the tranquillity of the area; however, it is considered that, subject to the conditions set out above, the additional use would not significantly diminish tranquillity beyond the application site."

84   Under the heading "Other Material Considerations", the OR gave Members the following advice on the AONB:

"2.142 Throughout the assessment of this application, regard must be had for the duty contained within Section 85 of the Countryside and Rights of Way Act 2000 which requires that in exercising or performing any functions in relation to, or so as to affect, land in an Area of Outstanding Natural Beauty (AONB), local planning authorities shall have regard to the purpose of conserving or enhancing the natural beauty of the AONB.
2.143 As set out at paragraph 2.21, paragraph 172 of the NPPF requires that 'major' development within the AONB should be refused unless exceptional circumstances exist, and it can be demonstrated that the development is in the public interest. The NPPF goes on to advise that that these considerations should include an assessment of:

a) the need for the development, including in terms of any national considerations, and the impact of permitting it, or refusing it, upon the local economy;
b) the cost of, and scope for, developing outside the designated area, or meeting the need for it in some other way; and
c) any detrimental effect on the environment, the landscape and recreational opportunities, and the extent to which that could be moderated.

2.144 The application relates to an existing racing circuit, which already has a visual and aural character which is distinct from that of the surrounding AONB. The proposed development would have a minor adverse effect on views of the site, albeit this effect relates to views which are already impacted by views of the buildings, structures, track and parked vehicles within the circuit and/or the A2. However, this minor adverse effect must attract great weight.
2.145 The development would significantly increase the use of the circuit, increasing its utility as a leisure and sporting venue. The provision of additional social and recreational uses and the enhancement of the facilities at the site is considered to carry some weight in favour of the development.
2.146 Whilst the application proposes significant additional use of the circuit which would generate noise, the noise generated by the additional uses would be limited. Mitigation could be secured by condition to ensure that, overall, the noise generated from the site would be no more disruptive (possibly less disruptive) than the existing use. As such, the impact is considered to be neutral."

85   When considering alternative sites, the OR advised:

"2.152 Returning to the NPPF paragraph 172 test, it is considered that, there is no realistic scope for developing outside of the AONB. The applicant has sought to moderate impacts of the development by significantly amending the scheme following the determination of the previous application. The development relates to an established race circuit within the AONB which provides recreational opportunities to participate or otherwise engage (spectate) in motorsport — the facilities for which are sparse. Despite being within the AONB, and notwithstanding the need to attribute great weight to conserving and enhancing the AONB, the adverse impacts of the development would be minor. The applicant has proposed mitigation in the form of landscaping to moderate these impacts. As such, it is concluded that there are exceptional circumstances in this instance. Furthermore, it is considered that the development would bring substantial economic benefits which provide a compelling public interest. As such, it is resolved that the 'paragraph 172 test' has been met."

86   The OR then went on to consider whether the material considerations outweighed the conflict with local policies:

"2.153 Finally, it is necessary to consider whether the material considerations of this case indicate that the conflict with policies DM11 and AS13 should be set aside and permission be granted.

2.154 The development would provide a short-term economic benefit, by providing employment during the construction phase. The application advises that the cost of the construction works would be around £5.5 million. In the longer term, the development (provided it is fully built out) would increase visitor numbers and increase the range and quality of facilities and services available on site which would, correspondingly, increase spend and the number of jobs which could be supported, supporting a significant increase in the number of employees both at the site and beyond. It is considered that substantial weight should be attached to this benefit. The development would include the provision of highways and drainage infrastructure to meet the needs of the development without causing harm on-site or elsewhere. Overall, it is considered that the development would provide short term and long term economic benefits which must be attributed substantial weight in favour of the development.

2.155 The development would provide an enhanced leisure and recreation offer at the site which would help to create and foster recreational communities with shared interests (albeit these communities may be from diverse locations). The proposed Pavilion building is considered to be of a reasonable architectural quality, being reminiscent of other motorsport buildings in the UK whilst also referencing some of the agricultural buildings in the area. Overall, it is considered that the development would have a minor social benefit.

2.156 Turning to the environmental role, the development would cause harm to the natural environment, comprising major development in the AONB which would cause a minor adverse impact on the character of the landscape, whilst increasing the use of the site significantly. It is acknowledged that the tranquillity of this part of the AONB is already reduced (medium to medium/low) by virtue of the existing use of the circuit and by the busy A2. Subject to conditions, it is not considered that tranquillity would be significantly diminished. Subject to conditions, the development would cause no unacceptable impacts on biodiversity or protected species and would provide some enhancements. The development is not located such that it would promote or facilitate sustainable modes of transport; however, it is also acknowledged that race circuits necessarily draw people from a wide area and are not suited to built-up areas. Notwithstanding this, the site is not accessible by more sustainable modes of transport such as public buses or trains, although a shuttle bus service will be secured whilst four electric vehicle charging points will be provided, reducing the harm caused by the unsuitable location of the circuit when balanced against the existing use. The additional uses would generate noise, albeit at significantly lower levels than the existing uses. This would be balanced against the benefits of enhanced controls for the existing (and proposed) uses, to be secured by condition. Overall, attributing great weight to the harm caused to the AONB and having regard for all other environmental factors, it is considered that the development would cause a minor adverse impact.

2.157 Overall, the development would give rise to substantial economic benefits, minor beneficial social benefits and minor adverse environmental harm. It is concluded, applying a 'flat' balance, that the benefits of the development are compelling and indicate that the developments conflict with policies DM11 and AS13 should be set aside in this instance."

87   Turning to the Claimant's first ground, on the evidence before it, I consider that the Council was rationally entitled to conclude that the noise impacts arising from the additional days of activities would not significantly diminish the level of tranquillity in the AONB, for two main reasons. First, because events would be restricted to quieter uses, at or below the levels of noise in the area when there is no activity at the Race Circuit (the residual level). Second, because of the enhanced controls on noise from all activities (e.g. more frequent, and therefore more effective, noise monitoring and the implementation of a Noise Management Plan).

88   As to the Claimant's second ground, in my judgment, the legal and policy framework on AONBs was correctly set out in the OR, and properly applied by the planning officer and Members to the facts of this application. I consider that the Claimant's interpretation of the legal and policy framework is incorrect insofar as it seeks to import an unspecified obligation to abate a nuisance or to eliminate SOAELs. The approach set out in paragraph 172 of the Framework does not require permission to be granted only for development that reduces noise impacts to levels that are not a statutory nuisance, or below SOAELs, still less to zero.

89   The Council, as decision maker, was required to assess the tranquillity of that part of the AONB that was affected and then consider the likely impacts of the proposal. In this case tranquillity levels in areas around the Race Circuit were shown to be medium to medium to low. Subject to control by conditions, there was sufficient evidence upon which the Council could properly conclude that additional use would not significantly diminish tranquillity beyond the site.

90   For these reasons, Ground 2 does not succeed.

Ground 3

Submissions

91   The Claimant submitted that, in its statement under regulation 30 of Town and Country Planning (Environmental Impact Assessment) Regulations 2017 ("the EIA Regulations"), and the OR and Minutes, the Council failed to give adequate reasons for the Decision, and failed to grapple with the issues raised in the light of

the detailed letters of representation made by residents and other consultees in opposition to the proposed development. The Claimant further submitted that the Planning Committee was required to give reasons for granting permission at common law, as in the case of *R. (CPRE Kent) v Dover DC* [2017] UKSC 79; [2018] 1 W.L.R. 108.

92   In response, the Council submitted that it discharged its duty under regulation 30 of the EIA Regulations, and the *CPRE Kent* case was distinguishable.

Conclusions

93   Under regulation 30(1)(d) to the EIA Regulations, the Council was obliged to inform the public of its final decisions and make available for inspection a statement, containing: (i) details of the matters referred to in regulation 29(2), and (ii) the main reasons and considerations on which the decision is based including, if relevant, information about the participation of the public.

94   In considering the adequacy of the reasons given in a statement under the EIA Regulations, the guidance given by Lord Brown in *South Buckinghamshire DC v Porter (No.2)* [2004] 1 W.L.R. 1953 should be applied (*CPRE Kent*, per Lord Carnwath at [39]). Reasons must be adequate and intelligible but may be briefly stated with the "degree of particularity required depending entirely on the nature of the issues falling for decision". The reasons given must enable the reader to understand why the matter was decided as it was and what conclusions were reached on the principal important controversial issues. Reasons need refer only to the main issues in the dispute and not to every material consideration, and the reasons can be stated.

95   A claimant must show that the reasons advanced (or lack of reasons) leave room for genuine as opposed to forensic doubt as to what was decided and why (*CPRE Kent*, per Lord Carnwath at [42]).

96   In this case, the Council issued the requisite statement. The Planning Committee adopted the reasoning in the OR, and accurately and adequately summarised the reasons for doing so. It referred to the OR and the Minutes, which "set out the main considerations on which the decision is based, including the Environmental Statement and Addendums". It explained that "the mitigation and monitoring requirements are addressed by the conditions attached to the Decision Notice". It informed readers that all these documents were posted on the Council's website.

97   The main reasons for the decision were set out in paragraphs 1.6 to 1.9, including the effects on the AONB and noise generally. The decision to grant permission took into account consultees' views and representations (paragraph 1.9).

98   The representations of Terence O'Rourke consultants were contained in two letters, dated 6 August 2019 and 28 January 2020. The latter was sent directly to Members. The officer's reasoning was formulated taking into account the initial representations that were made in the August 2019 letter, which referred to tranquillity, and the unacceptability of noise impacts, evidenced by the existence of an abatement notice and potential breaches. The officer took into account those representations, summarised them in the report, and advised Members accordingly.

99   The 28 January 2020 letter raised two saved polices that had not been dealt with in the OR. The officer provided an oral update to the Committee at the meeting dealing with those policies. The 28 January 2020 letter also raised the erroneous legal approach to the issues of noise and tranquillity that are included in this claim

under Grounds 1 and 2. The correct legal approach to those issues was set out in the OR. Members were entitled to adopt the reasoning in the OR and the oral update at the meeting on the issues raised.

100   Detailed issues of compliance with the revised abatement notice were not a matter for Members to assess or reach a conclusion one way or the other; that is not what is required by under paragraph 183 of the Framework. In so far as the Committee was required to consider evidence alleging non-compliance, the advice from the officer was clear.

101   Where a local planning authority resolves to approve the recommendation of an officers report, it can be assumed that they accepted the reasoning of that report (*R. (Palmer) v Herefordshire Council* [2016] EWCA Civ 1061; [2017] 1 W.L.R. 411 per Lewison LJ at [7]). There was nothing to displace that assumption in this case.

102   In my judgment, the statement read together with the detailed OR, the Minutes and the Decision Notice, met the standard of reasons required for the statement under the EIA Regulations.

103   Aside from the duty under the EIA Regulations, a planning authority is generally not under a duty to give reasons for the grant of planning permission, following the repeal of the statutory obligation to do so in 2013. However, in *CPRE Kent*, the Supreme Court held that, in certain types of cases, openness and fairness to the objectors required members' reasons to be stated. Lord Carnwath described this category of case at [59]:

> "59. As to the charge of uncertainty, it would be wrong to be over-prescriptive, in a judgment on a single case and a single set of policies. However it should not be difficult for councils and their officers to identify cases which call for a formulated statement of reasons, beyond the statutory requirements. Typically they will be cases where, as in *Oakley* and the present case, permission has been granted in the face of substantial public opposition and against the advice of officers, for projects which involve major departures from the development plan, or from other policies of recognised importance (such as the "specific policies" identified in the NPPF - para 22 above). Such decisions call for public explanation, not just because of their immediate impact; but also because, as Lord Bridge pointed out (para 45 above), they are likely to have lasting relevance for the application of policy in future cases."

104   In my judgment, this application clearly did not fall within the *CPRE Kent* category of case. It can be assumed that Members accepted their officers' recommendation, which was explained in considerable detail in the OR, and further reasons were given in the Minutes of the meeting. The mitigation and monitoring requirements were set out in the Decision Notice. A statement of reasons was issued pursuant to the duty under the EIA Regulations. In my view, the objectors could not have had any genuine, as opposed to forensic, doubt as to why the Planning Committee granted permission. Members were not required to explain how Members attached different weight to material considerations. There was considerable support for the application, as well as opposition. Whilst there were some 85 letters of objection, as well as the objection from the Kent Downs AONB Unit and two parish councils, there were also 964 letters in support, and support from two other parish councils. The points made for and against the application were summarised in the OR.

105   For these reasons, Ground 3 does not succeed.

Ground 4

Submissions

106   The Claimant submitted that the level of noise, assessed as SOAEL, engaged Article 8 ECHR. Given the positive obligations under Article 8, and the requirement to apply the precautionary principle, the Council was required to take effective measures to secure respect for the rights of other local residents to peaceful enjoyment of their homes. The failure to do so amounted to a violation of Article 8.

107   The Claimant also submitted that the Council failed to consider its human rights obligations adequately or at all in reaching its Decision.

108   The Council submitted that the OR and Members had regard to Article 8, and the decision to grant planning permission was not a violation of Article 8. The precautionary principle was not relevant.

109   In the alternative, section 31(2A) of the Senior Courts Act 1981 applied.

Conclusions

110   Section 6(1) HRA 1998 provides:

"It is unlawful for a public authority to act in a way which is incompatible with a Convention right."

111   Article 8 ECHR provides:

"1. Everyone has the right to respect for his private and family life, his home and his correspondence.
2. There shall be no interference by a public authority with the exercise of this right except such as is in accordance with the law and is necessary in a democratic society in the interests of national security, public safety or the economic well-being of the country, for the prevention of disorder or crime, for the protection of health or morals, or for the protection of the rights and freedoms of others."

112   The right to respect for the home encompasses the right to enjoyment of a residence free from excessive environmental pollution, including noise nuisance. This may give rise to an obligation on the part of the State to take effective measures against noise. As to positive obligations, in *Botta v Italy* (1998) 26 E.H.R.R. 241, at 257-258, the ECtHR held:

"There may be positive obligations inherent in effective respect for private or family life....However, the concept of respect is not precisely defined. In order to determine whether such obligations exist, regard must be had to the fair balance that has to be struck between the general interest and the interests of the individual, while the state has, in any event, a margin of appreciation."

113   The precautionary principle is a core principle of EU environmental law, enshrined in Article 191(2) of the Treaty on the Functioning of the EU. The classic definition of 'a precautionary approach' comes from the 1992 Rio Declaration on Environment and Development, which states that "[w]here there are threats of

serious or irreversible damage, lack of full scientific certainty shall not be used as a reason for postponing cost-effective measures to prevent environmental degradation" (UNEP 1992). The precautionary principle was applied in *Tatar v Romania* (App. No.67021/01) unreported 27 January 2009 ECtHR, at paragraph 120, and it was expressed at paragraph 10 of the judgment as follows:

> "According to the case law of the ECJ, when uncertainties remain as to the existence or extent of risks to human health, the institutions may take measures without having to wait for the reality and seriousness of those risks to be fully demonstrated."

114   In *Lough v First Secretary of State* [2004] EWCA Civ 905, Pill LJ reviewed the authorities and concluded:

> "43. It emerges from the authorities:
> (a) Article 8 is concerned to prevent intrusions into a person's private life and home and, in particular, arbitrary intrusions and that is the background against which alleged breaches are to be considered.
> (b) Respect for the home has an environmental dimension in that the law must offer protection to the environment of the home.
> (c) Not every loss of amenity involves a breach of Article 8(1). The degree of seriousness required to trigger lack of respect for the home will depend on the circumstances but it must be substantial.
> (d) The contents of Article 8(2) throw light on the extent of the right in Article 8(1) but infringement of Article 8(1) does not necessarily arise upon a loss of amenity and the reasonableness and appropriateness of measures taken by the public authority are relevant in considering whether the respect required by Article 8(1) has been accorded."

115   In *R. (RLT Built Environment Ltd) v Cornwall CC* [2016] EWHC 2817 (Admin), Hickinbottom J summarised the principles to be applied when considering Article 8 in a planning context, at [81]:

> "81. The relationship between the domestic planning scheme and article 8 has been considered in a number of cases, notably (*Chapman v United Kingdom* (2001) 33 E.H.R.R. 18, *Lough v First Secretary of State* [2004] EWCA Civ 905 and *Stevens v Secretary of State for Communities and Local Government* [2013] EWHC 792 (Admin) at [47] and following (approved in *Collins v Secretary of State for Communities and Local Government* [2013] EWCA Civ 1193). These cases largely concerned planning control, e.g. decisions in respect of planning permission (often, in the cases, sought retrospectively) or enforcement, frequently in the context of caravans which had been sited without any cognisance of the planning regime. With regard to planning control, the following relevant propositions can be drawn from them.
>
> i) Article 8 does not give a right to a home, or to a home in any particular place.
> ii) However, where someone has a home in a particular dwelling, it may interfere with the article 8 rights of him and/or his family to require him/them to move.

iii) Whilst those rights demand "respect", they are of course not guaranteed. In this context, as much as any other, the public interest and/or the rights and interests of others may justify interference with an individual's article 8 rights.

iv) Where article 8 rights are in play in a planning control context, they are a material consideration. Any interference in such rights caused by the planning control decision has to be balanced with and against all other material considerations, the issue of justification for interference with article 8 rights effectively being dealt with by way of such a fair balance analysis.

v) That balancing exercise is one of planning judgment. Consequently, it may be amenable to more than one, perfectly lawful, result; and this court will only interfere if the decision is outside the legitimate range. Indeed, in any challenge, the court will give deference to the decision of the primary decision-maker, because he has been assigned the decision-making task by Parliament, and he will usually have particular expertise and experience in the relevant area. Such a decision-maker will be accorded a substantial margin of discretion. The deference and margin of discretion will be the greater if he has particular expertise and experience in the relevant area, and/or if he is acting in a quasi-judicial capacity (such as an inspector).

vi) If the decision-maker has clearly engaged with the article 8 rights in play, and considered them with care, it is unlikely that the court will interfere with his conclusion. Article 8 rights are, of course, important: but it is not to be assumed that, in an area of social policy such as planning, they will often outweigh the importance of having coherent control over town and country planning, important not only in the public interest but also to protect the rights and freedoms of other individuals. In practice, cases in which this court will interfere are likely to be few."

116   In this case, Members of the Planning Committee had received specific training on human rights in the context of the planning decision-making process. In a standard guidance document accompanying the OR, they were specifically advised of the need to consider the human rights of those affected, and to have regard to Article 8. Therefore, both the officer and Members had Article 8 well in mind.

117   The issue of noise from the Race Circuit, and its impact upon local residents in their homes, was extensively considered in the OR. The planning officer undertook a structured weighing up and balancing of the issues of noise and loss of amenity against the benefits of the development, and the wider community interest, within the relevant statutory and policy framework. It was, in effect, a proportionality assessment, though not expressed to be undertaken pursuant to Article 8.

118   On the facts of this case, the precautionary principle was not relevant. This was not a decision which relied upon an analysis of risk, and where preliminary scientific evidence and evaluation did not allow the risk to be determined with sufficient certainty. It was well known and accepted that noise at a certain level is capable of affecting amenity and/or constituting statutory nuisance. There was no uncertainty concerning the terms of the revised abatement notice. However, the Council did not accept the evidence and submissions by the Claimant and other residents as to

non-compliance with the revised abatement notice, preferring to rely on its own evidence of compliance. It was entitled to reach this view.

119   Alternatively, even if Article 8 was not adequately considered in the OR, it is highly likely that the Council's decision would not have been substantially different if it had specifically addressed Article 8 in the OR. Planning permission would still have been granted, for the reasons set out in the OR. Therefore, even if my primary conclusion on Article 8 is incorrect, and the Council did fail to give sufficient consideration to Article 8, I would refuse relief, applying section 31(2A) of the Senior Courts Act 1981.

120   For these reasons, Ground 4 does not succeed.

Final conclusion

121   The claim for judicial review is dismissed.

FCC CESKA REPUBLIKA SRO v MINISTERSTVO ZIVOTNIHO PROSTREDI

EUROPEAN COURT OF JUSTICE (FOURTH CHAMBER)

(C-43/21)

C. Lycourgos, President of the Chamber, S. Rodin, J. C. Bonichot (Rapporteur), L.S. Rossi and O. Spineanu Matei, Judges, J. Kokott, AG: 2 June 2022

[2023] Env. L.R. 4

LT Environmental permits; Extensions of time; EU law; Integrated pollution prevention and control; Landfill sites; Public participation

H1 *Waste—integrated pollution prevention and control—Industrial Emissions Directive—extension of time for landfill permit—no change to storage capacity or other physical aspects of site—public participation rights—whether a "substantial change" within meaning of art.3(9)*

H2   A request for a preliminary ruling was made in proceedings between a Landfill Operator and the Ministry of the Environment and others concerning a decision in 2015 amending the permit to operate a landfill in order to extend the duration of waste disposal from 31 December 2015 until 31 December 2017. The permit had been amended on several occasions, including twice in order to extend the duration of waste disposal at the landfill. The City Court annulled the decision on the ground that the extension of the permit for waste disposal at the landfill was a "substantial change", which gave rise to the right to public participation in accordance with Directive 2010/75. On appeal, the Landfill Operator argued that the mere extension of the duration of waste disposal at a landfill by two years could not in and of itself be qualified as "substantial change" within the meaning of art.3(9) if it did not involve works or interventions which altered the physical aspect of the site. It submitted that the extension changed neither the dimensions of the landfill nor the total waste storage capacity but was for the purpose of filling the landfill to the permitted capacity. If the extension of the permit was to have an environmental impact, it would not constitute a "substantial change". The Supreme Administrative Court stayed proceedings and referred a question asking whether, under art.3(9), the mere extension of the duration of waste disposal at a landfill, without any change in the maximum approved dimensions of the installation or its total capacity, constituted a "substantial change" within the meaning of that provision.

H3   **Held:**

H4   (1) Under art.3(9), a "substantial change" to the installation was "a change in the nature or functioning, or an extension, of an installation or combustion plant, waste incineration plant or waste co-incineration plant which may have significant negative effects on human health or the environment". It was apparent from that wording that a change had to be classified as "substantial" on two conditions, the first relating to the content of the change and the second to its potential consequences. Those two criteria were cumulative. A change in the nature or functioning, or an extension, of an installation was not "substantial" within the meaning of art.3(9) if it was not likely to have significant negative effects on human health or the environment. Conversely, it was not sufficient for a change to be able to have significant negative effects on human health or the environment for it to be "substantial" within the meaning of that Directive. If that were the case, the EU legislature would not have specified that a substantial change had to consist of a change in the nature or functioning, or an extension, of an installation.

H5   (2) Article 3(9) defined the first condition, alternatively, as "a change in the nature or functioning, or an extension, of an installation". The mere extension of the duration of waste disposal at a landfill did not, in itself, change the perimeter of the installation or the storage capacity as provided for in the initial permit, and did not therefore constitute an "extension" of the installation. The referring court had also been careful to clarify that the extension of the duration of waste disposal at the landfill at issue was provided for without the maximum approved dimensions of the landfill or its total capacity changing at the same time. The mere extension of the duration of waste disposal at the landfill did not constitute a change of the installation, be it in its nature or in its functioning. None of the provisions in Directive 2010/75 mentioned the duration of the landfill's operation as a feature of the installation's functioning which had to be included in the permit. As the Directive did not require the initial permit to specify the duration of operation of the landfill, it could not be interpreted as requiring the mere extension of its operation to be the subject of a new permit. The extension of the duration of waste disposal at a landfill did not constitute either a change in the nature or functioning, or an extension of an installation, within the meaning of art.3(9). Consequently, such an extension did not satisfy the first of the two cumulative conditions for classification as a "substantial change" under that provision.

H6   (3) Accordingly, there was no need to examine whether the second condition, that change may give rise to significant negative effects on human health or the environment, was satisfied.

H7   (4) It followed that art.20(2) of the Directive did not require the Member States to require the operator of a landfill to apply for a new permit where that operator intended to merely extend the duration of waste disposal of the landfill within the limits of the total storage capacity for which a permit has already been given.

H8 **Cases referred to:**
Association nationale pour la protection des eaux and rivières and OABA (C-473/07) EU:C:2009:30
Brussels Hoofdstedelijk Gewest v Vlaams Gewest (C-275/09) EU:C:2011:154; [2011] Env. L.R. 26; [2011] P.T.S.R. D37
Bund fur Umwelt und Naturschutz Deutschland, Landesverband Nordrhein-Westfalen eV v Bezirksregierung Arnsberg (C-115/09) EU:C:2011:289; [2011] 3 C.M.L.R. 15; [2011] Env. L.R. 29
Council and Commission v Stichting Natuur en Milieu and Pesticide Action Network Europe (C-404/12 P and C-405/12 P) EU:C:2015:5; [2015] 2 C.M.L.R. 31

Council v Vereniging Milieudefensie and Stichting Stop Luchtverontreiniging Utrecht (C-401/12 P-C-403/12 P) EU:C:2015:4; [2015] 2 C.M.L.R. 32
Dimos Kropias Attikis (C-473/14) EU:C:2015:582
Edwards v Environment Agency (C-260/11) EU:C:2013:221; [2013] 1 W.L.R. 2914; [2013] 3 C.M.L.R. 18
Friends of the Irish Environment Ltd v An Bord Pleanala (C-254/19) EU:C:2020:680; [2021] Env. L.R. 16
Gemeinde Altrip v Land Rheinland-Pfalz (C-72/12) EU:C:2013:712; [2014] P.T.S.R. 311
Gruber v Unabhangiger Verwaltungssenat fur Karnten (C-570/13) EU:C:2015:231; [2015] Env. L.R. D6
Inter-Environnement Wallonie ASBL v Conseil des Ministres (C-411/17) EU:C:2019:622; [2020] Env. L.R. 9
Krizan v Slovenska inspekcia zivotneho prostredia (C-416/10) EU:C:2013:8; [2013] Env. L.R. 28
LB v College van Burgemeester en Wethouders van de Gemeente Echt-Susteren (C-826/18) EU:C:2021:7; [2021] P.T.S.R. 735; [2021] 2 C.M.L.R. 18
Møller (C-585/10) EU:C:2011:847
Proceedings Brought by Folk (C-529/15) EU:C:2017:419; [2018] 1 C.M.L.R. 6; [2017] Env. L.R. 35
Pro-Braine ASBL v Commune of Braine-le-Chateau (C-121/11) EU:C:2012:225; [2012] P.T.S.R. D29
R. (on the application of Wells) v Secretary of State for Transport, Local Government and the Regions (C-201/02) EU:C:2004:12; [2004] Env. L.R. 27; [2004] 1 C.M.L.R. 31
Stichting Natuur en Milieu v College van Gedeputeerde Staten van Groningen (C-165/09–C-167/09) EU:C:2011:348; [2011] 3 C.M.L.R. 21; [2012] Env. L.R. 2
Valciukiene v Pakruojo rajono savivaldybe (C-295/10) EU:C:2011:608; [2012] Env. L.R. 11

H9 **Legislation referred to:**
TFEU art.267
Convention on access to information, public participation in decision-making and access to justice in environmental matters 1998 (Aarhus Convention) arts 1 and 6 and Annex I
Directive 1999/31 (Landfill) arts 2 and 7
Directive 2010/75 (Industrial Emissions) arts 1, 3, 4, 10, 12, 14, 20, 24 and 25 and Annex I
Directive 2011/92 (EIA) art.1

H10 *L. Dvořáková*, *M. Smolek* and *J. Vláčil*, acting as Agents, appeared on behalf of the Czech Government.
M. Noll-Ehlers, *P. Ondrůšek* and *C. Valero*, acting as Agents, appeared on behalf of the Commission.

OPINION[1]

I. Introduction

AG1   How is the term 'substantial change' to an installation to be understood for the purposes of the Industrial Emissions Directive?[2] More specifically, is an extension of the duration, during which additional waste may be shipped to a landfill, to be regarded as a substantial change to the landfill if there is no change either to the maximum permitted quantity of waste or to the total capacity of the landfill? This is the question that the Court is required to answer in the present proceedings.

AG2   The significance of the term 'substantial change', which the Court has to interpret for the first time, lies in the fact that a substantial change to an installation is subject to particular requirements, including in terms of public participation and the legal protection of third parties (Article 20(2) and Articles 24 and 25 of the Industrial Emissions Directive). That interpretation can be guided by the case-law on the Environmental Impact Assessment Directive[3] and by the Aarhus Convention,[4] the latter being transposed via the provisions of the Industrial Emissions Directive concerning public participation and legal protection.

II. Legal context

A. International law – Aarhus Convention

AG3   As the rules on public participation in the Industrial Emissions Directive transpose the Aarhus Convention, it is appropriate to recall its relevant provisions.

AG4   The purpose of the Aarhus Convention is set out in Article 1:

> 'In order to contribute to the protection of the right of every person of present and future generations to live in an environment adequate to his or her health and well-being, each Party shall guarantee the rights of access to information, public participation in decision-making, and access to justice in environmental matters in accordance with the provisions of this Convention.'

AG5   Article 6 of the Aarhus Convention regulates public participation in decisions on specific activities:

> '1. Each Party:
>> (a) Shall apply the provisions of this article with respect to decisions on whether to permit proposed activities listed in Annex I;
>>
>> …
>
> 4. Each Party shall provide for early public participation, when all options are open and effective public participation can take place.
>> …

---

[1] Original language: German.
[2] Directive 2010/75 of the European Parliament and of the Council of 24 November 2010 on industrial emissions (integrated pollution prevention and control) ([2010] OJ L334/17).
[3] Directive 2011/92 of the European Parliament and of the Council of 13 December 2011 on the assessment of the effects of certain public and private projects on the environment ([2012] OJ L26/1), last amended by Directive 2014/52 ([2014] OJ L124/1).
[4] 1998 Convention on access to information, public participation in decision-making and access to justice in environmental matters ([2005] OJ L124/4), approved by Council Decision 2005/370/EC of 17 February 2005 ([2005] OJ L124/1).

6. Each Party shall require the competent public authorities to give the public concerned access for examination … as soon as it becomes available, to all information relevant to the decision-making referred to in this article that is available at the time of the public participation procedure; …

…

10. Each Party shall ensure that, when a public authority reconsiders or updates the operating conditions for an activity referred to in paragraph 1, the provisions of paragraphs 2 to 9 of this Article are applied *mutatis mutandis*, and where appropriate.

…'

AG6   The other paragraphs of that article contain detailed rules on public participation and the assessment of the effects of the activity on the environment.

AG7   Annex I to the Aarhus Convention lists the activities which are subject to mandatory public participation under Article 6, paragraph 1(a). The fourth indent of point 5 of that annex lists 'landfills receiving more than 10 tons per day or with a total capacity exceeding 25 000 tons, excluding landfills of inert waste'.

AG8   According to the first sentence of point 22 of Annex I to the Aarhus Convention, 'any change to or extension of activities, where such a change or extension in itself meets the criteria/thresholds set out in this annex, shall be subject to Article 6, paragraph 1(a) of this Convention'.

B. European Union law – Industrial Emissions Directive

AG9   Recital 18 of the Industrial Emissions Directive explains the term 'substantial change':

'Changes to an installation may give rise to higher levels of pollution. Operators should notify the competent authority of any planned change which might affect the environment. Substantial changes to installations which may have significant negative effects on human health or the environment should not be made without a permit granted in accordance with this Directive.'

AG10   According to recital 27 of the Industrial Emissions Directive, the provisions on public participation and legal protection transpose the Aarhus Convention:

'In accordance with the Aarhus Convention …, effective public participation in decision-making is necessary to enable the public to express, and the decision-maker to take account of, opinions and concerns which may be relevant to those decisions, thereby increasing the accountability and transparency of the decision-making process and contributing to public awareness of environmental issues and support for the decisions taken. Members of the public concerned should have access to justice in order to contribute to the protection of the right to live in an environment which is adequate for personal health and well-being.'

AG11   The subject matter of the Industrial Emissions Directive is set out in Article 1:

'This Directive lays down rules on integrated prevention and control of pollution arising from industrial activities.

It also lays down rules designed to prevent or, where that is not practicable, to reduce emissions into air, water and land and to prevent the generation of waste, in order to achieve a high level of protection of the environment taken as a whole.'

AG12   Article 3(9) of theIndustrial Emissions Directive defines the term 'substantial change' as 'a change in the nature or functioning, or an extension, of an installation or combustion plant, waste incineration plant or waste co-incineration plant which may have significant negative effects on human health or the environment'.

AG13   Article 4(1) of the Industrial Emissions Directive establishes the need for a permit:

> 'Member States shall take the necessary measures to ensure that no installation … is operated without a permit.
> …'

AG14   According to Article 3(3) of the Industrial Emissions Directive, point 5.4 of Annex I thereto and Article 2(g) of the Landfill Directive,[5] a landfill receiving more than 10 tonnes of waste per day or with a total capacity exceeding 25,000 tonnes, excluding landfills of inert waste, is an installation within the meaning of Article 4 of the Industrial Emissions Directive.

AG15   Article 20 of the Industrial Emissions Directive concerns changes to installations:

> '1. Member States shall take the necessary measures to ensure that the operator informs the competent authority of any planned change in the nature or functioning, or an extension of the installation which may have consequences for the environment. Where appropriate, the competent authority shall update the permit.
> 2. Member States shall take the necessary measures to ensure that no substantial change planned by the operator is made without a permit granted in accordance with this Directive.
> The application for a permit and the decision by the competent authority shall cover those parts of the installation and those details listed in Article 12 which may be affected by the substantial change.
> 3. Any change in the nature or functioning or an extension of an installation shall be deemed to be substantial if the change or extension in itself reaches the capacity thresholds set out in Annex I.'

AG16   Article 24(1)(b) of the Industrial Emissions Directive requires the public concerned to be given early and effective opportunities to participate in the procedure for the granting of a permit for any substantial change. Article 25 allows the public concerned to demand a review of the substantive and procedural legality of a permit.

III. The facts and the request for a preliminary ruling

AG17   FCC Česká republika is a Czech company which operates a landfill in the borough of Ďáblice in Prague further to a permit granted under the Industrial Emissions Directive.

---

[5] Council Directive 1999/31 of 26 April 1999 on the landfill of waste ([1999] OJ L182/1), as amended by Council Directive 2011/97 of 5 December 2011 amending Directive 1999/31 as regards specific criteria for the storage of metallic mercury considered as waste ([2011] OJ L328/49).

AG18   The integrated operating permit for the landfill was granted in 2007 and subsequently amended several times. In particular, the duration of waste disposal was extended twice. At the end of 2015, FCC applied to the Magistrát hlavního města Prahy (Prague City Hall) for a 13th amendment to the integrated permit as, although the original planned capacity of the landfill had not yet been utilised, its current permit required waste disposal at the landfill to stop at the end of 2015. On 29 December 2015, Prague City Hall extended the duration of waste disposal at the landfill by two years. The decision did not change the total capacity of the landfill or its maximum dimensions.[6]

AG19   The borough of the City of Prague, in which the landfill is located, and an association, whose main mission is to protect nature and the landscape and ensure the participation of citizens in that protection, lodged a complaint against the decision of Prague City Hall. However, the defendant, the *Ministerstvo životního prostředí* (Ministry of the Environment, Czech Republic), dismissed the complaint as inadmissible, due to the fact that the complainants had not participated in the procedure to amend the integrated permit.

AG20   The two complainants then lodged an action challenging the defendant's decision. The *Městský soud v Praze* (Prague City Court, Czech Republic) admitted the action, annulled the decision by Prague City Hall and referred the case back to it for re-examination. It held that the key issue for the purpose of assessing the complainants' participation is whether the amendment to the integrated permit approved a 'substantial change' to the installation operated by FCC. That would then determine who can participate in the procedure.

AG21   The *Městský soud v Praze* (Prague City Court) inferred that the scope of a project may be defined temporally and that an extension of the term of operation of a plant must be seen as a change in the scope of the project; that, if the operation of a plant was originally permitted for a certain period only, its effects on the environment after its permitted time of operation has ended would not have been assessed, as its continued impact would not have been countenanced; and that an extension of the time of operation means an extension of the impact on the environment.

AG22   FCC lodged an appeal on a point of law against the judgment of the *Městský soud v Praze* (Prague City Court) with the *Nejvyšší správní soud* (Supreme Administrative Court, Czech Republic).

AG23   The *Nejvyšší správní soud* (Supreme Administrative Court) has therefore referred the following question to the Court of Justice:

> 'Should Article 3(9) of the Industrial Emissions Directive be interpreted such that a "substantial change" to a plant includes an extension of the duration of waste disposal at a landfill without the maximum approved dimensions of the landfill or its total potential capacity changing at the same time?'

AG24   The Czech Republic and the European Commission submitted written observations. The Court did not consider it necessary to hold a hearing.

---

[6] The contested permit appears to be accessible online at *https://ippc.mzp.cz/ippc/ippc.nsf/xsp/.ibmmodres/domino/OpenAttachment/ippc/ippc.nsf/215B32AAF47F72E0C1257F32002C2B15/Files/zmena%20IP.pdf*. Further information on the permits granted for the landfill is available at *https://www.mzp.cz/ippc/ippc4.nsf/$$OpenDominoDocument.xsp?documentId=4D88556E61533616C1257B82004CE066&action=openDocument*. According to the Commission, the duration of waste disposal at the landfill has been extended by two years at least once more since that date. However, the final change to the landfill identified as a substantial change was decided in 2009.

IV. Legal appraisal

AG25   The question referred for a preliminary ruling seeks to clarify whether an extension of the duration of waste disposal at a landfill, without the maximum approved dimensions of the landfill or its total potential capacity changing at the same time, is a substantial change to that installation within the meaning of the Industrial Emissions Directive.

AG26   It follows from the request for a preliminary ruling that the landfill site at issue was originally authorised under the Industrial Emissions Directive. Therefore, and on the basis of the information available online,[7] it must be assumed that the landfill is large enough to fall within the scope of the directive, that is to say, it has the capacity to receive more than 10 tonnes of waste per day or a total capacity exceeding 25 000 tonnes.

AG27   If the extension of the duration of waste disposal at the landfill at issue is a substantial change, it requires a permit pursuant to Article 20(2) of the Industrial Emissions Directive. In that case, the administrative procedure must include public participation (Article 24), and the members of the public concerned may demand judicial review of the permit (Article 25). The operator, on the other hand, need only notify the competent authority of other changes that may have consequences for the environment (Article 20(1)).

AG28   As the authorising authority assumed in the case in the main proceedings that there was no substantial change, no public participation took place. If that assumption was correct, it would appear that the applicants cannot challenge the contested permit under Czech law; moreover, the request for a preliminary ruling does not contain any evidence of more extensive rights of action under EU law. The referring court therefore needs to know whether the contested permit concerned a substantial change.

AG29   In order to answer that question, I shall start by examining the definition of substantial change in Article 3(9) of the Industrial Emissions Directive (Section A) and then turn to the Aarhus Convention (Section B). I shall then narrow down the interpretation made thus in the light of the circumstances of the present case (Section C).

A. *Article 3(9) of the Industrial Emissions Directive*

AG30   Article 3(9) of the Industrial Emissions Directive defines a substantial change as a change in the nature or functioning, or an extension, of an installation which may have significant negative effects on human health or the environment.

AG31   It is true that the referring court raises the question of whether it is possible, for the purpose of interpreting the Industrial Emissions Directive, to apply the case-law on the Environmental Impact Assessment Directive establishing that a new environmental impact assessment is not required for the renewal of an existing permit in the absence of any works or interventions involving alterations to the physical aspect of the site.[8] However, that case-law is based on the definition of a project in Article 1(2)(a) of the Environmental Impact Assessment Directive,[9]

---

[7] Cited in fn.6; see also points AG54–AG57 below.

[8] Judgments of 17 March 2011, *Brussels Hoofdstedelijk Gewest* (C-275/09) EU:C:2011:154 at [24], and of 19 April 2012, *Pro-Braine* (C-121/11) EU:C:2012:225 at [32].

[9] Judgments of 17 March 2011, *Brussels Hoofdstedelijk Gewest* (C-275/09) EU:C:2011:154 at [20] et seq., and of 19 April 2012, *Pro-Braine* (C-121/11) EU:C:2012:225 at [31].

which is more restrictive than the definition of a substantial change in the Industrial Emissions Directive.

AG32   According to Article 1(2)(a) of the Environmental Impact Assessment Directive, the term 'project' includes the execution of construction works or of other installations and other interventions in the natural surroundings and landscape including those involving the extraction of mineral resources. It therefore expressly refers to works or interventions.

AG33   By contrast, the definition of substantial change in Article 3(9) of the Industrial Emissions Directive uses more abstract terms, namely a change in the nature or functioning, or an extension, of an installation. Those concepts are open to broader interpretation.

AG34   Consequently, the case-law on the Environmental Impact Assessment Directive should not be applied directly.

AG35   Nevertheless, merely extending the duration of additional waste disposal at a landfill, without the maximum permissible dimensions of the landfill or its total potential capacity changing at the same time, does not alter the functioning or nature of the landfill.

AG36   Nor does the extension expand the site or the planned dimensions of the landfill. However, it does allow an increase in the volume of waste actually disposed of, probably by approximately 50,000 tonnes of additional waste,[10] which could not be disposed of there without the extension.

AG37   In any event, that extension is an extension in time of the operation of the landfill.[11] Although such a temporal change does not reflect the key meaning of the word 'extension', which is probably closer to the term 'enlargement', and not only in the German language version,[12] the meaning of the term does not necessarily prevent the extension of a permit from being seen as an extension in time of the operation of an installation.

AG38   That interpretation of the term 'extension' is justified by the purpose of the Industrial Emissions Directive. The purpose of the directive, as laid down in Article 1 thereof, is to achieve integrated prevention and control of pollution by putting in place measures designed to prevent or reduce the emissions, of the activities listed in Annex I to that directive, into the air, water and land in order to achieve a high level of protection of the environment.[13] Thus, since the purpose of the Industrial Emissions Directive is defined broadly,[14] the term 'substantial change' may not be interpreted narrowly. On the contrary, the objective of a high level of protection of the environment must be the determining factor.

AG39   This also follows from recital 18 of theIndustrial Emissions Directive, which describes substantial changes as changes which may have significant negative effects on human health or the environment. There is no mention of changes in the functioning or nature of the installation or of its extension. These other reference points for a change included in the definition in Article 3(9) of the Industrial

---

[10] Page 4 of the contested decision, cited in fn.6.

[11] See my Opinion in *Inter-Environnement Wallonie and Bond Beter Leefmilieu Vlaanderen* (C-411/17) EU:C:2018:972, AG101.

[12] The English and French versions each use the term 'extension'.

[13] Judgments of 22 January 2009, *Association Nationale pour la Protection des Eaux et Rivières and Association OABA* (C-473/07) EU:C:2009:30 at [25] and [40]; of 26 May 2011, *Stichting Natuur en Milieu* (C-165/09–C-167/09) EU:C:2011:348 at [72]; of 15 December 2011, *Møller* (C-585/10) EU:C:2011:847 at [29]; and of 15 January 2013, *Križan* (C-416/10) EU:C:2013:8 at [108].

[14] Judgments of 22 January 2009, *Association Nationale pour la Protection des Eaux et Rivières and Association OABA* (C-473/07) EU:C:2009:30 at [27] and of 15 December 2011, *Møller* (C-585/10) EU:C:2011:847 at [31].

Emissions Directive are therefore to be understood not restrictively, but broadly, as a comprehensive explanation of possible changes.

AG40   Any limitation on the meaning of substantial change must be sought primarily in the potential additional effects of the activity on the environment. Thus, the only changes that are not substantial are changes that cannot have additional significant negative effects on human health or the environment compared to the pre-existing situation, whereas changes that can have additional significant effects require greater attention in order to guarantee a high level of protection.

AG41   My interim conclusion, therefore, is that a simple extension of the duration of disposal of waste in a landfill, without the maximum permissible dimensions of the landfill or its total potential capacity changing at the same time, in the sense that the operation of the installation is extended in time, may be a substantial change under Article 3(9) of the Industrial Emissions Directive if it can have additional significant negative effects on human health or the environment.

B. Aarhus Convention

AG42   That interpretation is also consistent with the Aarhus Convention. As stated in Article 1 thereof, its objective is to guarantee public participation in decision-making. Article 6 of the convention lays down certain rules on public participation for that purpose. The fourth indent of point 5 of Annex I to the Aarhus Convention applies those rules to landfills receiving more than 10 tonnes per day or with a total capacity exceeding 25,000 tonnes.

AG43   As, according to recital 27 of the Industrial Emissions Directive, the directive seeks to transpose the provisions of the Aarhus Convention on public participation and the concept of substantial change determines the scope of public participation, regard must be had to the convention when interpreting that concept.[15]

AG44   Article 6, paragraph 10, of the Aarhus Convention requires each party to ensure that, when a public authority reconsiders or updates the operating conditions for an activity referred to in Article 6, the rules on public participation are applied *mutatis mutandis*, and where appropriate.

AG45   The decision-making practice of the Aarhus Convention Compliance Committee,[16] endorsed by the parties, including the European Union, provides important guidance on the interpretation of that provision.

AG46   The Compliance Committee considers that the permitted duration of an activity is clearly an operating condition for that activity, and an important one at that. Accordingly, any change to that duration, be it a reduction or an extension, is a reconsideration or update of that activity's operating conditions within the meaning of Article 6, paragraph 10, of the Aarhus Convention.[17]

---

[15] See, to that effect, judgment of 15 January 2013, *Križan* (C-416/10) EU:C:2013:8 at [77]. See also, with regard to the Environmental Impact Assessment Directive, judgments of 12 May 2011, *Bund für Umwelt und Naturschutz Deutschland, Landesverband Nordrhein-Westfalen* (C-115/09) EU:C:2011:289 at [41] and of 16 April 2015, *Gruber* (C-570/13) EU:C:2015:231 at [34].

[16] The Compliance Committee'; see, in that regard, my Opinion in *Edwards and Pallikaropoulos* (C-260/11) EU:C:2012:645, AG8, and the Opinions of Advocate General Cruz Villalón in *Gemeinde Altrip* (C-72/12) EU:C:2013:422, AG101; of Advocate General Jääskinen in joined cases *Council v Vereniging Milieudefensie and Stichting Stop Luchtverontreiniging Utrecht* (C-401/12 P–C 403/12 P) EU:C:2014:310 AG114, and in joined cases *Council and Commission v Stichting Natuur en Milieu and Pesticide Action Network Europe* (C-404/12 P and C-405/12 P) EU:C:2014:309 AG23; and of Advocate General Bobek in *Folk* (C-529/15) EU:C:2017:1, AG86 and in *Stichting Varkens in Nood* (C-826/18) EU:C:2020:514, AG77.

[17] Findings and recommendations of the Compliance Committee of 4 October 2018, Stichting Greenpeace *Netherlands v Netherlands* (Borssele nuclear power plant), ACCC/C/2014/104, ECE/MP.PP/C.1/2019/3, AG65; of 19 August 2019, *Cummins v Ireland* (Trammon quarry), ACCC/C/2013/107, ECE/MP.PP/C.1/2019/9, AG79; and of 26 July

AG47   Although Article 6, paragraph 10, of the Aarhus Convention only requires the rules on public participation to be applied *mutatis mutandis* and where appropriate, the Compliance Committee considers that derogations from Article 6 are appropriate only where a change to the permitted duration is for a minimal time only and obviously would have insignificant or no effects on the environment.[18]

AG48   Although, at first glance, that statement goes further than my interpretation of Article 3(9) of the Industrial Emissions Directive, the potential effects on the environment are certainly a key criterion also for the Compliance Committee.[19]

C. Assessment of potential significant effects on the environment

AG49   However, in order to answer the question referred for a preliminary ruling, additional significant effects on the environment as a result of the permit at issue still have to be assessed, as those effects will enable a distinction to be drawn between substantial and non-substantial changes to the installation.

AG50   As noted by the Czech Republic, the effects on the environment of a landfill are caused, on the one hand, by the storage of waste. In particular, if the landfill has design defects, the waste can affect groundwater or can contaminate other land if it is not properly covered. Also, types of waste improperly stored together can give rise to harmful chemical reactions or biological processes that have negative effects on the environment. However, those negative effects do not change on account of an extension of the use as long as the area and capacity of the landfill and the measures needed to prevent certain negative effects on the environment remain the same. Therefore, from that perspective, a mere extension of the permit does not entail additional effects on the environment.

AG51   On the other hand, as the Commission points out, even the shipment of waste to a landfill and any processing operations on site generate additional effects on the environment. One need only consider the traffic and the fact that a completely covered, state-of-the-art, closed landfill site probably produces fewer emissions into the air, especially nuisance odours or dust, than a landfill that is still being filled with waste. An extension of the duration for disposing of additional waste would increase such operational effects on the environment, in time at least. They would be covered by the definition of pollution in Article 3(2) of the Industrial Emissions Directive.

AG52   The question is how to determine whether those additional effects on the environment qualify as a substantial change to the landfill.

1. Capacity thresholds

AG53   First, it has to be noted in that regard that Article 20(3) of the Industrial Emissions Directive defines which changes always qualify as substantial changes. This covers

---

2021, *OEKOBUERO v Czech Republic* (Dukovany nuclear power plant), ACCC/C/2016/143, ECE/MP.PP/C.1/2021/28, AG97.

[18] Findings and recommendations of the Compliance Committee of 4 October 2018, Stichting Greenpeace *Netherlands v Netherlands* (Borssele nuclear power plant), ACCC/C/2014/104, ECE/MP.PP/C.1/2019/3, AG71; of 19 August 2019, *Cummins v Ireland* (Trammon quarry), ACCC/C/2013/107, ECE/MP.PP/C.1/2019/9, AG83; and of 26 July 2021, *OEKOBUERO v Czech Republic* (Dukovany nuclear power plant), ACCC/C/2016/143, ECE/MP.PP/C.1/2021/28, AG104.

[19] See the references in fn.18 and the findings and recommendations of the Compliance Committee of 12 May 2011, Global 2000 *Friends of the Earth Austria v Slovakia* (Mochovce nuclear power plant), ACCC/C/2009/41, ECE/MP.PP/2011/11/Add.3, AG57, and of 4 October 2018, *Fons de Defensa Ambiental v Spain* (Uniland Cementera), ACCC/C/2013/99, ECE/MP.PP/C.1/2017/17, AG85.

a change which of itself reaches the capacity thresholds set out in Annex I thereof. Point 22 of Annex I to the Aarhus Convention contains a similar rule. It must necessarily be assumed that such changes have significant effects on the environment.

AG54   For landfills, based on point 5.4 of Annex I to the Industrial Emissions Directive, the daily capacity would have to increase by at least 10 tonnes or the total capacity would have to increase by at least 25,000 tonnes in order to satisfy the requirement of Article 20(3).[20]

AG55   The effects of the delivery and disposal of waste over a prolonged period would appear to be irrelevant based on that criterion, as the permit at issue alters neither the dimensions nor the total capacity of the landfill. The Czech Republic therefore argues that the requirements of Article 20(3) of the Industrial Emissions Directive are not fulfilled.

AG56   However, there would be no further disposal of waste without the permit at issue. Consequently, the Commission proposes that the decision on the extension of disposal should be assessed based on the residual capacity of the landfill included in the original permit, as it was only possible to exhaust that residual capacity based on the extension decision.

AG57   It would appear that the landfill still had space for about 50,000 tonnes of waste at the time of the extension,[21] which is significantly higher than the capacity threshold of 25,000 tonnes laid down for landfills in point 5.4 of Annex I to the Industrial Emissions Directive. If that information is correct, which it is for the national court to verify, a substantial change would have to be admitted in keeping with the Commission's view.

2. Relevant decision-making practice and case-law

AG58   That consideration is consistent with the Compliance Committee's decision-making practice[22] and would also appear at first sight to be supported by the Court's case-law on the Environmental Impact Assessment Directive.

AG59   However, the judgment of the Court relied on by the Commission[23] is less sound than it would appear. The renewal of consent for a gas terminal examined in that case was in fact a prerequisite to the execution of construction works, as the previous consent was never used.

AG60   A similar situation was addressed in the judgment in *Wells*,[24] on which the Court relied in the aforesaid judgment. That case concerned a quarry which had been closed long since and which could not have been used again without the contested permit.

AG61   Both of those cases are therefore marked by the fact that the permits at issue allowed fundamentally new, previously non-existent, effects on the environment.

AG62   By contrast, the Court did not require an environmental impact assessment with public participation for the purpose of renewing permits to use existing infrastructure

---

[20] The same capacity thresholds are laid down in the fourth indent of AG5 of Annex I to the Aarhus Convention for the purposes of AG22 of that annex.
[21] Page 4 of the contested decision, cited in fn.6.
[22] Findings and recommendations of the Compliance Committee of 26 July 2021, *OEKOBUERO v Czech Republic* (Dukovany nuclear power plant), ACCC/C/2016/143, ECE/MP.PP/C.1/2021/28, AG99. See also my Opinion in *Inter-Environnement Wallonie and Bond Beter Leefmilieu Vlaanderen* (C-411/17) EU:C:2018:972, AG91 et seq.
[23] Judgment of 9 September 2020, *Friends of the Irish Environment* (C-254/19) EU:C:2020:680 at [43]–[47].
[24] Judgment of 7 January 2004, *Wells* (C-201/02) EU:C:2004:12 at [45] and [46].

in the absence of further works, such as the permit to operate an airport[25] or a landfill.[26]

AG63   Consequently, it would appear that the Court sees no need for an environmental impact assessment where the effects on the environment persist largely unchanged. The Court clearly considered the overall increase over time caused by the persistence of the effects on the environment to be irrelevant.

AG64   If this appraisal of the case-law on the Environmental Impact Assessment Directive is applied to theIndustrial Emissions Directive, it is doubtful that the mere possibility of utilising the remaining residual capacity of a previously authorised, operational landfill can substantiate the application of Article 20(3) of the Industrial Emissions Directive.

3. Scope of the initial permit

AG65   The Court's case-law on the Environmental Impact Assessment Directive can be explained based on assumptions as to the scope of the original permit, which will ultimately also suggest the interpretation to be given to Article 3(9) of the Industrial Emissions Directive.

AG66   After all, if certain effects on the environment have already been the subject of an environmental impact assessment in connection with the permit, there is in principle no need to repeat that assessment where the permit is subsequently extended.[27] If, on the other hand, the assessment required was not carried out for an earlier permit, it may be necessary to rectify that omission for a subsequent permit, irrespective of whether or not an environmental impact assessment is required for that subsequent permit, considered in isolation.[28]

AG67   There is also evidence of this in the Compliance Committee's decision-making practice. After all, the Compliance Committee has also relied on whether the public was informed of possible future extensions of the permit at the time of its original participation and therefore had the opportunity to comment on the associated effects on the environment.[29]

AG68   Where an operating permit is extended, the distinction between a simple change and a substantial change within the meaning of Article 3(9) of the Industrial Emissions Directive therefore depends on whether that longer duration can give rise to significant negative effects on the environment which were not covered by the initial permit and therefore require a new assessment.

AG69   In the present case, the Czech Republic and FCC argue in the main proceedings that the facility to grant the contested extension of the waste disposal permit was included in the permit for the landfill from the outset. That is because the duration of waste disposal was predicated on the total planned capacity, not the expiry date of the permit.

AG70   That contention is also supported by the fact that dispensing with an extension would apparently trigger the need for further changes in practice. The closure plan

---

[25] Judgment of 17 March 2011, *Brussels Hoofdstedelijk Gewest* (C-275/09) EU:C:2011:154 at [24].

[26] Judgment of 19 April 2012, *Pro-Braine* (C-121/11) EU:C:2012:225 at [32].

[27] See judgments of 22 September 2011, *Valčiukienė* (C-295/10) EU:C:2011:608 at [61] and [62] and of 10 September 2015, *Dimos Kropias Attikis* (C-473/14) EU:C:2015:582 at [58] both regarding Directive 2001/42 of the European Parliament and of the Council of 27 June 2001 on the assessment of the effects of certain plans and programmes on the environment ([2001] OJ L197/30).

[28] Judgment of 17 March 2011, *Brussels Hoofdstedelijk Gewest* (C-275/09) EU:C:2011:154 at [37].

[29] Findings and recommendations of the Compliance Committee of 19 August 2019, *Cummins v Ireland* (Trammon quarry), ACCC/C/2013/107, ECE/MP.PP/C.1/2019/9, AG85.

required under Article 7(g) of the Landfill Directive might need to be amended, as it presupposes that the landfill is completely full. It might even be necessary to backfill it with material other than waste in order to prevent negative effects on the environment.

AG71 Cases involving an extension of a permit granted for a specific limited period would have to be assessed differently. Thus, it is conceivable that the initial permit was based on a specified maximum operating time.[30] The same would have to apply for the purpose of maintaining a provisional or temporary solution. Even an extension of an old permit that did not require public participation at the time, the full effects of which were originally as yet unknown or the compatibility of which with current standards is questionable, would probably have to be regarded in principle as a substantial change.

AG72 To summarise, additional effects on the environment are characterised by the fact that they were not taken into account in an earlier permit for the activity and in the public participation carried out for that activity.

AG73 Ultimately, however, it is for the national court to appraise those specific circumstances.

V. Conclusion

AG74 In summary, I therefore propose that the Court answer the question referred for a preliminary ruling as follows:

> Article 3(9) of Directive 2010/75/EU of the European Parliament and of the Council of 24 November 2010 on industrial emissions is to be interpreted as meaning that a 'substantial change' to an installation includes an extension of the duration of waste disposal at a landfill without the maximum approved dimensions of the landfill or its total potential capacity changing at the same time, if the extension of the permit can give rise to additional significant effects on the environment. Additional effects on the environment are effects that were not taken into account in an earlier permit for the activity and in the public participation carried out for that activity.

JUDGMENT[31]

1 This request for a preliminary ruling concerns the interpretation of Article 3(9) of Directive 2010/75/EU of the European Parliament and of the Council of 24 November 2010 on industrial emissions (integrated pollution prevention and control) (OJ 2010 L 334, p. 17).

2 The request has been made in proceedings between FCC Česká republika, s.r.o., on the one hand, and, on the other, the Ministerstvo životního prostředí (Ministry of the Environment, Czech Republic), Městská část Praha-Ďáblice (the borough of Praha-Ďáblice, Czech Republic) and Spolek pro Ďáblice, concerning the decision of 29 December 2015 amending the permit to operate the Praha-Ďáblice landfill

---

[30] See findings and recommendations of the Compliance Committee of 4 October 2018, *Stichting Greenpeace Netherlands v Netherlands* (Borssele nuclear power plant), ACCC/C/2014/104, ECE/MP.PP/C.1/2019/3, AG65, 66 and 71, and of 26 July 2021, *OEKOBUERO v Czech Republic* (Dukovany nuclear power plant), ACCC/C/2016/143, ECE/MP.PP/C.1/2021/28, AG104. See also findings and recommendations of the Compliance Committee of 19 August 2019, *Cummins v Ireland* (Trammon Quarry), ACCC/C/2013/107, ECE/MP.PP/C.1/2019/9, AG79.
[31] Language of the case: Czech.

granted to FCC Česká republika, s.r.o., in order to extend the duration of waste disposal from 31 December 2015 until 31 December 2017.

Legal context

European Union law

3   Recital 2 of Directive 2010/75 is worded as follows:

'In order to prevent, reduce and as far as possible eliminate pollution arising from industrial activities in compliance with the "polluter pays" principle and the principle of pollution prevention, it is necessary to establish a general framework for the control of the main industrial activities, giving priority to intervention at source, ensuring prudent management of natural resources and taking into account, when necessary, the economic situation and specific local characteristics of the place in which the industrial activity is taking place.'

4   Recital 5 of that directive states:

'In order to ensure the prevention and control of pollution, each installation should operate only if it holds a permit …'

5   Recital 18 of that directive provides:

'Changes to an installation may give rise to higher levels of pollution. Operators should notify the competent authority of any planned change which might affect the environment. Substantial changes to installations which may have significant negative effects on human health or the environment should not be made without a permit granted in accordance with this Directive.'

6   Recital 27 of that directive states:

'In accordance with the Århus Convention on access to information, public participation in decision-making and access to justice in environmental matters [(OJ 2005 L 124, p. 4), concluded by Council Decision 2005/370/EC of 17 February 2005 (OJ 2005 L 124, p. 1)], effective public participation in decision-making is necessary to enable the public to express, and the decision-maker to take account of, opinions and concerns which may be relevant to those decisions, thereby increasing the accountability and transparency of the decision-making process and contributing to public awareness of environmental issues and support for the decisions taken. …'

7   Under Article 3(9) of Directive 2010/75, a '"substantial change" means a change in the nature or functioning, or an extension, of an installation or combustion plant, waste incineration plant or waste co-incineration plant which may have significant negative effects on human health or the environment'.

8   Article 4 of that directive requires Member States to take the necessary measures in order to ensure that no installation or combustion plant, waste incineration plant or waste co-incineration plant is operated without a permit.

9   Article 10 of that directive, entitled 'Scope', states:

'This Chapter shall apply to the activities set out in Annex I and, where applicable, reaching the capacity thresholds set out in that Annex.'

10   Article 12 of that directive, entitled 'Application for permits', is worded as
      follows:

> '1. Member States shall take the necessary measures to ensure that an
>   application for a permit includes a description of the following:
>   (a) the installation and its activities;
>   (b) the raw and auxiliary materials, other substances and the energy
>   used in or generated by the installation;
>   (c) the sources of emissions from the installation;
>   (d) the conditions of the site of the installation;
>   (e) where applicable, a baseline report in accordance with Article
>   22(2);
>   (f) the nature and quantities of foreseeable emissions from the
>   installation into each medium as well as identification of
>   significant effects of the emissions on the environment;
>   (g) the proposed technology and other techniques for preventing
>   or, where this is not possible, reducing emissions from the
>   installation;
>   (h) measures for the prevention, preparation for re-use, recycling
>   and recovery of waste generated by the installation;
>   (i) further measures planned to comply with the general principles
>   of the basic obligations of the operator as provided for in Article
>   11;
>   (j) measures planned to monitor emissions into the environment;
>   (k) the main alternatives to the proposed technology, techniques
>   and measures studied by the applicant in outline.
>   An application for a permit shall also include a non-technical summary
>   of the details referred to in the first subparagraph.
> 2. Where information supplied in accordance with the requirements
>   provided for in [Council] Directive 85/337/EEC [of 27 June 1985 on
>   the assessment of the effects of certain public and private projects on
>   the environment (OJ 1985 L 175, p. 40)] or a safety report prepared
>   in accordance with [Council] Directive 96/82/EC [of 9 December 1996
>   on the control of major-accident hazards involving dangerous
>   substances (OJ 1997 L 10, p. 13)] or other information produced in
>   response to other legislation fulfils any of the requirements of paragraph
>   1, that information may be included in, or attached to, the application.'

11   Article 14(1) and (2) of Directive 2010/75, entitled 'Permit conditions', states:

> '1. Member States shall ensure that the permit includes all measures
>   necessary for compliance with the requirements of Articles 11 and 18.
>   Those measures shall include at least the following:
>   (a) emission limit values for polluting substances listed in Annex
>   II, and for other polluting substances, which are likely to be
>   emitted from the installation concerned in significant quantities,
>   having regard to their nature and their potential to transfer
>   pollution from one medium to another;

(b) appropriate requirements ensuring protection of the soil and groundwater and measures concerning the monitoring and management of waste generated by the installation;

(c) suitable emission monitoring requirements specifying:

    (i) measurement methodology, frequency and evaluation procedure; and

    (ii) where Article 15(3)(b) is applied, that results of emission monitoring are available for the same periods of time and reference conditions as for the emission levels associated with the best available techniques;

(d) an obligation to supply the competent authority regularly, and at least annually, with:

    (i) information on the basis of results of emission monitoring referred to in point (c) and other required data that enables the competent authority to verify compliance with the permit conditions; and

    (ii) where Article 15(3)(b) is applied, a summary of the results of emission monitoring which allows a comparison with the emission levels associated with the best available techniques;

(e) appropriate requirements for the regular maintenance and surveillance of measures taken to prevent emissions to soil and groundwater pursuant to point (b) and appropriate requirements concerning the periodic monitoring of soil and groundwater in relation to relevant hazardous substances likely to be found on site and having regard to the possibility of soil and groundwater contamination at the site of the installation;

(f) measures relating to conditions other than normal operating conditions such as start-up and shut-down operations, leaks, malfunctions, momentary stoppages and definitive cessation of operations;

(g) provisions on the minimisation of long-distance or transboundary pollution;

(h) conditions for assessing compliance with the emission limit values or a reference to the applicable requirements specified elsewhere.

2. For the purpose of paragraph 1(a), emission limit values may be supplemented or replaced by equivalent parameters or technical measures ensuring an equivalent level of environmental protection.
…'

12   Article 20 of that directive, entitled 'Changes by operators to installations', provides:

'1. Member States shall take the necessary measures to ensure that the operator informs the competent authority of any planned change in the nature or functioning, or an extension of the installation which may have consequences for the environment. Where appropriate, the competent authority shall update the permit.

2. Member States shall take the necessary measures to ensure that no substantial change planned by the operator is made without a permit granted in accordance with this Directive.

    The application for a permit and the decision by the competent authority shall cover those parts of the installation and those details listed in Article 12 which may be affected by the substantial change.

3. Any change in the nature or functioning or an extension of an installation shall be deemed to be substantial if the change or extension in itself reaches the capacity thresholds set out in Annex I.'

13   Article 24(1) of that directive states:

'Member States shall ensure that the public concerned are given early and effective opportunities to participate in the following procedures:

…

(b) the granting of a permit for any substantial change;

…'

14   Article 25 of that directive, entitled 'Access to justice', is worded as follows:

'1. Member States shall ensure that, in accordance with the relevant national legal system, members of the public concerned have access to a review procedure before a court of law or another independent and impartial body established by law to challenge the substantive or procedural legality of decisions, acts or omissions subject to Article 24 when one of the following conditions is met:

    (a) they have a sufficient interest;

    (b) they maintain the impairment of a right, where administrative procedural law of a Member State requires this as a precondition.

2. Member States shall determine at what stage the decisions, acts or omissions may be challenged.

3. What constitutes a sufficient interest and impairment of a right shall be determined by Member States, consistently with the objective of giving the public concerned wide access to justice.

    To this end, the interest of any non-governmental organisation promoting environmental protection and meeting any requirements under national law shall be deemed sufficient for the purpose of paragraph 1(a). Such organisations shall also be deemed to have rights capable of being impaired for the purpose of paragraph 1(b).

4. Paragraphs 1, 2 and 3 shall not exclude the possibility of a preliminary review procedure before an administrative authority and shall not affect the requirement of exhaustion of administrative review procedures prior to recourse to judicial review procedures, where such a requirement exists under national law.

    Any such procedure shall be fair, equitable, timely and not prohibitively expensive.

5. Member States shall ensure that practical information is made available to the public on access to administrative and judicial review procedures.'

Czech law

The Law on integrated prevention

15   The Zákon č. 76/2002 Sb., o integrované prevenci a omezování znečištění, o integrovaném registru znečišťování a o změně některých zákonů (zákon o integrované prevenci) (Law No 76/2002 on integrated pollution prevention and control, on an integrated pollution register, and amending certain laws (Law on integrated prevention)), in the version in force at the time of the facts in the main proceedings, which transposes Directive 2010/75 into the Czech legal order, defines, in Paragraph 2(i) thereof, a 'substantial change' as follows:

> 'A change in the use, method of operation, or scope of an installation that may have significant negative effects on human health or the environment; the following shall always constitute a substantial change:
> 1. A change in the use, method of operation, or scope of an installation if it in and of itself reaches the limits specified in Annex 1 to this Law …'

16   Under Paragraph 7(1) of that law, the following parties are always party to the proceedings concerning the granting of an integrated permit:

> '(a) the operator of the installation;
> (b) the installation owner if not the same as the installation operator;
> (c) the municipality in whose territory the installation is or is to be located;
> …
> (e) civil associations, charitable organisations, employers' associations or chambers of commerce the line of business of which is the promotion and protection of professional interests or public interests pursuant to special legislation, as well as municipalities or regions in the territory of which the installation may have an environmental impact, provided that they report to the authority as parties in writing within eight days of the day of the publication of a brief summary of data from the application pursuant to Paragraph 8.'

17   Paragraph 19a of the Law on integrated prevention regulates procedures concerning amendments to integrated permits. If a change to an installation is not substantial, the parties to the procedure are, pursuant to Paragraph 19a(4) of that law, only 'the parties' identified in Paragraph 7(1)(a) and (b) of that law, namely the installation operator and owner. Decisions concerning the granting of and any amendments to an integrated permit are made by a regional authority. In Prague, this is done by the Magistrát hlavního města Prahy (Prague City Hall). It is the Ministry of the Environment, namely the appeal authority, which is competent to decide on administrative reviews against their decisions.

Law on environmental impact assessment

18   The zákon č. 100/2001 Sb., o posuzování vlivů na životní prostředí (Law No 100/2001 on environmental impact assessment), in the version in force at the time of the facts in the main proceedings, transposes Directive 2011/92/EU of the European Parliament and of the Council of 13 December 2011 on the assessment

of the effects of certain public and private projects on the environment (OJ 2012 L 26, p. 1).

19   Under Paragraph 3 of Law No 100/2001, in the version in force at the time of the facts in the main proceedings, for the purposes of that law:

'…

(c) the territory concerned is the territory whose environment and population could be subject to a significant effect in the event of the implementation of the project or plan;

(d) the self-governing territorial unit concerned is the self-governing territorial unit whose administrative district encompasses at least a part of the territory concerned;

…

(i) the part of public concerned

…

2. A legal entity under private law whose line of business is, pursuant to its legal deed of establishment, environmental protection or protection of public health and whose main line of business is not enterprise or another gainful activity, which was established at least three years prior to the date of the publication of information concerning the follow-up proceedings referred to in Paragraph 9b(1) or prior to the date of the adoption of a decision pursuant to Paragraph 7(6), or which is supported by the signatures of at least 200 persons.'

20   Paragraph 9c of that law is worded as follows:

'If it reports to the administrative authority conducting the follow-up proceedings by a written submission within 30 days of the publication of information pursuant to Paragraph 9b(1), the following shall become parties to the follow-up proceedings:

(a) the self-governing territorial unit concerned; or

(b) the part of the public concerned, as specified in the second subparagraph of Paragraph 3(i).'

The dispute in the main proceedings and the question referred for a preliminary ruling

21   FCC Česká republika operates a landfill site in the borough of Praha-Ďáblice, on the basis of a permit issued in 2007 pursuant to the Law on integrated prevention. That permit has been amended on several occasions, including twice in order to extend the duration of waste disposal at the landfill. At the end of 2015, FCC Česká republika applied to the Prague city administration, namely the competent authority, for a third postponement of the planned end date of operation, fixed at 31 December 2015. By a decision of 29 December of the same year, that administrative authority granted the request and postponed the date of discontinuation of waste disposal at the landfill to 31 December 2017.

22   The borough of Praha-Ďáblice and Spolek pro Ďáblice, an environmental protection association, lodged an administrative appeal against that decision with the Ministry of the Environment, which dismissed the appeal as inadmissible on

the ground that the applicants were not parties to the procedure for amending the integrated permit.

23   The applicants appealed against the decision of the Ministry of the Environment to the *Mestsky soud v Praze* (Prague City Court, Czech Republic), which annulled it on the ground that the extension of the permit for waste disposal at the landfill was a 'substantial change' within the meaning of Paragraph 2(i) of the Law on integrated prevention, which gave rise to the right to public participation in accordance with Directive 2010/75.

24   FCC Česká republika lodged an appeal against the judgment of the *Městský soud v Praze* (Prague City Court) before the Nejvyšší správní soud (Supreme Administrative Court, Czech Republic), the referring court. FCC Česká republika submits that, with a view to the case-law of the Court of Justice as cited by the *Městský soud v Praze* (Prague City Court), the mere extension of the duration of waste disposal at a landfill by two years cannot in and of itself be qualified as 'substantial change' within the meaning of Paragraph 2(i) of the Law on integrated prevention if it does not involve works or interventions which alter the physical aspect of the site.

25   According to FCC Česká republika, the extension of the permit changed neither the dimensions of the landfill nor the total waste storage capacity. It was for the purpose of filling the landfill to the permitted capacity that FCC Česká republika submitted an application for the extension of the duration of waste disposal at the landfill. Lastly, if the extension of the permit was to have an environmental impact, it would not, according to FCC Česká republika, constitute a 'substantial change' within the meaning of Paragraph 2(i) of the Law on integrated prevention.

26   The referring court notes that the Court of Justice has not yet ruled on the interpretation of the concept of 'substantial change' within the meaning of Directive 2010/75.

27   Even though neither the maximum permitted dimensions nor the total capacity of the landfill is changing in the case in the main proceedings, the referring court notes that waste will, however, be brought in for an additional two years due to the extension of the duration of waste disposal at the landfill. The referring court also notes that the objective of Directive 2010/75 is, pursuant to recital 12 and Article 1, to ensure a high level of protection of the environment as a whole. The referring court therefore sees no obstacle to the extension of the operation of an installation constituting a 'substantial change' in so far as that extension is likely to have a negative effect on human health or the environment, as required by Article 3(9) of that directive.

28   In those circumstances, the Nejvyšší správní soud (Supreme Administrative Court) decided to stay the proceedings and to refer the following question to the Court of Justice for a preliminary ruling:

> 'Should Article 3(9) of Directive 2010/75 … be interpreted such that a "substantial change" of a plant includes an extension of the duration of waste disposal at a landfill without the maximum approved dimensions of the landfill or its total potential capacity changing at the same time?'

Consideration of the question referred

29   By its question, the referring court asks whether Article 3(9) of Directive 2010/75 must be interpreted as meaning that the mere extension of the duration of waste disposal at a landfill, without any change in the maximum approved dimensions of the installation or its total capacity, constitutes a 'substantial change' within the meaning of that provision.

30   It should be noted, as a preliminary point, that landfills intended to receive more than 10 tonnes of waste per day or with a capacity exceeding 25 000 tonnes are among the activities listed in Annex I to Directive 2010/75 which, falling within the scope of Chapter II of that directive pursuant to Article 10 thereof, are subject to a permit in accordance with Article 4 thereof. The same applies to any 'substantial change' to the installation pursuant to Article 20(2) of that directive.

31   Where an authorisation is required, first, Article 24(1)(a) of Directive 2010/75 requires Member States to ensure that the public concerned are given the early and effective opportunity to participate in the procedure for granting that permit and, second, Article 25 of that directive grants members of that public the right to bring judicial review proceedings, inter alia, against that permit, if they have a sufficient interest in doing so.

32   Under Article 3(9) of Directive 2010/75, a 'substantial change' to the installation is 'a change in the nature or functioning, or an extension, of an installation or combustion plant, waste incineration plant or waste co-incineration plant which may have significant negative effects on human health or the environment'.

33   It is apparent from the wording of Article 3(9) that a change must be classified as 'substantial' on two conditions, the first relating to the content of the change and the second to its potential consequences.

34   Those two criteria are cumulative. A change in the nature or functioning, or an extension, of an installation is not 'substantial' within the meaning of Article 3(9) of Directive 2010/75 if it is not likely to have significant negative effects on human health or the environment. Conversely, it is not sufficient for a change to be able to have significant negative effects on human health or the environment for it to be 'substantial' within the meaning of that directive. If that were the case, the EU legislature would not have specified that a substantial change must consist of a change in the nature or functioning, or an extension, of an installation.

35   As for the first condition relating to the content of the substantial change, Article 3(9) of Directive 2010/75 defines it, alternatively, as 'a change in the nature or functioning, or an extension, of an installation'.

36   In that regard, it must be noted, in the first place, that the mere extension of the duration of waste disposal at a landfill does not, in itself, change the perimeter of the installation or the storage capacity as provided for in the initial permit, and does not therefore constitute an 'extension' of the installation. The referring court was also careful to clarify that the extension of the duration of waste disposal at the landfill at issue in the main proceedings is provided for without the maximum approved dimensions of the landfill or its total capacity changing at the same time.

37   It should be added that that provision defines 'substantial change' as 'change … of an installation'. That wording is all the more significant in that Directive 2010/75 is intended to regulate 'industrial activities giving rise to pollution', as is apparent, in particular, from the definition of its scope in Article 2 of that directive and from the title of Annex I to that directive, which lists the activities subject to

a permit under Chapter II thereof. The mere extension of the duration of waste disposal at the landfill does not constitute a change of the installation, be it in its nature or in its functioning.

38   In the second place, as the Advocate General noted in point 35 of her Opinion, the mere extension of the duration of waste disposal at a landfill changes neither the functioning nor the nature of the landfill.

39   That reading is supported by the context of Article 3(9) of Directive 2010/75.

40   In that regard, it must be observed that no provision of Directive 2010/75 mentions the duration of the landfill's operation as a feature of the installation's functioning which must necessarily be included in the permit.

41   Since Directive 2010/75 does not require the initial permit to specify the duration of operation of the landfill, it cannot be interpreted as requiring the mere extension of its operation to be the subject of a new permit.

42   It follows from the foregoing that the mere extension of the duration of waste disposal at a landfill does not constitute either a change in the nature or functioning, or an extension of an installation, within the meaning of Article 3(9) of Directive 2010/75. Consequently, such an extension does not satisfy the first of the two cumulative conditions, recalled in paragraphs 32 and 33 of the present judgment, for classification as a 'substantial change' under that provision.

43   Accordingly, there is no need to examine whether the second condition of a 'substantial change', namely that that change may give rise to significant negative effects on human health or the environment, is satisfied.

44   It follows that that extension does not constitute a 'substantial change' within the meaning of Article 3(9) of Directive 2010/75. Therefore, the first subparagraph of Article 20(2) of that directive does not require the Member States to oblige the operator of a landfill to apply for a new permit where that operator intends to merely extend the duration of waste disposal of the landfill within the limits of the total storage capacity for which a permit has already been given.

45   In the light of the foregoing observations, the answer to the question referred is that Article 3(9) of Directive 2010/75 must be interpreted as meaning that the mere extension of the duration of waste disposal at a landfill, without any change in the maximum approved dimensions of the installation or its total capacity, does not constitute a 'substantial change' within the meaning of that provision.

Costs

46   Since these proceedings are, for the parties to the main proceedings, a step in the action pending before the national court, the decision on costs is a matter for that court. Costs incurred in submitting observations to the Court, other than the costs of those parties, are not recoverable.

On those grounds, the Court (Fourth Chamber) hereby rules:

> Article 3(9) of Directive 2010/75/EU of the European Parliament and of the Council of 24 November 2010 on industrial emissions (integrated pollution prevention and control) must be interpreted as meaning that the mere extension of the duration of waste disposal at a landfill, without any change in the maximum approved dimensions of the installation or its total capacity, does not constitute a 'substantial change' within the meaning of that provision.

MDW HOLDINGS LTD v NORVILL

COURT OF APPEAL (CIVIL DIVISION)

Newey, Asplin and Whipple LJJ: 28 June 2022

[2022] EWCA Civ 883; [2023] Env. L.R. 5

Anticipatory breach; Breach of warranty; Dishonesty; Due diligence; Measure of damages; Misrepresentation; Non-compliance; Share purchases; Waste management

H1 *Waste management—contract—sale and purchase of shares in waste company— representations and warranties—environmental compliance—due diligence— breach of warranties—dishonesty—misrepresentation—non-compliance with environmental regulations—anticipatory breach—non-disclosure—remedies— measure of damages—correct approach to valuing shares when false warranties and misrepresentation in relation to environmental compliance*

H2   In October 2015, the claimant MDW bought, by way of a share purchase agreement (SPA), the share capital of GDE Environmental Services (GDE), from the defendant N. GDE was a waste management company dealing with different types of waste including hazardous waste. GDE required various consents and permits to continue to operate. These included environmental permits for the waste management operations and trade effluent discharge consents. In entering into the SPA, MDW relied on various warranties made by N in relation to GDE's compliance with these permits and consents and all relevant environmental laws and regulations.

H3   At the original trial, the judge found that the sellers had breached those warranties. The judge found that GDE had breached consents, improperly discharged waste into a public sewer, falsified records and had supplied false information to regulators prior to the purchase of the company by MDW. In addition, the judge found that N had made actionable misrepresentations in response to MDW's due diligence questions and was guilty of deceit. Damages were assessed by reference to the difference between the value of GDE had the warranties been true (warranty true) and the actual value of GDE given that the warranties were false (warranty false). In calculating the 'warranty false' value the judge had used a lower multiplier and multiplicand than had been used to calculate the 'warranty true' value, to reflect the reputational damage that the breaches were liable to cause to GDE.

H4   N appealed, arguing that whilst damages should be assessed as at the date of the SPA, the judge should not have reduced the 'warranty false' multiplier and multiplicand to take account of a risk that had not subsequently materialised.

H5   MDW cross-appealed, arguing that that having arrived at a 'warranty true' value which was less than the price it had actually paid for the shares, the judge should have applied the tortious measure of damages and awarded the difference between the price actually paid and the 'warranty false' value.

H6   **Held,** in dismissing N's appeal but allowing the cross-appeal from MDW:

H7   (1) On N's appeal relating to the correct approach to assessing damages, the trial judge was entitled to reduce the multiplier and multiplicand when considering the 'warranty false' value and had adequately explained the basis for doing so. The reduction in the multiplier and multiplicand was appropriate, unsurprising, and in no way a windfall for the buyer. Further, given that the judge had also found the sellers guilty of deceit, it was no defence for them to demonstrate that the contingency had not eventuated.

H8   (2) Where damages fell to be assessed in respect of an anticipatory breach of contract (but not an actual breach), it was appropriate to consider what would have happened had the breach not occurred. Events occurring after the breach might be relevant to that consideration. In reducing the "warranty false" value, the judge was essentially saying that a purchaser who was aware of how the company had been conducting its business would not have been willing to pay as much for the shares. The fact that GDE did not in fact suffer reputational damage did not mean that its value was not reduced as at the date of the SPA; its goodwill was, at that time, impaired.

H9   (3) On MDW's cross-appeal on the award of a tortious measure of damages, where a buyer had been induced by deceit to make a purchase which they would not otherwise have bought, the damages would normally be assessed as the difference between the actual value of the property and the amount they had paid. If had they known the truth, the buyer would have negotiated a lower price rather than abandoning the transaction, damages would be assessed by reference to the difference between what they had in fact paid and what they would otherwise have paid. The trial judge found that N's misrepresentations had induced MDW to enter into the SPA but made no finding as to what MDW would have done had it known the truth. While MDW might well have abandoned the purchase, there was some evidence that it might have gone ahead and paid more than the 'warranty false' value. Accordingly, the question of whether MDW was entitled to additional damages for deceit would therefore have to be remitted to the trial judge.

H10   **Cases referred to:**

Ageas (UK) Ltd v Kwik-Fit (GB) Ltd [2014] EWHC 2178 (QB); [2014] Bus. L.R. 1338; [2015] Lloyd's Rep. I.R. 1

Buckingham v Francis, Douglas & Thompson (1986) 2 B.C.C. 98984; [1986] P.C.C. 347 QBD (Comm)

Bunge SA v Nidera BV (formerly Nidera Handelscompagnie BV) [2015] UKSC 43; [2015] Bus. L.R. 987; [2015] 2 Lloyd's Rep. 469

Bwllfa and Merthyr Dare Steam Collieries (1891) Ltd v Pontypridd Waterworks Co [1903] A.C. 426 HL

Classic Maritime Inc v Limbungan Makmur Sdn Bhd [2019] EWCA Civ 1102; [2019] Bus. L.R. 2854; [2020] 1 Lloyd's Rep. 178

County Personnel (Employment Agency) Ltd v Alan R Pulver & Co [1987] 1 W.L.R. 916; [1986] 2 E.G.L.R. 246; (1987) 84 L.S.G. 1409 CA (Civ Div)

Downs v Chappell [1997] 1 W.L.R. 426; [1996] C.L.C. 1492 CA (Civ Div)

Fage UK Ltd v Chobani UK Ltd [2014] EWCA Civ 5; [2014] E.T.M.R. 26; [2014] F.S.R. 29

Golden Strait Corp v Nippon Yusen Kubishika Kaisha (The Golden Victory) [2007] UKHL 12; [2007] 2 A.C. 353; [2007] Bus. L.R. 997

Hut Group Ltd v Nobahar-Cookson [2014] EWHC 3842 (QB)

Lion Nathan Ltd v CC Bottlers Ltd [1996] 1 W.L.R. 1438; [1996] 2 B.C.L.C. 371; (1996) 93(24) L.S.G. 26 PC (NZ)

Livingstone v Rawyards Coal Co (1880) 5 App. Cas. 25; (1880) 7 R. (H.L.) 1 HL (SC)

McConnel v Wright [1903] 1 Ch. 546 CA

Miliangos v George Frank (Textiles) Ltd [1976] A.C. 443; [1975] 3 W.L.R. 758; [1975] 2 C.M.L.R. 585 HL

OMV Petrom SA v Glencore International AG [2016] EWCA Civ 778; [2016] 2 Lloyd's Rep. 432; [2016] 2 C.L.C. 651

Phillips (Liquidator of AJ Bekhor & Co) v Brewin Dolphin Bell Lawrie Ltd (formerly Brewin Dolphin & Co Ltd) [2001] UKHL 2; [2001] 1 W.L.R. 143; [2001] B.C.C. 864

Ruxley Electronics v Forsyth [1996] A.C. 344; [1995] 3 W.L.R. 118; [1995] C.L.C. 905 HL

Senate Electrical Wholesalers Ltd v Alcatel Submarine Networks Ltd (formerly STC Submarine Systems Ltd) [1999] 2 Lloyd's Rep. 423 CA (Civ Div)

Smith New Court Securities Ltd v Citibank NA [1992] B.C.L.C. 1104 Ch D

Smith New Court Securities Ltd v Citibank NA [1994] 1 W.L.R. 1271; [1994] 2 B.C.L.C. 212; [1994] C.L.C. 203 CA (Civ Div)

Smith New Court Securities Ltd v Citibank NA [1997] A.C. 254; [1996] 3 W.L.R. 1051; [1997] 1 B.C.L.C. 350 HL

Taylor v Caldwell 122 E.R. 309; (1863) 3 B. & S. 826; (1863) 2 New Rep. 198 KB

Tuke v Hood [2022] EWCA Civ 23; [2022] Q.B. 659; [2022] 2 W.L.R. 983

Yam Seng Pte Ltd v International Trade Corp Ltd [2013] EWHC 111 (QB); [2013] 1 Lloyd's Rep. 526; [2013] 1 C.L.C. 662

H11 **Legislation referred to:**
Waterworks Clauses Act 1847
Misrepresentation Act 1967 s.2
Insolvency Act 1986 s.238

H12 *H. Sims QC* and *J. Jagasia* (instructed by Blake Morgan LLP) appeared on behalf of the defendants/appellants.

A. Ayres QC and *L. Scher* (instructed by Morgan LaRoche) appeared on behalf of the claimant/respondent.

JUDGMENT

LORD JUSTICE NEWEY:

1   This case raises issues as to how damages should be assessed for breach of warranty and deceit in the context of a share sale.

Basic facts

2   On 14 October 2015, the claimant, MDW Holdings Limited ("MDW") bought the entire issued capital of G.D. Environmental Services Limited ("GDE") from the defendants, James Norvill and his parents Jane and Stephen Norvill (together, "the Norvills"), for £3,584,224 pursuant to a share purchase agreement ("the SPA") of that date. By clause 6.1, the Norvills acknowledged that MDW was entering into the agreement in reliance on the warranties set out in schedule 5, which, by clause 6.2, the Norvills warranted to be true and accurate on the date of the agreement except as disclosed by a disclosure letter. Schedule 5 included, among others, warranties that GDE had conducted its business in accordance with all applicable laws and regulations (paragraph 5.1); that GDE held the requisite consents and was not in breach of any of their terms and conditions (paragraphs 6.1 and 6.2); that no proceedings against GDE had been threatened and there were no circumstances likely to give rise to any such proceedings (paragraph 9.2); that GDE's accounts showed a true and fair view (paragraph 18.1); and that GDE had complied with environmental laws and permits and there were no facts or circumstances likely to lead to any breach of any such law, to the revocation, suspension, variation or non-renewal of such a permit or to any claims, investigations, prosecutions or other proceedings (paragraphs 29.2, 29.3 and 29.4).

3   GDE's business involved the collection, processing and disposal of waste. The company dealt with both "dry" and "wet" waste. The latter comprised cess waste; non-hazardous waste, such as gulley waste; hazardous waste, such as waste from garage forecourts or interceptor tanks; and leachate, which is the ammonia-rich liquid run-off from landfill sites.

4   The operation of GDE's business depended on consents and permits from environmental regulators. GDE's primary regulator was Natural Resources Wales ("NRW") (before April 2013, the Environment Agency), which was the regulator of the waste industry. GDE was also subject to regulation by Dŵr Cymru Welsh Water ("DCWW") as the relevant sewerage undertaker. GDE held an environmental permit the relevant iteration of which was issued on 3 July 2012. It had also been granted a consent to discharge trade effluent into DCWW's public sewers subject to conditions set out in a variation dated 5 December 2012 ("the 2012 Consent"). Misleading either NRW or DCWW could constitute a criminal offence.

5   In his careful and detailed judgment, His Honour Judge Keyser QC, sitting as a Judge of the High Court, identified occasions on which the regulators had been supplied with false information by GDE prior to the date of the SPA. In paragraph 45 of his judgment, Judge Keyser QC ("the Judge") concluded that there had been "a culture of lying to the regulators when it was convenient to do so" in which Mr James Norvill had been complicit.

6   The Judge also found there to have been repeated and persistent breaches of the 2012 Consent in relation to the discharge of leachates. The Judge said in paragraph 147 of his judgment:

> "The truth is simply that GDE found itself unable to contain the levels of contaminants within the permitted levels and on occasion resorted to falsification in order to conceal this from NRW. What is also true is that GDE was unwilling to take steps that might have enabled it to comply with the 2012 Consent but at a commercial cost."

7   The Judge found, too, that GDE had improperly discharged cess waste directly into a public sewer via an inspection chamber known as "the magic hole". He considered the extent of this practice to have been exaggerated by MDW, however. He arrived at these conclusions in paragraph 171 of his judgment:

> "1) MDW's case on this issue has been considerably exaggerated. The practice of discharge of cess waste down the magic hole was not a daily occurrence and tankers did not queue up, as has been alleged.
>
> 2) It is improbable that there was more than occasional discharge of cess waste down the magic hole after 2012 ….
>
> 3) There were probably occasional discharges in 2013; these would have taken place if a tanker had been unable to discharge at a DCWW facility during working hours and were required for an early start the following day. Such discharges would have been in the evening or at weekends. I find on the balance of probabilities that the discharge of cess waste into the magic hole took place on occasion after October 2013 and in early 2014; one such occasional discharge may have prompted the investigation in February 2014. However, these occasions will have been very few. Any discharges while Mr Doe was still employed (that is, up to April 2014) were probably authorised; if any took place after that date (they may have done, but I am unable to find that they did) they were probably unauthorised by management personnel and unknown to them.
>
> 4) I find that the practice had no significant impact on GDE's financial performance or accounts in the two years immediately preceding the SPA."

8   There was a further finding that hard solids had occasionally been dug out of the very bottom of separator tanks and disposed of as dry waste. The Judge said this on the subject in paragraph 192(1) of his judgment:

> "This was an improper practice, because the hard solids ought to have been disposed of as hazardous waste. James [Norvill]
> … knew that it was improper. However, this practice was rare—it involved only the hard deposits that were not sucked up with the sludge, and the practice of manually digging them out was recognised as unsafe for employees and was carried out infrequently. The impact of the practice on GDE's financial performance cannot be quantified accurately but will have been minimal."

9   In the light of his factual findings, the Judge held that the Norvills had breached each of the warranties I mentioned in paragraph 2 above: see paragraphs 212-214, 216-221 and 243 of the judgment. The Judge also concluded that the Norvills had been responsible for untrue representations on which MDW had relied. The representations in question were made in "Due Diligence Index and Responses" provided to MDW and were to the effect that DCWW had agreed that consent levels were too low, that there was nothing to disclose with respect to breaches of discharge consents and that there was nothing adverse to disclose as regards DCWW sampling results: see paragraphs 251-252 of the judgment. The Judge found that Mr James Norvill knew that the relevant representations were being made, that he knew too that the representations in respect of breaches and DCWW sampling results were false and that, having left matters to Mr James Norvill, his parents also bore responsibility for his fraud, though themselves innocent of it: see paragraphs 260-262 of the judgment.

10   Overall, the Judge arrived at the following conclusions on liability:

> "277. The defendants are liable for breach of warranty in respect of:
> 1) The persistent and continuing breaches of the 2012 Consent concerning the discharge of leachate;
> 2) The false information provided to DCWW;
> 3) The disposal of hard solids from the tank bottom waste on the Dry Side;
> 4) The disposal of cess waste down the magic hole;
> 5) The failure to disclose the misfeasances in respect of hard solids as pollution incidents;
> 6) The failure to disclose the misfeasances in respect of leachate, hard solids, cess waste, and provision of false information to DCWW as non-compliances with regulatory consents and permits;
> 7) The threat of prosecution by reason of the breaches of the 2012 Consent;
> 8) The likelihood of revocation of the 2012 Consent by reason of those breaches.
> 278. However, breaches of warranty in respect of cess waste and tank bottom waste were of no demonstrable significance, because it has not been proved that they had any causal relation to any loss and damage. Therefore, in short, the relevant breaches of covenant concerned only the discharge of leachate: the persistent discharge in breach of the 2012 Consent, the threat of prosecution for that reason, the likelihood that the breaches would result in revocation of the 2012 Consent, and the provision of false information to DCWW.
> 279. The actionable misrepresentations were those in the Due Diligence Index and Responses; there were no other actionable misrepresentations. They cover the same ground as the breaches of warranty. The misrepresentations constituted deceit on the part of James. Jane and Stephen are liable for the same misrepresentations, and to the same extent, on the basis of section 2(1) of the Misrepresentation Act 1967. They would also be liable in deceit because, although innocent themselves, they are liable for the fraud of their agent, James."

11   Turning to quantum, the Judge began by saying this in paragraph 280 of his judgment:

> "It is common ground that the proper measure of damages for breach of warranty is the difference between (a) the value of GDE on the basis that the warranties were true ('Warranty True') and (b) the actual value of GDE given that the warranties were false ('Warranty False'). No different measure has been suggested for any claim in respect of fraudulent or negligent misrepresentation, at least for the purposes of this case. I shall refer generally only to breach of warranty."

12   On this aspect of the case, the Judge had the benefit of expert evidence from two forensic accountants: Mr Seamus Gates, called by MDW, and Mr Geoff Mesher, called by the Norvills. Both acknowledged the "EV/EBITDA" method of valuation to be that more commonly used by professional business valuers. As the Judge explained in footnote 1 to his judgment, "EBITDA" is a shorthand for "Earnings Before Interest, Tax, Depreciation and Amortisation" and the "EV/EBITDA" method:

"involves three stages: first, calculation of the level of maintainable EBITDA which could reasonably be expected to be achieved during the average year; second, application of a suitable multiple, so as to calculate capitalised earnings, giving what is sometimes referred to as the 'Enterprise Value' ('EV') of the business; third, deduction of net debt from the Enterprise Value".

13 The Judge found the "Warranty True" value of GDE to be £3,341,276: see paragraph 285 of the judgment. He observed that "[t]he price paid may be a guide but it can be no more than that" and, using the "EV/EBITDA multiplier approach", decided that it was appropriate to adopt a multiplicand (i.e. maintainable EBITDA) of £1,153,000 and a multiplier of 4.2. He added, "Both experts regarded the EBITDA multiplier that would be required to justify the purchase price as being on the high side and I see no reason therefore to accept it as the correct multiplier".

14 The Judge took the figures he used from evidence given by Mr Mesher. In a report dated 16 October 2020, Mr Mesher assessed the EBITDA to be used in valuation calculations at £1,153,000 (paragraph 3.18) and considered "an appropriate multiplier to use in the valuation of GDE to be around 4.2" (paragraph 4.20). After adjusting for net debt, Mr Mesher went on in paragraph 4.24:

"I therefore consider that the equity value of [GDE] as at 14th October 2015 was £3.3 million. This is not dissimilar to, albeit slightly less than, the price actually paid for [GDE] of £3.5 million. Accepting that the market value to be the price paid, by my calculations, the resultant multiplier was in fact 4.34. This is not outside of a reasonable range and supports the contention that the price paid represented market value."

15 With regard to the "Warranty False" valuation, the Judge said in paragraph 287 of his judgment that, for reasons given by Mr Mesher, he considered the appropriate multiplicand to be £1,115,000. "This figure", the Judge explained, "reflects the additional costs that would have been incurred in the lawful operation of the leachate processing operations at the Site and, correspondingly, the reduced profits".

16 So far as the multiplier was concerned, the Judge decided that this should be reduced from 4.2 to 4. He explained this as follows:

"288. … I consider that some reduction in the multiplier is appropriate to reflect reputational damage (or, as it has been put, 'the fragility of the goodwill') that the breaches were liable to cause to the company and the jeopardy that they occasioned to the future of the business. Both experts were ultimately in agreement that such a reduction could be justified in principle; they disagreed as to its justification and, if justified, its amount in this case. There is obvious reason to be cautious before discounting the multiplier at all. The effect of the breaches on the value of the business will primarily be reflected in the multiplicand; as the EBITDA would have been adjusted to reflect sustainable levels of profitability, a further qualitative adjustment to the multiplier would present a risk of double counting. The risk is real, but it is not a conclusive reason not to discount the multiplier, as Mr Mesher accepted. An innocent accounting error that overstated the profits would be adequately and completely dealt with by a discount of the multiplicand. The breaches in the present case were of a different order, because they involved not only the running of a non compliant operation (which might be dealt with in the multiplicand) but the deceiving of the regulator in order to keep that operation afloat. The argument of [counsel for the Norvills] that no discount is appropriate because it is known that no risks to the business have been realised since the SPA is to be rejected, as it relies impermissibly on hindsight.

289. However, I consider that Mr Gates' suggestion of a 25% discount in the multiplier is greatly overstated. Mr Gates proposed a discount of that amount on the assumption that there had been systematic non-compliance across the three areas of the claim (cess waste, tank bottom waste, and leachate); the proposal was based on the view that, in those circumstances, 25% of the actual profits of GDE across the entire business (that is, including the Dry Side) were placed at risk because of the possibility of further concealed non-compliances. However, such past non-compliances as I find there to have been in respect of cess waste or tank bottom waste were either historic or very occasional, were not known to the regulators and were in my view very unlikely to become known by them, and (from a valuation point of view at the date of purchase) were unlikely to be continued or repeated by the new owners of the company; therefore I do not accept that they occasioned reputational damage that ought to be reflected in the valuation. Further, I am not persuaded that the breaches in respect of leachate and the misleading of the regulators created a genuine risk to the viability of the business of the Dry Side. Any discount would, in my view, properly relate only to the risks to the ongoing wet waste division, over and above the reduction in the leachate business. The change of ownership of the company would itself tend to minimise the risks of adverse consequences with the regulators. Again, I do not accept that it is justified to value a business on the basis of possible concealed breaches for which there is no evidence.

290. In my judgment, the discount of the multiplier is to be ascertained, as Mr Mesher suggested, by choosing a figure at an appropriate point within the range of acceptable multipliers for an EV/EBITDA valuation. Mr Mesher considered that the appropriate range was between 3.8 and 4.5; and, although the specific figures at either end of this range were suggested by a fairly limited examination of comparables, I accept his opinion as to range. Having regard to the matters that I have referred to above, I consider that the risk of 'reputational damage' is appropriately reflected by discounting the multiplier from 4.2 to 4."

17   The Judge continued in paragraph 291:

"This line of reasoning would give a valuation as follows: £1,115,000 x 4 = £4,460,000 - £1,501,324: a total of £2,958,676. On this basis, the difference between the Warranty True valuation and the Warranty False valuation is £382,600, which by my reckoning is about 11.5% of the purchase price."

18   There is now no dispute about liability. However, both sides challenge the Judge's assessment of damages. By their appeal, the Norvills take issue with the Judge's reduction in the multiplier when calculating the "Warranty False" value. On the footing that adjustment was erroneous, the Norvills contend that the damages should have been assessed at £159,600 rather than £382,600. For its part, MDW, while arguing that the Judge's assessment of damages for breach of warranty cannot be impugned, maintains by its cross-appeal that it should have been awarded a larger sum for fraudulent misrepresentation. The amount due in that regard,

according to MDW, was £3,584,224 (i.e. the purchase price) less £2,958,676 (i.e. the "Warranty False" valuation) or, in other words, £625,548.

The appeal

19   The Norvills' central complaint is that the Judge reduced the multiplier when calculating GDE's "Warranty False" value to take account of a risk which, by the time of the trial, was known not to have materialised. Mr Hugh Sims QC, who appeared for the Norvills with Mr Jay Jagasia, pointed out that the Judge explained that the reduction reflected "reputational damage … that the breaches were liable to cause to [GDE] and the jeopardy that they occasioned to the future of the business". In the event, Mr Sims said, no such damage was caused: no prosecution was brought, GDE did not lose its permits and licences, and there was no suggestion of wider reputational harm to GDE's wet waste division. While accepting that damages fell to be assessed as at 14 October 2015, the date of the SPA, Mr Sims argued that it was incumbent on the Judge to have regard to how matters had turned out. By failing to do so, Mr Sims submitted, the Judge gave MDW a windfall which was inconsistent with the principle that an award of damages should put the innocent party in the position it would have been in had the contract been performed and, more specifically, with case law relating to the significance of contingencies. Mr Sims further contended that the Judge was inconsistent, since he *did* take account of post-SPA evidence when assessing the multiplicand to be used in the "Warranty False" calculation. In any case, Mr Sims said, the Judge's reduction in the multiplier was arbitrary, unreasoned and unjustified.

20   In support of his submission that the Judge was inconsistent in his approach to post-SPA evidence, Mr Sims pointed out that the figure of £1,115,000 which the Judge used as the multiplicand when valuing GDE on a "Warranty False" basis reflected views of Mr Mesher to which the Judge referred in paragraph 139(4) of his judgment. The Judge explained in paragraph 139(4) that Mr Mesher had given evidence to the following effect:

> "On a Warranty False basis, the only relevant disposal costs could be those for leachate, on the basis that lawful operation of the Wet Side in the period 2013 to 2015 would have required sending approximately 60% of the leachate for processing by Tradebe Limited. This would result in an additional cost of approximately £38,400 p.a. (7,680 tonnes of leachate, at a cost of £5 per tonne). This would reduce the EBITDA multiplicand to £1,115,000 …."

21   Mr Mesher had said this on the subject in his report:

> "4.29 Mr Gates … notes that not all of the leachate was passed to Tradebe in the years 2016 and 2017. During 2016, 61% of the leachate was treated by Tradebe, and during 2017 54% was treated by Tradebe. One can therefore assume that the claim is such that around 60% of the leachate should have been treated by Tradebe in the year ended 2015. This would equate to 7,680 tonnes.
> 4.30 At a rate of £5 per tonne, the claimed base cost of processing the leachate through Tradebe in the year ended 31st October 2015 would have been £38,400. This is the figure that I consider reasonably represents the expected additional annual costs related to the breach of warranty on leachate disposal costs."

22   For his part, Mr Andrew Ayres QC, who appeared for MDW with Mr Laurie Scher, supported the Judge's reduction in the multiplier.

Legal principles

23   As Lord Blackburn noted in *Livingstone v Rawyards Coal Co* (1880) 5 App. Cas. 25, at 39, it is:

> "a general rule that, where any injury is to be compensated by damages, in settling the sum of money to be given for reparation of damages you should as nearly as possible get at that sum of money which will put the party who has been injured, or who has suffered, in the same position as he would have been in if he had not sustained the wrong for which he is now getting his compensation or reparation".

24   In contract, application of the principle involves asking what position the innocent party would have been in had the contract been performed. The point was encapsulated in these terms by Parke B in *Robinson v Harman* (1848) 1 Ex. 850, at 855:

> "The rule of the common law is, that where a party sustains a loss by reason of a breach of contract, he is, so far as money can do it, to be placed in the same situation, with respect to damages, as if the contract had been performed."

It is on this basis that damages for breach of a warranty given on a sale of shares are determined by comparing the actual value of the shares with the value they would have had if the warranty had been true (as to which, see e.g. *Lion Nathan Ltd v CC Bottlers Ltd* [1996] 1 W.L.R. 1438, at 1441).

25   In tort, in contrast, damages aim to restore the status quo ante. Thus, damages for deceit, for example, seek to put the claimant in the position he would have been in, not if the representation had been true, but if it had never been made.

26   The differing measures of damages in contract and tort can be seen in this passage from paragraph 49-002 of *McGregor on Damages*, 21st ed.:

> "The tort of deceit needs careful handling as far as damages are concerned because in the great majority of cases the action induced by the deceit is the entering into a contract by the claimant, either with the defendant tortfeasor or with a third party, and difference principles principles. It is important in such circumstances to stress the between a measure of damages based on tort and a measure of damages based on contract. Thus the correct measure of damages in the tort of deceit is an award which serves to put the claimant into the position the claimant would have been in if the representation had not been made, and not, as with breach of condition or warranty in contract, into the position the claimant would have been in if the representation had been true. In other words, if the claimant has been induced by the deceit to conclude a contract the claimant is not entitled, as would be the case in contract, to recover in deceit for the loss of the bargain."

27   "[A]s a general rule in English law damages for tort or for breach of contract are assessed as at the date of the breach": see *Miliangos v George Frank (Textiles) Ltd* [1976] A.C. 443, at 468, per Lord Wilberforce. In *County Personnel (Employment Agency) Ltd v Alan R Pulver & Co* [1987] 1 W.L.R. 916, Bingham

LJ said at 926 that this rule "should not be mechanistically applied in circumstances where assessment at another date may more accurately reflect the overriding compensatory rule". In the present case, however, it has always been common ground that damages should be assessed as at the date of the SPA.

28   There are, though, circumstances in which the Courts will take account of events subsequent to the date of assessment when determining contractual damages. In that connection, reliance has been placed on what has been called "the *Bwllfa* principle", which takes its name from the decision of the House of Lords in *Bwllfa and Merthyr Dare Steam Collieries (1891) Ltd v Pontypridd Waterworks Co* [1903] A.C. 426 ("*Bwllfa*"). What was at issue there was the amount of compensation payable to mine owners under the Waterworks Clauses Act 1847 where undertakers had objected to the mine owners working coal near their waterworks. Lord Macnaghten, with whom Lord Shand concurred, said at 431:

> "The counter-notice by the undertakers following a notice of the mine owners under s. 22 does not operate to make a contract or to transfer property. It is not even a step towards a contract or a step towards expropriation. The undertakers acquire no property in the minerals. The property remains where it was. The mine owner is prohibited from working, and the undertakers are bound to make full compensation. That is all. If the question goes to arbitration, the arbitrator's duty is to determine the amount of compensation payable. In order to enable him to come to a just and true conclusion it is his duty, I think, to avail himself of all information at hand at the time of making his award which may be laid before him. Why should he listen to conjecture on a matter which has become an accomplished fact? Why should he guess when he can calculate? With the light before him, why should he shut his eyes and grope in the dark? The mine owner prevented from working his minerals is to be fully compensated—the Act says so. That means that so far as money can compensate him he is to be placed in the position in which he would have been if he had been free to go on working. Here it has been proved to demonstration that if he had not been interfered with he would have made between 5000l. and 6000l. I cannot understand upon what principle it is maintained that he should be content with half, and that half is full compensation."

Likewise, Lord Robertson said at 432, "if, owing to the course of the procedure, the period required for the working out of the coal in question has come to be matter of history, then estimate and conjecture are superseded by facts as the proper media concludendi".

29   A similar approach was taken, without, it seems, *Bwllfa* being cited, in *Phillips v Brewin Dolphin Bell Lawrie Ltd* [2001] 1 W.L.R. 143 ("*Phillips*"). It was there alleged that a company which had since gone into liquidation had entered into a transaction at an undervalue and, hence, that relief was available under section 238 of the Insolvency Act 1986. One of the questions raised by the application was what, if any, value was to be attributed to a covenant given by a company referred to as "PCG" in a sublease dated 10 November 1989. Lord Scott, with whom the other members of the House of Lords agreed, valued the covenant at nil. Having observed in paragraph 25 that "PCG's covenant, which had been precarious at the outset, had become worthless by 23 February 1990 at the latest", Lord Scott said in paragraph 26:

"[Counsel for the defendants] submitted that these ex post facto events ought not to be taken into account in valuing PCG's sublease covenant as at 10 November 1989. I do not agree. In valuing the covenant as at that date, the critical uncertainty is whether the sublease would survive for the four years necessary to enable all the four £312,500 payments to fall due, or would survive long enough to enable some of them to fall due, or would come to an end before any had fallen due. Where the events, or some of them, on which the uncertainties depend have actually happened, it seems to me unsatisfactory and unnecessary for the court to wear blinkers and pretend that it does not know what has happened. Problems of a comparable sort may arise for judicial determination in many different areas of the law. The answers may not be uniform but may depend upon the particular context in which the problem arises. For the purposes of section 238(4) however, and the valuation of the consideration for which a company has entered into a transaction, reality should, in my opinion, be given precedence over speculation. I would hold, taking account of the events that took place in the early months of 1990, that the value of PCG's covenant in the sublease of 10 November 1989 was nil. After all, if, following the signing of the sublease, AJB had taken the sublease to a bank or finance house and had tried to raise money on the security of the covenant, I do not believe that the bank or finance house, with knowledge about the circumstances surrounding the sublease, would have attributed any value at all to the sublease covenant."

30   *Bwllfa* was followed, and *Phillips* cited, in *Golden Strait Corp v Nippon Yusen Kubishika Kaisha (The Golden Victory)* [2007] UKHL 12; [2007] 2 A.C. 353 ("*The Golden Victory*"). That case concerned a seven-year charterparty dated 10 July 1998 which, by clause 33, gave both parties the right to cancel if there were war between certain countries. In December 2001, the charterers repudiated the charter, and the owners accepted the repudiation a few days later. Subsequently, in March 2003, a war falling within clause 33 broke out. The House of Lords held, by a majority (Lords Bingham and Walker dissenting), that the outbreak of war fell to be taken into account in calculating the damages payable by the charterers and, accordingly, that the owners were not entitled to damages in respect of the period after March 2003.

31   Lord Scott said in paragraph 38 that the owners "are seeking compensation exceeding the value of the contractual benefits of which they were deprived" and that their arguments "offend the compensatory principle". Earlier in his speech, after referring to the "assessment at the date of breach rule", Lord Scott had said:

"35. In cases … where the contract for sale of goods is not simply a contract for a one-off sale, but is a contract for the supply of goods over some specified period, the application of the general rule may not be in the least apt. Take the case of a three-year contract for the supply of goods and a repudiatory breach of the contract at the end of the first year. The breach is accepted and damages are claimed but before the assessment of the damages an event occurs that, if it had occurred while the contract was still on foot, would have been a frustrating event terminating the contract, e.g. legislation prohibiting any sale of the goods. The contractual benefit of which the victim of the breach of contract had been deprived by the breach would not have extended beyond the date of the frustrating event. So on what principled basis could the victim claim compensation attributable to a loss of contractual benefit after that date? Any rule that required damages attributable to that period to be paid would be inconsistent with the overriding compensatory principle on which awards of contractual damages ought to be based.

36. The same would, in my opinion, be true of any anticipatory breach the acceptance of which had terminated an executory contract. The contractual benefit for the loss of which the victim of the breach can seek compensation cannot escape the uncertainties of the future. If, at the time the assessment of damages takes place, there were nothing to suggest that expected benefit of the executory contract would not, if contract had remained on foot, have duly accrued, then the quantum of damages would be unaffected by uncertainties that would be no more than conceptual. If there were a real possibility that an event would happen terminating the contract, or in some way reducing the contractual benefit to which the damages claimant would, if the contract had remained on foot, have become entitled, then the quantum of damages might need, in order to reflect the extent of the chance that possibility might materialise, to be reduced proportionately. The lodestar is that the damages should represent the value of the contractual benefits of which the claimant had been deprived by the breach of contract, no less but also no more. But if a terminating event had happened, speculation would not be needed, an estimate of the extent of the chance of such a happening would no longer be necessary and, in relation to the period during which the contract would have remained executory had it not been for the terminating event, it would be apparent that the earlier anticipatory breach of contract had deprived the victim of the breach of nothing."

32   Lord Carswell and Lord Brown expressed similar views to Lord Scott. Lord Carswell said in paragraph 66:

"If the second Gulf War had not broken out by the time the arbitration was held, the arbitrator would have had to estimate the prospect that it might do so and factor into his calculation of the owners' loss the chance that the charter would be cancelled at some future date under clause 33. The loss which would have been sustained over the full period of the charter would then have been discounted to an extent which would have reflected the chance, estimated at the time of the assessment, that it would be so terminated. As events happened, however, the arbitrator did not come to assess damages until after the outbreak of war, when, as he found, the charterers would have cancelled the charter. The outbreak of the second Gulf War was then an accomplished fact, which was highly relevant to the amount of damages, and in my opinion the arbitrator was correct to take it into account in assessing the owners' loss. As Lord Robertson put it in the *Bwllfa* case, at p 432, 'estimate and conjecture are superseded by facts'."

Lord Brown said in paragraph 78, "the breach date rule does not require contingencies – such as the likely effect of a suspensive condition – to be judged prior to the date when damages finally come to be assessed".

33   *The Golden Victory* was the subject of consideration by the Supreme Court in *Bunge SA v Nidera BV* [2015] UKSC 43; [2015] Bus. L.R. 987 ("*Bunge*"). Lord Sumption, with whom Lords Neuberger, Mance and Clarke agreed, expressed his

agreement with the principle seen in *The Golden Victory*, commenting in paragraph 23:

"There is no principled reason why, in order to determine the value of the contractual performance which has been lost by the repudiation, one should not consider what would have happened if the repudiation had not occurred. On the contrary, this seems to be fundamental to any assessment of damages designed to compensate the injured party for the consequences of the breach."

Lord Sumption also dismissed the suggestion that a distinction was to be drawn between a one-off sale and a contract for the supply of goods or services over a period of time, explaining in paragraph 22:

"Where the only question is the relevant date for taking the market price, the financial consequences of the breach may be said to 'crystallise' at that date. But where, after that date, some supervening event occurs which shows that neither the original contract (had it continued) nor the notional substitute contract at the market price would ever have been performed, the concept of 'crystallising' the assessment of damages at that price is unhelpful. The occurrence of the supervening event would have reduced the value of performance, possibly to nothing, even if the contract had not been wrongfully terminated and whatever the relevant market price. The nature of that problem does not differ according to whether the contract provides for a single act of performance or several successive ones."

Further, Lord Sumption said this in paragraph 21 about the reasoning in *The Golden Victory*

"The reasoning has to some extent been obscured by the focus on the implications of the so-called 'breach-date rule' and on the competing demands of certainty and compensation. The real difference between the majority and the minority turned on the question what was being valued for the purpose of assessing damages. The majority were valuing the chartered service that would actually have been performed if the charterparty had not been wrongfully brought to a premature end. On that footing, the notional substitute contract, whenever it was made and at whatever market rate, would have made no difference because it would have been subject to the same war clause as the original contract: see Lord Scott of Foscote at para [37], and Lord Brown of Eaton-under-Heywood at paras [76]–[78] and [82]. The minority on the other hand considered that one should value not the chartered service which would actually have been performed, but the charterparty itself, assessed at the time that it was terminated, by reference to the terms of a notional substitute concluded as soon as possible after the termination of the original. That would vary, not according to the actual outcome, but according to the outcomes which were perceived as possible or probable at the time that the notional substitute contract was made. The possibility or probability of war would then be factored into the price agreed in the substitute contract: see Lord Bingham of Cornhill at paras [22] and Lord Walker of Gestingthorpe at paras [45]–[46]. I think that the majority's view on this point was correct. Sections 50 and 51 of the Sale of Goods Act, like the corresponding principles of the common law, are concerned with the price of the goods or services which would have been delivered under the contract. They are not concerned with the value of the contract as an article of commerce in itself. As Lord Brown observed at paras [82]–[83], even if the charterparty rights could have been sold for a capital sum, this was not a proper basis for assessing loss, and an assessment which proceeded as if it were would 'extend the effect of the available market rule well beyond its proper scope'."

34   By the time *Bunge* was decided, attempts had already been made to rely on *The Golden Victory* in two share sale cases. In the earlier of them, *Ageas (UK) Ltd v Kwik-Fit (GB) Ltd* [2014] EWHC 2178 (QB); [2014] Bus. L.R. 1338 ("*Ageas*"), the seller had given a warranty in respect of a subsidiary's accounts when selling the subsidiary. It subsequently transpired that the warranties had been breached in the treatment of an item known as "time on cover bad debt" (or "TOCBD"). In the event, however, the impact of TOCBD turned out to be less than had been anticipated at the date of breach, and the company which had insured the warranty liability ("AIG") maintained that regard should be had to that fact when calculating what it had to pay.

35   Popplewell J concluded in paragraph 35 that "[t]he *Bwllfa* approach, as applied in *The Golden Victory* ..., supports the proposition that when assessing damages for breach of contract by reference to the value of a company or other property at the date of breach, whose value depends upon a future contingency, account can be taken of what is subsequently known about the outcome of the contingency as a result of events subsequent to the valuation date where that is necessary in order to give effect to the compensatory principle". Popplewell J went on:

"In an appropriate case, the valuation can be made with the benefit of hindsight, taking account of what is known of the outcome of the contingency at the time that the assessment falls to be made by the court. This is so not merely as a cross-check against the reasonableness of prospective forecasting, as Staughton J regarded as permissible in *Buckingham v Francis* [1986] 2 All ER 738. It is so whatever view might prospectively be taken at the breach date of the outcome of the contingency."

36   Popplewell J added, however, two qualifications. The first was that the approach he had outlined "can only be justified where it is necessary to give effect to the overriding compensatory principle": see paragraph 37. The second was that "it is important to keep firmly in mind any contractual allocation of risk made by the parties": see paragraph 38. In that connection, Popplewell J said in paragraph 38:

"Party autonomy dictates that an award of damages should not confound the allocation of risk inherent in the parties' bargain. It is not therefore sufficient merely that there is a future contingency which plays a part in the assessment. It is necessary to examine whether the eventuation of that contingency represents a risk which has been allocated by the parties as one which should fall on one or other of them. If the benefit or detriment of the contingency eventuating is a risk which has been allocated to the buyer, it is not appropriate to deprive him of any benefit which in fact ensues: it is inherent in the bargain that the buyer should receive such benefit."

37   On the facts, Popplewell J was not persuaded that the post-acquisition incidence of TOCBD should be used in valuing the subsidiary at the date of the acquisition.

In the first place, AIG had "simply not shown that the conventional prospective approach of assessment at the breach date offends the compensatory principle or results in a windfall to [the purchaser]": see paragraph 49. Secondly, the contractual allocation of risk made it inappropriate to take account of post-acquisition experience. As to that, Popplewell J said:

> "50. The SPA was for a fixed price based on what Ageas [i.e. the purchaser] was prepared to pay, and [the seller] to accept, for a business which was thereafter Ageas's to do what it wanted with. There was no provision, as there sometimes is in such agreements, for any post acquisition adjustment of the price based on subsequent trading performance. Each party would have to determine an acceptable price based on forecasts reached prior to completion in what was a fast moving and competitive market facing new challenges in the grip of a major recession whose effect on customers remained uncertain. Upon completion, the contract was fully executed. The outcome of all the contingencies inherent in the forecasts were risks conferred on Ageas. If the business did better than the parties projected when calculating a price, that was for Ageas's benefit. If it did worse, that was its loss. The bargain embodied in the SPA was the allocation of risk to Ageas of any benefit or loss arising either as a result of the way Ageas chose to run the business or as a result of external influences on the success of the business.
>
> …
>
> 52. What happened to TOCBD after the acquisition was … part and parcel of the way Ageas chose to run the business following acquisition and the interaction between those business decisions and the effect of the market and macro-economic conditions on the business. Those contingencies are all matters which the parties agreed are for Ageas's risk. The incidence of TOCBD was just one element inextricably bound up with the way the business was run and the external influences on its success, and was subject to the same allocation of risk."

38   In the second case, *The Hut Group Ltd v Nobahar-Cookson* [2014] EWHC 3842 (QB), it was again decided, applying principles derived from Ageas, that events since the date of breach should not be taken into account. In the course of his judgment, Blair J noted at paragraph 185:

> "For the avoidance of doubt, it is not suggested that the mere fact that shares sold in breach of warranty later recover their value because the business in fact does well has any effect on quantum assessed as at the date of breach. Any such argument would be insupportable, not least because the buyer is entitled to the benefit of the upside, having taken the risk of the downside."

39   There was also reference to Ageas in *OMV Petrom SA v Glencore International AG* [2016] EWCA Civ 778; [2016] 2 Lloyd's Rep. 432 ("*OMV Petrom*"), which, as Christopher Clarke LJ noted in paragraph 1, concerned the measure of damages for deceit. In *OMV Petrom*, the defendant ("Glencore") had contracted to sell particular grades of oil, but had in fact supplied a blend of oils which cost less and had created, or caused to be created, false documents which were designed to deceive, and did deceive, the purchaser. If the purchaser had known the true position, it "would probably have rejected the claim cargoes and purchased the relevant brand elsewhere": see paragraph 11.

40   When determining the value of what Glencore had supplied for the purpose of calculating damages, the trial judge had applied a discount on the basis that "any buyer invited to purchase a blend which contained obscure or unfamiliar components and with no history of their performance would have been looking for a further discount from the CIF price of the components because of the range of uncertainties that came into play when buying an unknown blend as opposed to a recognized grade": see paragraph 21. On appeal, Glencore challenged the discount on the basis which Christopher Clarke LJ summarised as follows in paragraph 31:

> "The discount is said to be wrong in principle. Its basis was that anyone buying one of the blends would want a substantial discount because of the risks of using an untried blend in a refinery. Use of such a blend could reduce the output of refined product below what would be expected of the relevant brand or affect the machinery of the refinery itself. At worst use of the blend might lead to a fire or, more likely, rust. But, in the events which happened, nothing untoward occurred. In those circumstances any discount is inappropriate. The measure of damages is the price paid less the benefit received being the real value of the goods. To make a deduction for risks which did not eventuate would be to attribute to the blends an unreal value and to compensate [the purchaser] for a loss which it might have suffered but did not. Moreover, if the crude supplied had had some effect on the machinery of the refinery [the purchaser] could have claimed against Glencore for that so that, effectively, Glencore was the guarantor of such risks."

41   Christopher Clarke LJ, with whom Black and Kitchin LJJ agreed, rejected the contention. He said in paragraph 40:

> "[T]hese cargoes were unique and had to be valued by a calculation of the total cif value of the component crudes discounted on account of the risks and uncertainties involved in buying these odd cargoes which were a mixture of crude oils, condensates and fuel oil. The amount by which the price paid exceeded a price calculated on that basis constitutes the measure of the buyer's loss, representing, as it does, the amount that he has overpaid on account of the seller's deceit. That loss arose when on account of the deceit he acquired the property, for which he had to overpay. The fact, if such it be, that, afterwards, none of the risks to which the discount related materialised cannot alter the fact that the buyer was induced to pay too much when he did so."

In paragraph 49, Christopher Clarke LJ said:

> "The valuation is to be carried out as at the bill of lading date, being the date upon which [the purchaser's] loss crystallized, and at which time any valuation would have to take account of the then risks. What happened after the bill of lading date does not affect the value of the blend *on that date*. A valuation without any discount would produce a figure which did not represent the market value at that date, at which time no one would have bought the blends without one."

42   Distinguishing Ageas, Christopher Clarke LJ said in paragraph 57 that he did not regard the trial judge's approach as inconsistent with the compensatory principle. He commented:

"Whatever may be the position in relation to contractual claims not based on fraud, the duped buyer is entitled to compensation for the excessive price that he has paid which is to be determined as at the date when he acquired the property. To require the deceiver to make such compensation is consistent with a policy of discouraging intentional wrongdoing."

43   *OMV Petrom* chimes with earlier authority. In *McConnel v Wright* [1903] 1 Ch. 546, the plaintiff had subscribed for shares in a company ("Standard") in reliance on a representation that the company held certain shares in another company ("Globe"). At the time, the Globe shares were not in fact held by Standard, but Standard acquired them subsequently. It was held that transfer did not defeat a claim for deceit. Collins MR said at 553-554:

"on the evidence as it now stands and the result of the learned judge's decision, it was not at all certain, at the time when the prospectus was issued, whether the Globe shares would be acquired or not. In point of fact they were not acquired till some time later, and therefore at the date when the prospectus was issued there was a misrepresentation, and damages might have been assessed there and then on the date on which this gentleman paid his money on the allotment of shares to him. That is clearly the time at which his damages must be assessed. He had paid his money, and he had got in return for it a property which did not contain the 200,000 Globe shares, in respect of which a profit of so large an amount is said to have been obtained. Therefore the position is this, and anybody assessing the damages will have to consider it: What is the difference between the value of the property as it was represented and the property without this large asset in it, having regard to the possibility, certainty, or uncertainty of that asset ever being in fact acquired? We now know, no doubt, that it was acquired afterwards; but that is not the material point. The damages have to be ascertained in view of the facts as they were at the time—in view of the central fact that this asset had not been acquired."

Similarly, Romer LJ said at 557-558:

"[The defendant's counsel] say, True, the company had not these shares at the date of the allotment, but it acquired them a few days afterwards, and they ask the Court to say that made good the representation. I need scarcely point out the fallacy of that contention. Unless they can establish that the risk which was run by this company, which had not got the shares at the date of allotment, and might never have got them, was unsubstantial, in my opinion that risk was not unsubstantial. The question has to be tried by looking at what was the true value of the shares, of course, at the date of allotment. To shew what was the value of the shares later on, after the company had got these 200,000 Globe shares, is not to the point, nor indeed is it relevant to inquire, because if one went on to inquire what was the condition of the shares some days later, when the 200,000 Globe shares were acquired, one ought also to inquire what were the other circumstances of the company at that time; for it would not follow of necessity that there were no other counterbalancing disadvantages at that later date. It must be pointed out that it is irrelevant to inquire into a state of circumstances after the date of allotment—that is to say, to inquire only as to one particular side of the matter. The proper inquiry is, What was the true value of these shares at the date of allotment? As I have pointed out, if the risk run was substantial, as I have said I think it was, then the shares were not worth what they were represented to be worth by the prospectus, which was the price paid for them by the plaintiff."

The third member of the Court, Cozens-Hardy LJ, said at 559:

"It is not to the point, it seems to me, to allege that shortly afterwards the Globe shares were allotted. Subsequent events cannot be looked at for this purpose. There was a material risk at the date when the plaintiff acquired his shares that the statement would not be made good."

44   Returning to contractual principles, in *Classic Maritime Inc v Limbungan Makmur Sdn Bhd* [2019] EWCA Civ 1102; [2019] Bus. L.R. 2854 ("*Classic Maritime*") Males LJ, with whom Haddon-Cave and Rose LJJ agreed, distinguished *The Golden Victory* and *Bunge* on the basis that they had been concerned with anticipatory breach rather than actual breach. *Classic Maritime* concerned a long-term contract of affreightment providing for shipments of iron ore pellets. The claim related to the charterer's failure to provide seven shipments. At first instance, the judge found that the failure of the Fundao dam in Brazil had made it impossible for the charterer to perform the contract in respect of the third to seventh shipments, but also that the charterer would have defaulted on those shipments even if the dam had not burst. The Court of Appeal held that the bursting of the dam did not absolve the charterer from liability for substantial damages. Males LJ explained:

"[80] Both *The Golden Victory* and *Bunge v Nidera* were concerned with the assessment of damages for an anticipatory breach by renunciation which required the court to value the innocent party's right to future performance, in the former case the right to performance of what was in effect an instalment contract with monthly hire payments and in the latter case the right to performance of a single supply of goods. In both cases the compensatory principle operated to reduce or extinguish the innocent party's claim for damages. That was because the value of the performance to which that party was entitled was adversely affected by events which occurred after the acceptance of the repudiation. However, the fundamental principle is clear.
[81] The present case is not concerned with an anticipatory breach, but with actual breaches as a result of the charterer's failure to supply cargoes for each of the five shipments in issue. It is common ground that, subject only to cl 32, the charterer's obligation to supply cargoes was an absolute obligation (see *Triton Navigation Ltd v Vitol SA, The Nikmary* [2003] EWCA Civ 1715; [2004] 1 All ER (Comm) 698; [2004] 1 Lloyd's Rep 55). Thus the performance to which the shipowner was entitled, once it was determined that cl 32 did not provide the charterer with a defence, was the supply of cargoes. The value of that performance was the freights which the shipowner would have earned if the cargoes had been supplied less the cost of earning them. In principle, therefore, the comparison which application of the compensatory principle required was between (1) the freights which the shipowner would have earned less the cost of earning them and (2) the actual position in which the shipowner found itself as a result of the breach. It is now agreed that this comparison would result in a damages award of over US$19m.
[82] The comparison which the judge carried out was different. It was between the shipowner's position if the charterer had been ready and willing to perform

and the shipowner's actual position. The judge said at [146] that undertaking this comparison did not involve 'an impermissible sleight of hand' but I do not agree. The [charterer's] obligation was not to be ready and willing to supply a cargo in each case, but actually to supply one. The charterer was not in breach because it was unwilling to perform, but because it failed to do so, even if the reason why it failed to do so was because it was unwilling.

[83] In the case of an anticipatory breach (i.e. a renunciation in advance of the time for performance), a party repudiates a contract if it demonstrates an unwillingness to perform, in which case (as in *The Golden Victory* and *Bunge v Nidera*) it may be necessary to consider whether, if it had not demonstrated that unwillingness, it would nevertheless have been excused from performance by later events. If so, that will affect the value of the rights which the innocent party has lost. But that is not so in the case of an actual breach, as in the present case. In the present case, where there is an absolute obligation to supply a cargo, whether the charterer was ready and willing to supply is neither here nor there. Nor is it relevant whether performance is impossible as (in the absence of a defence such as frustration or illegality) impossibility is not a defence: *Taylor v Caldwell* (1863) 3 B & S 826 at 833; (1863) 122 ER 309 at 312. The simple fact is that the charterer failed to do what it had promised to do and is thereby in breach."

45 I should also mention *Senate Electrical Wholesalers Ltd v Alcatel Submarine Networks Ltd* [1999] 2 Lloyd's Rep. 423 ("*Senate*"), on which Mr Sims relied. That case arose from a share sale in which the vendor warranted the accuracy of some 1990 management accounts. It transpired that the accounts did not show a true and fair view because "rebate reserves" were overstated by £1.7 million. The vendor, however, argued that there was in fact no difference between the warranted figure and actual profit, in part on the basis that a £750,000 overestimate of the 1989 rebate reserve was available to boost the 1990 profits: see paragraphs 10(c) and 38(B)(a). In that connection, Stuart-Smith LJ, giving the judgment of the Court of Appeal, said in paragraph 56:

"Although the 1990 management accounts did not show a true and fair view because rebate reserves were overstated by £1 7m, in order to see if the plaintiff has suffered any loss and, if so, how it should be quantified, it is necessary to establish the actual profit for that year. Thus, if some credit or profit has been omitted which can properly be taken into account in the 1990 profit, the apparent loss is pro tanto extinguished or diminished. For this purpose, in our judgment, it is permissible to take into account hindsight to arrive at the actual figures."

46 Having quoted this passage, Popplewell J said in Ageas at paragraph 25:

"I do not find it easy to understand from the report quite what hindsight was being referred to. In particular it is not apparent that what was meant by hindsight was the taking into account of matters which had not yet occurred at the time of the sale, rather than retrospective accounting treatment. Whilst para 60 addresses and dismisses a hindsight argument by reference to what was known or expected at the date of sale about actual payment of the 1990 rebates, para 57 appears to address the £750,000 overestimate of 1989 rebate reserve as giving rise to an understatement of profit in the 1990 accounts as a matter of accounting treatment. I have not therefore found this dictum of great assistance in resolving the current dispute."

47   I agree. Reading Stuart-Smith LJ's reference to it being "permissible to take into account hindsight to arrive at the actual figures" in its context, I do not think it is of any real help with the issues raised in the present case.

48   Reference to subsequent events to determine whether an event which was contingent at the date of assessment occurred must be distinguished from their use to cast light on events which had happened by the date of assessment. Take the present case. When assessing the multiplicand, it was relevant to consider the degree to which GDE's costs would have been increased if the company had disposed of all leachate lawfully in the period before GDE was sold to MDW. In that context, Mr Mesher relied on the extent to which leachate had been processed by Tradebe in the years immediately after the sale. Doing so did not involve application of the *Bwllfa* principle. What had happened since the SPA provided evidence as to how far GDE had increased its pre-SPA profits by the unlawful disposal of leachate and, thus, of GDE's maintainable EBITDA. That is quite different from invoking matters subsequent to the date of assessment in order to show that something that was then contingent did, or did not, happen in the event.

49   Drawing some of the threads together, it seems to me that the following can be said:

i) Where damages fall to be assessed in respect of an anticipatory breach of contract which was accepted, it is appropriate to consider what would have happened if the breach had not occurred and, in that context, events subsequent to the breach may be relevant;

ii) That principle has, however, no application where a party to a contract has, by failing to supply goods or services, committed an actual, rather than anticipatory, breach of contract;

iii) Further, where a claimant has been induced by deceit to buy something, the defendant cannot reduce its liability by showing that a contingency which served to reduce the value of the item at the date of assessment did not eventuate;

iv) There is a strong case for saying that, in general at least, the position should be similar in relation to warranties given on a share sale. Supposing the position to be that the true value of some shares is depressed by a contingency, someone buying them at a higher figure will have paid more than they were worth even if the contingency never happens. Events subsequent to the purchase cannot affect the value at the time of the transaction. The price of a share could typically be said to be a product of a number of contingencies. If a particular risk does, or does not, occur, the price may rise or fall, but that will not retrospectively change the value of the share at an earlier date. In *Bunge*, Lord Sumption thought that the minority in *The Golden Victory* had been wrong to focus on the value of the charterparty itself, as opposed to the chartered service which would have been performed, observing that sections 50 and 51 of the Sale of Goods Act 1891 and the common law were alike concerned with "the value of the goods or services which would have been delivered under the contract", not "the value of the contract as an article of commerce in itself". In contrast, a share sale relates to an existing asset which is recognised as "an article of commerce in itself";

v) If, none the less, there can be cases in which account can be taken of what happened subsequently as regards a contingency which existed on the date of assessment when determining what, if any, damages are payable for breach of a warranty on a share sale, they must be rare. They would doubtless involve situations in which the buyer might otherwise be said to have gained a "windfall", but the mere fact that the value of the relevant shares has increased since the date of assessment cannot demonstrate such a "windfall": it is inherent in the selection of a date of assessment that subsequent changes in value can fall to be disregarded. Still less could it be appropriate to categorise a post-assessment rise in value as a "windfall" if it were attributable to steps that the purchaser had itself taken since the transaction. Further, as Popplewell LJ said in Ageas , it would be "important to keep firmly in mind any contractual allocation of risk made by the parties"; and

vi) There is no similar bar on using events subsequent to the date of assessment to cast light on events which had happened by that date.

The present case

50   The Judge valued GDE on a "Warranty False" basis at £2,958,676. On the Norvills' case, the Judge ought to have arrived at a somewhat higher "Warranty False" figure. Either way, GDE was worth substantially more than its net assets excluding goodwill. The fact that purchasers would have been willing to pay a price in excess of the value of GDE's other net assets shows it to have had goodwill.

51   The Judge thought it appropriate to make a reduction in the multiplier used for his "Warranty False" calculations "to reflect reputational damage (or, as it has been put, 'the fragility of the goodwill') that the breaches were liable to cause to the company and the jeopardy that they occasioned to the future of the business". The Judge was essentially saying that a purchaser aware of how GDE had been conducting its business would not have been willing to pay as much for its shares or, expressed differently, would have thought the company's goodwill somewhat less valuable.

52   The Judge's approach was consistent with evidence given by both Mr Gates and Mr Mesher. Mr Gates explained that, in his view, "a systematically non-compliant business … would warrant a lower multiple as well [as a downward adjustment to profits]". For his part, Mr Mesher accepted that a "qualitative discount" to the multiplier could be appropriate. Expanding on this in oral evidence, he said:

> "let's say 25 per cent is the absolute maximum, or not necessarily the absolute maximum but a reasonable reduction in a business which is capable of being carried on but has really significant transgressions, you know, down to zero in a situation where there may be for example a series of minor issues or issues which for example haven't gone to prosecution and haven't been followed up in terms of enforcement action by the authorities. So there is, of course, a scale."

53   In the event, GDE did not suffer the damage that a well-informed purchaser might have feared at the date of the SPA. It remains the case, however, that the Judge was fully justified in lowering the multiplier as well as the multiplicand

when working out what GDE was worth on a "Warranty False" basis. Had GDE disposed of all leachate lawfully, its profits would have been reduced with implications for the multiplicand. As, however, the company had behaved improperly, its value was diminished by more than the cut in the multiplicand would alone have implied. Purchasers knowing the truth would not merely have factored in the prospect of lower maintainable earnings, but have brought down what they were prepared to pay to take account of the misconduct. In other words, the fact that, as matters turned out, GDE did not experience reputational damage does not mean that the value of the company was not reduced in the way the Judge found as at the date of the SPA. While reputational damage could be said to have been contingent when the SPA was entered into, there was good reason for the Judge to decide that the value of GDE had already been depreciated. Put differently, there was an impairment to goodwill as at the date of the SPA.

54   That the Judge considered a downward adjustment to the multiplier as well as the multiplicand appropriate is entirely unsurprising. In fact, as Mr Ayres observed, it would have been remarkable if GDE's misbehaviour had not had such a consequence. As a matter of common sense, a willing purchaser would not have been likely to pay as much for the company. On top of that, there is good reason to think that the fact that GDE did not in the event suffer the reputational damage to which its misconduct might have been expected to give rise is attributable to efforts which MDW made to put matters right after it had acquired GDE. In all the circumstances, the approach which the Judge adopted cannot fairly be said to give MDW a "windfall".

55   Further, there was, as I see it, no inconsistency between the Judge's use of post-SPA evidence when determining the multiplicand and his refusal to take into account post-SPA events when considering whether the multiplier should be discounted. The former involved using matters subsequent to the date of assessment to cast light on events which had happened earlier, which is legitimate.

56   It appears to me, therefore, that the Judge was right to disregard the fact that reputational risks did not in the event materialise when assessing damages on contractual principles. For good measure, the Judge held the Norvills to have been guilty of deceit as well as breach of warranty and cases such as *OMV Petrom* and *McConnel v Wright* show that where, as here, a claimant has been induced to buy something by deceit, it is no defence to demonstrate that a contingency which reduced value at the date of the assessment did not eventuate.

57   In short, the Judge was, in my view, correct when in paragraph 288 of his judgment he dismissed the "argument … that no discount is appropriate because it is known that no risks to the business have been realised since the SPA" as "rel[ying] impermissibly on hindsight".

Was the Judge's reduction in the multiplier arbitrary, unreasoned and unjustified?

58   Mr Sims said that, even if the Judge was justified in making some downward adjustment to the "Warranty False" valuation, the reduction in the multiplier from 4.2 to 4 was arbitrary, unreasoned and unjustified. Nowhere in the judgment, Mr Sims submitted, is there any analysis of why that particular cut was thought to be justified. It is to be remembered, Mr Sims argued, that the change in the multiplier was applied to the whole of the multiplicand, not just such of it as was attributable to GDE's wet waste division, let alone only that part of that division's business

which dealt with leachate. In the circumstances, the Judge needed to give specific reasons for choosing to lower the multiplier by 0.2 rather than a different figure, or not at all.

59   To my mind, however, the Judge was fully entitled to reduce the multiplier to the extent he did and explained the basis for doing so adequately. The Judge noted in paragraph 290 of his judgment that "the discount of the multiplier is to be ascertained, as Mr Mesher suggested, by choosing a figure at an appropriate point within the range of acceptable multipliers for an EV/EBITDA valuation" and that "Mr Mesher considered that the appropriate range was between 3.8 and 4.5". The Judge followed the course which Mr Mesher had proposed and selected a multiplier within Mr Mesher's range. Further, it can be seen from paragraph 289 of his judgment that the Judge had well in mind factors limiting the significance of GDE's misconduct and, from paragraph 291, that the Judge considered the overall effect which the reduction in the multiplier would have on the "Warranty False" valuation. It is not easy to identify what more the Judge could usefully have said. At any rate, he said enough.

Conclusion

60   I would dismiss the appeal.

The cross-appeal

61   Noting in paragraph 280 of his judgment that "[n]o different measure has been suggested for any claim in respect of fraudulent or negligent misrepresentation", the Judge assessed damages using what it was common ground was the proper measure of damages for breach of warranty, namely, the difference between GDE's "Warranty True" value and its "Warranty False" value. That approach would have been satisfactory, Mr Ayres said, if the Judge had accepted that the "Warranty True" figure equated to what MDW had paid for GDE's shares. In the event, however, the Judge found the "Warranty True" value to have been £242,948 less than the purchase price. That being so, Mr Ayres said, it became necessary for the Judge to differentiate between the tortious and contractual measures of damages. If the Judge had applied the tortious measure, as he needed to do, he would have increased the damages he awarded to £625,548, on the basis that what MDW had paid (viz. £3,584,224) had exceeded the "Warranty False" value (viz. £2,958,676) by that amount.

62   The issues arising from these submissions and Mr Sims' response to them can be addressed under the following headings:

    i) Is it open to MDW to contend for anything other than the contractual measure?

    ii) Implications of the tortious measure

    iii) The present case

Is it open to MDW to contend for anything other than the contractual measure?

63   Mr Sims argued that paragraph 280 of the judgment reflected the reality. MDW had not contended for anything other than the contractual measure of damages

before the Judge, and, so Mr Sims submitted, it should not be allowed to do so in this Court.

64 However, it is plain that MDW alleged misrepresentation as well as breach of warranty. Thus, paragraph 1.3 of the amended particulars of claim stated that MDW's claim was for "breach of contractual warranty, and for negligent misrepresentation, and … for damages for fraudulent misrepresentation" and MDW's skeleton argument for the trial began, "This is the trial of C's claim for damages for breach of warranty, misrepresentation, and deceit". Later in the skeleton argument, this was said about quantum in paragraph 115:

> "The well-established measure of damages in breach of warranty claims is the difference between (WV) the value of the shares if the warranties had been complied with (what C would have obtained if the contract had been performed), and (TV) the true value of the shares (what C in fact obtained) at the date of purchase:
>
> 115.1 The measure of damages in tort is the difference between (P) the price actually paid by C for the shares in reliance on the representations, and (TV) the true value of the shares, plus any recoverable consequential losses after the purchase.
>
> 115.2 C does not seek consequential losses, and both parties have proceeded on the basis that (P) the price actually paid by C and (WV) the value of the shares if the warranties had been complied with are the same.
>
> 115.3 So there is no relevant distinction here between the quantum of damages sought by C for breach of contract and in tort. C seeks the difference between P and TV."

65 That the price which MDW paid for GDE's shares was taken to be the same as the value which the shares would have had if the warranties given in respect of them had been true is confirmed by the expert evidence. Mr Mesher said in his report that it was "unlikely that the market value of the Company as at 14th October 2015 is anything other than that which was actually paid" (paragraph 4.9) and referred elsewhere in his report to support for "the contention that the price paid represented market value" (paragraph 4.24) and to "the market value of £3.5 million" (paragraph 4.32). Likewise, Mr Mesher said when giving oral evidence at the trial that the figure of £3.3 million which he had arrived at by an objective valuation was "close enough to 3.5 million to support the overall value", while Mr Gates described the figure in the SPA as "a market value".

66 In written closing submissions, it was explained in paragraph 1.8 that MDW "does not suggest that the measure of loss in this particular case is different from the contractual measure". However, it can be seen from paragraph 151, which replicated paragraph 115 of MDW's skeleton argument for the trial, that MDW saw no relevant distinction between the contractual and tortious measures of damages because "both parties have proceeded on the basis that (P) the price actually paid by C and (WV) the value of the shares if the warranties had been complied with are the same". The premise is borne out by the Norvills' written closing submissions, which stated at paragraph 133 that the experts "were agreed on the Warranty True figure of £3.5m and so the difference between them was assessing the Warranty False figure".

67 In the event, the Judge found that MDW had paid more for GDE than its value on a "Warranty True" basis. The Judge concluded in paragraph 285 of his judgment

that GDE's value on a "Warranty True" basis was £3,341,276, £242,948 less than the purchase price. As Mr Ayres explained, it was that (unexpected) development which led MDW to distinguish in this Court between the tortious and contractual measures of damages.

68   In the circumstances, I can see no objection to MDW relying on the tortious measure of damages before us. It always alleged misrepresentation and at trial both summarised what it said the effect of the tortious measure of damages was and explained why it saw no relevant distinction between the tortious and contractual measures on the facts. A potential distinction having emerged as a result of the Judge differing from what had been common ground at trial, it must be legitimate for MDW now to contend that the tortious measure entitles it to a higher figure than it was awarded by the Judge on contractual principles.

69   Mr Sims suggested that MDW had taken the risk that the Judge would find that it had paid more for GDE than its "Warranty True" value. At trial, however, neither the Norvills nor the Judge alerted MDW to the possibility of a departure from the shared assumption that "the price actually paid by [MDW] and … the value of the shares if the warranties had been complied with are the same".

Implications of the tortious measure

70   In keeping with what had been said in MDW's skeleton argument and written closing submissions at the trial, Mr Ayres argued that the measure of damages in tort is "the difference between (P) the price actually paid by C for the shares in reliance on the representations, and (TV) the true value of the shares, plus any recoverable consequential losses after the purchase" and that, since MDW has not sought consequential losses, it is entitled to the difference between the price it paid and the "Warranty False" value of GDE's shares.

71   Mr Ayres cited in support of his submissions *Smith New Court Securities Ltd v Citibank NA* [1997] A.C. 254 ("*Smith New Court*"), which, as Lord Browne-Wilkinson observed at 260, raised for the first time in the House of Lords "the question of the correct measure of damages where a plaintiff has acquired property in reliance on a fraudulent misrepresentation made by the defendant". At 266-267, Lord Browne-Wilkinson concluded that the following principles apply when assessing the damages payable where a plaintiff has been induced by fraudulent misrepresentation to buy property:

> "(1) the defendant is bound to make reparation for all the damage directly flowing from the transaction; (2) although such damage need not have been foreseeable, it must have been directly caused by the transaction; (3) in assessing such damage, the plaintiff is entitled to recover by way of damages the full price paid by him, but he must give credit for any benefits which he has received as a result of the transaction; (4) as a general rule, the benefits received by him include the market value of the property acquired as at the date of acquisition; but such general rule is not to be inflexibly applied where to do so would prevent him obtaining full compensation for the wrong suffered; (5) although the circumstances in which the general rule should not apply cannot be comprehensively stated, it will normally not apply where either (a) the misrepresentation has continued to operate after the date of the acquisition of the asset so as to induce the plaintiff to retain the asset or (b) the circumstances of the case are such that the plaintiff

is, by reason of the fraud, locked into the property. (6) In addition, the plaintiff is entitled to recover consequential losses caused by the transaction; (7) the plaintiff must take all reasonable steps to mitigate his loss once he has discovered the fraud."

For his part, Lord Steyn said at 284 that "the normal method of calculating the loss caused by the deceit is the price paid less the real value of the subject matter of the sale" and went on:

"There is in truth only one legal measure of assessing damages in an action for deceit: the plaintiff is entitled to recover as damages a sum representing the financial loss flowing directly from his alteration of position under the inducement of the fraudulent representations of the defendants. The analogy of the assessment of damages in a contractual claim on the basis of cost of cure or difference in value springs to mind. In *Ruxley Electronics and Construction Ltd. v. Forsyth* [1996] A.C. 344, 360G, Lord Mustill said: 'There are not two alternative measures of damages, as opposite poles, but only one; namely, the loss truly suffered by the promisee.' In an action for deceit the price paid less the valuation at the transaction date is simply a method of measuring loss which will satisfactorily solve many cases. It is not a substitute for the single legal measure: it is an application of it."

72   Mr Ayres stressed Lord Browne-Wilkinson's third and fourth propositions and Lord Steyn's reference to a plaintiff being "entitled to recover as damages a sum representing the financial loss flowing directly from his alteration of position under the inducement of the fraudulent representations of the defendants". He also relied on a passage at 283 where Lord Steyn said that "it is not necessary in an action for deceit for the judge, after he had ascertained the loss directly flowing from the victim having entered into the transaction, to embark on a hypothetical reconstruction of what the parties would have agreed had the deceit not occurred".

73   In the circumstances, it is clear that, where a claimant has been induced by deceit to buy property in circumstances where he would not otherwise have bought it, the damages will normally be no less than the difference between the price paid and the real value of the property. Should the claimant have suffered consequential losses, a higher figure may be payable.

74   What, however, if the claimant, had he known the truth, would not have pulled out of the transaction entirely but would rather have negotiated a better price? Can it still claim price paid less true value? Or should the damages be price actually paid less what the claimant would have paid but for the deceit?

75   At first sight, Lord Steyn's rejection of the need to "embark on a hypothetical reconstruction of what the parties would have agreed had the deceit not occurred" might be thought to resolve the question. I do not think it does, however. Lord Steyn made the remark in the course of the following discussion of Hobhouse LJ's judgment in *Downs v Chappell* [1997] 1 W.L.R. 426:

"[Hobhouse LJ] enunciated the following 'qualification' of the conventional rule, at p. 443:

'In my judgment, having determined what the plaintiffs have lost as a result of entering into the transaction—their contract with Mr. Chappell—it is still appropriate to ask the question whether that loss can properly be treated as having been caused by the defendants' torts, notwithstanding that the torts caused the plaintiffs to enter into the transaction.'

> That led Hobhouse L.J., at p. 444, 'to compare the loss consequent upon entering into the transaction with what would have been the position had the represented, or supposed, state of affairs actually existed.' The correctness of this proposition in a case of deceit was debated at the bar. Counsel for Citibank in whose interest it was to adopt this proposition felt some difficulty in doing so. In my view the orthodox and settled rule that the plaintiff is entitled to all losses directly flowing from the transaction caused by the deceit does not require a revision. In other words, it is not necessary in an action for deceit for the judge, after he had ascertained the loss directly flowing from the victim having entered into the transaction, to embark on a hypothetical reconstruction of what the parties would have agreed had the deceit not occurred. The rule in deceit is justified by the grounds already discussed. I would hold that on this point *Downs v. Chappell* was wrongly decided."

Lord Steyn was thus addressing whether it was appropriate to ask what a claimant would have done if the false representation had been *true*, not whether it is relevant to inquire into what the claimant would have done if the representation had not been made. In this respect, I agree with the comments of Leggatt J in *Yam Seng Pte Ltd v International Trade Corp Ltd* [2013] EWHC 111 (QB); [2013] 1 C.L.C. 662 at paragraph 217(2).

76   It is also to be noted that, when *Smith New Court* was before the House of Lords, it was not in issue that the claimant would not have bought the relevant shares but for the misrepresentations which were found proved. At first instance, the defendants had argued that "[i]f without the misrepresentation [the plaintiff] would still have bought the shares but at a lower price the measure of damages is the amount by which they have overpaid, i.e. the difference between the two prices" (see [1992] B.C.L.C. 1104, at 1133-1134). However, Chadwick J, the trial judge, held it to be "impossible to be satisfied, on the balance of probabilities, that an offer … at 78p per share [i.e. the price which the plaintiff would have offered] would have been accepted" (see 1134) and so "approach[ed] the question of damages on the basis that, without the relevant misrepresentation, [the plaintiff] would not have bought the … shares" (see 1135).

77   In *Smith New Court*, Lord Steyn noted at 280 that "[f]or more than 100 years at least English law has adopted a policy of imposing more extensive liability on intentional wrongdoers than on merely careless defendants". In a similar vein, Lord Mustill recognised at 269 that "in a case of fraud there are good reasons for departing in some respects from the ordinary rules". Even so, the better view seems to me to be that, in a case where it is apparent that a claimant would have proceeded with a transaction at a lower price had there been no deceit, damages should be assessed by reference to the difference between what the claimant would have paid and what it did pay.

78   In *Smith New Court*, Lord Browne-Wilkinson took as "the starting point" the passage from *Livingstone v Rawyards Coal Co* in which Lord Blackburn said that the "general rule" is that "you should as nearly as possible get at that sum of money which will put the party who has been injured, or who has suffered, in the same position as he would have been in if he had not sustained the wrong for which he

is now getting his compensation or reparation". To similar effect was Lord Steyn's emphasis on there being "in truth only one legal measure of assessing damages in an action for deceit: the plaintiff is entitled to recover as damages a sum representing the financial loss flowing directly from his alteration of position under the inducement of the fraudulent representations of the defendants". Where the claimant would not have entered into the relevant transaction at all but for the deceit, it makes sense that damages should be fixed by reference to the difference between purchase price and real value. Supposing, on the other hand, that the claimant would still have bought, but for less, putting it in "the same position as [it] would have been in if [it] had not sustained the wrong" or giving it "a sum representing the financial loss flowing directly from [its] alteration of position under the inducement of the fraudulent representations" would seem to require it to receive the difference between the actual price and what it would have paid.

79   Support for that view is to be found in *McGregor on Damages*. When discussing the damages payable for deceit in circumstances where the claimant contracted to buy shares, the authors say in paragraph 49-010 that "[t]he normal measure of damages is the purchase price of the shares less their actual value, if any, at the time of acquisition". However, they add in footnote 38:

> "This measure is based on the very likely assumption that had the claimant known the true facts he would never have bought the shares. Were it possible to show, as the defendants tried unsuccessfully to show at first instance in *Smith New Court Securities v Scrimgeour Vickers* [1992] B.C.L.C. 1104, that in the absence of the representation the claimant would have been able to buy, and would have bought, the shares but at a lower figure, then the measure would become the difference between the price the buyer paid and the price he would have paid. This appears to be implicitly accepted in the judgment at first instance in *Smith New Court*: see at 1133i to 1135b; the point is not touched upon in the Court of Appeal ([1994] 1 W.L.R. 1271) or in the House of Lords ([1997] A.C. 254)."

The present case

80   The Judge made a finding in paragraph 274 of his judgment that MDW "was induced to enter into the SPA by the misrepresentations in the Due Diligence Index and Responses". He did not make any finding as to what MDW would have done had it known the truth, but Mr Ayres pointed out that the Judge had before him a witness statement from Mr Mark Hazell, a director of MDW and its majority shareholder, in which this was said in paragraph 21:

> "At the time the company [i.e. GDE] was purchased, there wasn't a reason for us to doubt the information supplied and integrity of the company. If I had such reason, I would not have sanctioned the offer to purchase the company and would have dropped it. I have usually got a good instinct for these sort of things but there was nothing that came out during the due diligence and the reports from the acquisition team to put me off and the team were happy that everything seemed to be in order and GDE was a promising proposition."

81   When, however, Mr Mark Hazell made his statement, MDW's allegations against the Norvills were not limited to those which the Judge held to have been made out. I agree with Mr Sims that, without more, we cannot infer from Mr Hazell's statement that he would necessarily have decided against buying GDE even at a reduced price had he appreciated the matters which the Judge considered to have been proved. In this connection, Mr Sims reminded us with some justification of the dangers of "island hopping" to which Lewison LJ made reference in *Fage UK Ltd v Chobani UK Ltd* [2014] EWCA Civ 5; [2014] F.S.R. 29, at paragraph 114.

82   As I understand it, Mr Mark Hazell was not challenged on paragraph 21 of his witness statement in cross-examination. At the time, however, there would have been no reason to do so. Both sides were assuming that GDE's "Warranty True" value was the same as the amount MDW had paid for its shares. On that basis, damages stood to be assessed as the difference between the price and the "Warranty False" value. The Norvills could not improve their position by establishing that, had it been aware of GDE's misconduct, MDW would have bought at a lower figure rather than abandoning the transaction entirely.

83   In the circumstances, Mr Ayres rightly accepted that we are not in a position to say what course MDW would have taken if it had known the facts. There is, moreover, some reason to think that, supposing MDW still to have been interested in buying GDE, it might have been prepared to pay more than GDE's "Warranty False" value to secure the company. On the basis of the Judge's findings, after all, the £3,584,224 which MDW paid for GDE exceeded its worth on a "Warranty True" basis by £242,948. Moreover, it may possibly have made commercial sense for MDW to "overpay" because of synergies between GDE's business and that of MDW. In that connection, Mr Mark Hazell spoke of GDE having "strong synergies with MDW's transport, logistics capabilities and history of large scale bluechip and government contracts" and Mr Oliver Hazell said that it had been suggested to him that he should investigate GDE as a possible acquisition "given company synergies".

84   All in all, it seems to me that, while it may very well be the case that MDW would not have contemplated buying GDE at all if it had had knowledge of the previous misbehaviour, we cannot rule out the possibility that it would still have been prepared to purchase, would have offered a sum in excess of GDE's "Warranty False" value and would have had that offer accepted. That being so, we are not, I think, in a position to decide what damages should be paid applying the tortious measure and there is no viable alternative to remitting that matter to the Judge. It will be for him to determine whether, had it known the truth, MDW (a) would not have bought GDE, in which case damages should be assessed at £625,548 (i.e. the difference between the £3,584,224 purchase price and the "Warranty False" value of £2,958,676) or (b) would, despite GDE's past misconduct, have both made and had accepted an offer for the company, in which case damages should be assessed by reference to the difference between that offer and the £3,584,224 it in fact paid.

85   Mr Sims suggested that MDW would not be entitled to damages of £625,548 even if it would not have purchased GDE had it known the truth on the basis that, as indicated by Lord Browne-Wilkinson's third proposition in *Smith New Court*, MDW would have to give credit for all benefits it had received from its acquisition of GDE and, given the synergies between the businesses of MDW and GDE, those benefits went beyond the "Warranty False" value of GDE. I cannot accept this. I can see nothing in the authorities to indicate that, when assessing the damages that

would be due to MDW in respect of the Norvills' deceit, it could be appropriate to give the Norvills credit for anything more than the market value of the shares they sold. That is especially so since, as Andrews LJ noted in *Tuke v Hood* [2022] EWCA Civ 23; [2022] 2 W.L.R. 983, at paragraph 58, the authorities demonstrate that "a deliberate wrongdoer is not to be rewarded for the fruits of his own deceit".

Overall conclusions

86   I would dismiss the appeal and, accordingly, decline to set aside the existing judgment against the Norvills for £382,600 by way of damages. I would also, however, allow the cross-appeal to the extent of remitting to the Judge the question whether MDW is entitled to additional damages for deceit.

LADY JUSTICE ASPLIN:

87   I would dismiss the appeal and would allow the cross-appeal, remitting the question of whether MDW is entitled to additional damages for deceit, for all the reasons given by Newey LJ.

LADY JUSTICE WHIPPLE:

88   I agree.

NORTHERN GAS NETWORKS LTD v REVENUE AND CUSTOMS COMMISSIONERS

COURT OF APPEAL (CIVIL DIVISION)

Lewison, Baker and Dingemans LJJ: 1 July 2022

[2022] EWCA Civ 910; [2023] Env. L.R. 6

☞ Contaminated land; Corporation tax; Entitlement; Expenditure; Gas distribution networks; Land remediation relief; Pipelines

H1 *Contaminated land—land remediation relief—Finance Act 2001 Sch.22—requirement to update and improve networks of iron gas supply pipes—pipes liable to corrode or fracture with risk of escaping gas and explosions—whether such revenue expenditure qualifying for land remediation relief enhanced deduction—whether land in a 'contaminated state' wholly or partly as a result of acts or omissions of the company—whether qualifying land remediation expenditure incurred in respect of the land*

H2   The appellant (N) was the owner and operator of a regional gas distribution network which it had acquired in 2005, and thereby became responsible for, some 37,000km of gas pipeline, much of which was made of iron. Neither N nor any company connected with it originally laid the pipes. Those pipes were liable to corrode or fracture over time giving rise to the risk of escaping gas and gas explosions. In consequence, a compulsory requirement had been imposed in 2001 to update and improve the networks of iron pipes. N complied with this requirement by replacing certain of its iron pipes with high density polyethylene (HDPE) pipes or lining existing iron pipes with HDPE pipes. The issue was whether N was entitled to land remediation relief under the Finance Act 2001 Sch.22. That would allow a deduction of 150% of the relevant expenditure in the computation of profits for the purposes of corporation tax. At the relevant time, the relevant conditions for qualification under Sch.22 Pt 2 were that: (1) N acquired "land" in the United Kingdom (UK); (2) the land was acquired for the purposes of its trade; (3) at the time of acquisition, all or part of the land was in a "contaminated state"; (4) N incurred qualifying land remediation expenditure (QLRE) in respect of the land; (5) the QLRE was allowable as a deduction in computing the profits of N's trade; and (6) the land was not in a contaminated state wholly or partly as a result of anything done or omitted to be done at any time by N or a person with a relevant connection to it. It was common ground that Conditions (2) and (5) were satisfied. The First-tier Tribunal (FTT) determined that Conditions (1) and (3) were satisfied but that Conditions (4) and (6) were not. The Upper tribunal (UT) decided that Condition (6) was not satisfied with the result that the claim to land remediation relief failed but expressed the view that Condition (4) was not satisfied either. N challenged the UT's decision on Conditions (4) and (6). The respondent sought to challenge the decision of the FTT on Condition (3).

H3   **Held,** in dismissing the appeal:

H4   (1) The "polluter pays" principle was a broad general statement of policy and no substitute for the words of the Finance Act itself. Words and passages in a statute derived their meaning from their context and the words that Parliament had used in the Act left no room for doubt. Condition (6) was not satisfied if the land was in a contaminated state wholly or partly as a result of anything done or omitted to be done at any time by N. The provisions required consideration of the state of the land both at the date of acquisition and at the date when the expenditure was incurred. The use of the words "at any time" in para.12(4) also meant that it was not correct to concentrate on the moment when the pipes were laid. On the facts found by the FTT, the reason why the land was contaminated, both at the date of acquisition and at the date when the expenditure was incurred, was because gas was being pumped through the iron pipes. The entity responsible for the pumping of gas at the date of acquisition was National Grid Transco (NGT), which had a relevant connection with N, and the entity responsible for pumping gas between the date of acquisition and the date of the expenditure was N itself. The iron pipes themselves did not give rise to any harm, the possibility of which arose because N, and before it NGT, pumped gas through them and it was the continuing pumping of the gas through the pipes that gave rise to the need for the works. The reason why the land was contaminated was N's continued pumping of the gas. That was an "act" of N which gave rise to, or caused, the contamination. As N had not itself laid the iron pipes the contamination was not "wholly" as a result of its acts or omissions but it was "partly" the result of these. The facts of the case were quite different from a factual situation in which land was contaminated at the time of its acquisition and the new owner simply did nothing for a while. That was a situation in which the new owner was passive in the face of existing contamination, as opposed to a situation where the new owner actively perpetuated the contamination. On the findings of the FTT, it was not unfair to describe N as the "polluter", since the contamination would not exist but for its pumping the gas. That failure to satisfy Condition (6) meant that the appeal failed.

H5   (2) No views were required nor would be expressed on Conditions (3) and (4).

H6   **Cases referred to:**
Housden v Conservators of Wimbledon and Putney Commons [2008] EWCA Civ 200; [2008] 1 W.L.R. 1172; [2008] 2 E.G.L.R. 107
Inland Revenue Commissioners v McGuckian [1997] 1 W.L.R. 991; [1997] S.T.C. 908; (1997) 94(27) L.S.G. 23 HL (NI)
Pollen Estate Trustee Co Ltd v Revenue and Customs Commissioners [2013] EWCA Civ 753; [2013] 1 W.L.R. 3785; [2013] 2 P. & C.R. DG17
R. (on the application of O (A Child)) v Secretary of State for the Home Department [2022] UKSC 3; [2022] 2 W.L.R. 343; [2022] H.R.L.R. 9
R. (on the application of Spath Holme Ltd) v Secretary of State for the Environment, Transport and the Regions [2001] 2 A.C. 349; [2001] 2 W.L.R. 15; (2001) 33 H.L.R. 31 HL

H7   **Legislation referred to:**
Gas Act 1986 Sch.4

Finance Act 2001 Sch.22
Corporation Tax Act 2009

H8 *J. Peacock KC, N. Mehta* and *S. Black* (instructed by Enyo Law LLP) appeared on behalf of the appellant.
D. Yates KC (instructed by HMRC Solicitor's Office) appeared on behalf of the respondent.

JUDGMENT

LORD JUSTICE LEWISON:

Introduction

1   The issue on this appeal is whether Northern Gas Networks Ltd ("NGN") is entitled to land remediation relief under Schedule 22 to the Finance Act 2001. Both the FTT (Judge Beare and Mr Adrain) and the UT (Meade J and Judge Jonathan Richards) decided that it was not. The decision of the FTT is at [2020] UKFTT 101 (TC); and that of the UT is at [2021] UKUT 157 (TCC); [2021] S.T.C. 1776.

2   If NGN is entitled to land remediation relief, then it is entitled to a deduction of 150% of the relevant expenditure in the computation of its profits for the purposes of corporation tax. If it is not, then the deduction is limited to 100% of the expenditure. Since the expenditure in issue exceeded £100 million; and the issue is also relevant to other utility providers, the UT granted permission to appeal.

The facts

3   The facts are not in dispute and NGN accepts that the UT accurately summarised them.

4   NGN owns and operates one of the eight regional gas distribution networks in the UK. It acquired that network in 2005 and thereby obtained, and became responsible for, some 37,000 kilometres of gas pipeline much of which was made of iron. Iron pipes are liable to corrode or fracture over time and thus gave rise to the risk of escaping gas and gas explosions. In consequence, the Health and Safety Executive has, since 2001, introduced a compulsory requirement for gas distribution companies, such as NGN, to update and improve their networks of iron pipes. That programme was known as the "30/30 Programme" because it required the replacement or improvement, over a 30-year period, of "at risk" mains pipelines located within 30 metres of a building. Following its acquisition of the network in 2005, NGN complies with this requirement by replacing certain of its iron pipes with high density polyethylene ("HDPE") pipes or lining existing iron pipes with HDPE pipes.

5   NGN acquired its gas distribution business by means of a purchase of assets (referred to as the "hive down") from National Grid Transco plc ("NGT") in 2005. At the time of the hive down, NGN was a subsidiary of NGT. The relationship of parent and subsidiary is a "relevant connection" for the purposes of land remediation relief. A few months after the hive down, the shares in NGN were sold out of the NGT group with the result that, at that point, NGN ceased to be a subsidiary of NGT.

6   One category of assets that NGN purchased from NGT consisted of the pipes comprising a gas distribution network. Those pipes were laid underneath various pieces of land, some privately owned (including by NGN itself) and some publicly owned. It was common ground both before the FTT and the UT that the pipes themselves remained chattels and had not become part of the land. Although I have some doubts whether that common ground was correct, I do not seek to disturb it.

7   Accordingly, when NGN acquired its business and assets from NGT, it also obtained certain rights to locate those pipes on land owned by others, and to access those pipes. In relation to pipes located on private land (though not pipes located on private streets) NGN took an assignment of private law land rights that NGT had previously obtained from owners of the relevant land. In relation to pipes located on public land, NGN obtained its rights under Schedule 4 to the Gas Act 1986.

8   No new iron pipes have been laid since the 1970s for the purposes of transporting gas. It was common ground that neither NGN, NGT or any company connected with either of them had themselves originally laid the iron pipes that were the object of the expenditure in dispute.

9   The 30–30 Programme imposed statutory obligations on NGN to replace or renew its network of iron pipes. It was common ground that, when performing work on a particular pipe, NGN would ensure that the flow of gas through that pipe was suspended. It was also common ground that it would not have been practicable for NGN to pause all transmission of gas through iron pipes until those pipes were satisfactorily renewed or replaced. Such a pause would have lasted for several years at least, would have prevented many households in the North and North East of England from obtaining gas during that period, and would have caused NGN to be in breach of its statutory and regulatory obligations where necessary.

The legislation

10   The FTT explained that land remediation relief is now governed by the Corporation Tax Act 2009 (as amended). Although we were not taken to the details, it was common ground that the conditions that would now need to be satisfied are more stringent than they were at the time of the events with which we are concerned. At the relevant time, the relevant parts of Schedule 22 to the Finance Act 2001 (now repealed) provided:

> **"2 Qualifying land remediation expenditure**
> (1) For the purposes of this Schedule "qualifying land remediation expenditure" of a company means expenditure of the company that meets the conditions in sub-paragraphs (2) to (6).
> (2) The first condition is that it is expenditure on land all or part of which is in a contaminated state (see paragraph 3).
> (3) The second condition is that the expenditure is expenditure on relevant land remediation directly undertaken by the company or on its behalf (see paragraph 4).
> (4) The third condition is that the expenditure is incurred–
> > (a) on employee costs (see paragraph 5), or
> > (b) on materials (see paragraph 6),

or is qualifying expenditure on sub-contracted land remediation (see paragraphs 9 to 11).

(5) The fourth condition is that the expenditure would not have been incurred had the land not been in a contaminated state (see paragraph 7).

(6) The fifth condition is that the expenditure is not subsidised (see paragraph 8).

3 Land in a contaminated state

(1) For the purposes of this Schedule land is in a contaminated state if, and only if, it is in such a condition, by reason of substances in, on or under the land, that–

(a) harm is being caused or there is a possibility of harm being caused…

4 Relevant land remediation

(1) For the purposes of this Schedule relevant land remediation, in relation to land acquired by a company, means–

(a) activities falling within sub-paragraph (2), and

(b) if there are such activities, preparatory activity falling within sub-paragraph (4) which satisfies the condition in sub-paragraph (5).

(2) The activities referred to in sub-paragraph (1)(a) are the doing of any works, the carrying out of any operations or the taking of any steps in relation to–

(a) the land in question,

(b) any controlled waters affected by that land, or

(c) any land adjoining or adjacent to that land,

for the purpose described in sub-paragraph (3).

(3) The purpose referred to in sub-paragraph (2) is that of–

(a) preventing or minimising, or remedying or mitigating the effects of, any harm, or any pollution of controlled waters, by reason of which the land is in a contaminated state; or

(b) restoring the land or waters to their former state. …

12 Entitlement to relief

(1) This paragraph applies if–

(a) land in the United Kingdom is, or has been, acquired by a company for the purposes of a Schedule A business or a trade carried on by the company,

(b) at the time of acquisition all or part of the land is or was in a contaminated state, and

(c) the company incurs qualifying land remediation expenditure in respect of the land.

(2) A company is entitled to land remediation relief for an accounting period if the company's qualifying land remediation expenditure is deductible in that period.

(3) The company's qualifying land remediation expenditure is deductible in that period if it is allowable as a deduction in computing for tax purposes the profits for that period of a Schedule A business or a trade carried on by the company.

(4) A company is not entitled to land remediation relief in respect of expenditure on land all or part of which is in a contaminated state, if the

land is in that state wholly or partly as a result of any thing done or omitted to be done at any time by the company or a person with a relevant connection to the company.

31 Interpretation

In this Schedule–

(1) "harm" means–

(a) harm to the health of living organisms,

(b) interference with the ecological systems of which any living organisms form part,

(c) offence to the senses of human beings, or

(d) damage to property…

"land" means any estate, interest or rights in or over land…

"substance" means any natural or artificial substance, whether in solid or liquid form or in the form of a gas or vapour."

11   It was thus common ground that NGN is entitled to land remediation relief if all the following conditions were met:

i)   NGN acquired "land" in the UK.

ii) The land was acquired for the purposes of NGN's trade.

iii) At the time of acquisition, all or part of the land was in a "contaminated state".

iv) NGN incurred qualifying land remediation expenditure in respect of the land.

v)   The qualifying land remediation expenditure was allowable as a deduction in computing the profits of NGN's trade.

vi) The land must not have been in a contaminated state wholly or partly as a result of anything done or omitted to be done at any time by NGN or a person with a relevant connection to NGN.

The decisions below

12   It was common ground before the FTT that Conditions (2) and (5) were satisfied. The FTT determined, contrary to HMRC's submissions, that Conditions (1) and (3) were satisfied. For the purpose of Condition (1), although NGN only acquired a right to pass gas through the pipes (which was in the nature of an easement), it was a right in land and thus fell within the definition of "land". For the purpose of Condition (3), however, "land" meant the physical land over or under which the right subsisted (the servient land). That interpretation was necessary because it cannot be said that an incorporeal hereditament is contaminated; nor can one spend money on an incorporeal hereditament, as opposed to the servient land. That, in turn, meant that the word "land" could not, or could not necessarily, be given a consistent meaning throughout the schedule. The FTT also decided, contrary to NGN's submissions, that Condition (4) was not satisfied. That was enough to dispose of NGN's claim for land remediation since NGN needed to satisfy all of Conditions (1) to (6). However, the FTT went on to conclude that Condition (6) was not satisfied either.

13   On appeal, the UT decided that Condition (6) was not satisfied with the result that the claim to land remediation relief failed. But they went on to express the view that Condition (4) was not satisfied either.

14   NGN challenges the UT's decision on Conditions (4) and (6). HMRC wish to challenge the decision of the FTT on Condition (3).

Condition (6)

15   Condition (6) is:

> "A company is not entitled to land remediation relief in respect of expenditure on land all or part of which is in a contaminated state, if the land is in that state wholly or partly as a result of any thing done or omitted to be done at any time by the company or a person with a relevant connection to the company."

16   The FTT's relevant findings of fact were:

> i) The main problem with iron pipes is their potential to fracture. If a pipe fails while there is gas flowing through it then there is a risk of gas escaping and causing an explosion: paragraph [12] (11).
> ii) The iron pipes themselves pose no risk to persons or property; instead it is the presence of gas within those pipes that does so: paragraph [12] (12); and
> iii) The gas which flows through the pipes does not increase the risk of fracture or cause or contribute to the corrosion of the pipes: paragraph [12] (11).

17   NGN's argument is that the contamination (i.e. the possibility of harm due to an escape of gas) is not attributable to the iron pipes alone or to the gas alone. It is the combination of the two that gives rise to the harm. The possibility of harm arises from the fact that if the iron pipes are corroded or fractured the gas could escape. At [36] the UT proceeded on the assumption that that was correct. Nevertheless, the UT reasoned that the land was contaminated at least partly because gas was being pumped through the pipes. NGN pumped the gas through the pipes and the harm was, therefore, partly a result of acts of NGN, namely the pumping of the gas through the pipes. Since Condition (6) is not satisfied if the land is in a contaminated state "wholly or partly" as a result of anything done or omitted to be done by the company, Condition (6) was not satisfied.

18   They went on to say that Condition (6) is not concerned with the reason why NGN acted as it did. It is simply concerned with the question whether the land is in a contaminated state wholly or partly as a result of NGN's actions.

19   Mr Peacock QC, for NGN, argues that this is an over-literal approach to the legislation. Condition (6) is intended to express the principle that "the polluter pays". Relief should only be denied where the claimant or a related entity is the true original underlying cause of the contamination itself or has increased the contamination. In the present case neither NGN nor NGT installed the iron pipes; and the continued flow of gas through the pipes did not exacerbate the risk of harm. NGN acquired land that was already contaminated because it acquired land in which there were iron pipes and gas was being pumped through them. Neither NGN nor NGT was responsible for the land becoming contaminated. At best, NGN's action in pumping gas through the pipes continued the contamination that already existed at the date of acquisition. It did not in any sense add to the contamination. Indeed, as its replacement programme took effect, the level of contamination was progressively reduced. The real question is whether NGN (or

before it NGT) was responsible for the combined state of affairs consisting of the transport of gas through the iron pipes. The logical outcome of the UT's analysis is that if a company acquires contaminated land and does not immediately rectify the contamination; or if it only mitigates the contamination, then it is denied relief. That is inconsistent with the definition of relevant land remediation in paragraph 4 which expressly includes work for the purpose of "minimising ... or mitigating the effects of, any harm."

20   I do not accept this argument.

21   The principle that "the polluter pays" is a broad general statement of policy. It is no substitute for the words of the Finance Act itself. Words and passages in a statute derive their meaning from their context. A phrase or passage must be read in the context of the section as a whole and in the wider context of a relevant group of sections. Other provisions in a statute and the statute as a whole may provide the relevant context. They are the words which Parliament has chosen to enact as an expression of the purpose of the legislation and are therefore the primary source by which meaning is ascertained: *R. (Project for the Registration of Children as British Citizens) v Secretary of State for the Home Department* [2022] UKSC 3; [2022] 2 W.L.R. 343 at [29] . Thus statutory interpretation is an exercise which requires the court to identify the "*meaning borne by the words in question in the particular context*" (*R. v Secretary of State for the Environment Ex p. Spath Holme Ltd* [2001] 2 A.C. 349, 396). An appeal to a purposive interpretation of an enactment is of particular utility where there is no obvious meaning of the words that Parliament has used (*IRC v McGuckian* [1997] 1 W.L.R. 991, 999) but it still requires the court to interpret the language that Parliament has used (*Pollen Estate Trustee Co Ltd v Revenue and Customs Commissioners* [2013] EWCA Civ 753; [2013] 1 W.L.R. 3785 at [24]). In this case, I cannot see that the words that Parliament has used leave room for doubt.

22   Condition (6) is not satisfied if the land is in a contaminated state wholly or partly as a result of any thing done or omitted to be done at any time by the company. Land is in a contaminated state if there is a "possibility of harm". The purpose of land remediation relief is to give relief against tax where there is expenditure on land which "is" in a contaminated state: paragraph 2 (2). That directs attention to the condition of the land at the date when the expenditure is incurred. That land must also have been in a contaminated state at the date when it was acquired: paragraph 12 (1) (b). So one is required to consider the state of the land both at the date of acquisition and at the date when the expenditure was incurred. The use of the words "at any time" in paragraph 12 (4) also mean that it is not correct to concentrate on the moment when the pipes were laid. On the facts found by the FTT the reason why the land was contaminated both at the date of acquisition and at the date when the expenditure was incurred was because gas was being pumped through the iron pipes. The entity responsible for the pumping of gas at the date of acquisition was NGT (which had a relevant connection with NGN) and the entity responsible for pumping gas between the date of acquisition and the date of the expenditure was NGN itself.

23   The iron pipes themselves (whether or not corroded) do not give rise to any harm. The harm (or, more accurately the possibility of harm being caused) arises because NGN, and before it NGT, pumps gas through them. If no gas had been pumped, the land would not have been contaminated. NGN has done that since it acquired the land, and continues to do so; and it is the continuing pumping of the

gas through the pipes that gives rise to the need for the works. The reason why the land "is" contaminated is NGN's continued pumping of the gas. That is an "act" of NGN which gives rise to (or causes) the contamination. I accept that because NGN did not itself lay the iron pipes the contamination is not "wholly" as a result of its acts or omissions. But I cannot escape from the conclusion that it is "partly" the result of its acts or omissions. Even on NGN's argument it is continuing the contamination that existed when it acquired the land. So if one poses Mr Peacock's question: is NGN responsible for the combined state of affairs, namely the combination of iron pipes and the transmission of gas, I consider that the only possible answer is that it is partly responsible for that state of affairs. Mr Peacock also argued that the "thing done" which caused the contamination was the laying of the iron pipes. But that seems to me to be inconsistent with the finding of the FTT that the iron pipes themselves pose no risk to persons or property; instead it is the presence of gas within those pipes that does so.

24   The facts of this case are quite different from a factual situation in which land is contaminated at the time of its acquisition and the new owner simply does nothing for a while. That is a situation in which the new owner is passive in the face of existing contamination, as opposed to a situation where the new owner actively perpetuates the contamination. One example canvassed during argument was a petrol filling station from which hydrocarbons had been leaking into the ground. If it were acquired by a developer who wished to use it for, say, housing, the land would have been acquired in a contaminated state, for which the developer would not have been responsible. Mr Peacock argued that if the developer did not immediately remedy the contamination, but undertook a programme of investigation while considering what to do, it might be said against him that his omission to act was partly responsible for the continuing contamination. That example would, I think, call for a purposive interpretation of the word "omission" in paragraph 12 (4). In that context it would, I think, bear the first of the meanings given to it in the Oxford English Dictionary, namely:

> "The non-performance or neglect of an action which one has a moral duty or legal obligation to perform."

25   The same would be true even if during the period of investigation hydrocarbons under the land migrated into the aquifers. In neither case would the developer have caused the contamination. If, on the other hand, the petrol filling station were acquired by an oil company which continued to store hydrocarbons which leaked onto the land, there would then be a causal connection between the acts of the land owner and the contamination.

26   In addition, I do not consider that an appeal to the principle that "the polluter pays" is of any real help to NGN. On the findings of the FTT it is not unfair to describe NGN as the polluter, since the contamination would not exist but for its pumping the gas.

27   Mr Peacock made the fair point that on this interpretation a company in the position of NGN, that is to say a gas transporter, could never claim the enhanced deduction. That may well be right, but that is because NGN continued to pump gas through the pipes. Had it ceased to pump the gas, then the likelihood is that at the time when the expenditure was incurred it would not have been possible to say that the land "is" contaminated, as required by paragraph 2 (2).

28   In short, I agree with the conclusion of the UT at [43]:

"We quite accept that imperfect or partial land remediation is capable of attracting relief. However, we think it is a quite different issue from that which confronts us. The question before us is whether para 12(4) is engaged in NGN's factual situation. Paragraph 12(4) is concerned to ensure that a company should not obtain enhanced relief where the harm or risk of harm results, wholly or partly, from the actions of the company or a person with a relevant connection. In this case, NGN is seeking enhanced relief for expenditure incurred on remedying a 'harm' that results quite clearly in part from its activity, and the activity of NGT before it, of distributing gas. NGT is entitled to an ordinary trading deduction for that expenditure. However, both the policy behind the legislation and the clear words of para 12(4) disqualify it from entitlement to the enhanced deduction. There is no anomaly in a company having no responsibility for the contaminated state of land obtaining enhanced relief for imperfect remediation, while a company which had at least partial responsibility for the contamination obtains no such enhanced relief."

29   Because, in my judgment, NGN fails to satisfy Condition (6), the appeal fails. That conclusion is enough to dispose of the appeal. Anything else I say would be *obiter* and would not bind any subsequent tribunal. As Mummery LJ said in *Housden v Conservators of Wimbledon and Putney Commons* [2008] EWCA Civ 200; [2008] 1 W.L.R. 1172 at [31]:

"In general, it is unwise to deliver judgments on points that do not have to be decided. There is no point in cluttering up the law reports with *obiter dicta*, which could, in some cases, embarrass a court having to decide the issue later on."

Condition 4

30   The FTT held that the expenditure did not qualify because whether it was spent on lining an iron pipe with HDPE or was spent on replacing an iron pipe with an HDPE pipe, the expenditure was incurred in order to improve a chattel, rather than being expenditure on land. The UT did not find it necessary to deal with Condition 4 although they did make "some brief remarks" about it. Their discussion proceeded on the basis that the pipes remained chattels. They considered that although the (assumed) fact that the pipes remained chattels did not rule out the possibility of the expenditure being qualifying expenditure, the expenditure had to have "some real world" connection with land. The expenditure in this case was incurred with a view to providing NGN with safe, durable pipes which it could use in its business of transporting gas. Consequently, the requisite connection with land was not present. Since satisfaction or otherwise of Condition 4 is not relevant either to the appeal before the UT or the appeal to this court, and I have some doubt whether the basis of the discussion is correct, I prefer not to express a view about it. I should not be taken as endorsing the reasoning of the UT on this point.

31   NGN also applied to adduce fresh evidence on this point; but because I do not need to deal with the substantive point, I do not need to deal with that either.

Condition 3

32   For the same reason I prefer not to express a view about Condition 3, especially since we do not have the considered views of the UT on that issue, although my impression is that the reasoning of the FTT on this point is persuasive.

Result

33   I would dismiss the appeal.

LORD JUSTICE BAKER:

34   I agree.

LORD JUSTICE DINGEMANS:

35   I also agree.

R. (ON THE APPLICATION OF NEW EARTH SOLUTIONS (WEST) LTD) v ENVIRONMENT AGENCY

Queen's Bench Division (Administrative Court)

Thornton J: 19 July 2022

[2022] EWHC 1883 (Admin); [2023] Env. L.R. 7

⚖ Environment Agency; Hazardous waste; Recycling; Retained EU legislation; Statutory interpretation; Trans-frontier waste shipments; Waste disposal

H1 *Waste management—hazardous waste—transfrontier shipment of waste—Regulation 1013/2006—Directive 2008/98 Annex I and II—Transfrontier Shipment of Waste Regulations 2007/1711—waste disposal operation—waste recovery operation— definition of waste disposal or recovery operation—whether export of waste from thermal processes was for the purposes of waste recovery or disposal*

H2   The Claimant NES was a company that stored and processed hazardous waste described as 'Air Pollution Control Residue' (APCr) or fly-ash, prior to export to Norway or Germany. The APCr was produced following the removal of contaminants from gases produced in thermal processes. The processing and storage of the APCr was controlled under an environmental permit issued by the Defendant, EA. NES proposed exporting the APCr to Norway where it would be mixed with a separate waste stream from titanium works. The mixing of the wases reduced the alkalinity of the APCr and the acidity of the waste from the titanium works. The resultant sludge mixture would then be disposed of by way of landfill.

H3   NES applied for consent to export the APCr under the relevant controls laid down in relevant European legislation, Directive 2008/98, Regulation 1013/2006 and the Transfrontier Shipment of Waste Regulations 2007. Under the notification of export, NES specified that the purpose of the export was for waste recovery. EA initially granted consent for the export, then subsequently withdrew that consent on the basis that the APCr was being exported for the purposes of a waste disposal operation. In doing so, EA identified the specific operation described in Annex I of the Directive, namely 'physico-chemical treatment not specified elsewhere in the Annex which results in final compounds or mixtures which are discarded by means of the operations numbered in D1-D12'.

H4   NES applied for judicial review of that decision to withdraw consent for the export of the APCr to Norway arguing:

(1)   The EA had incorrectly taken into account the mixture with, and treatment of, the titanium waste and the subsequent disposal of the residual sludge to landfill in determining whether the APCr was subject to a recovery operation. Following the decision in *SITA EcoService Nederland BV (formerly Verol*

Recycling Limburg BV) v Minister van Volkshuisvesting, Ruimtelijke Ordening en Milieubeheer (C-116/01) EU:C:2003:193 (*SITA*), it was argued that the EA should have focused on the initial mixture stage alone rather than the process as a whole.

(2) The EA had been incorrect to focus on the lists of operations listed in the annexes to the Directive. The correct approach would have been to address the principal objective of the operations concerned, including whether the waste was serving a useful purpose by replacing raw materials in accordance with the definition of waste recovery.

H5   **Held,** in refusing the application:

H6   (1) The decision in *SITA* concerned a composite operation which could not be accurately described as falling within any of the listed operations in the annexes to the Directive. Further, in *United Utilities Water Plc v Environment Agency* [2007] UKHL 41, the House of Lords had rejected the application of the principle in *SITA* to a D9 operation, having analysed a D9 disposal operation as generically different from D1–D7 and D10–D12 operations in the list. A D9 disposal operation was characterised, not only in terms of its intermediate treatment activity, but by looking to the eventual destination of the waste when it was discarded.

H7   (2) The lists in the annexes represented the most common disposal and recovery operations in practice. It was only if the waste operation in question did not appear on the lists that the decision-maker had to classify it as a disposal or recovery operation, on a case-by-case basis, in light of the objectives and definitions in the Directive, which would include the definition of "recovery" in art.3(15) of the Directive. Cases of genuine uncertainty might include operations with elements of both recovery and disposal, in which case it might become necessary to look for the "principal result" in the case of recovery or the "secondary consequence" in the case of disposal. The EA, when coming to a view on the correct classification of the waste operations, had been required and entitled to take account of the lists of recovery and disposal operations in the annexes. This included looking across the entirety of the waste operation. Accordingly, there had been no error of law in the EA's assessment of the operation as a D9 disposal operation.

H8   (3) The EA had reached the conclusion that the waste operations fell squarely within the listed D9 operations, there had been no need to assess the operations by reference to the definition of "recovery" in art.3(15). The EA had, however, made a second decision that the principal result of the operations was disposal, not recovery. The EA had an expertise which made any decision as to whether a process was a waste disposal or recovery operation a matter of judgement and evaluation to which a court would afford a margin of appreciation. The EA had been entitled to exercise its judgement in that regard and had explained the basis for doing so. There were rational and evidence-based grounds for its view and there had been no error of law in the exercise of its judgement.

H9 **Cases referred to:**

Abfall Service AG (ASA) v Bundesminister fur Umwelt, Jugend und Familie (C-6/00) EU:C:2002:121; [2002] Q.B. 1073; [2002] 1 C.M.L.R. 53
Commission v Luxembourg (C-458/00) EU:C:2003:94
Edilizia Mastrodonato (C-147/15) EU:C:2016:292
R. (on the application of Mott) v Environment Agency [2016] EWCA Civ 564; [2016] 1 W.L.R. 4338; [2017] Env. L.R. 1

R. (on the application of Spurrier) v Secretary of State for Transport [2019] EWHC 1070 (Admin); [2020] P.T.S.R. 240; [2019] J.P.L. 1163

R. (on the application of Tarmac Aggregates Ltd) (formerly Lafarge Aggregates Ltd) v Secretary of State for Environment, Food and Rural Affairs [2015] EWCA Civ 1149; [2016] P.T.S.R. 491; [2016] Env. L.R. 15

R. v Director General of Telecommunications Ex p. Cellcom Ltd [1999] E.C.C. 314; [1999] Masons C.L.R. 41; [1999] C.O.D. 105 QBD

SITA EcoService Nederland BV (formerly Verol Recycling Limburg BV) v Minister van Volkshuisvesting, Ruimtelijke Ordening en Milieubeheer (C-116/01) EU:C:2003:193; [2004] Q.B. 262; [2003] 2 C.M.L.R. 4

United Utilities Water Plc v Environment Agency [2007] UKHL 41; [2007] 1 W.L.R. 2707; [2008] J.P.L. 590

H10 **Legislation referred to:**
Regulation 259/93 (Waste Shipments into and out of the EC) [1993] OJ L30/1
Directive 96/61 (Integrated Pollution Prevention and Control) [1996] OJ L257/26
Pollution Prevention and Control (England and Wales) Regulations 2000 (SI 2000/1973) Sch.1(c)(ii)
Regulation 1013/2006 (Transboundary Waste Shipments) [2006] OJ L190/1 art.2
Transfrontier Shipment of Waste Regulations 2007 (SI 2007/1711)
Directive 2008/98 (Waste Framework) [2008] OJ L312/3 art.3(15) and (19), Annexes I and II
Directive 2010/75 (Industrial Emissions) [2010] OJ L334/17
Directive 2018/851 (Waste) [2018] OJ L150/109
International Waste Shipments (Amendment) (EU Exit) Regulations 2019 (SI 2019/590)

H11 *C. Badger* (instructed by Mills & Reeve) appeared on behalf of the Claimant.
N. Westaway (instructed by the Environment Agency) appeared on behalf of the Defendant.

JUDGMENT

THE HON. MRS JUSTICE THORNTON:

Introduction

1   The Claimant, New Earth Solutions (West) Ltd, brings a claim for judicial review of the decision by the Defendant, the Environment Agency, to withdraw consent for the export of hazardous waste described as 'Air Pollution Control Residue' ("APCr"), also referred to as 'fly ash', to Norway. The decision was taken pursuant to the control regime for transfrontier shipment of waste laid down in EU Regulation 1013/2006 on shipments of waste and the domestic Transfrontier Shipment of Waste Regulations (2007/1711). The Environment Agency is the competent authority for England under the regime.

2   When notifying the Environment Agency of its proposal to export the APCr to Norway, New Earth Solutions specified the purpose of the shipment as waste recovery. The Agency initially granted consent but subsequently withdrew it on

the basis that the purpose of the shipment was waste disposal. In contrast, the Norwegian Environment Agency, the competent authority for the country of destination, consented to the import of the waste on the basis it was a shipment for recovery.

3   The core issue between the parties is the correct categorisation of the waste operations, which take place in Norway, as a disposal or recovery operation.

4   The Environment Agency withdrew consent on the basis of two related assessments, both of which are challenged in this claim. The first is that the waste operations in Norway are properly classed as a D9 disposal operation under Annex I of the Waste Framework Directive (2008/98 EC), namely 'physico-chemical treatment not specified elsewhere in this Annex which results in final compounds or mixtures which are discarded by means of any of the operations numbered D1 to D12 (e.g., evaporation, drying, calcination, etc.).' The second, and related, decision was that the principal purpose of the waste operations is waste disposal, not recovery.

5   New Earth Solutions contends that the waste operations comprise three separate and distinct waste processes: i) substitution of APCr for virgin limestone; ii) 'neutralisation' of sulphuric acid by mixing it (in colloquial terms) with the APCr; and iii) deposit of the neutralised mixture or treatment residue into landfill. It advances two grounds of challenge:

   a.   The Agency acted unlawfully in failing to classify the act of substitution of APCr for the raw material, pulverised limestone, as a recovery operation (Ground 1).
   b.   In the alternative, the Agency wrongly took into account the treatment of the sulphuric acid and subsequent disposal of the treatment residue in determining whether or not the substitution of APCr for pulverised limestone is, or is not, a recovery operation (Ground 2).

Factual Background

The parties

6   The Claimant is New Earth Solutions (West) Ltd ("New Earth Solutions"), a company which has developed and built a plant in Boston, Lincolnshire to collect and store APCr prior to export to Norway or Germany. New Earth Solutions holds an environmental permit, granted by the Agency, for the repackaging and temporary storage of hazardous waste that allows the acceptance of up to 100,000 tonnes of APCr per year.

7   The Defendant is the Environment Agency ("the Agency"), the environmental regulator and the competent authority for England, in this case, the country of dispatch, under the transfrontier shipment of waste regime.

8   The First Interested Party is NorskAv fall Shandtering AS (NOAH), the owner of the island of Langøya, situated in the Holmestrand Fjord and belonging to the Homestrand municipality of Vestfold and Telemark in Norway. The island is comprised of limestone. It was, for centuries, subject to quarrying including modern industrial quarrying of limestone for use in the cement industry starting in 1899. Quarrying ended in 1985 and the large craters created by the operations were later used for the deposit of hazardous and ordinary waste. In 1993, the island was

acquired by NOAH, today owned by Gjelsten Holding. The APCr was to have been exported to the island.

9   The Second Interested Party is the Norwegian Environment Agency and the competent authority for Norway, the country of destination under the transfrontier shipment of waste regime. The Norwegian Environment Agency consented to the import of the waste on the basis it was a shipment for recovery.

APCr and how it is produced

10   Air Pollution Control residue (APCr) is the waste generated after contaminants are removed from gases produced in thermal processes, typically the combustion of municipal waste. Lime is used to 'clean' the gases (i.e., to remove the contaminants) before they are emitted to the atmosphere. APCr comprises predominantly lime and is strongly alkaline. APCr is a hazardous waste.

Description of waste treatment process(es) in Langøya Norway

11   Pigment manufacture at a titanium plant local to the island of Langøya generates an industrial acid waste stream. The acid waste is a corrosive liquid and comprises predominantly sulphuric acid with metal contaminants in solution. Historically, the acid was deposited into a local river, causing significant harm to local marine life before the practice was banned.

12   As a liquid and corrosive waste, sulphuric acid does not meet the waste acceptance criteria for deposit to land. Historically, the acid waste was treated with virgin limestone. This treatment process resulted in neutralisation of the liquid acid waste together with associated reactions which resulted in a reduction in the solubility and mobility of the metal and other contaminants, enabling the sludge generated to meet the waste acceptance criteria, so as to be suitable for deposit to land.

13   Instead of virgin limestone, the waste acid is now mixed with APCr, reducing the alkalinity of the APCr and reducing the acidity of the sulphuric acid, producing a treated sludge with a high calcium sulphate content. The toxic metals from both waste streams remain in the treatment residue but become less soluble as a result of forming metal sulphate compounds and the dioxins bound to the activated carbon are encapsulated by the sulphate compounds.

14   The sludge generated is then pumped into the Langøya quarry below sea level and the excess water drained off, to enable the waste to harden.

Chronology of decision making

15   On 23 December 2020, New Earth Solutions notified the Agency of its proposal to export 100,000 tonnes of APCr to Norway. The purpose of the shipment was said to be waste recovery with the waste operation specified as 'recycling/reclamation of other inorganic materials' (R5 in Annex II of the Waste Framework Directive) and the technology to be employed was described as neutralisation. The reason for export was said to be that 'no facilities exist for this material in the UK'.

16   On 22 February 2021, the Norwegian Environment Agency consented to the export as an R5 recovery operation. On 24th February 2021, the Environment Agency also consented to the shipment. However, the Agency subsequently received

an email from a Norwegian citizen questioning the Agency's consent and querying whether there were facilities in the UK for the treatment and disposal of APCr. Accordingly, the Agency sought further information from NOAH, the Norwegian Environment Agency and New Earth Solutions.

17   On 10 June 2021, the Agency withdrew consent for the shipment on the basis New Earth Solutions had not supplied sufficient evidence to show that the deposit of the treated APCr in the quarry would meet the definition of a recovery operation and there were facilities for the material in the UK.

18   On 9 July 2021, New Earth Solutions requested an internal review of the Agency's decision. A letter from its solicitors referred to the Agency's 'mistaken impression' that APCr will be used as 'a form of pre-treatment prior to disposal to landfill'. The letter explained that APCr was to be used as a direct substitute for virgin limestone to neutralise sulphuric acid waste. The operation was said to be a recovery operation which is complete at the point that the sulphuric acid waste is treated. The Agency was said to have fallen into legal error in considering the subsequent backfilling of the treatment residue:

> "the fact that the treatment residue that is created is subsequently either backfilled or landfilled by the site operator is not a material part of this recovery operation. It is not necessary for NES to seek consent for the deposit of calcium sulphate in Langoya which is a separate and distinct waste operation conducted by NOAH."

19   The letter from New Earth Solutions was accompanied by a report from an environmental chemist, Leslie Heasman, on the use of APCr as a substitute treatment reagent. Ms Heasman is a Chartered Chemist and fellow of the Royal Society of Chemistry. Her report explained that APCr has been used at the Langøyasite since 1995 to treat the acid waste and to replace the use of virgin limestone. The APCr is used in the same way as the limestone and achieves the same treatment objectives. In her view, the use of APCr as a treatment reagent to substitute for virgin limestone meets the definition of recovery in Article 3(15) of the Waste Framework Directive. It is "*self-evident that the principal result is that the APCr serves a useful purpose as reagent substituting raw materials which would otherwise be used. I consider that the recovery of the APCr for use as a treatment reagent is likely to be categorised as an R5 operation... The APCr is not subject to, nor does it require, any pre-treatment prior to being used in the same way as limestone... The categorisation of the substitution of limestone by APCr should not be conflated with the separate categorisation of the use, or fate, of the treatment residue.*"

20   In the course of its internal review, the Agency sought further information from New Earth Solutions, stating that:

> "The additional information should, as a minimum, demonstrate why the mixing of the APC residue waste with discarded sulphuric acid can meet the criteria for a permanent deposit of waste into land, rather than be pre-treatment prior to disposal in a landfill. The information you have provided so far does not contain enough detail to allow me to fully understand this basis of the appeal." (letter dated 29 July 2021)

21   New Earth Solutions responded by letter dated 17 August 2021, objecting to the Agency's characterisation of matters:

"We would like to make it clear that this is not what our client is asking you to consider and not what it was asking the EA to consent. The operation at NOAH involving the use of air pollution control residues ("APCr") is not a deposit for recovery operation. The recovery operation that our client is asking the EA to consider and consent is simply the recovery of APCr for use as a treatment reagent to substitute the use of a raw material, namely lime, in order to neutralise the sulphuric acid and convert it into an environmentally benign gypsum. We have enclosed a flow diagram which sets out the recovery process for which our client is seeking consent together with details of the subsequent processes employed at Langøya."

22   A flow chart supplied with the letter identifies three stages of the process at NOAH's site. The first stage (Process 1) is shown as substitution, with reference to 'Alkaline treatment reagent. Lime or Air Pollution control residue'. An accompanying note states, "*This is the substitution process that comprises the recovery activity*". Process 2 is described as a treatment process, in particular, 'neutralisation of acid waste' with the accompanying description "*The treatment achieves neutralisation of the pH, the formation of less soluble contaminant compounds, which are precipitated out from solution and the physical and chemical binding of contaminants into the sludge residue*". The 'neutralised treatment residue' is then depicted moving into Process 3 for either recovery or disposal.

The decision under challenge

23   By letter, dated 10 September 2021, the Agency confirmed its decision to withdraw consent for the export on the basis that the proposed waste treatment operation is a disposal activity not a recovery operation. In summary, the reasons given were as follows:

   a.   The initial decision to consent to the shipment was an error on the part of the Agency arising from working arrangements during Covid.
   b.   The treatment of the waste sulphuric acid with APCr does not amount to a recovery operation within the meaning of Article 3(15) of the Waste Framework Directive. APCr is hazardous, as is the sulphuric acid. Whilst the resulting treatment residue is less hazardous than its component parts, it could not be considered benign, as New Earth Solutions had sought to suggest.
   c.   New Earth Solutions' position was contradictory. The company had initially identified two waste operations; neutralisation followed by disposal and proposed that the Agency should only consider the former, not the latter. The company had since then suggested there was a further, and pre-cursory, operation of substitution which was the only operation the Agency could consider in deciding on the classification as disposal or recovery.
   d.   As to substitution, the Agency did not accept "*that the mere decision to substitute one substance with another represents a recovery operation. Instead it is the substitution together with the reaction of APCr with sulphuric acid that forms a waste treatment operation. Annex 1 and II of the WFD appear to reference actual or concrete waste operations such as they occur in practice and not 'in principle' decisions to replace one substance with another.*"

    e. In order to classify the reaction of the APCr waste with the sulphuric acid it was necessary to take account of the wider circumstances and the fate of the high sulphate waste. Any waste treatment operation could either be recovery or disposal. Having an appreciation of the wider treatment was consistent with the WFD. The waste treatment operation is best described as pre-treatment prior to landfill and the D9 disposal code is the most appropriate code. This view aligns with the definition of disposal in the WFD as it recognises the beneficial use of waste in disposal operations as a secondary consequence of the primary treatment operation.

    f. Even if the 'mixing' operation is to be judged strictly in isolation, there is a clear argument to say that this ought to be considered a disposal operation given the continued hazards association with the mixture.

    g. The case of *SITA* relied on by New Earth Solutions concerns an energy from waste operation and is not identical with the facts of the present case.

    h. Any disagreement between the UK and Norwegian competent authorities does not matter (Article 28(3) TFS Regulation).

    i. Accordingly, the treatment of APCr and discarded acid will amount to a disposal operation. In these circumstances the EA was obliged to follow UK policy, pursuant to which, shipments of waste to and from the UK for disposal are prohibited, save for a small number of exceptions which do not apply.

The views of the Norwegian and Swedish competent authorities

24   The Norwegian and Swedish competent authorities hold different views on classification of the waste operation(s) at NOAH's facilities.

25   The Norwegian Environment Agency considers the waste operations to be a recovery operation. It has explained its decision on the basis that NOAH needs to use suitable materials to neutralise and stabilise the sulphuric acid before landfilling. Regardless of whether NOAH obtains access to APCr the acid must be landfilled, but the landfilling cannot take place until the acid is neutralised and stabilised. APCr is highly suitable for neutralising and stabilising the acid. NOAH can use limestone instead of APCr but it is less effective and large quantities of limestone must then be extracted. NOAH's use of APCr replaces the extraction and use of virgin materials (limestone) that would otherwise have been used. The principal result in this case is that the acid is neutralised and stabilised and this use of APCr is to be regarded as a recovery operation.

26   In contrast, the Swedish Environmental Protection Agency has expressed the view that APCr is used in a pre-treatment process (neutralizing and/or stabilizing other wastes) at NOAH's site. This process results in a new hazardous waste, which in turn is placed in a hazardous waste landfill. Although the APCr is useful in the pre-treatment, the treatment in its entirety is aimed for disposal of the waste (landfilling). The treatment should, therefore, be seen as disposal.

The legal framework

Introduction

27   International shipments of waste are strictly controlled by a framework of control
      laid down in the EU Transfrontier Shipment of Waste Regulation (Regulation
      1013/2006 on shipments of waste) ("The TFS Regulation") and the Waste
      Framework Directive (Directive 2008/98/EC, as amended by Directive 2018/851)
      ("the WFD"), the latter which provides the foundation of waste law in the EU. The
      objective of the transfrontier shipment of waste ("TFS") regime is the protection
      of the environment with the effects on international trade being only incidental
      (Recital 1).

28   The TFS Regulation continues to apply as retained EU law. The domestic
      regulations, the Transfrontier Shipment of Waste Regulations 2007 (2007/1711)
      were subject to a number of amendments in connection with the UK's departure
      from the European Union, in particular the International Waste Shipments
      (Amendment) (EU Exit) Regulations 2019/590 making the TFS Regulation operable
      in UK law. The Waste Framework Directive is not retained EU law but is
      incorporated by reference in retained EU law and is the source of many of the
      principles applying in this case. Any decisions of the European Court of Justice
      prior to 31 December 2020 on the interpretation of key concepts found in the Waste
      Framework Directive or the TFS Regulation remain binding on the High Court.

29   The precise procedures and controls on shipments of waste depend on the origin,
      destination and route of the shipment; the type of waste shipped and the type of
      treatment to be applied to the waste at its destination (Article 1 TFS Regulation).
      Control is established via a system of prior notification of shipments of waste to
      competent authorities, enabling them to be properly informed about the proposed
      movement so as to take all necessary measures for the protection of environment
      and human health, including the ability to object to particular shipments of waste
      (Article 9 of the TFS Regulation and Part 5 of the Transfrontier Shipment of Waste
      Regulations 2007).

30   In England, the Agency is the relevant competent authority of dispatch
      (Regulation 6(a) 2007 Regulations). The Agency must comply with the current
      UK Plan for Shipments of Waste published by the Department for Environment,
      Food and Rural Affairs (DEFRA) (Regulations 11A and 15 2007 Regulations)
      which prohibits shipments of waste to and from the UK for disposal save in certain
      exceptional cases, which do not arise in the present case. The Plan implements
      long-standing UK policy of self-sufficiency in the disposal of waste by strictly
      limiting and describing the exceptions under which waste can be shipped to or
      from the UK for disposal. Other countries in Europe do not have the same export
      policy as the UK and wastes can be exported from those countries for disposal.

31   For present purposes, the main relevant features of the TFS regime are set out
      below.

Distinction between waste shipped for recovery or for disposal

32   The distinction between the disposal and recovery of waste is of central
      importance in EU law on waste.

33   Article 4 of the Waste Framework Directive sets down a five-step waste
      hierarchy, in priority order, for waste legislation and policy as follows: (a) waste

prevention; (b) preparing for re-use; (c) recycling; (d) other recovery, e.g., energy recovery; and (e) disposal. In this hierarchy, disposal is in last place, being the worst option. Recovery is in fourth place. In principle therefore, recovery is to be preferred over disposal. Recovery serves as a sensible use of waste as the waste replaces other materials which would otherwise have been used to fulfil a particular function. The distinction between recovery and disposal is based on a genuine difference in environmental impact through the substitution of natural resources in the economy and recognising the potential benefits to the environment and human health of using waste as a resource (Recital 19 of the WFD 2008).

34   Two significant policy drivers for waste management include the principle of self-sufficiency, whereby the European community as a whole should become self-sufficient in waste disposal, and the proximity principle whereby waste is disposed of in one of the nearest appropriate installations, in order to ensure a high level of protection for the environment and public health. Both principles militate against the movement of waste for disposal across borders (Article 16 of the WFD). The preamble to the TFS Regulation also notes that shipments of hazardous waste must be reduced to a minimum, a manifestation of the policy of self-sufficiency (Recital 8).

35   In similar vein, the EU TFS Regulation draws a clear and fundamental distinction between shipments of waste destined for disposal operations and those destined for recovery operations. Shipments of waste for disposal are actively discouraged and, subject to the imposition of 'optimum supervision and control' (see Recitals 14 and 20). In contrast, shipments of certain types of waste destined for recovery operations are subject to a 'minimum level of supervision and control' (Recital 15). The principles of proximity and sufficiency do not apply to waste for recovery so the waste can move freely between member states (see reference in *SITA EcoService Nederland BV (formerly Verol Recycling Limburg BV) v Minister van Volkshuisvesting, Ruimtelijke Ordening en Milieubeheer* (C-116/01) ("*SITA*") at §25).

Definitions of recovery and disposal and lists of common operations

36   'Disposal' is defined in Article 2(4) of the TFS Regulation by cross-reference to Article 3(19) WFD, which provides as follows:

> "'disposal' means any operation which is not recovery even where the operation has as a secondary consequence the reclamation of substances or energy. Annex I sets out a non-exhaustive list of disposal operations."

37   'Recovery' is defined in Article 2(6) of the TFS Regulation, also by cross-reference to the WFD, (Article 3(15)), which provides as follows:

> "'recovery' means any operation the principal result of which is waste serving a useful purpose by replacing other materials which would otherwise have been used to fulfil a particular function, or waste being prepared to fulfil that function, in the plant or in the wider economy. Annex II sets out a non-exhaustive list of recovery operations."

38   Both definitions refer to a non-exhaustive list of the relevant operations. Annex 1 sets out a list of 15 disposal operations, including: D1 (deposit into landfill); D2 (land treatment); D3 (deep injection); D4 (surface impoundment); D5 (specially

engineered landfill); D6 (release into water body); D8 (biological treatment not specified elsewhere in this Annex which results in final compounds or mixtures which are discarded by means of any of the operations in D1-D12); D9 (physico-chemical treatment not specified elsewhere in this Annex which results in final compounds or mixtures which are discarded by means of any of the operations numbered D1- D12); D10 (incineration on land); and D15 (storage pending any of the operations numbered D1 to D14). Annex II sets out a list of recovery operations including: R1 (use principally as a fuel or other means to generate energy); R3 (recycling/reclamation of organic substances); R5 (recycling/reclamation of other inorganic materials) and R11 (use of waste obtained from any of the operations numbered R1 to R10).

39   The European Commission's guidance explains the key distinction between recovery and disposal operations in colloquial terms, as follows:

> "In a nutshell, disposal operations primarily result from waste management operations based on getting rid of waste, whereas the principal result of a recovery operation is 'waste serving a useful purpose by replacing other materials which would otherwise have been used to fulfil a particular function or waste being prepared to fulfil that function in the plant or the wider economy.'"

40   In a decision of the House of Lords in *United Utilities Water Plc v Environment Agency* [2007] UKHL 41, Lord Walker analysed the distinction as follows, at §15:

> "But before exploring their intricacies I should draw attention to the very important distinction which Community environmental law makes between disposal and recovery. Disposal means, in colloquial terms, getting rid of rubbish as something worthless typically by landfill or by incineration. Recovery means making use of it typically by recycling it in one way or another. The terms in the French text of the Framework Directive (elimination and valorisation) bring out the distinction more vividly. The clear policy of the Framework Directive (since its amendment in 1991) has been to prefer recovery to disposal."

The significance of the correct classification of a shipment of waste

41   Given the significance of the distinction between recovery and disposal and the variation in controls over such shipments, the correct classification of a waste operation as disposal or recovery is important. An incorrect categorisation is grounds for a competent authority to object to a shipment. One of the aims of the TFS Regulation, which is to render shipments of waste for recovery easier than shipments of waste for disposal by laying down less restrictive rules for the former type of shipment, would be jeopardised if the classification of the purpose of those shipments were not scrutinised. A single operation may not be classified simultaneously as both a disposal and a recovery operation. To do so would put at risk the coherence and effectiveness of the legislation (*Abfall Service AG (ASA) v Bundesminister fur Umwelt, Jugend und Familie* (C-6/00) [2002] 1 C.M.L.R. 53 ("*Abfall*") at §63).

A system of dual control

42   Prior notice of a shipment of waste must be provided to the competent authorities of dispatch and destination, via a notification document, which must include prescribed information laid down in Annex II of the TFS Regulation, including the purpose of the shipment (as either disposal or recovery) and:

> "If the waste is destined for an interim recovery or disposal operation similar information regarding all facilities where subsequent interim and non-interim recovery or disposal operations are envisaged shall be indicated." (Paragraph 5 Annex II Part 1)
> "If the waste is destined for recovery: …(d) the costs of recovery and the cost of disposal of the non-recoverable faction." (Paragraph 20 Annex II Part 1)

43   Each designated competent authority in the countries of dispatch and destination must check the classification by the notifier and object to a shipment which is incorrectly classified (Article 12 TFS Regulation).

44   The competent authority of dispatch is entitled to object to a shipment on the basis that it has been incorrectly classified as a recovery operation (Article 12(1)(h)), a provision of the TFS Regulation which was not in the 1993 version of the TFS Regulation. Both competent authorities must consent and neither bind each other (Article 28(3) TFS Regulation).

45   The judgment of each competent authority is determinative for the purposes of the statutory controls. That obligation derives, in particular, from Article 26 of the Regulation, which requires Member States to prohibit and punish any illegal traffic, in particular cases resulting from a knowingly false classification of the purpose of the shipment by the notifier, and from Article 30(1) of the Regulation, which expressly imposes a general duty on Member States to take the requisite measures to ensure that waste is shipped in accordance with the provisions of the Regulation (*Provincia di Bari v Edilizia Mastrodonato Srl* (C-147/15) at §39 – 41).

Submissions

46   On behalf of New Earth Solutions, it is submitted that the waste operations at NOAH's site in Langøya comprise three separate and distinct waste processes: i) substitution of APCr for virgin limestone; ii) 'neutralisation' of the sulphuric acid by mixing it (in colloquial terms), with the APCr; and iii) deposit of the neutralised mixture or treatment residue into landfill.

47   The APCr is recovered for use as a treatment reagent with the sulphuric acid, in substitution for the raw material, limestone, thereby conferring an environmental benefit. There is a process of assessment and selection to ensure the alkalinity content of the APCr is suitable for use in this way. Even after acceptance, the APCr is continually monitored to ensure its ongoing suitability. Substitution is not a theoretical or 'in principle' decision as the Agency suggests. If the alkalinity of the APCr falls below 20% it is not accepted for use and slaked lime is used instead. Whilst the APCr does not need to be treated to perform its reagent role it needs to be suitable. Waste operations do not need to be complicated. As an example, Recital (22) of WFD reads: "*For the purposes of reaching end-of-waste status, a recovery operation may be as simple as the checking of waste to verify that it fulfils the end-of-waste criteria.*" Article 3(16) states that recovery operations can include "checking, cleaning or repairing". Storage can amount to a waste operation.

Substitution is a recovery operation, as defined in Article 3(15) of the WFD. Its principal objective is that the waste serves a useful purpose in replacing other materials (virgin limestone) which would otherwise have had to be used for that purpose. Accordingly, the Agency acted unlawfully in failing to classify the act of substitution of APCr for pulverised limestone as a recovery operation (Ground 1).

48   The second stage of the waste processes, neutralisation, sees the reclamation of APCr (R5) followed by subsequent disposal in landfill as a third and separate stage. The Agency has elided all three stages. Pursuant to the judgment of the European Court in *SITA*, the Agency should only have focused on the first of the three processes (substitution) at the site for the purposes of classifying the operation under the Transfrontier Shipment of Waste regime. The Agency should not concern itself with neutralisation of the sulphuric acid or the subsequent landfill activity, which is regulated by the Norwegian competent authority, and for which New Earth Solutions does not seek consent. The Agency is adopting the same approach to classification in the present case as the UK Government adopted in *SITA*, namely that each of the elements of a waste operation must be taken into account and a conclusion drawn on the basis of the overall contribution of the waste to the process as a whole. However, the European Court in *SITA* rejected this approach. Accordingly, in the alternative to ground 1, the Agency wrongly took into account the treatment of sulphuric acid and subsequent disposal of the treatment residue in determining whether or not the substitution of APCr for pulverised limestone is, or is not, a recovery operation (Ground 2).

49   The lists of recovery and disposal operations in the Annexes to the WFD should not be the primary focus in considering the classification of a waste operation. The lists may be helpful in clear cut cases, but their breadth and consequent substantial leeway for interpretation means they are less helpful in cases of ambiguity. Any conclusion that an operation is a 'disposal' operation must first consider the correct definition of 'recovery' in Article 3(15). The primary focus should therefore be on the principal objective of that operation. There is no indication in this regard that the Agency applied its mind to the appropriate and legally correct definition of 'recovery' in Article 3(15) of the Directive. The 'principal result' of an operation should be considered from the perspective of the waste operator in Norway and the issue of whether a particular operation is 'recovery' or 'disposal' is an issue of law, to be determined by the Court. It is not a question of the reasonableness of the Agency's exercise of judgment.

50   On behalf of the Agency, it is submitted that the waste operations in Norway are correctly characterised as a D9 disposal operation (Annex 1 WFD Directive) and/or the main objective of the operations was the disposal of co-treated waste into landfill. The Agency was not confined to considering the selection of APCr in substitution for non-waste materials (Ground 1) or, alternatively, to the use of APCr as a neutralising reagent (Ground 2), in both cases ignoring the material fact that the resulting material is sent to landfill. The statutory terminology does not support New Earth's interpretation which artificially disregards the underlying reason for carrying out the neutralisation operation (to ensure the waste is suitable for disposal to landfill). The treatment of waste acids for landfill does not become a recovery operation simply because it is co-treated with another waste stream, APCr, that also requires treatment prior to landfill. This would have potentially wider ramifications and would undermine the waste hierarchy by treating disposal to landfill in the same way as genuine recovery operations. The Agency's

interpretation is consistent with the statutory language, the statutory purpose and the approach taken in other cases.

51   The case of *SITA* is confined to its particular facts which do not arise in the present case. The lists of recovery and disposal operations are a necessary and appropriate focus. They remain an important reference point, despite the introduction of the definition of recovery in Article 3(15) of the Directive, which New Earth Solutions is obliged to disregard in order to sustain its challenge. Only in cases of genuine uncertainty or overlap will additional criteria need to be brought into play to assist in the task of interpreting the lists in Annexes I and II and in categorising the operations in any particular case as recovery or disposal. Consideration of the 'principal result' of waste treatment, for the purposes of the application of the definition of a recovery operation is prima facie a matter of judgment for the expert regulator, subject to any obvious errors of law in the exercise of its judgment in this regard. As the competent authority of dispatch, the Agency was entitled to come to its own view on the matter and the domestic Court in a judicial review should give weight to its view.

Discussion

Introduction

52   The core issue between the parties is the correct classification of the waste operations at the Langøya site in Norway as either disposal or recovery operations.

53   The two grounds of challenge advanced by New Earth Solutions overlap to a considerable extent. Both grounds rely on the application of the judgment of the European Court in *SITA*.

54   In coming to its contrary view that the operations are disposal operations, the Agency made two related decisions. First, it identified the operations as a D9 disposal operation, listed in Annex II of the Waste Framework Directive, namely 'physico-chemical treatment not specified elsewhere in this Annex which results in final compounds or mixtures which are discarded by means of any of the operations numbered D1 to D12 (e.g., evaporation, drying, calcination, etc.)'. Its second and related decision was to identify the principal purpose of the waste operation as disposal, not recovery:

> "… On consideration … we believe that rather than recovery, the primary purpose of the proposed treatment operation is to safely dispose of the acid by way of neutralisation, using APCr … in our view this does not amount to "recovery" within the meaning of the WFD…" (decision letter of 10 September 2021)

55   As referenced in the last sentence of the extract cited above from the decision letter, the Agency's conclusion in this regard is material because the definition of recovery in the WFD is '*any operation the principal result of which* is waste serving a useful purpose by replacing other materials' (Article 3(15) WFD). The Agency contends that its assessment of the primary purpose of the treatment constitutes the application of judgment as competent authority under the TFS regime, to which this Court should afford deference.

56   In response, New Earth Solutions submits that, in considering the classification of the operations, the Agency should have not treated the lists of recovery and

disposal operations in the Annexes to the WFD as its primary focus given the advent of the definition of recovery in Article 3(15) of the WFD. Further, the classification of the shipment of waste is a question of law for the Court and not a matter for the exercise of the Agency's judgment.

57   Accordingly, the following issues arise for consideration by the Court:

    a. The application of *SITA*.
    b. The interpretation and application of D9 of Annex I of the WFD.
    c. The interrelationship between the lists of recovery and disposal operations in the Annex's and the definition of recovery in Article 3(15) WFD.
    d. The role of the exercise of judgment by the Agency in its assessment of the 'principal result' of the waste operations.
    e. Whether substitution of APCr for virgin limestone is a distinct waste (recovery) operation in its own right.

SITA and United Utilities v Environment Agency

58   New Earth Solutions places heavy reliance on *SITA* in support of its case that the Agency should only have taken account of the substitution of APCr for limestone in classifying the purpose of the shipment.

59   The claimant in *SITA* was a company in the Netherlands, which notified the relevant competent authority of its intention to ship two consignments of waste to be used in the cement industry in Belgium in a combined treatment process consisting of two stages. The first stage was combustion of the waste as fuel in cement kilns and the second stage was use of the ash residue as a raw material in the production of clinker which would be milled to make cement. Nothing would remain of the waste at the end of the process. The claimant described the consignment as waste intended for recovery, in particular, item R1 (use principally as a fuel or other means to generate energy) and R3/R5 (recycling/reclamation of organic/nonorganic substances). The competent authority rejected the use of the residue for the production of clinker as an R3/R5 recovery operation but accepted the purpose of the shipment could be considered a recovery operation, in particular an R1 operation (use principally as a fuel), but it should be subject to certain conditions. The claimant objected to the imposition of the proposed conditions.

60   In its judgment, the European Court introduced the issue of present relevance as follows:

> "By its first question the national court essentially asks whether, in the case where a waste treatment process includes several distinct stages, its classification as a disposal operation or recovery operation within the meaning of the [WFD] Directive must, for the purpose of implementing the TFS Regulation, be considered comprehensively, as constituting a single operation, or rather by examining each of the stages separately, as distinct operations." (§34)

61   The Court went on to hold that, for the purposes of the WFD and TFS Regulation, a waste treatment process comprising several distinct stages was to be classified as either a disposal or recovery operation by reference to the first operation that the waste was to undergo after shipment only and not to the process as a whole (§49).

62   New Earth Solutions relies, in particular, on the following paragraphs of the judgment which, it submits, set down generally applicable criteria for the process of classification for the purposes of consent to export under the TFS regime:

> "41. Nevertheless, while a single operation must be given a single classification in light of the distinction between a recovery operation and a disposal operation, a waste treatment process can in practice include several successive stages of recovery or disposal.
>
> 42. It follows from the Directive and the Regulation that, in such a case, the treatment process as a whole is not to be assessed as a single operation, but each phase must be classified separately for the purpose of implementing the Regulation when it constitutes a distinct operation in itself.
>
> 43. As is clear from the sixth indent of Article 6(5) and the fifth indent of Article 7(4) of the Regulation, an operation classified as waste recovery may be followed by a disposal operation of the non-recoverable fraction of that waste. In such a case, the classification of the first operation as a recovery operation is not affected by the fact that it is followed by an operation to dispose of the residual waste.
>
> 44. Moreover, point R11 of Annex IIB to the Directive makes clear that the use of residual waste obtained from any of the operations listed in that annex, in points R1 to R10, itself constitutes a recovery operation distinct from the recovery operation which precedes it. In accordance with the distinction thus laid down in the Annex, it must therefore be determined whether an operation falls under operations. R1 to R10 in that annex independently, without taking into account the possible subsequent use of the residual wastes obtained from any of those operations a use of which is itself covered by a separate operation.
>
> 45. As the Commission rightly points out, and as made clear by the Advocate General in paragraph 51 of his Opinion, when the question of classification of a waste treatment operation arises for the purpose of implementing the Regulation, only the classification of the first operation which that waste must undergo subsequent to its shipment is relevant in determining the purpose of that shipment.
>
> 46. When the Regulation refers to the shipment of waste and distinguishes between shipments of waste destined for disposal and those destined for recovery, it is directed at the treatment which that waste must undergo when it arrives at its destination, not the possible subsequent processing of waste which has been thus treated or its residues. Moreover, that processing may take place in a different treatment plant and following further shipment."

63   The waste operations in play in SITA were R1, D10, R3, R5 and R11, in particular R1. It is apparent from paragraph 5 of the Court's judgment that it had its mind on the relevant list entries:

> "5 Annex IIA, headed "Disposal operations", states "… D10 Incineration on land…"
>
> 6 Annex IIB, headed "Recovery operations", states
>
> "…R1 Use principally as a fuel or other means to generate energy… R3 Recycling/reclamation of organic substances which are not used as solvents

(including composting and other biological transformation processes) … R5 Recycling/reclamation of other inorganic materials…R11 Use of wastes obtained from any of the operations numbered R1 to R10…"".

64   The relevant entries do not include a D9 operation.

65   I accept that paragraphs 41, 42 and 46, relied on by New Earth Solutions, are phrased in general terms, at least in the English language version of the judgment (the Court was not shown other language versions). However, paragraph 43 refers to the sixth indent of Article 6(5) and the fifth indent of Article 7(4) of the predecessor TFS Regulation (Regulation 259/1993). The former refers to "*the planned method of disposal for the residual waste after recycling has taken place*". The latter provides that a competent authority may object to a shipment "*if the costs of the disposal of the non-recoverable fraction do not justify the recovery under economic and environmental considerations*". These references lead the Court to conclude at paragraph 43 that "*an operation classified as waste recovery may be followed by a disposal operation of the non-recoverable fraction of that waste. In such a case*, the classification of the first operation as a recovery operation is not affected by the fact that it is followed by an operation to dispose of the residual waste" (emphasis added).

66   At paragraph 44, the Court draws on R11 in the list of recovery operations, 'use of waste obtained from any of the operations numbered R1 – R10', as indicating that the <u>use</u> of residual waste obtained from operations listed in R1 - R10, itself constitutes a recovery operation distinct from the recovery operation which precedes it. This leads the Court to conclude that "*In accordance with the distinction thus laid down in the Annex, it must therefore be determined whether an operation falls under operations R1 to R10 in that annex independently, without taking into account the possible subsequent use of the residual wastes obtained from any of those operations a use of which is itself covered by a separate operation*".

67   Paragraph 45 of the judgment refers to paragraph 51 of the Advocate General's opinion, which refers, in turn, to a composite waste treatment process which does not fall within any of the listed operations:

"In the case of a composite process which – as in the present case – cannot be accurately described as one of those listed operations, I concur with the Commission that it is the assessment of the first operation in the process which determines whether a shipment of waste intended to be subjected to the process requires notification under the Regulation as waste for disposal or waste for recovery…".

68   It was nonetheless common ground that the waste operations under scrutiny comprised distinct operations:

"By its first question the national court essentially asks whether, in the case where a waste treatment process includes several <u>distinct</u> stages…" (§34) "in the case in the main proceedings it appears from the order for reference that the national court is of the view that the processing which the waste at issue must undergo comprises <u>two distinct operations</u>." (§47)

69   The decision of the House of Lords in *United Utilities Water Plc v Environment Agency* [2007] 1 W.L.R. 2707, is relied on by the Agency to dispute the application of SITA to the present case. *United Utilities* concerned the need for a Pollution

Prevention and Control (PPC) permit, pursuant to the Pollution Prevention and Control Regulations 2000 (2000/1973), for aspects of operations conducted by United Utilities as part of its waste sewerage operations. Although focused on pollution prevention and control rather than the transfrontier shipment of waste regime, the House of Lords was required to consider section 5.3(c)(ii) of Schedule 1 of the PPC Regulations, which provides that a PPC permit is required for the '*disposal of non-hazardous waste ... by... (ii) physico-chemical treatment, not being treatment specified in any paragraph other than paragraph D9 in Annex IIA to [the Framework Directive] which results in final compounds or mixtures which are discarded by means of any of the operations numbered D1-D12 in that Annex.*' Accordingly, the House of Lords considered the D9 listing.

70   Lord Hoffman posed the rhetorical question of why it was not sufficient for the Regulations to simply designate physico-chemical treatment of the waste as an activity requiring a permit before stating that:

> "the answer is that it was necessary to distinguish between such treatment for the purposes of disposal and the same treatment for the purposes of recovery…the exclusion of recovery processes from the permit regime was no doubt part of a policy of encouraging recovery". (§5)

71   In his analysis, Lord Walker distinguished D9 (and D8) operations from other operations listed in the Annexes of the WFD, describing them as 'generically different' from other of the operations. In particular, he acknowledged the necessity of identifying the destination of the waste following its physico-chemcial treatment:

> "19 The purpose underlying section 5.3(c).… and both sides agree, with varying degrees of enthusiasm, that a purposive construction is needed - cannot be understood without looking at the whole of Annex IIA and Annex IIB to the Framework Directive.
>
> …..
>
> 20 Annex IIA contains 15 items, D1 to D15. D1 to D7 and D12 are all types of disposal by landfill or specialised methods akin to landfill. D10 and D11 are incineration (on land or at sea). All these activities are methods by which waste is finally disposed of … <u>D8 and D9, by contrast, are activities of treatment which produces a physical result (a product) which is "discarded by means of any of the operations numbered D1 to D12"</u>. D13, D14 and D15 refer to ancillary activities (blending, repacking, and temporary storage).
>
> 21 …<u>If I am right in supposing that D8 and D9 are generically different from the group of activities consisting of D1 to D7 and D10 to D12</u> (because that group lists activities by which waste is finally disposed of or discarded) …
>
> 26 …<u>it becomes apparent that some activities (D8 and D9) are defined, not only in terms of their physical product, but also in terms of the final destination of that product.… its meaning is to be spelled out, … by looking to the product's eventual destination when it is discarded.</u>" (emphasis added)

72   Moreover, and significantly, Lord Walker specifically rejected the applicability of *SITA* to D8/9 disposal operations:

> "25 The SITA case …. does not seem to me to assist the appellant either. It concerned the shipment of waste glue and other substances from the Netherlands to Belgium for use in the cement industry by two sequential

processes: first burning as fuel in cement kilns, and then production of clinker from the residue for use in cement-making. The Court of Justice's decision that the first operation was decisive for classification purposes turned largely on the inclusion in Annex IIB of head R11 ("use of wastes obtained from any of the operations numbered R1to R10"). <u>There is no comparable provision applicable in this case. On the contrary, the possible interaction between D8 and D9 suggests that intermediate activities are relevant to the definition of "installation".</u>" (emphasis supplied)

73   On the basis of its analysis of the D9 listing, the House of Lords rejected the argument advanced by United Utilities, that a permit was not necessary for a site where domestic sewage and trade effluent was partially treated by biological or physico-chemical treatment before being transported by pipeline to a central site for further treatment prior to some of the final product being disposed or by incineration or landfill. The company had accepted that the central site required a permit but disputed the need for a permit for the separate site where the physico-chemical treatment took place. United Utilities advanced a similar argument before the House of Lords as New Earth Solutions seeks to advance before this Court, namely, to separate out consideration of the treatment of the waste before its final disposal. The House of Lords rejected the submission on the basis of an analysis of the characteristics of a D9 disposal operation.

74   Accordingly, I reach the following conclusions.

75   *SITA* concerned a composite operation which could not be accurately described as falling within any of the listed operations in Annexes 1 and II of the WFD. It was common ground the operations comprised two distinct operations. The R1 operation of burning waste as a fuel in cement kilns was the primary operation followed by the use of the residual fraction of the waste. Paragraphs 41, 42 and 46 of the judgment are phrased in general terms, suggesting support for New Earth Solutions' submission that the case lays down generally applicable criteria for the classification of successive operations for the purposes of the TFS. However, paragraphs 43 – 46 go on to develop the Court's analysis by reference to a composite operation which does not fall within any of the listed operations comprising the disposal of the non-recoverable fraction of waste after a primary operation of recovery. This then is the context in which the Court comes to the conclusion that: "*in such a case*, the classification of the first operation as a recovery operation is not affected by the fact that it is followed by an operation to dispose of the residual waste" (§43) (emphasis added).

76   In *United Utilities*, the House of Lords rejected, in clear terms, the application of the principle in *SITA* to a D9 operation. The Court analysed a D9 operation as generically different from D1- D7 and D10 – D12 operations. A D9 disposal operation is characterised, not only in terms of its intermediate treatment activity, but by looking to the eventual destination of the waste when it is discarded.

The interrelationship between the lists of operations and the definition of recovery

77   New Earth Solutions contends that the Agency should not have made the lists of operations (Annexes I and II WFD) its primary focus in considering the classification of the operations. It should instead have considered the principal objective of the operation, including whether the waste serves a useful purpose by replacing raw materials, as per the definition of recovery.

78   A body of case-law of the European Court of Justice, built up in relation to previous versions of the Directive, established that the lists are intended to represent the most common disposal and recovery operations carried out in practice. They were not however an exhaustive list (§60 *Abfall*). Only where waste could not be brought within one of the operations referred to in the Annexes to the Directive, was there a need for a case-by-case assessment (§64 *Abfall*).

79   The question that arises in the present case is whether, and how, the case law developed under previous versions of the Directive, which did not contain a definition of recovery, should be applied in the context of the introduction of the definition of recovery in Article 3(15) of the 2008 Directive.

80   In *R. (Lafarge Aggregates Ltd) v Secretary of State for Environment, Food and Rural Affairs* [2015] EWCA Civ 1149 ("*Lafarge*"), Lord Justice Sales (as he was then) acknowledged the potential differences between the 2008 Directive and previous versions. The Court noted that the recitals to the 2008 Directive are more extensive than and do not fully correspond with recitals to previous Directives (§6) before going on to state that:

> "10. The previous Directive did not include a general definition equivalent to Article 3(15), but simply set out lists of recovery operations and disposal operations in Parts A and B of Annex II to that Directive. These were treated as mutually exclusive categories, as they are in the Annexes to the WF Directive.
> …
> 12. A body of case-law of the ECJ built up in relation to the previous Directive which gave guidance on this. It is not altogether clear how directly this case-law should be transposed when dealing with the WF Directive."

81   However, *Lafarge* was decided before the decision of the European Court in *Provincia di Bari v Edilizia Mastrodonato Srl* (C-147/15), the latter which was decided after the adoption of the definition of recovery in Article 3(15) WFD Directive. The Court reached the following view as to the role of the lists:

> "37 Article 3(15) of Directive 2008/98 defines, inter alia, the 'recovery' of waste as an operation the principal result of which is that the waste in question serves a useful purpose by replacing other materials which would otherwise have been used to fulfil a particular function…
> 38 Thus, that definition corresponds to the definition developed in the Court's case-law, according to which the essential characteristic of a waste recovery operation is that its principal objective is that the waste serves a useful purpose in replacing other materials which would have had to be used for that purpose, thereby enabling natural resources to be preserved (judgment of 27 February 2002 in *ASA*, C-6/00, EU:C:2002:121, paragraph 69).
> 39 It follows that the main objective of the recovery operation must be the conservation of natural resources. Conversely, if the conservation of natural resources constitutes only a secondary effect of an operation the principal objective of which is the disposal of waste, this cannot affect the classification of that operation as a disposal operation (see, to that effect, judgment of 13 February 2003 in *Commission v Luxembourg*, C-458/00, EU:C:2003:94, paragraph 43).

40 In this regard, it is apparent from Article 3(15) and (19) of Directive 2008/98 that the purpose of Annexes I and II to the directive is to set out the most common disposal and recovery operations, not to provide an exhaustive list of all the disposal and recovery operations covered by the directive.

41 That being said, it must be possible to classify any waste treatment operation as either a 'disposal' or a 'recovery' operation, and, as is apparent from Article 3(19) of Directive 2008/98, a single operation may not be classified at the same time as both a 'disposal' and a 'recovery' operation. Consequently, as is the case in the main proceedings, in a situation where, having regard solely to the terms of the operations in question, a waste treatment operation cannot be brought within one of the operations or categories of operations referred to in Annexes I and II to the directive, such operations must be classified on a case-by-case basis in the light of the objectives and definitions set out in the directive (see, by analogy, judgment of 27 February 2002 in *ASA*, C-6/00, EU:C:2002:121, paragraphs 62 to 64).

42 It is a matter for the referring court, having regard to all the relevant factors of the dispute in the main proceedings, and taking into consideration the objective of protecting the environment pursued by Directive 2008/98, to determine whether the main purpose of the backfilling of the quarry at issue in the main proceedings is to recover waste other than extractive waste intended to be used during this operation."

82   Accordingly, the present position is the same as under previous versions of the Directive. The lists represent the most common disposal and recovery operations in practice. It is only if the waste operation in question does not appear on the list that the decision maker must classify it as disposal or recovery operation, on a case-by-case basis, in light of the objectives and definitions in the directive, which will include the definition of recovery in Article 3(15).

83   Cases of genuine uncertainty may include operations with elements of both recovery and disposal in which case it may become necessary to look for the 'principal result' (in the case of recovery) or the secondary consequence (in the case of disposal).

84   In *Lafarge*, the presenting difficulty for the Court was that the descriptions of items in Annex I and Annex II overlapped. In particular, the backfill operation could be characterised as falling within paragraph D1 in Annex I or within paragraph R10 in Annex II:

> "That drafting technique, however, gives rise to difficult questions of categorisation of operations, since the descriptions of items in Annex I and in Annex II can in certain cases overlap. For example, the use of waste for backfill in the present case could be described as "Deposit into or on to land" (D1) or as falling within R10, as "Land treatment resulting in … ecological improvement"." (§11)

85   Sales LJ concluded this meant that additional criteria were required to assist in the task of interpreting the items in the respective lists and in categorising the particular operations in any particular case as recovery or disposal of waste. This analysis is consistent with the position of the European Court in *Mastrodonato*.

86   There was also a dispute between the parties in this case as to the necessary conditions for an operation to meet the definition of 'recovery' in Article 3(15) of

the WFD. The Agency submitted that recovery is defined as an operation of which 'the principal result' meets two conditions 1) serving a useful purpose and ii) replacing other (non-waste) materials which would otherwise have been met. It relied on the analysis of the Advocate General in *Mastrodonato* in this regard (§53). New Earth Solutions submitted that the essential characteristic of a waste recovery operation is that its principal objective is that the waste serves a useful purpose in replacing other materials which would have had to be used for that purpose. No other benefit is necessary. For the reasons set out below, I am not however persuaded that this issue has a material bearing on the outcome of the case and I do not therefore address the issue further.

87   Accordingly, I reach the conclusion that the list of recovery and disposal operations in Annexes I and II to the WFD directive set out the most common disposal and recovery operations. Where, having had regard solely to the lists, there is genuine uncertainty or overlap such that the waste operation cannot be brought within one of the operations or categories of operations referred to in the lists, then the waste operation(s) must be classified on a case-by-case basis, using additional criteria, in the light of the objectives and definitions set out in the directive, which will include the definition of recovery in Article 3(15) of the WFD. Cases of difficulty will include where operations overlap (as in *Lafarge*) or contain elements of both disposal and recovery, whereby it may become necessary to identify the 'principal result' and/or 'secondary consequence' of the operation.

The legal principles applicable to the review of the Agency's assessment as to the principal result of the waste operations

88   The parties were in dispute as to the role of the exercise of judgment by the Agency in its position as competent authority in coming to the view that the principal purpose of the waste operations was disposal not recovery.

89   The following general principles of judicial review are well established. The scope of judicial review, in terms of both the intensity of the scrutiny and the weight to be given to any primary decision maker's view is acutely sensitive to the regulatory context (*R. (Spurrier) v Secretary of State for Transport* [2019] EWHC 1070 (Admin) at §147). The margin of appreciation afforded by the Court will depend on the circumstances but will be substantial where a decision is highly dependent upon the assessment of a wide variety of complex technical matters by those who are expert in such matters and/or who are assigned to the task of assessment (*R. (Mott) v Environment Agency* [2016] EWCA Civ 564). The Court should be slow to impugn decisions of fact made by an expert and experienced decision-maker (*R. v Director General of Telecommunications Ex p. Cellcom Ltd* [1999] E.C.C. 314 at §26 Lightman J). A court must assess whether a particular issue is a matter of technical or scientific judgment rather than legal analysis. (*Mott*, at §77 Beatson LJ). It is not the role of a court to resolve conflicts of expert evidence, particularly not in favour of a claimant on whom the burden of proof lies.

90   The legislative framework for TFS requires the Agency, as competent authority, to check the proposed classification of a shipment and object to a shipment which is classified incorrectly (Article 12h) TFS Regulation). Article 28 of the TFS Regulation which was also not in the previous version of the Regulation, specifically recognises the potential for the competent authorities of dispatch and destination

to disagree on the classification of the waste treatment operation and provides that in such a case the provisions regarding disposal shall apply. (Article 28(3)). Thus, the statutory regime recognises the exercise of discretion necessarily arising and available to competent authorities in the classification process. It is apparent from the nature of the information required in the notification document that the competent authority is required to form a judgment as to the correct classification of the operation (Paragraph 20 of Annex II, Part 2 (see paragraph 42 above)). Moreover, the Member State of dispatch may have a particular interest in preventing the export of hazardous waste for disposal since such disposal may have serious environmental consequences for the member state of dispatch by virtue of the burden; of ensuring that the waste is disposed of in close proximity and in accordance with the principle of self-sufficiency (Advocate General in *Abfall* at A51).

91   As the national specialist environmental regulator on waste, the Agency has an expertise that is beyond the province of the Court. The approach in *Lafarge*, is illustrative in this context. The case concerned the proper interpretation and application of the concepts of "recovery" and "recovery operations" in Article 3(15) WFD. The Environment Agency decided that the operations proposed by Tarmac/Lafarge did not constitute recovery operations for the purposes of the Waste Framework Directive and its decision was upheld by the Inspector on appeal on the basis of modified reasoning. The Court of Appeal was only prepared to intervene in the Agency's decision making on grounds of irrationality:

> "On the evidence before him and on the basis of findings made by him, the Inspector clearly should have found that the backfill operation to create the lakes and the land bridge at the Quarry site was a legitimate function which would have had to be carried out in any event, whether waste was used or not. All the evidence indicated that Tarmac would indeed be required by the Council to comply with the planning obligation to which it was subject to restore the Quarry site, whether waste was used for that purpose or not. There was no evidence to suggest otherwise. In the circumstances it was irrational for the Inspector to reach any conclusions other than that Tarmac would be required to comply with the planning obligation which it had assumed by accepting the restoration condition."

92   It follows that I accept the Agency's submission that the assessment of the 'principal result' of a waste operation is prima facie a matter of judgment and evaluation for the Agency as the expert regulator, to which the Court must afford a margin of appreciation.

Substitution as a distinct waste operation

93   The parties were in dispute as to whether the process of substitution is a distinct operation in its own right. The issue has the potential to go beyond the present case and beyond the transfrontier shipment of waste regime, to waste regulation as a whole. The Court was not addressed in detail on the definition or scope of 'operation' in EU waste legislation. There was no indication that the parties had undertaken a comprehensive assessment of other potentially relevant legislation or case law. The Court was not addressed in any detail on the wider ramifications said by the Agency to arise from any decision by the Court to the effect that the treatment of

waste acids for landfill becomes a recovery operation due to co-treatment with another waste stream, including what is said to be, the potential undermining of the waste hierarchy.

94   Accordingly, given the issue only becomes of relevance if New Earth Solutions succeeds on the other legal issues raised above, I simply note at this juncture that substitution is not listed as one of the common recovery operations in Annex 1 of the Directive. Further, Articles 11 and 12 of the TFS Regulation entitle a competent authority to object to a shipment of waste destined for disposal or recovery, respectively, if the waste will be treated in a facility *'which is covered by* Directive 96/61/EC *but which does not apply best available techniques, as defined in Article 9(4) of that Directive in compliance with the permit of the facility which does not apply best available techniques.'* (Directive 96/61/EC is now published as the Industrial Emissions Directive 2010/75/EU). The requirement for polluting industry to use Best Available Techniques (BAT) to reduce pollution is a central feature of the pollution prevention and control licencing regime. Using waste instead of raw materials for the treatment of other wastes, for both disposal and recovery, is considered BAT on the basis it is said to be an efficient use of materials and minimises environmental impacts. The relevant EU BAT Conclusions Decision on hazardous waste identifies BAT for the treatment of waste as substituting raw materials for other waste. This is also reflected in relevant DEFRA guidance. On this basis, operators of licenced installations should therefore be substituting waste for raw materials when treating other waste as an aspect of best practice for pollution control. I am inclined to accept the Agency's submission that this may be said to indicate that substitution is regarded as a characteristic of a waste treatment operation rather than a separate recovery operation in its own right.

Application of the law to the facts

95   I turn now to apply the legal principles set out above to the facts of the present case.

96   As the designated competent authority in the country of dispatch, the Agency was required to check the classification of the purpose of the shipment provided by New Earth Solutions and to form its own assessment (Article 12 TFS Regulation). The Agency was entitled to object, as it did, to the proposed shipments on the basis that they had been incorrectly classified as a recovery operation (Article 12(1)(h) TFS Regulation). The fact that the Norwegian Environment Agency takes a different view of the waste treatment operations and assesses the purpose of shipment as a recovery operation is of no consequence in this regard (Article 28(3) TFS Regulation). Similarly, the fact that the Norwegian operator, NOAH, considers the operations to be a recovery operation is not determinative. European Commission guidance makes clear that *"Generally it has to be stressed that just because an operation is given a description by the operator in line with the terminology of the definitions of the WFD this does not automatically make the operation such an operation"*. As the competent authority of the country of dispatch, the Environment Agency was justified in having a particular interest in preventing the export of hazardous waste for disposal on the grounds of the burden on the Agency to ensure that hazardous waste is disposed of in close proximity and in accordance with the principle of self-sufficiency (*Abfall* - Advocate General's opinion at A51).

97   In coming to its view as the correct classification of the waste operations, the Agency was required, and entitled, to take account of the lists of recovery and disposal operations on the basis they represent the most common recovery and disposal operations (*Abfall* and *Provincia di Bari v Edilizia Mastrodonato*).

98   It was common ground that the treatment residue (the neutralised sulphuric acid and APCr) was to be disposed of into landfill at NOAH's site in Norway. The Agency was entitled to look across the entirely of the waste operation, in particular, both the physico-chemical treatment followed by final disposal, to come to its view that the relevant listed operation was a D9 disposal operation. The principle of *SITA* that classification of waste operations for the purposes of transfrontier shipment is by reference to the first operation the waste undergoes has no application to a D9 operation (*SITA* and *United Utilities*). *SITA* concerned a composite operation which could not be accurately described as falling within any of the listed operations, whereas here, the competent authority has assessed the relevant operation as a D9 operation. It was common ground in *SITA* that there were two distinct operations where this is disputed by the competent authority in the present case. Accordingly, I am not persuaded of any error of law in the Agency's assessment of the operations as a D9 disposal operation.

99   On the basis of its view that the waste operations fell squarely within the listed D9 operations there was no need for the Agency to assess the operations by reference to the definition of recovery in Article 3(15) WFD (*Mastrodonato*). Nonetheless, the Agency adopted a belt and braces approach, and it made a second, related, decision that the principal result of the operations was disposal not recovery. It reached the same view as the Swedish Environment Agency that, in short, the APCr is useful in the pre-treatment of the sulphuric acid but the treatment in its entirety is aimed for disposal of the waste (landfilling).

100   The Agency was entitled to exercise its judgment in this regard, and it has explained the basis for doing so in the key decision-making documents, namely the letters of 12 April 2021, 10 June 2021, 1 July 2021 and 10 September 2021, which the Agency says must be read together. From a review of them it is apparent that the Agency made inquiries of the Norwegian Environment Agency, NOAH and New Earth Solutions seeking information about the waste operations in question. The Agency rejected the characterisation of the treatment residue as equivalent to gypsum and a construction material. Its assessment was that whilst the residue from the mixing of the sulphuric acid and APCr might be less hazardous than its component parts, it continued to contain various contaminants, could not be considered benign and should not be confused with products manufactured from gypsum or the mineral itself. The Norwegian Environment Agency and NOAH had confirmed that the objective of the operations was landfilling ('basically to fill in the hole in the ground that the quarry left behind and rehabilitate the landscape and infill in the empty quarries at Langøya' (email from the Norwegian Environment Agency)). The Agency explained that it generally regards the addition of APCr to sulphuric acid to reduce the leachability of metals as pre-treatment prior to landfill, a position it has taken in relation to other requests for shipments of APCr.

101   In its submissions to the Court, the Agency further explained that its assessment accords with DEFRA's 2011 *Guidance on applying the waste hierarchy to hazardous waste*, which addresses the treatment of gas treatment residues (including APCr), some of which may contain dioxins and heavy metals. The processing of the waste stream is said to be important for environmental protection. For landfills

the guidance states that the waste is likely to require some form of treatment to fulfil the waste acceptance criteria for deposit to landfill. The guidance advises that where possible, the operator of the treatment process should consider making use of the neutralisation capacity of the material, which has the potential to replace raw binder materials used in treatment such as lime (in for example neutralisation / precipitation treatment).

102   New Earth Solutions relied on the statement of Leslie Heasman but she was not put forward as an expert and her evidence was permitted before the Court on the basis it was before the Agency during its decision making. In any event, it is not for the Court to resolve disputes of expert evidence. Other than Ms Heasman, New Earth Solutions relied, in effect, for support for its case on the position of the Norwegian Environment Agency, which, by virtue of the legislative framework, cannot bind the Agency. Accordingly, in my judgment there were rational and evidence-based grounds for the Agency's view, and I am not persuaded of any error of law in the Agency's exercise of its judgment. There is a clear contrast in this regard with the Court of Appeal's decision in *Lafarge* where the Court concluded that the Inspector in that case could not rationally have come to the view on the evidence that he did.

103   In light of these conclusions, it is not necessary for the Court to address the question of whether substitution of APCr for virgin limestone may be regarded as a distinct waste recovery operation, particularly given the potentially wider ramifications of any Court ruling on the issue and the limited submissions before me on these wider aspects. Even if substitution of APCr for pulverised limestone is a distinct operation, any such finding does not have the significance contended for it by New Earth Solutions in light of the other conclusions I have reached on the law. It would still have been open to the Agency to look at the treatment and subsequent disposal of the waste in deciding the operations were a D9 disposal operation or to look at the principal purpose of the operations. As the Agency pointed out in its decision letter, it is entirely consistent with the definition of disposal for a disposal operation to have, as a secondary consequence, the beneficial use of waste.

Conclusion

104   For the reasons set out above, the claim fails.

JONES v CHAPEL-EN-LE-FRITH PARISH COUNCIL

HIGH COURT OF JUSTICE (QUEEN'S BENCH DIVISION)

Turner J: 25 July 2022

[2022] EWHC 1909 (QB); [2023] Env. L.R. 8

Abatement orders; Anti-social behaviour; Noise; Parks; Statutory nuisance; Use

H1 *Statutory nuisance—noise nuisance arising from anti-social behaviour—abatement notices—whether assessment of existence of nuisance limited to intended use of facilities—whether impacts of 'unintended use' to be considered in determining whether injurious to health—hypersensitivity resulting from anti-social behaviour could prevent a finding of statutory nuisance*

H2 The appellants (J) lived close to a Multi-Use Games Area (MUGA) and skate park for which the respondent local authority (C) was responsible. J alleged that noise emanating from the activities carried out on the MUGA and the skate park, including ball noises, skateboard use, shouting and music played, was such as to amount to a statutory nuisance. The appellants' application for an abatement notice under s.82 of the Environmental Protection Act 1990 was dismissed by the Magistrates' Court with the District Judge finding that there was a sharp legal distinction to be drawn between, on the one hand, noise which was generated as a result of the "intended use" of the MUGA and skate park and, on the other, "anti-social use", such as the playing of loud music and the continued use of the facilities after they were intended to be closed. He concluded that the latter did not fall to be taken into account in assessment as to whether the allegation of nuisance had been made out. The District Judge also found that J had been rendered hypersensitive by the anti-social behaviour elements of activities at the site but for which they would not have been so adversely affected by the noise arising from the intended use. Three questions were raised by way of case stated, whether: (i) it had been wrong not to deal with the issue of whether the noise was injurious to health given that it had been found that it was the anti-social behaviour, rather than the intended use of the MUGA and skate park, which led to sleeplessness; (ii) it had been wrong to distinguish between noise generated by the intended use of the premises and noise emanating from anti-social behaviour associated with the premises; and (iii) anti-social behaviour which included noise deriving from the nuisance causing premises could prevent a finding of statutory nuisance on the basis that such anti-social behaviour had resulted in the complainants being found to be hypersensitive due to the anti-social behaviour?

H3 **Held:**

H4   (1) The conduct covered by the 1990 Act and the Anti-social Behaviour, Crime and Policing Act 2014 were not mutually exclusive. It followed that there was no legal basis for drawing a distinction per se between noise emitted as a result of anti-social behaviour and "intended use" noise. Under the common law, responsibility for a nuisance was not necessarily limited to the direct perpetrator of any activity giving rise to the undue interference. A failure to act could sometimes give rise to liability in nuisance at common law. The District Judge fell into error by excluding from his consideration all "anti-social noise" from the outset. Neither the statutory regime nor the common law of nuisance proceeded on the basis that liability in nuisance was circumscribed by the use to which premises were intended to be put rather than those to which they came actually to be put.

H5   (2) The first question to be answered was whether the noise emanating from the MUGA and the skate park amounted to a nuisance with respect to J. C was clearly the owner and occupier of the MUGA and the skate park. If it were a necessary pre-condition to establish "responsibility" on the part of the defendant for the nuisance then s.82(4)(c) of the 1990 Act would be meaningless because it was premised on the assumption that proceedings may be brought against the owner or occupier of the premises only when the person responsible could not be found, i.e. the owner or occupier was not, himself, responsible. The District Judge concluded that the "intended use" noise did not amount to a nuisance but made no finding as to whether the noise as a whole amounted to a nuisance. It followed that he fell into error and left unanswered a question which ought to have been answered before he proceeded to reach his conclusions on the case.

H6   (3) On the issue of hypersensitivity, the question to be addressed was what, objectively, a normal person would find it reasonable to put up with. The hypersensitivity of any given claimant was not a defence in the event that it would also be unreasonable, in any event, to expect a person of normal resilience to tolerate it. Furthermore, it would normally be wrong to hold that where an actionable nuisance was, in itself, foreseeably causative of hypersensitivity in previously robust individuals that the party liable in respect of the nuisance was thereafter absolved from its consequences. Since the District Judge excluded from the scope of his consideration all anti-social noise, his attribution of hypersensitivity to anti-social behaviour including noise was not, without more, an answer to J's complaints.

H7   (4) The answers to the questions raised were, therefore: (i) consideration should have been given to the impact upon health of all noise emanating from the MUGA and the Skate Park, regardless as to whether it fell to be as a result of intended use or anti-social behaviour; (ii) any distinction between noise generated by the intended use of premises and noise emanating from anti-social behaviour associated with those premises was not one which fell to be made under the Statutory Nuisance regime; and (iii) anti-social behaviour which included noise deriving from the nuisance causing premises could not prevent a finding of statutory nuisance on the basis that such anti-social behaviour had resulted in J being found to be hypersensitive due to the anti-social behaviour in the circumstances of this case. Since it was impermissible to distinguish between intended and anti-social noise, it was also impermissible to treat anti-social noise, in part, as a cause of hypersensitivity such as to negate a finding of nuisance. In any event, the existence of hypersensitivity was not a defence where even a person of normal resilience would have found the noise to be unreasonable.

H8 **Cases referred to:**
Cocking v Eacott [2016] EWCA Civ 140; [2016] Q.B. 1080; [2016] Env. L.R. 26
Coventry (t/a RDC Promotions) v Lawrence [2014] UKSC 13; [2014] A.C. 822;
[2014] Env. L.R. 25
Frank A Smart & Son Ltd v Aberdeenshire Council [2022] SAC (Civ) 5; 2022
S.L.T. (Sh Ct) 57; [2022] L.L.R. 238 SAC
Gaunt v Fynney (1872–73) L.R. 8 Ch. App. 8 Lord Chancellor
Lambert v Barratt Homes Ltd [2010] EWCA Civ 681; [2010] B.L.R. 527; [2010]
Env. L.R. D8
Milne v Stuartfield Windpower Ltd [2019] SC ABE 25
R. v Carrick DC Ex p. Shelley [1996] Env. L.R. 273; [1996] J.P.L. 857; (1996)
160 J.P. Rep. 912 QBD
*Sedleigh-Denfield v O'Callagan (Trustees for St Joseph's Society for Foreign
Missions)* [1940] A.C. 880 HL

H9 **Legislation referred to:**
Senior Courts Act 1981 s.28A
Environmental Protection Act 1990 ss.79 and 82
Anti-social Behaviour, Crime and Policing Act 2014 s.2

H10 *P. Riley-Smith* (instructed by Richard Buxton Solicitors) appeared on behalf of the
appellant.
The respondent did not attend and was not represented.

JUDGMENT

THE HON MR JUSTICE TURNER:

Introduction

1   This is an appeal by way of case stated against the decision of District Judge
(Magistrates' Courts) McGarva to dismiss the appellants' application for an
abatement order in respect of an alleged statutory noise nuisance.

2   The appellants all live close to a Multi Use Games Area ("MUGA") and the
skate park both of which are located in the Chapel-en-le Frith Memorial Skate park
in Derbyshire and responsibility for which lies with the respondent.

3   They allege that the noise emanating from the activities carried out on the MUGA
and the skate park is such as to amount to a statutory nuisance. It includes:

- ball strikes, kicks and bounces from the MUGA;
- impact noise of skateboards and other equipment on the metal ramps and
  installations in the skate park;
- noise from shouting from users of the MUGA and the skate park; and
- noise from music played in the MUGA and the skate park.

4   In finding against the appellants, the District Judge held that there was a sharp
legal distinction to be drawn between, on the one hand, noise which was generated
as a result of the "intended use" of the MUGA and skate park and, on the other,
"anti-social use" (such as the playing of loud music and the continued use of the

facilities after they were intended to be closed). He concluded that the latter did not fall to be taken into account in his assessment as to whether the allegation of nuisance had been made out.

5   He also found that the appellants had been rendered hypersensitive by the anti-social behaviour elements of what had been going on at the MUGA and the skate park but for which they would not have been so adversely affected by the noise arising from their intended use.

6   The appellants challenge these findings on the basis that they are founded upon a misunderstanding of the law.

The Law

7   Section 79 of the Environmental Protection Act 1990 ("the 1990 Act") provides insofar as is material:

> "(1) … the following matters constitute "statutory nuisances" for the purposes of this Part, that is to say—…
>> (g) noise emitted from premises so as to be prejudicial to health or a nuisance…"

8   Under s.82 of the 1990 Act, a person aggrieved by a statutory nuisance can apply to the Magistrates' Court for an 'abatement order'.

9   Under s.82(2):

> "If the magistrates' court…. is satisfied that the alleged nuisance exists, or that although abated it is likely to recur on the same premises… the court….shall make an order for either or both of the following purposes—
>> (a) requiring the defendant….to abate the nuisance, within a time specified in the order, and to execute any works necessary for that purpose;
>> (b) prohibiting a recurrence of the nuisance, and requiring the defendant…, within a time specified in the order, to execute any works necessary to prevent the recurrence;
> and, in England and Wales, may also impose on the defendant a fine not exceeding level 5 on the standard scale."

10   Under s.82(4):

> "Proceedings for an order under subsection (2) above shall be brought—
>> (a) … against the person responsible for the nuisance;…
>> (c) where the person responsible for the nuisance cannot be found, against the owner or occupier of the premises."

11   In *R. v Carrick DC* [1996] Env. L.R. 273 it was held in the context of statutory nuisance:

> "In principle "nuisance" has its common law meaning, either a public or a private nuisance."

12   The question therefore arises as to whether the noises generated by the anti-social behaviour complained of by the appellants falls within the scope of this regime. This issue is reflected in the first two of the three cases stated by the District Judge:

"1. Was I wrong not to deal with the issue of whether the noise was injurious
to health given that I found that it was the antisocial behaviour rather than the
intended use of the MUGA and skate park which led to sleeplessness?
2. Was I wrong to distinguish between noise generated by the intended use
of the premises and noise emanating from antisocial behaviour associated
with the premises?"

13   With respect to the second main issue, concerning hypersensitivity, the authority
of greatest relevance is of some vintage. In *Gaunt v Fynney* (1872–73) L.R. 8 Ch.
App. 8 the plaintiffs lived next to a property in which machinery, which included
a boiler, was operated. On one occasion, a sudden noise had alarmed members of
the plaintiffs' household and, since that time, the plaintiffs were convinced that the
boiler was dangerous. As a result, the noises which it made thereafter became a
permanent source of irritation and uneasiness to them. Against this background,
the court held:

"…a nervous, or anxious, or prepossessed listener hears sounds which would
otherwise have passed unnoticed, and magnifies and exaggerates into some
new significance, originating within himself, sounds which at other times
would have been passively heard and not regarded."

Against this background, the plaintiffs' claim in nuisance failed.

14   The issue of hypersensitivity arises in the third question raised by way of case
stated:

"Can antisocial behaviour which includes noise that derives from the nuisance
causing premises prevent a finding of statutory nuisance on the basis that such
antisocial behaviour has resulted in the complainants being found to be
hypersensitive due to the antisocial behaviour?"

The Central Distinction

15   In paragraph 45 of his judgment the District Judge held:

"There is in my view a distinction between noise amounting to anti-social
behaviour which is consequential to the presence of the MUGA alone and
noise which comes from the intended use of the MUGA which is playing ball
games. I do not think the parish council should be held responsible for
anti-social behaviour."

16   The District Judge reiterated this approach in paragraph 2 of his case stated:

"Having made those findings of fact I concluded that I should distinguish
between noise created by the use of the skate park and MUGA for their
intended uses; i.e. skateboarding and playing football and the use of the areas
for anti-social behaviour. I concluded that the parish council should not be
responsible for noise which emanated from acts of antisocial behaviour
including the use of the MUGA and skate park after dark. The skate park as
with any public open space can be a magnet for antisocial behaviour; the
removal of the skate park or MUGA would not necessarily remove the
antisocial behaviour. It is important to bear in mind a finding of nuisance
confers criminal liability and can give rise to a fine; the Parish council should

not be responsible for acts outside its control. It was contended by the complainants that I should not draw that distinction. Effectively the complainants are contending that section 82 confers absolute liability."

17   Although the District Judge thus articulated his reasons for concluding that it would be a generally good thing that "anti-social noise" should be distinguished from "intended use noise", he did not clearly explain the legal basis upon which this distinction fell be to made. It is therefore necessary to explore whether such a legal foundation can be established.

18   Furthermore, the respondent to this appeal chose, as they had every right to do, not to appear on this appeal. Although they had earlier indicted that a skeleton argument would be provided, it, unfortunately, never materialised. Accordingly, this Court has been driven to do its best to consider the merits of what may have been contended on behalf of the respondent without the benefit of its input.

19   It is also to be noted that the "intended noise"/"anti-social noise" distinction drawn by the District Judge was not one which had been relied upon or referred to by either party before him. It was, I am informed, entirely the product of his own creative input.

20   In this context, I am grateful to Mr Riley-Smith acting on behalf of the appellants for the care with which he has sought, in fulfilment of his duty of candour, to articulate what contentions may have been raised on behalf of the respondents to this appeal had they chosen to make an appearance.

Public Nuisance and Anti-Social Behaviour

21   The respondent made the point in its skeleton below that some of the matters about which the appellants were complaining did not fall within the scope of section 79(1)(g) of the 1990 Act because they comprised anti-social behaviour which was unrelated to the emission of noise. These included, for example: the throwing of eggs; verbal abuse and acts of trespass. Such conduct fell within the scope of the anti-social behaviour regime provided under the Anti-social Behaviour, Crime and Policing Act 2014 ("the 2014 Act").

22   The appellants have readily conceded the strength of this point and do not seek to argue that anti-social behaviour not involving the emission of noise falls to be considered by the court.

23   However, the District Judge went further than this holding, as he did, that even anti-social behaviour which *did* involve the emission of noise was excluded from his consideration.

24   The conduct covered by the 1990 Act and the 2014 Act are not mutually exclusive. Section 2 of the 2014 Act provides:

"(1) In this Part "anti-social behaviour" means—
(a) conduct that has caused, or is likely to cause, harassment, alarm or distress to any person,
(b) conduct capable of causing nuisance or annoyance to a person in relation to that person's occupation of residential premises, or
(c) conduct capable of causing housing-related nuisance or annoyance to any person."

25   The point is made in the publication *Home Office Anti-social behaviour powers: Statutory guidance for frontline professionals (June 2022)* which explains in respect

of Community Protection Notices under section 43 of the 2014 Act the relationship between the two regimes:

> "**Community Protection Notices and statutory nuisance**: Issuing a Community Protection Notice does not discharge the council from its duty to issue an Abatement Notice where the behaviour constitutes a statutory nuisance for the purposes of Part 3 of the Environmental Protection Act 1990. A statutory nuisance is one of the matters listed in section 79(1) of that Act which, given all the circumstances, is judged to be 'prejudicial to health or a nuisance'…
>
> While a Community Protection Notice can be issued for behaviour that may constitute a statutory nuisance, the interaction between the two powers should be considered. It remains a principle of law that a specific power should be used in preference to a general one."

26   It follows that there is no legal basis for drawing a distinction *per se* between noise emitted as a result of anti-social behaviour and "intended use" noise.

Intended Use

27   The District Judge sought to define the limits of the respondent's duties and responsibilities to the noise emitted as a result of the intended use of the MUGA and skate park.

28   Under the common law, responsibility for a nuisance is not necessarily limited to the direct perpetrator of any activity giving rise to the undue interference. A failure to act may sometimes give rise to liability in nuisance at common law. As Lord Neuberger observed in *Coventry v Lawrence* [2014] UKSC 13 at paragraph 3:

> "A nuisance can be defined, albeit in general terms, as an action (or sometimes a failure to act) on the part of a defendant, which is not otherwise authorised, and which causes an interference with the claimant's reasonable enjoyment of his land, or to use a slightly different formulation, which unduly interferes with the claimant's enjoyment of his land."[1]

29   The leading case on liability in nuisance for failing to act is *Sedleigh-Denfield v O'Callagan* [1940] A.C. 880. In which Lord Wright held at page 904:

> "If the defendant by himself or those for whom he is responsible has created what constitutes a nuisance and if it causes damage, the difficulty now being considered does not arise. But he may have taken over the nuisance, readymade as it were, when he acquired the property, or the nuisance may be due to a latent defect or to the act of a trespasser or stranger. Then he is not liable unless he continued or adopted the nuisance, or, more accurately did not without undue delay remedy it when he became aware of it, or with ordinary and reasonable care should have become aware of it."

30   A recent example of liability in nuisance caused by noise arising through omission to act can be found in *Cocking v Eacott* [2016] Q.B. 1080. In that case, the defendant was the owner of a house in which she allowed her daughter to live.

---

[1] I note, in passing, that the need for any given claimant to have an interest in land is not a prerequisite to establishing a statutory nuisance as opposed to a common law.

The defendant, herself, lived elsewhere. The constant barking of her daughter's dogs prompted the claimant, who lived next door, to sue the defendant in nuisance. The Court of Appeal concluded that the defendant was liable holding at paragraph 25:

> "An occupier... will normally be responsible for a nuisance even if he did not directly cause it, because he is in control and possession of the property. The cases show that an owner may be regarded as an occupier of property for these purposes even if he has allowed others to live or undertake activities on his land. In the *Sedleigh-Denfield case* [1940] AC 880, 903, 905 Lord Wright made clear that the liability attaches to an occupier because he has possession and control over the property. There was a debate before us as to whether the principle to be extracted from the *Sedleigh-Denfield* case was either (i) that an occupier is liable if he continues or adopts the nuisance by failing to abate it without undue delay after he became aware of it or with reasonable care should have become aware of it (as Lord Wright said, at pp 904–905), or (ii) that an occupier is liable if he continues the nuisance by failing to take any reasonable means to abate it after he became aware of it or should have done so (which was how Viscount Maugham, at p 894, and Lord Romer, at p 913, put the matter). In fact, both Lord Atkin, at p 899, and Lord Porter, at p 919, formulated their propositions in a similar way to Lord Wright, so I think that Mr MacBean's submission that the obligation on an occupier was limited to taking "reasonable means" to abate the nuisance was ill-founded. Rather, Ackner LJ was right in the *Page Motors case* 80 LGR 337, 345–346 to cite only Lord Wright's formulation, since he was in the majority."

There was no suggestion that the defendant could have escaped liability on the basis that she had not intended that her daughter should keep a dog which barked excessively.

31   The statutory regime is similar to the common law approach in that section 82(4)(c) of the 1990 Act provides for proceedings for an abatement order being brought "where the person responsible for the nuisance cannot be found, against the owner or occupier of the premises." The common law may, however, be broader in its application to the extent to which it is not necessary (but may nonetheless be a highly material factor) to establish that the person responsible for the nuisance cannot be found. (see, for example *Lambert v Barratt Homes Ltd* [2010] EWCA Civ 681).

32   The first stage of the statutory process requires the magistrates' court to determine whether the nuisance exists. If there is a nuisance then only those parties falling within the scope of section 82(3) of the 1990 Act are liable to be required to abate the nuisance. Once the magistrates' court is satisfied that a nuisance exists the wording of section 82(2) requires the court to make an order. There is no discretion to decline to make an order.

33   However, it is open to the court to postpone making an abatement order to give the parties an opportunity to assist the court in determining what steps are needed to achieve the objectives of s82(2) (see *Milne v Stuartfield Windpower Ltd* [2019] SC ABE 25). This because abatement in the case of noise nuisance does not automatically involve a requirement to cease all noise at all times. As was recently pointed out in *Frank A Smart & Son Ltd v Aberdeenshire Council* [2022] WL 00309248:

"…we note the inherent flexibility in the words "abate" and "nuisance". The notice does not, as the appellant fears, force shutting down of the turbines on the basis that it is the only guaranteed method of stopping the noise. Not all noise amounts to a nuisance. Abatement does not necessarily require elimination."

I note in passing that Scottish law is, in substance, identical to that in England and Wales with respect to the operation of the statutory scheme.

34   In my view, the District Judge fell into error by excluding from his consideration all "anti-social noise" from the outset. Neither the statutory regime nor the common law of nuisance proceeds on the basis that liability in nuisance is circumscribed by the use to which premises were intended to be put rather than those to which they came actually to be put.

35   The first question to be answered was, therefore, whether the noise emanating from the MUGA and the skate park amounted to a nuisance with respect to the appellants. The appellants contend that the respondent did not dispute that it was responsible for the nuisance before the District Judge. But even if that concession had not been made, the respondent was clearly the owner and occupier of the MUGA and the skate park. If it were a necessary pre-condition to establish "responsibility" on the part of the defendant for the nuisance then s. 82(4)(c) of the 1990 Act would be meaningless because it is premised on the assumption that proceedings may be brought against the owner or occupier of the premises only when the person responsible cannot be found i.e. the owner or occupier is not, himself, responsible.

36   The District Judge concluded that the "intended use" noise did not amount to a nuisance but he made no finding as to whether the noise as a whole amounted to a nuisance. It follows that, in my view, he fell into error and left unanswered a question which ought to have been answered before he proceeded to reach his conclusions on the case.

37   As to the issue of hypersensitivity, I am satisfied that the question to be addressed was what, objectively, a normal person would find it reasonable to put up with. The hypersensitivity of any given claimant is not a defence in the event that it would also be unreasonable, in any event, to expect a person of normal resilience to tolerate it. Furthermore, it would normally be wrong to hold that where an actionable nuisance is, in itself, foreseeably causative of hypersensitivity in previously robust individuals that the party liable in respect of the nuisance is thereafter absolved from its consequences. Since the District Judge excluded from the scope of his consideration all anti-social noise, his attribution of hypersensitivity to anti-social behaviour including noise was not, without more, an answer to the appellants' complaints.

Answers To the Questions Raised By the District Judge

38   The answers to the questions raised by the District Judge are to be answered thus:

1. Was I wrong not to deal with the issue of whether the noise was injurious to health given that I found that it was the antisocial behaviour rather than the intended use of the MUGA and the skate park which led to sleeplessness?

Yes. Consideration should have been given to the impact upon health of all noise emanating from the MUGA and the Skate park regardless as to whether it fell to be as a result of intended use or anti-social behaviour.

2. Was I wrong to distinguish between noise generated by the intended use of the premises and noise emanating from antisocial behaviour associated with the premises?

Yes. This is not a distinction which falls to be made under the statutory regime.

3. Can antisocial behaviour which includes noise that derives from the nuisance causing premises prevent a finding of statutory nuisance on the basis that such antisocial behaviour has resulted in the complainants being found to be hypersensitive due to the antisocial behaviour?

Not in the circumstances of this case. Since it was impermissible to distinguish between intended and anti-social noise, it was also impermissible to treat anti-social noise, in part, as a cause of hypersensitivity such as to negate a finding of nuisance. In any event, the existence of hypersensitivity is not a defence where even a person of normal resilience would have found the noise to be unreasonable.

Remedy

39   The Court's powers on a case stated are set out at section 28A (3) of the Senior Courts Act 1981:

> "The High Court shall hear and determine the question arising on the case (or the case as amended) and shall—
> (a) reverse, affirm or amend the determination in respect of which the case has been stated; or
> (b) remit the matter to the magistrates' court, or the Crown Court, with the opinion of the High Court, and may make such other order in relation to the matter (including as to costs) as it thinks fit."

40   At the conclusion of his submissions, Mr Riley-Smith requested that I should reserve my decision on the choice of remedy to allow all parties time to consider the implications of my findings. I am content with this course. The matter can be relisted for further consideration of the way forward in due course or, if appropriate, be decided on the papers.

ARMSTRONGS AGGREGATES LTD v NATURAL ENGLAND

QUEEN'S BENCH DIVISION (ADMINISTRATIVE COURT)

Fordham J: 28 July 2022

[2022] EWHC 2009 (Admin); [2023] Env. L.R. 9

⊕ Abuse of process; Appeals; Declarations of incompatibility; Delay; Environmental damage; Judicial review; Protection of property; Quarries; Remediation notices; Sites of Special Scientific Interest

H1 *Nature conservation—Site of Special Scientific Interest—quarries—planning permission Review of Old Minerals Permissions—Environment Act 1995— environmental damage—Environmental Damage (Prevention and Remediation) (England) Regulations 2015—Environmental Damage Notices—right of appeal against notices—CPR Pt 8—ECHR Protocol 1, art.1—right to property—claim relating to declaration of incompatibility of 2015 Regulations with the right to property—parallel proceedings—abuse of process—procedural exclusivity— alternative remedies—possible delay—whether a claim for judicial review parallel to statutory appeals was an abuse of process*

H2   The Claimant AA was the operator of a quarry in a designated Site of Special Scientific Interest (SSSI). Activities at the quarry were the subject of an extant, deemed planning permission under a scheme for the Review of Old Minerals Permission (ROMP) under the Environment Act 1995. The Defendant NE was the statutory body with responsibility for regulating activities on SSSIs. In June and December 2020, NE issued statutory 'environmental damage' notices (the ED Notices) pursuant to reg.18 of the Environmental Damage (Prevention and Remediation) (England) Regulations 2015 (the 2015 Regulations). The ED Notices required AA to submit proposals for the 'remediation' of the permanent loss of the notified habitats in the SSSI based on NE's assessment that the 'environmental damage' to the habitats had been caused by AA's activities. AA lodged two separate appeals with the Secretary of State against the ED notices in July 2020 and January 2021. These appeals were linked and an inquiry scheduled for November 2021.

H3   In October 2021, AA issued a claim under the CPR Pt 8, seeking a determination by the High Court of two questions of law. The questions were linked generally to whether the 2015 Regulations were incompatible with rights to property under art.1 of Protocol 1 of the ECHR (right to property) in circumstances where extant planning permissions under ROMP exist. The first question was whether the 2015 regulations were applicable in such circumstances (the 'applicability question')? The second question was whether it was unlawful to take action under the 2015 Regulations in such circumstances (the 'invocability question')? AA argued that the 2015 Regulations were inapplicable and that any action taken under them was unlawful where a ROMP existed because quarrying activities covered under a ROMP constituted lawful economic activity whose curtailment would be compensatable under the ROMP regime itself. Thus, without compensation, regulatory intervention under the 2015 Regulations, without compensation would breach the right to property.

H4   NE argued that on both questions there was no question of an interference with the right to property in the context of issuing ED Notices under the 2015 Regulations. Such notices required the submission of proposals based on conclusions drawn by NE which were, in turn, the subject of rights of appeal by an operator. It was only at the stage when a remediation notice was issued under reg.20 of the 2015 regulations that the question of any interference with a right to property would crystallise. NE sought to strike out AA's claim on the basis that the court had no jurisdiction or should not exercise its jurisdiction to entertain a claim under Pt 8 of the CPR.

H5   **Held,** in dismissing AA's claim and granting NE's application:

H6   (1) The possibility of a declaration of incompatibility between the 2015 Regulations and the right to property would only arise where the primary legislation pursuant to which the regulations were made prevented removal of any such incompatibility. No such provision in any primary legislation had been identified. If compatibility could not be achieved through the application of the 2015 Regulations alongside NE's duties as a public authority under the Human Rights Act 1998 s.6 or by interpreting them in accordance with s.3 of the 1998 Act, the issue would be one of invalidity. A claim brought under CPR Pt 8 could not seek an order to quash a decision as that was an exclusive remedy under judicial review.

H7   (2) AA's arguments in relation to the meaning, applicability and validity of the 2015 Regulations had been accepted by NE and could still be raised in subsequent proceedings for judicial review. Moreover, NE had not sought to raise any argument based around delay on the basis that those points were not being pursued by way of judicial review. Public law issues raised as a claim outside judicial review might constitute an abuse of process if the purpose of the claim was to circumvent or flout protections by reference to which permission for judicial review would be refused. These protections included delay and the availability of an alternative remedy.

H8   (3) It was not in the interests of justice or the public interest for judicial review to take precedence over the appeals process under the 2015 Regulations. If AA had commenced a judicial review with an application to stay any appeals under the 2015 Regulations instead of bringing a separate claim under CPR Pt 8, permission would have been refused on the ground that the right of appeal under the 2015 Regulations was a suitable alternative remedy.

H9   (4) If AA had applied for judicial review in October 2021, the court would have concluded that there was prejudice arising from a lack of promptness which, when taken together with the availability of a suitable alternative remedy, would have made any defence based upon delay irresistible. Accordingly, it was appropriate to strike out the claim under Pt 8 as an abuse of process.

H10   (5) AA had not argued that the points of law fell outside the scope of the appeals or raised any concerns over whether NE would be taking a point in relation to a lack of promptness or delay. AA had set about trying to stay the appeals under the 2015 Regulations and having the Pt 8 claim heard. In circumstances where an individual wanted to ensure they could raise a point about the actions of a public authority at an appropriate time where there were alternative avenues of redress, they should write, candidly and openly, to the public authority and any interested party to enquire of the authority's position and whether they would take any point on delay if a challenge was raised at a later date. In the absence of a positive reply, a court would understand why a claimant had issued proceedings protectively at an earlier stage. If the public authority accepted the reasonableness of waiting until a later stage, such a response would be relied upon as a 'shield' against criticism and as a good reason for an extension of time for any proceedings.

H11 **Cases referred to:**
Arkin v Marshall [2020] EWCA Civ 620; [2020] 1 W.L.R. 3284; [2020] H.L.R. 32
Caine v Advertiser and Times Ltd [2019] EWHC 39 (QB)
Clark v University of Lincolnshire and Humberside [2000] 1 W.L.R. 1988; [2000] Ed. C.R. 553; [2000] E.L.R. 345 CA (Civ Div)
O'Reilly v Mackman [1983] 2 A.C. 237; [1982] 3 W.L.R. 1096; (1982) 126 S.J. 820 HL
R. (on the application of Archer) v Revenue and Customs Commissioners [2019] EWCA Civ 1021; [2019] 1 W.L.R. 6355; [2019] S.T.C. 1353
R. (on the application of Glencore Energy UK Ltd) v Revenue and Customs Commissioners [2017] EWCA Civ 1716; [2017] 4 W.L.R. 213; [2018] S.T.C. 51
Richards v Worcestershire CC [2017] EWCA Civ 1998; [2018] P.T.S.R. 1563; (2018) 21 C.C.L. Rep. 376
St George's, University of London v Rafique-Aldawery [2018] EWCA Civ 2520; [2019] P.T.S.R. 658; [2019] E.L.R. 119
Trim v North Dorset DC [2010] EWCA Civ 1446; [2011] 1 W.L.R. 1901; [2011] P.T.S.R. 1110

H12 **Legislation referred to:**
CPR rr.3.4, 7.5, 11(1)(6), 54.2, 54.8 and 54.10
ECHR Protocol 1 art.1
Environment Act 1995
Human Rights Act 1998 ss.3, 4, 6 and 7
Directive 2004/35 (Prevention and Remedying of Environmental Damage) [2004] OJ L143/56
Environmental Damage (Prevention and Remediation) (England) Regulations 2015 (SI 2015/810) regs 18 and 19

H13 *C. McNall* (instructed by Fielden Marshall Glover Strutt) appeared on behalf of the Claimant.
J. Burton (instructed by Browne Jacobson) appeared on behalf of the Defendant.

JUDGMENT

MR JUSTICE FORDHAM:

Introduction

1   This case is about "procedural exclusivity", delay and alternative remedies. The Claimant is the operator of a quarry (Shap Pink Quarry) in a designated Site of Special Scientific Interest ("SSSI") where there are notified habitats. It has an extant, deemed planning permission (dated 12 June 2000). Its quarry is one to which the review of old minerals permissions ("ROMP") regime of the Environment Act 1995 applies. By statutory "environmental damage" notices ("the ED Notices") dated 11 June 2020 and 23 December 2020, issued pursuant to regulation 18 of the Environmental Damage (Prevention and Remediation) (England) Regulations 2015 SI 2015 No.810 ("the 2015 Regulations"), the Defendant has required proposals from the Claimant for the "remediation" of the permanent loss of notified habitats, the Defendant having assessed that "environmental damage" existed, which had been caused by the Claimant's operating activity. The Claimant has lodged appeals to the Secretary of State against the environmental damage notices, pursuant to regulation 19. The Claimant's appeal against the first ED notice was filed on 9 July 2020, a detailed statement of case in support of the appeal was filed on 1 December 2020 and the defendant's written response to the appeal was filed on 29 January 2021. The appeal against the second ED notice was filed in January 2021. The Claimant's detailed statement of case in support of that appeal was filed on 11 May 2021. The Defendant's written response to that appeal was filed on 5 July 2021. The two appeals were linked. Experts were instructed. Proofs of evidence were prepared. A joint site visit took place in September 2021. A four-day inquiry was fixed for 30 November 2021. The two appeals are pending.

The Part 8 Claim

2   Foreshadowed by a letter from the Claimant's new solicitors dated 11 October 2021, the Claimant issued a CPR Part 8 Claim on 25 October 2021. By that Claim, the Claimant seeks determination by the High Court of two questions ("the Two Questions"). It is that Part 8 Claim with which I am dealing. The Two Questions are questions of law. They are closely linked. They concern the position of any quarry within an SSSI, with an extant planning permission, and to which the ROMP regime is applicable (which I will call "a Qualifying Quarry"). In essence, the Two Questions ask whether a Qualifying Quarry can lawfully be the subject of any regulatory intervention by the Defendant pursuant to the 2015 Regulations, in light of A1P1 (the right to property) protected by the Human Rights Act 1998 ("HRA"). The first question (i) is whether, in the light of A1P1 rights, the 2015 Regulations have any applicability to Qualifying Quarries. The second question (ii) is whether, in the light of A1P1 rights, it is unlawful to take action under the 2015 Regulations. I will call (i) 'applicability'. I will call (ii) 'invocability'. The Claimant's position is that the answers are (i) "no" or, alternatively, (ii) "yes". In support of its position the Claimant relies, inter alia, on quarrying activities covered by an extant planning permission as "lawful economic activity", whose curtailment would be compensatable under the ROMP regime. It says that regulatory intervention pursuant to the 2015 Regulations, without compensation, would breach A1P1 rights.

3   The Grounds of the Part 8 Claim refer to the statutory appeals. They acknowledge that the issues in the Part 8 claim arise out of the two statutory notices. They contend that the High Court has "jurisdiction" to deal with the Part 8 claim, that the High Court is the appropriate "forum" to do so, and that "stays" of the statutory appeals are appropriate pending the High Court's determination of the two questions of law. In the Part 8 Claim, the Two Questions unmistakeably arise out of the ED Notices viewed alongside the 2015 Regulations. The Part 8 Details of Claim say this:

> 13. *The [ED] Notices and the 2015 Regulations, if valid, ostensibly create the situation where lawful and permitted activity can be terminated without the payment of any compensation which would otherwise be available under the ROMP provisions. ... 19. The [ED] Notices, and the legislation under which they are purportedly given, are impermissible and unlawful derogations of the Claimant's rights under the Permissions, and is outside the proper margin of appreciation afforded to the Defendant under A1P1, and are contrary to A1P1 insofar as: 19.1 The Notices and/or the 2015 Regulations operate so as to deprive the Claimant of its public and private law rights, under the Permissions, to peacefully enjoy and exploit its property; 19.2 The Notices and/or the 2015 Regulations operate so as to deprive the Claimant of its public and private law rights, under the Permissions, to extract minerals up to the Extraction Boundary; 19.3 The 2015 Regulations contain no derogation for any activity conducted after 2009; 19.4 The 2015 Regulations conflict with the Permissions. 20. The Defendant, in the giving of the Notices, is acting incompatibly with the Claimant's A1P1 rights. 21. If, without prejudice to the foregoing, and contrary to the Claimant's case, the 2015 Regulations are valid and operate without modification in relation to all SSSIs, regardless of planning status and/or the existence of valid Permissions granted or deemed granted by the competent planning authority, and so as to render unlawful (as contrary to the 2015 Regulations, which carry criminal sanctions) then the 2015 Regulations are incompatible with the Claimant's A1P1 rights.*

4   The Part 8 Claim seeks declaratory remedies. It also includes a claim for a "declaration of incompatibility" ("DOI") pursuant to section 4 of the HRA. It is unclear to me how the remedy of a DOI could arise. The 2015 Regulations are "subordinate legislation". Under the HRA, a DOI would only arise in the last resort where there is an incompatibility with a Convention right (here, A1P1) and where the primary legislation, pursuant to which the subordinate legislation was made, prevents removal of the incompatibility: see HRA s.4(4)(b). Neither Counsel was able to show me any "provision of primary legislation" which would "prevent removal of any incompatibility" between the 2015 Regulations and A1P1 rights, were such an incompatibility to arise. Mr Burton told me that the reach of the 2015 Regulations to SSSIs was not mandated by the Directive 2004/35/EC which was their origin. If compatibility could not be secured by reading and applying the 2015 Regulations alongside the Defendant's HRA section 6 duties, or by interpreting them in accordance with the HRA section 3 interpretative imperative, the conclusion would – as it seems to me – be a matter of invalidity, whether expressed in terms of a declaration or actioned by a quashing order. The Part 8 Claim does not – and could not – seek a quashing order, that being a judicial review remedy (CPR 54.2).

Crystallisation

5   It is appropriate that I record here that the Defendant takes the firm position that, insofar as any issue arises under the 2015 Regulations relating to interference with Qualifying Quarry operators' A1P1 rights, it would not and could not arise in the context of regulation 18 ED Notices. The Defendant submits that a regulation 18 ED Notice does not involve an incursion or intrusion into economic activity. Rather, an ED Notice requires the submission of proposals, based on conclusions by the Defendant which are appealable on prescribed grounds (regulation 19). Only at the stage of a regulation 20 remediation notice, says the Defendant, could there be specified mandatory action by the operator with penal consequences for default. If there were an interference with A1P1 rights, that is when it would crystallise. Other provisions in the 2015 Regulations could be characterised as interferences in A1P1 rights: e.g. a regulation 14 'stop notice'.

The Defendant's Applications

6   By an application issued on 23 November 2021, the Defendant asks the Court to rule that it has "no jurisdiction" or "should not exercise its jurisdiction": see CPR Part 11. By an Order by HHJ Bird dated 25 November 2021 the Part 8 Claim was transferred to the Planning Court in Manchester and directions were made for the one-day hearing of the Defendant's application. By an amended application dated 27 May 2022 the Defendant asks the Court, in the further alternative, to strike out the Part 8 Claim: CPR 3.4(2). By an application dated 19 July 2022 the Defendant seeks an extension of time for the application issued on 23 November 2021, which was made 'one day' outside the prescribed 14 days after the Acknowledgement of Service: CPR 11(4)(a). I can deal here with extensions of time. So far as concerns the Defendant's application of 27 May 2022 to amend the application of 23 November 2021, I granted permission on 1 July 2022. I did so because ample opportunity had been given to the Claimant's representatives to respond. They had identified no prejudice. I could identify none. The Defendant's Summary of Reasons (8 November 2021) had referred to the intention to apply to "strike out", but this had been omitted in error from the application subsequently made (23 November 2021). So far as concerns the application for the 'one-day' extension of time, I have decided to grant that application too. An email of 23 November 2021 had acknowledged the one day delay in filing the application and had apologised referring to the absence of any prejudice. What happened next was the order of HHJ Bird. The Claimant has insisted that the Defendant regularise the position by making a formal application to this Court, supported by a witness statement. Mr McNall for the Claimant did not oppose the application but adopted a neutral position. I am quite satisfied that the reasons given in the application and supporting witness statement amply justify the one-day extension by reference to the criteria governing relief from sanctions.

Jurisdiction

7   Mr Burton for the Defendant accepts, for the purposes of the present case, that "jurisdiction" in CPR Part 11 means "the court's power or authority to try the claim" (White Book §11.1.3). He says the "procedural exclusivity" principle – where applicable by reference to delay which would lead to a judicial review claim being

declined – would means the Court has no "jurisdiction" in this sense. He suggested an analogy with CPR Part 7 claims and a failure to serve claim within time (CPR 7.5), citing *Caine v Advertiser and Times Ltd* [2019] EWHC 39 (QB). His skeleton argument raised the further suggestion that regulation 19 appeals constitute an "implied ouster" of the High Court's jurisdiction, a point which he decided against developing orally. In my judgment, there is no basis for concluding that this court lacks the "power or authority" to try the issues raised in the Part 8 Claim, answering the Two Questions. The real questions are all about whether the Court should exercise the undoubted "jurisdiction" that it does have.

Procedural exclusivity

8   Procedural exclusivity was once thought of as a principle which requires that 'public law issues are ventilated only by way of judicial review'. It is now a much more focused, narrow principle. It requires that 'public law issues raised as a claim outside judicial review may constitute an abuse of process, if the claim serves to circumvent or flout protections by reference to which permission for judicial review would be refused'. The obvious example of such a protection is delay. Reduced to its simplest form, the point is this. If I know that I would be refused permission for a CPR Part 54 judicial review by reason of some principled protection for public authorities, I cannot expect to be able to proceed instead and get the issues resolved by a High Court Judge, by using a CPR Part 8 Claim Form and seeking declarations of unlawfulness. If I choose to do that, I can expect to be met by an application to strike out the claim, based on the principled protection which I am sidestepping. It could be delay. Or it could in principle be some other ground on which permission for judicial review would be refused (see <u>Administrative Court Judicial Review Guide 2021</u> §§6.3.3, 6.3.4) such as alternative remedy, or the claim being "academic".

9   When procedural exclusivity was born in *O'Reilly v Mackman* [1983] 2 A.C. 237, the principled protections (now in CPR Part 54) were in RSC Order 53, where "permission" was called "leave". Lord Diplock spoke (at 284E) of not allowing a claim whose pursuit would "defeat the public policy that underlies the grant of [the] protections" in judicial review. Lord Diplock's cardinal principle was this (285E): as a general rule, it would be "contrary to public policy and an abuse of the process of the court" to permit a person, seeking to establish that a decision of a public authority infringed rights to which they were entitled to protection in public law, to proceed by way of an ordinary action "and by this means to evade the provisions of Order 53 for the protection of such authorities".

10   This same, narrow principle – about protecting against circumvention or flouting of protections – can be found in subsequent cases. Counsel showed me two recent examples. One was *Richards v Worcestershire CC* [2017] EWCA Civ 1998; [2018] P.T.S.R. 1563. There, Rupert Jackson LJ (for the Court of Appeal) identified at the heart of the procedural exclusivity principle the "safeguards for public authorities in Order 53, namely the requirement for leave and a strict time limit for commencing proceedings". He cited (§63) *Clark v University of Lincolnshire and Humberside* [2000] 1 W.L.R. 1988 at §39, where Lord Woolf MR said that what was likely to be important was "not whether the right procedure has been adopted" but rather "whether the protection provided by Order 53 has been flouted". Rupert Jackson LJ derived this proposition from the caselaw (§65): "The exclusivity principle

applies where the claimant is challenging a public law decision or action and (a) his claim affects the public generally or (b) justice requires some other reason that the claimant should proceed by way of judicial review". The other recent case was *Arkin v Marshall* [2020] EWCA Civ 620; [2020] 1 W.L.R. 3284. There, the Court of Appeal addressed whether the procedure by which the issues had been raised involved "circumventing a number of important procedural steps" (§13) and concluded that it did not, since "it is inevitable that permission to apply for judicial review would have been granted" which meant that the party who has raised the issues by the chosen procedural route had "not stolen a procedural march".

The Defendant's position

11   Mr Burton says the Court should strike out the Part 8 Claim (CPR 3.4(2)(b)) as an abuse of the court process or alternatively should rule that it will not exercise its jurisdiction and set aside the claim form (CPR 11(1)(b) and (6)(a)). He puts procedural exclusivity at the heart of his argument. He submits in essence, as I saw it, as follows.

    i) The Defendant's service of the regulation 18 ED Notices, which feature heavily on the Part 8 Claim, and are plainly its trigger. They are "a purely public law act" just as was the service of the breach of condition notice in *Trim v North Dorset DC* [2010] EWCA Civ 1446; [2011] 1 W.L.R. 1901 at §26 (cited with approval in *Richards* at §64). Moreover, the meaning and application of the 2015 Regulations, questions about A1P1-compatibility, applicability and invocability (and for that matter validity) are all classic public law questions. The fact that the claim raises the Claimant's enjoyment of private property rights, in the context of planning control, does not alter that position: see *Trim* §27.

    ii) Whether the Part 8 Claim is an abuse of process (or the Court should rule that it will not exercise its jurisdiction), by reference to procedural exclusivity, focuses on the protective safeguards for public authorities arising in Part 54 judicial review proceedings: including delay and alternative remedy. The way to test whether there is an abuse of process viewed against those safeguarding principles is to ask the question what the judicial review Court would have done, by reference to such principles, had the Part 8 Claim instead been brought by judicial review under Part 54. That is why the Court of Appeal in *Trim* was considering whether – viewed as a judicial review case – there would have been a "good reason to extend time" (§38).

    iii) Had the Part 8 Claim been filed in October 2021 as a claim for judicial review, permission for judicial review would have been refused. The delay alone would have been fatal. The 'target' public authority action would have been the regulation 18 ED Notices of 11 June 2020 and 23 December 2020. It was those Notices, read with the 2015 Regulations, which gave rise to the Two Questions and the Claimant's arguments as to impugning A1P1 incompatibility and securing A1P1 compatibility. There was a straightforward and substantial lack of promptness, comparable to *Trim*. Reliance on the December 2020 Notice and the "one year" rule for a claim under the HRA section 7(5) would not save the Claimant because section 7(5) contains the caveat of being subject to any stricter rule under the procedure in question. Here, that means the 3 month time-frame in judicial review. The Claimant would have needed an extension of time and would have been unable to secure one. The delay has been highly prejudicial and detrimental to good administration. Had judicial review been commenced promptly after the receipt of the ED Notices, there would have been orderly case-management of the extant appeals. The delay meant very substantial steps and progress were made in relation to the appeals. By reason of delay alone, just as in *Trim*, the Part 8 Claim clearly offends the procedural exclusivity principle.

iv) But even leaving all of that to one side, there is the safeguard of the discretionary bar of alternative remedy, applicable at the permission stage in judicial review, which the Part 8 route serves to circumvent and flout. This is a classic case where there is an alternative remedy, applying the principle described by Sales LJ in *R. (Glencore Energy UK Ltd) v Revenue and Customs Commissioners* [2017] EWCA Civ 1716; [2017] 4 W.L.R. 213 at §§54-61. The statutory appeal remedy under regulation 19 is a suitable "alternative remedy" for pursuit. Judicial review is a remedy of last resort. Appeals were filed. They are capable of being dispositive. The Claimant can raise A1P1 arguments in the appeal, as to the legally correct interpretation and application of the 2015 Regulations (as it has done). The scope of the appeal jurisdiction (see regulation 19) allows the Inspector to address any and all points of substance raised, as to: whether the Defendant has "acted unreasonably" in "deciding that the damage is environmental damage" (including hotly disputed questions about whether there has been an "adverse effect" on the "integrity" of the site: 2015 Regulations Sch 1 §4); whether the Claimant's activity is "a cause of the environmental damage"; whether the Claimant as responsible operator has been "at fault or negligence". There is no reason to suppose that the inspector dealing with appeals would not be able to deal with any question of law including under the HRA. Judicial review – if needed – could be pursued in the future and all arguments could be advanced and decided for whatever legal merit they may have. The Claimant would be able to choose to seek judicial review of any decision refusing the regulation 19 appeals. Or the Claimant could (and should) await any regulation 20 Remediation Notice and the outcome of any regulation 21 appeal (§5 above). Judicial review at an appropriate later stage could raise any public law point, including A1P1, relating to the applicability or invocability of the 2015 Regulations. It could also raise the remedy of a quashing order in respect of the 2015 regulations (which a Part 8 claim cannot), and the fallback remedy of a DOI. Nobody could shut out any A1P1 argument, and the Claimant could point to the reasonableness of its pursuit of alternative remedies. Importantly, the Court would be considering A1P1 not in the abstract or in a vacuum, but with the crystallised and concrete picture which an A1P1 analysis requires. Viewed in terms of alternative remedy, a judicial review claim filed in October 2021 would be refused permission for judicial review and the appeals – by then so well advanced – allowed to run their course. But, viewed in alternative remedy terms, even a judicial review claim filed promptly after the ED Notices would also have been refused permission for judicial review, because of the appropriateness of the pursuit of the appeals.

Nothing is being shut out

12   An important feature of this case is that the Defendant specifically accepts that any and all of the Claimant's A1P1 arguments – concerning the meaning, applicability and validity of the 2015 Regulations – could, if still needed, be raised in subsequent judicial review proceedings. The Defendant says the appropriate time would be after any remediation Notice under regulation 20 (and any regulation 21 appeal): §5 above. But the important point is that there is no question of the Defendant raising a delay objection, on the basis that the points were not pursued by judicial review (now, or before now). It is important, in my judgment, that the Court should have clarity as to the implications of the Defendant's applications and whether the Defendant is storing up a delay point.

The Claimant's position

13   Mr McNall's arguments in response were, in essence as I saw it, as follows.

i) Procedural exclusivity requires handling with care. Technical debates about forum are to be avoided. The *Trim* case is distinguishable because it was a different species of statutory notice, and the discussion of property rights did not extend to A1P1. The Two Questions arise squarely out of private law rights to property. Having said that, the safeguarding principles of delay and alternative remedy are the proper focus for consideration of whether thePart 8 Claim is an abuse of process, or the Court should decide not to exercise its jurisdiction. It is really a question of identifying the right judicial forum and at the right time. That is the High Court, and now.

ii) The Part 8 Claim raises important HRA-based questions. The Two Questions are questions of law. They belong in Court. They can be determined, authoritatively, now. If either of the Two Questions is answered in the Claimant's favour that would be dispositive of these matters. No regulation 19 appeals would be needed; no regulation 20 Remediation Notice could be issued; no regulation 21 appeal would be needed. There is a 'penumbra of uncertainty' as to the jurisdictional reach of the regulation 19 appeals, and whether the Inspector on an appeal would deal with the questions of law regarding A1P1 and the 2015 Regulations. Those questions, even if an inspector on appeal is to answer them, are questions par excellence for a Court and specifically for the High Court. There is every reason why the Part 8 claim should proceed and be dealt with before the Court, and that substantial further costs in conjunction with the regulation 19 appeals should be avoided, if they can be. If judicial review had been commenced straight after the ED notices were issued in June and/or December 2020 – or if judicial review had been commenced in October 2021 – the "alternative remedy" principle would not have been a proper or clear basis for the judicial review court to refuse permission. There is no circumvention or flouting of that principle.

iii) In relation to the delay rule, a judicial review court dealing with a judicial review claim issued on 25 October 2021 would not have dismissed it on the grounds of delay. There has been no lack of promptness. Alternatively, an extension of time would be appropriate. There is the 'penumbra of uncertainty' about the jurisdictional reach of the appeal. There is the "one year" rule under section 7(5) of the HRA. That provision is important because it recognises that claims invoking HRA rights can be pursued other than by way of judicial review, within one year. It is also relevant to how strict the judicial review Court should be in an HRA case. Then there is the fact that the Defendant has been on clear notice, from the regulation 19 appeal documents filed by the Claimant, of the A1P1 arguments sought to be raised. That includes as to the applicability and invocability of the 2015 Regulations in the context of a Qualifying Quarry. The Defendant has known all along that the Claimant would wish to ventilate those human rights points. It has known all along that it would need to deal with them. Indeed, the same A1P1 points could in principle be raised by way of defence, were proceedings to be taken against the Claimant to penalise it for non-compliance with a Remediation Notice. Its answer includes the point that those arguments can properly be raised in the future and do not even need to be raised now. So there is no delay-based objection. Nor is there any prejudice from the Defendant now dealing with the Two Questions. After all, if the Part 8 Claim were to fail, the Defendant would be protected by a costs order made in the Part 8 proceedings.

Discussion

14   In my judgment, this is a classic alternative remedy case. The Court can readily posit the Claimant's representatives in October 2021, instead of choosing to raise the Two Questions by way of a Part 8 Claim, having commenced a claim for judicial review. That claim would have included an application for a stay of the appeal proceedings before the Inspectorate (CPR 54.10(2)(a)). Permission would have been refused, in light of the suitable alternative remedy available to the Claimant and being pursued. As the <u>Administrative Court Judicial Review Guide 2021</u> explains at §6.3.3.

> *Adequate alternative remedy. Judicial review is often said to be a remedy of last resort. If there is another route by which the decision in issue can be challenged, which provides an adequate remedy for the claimant, that alternative remedy should generally be used before applying for judicial review. The alternative remedy may come in various forms. Examples include an internal complaints procedure, review mechanism or appeal (whether statutory or non-statutory). If the Court finds that the claimant has (or had) an adequate alternative remedy, it will generally refuse permission to apply for judicial review.*

The appeals are an adequate alternative remedy in the circumstances. They should run their course. They may be dispositive. There was no good reason for avoiding or curtailing those avenues, and every good reason for their pursuit. If and insofar as the Claimant considers that it has points falling within the appellate jurisdiction of a regulation 19 appeal, it should be advancing those points before the appropriate decision-maker dealing with the appeal. That includes all of the arguments – which indeed can be found within the Claimant's appeal documents – about A1P1 and Qualifying Quarries and about whether and how the 2015 Regulations are to be interpreted and applied as a matter of law. The Claimant is fully protected so far as future ventilation and vindication in the High Court is concerned. A clear shortcoming in a Court considering A1P1 arguments at this stage is that they arise in a vacuum and without clarity about any settled, concrete regulatory action or its impacts. Overall, it would not be in the interests of justice or in the public interest for judicial review to take precedence over the appeal process, rather than the other way round. For these reasons, the Court would refuse permission for judicial review.

15   The alternative remedy point goes further. If there had been a judicial review filed promptly after 11 June 2020 and/or after 23 December 2020, permission would also have been refused because of the alternative remedy. Again, that is because of the last resort nature of judicial review, the primacy given to the statutory appeal before a specialist appellate decision-maker, the availability of the points in arguments on which the Claimant wishes to rely, the possibility – if needed – of resort to the High Court to make the arguments at an appropriate future stage, and all of the other virtues to which I have referred. In any event, the claim is not a 'protective' claim. Moreover, a focused judicial review pre-action letter – and the judicial review Acknowledgement of Service – would have put the Claimant and the permission judge in the same informed position as I am in. The Claimant is not being shut out (§12 above). The Defendant is not storing up delay objections to roll out at some later stage if arguments are raised before the High Court.

16   There is also the delay problem. In my judgment, a judicial review Court dealing with an application for permission for judicial review filed on 25 October 2021 would have concluded that the Claimant had acted with a conspicuous lack of promptness, that an extension of time would be needed, and that there is prejudice. The combination of the alternative remedy and the time-consuming and costly steps taken, the prejudice of then seeking to switch to Court proceedings, all in the context of issues raised in the appeal but then said to be regarded by the Claimant's new solicitors as "more suitable" for determination by a High Court Judge (letter of 11 October 2021), would have made the delay objection irresistible.

17   These conclusions are, in my judgment, very clear-cut. What follows, in my judgment, in the circumstances of the present case, is that this is one of those cases where – applying the true, narrow procedural exclusivity principle – it is appropriate to strike out the Part 8 Claim. I will strike out the claim as an abuse of process. I would, in the alternative and in any event, have decided for the same reasons that the Court should not exercise its jurisdiction pursuant to CPR 11(1)(b) and (6). The Part 8 Claim is dismissed. The Appeals can now run their course.

'Shield Letters'

18   I add this end-note. Questions and sometimes dilemmas can arise when a person affected by a public authority's ongoing actions wants to make sure they can raise a point with the Court at an appropriate time. Especially if there are alternative avenues which can be pursued. When is a challenge in Court going to be too soon, or too late? The parties cannot agree that there will be an extension of time: CPR 54.8(3). There may be third parties who would take a time point. One familiar practical step is to write – candidly and openly – asking the public authority (and any interested party) what their position would be about the appropriate time to raise identified point(s) and whether they will take a delay point if a challenge is raised at a later stage. If the answer is unresponsive or negative, the Court will understand why the Claimant proceeds protectively at that earlier stage. If clear letters are written accepting the reasonableness of waiting for a later stage, these

can properly be relied on as a 'shield' against criticism and as good evidence of reasonableness of action and good reason for any extension of time. In *R. (Archer) v Revenue and Customs Commissioners* [2019] EWCA Civ 1021; [2019] 1 W.L.R. 6355 at §92 Henderson LJ explained that "the sensible course" for a taxpayer pursuing "a potential alternative remedy" was to "seek HMRC's agreement that time for judicial review purposes should not begin to run until the … procedure has been completed", so that the Court could then "adopt a flexible and pragmatic approach" to timing, could "if necessary ensure that the taxpayer is not prejudiced", and could give "short shrift" to any refusal to agree "without justification". In *R. (Rafique-Aldawery) v St George's, University of London* [2018] EWCA Civ 2520; [2019] P.T.S.R. 658 at §21 Nicola Davies LJ said that where a claimant is "uncertain as to the course to be taken" it is open to them "to write to [the proposed defendant] stating that they do not, at that time, wish to institute proceedings for judicial review but putting [the defendant] on notice of the detail of the complaint and indicating that it may be necessary to apply for judicial review in the event that the [alternative] procedure does not provide a suitable remedy". She added that: "If in those circumstances the [defendant] later sought to take a time bar point in any subsequent judicial review proceedings the … letter could be filed in the proceedings. The fact that the [defendant was] on notice of the detail of the complaint from the outset would be a significant factor of which the court could take account in exercising its discretion to extend time". She said the course she had outlined "would likely serve to protect the legal position of the [claimant]".

19   In the present case, I have recorded the Defendant's clear position that nothing is shut out (§12 above). Mr McNall says this has had to be "teased out" of the Defendant at the hearing. But I cannot regard that as a fair criticism when no letter was written, at any stage, on behalf of the Claimant ventilating this topic with the Defendant. No letter was written seeking clarity or reassurance. Instead, the Claimant's new solicitors simply wrote on 11 October 2021 saying: "it appears to us that this matter turns on points of law which we believe are more suitable for determination by a High Court Judge". On that basis, they set about trying to get a Part 8 Claim heard, with the regulation 19 appeals stayed. They did not say the points of law were outside the scope of the appeals. They raised no concern about whether, if they were pursued after the alternative remedy of the appeals, the Defendant would be taking a time point.

Disposal

20   Circulating this judgment as a confidential draft enables me to deal here with consequential matters. The parties were agreed that the appropriate substantive orders to give effect to the judgment are: (1) the Defendant's application dated 19 July 2022 for a retrospective extension of time is granted; (2) the Claimant's Part 8 claim is dismissed; and (3) the Defendant shall provide the Inspector charged with determination of the Regulation 19 appeals with a copy of the Judgment. Costs were contentious in part. I am satisfied of the following. The Defendant should in principle have its costs of the Part 8 proceedings. That shall be on the "standard" basis: nothing in the Claimant's conduct justifies the "indemnity" basis. The exceptions are that the Claimant should not have to pay the Defendant's costs of drafting the application notices dated 27 May 2022 ('strike-out') and 19 July 2022 (the 'one-day' extension of time), the application fees incurred in making

those two applications, or the witness statement in support of the one-day extension application. These steps were necessitated by mistakes for which – in the circumstances of this case – the Defendant should, to that extent, bear its own costs. These are the only exceptions. There is no basis for any costs order in favour of the Claimant. My Order will make clear that the Claimant should have to pay the costs of the witness statement accompanying the 'strike-out' application. That is because an equivalent witness statement would likely have accompanied 'strike-out' if included in the original application, as it should have been.

HARRIS v ENVIRONMENT AGENCY

QUEEN'S BENCH DIVISION (ADMINISTRATIVE COURT)

Johnson J: 6 September 2022

[2022] EWHC 2264 (Admin); [2023] Env. L.R. 10

☞ Abstraction licences; Abstraction of water; Brexit; Conservation; Environment Agency; Investigations; Irrationality; Norfolk; Retained EU legislation; Risk; Sites of Special Scientific Interest; Special Areas of Conservation

H1 *Nature conservation—EU law-water abstraction—Habitats Directive—Water Resources Act 1991—Conservation of Habitats and Species Regulations—European Union (Withdrawal) Act 2018—review of abstraction licences—whether scope of review too narrow—whether breach of art.6(2) of Directive—whether breach of reg.9(3) of regulations—meaning of requirement to "have regard" to Directive— whether art.6(2) enforceable by domestic courts—whether decision irrational*

H2 The claimants (H) were residents who had been instrumental in the decision of the defendant (EA) not to renew two abstraction licences in the Norfolk Broads. They brought judicial review proceedings challenging EA's refusal to expand the scope of an investigation that it conducted into the effect of 240 licences for abstraction. That investigation concerned the effect of abstraction on just three Sites of Special Scientific Interest (SSSIs) and H argued that EA ought to review more broadly the impact of water abstraction to decide whether other licences should also be withdrawn or altered. Twenty-eight individual SSSIs together made up the Broads Special Area of Conservation (SAC) and 25 SSSIs made up the Broadlands Special Protection Area for Birds (SPA). The SAC and SPA were each designated as a "European site" protected under the Habitats Directive art.6, as was the Broadland Ramsar site. EA's Restoring Sustainable Abstraction (RSA) Programme began in 1999 to identify, investigate and resolve environmental damage caused by unsustainable water abstraction. Each RSA investigation addressed the impact of abstraction on a particular site, area or river, rather than on abstraction licences. This was in contrast with a Review of Consents (ROC) programme completed in 2010 that had focussed on licences. Under the RSA, once a site was identified as being at risk from abstraction, EA appraised the options, including using statutory powers to vary or revoke abstraction licences. The challenge was to the decision to limit the investigation to the three SSSIs and not to expand the coverage of the RSA investigation to other SSSIs within the SAC. The grounds for the claim were that: (1) EA was in breach of an obligation under the Habitats Directive to avoid the deterioration of protected habitats and disturbance of protected species; (2) that obligation had effect in domestic law by reason of the Conservation of Habitats and Species Regulations 2017 reg.9(3) which required EA to "have regard" to the Habitats Directive; (3) irrespective of the effect of reg.9(3), art.6(2) was enforceable by the domestic courts; and (4) EA's decision not to conduct a more expansive investigation into the impact of licenced water abstraction was irrational. It was common ground that reg.9(3) obliged EA to have regard to the requirements of art.6(2).

H3   **Held,** in allowing the claim:

H4   (1) The obligation to "have regard" to art.6(2) did not amount to an obligation to secure compliance with that article. It was striking that the statutory language for the duties imposed by regs 9(1) and 9(3) differed. Regulation 9(1) did not require the Secretary of State merely to have regard to the Habitats Directive but to secure compliance with the requirements of the Directive. Regulation 9(3) stated only that regard must be had to their requirements. The natural and conventional approach to the "have regard" duty was that it meant that EA was obliged to take account of the requirements of the Habitats Directive but may depart from its requirements if there was good reason to do so. In other words, it had to take account of the Habitats Directive but was entitled not itself to discharge all the requirements of the Directive where that could be justified. In the statutory context, the duty on EA to have regard to the requirements of the Habitats Directive meant that it had to take those requirements into account, and, insofar as it was the relevant public body with responsibility for fulfilling those requirements, then it had to discharge those requirements. In other words, the scope for departure that was ordinarily inherent in the words "have regard to" was considerably narrowed. That was entirely consistent with the approach that EA had sought to take. It was clear that it had regarded itself as bound by the Directive and sought to act in compliance with its requirements. Whether or not it had succeeded in discharging the requirements of art.6(2) was a separate issue.

H5   (2) It was agreed that the question of whether art.6(2) was enforceable by a United Kingdom (UK) court, irrespective of reg.9(3), turned on the application of s.4(2)(b) of the European Union (Withdrawal) Act 2018, namely whether the obligations under art.6(2) were of a kind recognised by the CJEU, or any court or tribunal in the UK, in a case decided before 11pm on 31 December 2020. Although the court in *Waddenzee* did not rule on the question of whether art.6(2) had direct effect, s.4(3) did not require that the particular provision in issue had been held to have direct effect. It only required that it was "of a kind" that had been held to have direct effect. There was a close relationship between art.6(2) and (3) and the former was "of a kind" that was recognised in *Waddenzee* as having direct effect. Further, the question of whether art.6(2) had legal effect in domestic proceedings had been addressed by the decision of the Upper Tribunal in *Natural England v Warren*. Accordingly, by reason of s.4 of the 2018 Act, art.6(2) continued to be recognised and available in domestic law and was to be enforced accordingly.

H6   (3) All permanent licences had been scrutinised during the ROC process. *Waddenzee* recognised that if such review was adequate, that satisfied art.6(3), and that art.6(2) had no role to play at that point. All time-limited licences were scrutinised when they fell to be renewed and the process, in principle, satisfied art.6(3), with art.6(2) having no role to play at that point. The process was, in principle, capable of complying with the requirements of Habitats Directive art.6. There was no general obligation proactively to review a licence unless there was some reason to do so. The fact that EA reviewed the impact of abstraction on three sites did not, in itself, mean that it was obliged to review the impact on all sites. On the other hand, the authorities were clear that it was not sufficient to wait until damage to a site occurred before taking remedial action. If there was reason to believe that there was a risk of damage, then it was necessary to take remedial steps. EA did not suggest that there was no risk of damage to other sites, besides the three SSSIs, and accepted that there was a potential risk.

H7   (4) EA may have reacted appropriately where it became aware of evidence of a specific risk to a particular site. However, the evidence showed that the ROC was not effective in ensuring that abstraction did not cause damage to protected sites and there thus remained a generalised risk from abstraction across the entire SAC. Having regard to the precautionary principle, that was sufficient to trigger the art.6(2) duty. It would be contrary to the precautionary principle and the reasoning in *Grune Liga Sachsen* if art.6(2) could only be triggered once it became clear that a particular site was at risk by an identified mechanism from abstraction at a specific location. It was sufficient that a generalised risk had been established, as a result of the demonstration of flaws in the ROC process, to require "appropriate steps" to be taken. A court would be slow to question EA's expert assessment as to the steps that should be taken. It was, however, not open to EA to take no steps: that was a breach of art.6(2). The process adopted in respect of time limited licences was, in principle, capable of securing compliance with art.6. The same applied to new licence applications. However, there were significant limitations to the ongoing work being done in respect of permanent licences. It followed that EA had not taken sufficient steps in respect of the risks to sites in the SAC, beyond the three SSSIs, posed by abstraction in accordance with permanent licences. As it was only EA that could vary or revoke permanent licences, it could not absolve itself from compliance with art.6 by pointing to work done by other public authorities. It had not therefore complied with art.6(2). Although it had taken account of art.6, it had not justified its failure to take steps in respect of the risks and was therefore in breach of its obligation under reg.9(3).

H8   (5) The explanation for not expanding the RSA programme to cover additional sites was coherent, amounting to a rational cost-benefit analysis. The problem for EA was that, for the reasons given, the programme of works would not discharge the art.6(2) obligation. Having committed itself to discharge that obligation, it was irrational not to expand the RSA programme without having any alternative mechanism in place that could ensure compliance with art.6(2). It followed that even if art.6(2) was not enforceable by the High Court, EA's decision was flawed on common law grounds. On that basis, H's rationality challenge also succeeded.

H9 **Cases referred to:**

Commission v Ireland (C-418/04) EU:C:2007:780

Commission of the European Communities v United Kingdom (C-6/04) EU:C:2005:626; [2006] Env. L.R. 29

Grune Liga Sachsen eV v Freistaat Sachsen (C-399/14) EU:C:2016:10; [2016] P.T.S.R. 1240; [2016] Env. L.R. 32

Landelijke Vereniging tot Behoud van de Waddenzee v Staatssecretaris van Landbouw, Natuurbeheer en Visserij (C-127/02) EU:C:2004:482; [2005] 2 C.M.L.R. 31; [2005] Env. L.R. 14

Natural England v Warren [2019] UKUT 300 (AAC); [2020] P.T.S.R. 565

R. (on the application of Boggis) v Natural England [2009] EWCA Civ 1061; [2010] P.T.S.R. 725; [2010] Env. L.R. 13

R. (on the application of Friends of the Earth Ltd) v Environment Agency [2003]
EWHC 3193 (Admin); [2004] Env. L.R. 31; [2004] A.C.D. 27
R. (on the application of London Oratory School Governors) v Schools Adjudicator
[2015] EWHC 1012 (Admin); [2015] E.L.R. 335
R. (on the application of Mott) v Environment Agency [2016] EWCA Civ 564;
[2016] 1 W.L.R. 4338; [2017] Env. L.R. 1

H10 **Legislation referred to:**
TFEU art.191
Ramsar Convention on Wetlands of International Importance Especially as
Waterfowl Habitat 1971
European Communities Act 1972 s.2
Water Resources Act 1991 ss.24, 38, 52 and 53
Directive 92/43 (Habitats) [1992] OJ L206/7 arts 2, 4 and 6, Annexes 1 and 2
Conservation (Natural Habitats, &c.) Regulations 1994 (SI 1994/2716) regs 3 and
50
Environment Act 1995 ss.1 and 6
Conservation of Habitats and Species Regulations 2010 (SI 2010/490)
Conservation of Habitats and Species Regulations 2017 (SI 2017/1012) regs 9, 65
and 102
European Union (Withdrawal) Act 2018 ss.1A, 1B, 2, 3, 4, 6 and 20
European Union (Withdrawal) Act 2020 s.39

H11 *R. Wald KC* (instructed by Freeths LLP) appeared on behalf of the claimants.
M. Dale-Harris (instructed by Environment Agency) appeared on behalf of the
defendant.

JUDGMENT

MR JUSTICE JOHNSON:

1   The claimants, Angelika and Timothy Harris, live in the Norfolk Broads. They
are concerned that water abstraction is causing irremediable damage to the
environment, including ecosystems that are legally protected. Their intervention
was instrumental in the decision of the defendant, the Environment Agency, not
to renew two abstraction licences. The claimants believe that the Environment
Agency ought to review more broadly the impact of water abstraction to decide
whether other licences should also be withdrawn or altered. They challenge, by
judicial review, the Environment Agency's refusal to expand the scope of an
investigation that it conducted into the effect of 240 licences for abstraction. That
investigation concerned the effect of abstraction on just three Sites of Special
Scientific Interest ("the three SSSIs").

2   The claimants' case is that:

(1) the Environment Agency is in breach of an obligation under article 6(2) of
the EU Habitats Directive (92/43/EEC) ("the Habitats Directive") to avoid
the deterioration of protected habitats and disturbance of protected species.

(2) The obligation under article 6(2) of the Habitats Directive has effect in
domestic law by reason of regulation 9(3) of the Conservation of Habitats

and Species Regulations 2017 ("the Habitats Regulations") which requires the Environment Agency to "have regard" to the Habitats Directive.

(3) Irrespective of the effect of regulation 9(3) of the Habitats Regulations, article 6(2) of the Habitats Directive is enforceable by the domestic courts.

(4) The Environment Agency's decision not to conduct a more expansive investigation into the impact of licenced water abstraction is irrational.

3   The Environment Agency accepts that it must have regard to article 6(2) of the Habitats Directive. It maintains that it has done so and that it has, after taking it into account, reasonably decided to limit its investigation of the impact of the 240 licences to the three SSSIs. It disputes that article 6(2) has direct effect in domestic law beyond the obligation to "have regard" to it. In any event, it maintains that it is acting compatibly with the requirements of article 6(2).

4   Permission to claim judicial review was granted by Chamberlain J. The parties have cooperated closely in identifying areas of agreement and dispute and focussing argument on the latter. They agree that the outcome of the claim depends on the resolution of the following issues:

(1) The ambit of the obligation, under regulation 9(3) of the Habitats Regulations, to "have regard" to the requirements of the Habitats Directive, including whether that mandates compliance with article 6(2) of the Habitats Directive (paragraphs 73-88 below).

(2) Whether article 6(2) of the Habitats Directive imposes an obligation of a kind recognised by the Court of Justice of the European Union ("CJEU") or any court or tribunal in the United Kingdom in a case decided before 2021 (paragraphs 89-94 below).

(3) Whether the Environment Agency has breached article 6(2) of the Habitats Directive by limiting its investigation of water abstraction to the three SSSIs (paragraphs 95-106 below).

(4) Whether the Environment Agency acted irrationally by limiting its investigation of water abstraction to the three SSSIs (paragraphs 107-109 below).

5   There is also a dispute between the parties as to the relevance (when determining issues (3) and (4)) of (a) funding constraints on the Environment Agency and (b) the possibility that it might undertake further work in respect of the impact of water abstraction, outside the ambit of the programme that examined the three SSSIs.

The factual background

The parties

6   The Environment Agency was established by section 1 of the Environment Act 1995. By section 6(1)(b) of the 1995 Act, its duties include the promotion of the conservation of flora and fauna which are dependent on an aquatic environment. It is responsible for the grant (and variation and revocation) of licences for the abstraction of water.

7   The claimants own and reside at Catfield Hall, Norfolk. That is within the area of Catfield Fen which is, itself, within the area of the 240 licences that were considered in the Environment Agency's investigation. The claimants also own land in Hickling and Potter Heigham which is also within the area covered by the

240 licences. They have been concerned for many years about the condition of fenland in the area where they live and own land. They are particularly concerned about the impact of the abstraction of groundwater for agricultural and other purposes. They have been raising those concerns with the Environment Agency for well over a decade. They successfully supported the Environment Agency's decision to vary two licences when that decision was challenged on appeal.

Impact of water abstraction on ecosystems

8   Groundwater is water that is present in the ground. Many ecosystems are dependent on a supply of groundwater. Groundwater may be abstracted (in the Norfolk Broads, from either the chalk, the crag, or the Sandringham sands) for use by the public water supply, industry, and agriculture. A licence is required to extract groundwater. Such licences may either be permanent (with no requirement to renew) or time limited (with the possibility of periodic renewal). The Environment Agency has power to revoke abstraction licences: sections 52 and 53 of the Water Resources Act 1991 (see paragraph 41 below).

9   The abstraction of groundwater has an impact on the supply of water to wetland habitats. The precise mechanism is complex. There are many unknowns, particularly in respect of the pathways by which water travels between the aquifer (underground permeable rock, from which abstraction generally takes place) and the shallow water table (from which it is accessed by flora). Changes to groundwater flows can also influence the chemistry within the ground and this can impact on the surface ecology. This all means that it is difficult to predict the locations where water abstraction from a particular area might have an impact, or to predict what the impact might be. It is known that there can be an impact over a considerable distance: abstraction from one location may affect an ecosystem several kilometres away. It is also known that it can take many years for the impact of abstraction to become fully apparent. Changes to ecosystems can, initially, be too subtle to be detected by routine monitoring (for example, loss of specialist invertebrates, or plants that only naturally occur in low densities). Once changes to an ecosystem are apparent, it may be too late to put matters right; by that stage, irremediable damage may have occurred.

10   For this reason, the interested party ("Natural England") (which has statutory responsibility for providing advice to the Environment Agency and others), advised the Environment Agency in October 2020 that it was necessary to consider water supply in the Broads and to take any necessary action to restore ground and surface water levels. For the same reason, the Environment Agency itself recognises an obligation to apply a "precautionary approach to dealing with adverse effects" such that it must take appropriate and proportionate action to ensure that licenced water abstraction does not lead to adverse effects.

The Norfolk Broadland river valleys

11   The Norfolk Broads is, in terms of rainfall, one of the driest parts of the country. Long-term average annual rainfall is between 600mm and 730mm. The low rainfall is exacerbated by periods of drought. The Broads also lie within an area where a great deal of irrigated fruit and vegetable production takes place. This is reliant on water abstraction. In the Bure and Thurne Reporting Area alone, more than 60 million litres of ground water and surface water are abstracted each day. So, there

is a relatively small amount of rainfall, but a considerable amount of water is taken from the ground.

12   The exceptional biodiversity in the Norfolk Broads has resulted in it having the highest level of national and international nature conservation protection. There are 28 individual SSSIs which together make up The Broads Special Area of Conservation ("SAC"). There are 25 SSSIs that make up the Broadlands Special Protection Area for birds ("SPA").

13   The SAC and SPA are each designated as a "European site" protected under article 6 of the Habitats Directive, as is the Broadland Ramsar site which is designated under the Ramsar Convention. The area supports water and wetland habitats which host the most diverse areas of fen vegetation in Western Europe. They support many rare animal and plant species. The features of the SAC which give rise to its status include types of calcareous fens and alluvial forests which are priority natural species and habitats respectively (listed in Annex 1 and Annex 2 of the Habitats Directive). The SPA's qualifying features include the great bittern, the ruff, and the Eurasian marsh harrier. The claimants' case applies to the entirety of all three European sites, but it is sufficient to focus on the SAC in order to resolve the claim.

14   The 28 SSSIs within the SAC include the Ant Broads and Marshes SSSI, Alderfen Broad SSSI, and Broad Fen, Dilham SSSI. These are the three SSSIs which were the subject of the Environment Agency's investigation.

15   There has been a measurable decline in some habitats in the SAC over recent decades. The Environment Agency believes that the abstraction of water has contributed to this decline. For example, the Ant Broads and Marshes hosts the largest population of fen orchid in England, but there has been a decline in the habitats that it needs to thrive. This is due to water abstraction.

16   In 2019 Natural England provided the following advice to the Environment Agency:

> "Given that the Broads is the major site in the UK for some of the Annex 1 habitats classified as Endangered and Vulnerable within Europe, the importance of maintaining the existing habitat extent and improving the integrity of supporting processes (e.g. the supply of low-nutrient base-rich water) cannot be [overstated].
>
> …
>
> Experimental work on abstraction effects on calcareous fens (Johansen *et al* 2011) clearly shows abstraction has impacts on water flows through a fen at distances of kilometres from the abstraction point. This effect occurs even whilst water level changes are indistinguishable from natural level variations. Water source and flows are intrinsic features of the hydrological regime of all wetland sites. As a result hydrological modelling of flows through sites is necessary to determine effects of abstraction."

The Review of Consents

17   Regulation 50 of the Conservation (Natural Habitats etc) Regulations 1994 ("the 1994 Habitats Regulations") required the Environment Agency to review, as soon as reasonably practicable, all licences for the abstraction of water that were granted before 30 October 1994 and which were likely to have a significant effect on any

European site. In order to discharge that obligation, the Environment Agency reviewed those licences between 2002 and 2010. This resulted in licences being affirmed, amended, or revoked, as appropriate.

18   The review identified four SSSIs in the Norfolk Broads where it was assessed that the risk associated with water abstraction was unacceptable. Licence changes were implemented to address the risks. The Environment Agency concluded that abstraction at other SSSIs (including the three SSSIs) was sustainable and that no further licence changes were required.

19   Following the completion of the Review of Consents programme, a "Renewals Communique" process was established between the Environment Agency and Natural England. This enables Natural England to indicate any concerns in relation to the renewal of particular licences. In a number of cases Natural England has expressed concerns about the renewal of licences which were approved during the Review of Consents.

Restoring Sustainable Abstraction ("RSA") Programme

20   The RSA programme began in 1999. Its purpose is to identify, investigate, and resolve environmental damage caused by unsustainable water abstraction. The focus was on sites, with each RSA investigation addressing the impact of abstraction on a particular site, area, or river (by contrast, the Review of Consents had focussed on abstraction licences).

21   The RSA programme began with the identification of sites at potential risk. Once a site was identified as being at risk from abstraction, the Environment Agency appraised the options. These included using statutory powers under the 1991 Act to vary or revoke abstraction licences.

22   By 2012, approximately 500 sites had been identified throughout England as being at risk. Most of these were SSSIs. In 2012 a decision was made to close the programme to new sites. This enabled the Environment Agency to plan the workload, timescales, and costs to complete the programme. The Environment Agency stresses that its decision did not mean that no new sites could be investigated, just that any further investigation would not take place under the RSA programme and would instead take place through the Environment Agency's "River Basin Management Plans." Conversely, the Environment Agency does not suggest that all sites at risk were captured by the RSA programme. It recognises that further sites are likely to be at risk.

Ant Broads and Marshes RSA Investigation

23   At a meeting with the Environment Agency in 2010 the claimants expressed concern about the impact of abstraction on Catfield Fen and the Environment Agency's "apparent lethargy and indifference". For example, they said that Milkweed (which is an important food source for the swallowtail butterfly) was suffering due to lack of groundwater. They made particular reference to abstraction at Plumsgate Road. They said that work undertaken by the Environment Agency indicated that abstraction at Plumsgate Road was having an effect more than 1km to the west, beyond Catfield Fen. They asked the Environment Agency to "stop the abstraction" (i.e. to revoke the licence).

24   The Environment Agency initiated a new investigation under the RSA programme, partly as a result of the information provided by the claimants. Initially,

the investigation was focussed on the evidence that had been presented in respect of Catfield Fen, but it also covered the Ant Broads and Marshes SSSI. In 2011, Natural England and the claimants compiled and presented a compendium of evidence documenting changes to the ecology of Catfield Fen which were caused by changes in the hydrological regime. The Environment Agency responded by commissioning a report on Catfield Fen's hydrology and hydrogeology. The report did not identify any definitive impact from abstraction, but there was broad agreement that abstraction, in combination with other factors, might be the cause of observable ecological changes. Modelling assessments were undertaken in 2014. These indicated that abstraction was reducing the upward flow of groundwater to the shallow surface water table. This had an impact on surface water levels.

25   In July 2017 an interim investigation report was produced. This raised concerns about changes to (and risk to) certain flora, including the calcareous fen habitat and the fen orchid populations. It summarised the work that had been undertaken by the RSA programme.

The Plumsgate Road and Ludham Road licences

26   Licences for the abstraction of water from sites at Plumsgate Road and Ludham Road (which are close to Catfield Fen) were granted in the late 1980s. They were subject to periodical renewal. They each permitted the abstraction of water from the crag aquifer for spray irrigation, with annual limits of 68,000m^3 and 22,700m^3 respectively. The licences continued to be renewed after the Review of Consents.

27   In May 2015 the Environment Agency refused to renew these two licences, in part because of the potential impact on flora at Catfield Fen which had been demonstrated by the RSA investigation and by the evidence produced by Natural England, the Royal Society for the Protection of Birds ("RSPB"), and the claimants. The Environment Agency was particularly concerned about the impact on calcareous fen and the fen orchid. The Environment Agency's decision was upheld on appeal by Elizabeth Hill, a Planning Inspector appointed by the Secretary of State. In her decision of 16 September 2016, Ms Hill charts the evidence of ecological change at Catfield Fen. The RSPB measured a 50% decline of calcareous fen between 1991 and 2015. This was corroborated by other evidence. There were also increasing acidity values and greater evidence of drier conditions across Catfield Fen. There was also evidence of a one third reduction of the population of fen orchid. Ms Hill concluded that the possibility that this was due to water abstraction pursuant to the two licences could not be ruled out.

28   At the end of her written decision, Ms Hill said:

"I… acknowledge that Mr and Mrs Harris have committed their time and resources into managing [part of Catfield Fen] in accordance with the [Higher Land Stewardship scheme] to maintain and improve its conservation value. Mr and Mrs Harris have… said that the outcome of the appeals should influence the EA's RSA programme more generally. However, that is a matter for the EA and these decisions cover only the submitted appeals."

29   This claim picks up where Ms Hill left off.

Natural England's Site Improvement plan

30   On 8 March 2018 Natural England provided the second version of a Site Improvement Plan for the SAC. It identified the risk of water abstraction as "a key issue potentially affecting the full range of Broads' habitats and species." It said that there was a need to "[i]nvestigate and restore sustainable abstraction" at sites where abstraction might be impacting on a particular site, and "to review licences in the context of a changing climate." Nothing within the Site Improvement Plan suggests that the need for such action was limited to the three SSSIs.

Limitation of Ant Broads and Marshes RSA to the three SSSIs

31   In 2018, the Environment Agency conducted an external consultation. Consultees suggested extending the Ant Broads and Marshes RSA investigation so as to cover other SSSIs. The Environment Agency initially rejected the suggestion because the RSA programme was closed to the addition of new sites. However, it then decided to add two further sites immediately adjacent to the Ant Broads and Marshes SSSI - Broad Fen, Dilham SSSI and Alderfen Broad SSSI.

32   It is the decision to limit the investigation to the three SSSIs and not to expand the coverage of the RSA investigation to other SSSIs within the SAC, which is the decision that is under challenge in these proceedings.

33   Ian Pearson, the Environment Agency's Lead Officer for the Ant Broads and Marshes RSA investigation, explains the reasons for the decision in his witness evidence. They are that:

   (1)   The RSA programme was closed to new sites.
   (2)   The Environment Agency's limited resources did not enable it to embark on further investigations.
   (3)   However, Broad Fen, Dilham SSSI and Alderfen Broad SSSI could be added without incurring significant additional expense.
   (4)   Those two sites were the most immediately adjacent to the Ant Broads and Marshes SSSI and supported similar SAC habitats.
   (5)   The inclusion of these two sites would inform pending licence renewal applications.
   (6)   There were no new concerns at these two sites which had not already been recognised and addressed through the Review of Consents process.

34   Insofar as Natural England had identified concerns in relation to other sites, the Environment Agency indicated that additional modelling work would be undertaken outside the RSA programme.

Natural England's October 2020 advice

35   On 28 October 2020 Natural England advised the Environment Agency on the assessment of abstraction licences. It said that knowledge had evolved since the Review of Consents process. This evolving knowledge needed to inform the approach. The Environment Agency should, when determining licences for other protected sites, act consistently with the approach taken in the Ant Broads and Marshes and should conduct a "systematic assessment of the evidence of ecosystem dependence on the supporting groundwater body or surface water system and the level of impact on these water bodies and systems…"

The Ant Broads and Marshes RSA Report

36   The Ant Broads and Marshes RSA Report was published on 14 June 2021. It addresses in considerable detail (and on the basis of extensive modelling and other work) the effect on the three SSSIs of abstractions under 240 licences in a screening area which covered, and extended well beyond, those SSSIs. It does not consider the effect of abstraction on other SSSIs within, or adjacent to, the screening area.

37   The Report concludes that it is not possible to rule out abstraction of water as a cause for adverse effects across the Broads SAC. It recognises that the Habitats Regulations require it to apply a precautionary approach and to take action to reduce abstraction where there was a risk that abstraction might cause such adverse effects. It identifies a number of options to achieve sustainable levels of abstraction so far as the three SSSIs are concerned. The preferred option entails the revocation or modification of 21 permanent abstraction licences, the expiry (without further renewal) of 10 time-limited licences, and the refusal of 4 further pending licence applications.

38   The modelling that was conducted for the RSA investigation shows that there are risks to other sites within the SAC, beyond the three SSSIs that were the focus of the investigation. Advice from Natural England is that seemingly small changes in the proportion of water supply, and consequential effects on water chemistry, can be significant to cause adverse effects to the habitats and species for which the SAC is recognised. The Environment Agency applies a threshold for water flow of a 5% deviation from that which would occur under natural conditions (i.e. without abstraction). It can only safely be concluded that abstraction has no adverse effect on site integrity if that threshold is not breached. The modelling shows that this threshold is exceeded in many areas across the SAC, including (but not limited to) the three SSSIs.

Further work following RSA Report

39   The work undertaken by the Environment Agency as part of its RSA programme was valuable in identifying new assessment tools and refinements to existing models. These are documented in a technical report. The Environment Agency accepts that the application of these new tools and refined models may demonstrate that there is a risk of harm to other sites. It is, accordingly, conducting further work. This includes work on the implications of the conclusions of the technical report for three further SSSIs. Preliminary indications are that the hydrological criteria that were used in the Ant Broads and Marshes RSA report are not currently met at two of those three further SSSIs (but there is an outstanding question as to whether those criteria are appropriate for the three further SSSIs). The Environment Agency is also using the new tools and refined models when considering applications for new licences, and applications to renew existing licences.

40   Natural England has indicated that "further work is needed to assess the impacts of water supply on protected sites and priority habitats out-with the Ant Valley and action taken as necessary." The Environment Agency emphasise that Natural England has not said in terms that this work is required "urgently" or "without delay".

Legal framework

Water Resources Act 1991

41   Chapter 2 of Part 2 of the Water Resources Act 1991 regulates the licensing of
water abstraction. Section 24 prohibits water abstraction without a licence. Section
38 makes provision for the Environment Agency to determine licence applications
(requiring that it has regard to all relevant circumstances). Section 52 permits the
Environment Agency to formulate proposals for revoking or varying existing
licences. Section 53 permits the Environment Agency to revoke or vary a licence
pursuant to such proposals.

The precautionary principle

42   Article 191(2) of the Treaty on the Functioning of the European Union provides
that Union policy on the environment shall aim at a high level of protection and
shall be based on the precautionary principle, and on the principle that preventive
action should be taken, and that environmental damage should, as a priority, be
rectified at source.

Habitats Directive

43   The Habitats Directive concerns the conservation of natural habitats and wild
fauna and flora. Its aim is to contribute to biodiversity in Member States through
the conservation of natural habitats, wild fauna, and flora: article 2.
44   It defines "natural habitat types of Community interest" to include those that
present outstanding examples of typical characteristics of the Continental region
and are listed in Annex 1. It defines "priority natural habitat types" to mean natural
habitat types that are in danger of disappearance (where certain other conditions
are also fulfilled). Again, they are listed in Annex 1. They include calcareous fens
with *Cladium mariscus* and species of the *Caricion davallianae*, and alluvial forests
with *Alnus glutinosa* and *Fraxinus excelsior*. It defines "special area of
conservation" to mean a site that is designated by the Member State where
conservation measures are applied for the maintenance or restoration of the natural
habitats or species for which the site is designated. It defines "species of Community
interest" to include species that are endangered, vulnerable, rare, or endemic and
requiring particular attention. They are listed in Annex 2. They include fen orchid
Liparis loeselii.
45   Article 4 prescribes a process for designating a site as a special area of
conservation. It requires Member States to establish priorities for the maintenance
or restoration of those habitats listed in Annex 1, and those species listed in Annex
2, in the light of any threats of degradation or destruction to which those sites are
exposed.
46   Article 6 states:

> "…2. Member States shall take appropriate steps to avoid, in the special areas
> of conservation, the deterioration of natural habitats and the habitats of species
> as well as disturbance of the species for which the areas have been designated,
> in so far as such disturbance could be significant in relation to the objectives
> of this Directive.

3. Any plan or project not directly connected with or necessary to the management of the site but likely to have a significant effect thereon, either individually or in combination with other plans or projects, shall be subject to appropriate assessment of its implications for the site in view of the site's conservation objectives. In the light of the conclusions of the assessment of the implications for the site and subject to the provisions of paragraph 4, the competent national authorities shall agree to the plan or project only after having ascertained that it will not adversely affect the integrity of the site concerned and, if appropriate, after having obtained the opinion of the general public.
..."

47   In *Landelijke Vereniging tot Behoud van de Waddenzee v Staatssecretaris van Landbouw, Natuurbeheer en Visserij* (C-127/02) [2005] 2 C.M.L.R. 31, the Grand Chamber of the European Court of Justice addressed the relationship between articles 6(2) and 6(3), in the context of the grant of annual licences for mechanical cockle fishing. The following principles emerge from the judgment:

   (1) The Habitats Directive must be interpreted in accordance with the precautionary principle: [44].
   (2) An activity such as mechanical fishing is within the concept of a "plan or project" within the meaning of article 6(3): [27].
   (3) Each annual grant of a licence is properly considered as a "plan or project" within the meaning of article 6(3): [28].
   (4) Where a licence has been granted in a manner compatible with article 6(3) (so only after ascertaining that it will not adversely affect the integrity of the site concerned, and consequently not likely to give rise to deterioration or significant disturbance) article 6(2) is (at that point) superfluous: [35]-[36].
   (5) But if the plan or project subsequently proves likely to give rise to deterioration of habitats or significant disturbance of species, article 6(2) provides a mechanism for ensuring the conservation of natural habitats and fauna and flora: [37].
   (6) Thus, article 6(3) ensures, prospectively, that a relevant plan or project is authorised only if it will not adversely affect the integrity of the site, whereas article 6(2) imposes a general protection obligation to avoid deterioration and significant disturbance: [38].

48   Article 6(2) therefore imposes a proactive preventive requirement: Commission notice "Managing Natura 2000 sites: The provisions of article 6 of the Habitats' Directive 92/43/EEC" at paragraphs 3.2 and 4.5.1. Compliance with article 6(2) cannot be achieved by reacting to demonstrable deterioration. Anticipatory measures are required to prevent deterioration before it occurs: *Commission v Ireland* (C-418/04) EU:C:2007:780 at [207]-[208]. This is an aspect of the precautionary principle.

49   Thus, where it appears that there is a risk of deterioration of a protected habitat, article 6(2) of the Habitats Directive requires that "appropriate steps" are taken to avoid that deterioration: *Grune Liga Sachsen eV v Freistaat Sachsen* (C-399/14) EU:C:2016:10; [2016] P.T.S.R. 1240 at [41]-[44]a.

50   This means that where it becomes apparent that there may be a risk to a protected habitat or species as a result of the licenced abstraction of water, article 6(2) imposes an obligation to review the applicable licences: *Grune Liga* at [44]. The review must be sufficiently robust to guarantee that the abstraction of water will not cause significant damage to ecosystems that are protected under the Habitats Directive: *Grune Liga* at [53].

Habitats Regulations

51   The 1994 Habitats Regulations transposed the Habitats Directive in England and Wales. They were consolidated and updated by the Conservation of Habitats and Species Regulations 2010 which, in turn, were consolidated and updated by the Conservation of Habitats and Species Regulations 2017. As explained below, the Habitats Regulations continue to have effect in domestic law because they are EU-derived domestic legislation: sections 1B(7) and 2(1) of the European Union (Withdrawal) Act 2018. The Habitats Regulations are thus retained EU Law: section 6(7) of the 2018 Act. It follows that they must be interpreted in accordance with retained EU case law and retained principles of EU law: section 6(3) of the 2018 Act.

52   Regulation 9 of the Habitats Regulations states:

> "9 Duties relating to compliance with the Directives
> (1) The appropriate authority, the nature conservation bodies and, in relation to the marine area, a competent authority must exercise their functions which are relevant to nature conservation, including marine conservation, so as to secure compliance with the requirements of the Directives.
> …
> (3) Without prejudice to the preceding provisions, a competent authority, in exercising any of its functions, must have regard to the requirements of the Directives so far as they may be affected by the exercise of those functions."

53   The "appropriate authority" means the Secretary of State; the "nature conservation bodies" means (in relation to England) Natural England; a "competent authority" includes any public body (and so, in particular, includes the Environment Agency); the "Directives" include the Habitats Directive: regulation 3.

54   Regulation 65(1), read with regulation 102(5) and (6), requires that when a site which has a water abstraction licence becomes a European site, the Environment Agency must, as soon as is reasonably practicable, undertake a review of the licence (and, if necessary, vary or revoke the licence following the review).

Withdrawal from European Union: the European Union (Withdrawal) Act 2018

55   The 2018 Act repeals the European Communities Act 1972 and converts EU law, as it stood at the end of 2020, into domestic law.

56   Legislation (such as the Habitats Regulations) passed under section 2(2) of the 1972 Act is EU-derived domestic legislation and continues to have effect in domestic law: section 2(1).

57   Section 3 provides that "direct EU legislation" forms part of domestic law. The Habitats Directive is not direct EU legislation (see section 3(2) and the definition of "EU tertiary legislation" in section 20, which excludes EU directives).

58   Section 4 (as amended by the European Union (Withdrawal) Act 2020) states:

> "4 Savings for rights etc. under section 2(1) of the ECA
>> (1) Any… obligations… which, immediately before IP completion day —
>>> (a) are recognised and available in domestic law by virtue of section 2(1) of the European Communities Act 1972, and
>>> (b) are enforced… accordingly,
>>
>> continue on and after IP completion day to be recognised and available in domestic law (and to be enforced… accordingly).
>> (2) Subsection (1) does not apply to any… obligations… so far as they—
>>> …
>>> (b) arise under an EU directive (including as applied by the EEA agreement) and are not of a kind recognised by the European Court or any court or tribunal in the United Kingdom in a case decided before IP completion day (whether or not as an essential part of the decision in the case).
>
> …"

59   Questions as to the meaning and effect of retained EU law (so, including the Habitats Regulations, and the obligation under article 6(2) which continues to have effect under section 4) must be decided in accordance with retained general principles of EU law: section 6(3)(a). The precautionary principle is a retained general principle of EU law: section 6(7).

60   IP completion day is 11pm on 31 December 2020: section 1A(6) of the 2018 Act and section 39(1) of the 2020 Act.

The claim for judicial review

61   The claimants say that, so far as the three SSSIs are concerned, the Environment Agency has acted lawfully and in accordance with article 6 of the Habitats Directive. The work done by the Environment Agency (and the resultant licensing changes) will ensure that there is no prospect that water abstraction will cause deterioration of the habitats or significant disturbance of the species at the three SSSIs. The claimants are not critical of the RSA investigation or report so far as it addresses the three SSSIs.

62   The claimants' case is that the Environment Agency acted unlawfully by limiting its investigation to the three SSSIs. They say that once it decided to review the 240 abstraction licences, it was required to consider their impact across the entirety of the SAC. Further, once the Environment Agency was aware of potential risks to other sites, it was obliged to address those potential risks.

63   The legal foundation for the claimants' claim is article 6(2) of the Habitats Directive. Their submission is that article 6(2) has effect in domestic law by virtue of regulation 9(3) of the Habitats Regulations. Although that regulation imposes an obligation only to "have regard" to the requirements of the Habitats Directive, in context this requires compliance with the Habitats Directive. This (say the claimants) was the finding of Sullivan J in *R. (Friends of the Earth) v Environment Agency* [2003] EWHC 3193 (Admin) at [57]. This interpretation is also mandated by a concession made by the Government in *Commission v United Kingdom* (C-6/04) [2006] Env. L.R. 29. Further, the claimants rely on the fact that regulation 9(1) imposes an obligation on Natural England to secure compliance with the

Habitats Directive, together with the fact that the Environment Agency acts on advice from Natural England. This means, they say, that the Environment Agency thereby itself comes under an obligation to secure compliance with the Directive.

64   Irrespective of the correct application of regulation 9(3), the claimants contend that article 6(2) is enforceable in domestic legal proceedings. That is because article 6 was recognised as having direct application in domestic law by the European Court of Justice in *Waddenzee* and by the Upper Tribunal (Administrative Appeals Chamber) in *Natural England v Warren* [2019] UKUT 300 (AAC); [2020] P.T.S.R. 565, and because section 4(2)(b) of the 2018 Act preserves that recognition.

65   The claimants' substantive case is that the decision to limit the RSA investigation to the three SSSIs was in breach of article 6(2) and was irrational.

66   The RSA programme amounts to the Environment Agency's purported compliance with article 6(2) in respect of the SAC. The "appropriate steps" comprise the review of the 240 licences in the screening area so as to ensure that abstraction does not give rise to a risk of deterioration or significant disturbance. The problem is that the Environment Agency has not conducted the review across the entirety of the SAC but only in respect of three SSSIs. Further, the evidence shows that the Review of Consents was flawed. It can no longer be relied on as demonstrating that there is no risk to sites within the SAC. It is therefore necessary to conduct a review across the entirety of the SAC. The failure to do so amounts to a breach of article 6(2).

67   Irrespective of the question of the enforceability of article 6(2) in domestic proceedings, the Environment Agency has decided to comply with article 6(2) and has devised a programme of work to discharge that obligation. Its decision making as to the work required was irrational, because there was no good reason to limit the RSA investigation to just three SSSIs. The potential risks apply across all the SSSIs within the screening area. Alderfen Broad SSSI and Broad Fen Dilham SSSI were not, on the available evidence, at any greater risk than other SSSIs. The Environment Agency recognised that there are priority natural habitats, protected under Annex 1 to the Habitats Directive, at those two SSSIs. But the same priority habitats can be found within 16 further SSSIs which were not part of the RSA programme. It was therefore irrational to limit the investigation to the three SSSIs. The Environment Agency could not rationally conclude that it could comply with article 6(2) without conducting a broader investigation.

The Environment Agency's response to the claim

68   The Environment Agency contends that the claim is based on a misunderstanding as to the nature of the RSA programme. It was never intended that the programme would be a comprehensive assessment of the impact of abstraction across the entirety of all European sites. The Ant Broads and Marshes RSA investigation was not intended to review the impact of all 240 licences across every protected species and habitat in the SAC. The intention of the RSA programme was to focus only on sites that had been assessed to be at risk. The Ant Broads and Marshes investigation was initially concerned only with the Ant Broads and Marshes SSSI, but this was expanded to two further SSSIs as a result of public consultation and for the reasons that Mr Pearson explains (see paragraph 33 above). The Environment Agency recognises that there may be risks to other sites, but these can be addressed by additional work outside the scope of the RSA programme. This work is ongoing

and iterative. The tools and modelling that were developed in the course of the RSA programme are being deployed when deciding whether new licence applications should be granted or whether time-limited licences should be renewed (and, in each case, what terms should be applied).

69   Regulation 9(3) of the Habitats Regulations requires only that the Environment Agency "has regard" to the Habitats Directive. It does not impose an obligation on the Environment Agency to comply with the Habitats Directive. If that had been the intention then regulation 9(3) would have been drafted in the same way as regulation 9(1) which imposes an obligation (but on the Secretary of State, not the Environment Agency) to secure compliance with the requirements of the Habitats Directive. The Environment Agency plainly had regard to the requirements of the Habitats Directive: the contemporaneous documentation, including the Ant Broads and Marshes RSA report, shows in terms that it took the requirements of the Habitats Directive into account at every stage of its decision making.

70   Article 6(2) has not been recognised by the courts as having direct effect in domestic law. The decision in *Waddenzee* was concerned with article 6(3), not article 6(2), and the court explicitly did not address the question of whether article 6(2) has direct effect. The court in *Warren* recognised that article 6(2) is binding, but that is a different matter. In any event, *Warren* was decided *per incuriam* because the court had not appreciated that *Waddenzee* did not rule on the question of whether article 6(2) has direct effect in domestic law.

71   The Environment Agency contend that it has not been shown that it has breached article 6(2): "there is no proper evidence before the court to demonstrate that a specific risk has been established which is not being acted upon." As and when risks are identified, they are appropriately addressed by the Environment Agency, acting on advice from Natural England. It was reasonable to limit the Ant Broads and Marshes RSA investigation to the three SSSIs. It was not necessary, practicable or reasonable to expand it to cover all other SSSIs in the screening area. On the contrary, it was reasonable to close the RSA programme to new sites so as to allow the programme to be completed and for the lessons learned from the programme then to be applied to future work. Notwithstanding that the programme had, in principle, been closed to new sites it was reasonable to expand it to cover the two additional sites for the reasons given by Mr Pearson (see paragraph 33 above). The Environment Agency has therefore acted rationally.

72   The decision as to how to discharge its statutory functions is for the Environment Agency, not the court: *Boggis v Natural England* [2010] P.T.S.R. 725 at [37]. The Environment Agency's judgement on questions of scientific, technical, and predictive assessments can only be challenged on a *Wednesbury* basis, acknowledging that an enhanced margin of appreciation is to be applied: *R. (Mott) v Environment Agency* [2016] 1 W.L.R. 4338. Further, in determining the level of resources to deploy in investigating potential risks, the Environment Agency is entitled to take account of funding pressures and competing demands on resources.

Issue 1: The requirement to "have regard" to the Habitats Directive

73   It is common ground that regulation 9(3) of the Habitats Regulations obliges the Environment Agency to have regard to the requirements of article 6(2) of the Habitats Directive.

74　　The claimants argue that the obligation to "have regard" to article 6(2) amounts to an obligation to secure compliance with article 6(2). They rely on what was said by Sullivan J in respect of regulation 3(4) of the 1994 Habitats Regulations (the predecessor of regulation 9(3) of the Habitats Regulations, and in materially identical terms) in *Friends of the Earth* at [57]:

> "Regulation 3(4) requires the Agency… to have regard to [the requirements of the Habitats Directive] in so far as they are relevant… when exercising any of its functions. … Even if the meaning of reg 3(4) was uncertain, which it is not, it would be necessary to construe it so as to impose such an obligation upon the Agency in order to give effect to the Directive (Case C-106/89) *Marleasing SA v La Comercial Internacional de Alimentacion SA* [1990] ECR I-4135 p 4159 para 8."

75　　I do not accept that this supports the claimant's argument. Sullivan J does not, in this passage, suggest that the words "have regard to" mean "secure compliance with". Sullivan J instead points out that in order to give effect to the Habitats Directive it is necessary to construe regulation 3(4) in a way which requires the Agency to "have regard" to the Habitats Directive when it exercises its functions (which is, anyway, what regulation 3(4) plainly requires). The claimants thus read far too much into this passage.

76　　Even if the meaning of Sullivan J's observation (read in isolation) is uncertain, which it is not, it is necessary to consider it in context. The meaning is clear when the passage is considered in the context of the issue that he was addressing, and the argument that was advanced. The case concerned a decision of the Environment Agency to modify a waste management licence. The Environment Agency and Friends of the Earth agreed that regulation 3(4) imposed an obligation on the Environment Agency to have regard to the requirements of the Habitats Directive when deciding whether the waste management licence should be modified: [41], [51]. The beneficiary of the licence disagreed, contending that the word "they" in regulation 3(4) referred to "every competent authority" rather than the requirements of the Habitats Directive: [55]. Thus, the argument that was advanced was that the obligation to "have regard" to the Habitats Directive arose where a public authority might be affected by the exercise of its functions rather than where the requirements of the Directive might be affected by the exercise of the authority's functions. The passage quoted at paragraph 74 above is immediately preceded by the sentence "FoE and the Agency are plainly correct that "they" is a reference to the requirements of the Habitats Directive." Thus, Sullivan J was not determining the meaning of the words "have regard to." He was instead determining the issue between the parties, namely which noun (as between "authority" and "Directive") was referenced by the pronoun "they".

77　　The claimants further rely on an argument advanced by the Government in Case C-6/04. In that case the Commission contended that the UK had not adequately transposed the Habitats Directive. In response, the Government submitted:

> "The relevant competent authorities are under a statutory obligation to exercise their functions so as to secure compliance with the Habitats Directive. This results… from regulations 3(2) and (4)…"

78　　Again, I do not accept the claimants' argument. The Government's submission as to the effect of the regulations is not, in itself, an aid to interpretation. Further, the Government's submission was based on the combination of regulations 3(2) and 3(4), rather than the effect of regulation 3(4) in isolation. Regulation 3(2) (the predecessor of regulation 9(1) of the current regulations) itself imposes an obligation "to secure compliance with the requirements of the [Habitats Directive]". The Government did not therefore submit that regulation 3(4) in isolation imposed an obligation to secure compliance with the Habitats Directive. Further, it may be noted that the court was not satisfied that regulation 3(4) was sufficient to "ensure that the provisions of the Habitats Directive... are transposed satisfactorily": [28].

79   The claimants are correct that regulation 9(1) imposes an obligation, on Natural England, to "secure compliance with the requirements of the Directives." They point out that the Environment Agency has not purported to depart from the advice that has been given by Natural England. They contend that it follows that the Environment Agency is itself under a legal obligation to secure compliance with the requirements of the Directives. I disagree. It does not follow. The claimants' argument assumes that the advice was a comprehensive distillation of the steps required to comply with the Directives. Even if that assumption is correct (and I do not think it is), it further assumes, wrongly, that the Environment Agency's decision to accept the advice means that the Environment Agency itself falls under the same legal obligation as the author of the advice.

80   A statutory obligation to "have regard" to something arises in many different contexts. It is usually imposed in respect of advice or guidance or a code of practice. It means that the advice or guidance or code must be considered when exercising the function or making the decision in question. That does not mean that it must be "followed" or "slavishly obeyed"; a decision maker may depart from such advice or guidance or code if there is good reason to do so – *R. (London Oratory School Governors) v Schools Adjudicator* [2015] EWHC 1012 (Admin) *per* Cobb J at [58].

81   The duty to "have regard" to X (where X is advice or guidance) is therefore different from a duty to act in accordance with X. In the present context, it is striking that the statutory language for the duties imposed by regulations 9(1) and 9(3) differ. Regulation 9(1) applies to the Secretary of State. It does not require the Secretary of State merely to have regard to the Habitats Directive. It requires the Secretary of State to secure compliance with the requirements of the Directive. Different statutory language is used in regulation 9(3). Instead of mandating compliance with the Directives it states only that regard must be had to their requirements. There is some force in Mr Dale-Harris' submission that this must impose a less onerous obligation than regulation 9(1).

82   Here, the natural and conventional approach to the "have regard" duty is that it means that the Environment Agency is obliged to take account of the requirements of the Habitats Directive but may depart from its requirements if there is good reason to do so. In other words, it must take account of the Habitats Directive but is entitled not itself to discharge all of the requirements of the Directive where that can be justified.

83   It is, however, relevant (when considering whether a departure can be justified) that the object of the "have regard" duty is "requirements" rather than advice or guidance. Advice or guidance is not, ordinarily, mandatory. "Requirements" more usually are mandatory. The "requirements" are set out, in mandatory terms, in a Directive which the Regulations themselves transposed. In this context, there is

not the same broad scope for taking something into account, but then deciding for good reason to depart from it, as there is in the case of non-binding guidance.

84   There is an important part of the regulatory context which helps explain the different language as between regulations 9(1) and 9(3). Regulation 9(3) is concerned with a "competent authority". That has a broad meaning (including every public body). In some contexts, different competent authorities may have overlapping roles that are relevant to the discharge of the requirements of the Habitats Directive. In such cases, it would not be meaningful or appropriate to impose on one single competent authority (or on every competent authority) an obligation to secure compliance with the Habitats Directive. Instead, what is required is that all competent authorities have regard to the Habitats Directive so as to ensure that, in the result, compliance with the Directive is achieved.

85   Conversely, regulation 9(1) is concerned with the Secretary of State and the nature conservation bodies, who each have overarching responsibility for compliance with the Habitats Directive. That seems to me to explain the difference in language. This implies that the duty to "have regard" here does not implicitly permit the Environment Agency to act in a way that is inconsistent with the Habitats Directive (in other words to have regard to the requirements of the Directive but then deliberately decide to act in a way that is inconsistent with those requirements). Rather, it recognises that the Environment Agency is one part of a complex regulatory structure and, depending on the issue, it may have a greater or lesser role to play.

86   In the present context the Environment Agency is effectively the sole (and certainly the principal) public body that is responsible for determining whether abstraction licences should be granted, varied, or revoked. If it does not secure the requirements of article 6(2) in respect of those decisions, then no other public body is capable of filling the gap.

87   For these reasons, in this context, the duty on the Environment Agency to have regard to the requirements of the Habitats Directive means that the Environment Agency must take those requirements into account, and, insofar as it is (in a particular context) the relevant public body with responsibility for fulfilling those requirements, then it must discharge those requirements. In other words, the scope for departure that is ordinarily inherent in the words "have regard to" is considerably narrowed.

88   This is all entirely consistent with the approach that the Environment Agency has sought to take. It is clear from all of the contemporaneous evidence (including internal emails) that the Environment Agency has regarded itself as bound by the Habitats Directive and has sought to act in compliance with its requirements. Thus, in a "Q&A" document, prepared in 2021 and published as part of the RSA report, it states: "The Environment Agency has a legal obligation to… avoid adverse effects on habitats and species…" Whether or not it has succeeded in discharging the requirements of article 6(2) is the subject of issues 3 and 4.

Issue 2: Are the obligations under article 6(2) of a kind recognised by a court before 2021?

89   The parties agree that the question of whether article 6(2) is enforceable by a UK court (irrespective of regulation 9(3) of the Habitats Regulations) turns on the application of section 4(2)(b) of the 2018 Act, namely whether the obligations

under article 6(2) are of a kind recognised by the CJEU, or any court or tribunal in the United Kingdom, in a case decided before 11pm on 31 December 2020.

90   In *Waddenzee*, conservation bodies in The Netherlands challenged a government decision to issue licences for mechanical cockle fishing. The court made a reference to the European Court of Justice. One of the questions that was referred was whether article 6(2) and 6(3) of the Habitats Directive "have direct effect in the sense that individuals may rely on them in national courts and those courts must provide the protection afforded to individuals by the direct effect of Community law…". In the light of the Court's analysis of the relationship between article 6(2) and article 6(3), and its conclusion that only article 6(3) was relevant in the context of the reference, it was not necessary for the court to consider the direct effect of article 6(2). It did not do so. It held that article 6(3) had direct effect. Its reasons for doing so were that it is binding ([65]), that its binding effect would be weakened if individuals could not rely on it before national courts ([66]), that it requires certainty that there will be no adverse effect before a licence is granted ([67]), and it may therefore be taken into account where the national court is determining whether the grant of a licence has kept within the limits of article 6(3) ([69]-[70]).

91   The court did not rule on the question of whether article 6(2) has direct effect. Section 4(3) does not, however, require that the particular provision in issue (here article 6(2)) has been held to have direct effect. It only requires that it is "of a kind" that has been held to have direct effect. There is a close relationship between article 6(2) and 6(3). They both require the national authorities to take steps to achieve the aims of the Habitats Directive and, in particular, to avoid deterioration of habitats and significant disturbance of species in the special areas of conservation. Article 6(3) applies prospectively. Article 6(2) enables a retrospective check that the article 6(3) steps remain adequate. Article 6(2) is thus "of a kind" that was recognised in *Waddenzee* as having direct effect.

92   Further, the question of whether article 6(2) has legal effect in domestic proceedings was addressed by the decision of the Upper Tribunal in *Warren*. Upper Tribunal Judge Markus QC held (in a judgment given on 2 October 2019), at [88], that the duties on member states under article 6(2) are binding on all public authorities of a member state, including the courts:

> "The tribunal was bound to act consistently with the precautionary principle because the duties on member states under article 6(2) are binding on all authorities of a member state including the courts…"

93   Judge Markus cited *Waddenzee* at [65]–[66]. Mr Dale-Harris argues that Judge Markus was saying only that article 6(2) was binding, without expressly stating in terms that it had direct effect in domestic law. That is correct so far as it goes, but the effect of Judge Markus' judgment was to recognise and enforce the precautionary principle that is inherent in article 6(2). This is sufficient to satisfy the test in section 4(3) of the 2018 Act. Mr Dale-Harris further argues that *Warren* was decided *per incuriam* because the judge had not appreciated that *Waddenzee* only decided that article 6(3) had direct effect and had made no such finding in respect of article 6(2). I disagree. There is no indication in *Warren* that Judge Markus had misunderstood the ambit of the court's finding in *Waddenzee*. Her citation of *Waddenzee* at [65]–[66] was entirely apt. Although those passages only concern article 6(3), their rationale reads across to article 6(2). They therefore provide support for Judge Markus' conclusion. In addition, even if *Warren* was decided

per incuriam, that is not relevant to the section 4(2) test. That test is satisfied once a case is identified that recognises article 6(2) as being enforceable in domestic proceedings. The statute expressly provides that it is not necessary for that to be an essential part of the court's decision. It is not relevant to the section 4(2) test to enquire as to whether the case was correctly decided or was decided *per incuriam*. The position might be different if the decision had been overturned on appeal, or later overruled, but that is not the case here.

94   Accordingly, by reason of section 4 of the 2018 Act, article 6(2) continues to be recognised and available in domestic law and is to be enforced accordingly.

Issue 3: Has the Environment Agency breached article 6(2) of the Habitats Directive?

95   The RSA investigation focusses on the impact of abstraction on specific sites, rather than the effect (across all sites) of specific licences. That answers the claimants' narrow argument that having elected to investigate the effects of 240 abstraction licences, it was not open to the Environment Agency to limit that investigation to the impact on just three SSSIs. The narrow argument overlooks the fact that the RSA investigation was always intended to be focussed on sites (and, in particular, sites which had been assessed as being at risk) rather than a comprehensive analysis of the impact of abstraction across every SSSI. The claimants have not identified any principled objection to the Environment Agency's decision to take a site-centric (rather than licence-centric) approach.

96   All permanent licences were scrutinised during the Review of Consents process (see paragraphs 17-19 above). *Waddenzee* recognises that (assuming the review is adequate) this satisfies article 6(3), and that article 6(2) has no role to play at that point (see paragraph 47(4) above). All time-limited licences are scrutinised when they fall to be renewed. The evidence indicates that the lessons learned during the RSA programme, including the new assessment tools and the refined models, are deployed when renewal decisions are made. Again, that process in principle satisfies article 6(3), and article 6(2) has no role to play at the point that licences are reviewed. This process is, in principle, capable of complying with the requirements of article 6.

97   Further, there is no general obligation proactively to review a licence unless there is some reason to do so. The fact that the Environment Agency reviewed the impact of abstraction on three sites does not, in itself, mean that it was obliged to review the impact on all sites.

98   On the other hand, the authorities are clear that it is not sufficient to wait until damage to a site occurs before taking remedial action (see paragraphs 47-48 above). If there is reason to believe that there is a risk of damage then it is necessary to take remedial steps: *Waddenzee* at [37], and *Grune Liga* at [42].

99   Here, the Environment Agency do not suggest that there is no risk of damage to other sites (besides the three SSSIs). They accept that there is a potential risk. The Environment Agency is right to make that concession:

(1) As the Environment Agency recognise in its RSA report, one of the key characteristics of the SAC is the through-flow of base-rich water that derives from the underlying aquifers.

(2) Water abstraction involves the taking of water from the underlying aquifers and thereby potentially reduces the through-flow of base-rich water which

is a key characteristic of the SAC. It also potentially changes the ground chemistry, impacting on surface ecology.

(3) There is therefore the clear potential for water abstraction to cause damage to wetland ecosystems.

(4) It is thus necessary to address the question whether abstraction of water in the area of a protected site is damaging to that site.

(5) This was done by the Review of Consents. That process was, in principle, capable of complying with the Environment Agency's obligations under article 6.

(6) However, as Mr Dale-Harris put it, the science of understanding the impact on SSSIs has "moved on". It has become clear, as a result of the evolving knowledge gained from the RSA programme, that the Review of Consents was flawed. It did not identify the risks posed by the Plumsgate Road and Ludham Road licences which are explained in the decision of Ms Hill. Nor did it identify the risks posed to the three SSSIs. Those risks were identified subsequently, as a result of the more developed work that was undertaken in the course of the RSA programme.

(7) The Environment Agency has itself recognised in a number of places that the Review of Consents has since been shown to be flawed. For example, in its pre-action protocol letter it accepted that by 2009/10 there was credible evidence that abstraction could be having adverse effects on Catfield Fen (even though the Review of Consents had not identified that the Plumsgate Road and Ludham Road licences posed any risks). The RSA report shows that there are other SSSIs where there are significant risks (see paragraph 39 above).

(8) Moreover, the Review of Consents process took place more than a decade ago. Natural England has identified the need to review licences in the context of a changing climate.

(9) Natural England has advised that further assessment work is needed (see paragraph 40 above). The Environment Agency has not provided any basis for disagreeing with this advice.

(10) Natural England does not consider that the Renewals Communique process is sufficient to address the risks. Nikolas Bertholdt, a freshwater senior adviser with Natural England, has provided evidence that Natural England considers that a "more strategic approach is needed, and investigation and actions taken where there is a credible risk to sites." This reflects the advice it provided in October 2020 (see paragraph 35 above).

100   The Environment Agency may well be right that it is reacting appropriately where it becomes aware of evidence of a specific risk to a particular site. However, the factors set out in the previous paragraph show that the Review of Consents was not effective in ensuring that abstraction does not cause damage to protected sites and there thus remains a generalised risk from abstraction (particularly abstraction under permanent licences) across the entire SAC. Having regard to the precautionary principle, that is sufficient to trigger the article 6(2) duty (see paragraphs 42 and 48-49 above). It would be contrary to the precautionary principle and the reasoning in *Grune Liga* if article 6(2) were not triggered by the factors set out in the previous paragraph and could only be triggered once it becomes clear that a particular site is at risk by an identified mechanism from abstraction at a specific location. It is

sufficient that a generalised risk has been established (as a result of the demonstration of flaws in the Review of Consents process) to require "appropriate steps" to be taken. What those steps might be depends on the particular circumstances, the expert advice of Natural England and the expert judgement of the Environment Agency. In some cases, very little may be necessary. For example, it might be possible to rule out any risk at a particular site by showing that it is sufficiently far from any location where abstraction takes place under a permanent licence for abstraction to have any impact. Or it might be possible to rule out the prospect that abstraction at a particular location has any impact by applying the tools and models that were developed during the RSA programme. The steps taken must, however, be sufficiently robust to guarantee that abstraction of water does not cause damage to ecosystems that are protected under the Habitats Directive: *Grune Liga* at [53].

101   Further, the Environment Agency has a broad discretion as to the steps that should be taken to achieve that end. The cost of different options is a relevant factor that can legitimately be considered. A court will be slow to question the Environment Agency's expert assessment as to the steps that should be taken. It is, however, not open to the Environment Agency to take no steps – that is a breach of article 6(2).

102   In respect of time limited licences, the Renewals Communique process (see paragraph 19 above) together with the application of the lessons learned from the RSA programme when considering the renewal of licences, is in principle capable of securing compliance with article 6 of the Directive. The same applies to new licence applications.

103   That leaves over the question of permanent licences. In his witness statement, Mr Pearson says that the ongoing work includes "adjusting permanent licences shown to be seriously damaging, either through voluntary action or by using our powers provided under s52 of the Water Resources Act 1991." This shows that there are significant limitations to the ongoing work that is being done in respect of permanent licences. First, Mr Pearson does not suggest that any systematic programme is in place to investigate permanent licences so as to establish whether abstraction under those licences is risking damage to protected sites. The deficiencies in the Review of Consent process, and the Environment Agency's recognition of the risks of such damage, means that some form of review is required. Absent such a review there is no secure basis for identifying a need for adjustments to licences. Second, the test that is applied before an adjustment is applied (that is, that the licence is shown to be "seriously damaging") is contrary to the precautionary principle. A much lower threshold for intervention is required. The Environment Agency must act unless it is satisfied that there is no risk of significant damage. Mr Pearson has, elsewhere, recognised that the flaws in the Review of Consents process necessitate further work to review permanent licences. In an internal email, in May 2021, he said the assessments made during the Review of Consents were called into question by the subsequent work but that there was "no plan or resourcing to look at these sites again other than through the occasional licence renewals process, and the chances are that time-limited licences are not the main cause of any concerns."

104   It follows that the Environment Agency has not taken sufficient steps in respect of the risks to sites in the SAC (beyond the three SSSIs) posed by abstraction in accordance with permanent licences. It is only the Environment Agency (albeit

with advice from Natural England) that may vary or revoke permanent licences. No other authority can do so. So, the Environment Agency cannot absolve itself from compliance with article 6 by pointing to work done by other public authorities. It has not therefore complied with article 6(2). Although it has taken account of article 6, it has not justified its failure to take steps in respect of the risks (particularly risks posed by abstraction in accordance with permanent licences), and it is therefore in breach of its obligation under regulation 9(3) of the Habitats Regulations. The claimed lack of resource does not justify these breaches. Resources may be relevant to the decision as to how to discharge the article 6(2)/regulation 9(3) obligations, but they are not relevant to the question of whether to discharge those obligations. The Environment Agency say that "other strands of work may be added.... in due course" but that is too vague and too late.

105   It was not essential for the risks to other sites to be addressed in the course of the RSA programme. It was open to the Environment Agency (within the bounds of rational decision making) to focus the RSA programme on a small number of sites, so long as adequate steps were taken, outside the RSA programme, to address the risks to other sites. The Environment Agency is entitled to exercise its scientific expertise in assessing what steps should be taken. I agree with the submission advanced on its behalf that relevant factors may include the degree of risk, the extent to which the risk is already being addressed, and the availability of resources. It may also take account of technical constraints (so, for example, it is said that a single RSA programme could not practically address disparate European sites featuring different habitat types). I also accept the submission that a court should be slow to second guess expert scientific and technical assessments that are made by the Environment Agency. So far, however, the Environment Agency has not undertaken any sufficient analysis of the steps needed to address the impact of abstraction in accordance with permanent licences.

106   The claimants have therefore demonstrated a breach of article 6(2) of the Habitats Directive and a breach of regulation 9(3) of the Habitats Regulations.

Issue 4: Has the Environment Agency acted irrationally?

107   Mr Pearson has explained why the Environment Agency did not expand the RSA programme to cover additional sites. The explanation is coherent. It amounts to a rational cost:benefit analysis. It was reasonable to close the RSA programme to new sites so as to enable the programme to be completed in a timely and planned manner. Likewise, it was reasonable, for the reasons Mr Pearson gives, to expand the programme (notwithstanding that it had been closed to new sites) to cover Broad Fen, Dilham SSSI and Alderfen Broad SSSI but not other sites. I do not accept the claimants' submission that having added those two additional sites it was irrational not to extend the programme further. Although one or more of the reasons for including those sites also applied to other SSSIs, the full constellation of reasons did not do so. The whole point was that this was a limited exception to the principle that the programme had been closed to new sites. Any significant expansion of the programme would itself have been inconsistent with that rational and legitimate policy choice.

108   The decision not to expand the Ant Broads and Marshes investigation further was not necessarily inconsistent with article 6(2). I agree with the submission advanced by the Environment Agency that the RSA programme was not the only

means by which the Environment Agency could legitimately discharge the obligations arising under article 6(2). In particular, I agree with the submission that it would be open to the RSA to discharge those obligations by reviewing individual licences, rather than by expanding the RSA programme so that every site within the SAC was investigated.

109   The problem for the Environment Agency is that, for the reasons given above in connection with issue (3), its programme of works will not discharge the article 6(2) obligation. Having committed itself to discharge that obligation, it was irrational for the Environment Agency not to expand the RSA programme without having any alternative mechanism in place that could ensure compliance with article 6(2). It follows that even if (contrary to the findings I have made in respect of issues (1) and (2)) article 6(2) is not enforceable by the High Court, the Environment Agency's decision is flawed on common law grounds. On this basis, the claimants' rationality challenge also succeeds.

Relief

110   The claimants seek an order that requires the Environment Agency to undertake a further RSA report forthwith. The Environment Agency contends this is unworkable. In any event, the relief sought by the claimants is not consistent with my finding that the Environment Agency can, in principle, discharge its obligations under article 6(2) in other ways. The parties did not make any submissions as to the form of relief in the course of the hearing. They agree that the question of relief is best determined following judgment on the substantive claim. I will make directions accordingly.

Outcome

111   The claimants have shown that water abstraction may be causing deterioration of protected habitats or significant disturbance of protected species within The Broads Special Area of Conservation (see paragraph 99 above).

112   The Environment Agency must (by reason of regulation 9(3) of the Habitats Regulations) have regard to the requirements of article 6(2) of the Habitats Directive. It must therefore be in a position to justify any departure from those requirements. The Environment Agency's obligation under article 6(2) continues to be enforceable in domestic law: section 4 of the 2018 Act. That obligation must continue to be interpreted in accordance with the precautionary principle: section 6 of the 2018 Act.

113   It follows that the Environment Agency must take appropriate steps to ensure that, in the SAC, there is no possibility of the deterioration of protected habitats or the significant disturbance of protected species as a result of licensed water abstraction. The Environment Agency has discharged that obligation in respect of three sites of special scientific interest. But it has not done so in respect of all sites within the SAC. That is because its review of abstraction licences was flawed and (at least in relation to permanent licences) it has not conducted a sufficient further review to address those flaws. It is therefore in breach of regulation 9(3) of the Habitats Regulations and article 6(2) of the Habitats Directive.

114   In addition, having decided to comply with article 6(2), it was not rational for the Environment Agency to limit its investigation to just three sites without

undertaking further work to ensure compliance with article 6(2) across the entire SAC.

115   The claim therefore succeeds.

ET v MINISTERSTVO ŽIVOTNÍHO PROSTŘEDÍ

European Court of Justice (Fourth Chamber)

(C-659/20)

C. Lycourgos, President of the Chamber, S. Rodin (Rapporteur),
J.-C. Bonichot, L.S. Rossi and O. Spineanu-Matei, Judges: L.
Medina, AG: 8 September 2022

[2023] Env. L.R. 11

☞ Birds; Breeding; Conservation; Endangered species; EU law; International
trade; Statutory interpretation

H1 *EU law—nature conservation—Convention on International Trade in Endangered
Species of Wild Fauna and Flora—Regulations 338/97 and 865/2006—exemptions
from prohibition of commercial activities—meaning of specimens born and bred
in captivity in art.8(3) of Regulation 865/2006—whether concept of 'breeding
stock' included only parents and offspring—whether permissible to examine origin
of ancestors never owned or kept by breeders*

H2   A parrot breeder applied for an exemption from the prohibition of trade in
endangered species for five specimens of hyacinth macaw. The grandparents of
those parrots had initially been imported in circumstances incompatible with the
Convention on International Trade in Endangered Species of Wild Fauna and Flora
(CITES). The exemption was refused on the basis that it could not be stated with
certainty that that stock had been established in accordance with the legal provisions.
On appeal, the breeder claimed that the competent regional authority had
misinterpreted the concept of "breeding stock" in art.1 of Regulation 865/2006,
which should be established only by the parent pair and the offspring of those
parents, so that the authority had not been authorised to examine the origin of the
grandparent pair. The Supreme Administrative Court stayed proceedings and
referred questions asking, essentially, whether:

(1) The term "breeding stock" covered the ancestors of specimens bred in a
     breeding operation which had never been owned or kept by that operation;
     and

(2) Article 54(2) of the Regulation, together with art.17 of the Charter of
     Fundamental Rights and the principle of protection of legitimate
     expectations, precluded a specimen of an animal species referred to in Annex
     A to the Regulation kept by a breeder from being regarded as born and bred
     in captivity, within the meaning of art.8(3), where the ancestors of that
     specimen that were not part of the breeding stock of that breeder, were
     acquired by a third party before the entry into force of those regulations, in

disregard of the applicable legal provisions or in a manner which was detrimental to the survival of the species concerned in the wild.

H3   **Held:**

H4   (1) The purpose of Regulation 865/2006 was to ensure the implementation of Regulation 338/97 and to ensure full compliance with the provisions of CITES, thereby guaranteeing the broadest possible protection for species of wild fauna and flora by regulating trade. It was apparent that, under CITES, the registration of a captive-breeding operation required the precise identification of such an operation, its owner and manager, and the facilities intended to house the stock. Therefore, the concept of "operation" could not be understood, in the context of Regulation 865/2006, as referring to a simple breeding process, detached from any concrete physical installation. It followed that the term "breeding stock" in art.1(3) did not include the ancestors of specimens bred in a breeding operation, which had never been owned or kept by that operation.

H5   (2) Insofar as it constituted an exception to the general rule prohibiting all commercial use of specimens of the species listed in Annex A, art.54(2) of Regulation 338/97 had to be interpreted strictly. Therefore, the conditions under which art.54(2) permitted the inference that a specimen of an animal species had been born and bred in captivity had also to be interpreted strictly, insofar as that provision sought to clarify the scope of art.8(3). Article 54(2) referred to the concept of "establishment" of the breeding stock. That concept had a broad scope and allowed account to be taken, when examining whether such a breeding stock complied with the requirements imposed by that provision, of events prior to the actual acquisition of the breeding stock by the breeder. Furthermore, the objective pursued by Regulation 865/2006 supported the interpretation that the competent authorities had the power to examine the ancestry of a breeding stock in the context of an application for an exemption certificate for the sale of specimens born and bred in captivity. Accordingly, the interpretation according to which the competent national authorities had the power to examine the ancestry of a breeding stock was consistent with the objective pursued by CITES of strengthening control of the ancestry of specimens born and bred in captivity. It followed that art.54(2), read in conjunction with art.17 of the Charter and the principle of protection of legitimate expectations, precluded a specimen, kept by a breeder, of a species of animal referred to in Annex A to Regulation 338/97 from being regarded as having been born and bred in captivity, within the meaning of art.8(3), where the ancestors of that specimen, which did not form part of the breeding stock of that breeder, were acquired by a third party before the entry into force of those regulations in a manner which was detrimental to the survival of the species concerned in the wild.

H6   **Cases referred to:**

A (C-950/19) EU:C:2021:230

Criminal Proceedings against Rubach (C-344/08) EU:C:2009:482; [2009] 3 C.M.L.R. 48; [2010] Env. L.R. 23

Criminal Proceedings against Tridon (C-510/99) EU:C:2001:559; [2003] 1 C.M.L.R. 2; [2002] Env. L.R. D5

Hauptzollamt B v XY (C-87/20) EU:C:2021:382; [2022] Env. L.R. 10

Klaipedos Regiono Atlieku Tvarkymo Centras UAB v Ecoservice Klaipėda UAB (C-927/19) EU:C:2021:700; [2022] P.T.S.R. 294

Krizan v Slovenska inspekcia zivotneho prostredia (C-416/10) EU:C:2013:8; [2013] Env. L.R. 28

Ledra Advertising Ltd v European Commission (C-8/15 P)–(C-10/15 P) EU:C:2016:701; [2017] 1 C.M.L.R. 35

Nationale Raad van Dierenkwekers en Liefhebbers VZW v Belgium (C-219/07) EU:C:2008:353; [2009] Env. L.R. D2

Skarb Państwa (Couverture de l'assurance automobile) (C-428/20) EU:C:2021:1043

Sofia Zoo (C-532/13) EU:C:2014:2140

Staatsanwaltschaft Wien (Ordres de virement falsifiés) (C-584/19) EU:C:2020:587

H7 Legislation referred to:
TFEU art.267
EU Charter of Fundamental Rights arts 17 and 47
Convention on International Trade in Endangered Species of Wild Fauna and Flora 1973 (CITES) arts II, IV, VII and XIV, Appendices I and II
Regulation 3626/82 (CITES) [1982] OJ L384/1
Regulation 338/97 (CITES) [1997] OJ L61/1 arts 1, 2, 5 and 8, Annexes A and B
Regulation 865/2006 (CITES Implementation) [2006] OJ L166/1 arts 1, 54 and 55
Regulation 2016/1012 (Breeding) [2016] OJ L171/66

H8 *L. Dvořáková, M. Smolek* and *J. Vláčil*, acting as Agents, appeared on behalf of the Czech Government.
S. Ondrášiková, acting as Agent, appeared on behalf of the Slovak Government.
P. Ondrůšek and *C. Valero*, acting as Agents, appeared on behalf of the Commission.

OPINION[1]

Introduction

AG1　'Wild fauna and flora in their many beautiful and varied forms are an irreplaceable part of the natural systems of the earth which must be protected for this and the generations to come'. That fundamental statement is made in the preamble to the Convention on International Trade in Endangered Species of Wild Fauna and Flora ('CITES').[2]

AG2　CITES is an international environmental treaty pursuing the objective of protecting certain species of wild fauna and flora from over-exploitation through international trade. Commentators have described it as 'arguably the most successful of all international treaties concerned with the conservation of wildlife', while nevertheless acknowledging that 'problems most certainly still exist'.[3] More particularly, illegal wildlife trafficking 'continues to be a major concern'.[4] The value of illegal trade worldwide is estimated by some to be between 7 and 23

---

[1] Original language: English.
[2] Signed in Washington (United States), on 3 March 1973 (*United Nations Treaty Series*, Vol. 993, No I-14537).
[3] Bowman, M., 'A Tale of Two CITES: Divergent Perspectives upon the Effectiveness of the Wildlife Trade Convention', *Review of European, Comparative & International Environmental Law*, Vol. 22, 2013, p. 228, citing Davies, P., in Bowman, M., Davies, P. and Redgwell, C., *Lyster's International Wildlife Law*, 2nd edition, Cambridge University Press, Cambridge, 2010, pp. 484 and 533.
[4] As recognised by the Resolution of the Conference of the Parties 11.3 'Compliance and enforcement'.

thousand million United States dollars (USD) per year.[5] The most recent UN World Wildlife Crime Report shows wildlife crime to be a business that is 'global; lucrative, with high demand driving high prices; and extremely widespread'.[6] That same report highlights the links between the global health crisis and the illegal exploitation of wildlife and considers the end to wildlife crime to be an 'essential part of building back better from the COVID-19 crisis'.[7]

AG3   It is against the backdrop of those general considerations that I intend to pursue the analysis of the request for a preliminary ruling submitted by the Nejvyšší správní soud (Supreme Administrative Court, Czech Republic). That request concerns the interpretation of two EU regulations pursuing the objective of protecting species of wild fauna and flora and guaranteeing their conservation through controls on international trade in specimens of those species, namely Council Regulation (EC) No 338/97[8] and Commission Regulation (EC) No 865/2006.[9]

AG4   Regulation No 338/97 lays down certain derogating provisions applicable to captive-born and -bred specimens of animal species listed in Annex A to that regulation. The main issue raised in the present case is essentially whether, for the purpose of determining whether specimens qualify for an exemption from the prohibition of trade applicable to captive-bred specimens of an animal species, the competent authorities may verify the origin of the breeding stock even where that examination extends beyond the specimens which the breeder lawfully acquired. As I intend to demonstrate in my analysis, the authorities should have the power to do so in order to determine whether the exemption should be granted.

Legal framework

International law

CITES

AG5   The object of CITES is to protect certain endangered species of wild fauna and flora by regulating international trade. It lays down separate rules protecting different species, divided into three categories corresponding to the three appendices to the convention and according to how great the threat of extinction is for them.

AG6   That convention, to which the European Union became a party on 8 July 2015, was implemented in the European Union as from 1 January 1984 by virtue of Council Regulation (EEC) No 3626/82.[10] That regulation was repealed by Regulation No 338/97.

---

[5] Nellemann, C. et al. (ed.), *The Rise of Environmental Crime – A Growing Threat to Natural Resources, Peace, Development and Security, A UNEP-Interpol Rapid Response Assessment*, UNEP, 2016, p. 7.
[6] United Nations Office on Drugs and Crime, *World Wildlife Crime Report 2020: Trafficking in protected species*, United Nations, New York, 2020, p. 3.
[7] Ibid.
[8] Council Regulation of 9 December 1996 on the protection of species of wild fauna and flora by regulating trade therein ([1997] OJ L61/1), as amended by Commission Regulation (EU) No 1320/2014 of 1 December 2014 ([2014] OJ L361/1).
[9] Commission Regulation of 4 May 2006 laying down detailed rules concerning the implementation of Council Regulation No 338/97 ([2006] OJ L166/1), as amended by Commission Regulation (EU) 2015/870 of 5 June 2015 ([2015] OJ L142/3).
[10] Council Regulation of 3 December 1982 on the implementation in the Community of the Convention on international trade in endangered species of wild fauna and flora ([1982] OJ L384/1).

AG7 Appendix I to CITES includes the most endangered species, with the strictest rules on protection. Pursuant to Article II(1) of CITES, trade in specimens of those species must be authorised only in 'exceptional circumstances'.

AG8 Pursuant to Article II(2)(a) of CITES, Appendix II to that convention includes 'all species which although not necessarily now threatened with extinction may become so unless trade in specimens of such species is subject to strict regulation in order to avoid utilisation incompatible with their survival'. The requirements for imports of Appendix II species are less stringent compared to those which apply to Appendix I species.

AG9 Article VII(4) of CITES provides that specimens of an animal species included in Appendix I and bred in captivity for commercial purposes are to be deemed to be specimens of species included in Appendix II.

European Union law

Regulation No 338/97

AG10 Article 1 of Regulation No 338/97 states that its object is to protect species of wild fauna and flora and to guarantee their conservation by regulating trade therein. It also states that it is to apply in compliance with the objectives, principles and provisions of CITES.

AG11 Article 2 of that regulation contains the following definitions:

> '…
>
> (g) "management authority" shall mean a national administrative authority designated, in the case of a Member State, in accordance with Article 13(1)(a)…
>
> …
>
> (s) "species" shall mean a species, subspecies or population thereof;
> (t) "specimen" shall mean any animal or plant, whether alive or dead, of the species listed in Annexes A to D …
>
> …'

AG12 Article 8 of Regulation No 338/97 provides:

> '1. The purchase, offer to purchase, acquisition for commercial purposes, display to the public for commercial purposes, use for commercial gain and sale, keeping for sale, offering for sale or transporting for sale of specimens of the species listed in Annex A shall be prohibited.
>
> …
>
> 3. In accordance with the requirements of other Community legislation on the conservation of wild fauna and flora, exemption from the prohibitions referred to in paragraph 1 may be granted by issuance of a certificate to that effect by a management authority of the Member State in which the specimens are located, on a case-by-case basis where the specimens:
>
> ….
>
> (d) are captive-born and bred specimens of an animal species or artificially propagated specimens of a plant species or are parts or derivatives of such specimens; …
>
> …'

Regulation No 865/2006

AG13   Article 1(3) of Regulation No 865/2006 contains the following definition:

'"breeding stock" means all the animals in a breeding operation that are used for reproduction;'

AG14   Article 54 of Regulation No 865/2006, headed 'Specimens born and bred in captivity of animal species', provides:

'Without prejudice to Article 55, a specimen of an animal species shall be considered to be born and bred in captivity only if a competent management authority, in consultation with a competent scientific authority of the Member State concerned, is satisfied that the following criteria are met:

…

(2) the breeding stock was established in accordance with the legal provisions applicable to it at the time of acquisition and in a manner not detrimental to the survival of the species concerned in the wild;
…'

Facts, procedure and the questions referred

AG15   The applicant is a parrot breeder. He applied, on 21 January 2015, for an exemption from the prohibition of trade in respect of five specimens of the hyacinth macaw (*Anodorhynchus hyacinthinus*) bred by the applicant and born in 2014. That species is listed in Annex A to Regulation No 338/97 and in Appendix I to CITES. The competent management authority refused to grant the application, based on an opinion of the competent scientific authority.

AG16   For the purpose of its assessment, the competent management authority made the following findings regarding the origin of the parrots subject to evaluation. The grandparents of the parrots ('the grandparent specimens') were imported by a Uruguayan national to Bratislava (Slovakia) in June 1993 under suspicious circumstances. The grandparent specimens were subsequently transferred by car to the Czech Republic by FU. At the border, the car was stopped by customs authorities and the grandparent specimens were confiscated from FU by means of an administrative decision. That administrative decision was, however, overturned by the Vrchní soud v Praze (High Court, Prague, Czech Republic) in 1996.

AG17   The authorities returned the grandparent specimens to FU who then lent them to GV. GV bred the parents of the parrots in question (the 'parent specimens') in 2000 and subsequently returned the grandparent specimens to FU, who in turn handed them over to the Zlín Zoo (Zlín, Czech Republic). The applicant obtained the parent specimens from GV in 2000. The validity of the transfer of ownership of the parent specimens to the applicant is not contested.

AG18   The scientific authority assessed whether the parent specimens qualified for exemption from the prohibition of trade applicable to captive-bred specimens of an animal species in accordance with the conditions laid down in Article 54(2) of Regulation No 865/2006. According to that provision, the breeding stock has to be established 'in accordance with the legal provisions applicable to it at the time of acquisition and in a manner not detrimental to the survival of the species concerned in the wild'. The scientific authority recommended that the exemption not be granted. In its view, there were discrepancies in the registration documents pertaining to the grandparent specimens and, furthermore, no information about the origin of the parent specimens was provided.

AG19   Based on the opinion of the scientific authority, the competent management authority refused to grant an exemption permitting the trade of the specimens in question. The applicant brought an appeal against that decision before the Ministerstvo životního prostředí (Ministry of the Environment, Czech Republic). In his appeal, he claimed that the concept of 'breeding stock' had been misinterpreted. In his view, that concept comprises only the parent specimens and their offspring. Hence, the authorities did not have the power to verify the origin of the grandparent specimens. The Ministerstvo životního prostředí (Ministry of the Environment) rejected the appeal, considering that the method of acquisition of the first reproducing pair is decisive in order to assess whether the breeding stock has been established in accordance with the applicable rules. Given that the applicant was not able to prove the origin of the grandparent specimens, it was impossible to grant the exemption permitting the trade of the specimens in question.

AG20   The applicant challenged the decision of the Ministerstvo životního prostředí (Ministry of the Environment) before the Krajský soud v Hradci Králové (Regional Court, Hradec Králové, Czech Republic). The judgment delivered by that court stated that trade in parrots of the *Anodorhynchus* species is prohibited and may be permitted only in exceptional circumstances as set out in Article 54(2) of Regulation No 865/2006, which were not the circumstances in which the applicant found himself. That court pointed out that, at the time of acquisition of the grandparent specimens, CITES was already in force in the Czech Republic and had been implemented into national law. It considered that, according to the legislation implementing CITES, an examination into the origin of the breeding stock is permitted and can be extended to the grandparent specimens. Therefore, the concept of 'breeding stock', as defined by Regulation No 865/2006, covers all three generations of parrot.

AG21   The applicant lodged an appeal on a point of law against the judgment of the Krajský soud v Hradci Králové (Regional Court, Hradec Králové) before the Nejvyšší správní soud (Supreme Administrative Court), the referring court. He claimed that the judgment under appeal erred in law by taking the view that the concept of 'breeding stock' covers the parent and the grandparent specimens concerned. According to the applicant, such an interpretation places an unreasonable burden of proof on him. Moreover, he claims that it is incorrect in the light of the scope of the concept of 'breeding stock'. That concept, in the applicant's submission, includes all animals located in one specific breeding operation and not their ancestors kept in other operations or by other breeders. The applicant also claims that the contested decision infringed his right to property and his legitimate expectations given that he had lawfully acquired the parent specimens.

AG22   In its response to the applicant's appeal on a point of law, the Ministerstvo životního prostředí (Ministry of the Environment) referred to the wording of Article 54(2) of Regulation No 865/2006, which employs the term '[establishment]' of breeding stock. The term 'establishment' clearly refers to the past and thereby to the beginning of the breeding line. Furthermore, the Ministerstvo životního prostředí (Ministry of the Environment) stated that the definition of breeding stock is secondary, whereas the manner in which the stock was established is decisive for the purposes of granting an exemption. With respect to the burden of proof, the Ministerstvo životního prostředí (Ministry of the Environment) stated that it was not unreasonable, given that an owner would be required to prove the origin of the breeding stock only if he or she intended to trade subsequent generations. The authorities examine the origin of the breeding stock in compliance with established practice in the European Union. However, the opposite view, advanced by the applicant, makes it easier to legitimise the breeding stock bred from specimens obtained from the wild. With regard to the right to property, the Ministerstvo životního prostředí (Ministry of the Environment) noted that the legal ownership of the grandparent specimens and their offspring is not contested. Thus, the applicant's right to property is not infringed, only restricted.

AG23   The referring court points out that the decisive issue in the present case is whether the definition of 'breeding stock' under Article 1(3) of Regulation No 865/2006 comprises all the animals in a specific breeding operation that are used for reproduction. If the Court were to interpret that definition broadly, including the grandparent specimens not kept by the applicant, then the second question referred becomes devoid of purpose.

AG24   However, should the Court give a narrow interpretation of the concept of 'breeding stock', restricted to the specimens within a specific breeding operation, then it would be necessary to answer the second question referred. By that question, the referring court seeks to ascertain whether the concept of '[establishment]' of the breeding stock, referred to in Article 54(2) of Regulation No 865/2006, covers only the lawful acquisition of the specimens concerned or whether it also covers the beginning of the breeding line.

AG25   In that regard, the referring court considers that the interpretation according to which the concept of 'establishment' covers the beginning of the breeding line of the specimens concerned prevents the legitimisation of 'questionable' stocks by means of 'dishonest' transfers. On the other hand, that court notes that a 'dishonest' transfer is not possible within the European Union. Indeed, it takes the view that under the legislative framework currently in force it is impossible lawfully to acquire specimens of the animals listed in Annex A to Regulation No 865/2006 without obtaining an exemption. Furthermore, if the examination of the entire breeding line were permitted, it would place unrealistic requirements on owners of protected animals, obliging them to prove the legitimacy of a long and undefined genealogical line.

AG26   By its third question, the referring court seeks to ascertain whether individual circumstances, such as the lawful acquisition of the parent specimens by the applicant and his legitimate expectations that he could trade the offspring, at least in the Czech Republic, may be taken into account. The referring court notes, in that regard, that even if CITES were applicable in the Czech Republic at the time of the acquisition, the national implementing legislation did not require the issuance of a certificate in the event of a national transfer. Moreover, the stricter EU legislation, which requires the issuance of such a certificate in the case of a transfer within the European Union as well as within the same Member State, was not applicable at the time when the transfer of the parent specimens took place.

AG27   Under these circumstances, the Nejvyšší správní soud (Supreme Administrative Court) decided to stay the proceedings and to refer the following questions to the Court of Justice for a preliminary ruling:

'(1) Does "breeding stock", as defined by [Regulation No 865/2006], include specimens that are the parents of specimens bred by a given breeder, even though that breeder never owned or kept them?

(2) If the answer to the first question is that such parent specimens do not constitute a part of the breeding stock, are competent bodies authorised to verify, in examining compliance with the condition set out in Article 54(2) of [Regulation No 865/2006], consisting of the establishment of stock lawfully and, at the same time, in a manner not detrimental to the survival of wild specimens, the origin of those parent specimens and to infer on that basis whether the breeding stock has been established in accordance with the rules set out in Article 54(2) of the Regulation?

(3) In examining compliance with the condition set out in Article 54(2) of [Regulation No 865/2006], consisting of the establishment of stock legally and, at the same time, in a manner not detrimental to the survival of wild specimens, can further circumstances of the case be taken into consideration (in particular, good faith in the transfer of the specimens and the legitimate expectation that trading in their potential offspring will be permitted, and potentially also the less stringent legislation applicable in the Czech Republic prior to the country's accession to the European Union)?'

Analysis

Question 1

AG28   By its first question, the referring court is asking, in essence, whether the concept of 'breeding stock', within the meaning of Article 1(3) of Regulation No 865/2006, covers the parents of specimens bred by a given breeder that he or she did not own or keep.

AG29   In that regard, I note, as a preliminary point, that qualifying animal specimens as having been 'born and bred in captivity' has important consequences with regard to their protection status. Indeed, whereas, pursuant to Article 8(1) of Regulation No 338/97, the trade of specimens of species listed in Annex A to that regulation is *prohibited*, Article 8(3)(d) of that regulation provides that captive-born and -bred specimens of an animal species may qualify for an *exemption* from the prohibition of trade (the 'captive-bred exemption'). The competent management authority issues a certificate to that effect (the 'sales exemption certificate').

AG30   Article 54 of Regulation No 865/2006 sets out a number of conditions that have to be satisfied in order for the management authority to consider that the specimens are born and bred in captivity. According, more particularly, to Article 54(2) of that regulation, that authority has to be satisfied that 'the breeding stock was established in accordance with the legal provisions applicable to it at the time of acquisition and in a manner not detrimental to the survival of the species concerned in the wild'.

AG31   In the present case, it is undisputed that the parents of the specimens acquired by the applicant (in other words, the grandparents of the youngest generation of parrots) do not satisfy the conditions set out in Article 54(2) of Regulation No 865/2006. Indeed, the grandparent specimens were caught in the wild and were imported into the Czech Republic under suspicious circumstances. However, the applicant states that the concept of 'breeding stock' should not include specimens which were never owned by him or kept in his breeding operation. It is his submission that the authorities should examine the requirements for granting an exemption from the prohibition of trade in view of the legal status of only the specimens kept in his own breeding operation.

AG32   It is in that context that the referring court seeks to ascertain the *scope* of the concept of 'breeding stock' within the meaning of Article 1(3) of Regulation No 865/2006. Should that concept be interpreted as covering all specimens used for the purposes of breeding that line irrespective of the operation in which they are kept, then the other two questions need not be considered. The authorities must take into account by definition the ancestry of the breeding stock when they examine its establishment, within the meaning of Article 54(2) of that regulation.

AG33   According to the Court's settled case-law, for the purpose of interpreting a provision of EU law it is necessary to consider not only its wording but also the context in which it occurs and the objectives pursued by the rules of which it is part.[11]

AG34   As far as concerns the wording of Article 1(3) of Regulation No 865/2006, it defines the concept of 'breeding stock' as 'all the animals in a breeding operation that are used for reproduction'.

AG35   The referring court, as well as the European Commission in its observations, takes the view that the wording of the definition of 'breeding stock' covers exclusively the animals held in a *specific* breeding operation. Indeed, the definition refers to animals kept in '*a*' breeding operation and not in *any* breeding operation.

AG36   A comparative examination of various language versions lends support to that interpretation. The French version refers to '*un* établissement d'élévage', the Spanish version to '*un* establecimiento', the German version to '*einem* Zuchtbetrieb' and the Latvian version to 'dzīvnieki *audzētavā*'.[12]

AG37   However, the textual interpretation is not conclusive to the extent that some other language versions of Article 1(3) of Regulation No 865/2006 suggest that the concept of 'breeding stock' means all the animals in a breeding 'process'.[13] Moreover, the Slovak Republic considers that the term 'operation' used in the English version connotes a 'reproduction process' and not a specific breeding operation.

AG38   In view of the apparent disparity between the equally authentic language versions of Article 1(3) of Regulation No 865/2006, it is necessary to examine the context in which that provision is set out, as well as the objectives pursued by it and the legislation of which it forms part.[14]

AG39   With regard to the context of Article 1(3) of Regulation No 865/2006, it must be recalled that, as follows from the first recital of that regulation, its objective is, inter alia, to ensure full compliance with the provisions of CITES. Therefore, for the purpose of interpreting that regulation, it is necessary to consider the provisions of CITES, including the resolutions adopted by the Conference of the Parties to CITES ('Resolution Conf.'), which help to clarify the interpretation of the provisions of that convention.[15]

---

[11] Judgment of 8 December 2020, *Staatsanwaltschaft Wien (Ordres de virement falsifiés)* (C-584/19) EU:C:2020:1002 at [49].
[12] Emphasis added.
[13] I refer, more particularly, to the Slovenian, Greek and Croatian versions.
[14] See, to that effect, judgment of 24 March 2021, *A* (C-950/19) EU:C:2021:230 at [37] and [38].
[15] See, by analogy, judgment of 12 May 2021, *Hauptzollamt B (Sturgeon caviar)* (C-87/20) EU:C:2021:382 at [30] and [31].

AG40   In that regard, I would make the following observations. On the one hand, the definition of the concept of 'breeding stock' under Regulation No 865/2006 is almost identical to the definition adopted by Resolution Conf. 10.16. That resolution specifies that 'the "breeding stock" of an operation means the ensemble of the animals in the operation that are used for reproduction'.[16] The use of the definite article 'the' before the nouns 'animals' and 'operation' would seem to suggest that the concept of 'breeding stock' should be understood to cover all animals used for reproduction *in a specific breeding operation* and not by various breeders in an indefinite number of operations.

AG41   On the other hand, under the terms of Resolution Conf. 12.10,[17] an 'operation' may only be registered according to the procedure it sets out if specimens produced by that operation qualify as having been 'bred in captivity' according to the provisions of Resolution Conf. 10.16.[18] The terms of the former resolution and its annexes provide sufficiently clear indications that the captive-breeding operation cannot be understood as meaning a 'process'.[19]

AG42   For the sake of completeness, it may be helpful to observe that even in other fields of law, and more particularly in EU agricultural law, the term 'breeding operation' is understood in a similar way. Regulation (EU) 2016/1012[20] defines the term 'breeding operation' as 'any breeders' association, breeding organisation, private undertaking operating in a closed production system or public body'.

AG43   Consequently, consideration of the context of which Regulation No 865/2006 forms part confirms the interpretation that the concept of 'breeding stock', within the meaning of Article 1(3) of that regulation, covers all the animals in a specific breeding operation. That same concept does not cover the parents of specimens bred by a given breeder which he or she did not own or keep.

AG44   As regards the objective pursued by Article 1(3) of Regulation No 865/2006 and the legislation of which it forms part, those also support a more restrictive understanding of the term 'breeding stock'. The definition of the scope of that concept has repercussions on the determination of the object of the evaluation by the authorities when they carry out the assessment as to whether the breeding stock was established in accordance with the conditions set out in Article 54(2) of Regulation No 865/2006. The object of the evaluation should be specific, precise and concrete.

AG45   From that perspective, even if the interpretation put forward by the Slovak Republic – that the English term 'breeding operation' connotes a 'process' – were accepted, *quod non*, it seems clear to me that such a process could not be unlimited, but should be understood as having *definite boundaries* within a specific operation.

---

[16] Resolution Conf. 10.16, paragraph 1(c).

[17] That resolution is headed 'Registration of operations that breed Appendix-I animal species in captivity for commercial purposes'. It is not implemented in the European Union, which means that registration of commercial captive-breeding operations with the CITES Secretariat is not a requirement to trade in the European Union. That being said, that resolution can be used as a reference point with regard to the understanding of the term 'breeding operation'.

[18] Resolution Conf. 12.10, paragraph 5(a).

[19] By way of example, Annex 1 to Resolution Conf. 12.10 sets out the information to be provided to the Secretariat by the management authority on operations to be registered, which includes the name and address of the owner and manager of the captive-breeding operation, the date of establishment, and the description of the facilities to house the stock. Annex 3 to that same resolution provides a sample application form, which requires, inter alia, an indication of the contact details of the owner and manager of the captive-breeding operation.

[20] Regulation of the European Parliament and of the Council of 8 June 2016 on zootechnical and genealogical conditions for the breeding, trade in and entry into the Union of purebred breeding animals, hybrid breeding pigs and the germinal products thereof and amending Regulation (EU) No 652/2014, Council Directives 89/608/EEC and 90/425/EEC and repealing certain acts in the area of animal breeding ('Animal Breeding Regulation') ([2016] OJ L171/66).

AG46   The Slovak Republic argues, however, that the consideration of the overall objective pursued by Regulation No 865/2006, consisting in the protection of endangered species, should lead to a different conclusion. In my view, the objective pursued by that regulation cannot lead to an interpretation of the concept of 'breeding stock' which would be inconsistent with the meaning of such a concept in the legislative context of which it forms part. In any event, the interpretation I propose of the concept of 'breeding stock' does not compromise the realisation of the objective of the protection of endangered species. As I will develop in the framework of the second and third questions, that objective is taken into account in order to acknowledge that the competent management authority has the power to examine the ancestry of the breeding stock when it determines whether a specimen of an animal species qualifies for the captive-bred exemption.

AG47   In the light of the above, I conclude that the concept of 'breeding stock', within the meaning of Article 1(3) of Regulation No 865/2006, covers all the animals kept in a specific breeding operation. Therefore, that concept does not cover, as such, the parents of specimens bred by a given breeder that he or she did not own or keep.

Questions 2 and 3

AG48   By its second and third questions, the referring court asks, in essence, on the one hand, whether the competent management authority has the power to verify the origin of the breeding stock in order to satisfy itself that it was established lawfully and in a manner not detrimental to the survival of the species concerned in the wild, within the meaning of Article 54(2) of Regulation No 865/2006. On the other hand, it asks whether, in the framework of that assessment, the specific circumstances of the case, such as the good faith of the breeder and his legitimate expectations that trading in offspring will be permitted, as well as the less stringent legislation applicable in the Czech Republic prior to that country's accession to the European Union, are decisive.

AG49   As I will attempt to demonstrate in my analysis, the authorities should have the power to verify the origin of the breeding stock. In circumstances where they are not satisfied that the conditions set out in Article 54(2) of Regulation No 865/2006 are met, the authorities should then have the power to refuse to grant an exemption from the prohibition of trading. In my view, considering the general rule of prohibiting the trade of endangered species, the authorities should have every means at their disposal in order to investigate where there are risk indicators and not to turn a blind eye.

(a) On the power of the management authority to establish the ancestry of the breeding stock

AG50   It should be borne in mind at the outset that, according to the Court's settled case-law,[21] for the purpose of interpreting a provision of EU law it is necessary to consider not only its wording but also the context in which it occurs and the objectives pursued by the rules of which it is part.

AG51   As regards, in the first place, the *text* of Article 54(2) of Regulation No 865/2006, it should be noted that that provision uses the concept of '[establishment]' of the

---

[21] See fn.11 above.

breeding stock, which is quite broad. It can, therefore, be understood as involving the examination of events that occurred in the past and, more particularly, the *ancestry* of the specimens.

AG52   As regards, in the second place, the *context* of that provision, it is important to recall, firstly, that Article 8(1) of Regulation No 338/97 sets out a *general rule prohibiting* all commercial use of specimens of the species listed in Annex A to that regulation. The exemptions provided for under Article 8(3) of that regulation, including the exemption in relation to captive-born and -bred specimens of an animal species, *may be granted, on a case-by-case basis*. The prohibition of trading endangered species reflects a fundamental principle of CITES, according to which trade in specimens of species threatened with extinction must be authorised only 'in exceptional circumstances'.[22] Given that the prohibition of trading endangered species is the rule, whereas the granting of an exemption from that rule with regard to captive-born species is the exception, that exception must be *interpreted strictly*.

AG53   Next, Article 8(3)(d) of Regulation No 338/97 *authorises, but does not require*, exemptions from the prohibition it lays down.[23] It clearly follows from that provision that the granting of the captive-bred exemption is only an *option* for the Member States.[24]

AG54   In that regard, it is important to point out that it follows from the case-law of the Court that, as regards species covered by Annex A to Regulation No 338/97, the Member States are allowed to lay down a *general prohibition* in their territory of all commercial use of captive-born and -bred specimens.[25] If that is so, it should a fortiori be considered that where exemptions from the prohibition of trade of listed species are authorised, the authorities enjoy a wide margin of discretion as to the methods they use in order to examine whether specimens qualify for exemption.

AG55   Lastly, it should be pointed out that Article 55 of Regulation No 865/2006 provides that a competent authority is to have the discretion to require the analysis of samples in circumstances where, *for the purposes of Article 54*, it considers it necessary to establish the *ancestry* of a specimen through the analysis of blood or other tissue. That provision lends support to the conclusion that the authorities have the power to examine the ancestry of the breeding stock in order to reach their finding with regard to the fulfilment of the conditions set out under Article 54(2) of that regulation.

AG56   As regards, in the third place, the *objective* of Regulation No 865/2006, it must be borne in mind that it implements Regulation No 338/97. The purpose of the arrangements introduced by those regulations in order to protect specimens of species listed in Annex A to Regulation No 338/97 is to ensure the fullest possible protection for species of wild fauna and flora through controls on trade in such species, in compliance with the objectives, principles and provisions of CITES.[26] The interpretation according to which the authorities have the power to examine the ancestry of the specimens in the framework of an application for a sales exemption certificate contributes to the attainment of the objective pursued by those regulations.

---

[22] Article II(1) of CITES.
[23] Judgment of 23 October 2001, *Tridon* (C-510/99) EU:C:2001:559 at [34].
[24] See, to that effect, judgment of 23 October 2001, *Tridon* (C-510/99) EU:C:2001:559 at [30].
[25] See, to that effect, judgment of 23 October 2001, *Tridon* (C-510/99) EU:C:2001:559 at [41].
[26] See, to that effect, judgment of 4 September 2014, *Sofia Zoo* (C-532/13) EU:C:2014:2140 at [34].

AG57   I also find it particularly relevant to point out that the conditions for the qualification of a specimen of an animal species as having been born and bred in captivity, as set out in Article 54(2) of Regulation No 865/2006, correspond to the ones set out in paragraph 2(b)(ii)(A) of Resolution Conf. 10.16. That resolution was adopted in view of the concern that 'much trade in specimens declared as bred in captivity remains contrary to [CITES] and to Resolutions of the Conference of the Parties, and may be detrimental to the survival of wild populations of the species concerned'. The interpretation according to which the authorities have the power to verify the origin of the breeding stock is consistent with the intentions of the Conference of the Parties to CITES to strengthen the protection of specimens bred in captivity.

AG58   Any other interpretation would be liable to run counter to the objectives mentioned above. As the referring court, the European Commission, the Czech Republic and the Slovak Republic have pointed out in their written observations, it is necessary to prevent the risk of an easy 'legitimisation' or 'laundering' of illegally traded specimens. Indeed, it would suffice for a breeder to acquire the offspring of a specimen caught in the wild for their future trade to be rendered lawful.[27] From that perspective, I do not find the statement of the referring court convincing in that a 'dishonest' transfer is not possible within the European Union.

AG59   In the light of the above, I take the view that the authorities have the power to examine the ancestry of the breeding stock for the purpose of determining its establishment within the meaning of Article 54(2) of Regulation No 865/2006.

(b) On the practical aspects and the burden of proof for establishing the ancestry of the breeding stock

AG60   It is important to address, at this stage, the concerns expressed by the referring court with regard to practical aspects of the examination by the authorities of the ancestry of the breeding stock. Those doubts correspond, to some extent, to the arguments put forward by the applicant in his written observations.

AG61   I agree with the Czech Republic and the Commission, which point out in their written observations and in answer to a question put by the Court, that that examination by the authorities may be extended to cover the moment when the first specimens were removed from the wild. As observed in point 51 of the present Opinion, the term '[establishment]' of the breeding stock employed in Article 54(2) of Regulation No 865/2006 is very broad. Its scope can therefore include the examination of the *entire breeding line* up to the specimens taken from the wild. Moreover, as the Commission rightly points out in its response to a question put by the Court, the term 'ancestry' employed in Article 55 of Regulation No 865/2006 is broader than the term 'parents' employed in Article 54(1)(a) of that regulation. The term 'ancestry' would seem, therefore, to suggest that the authorities should have the power to extend their investigation to the point in time when specimens

---

[27] See Lieberman, S., 'Procedures used by the United States of America in making CITES non-detriment findings', in Rosser, A., Haywood, M., *Guidance for CITES Scientific Authorities: Checklist to Assist in Making Non-detriment findings for Appendix 11 Exports*, IUCN – The World Conservation Union, Gland, Switzerland and Cambridge, UK, 2002, p. 32, who observes, in relation to the procedures used in the United States: 'there are … all-too-many cases where animals may themselves be bred in captivity, but the founder stock was not obtained legally, and therefore export of even the progeny would be detrimental to the survival of the species (in that it increases demand and facilitates detrimental trade)'.

were removed from the wild, as was the case with the grandparent specimens in question.

AG62   The length of time that may have lapsed since the founder stock was removed from the wild is not, in my view, decisive as such in circumstances where the proposed activity involves trade. Regulation No 338/97 already provides for a specific situation under which the authorities may decide to grant an exemption in view of the lapse of time. That situation concerns 'worked specimens that were acquired more than 50 years previously'[28] within the meaning of Article 2(w) of Regulation No 338/97. However, the specimens in question do not fall within the scope of that provision.

AG63   The applicant contends that the requirement to prove the legitimacy of the entire breeding line gives rise to an unreasonable burden of proof. I am not convinced that that is the case.

AG64   In that regard, it should be recalled, as was stated in point 30 of the present Opinion, that Article 54(2) of Regulation No 865/2006 sets out two conditions with regard to the establishment of the breeding stock which the administrative authorities have to assess. The first one relates to the establishment of the breeding stock 'in accordance with the legal provisions applicable to it at the time of the acquisition' (the 'legal acquisition finding'). The second one relates to the establishment of the breeding stock 'in a manner not detrimental to the survival of the species concerned in the wild' (the 'non-detriment finding'). Those two determinations are not specific to the question as to whether specimens are to be considered as having been born and bred in captivity; they reflect a general approach to the regulation of trade set out by Regulation No 338/97 and CITES.[29]

AG65   In the framework of the determinations carried out by the authorities, according to Article 54(2) of Regulation No 865/2006, it is important to observe that an examination of ancestry appears to be *common practice*, as the Czech Republic and the European Commission have underlined in their written observations.

AG66   The Czech Republic and the European Commission explain, in essence, that breeders do not *systematically* have to prove the legitimacy of the entire ancestry of the breeding stock. The authorities carry out a *risk assessment* depending on the circumstances of each case.[30] In carrying out such an assessment, 'the degree of risk to the species (risk of detriment, illegal trade involvement etc.)' should 'determine[…] the degree of scrutiny'.[31] The European Commission, in its written response to a question put by the Court, gives certain examples of relevant *risk indicators* on the basis of which the authorities should pay particular attention. Such risk indicators include the following: a sudden increase in or significant volume of trade in specimens declared in captivity; a declaration of specimens as bred in captivity from operations the level of annual production of which exceeds the normal level taking into account the size of the parental population and the potential for reproduction of the species concerned; specimens whose size and condition do not comply with the reproduction data supplied; or the existence of

---

[28] Article 8(3)(b).

[29] See Article 5(2)(a) and (b) of Regulation No 338/97 and Article IV(2)(a) and (b) of CITES with regard to the conditions for the issuance of an export permit of listed species. See also Resolution Conf. 18.7 'Legal acquisition findings' and Resolution Conf. 16.7 'Non-detriment findings'.

[30] In the specific context of the legal acquisition finding for the export of CITES-listed species, Resolution Conf. 18.7 defines the term 'risk assessment' as the 'evaluation of the likelihood that a specimen of a CITES-listed species was not legally acquired'.

[31] Lieberman, S., op. cit., p. 30.

doubts with regard to the legal origin of the founder stock which could have been acquired before the country in which it is located became a party to CITES. The European Commission also submitted that it is currently cooperating with the Member States in drawing up a guidance document with relevant examples of risk indicators.

AG67   The European Commission also pointed out that when the authorities assess whether to grant a sales exemption certificate, they take into account the *chain of custody* requirements.[32] That examination involves the documentation regarding the lawfulness of the acquisition of the breeding stock. In that context, it does not appear unreasonable to require the breeder to be able to prove the lawfulness of the acquisition on the basis of breeding records. What is more, the European Commission explained, in reply to a question put by the Court, that if the documentation does not exist, the proof of lawfulness of the chain of custody remains possible by other means.

AG68   It should also be borne in mind that with regard to specimens of species listed in Annex B to Regulation No 338/97, the Court has ruled that the task of determining what *evidence* may establish that the condition of lawful acquisition of those specimens has been met is left to the competent authorities of the Member States.[33] I consider that the same reasoning should apply *by analogy* with regard to specimens of species listed in Annex A to that same regulation, taking into account the fact that the latter does not specify what evidence may establish the lawful acquisition of those specimens.

AG69   With regard to the *point of reference* for the legal acquisition finding, it follows from the terms of Article 54(2) of Regulation No 865/2006 that the authorities would need to take into account the legal provisions that were applicable *at the date of acquisition of each specimen* as they move from generation to generation. With regard to the point of reference for the non-detriment finding, it must be observed that it is not specifically determined in that provision. In the absence of such a determination, the point of reference could be considered to be the same as for the legal acquisition finding, that is to say, the date of acquisition of the original specimens. However, the non-detriment finding is quite broad and may include a number of methods of assessment.[34] The nature of the determination involved appears to be more compatible with a consideration of the *evolution* of the species over a period of time, instead of a specific date. From that perspective, it seems more appropriate to avoid setting limits. I would, therefore, agree with the Commission's approach set out in a response to a question put by the Court, that in order to make a valid finding, the authorities should be able to take into account the status of the species *at the time of the assessment*. Such an interpretation ensures that the 'best available scientific information is the basis for non-detriment findings'.[35]

AG70   My final remark with regard to the determinations carried out by the authorities is that they must, in any event, comply with the principle of EU law relating to *good administration*, which entails requirements that must be met by the Member

---

[32] In the specific context of the legal acquisition finding for the export of CITES-listed species, Resolution Conf. 18.7 defines the term 'chain of custody' as follows: 'chronological documentation, to the extent practicable and in accordance with applicable laws and records, of the transactions pertaining to the removal from the wild of a specimen and the subsequent ownership of that specimen'.
[33] Judgment of 16 July 2009, *Rubach* (C-344/08) EU:C:2009:482 at [27].
[34] See Resolution Conf. 16.7 (Rev. CoP17) 'Non-detriment findings'.
[35] Resolution Conf. 14.2 'CITES Strategic Vision: 2008-2013', Objective 1.5.

States when they implement EU law. Among those requirements, the obligation to *state reasons* for decisions adopted by the national authorities is particularly important, since it puts their addressee in a position to defend his or her rights and decide in full knowledge of the circumstances whether it is worthwhile to bring an action against those decisions. It is also necessary in order to enable the courts to review the legality of those decisions and it is therefore a requirement for ensuring that the judicial review guaranteed by Article 47 of the Charter of Fundamental Rights of the European Union ('the Charter') is effective.[36] In the present case, there are no elements in the file demonstrating a breach of the obligation to state reasons or any other irregularity in the procedure followed by the competent management authority. That authority refused to grant an exemption to the trade of the specimens in question, relying on the recommendation by the scientific authority that that exemption not be granted.

AG71   In view of the above, I consider that acknowledging that the competent management authority has the power to examine the origin of specimens when it assesses whether to grant a sales exemption certificate does not amount to imposing on the breeders an unreasonable burden of proof.

(c) The relevance of the particular circumstances of the case on the assessment of the conditions set out in Article 54(2) of Regulation No 865/2006

AG72   The last point of my analysis will address the issue raised by the third question of the referring court in relation to the relevance of the particular circumstances of the case on the assessment of the conditions set out in Article 54(2) of Regulation No 865/2006. According to the referring court, such particular circumstances include the (ostensible) legitimate expectations of the breeder as to his right to trade the offspring of the grandparent specimens, his good faith as to the lawfulness of the acquisition and the less stringent legislation applicable in the Czech Republic prior to the country's accession to the European Union.

AG73   In my view, none of the abovementioned circumstances justify, by themselves, the management authority adopting a more lenient approach and granting an exemption that would allow the specimens in question to be traded.

AG74   To begin with, the conditions set out in Article 54(2) of Regulation No 865/2006 that the authorities have to assess in order to qualify specimens as having been born and bred in captivity do not relate to the breeder but to the establishment of the breeding stock. Moreover, those conditions are *cumulative*. Even if the authorities conclude that the establishment of the breeding stock was lawful at the time of the acquisition, that finding alone does not suffice to grant an exemption. What is more, as I pointed out above,[37] in order for the management authority to make a valid non-detriment finding it needs to take into account *updated* evidence on the state of the species.

AG75   Under those conditions, I am of the view that the existence of a less stringent applicable legislative framework at the time of the acquisition of the breeding stock prior to the country's accession to the European Union[38] is not a reason for the management authority to grant an exemption from the prohibition of trading the specimens in question. It should also be pointed out that, at the time of the

---

[36] Judgment of 7 September 2021, *Klaipėdos regiono atliekų tvarkymo centras* (C-927/19) EU:C:2021:700 at [120].
[37] Point 69.
[38] See the explanations of the referring court in that regard in [26] of the present opinion.

acquisition of the specimens in question, CITES was already applicable in the Czech Republic. Furthermore, the applicant did not claim that the specimens in question qualify for the exemption applicable to 'pre-convention specimens', that is to say, specimens of listed species acquired before CITES applied to them.[39]

AG76   More particularly, as regards the alleged legitimate expectations of the breeder, CITES 'in no way' affects the right of the parties to adopt stricter domestic measures regarding the conditions for the trade of species included in Appendix I to that convention 'or [even] the complete prohibition thereof'.[40] Therefore, traders should not be entitled to expect that the legislative framework will remain the same when they decide to trade specimens that fall under the general rule establishing a prohibition set out in CITES. Instead, the breeders have to demonstrate *due diligence* when they intend to engage in such trade.[41]

AG77   The referring court asks whether the fact that the applicant cannot trade the specimens in question interferes with his right to property within the meaning of Article 17 of the Charter. However, according to settled case-law,[42] the right to property is not an absolute right and must be viewed in relation to its social function. Consequently, its exercise may be restricted, provided that those restrictions in fact correspond to objectives of general interest and do not constitute, in relation to the aim pursued, disproportionate and intolerable interference, impairing the very substance of the right guaranteed. As regards the general interest objectives referred to above, the protection of wildlife is one of them[43] and is therefore capable of justifying a restriction on the exercise of the right to property. As regards the principle of proportionality, it is sufficient to state that Regulation No 338/97 and Regulation No 865/2006 operate a balance between the requirements of that right and the requirements linked to the protection of wildlife. Consequently, I take the view that the applicant's right to property is not infringed.

AG78   It is also relevant to point out that the applicant was permitted to keep the specimens and that he was not subject to any kind of administrative or criminal sanction. The present case does not seem to require, therefore, further analysis with regard to the respect of the principle of proportionality.

AG79   Nevertheless, the applicant claims that his breeding activity has a positive impact on the environment. In his view, the trade of the captive-bred specimens in question leads to a decrease in the demand for the illegal acquisition of specimens caught in the wild. That is, in my view, an unsubstantiated claim. Article 8(3)(f) of Regulation No 338/97 provides, in particular, that an exemption may be granted from the prohibition of trade where the specimens 'are intended for breeding or propagation purposes from which conservation benefits will accrue to the species concerned'. However, it does not appear from the file nor has it been argued before the Court that the breeder asked the authorities for an exemption based on that provision. In any event, as the Czech Republic has observed in its written response to a question put by the Court, that provision presupposes that the proposed activity has *concrete conservation benefits*, such as where there is participation in

---

[39] The exemption for pre-convention specimens is provided under Article 8(3)(a) of Regulation No 338/97. See Davies, P., op. cit. p. 510.

[40] Article XIV(1)(a) of CITES.

[41] Another matter entirely is whether the authorities would potentially have to provide for transitional measures to allow the traders to adapt. However, the applicant did not claim that his legitimate expectations were infringed on that ground.

[42] See judgment of 15 January 2013, *Križan* (C-416/10) EU:C:2013:8 at [113].

[43] See, to that effect, judgment of 19 June 2008, *Nationale Raad van Dierenkwekers en Liefhebbers and Andibel* (C-219/07) EU:C:2008:353 at [27].

conservation projects operated by zoos or where the specimens are returned to the wild.

AG80 My final remark concerns the relevance of the length of time that has lapsed since the founder stock was removed from the wild. As alluded to in point 62 of the present Opinion, that factor should not be decisive as such where the risk assessment has led the authorities to conclude against the granting of an exemption. The general rule prohibiting commercial activities involving listed specimens is not limited in time. For the sake of completeness, I wish to point out once more that the present case does not involve criminal proceedings; were that to be the case, the principle of limitation would apply. What is more, from the perspective of civil law, it must be observed that the lawfulness of acquisition of the specimens in question is not contested.

AG81 In view of the above, I do not consider that the specific circumstances of the case, such as the ones exposed by the referring court, are relevant in the context of the examination by the authorities of the conditions set out under Article 54(2) of Regulation No 865/2006.

Conclusion

AG82 In the light of the foregoing, I propose that the questions referred be answered as follows:

(1) The concept of 'breeding stock', within the meaning of Article 1(3) of Commission Regulation No 865/2006 of 4 May 2006 laying down detailed rules concerning the implementation of Council Regulation No 338/97, as amended by Commission Regulation (EU) 2015/870 of 5 June 2015, covers all the animals kept in a specific breeding operation. That concept does not cover the parents of specimens bred by a given breeder that he or she did not own or keep.

(2) The competent management authority has the power to verify the origin of the breeding stock in order to satisfy itself that it was established lawfully and in a manner not detrimental to the survival of the species concerned in the wild, within the meaning of Article 54(2) of Commission Regulation (EC) No 865/2006. For the purpose of that assessment, the specific circumstances of the case, such as the good faith of the breeder and his or her legitimate expectations that trading in offspring will be permitted, as well as the less stringent legislation applicable in the Czech Republic prior to that country's accession to the European Union, are not decisive.

JUDGMENT[44]

1 This request for a preliminary ruling concerns the interpretation of Article 1(3) and Article 54(2) of Commission Regulation (EC) No 865/2006 of 4 May 2006 laying down detailed rules concerning the implementation of Council Regulation (EC) No 338/97 on the protection of species of wild fauna and flora by regulating trade therein (OJ 2006 L 166, p. 1).

---

[44] Language of the case: Czech.

2   The request has been made in the course of an appeal on a point of law between ET and the Ministerstvo životního prostředí (Ministry of the Environment, Czech Republic) concerning the grant of an exemption from the prohibition of trade for five specimens of the hyacinth macaw (*Anodorhynchus hyacinthinus*).

Legal context

International law

3   The Convention on International Trade in Endangered Species of Wild Fauna and Flora, signed in Washington on 3 March 1973 (*United Nations Treaty Series*, vol. 993, No I-14537, 'CITES') seeks to ensure that international trade in species listed in its appendices, and in parts and derivatives thereof, does not damage the conservation of biodiversity and is based on a sustainable use of wild species.

4   CITES, to which the European Union became a party on 8 July 2015, was implemented in the European Union as from 1 January 1984 under Council Regulation (EEC) No 3626/82 of 3 December 1982 on the implementation in the Community of the Convention on international trade in endangered species of wild fauna and flora (OJ 1982 L 384, p. 1). That regulation was repealed by Council Regulation (EC) No 338/97 of 9 December 1996 on the protection of species of wild fauna and flora by regulating trade therein (OJ 1997 L 61, p. 1), the second paragraph of Article 1 of which provides that that regulation is to apply in compliance with the objectives, principles and provisions of CITES.

5   Article II(1) of CITES, entitled 'Fundamental principles', provides:

'Appendix I shall include all species threatened with extinction which are or may be affected by trade. Trade in specimens of these species must be subject to particularly strict regulation in order not to endanger further their survival and must only be authorised in exceptional circumstances.'

6   Since 22 October 1987, the hyacinth macaw species has been included in Appendix I to CITES.

7   Paragraph 1(c) of Resolution 10.16 of the Conference of the Parties to CITES ('Resolution Conf. 10.16') entitled 'Regarding terminology' provides:

'[The Conference of the Parties to CITES] ADOPTS the following definitions of terms used in this Resolution:

…

(c)   the "breeding stock" of an operation means the ensemble of the animals in the operation that are used for reproduction;'

8   Paragraph 2(b)(ii)(A) of that resolution, entitled 'Regarding the term "bred in captivity"', provides:

'[The Conference of the Parties to CITES] DECIDES that:

…

(b)   the term "bred in captivity" shall be interpreted to refer only to specimens, as defined in Article I, paragraph (b), of [CITES], born or otherwise produced in a controlled environment, and shall apply only if:

…

(ii) the breeding stock, to the satisfaction of the competent government authorities of the exporting country:
    A. was established in accordance with the provisions of CITES and relevant national laws and in a manner not detrimental to the survival of the species in the wild;'

9   Paragraph 5(a) of Resolution 12.10 of the Conference of the Parties to CITES ('Resolution Conf. 12.10'):

'[The Conference of the Parties to CITES] RESOLVES that:
    (a) an operation may only be registered according to the procedure in this Resolution if specimens produced by that operation qualify as "bred in captivity" according to the provisions of Resolution Conf. 10.16 (Rev.).'

10   Annex 1 to Resolution Conf. 12.10, entitled 'Information to be provided to the Secretariat by the Management Authority on operations to be registered', lists 16 categories of data which must be communicated to the Secretariat of CITES, which include, inter alia, the name and address of the owner and manager of the captive-breeding operation, the date of that operation and the description of facilities to house the captive stock and to prevent the escape of specimens.

European Union law

Regulation No 338/97

11   Recital 10 of Regulation No 338/97 provides:

'Whereas there is a need, in order to ensure the broadest possible protection for species covered by this Regulation, to lay down provisions for controlling trade and movement of specimens within the Community, and the conditions for housing specimens; whereas the certificates issued under this Regulation, which contribute to controlling these activities, must be governed by common rules on their issue, validity and use'.

12   Under the first paragraph of Article 1 of Regulation No 338/97, entitled 'Object':

'The object of this Regulation is to protect species of wild fauna and flora and to guarantee their conservation by regulating trade therein in accordance with the following Articles.'

13   Article 8(1), (2) and (3)(d) of that regulation, entitled 'Provisions relating to the control of commercial activities', provides:

'1.   The purchase, offer to purchase, acquisition for commercial purposes, display to the public for commercial purposes, use for commercial gain and sale, keeping for sale, offering for sale or transporting for sale of specimens of the species listed in Annex A shall be prohibited.
2.   Member States may prohibit the holding of specimens, in particular live animals of the species listed in Annex A.
3.   In accordance with the requirements of other Community legislation on the conservation of wild fauna and flora, exemption from the prohibitions referred to in paragraph 1 may be granted by issuance of

a certificate to that effect by a management authority of the Member State in which the specimens are located, on a case-by-case basis where the specimens:

...

(d) are captive-born and bred specimens of an animal species or artificially propagated specimens of a plant species or are parts or derivatives of such specimens'.

14   The species *Anodorhynchus*, which includes animals with the common names 'hyacinth macaw, Lear's macaw, glaucous macaw', appears in Annex A to that regulation.

Regulation No 865/2006

15   Recital 1 of Regulation No 865/2006 is worded as follows:

'Provisions are required to implement Regulation (EC) No 338/97 and to ensure full compliance with the provisions of [CITES].'

16   Article 1(3) of that regulation, entitled 'Definitions', provides:

'For the purposes of this Regulation, in addition to the definitions laid down in Article 2 of Regulation (EC) No 338/97, the following definitions shall apply:

...

(3) "breeding stock" means all the animals in a breeding operation that are used for reproduction'.

17   Article 54(2) of that regulation, entitled 'Specimens born and bred in captivity of animal species', states:

'Without prejudice to Article 55, a specimen of an animal species shall be considered to be born and bred in captivity only if a competent management authority, in consultation with a competent scientific authority of the Member State concerned, is satisfied that the following criteria are met:

...

(2) the breeding stock was established in accordance with the legal provisions applicable to it at the time of acquisition and in a manner not detrimental to the survival of the species concerned in the wild'.

18   Under Article 55 of Regulation No 865/2006, entitled 'Establishment of ancestry':

'Where, for the purposes of Articles 54, 62(1) or 63(1), a competent authority considers it necessary to establish the ancestry of an animal through the analysis of blood or other tissue, such analysis or the necessary samples shall be made available in a manner established by that authority.'

The dispute in the main proceedings and the questions referred for a preliminary ruling

19   ET breeds parrots in the Czech Republic. On 21 January 2015, he applied to the krajský úřad (Regional Authority, Czech Republic) responsible for granting an

exemption from the prohibition of trade for five specimens of hyacinth macaw (*Anodorhynchus hyacinthinus*) born during the year 2014 in his breeding.

20   The grandparents of those parrots ('the grandparent pair') were initially imported into Bratislava (Slovakia) by a Uruguayan citizen and then by car into the Czech Republic in June 1993, by FU, under circumstances incompatible with CITES.

21   While being transported to the Czech Republic, the car was stopped at the border by customs authorities and the grandparent pair was subsequently confiscated by means of an administrative decision. However, that decision was annulled by the Vrchní soud v Praze (High Court, Prague, Czech Republic) in 1996.

22   The competent administrative authority therefore returned the grandparent pair to FU, who then lent them to a third person called GV. GV obtained a pair in the year 2000, whom she raised ('the parent pair'). ET acquired that pair from GV in the course of that year, without the validity of the transfer of ownership having been contested.

23   The competent regional authority refused to grant the exemption sought, on 21 January 2015, by ET, on the basis of the opinion of the Agentura ochrany přírody a krajiny ČR (Nature Conservation Agency of the Czech Republic), which concerned the compatibility of the breeding stock by ET with Article 54(2) of Regulation No 856/2006. According to that opinion, it could not be stated with certainty that that stock had been established in accordance with the legal provisions, since the 1998 registers, mentioning the grandparent pair, contained numerous irregularities and did not reproduce other information concerning the origin of the specimens in question.

24   ET brought an administrative appeal against that refusal, in which he claimed that the competent regional authority had misinterpreted the concept of 'breeding stock', such a stock being established, in his view, only by the parent pair and the offspring of those parents, therefore that authority was not authorised to examine the origin of the grandparent pair.

25   The Ministry of the Environment rejected the appeal, considering that the method by which the grandparent pair was acquired was decisive and that an exemption could not be granted to ET, as he was unable to demonstrate the origin of that pair.

26   ET appealed against the decision rejecting his administrative appeal before the Krajský soud v Hradci Králové (Regional Court, Hradec Králové, Czech Republic).

27   That court dismissed the appeal on the ground that the trade in parrots of the *Anodorhynchus* species can only be authorised if the conditions laid down in Article 54 of Regulation No 865/2006 are satisfied. According to that court, neither of the conditions laid down in Article 54(2) of that regulation were satisfied in the present case.

28   More specifically, the Krajský soud v Hradci Králové (Regional Court, Hradec Králové) found in ET's appeal that, on the date on which the grandparent pair were imported into the Czech Republic, CITES was in force in that Member State and incorporated into the domestic order by national legislation. That court held that, first, according to the provisions for the transposition of CITES into Czech law, it is permissible to examine the origin of the breeding stock to the grandparent pair and, second, that the concept of 'breeding stock' within the meaning of Regulation No 865/2006 covers, in the present case, the three generations of parrots and that, therefore, the competent regional authority could require proof of the origin of the grandparent pair.

29   ET brought an appeal on a point of law against that judgment before the Nejvyšší správní soud (Supreme Administrative Court, Czech Republic), claiming that the Krajský soud v Hradci Králové (Regional Court, Hradec Králové) had misinterpreted the concept of 'breeding stock' within the meaning of Regulation No 865/2006.

30   The Nejvyšší správní soud (Supreme Administrative Court) notes that it is not disputed by the parties to the main proceedings, first, that the parent pair was born in captivity in 2000 in the Czech Republic and that its acquisition by ET was, as such, lawful, and second, that the origin of the grandparent pair is suspicious. Accordingly, that court asks, in the first place, whether the concept of 'breeding stock', within the meaning of Article 54(2) of Regulation No 865/2006, also includes relatives in the ancestry of such animals situated in the territory of a Member State.

31   In the second place, if the concept of 'breeding stock' were to be interpreted strictly, the question would arise as to whether the concept of 'establishment' of such stock, which appears in Article 54(2) of Regulation No 865/2006, refers only, in the present case, to the acquisition of the parent pair used for the reproduction or, on the contrary, to the beginning of the breeding line, namely, in the present case, the acquisition of the grandparent pair.

32   In the third place, the referring court asks whether certain specific circumstances should still be taken into account in the examination of the application for exemption sought by ET.

33   In that regard, the referring court points out that ET acquired the parent pair lawfully and that, at the time of that acquisition, first, the Czech Republic was not part of the European Union and, secondly, if CITES was in force there, the national legislation implementing that law did not require a certificate, within the meaning of CITES, to be issued in the case of a transfer within the same State. Accordingly, that court is of the opinion that ET could have had a legitimate expectation that the trade in the offspring of that parent pair would be permitted, at least in the Czech Republic.

34   Furthermore, the referring court states that the fact that the grandparent pair was returned to FU pursuant to a judicial decision may have to be taken into consideration in the examination of an application for exemption, as well as ET's argument that trade in specimens born in captivity would reduce market demand for illegal purchases of specimens captured in the wild. Finally, that court points out that, in the event that the exemption sought by ET is not granted, his right to property would be reduced to the right to have the parent pair and, possibly, their offspring, without being able to dispose of them legally.

35   In those circumstances, the Nejvyšší správní soud (Supreme Administrative Court) decided to stay the proceedings before it and refer the following questions to the Court for a preliminary ruling:

> '(1) Does "breeding stock", as defined by Regulation [No 865/2006], include specimens that are the parents of specimens bred by a given breeder, even though that breeder never owned or kept them?
> (2) If the answer to the first question is that such parent specimens do not constitute a part of the breeding stock, are competent bodies authorised to verify, in examining compliance with the condition set in Article 54(2) of [Regulation No 865/2006], consisting of the establishment of stock legally

and, at the same time, in a manner not detrimental to the survival of wild specimens, the origin of those parent specimens and to infer on that basis whether the breeding stock has been established in accordance with the rules set out in Article 54(2) of the regulation?

(3) In examining compliance with the condition set out in Article 54(2) of [Regulation No 865/2006], consisting of the establishment of stock legally and, at the same time, in a manner not detrimental to the survival of wild specimens, can further circumstances of the case be taken into consideration (in particular, good faith in the transfer of the specimens and the legitimate expectation that trading in their potential offspring will be permitted, and potentially also the less stringent legislation applicable in the Czech Republic prior to the country's accession to the European Union)?'

Consideration of the questions referred

The first question

36   By its first question, the referring court asks, in essence, whether Article 1(3) of Regulation No 865/2006 must be interpreted as meaning that the term 'breeding stock', within the meaning of that provision, covers the ancestors of specimens bred in a breeding operation which have never been owned or kept by that operation.

37   According to settled case-law, when interpreting a provision of EU law, it is necessary to consider not only its wording but also the context in which it occurs and the objectives pursued by the rules of which it is part (judgment of 8 December 2020, *Staatsanwaltschaft Wien (Falsified transfer orders)* (C-584/19) EU:C:2020:1002, paragraph 49 and the case-law cited).

38   In that regard, in the first place, as regards the literal interpretation of Article 1(3) of Regulation No 865/2006, it follows from that provision that the concept of 'breeding stock' includes all the animals of a breeding operation which are used for reproduction.

39   As the Advocate General observed, in points 36 and 37 of her Opinion, the wording of Article 1(3) of Regulation No 865/2006 is not sufficient, in itself, to remove the ambiguity as to the interpretation to be given to that provision, since the various language versions of that provision suggest various meanings. Whereas it follows from several language versions, such as the Spanish, German, French or Latvian versions, that only animals present in a breeding operation, that is to say, a specific site with structures suitable for breeding animals, come within the concept of 'breeding stock', within the meaning of that provision, other language versions, such as the Greek, English, Croatian or Slovenian, refer more broadly to all animals in a breeding process and which may potentially cover the ancestors of specimens which have never been owned or kept in a breeding operation.

40   It is common ground that the wording used in one language version of a provision of EU law cannot serve as the sole basis for the interpretation of that provision or be made to override the other language versions. Provisions of EU law must be interpreted and applied uniformly in the light of the versions existing in all languages of the European Union (see, to that effect, judgment of 24 March 2021, *A* (C-950/19) EU:C:2021:230, paragraph 37 and the case-law cited).

41   In those circumstances, it is necessary to examine, in the second place, the context of Article 1(3) of Regulation No 865/2006 as well as the objectives pursued by that provision and the rules of which it forms part.

42   In that regard, it should be noted, as stated in recital 1 of Regulation No 865/2006, that the purpose of that regulation is, first, to ensure the implementation of Regulation No 338/97 and, second, to ensure full compliance with the provisions of CITES, thereby guaranteeing, as stated in recital 10 of the latter regulation, the broadest possible protection for species of wild fauna and flora by regulating trade therein.

43   As the Advocate General pointed out in footnote 19 of her Opinion, it is apparent from Annex 1 to Resolution Conf. 12.10 that, under CITES, the registration of a captive-breeding operation requires the precise identification of such an operation, its owner and manager, and the facilities intended to house the stock. Therefore, the concept of 'operation' cannot be understood, in the context of Regulation No 865/2006, as referring to a simple breeding process, which is detached from any concrete physical installation.

44   It follows from the foregoing considerations that Article 1(3) of Regulation No 865/2006 must be interpreted as meaning that the term 'breeding stock', within the meaning of that provision, does not include the ancestors of specimens bred in a breeding operation, which have never been owned or kept by that operation.

The second and third questions

45   As a preliminary point, it should be noted, first, that, under Article 8(1) of Regulation No 338/97, it is prohibited to sell specimens of the species listed in Annex A to that regulation. However, Article 8(3) of that regulation allows Member States to derogate from such a prohibition, inter alia, where the specimens of an animal species listed in Annex A and which are for sale are specimens born and bred in captivity. According to Article 54 of Regulation No 865/2006, a specimen of an animal species is considered to be born and bred in captivity only if a management authority is satisfied that, inter alia, the breeding stock was established in accordance with the legal provisions applicable to it at the time of acquisition and in a manner not detrimental to the survival of the species concerned in the wild.

46   Secondly, it is apparent from the file before the Court that ET was refused authorisation to sell the parrots at issue in the main proceedings, on the ground that they could not be considered to have been born and bred in captivity, within the meaning of Article 8(3) of Regulation No 338/97, because the grandparent pair had been unlawfully imported into the Czech Republic by a third party. In accordance with what has been stated in paragraph 44 of the present judgment, that pair cannot be regarded as belonging to the breeding stock kept by ET, since ET has never owned or kept them.

47   Thirdly, it is also clear from the order for reference that it is possible to determine, among the ancestry of the parrots at issue in the main proceedings, the specimens removed from the wild, since it is common ground between the parties to the main proceedings that they are, in the present case, the grandparent pair.

48   It is in the light of those factors that the Court answers the second and third questions.

49   Accordingly, it must be held that, by its second and third questions, which it is appropriate to examine together, the referring court asks, in essence, whether Article 54(2) of Regulation No 865/2006, read in conjunction with Article 17 of the Charter of Fundamental Rights of the European Union ('the Charter') and the principle of protection of legitimate expectations, must be interpreted as meaning that it precludes a specimen, kept by a breeder, of an animal species referred to in Annex A to Regulation No 338/97, from being regarded as born and bred in captivity, within the meaning of Article 8(3) of that regulation, where the ancestors of that specimen, which do not constitute a part of the breeding stock of that breeder, were acquired by a third party before the entry into force of those regulations, in disregard of the applicable legal provisions or in a manner which is detrimental to the survival of the species concerned in the wild.

50   In the first place, it should be borne in mind that, in accordance with the case-law referred to in paragraph 37 of the present judgment, it is necessary to consider not only the wording of Article 54(2) of Regulation No 865/2006 but also the context in which it occurs and the objectives pursued by the rules of which it is part.

51   In addition, it is important to point out that Article 8(3) of Regulation No 338/97, in so far as it constitutes an exception to the general rule prohibiting all commercial use of specimens of the species listed in Annex A to that regulation, must be interpreted strictly. Therefore, the conditions under which Article 54(2) of Regulation No 865/2006 permits the inference that a specimen of an animal species born and bred in captivity must also be interpreted strictly, in so far as that provision seeks to clarify the scope of Article 8(3).

52   As the Advocate General pointed out in point 52 of her Opinion, that finding is borne out by Article II(1) of CITES, according to which trade in specimens of species threatened with extinction must be subject to particularly strict regulation in order not to further endanger their survival and must only be authorised in exceptional circumstances.

53   In the second place, as the Advocate General noted, in essence, in point 51 of her Opinion, Article 54(2) of Regulation No 865/2006 refers to the concept of 'establishment' of the breeding stock. That concept has a broad scope and allows account to be taken, when examining whether such a breeding stock complies with the requirements imposed by that provision, of events prior to the actual acquisition of the breeding stock by the breeder.

54   That finding is supported by Article 55 of Regulation No 865/2006, under which the competent authorities may examine the ancestry of an animal for the purposes of the application of Article 54 of that regulation. It follows, as the Advocate General stated in point 55 of her Opinion, that that provision allows the competent authorities to examine the ancestry of breeding stock in order to verify that the conditions laid down in Article 54(2) of Regulation No 865/2006 have been fulfilled.

55   Furthermore, the objective pursued by Regulation No 865/2006, as set out in paragraph 42 of the present judgment, supports the interpretation that the competent authorities have the power to examine the ancestry of a breeding stock in the context of an application for an exemption certificate for the sale of specimens born and bred in captivity.

56   In that respect, as the Advocate General pointed out in paragraph 57 of her Opinion, the conditions set out in Article 54(2) of Regulation No 865/2006 correspond to the ones set out in paragraph 2(b)(ii) of Resolution Conf. 10.16. That resolution was adopted in view of the concern that much trade in specimens declared

as born and bred in captivity remains contrary to CITES and to the resolutions of the Conference of the Parties to CITES, and may be detrimental to the survival of wild populations of the species concerned.

57   Thus, the interpretation according to which the competent national authorities have the power to examine the ancestry of a breeding stock is consistent with the objective pursued by CITES of strengthening control of the ancestry of specimens born and bred in captivity.

58   That being so, while Article 54(2) of Regulation No 865/2006 requires those authorities to check the manner in which the ancestry of the breeding stock were removed from their natural environment in order to ensure that that removal did not take place in a manner detrimental to the survival of the species in the wild, it is apparent, by contrast, from the very wording of that provision that it does not require those authorities to check whether the ancestry of the breeding stock has been acquired in accordance with the legal provisions applicable at the date of their acquisition, but only to ensure that the legal provisions applicable to the acquisition of the breeding stock have been complied with.

59   In addition, in order to determine whether the breeding stock was not established in a manner detrimental to the survival of the species concerned in the wild because of the removal of an ancestor of that stock from its natural environment, account must be taken of the status of the species concerned at the time of that removal. Where, on that date, as in the present case, that species fell within Appendix I to CITES, its removal must, in any event, be regarded as detrimental to the survival of the species concerned in the wild and no Member State must be able to grant an exemption from the prohibition on the sale of specimens originating from that ancestor pursuant to Article 8(3) of Regulation No 338/97.

60   As regards, in the third place, the practical aspects of the examination under Article 54(2) of Regulation No 865/2006, in so far as that provision, first, requires the competent authority to establish with certainty that the criteria set out therein are met and, second, does not lay down the detailed rules for such an examination or the means of proving that those criteria are met, it must be held that the task of laying down such detailed rules and means of proof is left to the competent authorities of the Member States. That evidence includes the licences or certificates provided for in that regulation or any other appropriate document which may be deemed useful by the competent national authorities (see, by analogy, judgment of 16 July 2009, *Rubach* (C-344/08) EU:C:2009:482, paragraph 27).

61   Consequently, such rules of examination may, in particular, as the Advocate General stated, in essence, in points 66 and 67 of her Opinion, depend on the risk assessment pertaining to the circumstances of each case and also include an examination of the documentation regarding the acquisition of the breeding stock.

62   In the fourth place, it should be noted that the prohibition on selling specimens of which one of the ancestors has been acquired in a manner that is detrimental to the survival of the species in the wild, resulting from a combined reading of Article 8(1) and (3) of Regulation No 338/97 and Article 54(2) of Regulation No 865/2006, is not incompatible with the right to property, as enshrined in Article 17 of the Charter.

63   It must be remembered that the right to property is not absolute and that its exercise may be subject to, under the conditions laid down in Article 52(1) of the Charter, restrictions justified by objectives of general interest pursued by the European Union (judgment of 20 September 2016, *Ledra Advertising v Commission*

and ECB(C-8/15 P–C-10/15 P) EU:C:2016:701, paragraph 69 and the case-law cited).

64   It should be noted that the protection of wild species constitutes such a legitimate objective in the public interest (see, to that effect, judgment of 19 June 2008, *Nationale Raad van Dierenkwekers en Liefhebbers and Andibel* (C-219/07) EU:C:2008:353, paragraph 27 and the case-law cited).

65   Furthermore, as the Advocate General observed in point 77 of her Opinion, Regulations No 338/97 and No 865/2006 operate a balance between that right and the requirements linked to the protection of wildlife. It should also be pointed out that such requirements make it possible to justify the fact that the placing on the market of specimens of endangered species is, in principle, prohibited. As regards, more specifically, ET's argument that that placing on the market may reduce the number of specimens of those species caught in the wild, it is sufficient to note that such placing on the market contributes to the creation, maintenance or extension of a market for the acquisition of such specimens. The EU legislature was entitled to take the view that the very existence of such a market constitutes, to a certain extent, a threat to the survival of endangered species.

66   Lastly, the factors mentioned by the referring court relating to the protection of ET's legitimate expectations in the fact that they could market the offspring of his breeding stock cannot lead to any other conclusion.

67   First, as the Advocate General observed in point 74 of her Opinion, even if the competent authority were to conclude that the establishment of the breeding stock was lawful at the date of its acquisition, that finding alone does not suffice to allow derogation from the prohibition on selling specimens of that stock in so far as, as has been pointed out in paragraph 59 of the present judgment, it would still be necessary to ensure that the establishment of that breeding stock was not detrimental to the survival of the species concerned in the wild.

68   Secondly, the fact that the regulatory framework in force was less stringent when ET purchased his breeding stock in 2000, since the Czech Republic was not yet a member of the European Union at that time, is also irrelevant.

69   In that regard, it is sufficient to note that the scope of the principle of protection of legitimate expectations cannot be extended to the point of generally preventing new rules from applying to the future effects of situations which arose under the earlier rules (judgment of 21 December 2021, *Skarb Państwa (Motor insurance cover)* (C-428/20) EU:C:2021:1043, paragraph 45 and the case-law cited).

70   Thirdly, as regards the fact that the grandparent pair was, in the present case, handed over to its importer, pursuant to a judicial decision, it is sufficient to note that, because of the date on which that decision was delivered, namely prior to the accession of the Czech Republic to the European Union, such a decision cannot, in any event, constitute a factor to be taken into consideration in order to determine whether the breeding stock at ET's disposal was established in accordance with Article 54(2) of Regulation No 865/2006.

71   It follows from all the foregoing considerations that Article 54(2) of Regulation No 865/2006, read in conjunction with Article 17 of the Charter and the principle of protection of legitimate expectations, must be interpreted as precluding a specimen, kept by a breeder, of a species of animal referred to in Annex A to Regulation No 338/97 from being regarded as having been born and bred in captivity, within the meaning of Article 8(3) of that regulation, where the ancestors of that specimen, which do not form part of the breeding stock of that breeder,

were acquired by a third party before the entry into force of those regulations in a manner which is detrimental to the survival of the species concerned in the wild.

Costs

72   Since these proceedings are, for the parties to the main proceedings, a step in the action pending before the national court, the decision on costs is a matter for that court. Costs incurred in submitting observations to the Court, other than the costs of those parties, are not recoverable.

On those grounds, the Court (Fourth Chamber) hereby rules:

1. Article 1(3) of Commission Regulation (EC) No 865/2006 of 4 May 2006 laying down detailed rules concerning the implementation of Council Regulation (EC) No 338/97 on the protection of species of wild fauna and flora by regulating trade therein, must be interpreted as meaning that:

   the concept of 'breeding stock', within the meaning of that provision, does not include the ancestors of specimens bred in a breeding operation which have never been owned or kept by that operation.

2. Article 54(2) of Regulation No 865/2006, read in conjunction with Article 17 of the Charter of Fundamental Rights of the European Union and the principle of protection of legitimate expectations, must be interpreted as:

   precluding a specimen, kept by a breeder, of a species of animal referred to in Annex A to Council Regulation (EC) No 338/97 of 9 December 1996 on the protection of species of wild fauna and flora by regulating trade therein, from being regarded as having been born and bred in captivity, within the meaning of Article 8(3) of that regulation, where the ancestors of that specimen, which do not form part of the breeding stock of that breeder, were acquired by a third party before the entry into force of those regulations in a manner which is detrimental to the survival of the species concerned in the wild.

JAKAB v REGIONAL COURT OF ZALAEGERSZEG, HUNGARY

QUEEN'S BENCH DIVISION (ADMINISTRATIVE COURT)

Dove J: 27 May 2022

[2022] EWHC 1308 (Admin); [2023] Env. L.R. 12

☞ Brexit; Controlled waste; Environmental offences; Extradition offences; Extradition orders; Fugitive offenders; Pollution; Proportionality; Right to respect for private and family life

H1 *Environmental crime—waste offences—Human Rights—extradition appeal—Extradition Act 2003 s.26—European Arrest Warrant—whether conduct would have been an offence if taken place in the UK—whether judge wrong in consideration of balancing exercise under art.8—whether relevant materials "controlled waste"—whether conduct an offence contrary to Environmental Protection Act 1990 s.33(i)(c) and 33(6)—whether an offence under Control of Pollution (Amendment) Act 1989 s.1 or the Hazardous Waste (England and Wales) Regulations 2005—whether premises from which hazardous waste was removed had to be in England and not outside it—whether evidence of acting in the course of a business or with a view to a profit*

H2   The appellant (J) appealed under the Extradition Act 2003 s.26. The European Arrest Warrant concerned sought his extradition in respect of convictions including for the transportation of various types of lead-acid batteries, used radiator grilles and multi-core aluminium wires without holding any official permit for waste management. The District Judge ruled that had the alleged conduct taken place in the UK, if proved, it would have amounted to an offence contrary to the Environmental Protection Act 1990 s.33(i)(c) and 33(6). The act of transporting the batteries was considered to constitute storing them temporarily, thereby contravening the 1990 Act, by keeping the batteries, which were controlled waste, in a manner likely cause pollution of the environment or harm to human health. The District Judge further rejected a challenge to extradition under the ECHR art.8, setting out his reasoning, and in particular the balancing exercise required by the authorities. The appeal was made on the grounds that the District Judge had been wrong: (1) to conclude that the conduct would have amounted to an offence within the UK; and (2) in the conclusions made in relation to art.8. The District Judge's conclusions on the offence had been reached in relation to s.33 of the 1990 Act. The respondent submitted that in the alternative to s.33, the conduct amounted to an offence under the Control of Pollution (Amendment) Act 1989 s.1 of transporting controlled waste without being a registered carrier, or the Hazardous Waste (England and Wales) Regulations 2005. In relation to s.33, J submitted that the District

Judge's view that such an offence could be made out by the temporary storage of the material whilst being transported and that such temporary storage could amount to an offence under those provisions was misconceived. There was no information to justify the conclusion that J's conduct amounted to treating or disposing of the waste in a manner likely to cause pollution of the environment or harm to human health. Nor could the District Judge have been satisfied to the criminal standard that the waste was "controlled waste". In relation to offences under the 1989 Act and 2005 Regulations, J also argued that the premises from which hazardous waste was removed had to be in England and not outside it, and as the batteries were removed from premises in Austria outside the territory of Hungary there could not, by analogy or transposition, be an offence under those provisions. Nor was there evidence that J had been acting in the course of a business or with a view to a profit.

H3   **Held:**

H4   (1) The issue of whether the materials could properly amount to controlled waste was common to each of the three sets of offences. It was agreed that the used radiator grills and aluminium wires were controlled waste. The question of whether or not the used lead-acid batteries were controlled waste depended upon the application of the Scrap Metal Dealers Act 1964. The definition under s.9(2) of the 1964 Act was broad in its reach and included the used lead-acid batteries. Those items were manufactured articles made at least partly out of metal and were broken or worn out. They therefore fell within the definition of scrap metal and as such were properly to be regarded as controlled waste for the purposes of the 1990 Act. In relation to s.33(1)(c), transporting the materials in a car did not amount to keeping the controlled waste. The context for understanding the parameters of that section were in s.29(3) of the 1990 Act which, in connection with pollution of the environment, dealt exclusively in s.29(3)(a)–(c) with waste being treated, kept, or deposited on land, as was appropriate within a part entitled "Waste on Land". It followed that the conduct identified did not fulfil the definition of s.33(1)(c), and had J been charged with an offence under that section for the conduct described in the UK he would have been entitled to be acquitted. The District Judge therefore fell into error in concluding that s.10 of the 2003 Act could be satisfied on the basis that there was an offence under s.33 of the 1990 Act. Those findings that the materials comprised controlled waste applied to the 1989 Act. J did not hold an official permit for the waste management operation upon which he was engaged, and so that element of the offence was made out.

H5   (2) On the question of whether J was acting in the course of any business or otherwise with a view to profit, given the quantity and nature of the materials being transported it was clear that they were being transported at the very least with a view to profiting from their disposal in due course. That conclusion was reinforced by the point that another offence involved the unlawful appropriation of used batteries and profiting from that theft. It followed that albeit the District Judge's reasons could not be sustained there was a further basis upon which the conclusion that s.10 was satisfied, namely the fact that the conduct described would substantiate an offence under s.1 of the 1989 Act.

H6   (3) There was no merit in the suggestion that because the hazardous waste described in the conduct originated in Austria the transposition exercise would fail. A consignment of waste being transported through England which had arrived by sea at the UK border could not be exempt from the 2005 Regulations. Once a practical and purposive approach was taken to the transposition exercise it was clear that those regulations would apply for the purposes of the s.10 exercise and that was a further basis upon which the requirements of s.10 were satisfied.

H7   (4) The sentencing powers for the offences relied upon in the alternative to that under s.33(1)(c) were more limited, albeit the possibility of imprisonment existed in relation to the offence under the 2005 Regulations. Whilst that point did not assist J in relation to the s.10 arguments, the conclusion supported the suggestion that less weight should attach to the seriousness of the offending in assessing the arguments under art.8. With the exception of the judge's approach to the question of the length of sentence which J still had left to serve on return and the failure to account for the offences for which he had been discharged from extradition, and also the lesser weight to be given to the seriousness of the offending, there was no flaw in the balancing exercise in relation to art.8 which the District Judge undertook. Rebalancing matters to take account of those factors, the District Judge had not reached a conclusion which was wrong. Whilst it was clear that the District Judge had not taken into account any question of "Brexit Uncertainty" this had not had any material impact upon the decision.

H8 **Cases referred to:**
Antochi v Germany [2020] EWHC 3092 (Admin); [2021] A.C.D. 15
Pink v Poland [2021] EWHC 1238 (Admin)
Poland v Celinski [2015] EWHC 1274 (Admin); [2016] 1 W.L.R. 551; [2015] A.C.D. 125
Rybak v Poland [2021] EWHC 712 (Admin); [2021] 1 W.L.R. 3993; [2021] A.C.D. 61

H9 **Legislation referred to:**
ECHR arts 3 and 8
Scrap Metal Dealers Act 1964 s.9
Control of Pollution (Amendment) Act 1989 s.1
Environmental Protection Act 1990 ss.29, 33 and 75
Directive 91/689 (Hazardous Waste) art.1 and Annexes I and II
Extradition Act 2003 ss.10, 14, 26, 64 and 65
Hazardous Waste (England and Wales) Regulations 2005 (SI 2005/894) regs 1, 12, 35, 36 and 65
List of Wastes (England) Regulations 2005 (SI 2005/895)
Controlled Waste (England and Wales) Regulations 2012 (SI 2012/811) reg.4 and Sch.1

H10 *J. Stansfield* (instructed by Lawrence & Co) appeared on behalf of the appellant. *B. Joyes* (instructed by Crown Prosecution Service) appeared on behalf of the respondent.

JUDGMENT

MR JUSTICE DOVE:

1   This is an appeal under section 26 of the Extradition Act 2003. It has a somewhat lengthy history as an appeal, following the ordering of the Appellant's extradition by the District Judge on 17th May 2019. Permission to appeal was refused on the

papers by Sir Wyn Williams on 27th September 2019. The Appellant renewed his application orally, and permission to appeal was granted by Holman J on 23rd January 2020. Permission was granted on two grounds, the first based upon section 10 of the 2003 Act relating to what is referred to below as offence 4, and the second in relation to article 8.

2   The Appellant then made an application to amend his grounds of appeal and stay the appeal proceedings on the basis of an argument under article 3 and prison conditions in Hungary. On 13th October 2020 Swift J granted permission to amend the grounds of appeal to include the article 3 ground, and stayed the proceedings until the Supreme Court handed down judgment in the case of *Zaboltnyi v Mateszalka District Court, Hungary*. He made directions as to the requirement for further written submissions once the outcome of that case was known. In the event, following the handing down of its judgment by the Supreme Court in *Zabolotnye*, the Appellant decided not to pursue the article 3 ground. The matter then came on for hearing on the two grounds for which the Appellant had permission on 14th October 2021.

3   At the hearing on 14th October 2021, it became clear that there was an important issue in relation to offence 4 which the parties had not addressed in their submissions either before the District Judge or before this court. That issue is investigated in greater detail below, but it relates to the question of whether or not the requirements of section 10 of the 2003 Act are satisfied in respect of offence 4 on the basis of an offence of transporting or transferring controlled waste without a permit to do so. The hearing therefore adjourned part heard in order to enable the parties to address this issue. Directions were given in relation to further submissions on this issue which were to be concluded by the end of 2021.

4   In the event the matter was again listed for hearing on 1st March 2022. In addition to addressing the further point in respect of offence 4, the Appellant addressed further submissions which had been raised since the commencement of the appeal in respect of suggested article 8 implications of the UK leaving the EU as a further basis for advancing the Appellant's article 8 claim. Again, this was not a matter which had been fully addressed in the parties' submissions at the hearing, and so further time was afforded until 21st March 2021 for further written material and submissions to be received in connection with this issue. In the event the exchange of these submissions concluded on 22nd March 2022, thereby enabling the court to proceed to preparing its judgment in this matter.

5   I wish to place on record my thanks to counsel in relation to the written and oral submissions which were prepared to assist the court, and which have been of considerable value in enabling me to reach my decision.

The EAW.

6   The EAW in the present case seeks the extradition of the Appellant in respect of two separate judgments and convictions. It was issued on 7th March 2017 and was certified on 9th June 2017. Conviction 1 arises from a judgment of the Municipal Court of Sopron dated 12th June 2007 in respect of an offence committed on 2nd February 2006 at the Sopron Border when the Appellant wished to enter Hungary using the passport of another thereby avoiding revealing his true identity since he was aware there was a search warrant in existence for him. The EAW records that the Appellant accepted he had taken the passport without the knowledge

of its true holder when interviewed, and that he was present when he was later sentenced to 8 months imprisonment, all of which remains outstanding. This was a suspended sentence which was activated according to the Respondent because the Appellant had committed criminal offences during the currency of the term of suspension.

7   Conviction 2 relates to a judgment issued on 12th May 2014, which became final on 3rd November 2015. In respect of this judgment the Appellant's return is sought to serve the entirety of a cumulative sentence of 3 years 6 months for a total of six offences. It is unnecessary to dwell on four of these offences which were not committed in Hungary, and therefore the District Judge concluded did not amount to extradition offences and the Appellant was discharged in respect of them. The two offences for which extradition was ordered were, firstly, an allegation of fraud by false representation committed on 1st August 2010, when along with another the Appellant obtained a quantity of Swiss francs and US dollars together with gold jewellery from a vulnerable individual for the purported treatment of a sick child when, in truth, no such child existed. The second offence is the contentious offence 4. It is necessary for the purposes of this judgment to set out the description of offence 4 in greater detail. Within the EAW it is described as follows:

> "The Ford Transit car with the number plate HZJ-782 was pulled over on 22 May 2012 at 3:30pm in Zalaegerszeg in front of the building located at 11 Egervari Street by an officer of the Criminal Investigations Department of Zalaegerszeg Police Department, in which vehicle defendants Zoltan Lakatos and Sandor Milan Jakab were transporting 17 various types of lead- acid batteries, 2 used radiator grilles and approximately 230 kg of multi-core aluminium wires without holding any official permit for waste management."

8   Further Information was sought from the Respondent in relation to whether or not the Appellant was treating, keeping, or disposing of the material being transported in a manner likely to cause pollution of the environment or harm to human health. The response to that request was provided by the Respondent in the following terms:

> "(ii)
>
>> (a) After obtaining the inoperative lead-batteries, Sandor Milan Jakab and his co-actor did not comply with environmental regulations; they improperly handled and transported the batteries. Lead batteries – due to their components – were capable of endangering the physical integrity and health of humans, the soil, the water, the air, and the components thereof, as well as the living organisms.
>>
>> (b) According to the "List of hazardous waste" in Article 1 (4) of Council Directive 91/689/EEC on hazardous waste, lead battery shall be considered as hazardous waste.
>
> In accordance with annex 1.B, wastes consisting of batteries and other electrical cells which contain lead or lead components listed in Annex II, points H6 and H7 respectively."

9   The District Judge set out the provisions of sections 64 and 65 of the 2003 Act to provide the context for the challenge under section 10 of the 2003 Act. In essence the District Judge noted that pursuant to those provisions "conduct" was part of

the definition of an extradition offence, and that it was necessary for the Respondent to demonstrate that the conduct amounted to an offence punishable under the law of the relevant part of the UK if that conduct had occurred in the relevant part of the UK. The District Judge set out his ruling on these issues in the following terms:

"45. s.10 Ruling:

The Judicial Authority submits that the criminal conduct therein constitutes an offence under s.33(i)(c) and 33(6) of the Environmental Protection Act 1990 ("EPA").

46. s.75(4) of the EPA defines controlled waste as being household, industrial or commercial waste "or any such waste". The further information states that SJ "improperly handled and transported the batteries" in question.

47. Mr Joyes, having carried out admirable researches, has directed the court to a passage in Wolf and Stanley on Environmental Law (6th edition) 2014, Routledge, p.222 which describes "keeping" as referring to "storing waste whether permanently or temporarily" and he submits that the carriage of said batteries in his vehicle during transportation is equivalent of temporary storage.

48. The further information provided by the Judicial Authority states that SJ improperly handled and transported the batteries and that the lead batteries - due to their components - were capable of endangering the physical integrity and health of humans, the soil, the water, the air... as well as... living organisms and that the said batteries were... "hazardous waste" within the meaning of Article 1(4) of the Council Directive 91/689/EEC.

49. The defence submit that there is no (or insufficient) evidence that SJ had "kept", "treated" or "disposed of" the items in question. Mr Stansfeld adds that transporting such waste, if indeed that was what SJ was doing, is clearly quite different from keeping it.

Counsel asserts that this provision of law is specifically designed to prevent waste from being kept on a particular site and does not cover its transportation.

50. Further and in the alternative the defence take issue with the suggestion that the materials set out in charge (iv) of Conviction 2 can properly be considered to fall within the accepted definition of "controlled waste" per s.75 (4) of the 1990 Act.

51. Having considered the able submissions made by the parties, I am entirely satisfied that, had the alleged conduct (in respect of charge (iv) of Conviction 2) taken place in the UK, if proved, it would have amounted to an offence contrary to s.33 (i)(c) and 33(6) of the EPA and I accept Mr Joyes' interpretation of the law in respect thereof as it relates to this case.

52. I am satisfied that the act of transporting the batteries in question on 22 May 2012, the requested person's conduct constituted storing them temporarily, thereby contravening the EPA, by keeping the batteries - controlled waste - in a manner likely cause pollution of the environment or harm to human health. Accordingly, this challenge must fail."

10   The District Judge went on to consider objections to extradition, firstly based on section 14 of the Extradition Act 2003. The District Judge concluded that the Appellant was properly to be regarded as a fugitive in respect of both of the judgments or convictions for which he was wanted. The District Judge further rejected the article 8 challenge to extradition, setting out his reasoning, and in

particular the balancing exercise required by the authorities and in particular *Poland v Celinski* [2015] EWHC 1274 (Admin), in the following terms:

"93. Article 8 Balancing Exercise:
  (a) Factors said to be in favour of Granting Extradition:
      (i) There is a strong and continuing important public interest in the UK abiding by its international extradition obligations.
      (ii) The seriousness of the offences in respect of which he has been convicted and sentenced. There remains a global sentence of 4 years 2 months outstanding (less the period of circa 3 months spent in the UK on remand).
      (iii) The assertion by the Judicial Authority and the finding by this court that the requested person is a fugitive from Justice in respect of both convictions.
      (iv) SJ is not a man of good character. Apart from the matters for which his return is sought he has the following matters recorded against him in the UK.
  (a) 27 January 2009 Conviction:
      (i) Making off without payment (ii) Driving without a license (iii) No insurance: offences all committed on 24th September 2008 - Fined and Penalty points imposed.
  (b) 31 January 2009: Caution for theft (Shoplifting)
      It is also to be noted that these offence dates do not sit comfortably with SJ's recollection of events, as according to him, he was in Hungary from 2007 through to 2013 and he made no mention of being in the UK when the above crimes were committed.
  (v) I have found him to be a fugitive in respect of both Convictions.
94. b Factors said to be in favour of refusing extradition.
  (i) SJ says that he has been settled in the UK since 2013.
  (ii) He states that he has been in regular employment and has fixed accommodation where he resides with his long-term partner, their children and his father.
  (iii) SJ says that, in the main, he has led a law-abiding life since settling in the UK.
  (v) He asserts that he is not a fugitive from justice in relation to either conviction.
95. Article 8 Findings and Ruling
I find that it will not be a disproportionate interference with the Article 8 rights of the requested person for extradition to be ordered.
My reasons and findings are as follows:
It is very important for the UK to be seen to be upholding its international extradition obligations. The UK is not to be considered a "safe haven" for those sought by other Convention countries either to stand trial or to serve a prison sentence.
  (ii) In my opinion, the offences set out in the EAW are serious and, in the event of a conviction in the UK for like criminal conduct, a prison sentence may well be imposed.

(iii) This court finds that the requested person is unlawfully at large and has acquired fugitive status in respect of both convictions for which his return is sought. The reasons for this finding are set out heretofore.

(iv) It is appreciated that there will be hardship caused to SJ and to his partner, their children and to his father. However, that of itself is not sufficient to prevent an order for extradition from being made. The 2 older children were born in Hungary and, until 2016, the father lived in Hungary.

(V) As this court has found as a fact that SJ is a fugitive from justice, this finding brings paragraph 39 of the decision in *Celinksi* above into consideration. I do not find that there are such strong counter balancing factors as would render extradition Article 8 disproportionate in this case."

11   It is convenient to consider the relevant submissions under each ground upon which this appeal is brought separately.

Ground 1: section 10 and offence 4.

12   On behalf of the Appellant Mr Stansfeld submits that the District Judge was wrong to conclude that the conduct described in the EAW and Further Information would have amounted to an offence contrary to section 33(1)(c) and section 33(6) of the Environmental Protection Act 1990. In particular, the District Judge's conclusion that such an offence could be made out by the temporary storage of the material whilst being transported and that such temporary storage could amount to an offence under these provisions was misconceived. In detail Mr Stansfeld submits as follows. Firstly, section 33 of the 1990 Act appears within Part II of the 1990 Act which is entitled "Waste on Land". The relevant parts of section 33 of the 1990 Act are as follows:

> "33. Prohibition on unauthorised or harmful deposit, treatment, or disposal of waste.
>
> 1. Subject to [subsections (1A), (1B), (2) and (3) below] and, in relation to Scotland, to subsection 54 below, a person shall not -
>
> (a) deposit controlled waste or extractive waste, or knowingly cause or knowingly permit controlled waste or extractive waste to be deposited in or on any land unless an environmental permit authorising the deposit is in force and the deposit is in accordance with the permit;
>
> (b) submit controlled waste, or knowingly cause or knowingly permit controlled waste to be submitted, to any listed operation (other than an operation within subsection (1A) that -
>
> (i) is carried out in or on any land, or by means of any mobile plant, and
>
> (ii) is not carried out under and in accordance with an environmental permit;
>
> (c) treat, keep, or dispose of controlled waste or extractive waste in a manner likely to cause pollution of the environment or harm to human health.
>
> …
>
> 5. Where controlled waste is carried in and deposited from a motor vehicle, the person who controls or is in a position to control the use of the vehicle

shall, for the purposes of subsection (1A) above, be treated as knowingly causing them to be deposited whether or not he gave any instructions for this to be done.

6. A person who contravenes subsection 1 above commits an offence."

13   The context for section 33(1)(c) is provided by section 29(3) of the 1990 Act which provides as follows:

> "(3) "Pollution of the environment" means the pollution of the environment due to release or escape (into any environmental medium) from -
> (a) the land on which controlled waste or extractive waste is treated,
> (b) the land on which controlled waste or extractive waste is kept,
> (c) the land in or on which controlled waste or extractive waste is deposited,
> (d) fixed plant by means of which controlled waste or extractive waste is treated, kept or disposed of."

14   Mr Stansfeld points out that the phrase in section 33(1)(c) of the 1990 Act "likely to cause pollution of the environment" needs to be understood in the context of section 29(3)(a) to (c), which expressly refers to land upon which controlled or extracted waste is treated, kept, or deposited. Mr Stansfeld submits that there is no information in the EAW or the Further Information which could justify the conclusion reached by the District Judge that the conduct upon which the Appellant was engaged amounted to treating or disposing of the waste in a manner likely to cause pollution of the environment or harm to human health. Firstly, there was no information before the court that the way in which the material was being handled would give rise to the likelihood of pollution or harm to human health. Secondly, Mr Stansfeld submits that transporting is to be regarded as distinct from keeping for the purpose of section 33(1)(c) of the 1990 Act.

15   In addition to these submissions Mr Stansfeld submits that the District Judge could not have been satisfied to the criminal standard that the waste was "controlled waste". The definition of controlled waste is to be found in section 75 of the 1990 Act. The relevant provision of section 75 provide as follows:

> "75. Meaning of "waste" and household, commercial and industrial waste and hazardous waste...
> (2) "waste" means anything that is waste within the meaning of Article 3(1) of Directive 2008/98/EC of the European Parliament and of the Council on waste
> ...
> (4) "controlled waste" means household, industrial and commercial waste or any such waste.
> ...
> (8) Regulations made by the Secretary of State made provide that waste of a description prescribed in the regulation shall be treated for the purposes of provisions of this Part prescribed in the regulations as being or not being household waste or industrial waste or commercial waste; and reference to waste in subsection (7) above and this subsection do not include sewage (including matter in or from a privy) except so far as the regulations provide otherwise."

16   The regulations produced in this connection are the Controlled Waste (England and Wales) Regulations 2012 which provide by regulation 4 that schedule 1 of the Regulations has effect in relation to the definition of waste. In particular, under paragraph 3 of schedule 1 of the Regulations it is provided that waste is to be treated as household waste, commercial waste or industrial waste because of the nature or the activity which produces it notwithstanding the place where it is produced. Classification number 8 relates to "waste oil, waste solvent or scrap metal" and classifies this as industrial waste. Mr Stansfeld submits that the lead acid batteries could not come within the definition of waste oil, waste solvent or scrap metal. He draws attention to the reliance of the 2012 Regulations on the definition of "scrap metal" under the Scrap Metal Dealers Act 1964 as being as follows:

> "scrap metal includes any old metal, and any broken, worn out, defaced or partly manufactured articles made wholly or partly of metal, and any metallic waste, and also includes old, broken, worn out or defaced tool tips or dies made of any of the materials commonly known as hard metal or cemented or sintered metallic carbides."

17   Thus, it is submitted on behalf of the Appellant that the offence under section 33(1)(c) of the 1990 Act could not be made out on the conduct described in the EAW and the Further Information.

18   The first alternative basis relied upon by the Respondent to contend that the conduct identified amounts to an offence depends upon reliance on the offence created by section 1 of the Control of Pollution (Amendment) Act 1989 which makes it an offence "for any person who is not a registered carrier of controlled waste, in the course of any business of his or otherwise with a view to profit to transport any controlled waste to or from any place in Great Britain". In respect of this alternative basis Mr Stansfeld accepts that the "two used radiator grills and approximately 230kg of multi-core aluminium wires" would fall within the definition of scrap metal, and therefore amount to controlled waste for the purposes of this offence. However, he continues to submit that the absence of information as to the origin of the lead acid batteries precludes them being included within the definition of controlled waste. Furthermore, it appears that they originated from outside Hungary, and the offence could only be committed if they were being taken to somewhere in Hungary, as to which there was no evidence. Finally, he submits that there is no evidence to support the contention that the Appellant was acting in the course of a business in connection with this or with a view to profit. Thus, he submits that this alternative basis does not satisfy the requirements to support extradition either.

19   The final alternative basis advanced by the Respondent is that the conduct specified in the EAW and the Further Information amounted to a breach of the Hazardous Waste Regulations 2005. Regulations 35 and 36 of the 2005 Regulations set out legal requirements for a consignment note to be completed when hazardous waste is removed from any premises (see regulation 35), and set out formal requirements in relation to the consignment note including ensuring that a copy of the consignment note travels with the consignment when it is in transit. Regulation 65 of the 2005 Regulations creates an offence of failure to comply with these requirements. By virtue of the provisions of the List of Wastes (England) Regulations 2005 it is accepted that lead acid batteries fall within the definition of hazardous waste. Thus, it is submitted on behalf of the Respondent that the offence

created by section 65 of the 2005 Regulations was committed as a consequence of the conduct specified for reasons set out below.

20   In response to this submission Mr Stansfeld on behalf of the Appellant places reliance on regulations 1(2) and (3) of the Hazardous Waste Regulations as extending only to England and Wales. Furthermore regulation 12 of the Hazardous Waste Regulations provides as follows:

> "12
>
> (4) These Regulations apply to hazardous waste in England notwithstanding that the waste -
>
> > (a) was produced on or removed from premises in Scotland, Wales, Northern Ireland or Gibraltar; or
> >
> > (b) is, or is to be, transported from premises in England to premises located in one of those places.
>
> (5) For the avoidance of doubt, in their application to -
>
> > (a) ships' waste, these Regulations apply to any ship;
> >
> > (b) the internal waters and the territorial sea of the United Kingdom adjacent to England, these Regulations apply, without prejudice to paragraph (3), to a consignment of waste transported in any ship,
>
> in each case (whether the ship is a United Kingdom ship or otherwise and if a United Kingdom ship, whether registered in England or otherwise)."

21   In the light of this Mr Stansfeld submits that, for the regulations to apply, the premises from which hazardous waste is removed must be in England and not outside it, and as it is the Respondent's case that the lead-acid batteries were removed from premises in Austria outside the territory of Hungary there could not, by analogy or transposition, be an offence under the Hazardous Waste Regulations on the basis of the conduct contained in the EAW and the Further Information.

22   In response to these submissions Mr Joyes on behalf of the Respondent sustains the contention that the District Judge was correct to conclude the conduct could amount to an offence under section 33(1)(c) of the 1990 Act. He submits that the materials were being kept by the Appellant inside his van and keeping materials amounting to waste is the equivalent of temporary storage for the purposes of the legislation, an interpretation which sustains the findings of the District Judge. The contention that section 33(1)(c) of the 1990 Act includes both permanent and temporary storing of waste is, Mr Joyes submits supported by a passage from Wolf and Stanley on Environmental Law (sixth edition).

23   Mr Joyes submits that all of the materials were controlled waste. It is not disputed that the radiator grills and aluminium wires were within the definition of industrial waste set out above. Additionally, Mr Joyes submits that the lead-acid batteries were also scrap metal since they amount to "broken…articles made wholly or partly of metal". Thus, the offence under section 33(1)(c) of the 1990 Act is made out.

24   Mr Joyes' alternative submission in relation to transporting controlled waste without registration as a carrier, Mr Joyes for the reasons already given, submits that the materials comprised in the conduct were controlled waste. The information contained within the EAW and Further Information makes plain that the basis of the Appellant's conviction was that he did not hold any official permit for the purposes of this activity. Finally, bearing in mind the extensive quantity and nature of the waste materials being transmitted, Mr Joyes contends that it is a clear inference that this was an activity where the Appellant was acting either in the

course of his business or otherwise with a view to profit. Mr Joyes notes that offence 5 within conviction 2 within the EAW (which is not an extradition offence because it was committed in Austria) is an offence related to the Appellant profiting from the theft of used batteries.

25   Turning finally to the further alternative of the conduct amounting to offences under the Hazardous Waste Regulations, Mr Joyes responds to the Appellant's submissions resisting this contention by drawing attention to the detailed provisions of regulation 12, which clearly apply to waste transiting into the UK, for instance by way of consignments transported by sea, as a consequence of regulation 12(5). Thus, the provisions of the regulations apply to consignments of waste being transported or transferred within the UK even if they have come from abroad by sea, that being the most likely means of waste being brought to the UK. Thus, Mr Joyes submits that the Appellant's objection to the Hazardous Waste Regulations applying to the conduct in this case by analogy is incorrect.

26   My conclusions in relation to the submissions under ground 1 are as follows. It appears a point which is in common to each of the three ways in which the Respondent puts its case that the Appellant contends the materials described in the EAW and the Further Information could not properly amount to controlled waste, and in particular that the used lead-acid batteries could not amount to controlled waste. I am unable to accept that submission. I note that it was not a matter which was addressed directly by the District Judge, however it is clear to me that the following can be recorded. Firstly, there is no dispute but that the two used radiator grills and 230 kilos of multi-core aluminium wires are, it is agreed, controlled waste. The question of whether or not the used lead-acid batteries are controlled waste depends upon the application of section 9(2) of the Scrap Metal Dealers Act 1964 which has been set out above. In my view the definition under section 9(2) of the 1964 Act is broad in its reach, and I have no difficulty in accepting the submission made by Mr Joyes that it includes the used lead- acid batteries. These items are manufactured articles made at least partly out of metal and are broken or worn out. They therefore fall within the definition of scrap metal and as such are properly to be regarded as controlled waste for the purposes of the 1990 Act.

27   The next question is whether or not the facts contained in the EAW and the Further Information relating to the conduct of the Appellant are capable of satisfying the provisions of section 33(1)(c). The conduct describes the Appellant being pulled over in his car by the police, and them discovering that which he was "transporting" in his car, namely the materials which have been set out above. I am unable to accept that transporting these materials in a car amounts to keeping the controlled waste for the purposes of section 33(1)(c). As Mr Stansfeld points out, the context for understanding the parameters of this section are to be found in section 29(3) of the 1990 Act which, in connection with pollution of the environment, deals exclusively in section 29(3)(a) to (c) with waste being treated, kept, or deposited on land, as is appropriate bearing in mind that these sections appear within a part entitled "Waste on Land". It follows that the conduct identified does not in my judgment fulfil the definition of section 33(1)(c), and had the Appellant been charged with an offence under this section for the conduct described in the UK he would be entitled to be acquitted. The District Judge therefore fell into error in concluding that section 10 of the 2003 Act could be satisfied on the basis that there was an offence under section 33 of the 1990 Act.

28   I turn to the second basis upon which the Respondent puts its case under section 10, namely reliance upon an offence under section 1 of the Control of Pollution (Amendment) Act 1989 in respect of transporting controlled waste without being a registered carrier. Firstly, my conclusions set out above deal with the question of whether or not all the materials described in the conduct amount to controlled waste: they did. Secondly, the terms of the EAW itself specify that the Appellant did not hold an official permit for the waste management operation upon which he was engaged, and therefore this element of the offence is made out. The final area of dispute is the question of whether or not there was evidence to suggest that the Appellant was acting in the course of any business or was acting otherwise with a view to profit.

29   In my judgement this question is one which can be answered on the basis of the very clear inference that given the quantity and nature of the materials that were being transported it is clear, and I have no difficulty in finding that I am sure, that they were being transported at the very least with a view to profiting from their disposal in due course. My confidence in this conclusion is reinforced by the point made by the Respondent in relation offence 5, which albeit not an extradition offence is nevertheless part of the evidential framework, and which relates to another offence involving the unlawful appropriation of used batteries, and the Appellant, along with others, profiting from that theft. It follows that albeit the District Judge's reasons cannot be sustained there is a further basis upon which the conclusion that section 10 is satisfied, namely the fact that the conduct described would substantiate an offence under section 1 of the 1989 Act.

30   The final element of ground 1 relates to the contentions in respect of the Hazardous Waste Regulations 2005. This submission is confined to the element of the materials which were lead-acid batteries and therefore, it is conceded, within the definition of hazardous waste. The Appellant's objection to reliance upon the Hazardous Waste Regulations relates to regulation 12 which has been set out above. I am unable to accept that there is merit in the suggestion that because the hazardous waste described in the conduct originated in Austria the transposition exercise would fail as a result of the provisions of regulation 12. It is clear in my view when regulation 12 is read as a whole that such a narrow interpretation is not justified. I am unable to accept the inference of Mr Stansfeld's submission that a consignment of waste being transported through England which had arrived by sea at the UK border could be exempt from these regulations. Once a practical and purposive approach is taken to the transposition exercise it becomes clear that the Hazardous Waste Regulations would apply for the purposes of the section 10 exercise and that this is a further basis upon which the requirements of section 10 are satisfied. In any event, my conclusions in relation to the offence under the 1989 Act is sufficient to dispense with ground 1.

31   It needs to be borne in mind that in relation to the offences relied upon in the alternative to the offence under section 33(1)(c) of the 1990 Act the sentencing powers are more limited, albeit the possibility of imprisonment exists in relation to the offence under the Hazardous Waste Regulations. Whilst this point does not assist the Appellant in relation to the section 10 arguments, it is relevant to the article 8 arguments on the basis that this conclusion supports the suggestion that less weight should attach to the seriousness of the offending in relation to Conviction 2 in assessing the arguments under article 8. I have taken this into account in assessing Ground 2 below.

Ground 2: Article 8.

32   On behalf of the Appellant Mr Stansfeld submits that there are 5 points which demonstrate that the conclusions of the District Judge in relation to article 8 are wrong. The first point is that the District Judge fails to make any reference at all to delay in the case and, secondly, makes no mention of the conduct of the Respondent in seeking to take proceedings for the extradition of the Appellant.

33   The Appellant submits that in relation to the first judgment, which was handed down in 2007, there was a very substantial period of time which elapsed prior to proceedings being brought in connection with those proceedings. Whilst the sentence was activated in 2012, extradition was not sought until 2017. Indeed, on the 27th November 2012 an earlier EAW was issued against the Appellant under which he was arrested on 30th June 2014 and discharged on 11th September 2014. It is submitted that not only is the period up to 2017 not explained, but also that it is of note that having been arrested in the UK in 2014 it is not explained why it was not until 2017 that the present EAW was issued. This significant passage of time is unexplained.

34   Further, the District Judge failed to give consideration to how the public interest in the extradition of the Appellant had reduced as a consequence of the Respondent's conduct. When the Appellant was arrested in June 2014 the Appellant was arrested pursuant to an accusation warrant in respect of one of the six offences for which he is currently wanted following conviction. The Appellant submits that it is unexplained as to why the Respondent continued to pursue that request for which the Appellant was arrested, rather than withdrawing that warrant and seeking an accusation warrant in respect of all six of these offences. Instead of seeking an accusation warrant for all six offences the Respondent proceeded to confirm the convictions as final and binding in November 2015 in the continued absence of the Appellant. This conduct has led, it is submitted, to further inexplicable delay consequently lessening the weight to be attached to the public interest in this case.

35   Thirdly, it is submitted on behalf of the Appellant that the District Judge placed weight on the global outstanding sentence for which he was wanted of 4 years 2 months in total, rather than recognising the more limited number of offences for which he fell to be extradited as a result of the District Judge's decision and the impact that his discharge from four of the offences would have upon the length of his sentence.

36   Fourthly, the District Judge was in error when he concluded that the offences were serious, and a prison sentence would be imposed if the matter had been tried in this jurisdiction. The value involved was the equivalent of £10,675, which should have led to an assessment that a custodial sentence was not inevitable.

37   Finally, the District Judge failed to take any account of the impact of the UK leaving the European Union. This submission relates to the difficulties which the Appellant would have were he to be extradited and then, having served his sentence, seek to return to the UK as a consequence of the change in immigration regulation that has arisen resulting from the UK withdrawing from the European Union.

38   In response to these submissions Mr Joyes on behalf of the Respondent submits that the starting point in relation to the Appellant's contentions in relation to delay is the clear and robust finding made by the District Judge that the Appellant is a fugitive. This finding was made in respect of both convictions on the basis, firstly, that the Appellant accepted he was aware of the obligation not to reoffend during

the suspended sentence term, but he did nonetheless offend as recorded by the Respondent. This led to the conclusion of the District Judge that "it could have come thus as no real surprise to [the Appellant] when they came looking for him in relation there to".

39   The District Judge also accepted the Respondent's assertion that the Appellant had an ongoing obligation to notify the Respondent of any change of address, but he failed to do so. Indeed, within the Further Information provided by the Respondent it is noted that notwithstanding the instruction which the Appellant had been given to notify of any change of his place of residence the Appellant changed his registered addresses, and subpoenas and requests sent to him were all returned with an indication that he was unknown at that address. In particular, the Further Information observes as follows as to why the nature of the proceedings and the evasiveness of the Appellant lead to the passage of time:

> "(15) In the procedure No B.491.2006 a European arrest warrant was issued indeed against Sandor Milan Jakab but the procedure aimed at adjudicating on the charge therefore after the court had adopted a verdict i.e. had taken a position regarding guilt, the European arrest warrant was withdrawn since it was issued for the purpose of ensuring the attendance of the defendant in the procedure so it was no longer relevant after the adoption of the verdict. Then in 2016 Sandor Milan Jakab submitted a motion for review to the Curia which obviously shows that this time he stayed in Hungary. After the motion for review had been adjudicated the BVOP began to carry out such measures which aimed to ensure that the defendant enlisted in the penal institution to serve his sentence. For this purpose, the BVOP sent a request to the defendant which he did not receive due to his stay at an unknown location - despite the fact that pursuant to the Criminal Procedures Act he shall report any change in his place of residency or stay, then the competent authority carried out several measures in order to deliver the request to the defendant. Since no measure yielded any positive result, the BVOP sent several requests to the police for finding the defendant and once it established that all measures taken to find the defendant were unsuccessful, pursuant to the provisions of law it sent a request to the court for issuing a European arrest warrant to ensure the execution of the sentence which was later issued by the court.
>
> In the procedure No. 14.B.861.2012 no arrest warrant could be requested due to the sentence No. B.491.2006 until the final decision because the procedure in 2006 concluded with the imposition of a suspended imprisonment the execution of which was ordered by a later verdict in 2012. The procedure in 2012 is more complicated which was conducted by consolidating several cases initiated separately therefore the court could not modify the European arrest warrant in accordance with the current state of the case every time when a case was consolidated. However, regarding that Sandor Milan Jakab was interrogated in the course of the investigation when he was advised of his obligation to immediately notify the acting authority of any change in his place of residence or stay in accordance with the

provisions of the Criminal Procedures Act. Therefore, he did not exercise his right of defence on his own initiative though he was aware of the procedure, the court attempted to summon him to every procedural action, and after the conclusion of the appellate procedure he filed in person a motion for review. The statutory provisions of the procedure in the absence of the defendant did not allow that the procedure be suspended."

40   The fact that the Appellant gave a Hungarian address as his place of residence in a review request is recorded in additional Further Information. The review request was dated 27th March 2016. Thus, Mr Joyes submits that a significant amount of the delay in the present case is attributable to the Appellant.

41   Mr Joyes submits that, even following disaggregation, the remaining offences for which the Appellant falls to be extradited clearly pass the custody threshold. The use of a false passport is a serious offence which would attract a custodial sentence. The fraud, on any proper analysis, would attract a custodial sentence in the light of the fact that it involved a vulnerable victim. Under the relevant guideline the starting point would be 26 weeks imprisonment. Thus, the District Judge was correct to conclude that a significant prison sentence would remain to be served.

42   In relation to the impact of the UK leaving the European Union it is submitted by Mr Joyes that in truth any adverse consequence arises from the Appellant being convicted of criminal offences rather than any other factor. Finally, Mr Joyes observes that the District Judge was entitled to note that the Appellant's wife has been, and is capable of continuing to, provide care for both their children and the Appellant's father. Mr Joyes also notes the Appellant's convictions for offences in the UK which were recorded by the District Judge along with the caution.

43   My conclusions in relation to the submissions made under ground 2 are as follows. Firstly, whilst it is correct to observe that the District Judge did not deal in detail with the questions of delay which are raised by the submissions in the current appeal, the judge did set out, in the context of his conclusions as to whether or not the Appellant was a fugitive, the factual background which led to the conclusion that the Appellant had been evading the criminal justice system in Hungary and seeking to put himself beyond the reach of the Respondent authorities. The Further Information which has been set out above provides further detail of the complexities of the processes facing the Respondent in the light of the need to adjust and perfect the extradition process, and also the Appellant giving them reason to believe that he was residing in Hungary leading to unanswered correspondence and a failure to progress the litigation. Taking the matter overall, and bearing in mind the District Judge's unassailable finding that the Appellant was a fugitive, I am unconvinced that there was significant material delay which was caused by the actions of the Respondent in this case. In reality the need for extradition proceedings arose in 2012, and given the explanations provided in the Further Information as to the procedural complexities and the difficulties caused by the Appellant not, as he was required to, advising directly of any change in his address, I do not consider that the Appellant's criticisms of the Respondent are warranted. Indeed, on the basis that the Appellant positively suggested at one point that he remained in Hungary, it is clear that the Appellant made a significant contribution to any delay in this case. I am unable to accept the Appellant's

arguments in connection with delay, or accept that the Respondent was dilatory in taking the procedural steps required to bring the Appellant before the court.

44   In relation to the point taken about a global sentence, I accept that it appears that the District Judge included as a factor favouring the grant of extradition the fact that there was a sentence of 4 years 2 months still to serve. It appears that no adjustment was made on the basis that he had concluded that four out of the six offences for which extradition was sought in relation to the second judgment had been dismissed by him as a basis upon which extradition could be ordered. Some adjustment ought to have been made to the weight attaching to this factor to recognise that the whole of that term could not be attributed to those offences for which the Appellant was legitimately wanted. In addition to this is the allied point that the offences relied upon in respect of the Respondent's successful argument under section 10 are less serious and with lesser sentencing powers than the offence under section 33(1)(c). This further lessens the weight that can attach to the nature of the offences in striking the article 8 balance. Thus, the District Judge was wrong in relation to paragraph 93(ii) of the judgment and there are grounds for restriking the balance in that respect.

45   Having said that, and made the necessary adjustments arising from the reduction in sentence from that which was imposed, in my judgment the offences for which the Appellant is to be extradited are serious offences which still give rise to a significant term of imprisonment will need to be served. I accept the submissions made on behalf of the Respondent that both the offence of use of a false passport and also the offence of fraud in the particular circumstance in which it was committed will give rise to a significant term of imprisonment. The outstanding sentence to be served is therefore still a matter to which significant weight attaches, albeit less than that attached by the District Judge.

46   The final point to be addressed is the one related to the impact on the Appellant's prospect of returning to the UK, following serving his sentence, as a consequence of the changes which have occurred as a result of the UK leaving the European Union. The former provisions in relation to free movement when the UK was part of the European Union no longer apply. As indicated above, at the time of the hearing there was limited material before the court engaging directly with the current position in relation to the Immigration Rules, and the position of the Appellant were he to be seeking to return to the UK having served his sentence of imprisonment on the basis of the Immigration Rules as they currently stand.

47   An agreed note on these issues was provided to the court after the hearing. Prior to dealing with those provisions, it is necessary to say a little about other cases which have considered this point thus far. In the case of *Antochi v Richterin am Amstergericht of the Amstergericht Munchen (Munich), Germany* [2020] EWHC 3092 (Admin) Fordham J concluded in paragraphs 50 - 52 of his judgment that what he described as "Brexit uncertainty" should appropriately be factored into the article 8 analysis, and taken account of both as a subjective matter in relation to the anguish which would be caused to the Appellant and the Appellant's family, as well as an objective factor founded upon the risk that the Appellant would not be able to return to the UK and the family home after serving the sentence for which the Appellant was wanted. It is to be noted that Fordham J had already concluded that the Appellant would succeed even if all of the issues relating to the UK leaving the EU were left to one side.

48   In *Rybak v District Court in Lublin, Poland* [2021] EWHC 712 (Admin); [2021] 1 W.L.R. 3993 Sir Ross Cranston followed the decision of Fordham J in *Antochi.* He concluded that the District Judge in that case ought to have taken account of the potential difficulties for the Appellant returning to the UK as an express factor in the article 8 balancing exercise which weighed against the ordering of extradition.

49   By contrast with these decisions, Chamberlin J in the case of *Pink v Regional Court in Elblag, (Poland)* [2021] EWHC 1238 (Admin) concluded, at paragraph 52, that whilst there was a prospect that if extradited the Appellant may not be readmitted to the UK after completing his sentence, and that this would put his current partner who had settled status in a difficult position, this position was not properly to be regarded as a consequence of extradition. He concluded the situation was rather a consequence of the Appellant's criminal convictions in *Poland,* coupled with changes to the Immigration Rules as a result of the UK leaving the European Union. There was no evidence to support the submission made to him that if the Appellant were discharged from extradition, he could be expected to acquire settled status.

50   Finally, in further additional submissions, Mr Stansfeld has drawn attention to an unreported decision of Choudhury J in *Gorak v Poland* in which Choudhury J observed that the District Judge should have taken account of the potential difficulties and uncertainties which the Appellant would face in returning to the UK after serving his sentence as a consequence of the UK leaving the European Union.

51   As set out above, it was agreed at the hearing that further time should be afforded to the parties to investigate in greater detail the position in relation to the impact on the prospect of the Appellant returning to the UK in the absence of a right to free movement as a result of the UK leaving the European Union. A detailed note has been agreed between the parties in relation to the assessment of the Appellant's case measured against the Immigration Rules, since at the end of his sentence in Hungary the Appellant would have to make an application for leave to enter and remain in the UK. Clearly, the agreed note proceeds, and can only proceed, to evaluate such an application on the basis of an understanding of the Immigration Rules as they currently stand, and an assessment of the Appellant and his family's current circumstances. It appears that this level of detail in relation to the provisions of the Immigration Rules and the merits of a future application by the Appellant for leave to enter were not available to the court in the earlier decisions set out above.

52   The agreed note sets out in extensive and helpful detail the particular provisions of the Immigration Rules and how they would govern the Appellant's application. For the purposes of this judgment, it suffices to summarise the effect of the agreed note and its principal points before analysing the impact which it has upon this appeal.

53   The first point to note is that any application made by the Appellant to re-join his family in the UK would be governed solely by Appendix FM of the Immigration Rules. The agreed note points out that as a consequence of the provisions of Appendix FM the Appellant would not meet the requirements for leave to enter as a parent of a child in the UK on the basis that he does not have sole parental responsibility for his three children. The provisions of Appendix FM would however enable him to make an application for entry clearance as a partner however, one of the requirements for entry clearance as a partner is that the application must not

fall for refusal under any of the grounds specified in section S-EC, the section of the Immigration Rules which deal with suitability criteria.

54   Paragraph S-EC provides that an applicant will be refused entry clearance on the grounds of suitability if certain criteria apply. Under paragraph S-EC 1.4 it is provided that exclusion of an applicant from the UK will be conducive to the public good if they have:

> "(b) been convicted of an offence for which they have been sentenced to a period of imprisonment of at least 12 months but less than 4 years, unless a period of 10 years has passed since the end of the sentence."

55   It is agreed that the Appellant will have served a prison sentence in Hungary of at least 12 months but less than 4 years, and therefore his application would fall for refusal if he made it within 10 years from the end of his sentence in Hungary. In addition to this it would be necessary for the Appellant to satisfy the income requirements set out in section E-CP of Appendix FM, as well as passing an English language test which is another requirement under the Immigration Rules. It is accepted within the agreed note that as a consequence of these requirements, and in particular the suitability requirements, the Appellant's application at the end of his sentence for leave to enter and remain in the UK would be refused, and the Appellant could only be granted leave to enter the UK under Appendix FM if he could satisfy the Entry Clearance Officer that there are exceptional circumstances which would render refusal of entry clearance at breach of article 8 "because such refusal would result in unjustifiably harsh consequences for the Applicant, their partner, a relevant child or another family member whose article 8 rights it is evident from that information would be effected by the decision to refuse the application".

56   The Home Office has a published policy "Family Life (as a partner or parent), Private Life and Exceptional Circumstances version 16.0" which provides policy in relation to addressing the question of exceptional circumstances. The policy defines "unjustifiable harsh consequences" in the following terms:

> "Ones which involve a harsh outcome(s) for the Applicant or their family which is not justified by the public interest, including in maintaining effective immigration controls, preventing burdens on the taxpayer, promoting integration and protecting the public and the rights and freedoms of others."

57   The policy identifies relevant factors to consider as including the ability of the members of the family unit to lawfully remain in or enter another country. It provides that the onus is on the applicant to show that it is not feasible for the family to remain in or enter another country: a mere wish, desire or preference to live in the UK is insufficient. It explains that an example of where it might not be feasible for a family to relocate elsewhere as being when the sponsor has gained settled status in the UK as a refugee, and the Applicant's spouse is of the same nationality. Other factors to be considered are whether there are any reasons why a partner or child in the UK cannot join or re-join the Applicant overseas, on the basis that it would be unjustifiably harsh for them to do so. The policy advises that cumulative factors should be considered, weighing those in favour of the Applicant and balancing them against the public interest, in order to determine the question of whether or not it would be unjustifiably harsh for the Applicant or a relevant family member for the application to be refused. The policy concludes:

"Where the applicant's partner is in the UK, the question of whether refusal of entry clearance could or would result in unjustifiably harsh consequences equally requires a very stringent assessment. For example, a British citizen partner who has lived in the UK all their life, has friends and family here, works here and speaks only English may not wish to uproot and relocate halfway across the world, and it may be very difficult for them to do so. However, a significant degree of hardship or inconvenience does not amount to an unjustifiably harsh consequence in this context. ECHR Article 8 does not oblige the UK to accept the choice of a couple as to which country they would prefer to reside in."

58   In assessing this issue, I have no doubt that the question of the prospects of the Appellant returning to the UK at the end of his sentence is a material consideration in relation to article 8. This is because it is related to the impact of the extradition decision upon his right to private and family life, as well as the right to private and family life of those with whom he shares those rights. Undoubtedly the best evidence of the prospects that is available is the application of the rules as they stand now in relation to the current circumstances of the Appellant and his family, albeit that both the Immigration Rules and the circumstances of the Appellant and his family may change between the time of the decision and the time when any application is to be made.

59   Applying that approach to the present case it is, in effect, an agreed position that there is in reality no "Brexit uncertainty" about the situation, but a clear and very strong likelihood that, unless something amounting to exceptional circumstances arises in the meantime, the removal of the Appellant from the UK is likely to lead to a long term separation from his wife and family unless his wife and family decide to relocate to Hungary in order to re-join him at the end of his sentence. This situation arises as a result of the application of the Immigration Rules and the Appellant being wanted under a conviction warrant. It undoubtedly presents the family with a very significant and difficult decision to face if extradition is granted affecting both the Appellant and his family in relation to the continuation of their family life.

60   This consideration has to be put into context. Firstly, it is not an uncommon situation in extradition and immigration cases for a consequence of a decision to be the separation of the person who is the subject of the decision from their family, either through the removal of an individual or the refusal to permit their permanent reunion with their family. This is evidenced by the fact that detailed Home Office policy and complex provisions of the Immigration Rules have been prepared to assist in decision making in these situations. It is important to observe that the provisions of the Immigration Rules, as amplified by the Home Office policy, are themselves designed to provide rules and guidance for the determination of applications for entry clearance and leave to remain which are compliant with the provisions of article 8, and ensure the making of proportionate decisions when those rights are affected. In other words, decisions which are made applying the Immigration Rules and the relevant policy guidance are decisions which will themselves have been intended to be made in compliance with the requirements and obligations contained within article 8. In broad terms, the provisions of the Immigration Rules in relation to suitability criteria reflect article 8(2), and interference with article 8 rights only where it is necessary in a democratic society

to do so. Thus, the circumstances in which the Appellant and his family would find themselves at the end of his sentence, and the prospects of the Appellant making a successful application for leave to enter, are reflective of the Immigration Rules' application of article 8 to cases of his kind. It is a further feature of the context that the placing of European Union citizens in the same circumstances so far as the Immigration Rules are concerned as non-European Union citizens is not accidental, but undoubtedly a deliberate consequence of the UK's decision to leave the European Union.

61   Further context is provided by the observations of Chamberlin J in *Pink,* namely that there is a strong sense in which this situation arises as a result of the Appellant's convictions for crimes in Hungary for which there are sentences to be served. I do not read Chamberlain J as suggesting that the position in which the Appellant and his family would find themselves as being irrelevant to article 8, but rather that the assessment of proportionality cannot overlook the real and obvious causes of that position, namely the Appellant's convictions for crimes in Hungary and the change in the Immigration Rules as a result of the UK leaving the European Union. This reinforces the point that the effect of him finding himself in this position in relation to the need to satisfy the Immigration Rules is not one which has arisen by accident. In short, what is material to the article 8 decision is an understanding that, as a consequence of the provisions of the Immigration Rules and the returning of the Appellant to serve the sentences outstanding in Hungary, the impact on family life were his family to remain in the UK will be of a very longstanding character and this feature, or the alternative of his family relocating to Hungary to re-join him at the end of his sentence, is a factor which should be taken into account in assessing the article 8 implications of ordering the Appellant's extradition.

62   Applying these conclusions to the present case, whilst it is clear that the District Judge did not take into account any question of "Brexit Uncertainty" I am unconvinced that that had any material impact upon the decision. As set out above, on the basis of a current understanding of the implications of the Immigration Rules for an application made by the Appellant to return to the UK at the end of this sentence there is little if any uncertainty, but rather an extremely strong likelihood, that either the Appellant will be separated from his family, or his family will have to relocate to Hungary in order to continue their family life together.

63   When the evidence in the present case and the District Judge's decision are analysed that is in effect the approach which was taken by the District Judge. The witness statements of the Appellant and his wife engaged with the impact upon the family upon either on the basis that the Appellant would be separated from his wife and daughters and his father and the impact that that would have upon them or, alternatively, that the family would have to relocate to Hungary. Indeed, at paragraphs 35 and 36 of the District Judge's decision, having noted the difficulties that the Appellant's wife and children would have had and had had when parted from the Appellant, the District Judge noted that in her proof of evidence the Appellant's wife had stated that if extradited she and the children would have to return to Hungary, with negative impacts on the children's upbringing and future, whilst in her evidence she stated that upon reflection she would remain in the UK, as her ties to Hungary had been severed. If she was to return to Hungary the Appellant's father would have to return and enter a care home as he would be unable to stay in the UK on his own.

64   In paragraph 94 and 95 (in particular at paragraph 95(iv)) of the judgment, the question of this hardship to the Appellant and his family arising from ordering extradition was directly addressed by the District Judge, and he concluded that it would be insufficient to prevent an order for extradition being made in the present case. That is a conclusion which I am unable to find was in any way wrong in the circumstances, even as amplified by the further material now before the court in this appeal bearing upon the impact of the Immigration Rules. The substance of the decision which the District Judge made reflected the reality of the application of those Immigration Rules, namely that the Appellant and his family would be caused hardship as a consequence either of being separated from the Appellant or, alternatively, as a consequence of the decision the Appellant's wife, children and father having to relocate to Hungary to be reunited with him. No doubt relocation would have significant consequences for the Appellant's family which the judge took into account having noted that the two older children were born in Hungary and the Appellant's father had lived there prior to 2016. This was therefore no doubt a matter to be placed in the balance as a factor in favour of refusing extradition, but the approach taken to it by the District Judge was in substance appropriate.

65   For the reasons given above, with the exception of the judge's approach to the question of the length of sentence which the Appellant still has left to serve on return and the failure to account for the offences for which he had been discharged from extradition, and also the lesser weight to be given to the seriousness of the offending for the reasons already given, there was in my judgment no flaw in the balancing exercise in relation to article 8 which the District Judge undertook. Rebalancing matters to take account of these factors, I am unconvinced that the District Judge reached a conclusion which was wrong. Even adjusting the sentence downwards, and taking account of the 3 months spent in the UK on remand, I am unable to conclude that the overall balance of the factors both favouring and opposed to the grant of extradition should lead to a different conclusion. In my judgment the factors in favour of granting extradition, and in particular the public interest in the UK abiding by international extradition obligations and the factors set out in paragraph 93, with the exception of the length of sentence to be served, clearly outweigh those factors which are opposed to extradition, including, as the District Judge did, the impact upon the Appellant and his family as a consequence of the decision. I do not consider therefore that ground 2 has been made out.

Conclusion.

66   For the reasons which have been set out above I do not consider that either ground 1 or ground 2 are made out in this case and the appeal must be dismissed.

MANCHESTER SHIP CANAL CO LTD v UNITED UTILITIES WATER LTD

COURT OF APPEAL (CIVIL DIVISION)

Asplin, Arnold and Nugee LJJ: 27 June 2022

[2022] EWCA Civ 852; [2023] Env. L.R. 13

⟲ Breach of statutory duty; Canals; Contamination; Nuisance; Sewage effluent; Sewerage undertakers; Trespass; Ultra vires

H1   *Water resources—sewerage—sewerage and water undertaker—discharge untreated effluent after heavy rainfall from sewerage undertaker's outfalls into canal—whether owner of canal had right of action against sewerage undertaker—whether right of action inconsistent with statutory enforcement of the duties of sewerage undertaker—discharge of water into canal—agreement between owner of canal and sewerage undertaker providing right to discharge water—right terminable on notice from owner of canal—whether agreement void as ultra vires—whether sewerage undertaker had continuous statutory right to discharge water into canal following termination of agreement*

H2   The Claimant/Appellant was the owner of the Manchester Ship Canal (MSC) and appealed two separate decisions made in favour of the Claimant/Respondent statutory sewerage undertaker (UU) in separate proceedings.

H3   The first (and subsidiary) appeal related to proceedings brought in 2010 (the 2010 Proceedings). In the 2010 Proceedings, MSC had claimed that all UU's discharges of water from its outfalls were a form of trespass. The Supreme Court subsequently held that UU had an implied statutory right to discharge surface water and treated effluent into the canal without the canal owner's consent, which right had arisen prior to the coming into force of the Water Industry Act 1991 (the 1991 Act) and had survived under that Act. Following re-amended particulars of claim and the settlement of the majority of the claims in trespass, a dispute remained regarding a small number of outfalls that were permitted by license agreements that MSC claimed were terminable on notice. In a preliminary hearing in respect of these, the judge ruled that if MSC terminated or purported to terminate these agreements, UU had a continued statutory right to drain through the outfalls, because the relevant termination provisions in the agreement were ultra vires and void.

H4   In a second set of proceeding brought in 2018 (the 2018 Proceedings), MSC threatened to bring a claim in trespass and nuisance against UU due to discharges of untreated effluent into the canal, which had been caused by heavy rainfall resulting in flooding and exceeding the capacity of the extant sewerage system. In response, UU brought a claim seeking a declaration that MSC could not bring a claim in trespass or nuisance in respect of a discharge which contravened relevant provisions of the 1991 Act. The judge in the 2018 Proceedings rejected the claim, applying the decision in *Marcic v Thames Water Utilities Ltd* [2003] UKHL 66; [2004] Env. L.R. 25. The judge noted that UU had a duty under the s.94 of the 1991 Act to effectively deal with the contents of the sewers and that the enforcement machinery in the Act precluded private tortious remedies.

H5   MSC appealed both decisions.

H6   **Held,** in **allowing** the appeal in the 2010 Proceedings, but **dismissing** the appeal in respect of the 2018 Proceedings:

H7   (1) The 2010 Proceedings: The judge had erred in finding that the licences for the outfalls were an unlawful fetter on the relevant powers and duties of the local authorities found in for example, the Public Health Acts 1875 and 1936. The judge had held that if the licences were valid, but the termination provisions were not, the practical effect would be to convert a precarious grant into a permanent deprivation of property. The ultra vires doctrine, however, had not been held to have the effect of converting a limited and determinable contractual right into a permanent one. It was impossible to see how an implied statutory right to discharge from the outfall could exist consistently with a contractual obligation to remove the pipe. It could not be right to say that once MSC had granted a limited and determinable right, UU had somehow acquired a permanent and indefeasible right to maintain its pipes despite agreeing the very opposite.

H8   (2) The 2018 Proceedings: It would be inconsistent with the scheme of the 1991 Act for MSC to be able to bring an action in trespass or nuisance against UU in respect of the discharge of untreated sewage into the canal, in breach of the foul water provisos of ss.117(5) and 186(3) of the 1991 Act, if the only way in which the discharge could have been prevented was for UU to have built more sewerage infrastructure. MSC's complaint was that the discharges into the canal were either a trespass or a nuisance which, in practical terms, could only be prevented by requiring the UU to build more sewerage infrastructure. It was irrelevant that the MSC's aim in threatening its private law action was not to compel UU to build more sewers but rather to be able to charge UU a rent or fee for the right to discharge into the canal and that, accordingly, the judge had been right to find that, absent any finding of negligent or deliberate wrongdoing on the part of the UU, a private law claim was inconsistent with the statutory scheme and so could not be brought.

H9   **Cases referred to:**

Allen v Gulf Oil Refining Ltd [1981] A.C. 1001; [1981] 2 W.L.R. 188; [1981] J.P.L. 353 HL

British Waterways Board v Severn Trent Water Ltd [2001] EWCA Civ 276; [2002] Ch. 25; [2001] Env. L.R. 45

Dobson v Thames Water Utilities Ltd [2007] EWHC 2021 (TCC); [2008] Env. L.R. 21; [2007] H.R.L.R. 45

Durrant v Branksome Urban DC [1897] 2 Ch. 291 CA

Dwr Cymru Cyfyngedig (Welsh Water) v Barratt Homes Ltd [2013] EWCA Civ 233; [2013] Env. L.R. 30; [2013] 1 W.L.R. 3486

Glossop v Heston and Isleworth Local Board (1879) 12 Ch. D. 102 CA

Manchester Ship Canal Co Ltd v United Utilities Water Plc [2014] UKSC 40; [2014] 1 W.L.R. 2576; [2014] 3 E.G.L.R. 81

Marcic v Thames Water Utilities Ltd [2003] UKHL 66; [2004] 2 A.C. 42; [2004] Env. L.R. 25

Pride of Derby and Derbyshire Angling Association Ltd v British Celanese Ltd [1953] Ch. 149; [1953] 2 W.L.R. 58; (1953) 117 J.P. 52 CA

Public Transport Commission of NSW v Perry 137 C.L.R. 107 HC (Aus)

R. (on the application of Child Poverty Action Group) v Secretary of State for Work and Pensions [2010] UKSC 54; [2011] 2 A.C. 15; [2011] 2 W.L.R. 1

R. v Somerset CC Ex p. Fewings [1995] 1 W.L.R. 1037; (1995) 7 Admin. L.R. 761; [1996] C.O.D. 76 CA (Civ Div)

Radstock Cooperative & Industrial Society v Norton-Radstock Urban DC [1968] Ch. 605; [1968] 2 W.L.R. 1214; (1968) 132 J.P. 238 CA (Civ Div)

Smith v Stone 82 E.R. 533; (1647) Sty. 65 KB

Stourcliffe Estates Co Ltd v Bournemouth Corp [1910] 2 Ch. 12 CA

Sunderland Corp v Priestman [1927] 2 Ch. 107 Ch D

H10 **Legislation referred to:**
Public Health Act 1848
Public Health Act 1875 ss.13–18, 21, 22, 30, 34, 67, 69 and 332
Manchester Ship Canal Act 1885
Derby Corporation Act 1901
Public Health Act 1936 ss.14–16, 22, 67 and 331
Landlord and Tenant Act 1954
Water Act 1973 s.14
Control of Pollution Act 1974
Water Act 1989
Land Drainage Act 1991
Water Industry Act 1991 ss.2, 18, 19, 94, 106, 116, 117, 159, 186 and 219
Water Resources Act 1991
Human Rights Act 1998 s.18
Environmental Permitting (England and Wales) Regulations 2016 (SI 2016/1154)

H11 *D. Hart QC, C. Morgan* and *N. Ostrowski* (instructed by BDB Pitmans LLP) appeared on behalf of The Manchester Ship Canal Co Ltd.
J. Karas QC, R. Moules and *J. McCreath* (instructed by Pinsent Masons LLP) appeared on behalf of United Utilities Water Ltd.
T. de la Mare QC and *G. Molyneaux* (instructed by Hausfield & Co LLP) appeared by way of written submissions only for the Interveners.

JUDGMENT

LORD JUSTICE NUGEE:

Introduction

1   There are two appeals before the Court brought by The Manchester Ship Canal Company Ltd (**"MSCC"**) against decisions of Fancourt J on issues arising in a long-running dispute between MSCC and United Utilities Water Ltd (**"UU"**) concerning discharges by UU into the Manchester Ship Canal (**"the canal"**).

Fancourt J decided both issues in favour of UU for the reasons contained in a single judgment handed down by him on 15 June 2021 at [2021] EWHC 1571 (Ch) (**"the Judgment"** or **"Jmt"**).

2   MSCC, originally incorporated pursuant to the Manchester Ship Canal Act 1885 as the Manchester Ship Canal Company, is the owner of the canal. It is admitted on the pleadings that it is the freehold owner of, and entitled to possession of, the beds and banks of the canal; there is a dispute whether it has any proprietary right in the waters of the canal, but we have heard no argument on the point and nothing turns on it for present purposes. The canal, constructed pursuant to the 1885 Act, is over 35 miles long and runs from east of Salford Quays in Greater Manchester to Eastham. In its upper reaches the canal is a canalisation of the Rivers Irwell and Mersey, and it drains into the Mersey estuary and hence the sea.

3   UU is the sewerage undertaker for the North West of England, having been appointed as such in 1989 under the provisions of the Water Act 1989. It owns an extensive network of sewers and drains, much of it inherited from its predecessors (local authorities and, under the Water Act 1973, the regional water authority). This includes in the region of 100 outfalls of various types which discharge directly or indirectly into the canal.

4   In 2010 MSCC brought a claim against UU which in summary alleged that all discharges from UU's outfalls constituted a trespass (**"the 2010 proceedings"**). Most of this claim had already been determined in UU's favour, or discontinued, by the time of the hearing before Fancourt J, but there remained a small number of outfalls in issue where the outfall had originally been permitted by MSCC by way of an agreement that on its face was terminable by MSCC. A preliminary issue was ordered as to whether UU would have any continued statutory right to drain through the outfalls if MSCC terminated (or purported to terminate) the agreements. Fancourt J decided this issue in favour of UU. In appeal CA-2021-000674 MSCC appeals this decision with permission of Arnold LJ granted on 6 September 2021. I will refer to this appeal as **"the 2010 appeal"**. Before us the parties treated the 2010 appeal as very much the subsidiary of the two questions, arguing it after the other appeal and more briefly, and I also propose to consider it after the other appeal.

5   This arises in a second set of proceedings, this time brought in 2018 by UU by way of Part 8 claim (**"the 2018 proceedings"**). The issue raised by this claim was whether MSCC has any private law claim in trespass or nuisance against UU in respect of discharges from outfalls that are not authorised by statute (in effect untreated foul water discharges that prejudicially affect the quality of the water in the canal). UU accepted that if there had been any such discharges it would have acted in breach of its statutory duty, but said that the only remedy available was regulatory enforcement under the relevant statutory provisions, not a private law action by the landowner affected. Again Fancourt J decided this issue in favour of UU and MSCC appeals, in this case with permission granted by Fancourt J himself. This is appeal CA-2021-000675 and I will refer to it as **"the 2018 appeal"**.

6   By Order dated 19 January 2022, Arnold LJ gave permission to a number of bodies with an interest in the environmental health of waterbodies to intervene in the 2018 appeal, by way of written submissions only.

Brief history of the statutory regulation of sewerage

7   It is helpful to start with a brief overview of the history of the statutory provisions regulating sewerage. I do not set out the text of the relevant provisions here, but simply identify the succession of principal statutes and some of their features.

8   Although provision was made by the Public Health Act 1848 for Local Boards of Health to be established with various powers in relation to drainage and sewers, we were not referred to its provisions and the first Act of Parliament to which we were referred was the Public Health Act 1875 (**"PHA 1875"**). This divided England (other than the metropolis) into districts (either urban sanitary districts or rural sanitary districts), each being subject to the jurisdiction of a "local authority" (either an urban sanitary authority or a rural sanitary authority) (s. 5). It vested all existing and future sewers within a district in the relevant local authority, subject to some limited exceptions (s. 13), "sewer" being given a wide definition which included almost all sewers and drains other than drains for draining one building only (s. 4). Various powers in connection with sewers were conferred on the local authorities, some of which I will have to look at in due course.

9   The PHA 1875 also contained a number of provisions which, in various forms, have been reiterated in later legislation. These included a statutory obligation on a local authority to cause to be made such sewers as might be necessary for effectually draining their district (s. 13); a right on owners and occupiers of premises within the district to connect to and use the local authority's sewers (s. 21); a power for a local authority to discontinue a sewer, but only on condition of providing a substitute for anyone lawfully using the sewer (s. 18); and a declaration that nothing in the Act should authorise a local authority to discharge sewage or filthy water into a watercourse (including a canal) without it first being treated to free it from foul matter (s. 17). The Act also contained, in s. 299, a particular statutory procedure for enforcing a local authority's obligations which was by way of complaint to the Local Government Board, which could make an order requiring compliance. Again I will have to come back to the detail of some of these provisions in due course.

10   On 1 October 1937 the Public Health Act 1936 (**"PHA 1936"**) was brought into force. This was a consolidating Act and superseded the PHA 1875 as the principal statute governing sewerage. By that stage there had been some change in the identity of the relevant local authorities, but it remained the case that it was the duty of a local authority to provide such public sewers as might be necessary for effectually draining their district (and in addition a local authority was by then also under a duty to make such provision, by means of sewage disposal works or otherwise, as might be necessary for effectually dealing with the contents of their sewers) (s. 14); that owners and occupiers had a right to connect to and use such public sewers (s. 34); that a local authority had power to discontinue a sewer but before depriving any person of the use of a sewer had to provide a sewer that was equally effective (s. 22); and that nothing in the Act authorised a local authority to use a sewer for the purpose of conveying foul water into a watercourse (or canal) until it had been treated (s. 30). And the Act again contained a particular statutory procedure for enforcing a local authority's obligations, in this case by complaint to the Minister who might (if satisfied, after holding a local inquiry, that there had been a default) make an order directing them to remedy it (s. 322).

11   On 1 April 1974 the principal provisions of the Water Act 1973 came into force. This established 10 regional water authorities in England and Wales (one of which

was the North West Water Authority) with responsibility both for water supply and for sewerage. So far as sewerage is concerned, it imposed on them the duty to provide such public sewers as might be necessary for effectually draining their area and to make provision for effectually dealing with the contents of their sewers (s. 14(1)), and provided that they should exercise the functions conferred on local authorities by the relevant sections of the Public Health Act 1936 (s. 14(2)).

12   In 1986 the Government decided to privatise the water industry. It set out its reasons for the decision in a White Paper published in February 1986: Privatisation of the Water Authorities in England and Wales (Cmnd. 9734). In July 1987 the Government supplemented this proposal with a proposal for a new public regulatory body, the National Rivers Authority (**"the NRA"**), in a document entitled The National Rivers Authority – The Government's proposals for a public regulatory body in a privatised water industry. Effect was given to these proposals by the Water Act 1989. A successor company, initially publicly owned, was nominated for each regional water authority, and on the transfer date (1 September 1989) the successor company was appointed to be the sewerage undertaker for the relevant area and the relevant assets of the water authority were transferred to it. UU was the successor company for the North West Water Authority and duly appointed as sewerage undertaker for the North West.

13   The general sewerage functions of a sewerage undertaker were set out in s. 67, which imposed a duty on such an undertaker to provide a system of public sewers so as to ensure that its area was and continued to be effectually drained, and to make provision for effectually dealing with the contents of those sewers. By s. 69 and sch 8, the functions of water authorities relating to sewerage services were transferred to sewerage undertakers, and the relevant provisions of the Public Health Act 1936 were to be read as referring to sewerage undertakers in place of water authorities. The Act again contained a special statutory regime for enforcement of the general s. 67 duty, in this case by the Secretary of State, or the Director General of Water Services (**"the Director"**), making orders under s. 20 for the purpose of securing compliance.

14   The final Act which I should refer to here is the Water Industry Act 1991 (*"WIA 1991"*), which consolidated various enactments with amendments. It came into force on 1 December 1991, and (as subsequently amended) remains the principal Act regulating sewerage. The general duty of a sewerage undertaker to provide a sewerage system to ensure that its area is effectually drained and to make provision for effectually dealing with the contents of its sewers is now found in s. 94; the right of any owner or occupier of premises to connect to a public sewer is now found in s. 106; and the right of the undertaker to discontinue a sewer, subject to providing an equally effective sewer for anyone lawfully using it, is now found in s. 116. The special statutory regime for enforcement of a sewerage undertaker's duties, including the general duty under s. 94, is now found in s. 18, which empowers the Secretary of State or the Water Services Regulation Authority (which has replaced the Director, and is commonly known as Ofwat) to make orders for the purpose of securing compliance.

15   The WIA 1991 also contains, in s. 117(5) and s. 186(3), two provisions which can be called the "foul water provisos". They are to the effect that nothing in specified provisions of the Act authorises a sewerage undertaker (i) to use a sewer or outfall for the purpose of conveying foul water into any watercourse or canal without the water having been so treated as "not to affect prejudicially the purity

and quality of the water" in the watercourse or canal, or (ii) "injuriously to affect … the … quality … of water" contained in a canal. The effect of these provisions lies at the heart of the 2018 appeal, and I will consider them in more detail below.

The 2018 proceedings – facts

16   UU served evidence in support of the 2018 proceedings from two witnesses: Mr James Haslett, a senior employee responsible for the operation of UU's wastewater network and treatment works, and Dr Keith Hendry, an aquatic scientist with particular experience of the Mersey basin and the canal. MSCC, while not accepting that evidence, did not serve any evidence of its own, nor was there any oral evidence or cross-examination, MSCC's position being that factual evidence was not necessary to resolve what was in essence a question of statutory construction. Fancourt J did not fully accept that, saying that the evidence of Mr Haslett and Dr Hendry was an important basis for the declaration that UU sought, and that while MSCC might not have agreed it, it was the only evidence before the Court (Jmt at [45]-[47]). He said that it was not intended to disprove any incident of negligence or misfeasance on the part of UU (UU having accepted that the declaration it sought was not intended to prevent MSCC alleging negligence against UU and that in such a case it might have a valid claim); the purpose of the evidence was to make it clear that, subject to such a case being alleged and proved, the unlawful discharges complained of were involuntary and could only be remedied in the way that the evidence explained. Fancourt J said that he accepted the evidence of Mr Haslett and Dr Hendry on that basis (Jmt at [47]).

17   With that introduction I can summarise their evidence as follows. Starting with Dr Hendry's, his evidence, drawn from his own personal experience over many years, was directed to the improvement in the water quality of the canal since the 1980s. He described the canal during the 1980s as being like an open sewer, virtually uninhabitable to fish. He attributed this to sustained underinvestment over successive generations in improvements to sewerage infrastructure, referring to the fact that although there was environmental regulation through the Control of Pollution Act 1974, the bodies charged with regulating discharges were the regional water authorities who were themselves operating the sewerage system, so that there was no genuinely independent regulation. On privatisation an independent regulator was established, initially the NRA and then from 1996 the Environment Agency ("the EA"). To meet the regulator's requirements, there had been substantial investment since privatisation by the water industry, including UU, and this had led to a transformation in water quality both nationally and specifically in the canal; fish were now common, with salmon, one of the most pollution-intolerant species, observed in the upper reaches of the Mersey (which requires them to have traversed part of the canal).

18   Dr Hendry also explained how a strategic approach had been taken to addressing environmental concerns which involves identifying spending priorities. He said that there was no point, for example, in addressing discharges into a body of water such as the canal on its own, without addressing discharges into the water bodies upstream which feed into it. The strategy for the Mersey basin adopted by the NRA was to start at the periphery of the basin, first improving water quality upstream, and then to move in. Dealing first with direct discharges into the canal would have required additional and costly effort to compensate for poor quality water still

coming from upstream, and the environmental benefits would have been considerably reduced.

19   Dr Hendry also gave evidence intended to demonstrate that it was not a simple question to assess whether UU's discharges into the canal were such as to "affect prejudicially" or "injuriously affect" the quality of water in the canal within the meaning of the foul water provisos in s. 117(5) and s. 186(3) WIA 1991. (I will use the term "unauthorised discharge" to refer to discharges which are in breach of the foul water provisos in this way). It is not necessary to give the detail, as UU did not ask the Court on the hearing of this claim to make any decision on these questions; the evidence was merely put forward to illustrate that it should not be assumed that UU's discharges were in fact unauthorised, and that there are technical arguments that by adding oxygen to the water in the canal (which by its design tends to suffer from oxygen depletion), and by adding to the volume of water in the canal, the discharges in fact benefit the canal.

20   The thrust of Mr Haslett's evidence was that improvements to sewerage infrastructure are the subject of a sophisticated regulatory regime which seeks to identify priorities for environmental improvements, and to balance the benefits of those against the cost of those improvements, which has to be borne by a sewerage undertaker's customers; and that if it were open to a litigant such as MSCC to force improvements to UU's infrastructure by bringing a private law claim in tort in respect of unauthorised discharges, that would be inconsistent with and undermine that regime.

21   He gave some detail of UU's sewerage infrastructure. The vast majority of it was not constructed by UU itself but inherited by UU in 1989, some of it dating back to Victorian times. It includes four types of outfalls which MSCC contend are responsible for unauthorised discharges, as follows:

> (1) Combined sewer overflows
> Almost all new sewer systems are separate systems in which there are separate sewers for surface water and foul water. But historically combined systems were used in which both surface water and foul water (from domestic and business premises) enter a single pipe system; such combined systems are very common in UU's network and across the UK. This means that in times of heavy rainfall the combined flow may exceed the capacity of the system. In the absence of an overflow this will back up and cause flooding and pollution (either of highways, external to customers' premises or, more distressingly, internal to such premises). A combined sewer overflow is designed to prevent such flooding by diverting excess flow to an appropriate watercourse. Such flow has by definition not been through any wastewater treatment works, and therefore has the effect of discharging untreated sewage into the watercourse (although it is diluted by stormwater and usually screened to prevent solid matter). At the time of privatisation the system inherited by UU included some 2817 combined sewer overflows. By 2018 that had been reduced to 2047.
>
> (2) Storm tank overflows
> UU treats sewage at wastewater treatment works. About a third of these have storm tanks. They are not needed for small treatment works, but for treatment works of any size, which will inevitably receive considerable volume from combined sewer systems, the rate of flow will increase significantly in times

of rainfall, and flows may exceed the capacity of the treatment works, the industry standard being that treatment works should be able to treat flows up to three times the dry weather flow. Storm tanks are used to store flow in excess of this capacity. But they too have a finite capacity which may be inadequate in times of heavy rainfall, in which case the excess is diverted to an overflow. UU has 197 such storm tank overflows in its system (a number which is unlikely to have changed much since privatisation since treatment works either have storm tanks, and hence overflows, or not).

(3) Emergency overflows

Emergency overflows operate in times of emergency, most commonly at pumping stations. If pumps suffer mechanical failure or loss of power, the sewage entering the pumping station will back up and flood the station and surrounding area; emergency overflows prevent this by allowing overflows into nearby watercourses. At the time of privatisation there were 630 such overflows in UU's system; in 2018 there were 585 (and another 396 which discharge into a combined sewer overflow).

(4) Discharges from wastewater treatment works

UU operates 568 treatment works, ranging from the very small (serving around 15 people) to the very large (the largest serving a population equivalent of some 1,200,000). After treatment the final effluent is discharged into a watercourse or other body of water, and the treatment processes vary with the size of the works and the environmental needs of the water body receiving the effluent.

22   Mr Haslett explained what would be necessary to prevent or reduce such discharges. In the case of a combined sewer overflow, one could in theory replace the combined sewer system with new separate systems; or install detention tanks to store storm flow until the sewers had sufficient capacity. In the case of storm tank overflows one could in theory install larger storm tanks or increase the capacity of the treatment works so that increased flows proceeded to treatment rather than being diverted to storm tanks. In the case of emergency overflows, better maintenance of equipment, installation of more modern and reliable equipment, and new telemetry informing UU when equipment has failed can contribute (and indeed have contributed) to the emergency overflows being used less frequently. In the case of discharges from treatment works, improvements in treatment processes can reduce the level of pollutants in the final effluent. It can be seen that all of these measures would require expenditure, usually on capital projects, and Mr Haslett gave details of the large amounts of capital expenditure undertaken by UU since privatisation.

23   Mr Haslett explained that under the WIA 1991 sewerage undertakers are subject to two regulators, an economic regulator (formerly the Director and now Ofwat) and an environmental regulator (formerly the NRA and now the EA). (To describe the Director and Ofwat as merely economic regulators to my mind rather underplays their role which is more extensive but it is not necessary to go into the details). In very broad terms the EA (which has a much broader remit than simply the water industry) has a duty to improve and maintain the quality of surface and ground waters, and as such is responsible for monitoring the quality of waters, and discharges into them. Among other things it controls discharges from individual outfalls through a regime of permits, and has a variety of enforcement tools if

discharges are not in compliance with permits. It also works with undertakers to identify capital works that are required to effect improvements. Some such works are required to meet legislative requirements. But where there is no legislative requirement this involves balancing the benefits of schemes for improvement against their costs.

24   Ofwat is responsible for setting the price framework for the charges which undertakers can charge consumers. It undertakes periodic price reviews, intended to ensure that undertakers can perform their functions, including necessary investment in infrastructure, without undue cost to their customers. This process can involve Ofwat in challenging schemes designed to deliver environmental improvements on the basis that the costs outweigh the benefits, leading to further liaison between Ofwat, the EA and the undertaker. At the end of the process Ofwat issues a final determination which sets the level of charges the undertaker can make.

25   Mr Haslett's evidence goes into these matters in considerable detail, but it is unnecessary to do so here. He summarises the position as follows. A key element of the operation of a sewerage undertaker such as UU since privatisation has been liaison with its regulators, working closely with the EA to determine the environmental improvement schemes that are necessary, and with Ofwat to set the consequential price levels to deliver such schemes. Funding for any particular project can only be raised by either increasing bills or by diverting resources from other projects, and (he believes) this regulatory regime provides a sophisticated way for identifying which projects should be prioritised.

Implied rights of discharge

26   We were referred to a large number of authorities, dating back to the PHA 1875. I do not propose to refer to them extensively here, but it is helpful to identify some decisions which form the backdrop to the present dispute.

27   I can start with *Durrant v Branksome Urban DC* [1897] 2 Ch. 291 ("*Durrant*"). The plaintiffs were owners of a stream called the Bourne. The defendant council was the local authority for the purposes of the PHA 1875 and had constructed drains which drained surface water from roads in their district into the Bourne. These were not foul water drains and did not convey sewage, but they were "sewers" for the purposes of the PHA 1875, and they carried sand or silt into the Bourne, which was what the plaintiffs complained of. The plaintiffs claimed that the defendant had no right to discharge into their stream, but both North J and, on appeal, this Court held that on the true construction of the PHA 1875, they had a statutory right to do so. The relevant provisions were as follows: (i) s. 15 which provided that "Every local authority … shall cause to be made such sewers as may be necessary for effectually draining their district for the purposes of this Act"; (ii) s. 16 which provided that "Any local authority may carry any sewer … into … any lands whatsoever in their district"; and (iii) s. 17 which provided as follows:

> **"17 Sewage to be purified before being discharged into streams**
> Nothing in this Act shall authorise any local authority to make or use any sewer drain or outfall for the purpose of conveying any sewage or filthy water into any natural stream or water course, or into any canal pond or lake until

such sewage or filthy water is freed from all excrementitious or other foul or noxious matter such as would affect or deteriorate the purity and quality of the water in such stream or watercourse or in such canal pond or lake."

This Court held that the inference from reading ss. 16 and 17 together was that s. 16 conferred a right on the local authority to discharge water into any stream or watercourse ("lands" in s. 16 including land covered with water) as long as it was free from the things referred to in s. 17, and the fact that the water here carried down sand and silt was not a breach of s. 17: see per Lindley LJ at 301-2, Lopes LJ at 303 and Chitty LJ at 304-5.

28   Durrant therefore established that under the PHA 1875 a local authority had a general statutory right to discharge water into watercourses so long as it was either clean, or had been treated so as not to fall foul of the restriction in s. 17. The same applied under the equivalent provisions in the PHA 1936, namely s. 15 which conferred power on a local authority to construct a public sewer in, on or over any land, and s. 30 which provided as follows:

> **30 Sewage, and &c, to be purified before being discharged into streams, canals and &c.**
> Nothing in this Part of this Act shall authorise a local authority to construct or use any public or other sewer, or any drain or outfall, for the purpose of conveying foul water into any natural or artificial stream, watercourse, canal pond or lake, until the water has been so treated as not to affect prejudicially the purity and quality of the water in such stream, watercourse, canal pond or lake."

These provisions of the PHA 1936 continued to apply to regional water authorities under the Water Act 1973, and to sewerage undertakers under the Water Act 1989.

29   In *British Waterways Board v Severn Trent Water Ltd* [2001] EWCA Civ 276 (**"BWB"**) the question was raised whether the position was the same under the WIA 1991 which replaced the PHA 1936. Severn Trent Water Ltd (**"STW"**) was the sewerage undertaker for its area, having been appointed under the Water Act 1989 as successor to the Severn-Trent Water Authority. It inherited a pipe which discharged surface water into the Stourbridge canal, owned by the British Waterways Board (**"BWB"**). The question raised was whether STW had a right under the WIA 1991 to discharge into the canal without BWB's permission. Arden J held that it did, finding (largely by analogy with *Durrant*) that such a right was implicit in s. 159 WIA 1991 which provides that a sewerage undertaker has power to lay pipes: see [2001] Ch. 32. On appeal however this Court held that there was no implied right in the WIA 1991 for a sewerage undertaker to discharge onto the land of another without consent and without compensation, and that *Durrant* was of little relevance: see per Peter Gibson LJ at [32] and [43], Chadwick LJ at [71] and [75] and Keene LJ at [78].

30   It was the decision in *BWB* which prompted MSCC to assert that all of UU's discharges into the canal were acts of trespass, and ultimately to bring the 2010 proceedings. One of UU's defences to the claim was that *BWB* did not apply to outfalls which had vested in UU before 1 December 1991 when the WIA 1991 came into force. That issue was heard successively by Newey J, who held in favour of UU at [2012] EWHC 232 (Ch); this Court, which allowed an appeal by MSCC at [2013] EWCA Civ 40; and the Supreme Court, which allowed UU's further

appeal at [2014] UKSC 40 (**"*MSCC* (2014)"**). The Supreme Court rejected UU's submission that *BWB* was wrongly decided, holding that the reasoning in *BWB* was compelling and unanswerable on the question put before the Court in *BWB* about the effect of s.159: see per Lord Sumption JSC at [15], Lord Toulson JSC at [26] and Lord Neuberger PSC at [57]. But it accepted UU's submission that Parliament cannot have intended by enacting the WIA 1991 to take away overnight the sewerage undertakers' rights to discharge from existing outfalls, and that they therefore continued to have a statutory right to discharge from any outfalls constructed before 1 December 1991: see per Lord Sumption JSC at [18]-[19], Lord Toulson JSC at [29ff], and Lord Neuberger PSC at [58ff]. The essential reasoning, as expressed by Lord Sumption, is that when the WIA 1991 imposed on sewerage undertakers duties which they could only perform by continuing to discharge from existing outfalls and at the same time applied to them the statutory restrictions on discontinuing the use of existing sewers (now found in s. 116 WIA 1991), it implicitly authorised the continued use of existing sewers.

31   The effect of the decision was to put an end to MSCC's contention that the mere continued discharge after 1991 by UU into the canal from any pre-existing outfall was a trespass. It did not however deal with the position in relation to unauthorised discharges in breach of the foul water provisos, which is the subject of the 2018 appeal. (Nor did it deal with the position where discharges had initially been by consent in the form of a terminable licence and the licence is terminated, which is the subject of the 2010 appeal).

Marcic

32   Before coming to the Judgment, it is convenient to refer to one other authority, which is the decision of the House of Lords in *Marcic v Thames Water Utilities Ltd* [2003] UKHL 66 (**"*Marcic*"**). Mr Marcic was the owner of a house in Old Church Lane, Stanmore. Thames Water Utilities Ltd (**"Thames"**) was the sewerage undertaker for the area. In times of heavy rainfall, surface water caused a foul water sewer under Old Church Lane to become overloaded and cause (external) foul water flooding to Mr Marcic's property. This happened repeatedly and Mr Marcic spent £16,000 constructing a flood defence system in his front garden. He sued Thames for an order requiring Thames to improve the sewerage system and for damages, basing his claim on the tort of nuisance and alternatively on the Human Rights Act 1998. Both claims were upheld by this Court ([2002] EWCA Civ 64) but rejected by the House of Lords. Nothing need be said about the Human Rights Act claim which is not relevant to the present appeal, but the rejection of the claim in nuisance is relied on by UU as demonstrating that MSCC equally has no claim in the present case in tort for unauthorised discharges in breach of the foul water provisos.

33   Reasoned judgments on this question were given by Lord Nicholls and Lord Hoffmann, Lords Steyn and Scott agreeing with both judgments and Lord Hope with that of Lord Nicholls.

34   Both Lord Nicholls and Lord Hoffmann explain that Thames was under a statutory duty (by s. 94 WIA 1991) to cause its area to be "effectually drained" and Lord Nicholls certainly proceeded on the basis that the flooding suffered by Mr Marcic indicated that Thames was in breach of that duty. But that duty was not directly enforceable by Mr Marcic as the only person who could enforce it in the

first instance was the Director, who could make an enforcement order under s. 18 WIA 1991, and the effect of s. 18(8) WIA 1991 was to make it clear that the only remedies for breach of the s. 94 duty were the statutory remedies (at [21] and [51]). But s. 18(8) did not exclude any remedies available in respect of an act or omission "otherwise than by virtue of its constituting a contravention" of such a duty. So the question was whether Mr Marcic had a common law claim in nuisance (at [22] and [52]).

35   Both Lord Nicholls and Lord Hoffmann concluded that he did not. Lord Nicholls' reasoning was as follows. This Court had found liability in nuisance on the basis of the general obligation on a landowner to take reasonable steps to prevent hazards on his land from causing damage to his neighbour (at [32]). But Thames was no ordinary occupier of land: it was a sewerage undertaker, and its obligations regarding its sewers could not sensibly be considered without regard to the elaborate statutory scheme under the WIA 1991. The common law of nuisance should not impose on Thames obligations inconsistent with that scheme (at [33]). Mr Marcic's claim in nuisance was inconsistent. However expressed, it always came down to this: Thames ought to build more sewers (at [34]). But it was abundantly clear that one important purpose of the enforcement scheme in the WIA 1991 was that individual householders should not be able to launch proceedings in respect of failure to build sufficient sewers. When flooding occurred, the Director would consider whether to make an enforcement order; and the existence of a parallel common law right whereby individual householders who suffer sewer flooding might themselves bring court proceedings when no enforcement order had been made would set at nought the statutory scheme (at [35]).

36   Lord Hoffmann's reasoning was as follows. The question was whether the failure by Thames to improve the sewers to meet the increased demand gave rise to a cause of action at common law (at [52]). But there was a consistent line of authority dating back to *Glossop v Heston and Isleworth Local Board* (1879) 12 Ch. D. 102 to the effect that the failure of a sewerage authority to construct new sewers did not constitute an actionable nuisance. These cases did not, as this Court had thought, turn on general principles about the law of nuisance; they were cases about sewers (at [54]-[59]). Sewers are different because they do not just involve two neighbouring landowners: if one customer is given a certain level of services then others in the same circumstances should receive the same. That raises questions of the public interest: capital expenditure has to be financed, interest must be paid on borrowings and undertakers must earn a reasonable return, and the expenditure can only be met by charges on consumers (at [63]). These are decisions which courts are not equipped to make in ordinary litigation (at [64]). The WIA 1991 contained an elaborate enforcement procedure. The Director was under a duty to consider complaints but was required to exercise his powers in the manner best calculated to achieve certain objectives (at [65]). Pursuant to these duties he had formulated certain policies, and made decisions whether capital expenditure was reasonable (in which case it is taken into account in assessing the charges which would give the undertaker a reasonable return on capital) or not. It was plain that this Court, in deciding that better sewers should have been laid to serve Mr Marcic's property, was in no position to take into account the wider issues which Parliament required the Director to consider (at [68]). The WIA 1991 made it even clearer than earlier legislation that Parliament did not intend the fairness of priorities to be decided by a judge. It intended the decision to rest with the Director, subject

only to judicial review. It would subvert the scheme of the WIA 1991 if the courts were to impose upon the sewerage undertakers, on a case by case basis, a system of priorities different from that which the Director considered appropriate (at [70]).

37   It can be seen that although their analysis is not in all respects identical, there is very little, if any, difference of substance between them. Both considered that the relationship of a sewerage undertaker to landowners is not to be equated with that of two private parties, but had to be considered in the light of the statutory scheme in the WIA 1991 for enforcement of a sewerage undertaker's duties. Both considered that it would subvert that scheme to allow landowners to bring common law claims for nuisance which, however framed, amounted to a complaint that the undertaker should have built more sewers.

38   It is also to be noted that the decision in *Marcic* was not just that no mandatory order should be made against Thames. Indeed by the time of the hearing in the House of Lords work had been carried out to alleviate the flooding, and the live issue was whether Mr Marcic could recover damages (see at [28]). The decision of the House of Lords was that there was no liability in nuisance at all, so that the damages claim was also unsustainable.

39   UU's position in the 2018 proceedings is that the same principles apply to MSCC's claims for trespass or nuisance in relation to unauthorised discharges. MSCC's position is that *Marcic* was concerned with different statutory provisions and should be distinguished.

The 2018 proceedings: Fancourt J's Judgment

40   In the Judgment, Fancourt J referred to the decisions in *BWB*, *Marcic* and *MSCC* (2014) (Jmt at [7]-[13]); reviewed the scheme of the WIA 1991 (Jmt at [14]-[28]); explained the nature of UU's claim in the 2018 proceedings (Jmt at [29]-[52]); analysed *Marcic* in detail (Jmt at [53]-[61]); and set out the parties' respective contentions (MSCC's at Jmt [62]-[73]) and (UU's at [74]).

41   At [75] he gave his conclusion that UU's argument was to be preferred. He gave his reasons for this conclusion at [76]-[90] in a series of numbered points. The central reasoning is found in his third and fourth points as follows:

"79. Third ... the reason (on the evidence) for such contaminated damage as has occurred is the effect of sudden heavy rainfall, which causes flooding and results in the capacity of the existing system being exceeded. It has occurred without UU doing anything to cause it, or being able to do anything lawfully to stop it, except by spending money on large-scale capital improvements. Any breach of duty by UU is therefore not a breach of one or more of the relevant sewerage provisions but a breach of the s.94 duty to make provision as is necessary from time to time for effectually dealing with the contents of the sewers in the area. In the absence of an allegation of negligence, malfunction or misconduct, the fact that insufficiently treated effluent is discharging into the Canal means that there must be a breach of the general duty in s.94(1)(b): see, by analogy, *Dobson v Thames Water Utilities Ltd* [2007] EWHC 2021 (TCC); [2008] Env. L.R. 21 ("*Dobson*") at [74]-[77], [81], [82] (malodours and mosquito infestation caused by sewage treatment works: contents of sewers therefore not being effectually dealt with; breach of s.94(1)(b)).

80. Fourth, the facts of this case, although different, are materially indistinguishable from the relevant facts of *Marcic*. The complaint, whether it is pleaded as a trespass, a nuisance or a breach of statutory duty, is of uncontrolled escape of untreated sewage, the only remedy for which is the construction of a better sewerage system. It is the substance of the complaint that is made that determines the question, not whether the claim is brought in trespass, nuisance or breach of statutory duty: see *Marcic* and *Barratt Homes Ltd v Dwr Cymru Cyfyngedig (No.2)* [2013] EWCA Civ 233; [2013] 1 W.L.R. 3486."

42   By his Order dated 15 June 2021 he therefore made a declaration that upon the true construction of the WIA 1991, where a discharge into the canal from sewers vested in UU contravenes s. 117(5) and/or s. 186(3) of the Act, MSCC may not bring an action in trespass or nuisance against UU in respect of such discharge absent an allegation of negligence or deliberate wrongdoing on the part of UU leading to the said discharge.

The 2018 appeal: Grounds of appeal

43   MSCC advances 5 grounds of appeal. In summary they are as follows:

(1) Fancourt J was wrong to conclude that unauthorised discharges necessarily involved a breach of s. 94 WIA 1991, and that the s. 18 machinery operated to the exclusion of private tortious remedies.

(2) Fancourt J adopted an over-broad reading of *Marcic*.

(3) On Fancourt J's interpretation there is little or no point to the foul water provisos.

(4) Fancourt J was wrong to find that the unauthorised discharges were involuntary.

(5) Fancourt J was wrong to find that a purely involuntary act is not an act of trespass. The 2018 appeal: preliminary.

44   Although Mr David Hart QC (who appeared with Mr Charles Morgan and Mr Nicholas Ostrowski for MSCC) argued the appeal under these various grounds of appeal, it seems to me that there is really only one issue in the 2018 appeal. This is whether Fancourt J was right to hold that the principle in *Marcic* applied to the unauthorised discharges in the present case. If he was, then any private law claims that MSCC would otherwise have cannot succeed as they are inconsistent with the statutory scheme.

45   I will say straightaway that I think Fancourt J was right on this question. Reducing the case to its simplest, Mr Marcic's complaint was that Thames was flooding his property with sewage. I do not think it was disputed that that was an interference with the reasonable enjoyment of his land, and anyone responsible for it would therefore have normally been liable for nuisance. But the House of Lords held that no action in nuisance lay because of Thames' special position as a sewerage undertaker, and because it would undermine the statutory scheme applicable to the enforcement of sewerage undertakers' duties in relation to sewage if such an action could be brought. Similarly, reducing MSCC's complaint to its simplest, it is that UU's outfalls are discharging untreated sewage into the canal without either the consent of MSCC or statutory authority. I will assume that MSCC is right that anyone responsible for such a discharge would normally have been liable for

trespass (or alternatively nuisance). But it seems to me that the principle of *Marcic* applies equally to this situation. To hold UU liable for trespass (or nuisance) for unauthorised discharges into the canal would be equally inconsistent with the statutory scheme applicable to it as sewerage undertaker.

46   My conclusion therefore is that the appeal should be dismissed. But I will consider the arguments advanced by Mr Hart in support of each of MSCC's grounds of appeal in turn.

Ground 1 – private remedies in tort are not ousted by s.18 of the Act

47   Mr Hart's overall submission was as follows. It is common ground that discharges in breach of the foul water provisos are not authorised by the WIA 1991. Given that lack of statutory authority, MSCC retains its ordinary common law remedies in trespass and nuisance. It does not matter that such an unauthorised discharge may or may not involve a breach of the sewerage undertaker's general duty in s. 94 WIA 1991; if it does, that may have other consequences, but it does not affect the lack of statutory authority, and consequential liability in tort, which arises from the discharges being in breach of the foul water provisos.

48   This argument turns on the proper construction of the relevant provisions of the WIA 1991. Starting with s. 94, this provides, so far as relevant, as follows:

> **"94 General duty to provide sewerage system.**
>   (1) It shall be the duty of every sewerage undertaker—
>   (a) to provide, improve and extend such a system of public sewers (whether inside its area or elsewhere) and so to cleanse and maintain those sewers and any lateral drains which belong to or vest in the undertaker as to ensure that that area is and continues to be effectually drained; and
>   (b) to make provision for the emptying of those sewers and such further provision (whether inside its area or elsewhere) as is necessary from time to time for effectually dealing, by means of sewage disposal works or otherwise, with the contents of those sewers.
>   …
>   (3) The duty of a sewerage undertaker under subsection (1) above shall be enforceable under section 18 above—
>   (a) by the Secretary of State; or
>   (b) with the consent of or in accordance with a general authorisation given by the Secretary of State, by the Authority.
>   …"

49   As can be seen, this imposes a general duty on a sewerage undertaker to provide a sewerage system, including by s. 94(1)(b) a duty to make such provision as is necessary from time to time for effectually dealing with the contents of its sewers, by means of sewage disposal works or otherwise. It also provides by s. 94(3) that that duty shall be enforceable under s. 18 by the Secretary of State or by "the Authority" (that is, Ofwat).

50   The relevant provisions of s. 18 are as follows:

"18. Orders for securing compliance with certain provisions.
(1) Subject to subsection (2) and sections 19 and 20 below, where in the case of any company holding an appointment under Chapter I of this Part or any person holding a licence under Chapter 1A of this Part the Secretary of State or the Authority is satisfied—

  (a) that that company or that person is contravening—

    (i) any condition of the company's appointment or the person's licence in relation to which he or it is the enforcement authority; or

    (ii) any statutory or other requirement which is enforceable under this section and in relation to which he or it is the enforcement authority;

  or

  (b) that that company or that person is likely to contravene any such condition or requirement,

he or it shall by a final enforcement order make such provision as is requisite for the purpose of securing compliance with that condition or requirement.
…
(2) Subject to section 19 below, where in the case of any company holding an appointment under Chapter I of this Part or any person holding a licence under Chapter 1A of this Part —

  (a) it appears to the Secretary of State or the Authority as mentioned in paragraph (a) or (b) of subsection (1) or (1A) above; and

  (b) it appears to him or it that it is requisite that a provisional enforcement order be made,

he or it may (instead of taking steps towards the making of a final order) by a provisional enforcement order make such provision as appears to him or it requisite for the purpose of securing compliance with the condition or requirement in question.

(3) In determining for the purposes of subsection (2)(b) above whether it is requisite that a provisional enforcement order be made, the Secretary of State or, as the case may be, the Authority shall have regard, in particular, to the extent to which any person is likely to sustain loss or damage in consequence of anything which, in contravention of any condition or of any statutory or other requirement enforceable under this section, is likely to be done, or omitted to be done, before a final enforcement order may be made.
…
(5) An enforcement order—

  (a) shall require the company to which it relates (according to the circumstances of the case) to do, or not to do, such things as are specified in the order or are of a description so specified;

  (b) shall take effect at such time, being the earliest practicable time, as is determined by or under the order; and

  (c) may be revoked at any time by the enforcement authority who made it.
…
(8) Where any act or omission–

(a) constitutes a contravention of a condition of an appointment under Chapter 1 of this Part or of a condition of a licence under Chapter 1A of this Part or of a statutory or other requirement enforceable under this section; or

(b) causes or contributes to a contravention of any such condition or requirement,

the only remedies for, or for causing or contributing to, that contravention (apart from those available by virtue of this section) shall be those for which express provision is made by or under any enactment and those that are available in respect of that act or omission otherwise than by virtue of its constituting, or causing or contributing to, such a contravention."

51   As can be seen this by s. 18(1) prima facie requires the Secretary of State or Ofwat to make a final enforcement order against a company holding a licence under Chapter I (which includes a sewerage undertaker) if satisfied that it is contravening any statutory requirement enforceable under the section. That (by s. 94(3)) includes the general s. 94 duty. The section also by s. 18(2) empowers the Secretary of State or Ofwat to make a provisional enforcement order and by s. 18(3) requires them in determining whether to do so to have regard to the damage likely to be caused to anyone before a final enforcement order can be made. It may be noted that s. 18(1) which, by using the words "shall make a final enforcement order", appears to impose a mandatory obligation on the Secretary of State or Ofwat, is expressly subject to s. 19. This provides in s. 19(1) a number of exceptions to the duty to enforce, including the case where the Secretary of State or Ofwat is satisfied that the contraventions were of a trivial nature (s. 19(1)(a)), or satisfied that the duties imposed on them by Part I of the Act preclude the making of the order (s. 19(1)(c)). I will come back to the Part I duties below.

52   Once an enforcement order is made, the obligation to comply with it is a duty owed to anyone who might be affected by a contravention of the order, and a breach of that duty which causes loss or damage is actionable by that person: s. 22(1) and (2). But unless and until such an order is made, the obligation on a sewerage undertaker to comply with its general duty under s. 94 is not actionable as such. This is the effect of s. 18(8) which makes it clear that the only remedies for a contravention of a statutory requirement enforceable under the section as such are those under s. 18 itself, or those expressly provided for in statute, so that no action lies in tort for breach of statutory duty.

53   But s. 18(8) also provides that this does not affect remedies available in respect of an act "otherwise than by virtue of its constituting … such a contravention." As Mr Hart put it, you cannot sue for breach of the s. 94 duty in terms, but if you have another claim, that may subsist. One might have thought, on an untutored reading of s. 18(8), that by enacting it Parliament had provided that if an act was both a contravention of the s. 94 duty and also something that would, apart from the Act, give rise to common law claims in tort, then the common law claims could still be sued on. But in the light of the analysis in *Marcic* this is clearly not the position (and indeed Mr Hart did not suggest as much, making the more modest submission that it was one of a number of pointers suggesting that common law claims may survive). Both Lord Nicholls at [22] and Lord Hoffmann at [52] referred to the effect of s. 18(8) as not ruling out or excluding Mr Marcic's claims, but went on to hold that this did not answer the question whether his common law claims in

nuisance survived. That depended on whether they would be consistent with the statutory scheme, and both held that they would not be.

54   As noted above, part of that statutory scheme is that the apparently mandatory nature of the obligation in s. 18(1) to make a final enforcement order is qualified by s. 19(1)(c) where the Secretary of State or Ofwat is satisfied that their Part I duties preclude them from making an order. Part I of the Act establishes Ofwat and imposes various duties on it and the Secretary of State. This includes, by s. 2, general duties with respect to the water industry. So far as relevant s. 2 provides as follows:

> **"2. General duties with respect to water industry.**
> (1) This section shall have effect for imposing duties on the Secretary of State and on the Authority as to when and how they should exercise and perform the powers and duties conferred or imposed on the Secretary of State or the Authority by virtue of any of the relevant provisions.
> (2A) The Secretary of State or, as the case may be, the Authority shall exercise and perform the powers and duties mentioned in subsection (1) above in the manner which he or it considers is best calculated–
> > (a) to further the consumer objective;
> > (b) to secure that the functions of a water undertaker and of a sewerage undertaker are properly carried out as respects every area of England and Wales;
> > (c) to secure that companies holding appointments under Chapter 1 of Part 2 of this Act as relevant undertakers are able (in particular, by securing reasonable returns on their capital) to finance the proper carrying out of those functions;
> > (d) to secure that the activities authorised by the licence of a water supply licensee or sewerage licensee and any statutory functions imposed on it in consequence of the licence are properly carried out; and
> > (e) to further the resilience objective.
> (2B) The consumer objective mentioned in subsection (2A)(a) above is to protect the interests of consumers, wherever appropriate by promoting effective competition between persons engaged in, or in commercial activities connected with, the provision of water and sewerage services.
> …
> (2DA) The resilience objective mentioned in subsection (2A)(e) is—
> > (a) to secure the long-term resilience of water undertakers' supply systems and sewerage undertakers' sewerage systems as regards environmental pressures, population growth and changes in consumer behaviour, and
> > (b) to secure that undertakers take steps for the purpose of enabling them to meet, in the long term, the need for the supply of water and the provision of sewerage services to consumers, including by promoting—
> > > (i) appropriate long-term planning and investment by relevant undertakers, and

(ii) the taking by them of a range of measures to manage water resources in sustainable ways, and to increase efficiency in the use of water and reduce demand for water so as to reduce pressure on water resources.

...

(4) In exercising any of the powers or performing any of the duties mentioned in subsection (1) above in accordance with the preceding provisions of this section, the Secretary of State and the Authority shall have regard to the principles of best regulatory practice (including the principles under which regulatory activities should be transparent, accountable, proportionate, consistent and targeted only at cases in which action is needed).

..."

55   This means, as noted by Lord Nicholls in *Marcic*, that the duties imposed by Part I may preclude the making of an order. This would cover a case where Ofwat considered that making an order would be incompatible with the policy objectives mentioned in s. 2, such as securing that an undertaker is able, by securing a reasonable return on its capital, to finance the proper discharge of its functions: *Marcic* at [15]. A contravention of a statutory requirement to which s. 18 applies does not therefore necessarily result in an enforcement order; other considerations which Ofwat is obliged to have regard to may be inconsistent with it making an enforcement order: *Marcic* at [16]. (The wording of s. 2 has been amended since the decision in *Marcic* but not so as to affect the points Lord Nicholls there makes).

56   The other provisions of the WIA 1991 to which reference should be made are those containing the foul water provisos. The first of these is s. 117(5), which provides as follows:

"(5) Nothing in sections 102 to 109 above or in sections 111 to 116 above shall be construed as authorising a sewerage undertaker to construct or use any public or other sewer, or any drain or outfall—
(a) in contravention of any applicable provision of the Water Resources Act 1991 or the Environmental Permitting (England and Wales) Regulations 2016 (S.I. 2016/1154); or
(b) for the purpose of conveying foul water into any natural or artificial stream, watercourse, canal, pond or lake, without the water having been so treated as not to affect prejudicially the purity and quality of the water in the stream, watercourse, canal, pond or lake."

57   The second is s. 186(3), which provides as follows:

"(3) Nothing in the relevant sewerage provisions shall authorise a sewerage undertaker injuriously to affect—
(a) any reservoir, canal, watercourse, river or stream, or any feeder thereof; or
(b) the supply, quality or fall of water contained in, or in any feeder of, any reservoir, canal, watercourse, river or stream,
without the consent of any person who would, apart from this Act, have been entitled by law to prevent, or be relieved against, the injurious affection of, or of the supply, quality or fall of water contained in, that reservoir, canal, watercourse, river, stream or feeder."

58   There is a definition of relevant sewerage provisions in s. 219(1). It is not
necessary to set it all out. Mr Hart relied in particular on the fact that it includes
both s. 106 and s. 116 (both of which are also among the provisions referred to in
s. 117(5)): s. 106 is the section which now provides for the right of an owner or
occupier of premises to have his drains or sewer communicate with the public
sewer of any sewerage undertaker and thereby to discharge foul or surface water
from his premises, and s. 116 is the section which now prevents a sewerage
undertaker from discontinuing a sewer used by anyone without providing a
substitute, as follows:

> **"116. Power to close or restrict use of public sewer.**
>
> (1) Subject to subsection (3) below, a sewerage undertaker may discontinue
> and prohibit the use of any public sewer which is vested in the undertaker.
>
> (2) A discontinuance or prohibition under this section may be for all
> purposes, for the purpose of foul water drainage or for the purpose of surface
> water drainage.
>
> (3) Before any person who is lawfully using a sewer for any purpose is
> deprived under this section by a sewerage undertaker of the use of the sewer
> for that purpose, the undertaker shall—
>
>> (a) provide a sewer which is equally effective for his use for that
>> purpose; and
>>
>> (b) at the undertaker's own expense, carry out any work necessary to
>> make that person's drains or sewers communicate with the sewer
>> provided in pursuance of this subsection.
>
> (4) Any dispute arising under subsection (3)(a) above between a sewerage
> undertaker and any other person as to the effectiveness of any sewer
> provided by the undertaker for that person's use may be referred to the
> Authority for determination under section 30A above by either party to the
> dispute."

59   It is now possible to consider the submissions advanced by Mr Hart under Ground
1. His argument was that Fancourt J was wrong to hold (i) that any breach of the
foul water provisos necessarily involved a breach of the general duty in s. 94(1)(b),
and (ii) that that breach meant that the s. 18 enforcement procedure operated to the
exclusion of private law remedies.

60   As to the first part of this submission, Mr Hart asserted it but did not really
explain it. The complaint that MSCC makes is that UU is discharging sewage into
the canal which is either entirely untreated (in the case of combined sewer
overflows, storm tank overflows and emergency overflows) or inadequately treated
(in the case of discharges from sewage works) in breach of the foul water provisos.
By definition it is MSCC's case that each such discharge, even if diluted by
rainwater and/or screened, is such as to affect prejudicially or injuriously affect
the purity or quality of the water in the canal. The duty on a sewerage undertaker
under s. 94(1)(b) includes a duty to make such provision as is necessary from time
to time for effectually dealing with the contents of its sewers. As a matter of
ordinary language it is difficult to see how it can be said that this duty has been
complied with if the contents of the sewers are allowed to discharge into the canal
in breach of the foul water provisos.

61   A similar view was taken by Ramsey J in *Dobson v Thames Water Utilities Ltd*
[2007] EWHC 2021 (TCC) ("*Dobson*") which concerned a complaint by local

residents arising from the operation by Thames of its Mogden sewage works. Ramsey J held that on the natural meaning of the phrase the contents of sewers had not been effectually dealt with when they caused odours and mosquitoes, one of the purposes of the requirement being to treat the sewage in such a way as to render it reasonably harmless and inoffensive: see at [73]-[74]. We received little argument on this aspect of the case but that seems to me to be right. At any rate, we were not given any example of a discharge which could be at the same time a breach of the foul water provisos but nevertheless an effectual dealing with the contents of the sewers.

62   Mr Hart had another way of putting the point when he said that if the discharges were unauthorised UU could hardly say that it was performing, albeit imperfectly, its s. 94 duties so as to exclude all consideration of its lack of authority. But I have not understood that point. UU is under duties under s. 94 to provide a system of public sewers, to maintain the sewers to ensure that the area is and continues to be effectually drained, to make provision for the emptying of the sewers, and to make such provision as is necessary for effectually dealing with their contents. The sewerage system which UU inherited on privatisation, including the outfalls in question, together with such improvements as it has made since, is the means by which UU seeks to perform those duties. That may or may not lead to unauthorised discharges in breach of the foul water provisos. But if it does, I do not see why it follows that this is not an imperfect performance of its s. 94 duties. That seems to me precisely what it is. UU may be (and as I have already said in my view would be) in breach of its s. 94 duties if there are unauthorised discharges, but that does not mean that the discharges are not part, albeit an inadequate part, of the way it seeks to carry out its duties.

63   But I do not think it is necessary to reach a definitive conclusion on the first part of Mr Hart's submissions on Ground 1. Even if it were the case that there were some unauthorised discharges which did not put UU in breach of its s. 94 duty, that does not answer the real question which is whether a claim in tort is inconsistent with the statutory scheme as a whole. Mr Hart accepted that an unauthorised discharge might well be a breach of s. 94 but said that the same act might give rise to two separate wrongs with two separate legal consequences, one a failure to deal with the contents of sewers (a matter for Ofwat under s. 18), and the other a discharge in breach of the foul water provisos (a matter of which MSCC could complain). He said that there was no essential clash between the common law position and the statutory position.

64   The difficulty that I have with this submission is that it seems to me to fly in the face of the decision in *Marcic*. The very essence of the decision is that there was a clash between permitting Mr Marcic to sue a sewerage undertaker at common law and the statutory scheme. I do not see why it is any less inconsistent to allow MSCC to sue UU for trespass (or nuisance) for operating a sewerage system that discharges untreated sewage into the canal in breach of the foul water provisos than it was to allow Mr Marcic to sue Thames for nuisance for operating a sewerage system that flooded his garden with untreated sewage. I will revert below to how Mr Hart sought to distinguish *Marcic* but to say that an act may be both a breach of statutory duty and a separate tort, each with their own legal consequences, does not seem to me to provide an answer to the question. Of course it may, but the question is whether it is consistent with the statute for the tortious remedy to be

available. Unless the case can be sufficiently distinguished from *Marcic*, the answer must be that it is not.

65   Mr Hart referred to a number of authorities with a view to persuading us that there was an established line of authority under the previous legislation to the effect that a discharge in breach of the (then) foul water provisos, or analogous provisos, was tortious. I can deal with these relatively briefly, as none of them discusses the *Marcic* question, that is whether a claim in tort was inconsistent with the statutory scheme.

66   In *Pride of Derby and Derbyshire Angling Association Ltd v British Celanese Ltd* [1953] Ch. 149 the plaintiffs succeeded at trial in a claim in nuisance against, among others, the Derby Corporation on the ground that it was discharging insufficiently treated sewage into the River Derwent from sewage works which it had constructed under a private Act, the Derby Corporation Act 1901. An appeal to this Court was dismissed. Evershed MR said (at 163) that if a public authority so exercises any of its functions as to cause a private nuisance it is liable to be sued unless it can rely on some statute as providing by express language or necessary or proper inference a defence to such an action. The defence that was set up was the 1901 Act. But this contained, in s. 113, a proviso that nothing in that part of the Act should authorize the corporation to construct any works or do any thing in contravention of s. 17 PHA 1875 (set out at paragraph 27 above), and all three judges said that there would in those circumstances be no defence of statutory authority available to the corporation: see per Evershed MR at 180, Denning LJ at 191 and Romer LJ at 193.

67   That illustrates that if an Act says that nothing in it authorises the discharge of untreated sewage into a watercourse, then it cannot be said that the Act confers statutory authority to do exactly that. But that is not the defence relied on here. UU does not say that it has statutory authority to discharge foul water in breach of the provisos, any more than Thames said it had statutory authority to flood Mr Marcic's garden. UU accepts that discharges in breach of the provisos are unauthorised. UU's defence is that to permit MSCC to sue in tort would be inconsistent with the statutory scheme. This point was not run in *Pride of Derby* and unsurprisingly the case says nothing about it.

68   In *Radstock Co-Operative and Industrial Society Ltd v Norton-Radstock UDC* [1968] 1 Ch. 605, the plaintiffs owned a bridge over the river Somer. A sewer vested in the defendant authority which had been laid in the bed of the river had become exposed due to increased flow in the river, and the resulting turbulence damaged the plaintiffs' bridge. They brought a claim relying on a number of causes of action, one of which was breach of s. 331 PHA 1936. This section (the predecessor of s. 186(3) WIA 1991) provided:

> "Nothing in this Act shall authorise a local authority injuriously to affect any reservoir, canal, watercourse, river or stream, or any feeder thereof, or the supply, quality or fall of water contained in, or in any feeder of, any reservoir, canal, watercourse, river or stream without the consent of any person who would, if this Act had not been passed, have been entitled by law to prevent, or be relieved against, the injurious affection of, or of the supply, quality or fall of water contained in, that reservoir, canal, watercourse, river, stream or feeder."

All three members of this Court held that this section did not confer a cause of action. Harman LJ said that it "merely preserves the common law rights of persons injuriously affected and does not arise in the absence of nuisance" (at 628); Russell LJ that a claim cannot be founded on s. 331 "for that section is a mere saving of common law rights" (at 631); and Sachs LJ (in a dissenting judgment) that the section "manifestly preserves the relevant rights of riparian owners as regards nuisance" (at 640). But none of them was dealing the question whether a claim in nuisance would be inconsistent with the statutory scheme, something that was not suggested in that case.

69   Similarly, in *BWB* Mr Hart pointed to the statement by Keene LJ at [84] that the foul water provisos in s. 117(5) and s. 186(3) "are there to make it clear that their common law remedies [i.e. those of persons affected by a discharge], particularly in nuisance, are not affected by the exercise of the statutory powers referred to." But this was another case decided before *Marcic* and Keene LJ was not considering the present question. He was considering whether the existence of the provisos supported an argument that the pipe-laying power in s. 159 WIA 1991 conferred an implied power to discharge. The question of quite what the consequences would be of a discharge in breach of the provisos was not before him.

70   Finally on this aspect of the appeal, Mr Hart referred to the decision of the Supreme Court in *MSCC* (2014). There Lord Sumption at [2] said that discharge into a private watercourse is an unlawful trespass unless authorised by statute, and at [17] that unless entitlement to discharge from existing outfalls into private watercourses survived the transfer to privatised water undertakers, the consequence is that in law such discharge must cease forthwith on 1 December 1991 and any continuing discharge thereafter would become tortious from that date. That undoubtedly proceeds on the basis that a discharge without either consent of the landowner or statutory authority is tortious and a trespass, and as a general proposition that is no doubt the case. It does not address the *Marcic* question whether any liability that would otherwise subsist in tort is inconsistent with the statutory scheme, and although *Marcic* is recorded as having been cited in argument, there is no trace in the judgments of there having been any argument about the principle.

71   Mr Hart also pointed to the fact that Lord Sumption referred in his judgment at [22] to the WIA 1991 as containing a large number of protections against the abusive or harmful use by undertakers of their statutory powers, the most important being those in s. 117(5) and s. 186(3), and submitted that on UU's argument the provisos do not in fact confer any significant protection on third parties such as MSCC. But Lord Sumption also said that that was not the place to examine them, and I do not think much can be derived from what he said. What can be said is that UU's argument is not concerned with deliberate abuse of powers (for example taking positive steps to divert untreated sewage into water) nor with the negligent exercise of powers. UU's argument is that it cannot be held responsible for unauthorised discharges where these happen without any deliberate or negligent action on its part.

72   Mr Hart said that the authorities established that the effect of the provisos in the pre-1991 legislation was that the person affected could bring common-law claims, and that in those circumstances it would be surprising if the WIA 1991, a consolidation Act, had altered the position to take this right away, without saying so expressly. But this is an example of the truism that a case is only authority for

what it decides. Since none of these cases considered the *Marcic* question, none of them is authority as to whether claims in tort were in fact consistent with the pre-1991 statutory schemes. That is a question which does not arise in the present case (and is unlikely now ever to do so). But whatever the position under the pre-1991 legislation, the *Marcic* principle undoubtedly does exist under the WIA 1991 as that is what the House of Lords decided in *Marcic*. The question is whether it applies to the unauthorised discharges, and that is a question of how broad a principle it is, which is the subject of Ground 2.

73   Before turning to that ground, I will summarise my conclusions on Ground 1. Had it not been for the decision in *Marcic*, Mr Hart's arguments – namely (i) that a discharge into a private watercourse in breach of the foul water proviso without the consent of the owner was unauthorised by statute and a common law wrong and (ii) that s. 18(8) WIA 1991 preserved the owner's right to sue in tort for that wrong even if the discharge was also a breach of s. 94 – would have appeared to have considerable force. But *Marcic* shows that in certain cases the existence of a private law right to sue a sewerage undertaker in tort is inconsistent with the statutory scheme and such a right must be regarded as impliedly ousted. The question is whether this is one of those cases. I do not see that that question is answered, as Mr Hart submitted it was, by the fact that in the present case we are concerned with a breach of the foul water provisos which were not in issue in *Marcic*. That breach establishes that the discharges are not authorised by statute, thereby negating any suggestion that the WIA 1991 conferred statutory authority on UU to discharge foul water into the canal. But it can scarcely be suggested that Thames had statutory authority to flood Mr Marcic's garden with sewage. That was not their defence to his claim (as Fancourt J noted at Jmt [82]). Their defence was that any claim in tort was ousted by the statute as being inconsistent with the statutory scheme.

74   Mr Hart submitted that a case where an undertaker was acting outside the powers set out in the statute was an entirely different legal situation from a case where an undertaker was simply in breach of s. 94. But I do not see that there is any fundamental difference. In each case the undertaker is doing something in breach of its obligations under the WIA 1991. In *Marcic* Thames was required by statute to ensure that its area was effectually drained and failed to do so with the result that sewage was discharged onto Mr Marcic's property. In the present case UU is required by statute not to act in breach of the foul water provisos but did so (or may have done so) with the result that sewage was discharged into MSCC's canal. In each case the explanation put forward by the undertaker is the same: this is the result of the infrastructure we have inherited and not something for which we can be made responsible (at any rate by way of a claim in tort). I do not see the two situations as entirely different. Whether there are any relevant differences at all turns in my view on the breadth of the *Marcic* principle (which is the subject of Ground 2) and not simply on the fact that this is a case concerned with the provisos and *Marcic* was not.

75   I would dismiss this ground of appeal.

Ground 2 – breadth of the Marcic principle

76   Fancourt J held (Jmt at [83]) that *Marcic* stood as authority for a broad principle as follows: "83. Seventh, *Marcic* was clearly decided as a matter of construction

of the 1991 Act, not simply affirming the old sewerage authorities. Both Lord Nicholls and Lord Hoffmann conclude that a claim in nuisance – where the only remedy for the nuisance is the construction of a better sewerage system – cannot co-exist with the statutory scheme in that Act. *Marcic* therefore stands for a broad principle derived from the structure of the 1991 Act, not a narrow principle that there is no claim in nuisance for failure to build more sewers."

77   Mr Hart criticised this statement. He said that the ratio of the decision in *Marcic* was to be found in Lord Hoffmann's speech at [52]-[54] where he referred to a line of authority that consistently held that failure to construct new sewers was not a nuisance, and that Lord Nicholls took things no wider.

78   I have had some difficulty in understanding the distinction that Mr Hart sought to draw. It is true that both Lord Hoffmann (at [52]-[54]) and Lord Nicholls (at [34]-[35]) characterised Mr Marcic's claim as being in effect that Thames should have built more sewers. But that was not his complaint in legal terms. His complaint was that the flooding of his garden with sewage was an interference with the reasonable enjoyment of his land and hence a nuisance. What both Lord Hoffmann and Lord Nicholls meant was that in practical terms the only way to stop that was to build more sewers: see per Lord Nicholls at [34]:

> "Mr Marcic's claim is expressed in various ways but in practical terms always comes down to this: Thames Water ought to build more sewers."

I do not see that it is any different here. MSCC's complaint is that the discharges into its canal are either a trespass or a nuisance. But in practical terms the only way to prevent that is for UU to build more infrastructure. This was the conclusion that Fancourt J reached on the evidence, as expressed by him as follows (Jmt at [49]):

> "49. It is important to appreciate that any such occurrences of unlawful discharge are not the result of anything done by UU: they are the result of heavy rainfall that causes the capacity of the sewerage infrastructure to be exceeded. That is the effect of the evidence that I have accepted. UU cannot refuse to allow surface or foul water to enter its sewers and it cannot simply close off the outfalls; nor can it lawfully store or release the excessive contents elsewhere, except by constructing a new, more capacious system at huge cost. The entry of foul discharge rather than adequately treated effluent into the Canal is therefore involuntary. UU has done nothing to cause or permit it to happen except abstain from building a more capacious or different system."

79   There is no challenge to that factual conclusion, and indeed in answer to a question from the Court, Mr Hart accepted in terms that in effect his complaint was that UU should build more sewers. He later qualified that by saying that although that was the nub of it, MSCC was not in fact seeking to compel UU to build more sewers; its aim was to be able to charge UU a rent or fee for the right to discharge into the canal. I accept that that is what MSCC hopes to achieve by the proceedings. But that does not affect the fact that what MSCC complains of is that UU's existing sewerage system is inadequate. It is in that sense that in effect what MSCC is saying is that UU should have built a larger or better system. I do not see that that is materially different from *Marcic*. And the fact that all MSCC actually wants is money, and the claim in trespass is a means of putting itself in a commercial position to negotiate a fee, does not seem to me to change the position. Indeed as I have mentioned (paragraph 38 above) by the time *Marcic* reached the

House of Lords, all Mr Marcic wanted was money (in his case compensation for past flooding and for the costs he had incurred), but his claim still failed.

80   I would therefore dismiss Ground 2.

Ground 3 – effect of foul water provisos

81   Ground 3 is that on Fancourt J's interpretation there is little or no point to the foul water provisos.

82   Fancourt J dealt with this point in two places. First (Jmt at [76]) he said this:

> "76. First, ss. 117(5) and 186(3), on which MSC principally relies, do not confer or preserve a distinct right of action for a person affected by unlawful discharge of foul water into a watercourse. They provide that the exercise by a sewerage undertaker of any of the powers identified in those subsections does not of itself confer on the undertaker an immunity from private law action. That is to say, the specified powers are not to be construed as providing that an undertaker may (without fault) commit a nuisance. The purpose of the subsections is accordingly to remove any argument based on the principle in *Allen v Gulf Oil Refining Ltd* [1981] A.C. 1001 that an undertaker has a defence of statutory authority. They are, to that extent, provisions that can be said in broad terms to preserve rights of those riparian owners intended to be protected, but they are not an answer to the question whether, as a matter of construction of the 1991 Act, a private law claim in nuisance can be maintained on the facts of individual cases, any more than the preservation of other remedies by s. 18(8) gave Mr Marcic a valid claim in nuisance." Then (Jmt at [89]) he said this:

>> "89. Finally, UU's interpretation of the 1991 Act might be said to be vulnerable to the argument that the statutory provisos are ineffective if claims in nuisance (or trespass) are ousted on a true construction of the Act. Clearly, the statutory provisos were intended to have some effect beyond signalling that an undertaker would have no defence of implied authority to a claim that an owner had no entitlement to bring. A defence of implied authority would only avail an undertaker that had taken reasonable care to exercise its powers so as not to cause the harm in question, not an undertaker that had acted negligently. However, as indicated in *Dobson*, there might be cases of non-negligent failures where a defence of implied authority could avail an undertaker and where the claim in nuisance might not be excluded as conflicting with the statutory machinery for enforcement of its s.94 duty. There is therefore scope for the statutory provisos to have some effect. In any event, one purpose of them is to make clear to an undertaker that it is not permitted to pollute watercourses."

83   Mr Hart said of the first passage that the problem with it was that there is little point in removing any argument based on *Allen v Gulf Oil Refining* [1981] A.C. 1001 if there could never be a civil claim in which that defence could arise in any event. The *Allen v Gulf Oil* principle was expressed by Lord Wilberforce at 1011E-H as being that when Parliament authorised the construction and use of an undertaking or works, then that carried with it an authority to do what is authorised, with immunity from any action based on nuisance. It is a condition of the principle that

the statutory powers are exercised without "negligence", here meaning that the undertaker is required, as a condition of obtaining immunity from action, to carry out the work and conduct the operation with all reasonable regard and care for the interests of other persons. The defence of statutory authority therefore only applies to nuisance committed without negligence (in this particular sense). But, Mr Hart said, UU's case is that all such claims are precluded by the *Marcic* principle in any event in which case the provisos achieved nothing.

84   Fancourt J was clearly alive to this point, as this is what he addresses in the second passage, where he identifies that a defence of implied authority only applies to an undertaker that has acted non-negligently. Here he tentatively suggested that there might be non-negligent failures that did not benefit from the *Marcic* principle, as suggested by Dobson. Mr Hart said that was difficult to understand as in *Dobson* all the claims were in fact based on negligence. But I do not think that was what Fancourt J was referring to. What he was referring to (as is clear from Jmt [87]-[88]) is the distinction suggested by Ramsey J in *Dobson* at [140] between "policy" or "capital expenditure" matters or decisions on the one hand (to which the *Marcic* principle would apply) and "operational" or "current expenditure" matters (to which it would not). It seems tolerably clear to me that what Fancourt J had in mind was that despite *Marcic* there might be room for an allegation in relation to an operational as opposed to a policy matter where the defence of statutory authority might have been argued to be available were it not for the provisos.

85   We heard no argument on this suggested distinction between policy and operational matters, and it was not suggested that the allegations that MSCC makes of trespass in fact fall on the operational side of the line. In those circumstances it is not necessary to express any concluded views on it, and I would be reluctant to do so. But for the reasons I have given I do not think this particular criticism of Fancourt J is made out.

86   Mr Hart said that even so there remained the general point that UU's case gave the provisos a more limited effect than they had had under the pre-1991 legislation and there was no indication that the WIA 1991 had been intended to have this effect: the provisos were in effect the same old provisos, and with the exception of the more complex enforcement procedures, the structure of the WIA 1991 was effectively the same.

87   I accept that the application of the *Marcic* principle to the unauthorised discharges in question does diminish the role of the provisos and leave it rather unclear what the practical effect of them now is. But Parliament has included similar provisions in the legislation governing sewerage authorities since 1875 and has thereby consistently made it clear that it does not wish them to discharge foul water into watercourses and is not authorising them to do so. As the facts of this and other cases illustrate, Parliament's expectations in that respect have been regularly disappointed as a result of lack of capacity in the sewerage system to cope with increased demand. But there is no reason to think that when the water industry was privatised in 1989, or when the legislation was consolidated in 1991, Parliament's concerns in this respect had diminished. On the contrary, the February 1986 White Paper set out the Government's intention to provide a "clearer strategic framework for the protection of the water environment" and in its July 1987 proposal for the NRA the Government referred to its commitment to ensure that arrangements for privatisation "should also provide for the effective maintenance or, where practicable and necessary, enhancement of the quality of our rivers" and other watercourses.

88   In those circumstances it seems to me entirely understandable that Parliament should wish to reproduce the provisos in the WIA 1991, a consolidation Act, rather than remove them. To deliberately remove them as part of the consolidation exercise would suggest that Parliament was no longer concerned to prevent such discharges, which would have been an odd thing to do. It is not difficult to believe that the precise legal effect of the provisos in the WIA 1991 Act was not something that was actively considered at the time: it is only the decision in *Marcic*, some years later, and its application to unauthorised discharges in the present case, that has exposed the limited continuing role of the provisos. That does not seem to me to be a sufficient basis on which to infer that Parliament intended that common law claims should survive, or a sufficient reason not to apply the *Marcic* principle.

89   I would therefore dismiss Ground 3.

Grounds 4 and 5 – trespass

90   Grounds 4 and 5 can be taken together. Ground 4 is that Fancourt J was wrong to find that the unauthorised discharges were involuntary. Ground 5 is that he was wrong to find that a purely involuntary act is not an act of trespass.

91   In the light of the conclusions I have already come to, I do not think these grounds assist MSCC in any event, as even if UU's discharges would otherwise have been actionable as trespasses, the application of the *Marcic* principle prevents MSCC from suing on them. But I will briefly address the issues on the assumption that the *Marcic* principle does not apply.

92   The starting point is that if A deliberately discharges water onto B's land that is (absent B's consent or any statutory or other right to do it) a trespass. To take an example discussed in argument, if A throws a bucket of water into B's garden, or points his hose at it, that is a trespass. Next, if A builds on his land in such a way that water will from time to time be discharged onto B's land, that would seem equally clearly a trespass. So if A builds his house so that the roof discharges rainwater onto B's land that would seem to be a trespass, even though the rain is intermittent, and even though once A has built it, A is not actively doing anything. Third, some trespasses are continuing. If A parks his car on B's land that is a trespass on the day it is parked, but it is also a trespass every day that A leaves the car there. If it were not so, it is difficult to see how B could obtain an injunction to have A remove the car, or indeed damages for each day it remains, but it seems obvious that in principle B could claim both. Similarly if A builds his house in such a way that part of it is built over the boundary on B's land, that is a trespass on the day it is built, but it is also a trespass every day that A leaves it there, and I would have thought there was no doubt that B could claim damages for each day the building remained on his land and (subject to discretionary considerations) obtain an injunction to have it removed. So too if A builds his house in such a way as to discharge rainwater onto B's land, it seems to me that there will be a trespass on each day that the water is so discharged even if A does nothing positive on those days.

93   The next question is whether a successor in title to A is also liable for trespass even if he does nothing. Suppose for example that A dies and leaves his house to C, or that A sells it to C, is C liable for trespass? The answer here is not quite so obvious, as C has neither built the house nor done anything at all; he has merely acquired an infringing structure. Again however it seems to me that C would be

liable. Otherwise B would simply have to put up with a continuing trespass on his land, which does not seem right, and might even lead to C in due course acquiring either a title to adverse possession (in the case of the house being built over the boundary) or an easement of eavesdrop by prescription (in the case of the roof discharging water). I consider that B could obtain an order requiring C to remove the building (or modify it so as to prevent it discharging water onto B's land), and that this could only be so if C were guilty of a trespass by leaving it there.

94   If that is right, the question is whether (on the assumption the *Marcic* principle does not apply) UU is in any different position. It too has acquired an existing structure which repeatedly discharges onto MSCC's property without MSCC's consent or any statutory authority. Why is UU not equally liable as C would be?

95   The answer that Fancourt J gave can be seen from the Judgment at [49] (cited at paragraph 78 above), namely that UU cannot refuse to allow surface or foul water to enter its sewers and it cannot simply close off the outfalls. That is a reference to the provision now found in s. 116 WIA 1991 (set out at paragraph 58 above). Fancourt J characterised UU's position as "involuntary" and held that as a matter of law a purely involuntary act is not an act of trespass, citing Clerk & Lindsell on Torts (23rd ed) at §18-07 (Jmt at [50]). The examples there given are of a person being forcibly carried onto the plaintiff's land (*Smith v Stone* (1647) Sty. 65) or falling onto railway tracks in an epileptic fit (*Public Transport Commission v NSW v Perry* 137 C.L.R. 107). Mr Hart said that those cases were a long way from the present case where UU's system is designed in such a way that it will regularly discharge untreated effluent into the canal in certain circumstances.

96   Nevertheless Mr Hart accepted that UU's system had (as all such systems must do) a finite capacity, and he accepted that there would be occasions when there would be exceptional flows which exceeded the capacity. He said that it should not be assumed that all the discharges from the outfalls were of the same character: there were a series of different outfalls (combined sewer overflows, storm tank overflows, emergency overflows and outfalls from treatment works) and it should not be thought that all the discharges from each outfall were on every occasion necessarily involuntary in the sense used by Fancourt J. But he did not dispute that some of them at least would be.

97   It is not necessary to reach any final conclusion on the point as it makes no difference to the outcome of the appeal but I think Fancourt J was right that in circumstances where UU cannot lawfully do anything to prevent the discharges they are to be regarded as involuntary and not trespasses at all. It is not like the case of the house acquired by C where C can always pull down or modify the house. If UU did not build the outfalls and cannot remove them (and assuming on the facts the discharges are not the result of any deliberate decisions made by UU or any negligence) then that does seem to me to be an involuntary invasion of MSCC's rights in the canal.

98   In those circumstances I would dismiss these grounds of appeal as well.

Interveners' submissions

99   The interveners made written submissions in support of the appeal. They summarised their points as follows:

(1) The natural reading of the foul water provisos is that they preserve common law rights in relation to polluting discharges into watercourses.

I have already in effect addressed this submission above when considering MSCC's Ground 1: see in particular paragraph 73 above.

(2) On Fancourt J's interpretation the provisos would be otiose. I have addressed this under MSCC's Ground 3 above.

(3) *Marcic* does not compel the conclusion that Fancourt J reached. I have addressed this under MSCC's Ground 2 above.

(4) There is a critical difference between *Marcic* and the present case in that there exists a parallel regime of criminal law environmental regulation under which an undertaker may need to invest in infrastructure.

100   The last is a point I have not yet addressed. I do not think it is sufficient to distinguish *Marcic*. The question that *Marcic* requires to be asked is whether the existence of common law remedies in tort "would be incompatible with the statutory scheme and therefore could not have been intended [to] co-exist with it": *R. (Child Poverty Action Group) v Secretary of State for Work and Pensions* [2010] UKSC 54 at [34] per Dyson JSC. In *Marcic* that incompatibility was found where in effect the complaint was that Thames should have built more sewers, because "it would subvert the scheme of the 1991 Act if the courts were to impose upon sewerage undertakers, on a case by case basis, a system of priorities which is different from that which the director considers appropriate" (per Lord Hoffmann at [70]). I do not see that the fact that the statutory scheme also includes a system of criminal regulation (with various remedies for breaches of the relevant regulations) weakens or makes inapplicable this incompatibility.

Conclusion on 2018 appeal

101   Neither the grounds of appeal advanced by MSCC nor such additional points as were made by the interveners persuade me that Fancourt J was wrong. I would dismiss the 2018 appeal.

102   UU served a Respondent's notice seeking to uphold the judgment on alternative grounds, but in the light of my conclusion it is not necessary to consider it.

Facts – the 2010 proceedings

103   There are 5 outfalls where MSCC's case is that they were the subject of contractual agreements which have now been terminated. These are as follows:

(1) Outfall 23 – agreement dated 5 September 1939
By agreement between MSCC and the Runcorn Rural District Council the Council agreed to pay MSCC the annual rent or sum of £1.1.0 in consideration of MSCC permitting the Council to lay and maintain an outfall pipe for the purpose of discharging storm water into the canal and on 6 months' notice to entirely remove or put an end to, or permit MSCC at the Council's expense to remove or put an end to, such privilege.

(2) Outfall 26 – agreement dated 2 March 1916
By agreement made between MSCC and the Runcorn Rural District Council, MSCC permitted the Council to lay a storm overflow into the canal, the Council agreeing to pay MSCC an annual rent of 5/- so long as the easement was allowed to remain. The Council also undertook to remove and put an end

to the easement, or allow MSCC to do so, and to discontinue to exercise the same, on 6 months' notice in writing being given by MSCC.

(3) Outfall 35 – agreement dated 24 June 1955

By agreement between MSCC and the Warrington Corporation MSCC demised to the Corporation the right and liberty to construct and maintain a storm overflow drain and use it for discharging stormwater into the canal, paying an annual rent or sum of £3.3.0, until determined by 6 months' notice in writing by either party, with a covenant by the Corporation to remove the works on termination and a provision that in default it should be lawful for MSCC to remove them at its expense.

(4) Outfall 36 – agreement dated 17 November 1987

By agreement between MSCC and Warrington Borough Council MSCC granted licence and authority to the Council to discharge water into the canal from specified works for a term of 15 years and thereafter until determined by either party on not less than 12 months' notice in writing, paying a yearly sum of £1907. The Council agreed to remove the works on the determination of the licence, and that in case of any default by the Council MSCC should be entitled to carry out any required works at the Council's expense.

(In relation to this outfall there is in fact a dispute whether this agreement governs it, as MSCC contends, or whether it is governed by an agreement dated 21 December 1934 for a term of 99 years from 1 January 1935. Nothing turns on this for present purposes.)

(5) Outfall 67 – agreement dated 24 April 1933

By agreement made between MSCC and the Eccles Corporation, it was agreed that the Corporation should be at liberty to construct a stormwater overflow sewer into the canal, paying a yearly rent of £8. It provided that this privilege and licence should be determinable by MSCC at any time after 1 January 1963 on giving 6 months' notice in writing, on receipt of which the Corporation should remove such stormwater overflow sewer and reinstate MSCC's land, in default of which MSCC would be at liberty to do so at the Corporation's expense.

104   It may be noted that the wording of the agreements varies, being variously expressed as the grant of a privilege, licence, right or liberty, an easement or a demise. UU's pleaded case asserts that each of them takes effect as a tenancy subject to the Landlord and Tenant Act 1954 but we have heard no argument on this question. I will refer to them (as they were referred to in argument) as licences without prejudice to the question whether any or all of them in fact takes effect by way of a tenancy.

105   It may also be noted that not all these outfalls are of the same type. It is common ground on the pleadings that outfalls 35 and 36 are combined sewer overflows discharging foul water and surface water, but that outfalls 23 and 26 are surface water overflows discharging surface and rain water. There appears to be a dispute as to outfall 67: UU's pleaded case is that it is a surface water sewer but MSCC's pleaded case is that it is used as a combined sewer overflow.

106   MSCC has given notices terminating, or purporting to terminate, each of these licences, some in 2008 (outfalls 26, 35 and 67) and the others in 2010 (outfalls 23 and 36).

107   *MSCC*'s case is that the continued use of each outfall after termination of the relevant licence is a trespass. Various defences have been raised by UU, most of which we are not concerned with on this appeal, but UU has also pleaded in relation to each of these outfalls that insofar as the relevant licence requires it to stop up or remove any pipe that constitutes a public sewer then it is unenforceable.

108   It was agreed that this point should be heard as a preliminary issue and it was this that came before Fancourt J and which he determined in favour of UU. It is common ground that if the appeal is allowed, UU's other defences will have to be determined.

The 2010 proceedings: Fancourt J's decision

109   Fancourt J first decided that MSCC were not entitled to take a point that the licences were the grant of additional rights to pollute rather than agreements to document consensual drainage, on the basis that it was too late to do so (Jmt at [105]-[106]).

110   He then considered the substantive question, concluding that UU has the right to continue to drain through the relevant outfalls notwithstanding the notices to terminate that had been given (Jmt at [113]). His essential reasoning can be found in the following passage:

> "107. Mr Hart argued, alternatively, that there was no incompatibility between terminable rights conferred by the licences and performance of the authorities' statutory drainage duties, nor any fettering of their statutory powers. An authority had power to contract on terms that are of benefit to its activities but which make the contract terminable. Alternatively, it is not possible to sever the terms of the licences and enforce the agreement without the provisions for termination.
>
> 108. The licensed drainage therefore overlapped the historic implied statutory right to drain into a watercourse, but in my judgment once the outfalls had been built and were being used as a public sewer (which it is common ground the licensed outfalls are), the absolute obligation to cease use and reinstate (albeit on notice in most cases) is inconsistent with the duty on an authority to permit and facilitate drainage through public sewers with limited power to discontinue use.
>
> 109. I therefore consider that the termination and reinstatement provisions of the licences were void…"

111   It was common ground that this conclusion was dispositive of the claims. By his Order dated 15 June 2021 he therefore made a declaration in the following terms:

> "Notwithstanding the purported termination by the Canal Company of agreements or alleged agreements dated 5 September 1939, 2 March 1916, 24 June 1955, 17 November 1987 and 24 April 1933, United Utilities is and continues to be entitled to discharge water and/or other matter into the Manchester Ship Canal … from each of the outfalls numbered 23, 26, 35, 36 and 67 in Schedule 1 to the Defence and Counterclaim in the 2010 Proceedings."

The 2010 appeal: Grounds of appeal

112   There are two grounds of appeal, as follows:

> (1) Ground 1 is that Fancourt J erred in holding that MSCC was not entitled on the pleadings to take the point that the licences were the grant of additional rights to pollute rather than agreements to document consensual drainage.
>
> (2) Ground 2 is that Fancourt J erred in holding that the effect of the licences was to constitute an unlawful fetter on the exercise of relevant powers and duties by the respective local authority parties.

113   UU has served a Respondent's notice in which it seeks to uphold the order on the alternative ground that UU has an implied statutory right to discharge from the outfalls in question which survives the termination of the licences.

Ground 2 – ultra vires

114   Ground 1, a procedural point, was not argued extensively. I prefer to start with Ground 2 which was the focus of the oral argument.

115   The argument for upholding the decision of Fancourt J which was put forward by Mr Jonathan Karas QC (who appeared with Mr Richard Moules and Mr James McCreath for UU) proceeded by a series of steps. The first was that a local authority can only do that which they are authorised, expressly or by implication, to do. This is a well-established principle: see for example *R. v Somerset CC ex p. Fewings* [1995] 1 W.L.R. 1037 per Sir Thomas Bingham MR at 1042G-H. I did not understand it to be disputed by Mr Morgan (who argued the 2010 appeal for MSCC).

116   Second, it follows that in order to enter into the licences the local authorities here must have been granted statutory powers to do so either expressly or by implication. Again I did not understand the principle to be disputed, although there was some debate as to whether the relevant powers here were express or implied. It is common ground (and clearly the case) that the question has to be considered by reference to the statute in force when each licence was entered into which, as can be seen from their dates (paragraph 103 above), was either the PHA 1875 or the PHA 1936. Mr Morgan submitted that express powers to enter into them were to be found in s. 14 PHA 1875 and s. 15 PHA 1936.

117   s. 14 PHA 1875 provided as follows:

> **"14 Power to purchase sewers**
> Any local authority may purchase or otherwise acquire from any person, any sewer, or any right of making or of user or other right in or respecting a sewer (with or without any buildings works materials or things belonging thereto), within their district, and any person may sell or grant to such authority any such sewer right or property belonging to him; and any purchase money paid by such authority in pursuance of this section shall be subject to the same trusts (if any) as the sewer right or property sold was subject to.
> But any person who, previously to the purchase of a sewer by such authority, has acquired a right to use such sewer shall be entitled to use the same, or any sewer substituted in lieu thereof, to the same extent as he would or might have done if the purchase had not been made."

The primary purpose of this section (as the headnote, and the final sentence, suggest) was no doubt to confer power on local authorities to acquire existing sewers, but Mr Morgan submitted that the power to "acquire … any right of making … a sewer" was wide enough to enable them to enter into licences granting them permission to construct a new sewer with an outfall into the canal. As a matter of language I agree, and I am inclined to think that this section did confer a sufficient express power.

118   s. 15 PHA 1936 provided as follows:

> **"15 Provision of public sewers and sewage disposal works**
> (1) A local authority may within their district, and also, subject to the provisions of the next succeeding section, without their district—
>> (i) construct a public sewer—
>>> (a) in, under or over any street, or under any cellar or vault below any street, subject, however, to the provisions of Part XII of this Act with respect to the breaking open of streets; and
>>> (b) in, on or over any land not forming part of a street, after giving reasonable notice to every owner and occupier of that land;
>> (ii) construct sewage disposal works, on any land acquired, or lawfully appropriated, for the purpose;
>> (iii) by agreement acquire, whether by way of purchase, lease or otherwise, any sewer or sewage disposal works or the right to use any sewer or sewage disposal works."

Mr Morgan relied on s. 15(1)(iii) as the equivalent of s. 14 PHA 1875 and as conferring an express power on the local authorities to enter into the licences in question. That I think is a less promising submission as the sub-section only in terms confers a power to acquire by agreement a right to use a sewer, not a right to make a sewer, which is a noticeable omission given that s. 15(1)(i) and (ii) do both confer powers to construct.

119   But I do not think it ultimately matters. Mr Karas accepted that whether by virtue of an express power or an implied power the local authorities did have power to enter into agreements permitting them to construct sewers with outfalls into the canal. That was on the basis that it is a general principle that local authorities have an implied power to do anything reasonably necessary or incidental to the powers and duties expressly conferred on them, and that entering into contractual agreements permitting construction of sewers can properly be described as reasonably necessary to the performance of their duties (that is, the duty under s. 15 PHA 1875 and s. 14 PHA 1936 respectively to "cause to be made such sewers" (or in the case of the PHA 1936 "provide such public sewers") "as may be necessary for effectually draining their district").

120   I agree that there is no difficulty in implying the necessary power to construct sewers by agreement. Both under the PHA 1875 and under the PHA 1936 the local authorities had a statutory power to lay sewers. In the PHA 1936 that was found in s. 15(1)(i) (set out above). In the PHA 1875 it was found in s. 16 which was as follows:

> **"16 Powers for making sewers**
> Any local authority may carry any sewer through across or under any turnpike road, or any street or place laid out as or intended for a street, or under any

cellar or vault which may be under the pavement or carriageway of any street, and, after giving reasonable notice in writing to the owner or occupier (if on the report of the surveyor it appears necessary), into through or under any lands whatsoever within their district.

They may also (subject to the provisions of this Act relating to sewage works without the district of their local authority) exercise all or any of the powers given by this section without their district for the purpose of outfall or distribution of sewage."

But it would I think be surprising if the local authorities had been obliged to resort to compulsory powers (entailing the payment of compensation for any diminution in value) and could not have negotiated for a contractual licence instead. The licences contain more or less detailed provisions on a range of matters (the size and location of the pipe, the rights of MSCC and the like) as well as agreed annual payments, and it seems self-evident that it is preferable for such matters to be dealt with by consensual agreement rather than by the unilateral exercise of statutory powers. In *BWB* the Severn-Trent Water Authority had entered into a licence in 1976 and Chadwick LJ said (at [48]):

"It is not, I think, open to doubt – nor is it in dispute – that the water authority entered into the licence of 22 April 1976 for the purpose of enabling them to perform the duty imposed by section 14(1) of the 1973 Act."

The water authority's duty under s. 14 of the Water Act 1973 was again to "provide … such public sewers as may be necessary for effectually draining their area" and as can be seen Chadwick LJ thought it obvious that the agreement was entered into in performance of that duty. See too *MSCC* (2014) at [17] and [21] per Lord Sumption where he contemplated new rights of discharge being acquired by negotiation.

121   Mr Karas did not dispute that the local authorities had power to enter into the licences here: his contention, at any rate initially, was not that they were ultra vires and void from the outset, but that the provisions for stopping up the sewer on termination were void. The third step in his argument was that the local authorities could only agree to such provisions if they had power to do so under the legislation, and power to do that could only be implied if it was consistent with the legislation and specifically with the limitations on the powers of local authorities to discontinue sewers. These were found in s. 18 PHA 1875 and s. 22 PHA 1936 respectively.

122   s. 18 PHA 1875 provided as follows:

"18 Alteration and discontinuance of sewers
Any local authority may from time to time lessen alter the course of cover in or otherwise improve any sewer belonging to them, and may discontinue close up or destroy any such sewer that has in their opinion become unnecessary, on condition of providing a sewer as effectual for the use of any person who may be deprived in pursuance of this section of the lawful use of any sewer: Provided that the discontinuance closing up or destruction of any sewer shall be so done as not to create a nuisance."

123   s. 22 PHA 1936 provided as follows:

"22 Power of local authority to alter, or close, public sewers

A local authority may alter the size or course of any public sewer vested in them, or may discontinue and prohibit the use of any such public sewer, either entirely or for the purpose of foul water drainage, or for the purpose of surface water drainage, but, before any person who is lawfully using the sewer for any purpose is deprived by the authority of the use of the sewer for that purpose, they shall provide a sewer equally effective for his use for that purpose and shall at their expense carry out any work necessary to make his drains or sewers communicate with the sewer so provided."

124   Mr Karas said that the problem was that the licences contained an absolute obligation to discontinue and remove the relevant sewer. That he said was inconsistent with the obligations in s. 18 PHA 1875 and s. 22 PHA 1936 which only permitted a local authority to discontinue a sewer that was being used by anyone if another equally effectual were provided. Mr Morgan accepted that where a householder's sewage drained into the system and was discharged, even on an intermittent basis, through an overflow, that person could be said to be lawfully using the overflow. (I suppose it might have been argued that it was different where the overflow was not a combined sewer overflow but merely a surface water overflow which did not drain sewage, but we did not in fact hear any argument to that effect).

125   I have no difficulty with the proposition that it would have been ultra vires and beyond the powers of a local authority simply to agree to discontinue an existing sewer other than in accordance with these statutory provisions. Suppose for example a local authority had laid a sewer under its power in s. 16 PHA 1875. On the authority of Durrant that would have given it a right to discharge from the sewer into a watercourse (see paragraph 27 above). Neither the right to keep the sewer physically in place nor the right to discharge from it would be limited in time. If the local authority then purported to agree that it would discontinue and remove the sewer on being requested to do so and without regard to its obligations under s. 18 PHA 1875, I accept that that would have been inconsistent with its statutory obligations. Under s. 18 the local authority would have had power to discontinue the sewer but only on condition of providing a sewer that was as effectual for the use of any person who might be deprived of the user of it (and moreover, as Asplin LJ pointed out in argument, only if in their opinion it had become unnecessary, at any rate under the PHA 1875). To discontinue it without providing an equally effectual sewer (and in circumstances where they did not consider it had become unnecessary) would therefore be contrary to their statutory powers, and to agree to do so would be to agree to do something beyond their powers.

126   Where I have more difficulty however is seeing that this is an adequate account of what the local authorities have done by entering into the licences. On the primary way in which Mr Karas put his case, which was that the licences were valid but the termination provisions were not, the practical effect would be, as Mr Morgan said, to convert what was a precarious grant into a permanent deprivation of property. That seems to me to be a very striking consequence. It is of course the case that statute may confer on statutory bodies the right to acquire property rights compulsorily, albeit usually at the price of paying appropriate compensation. It is also the case that the ultra vires doctrine may have the effect of preventing local authorities from entering into certain contracts, and the risk that a purported contract

with a local authority may turn out to be beyond their powers and void is a risk that anyone dealing with local authorities takes. But I am not aware that it has previously been held (or even suggested) that the ultra vires doctrine can have the effect of turning a limited and determinable contractual right into a permanent one, and as far as I can see without any compensation being payable. That seems a new and different type of risk, namely that a person dealing with a local authority may find that they are bound by a contract they have entered into, but one with a much more far-reaching effect than they ever agreed. I would be very reluctant to reach the conclusion that this was the law unless compelled by authority to do so; but no authority was I think put before us where anything similar had been held to have taken place.

127   There is an analogy (although I accept it is quite a distant one) with *Stourcliffe Estates Co Ltd v Corporation of Bournemouth* [1910] 2 Ch. 12 where the Corporation acquired by agreement land for a public park subject to a covenant restricting them from erecting buildings. It was argued that the covenant was void as inconsistent with a statutory power that the Corporation had to build conveniences in public parks, but the argument was rejected. Cozens-Hardy MR said at 18:

> "But, further, if they have taken this conveyance of this land in terms subject to these restrictive covenants, can they hold it free from those restrictions? That again is a proposition which seems to me to be startling. If the deed is wholly ultra vires I can understand it, but to suppose that the corporation could be allowed to retain the land and to repudiate the consideration or part of the consideration for it is a proposition to which certainly I could not give my adhesion."

128   Similarly, once it is accepted, as Mr Karas did accept, that the local authorities had the power to acquire rights to construct sewers by agreement, then in my judgment there is no reason why they could not agree to acquire limited and determinable rights if that is what they were offered. They did not need to contract on those terms and could have relied on their statutory powers instead; but having chosen to contract on terms that they acquired a determinable, not a permanent, right, that in my view is all they acquired. If such a right is then determined in accordance with its terms, that is not in my view a case of the local authority choosing to exercise a discretionary power in s. 18 PHA 1875 (or its successors) to discontinue the sewer; it is simply the consequence of only having acquired a limited right in the first place. The point can be illustrated by the fact that in each of the licences MSCC reserved the right, if the local authority did not do so, to remove the sewer itself at the authority's expense. What is there to stop it from doing so? On its face s. 18 PHA 1875 merely imposed restrictions on the exercise of powers on local authorities, not on anybody else.

129   When it was put to Mr Karas that he was trying to say that the licences were good in parts and bad in parts, he said that he was content to contend in the alternative that the licences were wholly void from the outset, in which case he would claim that UU had acquired rights by prescription. I need not consider if they would have been able to do so (I can see certain difficulties in claiming a right by prescription if the putative grantee has been making annual payments in respect of it), as I do not accept the premise. Not only was this not the case advanced by Mr Karas before Fancourt J (and accepted by him), nor indeed initially before us, but it seems to me inconsistent with the acceptance that the local authorities had

power to acquire rights by agreement. It would amount to a contention that they had no power to acquire anything less than a permanent right. That would mean, for example, that even the 99 year licence would be of no effect at all. That is another proposition that I find surprising. As I have said I do not see why local authorities could not choose to accept a limited right if they wanted to. If they had thought such a right inadequate, they could have resorted to their statutory powers instead, but they might have thought that it was perfectly acceptable, and in some respects preferable, to have an agreed right, even if determinable, in the first instance in the knowledge that if it were ever determined they could always fall back on statutory powers later. Mr Karas suggested that 6 months was far too short for that purpose, but it is not self-evident that it would have been thought too short at the dates the licences were entered into.

130   In those circumstances I would accept that Ground 2 of this appeal is well founded, and, subject to the Respondent's notice point, allow the appeal. It is not necessary in those circumstances to consider Ground 1.

Respondent's notice – statutory right to continue discharging

131   By its Respondent's notice UU seeks to uphold the decision of Fancourt J on the alternative ground that it has an implied right under WIA 1991 to continue discharging from the outfalls. That is put in two ways:

(1) prior to the commencement of the WIA 1991 on 1 December 1991 UU as sewerage undertaker also benefited from a concurrent implied right of statutory discharge from the outfalls in question, which continued notwithstanding the termination of the licences; and/or

(2) such a right arose as a matter of implication on the commencement of the WIA 1991 and continued notwithstanding the termination.

132   Mr Karas relied on the decision of the Supreme Court in these proceedings in *MSCC* (2014). There the leading judgment was given by Lord Sumption (with whom Lords Clarke and Hughes agreed; Lord Toulson gave a concurring judgment in which he described his reasons as according essentially with those of Lord Sumption). Lord Sumption's analysis was as follows. By the time of the WIA 1991 there had been well over a century in which sewerage authorities were entitled as of right to construct and discharge from outfalls into private watercourses (that is under the powers initially in the PHA 1875, as interpreted in *Durrant*), and one would expect the degree of dependence to be significant. In those circumstances:

"unless the entitlement to discharge from existing outfalls into private watercourses survives the transfer to privatised water undertakers the consequence is that in law such discharge must cease forthwith on 1 December 1991"

(at [17]). When therefore the WIA 1991 imposed on the privatised sewerage undertakers duties which they could perform only by continuing for a substantial period to discharge from existing outfalls, and at the same time applied to them the statutory restriction (now in s. 116 WIA 1991) on discontinuing the use of existing sewers, it implicitly authorised the continuing use of them. The inescapable inference is that:

> "those rights of discharge which had already accrued in relation to existing outfalls under previous statutory regimes survived."

(at [19]).

133   As can be seen, this analysis rests upon the survival of existing rights of discharge. I do not see that it can have the effect of creating new rights of discharge on the coming into force of the WIA 1991. Nothing in Lord Sumption's analysis suggests that he contemplated any such new rights springing up on 1 December 1991.

134   Nor is there any support for such an idea in the judgment of Lord Neuberger (with whom Lord Clarke and Lord Hughes again agreed). His analysis was that the right to discharge that water authorities had had prior to privatisation had passed to the new privatised undertakers under the Water Act 1989 and that the WIA 1991 did not remove them. As can be seen that analysis too rested on the survival of pre-1991 rights, not the creation of new rights in 1991. Indeed he himself made the point that a court should not be easily persuaded that a new right has been created by implication, particularly where that right interferes with the private rights of third parties and arises out of a long and detailed statute (at [58]).

135   I would therefore reject the second way in which Mr Karas put this point, namely that new implied rights to discharge from the outfalls in question arose on the coming into force of the WIA 1991. In my judgment it is necessary for UU to establish that it had a pre-existing implied statutory right of discharge before the WIA 1991.

136   The difficulty however with that is that I do not think that it did. What it had were rights to discharge under licences that were terminable. If the argument that those licences were wholly or partially ultra vires is rejected (as I have done), then on their face they obliged the local authorities (and UU as their successor) to remove the pipes on their termination. I do not see how an implied statutory right to discharge from the pipe can exist consistently with a contractual obligation to remove the pipe. In truth this is simply another way of saying that once MSCC has granted a limited and determinable right, the sewerage undertaker has somehow acquired a permanent and indefeasible right to maintain its pipes despite agreeing the very opposite. I do not think that can be right.

137   Nor do I think that there is anything in *MSCC* (2014) which would support it. Indeed Lord Sumption was careful to say, for the avoidance of doubt, that his conclusion:

> "in no way affects any binding agreement under which the parties may have regulated for themselves the use of particular outfalls. We were informed that there may be such agreements with some proprietors, but we have not been concerned with them."

(at [23]).

138   I would reject the argument put forward in the Respondent's notice.

Conclusion on 2010 appeal

139   I would allow the appeal and substitute a suitable declaration for that in Fancourt J's order. That will not determine the issue in relation to these outfalls as it is common ground that the proceedings will have to continue to enable UU's other defences to be considered. Nor have we been addressed on the practical

consequences for the parties if UU's other defences fail. But it appears from the pleadings that MSCC is not seeking injunctive relief, merely declarations and damages, so there would seem to be no question of its claim actually preventing use of the overflows.

LORD JUSTICE ARNOLD:

140   I agree.

LADY JUSTICE ASPLIN:

141   I also agree.

R. (ON THE APPLICATION OF WYATT) v FAREHAM BC

COURT OF APPEAL (CIVIL DIVISION)

Sir Keith Lindblom P (Senior President of Tribunals) and Singh and Males LJJ: 15 July 2022

[2022] EWCA Civ 983; [2023] Env. L.R. 14

⚖ Assessment; Development plans; Habitats; Irrationality; Local authorities' powers and duties; Planning permission; Protected areas; Residential development; Wetlands

H1 *Judicial review—nature conservation—Town & Country Planning—Habitats Regulations—Natural England Advice Note on risk to protected habitats from new development wastewater nutrient outputs—'nutrient neutrality' principle—whether reg.63 duty performed lawfully—whether planning application determined appropriately—whether judge erred in approach to "precautionary principle"—whether "reasonable worst-case scenario" had to be assessed where data was uncertain*

H2   The appellant (W) appealed against dismissal of his claim for judicial review of the grant by the respondent (F) of outline planning permission for a development of eight detached houses with four or more bedrooms in each indicated. The site was close to a Special Protection Area and excess nutrient deposits from new housing development, especially nitrogen from wastewater, could harm the integrity of the protected site if suitable mitigation measures were not put in place. Between the resolution to grant permission and decision notice being issued, Natural England (NE) published a technical guidance note. The application was amended to include mitigation measures and NE approved the nitrogen budget. In undertaking an "appropriate assessment" under reg.63 of the Habitats Regulations to ensure that the development would not adversely affect the integrity of the protected site, F had regard to NE's advice about "nutrient neutrality" in the technical guidance note. It used average land use figures in calculating the baseline nitrogen deposition from the site, based its calculation of how much nitrogen the proposed development would produce on a national average occupancy rate for new dwellings of 2.4 persons per dwelling, and applied a 20% "precautionary buffer". On appeal, the two issues were whether F: (1) lawfully performed its duty under reg.63; and (2) complied with its duty under s.38(6) of the Planning and Compulsory Purchase Act 2004 to determine the application in accordance with the development plan unless material considerations indicated otherwise? On the first issue, W submitted that the judge made two fundamental errors in his approach to the legal framework governing appropriate assessment. First, he accepted NE's evidence on the soundness of the method used by F in conducting the appropriate assessment but should have looked at the underlying evidence and considered, for himself, whether the figures used were sound, relying on the *Dutch Nitrogen* case. Secondly, the judge had erred in his approach to the "precautionary principle" in that he should have accepted that where data was uncertain, the "reasonable worst-case scenario" had to be assessed.

H3   **Held,** in dismissing the appeal:

H4   (1) F's conclusion on the crucial question under reg.63(5) was, ultimately, an evaluative judgment for it to make as "competent authority". The conclusion it reached, as a matter of evaluative judgment, had been legally sound.

H5   (2) The judge's self-direction on the relevant legal principles could not be faulted and he went on to apply those principles appropriately. Nor had he simply accepted NE's evidence without question. On the contrary, he examined in appropriate depth and detail the evidence of the expert witnesses on either side. Occupancy rates and the 20% precautionary buffer had been considered with care. More generally, the judge adopted the correct approach in his consideration of F's appropriate assessment as a whole. He applied an appropriately intense standard of scrutiny, consistent with the proper application of *Wednesbury* principles in the light of the jurisprudence to which he had referred.

H6   (3) The submission that the judge ought to have given greater weight than he did to the unfavourable status of the water environment in parts of the Solent was rejected. That fact was explicitly acknowledged and taken into account by NE when issuing the advice in its technical guidance note. There was no support either in the habitats legislation itself or in the relevant authorities for the proposition that the unfavourable status of a protected site raised the level of certainty which had to be achieved if the proposed development was to be approved, or for the proposition that the standard of review the court should adopt in those circumstances was more demanding. Whatever the particular circumstances in a given case, the basic duty of the competent authority under reg.63 was to grant planning permission only if satisfied that the proposed development "will not adversely affect the integrity" of the European protected site. The duty of the court was, and remained, to ensure that the authority's evaluative judgment on that question was lawfully exercised.

H7   (4) The judge had not adopted too lax an understanding of the precautionary principle, or wrongly discounted the concept of the "reasonable worst-case scenario". It had been legitimate for him to conclude that, at least in the present case, the "reasonable worst-case scenario" did not have to be assessed if the precautionary principle was to be satisfied.

H8   (5) There could not be any proper challenge to the lawfulness of the advice given by NE in its technical guidance note, which was an advisory document; neither mandatory in effect nor prescriptive of a single correct procedure to be followed. Nor did it misstate the legal position under reg.63.

H9   (6) Criticisms of F's use of the 2.4 occupancy rate, average land use figures and the 20% precautionary buffer were also rejected. Although an appropriate assessment had to be based on "best scientific knowledge", the question for the court was not whether each individual figure used in it was intrinsically the "best scientific knowledge" when considered on its own, divorced from the full context in which it was used. The court had to take a "holistic" view on the question whether the assessment methodology as a whole represented "best scientific knowledge".

When that was done, there was no *Wednesbury* error in F's approach. Nothing said in *Dutch Nitrogen* implied that the use of averages was inherently objectionable. Although their use would necessarily involve the exercise of judgment on their validity in the particular context, that did not mean that using them was, in principle, contrary to the requirement for the necessary degree of certainty. The use of average figures may sometimes be conducive to sufficient certainty, sometimes not. Whether that was so in a particular case would be a matter of judgment for the competent authority. The fact that the 20% precautionary buffer was not the product of arithmetic, but of judgment, did not mean that it lacked an adequate basis.

H10   (7) The officer's assessment under s.38(6), regarded with realism and common sense, was not flawed by any error of law. There was no misunderstanding or unlawful misapplication of development plan policy, and the path had been open to the officer to reach the conclusion that, "on balance", when it was "considered against the development plan as a whole", the proposal ought to be approved. The officer's conclusions on other material considerations were predicated on that conclusion and were sufficient to comply with the second limb of s.38(6).

H11   **Cases referred to:**

Bayer CropScience v Commission (T-429/13) EU:T:2018:280

BDW Trading Ltd (t/a David Wilson Homes (Central, Mercia and West Midlands)) v Secretary of State for Communities and Local Government [2016] EWCA Civ 493; [2017] P.T.S.R. 1337

Braintree DC v Secretary of State for Communities and Local Government [2018] EWCA Civ 610; [2018] 2 P. & C.R. 9; [2018] J.P.L. 1036

Compton Parish Council v Guildford BC [2019] EWHC 3242 (Admin); [2020] J.P.L. 661

Cooperatie Mobilisation for the Environment UA v College van Gedeputeerde (C-293/17) EU:C:2018:882; [2019] Env. L.R. 27

Craeynest v Brussels Hoofdstedelijk Gewest (C-723/17) EU:C:2019:533; [2020] Env. L.R. 4; [2020] 1 C.M.L.R. 7

Edinburgh City Council v Secretary of State for Scotland [1997] 1 W.L.R. 1447; 1998 S.C. (H.L.) 33; 1997 S.C.L.R. 1112 HL (SC)

Heard v Broadland DC [2012] EWHC 344 (Admin); [2012] Env. L.R. 23; [2012] P.T.S.R. D25

Holohan v An Bord Pleanala (C-461/17) EU:C:2018:883; [2019] P.T.S.R. 1054; [2019] Env. L.R. 16

Inclusion Housing Community Interest Co v Regulator of Social Housing [2020] EWHC 346 (Admin)

Kennedy v Information Commissioner [2014] UKSC 20; [2015] A.C. 455; [2014] 2 W.L.R. 808

Landelijke Vereniging tot Behoud van de Waddenzee v Staatssecretaris van Landbouw, Natuurbeheer en Visserij (C-127/02) EU:C:2004:482; [2005] 2 C.M.L.R. 31; [2005] Env. L.R. 14

Mansell v Tonbridge and Malling BC [2017] EWCA Civ 1314; [2019] P.T.S.R. 1452; [2018] J.P.L. 176

People Over Wind v Coillte Teoranta (C-323/17) EU:C:2018:244; [2018] P.T.S.R. 1668; [2018] Env. L.R. 31

R. (on the application of Plan B Earth) v Secretary of State for Transport [2020] EWCA Civ 214; [2020] P.T.S.R. 1446; [2020] J.P.L. 1005

R. (on the application of Friends of the Earth Ltd) v Heathrow Airport Ltd [2020] UKSC 52; [2021] P.T.S.R. 190; [2021] J.P.L. 905

R. (on the application of A) v Secretary of State for the Home Department [2021] UKSC 37; [2021] 1 W.L.R. 3931; [2021] H.R.L.R. 17

R. (on the application of BACI Bedfordshire Ltd) v Environment Agency [2019] EWCA Civ 1962; [2020] Env. L.R. 16

R. (on the application of Champion) v North Norfolk DC [2015] UKSC 52; [2015] 1 W.L.R. 3710; [2016] Env. L.R. 5

R. (on the application of Corbett) v Cornwall Council [2020] EWCA Civ 508; [2020] J.P.L. 1277

R. (on the application of Hampton Bishop PC) v Herefordshire Council [2014] EWCA Civ 878; [2015] 1 W.L.R. 2367

R. (on the application of Mahmood) v Secretary of State for the Home Department [2001] 1 W.L.R. 840; [2001] H.R.L.R. 14; [2001] A.C.D. 38 CA (Civ Div)

R. (on the application of McMorn) v Natural England [2015] EWHC 3297 (Admin); [2016] P.T.S.R. 750; [2016] Env. L.R. 14

R. v Ministry of Defence Ex p. Smith [1996] Q.B. 517; [1996] 2 W.L.R. 305; [1996] I.C.R. 740 CA (Civ Div)

R. (on the application of Morge) v Hampshire CC [2011] UKSC 2; [2011] 1 W.L.R. 268; [2011] Env. L.R. 19

R. (on the application of Mott) v Environment Agency [2016] EWCA Civ 564; [2016] 1 W.L.R. 4338; [2017] Env. L.R. 1,

R. (on the application of Pearce) v Parole Board of England and Wales [2022] EWCA Civ 4; [2022] 1 W.L.R. 2216

R. (on the application of Preston) v Cumbria CC [2019] EWHC 1362 (Admin); [2020] Env. L.R. 3

R. (on the application of Prideaux) v Buckinghamshire CC [2013] EWHC 1054 (Admin); [2013] Env. L.R. 32; [2013] P.T.S.R. D39

R. v Rochdale MBC Ex p. Milne (No.2) [2001] Env. L.R. 22; (2001) 81 P. & C.R. 27; [2001] J.P.L. 229 (Note) QBD

R. (on the application of United Trade Action Group Ltd) v Transport for London (TfL) [2021] EWCA Civ 1197; [2022] R.T.R. 2; [2022] L.L.R. 141

R. v Westminster City Council Ex p. Ermakov [1996] 2 F.C.R. 208; (1996) 28 H.L.R. 819; (1996) 8 Admin. L.R. 389 CA (Civ Div)

R. (on the application of Spurrier) v Secretary of State for Transport [2019] EWHC 1070 (Admin); [2020] P.T.S.R. 240; [2019] J.P.L. 1163

Smyth v Secretary of State for Communities and Local Government [2015] EWCA Civ 174; [2015] P.T.S.R. 1417; [2016] Env. L.R. 7

St Modwen Developments Ltd v Secretary of State for Communities and Local Government [2017] EWCA Civ 1643; [2018] P.T.S.R. 746; [2018] J.P.L. 398

Sweetman v An Bord Pleanala (C-258/11) EU:C:2013:220; [2014] P.T.S.R. 1092; [2015] Env. L.R. 18

Tesco Stores Ltd v Dundee City Council [2012] UKSC 13; [2012] P.T.S.R. 983; 2012 S.C. (U.K.S.C.) 278

Tiviot Way Investments Ltd v Secretary of State for Communities and Local Government [2015] EWHC 2489 (Admin); [2016] J.P.L. 171

H12 **Legislation referred to:**
Town and Country Planning Act 1990 s.54A
Directive 92/43 (Habitats) art.6
Planning and Compulsory Purchase Act 2004 s.38
Conservation of Habitats and Species Regulations 2017 (SI 2017/1012) regs 5, 7,
63 and 64

H13 *G. Jones KC* and *C. Fegan* (instructed by Fortune Green Legal Practice) appeared
on behalf of the appellant.
T. Mould KC (instructed by Southampton & Fareham Legal Services Partnership)
appeared on behalf of the respondent.
D. Elvin KC and *L. Wilcox* (instructed by Browne Jacobson LLP) appeared on
behalf of Natural England.

JUDGMENT

THE SENIOR PRESIDENT OF TRIBUNALS:

Introduction

1   There are two basic questions in this case. First, was the duty to make an
"appropriate assessment" under regulation 63 of the Conservation of Habitats and
Species Regulations 2017 ("the Habitats Regulations") lawfully performed by a
local planning authority when it granted planning permission for housing
development on land near a European protected site in the Solent? Second, did the
authority comply with its duty under section 38(6) of the Planning and Compulsory
Purchase Act 2004 to determine the application in accordance with the development
plan unless material considerations indicated otherwise? Neither question involves
any novel issue of law. The relevant legal principles are well established and clear.

2   With permission granted by Lord Justice William Davis, the appellant, Ronald
Wyatt, as Chairperson of Brook Avenue Residents Against Development
("BARAD"), appeals against the order of Mr Justice Jay dated 28 May 2021
dismissing his claim for judicial review of the decision of the respondent, Fareham
Borough Council on 1 October 2020 to grant outline planning permission for a
development of eight detached houses on land at Egmont Nurseries, Brook Avenue,
Warsash. The council is the local planning authority, and the "competent authority"
under regulation 7 of the Habitats Regulations. It has filed a respondent's notice.
The fourth interested party is Natural England, the "appropriate nature conservation
body" under regulation 5. It too has filed a respondent's notice. The first, second
and third interested parties – Lorraine, Michael and Thomas Hanslip – are the
landowners. They filed detailed grounds of resistance opposing the claim but have
played no part in the appeal.

The main issues in the appeal

3   The judge rejected Mr Wyatt's challenge on all eight grounds. Permission to
appeal was granted on four of the five grounds in the appellant's notice (grounds
1, 2, 4 and 5). The issue arising from grounds 1, 2 and 4 and the council's
respondent's notice is whether the council failed to make a lawful "appropriate

assessment" of the proposed development under regulation 63 of the Habitats Regulations, in part because it relied on the technical guidance note published by Natural England, entitled "Advice on Achieving Nutrient Neutrality for New Development in the Solent Region (Version 5 – June 2020)", which Mr Wyatt contends is legally flawed. The issue arising from ground 5 is whether the council failed lawfully to perform its duty under section 38(6) of the 2004 Act. These two main issues are distinct and can be dealt with separately.

The application for planning permission and the council's decision

4   The site of the proposed development lies a little to the east of the mouth of the River Hamble and about 5.5km from the Solent and Southampton Water Special Protection Area ("the SPA"), which is a European protected site. Aquatic habitats for many species of plants and birds within the protected site, including the Brent Goose, are vulnerable to the excess deposition of nutrients – in particular nitrogen compounds in wastewater, which cause algal growth. New housing development can thus harm the integrity of the protected site if suitable mitigation measures are not put in place.

5   The application for outline planning permission was submitted in June 2018. The proposed development was the "[demolition] of existing buildings, [the construction] of eight detached houses [and the creation] of [a] paddock". The existing use was described as "[redundant] glasshouses and nursery buildings". The application form indicated that each dwelling would have four or more bedrooms. When the council's Planning Committee considered the proposal in December 2018, it resolved that planning permission should be granted. Before the required section 106 agreement had been entered into and a decision notice issued, Natural England published its technical guidance note. The application came back to the committee on 19 August 2020. By then it had been amended to include mitigation measures, and Natural England had approved the nitrogen budget.

6   As competent authority, the council was required by regulation 63 of the Habitats Regulations to undertake an "appropriate assessment" to ensure that the development would not adversely affect the integrity of the protected site. In undertaking the "appropriate assessment" it had regard to Natural England's advice about "nutrient neutrality" in its technical guidance note. It used average land use figures in calculating the baseline nitrogen deposition from the site, based its calculation of how much nitrogen the proposed development would produce on a national average occupancy rate for new dwellings of 2.4 persons per dwelling, and applied a 20% "precautionary buffer".

The legislative provisions for "appropriate assessment"

7   Article 6(3) of Council Directive 92/43/EEC on the Conservation of Natural Habitats and of Wild Flora and Fauna ("the Habitats Directive") states:

"3. Any plan or project not directly connected with or necessary to the management of the site but likely to have a significant effect thereon, either individually or in combination with other plans or projects, shall be subject to appropriate assessment of its implications for the site in view of the site's conservation objectives. In the light of the conclusions of the assessment of the implications for the site and subject to the provisions of paragraph 4, the competent national authorities shall agree to the plan or project only after having ascertained that it will not adversely affect the integrity of the site concerned and, if appropriate, after having obtained the opinion of the general public."

8   That provision was transposed into domestic law by regulation 63 of the Habitats Regulations, "Assessment of implications for European sites and European offshore marine sites", which states:

> "(1) A competent authority, before deciding to undertake, or give any consent, permission or other authorisation for, a plan or project which –
>> (a) is likely to have a significant effect on a European site or a European offshore marine site (either alone or in combination with other plans or projects), and
>> (b) is not directly connected with or necessary to the management of that site,
>
> must make an appropriate assessment of the implications of the plan or project for that site in view of that site's conservation objectives.
>
> …
>
> (3) The competent authority must for the purposes of the assessment consult the appropriate nature conservation body and have regard to any representations made by that body within such reasonable time as the authority specifies.
>
> …
>
> (5) In the light of the conclusions of the assessment, and subject to regulation 64, the competent authority may agree to the plan or project only after having ascertained that it will not adversely affect the integrity of the European site or the European offshore marine site (as the case may be).
>
> (6) In considering whether a plan or project will adversely affect the integrity of the site, the competent authority must have regard to the manner in which it is proposed to be carried out or to any conditions or restrictions subject to which it proposes that the consent, permission or other authorisation should be given."

An exception to the obligation in paragraph (5) arises under regulation 64, where the authority is satisfied that there are "no alternative solutions" and that there are "imperative reasons of overriding public interest" for the project to be carried out.

9   There is a wealth of case law relevant to article 6(3) and regulation 63, both in the Court of Justice of the European Union ("the CJEU") and in the domestic courts. Some basic points emerge:

(1) The duty imposed by article 6(3) of the Habitats Directive and regulation 63 of the Habitats Regulations rests with competent authorities, not with the courts. Whether a plan or project will adversely affect the integrity of a European protected site under regulation 63(5) is always a matter of judgment for the competent authority itself (see the judgment of the CJEU in *Holohan v An Bord Pleanála* (C-461/17) [2019] P.T.S.R. 1054 at paragraph 44). That is an evaluative judgment, which the court is neither entitled nor equipped to make for itself (see the judgment of Lord Carnwath in *R. (on the application of Champion) v North Norfolk DC* [2015] UKSC

52; [2015] 1 W.L.R. 3170 at paragraph 41, and the judgment of Lord Justice Sales, as he then was, in *Smyth v Secretary of State for Communities and Local Government* [2015] EWCA Civ 174; [2015] P.T.S.R. 1417 at paragraph 83). In a legal challenge to a competent authority's decision, the role of the court is not to undertake its own assessment, but to review the performance by the authority of its duty under regulation 63. The court's function is supervisory only. This has been emphasised often in the domestic cases (see, for example, the recent first instance judgment in *Compton Parish Council v Guildford BC* [2020] J.P.L. 661 at paragraph 207).

(2) In *Coöperatie Mobilisation for the Environment UA, Vereniging Leefmilieu v College van Gedeputeerde Staten van Limburg* (C-293/17) [2019] Env. L.R. 27 ("*Dutch Nitrogen*"), the CJEU said that it is "for the national courts to carry out a thorough and in-depth examination of the scientific soundness of the "appropriate assessment"…" (paragraph 101 of the judgment), which "makes it possible to ensure that there is no reasonable scientific doubt as to the absence of adverse effects of each plan or project on the integrity of the site concerned, which it is for the national court to ascertain" (paragraph 104). The force of these statements is that the court, for its part, must be wholly satisfied in the exercise of its supervisory jurisdiction that the competent authority's performance of its obligations under article 6(3) was lawful. It must satisfy itself of the lawfulness of the authority's consideration of the scientific soundness of the appropriate assessment. But there is nothing in the CJEU's judgment to suggest that it intended to transform the respective roles of the competent authorities and the domestic courts by giving the court the job of undertaking an alternative appropriate assessment of its own.

(3) When reviewing the performance by a competent authority of its duty under regulation 63, the court will apply ordinary public law principles, conscious of the nature of the subject-matter and the expertise of the competent authority itself. If the competent authority has properly understood its duty under regulation 63, the court will intervene only if there is some *Wednesbury* error in the performance of that duty (see the judgment of Sales L.J. in *Smyth*, at paragraph 80, and the judgment of this court in *Plan B Earth v Secretary of State for Transport* [2020] P.T.S.R. 1446, at paragraphs 68 and 75 to 79, which were not doubted by the Supreme Court in the same proceedings ([2021] P.T.S.R. 190)). When exercising its supervisory function, the court will apply the normal *Wednesbury* standard, not a heightened standard such as "anxious scrutiny" (cf. *R. v Ministry of Defence Ex p. Smith* [1996] Q.B. 517, and *R. (on the application of Mahmood) v Secretary of State for the Home Department* [2001] 1 W.L.R. 840). It is well-established that such a heightened standard will apply only where fundamental rights or constitutional principles are at stake (see the judgment of Lord Carnwath in *Kennedy v Charity Commission* [2014] UKSC 20, at paragraph 245, and the first instance decision in *R. (on the application of McMorn) v Natural England* [2015] EWHC 3297 (Admin) at paragraphs 204 and 205). Given the demanding requirement inherent in regulation 63(5) – for the competent authority to ascertain that the project "will not adversely affect the integrity of the European site" – the court's examination of the authority's performance of its duty will be suitably exacting within

the bounds of its jurisdiction. But it should be remembered that the autonomous approach of the domestic courts in judging the lawfulness of such action has been explicitly approved by the CJEU (see the judgment of this court in *Plan B Earth*, at paragraphs 74, 75 and 137, discussing the CJEU's decision in *Craeynest v Brussels Hoofdstedelijk Gewest* (C-723/17) [2020] Env. L.R. 4).

(4) A competent authority is entitled, and can be expected, to give significant weight to the advice of an "expert national agency" with relevant expertise in the sphere of nature conservation, such as Natural England (see the judgment of Sales L.J. in *Smyth*, at paragraph 84, and the first instance judgment in *R. (on the application of Preston) v Cumbria CC* [2019] EWHC 1362 (Admin) at paragraph 69). The authority may lawfully disagree with, and depart from, such advice. But if it does, it must have cogent reasons for doing so (see the judgment of Baroness Hale in *R. (on the application of Morge) v Hampshire CC* [2011] 1 W.L.R. 268 at paragraph 45, the judgment of Sales L.J. in *Smyth*, at paragraph 85, and the first instance judgment in *R. (on the application of Prideaux) v Buckinghamshire CC* [2013] Env. L.R. 32 at paragraph 116). And the court for its part will give appropriate deference to the views of expert regulatory bodies (see, for example, the judgment of Lord Justice Beatson in *R. (on the application of Mott) v Environment Agency* [2016] 1 W.L.R. 4338 at paragraphs 69 to 77).

(5) When provided with expert evidence in a claim for judicial review, the court will not substitute its own opinion for that of the expert. As this court emphasised in *R. (on the application of BACI Bedfordshire) v Environment Agency* [2020] Env L.R. 16 at paragraph 87, "[unless] there is clear evidence revealing a failure of ... expertise – for example, some conspicuous factual or scientific error – the court is entitled to conclude there was no such failure". Experts may be expected to provide enough explanation to enable the court to decide whether the views they have stated are based on a conspicuous error (see the judgment of Sales L.J. in *Smyth*, at paragraph 83). But the court will bear in mind that decisions which entail "scientific, technical and predictive assessments by those with appropriate expertise" and which are "highly dependent upon the assessment of a wide variety of complex technical matters by those who are expert in such matters and/or who are assigned to the task of assessment (ultimately by Parliament)" should be accorded a substantial margin of appreciation (see the judgment of this court in *Plan B Earth*, at paragraph 68, and, at first instance in the same case, *Spurrier v Secretary of State for Transport* [2020] P.T.S.R. 240 at paragraphs 176 to 180).

(6) The requirement in the second sentence of article 6(3) of the Habitats Directive and in regulation 63(5) of the Habitats Regulations embodies the "precautionary principle, and makes it possible effectively to prevent adverse effects on the integrity of protected sites as a result of the plans or projects being considered" (see the judgment of the CJEU in *Landelijke Vereniging tot Behoud van de Waddenzee v Staatssecretaris Van Landbouw, Natuurbeheer en Visserij (Coöperatieve Producentenorganisatie van de Nederlandse Kokkelvisserij UA intervening)* (C-127/02) [2005] 2 C.M.L.R. 31) ("*Waddenzee*"), at paragraph 58). The "precautionary principle" requires

a high standard of investigation (see the judgment in *Waddenzee*, at paragraphs 44, 58, 59 and 61).

(7) The duty placed on the competent authority by article 6(3) and regulation 63 is to ascertain that there will be no adverse effects on the integrity of the protected site, but that conclusion does not need to be established to the standard of "absolute certainty". Rather, the competent authority must be "satisfied that there is no reasonable doubt as to the absence of adverse effects on the integrity of the site concerned" (paragraphs 44, 58, 59, and 61 of the CJEU's judgment and paragraphs 107 and 108 of the Advocate General's opinion in *Waddenzee*, and the judgment in *Holohan*, at paragraphs 33 to 37). In *Waddenzee* (at paragraph 59), the CJEU emphasised the responsibility of the competent authority, having taken account of the conclusions of the appropriate assessment, to authorise the proposed development "only if [it] has made certain that it will not adversely affect the integrity of that site". That, it said, "is the case where no reasonable scientific doubt remains as to the absence of such effects". But as Advocate General Kokott explained in *Waddenzee* (in paragraphs 102 to 106 of her opinion), a requirement of "absolute certainty" would be "disproportionate". As she said (at paragraph 107), "the necessary certainty cannot be construed as meaning absolute certainty ...", the conclusion of an appropriate assessment is, "of necessity, subjective in nature", and "competent authorities can, from their point of view, be certain that there will be no adverse effects even though, from an objective point of view, there is no absolute certainty". Similar observations appear in the judgment itself (in paragraphs 44, 58, 59 and 61). As the Supreme Court acknowledged in *Champion*, adopting the approach in *Waddenzee*, "while a high standard of investigation is demanded, the issue ultimately rests on the judgment of the authority" (see the judgment of Lord Carnwath, at paragraph 41). This approach is, in essence, what the "precautionary principle" requires in the context of article 6(3) of the Habitats Directive and regulation 63 of the Habitats Regulations.

(8) The requirement that there be "no reasonable doubt as to the absence of adverse effects on the integrity of the site concerned" does not mean that the "reasonable worst-case scenario" must always be assessed. In the European Commission guidance document entitled "Communication on the precautionary principle" (2000) it is stated in Annex III that "[when] the available data are inadequate or non-conclusive, a prudent and cautious approach to environmental protection, health or safety could be to opt for the worst-case hypothesis". That guidance, however, is not law (see *Heard v Broadland DC* [2012] Env. L.R. 23, at paragraph 69, and *Prideaux*, at paragraph 112), nor is it in mandatory terms. What is required in law is a sufficient degree of certainty to ensure that there is "no reasonable doubt" on the relevant question. It may sometimes be useful to consider a "reasonable worst-case scenario" when assessing whether the necessary degree of certainty has been achieved. But whether there are grounds for "reasonable doubt" will always be a matter of judgment in the particular case.

(9) An appropriate assessment must be based on the "best scientific knowledge in the field" (see *Holohan*, at paragraph 33). Such knowledge must be both up-to-date and not merely an expert's bare assertion (see the judgment of

Sales L.J. in *Smyth*, at paragraph 83). And the concept of "best scientific knowledge" is not a wholly free-standing requirement, separate from the precautionary principle itself. It is inherent in the precautionary principle, and in the concept of "no reasonable doubt".

(10) What is required of the competent authority, therefore, is a case-specific assessment in which the applicable science is brought to bear with sufficient rigour on the implications of the project for the protected site concerned. If an appropriate assessment is to comply with article 6(3) of the Habitats Directive it "cannot have lacunae and must contain complete, precise and definitive findings and conclusions capable of removing all reasonable scientific doubt as to the effects of the works proposed on the protected site concerned" (see the judgment of the CJEU in *Sweetman v An Bord Pleanála* (C-258/11) [2014] P.T.S.R. 1092, at paragraph 44, and its judgment in *People Over Wind and Sweetman v Coillte Teoranta* (C-323/17) [2018] P.T.S.R. 1668, at paragraph 38).

Natural England's technical guidance note

10   Natural England's technical guidance note was issued under section 4 of the Natural Environment and Rural Communities Act 2006, which provides, in subsection (4), that "Natural England may give advice to any person on any matter relating to its general purpose … (b) if [it] thinks it appropriate to do so, on its own initiative".

11   The technical guidance note advocated the calculation of a "nutrient budget" for a proposed development. If this showed that the development was likely to generate greater levels of nitrogen than would the existing lawful use of the site, the thrust of the advice given was that the local planning authority, when granting planning permission, would have to secure appropriate mitigation measures to avoid any residual increase in nutrient levels in the Solent.

12   In its opening paragraph the technical guidance note recognised that the water environment of the Solent is highly protected for its habitats and species of international importance. It acknowledged that the high levels of nitrogen input to this water environment were causing excessive plant growth – "eutrophication" – in the designated sites, and that the resulting mats of green algae and other impacts on the marine ecology were affecting protected habitats and bird species (paragraph 1.1). It referred to the "potential for future housing developments across the Solent region to exacerbate these impacts, [which] creates a risk to their potential future conservation status". It introduced "nutrient neutrality" as "a means of ensuring that development does not add to existing nutrient burdens", adding that "this provides certainty that the whole of the scheme is deliverable in line with the requirements of [the Habitats Regulations]" (paragraph 1.3). It advocated a practical method for calculating how nutrient neutrality could be achieved, based on "best scientific knowledge" but subject to revision as further evidence was obtained (paragraph 1.4).

13   The "best available up-to-date evidence" indicated that some of the protected sites were "widely in unfavourable condition due to existing levels of nutrients" and "at risk from additional nutrient inputs" (paragraph 2.3). In Natural England's view, there were likely significant effects on several internationally designated sites "due to the increase in wastewater from the new developments coming

forward" (paragraph 2.4). Nutrient neutrality would allow local planning authorities to comply with their duties under regulation 63 (paragraph 2.5), and provide "a means of ensuring that development does not add to existing nutrient burdens" (paragraph 2.6).

14   In section 4, "Nutrient Neutrality Approach for New Development", it was stated that "[achieving] nutrient neutrality is one way to address the existing uncertainty surrounding the impact of new development on designated sites", and that "[this] practical methodology provides advice on how to calculate nutrient budgets and options for mitigation, should this be necessary" (paragraph 4.1). It suggested this approach to calculating "nutrient budgets" (in paragraphs 4.6 to 4.9):

> "4.6 For those developments that wish to pursue neutrality, Natural England advises that a nitrogen budget is calculated for new developments that have the potential to result in increases of nitrogen entering the international sites. A nutrient budget calculated according to this methodology and demonstrating nutrient neutrality is, in our view, able to provide sufficient and reasonable certainty that the development does not adversely affect the integrity, by means of impacts from nutrients, on the relevant internationally designated sites. This approach must be tested through the 'appropriate assessment' stage of the Habitats Regulations Assessment. The information provided by the applicant on the nutrient budget and any mitigation proposed will be used by the local planning authority, as competent authority, to make an appropriate assessment of the implications of the plan or project on the designated sites in question. …
>
> 4.7 The nutrient neutrality calculation includes key inputs and assumptions that are based on the best-available scientific evidence and research. It has been developed as a pragmatic tool. However, for each input there is a degree of uncertainty. For example, there is uncertainty associated with predicting occupancy levels and water use for each household in perpetuity. Also, identifying current land/farm types and the associated nutrient inputs is based on best-available evidence, research and professional judgement and is again subject to a degree of uncertainty.
>
> 4.8 It is our advice to local planning authorities to take a precautionary approach in line with existing legislation and case-law when addressing uncertainty and calculating nutrient budgets. This should be achieved by ensuring nutrient budget calculations apply precautionary rates to variables and adding a precautionary buffer to the [total nitrogen] calculated for developments. A precautionary approach to the calculations and solutions helps the local planning authority and applicants to demonstrate the certainty needed for their assessments.
>
> 4.9 By applying the nutrient neutrality methodology, with the precautionary buffer, to new development, the competent authority may be satisfied that, while margins of error will inevitably vary for each development, this approach will ensure that new development in combination will avoid significant increases of nitrogen load to enter the internationally designated sites."

15   For development which would drain to the mains network, the suggested method would involve four stages. In the first stage, which was to calculate the total nitrogen derived from the development which would leave wastewater treatment works, the

first step was to "Calculate [the] additional population" arising from the development. Relevant here is the advice given on occupancy rates:

"4.18 New housing and overnight accommodation can increase the population as well as the housing stock within the catchment. This can cause an increase in nitrogen discharges. To determine the additional population that could arise from the proposed development, it is necessary that sufficiently evidenced occupancy rates are used. Natural England recommends that, as a starting point, local planning authorities should consider using the average national occupancy rate of 2.4, as calculated by the Office for National Statistics (ONS), as this can be consistently applied across all affected areas.

4.19 However competent authorities may choose to adopt bespoke calculations tailored to the area or scheme, rather than using national population or occupancy assumptions, where they are satisfied that there is sufficient evidence to support this approach. Conclusions that inform the use of a bespoke calculation need to be capable of removing all reasonable scientific doubt as to the effect of the proposed development on the international sites concerned, based on complete, precise and definitive findings. The competent authority will need to explain clearly why the approach taken is considered to be appropriate. Calculations for occupancy rates will need to be consistent with others used in relation to the scheme (e.g. for calculating open space requirements), unless there is a clear justification for them to differ."

16   The second step in the first stage was to "Confirm water use". In Natural England's view, planning authorities ought to impose conditions for maximum water usage of "110 litres per person per day" on new developments (paragraphs 4.11 and 4.22). The advice here was that "[the] water use figure is a proxy for the amount of wastewater that is generated by a household", that "[new] residential development may be able to achieve tighter water use figures" (paragraph 4.23), and that "while new developments should be required to meet the 100 litres per person a day standard, the risk of standards slipping over time and the uncertainty inherent in the relationship between water use and sewage volume should be addressed by the use in the calculation of 110 litres per person per day figure" (paragraph 4.25).

17   The third step in the first stage involved identifying the "[wastewater] treatment works" into which water from the development would drain. Natural England adopted a precautionary approach, stating that "[where] there is a permit limit for Total Nitrogen, the load calculation will use a worst case scenario that the [wastewater treatment works] operates at 90% of its permitted limit" (paragraph 4.29).

18   The fourth step in the first stage was to "Calculate Total Nitrogen (TN) in Kg per annum that would exit the [wastewater treatment works] after treatment derived from the proposed development". It was noted that "[natural] reductions in nitrogen concentrations, mainly through de-nitrification processes, also occur within watercourses". But there was "[insufficient] evidence ... to properly evaluate de-nitrification rates within the greater Solent catchments"; so that factor was not included. Natural England took the view that this provided "an additional precautionary factor for the methodology" (paragraph 4.42).

19   The second stage was to "Adjust nitrogen load to account for existing nitrogen from current land use". This advice was given:

"4.45 This next stage is to calculate the existing nitrogen losses from the current land use within the redline boundary of the scheme. The nitrogen loss from the current land use will be removed and replaced by that from the proposed development land use. The net change in land use will need to be subtracted from or added to the wastewater Total Nitrogen load.

4.46 Nitrogen-nitrate loss from agricultural land can be modelled using the Farmscoper model. …

4.47 If the development area covers agricultural land that clearly falls within a particular farm type used by the Farmscoper model then the modelled average nitrate-nitrogen loss from this farm type should be used. …

…

4.51 It is important that farm type classification is appropriately precautionary. It is recommended that evidence is provided of the farm type for the last 10 years and professional judgement is used as to what the land would revert to in the absence of a planning application. In many cases, the local planning authority, as competent authority, will have appropriate knowledge of existing land uses to help inform this process.

4.52 There may be areas of a greenfield development site that are not currently in agricultural use and have not been used as such for the last 10 years. In these areas as there is no agricultural input into the land a baseline nitrogen leaching value of 5 kg/ha should be used. This figure covers nitrogen loading from atmospheric deposition, pet waste and nitrogen fixing legumes."

20   The third stage was to adjust the nitrogen load to account for land uses in the proposed development.

21   The fourth stage was to "Calculate the net change in the Total Nitrogen load that would result from the development". The advice was this:

"4.67 It is necessary to recognise that all the figures used in the calculation are based on scientific research, evidence and modelled catchments. These figures are the best available evidence but it is important that a precautionary buffer is used that recognises the uncertainty with these figures and in our view ensures the approach prevents, with reasonable certainty, that there will be no adverse effect on site integrity. Natural England therefore recommends that a 20% precautionary buffer is built into the calculation.

4.68 There may be instances where it is the view of the competent authority that an alternative precautionary buffer should be used on a site-specific basis where sufficient evidence allows the legal tests to be met."

22   Since the judge's decision in the court below, Natural England has, in March 2022, issued further guidance. This does not bear on the claim with which we are concerned.

Natural England's response to consultation on the application for planning permission

23   On 9 June 2020, as statutory consultee under regulation 63(3), Natural England gave its advice to the council on "nutrient neutrality" for the proposed development. It did so in the light of the council's "Nitrogen Budget", dated 11 May 2020. The "Nitrogen Budget" was based on an occupancy rate of 2.4 persons per dwelling and included a precautionary buffer of 20%, both of which were subsequently used

in the council's appropriate assessment. Natural England said that "[provided] the council, as the competent authority, [was] assured and satisfied [that] the site areas [were] correct and that the existing land uses [were] appropriately precautionary", it raised "no further concerns with regard to the nutrient budget". Nor did it raise concern about the use of average land use figures for calculating the baseline nitrogen deposition from the site, about the 2.4 occupancy rate, or about the 20% precautionary buffer applied.

Mr Wyatt's objection

24   Mr Wyatt and his wife submitted several letters of objection to the council. In his "further comments" dated 15 June 2020, Mr Wyatt addressed the use of the 20% precautionary buffer, arguing that it appeared "irrational" because there was "no evidential basis explaining why a 20% buffer has been used". He also expressed his concern about the use of the occupancy rate of 2.4 persons per dwelling. He noted that the council had used its "discretion to vary this figure" when considering a proposal of "16 age related apartments" in Station Road, Portchester, for which it had "used what [it] termed an overall "cautious average" occupancy rate of 2", which was "in line with the 2011 Census figure". He expected the council to be consistent. The 2011 Census gave an average occupancy rate of 3.4 persons per household for houses of the size proposed, which would be "a more appropriate figure". If the council was "consistent" and used "the correct land use figures and a more realistic occupancy rate", it would "reject the application on the grounds that it will be in deficit and therefore cannot meet the nitrate neutrality regulations".

Natural England's further advice

25   Natural England gave further advice to the council on 18 August 2020, now in the light of the council's draft appropriate assessment. It did not doubt the conclusions of the draft appropriate assessment or the likely efficacy of the proposed mitigation measures. Again, it raised no concerns about the use of average figures, the occupancy rate of 2.4 persons per dwelling, or the use of the 20% precautionary buffer.

The appropriate assessment

26   In the appropriate assessment presented to the council's Planning Committee on 19 August 2020, it was acknowledged (on p.2) that "[all] new housing development within 5.6 km of the Solent SPAs is considered to contribute towards an impact on the integrity of the Solent SPAs", and (on p.4) that "[the] proposed development is within 5.6 km of the Solent & Southampton Water SPA". The likely nitrogen output of the proposed development was identified, and the proposed mitigation measures described and considered. These conclusions were stated (on p.17):

"The project being assessed will result in a positive nitrogen output of 10.5 kg/TN/yr and therefore the waste water from the development will add to the nitrogen levels within the Solent. ... The pathway is via the wastewater treatment works. Therefore, the surplus in the nitrogen output would need to be mitigated. ... In order for the development proposal to demonstrate nitrogen neutrality, an on-site wetland will be created on site. The proposed wetland would remove nitrates from surface water and roof water drainage through a combination of physical, chemical and biological processes via interactions between the water, substrate and micro-organisms such as algae. The wetland would in turn provide a reduction of 11.51 kg/N/yr meaning there would be an overall reduction in nitrates being discharged from the site. The mitigation will be secured through a Section 106. ...".

and (on p.18):

"In conclusion, the application will have a likely significant effect in the absence of avoidance and mitigation measures on [the protected sites] ... This represents the authority's Appropriate Assessment as Competent Authority in accordance with requirements under Regulation 63 of the [Habitats Regulations], [and] Article 6 (3) of the Habitats Directive ... .
The authority has concluded that the adverse effects arising from the proposal are wholly consistent with, and inclusive of the effects detailed in the Solent Recreation Mitigation Strategy. The authority's assessment is that the proposed mitigation package complies with this Strategy and that it can therefore be concluded that there will be no adverse effect on the integrity of the Solent and Southampton Water SPA."

The officer's advice on the appropriate assessment

27   In his report to the committee, the officer considered the possible impact of the development on the European protected sites in the Solent, under the requirements in regulation 63 of the Habitats Regulations and in the light of the appropriate assessment. He reminded the members that "[regulation 63] provides that planning permission can only be granted by a 'competent authority' if it can be shown that the proposed development will either not have a likely significant effect on designated [protected sites] or, if it will have a likely significant effect, that effect can be mitigated so that it will not result in an adverse effect on the integrity of the designated [protected sites] ..." (paragraph 8.26). He referred to Natural England's advice, explaining the concept of "nutrient neutrality" and the need for local planning authorities to take a "precautionary approach" (paragraphs 8.32 and 8.33); to the "nutrient budget" (paragraph 8.34); and to the existing land use (paragraphs 8.35 to 8.37).

28   He then came to the "assumed occupancy rate" (in paragraphs 8.38 to 8.42):

"8.38 Natural England recommends that, as a starting point, local planning authorities should consider using the average national occupancy rate of 2.4 persons per dwelling as calculated by the Office for National Statistics (ONS), as this can be consistently applied across all affected areas. However competent authorities may choose to adopt bespoke calculations where they are satisfied that there is sufficient evidence to support this approach.
8.39 Concern has been raised by third parties over the use of the average occupancy rate of 2.4 for this development of eight houses. Some have expressed the view that a higher occupancy rate ought to be applied since the houses are likely to be larger than average dwellings (although it should be noted that the application is in outline form and scale and layout of the

development are reserved matters). Third parties have noted that the Council used bespoke calculations when determining a recent planning application for a sheltered housing development elsewhere in the Borough.

8.40 It is acknowledged that some houses will have more than the average number of occupants. It is also of course the case that some will have less. The figure of 2.4 is an average based on a well evidenced source (the ONS) and which has been shown to be consistent over the past ten years. As stated above the Natural England methodology allows bespoke occupancy rates however to date the Council has only done so to lower, not raise, the occupancy rate and where clear evidence has been provided to demonstrate that the proposed accommodation has an absolute maximum rate of occupancy. In the case of sheltered housing which is owned and managed by the Council for example it has been previously been considered appropriate to apply a reduced occupancy rate accordingly.

8.41 In all instances it is the case that the Natural England methodology is already sufficiently precautionary because it assumes that every occupant of every new dwelling (along with the occupants of any existing dwellings made available by house moves) is a new resident of the Borough of Fareham. There is also a precautionary buffer of 20% applied to the total nitrogen load that would result from the development as part of the overall nutrient budget exercise.

8.42 Taking the above matters into account, Officers do not consider there to be any specific justification for applying anything other than the recommended average occupancy rate of 2.4 persons per dwelling when considering the nutrient budget for the development."

The evidence before the judge

29   The judge had before him in evidence a witness statement, dated 25 February 2021, of Dr James O'Neill on behalf of Mr Wyatt, and three witness statements, dated 9 December 2020, 4 February 2021 and 12 April 2021, of Ms Allison Potts on behalf of Natural England. Dr O'Neill is the Principal of James O'Neill Associates, an environmental consultancy. Ms Potts is the Acting Area Manager of Natural England's Thames Solent team.

30   In his witness statement, Dr O'Neill said that "[if] an incorrect occupancy rate is used then it will cause the total nitrogen figure … to be wrong", and lead to a figure "which has a real risk of significantly underestimating and therefore downplaying the actual nitrogen output of the development in question". Natural England suggested that an occupancy rate of 2.4 persons per dwelling should be used as a starting point, but that a "bespoke calculation" would be appropriate in some cases (paragraph 20). However, in Dr O'Neill's view, as the proposed dwellings would have four or five bedrooms, the national average occupancy rate would not represent best scientific evidence available. A "specific dataset for four to five bedroom dwellings" was available for Fareham, which would have given an average occupancy rate of 3 for such dwellings, not 2.4, broadly in alignment with the national average of 3.14. The use of the national average was not, therefore, justifiable (paragraphs 23 to 29).

31   On the "use of averages in the land classification", Dr O'Neill said the "selection of the correct land use for the site is a matter of judgement which [he was] not

qualified to make an assessment of here" (paragraph 36). But he made four points: first, existing land use figures should be "sufficiently precautionary" (paragraph 38); second, there was "reasonable doubt in respect of the land classification employed" in the appropriate assessment (paragraph 39); third, the "Farmscoper model" relied on average data, rather than using site-specific data; and fourth, the inaccuracy introduced by the use of the 2.4 occupancy rate would be compounded by the use of average land use figures (paragraph 42).

32   Finally, he addressed the 20% precautionary buffer. He said that, "for such a buffer to be valid, the level of uncertainty associated with each step of the calculation must be known" (paragraph 47). There was a range of statistical methods for quantifying that uncertainty, but "no evidence that they have been applied in respect of the impugned calculation". The buffer applied was "insufficiently precautionary" (paragraph 48).

33   Ms Potts did not agree with Dr O'Neill's opinion. In her evidence she said that his "focus on the 2.4 figure takes no account of the precaution that is built into the methodology as a whole" (third witness statement, paragraph 5). Natural England had considered the available data and concluded that the national average occupancy rate was "the best available scientific evidence for use in the methodology when applied to development within the Solent catchments." (third witness statement, paragraph 7).

34   Seven reasons were given for that conclusion. First, the 2.4 figure was often used, and it would only be necessary for a local planning authority to adopt bespoke figures in an "extreme occupancy scenario". The fact that a development consisted of larger houses was not in itself enough to warrant the adoption of a bespoke rate (second witness statement, paragraphs 23 to 25). Second, Natural England had concluded that reliance on the "finer grain detail" would have introduced "unnecessary and unwieldy complication". It "would have required using 65 different occupancy rates across the area (13 ONS areas x 1-5+ bedroom rates)", and it would also have been "necessary to use a per bedroom water usage rate". These figures were "not easily obtainable" (third witness statement, paragraph 8). Third, Natural England had assumed "100% inward migration", whereas in reality "some occupants of new dwellings will be moving within the affected catchments, so do not represent an entirely new burden" (second witness statement, paragraph 31, and third witness statement, paragraph 9). Fourth, "while larger properties tend towards having more occupants than smaller properties (but not in a linear relationship to the number of bedrooms), occupancy and dwelling size are not very highly correlated" (second witness statement, paragraph 26). Fifth, the occupancy rate of 2.4 persons per dwelling was part of a broader "strategic solution", and a "standardised approach" (second witness statement, paragraphs 32 and 33). Sixth, the data showed that houses with higher occupancy rates had significantly lower water use figures per occupant (second witness statement, paragraph 27). And seventh, the data was "suggestive of a decline in average occupancy over time". The 2.4 occupancy rate was meant to account for "the nutrient impact arising from the proposed development in perpetuity" (second witness statement, paragraphs 28 to 30).

35   Ms Potts drew attention to three "precautionary" elements in the method used for estimating "water use": first, "[the] water use figure used (110 l/p/d) is 10% higher than Southern Water's target required ..."; second, "[all] new build development will have meters and water use in metered properties is significantly

lower than non-metered properties"; and third, "[water] supply is less than water return to [wastewater treatment works] reflecting use of water to wash cars, water gardens". She also referred to two "precautionary" elements in the consideration of "Wastewater Treatment Work Operations": first, that it "[assumes wastewater treatment works with total nitrogen] permits operate at the maximum possible within legal limits", whereas the "Solent [wastewater treatment works] with [a total nitrogen] permit are currently on average performing 25% more effectively than [the] assumed level"; and second, that "[an] unknown proportion of nitrogen discharged seaward of the international sites will be lost to sea and will not affect the designated sites" (second witness statement, Table 1).

36   Ms Potts also referred to the 20% precautionary buffer, and explained in detail how the correct figure was arrived at. She said the development of the buffer had "involved consideration of the likelihood, severity, duration and tendency of potential impacts", and "in determining the level of the buffer, each component was assessed individually, as well as evaluating the relationships between each component, the risk of exceedances and the severity of such exceedance". Among the factors taken into account were "the degree of known variability for each component" and "the fact that not all risks are fully known". Ms Potts emphasised that defining the buffer had involved "expert judgement", and the choice of 20% as the appropriate figure was considered to be commensurate with "no reasonable doubt" about the absence of adverse effects on the integrity of the protected site (second witness statement, paragraphs 56 to 64, and third witness statement, paragraphs 19 to 21).

The judge's conclusions on the "appropriate assessment" grounds

37   Jay J. was critical of the approach to occupancy rates in Natural England's technical guidance note, and of the council's use of an occupancy rate of 2.4 persons per dwelling in this case. But adopting the degree of deference he thought right in the circumstances, and approaching the matter on a *Wednesbury* basis, he concluded that the use of the 2.4 occupancy rate was sufficiently precautionary. He concentrated, in particular, on two "precautionary elements" of the appropriate assessment that could "legitimately be brought into account": first, that "the relationship [between occupancy rates and water usage] is not one of direct proportionality", and second, that "the algorithm assumes 100% migration to the area" (paragraph 84 of his judgment). He was "satisfied that there was an adequate precautionary leeway afforded by [these] two key factors" (paragraph 86). He added, however, that the technical guidance note would need to be reviewed in the light of his judgment (paragraph 87).

38   The judge did not accept that the use of average land use figures was inappropriate, or that site specific measurements should have been taken. He thought that site specific measurements would provide "no more than a snapshot of existing land use", and it was not clear that "the overly rigorous approach recommended by Dr O'Neill would in fact yield more protective data" (paragraph 110).

39   On the use of the 20% precautionary buffer, the judge concluded that the lack of "any arithmetical calculation or other algorithm" in the calculation of the buffer was not fatal to it. He thought that there was "room for debate between reasonable scientists, using their judgment, expertise and experience, as to whether the figure

should be, say, 10%, 20% or 30%". And he found "no place for judicial intervention on any *Wednesbury* basis" (paragraph 111).

40   Those were the judge's principal conclusions on this part of the case. I shall also refer to some other passages in his judgment when I come to the argument put forward on the first main issue.

Did the council fail to comply with regulation 63 of the Habitats Regulations?

41   Mr Gregory Jones Q.C., for Mr Wyatt, submitted that the judge made two fundamental errors in his approach to the legal framework governing appropriate assessment. First, he accepted Ms Potts' evidence on the soundness of the method used by the council in conducting the appropriate assessment. He ought to have looked at the underlying evidence and considered, for himself, whether the figures used were sound. This, submitted Mr Jones, follows from the CJEU's judgment in *Dutch Nitrogen*, in particular at paragraph 101. He accepted that the court must adopt a *Wednesbury* approach, but he submitted that the approach should be more stringent given the high level of certainty required under regulation 63. Given that much of the water environment in the Solent was in unfavourable or failing status, the level of certainty required was higher. A distinction must be made between evidence considered by decision-makers at the time, and expert evidence produced later in explanation. Secondly, the judge had erred in his approach to the "precautionary principle". He should have accepted that where data is uncertain, the "reasonable worst-case scenario" must be assessed. This follows from the European Commission's guidance on the precautionary principle, cited with approval in *Bayer CropScience v Commission* (T-429/13), and it would be consistent with the approach taken in environmental impact assessment (see *R. v Rochdale Metropolitan Borough Council, ex parte Milne (No.2)* (2001) 81 P. & C.R. 27).

42   On ground 1 of the appeal Mr Jones argued that Natural England's technical guidance note invited error when it said local authorities "may choose to adopt bespoke calculations" for occupancy rates. In particular, he criticised the first sentence of paragraph 4.7 of the technical guidance note, the first sentence of paragraph 4.19, and paragraph 4.42. It would never be permissible for an authority to adopt the national average occupancy rate unless it was the correct occupancy rate for the development proposed. Authorities must adopt bespoke calculations. Otherwise, their decisions will not be based on the "best scientific knowledge". The correct occupancy rate was not a matter of expert judgment; it was a simple and readily ascertainable fact. In this case it was common ground that the occupancy rate of 2.4 persons per dwelling was inaccurate, and that an occupancy rate of 3 would have been accurate for the four-bedroom houses proposed. The council's decision to adopt an occupancy rate of 2.4 was therefore wrong, and unlawful. Each factor in the calculation of the nitrogen budget had to be precautionary, and based on the best available evidence. It was not permissible to rely on the precautionary nature of other factors, or on the precautionary buffer applied at the end, to justify using an insufficiently precautionary occupancy rate. Once the judge had concluded that using an occupancy rate of 2.4 did not represent the "best scientific knowledge", he could not hold that its use was lawful (see *Holohan*, at paragraph 33). He should not have found it sufficiently precautionary on the strength of the two factors mentioned by Ms Potts; there was no evidence that they would counteract the error. It was also inconsistent to conclude, as he did, that Natural

England's technical guidance note would need to be reviewed in the light of his judgment but that the decision in this case, based on the advice given in that document, was nonetheless sound.

43   On ground 2 Mr Jones criticised the use of average figures, and, in particular, the use of "average land use figures" in calculating the baseline nitrogen deposition from the site. Average figures relied on speculation about what might happen in the future, and so were necessarily contrary to the requirement for certainty under regulation 63. In *Dutch Nitrogen* the CJEU had made it clear that reliance on average values was impermissible (paragraphs 55 and 147 of the Advocate General's opinion, and paragraph 119 of the judgment). Using average land use figures to calculate the baseline nitrogen deposition from the site was insufficiently precautionary. Both in adopting these average figures and in its use of the Farmscoper model, Natural England's advice in paragraphs 4.45 to 4.52 of the technical guidance note was flawed, and so was the council's application of that advice in the appropriate assessment.

44   On ground 4 Mr Jones argued that the 20% precautionary buffer applied by the council was unlawful, because it lacked any evidential basis. The purpose of the buffer was not merely to provide an extra level of protection but to ensure that the whole exercise met the required standard of scientific certainty. To remove "all reasonable scientific doubt" about the effects of the proposed works on the protected site concerned", the uncertainty inherent in the initial steps must first be quantified, and then an appropriate buffer applied in light of that uncertainty (see *People Over Wind*, at paragraph 38). Natural England's relevant advice (in paragraphs 4.8, 4.9 and 4.67 of the technical guidance note) was flawed, and so was the council's application of that advice in the appropriate assessment.

45   Those arguments all go to the contention that the council erred in law when performing its duty under regulation 63(5) of the Habitats Regulations not to grant planning permission unless it had ascertained that the proposed development would "not adversely affect the integrity of the European site". I do not accept that contention. The council's conclusion on the crucial question under regulation 63(5) was, ultimately, an evaluative judgment for it to make as "competent authority". And in my view the conclusion it reached, as a matter of evaluative judgment, was legally sound. I therefore agree with the decision in the court below on this part of the claim.

46   I cannot fault the judge's self-direction on the relevant legal principles (in paragraphs 29 to 39 of his judgment), and in my opinion he went on to apply those principles appropriately. I do not think he made the fundamental errors of which he is accused.

47   The first of those alleged errors, essentially, is that the judge simply accepted the evidence of Ms Potts without question. I do not think he did that. On the contrary, he examined in appropriate depth and detail the evidence of the expert witnesses on either side (in paragraphs 58 to 72, and paragraphs 106 to 111).

48   On occupancy rates, he approached the evidence before him with care. He expressed his own concerns about some of that evidence (in paragraphs 75 to 80). He did not rely on the parts he found less than convincing (paragraph 84). He reminded himself of "[the] need for judicial deference in a domain of technical and scientific expertise" (paragraph 81). He acknowledged that the figures used by the competent authority must "have the effect of removing all scientific doubt "based on complete, precise and definitive findings"" (paragraph 79).

49   Nor did he accept unquestioningly the use of the 20% precautionary buffer, in the way in which it had been applied, merely because Ms Potts said that this was appropriate. In her evidence, she had explained, at length, the justification for using the 20% buffer (her second witness statement, paragraphs 56 to 64, and her third witness statement, paragraphs 18 to 21). She did not simply assert that its use was correct. And the judge, for his part, did not simply take her evidence at face value. He considered the reasons she had given in support of the 20% buffer, and he concluded, in the light of that evidence, that there was no justification for the court's intervention "on any *Wednesbury* basis" (paragraph 111). I agree.

50   More generally, it seems to me that the judge adopted the correct approach in his consideration of the council's appropriate assessment as a whole. He understood that the *Wednesbury* standard of review had to be deployed with suitable rigour in the legislative context here. He knew that he had to establish whether, in all the circumstances, the council had reached a reasonable and lawful conclusion, as a matter of its own exercise of evaluative judgment, in ascertaining whether the high threshold set by regulation 63(5) had been surmounted. He applied an appropriately intense standard of scrutiny, consistent with the proper application of *Wednesbury* principles in the light of the jurisprudence to which he had referred.

51   I reject the submission that the judge ought to have given greater weight than he did to the unfavourable status of the water environment in parts of the Solent. This was a fact explicitly acknowledged and taken into account by Natural England when issuing the advice in its technical guidance note – advice on which the council relied in its appropriate assessment. And there is no support either in the habitats legislation itself or in the relevant authorities for the proposition that the unfavourable status of a protected site raises the level of certainty which has to be achieved if the proposed development is to be approved, or for the proposition that the standard of review the court should adopt in those circumstances is more demanding. In this case, Natural England's technical guidance note, to which the council had regard in undertaking the appropriate assessment, took into account the fact some of the protected sites in the Solent were "widely in unfavourable condition due to existing levels of nutrients" and "at risk from additional nutrient inputs" (paragraph 2.3).

52   Whatever the particular circumstances in a given case, the basic duty of the competent authority under regulation 63 is, and remains, to grant planning permission only if satisfied that the proposed development "will not adversely affect the integrity" of the European protected site. The duty of the court is, and remains, to ensure that the authority's evaluative judgment on that question was lawfully exercised.

53   In doing that, the court must keep in mind the difference between evidence of what was considered by a decision-making authority at the time of its decision and evidence put forward after the event to explain or justify that decision (see *R. (on the application of United Trade Action Group Ltd.) v Transport for London* [2021] EWCA Civ 1197). It is trite, for example, that later evidence of a decision-maker's thinking cannot be used to contradict the original reasons given or to provide wholly new reasons (see *R. v Westminster City Council, ex parte Ermakov* [1996] 2 All E.R. 302, and *Inclusion Housing Community Interest Company v Regulator of Social Housing* [2020] EWHC 346 (Admin), at paragraph 78). But that has not been done in this case. Ms Potts' evidence goes no further than to amplify the reasons why Natural England decided to adopt the approach it did, and reached

the view it did, at the time of its consultation by the council. The evidence was properly admitted, and the judge was entitled to rely on it as he did.

54   As for the second fundamental error of which the judge is accused, I do not think he adopted too lax an understanding of the precautionary principle, either generally or as it applied in this case, or that he wrongly discounted the concept of the "reasonable worst-case scenario", contrary to the CJEU's reasoning in Bayer CropScience and the High Court's in *ex parte Milne*. In *Bayer CropScience* the CJEU cited the European Commission's guidance, "Communication on the precautionary principle" (2000) Annex III, which advises that in cases of doubt a "worst-case" hypothesis "could" – not must – be assessed (paragraph 114 of the judgment). But it did not treat the guidance as if it had the status of law. It adopted the established approach, consistent with its own judgment in *Waddenzee*. Nor does the principle referred to in *ex parte Milne* – that a proposal requiring environmental impact assessment must be sufficiently detailed to allow for proper assessment – bear on the question here, which is whether any uncertainty in the data involved in an appropriate assessment under regulation 63 must always be resolved by using a "reasonable worst-case scenario". In *Waddenzee*, as Jay J. said (in paragraph 32 of his judgment), the CJEU accepted that national authorities do not need to be "absolutely certain" that there will not be adverse effects on the integrity of the protected site, but must be "satisfied that there is no reasonable doubt as to the absence of adverse effects". The judge asked himself "whether "reasonable worst case scenario" is an apt synonym for "precautionary"", but he did not think it was necessary to come to a decisive view on the point (paragraph 47). I do not think he needed to do so. In my view it was legitimate for him to conclude that, at least in this case, the "reasonable worst-case scenario" did not have to be assessed if the precautionary principle was to be satisfied.

55   Turning to ground 1 of the appeal, I do not think there can be any proper challenge in these proceedings to the lawfulness of the advice given by Natural England in its technical guidance note, which seems to have been the real target for much of the argument advanced on behalf of Mr Wyatt.

56   It should be remembered that the technical guidance note is not statute. It does not create some additional legal requirement or test. It is an advisory document, which is neither mandatory in effect nor prescriptive of a single correct procedure to be followed. It contains guidance, whose purpose is to assist competent authorities in performing their functions under the habitats legislation. It does not assert that the approach it suggests is the only means of conducting an appropriate assessment. On the contrary, it expressly acknowledges that this approach is only "a means" or "one way" of undertaking that task (paragraphs 1.3, 2.6 and 4.1).

57   The Supreme Court has recently confirmed that there are only limited grounds on which a policy can be challenged as itself being unlawful (see *R. (on the application of A) v Secretary of State for the Home Department* [2021] UKSC 37, and also the recent decision of this court in *R. (on the application of Pearce) v The Parole Board* [2022] EWCA Civ 4). In *R. (on the application of A)* Lord Sales and Lord Burnett C.J. stressed that it is "not the role of policy guidance to eliminate all uncertainty regarding its application and all risk of legal errors" (paragraph 34). The appropriate question for the court is this: "does the policy in question authorise or approve unlawful conduct by those to whom it is directed?" (paragraph 38).

58   Where Natural England's advice on the appropriate occupancy rate is concerned, the answer to that question would clearly be "No". At the level of generality at

which the technical guidance note was suggesting it, the use of an occupancy rate of 2.4 persons per dwelling cannot be said to be unlawful on the ground that it is inconsistent with the "best scientific evidence". The technical guidance note did not misstate the legal position under regulation 63 (see *R. (on the application of A),* at paragraphs 46 and 47). It did not "authorise or approve", let alone prescribe, the use of that occupancy rate by all local planning authorities in every case, regardless of the circumstances. It did not remove or reduce the onus on those authorities to be sure, beyond "all reasonable scientific doubt", that the integrity of the protected site would not be adversely affected (see paragraphs 1.4, 2.5, 4.6 to 4.9, and 4.18 to 4.19 of the technical guidance note).

59   Nor do I accept the criticism made of the council's use of an occupancy rate of 2.4 persons per dwelling in the particular circumstances of this case. Although an appropriate assessment must be based on "best scientific knowledge", the question for the court is not whether each individual figure used in it is intrinsically the "best scientific knowledge" when considered on its own, divorced from the full context in which it is used. As Mr David Elvin Q.C. submitted for Natural England, the court must take a "holistic" view on the question whether the assessment methodology as a whole represents "best scientific knowledge".

60   When that is done here, it is, I think, plain that the council understood its duty under regulation 63 correctly. This much is clear from the summary of the law which the officer set out in his report (in particular, at paragraph 8.26), and from the equivalent summary in the appropriate assessment itself (in particular, at pp.15 to 19).

61   The council consulted Natural England twice. As the judge said (in paragraph 81 of his judgment), Natural England had specifically considered "the application of more size-sensitive datasets but rejected the need for [that]". It does not seem to have intended that the occupancy rate of 2.4 persons per dwelling should always be only a "starting point". It evidently took the view that there were sound reasons in consistency, given the nature and availability of other datasets, to use that occupancy rate for development in the Solent (Ms Potts' third witness statement, paragraphs 7 and 8). This was, on the face of it, a carefully considered judgment. And in any event, the council's committee considered objections to the use of an occupancy rate of 2.4 for the proposed development, but rejected them in the light of Natural England's response to consultation. Tellingly, Natural England did not oppose the use of that occupancy rate in this particular case, rather than the adoption of a bespoke figure. It had seen the council's nitrogen budget before responding to consultation, and it knew therefore that an occupancy rate of 2.4 was being used in that nitrogen budget. Had it been concerned about this, one would have expected it to make that clear, but it raised no such concern. And as Mr Timothy Mould Q.C. submitted for the council, compelling reasons would have been required for the council to depart from Natural England's position.

62   In the circumstances it was, I think, open to the council to rely on the precautionary nature of several factors in the nitrogen budget to ground its own judgment that the use of an occupancy rate of 2.4 persons per dwelling was consistent with a sufficiently precautionary approach in this instance.

63   The judge recognised the strength in two of the points made by Ms Potts in her evidence – that the relationship between occupancy rates and water usage was "not one of direct proportionality", and that the algorithm "assumed 100% migration to the area" (paragraph 84 of the judgment). He did not confine himself to reliance

on these two reasons alone – he merely said (in the same paragraph) that these two reasons "have force" and that he found the other reasons "less persuasive".

64   There were, I think, at least six other factors identified by Ms Potts in her second witness statement which, in combination with the two considerations on which the judge focused, were capable of justifying the conclusion that the use of the 2.4 occupancy rate would be consistent with the precautionary principle here. First, the water use figures for the proposed development were themselves precautionary. They were "10% higher than Southern Water's target required", and they did not take into account the fact that "[all] new build development will have meters and water use in metered properties is significantly lower than non-metered properties". Second, the water use figures were based on "water supply", which would in fact be "less than water return to [wastewater treatment works] reflecting use of water to wash cars, [and] water gardens". Third, the wastewater treatment works were "performing 25% more effectively" than the level assumed in the nitrogen calculations (see also paragraph 4.29 of Natural England's technical guidance note). Fourth, there would be natural reductions in nitrogen concentrations, mainly through de-nitrification processes, which were unquantifiable and so were not taken into account in the calculation (see also paragraph 4.42 of the technical guidance note). Fifth, there was not a high degree of correlation between occupancy rates and dwelling sizes. And sixth, an unknown proportion of the nitrogen discharged to the sea would not affect the protected sites.

65   The council was also entitled to rely, as the planning officer did in paragraph 8.41 of his report, on the use of the 20% precautionary buffer applied at the end of the calculation to strengthen the conclusion that the use of the 2.4 occupancy rate was appropriate in the particular circumstances of this case. Obviously, the application of such a buffer at the end of a calculation would not excuse a general lack of precaution in the figures used in the calculation itself. This could lead to impermissible "double-counting". But that is not what happened here. Even though, in this respect, the approach adopted by the council seems not to have been what the technical guidance note contemplated, the precautionary buffer was not used here to justify a general lack of precaution in the exercise, but to strengthen the justification for using an occupancy rate of 2.4 in the calculation. As Mr Mould submitted, it was not *Wednesbury* unreasonable to use it in this way. It was not the sole justification for the council's conclusion, as a matter of judgment, that an occupancy rate set at this level was consistent with a sufficiently precautionary approach in the appropriate assessment for this proposed development. It was one element in the broader justification for the use of that occupancy rate, to be seen in the context of the assessment methodology as a whole.

66   It would not be right for the court to intervene in a case of this kind simply because there is a divergence of expert opinion on some of the figures used in the appropriate assessment. Sometimes, perhaps often, there may not be a consensus of expert opinion. If that is so, there is nothing in law to compel the competent authority in making an appropriate assessment, or the court in reviewing the authority's decision taken in the light of that appropriate assessment, to default to the most conservative or cautious view propounded.

67   The argument advanced by Mr Jones does not demonstrate that in this case it was inappropriate or unlawful for the council to adopt the occupancy rate of 2.4 persons per dwelling on the ground that it was, in one expert's view, insufficiently precautionary – or for any other reason. As Mr Elvin submitted, this is a paradigm

case of expert witnesses differing on matters of scientific judgment, in which the court would need to be shown some conspicuous error in the competent authority's own evaluation of the expert advice it received at the time of its decision before that decision could properly be overturned. For the court to upset a decision when it has not been shown that the competent authority's own exercise of evaluative judgment was so defective as to be *Wednesbury* unreasonable but where there is disagreement between experts on the correct ingredients of the appropriate assessment, would involve the court stepping beyond its proper supervisory jurisdiction into the realm of the competent authority's own remit under the habitats legislation.

68   I think Mr Jones' criticism of the judge's reasoning on this issue is mistaken. The judge accepted that "[an] occupancy rate of 3 would be the best available scientific evidence for 4-5 bedroom houses in the Fareham region" (paragraph 83). This, however, was not fatal to his essential analysis. Reading the relevant passage of his judgment fairly as a whole, I do not think it can be said that he fell into error. He was recognising the fact that, taken in isolation, an occupancy rate of 3 would generally be appropriate for four and five-bedroom houses in the area. Nowhere did he suggest, however, that in this case the appropriate assessment as a whole was inconsistent with "best scientific knowledge". He found that the method used in the appropriate assessment, taken in its entirety and thus including the occupancy rate of 2.4, complied with the precautionary principle. He accepted as lawful the council's conclusion, as a matter of its own judgment, that in the circumstances here an assessment using that occupancy rate was sufficiently precautionary. And in my view he was right to do so.

69   Lastly on this ground, I do not think the judge's view that Natural England's technical guidance note would have to be reviewed in the light of his judgment is inconsistent with his view that the approach taken to the occupancy rate in this case was legally defensible. In effect, he was pointing out that the technical guidance note, as drafted, could be liable to misinterpretation or misapplication in other cases, and suggesting that Natural England might describe more clearly the general approach it suggested to this part of the calculation.

70   Ground 2 is also, in my view, unmeritorious – for two reasons. First, I see no objection in principle to the use of average land use figures to calculate the baseline level of nitrate deposition from the site of the proposed development.

71   And secondly, I cannot agree with the reading of the CJEU's judgment in *Dutch Nitrogen* urged on us by Mr Jones. That case concerned the question of whether "programmatic legislation" – where the appropriate assessment for certain types of project was carried out in advance at a general level and those projects would then be exempt from the requirement for individual assessment – was compatible with article 6(3) of the Habitats Directive. This was the issue to which the observations of the court and Advocate General Kokott on the use of average figures were directed. When the Advocate General said (in paragraph 55 of her opinion), that "[it] would not be sufficient merely to show rough averages and to ignore local or temporary peak load values where those peak values are likely adversely to affect the conservation objectives of the site", she meant, I think, that it was not appropriate to use averages for all projects of a certain type where some projects of that type might exceed those averages and thus damage the integrity of the protected site. She made clear (in paragraph 147 of her opinion) that the difficulty with using an average value for a number of sites was that it might fail

to "guarantee that there are no significant effects on any single protected site". To the same effect, the court said (in paragraph 119 of its judgment) that "[an] average value is not, in principle, capable of ensuring that there are no significant effects on any single protected site".

72   Those statements about the use of average values in that context must be viewed with care in a case such as this, which is not concerned with "programmatic legislation" but with the individual assessment of the particular effects of a specific project. Nothing said in *Dutch Nitrogen* implies that in this situation the use of averages is inherently objectionable. It is true that the use of average figures will necessarily involve the exercise of judgment on their validity in the particular context. But this does not mean that using them is, in principle, contrary to the requirement for the necessary degree of certainty, as amplified in Waddenzee . The use of average figures may sometimes be conducive to sufficient certainty, sometimes not. Whether that is so in a particular case will be a matter of judgment for the competent authority.

73   Nothing suggests that in this case either Natural England or the council misunderstood the degree of certainty required by the precautionary principle. Nor is there any evidence to show some justiciable error in the conclusion reached, as a matter of judgment, that the use of average land use figures was, in this case, suitable for the appropriate assessment, and sufficiently robust. Dr O'Neill's evidence does not demonstrate that there was such an error. Indeed, he recognised (in paragraph 36 of his witness statement) that the selection of the correct land use for the site was "a matter of judgement", on which he "did not feel qualified to make an assessment".

74   I do not accept that the judge held that the use of average land use figures was impermissible but failed to carry that conclusion through to a finding of legal error. What he did (in paragraphs 75 to 77 of his judgment) was to point out that the relevant advice in Natural England's technical guidance note might be misconstrued in some other case in which the circumstances were different. One should not infer from what he said that in his view the use of average figures would always be impermissible, or that this was so in the circumstances here.

75   Coming finally to ground 4, I do not think there can be any serious dispute that, in a particular case, the use of a 20% precautionary buffer can ensure that the appropriate assessment meets the required standard of scientific certainty. As the judge said (in paragraph 111 of his judgment), the 20% figure is "not derived from any arithmetical calculation or other algorithm". There is, however, no legal requirement that every element of an appropriate assessment be based on arithmetic or algorithm. That would be a fallacy. If a precautionary buffer is employed, it should be set at a reasonable level, to help achieve adequate certainty that the high threshold in regulation 63 is crossed. But as Mr Mould submitted, to think that reasonable scientific judgments in undertaking an appropriate assessment can only be reached through arithmetical calculation would be to take too narrow a view of rational enquiry. Such judgments can be formed, and sometimes will best be formed, without resort to arithmetic. This will not, in principle, expose the appropriate assessment to the charge that it suffers from "lacunae" or that it lacks "complete, precise and definitive findings", as required by the CJEU (see the CJEU's observations in *People Over Wind,* at paragraph 38).

76   The fact that the 20% precautionary buffer was not the product of arithmetic, but of judgment, does not mean that it lacked an adequate basis. As Ms Potts made

clear, the appropriate figure to adopt as a buffer was considered carefully by Natural England, knowing the nature of the risks and uncertainties involved (second witness statement, paragraphs 56 to 64, and third witness statement, paragraphs 19 to 21).

77   Once again, the essence of the complaint is that there is an expert witness – Dr O'Neill – who, in his evidence to the court, has disagreed with a particular figure used in the calculation. That disagreement does not automatically equate to evidence of serious scientific doubt about an appropriate figure for a precautionary buffer. No doubt Dr O'Neill's evidence shows that, for the reasons he gave, some experts might have adopted a more generous buffer than 20%. This does not mean, however, that the court is bound to find that the buffer actually chosen by Natural England and applied by the council as competent authority was insufficiently precautionary. As Ms Potts' evidence effectively confirmed, the choice of 20% as the appropriate figure represented the expert regulatory body's judgment on the level of precautionary buffer consistent with "no reasonable doubt" that the integrity of the protected site would not be adversely affected. It was made with that level of certainty explicitly in mind (third witness statement, paragraph 21). Neither the selection of that figure in Natural England's technical guidance note nor its use in the appropriate assessment undertaken by the council in this case is open to attack on any legal grounds.

Section 38(6) of the 2004 Act

78   Section 38(6) of the 2004 Act provides:

> "(6) If regard is to be had to the development plan for the purpose of any determination to be made under the Planning Acts, the determination must be made in accordance with the plan unless material considerations indicate otherwise."

79   This provision and its predecessor, section 54A of the Town and Country Planning Act 1990, are the subject of ample authority, including several decisions at the highest level and in this court. The relevant principles do not need to be set out at length yet again. They have been stated and restated many times (see, for example, the decision of this court in *Secretary of State for Communities and Local Government v BDW Trading Ltd. (trading as David Wilson Homes (Central, Mercia and West Midlands)* [2017] P.T.S.R. 1337 at paragraphs 19 to 23). A decision-maker must always heed the statutory priority given to the development plan, but is free to assess what weight to give to its policies and to all other material considerations in deciding whether the decision should be made, as the statute presumes, in accordance with the plan (see the speech of Lord Clyde in *City of Edinburgh v Secretary of State for Scotland* [1997] 1 W.L.R. 1447 at pp.1458 and 1459). If the decision-maker fails to have regard to a relevant policy in the plan or to interpret it properly, conscious that relevant policies in the plan may pull in different directions, the court can act (Lord Clyde's speech in *City of Edinburgh* at p.1459D-F, and the judgments of Lord Reed and Lord Hope of Craighead in *Tesco Stores Ltd v Dundee City Council* [2012] P.T.S.R. 983 at paragraphs 19 and 34 respectively). But there is no prescribed method for discharging the section 38(6) duty, such as a two-stage approach. This is left to the decision-maker's good sense in the particular circumstances of the case in hand (Lord Clyde's speech in *City of Edinburgh* at pp.1459 and 1460).

80   In *R. (on the application of Hampton Bishop Parish Council) v Herefordshire Council* [2014] EWCA Civ 878, Lord Justice Richards said (in paragraph 28) that "[it] is up to the decision-maker how precisely to go about the task, but if he is to act within his powers and in particular to comply with the statutory duty to make the determination in accordance with the development plan unless material considerations indicate otherwise, he must as a general rule decide at some stage in the exercise whether the proposed development does or does not accord with the development plan". As Mrs Justice Patterson emphasised in *Tiviot Way Investments Ltd v Secretary of State for Communities and Local Government* [2015] EWHC 2489 (Admin) (at paragraphs 27 to 36), with the later endorsement of this court in *BDW Trading Ltd* (at paragraph 21), the decision-maker must ascertain whether there is compliance or conflict with the development plan "as a whole".

81   It is axiomatic that the interpretation of a development plan policy is ultimately a matter for the court, but that the application of policy is for the decision-maker, subject to the court's review on public law grounds. The court will intervene on a misconstruction of policy by the decision-maker if satisfied that this has had a material bearing on the decision. But it will only upset a local planning authority's decision based on an officer's exercise of planning judgment in assessing compliance with policy if it is convinced that a public law error has been committed (see the judgment of Lord Reed in *Tesco v Dundee City Council* at paragraph 19).

The policies of the development plan

82   At the time of the decision to grant planning permission, the development plan for the borough of Fareham comprised the adopted Fareham Borough Core Strategy and the adopted Fareham Local Plan Part 2: Development Sites and Policies Plan. In his report to the committee the officer identified a number of relevant policies, including Policy CS2 ("Housing Provision"), Policy CS6 ("The Development Strategy") and Policy CS14 ("Development Outside Settlements") of the core strategy, and Policy DSP6 ("New Residential Development Outside of the Defined Urban Settlement Boundaries") and Policy DSP40 ("Housing Allocations") of the local plan (paragraph 4.1 of the officer's report).

83   Policy CS14 of the core strategy says that "[built] development on land outside the defined settlements will be strictly controlled to protect the countryside and coastline from development which would adversely affect its landscape character, appearance and function", and that "[acceptable] forms of development will include that essential for agriculture, forestry, horticulture and required infrastructure ...".

84   The first part of Policy DSP40 of the local plan refers to the sites allocated for residential development, sites with planning permission for residential development, and sites safeguarded from other forms of development. The second part of the policy deals with the situation where the requisite five-year supply of land for housing is lacking. It states:

> "Where it can be demonstrated that the Council does not have a five year supply of land for housing against the requirements of the Core Strategy (excluding Welbourne) additional housing sites, outside the urban area boundary, may be permitted where they meet all of the following criteria:
>
> > i. The proposal is relative in scale to the demonstrated 5 year housing land supply shortfall;

ii. The proposal is sustainably located adjacent to, and well related to, the existing urban settlement boundaries, and can be well integrated with the neighbouring settlement;

iii. The proposal is sensitively designed to reflect the character of the neighbouring settlement and to minimise any adverse impact on the Countryside and, if relevant, the Strategic Gaps;

iv. It can be demonstrated that the proposal is deliverable in the short term; and

v. The proposal would not have any unacceptable environmental, amenity or traffic implications."

The officer's advice on section 38(6) of the 2004 Act

85   When considering the implications of the five-year housing land supply, the officer advised the members that section 38(6) of the 2004 Act was the "starting point for the determination of this planning application" (paragraph 8.8 of the report), and that "there is a presumption in favour of policies of the extant Development Plan, unless material considerations indicate otherwise". He also reminded them that "[material] considerations include the planning policies set out in the [National Planning Policy Framework ("NPPF")]" (paragraph 8.9).

86   He then referred to several policies of the NPPF, including the policy for the "presumption in favour of sustainable development" in paragraph 11 (paragraph 8.12), and the policy in paragraph 177, which states that "[the] presumption in favour of sustainable development does not apply where the plan or project is likely to have a significant effect on a habitats site (either alone or in combination with other plans or projects), unless an appropriate assessment has concluded that the plan or project will not adversely affect the integrity of the habitats site" (paragraph 8.14).

87   On the question of the proposal's acceptability as residential development in the countryside, the officer concluded that it was in conflict with Policy CS14 and several other policies of the development plan, stating "[the] site is clearly outside of the defined urban settlement boundary and the proposal is therefore contrary to Policies CS2, CS6 and CS14 of the adopted Core Strategy and Policy DSP6 of the adopted Local Plan Part 2: Development Sites and Policies Plan" (in paragraph 8.22).

88   The officer quoted Policy DSP40 of the local plan in full (in paragraph 8.52) and then dealt with it in a series of paragraphs (paragraphs 8.53 to 8.65), in which he addressed each of the five criteria in the second part of the policy. On the second criterion, he said this (in paragraph 8.55):

"8.55 The site is considered to be sustainably located within a reasonable distance of local schools, services and facilities at nearby local centres (Warsash and Locks Heath). This part of the northern arm of Brook Avenue is located outside of the urban area, the existing urban settlement boundary being approximately 140 metres east of the site. The proposal is not therefore adjacent to the urban settlement boundary."

He found compliance with each of the other four criteria (paragraphs 8.54 and 8.56 to 8.65.).

89   When he came to the "planning balance", the officer said (in paragraph 8.78):

"8.78 Section 38(6) of [the 2004 Act] sets out the starting point for the determination of planning applications …".

He then quoted section 38(6), and continued (in paragraphs 8.79 to 8.83):

"8.79 This application has previously been the subject of a favourable Committee resolution to grant planning permission. The revised application proposes additional measures to address the matter of nutrient neutrality but is otherwise the same.

8.80 The site is outside of the defined urban settlement boundary and the proposal does not relate to agriculture, forestry, horticulture and required infrastructure. The principle of the proposed development of the site would be contrary to Policies CS2, CS6 and CS14 of the Core Strategy and Policy DSP6 of Local Plan Part 2: Development Sites and Policies Plan.

8.81 Officers have carefully assessed the proposals against Policy DSP40: Housing Allocations which is engaged as this Council cannot demonstrate a 5YHLS. In weighing up the material considerations and conflicts between policies; the development of a greenfield site weighted against Policy DSP40, Officers have concluded that the proposal is relative in scale to the demonstrated 5YHLS shortfall (DSP40(i)), can be delivered in the short-term (DSP40(iv)), and would not have any unacceptable environmental, traffic or amenity implications (DSP40(v)). Whilst there would be harm to the character and appearance of the countryside the unsightly derelict buildings currently on the site would be demolished. Furthermore, it has been shown that the site could accommodate eight houses set back from the Brook Avenue frontage and an area of green space to sensitively reflect nearby existing development and reduce the visual impact thereby satisfying DSP40(iii). Officers have however found there to be some conflict with the second test at Policy DSP40(ii) since the site is acknowledged to be in a sustainable location but is not adjacent to the existing urban area.

8.82 In balancing the objectives of adopted policy which seeks to restrict development within the countryside alongside the shortage in housing supply, Officers acknowledge that the proposal could deliver 8 dwellings, as well as an off-site contribution towards affordable housing provision, in the short term. The contribution the proposed scheme would make towards boosting the Borough's housing supply would be modest but is still a material consideration in the light of this Council's current 5YHLS.

8.83 There is a clear conflict with development plan policy CS14 as this is development in the countryside. Ordinarily, officers would have found this to be the principal policy such that a scheme in the countryside should be refused. However, in light of the Council's lack of a 5YHLS, development plan policy DSP40 is engaged and officers have considered the scheme against the criteria therein. The scheme is considered to satisfy four of the five criteria and in the circumstances, officers consider that more weight should be given to this policy than CS14 such that, on balance, when considered against the development plan as a whole, the scheme should be approved."

90   The officer went on to consider relevant policies in the NPPF (in paragraphs 8.84 to 8.87). He referred to the fact that an appropriate assessment had been undertaken and had "concluded that the development would not have an adverse

effect on the integrity of the sites"; noted that in these circumstances paragraph 177 of the NPPF said "the presumption in favour of sustainable development imposed by paragraph 11 … is applied" (paragraph 8.84); confirmed that officers had "therefore assessed the proposals against the 'tilted balance' test set out at paragraph 11 of the NPPF" (paragraph 8.85), and considered there to be "no policies within the [NPPF] that protect areas or assets of particular importance which provide a clear reason for refusing the development proposed" and that "any adverse impacts of granting permission would not significantly and demonstrably outweigh the benefits, when assessed against the policies in the [NPPF] taken as a whole" (paragraph 8.86). He recommended that planning permission be granted, subject to a section 106 obligation and suitable conditions (paragraph 8.87).

The judge's conclusions on the section 38(6) grounds

91   Jay J. found it clear that the officer had advised the committee that the proposed development did not accord with the development plan in a number of respects. However, paragraph 8.83 of the report gave rise, in his view, to "a degree of interpretative challenge", and "its various strands are difficult to identify and disentangle" (paragraph 159). That paragraph, he thought, was "somewhat elliptical" and "a degree of benevolence" was required. The issue was "how much?" (paragraph 160).

92   On that question the judge said that in paragraph 8.83 the officer "was dealing with the first stage of the s.38(6) analysis", and "considering the extent of compliance with the development plan and the ordering of policies within that plan". The officer had "found, as he was entitled to, that policy DSP40 was more important in this case than CS14, owing to the shortfall in housing supply, and that the failure to satisfy the second criterion did not undermine this conclusion". In the judge's view, "[the] final clause in para 8.83 could be better worded, but it sets out the planning officer's conclusion on the first stage". It was "not a conclusion on the s.38(6) issue tout court, still less the planning application as a whole" (paragraph 160).

93   Having concluded that paragraphs 8.84 to 8.87 of the officer's report dealt with "the second stage of the s.38(6) exercise", the judge described paragraph 8.86 of the report as a "composite conclusion on all remaining material considerations in the light of the tilted balance [in NPPF policy]". The officer's "overall conclusion" in paragraph 8.87 was, he said, was "legally unexceptionable" (paragraph 161).

Did the council lawfully discharge its duty under section 38(6)?

94   Mr Jones submitted, as he did before the judge, that the council had failed to comply with section 38(6). The officer's advice in paragraphs 8.78 to 8.87 of his report did not contain a conclusive view on the question of whether the proposed development was in accordance with the development plan as a whole – an essential part of the decision-making process, as Patterson J. had said in *Tiviot Way Investments* (paragraph 27). There was at least "substantial doubt" over the council's performance of its duty (see the judgment of Lord Justice Elias in *Secretary of State for Communities and Local Government v Calderdale MBC* [2011] J.P.L. 412 at paragraph 46). The officer had not dealt properly with the "nature and extent" of the proposal's conflict with the plan, and the significance of that conflict (see the judgment of Lord Reed in *Tesco v Dundee City Council* at paragraph 22). In

the final sentence of paragraph 8.83 of the report, it was not clear whether he was saying that the proposal accorded with the plan as a whole, or that, despite not being in accordance with the plan, it should be approved because "other material considerations [indicated] otherwise". Having recognised the ambiguity in the officer's assessment, the judge should have found there was "substantial doubt" sufficient to justify his quashing the planning permission. He went beyond the "benevolence" appropriate in the reading of a planning officer's report.

95   Mr Mould supported the judge's analysis. The court, he submitted, should not read the officer's report with undue rigour, but with "reasonable benevolence" and bearing in mind it was written for councillors with local knowledge (see *R. (on the application of Mansell) v Tonbridge and Malling BC* [2019] P.T.S.R. 1452; [2017] EWCA Civ 1314 at paragraph 42). Reading the report fairly, it could not conclude that the members had been materially misled. The officer understood the priority to be given to the development plan. He was clearly satisfied that, on balance, the proposal was in accordance with the plan. Because of the shortfall in the housing land supply, he gave more weight to Policy DSP40 of the local plan than to Policy CS14 of the core strategy. In paragraph 8.83 of the report he concluded, in effect, that the limited conflict with Policy DSP40, a partial conflict with only one of its five criteria, when added to the conflict with other plan policies, did not prevent him from finding the proposal in accordance with the plan "as a whole". This was a reasonable and lawful exercise of planning judgment. The following four paragraphs of the report, paragraphs 8.84 to 8.87, were devoted to "other material considerations" arising from the NPPF, which, again as a matter of planning judgment, the officer found not to indicate the refusal of planning permission. Both limbs of section 38(6) were properly dealt with. And the officer's ultimate conclusion on the "planning balance", in paragraph 8.87, was not irrational or otherwise unlawful.

96   This is an issue to be dealt with in the spirit of realism and common sense to which this court has often referred (see, for example, what was said in *Mansell*, at paragraph 42; and in *St Modwen Developments Ltd v Secretary of State for Communities and Local Government* [2017] EWCA Civ 1643 at paragraph 7).

97   Like the judge, I am not persuaded by Mr Jones' argument here. On a fair reading of the officer's report, in particular the passages which embody the performance of the decision-maker's duty under section 38(6), I would accept that the assessment may, in part, be infelicitously expressed, but not that it is, in substance, unlawful. This is not to ignore the well-known principles governing the approach to planning officers' reports to committee stated by this court in *Mansell*, but only to apply those principles sensibly in the circumstances here. When that is done, I do not think one can conclude that there was any "material defect" in the officer's advice justifying interference by the court (see *Mansell*, at paragraph 42(3)).

98   Unlike several cases which have recently found their way to the Court of Appeal or above (see, for example, *Braintree District Council v Secretary of State for Communities and Local Government* [2018] EWCA Civ 610), there is no issue of policy interpretation for the court to resolve here. The meaning and effect of the relevant policies of the development plan are uncontentious.

99   In any event, I do not think it can be said that this is one of those cases in which the officer, or the members, misinterpreted any of the relevant policies (see *R. (on the application of Corbett) v The Cornwall Council* [2020] EWCA Civ 508 at paragraphs 65 to 67). The officer recognised that the proposal was in conflict with

Policy CS14 of the core strategy because it would be development in the countryside which did not fall into any of the acceptable forms of development identified in that policy. Indeed, he accepted that there was a "clear conflict" with that policy, "as this is development in the countryside", and that this conflict would "ordinarily" have led to the refusal of planning permission (paragraph 8.83 of his report).

100   I agree with Mr Jones that we can put to one side the general quality of the officer's report, and the obvious care he took in other parts of his planning assessment. As Mr Jones submitted, the judge's observations praising the officer for the way in which he dealt with other matters could not override a finding that he went wrong in handling the requirements of section 38(6). But I also accept Mr Mould's submission that those observations of the judge played no part in his conclusions on those parts of the officer's report where the officer applied the policies of the development plan and took other material considerations into account.

101   It cannot be suggested that either the officer or the committee was unaware of section 38(6) and the need to perform the duty it states. The officer quoted that provision at the beginning of his consideration of "the planning balance", in paragraph 8.78 of his report. He obviously had it in mind as he went about that assessment. So this is not a case where it is unclear whether the decision-maker had in mind the words of the statute and proceeded in the light of them. Here, the officer plainly did that. The question is whether he did so lawfully.

102   As Mr Mould submitted, the structure of the officer's section 38(6) assessment, in paragraphs 8.78 to 8.87 of his report, is divided into two parts. In the first, comprising paragraphs 8.78 to 8.83, the officer addressed the first limb of the duty – to ascertain whether the proposal was or was not "in accordance with the development plan". In the second part, which comprises paragraphs 8.84 to 8.87, he turned to "other material considerations", in particular the policy for the "presumption in favour of sustainable development" in paragraph 11 of the NPPF. He did not have to split the assessment in this way, there being no statutory requirement to do so. But he was entitled to do it, and was thus able to divide his conclusions on the two limbs more distinctly than if he had combined them in a single sentence or paragraph.

103   I consider, as the judge did, that the officer reached a clear conclusion on the compliance of the proposal with the development plan as a whole. That conclusion appears in the final sentence of paragraph 8.83 of the report. It is true that the officer did not express it in the language used in the first limb of the section 38(6) duty. He did not say, explicitly, that the proposal was "in accordance with the development plan". He said that "on balance, when considered against the development plan as a whole, the scheme should be approved". This corresponds to the first limb of the statutory duty. In the context of the officer's consideration of the four policies of the development plan to which he referred in paragraph 8.80 and his consideration of Policy DSP40 of the local plan and Policy CS14 of the core strategy in paragraphs 8.81 to 8.83, it was, in my view, a sufficiently clear conclusion that the proposal was in accordance with the plan as a whole. To hold otherwise would be to rob the officer's conclusion of its real meaning, and to undo the committee's acceptance of it in resolving as it did.

104   Was the officer lawfully entitled to reach the conclusion that the proposed development accorded with the development plan as a whole? In my view he was. So long as he did not lapse into a misunderstanding of any relevant policy of the

plan – which he did not – the accordance of the proposal with the plan as a whole was a matter of planning judgment for him.

105   What the planning officer did here, as one sees in paragraph 8.22 of the report, was to acknowledge that the application site was "clearly outside … the defined urban settlement boundary", so that the proposal was "contrary to" several policies of the core strategy and also Policy DSP6 of the local plan. However, because of the absence of a five-year supply of housing land under the requirements of the core strategy it was Policy DSP40 of the local plan on which the officer focused, as the policy of central relevance to the proposal. There can be no complaint about that. This was a classic case of two policies of the development plan pulling in different directions: Policy CS14 of the core strategy pointing to a refusal of planning permission for housing development in the countryside, and Policy DSP40 creating, in its second part, a different and permissive approach to such proposals in the absence of a five-year supply of housing land, subject to the criteria set out. In those circumstances the two policies would obviously be in tension with each other. A proposal satisfying the criteria in the second part of Policy DSP40 would accord with the policy formulated specifically for the situation which arose here, but would likely be in conflict with Policy CS14. In that situation, the decision-maker would have to consider which of these two policies should prevail, the general policy for development in the countryside or the policy deliberately crafted for housing development in the countryside where there is not a five-year supply of housing land. In this case the officer effectively gave precedence to Policy DSP40, as he was clearly entitled to do.

106   The part of Policy DSP40 which fell to be applied here, because of the absence of a 5-year supply of housing land, sets out what is, in effect, a self-contained policy approach to the determination of applications for planning permission for housing development in those circumstances. The five criteria in the policy encapsulate considerations to which the council will need to have regard when determining such an application.

107   The officer quoted the relevant part of Policy DSP40 in paragraph 8.52 of his report, and then went through the five criteria, one by one, in paragraphs 8.53 to 8.65. He did not suggest that any of those criteria could be left out of account. He found that four of them – the first, third, fourth, and fifth – were fully complied with. There is no criticism of his consideration of those four criteria. The other criterion – the second – he dealt with in paragraph 8.55, reaching the significant conclusion that the site was "sustainably located within a reasonable distance of local schools, services and facilities at nearby local centres …". But because the urban settlement boundary was "approximately 140 metres east of the site", the development would "not … [be] adjacent to [that] boundary". Thus the proposal complied partially with the second criterion, though not totally. It was non-compliant only to the extent that the site was 140 metres from the urban settlement boundary, not "adjacent" to it. There is, however, no definition of the concept of adjacency in the policy. This is left to the decision-maker's planning judgment on the facts of the particular case. In summary, therefore, the proposal was fully compliant with four of the five criteria in the policy and substantially compliant with the other.

108   Those conclusions were picked up later in the officer's report, and distilled in paragraph 8.81, where he concluded that there was compliance with the first, third, fourth and fifth criteria of Policy DSP40, but "some conflict" with the second

criterion, "since the site is acknowledged to be in a sustainable location but is not adjacent to the existing urban area". None of that part of the officer's assessment betrays any misunderstanding of Policy DSP40, nor any unlawful application of it.

109   The advice in the following paragraph (paragraph 8.82) is also unimpeachable. It refers to the contribution that the proposed development would make towards the provision of housing and affordable housing in the situation to which the second part of Policy DSP40 is directed – the absence of a five-year housing land supply.

110   In paragraph 8.83 the officer recognised the "clear conflict" with Policy CS14 of the core strategy, because this would be "development in the countryside". That policy, however, was not "the principal policy" because the lack of a five-year housing land supply meant that Policy DSP40 was engaged, and that the proposal was to be considered under the criteria in that policy. Having stated that position, the officer then returned to his assessment of the proposal's compliance with Policy DSP40. He concluded that "in the circumstances, … more weight should be given to this policy than CS14 such that, on balance, when considered against the development plan as a whole, the scheme should be approved".

111   That clearly was an expression of planning judgment, having regard to the role of Policy DSP40 as the main policy of relevance, and the degree of compliance the officer had found with it. One can readily infer that in his view some provisions of the development plan pulled in opposite directions (see Lord Clyde's speech in *City of Edinburgh* at p.1459 D-F, and the judgments of Lord Reed and Lord Hope in *Tesco v Dundee City Council* respectively at paragraphs 19 and 34, and the judgment of Mr Justice Sullivan, as he then was, in *ex parte Milne*, at paragraphs 48 to 50). Policy CS14 of the core strategy was in tension with Policy DSP40 of the local plan, but the latter prevailed because there was not a five-year supply of housing land. The proposal substantially complied with the relevant part of Policy DSP40, satisfying all five criteria save for its limited conflict with the second criterion. And that limited conflict with one element of a single criterion in the policy was not, in the officer's view, enough to prevent a finding of compliance with "the development plan as a whole". In other words, the degree of conflict with the policy was not, overall, of such significance as to prevent approval of the scheme being in accordance with the plan for the purposes of section 38(6). This conclusion too, was a matter of planning judgment for the officer and is not assailable on any public law grounds.

112   There was, in my view, no misunderstanding or unlawful misapplication of development plan policy, and the path was open to the officer to reach the conclusion he did in the final sentence of paragraph 8.83 – that, "on balance", when it was "considered against the development plan as a whole", the proposal ought to be approved. Though not perhaps expressed with perfect clarity, this was a rational conclusion in the exercise of planning judgment, consistent with the relevant passages of the officer's report read fairly together, and plain in its meaning in that context. In short, it was lawful.

113   The officer's conclusions on other material considerations in paragraphs 8.84 to 8.87 were predicated on his conclusion on the first limb of the section 38(6) duty – that a decision to grant planning permission for the proposed development would be in accordance with the development plan. Those conclusions, whose import was that "material considerations" did not indicate that planning permission should

be refused, were clearly stated, and are sufficient, in my view, to comply with the second limb of section 38(6). I agree with the judge's conclusions to that effect.

114   In my view, therefore, the officer's assessment under section 38(6), regarded with realism and common sense, is not flawed by any error of law. The reality here is that in the conscious performance of the section 38(6) duty, he undertook every necessary exercise of planning judgment for that duty to be complied with, and none of those planning judgments are infected by legal error. In substance, the officer's assessment, accepted by the members, was not materially defective.

Conclusion

115   For the reasons I have given, I would dismiss the appeal.

LORD JUSTICE SINGH:

116   I agree that this appeal should be dismissed for the reasons given by the Senior President of Tribunals.

LORD JUSTICE MALES:

117   I agree with the judgment of the Senior President of Tribunals on grounds two, four and five, concerned respectively with the use of average land use figures in the calculation of baseline nitrogen deposition, the use of a 20% buffer in the budget calculation, and section 38(6) of the Planning and Compulsory Purchase Act 2004. On those issues I have nothing to add.

118   On the first ground of appeal, which is concerned with the use of the average national occupancy rate of 2.4 persons per dwelling in calculating a nutrient budget for a development of 4-5 bedroom houses, I agree with what the Senior President has said and with his conclusion that the appeal should be dismissed. However, I think it necessary to spell out that, in my view at any rate, the Council's appropriate assessment was not in accordance with the procedure set out in the technical guidance issued by Natural England, but was nevertheless lawful because there was a good reason not to follow that procedure. In short, that good reason was that the Council consulted Natural England, making clear that it had used the 2.4 persons occupancy rate, and Natural England had no objection to this. I set out my reasoning in this judgment.

The legal framework

119   Council Directive 92/43/EC ("the Habitats Directive") was transposed into domestic law by the Conservation of Habitats and Species Regulations 2017 ("the Habitats Regulations"). In the case of a proposed development which is likely to have a significant effect on a protected site, Regulation 63 imposes three relevant obligations on a planning authority (referred to in the Regulations as a "competent authority"). It is common ground that the development here was likely to have such an effect, and that Regulation 63 is therefore engaged.

120   Those three obligations are as follows. They are mandatory. First, the planning authority must make an "appropriate assessment" of the implications of the proposed development for that site (para (1)). Second, it must consult the appropriate nature conservation body, in this case Natural England, and have regard to any representations made by that body (para (3)). Third, it must refuse planning permission if the conclusion of the "appropriate assessment" is that the proposed

development will adversely affect the integrity of the site in question (para (5): strictly, para (5) says that permission may only be granted if the development will not adversely affect the integrity of the site, but this amounts to the same thing.

121   This latter obligation is subject to an exception, not applicable here, if the planning authority is satisfied that there are "no alternative solutions" and that there are "imperative reasons of overriding public interest" for the grant of permission (see Regulation 64). But that is the only circumstance in which permission may be granted for a development when an "appropriate assessment" carried out by the planning authority indicates an adverse effect on the site in question. The existence of an exception in these very limited circumstances, but not otherwise, demonstrates the importance which the legislature has attached, as a matter of policy, to the protection of endangered habitats. Unless a proposed development qualifies as necessary for imperative reasons of overriding public interest, with no alternative solution, planning permission *must* be refused for a development which will adversely affect the integrity of the site. There is no balance to be undertaken, weighing protection of the environment against (for example) the need for housing, however acute that need may be. Unless Regulation 64 applies, the planning authority has no discretion to exercise once it has concluded, by means of an "appropriate assessment", that the effect of the proposed development will be adverse – and that is equally so even if the adverse effect is only modest.

122   Accordingly Fareham Borough Council had an obligation in the present case to carry out an appropriate assessment, to consult Natural England and to have regard to any representations which it made. The decision whether to grant permission in the light of that "appropriate assessment" remained that of the Council as the planning authority. But that decision was constrained by the outcome of the "appropriate assessment". If the assessment was unfavourable, permission had to be refused and the grant of permission would necessarily be unlawful. If the assessment was favourable, the Council would have to make a planning judgment in the usual way, with which the court would only interfere on *Wednesbury* grounds.

123   Thus in a case where Regulation 63 (but not Regulation 64) applies, the task for the planning authority is not merely to undertake an overall evaluation of all the circumstances, giving such weight to each as it thinks fit. Rather, a favourable "appropriate assessment" is a necessary gateway through which an application must pass before the grant of permission can be considered.

The nature of the "appropriate assessment"

124   Accordingly the nature of the "appropriate assessment" which a planning authority is obliged to carry out and the degree of rigour which it must bring to bear may be of critical importance. A more rigorous assessment may show an adverse effect which a less rigorous assessment would not. The question therefore arises, who decides what should be done by way of "appropriate assessment" and how it should be carried out? The answer is that, in general, it is left to the planning authority to decide for itself what steps should be taken to investigate the impact of the proposed development on the protected site. This was explained by Lord Carnwath, giving the judgment of the Supreme Court, in *R. (Champion) v North Norfolk DC* [2015] UKSC 52; [2015] 1 W.L.R. 3710:

"41. The process envisaged by article 6(3) should not be over-complicated. As Richards LJ points out, in cases where it is not obvious, the competent authority will consider whether the 'trigger' for appropriate assessment is met (and see paras 41-43 of *Waddenzee*). But this informal threshold decision is not to be confused with a formal 'screening opinion' in the EIA sense. The operative words are those of the Habitats Directive itself. All that is required is that, in a case where the authority has found there to be a risk of significant adverse effects to a protected site, there should be an 'appropriate assessment'. 'Appropriate' is not a technical term. It indicates no more than that the assessment should be appropriate to the task in hand: that task being to satisfy the responsible authority that the project 'will not adversely affect the integrity of the site taking account of the matters set out in the article. As the court itself indicated in *Waddenzee* the context implies a high standard of investigation. However, as Advocate General Kokott said in *Waddenzee* [2005] All E.R. (EC) 353, para 107:

> 'the necessary certainty cannot be construed as meaning absolute certainty since that is almost impossible to attain. Instead, it is clear from the second sentence of article 6(3) of the Habitats Directive that the competent authorities must take a decision having assessed all the relevant information which is set out in particular in the appropriate assessment. The conclusion of this assessment is, of necessity, subjective in nature. Therefore, the competent authorities can, from their point of view, be certain that there will be no adverse effects even though, from an objective point of view, there is no absolute certainty.'

In short, no special procedure is prescribed, and, while a high standard of investigation is demanded, the issue ultimately rests on the judgment of the authority."

125   Accordingly, and in general, so long as the planning authority makes rational choices as to the steps which it will take to investigate the impact of the proposed development, the court will not interfere. Those rational choices must include application of the precautionary principle, which is implicit in the Regulations, and must involve a high standard of investigation, but precisely what that means in practice in any given case is left to the judgment of the planning authority, subject only to review by the court on *Wednesbury* grounds.

Natural England's Advice to planning authorities

126   In the present context, however, Natural England as the appropriate nature conservation body has published specific guidance to planning authorities as to the nature of the "appropriate assessment" which they should carry out, which is precisely applicable to the proposed development in this case. The relevant Advice was its "Advice on Achieving Nutrient Neutrality for New Development in the Solent Region (Version 5 – June 2020)" ("the 2020 Advice").

127   The 2020 Advice sets out "a practical methodology to calculating how nutrient neutrality can be achieved", which is said to be "based on best available scientific knowledge". The methodology consists of calculating a "nutrient budget", by which the amount of nutrient deposition on protected sites resulting from a proposed development can be estimated. It is, however, important that the 2020 Advice states repeatedly that it is "one way" (or "one means") of addressing this question (see paras 1.3, 2.2 and 4.1). It does not purport to prescribe a calculation which planning

authorities in the Solent region *must* perform in all circumstances in order to carry out a lawful "appropriate assessment".

128   The 2020 Advice begins by explaining the importance for wildlife of the water environment within the Solent region and the existing (and in some cases increasing) deterioration of protected sites. The methodology which it sets out does not seek to reverse the deterioration. Rather, it has the more limited ambition that new developments should not make things worse. In that context it emphasises repeatedly that planning authorities should take a precautionary approach when addressing uncertainty and calculating nutrient budgets. For example:

> "1.4 … It is our advice to local planning authorities to take a precautionary approach in line with existing legislation and case-law when addressing uncertainty and calculating nutrient budgets."

129   The 2020 Advice goes on to explain that this precautionary approach must be adopted separately at two stages, first when determining each of the "key inputs and assumptions" underpinning a nutrient budget, one of which is the prediction of occupancy levels for a new development, and then again when adding a precautionary buffer to the Total Nitrogen ("TN") which has been calculated:

> "4.7 The nutrient neutrality calculation includes key inputs and assumptions that are based on the best-available scientific evidence and research. It has been developed as a pragmatic tool. However, for each input there is a degree of uncertainty. For example, there is uncertainty associated with predicting occupancy levels and water use for each household in perpetuity. Also, identifying current land / farm types and the associated nutrient inputs is based on best-available evidence, research and professional judgement and is again subject to a degree of uncertainty.
>
> 4.8 It is our advice to local planning authorities to take a precautionary approach in line with existing legislation and case-law when addressing uncertainty and calculating nutrient budgets. This should be achieved by ensuring nutrient budget calculations apply precautionary rates to variables and adding a precautionary buffer to the TN calculated for developments. A precautionary approach to the calculations and solutions helps the local planning authority and applicants to demonstrate the certainty needed for their assessments."

130   The 2020 Advice explains at para 4.12 that the proposed methodology "is for all types of development that would result in a net increase in population served by a wastewater system, including new homes, student accommodation, tourism attractions and tourist accommodation".

131   The methodology contains a number of stages for developments which will drain to the mains network. The first stage is to calculate the Total Nitrogen (measured in kilograms per annum) derived from the development that would exit the Wastewater Treatment Works after treatment. Within this first stage are three steps, the first of which is to calculate the additional population resulting from the proposed development. This is dealt with at paras 4.18 and 4.19, on which much of the argument focused:

> "**Stage 1** Step 1 Calculate additional population

4.18 New housing and overnight accommodation can increase the population as well as the housing stock within the catchment. This can cause an increase in nitrogen discharges. To determine the additional population that could arise from the proposed development, it is necessary that sufficiently evidenced occupancy rates are used. Natural England recommends that, as a starting point, local planning authorities should consider using the average national occupancy rate of 2.4, as calculated by the Office for National Statistics (ONS), as this can be consistently applied across all affected areas.

4.19 However competent authorities may choose to adopt bespoke calculation tailored to the area or scheme, rather than using national population or occupancy assumptions, where they are satisfied that there is sufficient evidence to support this approach. Conclusions that inform the use of a bespoke calculation need to be capable of removing all reasonable scientific doubt as to the effect of the proposed development on the international sites concerned, based on complete, precise and definitive findings. The competent authority will need to explain clearly why the approach taken is considered to be appropriate. Calculations for occupancy rates will need to be consistent with others used in relation to the scheme (e.g. for calculating open space requirements), unless there is a clear justification for them to differ."

132   As is apparent from these paragraphs, the occupancy rate of 2.4 persons per dwelling is the average national occupancy rate for all kinds of dwellings, calculated by the Office for National Statistics. It is derived from the 2011 Census.

133   I would make two observations on what is said in these paragraphs. First, Natural England's recommendation is that this occupancy rate should be "considered" by competent authorities, not that its use is in any way mandatory. It is described as no more than "a starting point". Second, the Advice states that competent authorities "may" choose to adopt a different rate, tailored to a particular area or particular scheme, but that where they do so, the occupancy rate adopted must be evidence-based, clearly explained and consistent with other calculations used in relation to the proposed development.

134   Mr Timothy Mould QC for the Council and Mr David Elvin QC for Natural England emphasised the use of the word "may", submitting therefore that competent authorities can be under no obligation to use another occupancy figure. Mr Gregory Jones QC for the appellant objectors submitted that the word "may" should be read as "must". I would not accept either of these submissions. In my judgment the advice to planning authorities is to begin ("a starting point") by considering whether the average national occupancy rate of 2.4 is appropriate to use for the development in question. As it is a national average rate over all kinds of dwelling, it is likely that it can appropriately be used where a development consists of mixed housing, including both larger and smaller properties. In such cases, the starting point may well also be the finishing point. But it is common sense that a new development consisting exclusively of larger houses is likely to have a higher occupancy rate than the national average. In such a case, there seems to me to be a powerful argument that it is not appropriate to use the 2.4 rate, which a planning authority needs to consider. I would read these paragraphs as encouraging planning authorities to consider whether there is an alternative evidence-based occupancy rate for which

a clear justification can be stated. In fact, such an alternative rate would not have been difficult to find in this case: the Office for National Statistics, which is the source of the 2.4 rate, also publishes an average occupancy rate for four-bedroom houses based on the same source (i.e. the 2011 Census), namely 3.14 persons per dwelling.

135   Once the occupancy rate for the nitrogen budget calculation has been determined, the next step is to determine the estimated water use for the proposed development. The 2020 Advice recommends using a figure, itself described as precautionary, of 110 litres per person per day. There was nothing to indicate any circumstances in which a lesser usage figure should be used, for example that some occupants of the new dwellings might already be residents within the catchment area.

136   Stages 2 to 4 of the calculation need not be considered in any detail for the purpose of this ground of appeal. Stage 2 is to adjust the nitrogen load to account for existing nitrogen from current land use; Stage 3 is to adjust the nitrogen load to account for land use with the proposed development; and Stage 4 is to calculate the net change in the Total Nitrogen load that would result from the development. It is at this last stage that a precautionary buffer is recommended:

> "4.67 It is necessary to recognise that all the figures used in the calculation are based on scientific research, evidence and modelled catchments. These figures are the best available evidence but it is important that a precautionary buffer is used that recognises the uncertainty with these figures and in our view ensures the approach prevents, with reasonable certainty, that there will be no adverse effect on site integrity. Natural England therefore recommends that a 20% precautionary buffer is built into the calculation."

137   Thus the 20% precautionary buffer is not a substitute for use of the best available evidence-based figures for the previous stages of the methodology. On the contrary, it is an additional protection which assumes that the best available figures have been used in those previous stages.

The status of the 2020 Advice

138   Mr Jones submitted that the guidance set out in the 2020 Advice was unlawful, although it is fair to say that his primary attack in this court was that it had not been properly applied. I would reject the submission that the 2020 Advice was itself unlawful. It is a rational methodology recommended by the appropriate nature conservation body.

139   The question then arises whether a planning authority in the Solent Region must carry out an "appropriate assessment" in accordance with the 2020 Advice – or to put it another way, whether any departure from the methodology set out in the 2020 Advice would render an "appropriate assessment" unlawful, such that a grant of planning permission based on such an assessment would be *Wednesbury* unreasonable. In my judgment that cannot be the case. The 2020 Advice itself makes clear that it is only one way of carrying out an "appropriate assessment" and that its use is not mandatory. The true position is that a planning authority ought to follow the methodology contained in the 2020 Advice unless it has good reason not to do so. That is for the same reason, explained by Lord Justice Sales in *Smyth v Secretary of State for Communities and Local Government* [2015] EWCA Civ 174; [2015] P.T.S.R. 1417, that a planning authority must place

considerable weight on the response of Natural England in response to a consultation under Regulation 63(3):

> "85. Moreover, the authorities confirm that in a context such as this a relevant competent authority is entitled to place considerable weight on the opinion of Natural England, as the expert national agency with responsibility for oversight of nature conservation, and ought to do so (absent good reason why not): *Hart*, supra, [49]; *R. (Akester) v DEFRA* [2010] Env. L.R. 33, [112]; *R. (Morge) v Hampshire County Council* [2011] UKSC 2; [2011] 1 W.L.R. 268, [45] (Baroness Hale); *R. (Prideaux) v Buckinghamshire County Council* [2013] EWHC 1054 (Admin); [2013] Env. L.R. 32 at [116]. The Judge could not be faulted in giving weight to this consideration in the present case, at para. [165] of her judgment."

140   One potentially good reason not to follow the methodology in the 2020 Advice precisely would be that Natural England itself has raised no concerns about a proposed development, despite appreciating that the methodology has not been precisely followed.

The obligation to consult Natural England

141   This brings me to the obligation, contained in Regulation 63(3), to consult Natural England and to have regard to its view. As explained in the passage from Lord Justice Sales' judgment in *Smyth* quoted above, the Council was both entitled and required to place considerable weight on the opinion of Natural England, unless there was good reason not to do so.

142   In this case the Council did consult Natural England. Although it did not draw specific attention to the use of the national average occupancy rate of 2.4 persons per dwelling for a development consisting of 4-5 bedroom houses, it provided information about the proposed development to Natural England from which the nature of the development and the use of the national average occupancy rate were both readily apparent. We can safely proceed on the basis that Natural England understood this. That is apparent from its stance and evidence in this action, opposing the claim for judicial review. Natural England made clear in its response to the consultation that it had no concerns about the proposed development, including the use of the average national occupancy rate, provided that certain conditions were imposed. That was so even though using the occupancy rate of 2.4 resulted in a nitrogen budget calculation which was only just positive, from which it would have been apparent that taking any higher occupancy rate would have meant that the assessment was negative and that permission would necessarily have had to be refused.

The Officers' Report

143   The Officers' Report for the proposed development, dated 19th August 2020, noted that the application was for eight detached dwellings which were likely to be larger than average. It summarised accurately the content of paras 4.18 and 4.19 of the 2020 Advice, noting that Natural England recommended that, as a starting point, local planning authorities should consider using the average national occupancy rate of 2.4 persons per dwelling, but that they might choose to adopt bespoke calculations where satisfied that there is sufficient evidence to support

this approach. Referring to the concern of objectors that a higher occupancy rate ought to be applied since the houses were likely to be larger than average dwellings, the Report concluded as follows:

> "8.40 It is acknowledged that some houses will have more than the average number of occupants. It is also of course the case that some will have less. The figure of 2.4 is an average based on a well evidenced source (the ONS) and which has been shown to be consistent over the past 10 years. As stated above the Natural England methodology allows bespoke occupancy rates however to date the Council has only done so to lower, not raise, the occupancy rate and where clear evidence has been provided to demonstrate that the proposed accommodation has an absolute maximum rate of occupancy. In the case of sheltered housing which is owned and managed by the Council for example it has previously been considered appropriate to apply a reduced occupancy rate accordingly.
>
> 8.41 In all instances it is the case that the Natural England methodology is already sufficiently precautionary because it assumes that every occupant of every new dwelling (along with the occupants of any existing dwellings made available by house moves) is a new resident of the Borough of Fareham. There is also a precautionary buffer of 20% applied to the total nitrogen load that would result from the development as part of the overall nutrient budget exercise.
>
> 8.42 Taking the above matters into account, Officers do not consider there to be any specific justification for applying anything other than the recommended average occupancy rate of 2.4 persons per dwelling when considering the nutrient budget for the development."

144   For my part, and without (I hope) reading the Report in an unduly legalistic way, I do not think that these paragraphs represent a correct application of the methodology contained in the 2020 Advice. The Report treats the average national occupancy rate as the rate "recommended" by Natural England, to be applied unless there is a "specific justification" for taking some other rate. But that is not what the 2020 Advice says. What it says is that the 2.4 rate should be considered, but it does not suggest that it is anything more than a starting point.

145   Moreover, the Report's justification for using the 2.4 figure was that the Natural England methodology "is already sufficiently precautionary". The first reason for this view was that the methodology assumes that every occupant of every new development would be a new resident of the borough. On this point the Report is mistaken. There is nothing to that effect in the 2020 Advice. It does not suggest, for example, that in the case of a mixed development where it might be expected that occupancy will be in line with the average national rate, some adjustment should be made to take account of this factor. The second reason was that there was also "a precautionary buffer of 20% applied to the total nitrogen load". But the existence of that buffer is not a justification for using anything other than the best available evidence-based occupancy rate for the development concerned. Rather, the 20% buffer is intended to be an additional protection, over and above the use of the best available evidence as to the "key inputs and assumptions" underpinning the nutrient budget. It is applied only after the four stages of the methodology have been completed. In my view, therefore, the Report departs from the methodology set out in the 2020 Advice on the question of occupancy rate.

Conclusion

146   Despite this, however, I consider that the use of the national average occupancy rate of 2.4 persons per dwelling did not render the "appropriate assessment" carried out by the Council unlawful. The question for the Council was not whether it had followed precisely the methodology set out in the 2020 Advice, but rather whether it had carried out a sufficient "appropriate assessment" for the purpose of the Habitats Regulations. It was not mandatory to follow precisely the methodology set out in the 2020 Advice and the use of the national average occupancy rate was not questioned by Natural England when consulted about the proposed development. Rather, Natural England stated that it had no concerns. That was a view to which the Council was entitled and required to have regard. It provided a good reason not to follow precisely the methodology set out in the 2020 Advice. In those circumstances we can only interfere with the conclusion of the Council, based on the assessment which it had undertaken, that the proposed development would not contravene Regulation 63 of the Habitats Regulations, if that conclusion was *Wednesbury* unreasonable. That is a demanding test and I am not persuaded that it is satisfied here.

Postscript – the 2022 Advice

147   I would add that we have been provided with the latest version of Natural England's Advice to planning authorities, issued in March 2022 and updated expressly in the light of (among other things) the judgment of Mr Justice Jay in this case. This Advice is not limited to the Solent region.

148   Interestingly, the 2022 Advice emphasises the importance of local conditions in selecting an occupancy figure, and the need to focus on the particular project being assessed. It recognises that the average national occupancy rate of 2.4 persons per dwelling (which it notes will be subject to change when the results of the 2021 Census become available) may not be appropriate for certain types of development:

> **"Occupancy rates based on dwelling type**
> Should the nature or scale of development associated with a particular project proposal suggest that the use of an average occupancy rate is not appropriate, then the Local Planning Authority may decide to adopt an occupancy rate based on the dwelling types proposed for that particular project, provided it meets the criteria outlined above ..."

Those criteria include that the rate selected reflects local conditions, is sufficiently robust and appropriate for the project being assessed, and is derived from a reliable source which can show trends over a protracted period of time, such as data from the Office for National Statistics.

149   For the future it is the 2022 Advice which planning authorities will need to consider.

R. (ON THE APPLICATION OF CATHIE) v CHESHIRE WEST AND CHESTER BC

QUEEN'S BENCH DIVISION (ADMINISTRATIVE COURT)

HH Judge Bird: 12 August 2022

[2022] EWHC 2148 (Admin); [2023] Env. L.R. 15

Agricultural buildings; Cattle; Dairying; Discharge; Odours; Planning conditions; Planning permission; Retrospective permission; Waste

H1 *Judicial review—Town and Country Planning—Statutory Nuisance—agricultural development—Planning Condition regarding odour management—abatement notice served previously—Condition discharged following submission of Odour Management Plan—whether decision to discharge on the erroneous basis of use of "Best Practicable Means" relevant to statutory nuisance regime rather than the correct test of "best means" for planning regime—whether regard had to immaterial considerations in form of business model and financial circumstances of applicants—whether irrational to find that the measures in Plan amounted to best practice on basis of business model and financial circumstances*

H2   The defendant council (CWC) had granted retrospective conditional planning permission for a reception pit and slatted yard at a farm. A Condition required the submission of an odour management plan (OMP) for approval which CWC discharged. The claimant (C) was a neighbour who sought to challenge that decision. The pit was designed to contain solid and liquid waste generated by cows at the farm. Around a year before the planning application, C complained about the foul smell generated by the dairy farming operation at the farm and CWC served a statutory nuisance abatement notice under the Environmental Protection Act 1990. The interested parties were required to abate the nuisance within 14 days and to provide an OMP to CWC which was to demonstrate "best practicable means" (BPM) to minimise the odours. There was no appeal against the notice. It was an offence under s.80(4) of the 1990 Act not to comply with an abatement notice. Section 80(7) provided that a person able to "prove that the best practicable means were used to prevent, or to counteract the effects of, the nuisance" had a defence. The interested parties had an OMP prepared to comply with the abatement notice, and the steps set out in it were implemented, following which there was no recurrence of the statutory nuisance and no fresh abatement notice was served. Review of the planning application identified "significant concerns as to whether residential amenity would be adequately and consistently protected from unacceptable impacts of odour"; the first OMP was good enough to satisfy the requirements of the abatement notice but not to deal with issues of residential amenity. The interested parties submitted a fresh application and submitted a new

Odour Impact Assessment (OIA) which recommended that the OMP should be revised and updated. The Planning Condition required such a revised OMP taking into account relevant matters raised in the OIA. Following submission of a third submission of a new OMP, the Condition was discharged. C sought judicial review on three grounds, that: (1) CWC made the decision on the basis that the relevant OMP demonstrated the exercise of BPM to avoid unacceptable odours arising from the farm, relevant to the statutory nuisance regime, rather than the correct test for the planning regime of whether it was the best means of ensuring that neighbouring properties continued to enjoy a high standard of amenity; (2) CWC had regard, and attached significant weight, to the business model and financial circumstances of the applicants which were immaterial considerations; and (3) the Condition required the OMP to include "details of all measures to be employed to minimise odorous emissions from the reception pit, slatted area about it and hard-standing adjacent to it, such measures demonstrating best practice", and it was irrational to find that the measures in the submitted OMP amounted to best practice on the basis of the business model and financial circumstances of the applicants. On the first ground, it was submitted that in misdirecting itself as to the relevant test, CWC wrongly focused on the efforts of the landowner rather than whether the result of those efforts was in fact the achievement of an acceptable standard of amenity.

H3   **Held**, in dismissing the claim:

H4   (1) There were two questions at the heart of the application. First, what did the Condition require the OMP to do? Secondly, did CWC apply the correct test when it decided to discharge the Condition? The need to demonstrate "best practice" in respect of "all measures to be employed to minimise odorous emissions from the reception pit, slatted area about it and hard standing adjacent to it" could not be read in a way that imposed unreasonable requirements on the interested parties.

H5   (2) There was nothing in the first ground. As set out, that proceeded on the basis that CWC ought to have asked itself if the OMP set out "the best means" of ensuring that neighbouring properties enjoyed an appropriate standard of amenity. In skeleton arguments, C adopted a different test suggesting that the appropriate question was whether the OMP was "satisfactory" and dropping all reference to "best means". The test for discharge in the present case was whether the OMP proposed a "satisfactory" solution to the impact of the farming operations on residential amenity. It was plain that a satisfactory solution did not need to be an ideal solution. CWC had concluded that the OMP showed that "all reasonably practicable measures in the operational management of the facilities to minimise adverse impacts" would be taken. Once it was understood that the Condition had to be read so as to impose no more than "reasonable" obligations, that formulation was sufficient to justify the conclusion that the steps set out in the OMP were sufficient. It followed that the Condition could lawfully be discharged. In any event, there was clear overlap between steps that employed BPM and steps that were satisfactory. At one extreme, it may be that BPM were wholly ineffective to mitigate problem odours and so not "satisfactory". On the other hand, BPM might be more than enough to meet the "satisfactory" criterion. Whether in a given case steps that complied with BPM were "sufficient" to discharge a Condition was a matter of fact and degree. It was plain that CWC had been entitled to conclude that the OMP was satisfactory.

H6   (3) The second ground would also be dismissed. CWC had been required to interpret the Condition so that it did not impose a disproportionate or unjustifiable financial burden on the interested parties. That required a consideration of such circumstances as far as they were material.

H7   (4) The use of the "best practice" qualifier in the Condition did not mean that CWC had been entitled to place an unjustifiable and disproportionate financial burden on the interested parties. The Condition could not be read to impose an obligation on the interested party to adopt a "gold-plated" solution. If the Condition was read in that way, it would fall foul of the National Planning Policy Framework and the Planning Practice Guidance. There was no basis to conclude, nor evidence to suggest, that the measures taken in respect of odorous emissions from the pit, the slatted area and the hard standing did not comply with "best practice". CWC had applied the correct test when considering the discharge of the Condition and no public law error had been identified.

H8 **Cases referred to:**
Proberun Ltd v Secretary of State for the Environment (1991) 61 P. & C.R. 77; [1990] 3 P.L.R. 79; [1991] J.P.L. 159 CA (Civ Div)
R. (on the application of Smith-Ryland) v Warwick DC [2018] EWHC 3123 (Admin)
Trump International Golf Club Scotland Ltd v Scottish Ministers [2015] UKSC 74; [2016] 1 W.L.R. 85; 2016 S.C. (U.K.S.C.) 25

H9 **Legislation referred to:**
Environmental Protection Act 1990 ss.79 and 80

H10 *R. Wald KC* and *K. Barns* (instructed by Birketts) appeared on behalf of the claimant.
P. Riley-Smith (instructed by Cheshire West & Chester Borough Council) appeared on behalf of the defendant.

JUDGMENT

HIS HONOUR JUDGE BIRD:

Introduction

1   On 6 April 2020, the defendant granted retrospective conditional planning permission (ref: 19/03679/FUL) for a reception pit and slatted yard at Hale Pastures Farm ("the Farm"). Condition 2 (set out at paragraph 28 below) required the interested parties to submit an odour management plan ("OMP") for approval. On 3 November 2021, the defendant discharged condition 2. This is the claimant's challenge to that decision.

The Background

2   Mr and Mrs Cathie live at Hales Pasture House ("the House") in Allostock in Cheshire. It has a paddock, stables and a garden. Until 1987 it was part of the Farm. Mr and Mrs Cathie bought the House in 1996 and have lived there since then. Until 2017 the Farm (which is owned by the interested parties) caused them no particular issue. In 2017 the farming business changed. A herd of 80 cows was acquired. They are housed, fed and milked in newly developed buildings.

3   The new buildings were constructed without planning permission. In planning terms, the new development comprised:

> "*a portal-framed shed with single-storey side extension for a mix of agricultural and B8 uses, change of use of an area of hardstanding to a mix of agricultural and B8 uses, construction of reception pit and erection of two adjoining buildings for dairy farming, with extensions and alterations to yard and access track.*"

4   The reception pit is covered by concrete slats and is 6m wide, 26m long and 2.2m deep. It therefore has a capacity of around 343 cubic metres. It sits southwest of the House, between 68.9m and 76.7m from it. It is between 81m and 101m from the garden (see Table 2 in the first OMP referred to below).

5   The pit is designed to contain both solid and liquid waste generated by the cows. The emptying regime for the pit has changed over time:

   a.   The pit is now emptied every week or so. This is a more regular pattern than was previously the case. The change was brought about as a result of the recommendations made by Smith Grant in their report of November 2019. Before the change, it would be emptied every 2 to 3 months all year round. The liquid slurry is then spread on fields which are some distance away. The emptying process including slurry spreading can take about 3 hours. It takes between 5 and 10 minutes to fill a tanker. The remaining time is taken driving to the fields and spreading the slurry.

   b.   Solids are emptied in the summer months only and at a frequency of between 2 and 5 times per year.

The Abatement Notice

6   Mr and Mrs Cathie found the foul smell generated by the dairy farming operation at the Farm difficult to put up with. They reported matters to the defendant in March 2018. On 12 September 2018, after on-site investigations and in accordance with its duties under section 80(1)(a) of the Environmental Protection Act 1990, the defendant served a statutory abatement notice on the interested parties. The defendant was satisfied that "a statutory nuisance" (see section 79(1)(d) of the 1990 Act which provides that "*any.... smell or other effluvia arising on industrial, trade or business premises and being prejudicial to health or a nuisance*" is a statutory nuisance) existed. The interested parties were required to abate the nuisance within 14 days and to provide an OMP to the Defendant which was to demonstrate "*best practicable means*" to minimise the odours. There was no appeal against the notice.

7   By section 80(4) of the 1990 Act it is an offence for any person served with an abatement notice (in the absence of a reasonable excuse) not to comply with it. Section 80(7) of the Act provides that a person able to "*prove that the* best practicable means *were used to prevent, or to counteract the effects of, the nuisance*" (emphasis added) has a defence.

The first OMP

8   The interested parties instructed Resource and Environmental Consultants Limited ("REC") to prepare an OMP to comply with the abatement notice. As a preliminary step REC carried out an odour impact statement. The results were then used to

inform the OMP, which set out steps to put an end to the statutory nuisance. These include:

    a. Emptying the pit from a bottom feed pipe to reduce "agitation" on the surface of the slurry and so reduce the release of odours.
    b. Minimising the stirring and agitation of slurry.
    c. The use of a low protein diet for the cows to reduce the nitrogen and sulphur content of the manure which in turn would reduce odours.
    d. A regular cleaning regime.

9   Under the heading "prevailing meteorological conditions" the OMP accepts that wind direction is an important factor in considering the impact of odour emissions. The predominant wind direction was noted to be from the south.

10   The OMP concludes with an odour risk assessment. It considers the impact of odour (from stored slurry, from stirring, mixing and spreading the slurry, from discharging contents into tankers and from cow cubicles) at the House, its garden and the paddock once the proposed mitigation is in place. In each case the risk was assessed as "low" with the probability of exposure in each case assessed as "low" and the severity of the consequences of exposure in each case at "medium."

11   It is important to note that since the OMP was submitted, and the steps set out in it were implemented, there has been no recurrence of the statutory nuisance and no fresh abatement notice has been served. It seems therefore to follow that the mitigation measures put in place have had a positive impact on the lives of Mr and Mrs Cathie.

12   At or about the time the first OMP was prepared, the interested parties applied for retrospective planning permission in respect of the development at the Farm. It was accompanied by the first OMP.

The second Odour Impact Assessment ("OIA")

13   The second OIA was prepared by Redmore, not for the interested parties, but for Mr and Mrs Cathie. A copy was sent to the defendant on 5 November 2018 in support of their opposition to the grant of retrospective planning permission.

14   The report concludes that overall odour impacts at the House are "significant" and that odours "*attributable to existing sources at the farm have the potential to adversely affect currently and future amenity levels at [the House]*".

The first retrospective planning application

15   The Defendant's Environmental Protection team ("the Team") reviewed the application for planning permission on or about 1 February 2019 and raised "*significant concerns*". It was not satisfied that residential amenity would be "*adequately and consistently protected from unacceptable impacts of odour*".

16   The first OMP was good enough to satisfy the requirements of the abatement notice (to stop the statutory nuisance) but not good enough to deal with issues of residential amenity. The interested parties withdrew the application for planning permission on 25 March 2019.

The second retrospective planning application

17   The interested parties submitted a fresh application (this time in respect of the reception pit, the slatted yard above it and the erection of 2 robot milking sheds) on 4 October 2019. This time they were better prepared and did not rely on the first OMP. They submitted a new OIA dated November 2019 prepared by Smith Grant LLP.

18   The Smith Grant report is comprehensive and impressive. It expressly addresses planning issues. In addition to considering reports and information available at the time it was written, it is based on an "*odour dispersion modelling exercise.*" That exercise involved the collection of foul samples from various locations and an analysis of the "odour concentration" for each sample. That concentration was then used to calculate odour emission rates. The report therefore sets out an empirical analysis of the impact of odours.

19   The concrete slats that cover the pit are said to "*substantially reduce*" odour emissions from the pit itself. The primary source of odour is identified as cow waste on the slatted yard (see paragraph 6.1.4).

20   Having set out the mitigating measures included in the first OMP, at paragraph 7.7.3 the report notes:

> "*Key aspects that would serve to minimise the risk of odour impacts at [the House] due to the reception pit would be the* <u>regular</u> *emptying of the pit to minimise the anaerobic decomposition of the slurry and ensuring,* <u>when possible</u>*, pit emptying is not undertaken during conditions when dispersion would be towards the property.*" (emphasis added)

21   Two important points arise from this paragraph. First, the recommendation of "regular" emptying is a suggestion that the pit be emptied more often (paragraph 7.1.3 of the report describes the previous regime of emptying the pit typically every 2 months) and secondly, decisions about when to empty the pit should take account of weather conditions.

22   The report is summarised at section 8. The two points set out at paragraph 7.7.3 are repeated. The report accepts that odours will be generated at the site and may on occasion adversely impact the amenity of those at the House. It is however the author's view that:

> "*with* <u>appropriate management of the reception pit in accordance with the OMP and best practice</u> *and in particular the minimisation of disturbance of the pit contents,* <u>regular emptying of the pit liquid content</u> *and* <u>endeavouring to ensure liquid and solid removal are only undertaken during suitable weather conditions</u> (unless conditions mean this would not be possible such as during a prolonged adverse period of weather) the potential for odours to significantly impact the surrounding environment can be managed and mitigated." (emphasis added)

23   Finally, the report recommends that the OMP should be "revised and updated in light of this OIA".

The Officer's Report

24   The case officer (Mrs Reay) recommended the application for approval. Plainly, she was aware of the Smith Grant report and took its contents into account. From

her report, it appears the Team this time did not object to the application, and indeed (see paragraph 6.15) believed that the Smith Grant OIA "*robustly*" demonstrated that odour concentration levels at the House are unlikely to have a "*greater than slight adverse effect*".

25   At this stage, the pit and farming operation had been operating in accordance with recommendations set out in the first OMP and there had been no repetition of the statutory nuisance (see paragraphs 6.11 to 6.13 of the officer's report). The further mitigating steps suggested by Smith Grant, could only lead to further improvements.

26   At paragraph 6.25 of the report, the officer recommends that a condition, requiring a revised OMP taking into account relevant matters raised in the Smith Grant report, be imposed.

27   Planning permission was granted on 6 April 2020.

The condition

28   The permission was subject to 2 conditions. The first required the development be carried out in accordance with specified approved plans. The second was as follows:

> "*Within one month of the date of this permission, a revised Odour Management Plan shall be submitted to the Local Planning Authority. This Plan shall be agreed with and approved by the Local Planning Authority and should take into account relevant matters raised in the [Smith Grant report]. The OMP shall also include, but not be limited to, details of all measures to be employed to minimise odorous emissions from the reception pit, slatted area about it and hard-standing adjacent to it, such measures demonstrating best practice. Other aspects to be included include details of obtaining and recording meteorological details* to inform *removal of liquids and solids from the reception pit; odour mitigation measures to be employed in relation to emptying the reception pit; handling complaints; recording inventory (including feedstock) and process controls. As well as covering both normal operations, the OMP should anticipate and plan for abnormal events and foreseeable accidents and incidents. The OMP should also retain measures intended to monitor and control flies associated with the reception pit.*"
> (emphasis added)

29   The reason given for the condition was "*to protect the residential amenity that neighbouring occupiers can reasonably expect to enjoy.*" I deal with the proper interpretation of the condition below.

The Discharge of Condition 2

The first application

30   On 5 May 2020, the interested parties applied to discharge the condition. As required, they produced a new OMP. It was dated 1 May 2020 and was prepared by REC. The Team were far from impressed. They felt it was "*substantially similar to*" the first OMP. In essence it failed to take account of the Smith Grant report.

31   The Team note that the OMP makes no reference to wind conditions and that it would expect a full and proper OMP to specify that:

> "*the pit should only be emptied when winds are from directions other than south, south-west or west....this would seem to be one of the fundamental ways that the OMP can demonstrate best practice in minimising odour exposure.*"

32   It is important to note that these comments and expectations are at odds with paragraph 7.7.3 of the Smith Grant report (which stops short of requiring that the pit should be emptied in favourable weather conditions, instead advising this be done "*where possible*") and go beyond what the condition requires (that the weather conditions be monitored to "*inform*" – not "dictate" – when emptying will take place).

33   The application to discharge appears to have been withdrawn.

The second application

34   A new application was submitted on 3 May 2021. Another OMP was submitted on 4 May 2021 and commented on by the Team in an email dated 14 May 2021. They describe the OMP as "*a clear improvement.*" Nonetheless, they raise a number of queries.

35   A further OMP was submitted on or about 30 September 2021. Dealing with the slurry and solids removal process it says this:

> "*The slurry within the pit will be emptied into a tanker, approximately once a week, via a gravity-fed bottom pipe. This will reduce agitation to the top layer of slurry and as such, will minimise the release of odour emissions.*"

36   This partial emptying regime adopts the recommendation at paragraph 7.7.3 of the Smith Grant report and ensures (as the first OMP and the Smith Grant report recommend) that surface agitation is minimised.

37   Paragraphs 2.3 and 2.4 of the OMP (under the heading "operations" and "hygiene") deal with steps to be taken in respect of cow waste in and about the yard (identified as the primary source of odour in the Smith Grant report).

> "*The hardstanding and yard areas are scraped using specialist equipment twice daily.....Scraping of the hardstanding areas will be undertaken twice daily as noted above. The robotic equipment have timed wash sequences to ensure a sterile milking environment for the cows. The area will be kept in a tidy manner, washed down daily in addition to periodic deep cleans to ensure best practice. These processes are all in accordance with existing stringent Farm assurance requirements.*"

38   The OMP goes on (page 5) to note that the interested parties cannot dictate when the pit is emptied. The process requires contractors whose availability will depend on factors beyond the control of the interested parties.

> "*As with most dairy herds nowadays, but in particular smaller units, the farm is reliant on contractors to undertake most of the field and slurry removal work. The scale of the dairy unit, limited to just 80 milking cows, does not afford the investment in the modern machinery and extra permanent labour to allow the enterprise to operate commercially with owned equipment. As such, the contractors form an important part of the farm's team. This does limit the ability to determine the timings of all operations, with discretion*

needed by the contractors to allow them to efficiently serve all their customers'
needs, usually within small weather windows for specific activities required
of various farmers at the same time. On occasions, rented equipment may be
used from the contractors, with employees undertaking the processes, but this
still has a limitation in terms of availability of equipment."

39   It is therefore clear that the OMP did not meet the apparent expectation of the
Team expressed in respect of the 1 May 2020 OMP that "*the pit should only be*
emptied when winds are from directions other than south, south-west or west".

40   Dealing with weather conditions (see table 4) the OMP notes:

"Meteorological conditions i.e., wind direction to be obtained and recorded
on spreadsheet <u>to inform</u> solid removal of material from reception pit. Data
to be obtained from phone weather App. <u>If forecast indicates wind blowing</u>
<u>in the direction of receptors, a discussion will be undertaken between team</u>
<u>members to consider the operational options.</u> These considerations and the
decision-making process will be documented, to further evidence the informed
removal of solids from the reception pit." (emphasis added).

41   The OMP therefore mirrors the condition by making it clear that meteorological
conditions will be taken into account when decisions about emptying are made.

Team Comments October 2021

42   The Team commented on the latest version of the OMP in its report (written by
Jim Candlin a Senior Regulatory Services Officer) dated 15 October 2021. The
report was addressed to Mrs Reay who had delegated authority to deal with the
application to discharge the condition. At the time Mrs Reay considered the report
she was of course very familiar with the background and context of the matters
addressed.

43   The claimants point out that the report refers more than once to "best practicable
means" (or "BPM"). As this point is central to the present claim, I set out each
reference to BPM in the report:

   a. In the introductory section under the heading "Background" there is reference
      to the OMP required by the abatement notice to reflect BPM.
   b. Under the heading "purpose of the [latest version of the] OMP" the report
      suggests that the standard of BPM would be met if the interested parties
      carries out "<u>all reasonably practicable measures</u> in the operational
      management of the facilities" It notes that adverse impacts may occur even
      if BPM have been used. (emphasis added).
   c. Under the heading "conclusion" it notes that the OMP demonstrates that
      BPM will be employed. In other words, that the interested parties has
      adopted "*all reasonably practicable measures*" to comply with the condition.
   d. Under the heading "advisory 1" the report notes that the interested parties
      would be at risk of prosecution should they not be able to demonstrate a
      defence of BPM for any breach of the extant abatement notice.

44   In the section headed "chapter 2" the report comments on the removal of liquids
and solids from the pit. It notes that odours from liquid removal will be limited to
"*negligible emissions from the relief valve on the tanker*." It follows that the Team

is satisfied that unreasonable odour levels are not likely to occur during liquid removal.

45   As might be expected, the Team address the fact that the latest OMP does not provide for emptying of the pit only when the wind is blowing in the right direction. It squarely addresses the point raised in the OMP about reliance on contractors and refers to the fact that the interested parties have approached contractors to explore the possibility and concludes:

> "..... *this Unit considers that* it would be unreasonable to expect the OMP to commit to not undertaking solids removal during certain specified meteorological conditions. This Unit is satisfied that the farm is doing all that is reasonably possible and practicable to manage and minimise odour emissions during solids removal and has made reasonable additional enquiries to explore further minimising odour emissions."

46   It is important to see this point in context. As I have set out, the terms of the condition do not require the OMP to "*commit to not undertaking solids removal during certain specified meteorological conditions.*" The Team's view on the reasonableness of such a requirement is therefore of no relevance. It seems to me that this is simply a justification for the Team's change of view that it no longer "expected" the OMP to require emptying be carried out only in certain weather conditions (see paragraph 31 above).

47   The condition was discharged on 3 November 2021. The Defendant accepts that in reaching its decision, it relied on the Team's comments of October 2021.

The grounds

48   The claimants bring these proceedings for judicial review on 3 grounds:

> Ground 1: The Defendant made the Decision on the basis that the relevant odour management plan demonstrated that the First Interested parties ("the First IP") was exercising "best practicable means" ("BPM") to avoid unacceptable odours arising from the Farm. The Defendant misdirected itself in applying the BPM test since this does not form part of the planning regime but instead relates to the separate statutory nuisance regime (BPM is a defence to the criminal offence of failing to comply with an abatement notice). Rather, as per *Proberun Ltd v Secretary of State for Environment and Medina BC* (1991) 61 P. & C.R. 77 and paragraph 130(f) of the NPPF, the Defendant was required to consider whether the odour management plan under consideration was the best means of ensuring that neighbouring properties continued to enjoy a high standard of amenity. Therefore, in misdirecting itself as to the relevant test, the Defendant wrongly focussed on the efforts of the landowner rather than whether the result of those efforts was in fact the achievement of an acceptable standard of amenity. (Emphasis added).
>
> Ground 2: In making the Decision the Defendant had regard to (and went on to attach significant weight to) the business model and financial circumstances of the First IP landowner of the Farm. These factors are unrelated to the character of the use of the land and they were therefore immaterial considerations that the Defendant erred in taking into account.
>
> Ground 3: Condition 2 required the odour management plan to include "details of all measures to be employed to minimise odorous emissions from the

reception pit, slatted area about it and hard-standing adjacent to it, such measures demonstrating best practice." It was irrational for the Defendant to find that the measures in the submitted odour management plan amounted to best practice on the basis of the business model and financial circumstances of the First Interested Party. The latter are logically unrelated to best practice, the whole point of which is to impose a recognised and uniform standard against which the measures should be judged.

The Submissions

49   The claimant submitted that:

   a. The Team's report of 15 October approved the updated OMP only because it adopted BPM. This showed not only a "stunning *volte face*" on their part but also led the Planning Officer into error. She adopted a flawed approach by relying on the report (and so on BPM). BPM is not a relevant planning consideration.
   b. In any event the OMP does not set out BPM.
   c. The correct approach is derived from *Proberun*: was the OMP "satisfactory" in the context of the reason for the imposition of the condition? The only basis for the "*volte face*" of the environmental team was the introduction of the BPM test. This is a change of position not reflected in the grounds.
   d. The Defendant wrongly took into account the personal circumstances of the interested parties (the steps it could afford to take). Such circumstances, save in very limited circumstances, are not relevant planning considerations.

50   The Defendant submitted that the claimant's argument was predicated on the basis that the pit was only to be emptied in certain weather conditions (when "*the winds are from directions other than south, south-west or west*" see the Team's response to the OMP of 1 May 2020). The argument was misplaced; no such requirement was set out in the relevant condition. The condition required that "meteorological details" be used "to inform" (not dictate) removal of liquids and solids from the reception pit. In respect of the grounds, the Defendant submits:

   a. The Planning Officer took account of the October 2021 report. That was appropriate. In doing so she did not override or misapply the terms of the condition. The Officer exercised planning judgment in such a way that no valid challenge arises.
   b. The Defendant was entitled to take account of practical, on the ground difficulties that the interested parties would face when operating the development. This is clear from the 6 tests set out for conditions in the NPPF and from PPG 120. Imposing conditions about weather would impose an unreasonable burden. It is a material consideration that ignoring the on-the-ground position would prevent the condition from working.
   c. The Defendant's exercise of planning judgment cannot be criticised on the basis of irrationality.

Discussion

51   Two questions lie at the heart of this application. First, what does the condition require the OMP to do? Secondly, did the Defendant apply the correct test when it decided to discharge the condition?

52   The first question requires me to determine what the condition means (see the approach taken by Jay J in *R. (Smith-Ryland) v Warwick DC* [2018] EWHC 3123 (Admin) paragraph 40). The proper approach to that exercise is set out by the House of Lords in *Trump International v Scottish Ministers* [2016] 1 W.L.R. 85 and described by Jay J as "*an objective, purposive approach which cannot ignore the application of basic common sense*".

53   The second question requires some brief consideration of authority.

What does the condition mean?

The approach

54   Plainly the court will approach the exercise of interpretation on the basis that the condition imposes no greater obligation on the interested parties than the law allows. NPPF 55 and 56 sets out the 6 requirements that must be met by any condition: it must be necessary, relevant to planning and to the development to be permitted, enforceable, precise and reasonable in all other respects.

55   Further guidance on the imposition of (and so lawfulness of) conditions and the 6 requirements is set out in "Planning Practice Guidance" on the use of planning conditions. Under the heading "are there any circumstances in where planning conditions should not be used?" 6 principles are set out. Prohibited conditions include those that: "....*unreasonably impact on the deliverability of a development*". Further, conditions that "....*place unjustifiable and disproportionate financial burdens on an applicant will fail the test of reasonableness....*"

56   When considering the meaning of the condition I am also entitled to take account of the content of the Smith Grant report and of the stated purpose of the condition. The proper approach is an objective one. I am therefore not concerned with what the subjective views of the parties but with the view of an informed bystander possessed of all relevant background material available at the time the condition was formulated.

The meaning

57   Against the background I have set out, the following key points on interpretation can be made.

58   The condition makes it clear that decisions about emptying the pit will be "*informed*" by the weather. The condition therefore proceeds on the basis that other factors can properly be taken into account. There is nothing in the condition to suggest that the pit can only be emptied in certain weather conditions or when the wind is blowing in a particular direction. This is entirely in line with common sense (wind directions might change without notice) and with the Smith Grant report. Further, there is nothing in the condition which can be read so as to limit the factors that the interested parties are entitled to take into account.

59   The need to demonstrate "*best practice*" in respect of "*all measures to be employed to minimise odorous emissions from the reception pit, stated area about*

it and hard standing adjacent to it" cannot be read in a way that imposes unreasonable requirements on the interested parties.

What is the proper test to apply when considering discharge?

60   Ground 1 as set out above proceeds on the basis that the Defendant ought to have asked itself if the OMP set out "the best means" of ensuring that neighbouring properties enjoyed an appropriate standard of amenity.

61   As the Defendant points out, the claimants have now adopted a different test in their skeleton argument. They have re-phrased their ground 1 and dropped all reference to "best means". They now suggest that the appropriate question is whether the OMP was "satisfactory."

62   The grounds make it clear that the claimants rely on *Medina BC v Proberun* (1991) 61 P. & C.R. 77 in support of their original proposition that "*when considering whether to discharge a condition requiring the approval of details, the decision maker must ... ask whether the submitted details are "satisfactory". What is satisfactory must logically be assessed by reference to the purpose of the condition. If the decision maker does not consider the details to be satisfactory, he or she should consider whether they are nonetheless the best that can be achieved in light of the constraints of the site.*"

63   *Proberun* in my judgment does not support this approach. It concerned the discharge of a condition attached to an outline planning permission requiring approval of details of an access route to the development site. Outline planning permission had been granted by the Secretary of State on appeal notwithstanding the fact that no satisfactory access could be provided over land forming part of the site or otherwise in the ownership of the developer. The application to discharge the access condition was refused (by the Planning Inspector) because he considered "*the submitted design [was] seriously flawed.*" The Inspector's decision was appealed to the High Court and the appeal allowed. It considered that the "*proper test [of] whether the submitted details met the requirements of [the access] condition was whether the means of access shown on the plans was the best means of vehicular access that could be achieved on the site.*" The Court of Appeal upheld the decision of the High Court but explained the High Court decision in this way:

> "*In saying that the proper test was whether the means of access was the best that could be achieved on the site [the High Court] was obviously formulating that test in relation to the facts of this case. If a satisfactory access is proposed, nobody should be concerned to inquire whether it is the best that could be achieved. But here it was asserted by the county council and effectively, though not formally, accepted by the applicants that their proposals for the junction were less than satisfactory. Therefore, the test became: what is the best which can be achieved within the limits of the site?*"

64   *Proberun* makes the point that a planning authority must (as it was put in *Smith-Ryland* at paragraph 45) "*be strictly loyal to the terms of the parent permission*" at the subsequent approval stage. The Encyclopaedia of Planning Law and Practice (at P62.01) puts it in this way: "*the planning authority are not entitled to refuse to approve reserved matters on grounds going to the principle of the development itself and which are therefore already implicit in the grant of the outline permission.*" The decision provides an example of a situation where a

condition might be discharged even if the relevant solution proposed is insufficient. In that case, the applicant must make the solution as good as it can be. Using "best means" in this context does not change the "*satisfactory*" test for discharge, instead it requires the applicant to ensure that the (necessarily unsatisfactory) alternative is as good as it can be.

65   I am satisfied that the test for discharge in the present case is whether the OMP proposed a "satisfactory" solution to the impact of the farming operations on residential amenity at the House. It is plain that a satisfactory solution does not need to be an ideal solution.

66   I turn to the grounds.

Ground 1

67   The claimant now argues that the Defendant applied the wrong test. It should have asked if the OMP was satisfactory, but instead (directed by the Team's response to the OMP) it asked if the OMP employed BPM. In my view there is nothing in this ground.

68   I have set out above how the Team deals with BPM. It concludes that the OMP shows that "*all reasonably practicable measures in the operational management of the facilities to minimise adverse impacts*" will be taken. That is the basis on which the Defendant discharged the condition. In my judgment, once it is understood that the condition must be read so as to impose no more than "reasonable" obligations on the interested parties, this formulation is sufficient to justify the conclusion that the steps set out in the OMP are sufficient. It follows that the condition could lawfully be discharged.

69   In any event, there is clear overlap between steps that employ BPM and steps that are satisfactory. At one extreme it may be that BPM are wholly ineffective to mitigate problem odours and so are not "satisfactory". On the other hand, BPM might be more than enough to meet the "satisfactory" criterion. Whether in a given case steps that comply with BPM are "sufficient" to discharge a condition is a matter of fact and degree. Given the matters I have set out above it is in my judgment plain that the Defendant was entitled to conclude that the OMP was satisfactory. I am satisfied that the Defendant considered the substance of the Team's recommendation and not just the label the Team attached to their conclusion.

70   Further, the Team apply the BPM standard to the pit emptying regime. In my view, whilst useful context, that clearly goes beyond what the condition requires. It imposes no limit on the matters that can be taken into account when the decision to empty is made, it simply requires that weather conditions "inform" the decision. The BPM standard therefore applies to matters which are unconstrained by the condition.

71   In reaching the conclusion that the Defendant did not apply the wrong test and so was entitled to discharge the condition I take account of the fact that the Team was clearly aware that it was being asked to give a view on a planning matter. It had been involved in the matter for some considerable time and was well aware that it was not being asked to express a view on whether a section 80(7) defence would be available to the interested parties. There was never (at least since compliance with the first OMP) any question that there was a statutory nuisance capable of giving rise to a prosecution in any event.

72   The claimant suggests that the Defendant wrongly concentrated on the efforts of the interested parties rather than on the result of those efforts. But the latter is a function of the former and the condition requires actions to be taken.

73   If the claimant's position was correct it would mean that it in order to discharge the condition, the interested parties would take on a "disproportionate or unjustifiable financial burden" because the scale of the farming operation was such that it was simply not possible for the interested parties to invest it their own equipment to empty the pit. The condition would be unreasonable and so unlawful. It would have been wrong (an error of law in misdirecting itself) for the Defendant to conclude that it should read the condition so that it imposed an obligation that was impossible to meet.

74   The claimant also suggest that the discharge of the condition could only be legitimately achieved if it protected their amenity to a "high standard." She relied on NPPF 130 which appears in the "*achieving well designed places*" section of the NPPF. It provides that planning decisions should (see (f)) "*ensure that developments….create places that are safe, inclusive and accessible and which promote health and well-being, with a high standard of amenity for existing and future users.*" I cannot accept the claimant's argument.

75   Amenity is an important planning consideration. It is reflected in the Defendant's Local Plan (Part Two) Policy DM2 which requires that a development should not "*result in a significant adverse impact on the residential amenity of the occupiers of existing properties*". Paragraph 47 of the Defendant's PaP response (dated 6 December 2021) points out at paragraph 47 that at the time part 2 of the local plan was adopted it was found to be consistent with NPPF 130. In any event the claimants are not present or future users of the development. NPPF 130 is about encouraging practical design excellence and creating high amenity through design for those who will use the relevant development. DM2 is about others (non-users) who might be affected by a development.

Ground 2

76   There is in my view nothing in this ground.

77   For the reasons I have set out, the Defendant was required to interpret the condition so that it did not impose a disproportionate or unjustifiable financial burden on the interested parties. That requires a consideration of the claimant's circumstances as far as they are material.

78   The claimants make the point that the permission runs with the land so that the interested parties may sell. If he does so the purchaser may be immensely wealthy and so, may be able to afford to have his own equipment and staff so as to facilitate emptying the pit only when the wind was in the right direction. That new owner would be under no obligation to do so because (it is said) he could rely on the present OMP. I cannot accept that argument. The OMP (as required by the condition) requires that weather conditions be monitored and used to "inform" operations. As the OMP puts it at page 14, weather forecasts will provide additional information to inform "any planned potentially odorous activities". With additional resources and (perhaps) staff and equipment on hand, the result of this exercise is likely to be that operations will take place when conditions are favourable.

Ground 3

79   The use of the "best practice" qualifier in the condition does not mean that the Defendant is entitled to place on the interested parties an unjustifiable and disproportionate financial burden. The condition cannot be read to impose an obligation on the interested party to adopt a "gold-plated" solution. If the condition was read in that way, it would fall foul of the NPPF and the PPG.

80   At least 4 steps are taken to minimise emissions "from the pit" and its surrounds: first the aim is not to agitate or disturb the slurry. The main cause of agitation would be the process of draining the pit. To deal with that the pit is drained from a gravity fed bottom pipe and "stirring and agitation" is generally to be minimised. Secondly, steps are taken (subject to the primacy of animal health) to ensure that the cows' diet does not add to odour issues (see for example pages 6 and 11 of the latest OMP). Thirdly (see the latest OMP at paragraph 4.3) the slatted yard above the pit "*reduces mass exchange between the top layer of slurry and the surrounding air significantly minimising odour*" and finally the slatted and hardstanding areas will be "scraped using specialist equipment twice daily" (see the latest OMP at paragraphs 2.3 and 4.3).

81   I can see no basis to conclude (or evidence to suggest) that the measures taken in respect of odorous emissions from the pit, the slatted area and the hard standing do not comply with "best practice".

Conclusion

82   In my judgment, the Defendant applied the correct test when considering the discharge of condition two. No public law error has been identified. It follows that the claim must be dismissed.

83   The decision to discharge the condition must be seen in the context of steadily improving odour emissions at the Farm. The starting point, in 2018 before the abatement notice was served, represents rock-bottom. Then things improved after the steps outlined in the first OMP were implemented. The Smith Grant report sets out further steps leading to further improvements. Whilst improvement is not necessarily relevant to the discharge question it may offer some comfort to the claimants.

84   A failure to discharge the condition in this case would in my view have amounted to an indirect (and impermissible) attack on the grant of planning permission because it would have prevented the interested parties from making any use of the new (and now authorised) development.

85   I am grateful to counsel for their assistance. If an order can be agreed I will hand down this judgment in the absence of the parties.

R. v ANDERSON (GORDON)

COURT OF APPEAL (CRIMINAL DIVISION)

Sir Adrian Fulford and Cutts and Farbey JJ: 9 November 2022

[2022] EWCA Crim 1465; [2023] Env. L.R. 16

ᴸᴾ Conditions; Corporate personality; Directors disqualification orders; Disqualification periods; Environmental offences; Environmental permits; Good character; Non-compliance; Risk of harm; Sentencing guidelines; Suspended sentences; Waste disposal

H1 *Environmental crime—sentencing—waste—offences under Environmental Permitting (England and Wales) Regulations—sentence to suspended imprisonment, unpaid work and director disqualification—whether judge erred in assessment of level of harm under Sentencing Guideline—whether s.33B of the Environmental Protection Act 1990 limited assessment to clear-up costs arising from excess over the permitted amounts of waste—whether judge erred in approach to evidence—whether "corporate veil" wrongly "pierced"—whether incorrect in approach to complex liability issues—whether imposition of maximum disqualification period manifestly excessive*

H2   The appellant (GA) had pleaded guilty to two counts of failing to comply with or contravening an environmental permit condition, contrary to regs 38(2) and 41, and one count of operating a regulated facility otherwise than in accordance with an environmental permit, contrary to regs 38(1)(1), 12(1)(a) and 41 of the Environmental Permitting (England and Wales) Regulations 2016. The offences had been committed by a company (PCR) with the consent or connivance of, or were attributable to, the neglect of GA, who was a director of the company. He was sentenced to concurrent terms of 15 months' imprisonment suspended for 18 months together with 250 hours unpaid work, and disqualification from being a director for 15 years under the Company Directors Disqualification Act 1986 s.2, the maximum period that could be imposed. The first set of offences concerned premises in Deeside where waste was stored in excess of the permitted amount and in breach of storage conditions, and there had been a failure to submit a written fire prevention and mitigation plan for approval within the time specified in the environmental permit. Further offences concerned a site at Holyhead where PCR operated, or knowingly caused or permitted the operation of, a waste operation without an environmental permit. The Holyhead site was used to store waste when Deeside became full. GA knew that there was insufficient storage capacity at Deeside to accept the waste, which PCR had been paid to accept, and the Holyhead site was specifically procured as additional storage space. GA was given clear advice by his environmental consultant about the 500-tonne limit for a waste exemption for Holyhead and an application for a full permit had been rejected.

During the relevant period, PCR received a total of £2,132,234 from various companies for waste operations. The failure to comply with storage and other conditions at Deeside created the risk of a major fire with the potential to be extremely dangerous, causing serious and extensive harm to the environment and to human health. The cost to clear Deeside, excluding legal costs, was £1,850,000. GA appealed on six grounds. The first was that the judge erred at step 3 of the Sentencing Guideline relating to Environmental Offences when she assessed, vis-à-vis the level of harm, that the offending fell at the top of category 2 having taken into account the cost of the removal of the entirety of the waste at Deeside including the amounts permitted following the liquidation of PCR. It was argued that the judge should have limited the assessment to the clear-up costs arising from GA's offending, that being the excess over the permitted amounts, relying on s.33B of the Environmental Protection Act 1990. The remaining grounds were that the judge: erred in her approach to resolving evidential disputes; impermissibly "rejected/ignored" the defence expert report without warning or reason; wrongly "pierced the corporate veil" without legal argument; incorrectly attributed the liabilities of PCR to GA, and incorrectly took into account various complex liability issues; and that the 15-year period of disqualification was manifestly excessive.

H3   **Held:**

H4   (1) The judge had not been wrong to take into account the entirety of the clean-up costs. The court was neither dealing with confiscation proceedings nor an application for compensation. Section 33B of the 1990 Act was irrelevant. The present case involved an entirely separate exercise from assessing compensation. The judge was required by the Guideline to assess at Stage 3 whether the costs incurred through were major, significant or low, when considering the harm caused by the offending and this was not limited to loss and damage resulting from the offence. There was a clear and sufficient nexus between GA's offending as a director of PCR and the harm as reflected in the need to clear the entirety of the waste. The argument that there was no proper basis for determining that GA had committed the three offences "deliberately" was equally devoid of traction.

H5   (2) GA's submission that, in the absence of a Newton Hearing, all the disputed facts needed to be resolved in his favour was rejected. In any event, the court was unable to identify within the sentencing remarks any significant disputed factual issues in relation to which the judge accepted the evidence introduced by the prosecution in favour of evidence introduced by GA. Nor had the judge made any findings in her sentencing remarks which materially contradicted or rejected the contents of the defence expert's statement.

H6   (3) On the subject of "piercing the corporate veil", GA essentially asked the court to consider the impact of what was, in the context of the present appeal against sentence, an entirely irrelevant legal concept. The principle was essentially concerned with the limited circumstances in which the separate personality of the company could be disregarded in order to obtain a remedy against someone other than the company in respect of a liability which would otherwise be that of the company alone. It had no relevance to the fact-finding exercise that a judge undertook in passing sentence. The judge was assessing the correct punishment to be imposed as a consequence of admitted criminality and considering issues such as whether GA had intentionally breached or flagrantly disregarded the law, and the extent of the environmental impact, or risk thereof, including the costs of the clean-up operation. Those considerations did not involve "piercing the corporate veil" in the sense prohibited by the established jurisprudence. Instead, the judge had been assessing the extent of the punishment that was appropriate for GA's role as a director in what had taken place, bearing in mind the harm caused and his culpability. In a similar vein, the judge was required by the Guideline to take into account GA's motive as a director of the company; namely whether he was acting altruistically or for commercial advantage. GA's submissions in this context were misconceived.

H7   (4) The judge had not engaged with complex liability issues and instead analysed the matters that were relevant for determining the level of sentence, as required by the Guideline.

H8   (5) The court made an order under the Company Directors Disqualification Act 1986 s.2 for the maximum permitted period. The Crown candidly accepted this was a longer disqualification period than would have been expected in the case of a man of otherwise good character who, albeit late in the day, pleaded guilty and who had never previously been subject to a disqualification order. It was conceded that the order should have been within the middle bracket.

H9   (6) Accordingly, the judge's approach had been entirely correct, and the sentence was neither manifestly excessive nor wrong in principle, save as regards the sixth ground. The period of 15 year's disqualification would be quashed and substituted with a period of six years.

H10 **Cases referred to:**
Petrodel Resources Ltd v Prest [2013] UKSC 34; [2013] 2 A.C. 415; [2013] 3 W.L.R. 1
R. v Boyle Transport (Northern Ireland) Ltd [2016] EWCA Crim 19; [2016] 4 W.L.R. 63; [2016] B.C.C. 746
R. v Millard (Ray) (1994) 15 Cr. App. R. (S.) 445; [1994] Crim. L.R. 146 CA (Civ Div)
R. v Newton (Robert John) (1983) 77 Cr. App. R. 13; (1982) 4 Cr. App. R. (S.) 388 CA (Civ Div)
Sevenoaks Stationers (Retail) Ltd, Re [1991] Ch. 164; [1990] 3 W.L.R. 1165; [1990] B.C.C. 765 CA (Civ Div)

H11 **Legislation referred to:**
Company Directors Disqualification Act 1986 ss.2 and 6
Environmental Protection Act 1990 ss.33, 33B and 34
Environmental Permitting (England and Wales) Regulations 2016 (SI 2016/1154) regs 38 and 41

H12 *S. Riggs* (instructed by Weightmans LLP) appeared on behalf of the appellant.
C. Stables (instructed by Natural Resources Wales) appeared on behalf of the respondent.

JUDGMENT

SIR ADRIAN FULFORD:

History

1   On 8 March 2021, in the Crown Court at Mold before Judge Nicola Jones, the appellant (who is 67) pleaded guilty to two identically worded counts of failing to comply with or contravening an environmental permit condition, contrary to Regulations 38(2) and 41 of the Environmental Permitting (England and Wales) Regulations 2016 (counts 8 and 9). The particulars of the offence in each case were that between 1 January 2017 and 26 June 2018, in relation to land at Unit 1-1a & 2 Parkway, Deeside Industrial Park, Deeside, Clwyd, Paperback Collection and Recycling Limited ("PCR") had committed the offences in counts 1 and 2, and the offences reflected in counts 8 and 9 (respectively relating to counts 1 and 2) were committed with the consent or connivance of, or was attributable to, the neglect of the appellant, who was a director of the company (for the terms of counts 1 and 2, see [7] *et seq* below).

2   He pleaded guilty, additionally, to one count of operating a regulated facility otherwise than in accordance with an environmental permit, contrary to Regulations 38(1)(1), 12(1)(a) and 41 of the Environmental Permitting (England and Wales) Regulations 2016 (count 12). The particulars of the offence were that between 1 January 2017 and 26 June 2018, in relation to land at the former Anglesey Aluminium Works, Penrhos, Hollyhead, Anglesey, PCR had committed the offence in count 5, and this offence (*viz.* count 12) was committed with the consent or connivance of, or was attributable to the neglect of, the appellant, who was a director of the said company.

3   Counts 10, 11, 13 and 14 on the indictment were ordered to lie on the file in the usual terms.

4   On 18 August 2021, in the Crown Court at Caernarfon, Judge Jones sentenced the appellant on the three counts to concurrent terms of 15 months' imprisonment suspended for 18 months together with 250 hours unpaid work, and he was disqualified from being a director for 15 years under section 2 of the Company Directors Disqualification Act 1986. We note, *en passant*, that the maximum disqualification period that can be imposed is 15 years. The appellant now appeals against that overall sentence by leave of the single judge.

5   PCR was jointly charged with the appellant. The company, now in liquidation, entered guilty pleas on counts 1 – 7.

6   It is necessary to consider in greater detail the various counts faced by the appellant and PCR.

7   Counts 1 – 4 were charges against PCR of failing to comply with or contravening an environmental permit condition, contrary to Regulation 38(2) of the Environmental Permitting (England and Wales) Regulations 2016.

8   On count 1 it was charged that PCR, between 1 January 2017 and 26 June 2018, in relation to land at Units 1-1a and 2 Parkway, Deeside Industrial Park, Deeside, Clwyd, failed to comply with Condition 2.3.1(a) of its environmental permit by storing in excess of 12,000 tonnes of external waste (that being the limit set by the permit). Count 8 was a mirror of count 1 and related to the appellant as the director of PCR. As set out above, given the company had committed the offence in count

1, the appellant was guilty of count 8, since the offence was committed with his consent or connivance or was attributable to his neglect as the director of PCR. Natural Resources Wales ("NRW"), the prosecuting authority, did not accept that Count 8 occurred merely as a result of neglect, it being the prosecution's case that the defendant consented to the decisions reached in the name of the company (indeed, he had made them), and connived in the determination and carrying out of those decisions (as he had day-to-day operational control of the company and its activities).

9   On count 2, PCR was charged that between the same dates and at the same premises (Deeside), it failed to comply with the same condition by failing to ensure that the dimensions of waste stacks were in accordance with the guidance document TGN7.01, and by failing to ensure that the required minimum separation distances between waste stacks existed and/or were maintained. Count 9, relating to the appellant, was a mirror of Count 2. The Crown did not accept that the failings in relation to the waste stacks as to maximum height and separation distances occurred – as averred by the appellant – only "some of the time".

10   On count 3, again between the same dates and at the same premises (Deeside), PCR was charged with failing to comply with condition 2.1.1 of its environmental permit by storing plastic waste, of EWC Code 19 12 04, in or on external areas at the land.

11   On count 4, PCR was charged that between 17 November 2017 and 26 June 2018 at the same premises at Deeside it failed to comply with Condition 2.4.1 of its environmental permit by failing to submit a written fire prevention and mitigation plan to NRW for approval within the time specified in the environmental permit.

12   On count 5, PCR was charged with operating a regulated facility otherwise than in accordance with an environmental permit, contrary to Regulations 38(1)(a) and 12(1)(a) of the Environmental Permitting (England and Wales) Regulations 2016, in that between 01 January 2017 and 26 June 2018, in relation to land at the former Anglesey Aluminium Works, Penrhos, Hollyhead, Anglesey ("Penrhos"), PCR operated, or knowingly caused or permitted the operation of, a regulated facility, namely a waste operation, without the authority of an environmental permit. Count 12 to which the appellant pleaded guilty was a mirror of Count 5.

13   We note that the owner or the proprietor of Penrhos was a company called Orthios Eco Parks (Anglesey) Ltd ("Orthios"), based in Christleton, just outside Chester. The company had been the proprietor of the site since May 2016. In February 2018, following receipt of an anonymous letter at the NRW Bangor office, officers found a large quantity of film-wrapped baled waste inside an extremely large A frame building at Penrhos, comprised of plastics mixed with other waste, which had been attributed with waste code 19 12 04 (*viz.* plastics and rubber). This latter information was revealed in documents which were obtained during the investigation. The operation of Penrhos to store the baled waste was the basis of Counts 5 and 12 to which, as just set out, the company and the appellant pleaded guilty.

14   Copies of waste transfer notes showed the importation (*viz.* the deposit) of 8,686.3 tonnes, or 17,372 bales of waste, from Deeside to Penrhos. The A Frame building at Penrhos had been leased to PCR. There were no permits for either the importation of the waste or its storage. A waste exemption had been registered in respect of the waste stored at Penrhos, but the terms of the exemption were contravened, as it only allowed storage of up to 500 tonnes over a period of 12 months. A breach

of the exemption rendered it void. PCR provided a copy of the exemption certificate to Orthios. As the operation at Penrhos grew, the landlord was advised incorrectly by the appellant that the appropriate permits were in place.

15   The *modus operandi* adopted during this criminality was that Penrhos was used to store waste when Deeside became full. The appellant knew that there was insufficient storage capacity at Deeside to accept the waste, which the company had been paid to accept, and Penrhos was specifically procured as additional storage space. The appellant was given clear advice by his environmental consultant about the 500-tonne limit. In September 2017 an application was made for a full permit for a plastic-to-waste recovery operation, which included storage, in respect of Penrhos site, but this was rejected. Therefore, despite having received clear advice from his environmental consultant, the appellant continued to transport baled waste to Penrhos beyond the amount permitted. The operation of that facility was entirely illegal: as just rehearsed, the breached exemption was voided and an environmental permit was never granted.

16   On count 6, PCR was charged with depositing controlled waste otherwise than in accordance with an environmental permit, contrary to section 33(1)(a) and (6) of the Environmental Protection Act 1990, in that between 1 January 2017 and 26 June 2018 PCR deposited at Penrhos, or knowingly caused or permitted to be deposited, controlled waste, namely baled waste plastics mixed with other waste, otherwise than in accordance with an environmental permit.

17   We note in passing that although PCR pleaded guilty to counts 5 and 6 on a suggested basis, it was the prosecution's case that the 12,000 tonne waste limit was exceeded throughout most, if not all, of the indictment period and not, as suggested in the basis of plea, merely "on occasion".

18   Finally, on count 7, PCR was charged with failing to comply with relevant duty of care requirements, contrary to section 34(1)(a) and (6) of the Environmental Protection Act 1990, in that between 1 January 2017 and 26 June 2018, being a company which produced, carried, kept, treated or disposed of controlled waste, it failed to take all reasonable measures to prevent any contravention by any other person of section 33 of the Environmental Protection Act 1990. The company was sentenced to a nominal fine of £1 on each count.

19   The procedure, therefore, was that waste was treated and baled at Deeside prior to being transported to Penrhos. A company called UPM-Kymnene had transferred a total of 13,894 tonnes of waste to PCR between February 2017 and February 2018. During this period PCR received a total of £2,132,234 from various companies for waste operations. UPM-Kymnene alone paid £1,200,000 to PCR, which included extracting and baling the relevant waste.

20   Given Deeside was regulated and subject to a permit granted by NRW in September 2015, the site was the subject of regular visits by NRW officers. On 18 September 2017 officers found baled waste that was not stored in compliance with the fire prevention or the fire risk assessment plans. Stack heights were up to seven bales high, which was excessive. Distances between the stacks were inadequate at between one to two metres, and the boundary stacks were too close to neighbouring premises. Furthermore, PCR was in contravention of various permit conditions (including the limit for the storage of waste) and waste was stored contrary to the fire safety provisions in the fire safety plan which had been incorporated into the permit. After a variation of the permit in November 2017, PCR also failed to submit to NRW a new fire prevention mitigation plan as required by the permit conditions.

The risk at Deeside was one of a major fire. This would have had the potential to be extremely dangerous, causing serious and extensive harm to the environment and to human health. The cost to clear Deeside, excluding legal costs, was £1,850,000 (*per* the statement of Andrew Bird).

The Restraint Orders

21   On 10 February 2020, Judge Petts discharged restraint orders against the appellant and his wife which had been granted, on the papers, by Judge Rowlands on 16 May 2018 (following an application by NRW). Judge Petts was unpersuaded by the prosecution's submission that since the Andersons were the sole directors and shareholders, and Mr Anderson was the sole decision maker, the corporate veil could be pierced thereby enabling the court to conclude that there were reasonable grounds to suspect that Mr and Mrs Anderson had benefited from criminal conduct. The judge concluded there would need to be a stronger basis for reaching that conclusion.

The Sentencing Exercise

22   On 17 May 2021, the case was listed to determine if the sentencing hearing, then set for 21 May 2021, should be vacated. The prosecution informed the judge that a basis of plea had been submitted on behalf of the appellant, revealing a "substantial gap" between the parties relating to factual matters, which could not be resolved other than by a Newton hearing. NRW had that morning received a defence bundle running to 1,100 pages. The appellant submitted the hearing date should be maintained and that the sentencing hearing should proceed on the basis that PCR was a business that had been trading for 25 years with a significant business record and representations could be advanced simply on the basis of the contemporaneous paperwork. It is to be stressed, therefore, that the appellant encouraged the judge to resolve the relevant factual issues bearing in mind the parties' submissions, which were to be based on documents rather than on any oral evidence.

23   Although at the commencement of the hearing on 17 May 2021, Judge Jones expressed the view that a Newton/Fact Finding Hearing would be needed, having heard submissions she determined that it had not been established that this step was necessary, as she did not consider that the gap between the parties would make a material difference to the sentence. Whilst the judge recognised that there were significant differences between the prosecution and the defence, it was not, she suggested, the place of the court to iron out every detail that had not been agreed. The judge expressed the view that although the parties disagreed significantly, those disagreements would not affect the eventual outcome.

24   The sentencing hearing eventually took place on 18 August 2021. The court was not advised of any change of position as regards the approach to be taken to establishing the relevant facts. Indeed, in the document served on the court by Ms Riggs on 16 August 2021 entitled "Reference the Defence Bundle", there was no suggestion that witnesses should be called and instead it was simply indicated that relevant passages in the defence bundle, which included an expert report, would be drawn to the court's attention during the sentencing hearing on 18 August 2021.

25   Andrew Bird, a director of Tilstone Industrial Limited, landlords of Deeside had provided a victim impact statement dated 9 June 2021.

26   The judge took into account the appellant's lack of previous convictions and his previous good character. The judge was satisfied, as regards culpability, that the offences were deliberate, given the appellant was an experienced waste operator who had sole control of the company. He was aware it was his responsibility to ensure safety at Deeside. He was familiar with the regulations because of his experience in the industry and he nonetheless chose to ignore them. In relation to Penrhos, the appellant knew that there was a limited 500-ton exemption, but he continued to bring waste to Anglesey, thereby blatantly disregarding the regulations.

27   As to harm, the judge determined that count 8 straddled the two higher categories, but she applied category 2 on account of the appellant's mitigation. The judge assessed that the relevant cost of cleaning up the two sites came to a total of £2,631,740 which fell in her judgment within the significant cost category. She reached this conclusion on the basis that once PCR had gone into liquidation, it was necessary for the entirety of the site at Deeside to be cleared of waste. It was "nonsensical" in those circumstances to suggest that for the purposes of the Guideline the costs of the clear up at Deeside were to be confined to the excess waste stored at the site, namely that which was over the permitted levels. The starting point in consequence was 1 year's imprisonment, within a range of 26 weeks to 18 months. The offence was aggravated because it was committed for financial gain, and the business had not been run for altruistic reasons given it was a commercial venture. The judge determined that the appellant had sought to minimise his criminality. The judge took into account the impact of the proceedings on the appellant's mental health. She considered that the custody threshold had been crossed but an immediate custodial sentence was properly to be avoided on account of the impact of the COVID pandemic, the appellant's previous good character, the fact that he had not offended since the commission of these offences and his new employment. The judge found clear grounds for concluding that the appellant had a realistic prospect of rehabilitation.

28   Following a trial, in the judge's view the shortest possible term was 18 months' imprisonment, concurrent on each count, and applying 15% credit for the appellant's guilty plea, that resulted in a sentence of 15 months, which was suspended for 18 months. He was, additionally, required to undertake 250 hours of unpaid work. Given the extensive nature and seriousness of the offences, together with the fact that the appellant blatantly ignored the relevant provisions, the judge imposed the maximum period of disqualification.

The Grounds of Appeal

29   There are six grounds of appeal, albeit there is a high degree of overlap between them.

I. The Guideline

30   It is submitted the judge erred at step 3 of the Guideline relating to Environmental Offences entitled "Individuals: Unauthorised or harmful deposit, treatment or disposal etc of waste/illegal discharges to air, land and water" (the "Guideline") when she assessed, vis-à-vis the level of harm, that the offending fell at the top of category 2 having taken into account the cost of the removal of the entirety of the waste at Deeside (including the 12,000-tonne permitted external and 3,000-tonne permitted internal waste) following the liquidation of the company. It is submitted

the judge should have limited the assessment to the clear-up costs arising from the appellant's offending – the excess over 12,000 and 3,000 tonnes respectively – for which two brackets of costs were provided: £284,800 to £545,650 (see [3.2.8] of Simone Aplin's report dated 14 May 2021, based in turn on the Ashfield Solutions' report) and £231,650 to £310,750 (see [3.2.7] of the same report, based on the last reported tonnage). As the prosecution have indicated, the uncontradicted, albeit unagreed, evidence was that 17,410 tonnes of waste were removed from Deeside, at a cost exceeding £1.85 million (see the statement of Andrew Bird). The 8,686.3 tonnes of waste at Penrhos have yet to be removed, although the landlord is subject to an enforceable requirement to undertake this work. The estimated costs for removing this waste range between £781,740 (for disposal under the most favourable conditions) and significantly over £1m if the waste is sent to landfill.

31   The "Post Works Verification Report" concerning Deeside was served over 3 months before the sentencing hearing, and it was exhibited in the witness statement of Paul Challender dated 13 May 2021. The statement and the report were served on the defence on 14 May 2021. Although the appellant has called into question elements of this report, no request was made at any stage for the judge to conduct a Newton Hearing; indeed, as set out above, on 17 May 2021 the appellant encouraged the court to resolve any evidential issues on the basis of the documentary material before the court.

32   The essence of the appellant's argument, therefore, is that only part of the operation at Deeside was relevant (*i.e.* the excess waste, together with the close proximity of the stacks). The breach of the permit condition did not necessitate removing all the waste from the site. It is argued that section 33B of the Environmental Protection Act 1990 ("EPA"), albeit in the context of a claim for compensation, relates to the clean-up costs for breach of a permit condition specifically resulting from the offence. It is accepted that as regards Penrhos the entirety of the waste falls to be removed because the operation *in toto* was unlawful.

33   It is further submitted that the judge was wrong to conclude that the appellant had abandoned the sites. In making this and other determinations adverse to the appellant, there was, it is submitted, no justification for "piercing the corporate veil", given, *inter alia*, the appellant was not the permit holder. PCR was the permit holder and in consequence was the holder of the waste. It is averred that PCR, along with its liabilities, was sold to A & D Recycling Ltd, a company that had been identified as potential purchaser prior to PRC entering administration.

34   It is argued there was no proper basis for determining that Mr Anderson had committed these three offences "deliberately"; instead, it is suggested that he did not intentionally breach the law. He had actual foresight of the offending but nonetheless took the risk to try and trade through the problem within the confines of financial constraint. At the Penrhos site, whilst storage occurred in breach of the exemption, PRCL was seeking to regularise the site by submitting an application for an environmental permit, which took many months for NRW to process. At Deeside, efforts were being made to comply with the storage conditions and the company was appealing the regulator-led permit variation following a change in guidance which required a new fire prevention plan to be submitted. In due course the appeal was abandoned due to lack of finances.

35   In all the circumstances, it is contended that the starting point identified by the judge was excessively high.

II. The judge erred in her approach to resolving evidential disputes

36   It is submitted that once the judge had determined that a Newton Hearing was unnecessary and sentencing would proceed by way of submissions, she erred in relation to points of evidential conflict whenever she rejected elements of the factual basis relied on by the appellant. It is suggested this approach led her erroneously to conclude that the case was one of high category 2 harm for counts 8 and 9, and category 3 for count 12. In support of this submission, the appellant relies on the well-known authority of *R. v Newton* (1983) 77 Cr. App. R. 13, and particularly the latter part of the oft-quoted passage from the judgment of Lord Lane CJ when his lordship was dealing with the three approaches to conflicting evidence following a guilty plea by a defendant:

> "The third possibility in these circumstances is for him to hear no evidence but to listen to the submissions of counsel and then come to a conclusion. But if he does that, then [...] where there is a substantial conflict between the two sides, he must come down on the side of the defendant. In other words where there has been a substantial conflict, the version of the defendant must so far as possible be accepted."

37   In the appellant's skeleton argument, it is indicated that the principal factual disagreements that are of relevance were set out in the Basis of Plea document, dated 8 March 2020. We need not rehearse them in detail; instead, we highlight that in the main they are directed at evidence concerning Orthios, the owner or the proprietor of Penrhos (see [13] above): it was not accepted that Orthios was a "victim" of these offences or that it had provided reliable evidence, and the suggested disposal costs of £1,318,661.51 were disputed. It was set out that the witness statements of Philip McCormick (a chartered architect and a director of the Orthios Group) were challenged.

III. The judge impermissibly "rejecting/ignoring" the defence expert report without warning or reason

38   It is argued that at the time of the sentencing hearing there was no suggestion that the defence expert, Simone Aplin, was not a suitably qualified expert who could assist the court. It is suggested that her evidence was to be preferred to the position advanced by NRW as regards the risk of pollution, namely that she concluded there was only a risk of harm from fire. Ms Aplin had been instructed to review the evidence and to give an opinion on whether environmental harm resulted from the charges and, if so, to give an opinion as to the scale of harm.

IV. The judge wrongly "pierced the corporate veil"

39   The appellant submits that the judge "pierced the corporate veil", without legal argument, and incorrectly "attributed the liabilities of PCR to the appellant". It is emphasised that the appellant "did not have any liability independent of PCR". The latter was the tenant at both sites, the permit holder at Deeside, the exemption holder at Penrhos, the permit applicant at Penrhos, the holder of the waste (given the contracts were in the name of PCR) and the legal entity which engaged advisers to consider waste disposal. Against that background it is said that the judge "conflated" the position of the appellant with PCR, thereby "effectively piercing

the corporate veil". In particular, the appellant critically highlights the following observations by the judge: "you leased the premises in Deeside from Tilestone Limited. At that time you were only authorised to hold 12,000 tonnes on the outside of the site"; "you also took a lease in Penrhos on the old Anglesey Aluminium Site. You obtained an S2 exemption that allowed you to keep 500 tonnes of waste on the site"; "I know that you have made an application for [...] an environment permit to have more waste at the site"; "you had sole control of the company (*viz.* PCR)"; and "the aggravation here is that, in my judgment, this is for financial gain, you were not running that business for altruistic reasons, you were running that business as a commercial venture and, of course, the extent of the costs of the clean-up moves it up through the range". It is argued that the judge's approach had the result that "the liability of PCR was treated as a financial gain of the appellant personally and assessed as a major aggravating feature in effect extinguishing the mitigation".

40   The appellant relies on the positive submission that his financial gain was limited to his salary (*viz.* £27,000 before tax). Set against this modest benefit, it is emphasised that jointly with his wife he loaned the company £218,000 "to ensure its viability and long-term future". Furthermore, by way of mitigation the court is asked to have in mind that "(the appellant) had been involved in the management of PCRL since 1985. Neither the company, nor Anderson had any previous convictions. He had in place a proper management structure and a detailed environmental management system. In 2017, the Deeside site was assessed as a band C site which equates to a top performing site".

V. The judge incorrectly took into account complex liability issues.

41   During mitigation, the appellant advanced the position that A&D Recycling Ltd (who ultimately took over the lease at Deeside) was an investor who he had secured prior to the intervention the NRW. It was suggested that A&D Recycling purchased PRC from the liquidators and, at least potentially, a reduction was made to reflect the waste present on the site, along with the position of the landlord.

42   It is averred that the details of the contractual arrangements between the parties relating to the sale of PCR and its liabilities are unclear. Against that background, it is suggested these issues should not have been explored as part of the sentencing exercise. Additionally, submissions were made during the course of mitigation about the reliability of the figures appearing in the Post Verification Report in relation to the quantity of waste. The appellant relied on the report of Ms Aplin as to the absence of any evidence to substantiate actual harm and her assessment of the risk of harm. There was said to be no evidence before the court to make good the bare assertion by the prosecution relating to risk to the nearby water course which flows to the River Dee. Instead, the risk of harm of this kind would depend on the drainage at the site and the topography of the land, along with similar factors, and no such evidence was led by the prosecution.

43   The appellant argues that the judge erred in taking into account a victim impact statement from the landlord of Deeside, Tilstone (as provided by Andrew Bird) seeking compensation. It is suggested that this raised complex liability issues which should not be determined during a sentencing hearing. Having set out the difficulties that followed PCR entering voluntary liquidation on 14 June 2018, including particularly the final £1.85 million cost of clearing Deeside, at the conclusion of the statement, he states, "If possible, we would like to seek compensation from the

court". It is suggested that PCR alone was liable for any loss incurred and that the statement reveals that the reputational damage has been kept to a minimum.

VI. The 15-year period of disqualification was manifestly excessive

44   In arguing that the period of disqualification was unjustifiably long, the appellant relies on his age (now 67); his long-term and honourable involvement in the waste industry, running his own business for over 25 years with no previous convictions, cautions, warning letters or disqualification orders; the positive character evidence from his current employer; his guilty plea; and the absence of any pollution in the present case, as opposed to the risk of pollution, thereby indicating that this was less than a "particularly" serious case. It is highlighted that the administrators of PCR raised no concerns with the insolvency service as to the conduct of the appellant, who continued to provide assistance after PCR entered administration.

45   It is emphasised that *in Re Sevenoaks Stationers (Retail) Ltd* [1990] 3 W.L.R. 1165; [1991] Ch. 164 the Court of Appeal (Civil Division) identified the following three brackets in relation to disqualifications under section 6 of the Company Directors Disqualification Act 1986:

> i) the top bracket of disqualification for periods over 10 years should be reserved for particularly serious cases. These may include cases where a director who has already had one period of disqualification imposed on him falls to be disqualified yet again.
> ii) the middle bracket of disqualification for from six to 10 years should apply for serious cases which do not merit the top bracket.
> iii) the minimum bracket of two to five years' disqualification should be applied where, though the disqualification is mandatory, the case is, relatively, not very serious.

46   Since *R. v Millard* (1994) 15 Cr. App. R. (S.) 445, the criminal courts have consistently applied these brackets to disqualifications under section 2 of the 1986 Act.

Discussion

I. The Guideline

47   We are wholly unpersuaded that the judge was wrong to take into account the entirety of the clean-up costs. The court was neither dealing with confiscation proceedings nor an application for compensation. Section 33 B of the Environmental Protection Act 1990, relied on substantively by the appellant, is irrelevant for these purposes. The section, as potentially germane, provides that:

> "(2) The reference in section 133(a) of the Sentencing Code (**compensation orders**) to loss or damage **resulting from the offence** includes costs incurred or to be incurred by a relevant person in—
> (a) removing the waste deposited or disposed of in or on the land;
> (b) taking other steps to eliminate or reduce the consequences of the deposit or disposal; or
> (c) both."

(our emphasis)

48   The present case involves an entirely separate exercise from assessing compensation: the sentencing judge was enjoined by the Guideline to assess at Stage 3 whether the costs incurred through clean-up, site restoration or animal rehabilitation are major (category 1), significant (category 2) or low (category 3), when considering the harm caused by the offending. The judge's approach to this decision is not limited in the restricted way advanced by Ms Riggs (on behalf of the appellant) to loss and damage resulting from the offence, relying on section 33 B. We stress, therefore, that the application of the Guideline for the purposes of sentencing is an entirely separate exercise to any decision on compensation and the statutory provisions that relate to that exercise. Furthermore, we indicate that we are not expressing any view as to whether Ms Rigg's interpretation is correct as regards section 33 B in the context of an application for compensation.

49   Returning to the Guideline, there is in our judgment a clear and sufficient nexus between the appellant's offending as a director of PCR, on the one hand, and the harm as reflected in the need to clear the entirety of the waste, on the other. The appellant was guilty of count 8 on the basis that the offence in count 1 had been committed with his consent or connivance or was attributable to his neglect as a director of PCR. As Ms Riggs accepted in the course of her submissions, it was the appellant's case that PCR only became insolvent as a result of the NRW's investigation into these offences, which led to the present prosecutions. Put otherwise, it is the appellant's contention that absent this offending and the attendant prosecution, the necessity for the site to be cleared would not have arisen. The offending reflected in count 8, therefore, substantively contributed to the requirement for the landlords to clear the site at Deeside: as set out by Andrew Bird in his statement of 9 June 2021, following the demise of PCR, Tilstone was only able to grant a lease to AD Recycling Ltd – thereby once again being able to collect rent on the yard – after this critical step had been taken. Although it is suggested by Ms Riggs this was a complex scenario, no credible alternative option has been advanced by the appellant as regards this consequence of the appellant's criminality. It has not been suggested, furthermore, that the landlords expended this considerable sum of money (or part of it) needlessly, for instance because another body had, or credibly may have had, responsibility for undertaking this work of returning the yard to a state of being a commercially viable site. Any dispute as to the extent of the appellant's responsibility for what occurred, for instance vis-à-vis PCR, fell to be resolved by the judge when considering culpability. We note in that regard that Mr and Mrs Anderson were the only directors and shareholders during the period of the charges, and the appellant was the sole active director.

50   Although the judge suggested that PCR and the appellant had "abandoned" the sites, the reality of the situation has been described in the preceding paragraph: the result of this criminality was that the landlords were obliged to clear up the entirety of the site because there was no credible suggestion that the remedial work would be undertaken by someone else.

51   The argument that there was no proper basis for determining that the appellant had committed these three offences "deliberately" is equally devoid of traction. As the appellant is compelled to accept, he "had actual foresight of the offending", albeit he may well have hoped that, serendipitously, his criminality would be unremarked and have a trouble-free ending. Given his experience and his position in the company, it is inevitable that he was aware of each of the infringements, to

which he pleaded guilty, at the time they occurred. The "deliberate" nature of his actions was not extinguished by a wish that an environmental permit would in due course be granted (it was refused) or that an appeal against a permit variation would be successful (in the event, he did not pursue the appeal).

52   It follows that we reject the criticisms that are made to the judge's approach to the Guideline.

II. The judge erred in her approach to resolving evidential disputes

53   We reject unhesitatingly the submission that once the judge had determined that a Newton Hearing was unnecessary and sentencing would proceed by way of submissions, she erred when points of evidential conflict arose in rejecting elements of the factual basis relied on by the appellant. This argument is fundamentally flawed in two main respects.

54   First, although in advance of the hearing on 17 May 2021 there were clear areas of significant difference between the prosecution and the defence as to the facts, which led the judge to consider and the Crown to submit that a Newton Hearing was necessary, the appellant strongly encouraged the judge not to adopt that course and instead invited the court to resolve any disputes on the basis of the documents. The appellant, furthermore, did not change this stance at any juncture after 17 May 2021 (see [22] – [24] above). It is unsustainable for an appellant expressly to forgo the opportunity for a Newton Hearing, encouraging the judge to resolve contested facts on the documents, only thereafter to complain that the court failed to adopt the position preferred by the defendant. It had not been contended at any stage prior to sentence that the judge was, as a matter of course, required to resolve the disputed issues in the appellant's favour.

55   Second, the factual disagreements that had an impact on the sentencing exercise were few and far between. The appellant suggests that those of consequence were set out in the Basis of Plea document, dated 8 March 2020. For convenience, we summarise that in the main these related to the evidence concerning Orthios, the owner or the proprietor of Penrhos (see [13] above): it was not accepted that Orthios was a "victim" of these offences or that it had provided reliable evidence; furthermore, it was submitted that the suggested disposal costs for Penrhos of £1,318,661.51 were disputed. We note, however, that the judge adopted the bracket of £781,740 to over £1m and Ms Aplin (who provided the appellant's expert report) did not challenge a bracket of £781,740 to £894,658. Otherwise, there are no significant factors relating to Orthios that the appellant challenged and on which the judge placed any reliance.

56   The judge set out in relation to Deeside that "a fire at that site would have had the potential to be extremely dangerous, risking serious extensive harm to the environment, there is a nearby water course which flows into the River Dee [...]". This was consistent with the findings of Ms Aplin:

> "3.4.12 The parkway site is located within an industrial estate and there are other businesses located adjacent to it. Although the site is not within a groundwater source protection zone, the River Dee, Bala Lake SAC and the River Dee SSSI are 1km or more to the south west of the facility. There is a small watercourse to the rear of the facility, behind the public footpath which runs along the perimeter at points and a series of small lakes to the west, one within 200m of the site. [...]

3.4.14 Had there been a fire in the bales on the yard, it is likely that it would have been difficult to identify and control as the stack layout would have limited access to the seat of the fire and the ability to remove unaffected bales in order to limit the spread. This could result in a much larger and longer-burning fire than might have occurred if the stacks conformed with the FPP and were readily accessible. The CAR form generated following an inspection by Pal Challener and Gerraint Hugues a NWFRS officer confirms this stating "Should a fire occur towards the rear of the stack this would hinder firefighting operations as there is no vehicular access to the rear. North Wales Fire and Rescue Service would have to depend on hose lines operating from the cycle path with the need for an aerial appliance in the yard."

3.4.15 Given that some of the site surface was hardstanding and not impermeable, there was the potential for contaminated firewater to leave the site and enter the small watercourse running along the perimeter. This was mitigated slightly by a small soil bund running along parts of the perimeter. However, it alone would have been unlikely to be effective in containing a significant amount of contaminated run-off as it was not continuous and did not look to be engineered. […] As such they are likely to take measures to prevent any discharge where possible and mitigate harm if it does occur with pollution prevention equipment. Overall, the likelihood and severity of potential pollution would depend on the volume of water, local topography, and pollution control measures.

3.4.16 The potential impact of emissions to air is harder to estimate given that it will be determined by the scale of the fire, and weather conditions. Waste plastics are known to produce dark, noxious smoke and, depending on the wind direction, it would have the potential to impact on amenity, quality of life and if sustained, human health. This could have been exacerbated by the challenges of fighting a fire on site which, because of the stack sizes and lack of access, would have been more difficult to control and bring to an end."

57   In the context of the impact of the offence vis-à-vis fire, Ms Aplin assessed that both the excessive waste and the stockpile size and layout at Deeside put the case in either category 2 or category 3 (*i.e.* there was a risk of category 1 harm or there was a risk of category 2 harm, depending on the severity of the fire). The judge found that the risk of fire came within category 2 (*viz.* there was a risk of category 1 harm). This was not, therefore, inconsistent with Ms Aplin. We add that the drone footage of Deeside shows that the site fuel storage area was surrounded on three sides by waste stacks of excessive height, packed too closely together without separation distances/firebreaks.

58   As to the clear-up costs, the judge referred to the £1.85 million figure for Deeside, potentially allowing for a discount of @ £110,000. It is not disputed that this was the bill submitted by Lancashire Waste. As set out above, for Penrhos, the judge used the bracket of £781,740 - £1m for the clear-up costs. This led to a total sum of £2,631.740, which the judge considered to be significant. Although Ms Aplin touches on the costs of moving the excess waste, she does not materially dispute these figures.

59   We reject, therefore, the appellant's submission of principle (*viz.* that in the absence of a Newton Hearing all the disputed facts needed to be resolved in his favour) and in any event we are unable to identify within the sentencing remarks

any significant disputed factual issues in relation to which the judge accepted the evidence introduced by the prosecution in favour of evidence introduced by the applicant.

III. The judge impermissibly "rejecting/ignoring" the defence expert report without warning or reason

60   This submission in relation to Ms Aplin is without merit. The judge did not make any findings in her sentencing remarks which materially contradicted or rejected the contents of Ms Aplin's statement. It was for the judge to assess where within the Guideline these offences fell, but the facts on which the judge relied for her conclusions were not significantly inconsistent with the conclusions of Ms Aplin. In any event, for the reasons set out under the preceding ground of appeal, the judge was applying the defence suggestion that she should make decisions on the facts based on the documentary material.

IV. The judge wrongly "pierced the corporate veil"

61   The appellant in the lengthy submissions that he advanced on the subject of "piercing the corporate veil" has essentially asked the court to consider the impact of what is, in the context of the present appeal against sentence, an entirely irrelevant legal concept. There is a prohibition on "piercing the corporate veil" in the sense that ordinarily the courts will not disregard a company's separate legal personality in order to obtain a remedy against someone other than the company in respect of a liability which would otherwise be that of the company alone (see *Baroness Hale of Richmond JSC in Petrodel Resources Ltd v Prest* [2013] UKSC 34; [2013] 3 W.L.R. 1 at [92]). This principle can be avoided in limited circumstances, as described by Lord Sumption JSC in *Petrodel*:

> "35. I conclude that there is a limited principle of English law which applies when a person is under an existing legal obligation or liability or subject to an existing legal restriction which he deliberately evades or whose enforcement he deliberately frustrates by interposing a company under his control. The court may then pierce the corporate veil for the purpose, and only for the purpose, of depriving the company or its controller of the advantage that they would otherwise have obtained by the company's separate legal personality. The principle is properly described as a limited one, because in almost every case where the test is satisfied, the facts will in practice disclose a legal relationship between the company and its controller which will make it unnecessary to pierce the corporate veil. [...] But the recognition of a small residual category of cases where the abuse of the corporate veil to evade or frustrate the law can be addressed only by disregarding the legal personality of the company is, I believe, consistent with authority and with long-standing principles of legal policy."

62   The appellant had pleaded guilty to offences that he had committed as a Director of PCR. The judge stated in passing sentence as regards the appellant: "you leased the premises in Deeside from Tilestone Limited. At that time you were only authorised to hold 12,000 tonnes on the outside of the site"; "you also took a lease in Penrhos on the old Anglesey Aluminium Site. You obtained an S2 exemption that allowed you to keep 500 tonnes of waste on the site"; "I know that you have

made an application for [...] an environment permit to have more waste at the site"; "you had sole control of the company (*viz.* PCR)"; and "the aggravation here is that, in my judgment, this is for financial gain, you were not running that business for altruistic reasons, you were running that business as a commercial venture and, of course, the extent of the costs of the clean-up moves it up through the range". It is argued that the judge's approach had the result that "the liability of PCR was treated as a financial gain of the appellant personally and assessed as a major aggravating feature in effect extinguishing the mitigation". In this sense, the corporate veil had been impermissibly pierced.

63   We do not accept that contention. Given this principle is essentially concerned with the limited circumstances in which the "the separate personality of the company" can be disregarded in order to obtain a remedy against someone other than the company in respect of a liability which would otherwise be that of the company alone, it has no relevance to the fact-finding exercise that a judge undertakes in passing sentence. The judge was assessing the correct punishment to be imposed as a consequence of this criminality (see *R. v Boyle Transport (Northern Ireland) Ltd* [2016] EWCA Crim 19; [2016] 4 W.L.R. 63 at [90]), criminality which was admitted. The judge was considering, vis-à-vis culpability, issues such as whether the appellant had intentionally breached or flagrantly disregarded the law, and as regards harm, the extent of the environmental impact, or risk thereof, including the costs of the clean-up operation. These considerations do not involve piercing the corporate veil in the sense prohibited by the established jurisprudence; instead, the judge was assessing the extent of the punishment that was appropriate for the appellant's role as a director in what had taken place, bearing in mind the harm caused and his culpability. In a similar vein, the judge is enjoined by the Guideline to take into account the appellant's motive as a director of the company, namely whether he was acting altruistically or for commercial advantage (one of the non-statutory aggravating features of the offence is whether it was committed for financial gain).

64   The appellant's submissions in this context are misconceived.

V. The judge incorrectly took into account complex liability issues.

65   We have essentially dealt with this in the analysis set out above. The judge did not engage with complex liability issues and instead analysed the matters that were relevant for determining the level of sentence, as required by the Guideline.

VI. The 15-year period of disqualification was manifestly excessive

66   The court made an order under section 2 of the Company Directors Disqualification Act 1986 that the appellant should be disqualified from being a director of a company etc., for a period of 15 years. This is the maximum permitted. The Crown candidly accepts this was a longer disqualification period than would have been expected in the case of a man of otherwise good character who, albeit late in the day, pleaded guilty and who had never previously been subject to a disqualification order. It is conceded that the order should have been within the middle bracket (see [45] above). We agree.

Conclusion

67   For the reasons set out above we consider that the judge's approach was entirely correct and we have no doubt that the sentence was neither manifestly excessive nor wrong in principle, save as regards Ground VI. We quash the period of 15 year's disqualification and substitute a period of 6 years. To that extent only this appeal against sentence is allowed.

DEUTSCHE UMWELTHILFE (RÉCEPTION DES VÉHICULES À MOTEUR)

EUROPEAN COURT OF JUSTICE (GRAND CHAMBER)

(C-873/19)

K. Lenaerts, President, L. Bay Larsen, Vice-President, A. Prechal, K. Jürimäe, C. Lycourgos, E. Regan, P.G. Xuereb (Rapporteur), Presidents of Chambers, M. Ilešič, J.-C. Bonichot, A. Kumin, N. Jääskinen, N. Wahl and I. Ziemele, Judges: A. Rantos, AG: 8 November 2022

EU:C:2022:857; [2023] Env. L.R. 17

☞ Associations; Direct and individual concern; EU law; Emission limit values; Illegality; Non-compliance; Type approval

H1 *EU law—air pollution—access to justice—diesel engine 'defeat device'—Regulation 715/2007—challenge to authorisation of software for exhaust gas recirculation to reduce NOx emissions limited by a 'temperature window'—whether environmental association had right to standing under Aarhus Convention—whether "need" for defeat device under art.5(2)(a) of Regulation to be assessed in light of the state of the art as at the date of the EC type-approval—whether necessary to consider circumstances other than that "need" for purposes of examining the lawfulness of device*

H2   A request for a preliminary ruling was made in proceedings brought by an environmental association (D) regarding the decision to authorise the use of software reducing the recirculation of gaseous pollutants according to outside temperature in certain vehicles produced by Volkswagen AG (V). Those vehicles had a valve for exhaust gas recirculation (EGR) used to control and reduce NOx emissions. The vehicles originally had software installed in the electronic engine controller to operate the EGR system in two modes; 'mode 0', activated when the vehicle was driven on a road, and 'mode 1', which operated during the New European Driving Cycle approval test for pollutant emissions, conducted in a laboratory. When mode 0 was activated, the EGR rate was reduced. Under normal conditions of use, the vehicles were almost exclusively in mode 0 and did not comply with the emission limit values for NOx laid down in Regulation 715/2007 on type approval of motor vehicles. V did not notify the regulator (K) of the existence of such software in the EC type-approval procedure for those vehicles. K found that that software constituted a "defeat device" within the meaning of art.3(10) of the Regulation, which was not consistent with art.5, and ordered V to remove the device and take the necessary measures to ensure that the vehicles complied with the national and European Union (EU) legislation concerned. V then updated the software, setting the EGR valve such that the EGR rate was 0% when the outside temperature was below -9°C, 85% when it was between -9 and 11°C, and increased above 11°C to be 100% operational only at outside temperatures above 15°C. Thus, the exhaust-gas purification by that recirculation system was fully effective only if the external temperature was greater than 15°C; the 'temperature window'. K then granted authorisation for the software, taking the view that the defeat devices were lawful. D sought annulment of the decision, submitting that the defeat device was still unlawful as it became active when the average temperatures recorded in Germany were reached. Furthermore, it contended that car manufacturers were able to design engines which did not require a reduction, for technical reasons, of the performance of emission control systems at average temperatures, and which would, therefore, operate under normal conditions of use. The German Republic argued that the association did not have standing to bring proceedings against the contested decision and that the temperature window available to the vehicles after the updating of the software was compatible with EU law. The questions referred asked, essentially, whether: (1) D had to be given standing under art.9(3) of the Aarhus Convention; and (2) the "need" for a defeat device within the meaning of art.5(2)(a) of the Regulation had to be assessed in the light of the state of the art as at the date of the EC type-approval and whether it was necessary to take into consideration circumstances other than that "need" for the purposes of examining the lawfulness of that device.

H3   **Held:**

H4   (1) The decision fell within the material scope of art.9(3), since it constituted an "act" of a public authority alleged to contravene the provisions of "national law relating to the environment". An environmental association authorised to bring legal proceedings fell within the personal scope of the Aarhus Convention art.9(3) as a "member of the public" and meeting "the criteria, if any, laid down in … national law" and also being part of the "public concerned", within the meaning of art.2(5). The concept of "criteria laid down in … national law", within the meaning of art.9(3) permitted Member States to establish procedural rules setting out conditions that had to be satisfied in order to be able to pursue such review procedures. However, Member States could not reduce the material scope of art.9(3) by excluding certain categories of provisions of national environmental law. Accordingly, although art.9(3) did not have direct effect in EU law and could not, therefore, be relied on to disapply a provision of national law which was contrary to it, the primacy of international agreements concluded by the EU required that national law be interpreted, to the fullest extent possible, in accordance with the requirements of those agreements. Article 9(3), read in conjunction with art.47 of the Charter of Fundamental Rights, imposed an obligation to ensure effective judicial protection of the rights conferred by EU law, in particular the provisions of environmental law.

H5   (2) The right to bring proceedings provided for in art.9(3) would be deprived of all useful effect and substance if certain categories of "members of the public" were denied of any right to bring proceedings against acts and omissions that contravened certain categories of provisions of national law relating to the environment, by imposing criteria laid down by national law. Such criteria could not deprive environmental associations of the ability to verify compliance with EU environmental law, given that such rules were usually in the public interest, rather the interests of individuals, and that the objective of those associations was to defend the public. Although they implied that Member States retained discretion as to the implementation of that provision, the words "criteria, if any, laid down in its national law" could not allow States to impose criteria so strict that it would be effectively impossible for environmental associations to challenge the acts or omissions that were the subject of that provision. By thus denying environmental organisations any right to bring an action against such a decision granting or amending EC type-approval, the relevant national procedural law was contrary to the requirements flowing from art.9(3) of the Convention and art.47 of the Charter. It was for the referring court to interpret the national procedural rules in a manner consistent with both the objectives of art.9(3) and the objective of effective judicial protection of the rights conferred by EU law, in order to enable environmental associations to challenge a decision granting or amending EC type-approval, which may be contrary to art.5(2), before a court. If such a consistent interpretation were impossible, a national court hearing a case had the obligation to disapply any provision of national law preventing the challenge.

H6   (3) A defeat device could only be justified under art.5(2)(a) where that device strictly met the need to avoid immediate risks of damage or accident to the engine, caused by a malfunction of a component of the EGR system, of such a serious nature as to give rise to a specific hazard when a vehicle fitted with that device was driven. Furthermore, there was only a "need" for such a defeat device where, at the time of the EC type-approval of that device or of the vehicle equipped with it, no other technical solution made it possible to avoid immediate risks of damage or accident to the engine, which gave rise to a specific hazard when driving the vehicle.

H7 **Cases referred to:**
AK v Krajowa Rada Sadownictwa (C-585/18) EU:C:2019:982; [2020] 2 C.M.L.R. 10
CLCV (Dispositif d'invalidation sur moteur diesel) (C-693/18) EU:C:2020:1040
Deutsche Umwelthilfe (C-752/18) EU:C:2019:1114
DS v Porsche Inter Auto GmbH & Co KG (C-145/20) EU:C:2022:572; [2022] 4 W.L.R. 91; [2023] 1 C.M.L.R. 12
Fussl Modestrasse Mayr GmbH v SevenOne Media GmbH (C-555/19) EU:C:2021:89; [2021] 2 C.M.L.R. 29
GSMB Invest (C-128/20) EU:C:2022:570
Land Baden-Wurttemberg v DR (C-619/19) EU:C:2021:35; [2021] P.T.S.R. 1038; [2021] Env. L.R. 23
Lesoochranarske Zoskupenie VLK v Ministerstvo Zivotneho Prostredia Slovenskej Republiky (C-240/09) EU:C:2011:125; [2012] Q.B. 606; [2011] Env. L.R. 28
North East Pylon Pressure Campaign Ltd v An Bord Pleanala (C-470/16) EU:C:2018:185; [2018] 3 C.M.L.R. 6; [2018] Env. L.R. 28
Protect Natur-, Arten—und Landschaftsschutz Umweltorganisation (C-664/15) EU:C:2017:987
Stichting Varkens in Nood (C-826/18) EU:C:2021:7
Volkswagen (C-134/20) EU:C:2022:571
Wasserleitungsverband Nördliches Burgenland (C-197/18) EU:C:2019:824

H8   **Legislation referred to:**
EC Treaty arts 95 and 175
TFEU arts 114, 192 and 267
UNECE Convention on Access to Information, Public Participation in Decision-making and Access to Justice in Environmental Matters (Aarhus) arts 1, 2, 6 and 9
Charter of Fundamental Rights of the European Union arts 47 and 51
Directive 85/337 (EIA)
Directive 2003/35 (SEA)
Regulation 1367/2006 arts 1 and 2
Regulation 715/2007 arts 1, 3, 4 and 5 and Annex I
Directive 2007/46 arts 1 and 3 and Annexes IV and XI
Regulation 2018/858 art.88

H9   *R. Klinger*, Rechtsanwalt, appeared on behalf of Deutsche Umwelthilfe eV.
F. Liebhart, acting as Agent, appeared on behalf of the German Government.
B. Wolfers and *R.B.A. Wollenschläger*, Rechtsanwälte, appeared on behalf of Volkswagen AG.
A.C. Becker, *G. Gattinara* and *M. Huttunen*, acting as Agents, appeared on behalf of the European Commission.

OPINION¹

I. Introduction

AG1   In the case in the main proceedings, the national EC type-approval authority took the decision to authorise, for vehicles manufactured by the motor vehicle manufacturer Volkswagen AG and equipped with a Euro 5 generation diesel engine, software installed in the electronic engine controller which, under certain external temperature conditions, reduces the recirculation of exhaust gases, which results in an increase in nitrogen oxide (NOx) emissions.

AG2   Deutsche Umwelthilfe eV, an approved environmental association, brought an action against that decision before the Schleswig-Holsteinisches Verwaltungsgericht (Administrative Court, Schleswig-Holstein, Germany), claiming that that software constitutes an unlawful 'defeat device', for the purposes of Article 5(2) of Regulation (EC) No 715/2007.²

AG3   According to the referring court, Deutsche Umwelthilfe does not have standing to bring proceedings under national law to challenge that decision. The referring court therefore asks the Court, first, whether Article 9(3) of the Aarhus Convention,³ read in conjunction with Article 47 of the Charter of Fundamental Rights of the European Union ('the Charter'), requires that such an association be entitled to challenge, before the national courts, an administrative decision granting EC type-approval of vehicles in the light of Article 5(2) of Regulation No 715/2007.

---

¹ Original language: French.
² Regulation of the European Parliament and of the Council of 20 June 2007 on type approval of motor vehicles with respect to emissions from light passenger and commercial vehicles (Euro 5 and Euro 6) and on access to vehicle repair and maintenance information (OJ 2007 L 171, p. 1), as amended by Commission Regulation (EC) No 692/2008 of 18 July 2008 (OJ 2008 L 199, p. 1) ('Regulation No 715/2007').
³ Convention on access to information, public participation in decision-making and access to justice in environmental matters, signed in Aarhus (Denmark) on 25 June 1998 and approved on behalf of the European Community by Council Decision 2005/370/EC of 17 February 2005 (OJ 2005 L 124, p. 1; 'the Aarhus Convention').

AG4   Secondly, if the answer is in the affirmative, the referring court seeks to ascertain whether the 'need' for a defeat device, within the meaning of Article 5(2) of that regulation, is to be assessed according to the state of the art existing on the date of the EC type-approval of the vehicles concerned and whether account must be taken of other circumstances which may render such a defeat device permissible.

II. Legal framework

A. International law

AG5   Article 1 of the Aarhus Convention, entitled 'Objective', states:

> 'In order to contribute to the protection of the right of every person of present and future generations to live in an environment adequate to his or her health and well-being, each Party shall guarantee the rights of access to information, public participation in decision-making, and access to justice in environmental matters in accordance with the provisions of this Convention.'

AG6   Article 2 of that convention, entitled 'Definitions', provides in paragraphs 4 and 5 thereof:

> '4. "The public" means one or more natural or legal persons, and, in accordance with national legislation or practice, their associations, organisations or groups;
> 5. "The public concerned" means the public affected or likely to be affected by, or having an interest in, the environmental decision-making; for the purposes of this definition, non-governmental organisations promoting environmental protection and meeting any requirements under national law shall be deemed to have an interest.'

AG7   Article 9 of that convention, entitled 'Access to justice', reads as follows in paragraphs 2 and 3:

> '2. Each Party shall, within the framework of its national legislation, ensure that members of the public concerned
>   (a) Having a sufficient interest or, alternatively,
>   (b) Maintaining impairment of a right, where the administrative procedural law of a Party requires this as a precondition, have access to a review procedure before a court of law and/or another independent and impartial body established by law, to challenge the substantive and procedural legality of any decision, act or omission subject to the provisions of Article 6 and, where so provided for under national law and without prejudice to paragraph 3 below, of other relevant provisions of this Convention.
> What constitutes a sufficient interest and impairment of a right shall be determined in accordance with the requirements of national law and consistently with the objective of giving the public concerned wide access to justice within the scope of this Convention. To this end, the interest of any non-governmental organisation meeting the requirements referred to in Article 2(5), shall be deemed sufficient for the purpose

of subparagraph (a) above. Such organisations shall also be deemed to have rights capable of being impaired for the purpose of subparagraph (b) above.

...

3. In addition and without prejudice to the review procedures referred to in paragraphs 1 and 2 above, each Party shall ensure that, where they meet the criteria, if any, laid down in its national law, members of the public have access to administrative or judicial procedures to challenge acts and omissions by private persons and public authorities which contravene provisions of its national law relating to the environment.'

B. European Union law

1. Regulation (EC) No 1367/2006

AG8   Article 1 of Regulation (EC) No 1367/2006,[4] entitled 'Objective', states in paragraph 1 thereof:

'The objective of this Regulation is to contribute to the implementation of the obligations arising under the UNECE Convention on Access to Information, Public Participation in Decision-making and Access to Justice in Environmental Matters, hereinafter referred to as "the Aarhus Convention", by laying down rules to apply the provisions of the Convention to Community institutions and bodies, in particular by:

...

(d) granting access to justice in environmental matters at Community level under the conditions laid down by this Regulation.'

AG9   Article 2 of that regulation, entitled 'Definitions', provides in paragraph 1(f):

'For the purposes of this Regulation:

...

(f) "environmental law" means Community legislation which, irrespective of its legal basis, contributes to the pursuit of the objectives of Community policy on the environment as set out in the Treaty: preserving, protecting and improving the quality of the environment, protecting human health, the prudent and rational utilisation of natural resources, and promoting measures at international level to deal with regional or worldwide environmental problems'.

2. Regulation No 715/2007

AG10   Recitals 1, 6 and 7 of Regulation No 715/2007 state:

'(1) ... The technical requirements for the type approval of motor vehicles with regard to emissions should ... be harmonised to avoid requirements that differ from one Member State to another, and to ensure a high level of environmental protection.

---

[4] Regulation of the European Parliament and of the Council of 6 September 2006 on the application of the provisions of the Aarhus Convention on Access to Information, Public Participation in Decision-making and Access to Justice in Environmental Matters to Community institutions and bodies (OJ 2006 L 264, p. 13).

...

(6) In particular, a considerable reduction in nitrogen oxide emissions from diesel vehicles is necessary to improve air quality and comply with limit values for pollution. ...

(7) In setting emissions standards it is important to take into account the implications for markets and manufacturers' competitiveness, the direct and indirect costs imposed on business and the benefits that accrue in terms of stimulating innovation, improving air quality, reducing health costs and increasing life expectancy, as well as the implications for the overall impact on carbon dioxide emissions.'

AG11   Article 1 of that regulation, entitled 'Subject matter', provides in paragraph 1 thereof:

'This Regulation establishes common technical requirements for the type approval of motor vehicles (vehicles) and replacement parts, such as replacement pollution control devices, with regard to their emissions.'

AG12   Article 3 of that regulation, entitled 'Definitions', provides in point 10 thereof:

'For the purposes of this Regulation and its implementing measures the following definitions shall apply:

...

10. "defeat device" means any element of design which senses temperature, vehicle speed, engine speed (RPM), transmission gear, manifold vacuum or any other parameter for the purpose of activating, modulating, delaying or deactivating the operation of any part of the emission control system, that reduces the effectiveness of the emission control system under conditions which may reasonably be expected to be encountered in normal vehicle operation and use.'

AG13   Article 5 of that same regulation, entitled 'Requirements and tests', provides in paragraphs 1 and 2:

'1. The manufacturer shall equip vehicles so that the components likely to affect emissions are designed, constructed and assembled so as to enable the vehicle, in normal use, to comply with this Regulation and its implementing measures.

2. The use of defeat devices that reduce the effectiveness of emission control systems shall be prohibited. The prohibition shall not apply where:

(a) the need for the device is justified in terms of protecting the engine against damage or accident and for safe operation of the vehicle;

(b) the device does not function beyond the requirements of engine starting;
    or

(c) the conditions are substantially included in the test procedures for verifying evaporative emissions and average tailpipe emissions.'

AG14   Annex I to Regulation No 715/2007, entitled 'Emission limits', lays down NOx emission limit values, in particular for Euro 5 generation vehicles, which are set out in Table 1.

3. Directive 2007/46/EC

AG15   Directive 2007/46/EC[5] was repealed by Regulation (EU) 2018/858,[6] with effect from 1 September 2020, pursuant to Article 88 of the regulation. However, in view of the date of the facts at issue, that directive remains applicable to the dispute in the main proceedings.

AG16   Article 1 of the directive, entitled 'Subject matter', stipulated:

> 'This Directive establishes a harmonised framework containing the administrative provisions and general technical requirements for approval of all new vehicles within its scope and of the systems, components and separate technical units intended for those vehicles, with a view to facilitating their registration, sale and entry into service within the Community.
>
> …
>
> Specific technical requirements concerning the construction and functioning of vehicles shall be laid down in application of this Directive in regulatory acts, the exhaustive list of which is set out in Annex IV.'

AG17   Article 3 of that directive, entitled 'Definitions', provided in point 5:

> 'For the purposes of this Directive and of the regulatory acts listed in Annex IV, save as otherwise provided therein:
>
> …
>
> 5. "EC type-approval" means the procedure whereby a Member State certifies that a type of vehicle, system, component or separate technical unit satisfies the relevant administrative provisions and technical requirements of this Directive and of the regulatory acts listed in Annex IV or XI.'

AG18   Annex IV to that directive, entitled 'Requirements for the purpose of EC type-approval of vehicles' referred, in Part I, entitled 'Regulatory acts for EC type-approval of vehicles produced in unlimited series', to Regulation No 715/2007 with regard to 'emissions (Euro 5 and 6) light duty vehicles/access to information'.

C. German law

AG19   Paragraph 42 of the Verwaltungsgerichtsordnung (Administrative Court Rules),[7] in the version applicable to the dispute in the main proceedings ('the VwGO'), states:

---

[5] Directive of the European Parliament and of the Council of 5 September 2007 establishing a framework for the approval of motor vehicles and their trailers, and of systems, components and separate technical units intended for such vehicles (Framework Directive) (OJ 2007 L 263, p. 1), as amended by Commission Regulation (EU) No 214/2014 of 25 February 2014 (OJ 2014 L 69, p. 3) ('Directive 2007/46').

[6] Regulation of the European Parliament and of the Council of 30 May 2018 on the approval and market surveillance of motor vehicles and their trailers, and of systems, components and separate technical units intended for such vehicles, amending Regulations (EC) No 715/2007 and (EC) No 595/2009 and repealing Directive 2007/46/EC (OJ 2018 L 151, p. 1).

[7] BGBl. 1991 I, p. 686.

'1. An action may seek to have an administrative measure set aside (action for annulment) or to have the adoption of an administrative measure ordered in the event of a refusal or failure to act (action for enjoinder).

2. Except where otherwise provided by law, such an action is admissible only if the claimant asserts that his or her rights have been impaired by the administrative measure or by the refusal or failure to act.'

AG20   Paragraph 113(1) of the VwGO provides:

'In so far as the administrative measure is unlawful and the claimant's rights have thereby been impaired, the court shall set aside the administrative measure and, where appropriate, the decision following an appeal. …'

AG21   Paragraph 1(1) of the Gesetz über ergänzende Vorschriften zu Rechtsbehelfen in Umweltangelegenheiten nach der EG- Richtlinie 2003/35/EG (Umwelt-Rechtsbehelfsgesetz) (Law on supplementary provisions governing actions in environmental matters under Directive 2003/35/EC[8] (Law on actions in environmental matters)),[9] in the version applicable to the dispute in the main proceedings ('the UmwRG'), provides:

'This law shall apply to actions against the following decisions:
    …

5. administrative measures or public law contracts authorising projects other than those referred to in points 1 to 2b pursuant to environmental provisions of Federal law, *Land* law or directly applicable acts of EU law; and

6. administrative measures concerning supervisory or control measures taken in order to implement or enforce the decisions referred to in points 1 to 5, intended to ensure compliance with the environmental provisions of Federal law, *Land* law or directly applicable acts of EU law.

This law shall also apply where, contrary to the provisions in force, a decision referred to in the first sentence has not been taken. …
    …

The first and second sentences shall not apply where a decision within the meaning of this subparagraph has been adopted as a result of a decision of the administrative courts deciding a dispute.'

AG22   Paragraph 2(1) of the UmwRG is worded as follows:

'A domestic or foreign association recognised under Paragraph 3 may bring an action in accordance with the VwGO to challenge a decision within the meaning of the first sentence of Paragraph 1(1) or a failure to adopt such a decision, without being required to maintain an impairment of its own rights, where the association

(1) asserts that a decision referred to in the first sentence of Paragraph 1(1), or the failure to adopt that decision, is contrary to provisions which may be relevant for the purposes of the decision;

---

[8] Directive of the European Parliament and of the Council of 26 May 2003 providing for public participation in respect of the drawing up of certain plans and programmes relating to the environment and amending with regard to public participation and access to justice Council Directives 85/337/EEC and 96/61/EC (OJ 2003 L 156, p. 17).
[9] BGBl. 2017 I, p. 3290.

    (2) asserts that it is affected by a decision referred to in the first sentence of Paragraph 1(1), or by the failure to adopt that decision, within its statutory field of activity of helping to achieve the objectives of environmental protection, and

    (3) in the case of a procedure referred to in

        (a) points 1 to 2b of the first sentence of Paragraph 1(1), was entitled to participate in it;

        (b) point 4 of the first sentence of Paragraph 1(1), was entitled to participate in it and, in that context, it expressed a view on the substance in accordance with the provisions in force, or it was not given the opportunity to express its view, contrary to the provisions in force.

In the event of an appeal against a decision referred to in points 2a to 6 of the first sentence of Paragraph 1(1), or against the failure to take that decision, the association must also rely on an infringement of provisions relating to the environment.'

AG23   Under Paragraph 25(2) of the Verordnung über die EG-Genehmigung für Kraftfahrzeuge und ihre Anhänger sowie für Systeme, Bauteile und selbstständige technische Einheiten für diese Fahrzeuge (EG-Fahrzeuggenehmigungsverordnung) (Regulation on the EC type-approval for motor vehicles and their trailers, and for systems, components and separate technical units intended for such vehicles (EC motor vehicle type-approval regulation)),[10] in the version applicable to the dispute in the main proceedings ('the EG-FGV'):

    '1. If the Kraftfahrt-Bundesamt [(Federal Motor Transport Authority, Germany) ("the KBA")] finds that vehicles, systems, components or separate technical units do not conform to the approved type, it may take the necessary measures under that directive which is applicable to the type concerned out of Directives [2007/46], 2002/24/EC[11] or 2003/37/EC[12] to ensure that production conforms to the approved type.

    2. In order to remedy any deficiencies which have come to light and to ensure the conformity of vehicles already put into circulation, and of components or separate technical units, the Federal Motor Transport Authority may retroactively impose ancillary provisions.'

III. The dispute in the main proceedings, the questions referred for a preliminary ruling and the procedure before the Court

AG24   Volkswagen produced, inter alia, VW Golf Plus TDI motor vehicles, equipped with a Euro 5 generation EA 189-type diesel engine with a capacity of two litres ('the vehicles concerned'). Those vehicles have a valve for the recycling of exhaust gas.

AG25   The vehicles concerned initially contained software installed in the electronic engine controller which had a 'mode 0' and a 'mode 1' ('the switch system'). Mode

---

[10] BGBl. 2011 I, p. 126.
[11] Directive of the European Parliament and of the Council of 18 March 2002 relating to the type-approval of two or three-wheel motor vehicles and repealing Council Directive 92/61/EEC (OJ 2002 L 124, p. 1).
[12] Directive of the European Parliament and of the Council of 26 May 2003 on type-approval of agricultural or forestry tractors, their trailers and interchangeable towed machinery, together with their systems, components and separate technical units and repealing Directive 74/150/EEC (OJ 2003 L 171, p. 1).

1 was used for the approval test for pollutant emissions, called the 'New European Driving Cycle' (NEDC), which is conducted in a laboratory. If the characteristic conditions of that approval test did not exist, mode 0 was applied and, in that case, the exhaust gas recirculation rate decreased. In real-world operation, those vehicles were almost exclusively in mode 0, meaning that they did not comply with the NOx limit values laid down in Regulation No 715/2007. It is apparent from the order for reference that the switch system was therefore a prohibited defeat device within the meaning of Article 5(1) and (2) of that regulation. In the EC type-approval procedure for the vehicles concerned, Volkswagen did not notify the KBA of the existence of that system.

AG26   On 15 October 2015, the KBA adopted a decision, pursuant to Paragraph 25(2) of the EG-FGV, by which, inter alia, it ordered Volkswagen to ensure that the Euro 5 generation EA 189-type engines complied with the national and EU legislation in force. The KBA stated that the solutions had to be submitted to it for approval before they were implemented in practice.

AG27   In that context, Volkswagen updated the software installed in the electronic engine controller for the vehicles concerned ('the software at issue'). That software established a temperature window in which the exhaust gas recirculation rate, that is to say the portion of the exhaust gas redirected to the engine, is 0% when the external temperature is less than -9 °C, 85% when it is between -9 and 11 °C, and increases from 11 °C upwards to reach 100% from an external temperature of 15 °C ('the temperature window').

AG28   By decision of 20 June 2016 ('the contested decision'), the KBA granted authorisation for the software in question. In that regard, it held, inter alia, that there were no impermissible defeat devices, within the meaning of Regulation No 715/2007, taking the view that the defeat devices still present were permissible.

AG29   On 15 November 2016, Deutsche Umwelthilfe, an association which is entitled to bring legal proceedings under Paragraph 3 of the UmwRG, brought an administrative action against the contested decision, which had not yet been the subject of a decision on the date of the present request for a preliminary ruling.

AG30   On 24 April 2018, that association brought an action before the Schleswig-Holsteinisches Verwaltungsgericht (Administrative Court, Schleswig-Holstein), the referring court, seeking annulment of the contested decision. It argued that the software at issue created a defeat device which had to be regarded as unlawful for the purposes of Article 5(2) of Regulation No 715/2007 since it becomes active when the average temperatures existing in Germany, namely approximately 10.4 °C in 2018, are reached. According to the association, car manufacturers are, in principle, able to design engines which do not require a reduction, for technical reasons, of the performance of NOx emission control systems at average temperatures, that is to say under normal operating conditions.

AG31   The Bundesrepublik Deutschland (Federal Republic of Germany) has submitted that Deutsche Umwelthilfe does not have standing to bring proceedings against the contested decision and, consequently, that its action is inadmissible.

AG32   In the referring court's view, Deutsche Umwelthilfe does not, in the present case, have standing to bring proceedings under Paragraph 42(2) of the VwGO, under which, unless otherwise provided for by law, the action is admissible only if the applicant asserts that his or her rights have been impaired by the administrative measure at issue. There is no provision in the law which, unlike the system of individual actions on which that provision is based, may exceptionally confer standing on that association.

AG33   In particular, the case in the main proceedings does not fall within the scope of the UmwRG, as defined in Paragraph 1(1) of that law. Among the decisions which may be the subject of an action brought by an environmental organisation, the only category that could be envisaged in the present case is that referred to in Paragraph 1(1), first sentence, point 5, of the UmwRG, according to which that law is applicable to actions against administrative measures or public-law contracts authorising projects other than those referred to in Paragraph 1(1), points 1 to 2b, pursuant to environmental provisions of Federal law, *Land* law or directly applicable acts of EU law. In that regard, according to the referring court, Article 5(2) of Regulation No 715/2007 is linked to the environment and is not merely a technical provision intended to regulate the internal market, as is apparent from recitals 1, 4 and 7 of that regulation.

AG34   However, Paragraph 1(1), first sentence, point 5, of the UmwRG concerns only administrative measures authorising 'projects'. The term 'project', within the meaning of that provision, was adopted in connection with Directive 85/337/EEC,[13] Article 1(2) of which defines a 'project' as 'the execution of construction works or of other installations or schemes' (first indent) and 'other interventions in the natural surroundings and landscape including those involving the extraction of mineral resources' (second indent). In that context, the national legislation concerns only fixed installations or measures which constitute direct intervention. Both the EC type-approval of vehicles and the amendment of the EC approval covered by the contested decision relate to the 'authorisation' of a product and do not constitute a 'project' within the meaning of national law, in so far as they do not relate to a fixed installation and do not involve any direct intervention in the natural surroundings and landscape.

AG35   Moreover, in the referring court's view, a broad interpretation of 'project', within the meaning of Paragraph 1(1), first sentence, point 5, of the UmwRG, does not allow a different conclusion to be reached. It is true that the Court has noted that it is for the national court, in order to ensure effective judicial protection in the fields covered by EU environmental law, to interpret its national law in a way which, to the fullest extent possible, is consistent with the objectives laid down in Article 9(3) of the Aarhus Convention.[14] However, because of the clear definition of 'project' in national law, the referring court is prevented from extending that concept in the present case to the authorisation for updating the software at issue in order to bring the vehicles concerned into line with the legislation in force.

AG36   Furthermore, it is not possible to apply the provisions of the UmwRG by analogy, on the basis of an unintended lacuna in the national legislation, that is to say an instance where the legislature had not identified or could not identify the interest in question because of a subsequent change in circumstances. In the course of the legislative process which led to the amendment of the UmwRG in 2017, which sought, inter alia, to adapt the law to the requirements of public international law resulting from Article 9(3) of the Aarhus Convention and to take account of the

---

[13] Council Directive of 27 June 1985 on the assessment of the effects of certain public and private projects on the environment (OJ 1985 L 175, p. 40). That directive was repealed by Directive 2011/92/EU of the European Parliament and of the Council of 13 December 2011 on the assessment of the effects of certain public and private projects on the environment (OJ 2012 L 26, p. 1).

[14] Judgment of 8 March 2011, *Lesoochranárske zoskupenie* (C-240/09) EU:C:2011:125 at paragraph 50.

judgment of 8 March 2011, *Lesoochranárske zoskupenie* (C-240/09) EU:C:2011:125, the question of the application of the concept of a 'project', within the meaning of Paragraph 1(1), first sentence, point 5, of that law, to product approvals was identified and discussed. In that regard, it was expressly stated that that law does not concern the product sector, including with respect to vehicles. Moreover, the explanatory memorandum to that law expressly states that the national legislature has refrained from transposing Article 9(3) of the Aarhus Convention into a general provision on the ground that that would constitute a source of major difficulties with respect to delimitation and legal uncertainty.

AG37   Nor can Deutsche Umwelthilfe claim that it has standing to bring proceedings derived directly from Article 9(3) of the Aarhus Convention. Since that provision, in itself, has no direct effect in EU law, as stated in the judgment of 20 December 2017, *Protect Natur-, Arten—und Landschaftsschutz Umweltorganisation* (C-664/15) EU:C:2017:987; 'the judgment in *Protect*'; at paragraph 45, it does not constitute a legislative provision for the purposes of the first phrase of Paragraph 42(2) of the VwGO.

AG38   The referring court adds that Deutsche Umwelthilfe has no standing to bring proceedings against the contested decision under the second phrase of Paragraph 42(2) of the VwGO either, under which the applicant must assert that his or her rights have been impaired by the administrative measure at issue. The system of individual actions provided for in the VwGO is based on subjective rights. However, the case in the main proceedings does not appear to concern a subjective right of a natural person which has been infringed. Infringement of the prohibition on using defeat devices laid down in Article 5(2) of Regulation No 715/2007, which alone may be relevant in the present case, does not confer any subjective right on a natural person, since that provision is not intended to protect a group of persons who are decisively distinct from the general public.

AG39   According to the referring court, the outcome of the main proceedings therefore depends on whether Deutsche Umwelthilfe may claim standing to bring proceedings which is derived directly from EU law. In the light of the judgment in *Protect*, that standing to bring proceedings could result from the combined provisions of Article 9(3) of the Aarhus Convention and the first paragraph of Article 47 of the Charter. In that regard, the referring court points out that the case in the main proceedings does not fall within the scope of Article 9(2) of that convention since, first, the contested decision is not a decision governed by Article 6 of that convention and, secondly, there is no provision of national law, for the purposes of the first sentence of Article 9(2) of that convention, which would render other provisions of the convention applicable.

AG40   The referring court states that, as regards the consequences of the judgment in *Protect* for national procedural law, the national courts have given divergent decisions, which gives rise to its doubts as to whether EU law allows an approved environmental association to challenge, even beyond the possibilities of bringing an action already provided for by the UmwRG, an administrative authorisation for a product of the type at issue in the present case if the action of that association seeks to ensure compliance with provisions of EU environmental law which do not give rise to any subjective right.

AG41   In the event that the Court considers that an environmental association has standing to challenge the EC type-approval of vehicles, the referring court takes the view that the lawfulness of the contested decision depends crucially on the interpretation of Article 5(2) of Regulation No 715/2007, in particular with regard to the concept of the 'need' for a defeat device. That court asks whether vehicle manufacturers must take account of the current state of the art in order to ascertain whether a defeat device is in fact necessary in terms of protecting the engine against damage or accident and for the safe operation of the vehicle.

AG42   It was in those circumstances that the Schleswig-Holsteinisches Verwaltungsgericht (Administrative Court, Schleswig-Holstein) decided to stay the proceedings and to refer the following questions to the Court for a preliminary ruling:

> '(1) Is Article 9(3) of the [Aarhus Convention,] in conjunction with Article 47 of the [Charter], to be interpreted as meaning that it must in principle be possible for environmental associations to challenge before the courts a decision approving the manufacture of diesel passenger cars with defeat devices that are potentially in breach of Article 5(2) of Regulation [No 715/2007]?
>
> (2) If Question 1 is answered in the affirmative:
>
>> (a) Is Article 5(2) of Regulation [No 715/2007] to be interpreted as meaning that the yardstick for determining whether the need for a defeat device is justified in terms of protecting the engine against damage or accident and for safe operation of the vehicle is, in principle, the state of the art, in the sense of what is technically feasible at the time when the EC type approval is granted?
>>
>> (b) In addition to the state of the art, should account be taken of other circumstances which may lead to the permissibility of a defeat device, even though, according to the current state of the art alone, the "need" for such a device would not be "justified" within the meaning of Article 5(2)(a) of Regulation [No 715/2007]?'

AG43   Written observations were submitted by Deutsche Umwelthilfe, the KBA, Volkswagen, and by the European Commission. Those parties and interested parties also replied in writing to the questions put by the Court.

IV. Analysis

A. The first question referred for a preliminary ruling

AG44   By its first question, the referring court asks, in essence, whether Article 9(3) of the Aarhus Convention, read in conjunction with the first paragraph of Article 47 of the Charter, must be interpreted as meaning that an approved environmental association, which is entitled to bring legal proceedings under national law, must be able to challenge before a national court an administrative decision granting EC type-approval of vehicles which may be contrary to Article 5(2) of Regulation No 715/2007, a provision which prohibits, subject to certain exceptions, the use of defeat devices which reduce the effectiveness of emission control systems.

AG45   Under Article 9(3) of the Aarhus Convention, without prejudice to the review procedures referred to in Article 9(1) and (2), each party is to ensure that, where they meet the criteria, if any, laid down in its national law, members of the public have access to administrative or judicial procedures to challenge acts and omissions by private persons and public authorities which contravene provisions of its national law relating to the environment.

AG46   In order to answer this question, I shall examine the scope of Article 9(3) of the Aarhus Convention and then the implications of that provision when read in conjunction with the first paragraph of Article 47 of the Charter.

1. The scope of Article 9(3) of the Aarhus Convention

AG47   It should be noted at the outset that the case in the main proceedings concerns the possibility of *bringing legal proceedings to challenge the act of a public authority*, namely the EC type-approval of vehicles. Those conditions referred to in Article 9(3) of the Aarhus Convention are therefore satisfied. The other conditions relate to the scope *ratione materiae* and the scope *ratione personae* of that provision, which will be addressed in turn.

AG48   As far as its scope *ratione materiae* is concerned, Article 9(3) of the Aarhus Convention requires that the act in question contravene 'provisions of ... national law relating to the environment'. In the present case, the measure invoked by Deutsche Umwelthilfe is Regulation No 715/2007 and, in particular, Article 5(2) thereof. It must therefore be ascertained whether that provision falls within the scope of 'national law relating to the environment'.

AG49   In that regard, first, contrary to the KBA's submissions, I share the referring court's view that that regulation does fall within the scope of environmental law and must therefore not be regarded solely as a technical regulation intended to regulate the internal market. It seems to me that that issue was resolved by the judgment of 17 December 2020, *CLCV (Defeat device on diesel engines)* (C-693/18) EU:C:2020:1040; 'the judgment in *CLCV*'; at paragraph 113, which stated that the objective pursued by Regulation No 715/2007 is to ensure a high level of environmental protection and improve air quality within the European Union.

AG50   The KBA also states that that regulation is based on Article 95 EC (now Article 114 TFEU), which concerns measures for the approximation of the provisions laid down by law, regulation or administrative action in Member States which have as their object the establishment and functioning of the internal market. However, Article 95(3) EC provides that the Commission, in its proposals concerning health, safety, *environmental protection* and consumer protection, will take as a base a high level of protection, taking account in particular of any new development based on scientific facts. Consequently, the fact that that regulation is not founded on a specific legal basis relating to the environment, namely Article 175 EC, is not such as to exclude the link between that regulation and environmental law.

AG51   In any event, Article 2(1)(f) of Regulation No 1367/2006 defines 'environmental law' as 'Community legislation which, *irrespective of its legal basis*, contributes to the pursuit of the objectives of Community policy on the environment as set out in the Treaty: *preserving, protecting and improving the quality of the environment*, protecting human health, the prudent and rational utilisation of natural resources, and promoting measures at international level to deal with regional or worldwide environmental problems'.[15] That is indeed the case with Regulation No 715/2007.

AG52   With regard more specifically to Article 5(2) of that regulation, that provision concerns 'defeat devices' within the meaning of Article 3(10) thereof. Although

---

[15] Emphasis added.

that provision is of a technical nature, it forms part of that regulation and is intended to limit the emission of gaseous pollutants, thereby helping to protect the environment. More generally, as Deutsche Umwelthilfe has stated, it is inconceivable to separate environmental law and technical regulations as a matter of principle since an environmental provision is often of a technical nature. In that regard, I note that recital 1 of Regulation No 715/2007 states that the 'technical requirements for the type approval of motor vehicles with regard to emissions should therefore be harmonised to avoid requirements that differ from one Member State to another, and to ensure a high level of environmental protection'. That recital therefore expressly establishes a link between the technical rules concerning EC type-approval and environmental protection.

AG53   Secondly, the provision of EU law on which Deutsche Umwelthilfe relies, namely Article 5(2) of Regulation No 715/2007, is directly applicable in the Member States and must be regarded as forming part of the provisions of *national* law relating to the environment.[16]

AG54   As regards the scope *ratione personae* of Article 9(3) of the Aarhus Convention, that provision states that 'members of the public' who 'meet the criteria, if any, laid down in ... national law' have the rights set out in that provision. In that regard, it is clear from the order for reference that Deutsche Umwelthilfe is an approved environmental association which is entitled to bring legal proceedings in accordance with Paragraph 3 of the UmwRG and whose purpose, according to its articles of association, is to contribute to the protection of nature and the environment and also to health- and environment-related consumer protection, in particular by providing information and advice to consumers. Consequently, that association satisfies the conditions to bring legal proceedings before the national courts to promote environmental protection.

AG55   Accordingly, an association such as Deutsche Umwelthilfe falls not only within the scope of 'the public', within the meaning of Article 2(4) of the Aarhus Convention but also 'the public concerned', within the meaning of Article 2(5) of that convention. Under the latter provision, non-governmental organisations promoting environmental protection and meeting any requirements under national law must be deemed to have an interest.

AG56   Finally, the referring court asks whether the expression 'criteria ... laid down in ... national law', within the meaning of Article 9(3) of the Aarhus Convention, covers only criteria concerning those who have a right to bring proceedings since the national legislature has defined those criteria in a binding manner in Paragraph 3 of the UmwRG. In my view, that expression also concerns the subject matter of an action and those criteria must comply with EU law. That question will be examined below.

2. The implications of Article 9(3) of the Aarhus Convention when read in conjunction with the first paragraph of Article 47 of the Charter

AG57   According to the case-law of the Court, the review procedures referred to in Article 9(3) of the Aarhus Convention may be subject to 'criteria', from which it

---

[16] See, to that effect, Aarhus Convention Compliance Committee, findings and recommendations of 29 April 2008, Denmark (ACCC/C/2006/18, ECE/MP.PP/2008/5/Add.4, paragraph 27), according to which, in the context of Article 9(3) of the Aarhus Convention, EU law relating to the environment should be considered to be part of the national law of a Member State. The English-language version of that document can be found at: *https://unece.org/DAM/env /documents/2008/pp/mop3/ece_mp_pp_2008_5_add_4_e.pdf*.

follows that Member States may, in the context of the discretion they have in that regard, establish procedural rules setting out conditions that must be satisfied in order to be able to pursue such review procedures.[17] In that regard, as the referring court states, the reform of the UmwRG during 2017 was intended, inter alia, to bring the law into line with the requirements of public international law resulting from Article 9(3) of the Aarhus Convention.

AG58   According to the national court, Deutsche Umwelthilfe does not have standing to bring proceedings under national law to challenge an administrative decision granting EC type-approval.[18] Moreover, Article 9(3) of the Aarhus Convention, as such, has no direct effect in EU law.[19] In those circumstances, if the national law does not provide that an approved environmental association has standing to bring proceedings, that provision, by itself, cannot confer such standing on it.

AG59   However, the national court referred to the judgment in *Protect* to justify its request for a preliminary ruling. In that regard, that judgment makes the link between Article 9(3) of the Aarhus Convention and Article 47 of the Charter in respect of the right of access to justice of environmental organisations.[20] The reasoning adopted by the Court in that judgment seems to me to be readily transposable to the present case, as follows.

AG60   Under Article 3(5) of Directive 2007/46, EC type-approval means the procedure whereby a *Member State certifies* that a type of vehicle, system, component or separate technical unit satisfies the relevant administrative provisions and technical requirements of that directive and of the regulatory acts listed in Annex IV or XI to that directive. Annex IV referred to Regulation No 715/2007, Article 5(2) of which is binding in nature.

AG61   Therefore, where a Member State lays down rules of procedural law applicable to the matters referred to in Article 9(3) of the Aarhus Convention concerning the exercise of the rights that an environmental organisation derives from Article 5(2) of Regulation No 715/2007, in order for decisions of the competent national authorities to be reviewed in the light of their obligations under that provision, the Member State is implementing an obligation stemming from that provision and must therefore be regarded as implementing EU law, for the purposes of Article 51(1) of the Charter, with the result that the Charter is applicable.[21]

AG62   Although Article 9(3) of the Aarhus Convention, in itself, has no direct effect in EU law, the fact remains that that provision, read in conjunction with the first paragraph of Article 47 of the Charter, imposes on Member States an obligation to ensure effective judicial protection of the rights conferred by EU law, in particular the provisions of environmental law.[22]

AG63   The right to bring proceedings set out in Article 9(3) of the Aarhus Convention would be deprived of all useful effect, and even of its very substance, if it had to be conceded that, by imposing criteria laid down in national law, certain categories

---

[17] Judgment of 14 January 2021, *Stichting Varkens in Nood* (C-826/18) EU:C:2021:7 at paragraph 49 and the case-law cited.
[18] See AG 32 to 40 of this Opinion.
[19] Judgment of 20 December 2017, *Protect Natur-, Arten—und Landschaftsschutz Umweltorganisation* (C-664/15) EU:C:2017:987 at paragraph 45 and the case-law cited.
[20] With regard to the scope of Article 47 of the Charter, see Safjan, M. and Düsterhaus, D., 'A Union of Effective Judicial Protection: Addressing a Multi-level Challenge through the Lens of Article 47 CFREU', *Yearbook of European Law*, 2014, vol. 33, No 1, pp. 3-40.
[21] See, to that effect, the judgment in *Protect* at paragraph 44 and the case-law cited.
[22] See, to that effect, the judgment in Protect, paragraph 45, and judgment of 3 October 2019, *Wasserleitungsverband Nördliches Burgenland* (C-197/18) EU:C:2019:824 at paragraph 33.

of 'members of the public', a fortiori 'the public concerned', such as environmental associations that satisfy the requirements laid down in Article 2(5) of that convention, were to be denied any right to bring proceedings.[23] Those associations cannot be deprived of the possibility of verifying that the rules of EU environmental law are being complied with, given also that such rules are usually in the public interest, rather than simply in the interests of certain individuals, and that the objective of those associations is to defend the public interest.[24]

AG64   Although they imply that contracting States retain discretion as to the implementation of that provision, the words 'criteria, if any, laid down in its national law' in Article 9(3) of the Aarhus Convention cannot allow those States to impose criteria so strict that it would be effectively impossible for environmental organisations to contest the actions or omissions that are the subject of that provision.[25]

AG65   In the present case, it is apparent from the order for reference that Deutsche Umwelthilfe does not have standing to bring proceedings to challenge an administrative decision granting EC type-approval on the ground, inter alia, that that approval constitutes a 'product approval' and that, for such an approval, national law does not allow an environmental association, even if it falls within the scope of 'the public concerned', within the meaning of Article 2(5) of the Aarhus Convention, to bring proceedings before a national court against an administrative decision granting EC type-approval to vehicles. By thus denying environmental associations any right to bring an action against such a decision to grant a permit, the relevant national procedural law is contrary to the requirements flowing from a combined reading of Article 9(3) of the Aarhus Convention and the first paragraph of Article 47 of the Charter.[26]

AG66   In other words, the effectiveness of Article 5(2) of Regulation No 715/2007, seen from the viewpoint of the fundamental right to an effective judicial remedy, requires that the right to challenge an administrative decision granting EC type-approval be granted to approved environmental associations.[27]

AG67   It should be added that, while the freedoms guaranteed by the Charter may be limited, any limitation on their exercise must, in accordance with Article 52(1) thereof, be provided for by law and respect the essential content of those freedoms. Moreover, as is clear from that provision, in accordance with the principle of proportionality, limitations may be made only if they are necessary and actually meet objectives of general interest recognised by the European Union or the need to protect the rights and freedoms of others.[28] However, in the present case, I fail to see which objective of general interest recognised by the European Union could justify prohibiting an environmental association from having access to justice in order to challenge the EC type-approval of vehicles.[29]

---

[23] See, to that effect, the judgment in Protect, paragraph 46, and judgment of 3 October 2019, *Wasserleitungsverband Nördliches Burgenland* (C-197/18) EU:C:2019:824 at paragraph 34.
[24] See, to that effect, the judgment in *Protect*, paragraph 47 and the case-law cited.
[25] The judgment in *Protect*, paragraph 48.
[26] See, to that effect, the judgment in *Protect* at paragraph 52.
[27] See, to that effect, Opinion of Advocate General Sharpston in *Protect Natur-, Arten—und Landschaftsschutz Umweltorganisation* (C-664/15) EU:C:2017:760 at AG91.
[28] Judgment of 3 February 2021, *Fussl Modestraße Mayr* (C-555/19) EU:C:2021:89 at paragraph 84 and the case-law cited.
[29] The KBA submits that the Grundgesetz (German Basic Law) has made a systematic choice in favour of the protection of subjective rights.

AG68   According to the referring court, even a broad, or analogous, interpretation of national law does not make it possible to confer standing on an environmental association to challenge a decision granting EC type-approval. Nevertheless, I note that that court refers to a judgment of the Verwaltungsgericht Berlin (Administrative Court, Berlin, Germany) of 18 April 2018 concerning the lawfulness of the authorisation for the regular operation of certain megatrucks and the extension of the trial phase of certain other megatrucks, according to which the second phrase of Paragraph 42(2) of the VwGO confers standing to bring proceedings on an approved environmental association which seeks to enforce compliance with provisions based on EU environmental law. Moreover, as the KBA points out, Deutsche Umwelthilfe submitted in the main proceedings that its standing to bring proceedings was derived directly from Paragraph 1(1), first sentence, point 6, and from Paragraph 2(1) of the UmwRG.

AG69   It is for the referring court to interpret, to the fullest extent possible, the procedural rules relating to the conditions to be met in order to bring proceedings, in accordance with both the objectives of Article 9(3) of the Aarhus Convention and the objective of effective judicial protection of the rights conferred by EU law, in order to enable an environmental association, such as Deutsche Umwelthilfe, to challenge before a national court a decision that may be contrary to EU environmental law.[30]

AG70   However, if such a compliant interpretation were to be found to be impossible, it follows from the established case-law of the Court that a national court which is called upon, within the exercise of its jurisdiction, to apply rules of EU law is under a duty to give full effect to those rules, if necessary refusing of its own motion to apply any conflicting provision of national legislation, even if adopted subsequently, and it is not necessary for the court to request or await the prior setting aside of such provision by legislative or other constitutional means.[31]

AG71   The referring court asks whether Article 9(3) of the Aarhus Convention must be interpreted as meaning that, in view of the large number of decisions that are linked to the environment, the Member States may exempt certain administrative decisions from judicial review on the initiative of environmental associations, such as those relating to product approvals, the possibility of bringing an action being limited to certain decisions that are serious in terms of their environmental impact. However, I consider that such an approach finds no support, whether in the provisions of that convention or in the case-law of the Court. In any event, as Deutsche Umwelthilfe submits, a decision granting EC type-approval may concern a large number of vehicles and cannot therefore be regarded as being only of minor importance for environmental protection. In that regard, as stated in recital 6 of Regulation No 715/2007, a considerable reduction in NOx emissions from diesel vehicles is necessary to improve air quality and comply with limit values for pollution.

AG72   Moreover, the referring court notes that, unlike the facts which gave rise to the judgment in *Protect*, related to Austrian law, environmental associations, under German law, have the possibility, within the framework of the UmwRG, to have the approval of projects reviewed and therefore a total exclusion of the right of associations to bring proceedings does not exist. Procedural law does not therefore

---

[30] See, to that effect, the judgment in Protect, paragraph 54, and judgment of 19 December 2019, *Deutsche Umwelthilfe* (C-752/18) EU:C:2019:1114 at paragraph 39.
[31] See, to that effect, the judgment in *Protect* at paragraph 56.

contain a gap in legal protection which is comparable to that found in that judgment. However, as the referring court points out, an association such as Deutsche Umwelthilfe has no access to justice in order to challenge a decision granting EC type-approval. Therefore, I am of the opinion that the case-law in the judgment in *Protect* is fully applicable for the purpose of ensuring compliance with a rule of EU environmental law.

AG73   The KBA and Volkswagen submit that the *actio popularis* is structurally extraneous to German procedural law and that an environmental association must therefore always be able to claim that, as a result of action taken by the authorities, its rights may have been infringed. However, in the present case, the application of Article 9(3) of the Aarhus Convention, read in conjunction with the first paragraph of Article 47 of the Charter, does not lead to an *actio popularis*.[32] The right of access to justice in a case such as that in the main proceedings presupposes that national law has conferred on the association concerned the right to be a party to legal proceedings since its articles of association have been approved by the competent national authorities. Such an organisation therefore provides assurances of its reliability and competence in the performance of its duties.[33] Since the interest which those organisations have in environmental protection is recognised in law, they are concerned by an infringement of directly applicable provisions of EU environmental law to an extent sufficient to enable them to rely on those provisions before the national courts.[34]

AG74   In the light of all the foregoing, I propose that the answer to the first question should be that Article 9(3) of the Aarhus Convention, read in conjunction with the first paragraph of Article 47 of the Charter, must be interpreted as meaning that an approved environmental association, which is entitled to bring legal proceedings under national law, must be able to challenge before a national court an administrative decision granting EC type-approval of vehicles which may be contrary to Article 5(2) of Regulation No 715/2007, a provision which prohibits, subject to certain exceptions, the use of defeat devices which reduce the effectiveness of emission control systems.

B. The second question referred for a preliminary ruling

AG75   By its second question, which is raised in the event that the first question is answered in the affirmative, the national court asks, in essence, whether Article 5(2)(a) of Regulation No 715/2007 must be interpreted as meaning that the 'need' for a defeat device in terms of protecting the engine against damage or accident and for safe operation of the vehicle is to be assessed in the light of the state of the art at the time when the EC type-approval is granted to the vehicles concerned and

---

[32] In her Opinion in *Protect Natur-, Arten—und Landschaftsschutz Umweltorganisation* (C-664/15) EU:C:2017:760 at AG81, Advocate General Sharpston stated that the authors of the Aarhus Convention did not opt to introduce an *actio popularis* in environmental matters and that they decided to strengthen the role of environmental organisations. The Advocate General added that, in so doing, they steered a middle course between the maximalist approach (*actio popularis*) and the minimalist approach (a right of individual action available only to parties having a direct interest at stake).

[33] As Advocate General Sharpston noted in her Opinion in *Protect Natur-, Arten—und Landschaftsschutz Umweltorganisation* (C-664/15) EU:C:2017:760 AG74, environmental organisations promoting environmental protection and meeting objectively justified, transparent and non-discriminatory requirements facilitating access to justice under national law must be entitled to rely on Article 9(3) of the Aarhus Convention.

[34] See, to that effect, Opinion of Advocate General Kokott in *Lesoochranárske zoskupenie VLK* (C-243/15) EU:C:2016:491 at AG49.

whether it is necessary to take account of circumstances other than that 'need' in order to examine the lawfulness of a defeat device.[35]

AG76   Under Article 5(2) of Regulation No 715/2007, the use of defeat devices that reduce the effectiveness of emission control systems is prohibited. However, there are three exceptions to that prohibition, including that in point (a) of that provision, namely where the 'need for the device is justified in terms of protecting the engine against damage or accident and for safe operation of the vehicle'.

AG77   As a preliminary point, I note that, in its question, the referring court assumes that the temperature window constitutes a 'defeat device' within the meaning of Article 3(10) of Regulation No 715/2007. In the judgment in *CLCV*, the Court held that a device which detects any parameter related to the conduct of the approval procedures provided for by Regulation No 715/2007 in order to improve the performance of the emission control system during those procedures, and thus obtain approval of the vehicle, constitutes a 'defeat device' even if such an improvement may also be observed, occasionally, under normal conditions of vehicle use.[36]

AG78   The Court also held that the prohibition laid down in Article 5(2)(a) of that regulation would be devoid of substance and deprived of any effectiveness if car manufacturers were permitted to equip motor vehicles with such defeat devices with the sole aim of protecting the engine against clogging up and ageing.[37] That case-law was delivered in the context of the examination of the conformity of the switch system with EU law.

AG79   Cases *GSMB Invest* (C-128/20), *Volkswagen* (C-134/20) and *Porsche Inter Auto and Volkswagen* (C-145/20) however, concern a temperature window which is similar to that which is the subject of the present question. In my Joined Opinion in those three cases,[38] which I delivered on 23 September 2021, I proposed that the Court should take the view that Article 3(10) of Regulation No 715/2007, read in conjunction with Article 5(1) of that regulation, is to be interpreted as meaning that a device which, under real driving conditions of a motor vehicle, ensures exhaust gas recirculation in full only when the outside temperature is between 15 °C and 33 °C and the driving altitude is lower than 1000 m, whereas, outside that window, per 10 °C, and above an altitude of 1000 m, per 250 m of altitude, the exhaust gas recirculation rate decreases in a linear way down to zero, with the result that NOx emissions increase beyond the limit values laid down in the regulation, constitutes a 'defeat device'.[39] Those considerations can be transposed to the present case.

AG80   By Question 2(a), the referring court seeks to ascertain whether the 'need' for a defeat device in terms of protecting the engine against damage or accident and for safe operation of the vehicle must be assessed in the light of what is technically feasible at the time when the EC type-approval is granted to the vehicles concerned.

AG81   I agree with that court that, in order to answer that question, the date of the EC type-approval must be used as the basis. The EC type-approval concerns new vehicles which must comply with the regulatory acts in force at the time of approval,

---

[35] In its second question, the national court refers to 'defeat devices'. However, since the case in the main proceedings concerns the temperature window only, I shall refer to that single defeat device.
[36] The judgment in *CLCV* at paragraph 102.
[37] The judgment in *CLCV* at paragraph 113.
[38] Opinion in *GSMB Invest Volkswagen* and *Porsche Inter Auto* and *Volkswagen* (C-128/20), (C-134/20) and (C-145/20) EU:C:2021:758.
[39] AG104 of that Opinion.

including those referred to in Annex IV to Directive 2007/46, which include Regulation No 715/2007.

AG82   With regard to the technical requirements concerning that type-approval, I took the view in my Opinion in Cases *GSMB Invest* (C-128/20), *Volkswagen* (C-134/20) and *Porsche Inter Auto and Volkswagen* (C-145/20), that nowhere in Regulation No 715/2007 is it stated that a particular technology should be used for EC type-approval.[40] In other words, as Volkswagen submits, that regulation, like Directive 2007/46, is designed to be neutral from a technological perspective.

AG83   I also recalled that, as is stated in recital 7 of that regulation, 'in setting emissions standards it is important to take into account the implications for markets and manufacturers' competitiveness, the direct and indirect costs imposed on business and the benefits that accrue in terms of stimulating innovation, improving air quality, reducing health costs and increasing life expectancy, as well as the implications for the overall impact on carbon dioxide emissions'. Accordingly, when the EU legislature determined the limit values of pollutant emissions, account had already been taken of the interests of vehicle manufacturers. It is therefore for those manufacturers to adapt to and to apply the appropriate technical means to comply with those limit values, without the technology used *necessarily being the best possible or being required.*[41] To that effect, as the KBA points out, it may be sufficient to use modern medium technologies which are widely used on the market, provided that they comply with the requirements for EC type-approval.

AG84   I added that permitting a defeat device under Article 5(2)(a) of Regulation No 715/2007 solely because, for example, research costs are high, the technical device is expensive or vehicle maintenance is more frequent or more costly for the user would render the regulation meaningless.[42]

AG85   Again, I take the view that those considerations can be transposed to the present case. In that regard, I agree with the referring court that any exception under Article 5(2) of Regulation No 715/2007 should, as a matter of principle, be excluded where, for financial reasons, the manufacturer designs engines in such a way that, under normal operating conditions, the safety of the engine is not guaranteed by effective technology to control emissions and that feature is largely deactivated for that reason.

AG86   The 'need' for a defeat device exists only where no solution makes it possible to avoid immediate risks of damage which create a specific hazard when the vehicle is driven.[43]

AG87   In addition, by Question 2(b), the referring court asks whether, in addition to the state of the art, account should be taken of other circumstances which may lead to the permissibility of a defeat device, even though, according to the current state of the art alone, there is no 'need' for that device, within the meaning of Article 5(2)(a) of Regulation No 715/2007.

AG88   In that respect, with regard to the concept of 'need', it follows from the judgment in *CLCV* that, since Article 5(2)(a) of that regulation constitutes an exception to

---

[40] AG129 of that Opinion.
[41] Opinion in *GSMB Invest, Volkswagen* and *Porsche Inter Auto* and *Volkswagen* (C-128/20), (C-134/20) and (C-145/20) EU:C:2021:758 at AG129.
[42] Opinion in *GSMB Invest, Volkswagen* and *Porsche Inter Auto* and *Volkswagen* (C-128/20), (C-134/20) and (C-145/20) EU:C:2021:758 at AG130.
[43] See, to that effect, the judgment in *CLCV* at paragraph 114.

the prohibition on the use of defeat devices which reduce the effectiveness of emission control systems, it must be *interpreted strictly*.[44]

AG89   In those circumstances, in the absence of a 'need' for the defeat device at issue in the present case, as the referring court states in Question 2(b),[45] there are, in my view, no other circumstances which may lead to the permissibility of a defeat device. Since the other two exceptions provided for in Article 5(2)(b) and (c) of Regulation No 715/2007 are not applicable in the case in the main proceedings, that regulation does not provide any additional justification for authorising a defeat device.

AG90   Therefore, I propose that the Court answer the second question to the effect that Article 5(2)(a) of Regulation No 715/2007 must be interpreted as meaning that the 'need' for a defeat device in terms of protecting the engine against damage or accident and for safe operation of the vehicle is not to be assessed in the light of the state of the art at the time when the EC type-approval is granted and it is not necessary to take account of circumstances other than that 'need' in order to examine the lawfulness of a defeat device.

V. Conclusion

AG91   In the light of the foregoing considerations, I propose that the Court should answer the questions referred for a preliminary ruling by the Schleswig-Holsteinisches Verwaltungsgericht (Administrative Court, Schleswig-Holstein, Germany) as follows:

(1) Article 9(3) of the Convention on access to information, public participation in decision-making and access to justice in environmental matters, signed in Aarhus on 25 June 1998 and approved on behalf of the European Community by Council Decision 2005/370/EC of 17 February 2005, read in conjunction with Article 47 of the Charter of Fundamental Rights of the European Union, must be interpreted as meaning that an approved environmental association, which is entitled to bring legal proceedings under national law, must be able to challenge before a national court an administrative decision granting EC type-approval of vehicles which may be contrary to Article 5(2) of Regulation (EC) No 715/2007 of the European Parliament and of the Council of 20 June 2007 on type approval of motor vehicles with respect to emissions from light passenger and commercial vehicles (Euro 5 and Euro 6) and on access to vehicle repair and maintenance information, a provision which prohibits, subject to certain exceptions, the use of defeat devices which reduce the effectiveness of emission control systems.

(2) Article 5(2)(a) of Regulation No 715/2007 must be interpreted as meaning that the 'need' for a defeat device in terms of protecting the engine against damage or accident and for safe operation of the vehicle is not to be assessed in the light of the state of the art at the time when the EC type-approval is granted and it is not necessary to take account of circumstances other than that 'need' in order to examine the lawfulness of a defeat device.

---

[44] The judgment in *CLCV* at paragraph 112.
[45] This is a factual assessment which is a matter for the referring court.

JUDGMENT[46]

1   This request for a preliminary ruling concerns the interpretation of Article 9(3) of the Convention on access to information, public participation in decision-making and access to justice in environmental matters, signed in Aarhus (Denmark) on 25 June 1998 and approved on behalf of the European Community by Council Decision 2005/370/EC of 17 February 2005 (OJ 2005 L 124, p. 1; 'the Aarhus Convention'), of the first paragraph of Article 47 of the Charter of Fundamental Rights of the European Union ('the Charter') and of Article 5(2)(a) of Regulation (EC) No 715/2007 of the European Parliament and of the Council of 20 June 2007 on type approval of motor vehicles with respect to emissions from light passenger and commercial vehicles (Euro 5 and Euro 6) and on access to vehicle repair and maintenance information (OJ 2007 L 171, p. 1).

2   The request has been made in proceedings between Deutsche Umwelthilfe eV, an environmental association, and the Bundesrepublik Deutschland (Federal Republic of Germany), represented by the Kraftfahrt-Bundesamt (Federal Motor Transport Authority, Germany; 'the KBA'), concerning the decision by which the KBA authorised, for certain vehicles produced by Volkswagen AG, the use of software reducing the recirculation of gaseous pollutants according to outside temperature.

Legal context

International law

3   The eighteenth recital of the Aarhus Convention states:

> 'Concerned that effective judicial mechanisms should be accessible to the public, including organisations, so that its legitimate interests are protected and the law is enforced.'

4   Article 2 of that convention, entitled 'Definitions', provides in paragraphs 4 and 5:

> '4. "The public" means one or more natural or legal persons, and, in accordance with national legislation or practice, their associations, organisations or groups;
>
> 5. "The public concerned" means the public affected or likely to be affected by, or having an interest in, the environmental decision-making; for the purposes of this definition, non-governmental organisations promoting environmental protection and meeting any requirements under national law shall be deemed to have an interest.'

5   Article 9 of the Aarhus Convention, entitled 'Access to justice', provides in paragraphs 3 and 4:

> '3. In addition and without prejudice to the review procedures referred to in paragraphs 1 and 2 [of the present Article], each Party shall ensure that, where they meet the criteria, if any, laid down in its national law, members of the public have access to administrative or judicial

---

[46] Language of the case: German.

procedures to challenge acts and omissions by private persons and public authorities which contravene provisions of its national law relating to the environment.

4. In addition and without prejudice to paragraph 1 above, the procedures referred to in paragraphs 1, 2 and 3 above shall provide adequate and effective remedies, including injunctive relief as appropriate, and be fair, equitable, timely and not prohibitively expensive. Decisions under this Article shall be given or recorded in writing. Decisions of courts, and whenever possible of other bodies, shall be publicly accessible.'

European Union law

Regulation (EC) No 1367/2006

6   Article 1(1) of Regulation (EC) No 1367/2006 of the European Parliament and of the Council of 6 September 2006 on the application of the provisions of the Aarhus Convention on Access to Information, Public Participation in Decision-making and Access to Justice in Environmental Matters to Community institutions and bodies (OJ 2006 L 264, p. 13) provides:

'The objective of this Regulation is to contribute to the implementation of the obligations arising under the [the Aarhus Convention], by laying down rules to apply the provisions of the Convention to Community institutions and bodies, in particular by:

…

(d) granting access to justice in environmental matters at [European] Community level under the conditions laid down by this Regulation.'

7   Article 2 of that regulation, entitled 'Definitions', provides in paragraph 1(f):

'For the purpose of this Regulation:

…

(f) "environmental law" means Community legislation which, irrespective of its legal basis, contributes to the pursuit of the objectives of Community policy on the environment as set out in the Treaty: preserving, protecting and improving the quality of the environment, protecting human health, the prudent and rational utilisation of natural resources, and promoting measures at international level to deal with regional or worldwide environmental problems.'

The Framework Directive

8   Directive 2007/46/EC of the European Parliament and of the Council of 5 September 2007 establishing a framework for the approval of motor vehicles and their trailers, and of systems, components and separate technical units intended for such vehicles (Framework Directive) (OJ 2007 L 263, p. 1), as amended by Commission Regulation (EC) No 1060/2008 of 7 October 2008 (OJ 2008 L 292, p. 1) ('the Framework Directive'), was repealed by Regulation (EU) 2018/858 of the European Parliament and of the Council of 30 May 2018 on the approval and market surveillance of motor vehicles and their trailers, and of systems, components

and separate technical units intended for such vehicles, amending Regulations (EC) No 715/2007 and (EC) No 595/2009 and repealing Directive 2007/46/EC (OJ 2018 L 151, p. 1), with effect from 1 September 2020. However, in view of the date of the facts of the dispute in the main proceedings, the Framework Directive remains applicable to that dispute.

9   Article 1 of the Framework Directive provided:

> 'This Directive establishes a harmonised framework containing the administrative provisions and general technical requirements for approval of all new vehicles within its scope and of the systems, components and separate technical units intended for those vehicles, with a view to facilitating their registration, sale and entry into service within the Community.
>
> …
>
> Specific technical requirements concerning the construction and functioning of vehicles shall be laid down in application of this Directive in regulatory acts, the exhaustive list of which is set out in Annex IV.'

10   Article 3(5) of the Framework Directive provided:

> 'For the purposes of this Directive and of the regulatory acts listed in Annex IV, save as otherwise provided therein:
>
> …
>
> 5. "EC type-approval" means the procedure whereby a Member State certifies that a type of vehicle, system, component or separate technical unit satisfies the relevant administrative provisions and technical requirements of this Directive and of the regulatory acts listed in Annex IV or XI'

11   Annex IV to that framework directive, entitled 'Requirements for the purpose of EC type-approval of vehicles', referred, in Part I thereof, entitled 'Regulatory acts for EC type-approval of vehicles produced in unlimited series', to Regulation No 715/2007 in relation to 'Emissions (Euro 5 and 6) light-duty vehicles/access to information'.

Regulation No 715/2007

12   Recitals 1, 6, 7 and 12 of Regulation No 715/2007 state:

> '(1) … The technical requirements for the type approval of motor vehicles with regard to emissions should … be harmonised to avoid requirements that differ from one Member State to another, and to ensure a high level of environmental protection.
>
> …
>
> (6) In particular, a considerable reduction in [NOx] emissions from diesel vehicles is necessary to improve air quality and comply with limit values for pollution. …
>
> (7) In setting emissions standards it is important to take into account the implications for markets and manufacturers' competitiveness, the direct and indirect costs imposed on business and the benefits that accrue in terms of stimulating innovation, improving air quality, reducing health costs and increasing life expectancy, as well as the implications for the overall impact on carbon dioxide [(CO_2)] emissions.

...

(12) Efforts should be continued to implement stricter emission limits, including reduction of [CO2] emissions, and to ensure that those limits relate to the actual performance of vehicles when in use.'

13   Article 1(1) of that regulation provides:

'This Regulation establishes common technical requirements for the type approval of motor vehicles (vehicles) and replacement parts, such as replacement pollution control devices, with regard to their emissions.'

14   Article 3(10) of Regulation No 715/2007 provides:

'For the purposes of this Regulation and its implementing measures the following definitions shall apply:

...

10. "defeat device" means any element of design which senses temperature, vehicle speed, engine speed (RPM), transmission gear, manifold vacuum or any other parameter for the purpose of activating, modulating, delaying or deactivating the operation of any part of the emission control system, that reduces the effectiveness of the emission control system under conditions which may reasonably be expected to be encountered in normal vehicle operation and use.'

15   Article 4(1) and (2) of that regulation states:

'1. Manufacturers shall demonstrate that all new vehicles sold, registered or put into service in the Community are type approved in accordance with this Regulation and its implementing measures. Manufacturers shall also demonstrate that all new replacement pollution control devices requiring type approval which are sold or put into service in the Community are type approved in accordance with this Regulation and its implementing measures.

These obligations include meeting the emission limits set out in Annex I and the implementing measures referred to in Article 5.

2. Manufacturers shall ensure that type approval procedures for verifying conformity of production, durability of pollution control devices and in-service conformity are met.

In addition, the technical measures taken by the manufacturer must be such as to ensure that the tailpipe and evaporative emissions are effectively limited, pursuant to this Regulation, throughout the normal life of the vehicles under normal conditions of use. ...

...'

16   Article 5(1) and (2) of Regulation No 715/2007 provides:

'1. The manufacturer shall equip vehicles so that the components likely to affect emissions are designed, constructed and assembled so as to enable the vehicle, in normal use, to comply with this Regulation and its implementing measures.

2. The use of defeat devices that reduce the effectiveness of emission control systems shall be prohibited. The prohibition shall not apply where:

> (a) the need for the device is justified in terms of protecting the
> engine against damage or accident and for safe operation of the
> vehicle;
> ...'

17   Annex I to that regulation, entitled 'Emission limits', lays down, inter alia, emission limit values for NOx.

German law

18   Paragraph 42 of the Verwaltungsgerichtsordnung (Administrative Court Rules) of 21 January 1960 (BGBl. 1960 I, p. 17), in the version applicable to the dispute in the main proceedings (BGBl. 1991 I, p. 686) ('the VwGO'), sets out the conditions governing the admissibility of actions in the following terms:

> '1. An action may seek to have an administrative measure annulled (action for annulment) or to have the adoption of an administrative measure ordered in the event of a refusal or failure to act (action for enjoinder).
> 2. Except where otherwise provided by law, such an action is admissible only if the claimant asserts that his or her rights have been impaired by the administrative measure or by the refusal or failure to act.'

19   The first sentence of Paragraph 113(1) of the VwGO provides:

> 'In so far as the administrative measure is unlawful and the claimant's rights have thereby been impaired, the court shall annul the administrative measure and, where appropriate, the decision following an appeal.'

20   Paragraph 1(1) of the Gesetz über ergänzende Vorschriften zu Rechtsbehelfen in Umweltangelegenheiten nach der EG-Richtlinie 2003/35/EG (Umwelt-Rechtsbehelfsgesetz – UmwRG) (Law on supplementary provisions governing actions in environmental matters under Directive 2003/35/EC), of 7 December 2006 (BGBl. 2006 I, p. 2816), in the version applicable to the dispute in the main proceedings (BGBl. 2017 I, p. 3290) ('the UmwRG'), provides:

> 'This law shall apply to actions against the following decisions:
> ...
> (5) administrative measures or public law contracts authorising projects other than those referred to in points 1 to 2b pursuant to environmental provisions of Federal law, *Land* law or directly applicable acts of EU law, ...
> This law shall also apply where, contrary to the provisions in force, a decision referred to in the first subsubparagraph has not been taken.
> ...
> ...'

21   Paragraph 2(1) of the UmwRG states:

> 'A domestic or foreign association approved under Paragraph 3 may bring an action in accordance with the VwGO to challenge a decision within the meaning of the first subsubparagraph of Paragraph 1(1) or a failure to adopt such a decision, without being required to maintain an impairment of its own rights, where the association

(1) asserts that a decision referred to in the first subsubparagraph of Paragraph 1(1), or the failure to adopt that decision, is contrary to provisions which may be relevant for the purposes of the decision;

(2) asserts that it is affected by a decision referred to in the first subsubparagraph of Paragraph 1(1), or by the failure to adopt that decision, within its statutory field of activity of helping to achieve the objectives of environmental protection, …

…

In the event of an appeal against a decision referred to in points 2a to 6 of the first subsubparagraph of Paragraph 1(1), or against the failure to take that decision, the association must also rely on an infringement of provisions relating to the environment.'

22   Paragraph 3 of the UmwRG lays down the conditions which national or foreign associations must fulfil in order to be approved and to bring proceedings under that law, as well as the approval procedure. According to Paragraph 3(1) of the UmwRG, such an association is, on request, approved where: in essence, it promotes, in accordance with its statutes, ideally and not temporarily, mainly environmental protection objectives; it has been in existence for at least three years at the date of approval and has been active during that period; it offers a guarantee of proper performance of its tasks, in particular adequate participation in the decision-making procedures of the authorities; it pursues objectives of general interest; and it allows any person who supports its objectives to become a member.

23   Under Paragraph 25(2) of the Verordnung über die EG-Genehmigung für Kraftfahrzeuge und ihre Anhänger sowie für Systeme, Bauteile und selbstständige technische Einheiten für diese Fahrzeuge (EG-Fahrzeuggenehmigungsverordnung – EG-FGV) (Rules on the EC type-approval for motor vehicles and their trailers, and for systems, components and separate technical units intended for such vehicles (EC motor vehicle type-approval rules)), of 3 February 2011 (BGBl. 2011 I, p. 126), in the version applicable to the dispute in the main proceedings:

'1. If the [KBA] finds that vehicles, systems, components or separate technical units do not conform to the approved type, it may take the necessary measures under the directive which is applicable to the type concerned out of Directives [2007/46], 2002/24/EC [of the European Parliament and of the Council of 18 March 2002 relating to the type-approval of two or three-wheel motor vehicles and repealing Council Directive 92/61/EEC (OJ 2002 L 124, p. 1)] or 2003/37/EC [of the European Parliament and of the Council of 26 May 2003 on type-approval of agricultural or forestry tractors, their trailers and interchangeable towed machinery, together with their systems, components and separate technical units and repealing Directive 74/150/EEC (OJ 2003 L 171, p. 1),] to ensure that production conforms to the approved type.

2. In order to remedy any deficiencies which have come to light and to ensure the conformity of vehicles already put into circulation, and of components or separate technical units, the [KBA] may retroactively impose ancillary provisions.'

The dispute in the main proceedings and the questions referred for a preliminary ruling

24   Volkswagen is a car manufacturer which marketed motor vehicles, in particular VW Golf Plus TDI vehicles, which were equipped with a Euro 5 generation EA 189-type diesel engine. Those vehicles had a valve for exhaust gas recirculation ('the EGR valve'), which is one of the technologies used by car manufacturers, including Volkswagen, to control and reduce NOx emissions.

25   According to the information provided by the referring court, those vehicles originally had software installed in the electronic engine controller to operate the EGR system in two modes, namely mode 0, which is activated when the vehicle is driven on a road, and mode 1, which operates during the approval test for pollutant emissions, called the 'New European Driving Cycle' (NEDC), conducted in a laboratory. When mode 0 was activated, the EGR rate was reduced. Under normal conditions of use, the vehicles concerned were almost exclusively in mode 0 and did not comply with the emission limit values for NOx laid down in Regulation No 715/2007.

26   In the EC type-approval procedure for those vehicles, Volkswagen did not notify the KBA of the existence of such software.

27   On 15 October 2015, the KBA adopted a decision pursuant to Paragraph 25(2) of the Rules on the EC type-approval for motor vehicles and their trailers, and for systems, components and separate technical units intended for such vehicles (EC motor vehicle type-approval rules), in the version applicable to the dispute in the main proceedings, in which it found that that software constituted a 'defeat device' within the meaning of Article 3(10) of Regulation No 715/2007, which was not consistent with Article 5 of that regulation; the KBA ordered Volkswagen to remove that device and to take the necessary measures to ensure that the vehicles complied with the national legislation concerned and the EU legislation.

28   Following that decision, Volkswagen updated the software. The effect of that update was to set the EGR valve to regulate the EGR rate such that that rate was 0% when the outside temperature was below -9 °C, 85% when it was between -9 and 11 °C, and increased above 11 °C to be 100% operational only at outside temperatures above 15 °C. Thus, the exhaust-gas purification by that recirculation system was fully effective only if the external temperature was greater than 15 °C ('the temperature window').

29   By decision of 20 June 2016 ('the contested decision'), the KBA granted authorisation for the software at issue in the main proceedings. In that regard, it took the view that the defeat devices still present in the vehicles concerned ('the vehicles at issue in the main proceedings') were lawful.

30   On 15 November 2016, Deutsche Umwelthilfe, an association which is authorised to bring legal proceedings under Paragraph 3 of the UmwRG, lodged an administrative appeal against the contested decision, which has not yet been the subject of a decision.

31   On 24 April 2018, Deutsche Umwelthilfe brought an action before the Schleswig-Holsteinisches   Verwaltungsgericht   (Administrative   Court, Schleswig-Holstein, Germany), the referring court, seeking annulment of the contested decision. It submits that the vehicles at issue in the main proceedings were still equipped with an unlawful defeat device, within the meaning of Article 5(2) of Regulation No 715/2007, since that device becomes active when the average

temperatures recorded in Germany are reached. Furthermore, it submits that car manufacturers are able to design engines which do not require a reduction, for technical reasons, of the performance of emission control systems at average temperatures, and which would, therefore, operate under normal conditions of use.

32   The Federal Republic of Germany, the defendant in the main proceedings, contends, first, that Deutsche Umwelthilfe does not have standing to bring proceedings against the contested decision and that its action is, therefore, inadmissible. Secondly, the temperature window available to the vehicles at issue in the main proceedings after the updating of the software concerned is, in its view, compatible with EU law.

33   As regards the admissibility of the action in the main proceedings, the referring court considers, in the first place, that Deutsche Umwelthilfe does not have standing to bring proceedings under Paragraph 42(2) of the VwGO, under which, unless otherwise provided for by law, the action is admissible only if the applicant asserts that his or her rights have been impaired by the administrative measure at issue. That provision is thus an expression of the fact that the system of individual actions provided for in the VwGO is based on individual rights. However, the dispute in the main proceedings does not appear to concern an individual's right which has been infringed by the contested decision. The prohibition on using defeat devices which reduce the effectiveness of emission control systems, laid down in the first sentence of Article 5(2) of Regulation No 715/2007 and relied on by Deutsche Umwelthilfe, does not confer any individual right on a natural person, since that provision is not intended to protect citizens individually.

34   In the second place, the referring court considers that that association cannot derive standing to bring proceedings from Paragraph 2(1) of the UmwRG, read in conjunction with Paragraph 1(1) of the UmwRG, which provides for a statutory exemption from the requirement for an individual right, within the meaning of the first phrase of Paragraph 42(2) of the VwGO. That court states, in that regard, that only the decisions listed in Paragraph 1(1) are actionable by an environmental association pursuant to the UmwRG. Of those decisions, only those referred to in the first subsubparagraph, point 5, of that provision are relevant, namely 'administrative measures or public law contracts authorising projects … pursuant to environmental provisions of Federal law, *Land* law or directly applicable acts of EU law'.

35   However, the contested decision does not constitute a decision within the meaning of point 5 of the first subsubparagraph of Paragraph 1(1) of the UmwRG, since by that decision authorisation was granted to a 'product', not to a 'project'. The concept of 'project' within the meaning of that provision is derived from town and country planning law and was defined on the basis of Council Directive (85/337/EEC) of 27 June 1985 on the assessment of the effects of certain public and private projects on the environment (OJ 1985 L 175, p. 40), Article 1(2) of which provides that the term 'project' means 'the execution of construction works or of other installations or schemes' and 'other interventions in the natural surroundings and landscape including those involving the extraction of mineral resources'. In that regard, it is apparent from the national legislation at issue in the main proceedings that that concept relates only to fixed installations or measures which constitute direct interventions in the natural surroundings and landscape. Consequently, the EC type-approval of light passenger vehicles and the amendment of such EC approval which are the subject of the contested decision cannot be regarded as authorisation

for a 'project', within the meaning of the national law, since they do not relate to a fixed installation and do not involve any direct intervention in the natural surroundings and landscape.

36   Furthermore, the provisions of the UmwRG cannot be applied by analogy given that, during the proceedings which led to the amendment of the UmwRG, which took place in 2017, it was expressly stated that that amendment did not concern the product sector, including with regard to vehicles.

37   In the third place, according to the referring court, nor can Deutsche Umwelthilfe derive standing from Article 9(3) of the Aarhus Convention, since, as the Court held in the judgment of 20 December 2017, *Protect Natur-, Arten—und Landschaftsschutz Umweltorganisation* (C-664/15) EU:C:2017:987 at paragraph 45, that provision, in itself, has no direct effect. Accordingly, Article 9 does not constitute a statutory exemption from the requirement for an individual right, within the meaning of the first phrase of Paragraph 42(2) of the VwGO.

38   In those circumstances, the referring court considers that the admissibility of the action in the main proceedings depends on whether Deutsche Umwelthilfe may derive standing to bring proceedings directly from EU law. It notes in that regard that, in the light of the judgment of 20 December 2017, *Protect Natur-, Arten—und Landschaftsschutz Umweltorganisation* (C-664/15) EU:C:2017:987 at paragraph 45, Deutsche Umwelthilfe's standing to bring proceedings could result from the application of Article 9(3) of the Aarhus Convention in conjunction with the first paragraph of Article 47 of the Charter.

39   The referring court states that, in the light of the divergent case-law which exists between the national courts as to the inferences to be drawn from that judgment, it is necessary for it to ascertain whether Article 9(3) of the Aarhus Convention, read in conjunction with the first paragraph of Article 47 of the Charter, must be interpreted as meaning that it is possible for an environmental association, even beyond the possibilities of bringing proceedings already provided for in the UmwRG, to challenge the administrative authorisation for a product, such as the authorisation at issue in the main proceedings, if the action brought by that association seeks to ensure compliance with provisions of EU environmental law which do not give rise to any individual rights.

40   The referring court states that its doubts concern the interpretation of the concept of 'criteria laid down in national law' within the meaning of Article 9(3) of the Aarhus Convention. First, that concept could be interpreted as covering only criteria which serve to delimit those persons entitled to bring an action and, consequently, the Member States would have leeway only with regard to the question of to which environmental associations they wish to grant the right to defend the public interest in environmental matters. If that interpretation were to be followed, Deutsche Umwelthilfe would have standing to bring proceedings in the main proceedings, given that the German legislature laid down those criteria in Paragraph 3 of the UmwRG and Deutsche Umwelthilfe was approved in accordance with that provision.

41   Secondly, the concept of 'criteria laid down in national law' could be interpreted as meaning that Member States have the power to determine criteria also in relation to the subject matter of the action and, therefore, to exclude certain administrative decisions from any judicial review sought by environmental associations. According to the referring court, such a limitation of the standing of those associations to certain decisions, in particular decisions which have a serious environmental impact,

could be justified by reason of the large number of administrative decisions linked to the environment. As regards, more specifically, product approvals, the referring court notes that, admittedly, such approvals cannot be regarded as never being of major importance for the environment. However, in the light of the large number of individual product approvals, practical considerations also support the argument that Member States must be able, by way of categorising considerations, to avoid subjecting certain individual decisions to the uncertainty of being challenged by third parties, such as environmental associations.

42   Should the Court consider that an environmental association has standing to challenge the contested decision, the referring court raises the question of the interpretation to be given to Article 5(2)(a) of Regulation No 715/2007.

43   The referring court takes the view that the temperature window at issue in the main proceedings constitutes a defeat device within the meaning of Article 3(10) of Regulation No 715/2007. It considers that, even if the concept of 'conditions which may reasonably be expected to be encountered in normal vehicle operation and use', in that provision, is not defined by Regulation No 715/2007, it should be found, having regard to the objectives of that regulation, and in particular recitals 4 and 6 thereof, that only actual driving conditions can be regarded as normal operating conditions. In that regard, the referring court considers that the objective of reducing NOx emissions can be achieved only if those emissions are in fact reduced during actual vehicle use and not only in artificial conditions. It notes that, in Europe, temperatures below 15 °C form part of the 'normal conditions' which 'may reasonably be expected' within the meaning of that provision. Indeed, for the year 2018, the average annual temperature in Germany was 10.4 °C. Thus, the EGR rate of the vehicles at issue in the main proceedings was already reduced and the emissions control system partially deactivated, whereas the temperatures were entirely average.

44   The referring court is uncertain, however, whether the concept of 'need' for the defeat device, within the meaning of Article 5(2)(a) of Regulation No 715/2007, must be interpreted in the light of the current state of the art in order to ascertain whether a defeat device is actually necessary in terms of protecting the engine against damage or accident and for safe operation of the vehicle concerned. It is also uncertain whether other circumstances, such as costs for manufacturers and the impact on their competitiveness, should also be taken into account.

45   In those circumstances the Schleswig-Holsteinisches Verwaltungsgericht (Administrative Court, Schleswig-Holstein) decided to stay the proceedings and to refer the following questions to the Court of Justice for a preliminary ruling:

> '(1) Is Article 9(3) of the [Aarhus Convention], in conjunction with Article 47 of the [Charter], to be interpreted as meaning that it must in principle be possible for environmental associations to challenge before the courts a decision approving the manufacture of diesel passenger cars with defeat devices that are potentially in breach of Article 5(2) of Regulation [No 715/2007]?
>
> (2) If Question 1 is answered in the affirmative:
>
>> (a) Is Article 5(2) of Regulation [No 715/2007] to be interpreted as meaning that the yardstick for determining whether the need for a defeat device is justified in terms of protecting the engine against

damage or accident and for safe operation of the vehicle is, in principle, the state of the art, in the sense of what is technically feasible at the time when the EC type approval is granted?

(b) In addition to the state of the art, should account be taken of other circumstances which may lead to the permissibility of a defeat device, even though, according to the current state of the art alone, the "need" for such a device would not be "justified" within the meaning of Article 5(2)(a) of [Regulation No 715/2007]?'

Consideration of the questions referred

The first question

46   By its first question, the referring court asks, in essence, whether Article 9(3) of the Aarhus Convention, read in conjunction with the first paragraph of Article 47 of the Charter, must be interpreted as precluding a situation where an environmental association, which is authorised to bring legal proceedings under national law, is unable to challenge before a national court an administrative decision granting or amending EC type-approval which may be contrary to Article 5(2) of Regulation No 715/2007.

47   It is apparent from request for a preliminary ruling that the first question is based on the fact that, according to the referring court, the applicable national legislation does not confer on Deutsche Umwelthilfe standing to bring proceedings against an administrative decision granting or amending EC type-approval, such as that at issue in the main proceedings.

48   First of all, it should be borne in mind that the Court of Justice has jurisdiction to give preliminary rulings concerning the interpretation of the Aarhus Convention, which was signed by the Community and subsequently approved by Decision 2005/370, and the provisions of which therefore form an integral part of the EU legal order (judgments of 8 March 2011, *Lesoochranárske zoskupenie* (C-240/09) EU:C:2011:125 at paragraph 30, and of 15 March 2018, *North East Pylon Pressure Campaign and Sheehy* (C-470/16) EU:C:2018:185 at paragraph 46 and the case-law cited).

49   Under Article 9(3) of the Aarhus Convention, without prejudice to the review procedures referred to in paragraphs 1 and 2 of that article, each party must ensure that, where they meet the criteria, if any, laid down in its national law, members of the public have access to administrative or judicial procedures to challenge acts and omissions by private persons and public authorities which contravene provisions of its national law relating to the environment.

50   In the first place, it must be found that an administrative decision granting or amending EC type-approval which may be contrary to Article 5(2) of Regulation No 715/2007 falls within the material scope of Article 9(3) of the Aarhus Convention, since it constitutes an 'act' of a public authority which is alleged to contravene the provisions of 'national law relating to the environment'.

51   It should be borne in mind, first, that the Court has held, in the judgments of 17 December 2020, *CLCV (Defeat device on diesel engines)* (C-693/18) EU:C:2020:1040 at paragraphs 67, 86 and 87; of 14 July 2022, *GSMB Invest* (C-128/20) EU:C:2022:570, paragraph 43; and of 14 July 2022 *Volkswagen* (C-134/20) EU:C:2022:571 at paragraph 50, that the objective pursued by

Regulation No 715/2007, is, as is apparent from recitals 1 and 6 thereof, to ensure a high level of environmental protection and, more specifically, considerably to reduce the NOx emissions from diesel vehicles in order to improve air quality and comply with limit values for pollution.

52   The finding that Regulation No 715/2007, and in particular Article 5(2) thereof, has such an environmental objective and therefore forms part of the 'law relating to the environment', within the meaning of Article 9(3) of the Aarhus Convention, is not, contrary to what the KBA maintains, in any way undermined by the fact that that regulation was adopted on the basis of Article 95 EC, now Article 114 TFEU, which concerns measures for the approximation of the provisions laid down by law, regulation or administrative action in Member States which have as their object the establishment and functioning of the internal market.

53   In that regard, it must be recalled that Article 114(3) TFEU provides that the Commission, in its proposals for measures for the approximation of the provisions laid down by law, regulation or administrative action in Member States concerning environmental protection, is to take as a base a high level of protection, taking account in particular of any new development based on scientific facts. Consequently, as the Advocate General observed in point 50 of his Opinion, the fact that Regulation No 715/2007 was not adopted on the basis of a specific legal basis relating to the environment, such as Article 175 EC, now Article 192 TFEU, is not such as to exclude the environmental objective of that regulation and its belonging to the 'law relating to the environment'.

54   That finding is supported, first, by Regulation No 1367/2006, whose objective, in accordance with Article 1(1)(d) thereof, is to contribute to the implementation of the obligations arising under the Aarhus Convention, by laying down rules to apply the provisions of that convention to EU institutions and bodies, in particular by granting access to justice in environmental matters at EU level. Thus, Article 2(1)(f) of that regulation states that 'environmental law' means, for the purposes of that regulation, EU legislation which, 'irrespective of its legal basis', contributes to the pursuit of the objectives of EU policy on the environment as set out in the FEU Treaty, including preserving, protecting and improving the quality of the environment and protecting human health.

55   Secondly, the abovementioned finding is reinforced by the Aarhus Convention implementation guide, that is, the document published by the United Nations Economic Commission for Europe entitled 'The Aarhus Convention: An Implementation Guide' (Second Edition, 2014), which, according to settled case-law of the Court, may be regarded as an explanatory document, capable of being taken into consideration if appropriate among other relevant material for the purpose of interpreting that convention, even if the observations in the guide have no binding force and do not have the normative effect of the provisions of the convention (judgment of 20 January 2021, *Land Baden-Württemberg (Internal communications)* (C-619/19) EU:C:2021:35 at paragraph 51 and the case-law cited).

56   Indeed, that guide confirms the broad meaning to be given to the expression 'provisions of national law relating to the environment', as set out in Article 9(3) of the Aarhus Convention, in so far as, at page 197 of that guide, it is stated that 'national laws relating to the environment are neither limited to the information or public participation rights guaranteed by the Convention, nor to legislation where the environment is mentioned in the title or heading. Rather, the decisive issue is if the provision in question somehow relates to the environment. Thus, also acts

and omissions that may contravene provisions on, among other things, city planning, environmental taxes, control of chemicals or wastes, exploitation of natural resources and pollution from ships are covered by paragraph 3, regardless of whether the provisions in question are found in planning laws, taxation laws or maritime laws'.

57   Moreover, the allegedly technical nature of the first sentence of Article 5(2) of Regulation No 715/2007, which provides that the use of defeat devices that reduce the effectiveness of emission control systems must be prohibited, in no way alters the fact that that provision seeks, by means of such a prohibition, precisely to limit emissions of gaseous pollutants and thus to contribute to the environmental protection objective pursued by that regulation.

58   Furthermore, Article 5(2) of Regulation No 715/2007, as a provision of environmental law which, moreover, is directly applicable in all Member States, in accordance with Article 288(2) TFEU, must be regarded as forming part of 'national law' within the meaning of Article 9(3) of the Aarhus Convention.

59   In the second place, it should be noted that an environmental association authorised to bring legal proceedings falls within the personal scope of Article 9(3) of the Aarhus Convention. In that regard, it must be borne in mind that, in order to be entitled to the rights provided for in that provision, an applicant must, inter alia, be a 'member of the public' and meet 'the criteria, if any, laid down in … national law'.

60   In accordance with Article 2(4) of the Aarhus Convention, the term 'public' means one or more natural or legal persons, and, in accordance with national legislation or practice, their associations, organisations or groups. It therefore follows from Article 2(4) and Article 9(3) of that convention that the parties to the convention may lay down in their national law criteria which an environmental association must meet in order to enjoy the rights provided for in the latter provision.

61   It is apparent from the request for a preliminary ruling that, under German law, those criteria are laid down in Paragraph 3(1) of the UmwRG and that Deutsche Umwelthilfe – the object of which, according to its statutes, is to contribute to the protection of nature and the environment as well as to consumer protection in so far as it relates to the environment and health – meets those criteria and that it has indeed been approved as an environmental association authorised to bring legal proceedings in accordance with Paragraph 3 of the UmwRG.

62   It should be further noted that such an association is also part of the 'public concerned', within the meaning of Article 2(5) of the Aarhus Convention, which means the public affected or likely to be affected by, or having an interest in, the environmental decision-making. Thus, in the words of that provision, non-governmental organisations promoting environmental protection and meeting any requirements under national law are to be deemed to have such an interest.

63   In the third place, as regards the referring court's questioning, which seeks, more specifically, to determine whether the concept of 'criteria laid down in … national law', within the meaning of Article 9(3) of the Aarhus Convention, allows the parties to that convention to lay down such criteria not only in relation to those persons entitled to bring an action, but also with regard to the subject matter of the action, it must be borne in mind that the Court has held that it follows from that provision – and in particular from that fact that, in accordance with the wording thereof, the review procedures referred to therein may be made subject to 'criteria' – that Member States may, in the context of the discretion they have in that regard,

establish procedural rules setting out conditions that must be satisfied in order to be able to pursue such review procedures (judgments of 20 December 2017, *Protect Natur-, Arten—und Landschaftsschutz Umweltorganisation* (C-664/15) EU:C:2017:987 at paragraph 86, and of 14 January 2021, *Stichting Varkens in Nood* (C-826/18) EU:C:2021:7 at paragraph 49).

64   However, first, it must be noted that, according to the actual wording of Article 9(3) of the Aarhus Convention, such criteria relate to the determination of those persons entitled to bring an action, not to the determination of the subject matter of the action in so far as the latter concerns infringement of provisions of national environmental law. It follows that Member States may not reduce the material scope of Article 9(3) by excluding from the subject matter of the action certain categories of provisions of national environmental law.

65   Secondly, where a Member State lays down rules of procedural law applicable to the matters referred to in Article 9(3) of the Aarhus Convention concerning the exercise of the rights that an environmental organisation derives from Article 5(2) of Regulation No 715/2007, in order for decisions of the competent national authorities to be reviewed in the light of their obligations under that article, the Member State is implementing EU law for the purposes of Article 51(1) of the Charter and must, therefore, ensure compliance, inter alia, with the right to an effective remedy, enshrined in Article 47 thereof (see, to that effect, judgment of 20 December 2017, *Protect Natur-, Arten—und Landschaftsschutz Umweltorganisation* (C-664/15) EU:C:2017:987 at paragraphs 44 and 87 and the case-law cited).

66   Consequently, while it is true that Article 9(3) of the Aarhus Convention does not have direct effect in EU law and cannot, therefore, be relied on, as such, in a dispute falling within the scope of EU law, in order to disapply a provision of national law which is contrary to it, the fact remains that, first, the primacy of international agreements concluded by the European Union requires that national law be interpreted, to the fullest extent possible, in accordance with the requirements of those agreements and, secondly, that Article 9(3) of the Aarhus Convention, read in conjunction with Article 47 of the Charter, imposes on Member States an obligation to ensure effective judicial protection of the rights conferred by EU law, in particular the provisions of environmental law (judgment of 20 December 2017, *Protect Natur-, Arten—und Landschaftsschutz Umweltorganisation* (C-664/15) EU:C:2017:987 at paragraph 45).

67   However, the right to bring proceedings provided for in Article 9(3) of the Aarhus Convention, which is intended to ensure effective environmental protection (judgment of 8 March 2011, *Lesoochranárske zoskupenie* (C-240/09) EU:C:2011:125 at paragraph 46), would be deprived of all useful effect, and even of its very substance, if it had to be conceded that, by imposing criteria laid down by national law, certain categories of 'members of the public' – a fortiori 'the public concerned', such as environmental associations that satisfy the requirements laid down in Article 2(5) of the Aarhus Convention – were to be denied of any right to bring proceedings against acts and omissions by private persons and public authorities which contravene certain categories of provisions of national law relating to the environment (see, to that effect, judgment of 20 December 2017, *Protect Natur-, Arten—und Landschaftsschutz Umweltorganisation* (C-664/15) EU:C:2017:987 at paragraph 46).

68   Imposing those criteria must not deprive environmental associations in particular of the possibility of verifying that the rules of EU environmental law are being complied with, given also that such rules are usually in the public interest, rather than simply in the interests of certain individuals, and that the objective of those associations is to defend the public interest (judgment of 20 December 2017, *Protect Natur-, Arten—und Landschaftsschutz Umweltorganisation* (C-664/15) EU:C:2017:987 at paragraph 47 and the case-law cited).

69   Although they imply that Member States retain discretion as to the implementation of that provision, the words 'criteria, if any, laid down in its national law' in Article 9(3) of the Aarhus Convention cannot allow those States to impose criteria so strict that it would be effectively impossible for environmental associations to challenge the acts or omissions that are the subject of that provision (judgment of 20 December 2017, *Protect Natur-, Arten—und Landschaftsschutz Umweltorganisation* (C-664/15) EU:C:2017:987 at paragraph 48).

70   In the present case, it seems to follow from the information provided by the referring court, set out in paragraphs 33 to 35 above, that, under German law, since an environmental association lacks standing to bring proceedings against an approval decision for 'a product', it cannot, even if it meets the requirements laid down in Paragraph 3(1) of the UmwRG, bring an action before a national court in order to challenge a decision granting or amending an EC type-approval which may be contrary to the prohibition on the use of defeat devices which reduce the effectiveness of emission control systems, laid down in Article 5(2) of Regulation No 715/2007.

71   By thus denying environmental organisations any right to bring an action against such a decision granting or amending EC type-approval, the relevant national procedural law is contrary to the requirements flowing from a combined reading of Article 9(3) of the Aarhus Convention and Article 47 of the Charter (see, by analogy, judgment of 20 December 2017, *Protect Natur-, Arten—und Landschaftsschutz Umweltorganisation* (C-664/15) EU:C:2017:987 at paragraph 52).

72   In particular, the fact that an environmental association, although authorised for the purposes of having access to the judicial procedures referred to in Article 9(3) of the Aarhus Convention, cannot access justice in order to challenge a decision granting or amending EC type-approval which may be contrary to Article 5(2) of Regulation No 715/2007 and, therefore, contrary to a 'provision of national law relating to the environment' within the meaning of Article 9(3) of that convention, constitutes a limitation of the right to an effective remedy, guaranteed by Article 47 of the Charter. Such a limitation cannot be considered justified.

73   In that respect, as regards the argument that such a limitation of the standing of environmental associations to bring proceedings to certain decisions, in particular those having a serious environmental impact, could be justified on account of the large number of administrative decisions linked to the environment, it must be held that, as the Advocate General observed, in essence, in point 71 of his Opinion, first, it is not apparent from Article 9(3) of the Aarhus Convention that the right to bring an action provided for therein could be limited solely to decisions with significant consequences for the environment. Secondly, decisions granting or amending an EC type-approval are likely to concern many vehicles and cannot therefore, in any event, be regarded as being of only minor importance for the environment. In that regard, as is apparent from recital 6 of Regulation No 715/2007,

in particular, a considerable reduction in NOx emissions from diesel vehicles is necessary to improve air quality and comply with limit values for pollution. However, decisions granting or amending EC type-approval in breach of the prohibition on the use of defeat devices which reduce the effectiveness of emission control systems, laid down in Article 5(2) of that regulation, are liable to frustrate the attainment of those environmental protection objectives.

74   Furthermore, contrary to what the KBA contends, the fact that it is impossible for an environmental association, such as Deutsche Umwelthilfe, to bring an action against decisions granting or amending EC type-approval, is in no way necessary in order to avoid an *actio popularis*. As the Advocate General observed in point 73 of his Opinion, where an association has been approved in accordance with the criteria laid down by national law and has, therefore, been granted the right to be a party to legal proceedings in environmental matters, it must be regarded as being sufficiently concerned by the infringement of the provisions of EU environmental law in order to be able to rely on such an infringement before the national courts.

75   Consequently, it is for the referring court to interpret, to the fullest extent possible, the procedural rules relating to the conditions to be met in order to bring proceedings, in a manner consistent with both the objectives of Article 9(3) of the Aarhus Convention and the objective of effective judicial protection of the rights conferred by EU law, in order to enable an environmental association, such as Deutsche Umwelthilfe, to challenge before a court a decision granting or amending EC type-approval which may be contrary to Article 5(2) of Regulation No 715/2007 (see, by analogy, judgment of 20 December 2017, *Protect Natur-, Arten—und Landschaftsschutz Umweltorganisation* (C-664/15) EU:C:2017:987, paragraph 54).

76   In that regard, it should be noted that the referring court made reference, in its request for a preliminary ruling, to a judgment delivered in Germany following the judgment of 20 December 2017, *Protect Natur-, Arten—und Landschaftsschutz Umweltorganisation* (C-664/15) EU:C:2017:987, which recognised, by such a consistent interpretation of the second phrase of Paragraph 42(2) of the VwGO, that such an association has standing to bring proceedings when it seeks to ensure compliance with provisions based on EU environmental law. Thus, it does not seem a priori to be excluded that such standing could be granted to an environmental association, such as Deutsche Umwelthilfe, on the basis of an interpretation of German law which meets the requirements of Article 9(3) of the Aarhus Convention, read in conjunction with Article 47 of the Charter.

77   If such a consistent interpretation should prove impossible, it must be recalled that any national court, hearing a case within its jurisdiction, has, as a body of a Member State, the obligation to disapply any provision of national law which is contrary to a provision of EU law with direct effect in the case pending before it (judgment of 19 November 2019, *AK (Independence of the Disciplinary Chamber of the Supreme Court)* (C-585/18), (C-624/18) and (C-625/18) EU:C:2019:982 at paragraph 161 and the case-law cited).

78   As is apparent from paragraph 66 above, Article 9(3) of the Aarhus Convention does not, as such, have direct effect, with the result that that provision cannot compel the referring court to disapply a national provision which is contrary to it.

79   However, the discretion conferred on the Member States to lay down rules governing the right to bring proceedings, referred to in that provision, does not affect their obligation to ensure a right to an effective remedy enshrined in Article

47 of the Charter, as, moreover, also alluded to in Article 9(4) of the Aarhus Convention. Article 47 of the Charter is sufficient in itself and does not need to be made more specific by provisions of EU or national law in order to confer on individuals a right which they may rely on as such (judgment of 19 November 2019, *AK (Independence of the Disciplinary Chamber of the Supreme Court)* (C-585/18), (C-624/18) and (C-625/18) EU:C:2019:982 at paragraph 162 and the case-law cited). Thus, that article may be relied on as a limit on the discretion left to the Member States under Article 9(3) of the Aarhus Convention.

80   Accordingly, in the situation referred to in paragraph 77 above, it will be for the referring court to disapply the provisions of national law precluding an environmental association, such as Deutsche Umwelthilfe, from being able to challenge a decision granting or amending EC type-approval which may be contrary to Article 5(2) of Regulation No 715/2007.

81   In the light of all the foregoing, the answer to the first question is that Article 9(3) of the Aarhus Convention, read in conjunction with Article 47 of the Charter, must be interpreted as precluding a situation where an environmental association, authorised to bring legal proceedings in accordance with national law, is unable to challenge before a national court an administrative decision granting or amending EC type-approval which may be contrary to Article 5(2) of Regulation No 715/2007.

The second question

82   By parts (a) and (b) of its second question, which it is appropriate to examine together, the referring court asks, in essence, whether Article 5(2)(a) of Regulation No 715/2007 must be interpreted as meaning that the 'need' for a defeat device, within the meaning of that provision, must be assessed in the light of the state of the art as at the date of the EC type-approval and whether it is necessary to take into consideration circumstances other than that 'need' for the purposes of examining the lawfulness of that defeat device.

83   First of all, it must be recalled that Article 3(10) of Regulation No 715/2007 defines a 'defeat device' as being 'any element of design which senses temperature, vehicle speed, engine speed (RPM), transmission gear, manifold vacuum or any other parameter for the purpose of activating, modulating, delaying or deactivating the operation of any part of the emission control system, that reduces the effectiveness of the emission control system under conditions which may reasonably be expected to be encountered in normal vehicle operation and use'.

84   In the present case, it is apparent from the request for a preliminary ruling that the software at issue in the main proceedings has established a temperature window under which the EGR rate is 0% when the outside temperature is below -9 °C, 85% when it is between -9 and 11 °C, and increases above 11 °C to be 100% operational only at outside temperatures above 15 °C. As the referring court notes, the EGR rate is, therefore, reduced to 85% where the average temperatures recorded in Germany – which for 2018 would have been 10.4 °C – are reached.

85   In that regard, the Court has held, as regards a temperature window identical to that at issue in the main proceedings, that Article 3(10) of Regulation No 715/2007, read in conjunction with Article 5(1) of that regulation, must be interpreted as meaning that a device which ensures compliance with the emission limit values laid down by that regulation only where the outside temperature is between 15 °C and 33 °C and the driving altitude is below 1000 metres constitutes a 'defeat device'

within the meaning of Article 3(10) of that regulation (judgments of 14 July 2022, *GSMB Invest* (C-128/20) EU:C:2022:570 at paragraph 47, and of 14 July 2022, *Volkswagen* (C-134/20) EU:C:2022:571 at paragraph 54).

86   Under Article 5(2) of Regulation No 715/2007, the use of defeat devices that reduce the effectiveness of emission control systems must be prohibited. However, there are three exceptions to that prohibition, including the exception in Article 5(2)(a) of that regulation, namely where 'the need for the device is justified in terms of protecting the engine against damage or accident and for safe operation of the vehicle'.

87   In so far as it lays down an exception to the prohibition on the use of defeat devices that reduce the effectiveness of emission control systems, that provision must be interpreted strictly (judgments of 14 July 2022, *GSMB Invest* (C-128/20) EU:C:2022:570 at paragraph 50; of 14 July 2022, *Volkswagen* (C-134/20) EU:C:2022:571 at paragraph 63; and of 14 July 2022, *Porsche Inter Auto and Volkswagen* (C-145/20) EU:C:2022:572 at paragraph 61).

88   It is apparent from the very wording of Article 5(2)(a) of Regulation No 715/2007 that, in order to fall within the exception provided for in that provision, the need for a defeat device must be justified not only in terms of protecting the engine against damage or accident, but also in terms of the safe operation of the vehicle. Indeed, in view of the use of the coordinating conjunction 'and' in that provision, it must be interpreted as meaning that the conditions laid down therein are cumulative (judgments of 14 July 2022, *GSMB Invest* (C-128/20) EU:C:2022:570 at paragraph 61; of 14 July 2022, *Volkswagen* (C-134/20) EU:C:2022:571 at paragraph 73; and of 14 July 2022, *Porsche Inter Auto and Volkswagen* (C-145/20) EU:C:2022:572 at paragraph 72).

89   Consequently, in view of the strict interpretation to be given to that exception, a defeat device such as that at issue in the main proceedings can be justified under that exception only where it is established that that device strictly meets the need to avoid immediate risks of damage or accident to the engine, caused by a malfunction of a component of the EGR system, of such a serious nature as to give rise to a specific hazard when a vehicle fitted with that device is driven. However, such a determination is, in the main proceedings, part of the assessment of the facts which falls to the referring court alone (judgments of 14 July 2022, *GSMB Invest* (C-128/20) EU:C:2022:570 at paragraph 62; of 14 July 2022, *Volkswagen* (C-134/20) EU:C:2022:571 at paragraph 74; and of 14 July 2022, *Porsche Inter Auto and Volkswagen* (C-145/20) EU:C:2022:572 at paragraph 73).

90   Furthermore, as regards a temperature window identical to that at issue in the main proceedings, the Court has held that, while it is true that Article 5(2)(a) of Regulation No 715/2007 does not formally impose any further conditions for the application of the exception laid down in that provision, the fact remains that a defeat device which, under normal driving conditions, operated during most of the year in order to protect the engine from damage or accident and ensure the safe operation of the vehicle, would clearly run counter to the objective pursued by that regulation, from which that provision allows derogation only in very specific circumstances, and would result in a disproportionate infringement of the principle of limiting NOx emissions from vehicles (judgments of 14 July 2022, *GSMB Invest* (C-128/20) EU:C:2022:570 at paragraph 63; of 14 July 2022, *Volkswagen* (C-134/20) EU:C:2022:571 at paragraph 75; and of 14 July 2022, *Porsche Inter Auto and Volkswagen* (C-145/20) EU:C:2022:572 at paragraph 74).

91   The Court has therefore concluded that, in view of the strict interpretation that must be given to Article 5(2)(a) of Regulation No 715/2007, such a defeat device cannot be justified under that provision. Indeed, to accept that such a defeat device may fall within the exception provided for in that provision would result in that exception being applicable for most of the year under real driving conditions prevalent in the territory of the European Union, with the result that the principle of the prohibition of such defeat devices, laid down in Article 5(2) of Regulation No 715/2007, could, in practice, be applied less frequently than that exception (judgments of 14 July 2022, *GSMB Invest* (C-128/20) EU:C:2022:570 at paragraphs 64 and 65; of 14 July 2022, *Volkswagen* (C-134/20) EU:C:2022:571 at paragraphs 76 and 77; and of 14 July 2022, *Porsche Inter Auto and Volkswagen* (C-145/20) EU:C:2022:572 at paragraphs 75 and 76).

92   In that regard, the Court has stated, first, that it is apparent from recital 7 of Regulation No 715/2007 that, when the EU legislature determined the emission limits for pollutants, it took into account the economic interests of manufacturers and, in particular, the costs imposed on undertakings by the need to comply with those limits. It is thus for manufacturers to adapt and apply technical devices capable of complying with those limits as that regulation does not require the use of any particular technology (judgments of 14 July 2022, *GSMB Invest* (C-128/20) EU:C:2022:570, paragraph 67; of 14 July 2022, *Volkswagen* (C-134/20) EU:C:2022:571 at paragraph 79; and of 14 July 2022, *Porsche Inter Auto and Volkswagen* (C-145/20) EU:C:2022:572 at paragraph 78).

93   Secondly, the objective pursued by Regulation No 715/2007, which consists in guaranteeing a high level of protection of the environment and improving air quality within the European Union, means NOx emissions being effectively limited throughout the normal life of vehicles. Permitting a defeat device under Article 5(2)(a) of that regulation solely because, for example, research costs are high, the technical device is expensive or vehicle maintenance is more frequent or more costly for the user would jeopardise that aim (judgments of 14 July 2022, *GSMB Invest* (C-128/20) EU:C:2022:570 at paragraph 68; of 14 July 2022, *Volkswagen* (C-134/20) EU:C:2022:571 at paragraph 80; and of 14 July 2022, *Porsche Inter Auto and Volkswagen* (C-145/20) EU:C:2022:572 at paragraph 79).

94   In those circumstances, and in view of the fact that provision must be interpreted strictly, it must be held that the 'need' for a defeat device, within the meaning of that provision, exists only where, at the time of the EC type-approval of that device or of the vehicle equipped with it, no other technical solution makes it possible to avoid immediate risks of damage or accident to the engine, which give rise to a specific hazard when driving the vehicle (judgments of 14 July 2022, *GSMB Invest* (C-128/20) EU:C:2022:570 at paragraph 69; of 14 July 2022, *Volkswagen* (C-134/20) EU:C:2022:571 at paragraph 81; and of 14 July 2022, *Porsche Inter Auto and Volkswagen* (C-145/20) EU:C:2022:572 at paragraph 80).

95   Consequently, the answer to the second question is that Article 5(2)(a) of Regulation No 715/2007 must be interpreted as meaning that a defeat device can be justified under that provision only where it is established that that device strictly meets the need to avoid immediate risks of damage or accident to the engine, caused by a malfunction of a component of the exhaust gas recirculation system, of such a serious nature as to give rise to a specific hazard when a vehicle fitted with that device is driven. Furthermore, the 'need' for a defeat device, within the meaning of that provision, exists only where, at the time of the EC type-approval of that

device or of the vehicle equipped with it, no other technical solution makes it possible to avoid immediate risks of damage or accident to the engine, which give rise to a specific hazard when driving the vehicle.

Costs

96   Since these proceedings are, for the parties to the main proceedings, a step in the action pending before the national court, the decision on costs is a matter for that court. Costs incurred in submitting observations to the Court, other than the costs of those parties, are not recoverable.

On those grounds, the Court (Grand Chamber) hereby rules:

1. Article 9(3) of the Convention on access to information, public participation in decision-making and access to justice in environmental matters, signed in Aarhus on 25 June 1998 and approved on behalf of the European Community by Council Decision 2005/370/EC of 17 February 2005, read in conjunction with Article 47 of the Charter of Fundamental Rights of the European Union, must be interpreted as precluding a situation where an environmental association, authorised to bring legal proceedings in accordance with national law, is unable to challenge before a national court an administrative decision granting or amending EC type-approval which may be contrary to Article 5(2) of Regulation (EC) No 715/2007 of the European Parliament and of the Council of 20 June 2007 on type approval of motor vehicles with respect to emissions from light passenger and commercial vehicles (Euro 5 and Euro 6) and on access to vehicle repair and maintenance information.

2. Article 5(2)(a) of Regulation No 715/2007 must be interpreted as meaning that a defeat device can be justified under that provision only where it is established that that device strictly meets the need to avoid immediate risks of damage or accident to the engine, caused by a malfunction of a component of the exhaust gas recirculation system, of such a serious nature as to give rise to a specific hazard when a vehicle fitted with that device is driven. Furthermore, the 'need' for a defeat device, within the meaning of that provision, exists only where, at the time of the EC type-approval of that device or of the vehicle equipped with it, no other technical solution makes it possible to avoid immediate risks of damage or accident to the engine, which give rise to a specific hazard when driving the vehicle.

R. (ON THE APPLICATION OF HARDCASTLE) v BUCKINGHAMSHIRE COUNCIL

KING'S BENCH DIVISION (ADMINISTRATIVE COURT)

Sir Ross Cranston: 16 November 2022

[2022] EWHC 2905 (Admin); [2023] Env. L.R. 18

Authority; Breach of statutory duty; Delegated responsibility; Environmental impact assessments; Legitimate expectation; Local authorities' powers and duties; Local plans; Material considerations; Outline planning permission; Residential development; Screening opinions; Villages

H1   *Judicial review—Town and Country Planning—Environmental Impact Assessment Regulations—permission for "up to" 170 dwellings—site allocation in Local Plan for "at least" 170 dwellings—reduction resulting from revised Biodiversity Net Gain proposals—whether development in compliance with development plan—whether failure to take application back to committee in breach Town and Country Planning Act 1990 s.70(2)—whether a breach of 'Kides' principle—whether unlawful consideration of new Biodiversity Net Gain—whether breach of legitimate expectation—whether delegated authority exceeded—whether fundamental errors in screening opinion in breach of the EIA Regulations—whether unlawful failure to review the screening decision in light of changed circumstances and new information—whether officers' report contained misinterpretation/misdirection on National Planning Policy Framework*

H2   The claimant (H) sought judicial review of the grant of outline planning permission by the defendant (B) for a residential development including "up to 170 dwellings". The site allocation in the Local Plan was for "at least" 170 dwellings. A screening opinion under the Town and Country Planning (Environmental Impact Assessment) Regulations 2011 determined that the project was not an EIA development, and no environmental impact assessment was required. The reduction from "at least" to "up to" 170 dwellings resulted from revised Biodiversity Net Gain (BNG) proposals which H argued meant the development was not in compliance with the development plan. The claim was on a number of grounds: (1) a failure to take the planning application back to the committee in breach of the duty in the Town and Country Planning Act 1990 s.70(2) to have regard to all material considerations and the *Kides* principle and an unlawful misunderstanding and misapplication of that principle; (2) unlawful consideration of new BNG; (3) breach of legitimate expectation; (4) that the decision of B's officers to grant permission exceeded their delegated authority; (5) that there were fundamental errors in the screening opinion in breach of the 2011 Regulations, together with an unlawful failure to review the screening decision when circumstances had changed and new information emerged; and (6) that the officers' report contained misinterpretation/misdirection on the National Planning Policy Framework (NPPF) with regard to Best and Most Versatile agricultural land.

H3   **Held,** in dismissing the application:

H4   (1) None of changing factors submitted by H qualified as material considerations. The officer had been correct to conclude that there was no basis to revert to the committee taking account of those matters either individually or cumulatively. That approach had applied the *Kides* principle correctly. The arguments on consideration of new BNG added nothing.

H5   (2) On legitimate expectation, a letter from B's director for legal and democratic services had referred expressly to a decision to take the application back to committee. That was a clear and unambiguous statement that the matter would be remitted. The issue was then whether B could resile from its statement. Not remitting the matter to the committee was a proportionate response to a legitimate aim pursued in the public interest and there was no good reason for remission to occur. Moreover, there was no unfairness to H or others. Given that no new material considerations had arisen, it was difficult to see how further representations could have made a difference in any event. When the officers were later considering whether they should grant permission pursuant to their delegated authority, they were entitled to assess whether circumstances had changed in such a way as to require that the application be referred back to the committee. The officers gave careful and genuine consideration to whether the range of new material meant that they should do so. In doing this they were not engaged in matters outside the delegation but acting consistently with it through the exercise of their lawful discretion.

H6   (3) On the screening opinion, H had not shown that the change in the size of the proposal would make a difference to the outcome. Nor had he provided objective evidence to show that the screening opinion would not reasonably have been negative if potential cumulative effects had been considered. References to "substantial" and "substantive", rather than "significant", effects in the wording of the screening opinion did not mean that the wrong legal test had been applied. That was the kind of legalism and forensic analysis of language which was to be deprecated. In any event, at the outset the screening opinion stated that it was determining "the likelihood of significant effects" and it concluded that the proposal "would not have a significant impact". In other words, the screening opinion applied the correct legal test. Critique of the approach to absorption capacity resulted from a misreading of the issue. The screening opinion had contained adequate reasons. There were comments on each of the individual criteria in Sch.3 which, though crisp, were adequate in accord with their purpose. As to H's point that there were no reasons given for the overall conclusion there was, in short, no need for reasons for reasons. A reasonable planning officer would not have thought the changes argued by H to require a review could change the outcome of the 2015 screening individually or cumulatively. In other words, a further screening would have produced the same conclusion as the 2015 screening that the development would not have significant effects on the environment.

H7   (4) On the NPPF issue, the report could not be said to have contained material errors, failed to guide the members sufficiently, or significantly mislead them on a matter material to their decision.

H8 **Cases referred to:**

Baroness Cumberlege of Newick v Secretary of State for Communities and Local Government [2018] EWCA Civ 1305; [2018] P.T.S.R. 2063; [2018] Env. L.R. 34

Crystal Property (London) Ltd v Secretary of State for Communities and Local Government [2016] EWCA Civ 1265; [2017] J.P.L. 594

Finucane's Application for Judicial Review, Re [2019] UKSC 7; [2019] N.I. 292; [2019] H.R.L.R. 7

Hockley v Essex CC [2013] EWHC 4051 (Admin); [2014] Env. L.R. 24

Kenyon v Secretary of State for Housing, Communities and Local Government [2020] EWCA Civ 302; [2021] Env. L.R. 8; [2020] J.P.L. 1189

Mansell v Tonbridge and Malling BC [2017] EWCA Civ 1314; [2019] P.T.S.R. 1452; [2018] J.P.L. 176

Paponette v Attorney General of Trinidad and Tobago [2010] UKPC 32; [2012] 1 A.C. 1; [2011] 3 W.L.R. 219

R. (on the application of Bateman) v South Cambridgeshire DC [2011] EWCA Civ 157; [2011] N.P.C. 22

R. (on the application of CBRE Lionbrook (General Partners) Ltd) v Rugby BC [2014] EWHC 646 (Admin); [2014] Env. L.R. D3

R. (on the application of The Co-Operative Group Ltd) v West Lancashire BC [2021] EWHC 507 (Admin)

R. (on the application of Dry) v West Oxfordshire DC [2010] EWCA Civ 1143; [2011] 1 P. & C.R. 16; [2011] J.P.L. 579

R. (on the application of Flynn) v Southwark LBC [2021] EWCA Civ 827

R. (on the application of Friends of the Earth Ltd) v Heathrow Airport Ltd [2020] UKSC 52; [2021] P.T.S.R. 190; [2021] J.P.L. 905

R. (on the application of Hinds) v Blackpool BC [2012] EWCA Civ 466; [2012] J.P.L. 1365

R. (on the application of Hough) v Secretary of State for the Home Department [2022] EWHC 1635 (Admin)

R. (on the application of Kides) v South Cambridgeshire DC [2002] EWCA Civ 1370; [2003] 1 P. & C.R. 19; [2003] J.P.L. 431

R. (on the application of Leckhampton Green Land Action Group Ltd) v Tewkesbury BC [2017] EWHC 198 (Admin); [2017] Env. L.R. 28

R. (on the application of Lee Valley Regional Park Authority) v Epping Forest DC [2016] EWCA Civ 404; [2016] Env. L.R. 30; [2016] J.P.L. 1009

R. (on the application of Milton (Peterborough) Estates Co (t/a Fitzwilliam (Malton) Estate)) v Ryedale DC [2015] EWHC 1948 (Admin)

R. (on the application of Nadarajah) v Secretary of State for the Home Department [2005] EWCA Civ 1363

Secretary of State for Education and Science v Tameside MBC [1977] A.C. 1014; [1976] 3 W.L.R. 641; (1976) 120 S.J. 735 HL

Swire v Ashford BC [2021] EWHC 702 (Admin); [2021] Env. L.R. 29; [2022] 2 P. & C.R. 2

Wakil (t/a Orya Textiles) v Hammersmith and Fulham LBC [2013] EWHC 2833 (Admin); [2014] Env. L.R. 14

H9 **Legislation referred to:**
Town and Country Planning Act 1990 s.70

Planning and Compulsory Purchase Act 2004 s.38
Town and Country Planning (Environmental Impact Assessment) Regulations
2011 (SI 2011/1824) regs 3–7 and Sch.3

H10   *R. Honey KC, M. Golden* and *J. Welch* (instructed by Fortune Green Legal Practice)
appeared on behalf of the claimant.
A. Booth KC and *C. Streeten* (instructed by Buckinghamshire Council) appeared
on behalf of the defendant.
H. Mohamed (instructed by Dentons Solicitors) appeared on behalf of the interested
party.

JUDGMENT

SIR ROSS CRANSTON:

Introduction

1   This is a challenge to the grant earlier this year of outline planning permission
by the defendant, Buckinghamshire Council, for a residential development on a
site abutting Maids Moreton in Buckinghamshire. Maids Moreton is a village which
the 2011 census records as having 351 homes and 847 residents. The permission
granted to the interested party, which I call "the developer" in this judgment, relates
to "up to 170 dwellings, public open space and associated infrastructure." Last year
a planning inspector had reported on the Vale of Aylesbury local plan, and that
had been adopted on 15 September 2021. Site allocation D-MMO006 concerns
the site, which it allocates for "at least" 170 dwellings at a density that takes account
of the adjacent settlement character and identity and the edge of countryside
location.

2   The claimant is a resident and parish councillor of Maids Moreton and a member
of the Maids Moreton and Foscote Action Group, formed in 2019. He has objected
to the development since its inception in 2015. Over several years both he and the
action group have raised a number of objections to the development both orally
and in writing. In this judicial review the claimant raises six grounds of challenge.
When granting permission on 1 July 2022, Lang J observed that these raised
arguable grounds which merited consideration at a full hearing. Mr Honey KC
(with the assistance of Ms Golden and Mr Welch) advanced the grounds with
typical skill and thoroughness, but for the reasons explained in the judgment I have
concluded that the claim cannot succeed.

Background

3   Buckinghamshire Council ("the council") become a unitary local authority and
the planning authority for the county in April 2020. Until then these matters were
considered by the former Aylesbury Vale District Council ("Aylesbury"), which
became part of the new unitary authority. It was thus to Aylesbury that the developer
applied for outline planning permission in 2015.

The 2015 screening opinion

4   Prior to the developer's application, Aylesbury had a screening opinion prepared under regulations 4-7 of the Town and Country Planning (Environmental Impact Assessment) Regulations 2011 ("the 2011 Regulations"). That led to its decision on 19 November 2015 that this was not an EIA development, and no environmental impact assessment was required.

5   The screening opinion stated at the outset that its rationale was to determine "the likelihood of significant effects on the environment and whether an Environmental Impact Assessment (EIA) is necessary." It then proceeded by examining the relevant criteria set out in schedule 3 of the 2011 Regulations.

6   In setting out the characteristics of the proposed development, the screening opinion stated (a) that its size was "7.95ha, up to 155 dwellings, public open space and play area, landscaping and flood mitigation." As regards (b), cumulation with other development, it said that it related to an area of agricultural land and the proposal was not part of a larger scheme. Use of natural resources, (c), was stated as "greenfield site but none of substantive nature." Pollution and nuisance, (e), noted that following occupation the development would result in additional vehicle movements, but it was unlikely that this would be of a substantive nature.

7   Among aspects of location, the screening opinion stated at (a) that existing land use was "agricultural, countryside". Natural resources in area, (b) stated that the site "comprises open land in the countryside which would be lost as a result of the development, but any impacts would not be of more than local importance." At (c), absorption capacity of natural environment, the opinion stated that the proposal was "not considered to raise substantive issues relating to identified criteria, but this would be assessed during the consideration of any subsequent planning application."

8   As regards the characteristics of the potential impact, the screening opinion stated as regards its magnitude and complexity, (iii)(c) that it was "[u]nlikely to be substantive and would be localised impact, not anticipated to be complex." As regards the probability of impact of the proposed development, (iii)(d), the screening opinion stated that it was unlikely to be substantive. It added: "Possible visual impacts and potential for impact on highways, ecology, flood risk, drainage and archaeology, but would be a localised impact and therefore probability of impact is not considered substantial."

9   The conclusion and recommendation of the screening opinion were as follows: "It is considered in the light of available information that the proposal would not have a significant impact and as a result an EIA is not required."

Highways

10   In a letter dated 30 November 2018 to Aylesbury, Buckinghamshire County Council, then the highways authority, explained that in light of the planning application it was more appropriate to investigate deterring traffic resulting from the development from using College Farm Road (also known as Mill Lane) rather than improving the junction of the road with the A422. That would be by traffic calming measures. If these were successful the result would be additional traffic from the development travelling into Buckingham, which would require mitigation through the Buckingham traffic strategy.

Agricultural land quality

11   The developer had a report prepared by consultants about agricultural land classification relating to the site. Dated February 2019 the report stated that the proposed development would take approximately 8 ha of land affecting four relatively small fields used mainly for arable farming. Its overall impact locally was of only minor significance in terms of agricultural land quality. The land was mostly grade 3a which was identified as being BMV (best and more versatile). The report concluded that its loss did not represent a significant loss locally or regionally in terms of BMV.

12   The report concluded:

> "The loss of this site to development is therefore not significant to the supply of BMV agricultural land within the district and the Southeast as a whole with development on some BMV land in Aylesbury Vale being inevitable in most cases."

Permission deferred and delegated for approval, 2019

13   The developer's application for planning permission was considered by Aylesbury's strategic development management committee in early 2019. It resolved that permission be deferred and delegated for approval subject to the completion of a section 106 agreement and the conditions which officers considered appropriate.

14   In response to a letter in March 2019 from Mrs Kate Pryke of the Maids Moreton and Foscote Action Group, on 2 May 2019 Aylesbury replied, inter alia, that it would not refer the matter back to the planning committee. Officers would only do that, it explained, if there was a significant change in policy or circumstances that would influence the decision made and the committee would need to consider it – and that was not the position.

Contaminated land

15   The developer had a consultant prepare a report on contaminated land. The council's pollution control officer prepared comments in relation to the subject dated 9 November 2020. The report recorded that the ground investigation had identified that elevated levels of arsenic were present across the entire site. The consultant's report had stated that these occurred naturally. The report went on to say that this was not considered a significant risk to human health and was in line with the current guidance. However, the report recommended that further assessment be undertaken. The pollution control officer agreed with this recommendation, adding that it might be that based on the results remedial work may be necessary.

Anglian Water report

16   In early November 2020 there was a report in relation to the proposed development by Anglian Water. As to wastewater, there was not the capacity in the Buckingham centre to deal with it, but Anglian Water was obligated to accept the foul flows from the development if it had the benefit of planning consent and would therefore take the necessary steps to ensure that there was sufficient treatment capacity should the council grant it.

17   As to the used water network and unacceptable risk of flooding downstream, Anglian Water stated that it would need to work with the developer to ensure any infrastructure improvements, but a full assessment could not be made at that point due to a lack of information.

Natural England

18   Natural England had no overall objection to the development when it responded on 2 November 2020. It considered that without appropriate mitigation the application would damage or destroy the interest features of the Foxcote Reservoir & Wood SSSI. To mitigate that Natural England advised an appropriate planning condition or that an obligation be attached to any planning permission to ensure implementation of the measures the developer's consultants had recommended in their 2016 ecological enhancement plan.

The 2020 officer's report

19   In November 2020 the application was referred back to committee, this time the strategic sites planning committee of the now unified Buckinghamshire Council ("the committee"). An officer's report was prepared for consideration by that committee.

20   The officer's report, dated 19 November 2020, stated that the proposal was an outline application with all matters reserved except access for up to 170 dwellings, public open space and associated infrastructure.

21   Part 1 of the report first explained that previously the matter had been before Aylesbury's planning committee, which had resolved that permission be deferred and delegated for approval, subject to the matters referred to earlier. Since then, the report continued, work had been progressing on the section 106 agreement. Importantly, work on the Vale of Aylesbury Local Plan (VALP) had also progressed such that a number of policies within that plan could be given greater weight in decision making. In addition, further representations had been received. In that context it was considered appropriate for the application to be returned to committee for determination and to update the position including the evolving policy framework.

22   The report then noted that the application was for up to 170 dwellings. At various points in the report the officer refers to 170 dwellings, but that this is shorthand for "up to 170 dwellings" is clear, not least when, at paragraph 5.7 the report states, when considering that the development would increase the population of Maids Moreton by approximately 50 percent, that it is "of 170 dwellings (noting that the development is for up to 170 dwellings) ..."

23   The report at paragraph 1.5 noted that there would be harm to the character of the landscape and on the settlement character which would be of moderate negative weight. The development would also result in loss of BMV agricultural land which would be of limited negative weight.

24   At paragraph 1.14 the report stated:

"In considering the overall planning balance it is considered that the adverse impacts would not significantly and demonstrably outweigh the benefits of the proposal. It is therefore recommended that the application be approved subject to the completion of a s.106 legal agreement securing the matters outlined in section 6 below and subject to conditions as appropriate."

25 Part 2 of the report was a description of the proposed development.

26 Under the heading "Relevant planning history", part 3, the report stated "15/03562/SO – Screening Opinion for proposed development – Environmental Impact assessment not required."

27 The report at part 4 noted the significant number of representations received - set out in detail in Appendix A – "the key concerns" being development outside settlement boundaries, impact on landscape, impact on traffic and congestion, and impact on heritage assets, residential amenities and infrastructure.

28 Part 5 was the longest part of the report – "Policy considerations and evaluation" – and sub-divided.

29 After identifying relevant planning policy, under the sub-heading "Principle and location of development" the report noted that the site did not represent small scale development in that it was of 170 dwellings on a 8.649ha site.

30 Paragraph 5.5 of the report explained that:

"the site is proposed to be allocated in the emerging VALP for development as part of MMO006 and this supports the development of the site for 170 dwellings subject to a number of criteria. MMO006 (as proposed to be modified) anticipated delivery of the following: a provision of at least 170 dwellings at a density that takes account of the adjacent settlement character and identity and the edge of countryside location."

31 Later paragraph 5.7 stated that the development, with its 170 dwellings "(noting that the development is for up to 170 dwellings)", would increase the population of Maids Moreton by approximately 50 percent.

32 When considering the sub-heading "Housing supply, affordable housing and housing mix", the report concluded that the development would make a significant contribution to these. On that basis, the report said at paragraph 5.18, that the development would accord with the development plan policy, the NPPF and emerging policies, including MMO006. As such, the paragraph added, significant weight should be given to the development in respect of the contribution to housing supply and affordable housing, and considerable weight to the economic benefits in this regard.

33 Under the sub-heading "Transport matters and parking", the report noted that it was evident that the impact of the development traffic on College Farm Road (also known as Mill Lane) and its junction with the A422 needed to be mitigated. A mitigation package had been secured regarding (1) improvements on the A422 in the vicinity of the junction with College Farm Road to improve safety at the junction and (2) traffic calming works to the north-western end of College Farm Road at its junction with Church Street, to make College Farm Road a less attractive route: para. 5.33. If the traffic calming had the desired effect of deterring traffic from using College Farm Road, mitigation to the junction with the A422 might not be required: para. 5.35. The report showed with illustrations the proposed traffic calming in principle: para. 5.39. If the traffic calming was successful that would result in additional traffic in Buckingham, which would need to be mitigated: para. 5.44. The report later returned to the aim of making College Farm Road a less

attractive route from the beginning and deterring development traffic from using it: para. 5.122.

34   Under the sub-heading "Visual impact", the report stated that there were "significant adverse visual impacts from the development" but added at paragraph 5.78 that "these will be in the immediate vicinity of the site and there is scope for the existing relationship between the settlement and the open countryside to be visually enhanced in line with the Landscape Character Assessment guidance."

35   Regarding agricultural land, paragraph 5.80 of the report noted that paragraph 170 of the NPPF advised that local planning authorities

> "…should take into account the economic and other benefits of the best and most versatile agricultural land and, where significant development of agricultural land was demonstrated to be necessary, local planning authorities should seek to use areas of poorer quality land in preference to that of a higher quality."

36   The report observed that there was no definition as to what comprised "significant development" but the threshold above which Natural England was required to be consulted was set at 20 hectares and the site fell below that threshold.

37   The report went on at paragraph 5.81 to note that development would result in the loss of best and most versatile (BMV) agricultural land. Consideration had been given to the development of this agricultural land as required by the NPPF. However, having regard to the size of the site and the extent of BMV land lost, it was not considered that this would represent a significant development in the Aylesbury Vale area. As such, in considering that there would be some loss of BMV, "it is considered that this matter should be afforded very limited negative weight in the planning balance." This conclusion was reiterated in the overall assessment on the report.

38   Nine paragraphs were devoted to the biodiversity net gain calculation. The report noted that the council's biodiversity officer raised no objections subject to a condition to secure the various objectives and management of the site: para. 5.100. Further enhancements had been identified directly adjacent to the existing features and would need to be established in the enhancement plan. The ecological enhancement plan would be critical to ensure the concerns raised were appropriately addressed: para 5.101. Consequently, and with the mitigation proposed, the proposal would accord with emerging policy NE1 of the VALP: para. 5.102.

39   Part 6 dealt with developer contributions.

40   Part 7 was the overall assessment, with the weighing and balancing of issues.

41   The report concluded with the officer's recommendation: "The officer recommendation is that the application be Deferred and Delegated to officers for approval subject to the satisfactory completion of a s.106 agreement to secure the requirements set out in the report, subject to securing a District Licence to address protected species and subject to any conditions considered appropriate or refuse if a satisfactory S106 agreement cannot be completed for such reasons as officers considers appropriate."

42   A Corrigendum Report of the same date was produced incorporating further objections and comments from consultants.

November 2020 committee meeting and decision

43   The committee met on 19 November 2020. During its meeting, the committee heard a number of representations, including from both the claimant and the developer. There was then a motion to refuse the officer's recommendation, which was lost by one vote (with the chair casting a second, deciding, vote). Subsequently, by way of a split vote with the chairman casting the deciding vote, the committee resolved to accept the officer's recommendation, that permission be deferred and delegated for approval by officers, subject to (i) the satisfactory completion of the s.106 agreement, (ii) the securing of a district licence to address protected species, and (iii) conditions as considered appropriate. The resolution stated that if any of these "subject to" matters were not achieved, the application should be refused.

44   Later that month, on 30 November 2020, a draft s.106 agreement was published. The claimant lodged objections the following month.

45   The council delayed determining the application under delegated powers in the light of the inspector's decision to hold a further hearing in relation to the proposed allocation MMO006 and transportation. The background to this hearing is as follows.

The inspector's report on Vale of Aylesbury local plan, February 2018-September 2021

46   In February 2018 Aylesbury submitted the draft Vale of Aylesbury local plan (VALP) for examination by the inspector, Mr Paul Clark.

47   Aylesbury had proposed to delete the allocation in the draft plan of what in effect is the site for the development in the light of advice received from the former Buckinghamshire County Council, as the highways authority, concerning access to the site. Following further advice from the County Council, Aylesbury reviewed that decision shortly before the hearing session in July 2018 and the site was then allocated for housing.

48   In mid-2019 the Maids Moreton and Foscote Action Group had made representations to the inspector that the site was unsuitable for development.

49   In October 2019, the inspector issued his main modifications to the draft plan.

50   On 16 December 2020 he issued discussion document number 8, his initial consideration of representations on modifications. In it he explained his insertion of "at least" in front of proposed housing quantities. It introduced an element of uncertainty to a plan, he conceded, but the feasibility studies which provided the evidence for the figures did not demonstrate that more could not be achieved. Further, it was government policy to boost development, particularly the supply of housing. None of the representations indicated that the figures should be regarded as a maximum.

51   In the discussion document the inspector also announced that he intended to hold a further hearing session regarding what was the draft site allocation. That was because although he found the council's explanations and adjustments to modification acceptable, new transport evidence meant he would benefit from a further hearing session. As well the council's about-face, shortly before the 2018 July hearing session, meant that objectors about the site allocation did not receive notification in time to attend the hearing session at that point and they should now have the opportunity to be heard.

52   There was the further VALP hearing session as regards the site on 15 and 16 April 2021, which the inspector had foreshadowed. The claimant spoke at this session.

53   The inspector's final report was published on 2 September 2021.

The inspector's report

54   In his report the inspector at DL227 recorded that the 2015 HELAA (Housing and economic land availability assessment) regarded the site as unsuitable, but a later HELAA reversed that. In the 2017 sustainability appraisal it was the least suitable site in the village reflecting a lack of local employment (so leading to commuting but without adequate transport infrastructure), its status as a greenfield site (so leading to impacts on wildlife), its classification as best and most versatile (BMV) agricultural land, and an increase in flood risk.

55   The inspector noted that while residents of Maids Moreton clearly saw themselves as separate from Buckingham, to an independent observer the two settlements coalesced: DL229.

56   With respect to BMV agricultural land, the inspector noted that much land around Buckingham was of this classification, so that if growth at Buckingham was to be accommodated at all it was inevitable that some loss would occur. He had no reason to question the Council's advice that alternatives offered no advantage in terms of using poorer quality land: DL232.

57   At DL233 the inspector noted that any development of a greenfield site carried with it a risk of increased surface water flooding because of faster run-off from hard surfaces, but the risk was usually dealt with during consideration of a planning application. The submitted plan's policy for allocation MMO006 included criterion (e), which would require the submission of a surface water drainage scheme.

58   Turning to traffic matters, the inspector noted that discussions on access had been resolved to the satisfaction of the highway authority. There were "discontinuities", as he put it, in the transport advice given during the preparation of the plan and during concurrent consideration of the planning application: DL235. As regards the first, with housing allocations including MMO006, Milton Keynes to the east of Buckingham would be a main destination of traffic and routes avoiding the latter's town centre included the use of College Farm Road: DL239. The inspector observed that the current planning application to develop the MMO006 allocation gave the impression that traffic calming measures would be imposed on College Farm Road, which would dissuade traffic from using roads so treated. The inspector continued: "Be that as it may, I was given explicit assurance by the Council's representative at the hearing session that my understanding was correct that the traffic calming measures were intended to make sure that the roads concerned would accommodate the traffic generated from the MMO006 allocation in a safe way": DL240.

59   The inspector concluded:

"241...having examined the matter at considerable length and in considerable detail, I am convinced that, given the difficult decisions which the Council has had to face in determining Buckingham's future and taking all matters together in the round, this allocation is positively prepared and justified, although a modification is necessary [MM101] to make the allocation effective and consistent with government policy by reflecting the contribution which the allocation will need to make to the resolution of Buckingham's highway deficiencies, updating the site's expected time of delivery and to make it clear, in line with government policy, that the expected number of dwellings should be viewed as a minimum."

Vale of Aylesbury local plan, September 2021

60   The council adopted the VALP on 15 September 2021.

61   As to site MMO006, a size of 8.8ha, it was allocated for 170 homes, green infrastructure and surface water drainage. Site-specific requirements included the provision of "at least 170 dwellings at a density that takes account of the adjacent settlement character and identity and the edge of countryside location."

62   Plan T1 states that the council will seek to ensure that development proposals will deliver highway and transport improvements to ensure that new housing and employment development does not create a severe impact on the highway and public transportation network and encourages modal shift with greater use of more sustainable forms of transport. T4 states that new development will be permitted where there is evidence that there is sufficient capacity in the transport network to accommodate the increase in travel. As to T5, it provides that new development will only be permitted if the necessary mitigation is provided against unacceptable transport impacts.

Mr Elvin's opinion and emails relating to it, early 2021

63   While the inspector was considering the local plan, the council obtained a legal opinion from Mr David Elvin KC in early 2021 to examine what it considered were serious allegations made against council officers and what was said to be its unlawful handling of the planning application. Specifically, Mr Elvin was asked to advise on (i) whether officers misled members or wrongly advised them or made any other error in their role with the committee; and (ii) whether the council's constitution enabled the application to be considered by the strategic site committee rather than the area committee.

64   After detailed analysis of these issues Mr Elvin KC concluded that there was no error in the conduct of the officers and the matter was appropriately dealt with by the committee.

65   Under a final heading, "Issues for the council's further consideration", Mr Elvin referred to the inspector's 16 December 2020 decision to hold a further hearing, as explained earlier in the judgment. Mr Elvin said it would provide an opportunity for the soundness of the site allocation to be further tested. At paragraph 61, he said that the views of officers in the 2020 report and expressed to the committee had been overtaken by events. The view that no main modifications were required for MMO006 and therefore soundness was not in issue was no longer tenable, and the issue of moderate weight in it may require alteration. After referring to *Kides*, Mr Elvin went on to opine:

"63. Since the weight and significance to be attached to the VALP was a matter of some significance in the [officer's report] and the [committee] meeting, for the resolution to proceed to the issue of permission without further consideration of the above would open it to a serious risk of challenge on *Kides* principles unless it is reported back to [committee].

64. Whether the application should be fully reported back to members for reconsideration in the near future, or on a briefer basis with a view to taking the matter back once the Inspector has heard and reported on the [site] objections is a matter for the Council to decide having regard to the current circumstances and the changes that have occurred since the meeting."

66   On 25 January 2021 the council's director for legal and constitutional services, Mr Nick Graham, emailed Ms Kate Pryke of the Maids Moreton and Foscote Action Group. In the course of the email he referred to Mr Elvin's opinion, in particular the reference to the inspector's intention to hold the additional hearing session and the opportunity it provided for the soundness of the proposed allocation of the site to be further considered. Mr Graham continued:

"It is Mr Elvin's view, accepted by the Council, that this amounts to a material change in circumstances and which will now require at least some of the matters considered by the Committee to be considered further. That is not in any way to suggest that there was anything wrong with the original decision of the Committee, rather that the Inspector's further intervention since that decision warrants reconsideration. In the circumstances, it has been decided that a final decision on this application, will be deferred until the position of the VALP inspector is known. At the moment it is anticipated that a hearing to consider further representations about this site will take place in March/April and so we do not expect any referral back before that date. If there is any significant delay to this anticipated timetable this position may need to be revisited."

67   A month later, on 24 February 2021, Mr Graham wrote further to Ms Pryke in relation to some nine points she had raised in a letter of 16 February 2021. Regarding point 9 he said:

"[A]ll members of the Strategic Sites Committee have received an explanation regarding the decision to refer the application back to committee."

Three-member call-in request, September 2021

68   Following the inspector's report, three local councillors requested that the planning application be called back to the committee.

69   The request was advanced on two bases. First, there was the change of circumstances because of the discontinuities between the transport advice given to the inspector and that placed before the committee. Secondly, there were defects in the section 106 agreement.

Maids Moreton and Foscote Action Group letter, January 2022

70   On 3 January 2022 the Maids Moreton and Foscote Action Group wrote a carefully constructed letter to the council, stating that the application should be remitted to the committee under the *Kides* principle, majoring on traffic as a new material consideration and on deficiencies in the s.106 agreement. Councillors were copied in.

Biodiversity net gain assessments

71   The developer commissioned a biodiversity net gain assessment (BNG) in 2015, to accompany its application for planning permission. That went through various iterations in the following years. The different versions were accompanied by drawings of the site, showing its different features and indications of where housing was to be. There was a version dated January 2022.

72   In response to the January 2022 version, the council's interim ecology team leader identified a number of errors that the developer had submitted.

73   As a result the developer submitted a further BNG assessment in February 2022, noting that to demonstrate that the proposals could provide a 10 percent net gain to biodiversity, the development area had been reduced. The precise design would be through the submission of a reserved matters application.

74   The council's interim ecology team leader observed that the plans now showed a reduction in the number of houses to accommodate the BNG.

Officer's report and delegated decision, March 2022

75   Following the inspector's report, the council decided that the planning application could be determined under delegated powers without a further referral back to committee.

76   This was recorded in a decision memorandum of 24 March 2022 signed by the service director, planning and environment. The memorandum explained the history of the application, and the delay in making a decision - following the committee's determination on 19 November 2020 - because of the inspector's additional hearing in April 2021. Now the inspector had approved policy D-MMO006 and no modifications were required to be considered by the committee. There had been requests to have the matter returned to the committee, including a call-in request by local members, but the director for legal and democratic services had advised that since the application had already been heard at committee, the three-member call-in was not valid under the council's constitution.

77   The memorandum further explained that the determination process for the application had been made in consultation with the chair of the committee. The cabinet member for planning and regeneration had been notified. It had been concluded that the exercise of delegated powers in relation to this application was appropriate.

The 2022 officer's report

78   Following an introduction, part 2 of the officer's report of 24 March 2022 was entitled "Update".

79   The first update matter was the VALP. Paragraph 2.2 read, in part:

> "…at the time the planning application was reported to Committee on 19th November 2020, Policy D-MMO006 was worded as set out in full at paragraph 5.5 of the officer's report. The wording included the main and additional modifications as proposed at that time. The Inspector in his final report concluded that these modifications to the policy were required as set out in his Main Modification 101. The VALP Inspector found the allocation to be

sound and the site is allocated in the adopted VALP for development as part of MMO006 and this supports the development of the site for at least 170 dwellings subject to a number of criteria as set out in that policy."

80   Paragraph 2.3 stated that the VALP had been adopted on 15 September 2021 and could now be given full weight. Paragraph 2.4 added that as now adopted it formed part of the development plan,

> "which further justifies the Council's resolution to grant permission for the development."

81   The update section then mentioned the adoption of NPPF 2021 and the Council's new 2021 five-year housing land supply: paras.2.5, 2.6 respectively.

82   Under the heading "Additional information", the update noted the revisions of the biodiversity net gain submission (BNG). The report's "response", paragraph 2.8 explained:

> "The quantum of the development proposed remains up to 170 dwellings, however it is acknowledged that the number of dwellings could be less than previously indicated given that there is a reduction in the developed area to achieve the required biodiversity net gain as shown on the amended landscape masterplan and feasibility plan. This would still be consistent with the description of development for which outline permission is sought and considered by committee. Regard has been had to the mitigation indicated, the impact on the landscape character area, on the settlement character and the visual impact of the development itself whilst recognising this is an outline application and the details of appearance, landscaping, layout and scale are matters reserved for subsequent approval."

83   The report explained the updated BNG assessment dated February 2022, in particular the reduction in habitat units resulting in the 11.51 percent net gain becoming a 10.21 percent net gain. However, the report added at paragraph 2.11 that

> "this is not considered to be significant and would not require the application to be returned to committee for consideration by Members since it would not represent a material change to the original conclusions reached in this matter."

84   Turning to additional consultee responses, the officer reported at paragraph 2.12 on contaminated land, the naturally occurring arsenic which had been found in the soil. The report explained the position and noted that additional testing was being undertaken. It recommended a condition to planning permission to address any adverse results.

85   Part 3 of the officer's report dealt with representations and set out the officer's responses. (There was also a separate table with responses to the representations regarding the s.106 legal agreement.)

86   After considering the representations with respect to traffic mitigation measures on College Farm Road (sometimes called Mill Lane), the report's lengthy response was summarised at the end of paragraph 3.17:

> "[I]t is clear from the above that the proposals and advice put forward by the Council for both the planning application and during the VALP hearings result in the same conclusions that the Inspector reached in his report. It is the case

that the development is likely to result in additional traffic using Mill Lane, there are measures in place in the form of traffic calming that aim to dissuade traffic from using the road and at the same time will allow the traffic that does want to use the road to be accommodated and facilitated in a safer manner, and ultimately, if there are capacity issues at the Mill Lane junction with the A422 junction there is a scheme agreed to mitigate those issues. It is also important to confirm that the assessments carried out as part of the TA [transport assessment] submitted in support of the application did assume that additional development traffic will use Mill Lane and none of assessments relied upon any traffic being reassigned away from using Mill Lane and instead routing through Buckingham for the application to be acceptable; traffic uses both routes. Having regard to the above it is not considered that inconsistent highways advice has been given in respect of Mill Lane (also known as College Farm Road) and that the representations made do not raise any new material considerations on highways grounds to require the application to be returned to committee."

87   As to ecology, there had been further consideration and representations, with the background being the changes in the BNG assessment and the reduction in net gain (as explained earlier). The report's response at paragraph 3.31 was that this

"is not considered to be significant and would not require the application to be returned to committee for consideration by Members since it would not represent a material change to the conclusions reached in this matter."

88   The response at paragraph 3.31 continued that changes had been made to the BNG metric and report to ensure that they reflected the baseline and indicative proposals. It was an outline scheme with all matters reserved except for access. Therefore it would only be when the final layout was known that these matters would be subject to further scrutiny through the detailed design process. The paragraph added that planning conditions were to be imposed which would require the submission and approval of ecological details, including updated biodiversity net gain calculations, mitigation for losses, and also surveys, to the council's satisfaction. The council's ecology officer was satisfied that conditions would secure the net gain to biodiversity mentioned.

89   In considering the planning balance in part 4, the report observed that the proposal accorded with the development plan and there were no material considerations that indicated a determination otherwise. It added that the adoption of the VALP strengthened the decision made by the committee and reaffirmed that the delivery of this housing allocation played an important role in delivering the required growth in the Vale of Aylesbury area.

90   In the conclusion, part 5, the report stated:

"5.1. For these reasons the position remains as advised to members at Committee and as resolved upon by members. The additional representations made, and consultation responses received, since the application was considered by Committee do not give rise to any material change in circumstances and certainly none that might make a difference to the committee's conclusion that permission should be granted.

5.2. It is not considered necessary to refer this matter back to committee as there is no new material consideration that has arisen after the resolution to grant, which could affect or change the resolution reached by the Committee. It is concluded that were the application referred back to Committee the decision would be the same."

91   The conditions attached to the report included conditions 1 and 16, which provide that details of layout and housing mix were to be submitted and approved by the council, reflecting that this was for outline permission and the up-to-date position on housing need at the time of the submission of reserved matters.

92   Condition 20 is that the development shall be implemented in accordance with the objectives and management prescriptions detailed in the 2016 ecological enhancement plan, but that there were to be an updated ecological "walkover", and possibly further surveys prior to the commencement of development, to inform mitigation measures and site landscaping plans to maximise site biodiversity.

Ground 1: Failure To Return To Committee and/Or Error Re Kides Principle

93   The claimant contends that there are two errors of law under Ground 1, caused by the Council's failure to take the planning application back to the committee: (i) a breach of the Council's statutory duty in s.70(2) of the Town and Country Planning Act 1990 ("the 1990 Act") and the *Kides* principle; and (ii) an unlawful misunderstanding and misapplication of the *Kides* principle.

Legal principles

94   Section 70(2) of the 1990 Act provides that, in dealing with an application for planning permission, the planning authority shall have regard, inter alia, to (a) the provisions of the development plan, so far as material to the application and (c) any other material consideration.

95   In *R. (Kides) v South Cambridgeshire DC* [2002] EWCA Civ 1370 the Court of Appeal held that an authority's duty to "have regard to" material considerations is not to be elevated into a formal requirement that with every new material consideration arising after the passing of a resolution (in principle) to grant planning permission, but before the issue of the decision notice, there has to be a specific referral back to committee. The duty is discharged if, as at the date at which the decision notice is issued, the authority has considered all material considerations affecting the application with the application in mind—albeit that the application was not specifically placed before it for reconsideration: [122]. The court added that, where a delegated officer is to issue a decision and becomes aware (or ought reasonably to have become aware) of a new material consideration, s.70(2) requires that the authority have regard to that consideration before finally determining the application: [125].

96   The Court of Appeal added that in practice, where since the passing of the resolution some new factor has arisen of which the delegated officer is aware, and which might rationally be regarded as a material consideration for the purposes of s.70(2), the delegated officer can only safely proceed to issue the decision notice if he is satisfied (a) that the authority is aware of the new factor, (b) that it has considered it with the application in mind, and (c) that on a reconsideration the authority would reach (not might reach) the same decision: [126]. In passing I observe that (c) seems to go to materiality, rather than the "having regard to" aspect of s.70(2).

97   In *R. (Dry) v West Oxfordshire DC* [2010] EWCA Civ 1143, Carnwath LJ
observed that the guidance in paragraph [126] of *Kides* is only guidance as to what
is advisable and must be applied with common sense, and with regard to the facts
of the particular case: [16]. That dictum is not, however, a route to avoid the
statutory requirements: *R. (Hinds) v Blackpool BC* [2012] EWCA Civ 466 at [35].

98   The separate legal issue of what is a material consideration in s.70(2) was
identified in *Kides* as one which, when placed in the decisionmaker's scales, would
tip the balance to some extent, one way or another: [121]. In *Wakil (t/a Orya
Textiles) v Hammersmith and Fulham LBC* [2013] EWHC 2833 (Admin), Lindblom
J reviewed *Kides*, *Dry*, and *Hinds* and said this:

> "When a grant of planning permission is challenged on the ground that the
> local planning authority, having resolved to approve the development proposed,
> ought to reconsider that decision, the court will have to consider whether the
> new factor relied upon in the challenge would have been capable of affecting
> the outcome. What is required therefore is not merely some obvious change
> in circumstances but a change that might have had a material effect on the
> authority's deliberations had it occurred before the decision was made. The
> crucial question for the court to consider is whether the new factor might have
> led the authority to reach a different decision."

99   In my view what is a material consideration must be determined in line with the
contemporary jurisprudence on the subject (in as much as it differs from these
authorities), namely, that this is a consideration which the rational decision-maker
would regard as "so obviously material" that it must be taken into account: *R. (on
the application of Friends of the Earth Ltd) v Heathrow Airport Ltd* [2020] UKSC
52 at [116]-[11], per Lords Hodge and Sales (with whom other members of the
Supreme Court agreed) citing, inter alia, Lindblom LJ in *Baroness Cumberlege of
Newick v Secretary of State for Communities and Local Government* [2018] EWCA
Civ 1305 at [20]-[26], with whom Moylan and Peter Jackson LJJ agreed. In this
context it seems to me that a rational decision-maker would regard a new
consideration as "so obviously material" if it was realistically capable of causing
the authority to reach a different conclusion. Ultimately, this is a matter for the
court, although what officers regard as material may be accepted by the court when
conducting its own analysis: e.g., *R. (Leckhampton Green Land Action Group
Limited) v Tewkesbury* [2017] EWHC 198 (Admin) at [94], [112], per Holgate J.

100   In summary, the *Kides* principle is that "having regard to" material considerations
in s.70(2) is not a requirement that with every new material consideration arising
after the grant of planning permission, but before the decision notice, there has to
be a specific referral back to members. If at the date at which the decision notice
is issued the authority has considered all material considerations with the application
in mind there is no need to remit. As guidance, and in light of common sense and
the circumstances of the particular case, this means that a delegated officer must
be satisfied that the members are aware of the new consideration, and it has
considered it with the application in mind.

101   For these purposes, a material consideration is one where the court takes the
view that a rational decision-maker would regard it as "so obviously material" that
it must be taken into account. In the real world not every new consideration which
arises can be remitted to the authority. If no rational decision-maker would regard
a consideration as "so obviously material" that it must be taken into account, that

is the end of the matter. Given the practicalities of decision-making, a delegated officer will need to take a view as to whether something is a material consideration. Ultimately it is an issue for the court to decide, but the court may find the officer's view persuasive.

1: Alleged breach of s70(2) duty and the Kides principle

102   The claimant contends that new material considerations arose in the period between 19 November 2020 when the committee made its decision and 24 March 2022, when planning permission was granted, which were not considered by the committee. Each of these would tip the balance of the decision-maker's scales to some extent one way or the other. In the claimant's submission the changes were threefold.

(a) Reduction of developable area resulting from new BNG proposals

103   The claimant began with the developable area which the committee considered in November 2020 - to accommodate "up to" 170 dwellings and the adopted VALP for the site, which required it to deliver "at least" 170 dwellings. The officer's report 2022 stated that the revised biodiversity net gain (BNG) proposals led to a reduction in the amount of development and noted that updated plans showed a further reduction in the number of houses to accommodate it. That reduced amount of development was confirmed by the council's ecologist, first as a result of the fourth BNG proposal, and then in the fifth BNG proposal.

104   On the claimant's case this reduction was shown in the plans, which I was taken to at the hearing. Compared with the October 2015 feasibility plan and the September 2016 illustrative landscape masterplan there was a reduction in the number of dwellings shown in the plans accompanying the fourth BNG proposals (the January 2022 illustrative landscape masterplan and the January 2022 feasibility plan) and a yet further reduction in the plans accompanying the fifth BNG proposals (the February 2022 proposed habitats plan and the February 2022 urban street planting plan). In all it was submitted that there was a reduction of 11 buildings from the planned 170 dwellings.

105   This reduction, the claimant submitted, was important. VALP policy MMO006 required the site to be developed for at least 170 dwellings, and if that was not achieved there would be non-compliance with the development plan. Further, the number of homes to be delivered by the site was important as the contribution to housing delivery - a key benefit that had been relied on in permitting the development. Finally, there was national policy in the NPPF, that planning decisions support development that makes efficient use of land and optimal use of the potential of each site. All this needed to be considered and returned to the committee.

106   These submissions need to be considered against the background that this was an outline application which approved the principle of development but where layout and scale are reserved. The configuration of housing is yet to come; the plans available are simply illustrative of how this might be brought forward. The reality is that the developer will be keen, in line with planning policy, to maximise the number of dwellings on the site. A further background factor is that the BNG calculations were part of an ongoing assessment process, a process which will continue until the reserved matters stage. Thirdly, the inspector's fixing on "at least" 170 dwellings was in the context, as he explained at paragraph 241, quoted

earlier, that consistent with government policy the council had to increase the supply of housing.

107   The reduction in the habitat unit figure from 11.51 percent as advised to the committee in the 2020 report, to 10.21 percent at the time of the decision to grant planning permission, is not in my view one that a rational decision-maker would regard as so obviously material that the committee might have reached a different conclusion on the grant of permission if they had known. That was the conclusion in the 2022 officer's report, and in my view she was right. As to the change in developable area and the number of dwellings, the committee was told in the 2020 officer's report that the development would be "up to 170" dwellings. The committee also knew that the draft allocation policy in the VALP identified the 170 dwellings figure as a minimum. As we have seen the committee considered that the application complied with the emerging VALP, and also the NPPF. The grant of outline planning permission for 170 dwellings must be seen in that light and also in light of the reality that at that outline stage the layout and hence the exact number of dwellings were yet to be determined. As with the change in the BNG figures I agree with the 2022 officer's report that this would not represent a material change.

(b) VALP inspector re College Farm Road (Mill Lane) traffic mitigation measures

108   The impact of the development's traffic locally was a critical issue in the determination of the application, in particular on College Farm Road (Mill Lane). The claimant explains in his witness statement how controversial traffic was. The 2020 officer's report at paragraph 4.1 also noted that the impact on traffic and congestion was a key concern. The VALP inspector dealt with it, as we have seen. The three-member call-in request in September 2021 specifically referred to this issue as one of the reasons for requesting the matter to be called-in.

109   The claimant's case is that there was a change in the stance of the council regarding traffic, which as a new material consideration should have been returned to the committee. The advice in the 2020 officer's report was that the aim of the mitigation measures was to "deter" the development's traffic from using College Farm Road. However, the claimant submits, the Council's evidence before the VALP inspector was different, and on analysis the inspector concluded that rather than deter (or "dissuade") traffic from using College Farm Road, the aim of the mitigation measures was to accommodate development traffic: see DL240. (As we have seen, the inspector referred to "discontinuities" between the two sets of advice.) In the claimant's submission, it was wrong for the officer to seek to reconcile the two sets of advice in her 2022 report. The matter should have gone back to committee. Even if the correct position was that the works would both deter and accommodate development traffic, that position would still be different from the advice given to the committee in November 2020.

110   In my judgment there is not the degree of contradiction that the claimant presents. The context of the "deter" and "accommodate" advice was different. The "deter" advice to members in the 2020 officer's report was the concern which had been raised, including from the claimant and the Maids Moreton and Foscote Action Group, about the traffic which the development would generate, in particular the impact on College Farm Road and the need to deter traffic because of the junction of that road with the A422: see paras. 5.33, 5.35. By contrast the context of the advice to the inspector was his concern with plan making, taking account of this

and other allocated sites, and whether this allocation was sound in terms, inter alia, of accommodating the inevitable increase in traffic associated with any development. That is evident in his comments at DL239-241, referred to earlier.

111   As described earlier in the judgment, the 2022 officer's report grappled in detail with the issue of what the inspector later characterised as the discontinuities of advice. That report concluded that the proposal and the advice put forward by the council for both the planning application and during the VALP hearings resulted in the same conclusions, those the inspector reached in his report. In my view, the officer was correct when she said that there was no material change in the circumstances to justify a referral back to the committee. This is not surprising since there was never any suggestion in the 2020 officer's report that all development traffic would be deterred from College Farm Lane; obviously not. Members would appreciate that additional traffic from the development would be generated, and that was why the traffic calming measures were needed, to moderate (deter) it and also to accommodate it safely, as at the junction of College Farm Road and the A422.

112   The 2020 officer's report advised that as regards traffic, if highways improvements were secured the proposal would be compliant with the emerging VALP (with modifications). The VALP was then adopted. In as much as policies T1-T3 require additional traffic from developments to be accommodated, it is unrealistic to suggest that the inspector did not appreciate that as a result of the traffic measures (which might be added to), traffic would be accommodated on College Farm Road to an extent by being deterred from using it. Overall, there was a consistency between what the committee found to be necessary in 2020 and the now adopted policies of the VALP.

(c) Adoption of VALP

113   Here the claimant contends that section 38(6) of the Planning and Compulsory Purchase Act 2004 ("the 2004 Act") required the planning authority to reach a conclusion about the compliance of the amended proposed development with the new statutory development plan as a whole, as part of the statutory presumption in its favour. For these purposes the 2020 officer's report did not reach any conclusion on the development's compliance with the VALP taken as a whole. Moreover, the 2020 report decided the application using the "tilted balance" test in paragraph 11(d) of the NPPF. Regardless of whether the content of these policies had changed, their status and how they featured in the decision-making process set out in statute had changed radically.

114   In my view this submission has an air of unreality. Certainly section 38(6) of the 2004 Act requires that, if relevant, a determination must be made in accordance with the development plan unless material considerations indicate otherwise. But the reality is that this is what occurred. The VALP was at an advanced stage when considered by the committee. It details (as modified) were set out at paragraph 5.5 of the 2020 officer's report. Members in approving the officer's recommendation to grant planning permission in November 2020 were therefore deciding that the application was in accordance with the then emerging VALP, in particular the principle of development and that there was compliance with relevant policies. The VALP was then adopted without change.

115   For the reasons given earlier there were no materially different circumstances when permission was granted in 2022. The claimant has not identified any way in which the application before the committee in 2020 conflicts with the adopted VALP. On various occasions the 2020 officer's report explained expressly that the development was consistent with the VALP. Examples referred to earlier in the judgment were in paragraphs 5.5 (principles of development), 5.69 (transport), and 5.102 (ecology). It is clear to me that in accepting the recommendations in the 2020 officer's report members regarded the application as in accordance with the policies in the emerging VALP (as modified), which became the adopted plan. There is therefore only the issue of weight, which goes nowhere when the VALP was adopted and in fact reinforced the committee's conclusion that permission should be granted. All this was what the officer's report of 2022 rightly concluded.

(d) The overall position

116   The claimant contends that matters (a)-(c) if they did not qualify as a material consideration by themselves did so cumulatively. In my view this adds nothing. Looking at the position overall, the committee had resolved to grant planning permission in 2020, subject to the three conditions in the resolution. What the officer had to do was to ensure those conditions were met, in particular the completion of the legal agreement. She had also to consider, applying the principle in *Kides*, whether the application should be taken back to the committee. That was what she did in the 2022 report. In my view her conclusion was correct that there was no basis to revert to the committee taking the matters (a)-(c) either individually or cumulatively.

2: Alleged misunderstanding/misapplication of Kides principle

117   The claimant contends that the 2022 officer's report fundamentally misunderstood and misapplied the *Kides* test. In considering whether there was a material change to the conclusions reached in a matter in 2020, indeed in one case (at paragraph 5.2) asking whether a new material consideration could, in the officer's view, change the outcome of the committee's decision, the 2022 officer's report was incorrectly applying the test in *Kides* by invoking a much higher hurdle.

118   As ever it is necessary with this officer's report to eschew an unduly legalistic or unduly critical approach but rather to engage in a reasonably benevolent and fair reading, taking it as a whole: *Mansell v Tonbridge and Malling BC* [2017] EWCA Civ 1314 at [42], per Lindblom LJ; *R. (Lee Valley Regional Park Authority) v Epping Forest DC* [2016] EWCA Civ 404 at [31], per Lindblom LJ. In my view, on a fair, objective assessment of the 2022 Report (see especially paragraphs 2.11, 3.31, 5.1 and 5.2 referred to earlier in the judgment), the officer adopted an approach applying the *Kides* principle. Ultimately it is for the court when, as in this case, her decision is challenged. As I have explained, I have reached the same conclusions as she did.

Ground 2: Alleged Unlawful Consideration of New BNG

119   The claimant accepted that although this is a separate ground there is some overlap with ground 1 on the facts. In summary this ground is that the 2022 officer's report did not consider the extent of the reduction in the developable area proposed;

whether dwellings would be lost as a result; and whether the development might fall below the "at least 170" policy requirement in MMO006. This followed from the revisions to the BNG proposals and the reduction in the developable area proposed. As a matter of law, the claimant submitted, the officers failed to grapple with this issue, contrary to the *Tameside* duty (*Secretary of State for Education v Tameside MBC* [1977] A.C. 1014); left relevant material considerations out of account, in particular compliance or otherwise with the VALP; and failed to give reasons about the issue. Even with an application for outline planning permission, a developer had to provide sufficient information to enable the local planning authority to form a proper judgment of what is proposed; *Crystal Property (London) Ltd v Secretary of State for Communities and Local Government* [2016] EWCA Civ 1265 at [5], [34], per Lindblom LJ.

120   In my view none of this goes anywhere. The *Tameside* duty sets a high threshold, and that applies in the planning context as elsewhere: see *R. (Hough) v Secretary of State for the Home Department* [2022] EWHC 1635 (Admin) at [92], per Lieven J. The issue is whether the inquiry made by a planning authority is so inadequate that no reasonable planning authority could suppose it had sufficient material available to grant planning permission. That cannot be said in this case, where after the revision of the BNG in 2022 the council's ecologist was satisfied that the 10 percent BNG could still be achieved, but the exact layout and location of habitat and biodiversity sites would be subject to the detailed planning stage. It is not clear to me what relevant considerations the council did not take into account, but if it is the number of houses that has been addressed already, especially in the context of an outline planning application. *Crystal Property* was a different case involving one building and details in the application were specific by comparison. The issue of compliance with the VALP has been addressed earlier.

121   The claimant also challenges the standard of reasons on this matter. It is horn book law that officers' reports need not refer to every matter, and reasons need only be briefly stated. Only if there is a genuine as opposed to a forensic doubt as to what was decided and why will a reasons challenge succeed. Here paragraph 3.31 of the 2022 officer's report, referred to above, set out how the officers, including the council's ecology officer, were satisfied that the conditions imposed on the permission were sufficient to ensure a net gain to biodiversity. I accept the council's submission that this was a rational and clearly expressed conclusion.

Ground 3: Breach of A Legitimate Expectation

122   The claimant contends that the council had, through its express statements and past practice, made a commitment to local residents that the developer's planning application would be returned to the committee for reconsideration and the council should abide by that. There was the email of 25 January 2021 from the council's director for legal and democratic services to Ms Kate Pryke (acting on behalf of the Maids Moreton and Foscote Action Group), quoted earlier in the judgment, referring to Mr Elvin KC's legal advice stating that it was his view, accepted by the council, that some of the matters needed to be reconsidered. There was also the 24 February 2021 letter to Ms Pryke referring to the decision to refer the application back to committee. As to past practice the claimant refers to the application having been taken back to the committee in November 2020, and to the 2 May 2019 letter to Ms Pryke, that an application would be referred back to

committee if there was a significant change in policy or circumstances that would influence the decision made which the committee would need to consider.

123   To ground a legitimate expectation there needs to be a clear and unambiguous undertaking, and the authority giving the undertaking will not be allowed to depart from it unless it is fair to do so: *Finucane's Application for Judicial Review, Re* [2019] UKSC 7 at [62]. The council sought to argue that none of this amounted to a clear and unambiguous undertaking to remit matters to the committee. All these statements were in some way qualified. The statements of 25 January 2021 and 24 February 2021 were on the back of Mr Elvin's legal advice, not addressed to the public, and in any event unsolicited advice not germane to the issues he had been asked to address. It was the council's intention to take the matter back to committee, but that did not constitute a promise to do so. There was no past practice.

124   The first part of the email of 25 January 2021 does not, contrary to the claimant's opinion, contain a promise to remit the matter to members, only that further consideration would be given to the implications of the inspector's intention to have a further hearing. The second part of the email refers to "any reference" back, which is somewhat equivocal. However, the letter from the council's director for legal and democratic services to Ms Kate Pryke of 24 February 2021 referred expressly to the decision to take the application back to committee. That, to my mind, is a clear and unambiguous statement that the matter will be remitted to the committee. For completeness I should add that there is, in my judgment, nothing constituting a past practice to the effect that the matter would be remitted.

125   The issue then becomes whether the council could resile from its statement to remit matters to the committee. The claimant's case is that it was unfair for the council to do so and it could not be justified. In his witness statement the claimant states that he held back from making representations both as an individual and parish councillor on the basis that he would be able to do so to the committee in person. There was no time, he adds, to make representations on the 2022 officer's report since it appeared at the same time as the grant of planning consent. For the claimant it is submitted that there were very good reasons to return to the committee given how matters such as traffic and biodiversity had moved on in the 18 months since the 2020 decision. That was quite apart from the opportunity it would afford objectors in making oral representations directly to members.

126   Where a legitimate expectation is frustrated, it is for the authority to identify any overriding interest on which it relies to justify this, and it is then a matter for the court to weigh the requirements of fairness against that interest: *Paponette v Attorney General of Trinidad and Tobago* [2010] UKPC 32 at [37]. The court will ask whether that frustration was objectively justified as a proportionate measure in the circumstances: [38] (citing with approval Laws LJ in *R. (Nadarajah) v Secretary of State for the Home Department* [2005] EWCA Civ 1363 at [68]). The burden is on the authority to prove that its failure or refusal to honour its promises is justified in the public interest.

127   In my view not remitting the matter to the committee was a proportionate response to a legitimate aim pursued in the public interest. The intention to refer the application back to the committee expressed in the communications with Ms Pryke was in the context of the council's expectation that the position as regards the allocation of the application site in the VALP could change, following the further hearing the inspector had scheduled. The allocation was adopted without amendment. The premise that the application would need to be remitted in light

of an adverse finding on the inspector's part was removed. Given that, coupled with my findings that no material considerations had arisen in the eighteen months since the committee's decision in November 2020, there was no good reason for remission to occur.

128   Moreover, there was no unfairness to the claimant and to others such as the Maids Moreton and Foscote Action Group. It is no criticism, but the fact is that they have not missed an opportunity to make representations. The 2020 officer's report has in its appendix many pages of representations. Objectors to the application, including the claimant, made oral representations at the November 2020 meeting of the committee. The 2022 officer's report is replete with responses to representations, as well as consultant's reports, and the s.106 agreement attracted many representations as well. There was the three-member call-in request in September 2021 and the Maids Moreton and Foscote Action Group letter in early January 2022. In relation to the VALP, the inspector had convened the further hearing to which the claimant and others made representations. Finally, given that no new material considerations had arisen, it is difficult to see how further representations could have made a difference.

Ground 4: Delegated Authority Exceeded

129   The claimant raises an issue of *vires*, that the decision of the officers to grant planning permission in 2022 exceeded their delegation.

130   On his case the committee's 2020 resolution confined the officers' authority to approving the planning application subject to (i) the satisfactory completion of a legal agreement to secure various matters; (ii) the securing of a district licence to address protected species; and (iii) conditions as considered appropriate by officers; or, if any of these requirements were not achieved, the application was to be refused. In other words, the claimant submitted, the resolution meant that officers could only consider whether (i) to (iii) had been met and, if so, to approve, if not, to refuse the application.

131   Instead, the claimant continued, the 2022 officer's report showed that the officers had gone well beyond their delegated authority, indeed, had reassessed the proposal's planning merits. They had assessed compliance with the new statutory development plan following the adoption of the VALP and considered the 2021 NPPF. As well they had considered alterations to the scheme, for example, those resulting from the BNG revisions, and the basis of the inspector's conclusions relating to the College Farm Road traffic mitigation. They had also considered further consultee reports and representations, for example on BNG. Yet all these powers of dealing with the application had been retained by the committee.

132   The law as to delegation was addressed by the Court of Appeal in *R. (on the application of Flynn) v Southwark LBC* [2021] EWCA Civ 827. Sir Keith Lindblom SPT (with whom Baker and Lewis LJJ agreed) said that that there was nothing unusual in a local planning authority to proceed by delegating development control functions to planning officers: [40]. An objective and realistic approach had to be taken to understanding a planning committee's decision in this regard: [41]. He added:

"41 …The court will look for the members' intention as it appears from the words of the resolution. To grasp the meaning and effect of a committee's resolution to grant planning permission, one must read it in a straightforward way, keeping in mind the relevant context. Part of the context may be an officer's report recommending the grant of planning permission, and it can generally be assumed that if the members have accepted such a recommendation they will have done so following the officer's advice."

133   He considered what was implicit in the resolution in that case: [48]. However, he added, the delegation rested in the resolution itself: [49].

134   In my view an objective and realistic approach to understanding the planning committee's delegation was that when the officers were later considering whether they should grant permission pursuant to that delegated authority, they were entitled to assess whether circumstances had changed in such a way as to require that the application be referred back to the committee. That is the relevant context. What occurred was that the officers in the present case gave careful and genuine consideration to whether the range of new material – including the many representations and consultation responses - meant that they should remit the matter. In doing this they were not engaged in matters outside the delegation but acting consistently with it through the exercise of their lawful discussion. To put it another way, they were doing what was implicit in the 2020 resolution. They cannot be said to be reassessing the planning merits.

Ground 5: EIA Screening

135   The claimant advanced two broad errors in relation to the November 2015 screening opinion, the first, that there were fundamental errors in the opinion in breach of the 2011 regulations; the second, that there was an unlawful failure to review the screening decision when circumstances had changed, and new information emerged. Accordingly, the planning permission is unlawful as it was granted in breach of the 2011 Regulations.

The relevant legal principles

136   In *R. (on the application of Bateman) v South Cambridgeshire DC* [2011] EWCA Civ 157, Moore-Bick LJ approved earlier authority that the decision taken on a screening opinion must be carefully and conscientiously considered and based on sufficient and accurate information. The opinion need not be elaborate but must demonstrate that the issues have been understood and considered: [11]. The limited nature and scope of a screening opinion was emphasised. Moore-Bick LJ said that it was

> "[20] …important to bear in mind the nature of what is involved in giving a screening opinion. It is not intended to involve a detailed assessment of factors relevant to the grant of planning permission; that comes later and will ordinarily include an assessment of environmental factors, among others. Nor does it involve a full assessment of any environmental effects. It involves only a decision, almost inevitably on the basis of less than complete information, whether an EIA needs to be undertaken at all. [It is] important, therefore, that the court should not impose too high a burden on planning authorities in relation to what is no more than a procedure intended to identify the relatively small number of cases in which development is likely to have significant effects on the environment".

137   This passage was approved in *Kenyon v Secretary of State for Housing, Communities and Local Government* [2020] EWCA Civ 302 at [13], per Coulson LJ (with whom David Richards and Lewison LJJ agreed) emphasising the limited nature and scope of a screening opinion.

138   Moore-Bick LJ went on the say that when adopting a screening opinion, the planning authority must provide sufficient information to enable anyone interested in the decision to see that proper consideration has been given to the possible environmental effects of the development and to understand the reasons for the decision: [21]. Reasons for a decision of this nature need not be extensive, provided that they are clear: [23].

139   In this respect *Keynon* also approved the following passage in Mummery LJ's judgment in *Bateman*:

> "40. In my judgment, the decision not to have an EIA is a significantly different kind of decision from a refusal or grant of planning permission. The reasons for a preliminary administrative decision whether or not to have an EIA do not have to satisfy the same standards of information and reasoning as would apply to a substantive decision on a planning application. The degree of 'grappling' is different, more provisional and less exacting..."

(1) Errors in the screening opinion

140   The claimant identified what it contended were five separate errors of law and approach in the screening opinion, so that the decision based on it was in its submission unlawful, whether the errors were taken individually or cumulatively.

(a) Actual development not screened

141   The claimant contended firstly that what was screened was approximately 10 percent less than the actual development proposed, in terms of both site area and the number of dwellings – the screening was 7.95ha, up to 155 dwellings, whereas the permission covered 170 dwellings with a size of 8.7ha. The scale and therefore likely impact of the proposed development was under-estimated.

142   In *R. (on the application of CBRE Lionbrook (General Partners) Ltd) v Rugby BC* [2014] EWHC 646 (Admin) Lindblom J said that the concept of a development having been the subject of a screening opinion was broad enough to include a previous screening process for an earlier version of the proposal, so long as the nature and extent of any subsequent changes to the proposal did not give rise to a realistic prospect of a different outcome if another formal screening process were to be gone through: [47].

143   In my view the claimant has not demonstrated that there is such a prospect. Given what a screening opinion is designed to do, the claimant has not persuaded me that the change in the size of the proposal would make a difference to the outcome of the screening opinion. This was the situation envisaged by Lindblom J in *Lionbrook*, where there was no legal error found in relying on a screening decision relating to an earlier and different version of the proposal.

(b) Cumulative effects

144   Here the claimant contends that the screening opinion applied the wrong legal test for cumulative effects in that it only considered whether the development was part of a larger scheme, whereas it should have considered the possible cumulative effects with other existing, approved, or planned developments: 2011 EIA Regulations, reg,4(6), Sch.3, para.1. Quite apart from matters such as the inadequacy of Anglian Water's Buckingham centre to cope with wastewater, the inspector had noted the merging of Maids Moreton with Buckingham, and also the traffic, water, and sewerage issues which were similar in other housing allocation sites around Buckingham and had the potential for cumulative effects (in particular the Moreton Road scheme near Maids Moreton for 130 dwellings).

145   To my mind the answer to this submission is contained in what Lindblom J said in *Hockley v Essex CC* [2013] EWHC 4051 (Admin), which was approved in *Kenyon v Secretary of State for Housing, Communities and Local Government* [2020] EWCA Civ 302 at [15]. In that passage Lindblom J said:

> "102. There has to be a sensible limit to what a screening decision-maker is expected to do…Conjecture about future development on other sites that might or might not act with the development in question to produce indirect, secondary or cumulative effects is not in the screening decision-maker's remit. I do not think the precautionary approach extends to that. And when it is suggested in a claim for judicial review that a screening decision was deficient because some potential cumulative effect was left out, it is not enough for a claimant simply to point to other developments in the locality that have been or might be approved, and to leave it to the court to work out whether any aggregate effects were unlikely to be significant. Unless it is obvious that relevant and potentially significant effects on the environment have been overlooked, the court will need some objective evidence to show this was so. It will need to be satisfied that the authority responsible for the screening decision was aware, or ought to have been, of the potential cumulative effects; that the screening opinion could not reasonably have been negative if those potential effects had been considered; and that this was, or should have been, apparent to the authority at the time."

146   Here the claimant has not provided objective evidence to show that the screening opinion would not reasonably have been negative if these potential cumulative effects had been considered. As regards any cumulative effects with sewerage and wastewater, I note in passing that Anglian Water in its 5 November 2020 report had said that it was obligated and would take the necessary steps to deal with this, and also that the highways authority in November 2018 had indicated that it would mitigate additional traffic travelling into (and through) Buckingham in the Buckingham traffic strategy.

(c) Wrong test – substantial, not significant effects

147   The claimant submits that the wrong legal test was applied because of references to "substantial" and "substantive" effects in the wording of the screening opinion. I agree with the council and developer that this is the kind of legalism and forensic analysis of language which was to be deprecated. In any event at the outset the screening opinion stated that it was determining "the likelihood of significant

effects" and it concluded that the proposal "would not have a significant impact". In other words, the screening opinion applied the correct legal test.

(d) Absorption capacity wrongly deferred

148   Here the claimant submits that the wrong approach was adopted as regards issue (ii)(c) of the screening opinion, by saying in relation to absorption capacity that the impact would be assessed during consideration of the subsequent planning application. There was no careful and conscientious consideration of this issue, and the absence of sufficient information about the impact of the project to make an informed judgement meant the doubt should have been resolved in favour of requiring an EIA.

149   In my view the clause beginning "but" was an aside, not a qualification, recognising the reality that that the absorption capacity would need to be assessed during the consideration of any planning application. In the first part of that sentence the council stated a definite conclusion, that "the proposal is not considered to raise substantive issues relating to the identified criteria" in the 2011 Regulations. I accept the council's submission that the claimant's approach is a misreading of issue (ii)(c).

(e) Inadequate reasons

150   The claimant's last point was that the screening opinion did not contain adequate reasons explaining clearly and precisely the full reasons for its conclusion regarding whether the development was likely to have significant effects on the environment by virtue of factors such as its nature, size or location.

151   The claimant accepts, as indeed he must, that there were comments on each of the individual criteria in Schedule 3. In my view, albeit crisp, they were adequate, in accord with their purpose (as Mummery LJ explained at paragraph [40] of his judgment in *Bateman*). As to the claimant's point that there were no reasons given for the overall conclusion there is, in short, no need for reasons for reasons.

(2) Unlawful failure to review the screening decision

152   The first issue to consider under this head is the council's assertion at paragraph 57 of its summary grounds of defence, that it had considered whether any changes since 2015 necessitated a further screening process and concluded in 2020 that they did not. The claimant challenges the truth of that assertion. Despite the claimant having raised the matter in its Reply and subsequent correspondence, his case was that there was no evidence to support the council's assertion, either disclosure of any document under the duty of candour or a witness statement. The contemporaneous evidence, the 2020 officer's report, referred only to the 2015 screening, not to any reconsideration.

153   This is a troubling issue and it is better for me to proceed on the assumption that there was no consideration in 2020 whether the conclusion in the negative screening opinion of 2015 still held. However, I cannot accept that a solicitor, knowing her duties to this court, would sign the statement of truth to the summary grounds without having been assured about the assertion at paragraph 57.

Legal principles

154   In *Swire v Ashford BC* [2021] EWHC 702 (Admin) Sir Duncan Ouseley J held, in general terms, that for an issue under regulation 3 of the Town and Country Planning (Environmental Impact Assessment) Regulations 2017 to arise – prohibiting the grant of permission for EIA development without an EIA - there has to be a change in circumstances after a negative screening opinion and that change has to be rationally capable of leading to a change in the view that the development was not an EIA development: [79]-[84]. In coming to that conclusion, he drew on Dove J's judgment in *R. (Milton (Peterborough) Estates Co) v Ryedale DC* [2015] EWHC 1948 (Admin) at [40]-[43]. Specifically, where there has been no reconsideration of changes since a negative screening opinion, Ouseley J said:

> "82 …the grant will still be lawful and not in breach of Reg.3, if no reasonable planning officer, having reached the screening opinion that it did, would have thought that the changes could make the development EIA development, that is one likely to have significant environmental effects. If a reasonable planning officer could have so concluded, the grant of permission will be unlawful. What would be tested is not the rationality of a conclusion or planning judgment by the officer, because there is none, but the lawfulness of the grant, in the absence of a conclusion that it was not EIA development."

The claimant's changed circumstances

155   In this case the claimant contends that a reasonable planning officer could not have concluded that notwithstanding the changes since 2015 this development was not an EIA development. The changes which the claimant contends might have led to a real prospect of a different screening outcome were eightfold, two concerning issues already addressed, the increase from 155 to 170 in the number of dwellings and the increase in traffic. As to these it will be clear from what was said earlier that the claimant did not persuade me that the change in the size of the proposal would make a difference to the outcome of the screening opinion. As to traffic, the screening opinion had said that additional vehicle movements were unlikely to be of a substantive nature.

156   The other six changes were, on the claimant's case:

> (i) The site's status as best and most versatile (BMV) land was identified in the agricultural land classification report in February 2019. However, Natural England's high-level mapping in 2010, which the claimant accepts the Council relied on, indicated that the area was grade 3, good to moderate, and the Council's sustainability appraisal for the VALP classified it as 3a. More importantly, the classification report of 2019 concluded that loss of the land did not represent a significant loss locally or regionally in terms of BMV land. In my view none of this meant, as the claimant contends, a wholly different and incompatible conclusion was to be drawn from what the screening opinion had stated at paragraphs (i)(c) and (ii)(b).
> (ii) The 2020 officer's report recognised "significant adverse visual impacts from the development". But this of itself is misleading, since the 2020 officer's report at paragraph 5.78 went on to say that this would be in the immediate vicinity of the site – which is what the screening opinion had

said at (iii)(d). Indeed, the officer's report had added that there was scope for the existing relationship between the settlement and the open countryside to be visually enhanced.

(iii) The screening opinion omitted to mention the nearby Foscote Reservoir & Wood Site SSSI, and in its report of 2020 Natural England said that without suggested mitigation the development would damage or destroy the interest features for which the SSSI had been notified. It is hard to conceive that Aylesbury would not have been aware of such an important matter as the SSSI when preparing the screening opinion. In any event, Natural England was not objecting to the development: with appropriate mitigation it took the view, as seen earlier, that the SSSI could be protected, and advised that this might be achieved through an appropriate planning condition.

(iv) Contaminated land, omitted from the screening opinion, but contained in the report of the pollution control officer, who stated high levels of arsenic had been found. However, the council's pollution control officer, in commenting on the consultant's report, underlined that the arsenic was naturally occurring, and while recognising that further work might be undertaken made clear that it was not considered a significant risk to human health and the levels were in line with the current guidance.

(v) Anglian Water stated on 5 November 2020 that its treatment centre did not have capacity to deal with the development, and that the development would lead to an unacceptable risk of flooding. Again, this is only half the story. Anglian Water said it was obliged to deal with the foul flows from the development and would work with the developer to ensure any infrastructure improvements to address flooding risk.

(vi) Cumulative effects from other developments in the area, for which planning permission had been granted, particularly on traffic impacts. In my view the objective evidence which as regards cumulative effects Lindblom J referred to in *Hockley v Essex CC* [2013] EWHC 4051 (Admin) is not available, even as regards traffic impacts.

157   The upshot in my view is that a reasonable planning officer would not have thought these changes, such as they were, could change the outcome of the 2015 screening individually or cumulatively. In other words, a further screening would have produced the same conclusion as the 2015 screening that the development would not have significant effects on the environment.

Ground 6: Misinterpretation/misdirection on NPPF re BMV

158   Paragraphs 170 and 171 of the 2019 NPPF provided, as relevant:

"171. Planning policies and decisions should contribute to and enhance the natural and local environment by…
(b) recognising the intrinsic character and beauty of the countryside, and the wider benefits from natural capital and ecosystem services – including the economic and other benefits of the best and most versatile agricultural land…

> 171. Plans should: distinguish between the hierarchy of international, national and locally designated sites; allocate land with the least environmental or amenity value, where consistent with other policies in this Framework..."
>
> Footnote 53 to the paragraph 171 read: "Where significant development of agricultural land is demonstrated to be necessary, areas of poorer quality land should be preferred to those of a higher quality."

159   Paragraph 170(b) applied to both planning policies and decisions, whereas paragraph 171 applied to plans only.

160   The claimant contends that the 2020 officer's report at paragraphs 5.80-5.81, referred to earlier in the judgment, confused paragraphs 170(b) and 171, footnote 53, applying the significant development criterion – which the report said was greater than 20 hectares from paragraph 171 – although it had no place in relation to paragraph 170(b). In the claimant's submission the officer's report had consequently misinterpreted and misrepresented the NPPF policy and materially misled the committee. Members should have been advised that NPPF policy on BMV decisions should contribute to and enhance the natural and local environment by recognising its economic and other benefits. Instead, they were advised that the loss of BMV land was not a weighty material consideration in terms of NPPF policy as the development was less than 20 hectares and therefore not significant development. Overall this decision regarding planning permission was finely balanced, evident in the split vote in the committee. BMV was not a peripheral issue.

161   In considering these submissions, it is necessary to recall the well-known law regarding officer's reports and advice to members: first, planning officers' reports must be read not in an unduly critical way, but fairly and as a whole; and secondly, the question for the court is whether the officer has failed to guide the members sufficiently, or has significantly misled them on a material matter: *R. (Lee Valley Regional Park Authority) v Epping Forest DC* [2016] EWCA Civ 404 at [31], per Lindblom LJ (with whom Underhill and Treacy LJJ agreed); *R. (on the application of The Co-Operative Group Ltd) v West Lancashire BC* [2021] EWHC 507 (Admin) at [13], per Holgate J.

162   In this case members were told that loss of the site, 8ha of agricultural land, would be of limited weight. In two paragraphs, 5.80-5.81, they were advised that most of the site was BMV. They were also expressly advised that they needed to consider the role of what was then paragraph 170 of the NPPF, and that paragraph 170b meant that they should take into account the economic and other benefits of BMV. So far, so good. Footnote 53 to paragraph 171 was then quoted in the text of the report, without informing them that that it was a footnote, or that it related only to plan making. They were then referred to the threshold for consulting Natural England regarding significance and that this site was under it – both points correct.

163   The result was that members were not told the full story about the guidance proffered in the NPPF. But it is important that the inaccuracy was not as to a relevant fact (or facts), or as to a statutory requirement. Further, while the loss of agricultural land was not a peripheral issue, which at one point the council seemed to suggest, the reality was that it was overshadowed by other issues such as housing supply and biodiversity, in particular by transport and traffic matters which featured over many pages and many paragraphs of the report. The reality also was that the conclusion in the 2019 consultant's report assessing the land was that the loss of

the site to agriculture did not represent a significant loss locally or regionally in terms of BMV and was almost inevitable with any development in the area. In my view the report cannot be said to have contained material errors, failed to guide the members sufficiently, or significantly mislead them on a matter material to their decision.

Conclusion

164   For the reasons given I dismiss the claim. There is no need for me to consider the alternative way the council and developer put their case, that pursuant to section 31(2A) of the Senior Courts Act 1981 relief should be refused on the basis that it is highly likely that the outcome would not have been substantially different absent the alleged errors.

PORR BAU GMBH

EUROPEAN COURT OF JUSTICE (FIRST CHAMBER)

(C-238/21)

A. Arabadjiev (Rapporteur), President of the Chamber, L. Bay
Larsen, Vice-President of the Court, acting as Judge of the First
Chamber, P.G. Xuereb, A. Kumin and I. Ziemele, Judges: L. Medina,
AG: 17 November 2022

EU:C:2022:885; [2023] Env. L.R. 19

⚖ EU law; Excavation; National legislation; Soils; Statutory interpretation; Waste

H1 *EU law—waste—Directive 2008/98—concepts of "waste" and "by-product"—*
"end of waste" status—use by farmers of uncontaminated excavated material from
construction for soil adaptation or improvement—national law requiring such
material to be classified as "waste" even if falling within the concept of
"by-product"—such status as "waste" only lost when used directly as a substitute
and holder satisfied formal criteria irrelevant for the purposes of environmental
protection—whether national provisions in breach of Directive

H2   A request for a preliminary ruling was made in proceedings where a number of
farmers had approached a construction company (P) to obtain excavated materials
for the purpose of soil adaptation or improvement. P supplied uncontaminated
excavated materials of the highest quality class for excavated soil under Austrian
law. It sought a declaration that the excavated materials supplied did not constitute
"waste" and, in the alternative, that the proposed works did not constitute an activity
subject to an obligation to pay a contribution in respect of contaminated sites. The
Austrian authorities found that the materials in question did constitute "waste"
under national law and that their "end-of-waste" status had not been achieved,
primarily on the ground that formal criteria laid down in the Federal Waste
Management Plan had not been complied with. The referring court noted that the
materials had undergone a checking operation, with the result that they could be
used directly. It stated that they were used for the purpose of improving agricultural
structures, that there was a need for materials, that the technical requirements had
been complied with and that, in addition, there were no harmful effects on the
environment or on health. Moreover, the aim of such an approach was to prevent
waste and to substitute such materials for raw materials. Under Austrian law, only
two activities enabled "end-of-waste" status to be achieved; (1) preparing for re-use
by checking, cleaning or repairing; and (2) the actual use of the materials to
substitute raw materials. For excavated materials, the applicable criteria were more
restrictive, since preparing for re-use did not achieve their "end-of-waste" status.

Thus, that court took the view that "end-of-waste" status was restricted in a manner contrary to EU law.

H3   The questions referred asked, essentially, whether arts 3, 5(1) and 6(1) of Directive 2008/98 precluded national legislation under which uncontaminated excavated materials, in the highest quality class under national law; (1) had to be classified as "waste" even if it were determined that those materials fell within the concept of "by-product"; and (2) only lost that "waste" status when they were used directly as a substitute and their holder satisfied the formal criteria which were irrelevant for the purposes of environmental protection.

H4   **Held:**

H5   (1) Legislation classifying such materials as "waste" where their holder neither intended nor was required to discard them and those materials met the conditions laid down in art.5(1) for being classified as "by-products", was contrary to the Directive. It was for the referring court to determine whether P had in fact intended to "discard" the materials at issue, with the result that they would constitute "waste". In particular, that court should determine whether those materials constituted a burden which P sought to discard, with the result that there would be a risk that they would be discarded in a manner likely to cause harm to the environment, particularly by dumping them or disposing of them in an uncontrolled manner. In the present case, it was apparent that, even before the excavation of the materials, local farmers had made an express request for their supply. After appropriate construction projects had been found, those excavated materials were made available, alongside an agreement under which P would carry out works to adapt and improve the land and cultivation areas using those materials. Such factors, if proven, did not appear to be such as to establish the intention to discard those materials.

H6   (2) It was also for the referring court to ascertain whether the excavated materials had to be classified as a "by-product" within the meaning of art.5(1). That included verifying whether the farmers concerned had made a binding commitment to take delivery of the excavated materials, but also that those materials and the quantities supplied did in fact serve to carry out the works and were strictly limited for those purposes. If the materials were not supplied immediately, it was appropriate to allow temporary storage for a reasonable period, until the works for which they were intended were carried out. Although it was apparent that the excavated materials were subject to a quality control demonstrating that they were uncontaminated materials in the highest quality class and recognised as such under national law, it was for the referring court to satisfy itself that they did not require any processing or treatment before their further use. On the question whether the materials formed an integral part of P's production process, the excavated soil was the result of one of the first steps usually undertaken in a construction operation as an economic activity, the result of which was the transformation of land. The Federal Waste Management Plan, which laid down specific requirements for the reduction of waste quantities, their pollutants and their harmful effects on human health and the environment, also declared that the use of uncontaminated excavated materials in the highest quality class was suitable and authorised for land adaptation and improvement. That use was, in principle, consistent with the objectives of Directive 2008/98. The use of such excavated soil had a significant advantage for the environment because it contributed, as required by art.11(2)(b), to the reduction of waste, to the preservation of natural resources and to the development of a circular economy. In addition, use of such excavated materials made it possible to comply with the waste hierarchy defined in art.4.

H7   (3) National law providing that uncontaminated excavated materials of the highest quality class only lost that "waste" status when they were used directly as a substitute and their holder had satisfied formal criteria which were irrelevant for the purposes of environmental protection, were also contrary to the Directive if those criteria had the effect of undermining the attainment of its objectives. An examination seeking to determine the status and presence of pollution or of contamination in excavated materials could be classified as a "checking operation", covered by the concept of "preparing for re-use", as defined in art.3. Accordingly, waste which was the subject of such a "preparing for re-use" operation could be regarded as having undergone a recovery operation, within the meaning of art.6(1), if its re-use did not require any other pre-processing. It was for the referring court to assess whether the specific criteria defined in accordance with the conditions in that article were complied with following the checking operation. It was apparent that the assessment that the "end-of-waste" status of the excavated materials had not been achieved was essentially attributable to non-compliance with the formal criteria which were irrelevant for the purposes of environmental protection. If the excavated materials at issue were the subject of a recovery operation and satisfied all the specific criteria defined in accordance with the conditions laid down in art.6(1), it had to be held that the "end-of-waste" status of those materials had been achieved.

H8 **Cases referred to:**
Brady v Environmental Protection Agency (C-113/12) EU:C:2013:627; [2014] 2 C.M.L.R. 3; [2014] Env. L.R. 13
Commission v Spain (C-121/03) EU:C:2005:512
Commune de Mesquer v Total France SA (C-188/07) EU:C:2008:359; [2009] P.T.S.R. 588; [2009] Env. L.R. 9
Criminal Proceedings against Tronex BV (C-624/17) EU:C:2019:564; [2019] P.T.S.R. 2042; [2020] 1 C.M.L.R. 15
KVZ retec (C-176/05) EU:C:2007:123
Sappi Austria Produktion and Wasserverband 'Region Gratkorn-Gratwein' (C-629/19) EU:C:2020:824
Tallinna Vesi AS v Keskkonnaamet (C-60/18) EU:C:2019:264; [2019] Env. L.R. 30

H9 **Legislation referred to:**
TFEU art.267
Directive 75/442 (Waste)
Directive 2006/12 (Waste)
Directive 2008/98 (Waste) arts 1, 3, 4, 5, 6, 11, 13 and 28 and Annex II

H10 *M. Walcher*, Rechtsanwalt, appeared on behalf of Porr Bau GmbH.
F. Boldog, A. Kögl, A. Posch, J. Schmoll and *E. Wolfslehner*, acting as Agents, appeared on behalf of the Austrian Government.
S. Bourgois, C. Hermes and *M. Ioan*, acting as Agents, appeared on behalf of the European Commission.

OPINION

I. Introduction[1]

AG1   The present request for a preliminary ruling concerns the interpretation of the concept of 'waste' in Article 3(1) of Directive 2008/98[2] and the conditions under which excavated materials – namely uncontaminated top-quality soil – achieve end-of-waste status pursuant to Article 6 of that directive. The case follows on from judgments such as *Tallinna Vesi*[3] and *Sappi Austria Produktion and Wasserverband 'Region Gratkorn-Gratwein'*,[4] where the Court interpreted those same provisions respectively with regard to sewage sludge and waste water.

AG2   The request has been submitted in the course of the proceedings between Porr Bau GmbH and the Bezirkshauptmannschaft Graz-Umgebung (administrative authorities of the District of Graz and surrounding area; 'the respondent authority'). Those proceedings concern an administrative decision which found that the excavated soil ordered by certain farmers from a construction undertaking in Austria, for the purposes of levelling and restoring their cultivation areas, was to be considered waste, and thus subject to the payment of a contribution, even though it had been classified as uncontaminated material of the highest quality under Austrian law.

AG3   The referring court wishes mainly to ascertain whether Article 6 of Directive 2008/98, interpreted in the light of the objectives of that directive, precludes national legislation which grants end-of-waste status to uncontaminated top-quality excavated soil only (i) when it is used directly as a substitute for raw materials and (ii) when the holder fulfils certain formal requirements such as record-keeping and documentation obligations. As a preliminary issue, that court also wonders whether uncontaminated top-quality excavated soil, supplied by a construction undertaking for the purposes of improving the yields from cultivation land, constitutes 'waste' within the meaning of Article 3(1) of Directive 2008/98 or, alternatively, a 'by-product' within the meaning of Article 5(1) of that directive.

II. Legal framework

A. European Union law

AG4   According to Article 1 of Directive 2008/98, in the version applicable to the main proceedings,[5] that directive lays down 'measures to protect the environment and human health by preventing or reducing the adverse impacts of the generation and management of waste and by reducing overall impacts of resource use and improving the efficiency of such use'.

---

[1] Original language: English.
[2] Directive 2008/98/EC of the European Parliament and of the Council of 19 November 2008 on waste and repealing certain Directives (OJ 2008 L 312, p. 3).
[3] Judgment of 28 March 2019, *Tallinna Vesi* (C-60/18) EU:C:2019:264; 'the judgment in *Tallinna Vesi*'.
[4] Judgment of 14 October 2020, *Sappi Austria Produktion and Wasserverband 'Region Gratkorn-Gratwein'* (C-629/19) EU:C:2020:824; 'the judgment in *Sappi*'.
[5] Directive 2008/98 was last amended by Directive (EU) 2018/851 of the European Parliament and of the Council of 30 May 2018 amending Directive 2008/98/EC on waste (OJ 2018 L 150, p. 109). Its transposition period ended on 5 July 2020. In the order for reference, however, the referring court indicates that the applicable version of Directive 2008/98 in the main action is the one preceding the amendments introduced by Directive 2018/851. Since, according to settled case-law of the Court, the national court has sole jurisdiction to determine the legal framework applicable to those proceedings, I shall not question its assessment concerning the version of Directive 2008/98 to be applied in the present case.

AG5   Article 3 of Directive 2008/98, entitled 'Definitions', provides that, for the purpose of that directive, the following definitions in paragraphs 1, 15 and 16 of the terms 'waste', 'recovery' and 'preparing for re-use' are to apply:

> '1. "waste" means any substance or object which the holder discards or intends or is required to discard;
>
> …
>
> 15. "recovery" means any operation the principal result of which is waste serving a useful purpose by replacing other materials which would otherwise have been used to fulfil a particular function, or waste being prepared to fulfil that function, in the plant or in the wider economy. Annex II sets out a non-exhaustive list of recovery operations;
>
> 16. "preparing for re-use" means checking, cleaning or repairing recovery operations, by which products or components of products that have become waste are prepared so that they can be re-used without any other pre-processing;
>
> …'

AG6   Article 4 of Directive 2008/98, entitled 'Waste hierarchy', states:

> '1. The following waste hierarchy shall apply as a priority order in waste prevention and management legislation and policy:
>   (a) prevention;
>   (b) preparing for re-use;
>   (c) recycling;
>   (d) other recovery, e.g. energy recovery; and
>   (e) disposal.
>   …'

AG7   Article 5 of Directive 2008/98, under the heading 'By-products', reads as follows:

> '1. A substance or object, resulting from a production process, the primary aim of which is not the production of that item, may be regarded as not being waste referred to in [Article 3(1)] but as being a by-product only if the following conditions are met:
>   (a) further use of the substance or object is certain;
>   (b) the substance or object can be used directly without any further processing other than normal industrial practice;
>   (c) the substance or object is produced as an integral part of a production process; and
>   (d) further use is lawful, i.e. the substance or object fulfils all relevant product, environmental and health protection requirements for the specific use and will not lead to overall adverse environmental or human health impacts.
>   …'

AG8   Article 6 of Directive 2008/98, entitled 'End-of-waste status', provides:

> '1. Certain specified waste shall cease to be waste within the meaning of [Article 3(1)] when it has undergone a recovery, including recycling, operation and complies with specific criteria to be developed in accordance with the following conditions:

(a) the substance or object is commonly used for specific purposes;

(b) a market or demand exists for such a substance or object;

(c) the substance or object fulfils the technical requirements for the specific purposes and meets the existing legislation and standards applicable to products; and

(d) the use of the substance or object will not lead to overall adverse environmental or human health impacts.

The criteria shall include limit values for pollutants where necessary and shall take into account any possible adverse environmental effects of the substance or object.

…

4. Where criteria have not been set at Community level under the procedure set out in paragraphs 1 and 2, Member States may decide case by case whether certain waste has ceased to be waste taking into account the applicable case law. …'

AG9   The essential obligation and objective laid down by Directive 2008/98 is set out in Article 13:

'Member States shall take the necessary measures to ensure that waste management is carried out without endangering human health, without harming the environment …'

AG10   Article 28 of Directive 2008/98, under the title 'Waste management plans', states that Member States are to ensure that their competent authorities establish, in accordance inter alia with Articles 1, 4 and 13, one or more waste management plans.

B. Austrian law

1. The Law on waste management

AG11   The relevant provisions of the Abfallwirtschaftsgesetz 2002 (Austrian federal law of 2002 on waste management; 'the Law on waste management'), which transposes Directive 2008/98, are worded as follows:

'Definitions

Paragraph 2(1) For the purposes of [the Law on waste management], waste means any movable property,

1. which the holder intends to discard or has discarded, or

2. whose collection, storage, transport and treatment as waste is necessary in order not to harm public interests (Paragraph 1(3)).

…

(5) For the purposes of [the Law on waste management],

…

6. "preparing for reuse" means any checking, cleaning or repairing recovery operations, by which products or components of products that have become waste are prepared so that they can be reused without any other pre-processing;

…

End-of-waste status
Paragraph 5(1) Unless otherwise specified in a regulation referred to in Paragraph 5(2) or in a regulation referred to in Article 6(2) of Directive 2008/98/EC on waste, existing substances shall be deemed to be waste until they or substances directly obtained from them are used as a substitute for raw materials or for products obtained from primary raw materials. In the case of preparing for reuse within the meaning of point 6 of Paragraph 2(5), the end-of-waste status occurs at the end of that recovery operation.
…

Federal waste management plan
Paragraph 8(1) In order to achieve the objectives and to implement the principles set out in [the Law on waste management], the Federal Minister for Agriculture, Forestry, the Environment and the Management of Water shall draw up a federal waste management plan at least every six years.
…'

2. The Federal waste management plan

AG12   The Bundesabfallwirtschaftsplan 2011 (Austrian federal waste management plan of 2011; 'the Federal waste management plan'), adopted on the basis of Article 28 of Directive 2008/98 and Paragraph 8(1) of the Law on waste management, lays down specific requirements concerning the reduction of the quantities of waste, of its pollutants and of its harmful effect on the environment and health, as well as the environmentally sound and economically useful recovery of waste.

3. The Law on the rehabilitation of disused hazardous sites

AG13   Under Paragraph 1 of the Altlastensanierungsgesetz 1989 (Austrian federal law of 1989 on the rehabilitation of disused hazardous sites, as subsequently amended), that law aims 'to finance the safeguarding and rehabilitation of disused hazardous sites within the meaning of [that law]'. In particular, Paragraph 3 provides that the long-term deposit of waste on the surface or underground for, inter alia, filling uneven ground or land development, is to be subject to the payment of a contribution known as the 'Altlastenbeitrag' (disused hazardous site contribution). However, that waste is exempt from that obligation when, in essence, it is used in accordance with the requirements of the Federal waste management plan. The Law on the rehabilitation of disused hazardous sites also sets out, in Paragraph 10, a procedure the purpose of which is to clarify, by means of an administrative decision, whether the substantive conditions for the obligation to make a contribution in respect of contaminated sites are fulfilled.

III. Facts, procedure and the questions referred

AG14   Porr Bau, the applicant in the main proceedings, is a construction undertaking established in Austria. In July 2015, certain local farmers asked it to supply them with excavated soil and to distribute it over their properties. The purpose of the farmers' request was to level their agricultural land and improve their cultivation areas, thereby increasing yields.

AG15   On the date the farmers approached Porr Bau, it was not certain that that undertaking would be in a position to respond to their request. It was only after the selection of an appropriate construction project and the extraction of soil samples that Porr Bau supplied the requested material. For that purpose, the soil had been qualified as being of class quality A1, that is to say, the highest quality of uncontaminated excavated soil established in the Federal waste management plan. The use of that class of soil is, under Austrian law, suitable and authorised for land adaptation and land development. Porr Bau was also paid to carry out the works to improve the land and the cultivation areas concerned.

AG16   On 4 May 2018, pursuant to the Law on the rehabilitation of disused hazardous sites, Porr Bau asked the respondent authority to declare that the excavated soil supplied to the farmers did not constitute waste. In the alternative, it asked for that soil to be exempted from the obligation to pay the contribution on the use of waste.

AG17   On 14 September 2020, the respondent authority found that the excavated soil at issue constituted waste within the meaning of Paragraph 2(1) of the Law on waste management. That authority also considered that the soil had not achieved end-of-waste status, essentially due to the failure to comply with certain formal requirements laid down in the Federal waste management plan. It concluded therefore that the contribution on the use of waste could not be exempted.

AG18   The Landesverwaltungsgericht Steiermark (Regional Administrative Court, Styria, Austria), which is hearing the appeal against that decision, has doubts as to the view taken by the respondent authority.

AG19   In particular, the referring court questions the interpretation of the concept of 'waste' adopted by that authority and its application to uncontaminated excavated soil of the highest quality class, such as the soil at issue in the present case. In addition, the referring court observes that, under Austrian law, excavated materials can only achieve end-of-waste status when they have been used directly as a substitute for raw materials or for products made from primary raw materials. That raises the question whether the national legislation regulates the achievement of end-of-waste status more strictly than Article 6 of Directive 2008/98 in respect of uncontaminated soil of the highest quality. Moreover, the referring court points out that Austrian law requires, for the purposes of achieving end-of-waste status, the fulfillment of certain formal requirements, specifically record-keeping and documentation obligations. The referring court asks whether, where uncontaminated top-quality excavated soil is concerned, the obligation to comply with those requirements, which that court considers to have no environmental relevance, infringes Article 6 of Directive 2008/98.

AG20   In those circumstances the Landesverwaltungsgericht Steiermark (Regional Administrative Court, Styria) decided to stay the proceedings and to refer the following questions to the Court for a preliminary ruling:

> '(1) Does Article 6(1) of [Directive 2008/98] preclude national legislation under which end-of-waste status is achieved only once waste or existing substances or the substances obtained from them are used directly as a substitute for raw materials or for products made from primary raw materials or once they have been prepared for reuse?
> If Question 1 is answered in the negative:
> (2) Does Article 6(1) of [Directive 2008/98] preclude national legislation under which end-of-waste status in respect of excavated materials can be achieved at the earliest when they serve as a substitute for raw materials or for products made from primary raw materials?

If Question 1 and/or Question 2 is/are answered in the negative:

(3) Does Article 6(1) of [Directive 2008/98] preclude national legislation under which end-of-waste status in respect of excavated materials cannot be achieved if formal criteria (in particular record-keeping and documentation obligations) which have no environmentally relevant influence on the measure carried out are not complied with or are not complied with in full, even though the excavated materials demonstrably fall below the limit values (premium) to be complied with for the specific intended use?'

IV. Analysis

AG21   By its request, the referring court asks, in essence, whether Article 6(1) of Directive 2008/98 must be interpreted as precluding national legislation under which end-of-waste status is achieved, as a general rule, only when waste is used directly as a substitute for raw materials or is prepared for reuse and, in the particular case of excavated materials, only when the excavated materials have been used directly as a substitute for raw materials, and their holder has satisfied formal requirements such as record-keeping and documentation obligations.

AG22   As a preliminary point, I must observe that, in the order for reference, the referring court expresses doubts as to whether uncontaminated excavated soil, classified as top-quality under national law, constitutes waste within the meaning of Article 3(1) of Directive 2008/98. After all, the application of Article 6 of that directive is based on the premiss that a substance or object is qualified as waste beforehand. Although this particular issue is not expressly raised in the questions referred, I shall first examine whether the provision by a construction company of uncontaminated top-quality excavated soil, under the specific circumstances of a case such as that in the main proceedings, should be considered waste. In my analysis, I shall also address the issue, discussed by the parties during the hearing before the Court, of whether the soil supplied should be regarded instead as a by-product within the meaning of Article 5(1) of Directive 2008/98.

AG23   On the assumption that the material at issue in the main proceedings is considered waste, I shall examine the three questions referred together. Those questions must be read as inviting the Court to determine whether the national legislation in question is compatible with Article 6(1) of Directive 2008/98 when the sole possibility of recovery for uncontaminated top-quality excavated soil, in order to reach end-of-waste status, is its use as a substitute for raw materials and the fulfilment of certain formal requirements such as record-keeping and documentation obligations.

A. Uncontaminated top-quality excavated soil as waste or as a by-product

1. Scope of Directive 2008/98

AG24   Before examining whether uncontaminated top-quality excavated soil could be considered as waste or, alternatively, as a by-product, within the respective meanings of Article 3(1) and Article 5(1) of Directive 2008/98, I should briefly point out that Article 2(1)(c) of that same directive excludes, from its scope, uncontaminated soil and other naturally occurring material excavated in the course of construction activities where it is certain that the material will be used for the purposes of construction in its natural state on the site from which it was excavated.

AG25 Given that, in the light of the information set out in the order for reference, the excavated soil at issue in the main proceedings was deposited elsewhere than in its excavation location, it is not covered by Article 2(1)(c) of Directive 2008/98 and, consequently, it must be considered in accordance with the definition of waste and the provisions for by-products of that directive.[6]

2. The concepts of 'waste' and 'by-product'

AG26 Article 3(1) of Directive 2008/98 defines the concept of 'waste' as any substance or object which the holder discards or intends to discard (*subjective* waste) or which the holder is required to discard (*objective* waste). The concept of waste has been widely interpreted by the Court, which has defined relevant criteria for the purposes of determining whether a substance or object, including materials, is to be considered waste within the meaning of that provision.[7]

AG27 In particular, according to settled case-law, the classification of a substance or object as waste, in its subjective sense, is to be inferred primarily from the holder's actions and the meaning of the term 'discard'.[8] That term and the term 'waste' encompass concepts of EU law which, in view of the aim of Directive 2008/98 to minimise the negative effects of the generation and management of waste on human health and the environment, cannot be interpreted restrictively.[9]

AG28 The Court has also emphasised that, in order to assess whether a substance or an object is waste, account must be taken of all the circumstances of the specific case, regard being had to the aim of Directive 2008/98 and the need to ensure that its effectiveness is not undermined.[10]

AG29 Among the circumstances that may reveal the existence of waste is the fact, first, that a substance or an object is a production or consumption residue, that is to say a product which was not itself sought.[11] In addition, particular attention must be paid, according to the Court, to the fact that the substance or object in question is not or is no longer of any use to its holder, such that that substance or object constitutes a burden which that holder will seek to discard.[12] Moreover, neither the method of treatment reserved for a substance nor the use to which it is put determines conclusively whether or not the substance is to be classified as 'waste'. Finally, the concept of 'waste' does not exclude either substances or objects which are capable of economic reuse.[13]

AG30 In parallel with the previous case-law, the Court has also developed the concept of 'by-product', mostly on the basis of the interpretation of Directive 75/442.[14] That case-law is currently codified in Article 5(1) of Directive 2008/98, which, in essence, refers to a substance or object which the holder is not willing to discard, by reason of the financial advantage that might be obtained from its reuse, and

---

[6] See, in that regard, recital 11 of Directive 2008/98, *in fine*.
[7] For a recent outline of those criteria, see the judgment in *Sappi* at paragraphs 43 to 53 and the case-law cited.
[8] Judgment of 4 July 2019, *Tronex* (C-624/17) EU:C:2019:564 at paragraph 17 and the case-law cited.
[9] The judgment in *Sappi*, paragraph 43 and the case-law cited.
[10] Judgment of 4 July 2019, *Tronex* (C-624/17) EU:C:2019:564 at paragraph 20 and the case-law cited.
[11] Judgment of 24 June 2008, *Commune de Mesquer* (C-188/07) EU:C:2008:359 at paragraph 41.
[12] Judgment of 4 July 2019, *Tronex* (C-624/17) EU:C:2019:564 at paragraph 22 and the case-law cited.
[13] Judgment of 3 October 2013, *Brady* (C-113/12) EU:C:2013:627 at paragraph 42 and the case-law cited.
[14] Council Directive 75/442/EEC of 15 July 1975 on waste (OJ 1975 L 194, p. 39), subsequently amended by Council Directive 91/156/EEC of 18 March 1991 (OJ 1991 L 78, p. 32) and consolidated in Directive 2006/12/EC of the European Parliament and of the Council of 5 April 2006 on waste (OJ 2006 L 114, p. 9).

which cannot therefore be regarded as a burden and thus as a waste. In the Court's view, it would not be justified to make a substance or object which the holder intends to exploit or market on economically advantageous terms, within a subsequent recovery process, subject to the strict requirements of Directive 2008/98 on environment and human health protection.[15]

3. Uncontaminated top-quality excavated soil requested for the levelling and improvement of cultivation land

AG31   It is of course for the referring court, which alone has jurisdiction to assess the facts of the case before it, to verify, in the light of the case-law previously cited, whether a holder of excavated materials, namely uncontaminated top-quality soil, intends to discard them, giving rise to waste, or to exploit them in economically advantageous terms, giving rise to a by-product.[16] That being so, I would invite the Court to provide the referring court with the following guidance in order to resolve the dispute before it. This guidance is based on the specific circumstances that must not be disregarded in a case such as the one in the main proceedings.

(a) Top-quality excavated soil as waste

AG32   To begin with, I would like to point out that, according to the Austrian Government, the decision adopted by the respondent authority, which concludes that the excavated soil at issue has the status of waste, is based on the case-law developed by the Verwaltungsgerichtshof (Supreme Administrative Court, Austria) on the concept of 'waste' as laid down in Paragraph 2(1) of the Law on waste management.[17] According to that court, where materials are excavated or demolished during a construction project, the main purpose of the construction developer is usually to complete that project without being hampered by those materials. They are therefore removed from the site with the intention of discarding them.

AG33   I agree that the standard established by the Verwaltungsgerichtshof (Supreme Administrative Court), subsequently followed in the decision under appeal, can be employed, as a general rule, for the purposes of determining whether excavated materials resulting from construction activities are to be regarded as waste. However, as indicated in point 28 above, the assessment of the existence of waste, within the meaning of Article 3(1) of Directive 2008/98, requires, according to the Court's case-law, account to be taken of all the circumstances of a specific case.[18] That means that, for that general rule to be applied, the elements characterising the concrete intention of a holder of waste must not be disregarded.

AG34   In my opinion, contrary to the position taken by the Austrian Government and the Commission, there are factual elements in the present case that deserve to be taken into account in the assessment of the specific intention of a construction undertaking regarding the further use of the material which it previously excavated. Those elements may include, for instance, the prior demand for the material to be excavated by local operators when that material may be marketed after careful selection and sampling of its quality. In essence, it cannot be excluded that a construction company, instead of perceiving excavated material as a residue or a burden to be discarded, might instead seek ways to obtain a profit from its own

---

[15] Judgment of 4 July 2019, *Tronex* (C-624/17) EU:C:2019:564 at paragraph 24 and the case-law cited.
[16] The judgment in *Sappi* at paragraph 53 and the case-law cited.
[17] Article 2(1) of the Law on waste management transposes Article 3(1) of Directive 2008/98 into Austrian law.
[18] See, as a further example, judgment of 1 March 2007, *KVZ retec* (C-176/05) EU:C:2007:123 at AG64.

activity, especially when that material is classified as belonging to the highest quality class of uncontaminated soil.

AG35   Indeed, the present case illustrates how a construction undertaking may be inclined, not to discard material previously excavated, but to exploit it in economically advantageous terms. This is suggested by the fact that it was a group of local farmers who initially contacted Porr Bau in order to distribute excavated soil over their properties for the purposes of levelling and improving their agricultural land. While it was not certain, at the time when the farmers approached Porr Bau, that that undertaking would be in a position to satisfy their demand, the initiative of those farmers encouraged it to select an appropriate construction project and to extract soil samples. The order for reference further indicates that that soil was subject to a quality control and that it was subsequently classified as uncontaminated top-quality material, which, according to Austrian law, is suitable and authorised for land adaptation and land development. At the request of the farmers, Porr Bau was also paid to carry out the works to improve the land and the cultivation areas concerned.

AG36   It is then difficult to conclude that, under circumstances such as those of the present case, the intention of a construction undertaking is to discard excavated soil that has been carefully selected, subjected to a quality control and supplied as uncontaminated top-quality material in order to attend to a specific request from local operators in need of that material. I also think it should not be assumed that all excavated soil by a construction undertaking is by default to be discarded. After all, it cannot be excluded that that material might be used within the construction project concerned, which, as indicated in point 24 above, would take it outside the scope of Directive 2008/98.

AG37   In the light of the foregoing considerations, I think the Court should tend towards the view that, subject to the verifications to be made by the referring court, uncontaminated top-quality excavated soil should not be regarded, in a case like the present one, as waste within the meaning of Article 3(1) of Directive 2008/98.

(b) Excavated soil as a by-product

AG38   By contrast, a close analysis of the case makes it apparent, in line with Porr Bau's written observations, that the soil at issue in the main proceedings might satisfy the requirements laid down in Article 5(1) of Directive 2008/98 for a by-product.

AG39   I should point out, in that regard, that, according to Article 5(1) of Directive 2008/98, a substance or object resulting from a production process, the primary aim of which is not the production of that item, may be regarded as not being waste, but as being a by-product. For that to be so, that provision also requires the fulfilment of four conditions, namely (i) the further use of the substance or object is certain; (ii) the substance or object can be used directly without any further processing other than normal industrial practice; (iii) the substance or object is produced as an integral part of a production process, and (iv) the further use is lawful. I shall briefly examine all those elements in the light of the information arising from the Court file.

(1) Definition of by-product

AG40   As regards, first of all, whether excavated soil can be considered 'a substance or object resulting from a production process, the primary aim of which is not the production of that item', within the meaning of the first subparagraph of Article

5(1) of Directive 2008/98, it is important to bear in mind that the Court has traditionally held, in its settled case-law, that 'materials or raw materials resulting from an extraction or manufacturing process' may be not regarded as a residue, but as a by-product.[19] As already noted, that case-law is at the heart of the concept of 'by-product', which was subsequently codified in Article 5(1) of Directive 2008/98 using for that purpose, instead of the terms 'extraction or manufacturing process', the terms 'production process'.

AG41   In my view, contrary to the thesis defended, in essence, by the Austrian Government in its observations, no argument supports the view that the EU legislature, when codifying the case-law of the Court by using the terms 'production process', intended to restrain the consideration of by-products to secondary items resulting from an industrial production. On the contrary, a production process is commonly defined by economic scholars as the process in which the factors of production, namely capital, labour, technology and land (inputs), are turned into goods and services (output).[20] Land can therefore be the object of a production process, which means that a secondary product resulting from its transformation, including excavated soil, should be regarded as falling under the concept of 'by-product', provided it fulfils the additional conditions laid down in Article 5(1) of Directive 2008/98.

AG42   In that regard, I would like to draw the Court's attention to the judgment in *Brady*.[21] In it, the Court considered, when interpreting Directive 75/442, that slurry generated in farms as a secondary product and sold to other farmers for reuse as fertiliser could be regarded as a by-product. That demonstrates that, even before the adoption of Article 5(1) of Directive 2008/98, the Court has admitted, as by-products, outputs resulting from economic transformation activities that do not exclusively take place within an industrial context. On those bases, I would invite the Court to adopt an interpretation of the terms 'production process' which not only pairs the common definition of those terms, but also follows the understanding of the concept of 'by-product' in the Court's case-law before the adoption of Article 5(1) of Directive 2008/98.

(2) Further use is sufficiently certain

AG43   With regard to the condition that further use of the substance or object at issue must be certain, without prejudice to the specific checks which the national court will carry out, it is sufficiently conclusive in that regard that, prior to the excavation of the soil at issue in the main proceedings, there was an express request for the supply of that material from local operators. That request later resulted in an engagement to provide the requested soil, along with an agreement by which the construction undertaking would carry out, using that same material, the necessary works for the levelling and improvement of the agricultural land concerned. Even though, on the date the farmers initially approached Porr Bau, it was not certain that that undertaking could accommodate their request, that does not in itself mean, in the light of the Court's case-law, that further use of the excavated soil concerned

---

[19] See, inter alia, the judgment in *Sappi* at paragraph 51 and the case-law cited.
[20] Under classical economics, excavated materials are categorised as by-products of land. See, inter alia, Pearce, D. W., *Macmillan dictionary of Modern Economics*, London: Macmillan Education UK, pp. 311 320. See also, as a concrete illustration, Environmental Protection Agency of Ireland, *Guidance on Soil and Stone By-products*, June 2019, available at *https://www.epa.ie/publications/licensing--permitting/waste /Guidance_on_Soil_and_Stone_By_Product.pdf*
[21] See judgment of 3 October 2013, *Brady* (C-113/12) EU:C:2013:627 at paragraph 60.

was not certain.[22] Indeed, the requirement of certainty appears to be fulfilled at a sufficiently early stage in the present case.

AG44   Nonetheless, the Court has laid down useful criteria to assess more specifically whether the further use of material intended to be distributed over agricultural land, such as the excavated soil at issue, is sufficiently certain. The requirements established, for instance, in the judgment in *Brady*, already cited, are as follows:

- first, the farmers' plots of land where the material is to be supplied must be clearly identified from the outset;[23]
- second, the material – and the quantities to be delivered – must actually be intended and strictly limited to the needs of the specific use established;[24]
- third, the supply of the material concerned must actually be used or marketed on terms that are economically advantageous to its holder;
- fourth, in event that the material at issue is not supplied immediately, there is an obligation to use appropriate and sufficient storage to keep the soil during the period of storage; moreover, that period of storage must not exceed what is required in order for the undertaking to be able to meet its contractual commitments.[25]

AG45   To my mind, the Court should consider making applicable the requirements elaborated in *Brady*, concerning the further use of material to be distributed over agricultural land, to a case regarding excavated soil such as that at issue in the main proceedings. That would help to assess more specifically whether the further use of that material is sufficiently certain within the meaning of Article 5(1)(a) of Directive 2008/98. As a matter of fact, I would point out that the information shared by the referring court in the order for reference appears to reveal that the first three requirements are satisfied in the main action. By contrast, the order for reference does not contain any information concerning whether the excavated soil at issue in the main proceedings was – or was not – supplied immediately, which raises the question whether the requirement related to the storage of that material was at all applicable. In any event, I must stress, once again, that it is for the referring court to carry out that assessment and to determine ultimately whether the condition laid down in Article 5(1)(a) of Directive 2008/98 should be regarded as being satisfied.

(3) No further processing and part of an integral production process

AG46   With regard to the conditions laid down by Article 5(1)(b) and (c) of Directive 2008/98, according to which the substance or object must be used directly without any further processing other than normal industrial practice and the substance or object must be produced as an integral part of a production process, I think that it is clear that excavated soil supplied for the levelling of land does not require any processing or treatment before its further use. That is all the more so when, as repeatedly mentioned, that excavated soil has undergone a control declaring that it is uncontaminated top-quality material, recognised as such under national law.[26]

---

[22] See judgment of 3 October 2013, *Brady* (C-113/12) EU:C:2013:627 at paragraph 48.
[23] *Ibid.*, paragraph 53.
[24] *Ibid.*, paragraphs 52, 53 and 56.
[25] *Ibid.*, paragraphs 55 and 56.
[26] As Porr Bau explains in its observations, without being rebutted by the other parties before the Court, the soil supplied was 'virgin soil', taken from one agricultural site and directly delivered to another identical agricultural site.

AG47   Furthermore, I have already argued, in points 41 and 42 above, that the term 'production process', in the first subparagraph of Article 5(1) of Directive 2008/98, should be interpreted as encompassing economic transformation activities that go beyond those that take place exclusively within an industrial context. As to the present case, it is important to understand that excavated soil is the inevitable result of one of the first steps usually undertaken in a construction operation as an economic activity, the result of which is the transformation of land. For that reason, excavated soil should be regarded as an integral part of a production process within the meaning of Article 5(1)(c) of Directive 2008/98.

AG48   Finally, I consider it important that the Court also adopts a dynamic understanding of how regular a certain by-product is supplied as such by an undertaking, which is not, by the way, a condition expressly established by Article 5(1) of Directive 2008/98. Even if a material were not provided on a regular basis as a by-product – as could be the case with Porr Bau and the excavated soil at issue in the main proceedings – that should not lead to the conclusion that the supply of that material cannot evolve and be transformed into an activity capable of being performed on a more regular basis if that results into an economic benefit for an undertaking.

(4) Further lawful use

AG49   Lastly, with regard to the condition that the further use of the substance or object at issue must be lawful, Article 5(1)(d) of Directive 2008/98 requires, in particular, that the substance or object satisfies all relevant product, environmental and health protection requirements for its specific use and will not lead to overall adverse environmental or human health impacts.

AG50   In that respect, I have already mentioned that, according to the information provided by the referring court, the soil concerned by the main proceedings had been classified, following a quality analysis undertaken before its reuse, as belonging to the highest quality of uncontaminated excavated materials as defined by Austrian law, in particular under the Federal waste management plan. As indicated in point 12 above, that waste management plan lays down specific requirements concerning the reduction of the quantities of waste, of its pollutants and of its harmful effect on the environment and health. It also declares that the use of uncontaminated top-quality soil is suitable and authorised for land adaptation and land development.

AG51   It appears then that, inasmuch as a classification of the excavated soil at issue in the main proceedings highlights both its uncontaminated status and its suitability for the specific purpose of land adaptation, the fourth condition should also be regarded as having been satisfied in the circumstances of a case such as the one in the main proceedings.

(c) Final remark

AG52   It follows from the foregoing considerations that, subject to the checks to be carried out by the referring court, a construction undertaking which carefully selects soil, subjects it to a quality control and supplies it as uncontaminated top-quality material in order to attend to a specific request from local operators in need of that material does not intend to discard it, but rather seeks to exploit it under advantageous conditions for that undertaking. That excavated soil should not therefore, in the specific circumstances of the present case, be regarded as waste within the meaning of Article 3(1) of Directive 2008/98.

AG53   By contrast, I consider that Article 5(1) of Directive 2008/98 should be interpreted as meaning that uncontaminated top-quality excavated soil, supplied for the purposes of attending the specific request from local operators, after that soil has been selected and undergone a quality control, constitutes a by-product provided that the conditions laid down in that article are fulfilled in accordance with the guidance set out in the preceding points of this Opinion.

B. *Achieving end-of-waste status*

AG54   My previous analysis excludes the need to examine the three questions referred by the national court concerning the interpretation of Article 6 of Directive 2008/98. However, should the Court decide not to follow the conclusion that the excavated soil at issue in the main proceedings should be regarded as a by-product, but instead as waste, I present my analysis on those three questions below.

1. Article 6 of Directive 2008/98 and the case-law of the Court

AG55   Under Article 6(1) of Directive 2008/98, in the version applicable to the present proceedings,[27] certain specified waste ceases to be waste within the meaning of Article 3(1) when it has undergone a recovery, including recycling, operation.

AG56   Pursuant to that provision, end-of-waste status must also comply with specific criteria developed in accordance with the following conditions: first, the substance or object in question must be commonly used for specific purposes; second, a market or demand must exist for such a substance or object; third, the substance or object must fulfil the technical requirements for the specific purposes and meet the existing legislation and standards applicable to products, and, fourth, the use of the substance or object must not lead to overall adverse environmental or human health impacts.

AG57   According to Article 6(2) of Directive 2008/98, the definition of the specific criteria that allow end-of-waste status to be achieved are to be adopted primarily by the European Commission. However, in the absence of implementing legislation adopted at EU level, Article 6(4) of Directive 2008/98 allows Member States to decide case by case whether certain waste has ceased to be waste.

AG58   It also follows from the case-law of the Court, in particular from its judgment in *Tallinna Vesi*, that the exact nature of the measures relating to the end-of-waste status of a substance or object has not been specified by the EU legislature.[28] Member States may thus adopt generally applicable national legislation providing for the cessation of waste status concerning certain types of waste.[29] Alternatively, Member States may also adopt individual decisions, in particular on the basis of applications submitted by holders of the substance or object classified as waste.[30] Member States are even entitled, according to the case-law of the Court, to take the view that some waste cannot cease to be waste and to refrain from adopting legislation concerning the end-of-waste status of that waste.[31]

AG59   In those three contexts, Member States must, however, ensure that their national legislation – or the fact that such legislation has not been adopted – does not amount

---

[27] See footnote 5 above.
[28] The judgment in *Tallinna Vesi* at paragraph 22.
[29] Ibid., paragraphs 23 and 25.
[30] Ibid., paragraph 24.
[31] Ibid., paragraph 26.

to an obstacle to the attainment of the objectives set by Directive 2008/98. Those objectives have been defined by the Court as encouraging the application of the waste hierarchy laid down in Article 4 of that directive, and, as is stated in recitals 8 and 29, encouraging the recovery of waste and the use of recovered material in order to preserve natural resources and to enable the development of a circular economy.[32] In addition, the measures adopted on the basis of Article 6(4) of Directive 2008/98 must comply with the requirements laid down in Article 6(1)(a) to (d) thereof, and, in particular, take account of any possible adverse impact which the substance or object concerned may have on the environment and on human health.[33]

2. The end-of-waste status of uncontaminated top-quality excavated soil

AG60   In the present case, it is common ground for the parties that, in accordance with Article 5(1) of the Law on waste management, the referring court must determine when the uncontaminated top-quality excavated soil provided by Porr Bau to local farmers in the main action ceased to be waste. The answer to that issue is highly relevant given that the payment of a contribution for the deposit of waste, pursuant to the Law on the rehabilitation of disused hazardous sites, depends on the determination of the moment in which that material might have achieved end-of-waste status.[34]

(a) National provision and case-law applicable

AG61   Article 5(1) of the Law on waste management stipulates, in essence, that the substances or objects derived from waste do not achieve end-of-waste status until they are used as a direct substitute for raw materials or products obtained from primary raw materials, or until their preparation for reuse is completed.

AG62   That rule of the Law on waste management does not apply, however, in its entirety to excavated materials. Indeed, according to the order for reference, as corroborated by the Austrian Government,[35] excavated materials are considered to have achieved end-of-waste status only once they have been used as a direct substitute for raw materials or products obtained from primary raw materials. Recovery through preparation for reuse is therefore not available to them as a result of a decision adopted by Austria on the basis of the margin of discretion which Article 6(4) of Directive 2008/98 allows Member States. On top of that, for excavated materials to achieve end-of-waste status, formal requirements such as record-keeping or documentation obligations are to be fulfilled according to the Federal waste management plan.

AG63   The source of the present dispute mainly relates to the parties' disagreement as to when the excavated soil at issue in the main proceedings should be regarded as having undergone a recovery operation, as required by Article 6(1) of Directive 2008/98. Indeed, Porr Bau considers that the quality control carried out on that material, for the purposes of determining its uncontaminated top-quality class,

---

[32] Ibid., paragraphs 23 and 27.
[33] Ibid., paragraph 23. See also, in that regard, Article 13 of Directive 2008/98.
[34] In that respect, the Austrian Government explains that, according to the case-law of the Verwaltungsgerichtshof (Supreme Administrative Court), excavated materials considered as waste retain that status even at the moment when they are used for land development. That means that, even if those materials achieve end-of-waste status as a result of that specific use, that has no bearing on the obligation to pay a contribution under the Law on the rehabilitation of disused hazardous sites.
[35] See, in that regard, recitals of the Law on the waste management.

amounts to a 'preparing for reuse' operation and thus a recovery. In its view, which mirrors the view expressed by the referring court in the order for reference, a national provision limiting that possibility would be contrary to Article 6(1) of Directive 2008/98. By contrast, the Austrian Government submits that a quality control of excavated soil cannot be qualified as a 'preparing for reuse' operation. Consequently, that material cannot be considered to have gone through a recovery until it is used for the adaptation of agricultural land and the improvement of cultivation areas.

AG64   In that regard, I must point out, in the first place, that, according to recital 22 of Directive 2008/98, for the purposes of reaching end-of-waste status, a recovery operation may be 'as simple as the checking of waste to verify that it fulfils the end-of-waste criteria'.

AG65   That recital is given concrete expression in Article 3(16) of Directive 2008/98, which formally defines 'preparing for re-use' as an operation consisting in the 'checking, cleaning or repairing' of products or components of products that have become waste in order to prepare them so that they can be reused without any other pre-processing.[36] That same provision expressly qualifies 'preparing for re-use' operations as a recovery. Therefore, waste that undergoes such a 'preparing for re-use' operation must be regarded as having satisfied the first requirement laid down in Article 6(1) of Directive 2008/98 for the achievement of end-of-waste status.

AG66   It is also worth noting that Article 4 of Directive 2008/98, which defines the hierarchy to be applied in waste legislation and policy, places 'preparing for re-use' in second position in the order of priorities for waste management, right after prevention.

AG67   In the second place, for waste to achieve end-of-waste status, it must not only undergo a recovery process, such as checking, as mentioned above. After all, for a change of status of certain waste to take place, it is necessary to ensure that the product in question is not harmful.[37] That is all the more so given that, as the Court has recently indicated, end-of-waste status results in the end of the protection that the law governing waste guarantees as regards the environment and human health.[38] That is the reason why, during the recovery of waste, a high level of protection of the environment and human health must be guaranteed,[39] and why a specific recovery operation must ensure that the conditions in Article 6(1) of Directive 2008/98 are fully respected.

AG68   It is in the light of the above considerations that it must be ascertained whether national legislation which grants end-of-waste status to uncontaminated top-quality soil only when it has been used as a substitute for raw materials and after certain formal requirements have been satisfied, and not when its uncontaminated status and top-quality class have been defined, is compatible with Article 6(1) of Directive 2008/98, as interpreted by the Court.

(b) Quality control as recovery

AG69   On the one hand, I believe it is sufficiently clear that an examination capable of determining the quality and uncontaminated status of excavated soil is suitable,

---

[36] This provision has been transposed into Austrian law in those exact terms, in particular in Paragraph 2(5)(6) of the Law on waste management.
[37] The judgment in *Tallinna Vesi* at paragraph 23.
[38] The judgment in *Tallinna Vesi* at paragraph 23.
[39] The judgment in *Sappi* at paragraph 66.

from a formal perspective, to be considered as a 'checking operation', thus falling under the concept of 'preparing for re-use' as defined in Article 3(16) of Directive 2008/98. The Austrian Government argues that that type of operation is reserved, according to that provision, to 'products or components of products' and that the excavated soil concerned by the present case cannot be qualified as such. However, that argument should not be upheld on grounds similar to those set out in points 41 and 42 above, which invite the Court to consider land transformation activities, such as construction works, as a production process and, therefore, excavated soil as a product of that activity. Excavated soil can thus be subject to a preparing for reuse operation.

AG70   On the other hand, it is certainly for a national court to assess, when necessary on the basis of a scientific and technical analysis,[40] whether a quality and contamination control performed on excavated soil is appropriate for the purposes of excluding any harm to the environment and human health, and also appropriate to determining whether the conditions laid down in Article 6(1) of Directive 2008/98, as described in point 56 above, have been respected. The aim should be to ensure that excavated soil does not present a potentially greater risk than that of comparable raw materials for a specific use.

AG71   As regards those conditions, that appears to be the situation in the main proceedings in view of the facts established in the order for reference. That order indicates, first, that, before being excavated, it was established that uncontaminated top-quality soil would be used for a specific purpose, namely the levelling and restoration of agricultural lands. Second, there was a specific demand for excavated soil, in particular from the farmers, which addressed the holder of uncontaminated top-quality soil for that purpose. Third, the order for reference states that the excavated soil fulfilled the technical requirements and standards for the levelling and restoration of agricultural land and complied with the relevant legislation and standards. Forth, given the top quality of the excavated soil according to the Federal waste management plan, the use of the substance or object would not appear to lead to overall adverse environment or human health impacts. Let me recall, in that regard, that, in the order for reference, the referring court expressly indicates that the excavated soil at issue in the main proceedings was demonstrably below the limit values of contamination defined in the Federal waste management plan for the specific use of land adaptation and land development.

AG72   I would like to emphasise that the above interpretation of Article 3(16) and Article 6 of Directive 2008/98, granting end-of-waste status to excavated soil which has been subject to a control and classified as being in the top-quality class of material under national law, ensures that the effectiveness of Directive 2008/98 is not undermined, as prescribed by the case-law cited in point 59 above, which essentially requires Member States to grant end-of-waste status to substances or objects where that contributes to the achievement of the objectives of Directive 2008/98.

AG73   As to the present case, it must be considered that the use of top-quality excavated soil, for the purposes of levelling and restoring agricultural land, makes it possible to respect the waste hierarchy defined in Article 4 of Directive 2008/98 and, in particular, to respond to the encouragement to recover waste in order to conserve natural resources and promote the development of a circular economy.

---

[40] The judgment in *Sappi* at paragraph 67.

AG74   After all, as Porr Bau argues, if excavated uncontaminated material classified as top quality was not regarded as having achieved end-of-waste status following a quality control, that soil, whose properties can be used to improve agricultural structures, could have been disposed of in a landfill, in accordance with the obligations laid down in Directive 2008/98 and the Austrian national legislation. That would lead not only to the potential impairment of landfill capacity, but also to the contamination of that soil, which could no longer be used for useful purposes. Besides, instead of implementing the waste hierarchy and responding to the encouragement to recover waste in order to conserve natural resources, as already indicated, the holder of such waste would be required, under Austrian law, to pay a contribution in respect of contaminated sites, which would impair the polluter-pays principle that, according to recitals 1 and 26 of Directive 2008/98, is a guiding principle for European environmental law and policy.

AG75   Consequently, I am of the view that the grant of end-of-waste status to excavated soil once it has been subject to a control and defined as uncontaminated top-quality material can meet the objectives of Directive 2008/98. National legislation which provides that end-of-waste status may occur solely when that type of soil is used to replace raw materials directly, and which excludes preparation for reuse for it, exceeds the margin of discretion recognised to Members States and is therefore precluded by Article 6(1) of Directive 2008/98.

(c) Formal requirements

AG76   As regards the formal requirements, such as record-keeping and documentation obligations, which, according to the referring court, must be additionally satisfied by excavated materials in order to achieve the end-of-waste status, a similar understanding should apply. In particular, it is necessary to ensure that formal requirements do not compromise the effectiveness of Directive 2008/98. In other words, national legislation which provides that end-of-waste status of excavated materials cannot end in the event of non-compliance with formal obligations, even though the conditions laid down in Article 6(1) of Directive 2008/98 are fulfilled, prevents the objectives of Directive 2008/98 from being achieved and for that reason should be set aside.

AG77   Certainly, as the Austrian Government points out, the setting of formal requirements for end-of-waste status is not foreign to EU law. In that regard, Member States enjoy a margin of discretion when it comes to laying out the criteria of the end-of-waste status. Nevertheless, those formal requirements must be defined in a way that achieves their goals without compromising the objectives of Directive 2008/98.

AG78   That does not appears to be the case in the main action in the light of the description made by the referring court in the order for reference. Indeed, as the Austrian Government recognises in its observations, the decision under appeal before the referring court concluded that the excavated soil at stake had not achieved end-of-waste status essentially due to the failure to comply with certain formal requirements laid down in the Federal waste management plan. Yet, as repeatedly mentioned, the referring court indicates that the excavated soil at issue in the main proceedings had been classified as top-quality soil and was demonstrably below the limit values of contamination defined in the Federal waste management plan for the specific use of land adaptation and land development.

AG79   The formal requirements therefore led the respondent authority to consider uncontaminated top-quality soil as waste, encouraging disposal and the acquisition of new raw materials, instead of encouraging the reuse of pre-existing materials. Inasmuch as the reuse of uncontaminated top-quality materials could be discouraged, formal requirements which prove to have no environmental relevance must be regarded as undermining the promotion of the waste hierarchy defined in Article 4 of Directive 2008/98 and, as such, the effectiveness of that directive.

(d) Final remark

AG80   In the light of the foregoing considerations, Article 6(1) of Directive 2008/98 must be interpreted as precluding national legislation which grants end-of-waste status to uncontaminated excavated soil, classified as top-quality material for the specific purpose of land development under national law, only when it is used directly as a substitute for raw materials and inasmuch as it denies the end-of-waste status until the holder fulfils certain formal requirements with no environmental relevance such as record-keeping and documentation obligations.

V. Conclusion

AG81   On the basis of the analysis set out above, I propose that the Court answer the request for a preliminary ruling from the Landesverwaltungsgericht Steiermark (Regional Administrative Court of Styria, Austria) as follows:

> Article 6(1) of Directive 2008/98/EC of the European Parliament and of the Council of 19 November 2008 on waste and repealing certain Directives must be interpreted as precluding national legislation which grants end-of-waste status to uncontaminated excavated soil, classified as top-quality material for the specific purpose of land development under national law, only when it is used directly as a substitute for raw materials and inasmuch as it denies the end-of-waste status until the holder fulfils certain formal requirements with no environmental relevance such as record-keeping and documentation obligations.
>
> However, Article 6(1) of Directive 2008/98 should not be applied in a case such as the one in the main proceedings, inasmuch as Article 3(1) and Article 5(1) of Directive 2008/98 must be interpreted as meaning that uncontaminated top-quality excavated soil, supplied for the purposes of attending to a request from local farmers relating to land adaptation and land development, after that soil has been selected and undergone a quality control, constitutes not waste, but a by-product, provided that the conditions laid down in Article 5(1)(a) to (d) of Directive 2008/98 are fulfilled. It is for the referring court to carry out that assessment.

JUDGMENT[41]

1   This request for a preliminary ruling concerns the interpretation of Article 6(1) of Directive 2008/98/EC of the European Parliament and of the Council of 19 November 2008 on waste and repealing certain Directives (OJ 2008 L 312, p. 3).

---

[41] Language of the case: German.

2   The request has been made in proceedings between Porr Bau GmbH ('Porr Bau')
and the Bezirkshauptmannschaft Graz-Umgebung (administrative authorities of
the District of Graz and surrounding area) concerning the latter's finding that
excavated materials discharged on cultivation areas constituted waste.

Legal context

European Union law

3   The essential objective of Council Directive 75/442/EEC of 15 July 1975 on
waste (OJ 1975 L 194, p. 39), as amended by Council Directive 91/156/EEC of
18 March 1991 (OJ 1991 L 78, p. 32) ('Directive 75/442'), was, according to the
third recital thereof, the protection of human health and the environment against
harmful effects caused by the collection, transport, treatment, storage and tipping
of waste. Directive 75/442 was repealed and replaced by Directive 2006/12/EC of
the European Parliament and of the Council of 5 April 2006 on waste (OJ 2006 L
114, p. 9), which was itself repealed and replaced by Directive 2008/98.

4   Recitals 6, 8,11, 22 and 29 of Directive 2008/98 state:

> '(6)   The first objective of any waste policy should be to minimise the
> negative effects of the generation and management of waste on human
> health and the environment. Waste policy should also aim at reducing
> the use of resources, and favour the practical application of the waste
> hierarchy.
>
> …
>
> (8)   … Furthermore, the recovery of waste and the use of recovered
> materials should be encouraged in order to conserve natural resources.
>
> …
>
> …
>
> (11)   The waste status of uncontaminated excavated soils and other naturally
> occurring material which are used on sites other than the one from
> which they were excavated should be considered in accordance with
> the definition of waste and the provisions on by-products or on the end
> of waste status under this Directive.
>
> …
>
> (22)   … In order to specify certain aspects of the definition of waste, this
> Directive should clarify:
>
> > …
> >
> > – when certain waste ceases to be waste, laying down
> > end-of-waste criteria that provide a high level of environmental
> > protection and an environmental and economic benefit; possible
> > categories of waste for which "end-of-waste" specifications
> > and criteria should be developed are, among others, construction
> > and demolition waste … For the purposes of reaching
> > end-of-waste status, a recovery operation may be as simple as
> > the checking of waste to verify that it fulfils the end-of-waste
> > criteria.
>
> …

(29) Member States should support the use of recyclates, such as recovered paper, in line with the waste hierarchy and with the aim of a recycling society, and should not support the landfilling or incineration of such recyclates whenever possible.'

5   Chapter I of that directive, entitled 'Subject matter, scope and definitions', includes Articles 1 to 7 thereof.

6   Article 1 of that directive is worded as follows:

'This Directive lays down measures to protect the environment and human health by preventing or reducing the adverse impacts of the generation and management of waste and by reducing overall impacts of resource use and improving the efficiency of such use.'

7   Article 3 of that directive, entitled 'Definitions', provides:

'For the purposes of this Directive, the following definitions shall apply:
1. "waste" means any substance or object which the holder discards or intends or is required to discard;
…
15. "recovery" means any operation the principal result of which is waste serving a useful purpose by replacing other materials which would otherwise have been used to fulfil a particular function, or waste being prepared to fulfil that function, in the plant or in the wider economy. Annex II sets out a non-exhaustive list of recovery operations;
16. "preparing for re-use" means checking, cleaning or repairing recovery operations, by which products or components of products that have become waste are prepared so that they can be re-used without any other pre-processing;
…
19. "disposal" means any operation which is not recovery even where the operation has as a secondary consequence the reclamation of substances or energy. Annex I sets out a non-exhaustive list of disposal operations;
…'

8   Article 4 of Directive 2008/98, entitled 'Waste hierarchy', is worded as follows:

'1. The following waste hierarchy shall apply as a priority order in waste prevention and management legislation and policy:
  (a) prevention;
  (b) preparing for re-use;
  (c) recycling;
  (d) other recovery, e.g. energy recovery; and
  (e) disposal.
2. When applying the waste hierarchy referred to in paragraph 1, Member States shall take measures to encourage the options that deliver the best overall environmental outcome. …
…'

9   Article 5 of that directive, entitled 'By-products', states, in paragraph 1 thereof:

'A substance or object, resulting from a production process, the primary aim of which is not the production of that item, may be regarded as not being waste referred to in point 1 of Article 3 but as being a by-product only if the following conditions are met:

    (a) further use of the substance or object is certain;

    (b) the substance or object can be used directly without any further processing other than normal industrial practice;

    (c) the substance or object is produced as an integral part of a production process; and

    (d) further use is lawful, i.e. the substance or object fulfils all relevant product, environmental and health protection requirements for the specific use and will not lead to overall adverse environmental or human health impacts.'

10   Under Article 6 of Directive 2008/98, headed 'End-of-waste status':

'1. Certain specified waste shall cease to be waste within the meaning of point 1 of Article 3 when it has undergone a recovery, including recycling, operation and complies with specific criteria to be developed in accordance with the following conditions:

    (a) the substance or object is commonly used for specific purposes;

    (b) a market or demand exists for such a substance or object;

    (c) the substance or object fulfils the technical requirements for the specific purposes and meets the existing legislation and standards applicable to products; and

    (d) the use of the substance or object will not lead to overall adverse environmental or human health impacts.

    The criteria shall include limit values for pollutants where necessary and shall take into account any possible adverse environmental effects of the substance or object.

    …

4. Where criteria have not been set at Community level under the procedure set out in paragraphs 1 and 2, Member States may decide case by case whether certain waste has ceased to be waste taking into account the applicable case-law. …'

11   Article 11 of that directive, entitled 'Re-use and recycling', provides, in paragraph 2 thereof:

'In order to comply with the objectives of this Directive, and move towards a European recycling society with a high level of resource efficiency, Member States shall take the necessary measures designed to achieve the following targets:

    …

    (b) by 2020, the preparing for re-use, recycling and other material recovery, including backfilling operations using waste to substitute other materials, of non-hazardous construction and demolition waste excluding naturally occurring material defined in category 17 05 04 in the list of waste shall be increased to a minimum of 70% by weight.'

12   The recovery operations listed in Annex II to Directive 2008/98 include, inter alia, 'land treatment resulting in benefit to agriculture or ecological improvement'.

Austrian law

13   Paragraph 2(1) of the Abfallwirtschaftsgesetz 2002 (2002 Federal Law on Waste Management) provides:

> 'For the purposes of this Federal Law, waste means any movable property
> 1. which the holder intends to discard or has discarded, or
> 2. whose collection, storage, transport and treatment as waste is necessary in order not to harm public interests (Paragraph 1(3)).'

14   Under Paragraph 5(1) of that law:

> 'Unless otherwise specified in a regulation referred to in Paragraph 5(2) or in a regulation referred to in Article 6(2) of Directive 2008/98 on waste, existing substances shall be deemed to be waste until they or substances obtained from them are used directly as a substitute for raw materials or for products obtained from primary raw materials. In the case of preparing for re-use within the meaning of point 6 of Paragraph 2(5), the end-of-waste status occurs at the end of that recovery operation.'

The dispute in the main proceedings and the questions referred for a preliminary ruling

15   Several farmers approached Porr Bau to obtain excavated materials from it for the purpose of soil adaptation or an improvement in cultivation areas. At that time, it was not certain that that undertaking would be in a position to meet their request. That request led Porr Bau subsequently to select an appropriate construction project and to extract those materials from it. Porr Bau thus supplied the requested materials, namely uncontaminated excavated materials of quality class A1, which, under Austrian law, is the highest quality class for excavated soil. In accordance with that law, the use of those materials is appropriate for such terrain adjustments and is lawful.

16   On 4 May 2018, Porr Bau requested the administrative authorities of the District of Graz and surrounding area to declare that the excavated materials which it had supplied did not constitute waste and, in the alternative, that the proposed works did not constitute an activity subject to an obligation to pay a contribution in respect of contaminated sites.

17   By decision of 14 September 2020, those authorities found that the materials in question constituted waste, within the meaning of Paragraph 2(1) of the 2002 Federal Law on Waste Management and that their end-of-waste status had not been achieved, primarily on the ground that formal criteria laid down in the Federal Waste Management Plan had not been complied with.

18   Porr Bau brought an action against that decision before the Landesverwaltungsgericht Steiermark (Regional Administrative Court, Styria, Austria), which is uncertain whether the excavated materials at issue must be classified as 'waste' within the meaning of Directive 2008/98. Furthermore, that court notes that, if those materials are to be classified as waste, it will have to examine whether end-of-waste status has been achieved.

19   The referring court points out that those materials have undergone a checking operation, with the result that they can be used directly. It states that, in the present case, they were used for the purpose of improving agricultural structures, that there was a need for materials, that the technical requirements have been complied with and that, in addition, there were no harmful effects on the environment or on health. Moreover, the aim of such an approach is to prevent waste and to substitute such materials for raw materials.

20   That court states that, under Austrian law, only two activities enable end-of-waste status to be achieved, namely, first, preparing for re-use by checking, cleaning or repairing and, second, the actual use of the materials concerned to substitute raw materials. As regards excavated materials, the applicable criteria are more restrictive, since preparing for re-use does not achieve their end-of-waste status. Thus, that court takes the view that, according to the state of the law currently in force in Austria and according to generally adopted interpretation, end-of-waste status is restricted in a manner contrary to EU law.

21   Although the excavated materials at issue are in the highest quality class and are appropriate, at a technical and legal level, for the improvement of the cultivation areas in question, the formal criteria laid down in the Federal Waste Management Plan, interpreted strictly, could prevent those materials from ceasing to be waste.

22   Accordingly, in the referring court's view, an activity such as an improvement of cultivation areas with the aid of excavated materials, which is used to substitute raw materials and is necessary under the waste hierarchy laid down in Directive 2008/98, is prevented. That would create an incentive, contrary to the objectives pursued by that directive, to use primary raw materials and to dispose of secondary raw materials, such as excavated materials, which are perfectly suitable for recovery.

23   In those circumstances the Landesverwaltungsgericht Steiermark (Regional Administrative Court, Styria) decided to stay the proceedings and to refer the following questions to the Court of Justice for a preliminary ruling:

> '(1) Does Article 6(1) of Directive [2008/98] preclude national legislation under which end-of-waste status is achieved only once waste or existing substances or the substances obtained from them are used directly as a substitute for raw materials or for products made from primary raw materials or they have been prepared for re-use?
>
> If Question 1 is answered in the negative:
>
> (2) Does Article 6(1) of Directive 2008/98 preclude national legislation under which end-of-waste status in respect of excavated materials can be achieved at the earliest when they serve as a substitute for raw materials or for products made from primary raw materials?
>
> If Question 1 and/or Question 2 is/are answered in the negative:
>
> (3) Does Article 6(1) of Directive 2008/98 preclude national legislation under which end-of-waste status in respect of excavated materials cannot be achieved if formal criteria (in particular record-keeping and documentation obligations) which have no environmentally relevant influence on the measure carried out are not complied with or are not complied with in full, even though the excavated materials demonstrably fall below the limit values (premium) to be complied with for the specific intended use?'

Consideration of the questions referred

24   From the outset, it should be noted that, according to settled case-law, in the procedure laid down by Article 267 TFEU providing for cooperation between national courts and the Court of Justice, it is for the latter to provide the national court with an answer which will be of use to it and enable it to decide the case before it. To that end, the Court should, where necessary, reformulate the question referred to it. The Court may also find it necessary to consider provisions of EU law which the national court has not referred to in its question (judgment of 1 August 2022, *Uniqa Asigurari* (C-267/21) EU:C:2022:614 at paragraph 21 and the case-law cited).

25   It is also for the Court to answer the questions asked on the basis of the national legislation and the factual context defined by the referring court, which alone has jurisdiction in that regard, and to provide it with all the criteria for the interpretation of EU law which may enable it to assess whether that legislation is compatible with the provisions of the directive concerned (see, to that effect, judgment of 10 February 2022, *Philips Orastie* (C-487/20) EU:C:2022:92 at paragraph 21 and the case-law cited).

26   In the present case, the referring court is uncertain as to whether the excavated materials at issue in the main proceedings constitute 'waste' within the meaning of point 1 of Article 3 of Directive 2008/98. That court observes that one of the issues of the dispute before it is to ascertain whether uncontaminated excavated materials which, under national legislation, are in the highest quality class must be classified as 'waste'.

27   The Austrian Government contends that, under Austrian law, where materials are excavated or demolished in the course of a construction project, the main purpose of the construction developer is usually to carry out that project without being hindered by those materials, with the result that they are removed from the site in question with the intention of discarding them.

28   Porr Bau takes the view that that is not the case here and submits that the excavated materials at issue in the main proceedings could fulfil the conditions laid down in Article 5(1) of Directive 2008/98 and thus be classified as 'by-products'.

29   In the event that those materials were nevertheless to be classified as 'waste', the referring court states that it will be necessary to make them subject to a contribution in respect of contaminated sites and to examine whether and, if so when, the end-of-waste status of those materials has been achieved.

30   In that regard, it should be noted that, according to recital 11 of Directive 2008/98, the waste status of uncontaminated excavated soils and other naturally occurring material which are used on sites other than the one from which they were excavated should be considered in accordance with the definition of waste and the provisions on by-products or on the end-of-waste status under that directive.

31   Therefore, in order to provide a useful answer to the referring court, it must be held that, by its questions, which it is appropriate to consider together, that court asks, in essence, whether point 1 of Article 3, Article 5(1) and Article 6(1) of Directive 2008/98 must be interpreted as precluding national legislation under which uncontaminated excavated materials, which, pursuant to national law, are in the highest quality class, first, must be classified as 'waste' even if it were determined that those materials fall within the concept of 'by-product' and, second,

only lose that waste status when they are used directly as a substitute and their holder satisfies the formal criteria which are irrelevant for the purposes of environmental protection.

Classification of excavated materials as 'waste' or as a 'by-product'

32   Article 3 of Directive 2008/98 defines the concept of 'waste' as being any substance or object which the holder discards or intends or is required to discard.

33   In that regard, the Court has repeatedly held that the classification of a substance or object as 'waste' is to be inferred primarily from the holder's actions and the meaning of the term 'discard' (judgment of 14 October 2020, *Sappi Austria Produktion and Wasserverband 'Region Gratkorn-Gratwein'* (C-629/19) EU:C:2020:824 at paragraph 42 and the case-law cited).

34   As regards the meaning of the term 'discard', it follows from the Court's settled case-law that that term must be interpreted in the light of the aim of Directive 2008/98, which, in the words of recital 6 thereof, is to minimise the negative effects of the generation and management of waste on human health and the environment, having regard to Article 191(2) TFEU, which provides that EU policy on the environment is to aim at a high level of protection and is to be based, in particular, on the precautionary principle and the principle that preventive action should be taken. It follows that the term 'discard', and therefore the concept of 'waste' within the meaning of point 1 of Article 3 of Directive 2008/98, cannot be interpreted restrictively (judgment of 4 July 2019, *Tronex* (C-624/17) EU:C:2019:564 at paragraph 18 and the case-law cited).

35   More specifically, the existence of 'waste', within the meaning of Directive 2008/98, must be determined in the light of all the circumstances certain of which may constitute evidence that a substance or object has been discarded or of an intention or requirement to discard it within the meaning of point 1 of Article 3 of Directive 2008/98 (see, to that effect, judgment of 14 October 2020, *Sappi Austria Produktion and Wasserverband 'Region Gratkorn-Gratwein'* (C-629/19) EU:C:2020:824 at paragraph 45 and the case-law cited).

36   Among the circumstances that may constitute such evidence is the fact that a substance is a production or consumption residue, that is to say, a product which was not itself sought and for which special precautions must be taken if it is used owing to the environmentally hazardous nature of its composition (judgment of 14 October 2020, *Sappi Austria Produktion and Wasserverband 'Region Gratkorn-Gratwein'* (C-629/19) EU:C:2020:824 at paragraphs 46 and 47 and the case-law cited).

37   It is also clear from the Court's case-law that neither the method of treatment reserved for a substance nor the use to which that substance is put determines conclusively whether or not the substance is to be classified as 'waste' and that the concept of 'waste' does not exclude substances or objects which are capable of economic re-use. The system of supervision and control established by Directive 2008/98 is intended to cover all substances and objects discarded by their owners, even if they have a commercial value and are collected on a commercial basis for recycling, reclamation or re-use (judgment of 14 October 2020, *Sappi Austria Produktion and Wasserverband 'Region Gratkorn-Gratwein'* (C-629/19) EU:C:2020:824 at paragraph 48 and the case-law cited).

38   In addition, particular attention must be paid to the fact that the substance or object in question is not or is no longer of any use to its holder, such that that substance or object constitutes a burden which that holder will seek to discard. If that is indeed the case, there is a risk that that holder will dispose of the substance or object in his or her possession in a way likely to cause harm to the environment, particularly by dumping it or disposing of it in an uncontrolled manner. That substance or object, because it falls within the concept of 'waste' within the meaning of Directive 2008/98, is subject to the provisions of that directive, which means that the recovery or disposal of that substance or object must be carried out in such a way that human health is not endangered and without using processes or methods likely to harm the environment (judgment of 14 October 2020, *Sappi Austria Produktion and Wasserverband 'Region Gratkorn-Gratwein'* (C-629/19) EU:C:2020:824 at paragraph 49 and the case-law cited).

39   In that regard, the degree of probability that a substance or an object will be re-used without a prior processing operation constitutes a criterion relevant to assessing whether or not they constitute waste within the meaning of Directive 2008/98. If, beyond the mere possibility of re-using the substance or object in question, there is also a financial advantage for the holder in so doing, the likelihood of such re-use is high. In such circumstances, the substance or object in question must no longer be regarded as a burden which its holder seeks to 'discard', but as a genuine product (see, to that effect, judgment of 14 October 2020, *Sappi Austria Produktion and Wasserverband 'Region Gratkorn-Gratwein'* (C-629/19) EU:C:2020:824 at paragraph 50 and the case-law cited).

40   In certain situations, a substance or an object resulting from an extraction or manufacturing process the primary aim of which is not their production may be regarded not as a residue, but as by-products, which their holder does not seek to 'discard', within the meaning of point 1 of Article 3 of Directive 2008/98, but which he or she intends to exploit or market on terms advantageous to him or herself in a subsequent process – including, as the case may be, in order to meet the needs of economic operators other than the producer of those substances – provided that such re-use is not a mere possibility but a certainty, without any further processing prior to re-use and as part of the continuing process of production (see, to that effect, judgment of 14 October 2020, *Sappi Austria Produktion and Wasserverband 'Region Gratkorn-Gratwein'* (C-629/19) EU:C:2020:824 at paragraph 51 and the case-law cited).

41   As the Court has already held, it would indeed not be justified at all to make substances or objects which the holder intends to exploit or market on economically advantageous terms, whether or not there is to be a subsequent recovery process, subject to the requirements of Directive 2008/98, which seek to ensure that recovery and disposal operations will be carried out without endangering human health and without using processes or methods which could harm the environment. However, having regard to the requirement to interpret the concept of 'waste' widely, it is only situations in which the re-use of the substance or object in question is not a mere possibility but a certainty that are envisaged, which it is for the referring court to ascertain, without the necessity of using any of the waste recovery processes referred to in Annex II to Directive 2008/98 prior to re-use (see, to that effect, judgment of 14 October 2020, *Sappi Austria Produktion and Wasserverband 'Region Gratkorn-Gratwein'* (C-629/19) EU:C:2020:824 at paragraph 52 and the case-law cited).

42   It is apparent from Article 5(1) of Directive 2008/98 that a 'by-product' is a substance or object resulting from a production process the primary aim of which is not to produce that substance or object and which meets a number of conditions listed in Article 5(1)(a) to (d).

43   As follows from that provision, a substance or object, resulting from a production process, the primary aim of which is not the production of that substance or product, may be regarded as being not 'waste' as referred to in point 1 of Article 3 of that directive but as a 'by-product' only if the following cumulative conditions are met: first, further use of the substance or object must be certain; second, it must be possible to use the substance or object directly without any further processing other than normal industrial practice; third, the substance or object must be produced as an integral part of a production process; and fourth, further use must be lawful, that is to say the substance or object fulfils all relevant product, environmental and health protection requirements for the specific use and will not lead to overall adverse environmental or human health impacts.

44   A substance or object which constitutes a 'by-product', within the meaning of Article 5(1) of Directive 2008/98, is not regarded as being waste falling within the scope of that directive. Thus, according to that provision, the classification of 'by-product' and the status of 'waste' are mutually exclusive (see, to that effect, judgment of 14 October 2020, *Sappi Austria Produktion and Wasserverband 'Region Gratkorn-Gratwein'* (C-629/19) EU:C:2020:824 at paragraph 71).

45   In that regard, the Court has ruled that petroleum coke which is produced intentionally or in the course of producing other petroleum fuels in an oil refinery and is certain to be used as fuel to meet the energy needs of the refinery and those of other industries does not constitute waste within the meaning of that directive. Livestock effluent may, on the same terms, fall outside classification as 'waste', if it is used as soil fertiliser as part of a lawful practice of spreading on clearly identified parcels and if its storage is limited to the needs of those spreading operations (see, to that effect, judgment of 8 September 2005, *Commission v Spain* (C-121/03) EU:C:2005:512 at paragraphs 59 and 60 and the case-law cited).

46   It is for the referring court, which alone has jurisdiction to assess the facts of the case before it, to determine whether, in the light of the considerations set out in paragraphs 32 to 39 above, Porr Bau had in fact intended to 'discard' the excavated materials at issue in the main proceedings, with the result that they would constitute waste, within the meaning of point 1 of Article 3 of Directive 2008/98.

47   It is, in particular, for that court to determine whether those excavated materials constituted a burden which that construction undertaking sought to discard, with the result that there would be a risk that that undertaking would discard them in a manner likely to cause harm to the environment, particularly by dumping them or disposing of them in an uncontrolled manner.

48   That being so, it is for the Court to provide that referring court with any helpful guidance to resolve the dispute before it (see, to that effect, judgment of 14 October 2020, *Sappi Austria Produktion and Wasserverband 'Region Gratkorn-Gratwein'* (C-629/19) EU:C:2020:824 at paragraph 53 and the case-law cited).

49   In the present case, it is apparent from the information before the Court that, even before the excavation of the materials at issue in the main proceedings, local farmers had made an express request for the supply of such materials. After appropriate construction projects had been found, making the requested excavated materials available, that request, it is stated, led to a commitment by Porr Bau to

make those excavated materials available, alongside an agreement under which that undertaking would carry out, by means of those materials, the works to adapt and improve the land and cultivation areas duly identified. Such factors, if proven which it is for the referring court to determine, do not appear to be such as to establish the intention of the construction undertaking concerned to discard those materials.

50   It is, therefore, necessary to examine whether the excavated materials at issue in the main proceedings must be classified as a 'by-product' within the meaning of Article 5(1) of Directive 2008/98.

51   It is for the referring court to ascertain whether all the conditions laid down in that provision, referred to in paragraph 43 above, are fulfilled.

52   As regards, in the first place, the condition laid down in Article 5(1)(a) of that directive, according to which further use of the substance or object is certain, it will be for the referring court to verify in the present case that the farmers concerned have made a binding commitment to Porr Bau to take delivery of the excavated materials at issue in the main proceedings in order to use them for carrying out works to adapt and improve land and cultivation areas, but also that those materials and the quantities supplied did in fact serve to carry out those works and were strictly limited for those purposes.

53   If the materials were not supplied immediately, it is appropriate to allow temporary storage for a reasonable period, until the works for which they are intended are carried out. As is clear from the case-law referred to in paragraph 45 above, that period of storage must, however, not exceed what is required in order for the undertaking concerned to be able to meet its contractual obligations (see, to that effect, judgment of 3 October 2013, *Brady* (C-113/12) EU:C:2013:627 at paragraph 45 and the case-law cited).

54   As regards, in the second place, the condition laid down in Article 5(1)(b) of Directive 2008/98 that it must be possible to use the substance or object directly without further processing other than normal industrial practice, it is apparent from the order for reference that the excavated materials at issue in the main proceedings were subject to a quality control demonstrating that they are uncontaminated materials in the highest quality class and are recognised as such under national law. It is nevertheless for the referring court to satisfy itself that those materials did not require any processing or treatment before their further use.

55   In the third place, regarding the condition laid down in Article 5(1)(c) of Directive 2008/98 and the question whether those materials form an integral part of Porr Bau's production process, it should be noted, as the Advocate General observed in points 41 and 47 of her Opinion, that the excavated soil is the result of one of the first steps usually undertaken in a construction operation as an economic activity, the result of which is the transformation of land.

56   As regards, in the fourth place, the condition that the further use of the substance or object at issue must be lawful, Article 5(1)(d) of Directive 2008/98 requires, in particular, that the substance or object fulfils all relevant product, environmental and health protection requirements for the specific use and will not lead to overall adverse environmental or human health impacts.

57   It should be borne in mind in that regard that, according to the information in the order for reference, the excavated materials at issue in the main proceedings had been classified, following a quality analysis carried out before their re-use, as uncontaminated excavated materials in the highest quality class, as defined by

Austrian law, in particular in the context of the Federal Waste Management Plan, which lays down specific requirements for the reduction of waste quantities, their pollutants and their harmful effects on human health and the environment. That plan, it is contended, also declares that the use of uncontaminated excavated materials in the highest quality class is suitable and authorised for land adaptation and improvement.

58   That use is, in principle, consistent with the objectives of Directive 2008/98. It should be noted that the use of excavated soil, in the form of building materials, in so far as such soil meets strict quality requirements, has a significant advantage for the environment because it contributes, as required by Article 11(2)(b) of that directive, to the reduction of waste, to the preservation of natural resources and to the development of a circular economy.

59   In addition, as the Advocate General observed in point 73 of her Opinion, it must be held that the use of excavated materials in the highest quality class, for the purpose of adapting and improving cultivation areas, makes it possible to comply with the waste hierarchy defined in Article 4 of that directive.

60   If, conversely, the referring court were to conclude that the excavated materials at issue in the main proceedings constitute 'waste', within the meaning of point 1 of Article 3 of Directive 2008/98, it asks whether Article 6(1) of that directive must be interpreted as precluding national legislation under which the end-of-waste status of such materials is achieved only when they are used directly as a substitute and their holder satisfies the formal criteria which are irrelevant for the purposes of environmental protection.

The end-of-waste status of excavated materials

61   Under Article 6(1) of Directive 2008/98, certain specified waste ceases to be waste when it has undergone a recovery or recycling operation. End-of-waste status is also subject to specific criteria which must be defined in accordance with a number of conditions. First, the substance or object at issue must commonly be used for specific purposes. Second, a market or demand must exist for such a substance or object. Third, the substance or object must fulfil the technical requirements for the specific purposes and meet the existing legislation and standards applicable to products. Fourth, the use of the substance or object must not lead to overall adverse environmental or human health impacts.

62   The referring court observes that Paragraph 5(1) of the 2002 Federal Law on Waste Management provides that existing substances or substances obtained from them are to cease to be waste when those substances are directly used as substitutes for raw materials or products obtained from primary raw materials or at the end of their preparation for re-use.

63   However, as regards excavated materials, that court states that that end-of-waste status is achieved only when those materials have been used as substitutes for raw materials or for products obtained from primary raw materials.

64   In addition, that referring court notes, first, that recovery through preparation for re-use does not achieve end-of-waste status. Second, in order for that status to be achieved, formal requirements, such as record-keeping and documentation obligations which are irrelevant for the purposes of environmental protection, must be fulfilled, in accordance with the Federal Waste Management Plan.

65   It is, therefore, necessary to ascertain whether Article 6(1) of Directive 2008/98 precludes national legislation under which the end-of-waste status of uncontaminated excavated materials, which, pursuant to national law, are in the highest quality class, is achieved only when they have been used as a substitute for raw materials and after such formal requirements have been satisfied.

66   In the first place, it should be noted that, although the recovery operations listed in Annex II to Directive 2008/98 include 'land treatment resulting in benefit to agriculture or ecological improvement', it is apparent from recital 22 of that directive that, for the purposes of reaching end-of-waste status, a recovery operation may be as simple as the checking of waste to verify that it fulfils the end-of-waste criteria.

67   As the Advocate General observed in point 65 of her Opinion, that recital finds expression in point 16 of Article 3 of Directive 2008/98, which defines 'preparing for re-use' as any operation consisting in the 'checking, cleaning or repairing' of products or components of products that have become waste in order to prepare them so that they can be re-used without any other pre-processing. That same provision expressly classifies 'preparing for re-use' operations as a recovery.

68   Therefore, it must be held that an examination seeking to determine the status and presence of pollution or of contamination in excavated materials may be classified as a 'checking operation', covered by the concept of 'preparing for re-use', as defined in point 16 of Article 3 of Directive 2008/98. Accordingly, waste which is the subject of such a 'preparing for re-use' operation may be regarded as having undergone a recovery operation, within the meaning of Article 6(1) of that directive, if its re-use does not require any other pre-processing.

69   In the second place, it is for the referring court to assess whether, in the case in the main proceedings, the specific criteria defined in accordance with the conditions laid down in that Article 6(1) are complied with following the checking operation.

70   As regards the formal criteria laid down in the Federal Waste Management Plan to which the excavated materials at issue in the main proceedings were made subject, it should be noted that, in accordance with the second subparagraph of Article 6(1) of Directive 2008/98, the end-of-waste status criteria are to include limit values for pollutants where necessary and are to take into account any possible adverse environmental effects of the substance or object. Furthermore, Member States enjoy, within the framework laid down in Article 6(4) of that directive, discretion as regards the setting of those criteria.

71   Therefore, although formal criteria such as those mentioned by the referring court may prove necessary, in particular, in order to ensure the quality and safety of the substance at issue, they must be set in such a way as to attain their objectives without undermining the achievement of the objectives of Directive 2008/98.

72   In the present case, it is apparent from the file before the Court that, according to the decision referred to in paragraph 17 above, the assessment that the end-of-waste status of the excavated materials at issue in the main proceedings had not been achieved was essentially attributable to non-compliance with the formal criteria which are irrelevant for the purposes of environmental protection.

73   The objectives pursued by Directive 2008/98 would be likely to be disregarded if, notwithstanding the fact that the uncontaminated excavated materials in the highest quality class comply with the specific criteria defined in accordance with the conditions laid down in Article 6(1) of that directive, those materials – the properties of which serve to improve agricultural structures – were not regarded

as having lost their waste status following a quality control making it possible to ensure that their use was safe for the environment or human health.

74   If, as the referring court points out, the re-use of such excavated materials were hindered by formal criteria which are irrelevant for the purposes of environmental protection, those criteria would have to be regarded as running counter to the objectives pursued by Directive 2008/98, which, as is apparent from recitals 6, 8 and 29 of that directive, consist in encouraging the application of the waste hierarchy provided for in Article 4 of that directive as well as the recovery of waste and the use of recovered materials in order to conserve natural resources and to enable the development of a circular economy. Such measures would, as the case may be, undermine the effectiveness of that directive.

75   It cannot be accepted that such formal criteria have the effect of undermining the attainment of the objectives of Directive 2008/98. It is for the referring court, which alone has jurisdiction to interpret the provisions of its national law, to examine whether that is so in the present case.

76   It follows from those considerations that, if the excavated materials at issue in the main proceedings were the subject of a recovery operation and satisfy all the specific criteria defined in accordance with the conditions laid down in Article 6(1)(a) to (d) of Directive 2008/98, which it is for the referring court to ascertain, it must be held that the end-of-waste status of those materials has been achieved.

77   In the light of all the foregoing considerations, the answer to the questions referred is that point 1 of Article 3 and Article 6(1) of Directive 2008/98 must be interpreted as precluding national legislation under which uncontaminated excavated materials, which, pursuant to national law, are in the highest quality class:

- must be classified as 'waste' where their holder neither intends nor is required to discard them and those materials meet the conditions laid down in Article 5(1) of that directive for being classified as 'by-products', and
- only lose that waste status when they are used directly as a substitute and their holder has satisfied the formal criteria which are irrelevant for the purposes of environmental protection, if those criteria have the effect of undermining the attainment of the objectives of that directive.

Costs

78   Since these proceedings are, for the parties to the main proceedings, a step in the action pending before the referring court, the decision on costs is a matter for that court. Costs incurred in submitting observations to the Court, other than the costs of those parties, are not recoverable.

On those grounds, the Court (First Chamber) hereby rules:

Point 1 of Article 3 and Article 6(1) of Directive 2008/98/EC of the European Parliament and of the Council of 19 November 2008 on waste and repealing certain Directives, must be interpreted as precluding national legislation under which uncontaminated excavated materials, which, pursuant to national law, are in the highest quality class,

- must be classified as 'waste' where their holder neither intends nor is required to discard them and those materials meet the conditions laid down in Article 5(1) of that directive for being classified as 'by-products', and

— only lose that waste status when they are used directly as a substitute and their holder has satisfied the formal criteria which are irrelevant for the purposes of environmental protection, if those criteria have the effect of undermining the attainment of the objectives of that directive.

R. (ON THE APPLICATION OF SAHOTA) v HEREFORDSHIRE COUNCIL

COURT OF APPEAL (CIVIL DIVISION)

Singh, Arnold and Lewis LJJ: 13 December 2022

[2022] EWCA Civ 1640; [2023] Env. L.R. 20

⚓ Admissibility; Agricultural buildings; Assessment; Environmental impact; Habitats; Planning permission; Sites of Special Scientific Interest; Special Areas of Conservation; Watercourses

H1   *Judicial review—Town and Country Planning—nature conservation—Conservation of Habitats and Species Regulations 2017—agricultural runoff into nearby watercourses including Special Area of Conservation and Site of Special Scientific Interest—whether planning committee misled into believing no need for a Habitats Regulations Assessment—whether judge wrong to admit ecology officer's evidence and then dismiss claim—whether relied on erroneous and/or irrational interpretations of evidence and argument advanced—whether judge erred in law in finding compliance with Conservation of Habitats and Species Regulations 2017 reg.63*

H2   The appellant (S) brought a claim for judicial review to challenge the grant of planning permission by the respondent (H) for the erection of a cattle shed and an extension to an existing agricultural building. The concern was that, as the proposed development contemplated the expansion of livestock farming, this would increase manure production and the spreading of manure on the surrounding fields, which would run off into nearby watercourses, in particular the River Wye which was a Special Area of Conservation (SAC) and a Site of Special Scientific Interest. S also argued that H's planning committee had been misled into believing that there was no need for a Habitats Regulations Assessment. The claim was dismissed by the High Court which admitted evidence from H's ecology officer. The grounds of appeal were that: (1) the judge's decisions to admit the ecology officer's evidence and then dismiss the claim had been unjust and relied critically on erroneous and/or irrational interpretations of the evidence and of the argument advanced; and (2) the judge erred in law in deciding that, prior to granting planning permission, H had complied with the Conservation of Habitats and Species Regulations 2017 reg.63.

H3   **Held,** in dismissing the appeal:

H4   (1) The judge had not fallen into error with regard to the admission of evidence as a matter of principle. He had correctly directed himself as to the relevant principles and the authorities and reminded himself of the need for caution before admitting the evidence. Nor was the conclusion reached one which was not reasonably open to him. To the contrary, it had been helpful to admit the evidence in order to elucidate what had been before the committee.

H5   (2) The duty imposed by the Habitats Directive art.6(3) and reg.63 rested with competent authorities and not with the courts. Whether a plan or project would adversely affect the integrity of a European protected site was always a matter of judgment for the competent authority itself. That was an evaluative judgment, which the court was neither entitled nor equipped to make for itself. In a legal challenge to a competent authority's decision, the court's function was supervisory only, applying ordinary public law principles, conscious of the nature of the subject-matter and the expertise of the competent authority itself. If the competent authority had properly understood its duty, the court would intervene only if there was some *Wednesbury* error in the performance of that duty.

H6   (3) As pointed out in *R. (on the application of Champion) v North Norfolk DC*, there was an important distinction between the Habitats Directive/Habitats Regulations on the one hand and the Town and Country Planning (Environmental Impact Assessment) Regulations 2011 on the other: the former containing no equivalent to "screening" under the EIA Regulations. At least, in this country, the use of the term "screening" in relation to the Habitats legislation was potentially confusing, because of the technical meaning it had under the EIA Regulations. The formal procedures prescribed for EIA purposes, including "screening", preparation of an environmental statement, and mandatory public consultation, had no counterpart in the Habitats legislation. In cases where it was not "obvious", the competent authority would consider whether the "trigger" for appropriate assessment was met. But that "informal threshold decision" was not to be confused with a formal "screening opinion" in the EIA sense. All that was required was that, in a case where the authority had found there to be a risk of significant adverse effects to a protected site, there should be an "appropriate assessment".

H7   (4) The evidence made it clear that there were no relevant effects of the proposed development on the River Wye SAC, whether taken in isolation or in combination with other plans or projects. That was based on the ecology officer's own expert experience and on the methodology recommended by the expert body in the field, Natural England. S' real complaint was not so much that the planning committee had been misled by the officers' report, nor even that the ecology officer's evidence had been wrongly admitted by the judge, but rather that the advice had been wrong. In order to succeed in that argument, S would have to do more than show that others might take a different view. What had to be shown was that there were public law grounds which would entitle the court to intervene by way of judicial review, in particular that there was a demonstrable error in the reasoning process; or that the conclusion was irrational. Having regard to the appropriate standard of review and on the evidence, there were no such public law grounds in this case.

H8   **Cases referred to:**
Dover DC v Campaign to Protect Rural England (Kent) [2017] UKSC 79; [2018] 1 W.L.R. 108; [2018] Env. L.R. 17
Kenyon v Secretary of State for Housing, Communities and Local Government [2020] EWCA Civ 302; [2021] Env. L.R. 8; [2020] J.P.L. 1189
Mansell v Tonbridge and Malling BC [2017] EWCA Civ 1314; [2019] P.T.S.R. 1452; [2018] J.P.L. 176

No Adastral New Town Ltd v Suffolk Coastal DC [2015] EWCA Civ 88; [2015] Env. L.R. 28

R. (on the application of Champion) v North Norfolk DC [2015] UKSC 52; [2015] 1 W.L.R. 3710; [2016] Env. L.R. 5

R. (on the application of Lanner Parish Council) v Cornwall Council [2013] EWCA Civ 1290; [2013] 45 E.G. 75 (C.S.)

R. (on the application of Law Society) v Lord Chancellor [2018] EWHC 2094 (Admin); [2019] 1 W.L.R. 1649; [2018] 5 Costs L.R. 937

R. (on the application of Lee Valley Regional Park Authority) v Epping Forest DC [2016] EWCA Civ 404; [2016] Env. L.R. 30; [2016] J.P.L. 1009

R. v Mendip DC Ex p. Fabre [2017] P.T.S.R. 1112; (2000) 80 P. & C.R. 500; [2000] J.P.L. 810 QBD

R. (on the application of Morge) v Hampshire CC [2011] UKSC 2; [2011] 1 W.L.R. 268; [2011] P.T.S.R. 337

R. (on the application of Palmer) v Herefordshire Council [2016] EWCA Civ 1061; [2017] 1 W.L.R. 411

R. (on the application of Shasha) v Westminster City Council [2016] EWHC 3283 (Admin); [2017] P.T.S.R. 306; [2017] J.P.L. 539

R. (on the application of United Trade Action Group Ltd) v Transport for London (TfL) [2021] EWCA Civ 1197; [2022] R.T.R. 2; [2022] L.L.R. 141

R. (on the application of Watermead Parish Council) v Aylesbury Vale DC [2017] EWCA Civ 152; [2018] P.T.S.R. 43

R. v Westminster City Council Ex p. Ermakov [1996] 2 F.C.R. 208; (1996) 28 H.L.R. 819; (1996) 8 Admin. L.R. 389 CA (Civ Div)

R. (on the application of Wyatt) v Fareham BC [2022] EWCA Civ 983; [2023] Env. L.R. 14; [2022] J.P.L. 1509

Smyth v Secretary of State for Communities and Local Government [2015] EWCA Civ 174; [2015] P.T.S.R. 1417; [2016] Env. L.R. 7

Sweetman v An Bord Pleanala (C-258/11) EU:C:2013:220; [2014] P.T.S.R. 1092; [2015] Env. L.R. 18

H9 **Legislation referred to:**
Senior Courts Act 1981 s.31
Directive 92/43 (Habitats) art.6
Town and Country Planning (General Development Procedure) (England) (Amendment) Order 2003 (SI 2003/2047) art.5
Town and Country Planning (Development Management Procedure) (England) (Amendment) Order 2013 (SI 2013/1238) art.7
Town and Country Planning (Development Management Procedure) England Order (SI 2015/595) art.15
Conservation of Habitats and Species Regulations 2017 (SI 2017/1012) reg.63

H10 *A. Goodman* (instructed by Leigh Day LLP) appeared on behalf of the appellant.
M. Henderson (instructed by Herefordshire Council) appeared on behalf of the respondent.

JUDGMENT

LORD JUSTICE SINGH:

Introduction

1   This appeal arises from the Respondent's grant of planning permission, on 4 June 2020, to the Interested Party (Mr John Morgan), to which the Appellant (Mr David Sahota) objects. The Appellant brought a claim for judicial review to challenge the grant of planning permission but that claim was dismissed by HHJ Worster (sitting as a judge of the High Court) ("the judge"), in a judgment given on 25 August 2021.

2   The issues on this appeal are: (1) whether the judge erred in admitting the evidence of Mr James Bisset, the ecology officer at the Respondent authority; and (2) whether the Respondent's planning committee was misled into believing that there was no need for a Habitats Regulations Assessment ("HRA").

3   At the hearing we heard from Mr Alex Goodman for the Appellant and Mr Matthew Henderson for the Respondent. I express the Court's gratitude to them both for their written and oral submissions.

Factual Background

4   On 30 July 2019 the Interested Party applied to the Respondent for planning permission for the proposed development, which was for the erection of a cattle shed and an extension to an existing agricultural building. The site of the proposed development is located within the upper Golden Valley in western Herefordshire in the rural parish of Dorstone. The River Wye is a Special Area of Conservation ("SAC") and is also a Site of Special Scientific Interest ("SSSI").

5   The Appellant is concerned that, as the proposed development contemplates the expansion of livestock farming, this would increase manure production and the spreading of manure on the surrounding fields, which would run off into nearby watercourses, in particular the River Wye.

6   The Respondent's planning committee considered the application and resolved to grant planning permission following a meeting on 3 June 2020. The committee's resolution was in accordance with the recommendation of the Respondent's officers, as contained in their report to the committee.

7   On 20 August 2019, Mr Bisset had been consulted by the Respondent's case officer about the application for planning permission. Mr Bisset is a qualified ecology officer with over 35 years' professional experience. He provided written advice to the planning officer, which stated:

> "The additional cattle shed has a floor area of 465.5msq. This falls under any trigger sizes (500msq) for air pollution emissions in regards to any Sites of Special Scientific Interest as identified through [N]atural England's details SSSI Impact Risk Zone data set. Based on this information no detailed air emissions assessment is required for this specific development at this location. No likely significant effects on any relevant SSSI have been identified. There are no further ecology comments on this … development within an existing developed farm complex."

8   That advice was inserted verbatim into the officers' report to the planning committee, at para. 4.2. I will set out other relevant parts of the report below.

9   In the course of these proceedings in the High Court, the Respondent filed a witness statement from Mr Bisset, dated 23 October 2020. Objection was (and is) taken to the admission of that statement. I will refer to Mr Bisset's evidence in more detail below.

10   In his judgment the judge rejected the objection to the admission of the evidence of Mr Bisset. He then dismissed the claim for judicial review on its merits.

The planning officers' report

11   As I have mentioned, para. 4.2 of the officers' report set out verbatim the advice which had been received from the ecology officer.

12   At paras. 6.24-6.26, under the heading 'Ecology and Biodiversity', the report said:

> "6.24 Policy E1 of the DNDP [Dorstone Neighbourhood Development Plan] sets out that development proposals should not have any adverse impacts on the River Wye Special Area of Conservation (SAC), echoing the requirements set out in more detail at Policy SD3 and SD4 of the CS [Core Strategy].
> 6.25 The applicant has advised that given the building would be for the housing of cattle, all manure will be solid with no slurry given that the cattle would be on straw, as is standard practice.
> 6.26 The Council's Ecologist has commented that the additional cattle shed would have a floor area of 464.5msq. This falls under any trigger sizes (500msq) for air pollution emissions in regards to any Sites of Special Scientific Interest as identified though natural England's details SSSI Impact Risk Zone data set. Based on this information, there is no detailed air emissions assessment required for this development at this location. Noting that the site is outside the River Wye Special SAC, there are no other triggers for a Habitat Regulations Assessment (HRA) process and there are therefore no likely significant effects on any other relevant SSSI."

13   The report concluded, at para. 6.30, as follows:

> "The application would result in the modest expansion to a small scale rural enterprise, fulfilling economic objectives of sustainable development. The proposed buildings, by virtue of their design, scale and siting would positively respond to the existing and established complex of buildings and are not considered to cause harm to the wider landscape setting. Moreover, no harm to ecological networks or the local highway network is identified. Overall, the proposal is considered to accord with the provisions of the Dorstone Neighbourhood Development Plan, the Herefordshire Local Plan – Core Strategy and the National Planning Policy Framework. The proposal is therefore considered a sustainable form of development and is accordingly recommended for approval subject to the conditions as set out below."

14   It appears from the transcript of the meeting of the planning committee on 3 June 2020 that members of the committee asked questions of the planning officers about ecology matters. The answers in substance repeated what had been said in writing, that the advice from the ecology officer was that there was no cumulative

impact assessment of what the site could produce because the ecologist had taken the view that there is no objection to the proposal.

Material legislation

15   Regulation 63 of the Conservation of Habitats and Species Regulations 2017 (SI 2017 No. 1012) ("the Habitats Regulations") transposed article 6(3) of Council Directive 92/43/EEC (the Habitats Directive) into domestic law. The Habitats Regulations remain part of domestic law although the United Kingdom has now left the European Union.

16   Regulation 63 provides that:

> "(1) A competent authority, before deciding to undertake, or give any consent, permission or other authorisation for, a plan or project which—
> (a) is *likely to have a significant effect on a European site* or a European offshore marine site (either alone or in combination with other plans or projects), and
> (b) is not directly connected with or necessary to the management of that site, must make *an appropriate assessment* of the implications of the plan or project for that site in view of that site's conservation objectives. […]
> (3) The competent authority must for the purposes of the assessment consult the appropriate nature conservation body and have regard to any representations made by that body within such reasonable time as the authority specifies […]" (Emphasis added)

Grounds of Appeal

17   Although the initial grounds of appeal were not drafted in this way, the Appellant has adopted what was said by Stuart-Smith LJ in granting permission to appeal on 19 January 2022 and has formulated the issues which arise on this appeal in the following way:

> (1) The judge's decisions (a) to admit the evidence of Mr Bisset and then (b) to dismiss the claim relied critically on erroneous and/or irrational interpretations of the evidence (including the evidence of Mr Bisset itself) and of the argument advanced to the judge and further, his decision is unjust (see 52.21(3)(b)) in admitting Mr Bisset's evidence and in the reliance he placed on it ("Issue 1").
> (2) The judge erred in law in deciding that, prior to granting planning permission, the Respondent had complied with regulation 63 of the Habitats Regulations ("Issue 2").

Issue 1: the admissibility of Mr Bisset's evidence

18   The authorities on the admissibility of "*ex post facto*" evidence in judicial review proceedings were summarised by this Court (comprising Bean LJ, Sir Keith Lindblom SPT and Sir Stephen Irwin) in *R. (United Trade Action Group Ltd) v Transport for London* [2021] EWCA Civ 1197; [2022] R.T.R. 2 at para 125. The authorities, many of which were cited to us also, include *R. v Westminster City*

Council Ex p. Ermakov [1996] 2 F.C.R. 208; *R. (Lanner Parish Council) v Cornwall Council* [2013] EWCA Civ 1290; *R. (Watermead Parish Council) v Aylesbury Vale DC* [2017] EWCA Civ 152; [2018] P.T.S.R. 43; and *Kenyon v Secretary of State for Housing, Communities and Local Government* [2020] EWCA Civ 302; [2021] Env. L.R. 8. It is unnecessary to recite all of the seven principles which were identified by the Court in *United Trade Action Group* but several pertinent points can be derived from them.

(1) The court has a discretion whether to admit evidence that has come into existence after the decision under review was made, as a means of elucidating, correcting or adding to the contemporaneous reasons for it.

(2) Evidence directly in conflict with the contemporaneous record of the decision-making will not generally be admitted. The touchstone is whether the evidence is elucidation not fundamental alteration, confirmation not contradiction.

(3) Sometimes, even where the evidence is merely explanatory, the court will have to ask itself whether it would be legitimate to admit the explanation given. Circumstances will vary. For example, when the court is dealing with a challenge to a planning inspector's decision it will have in mind that there is an express statutory duty on the inspector to give reasons for his decision. As was common ground before us, there is no similar statutory duty on a local planning authority in a case such as the present. There was such a duty at one time but that has been abrogated: see the Town and Country Planning (General Development Procedure) (England) (Amendment) Order 2003 (SI 2003 No. 2047), article 5, which was brought into force on 5 December 2003 and was repealed with effect from 25 June 2013 by the Town and Country Planning (Development Management Procedure) (England) (Amendment) Order 2013 (SI 2013 No. 1238), article 7. The history is set out more fully in *Dover DC v Campaign to Protect Rural England (Kent)* [2017] UKSC 79; [2018] 1 W.L.R. 108, at paras. 28-30 (Lord Carnwath JSC).

19   It follows from what I have said so far that the basis on which this Court can interfere with the judge's decision to admit Mr Bisset's evidence in the present case is a limited one. As was common ground before us, the role of this Court is its usual one when sitting as an appellate court. It is not our function simply to substitute our own decision for that of the judge. We must ask ourselves whether the judge exercised his discretion wrongly. In particular, did the judge fall into error as a matter of principle? And, even if he did not, was the conclusion to which he came one that was not reasonably open to him?

20   When approached in that way, I am unable to accept Mr Goodman's submissions. In my view, the judge did not fall into error as a matter of principle. He correctly directed himself as to the relevant principles and the authorities on this topic. He reminded himself of the need for caution before admitting Mr Bisset's evidence. Furthermore, I do not think that the conclusion to which he came was one which was not reasonably open to him. To the contrary, I agree with the judge that it was helpful in this case to admit Mr Bisset's evidence in order to elucidate what had been before the committee. Indeed, as will become apparent later when I address Issue 2, it could be said that it is in the Appellant's interests, and not necessarily the Respondent's, for Mr Bisset's evidence to be admitted, since this enables Mr

Goodman to attack the reasoning in that evidence which would not have been apparent on the face of the officers' report to the planning committee.

21   Mr Goodman made three fundamental submissions before us in support of his argument on Issue 1. The first submission is that there was a structural defect in the judge's reasoning. By this Mr Goodman means that, since the decision-maker was the planning committee and not Mr Bisset, it was not open to the judge to admit his evidence by way of elucidation of the committee's reasons for granting planning permission. In support of that submission Mr Goodman relied on the decision of the High Court in *R. (Shasha) v Westminster City Council* [2016] EWHC 3283 (Admin); [2017] P.T.S.R. 306, in particular at paras. 42-43 and 56 (Mr John Howell QC, sitting as a deputy High Court judge).

22   This submission comes up against the problem that it is well established that, although one is concerned with the members' reasons and not the planning officer's, where a planning officer makes a recommendation which is followed by the members, the reasonable inference is that the members did so for the reasons advanced by the officer, unless there is some indication to the contrary: see *R. v Mendip DC Ex p. Fabre* (2000) 80 P. & C.R. 500, at 511 (Sullivan J), a passage cited with approval by this Court in *R. (Palmer) v Herefordshire Council* [2016] EWCA Civ 1061; [2017] 1 W.L.R. 411, at para. 7 (Lewison LJ). In the present case, I can see no reason to avoid drawing the reasonable inference that the planning committee did grant planning permission for the reasons advanced by the officers in their report to it. Accordingly, the suggested distinction between the committee's reasons and those of the officers (including Mr Bisset) falls away.

23   Mr Goodman's second submission is that Mr Bisset's evidence was not simply elucidation but rather contradicted what had been said to the committee in the officers' report. I disagree. In my view, it was open to the judge to conclude that the evidence of Mr Bisset simply set out his "workings", which helped to understand why he had reached the conclusion which he had, and which had been fairly and fully set out in the officers' report to the committee. In this context it is important to bear in mind what Sullivan J said in *Fabre*, at page 509: part of a planning officer's expert function in reporting to the committee must be to make an assessment of how much information needs to be included in the report in order to avoid burdening a busy committee with excessive and unnecessary detail. Furthermore, as was said in *Fabre* and has frequently been reiterated in similar cases, it should be borne in mind that the planning committee comprises local councillors, who are likely to be familiar with their own local area. In the present case that is clear from the transcript of the planning committee meeting which we have before us. For example, the local councillor in whose ward the proposed development site is located made detailed and pertinent remarks at that meeting.

24   In this context it is also important to bear in mind what was said by Lady Hale JSC in *R. (Morge) v Hampshire CC* [2011] UKSC 2; [2011] 1 W.L.R. 268, at paras. 35-36. As Lady Hale emphasised in that passage, in this country planning decisions are taken by democratically elected councillors, who are responsible to, and sensitive to the concerns of, their local communities. They have professional advisers who investigate and report to them. Those reports must be clear and full enough to enable them to understand the issues and make up their minds within the limits that the law allows them. But the court should not impose too demanding a standard upon such reports, for otherwise their whole purpose will be defeated: the councillors either will not read them or will not have a clear enough grasp of the

issues to make a decision for themselves. Lady Hale also emphasised that democratically elected bodies go about their decision-making in a different way from courts. It is their job, not the court's, to weigh the competing public and private interests involved.

25   Mr Goodman's third submission is that the judge's decision to admit Mr Bisset's evidence in this case goes "against the grain" both of the nature of judicial review proceedings; and the nature of planning decision-making in this country.

26   I do not agree that what the judge did in this case goes against the grain of judicial review proceedings. He was well aware of the need for caution before admitting this type of evidence but was entitled to do so consistent with the nature of judicial review proceedings. In this context Mr Goodman placed reliance on what was said by Coulson LJ in *Kenyon*, at para. 28, that in judicial review proceedings it is generally inappropriate to seek to rely on documents which were not available to the decision-maker. In my view, Coulson LJ's particular concern in that passage was that admitting *ex post facto* documents risks undermining the process of judicial review because the court will be asked to conduct a kind of "rolling review", in which nothing is ever finalised or settled. This serves only to encourage the attitude that it is always possible to "have another go." Although I agree with Coulson LJ about the risks of permitting a "rolling review" they do not arise on the facts of the present appeal. What Mr Bisset's evidence does is not to refer to information which has arisen after the decision under challenge was taken. Rather it refers to material which he had in his mind at the time and which helps to explain how he reached the conclusion which he did and which was then conveyed to the planning committee through the officers' report.

27   Turning to the "grain" of the planning system, I accept Mr Henderson's submission for the Respondent, that Mr Goodman has simply been unable to identify any legal obligation which was breached by the procedure adopted in this case. Although it is true that in a general lay-person's sense, the planning system is open to public scrutiny, there are specific legal obligations, for example to consult the public in certain contexts, which simply do not arise in the present context. By way of example, Mr Henderson showed us Article 15 of the Town and Country Planning (Development Management Procedure) England Order (SI 2015 No. 595). Article 15 requires a planning application to be publicised. That was done in the present case and has nothing to do with the admissibility of Mr Bisset's evidence.

28   Further, there is a provision in regulation 63(4) of the Habitats Regulations themselves which requires a competent authority to consult the public ("take the opinion of the general public") if it thinks it appropriate to do so: as Mr Henderson pointed out, this shows that, when the legislator wished to cater for public participation in the decision-making process, it did so. The fact that there is no specific provision which deals with the present situation is telling.

29   For the above reasons I would reject the Appellant's submissions on Issue 1.

Issue 2: whether an appropriate assessment was required

30   On behalf of the Appellant Mr Goodman submits that the officers' report misled the planning committee by advising that an HRA was not required in this case. He submits that regulation 63 of the Habitats Regulations requires a competent authority to undertake an "appropriate assessment" before giving consent to any project

likely to have a significant effect on a European site. It is common ground that the River Wye SAC is such a site. It is also common ground that an appropriate assessment did not take place; this is because it was considered to be unnecessary by the Respondent, on the advice of its officers.

31   Mr Goodman submits that the test under regulation 63 is whether scientific doubt can be excluded as to the possibility that the proposal could, in combination with other developments, have an adverse effect on the River Wye SAC. He submits that the officers' report did not properly advise the planning committee of that test, and the report's reasoning that, because the site was not itself within the SAC, there were "therefore no likely significant effects" was wrong in law. This was because the site and all run off from it is hydrologically connected to the River Wye SAC, so that the mere fact that the site was not within the SAC was not determinative of the potential impacts as the advice seemed to suggest. Furthermore, as Mr Goodman emphasised before us, the Appellant's fundamental complaint is that the officers, including Mr Bisset, did not consider what would be the *cumulative* impact of the increase in manure production at the proposed development site when combined with the manure produced and spread in other parts of the farmholding.

32   In this context Mr Goodman showed us the witness statement of Simon Maiden-Brooks. The judge permitted the Appellant to rely on that statement only to a limited extent, going to the issue under section 31 of the Senior Courts Act 1981 (which is no longer a live issue before this Court). The judge did not permit the Appellant to rely on the witness statement for wider purposes. Nevertheless, Mr Goodman referred us to that statement, in particular paras. 35-36, which state:

> "35. In simple terms, the whole issue is that when manure is spread within the hydrological catchment area, the rain causes that to run off, in part as surface run-off. The manure is nutrient-rich, and it is this increase in nutrients which causes the problem with the River Wye SAC. I have concluded that all of the land on which the manure is being spread is within the hydrological catchment area of the River Wye SAC.
> 36. Notwithstanding this, on the Council's case, some of the land is within the purple shaded area, which leads to the conclusion that (even on the Council's case) some of the manure spreading areas will potentially cause problems to the River Wye SAC. I am therefore unclear as to why an HRA wasn't carried out."

33   I will return to that evidence below when I set out my conclusions on Issue 2.

34   Before us particular reliance was placed by Mr Goodman on *Smyth v Secretary of State for Communities and Local Government* [2015] EWCA Civ 174; [2015] P.T.S.R. 1417, at para. 83, where Sales LJ said:

> "I agree with Mr Jones's submission, to the extent that he argued that it would not comply with the relevant standards of evidence indicated by the Court of Justice for a national competent authority simply to rely for its screening opinion or 'appropriate assessment' under article 6(3) on a mere assertion by an expert, unsupported by consideration of any background facts and without reasoning to explain the assertion made. If such a case arose, evidence of that character could fairly be described as merely subjective, and as material which failed to qualify as something which could be regarded as 'the best scientific

knowledge in the field'. However, *such a case will be rare*. Expert witnesses know that it is incumbent on them to refer to relevant underlying evidence and to explain their opinions, and typically do so." (Emphasis added)

35   Mr Goodman submits that the present case was not one of those "rare" cases in which it was "obvious" that no appropriate assessment was required. He also emphasised before us that the threshold for an HRA is a very low one. For that proposition he relied in particular on the Opinion of Advocate General Sharpston in *Sweetman v An Bord Pleanála* (C-258/11) EU:C:2013:220; [2014] P.T.S.R. 1092, at paras. 47-49, where she said that the "possibility" of there being a significant effect on a European site will generate the need for an appropriate assessment for the purposes of article 6(3) of the Habitats Directive.

Relevant legal principles

36   It was common ground before us that the principles which govern this kind of challenge were summarised by Lindblom LJ in *R. (Mansell) v Tonbridge and Malling BC* [2017] EWCA Civ 1314; [2019] P.T.S.R. 1452, at para. 42. As Lindblom LJ put it at para. 42(2):

> "The question for the court will always be whether, on a fair reading of the report as a whole, the officer has materially misled the members on a matter bearing upon their decision, and the error has gone uncorrected before the decision was made."

As Lindblom LJ emphasised in the same passage, the officers' report is not to be read with undue rigour but with reasonable benevolence and bearing in mind that it is written for councillors with local knowledge. Minor or inconsequential errors may be excused.

37   It is also important to keep in mind the points emphasised by Lindblom LJ in para. 41. First, the Planning Court (and this Court also) must always be vigilant against excessive legalism infecting the planning system. The courts must keep in mind that the function of planning decision-making has been assigned by Parliament, not to judges, but (at local level) to elected councillors with the benefit of advice given to them by planning officers. Further, they are entitled to expect good sense and fairness in the court's review of a planning decision, not the hypercritical approach which the court is often urged to adopt.

38   In the specific context of the Habitats Regulations, Lindblom LJ gave the following guidance in *R. (Lee Valley Regional Park Authority) v Epping Forest DC* [2016] EWCA Civ 404; [2016] Env. L.R. 30, at para. 65:

> "… It must be remembered, as Sullivan J said in *R. (on the application of Hart DC) v Secretary of State for Communities and Local Government* [2008] 2 P. & C.R. 16 (in para. [72] of his judgment), that the Habitats Directive is 'intended to be an aid to effective environmental decision making, not a legal obstacle course'. Judging whether an appropriate assessment is required in a particular case is the responsibility not of the court but of the local planning authority, subject to review by the court only on conventional *Wednesbury* grounds (see the judgment of Sales LJ, with whom Richards and Lewison LJJ agreed, in *R. (on the application of Dianne Smyth) v Secretary of State for Communities and Local Government* [2015] EWCA Civ 174, at [78]–[81]).,,,"

39   As Sir Keith Lindblom SPT pointed out in *R. (Wyatt) v Fareham BC* [2022] EWCA Civ 983, at para. 9, there is a wealth of case law relevant to article 6(3) of the Habitats Directive and regulation 63 of the Habitats Regulations, both in the Court of Justice of the European Union ("the CJEU") and in domestic courts. Some basic points emerge, which he then helpfully set out in ten sub-paragraphs. It is unnecessary for present purposes to recite those in full although I have them all in mind. Particular points arising from them deserve emphasis in the present appeal.

40   First, the duty imposed by article 6(3) and regulation 63 rests with competent authorities and not with the courts. Whether a plan or project will adversely affect the integrity of a European protected site is always a matter of judgment for the competent authority itself. That is an evaluative judgment, which the court is neither entitled nor equipped to make for itself. In a legal challenge to a competent authority's decision, the role of the court is not to undertake its own assessment, but to review the performance by the authority of its duty under regulation 63. The court's function is supervisory only.

41   As was said by Sir Keith Lindblom in *Wyatt*, at para. 9(3), when reviewing the performance by a competent authority of its duty under regulation 63, the court will apply ordinary public law principles, conscious of the nature of the subject-matter and the expertise of the competent authority itself. If the competent authority has properly understood its duty under regulation 63, the court will intervene only if there is some *Wednesbury* error in the performance of that duty.

42   As he continued, at para. 9(4), a competent authority is entitled, and can be expected, to give significant weight to the advice of an expert national agency with relevant expertise in the sphere of nature conservation, such as Natural England. Although the authority may lawfully disagree with, and depart from, such advice, if it does so, it must have cogent reasons for doing so. Further, the court for its part will give appropriate deference to the views of expert regulatory bodies.

43   In *R. (Champion) v North Norfolk DC* [2015] UKSC 52; [2015] 1 W.L.R. 3710, at para. 35, Lord Carnwath JSC pointed out that there is an important distinction between the Habitats Directive/Habitats Regulations on the one hand and the Environmental Impact Assessment ("EIA") Regulations on the other: the former contain no equivalent to "screening" under the EIA Regulations. As he pointed out at para. 39, at least in this country the use of the term "screening" in relation to the Habitats legislation is potentially confusing, because of the technical meaning it has under the EIA Regulations. The formal procedures prescribed for EIA purposes, including "screening", preparation of an environmental statement, and mandatory public consultation, have no counterpart in the Habitats legislation.

44   At para. 40 Lord Carnwath cited with approval the decision of this Court in *No Adastral New Town Ltd v Suffolk Coastal DC* [2015] EWCA Civ 88; [2015] Env. L.R. 28, at paras. 63-69. There Richards LJ considered the language of article 6(3) of the Habitats Directive and noted the absence in the Court's judgment in *Sweetman* of any support for the contention that there must be a screening assessment at an early stage in the decision-making process. At para. 41, Lord Carnwath continued that the process envisaged by article 6(3) should not be overcomplicated. As Richards LJ had pointed out, in cases where it is not "obvious", the competent authority will consider whether the "trigger" for appropriate assessment is met. But this "informal threshold decision" is not to be confused with a formal "screening opinion" in the EIA sense. The operative words are those of the Habitats Directive itself. All that is required is that, in a case where the authority has found there to

be a risk of significant adverse effects to a protected site, there should be an "appropriate assessment".

45   Before us Mr Goodman placed emphasis on the decision of the Divisional Court (Leggatt LJ and Carr J) in *R. (Law Society) v Lord Chancellor* [2018] EWHC 2094 (Admin); [2019] 1 W.L.R. 1649, in particular at para. 98, where, in giving the judgment of the Court, Carr J explained that a public authority's decision may be challenged on the basis that there is a demonstrable flaw in the reasoning which led to it, for example that a significant reliance was placed on an irrelevant consideration, or that there was no evidence to support an important step in the reasoning, or that the reasoning involved a serious logical or methodological error. Mr Goodman submits that this is just such a case, because both the officers' report to the planning committee and the evidence of Mr Bisset (if it is admissible) contain a demonstrable flaw in the reasoning process.

46   In order to assess that submission it is important to look at the guidance given by Natural England as to the methodology to be used, on which Mr Bisset relied when he considered the issues on which his advice was sought in the planning process.

Natural England's User Guidance on Impact Risk Zones for Sites of Special Scientific Interest

47   Although the guidance from Natural England, which is dated 3 June 2019, is expressly concerned with SSSIs it was common ground before us that it also covers European sites such as the SAC in the present case.

48   At page 2 the Guidance states as follows:

"The Impact Risk Zones (IRZs) are a GIS tool developed by Natural England to make a rapid initial assessment of the potential risks to SSSIs posed by development proposals. They define zones around each SSSI which reflect the particular sensitivities of the features for which it is notified and indicate the types of development proposal which could potentially have adverse impacts. The IRZs also cover the interest features and sensitivities of European sites, which are underpinned by the SSSI designation and 'Compensation Sites', which have been secured as compensation for impacts on European/Ramsar sites.

Local planning authorities (LPAs) have a duty to consult Natural England before granting planning permission on any development that is in or likely to affect a SSSI. The SSSI IRZs can be used by LPAs to consider whether a proposed development is likely to affect a SSSI and determine whether they will need to consult Natural England to seek advice on the nature of any potential SSSI impacts and how they might be avoided or mitigated. The IRZs do not alter or remove the requirements to consult Natural England on other natural environmental impacts or other types of development proposal under the Town and Country Planning (Development Management Procedure) (England) Order 2015 and other statutory requirements – see the gov.uk website for further information."

49   In a table, under the heading 'Important Notes', the Guidance states, at para. 2, that the IRZs seek to guide consultations relating to the likely impacts of

development on SSSIs under Schedule 4(w) to the Town and Country Planning (Development Management Procedure) (England) Order 2015.

50   Appendix 2 of the Guidance states that Natural England's local team staff have reviewed the IRZs and where necessary they have been varied to reflect specific local circumstances "such as known water quality issues".

51   Natural England also makes available information to local planning authorities which is not in the public domain. It is clear on the evidence before us that Mr Bisset relied on such non-public data in the present case. I turn to his evidence now.

The evidence of James Bisset

52   At para. 11 of his witness statement Mr Bisset said that:

"Amongst other matters, the non-public Natural England data shows IRZs as specific to a particular Special Area of Conservation or specified Site(s) of Special Scientific Interest – including the hydrological catchment area for the River Wye SAC where discharges may affect the SAC. As in the Council's earlier documents, I will refer to this latter area as 'the NE hydrological catchment area'."

53   At paras. 13-16 Mr Bisset continued as follows:

"13. This detailed IRZ provided the response for the location of the development as shown in (Exhibit JBB02). This response details the nature and scale of development that Natural England consider could affect the specified designated site in relation to specific types of potential effect. In this case, the response showed that the Site is outside of the NE hydrological catchment area, and therefore the information on the response relates to the River Wye's other designation as a SSSI.

14. This IRZ output provided a clear basis that allowed me to further assess any potential effects on the River Wye SAC/SSSI from the proposed development. The only relevant 'trigger' identified that _might_ relate to the Site was for air pollution. The IRZ identifies that Natural England only consider livestock and poultry units with an area over 500m2 as requiring further consideration (this includes all aspects related to air emissions including the stock themselves and any manure created within the development). In the Application the actual floor area of the shed holding stock that could potentially create any relevant air emissions is clearly identified in the application information as being only 464.5m2.

15. Having given this information from the statutory nature conservation body significant weight in my considerations, and based on the IRZ guidance published by Natural England (Exhibit JBB03) that clearly identifies that in these circumstances no consultation with Natural England was appropriate or required, *I was able to reach my own professional judgment that there was no effect on the River Wye SAC from the proposed development*. I considered this to be clear and obvious.

16. Having identified that there was no effect on the River Wye SAC from the proposed development, it was not necessary to consider any 'in

combination' or 'cumulative' effects as the development had no identified effects when considered 'alone'. *In short, there was no effect which could operate 'in combination' with another project.*" (Emphasis added)

The Respondent's position statement

54   It is also helpful in this context to refer to the Herefordshire Council position statement on development in the River Lugg catchment area (February 2020). In relation to Habitat Regulations Assessments, the position statement says that the Respondent (in its role as competent authority) must carry out such an assessment on any relevant planning application that falls within the red and purple areas shown on the attached plan. Where there is a likely significant effect the council must carry out an appropriate assessment.

55   It is common ground before us that the application site in the present case does not itself fall within either the red zone or the purple zone on the attached plan but that part of the farmholding does fall within the purple zone.

56   The position statement also states that, where certain criteria are in place, phosphates would be unlikely to reach the river as there is no pathway for impacts. With no pathway for impacts there is no need for a further Habitats Regulations Assessment. Before us Mr Henderson submitted that that is the situation in the present case.

The position statement of Natural Resources Wales

57   By way of contrast to the position in England, Mr Goodman drew our attention to the position statement of Natural Resources Wales in relation to SAC designated rivers and phosphates. There it is stated:

"New development within *any* part of the catchment which will increase the amount or concentration of wastewater effluent or organic materials discharged directly or indirectly into the catchment's waterbodies has the potential to increase phosphate levels within those waterbodies." (Emphasis added)

Under the heading of 'Habitats Regulations Assessment' it is stated:

"*Any* proposed development within the Wye catchment that *might* increase the amount of phosphate within the catchment could lead to additional damaging effects to the SAC features and therefore such proposals should be screened through a HRA to determine whether they are likely to have a significant effect on the SAC condition. Once issued by NRW, this position statement in combination with the Compliance Assessment Report, applies to all development that is yet to be determined by the relevant planning authority." (Emphasis added)

58   The summary of Natural Resources Wales's current position is as follows:

"A large number of water bodies on the Wye are failing their phosphate targets. Even where they are passing, there is generally little headroom. For this reason we are unable to rule out the possibility that additional phosphate input on any part of the River Wye SAC will further damage the SAC. We therefore recommend that *any* proposed new development that *might* otherwise result in increasing the amount of phosphate within the SAC either by direct or indirect discharges must be able to demonstrate phosphate neutrality or betterment." (Emphasis added)

59   Interesting though it is to be shown what the position would be if the proposed development site were on the other side of the border between England and Wales, this is simply not relevant to this appeal. It is inherent in the scheme of devolution that there may be different laws and policies in England and Wales.

My assessment

60   I accept Mr Henderson's submission (summarised at para. 56 above), essentially for the reasons which are set out in the evidence of Mr Bisset. In particular Mr Bisset's reasons at paras. 15-16 of his witness statement make it clear that there were no relevant effects of the proposed development on the River Wye SAC, whether taken in isolation or in combination with other plans or projects. As he expressly stated at para. 15 of his statement, Mr Bisset's conclusion was based on his own expert experience. Further, it was based on the methodology recommended by the expert body in this field, Natural England.

61   On analysis, the Appellant's real complaint on this appeal is not so much that the planning committee was misled by the officers' report (the advice of Mr Bissett was accurately relayed to the committee by it); nor even that Mr Bissett's evidence was wrongly admitted by the judge (the subject of Issue 1), since it may assist the Appellant if the court is able to have regard to Mr Bisset's evidence. It is rather that Mr Bissett's advice was wrong.

62   But in order to succeed in that argument the Appellant would have to do more than show that others (including other experts such as Mr Maiden-Brooks) might take a different view. What has to be shown is that there are public law grounds which would entitle the court to intervene by way of judicial review, in particular that there was a demonstrable error in the reasoning process; or that the conclusion was irrational.

63   Having regard to the appropriate standard of review and on the evidence which I have summarised above, I have reached the conclusion that there are no such public law grounds in this case. Accordingly, I would reject the Appellant's submissions on Issue 2.

Conclusion

64   For the reasons I have given I would dismiss this appeal.

LORD JUSTICE ARNOLD:
65   I agree.

LORD JUSTICE LEWIS:
66   I also agree.

DAVIES v BRIDGEND CBC

COURT OF APPEAL (CIVIL DIVISION)

Baker, Birss and Snowden LJJ: 3 February 2023

[2023] EWCA Civ 80; [2023] Env. L.R. 21

Causation; Diminution in value; Economic loss; Encroachment; Invasive species; Neighbouring land; Nuisance; Plants

H1 *Nuisance—Japanese Knotweed encroachment—into neighbouring property—breach of relevant duty in nuisance until reasonable and effective treatment programme started—"blight" claim for residual diminution in value of property even after knotweed treated so far as possible—court finding that damages for diminution in value due to knotweed irrecoverable in nuisance following 'Network Rail Infrastructure Ltd v Williams'—whether 'Williams' authority for such proposition—whether lack of causation of loss*

H2   The appellant (D) bought a property in 2004 adjoining land owned by the respondent council (B). Japanese Knotweed growing on B's land encroached into D's land. In D's claim for nuisance, the District Judge found that it was likely that knotweed had spread into D's land before 2004 and that B was in breach of the relevant duty in nuisance from 2013 until 2018 when a reasonable and effective treatment programme finally started. B argued that since the knotweed was already present on D's land, any damage arose before the breach of duty and so, since the fact the property was affected by knotweed was not due to any breach, the claim was fatally flawed on causation. The District Judge rejected that argument on the basis that there was a continuing nuisance and breach of duty as a result of persisting encroachment. While the initial encroachment was historic, any loss suffered by D in principle continued and would accrue by the continuation of the breach in B's failing to treat the knotweed. The judge also held that unless and until B treated the knotweed on its land, any attempt by D to eradicate knotweed on his own land would have been rendered futile. On the question of damages, the relevant head was a claim for £4,900 "blight" for the residual diminution in value of the property remaining even after the knotweed had been treated as best it could be. The District Judge held that, following the *Network Rail Infrastructure Ltd v Williams* case, all the diminution in value damages were irrecoverable and dismissed the claim. On appeal, D claimed that the damages were losses consequential on the nuisance found. The County Court dismissed the appeal. Though accepting that the diminution in value claimed was consequential on the nuisance, the court held that *Williams* was authority for the proposition that damages for diminution in value due to knotweed were irrecoverable in nuisance. In the Court of Appeal, the sole ground was that the judges below had erred in that they had misunderstood *Williams* which, properly understood, was not authority against D's case. B argued that the earlier judgments had been correct, and also contested causation, as well as making a submission about the quality of D's evidence of diminution in value itself.

H3   **Held,** in allowing the appeal:

H4   (1) In a case in which the knotweed was on the defendant's land, even if close to the boundary and at risk of invading the claimant's land, *Williams* held that the reduction in market value of the claimant's land caused did not result from physical damage nor from physical interference with the claimant's property and therefore did not amount to a nuisance. The purpose of the tort of nuisance was not *simply* to protect the value of property. *Williams* itself later recognised that if the value of the claimant's property was diminished as a result of an interference with the claimant's quiet enjoyment or amenity, due to physical encroachment of knotweed from the defendant's land into the claimant's land, damages including diminution in value of the property would be available. The reasoning in the relevant passages of *Williams*, relied on by the judges below, was nothing to do with recoverability of damages in a case in which the tort of nuisance was complete. Once it was accepted that there was damage leading to a loss, the diminution in value, which was consequential on the nuisance, there was no authority that consequential damage to the claimant's economic interests was irrecoverable. Though a trivial or de minimis encroachment of knotweed would not be actionable on that basis, there was no finding in the present case that the knotweed in D's land was merely trivial. The submission that proving a non-trivial encroachment of knotweed into land was not enough and that to establish nuisance a claimant also had to prove that the knotweed was also a risk to structures on the land or that there was a prospect of improving or altering the property which the knotweed interfered with, or something similar, was rejected. The references in *Williams* to future risk and increased difficulty in development were given simply as examples of interference with amenity in order to illustrate why knotweed could fairly be called a "pernicious weed" and a "natural hazard". The point being made was a distinction between "pure economic loss", loss without physical damage or physical interference which was not actionable, and cases in which there was physical change to the claimant's property as a result of the presence there of knotweed rhizomes. Once that natural hazard was present in the claimant's land (to a non-trivial extent), the claimant's quiet enjoyment or use of it, or the land's amenity value, had been diminished. For the purposes of the elements of the tort of nuisance that amounted to damage and it was the result of a physical interference. If consequential residual diminution in value could be proved, damages on that basis could be recovered. They were not pure economic loss because of the physical manner in which they had been caused.

H5   (2) B's submission that the residual diminution in value, the reduction in value left even after knotweed had been properly treated, could not have been caused by the nuisance because the knotweed encroachment had already happened before the breach of duty, was wrong. Viewed in 2018, after five years of breach by B failing to treat the knotweed on its own land adequately, the knotweed was still encroaching on D's land and any treatment by D would have been futile unless and until B complied with its duty as a good neighbour and dealt with its own knotweed. That was not an exception to the "but for" test. The harm to the quiet enjoyment and amenity suffered by D persisted in 2018 precisely because the nuisance was a continuing one. The harm then had been caused by the breach of duty. If B had acted properly within one month of being on notice of the problem, for example, there would be no breach of duty.

H6   (3) Despite B's arguments on the evidence, £4,900 would be a fair figure for the residual diminution in value.

H7 **Cases referred to:**

Blue Circle Industries Plc v Ministry of Defence [1999] Ch. 289; [1999] 2 W.L.R. 295; [1999] Env. L.R. 22 CA (Civ Div)

Delaware Mansions Ltd v Westminster City Council [2001] UKHL 55; [2002] 1 A.C. 321; [2001] 3 W.L.R. 1007 HL

Dennis v Ministry of Defence [2003] EWHC 793 (QB); [2003] Env. L.R. 34; [2003] J.P.L. 1577

Hunter v Canary Wharf Ltd [1997] A.C. 655; [1997] 2 W.L.R. 684; [1997] Env. L.R. 488 HL

Jan De Nul (UK) Ltd v Axa Royale Belge SA (formerly NV Royale Belge) [2002] EWCA Civ 209; [2002] 1 Lloyd's Rep. 583

Network Rail Infrastructure Ltd v Williams [2018] EWCA Civ 1514; [2019] Q.B. 601; [2018] Env. L.R. 35

H8   *T. Carter* (instructed by High Street Solicitors Ltd) appeared on behalf of the appellant.

M. White (instructed by Dolmans Solicitors) appeared on behalf of the respondent.

JUDGMENT

LORD JUSTICE BIRSS:

1   This case is about the role played by diminution in value in cases of nuisance involving the plant Japanese knotweed ("knotweed"). The appellant Mr Davies owns a property in Nant-y-moel, Bridgend, Wales at 10 Dinam Street. It adjoins land owned by the local council, the respondent. There is knotweed growing on the respondent's land. The knotweed encroached from the respondent's land into the appellant's land.

2   The appellant brought a claim in nuisance against the respondent. The claim was heard by DJ Fouracre in Swansea County Court with judgment given on 8th November 2021.

3   The District Judge found that the stand of knotweed on the respondent's land seemed to have been present for over 50 years. In 2004 the appellant bought the property at 10 Dinam Street as an investment. It is rented out. The District Judge found that it was likely that knotweed had spread from the respondent's land into the appellant's land before 2004.

4   In 2012 a RICS report on knotweed was published, describing the difficulties it can cause. It is fair to point out that more recently the 2012 RICS report was withdrawn and the RICS now says that knotweed is not the "bogey plant" it was once thought to be. Nevertheless neither side before us contended that this means knotweed is not capable of founding a claim in nuisance.

5   The appellant became concerned about knotweed in 2017. He raised it with the respondent in 2019.

6   The District Judge found that the respondent was in breach of the relevant duty in nuisance owed to the appellant as a neighbour, starting from 2013 and on until 2018 when a reasonable and effective treatment programme finally started. There has been no appeal from this conclusion about breach from 2013-2018.

7   The respondent contended that since the knotweed was already present on the appellant's land, any damage arose before the breach of duty and so, since the fact the property is affected by knotweed is not due to any breach, the claim was fatally flawed on causation. The District Judge rejected this argument (paragraph 24), holding that it was answered by the fact that there was a continuing nuisance and breach of duty as a result of persisting encroachment. While the initial encroachment was historic, any loss suffered by the appellant in principle continues and will accrue by the continuation of the breach in the respondent's failing to treat the knotweed. The judge also held (paragraph 27) that unless and until the respondent treated the knotweed on its land, any attempt by the appellant to eradicate knotweed on his own land would have been rendered futile.

8   Turning to damages, all the sums claimed were characterised as aspects of a diminution in the value of the appellant's property. The damages originally claimed were under various heads including a sum for the cost of treatment, a sum for disturbance and inconvenience, and other sums. The only head of damages left is a claim for £4,900 as what is sometimes called the "residual" diminution in value of the property, also called "blight", remaining even after the knotweed has been treated as best it can be. All the other heads have been dropped over the course of these proceedings for various reasons, or they failed and were not appealed.

9   The District Judge held that all the diminution in value damages were irrecoverable in law in a case like this, based on the decision of the Court of Appeal in *Network Rail Infrastructure Ltd v Williams* [2018] EWCA Civ 1514; [2019] Q.B. 601 (Sir Terence Etherton MR, Sharp and Legatt LJJ). Therefore the District Judge dismissed the claim.

10   On appeal, the main point was on diminution in value. The appellant claimed that the damages were losses consequential on the nuisance found. The Circuit Judge HHJ Beard dismissed the appeal on 27 May 2022. He accepted that the diminution in value claimed was consequential on the nuisance identified by the court below, but held that *Williams* was authority for the proposition that damages for diminution in value due to knotweed are irrecoverable in nuisance. As the Circuit Judge put it at paragraph 19:

> "The only actual *damage* in this case, which is not physical, is diminution in value. However I consider *Williams* is authority that such economic damage is not recoverable. The phrase "the purpose of the tort of nuisance is not to protect the value of property as an investment or a financial asset" could not be clearer. I accept [counsel for the appellant's] argument that this is damage leading to a loss which is consequential on the nuisance found. However, it is not recoverable damage, it is pure economic loss."

11   The Circuit Judge also rejected the appeal on causation (paragraph 22).

12   The appellant applied for permission to bring a second appeal and Arnold LJ gave permission because the point of principle about recoverability was important, not least given the number of knotweed cases.

13   As the sole ground of appeal the appellant contends the judges below have erred in that they have misunderstood *Williams*, whereas, properly understood, *Williams* is not an authority against the appellant's case. The respondent contends the judgments below are right, and also advances two points by a respondent's notice: one is a challenge to the causation point which it has lost up to now, and the other

is a submission about the quality of the appellant's evidence of diminution in value itself.

14   Before going further, I note that what is in issue in terms of damages here is £4,900. If that was all that was at stake, the proportionality of these proceedings having got this far would be questionable, but the principle is an important one, and no doubt (sadly) the costs are substantial.

The appeal – recoverability of diminution in value

15   *Williams* was an appeal concerning two properties in Maesteg, South Wales which were tried together. The claimants (Mr Williams and Mr Waistel) had brought a claim in nuisance against Network Rail Infrastructure Ltd ("NR") the proprietor of neighbouring land. Broadly speaking, the claimants won both at first instance and on the appeal. Notably for what follows, the damages awarded to the claimants included various items but one was damages for the residual diminution in value of the land (or stigma). These were summarised at paragraph 35 in the judgment in the Court of Appeal as follows:

> "35. The Recorder then addressed damages for the diminution in value of the claimants' properties arising from interference with their quiet enjoyment of their land. The Recorder held that, given that the claimants were entitled to recover damages to treat the knotweed in order to remove the nuisance, the appropriate diminution in value was the residual diminution in value once the treatment was completed. The Recorder held (at [243]-[259]) that Mr Williams was entitled to £10,500 and Mr Waistell was entitled to £10,000 for that reason."

16   Before the Recorder at first instance the claims in *Williams* had been examined in two ways: a first basis looking at the knotweed encroaching onto the claimant's land from NR's land, and a second basis looking at the presence of knotweed on the NR's land itself. The results were:

    i) On the first basis, characterised as an encroachment claim, there was no tort of nuisance because while knotweed had encroached onto the claimant's land from NR's land, and was not trivial (paragraph 53), nevertheless that knotweed on the claimant's land had caused no actual physical damage. The existence of physical damage was a necessary element of the tort put this way and so the claim put that way failed (see paragraphs 19 to 21). The fact the presence of the knotweed had resulted in a diminution in value of the properties did not constitute damage.

    ii) On the second basis, characterised as a quiet enjoyment/loss of amenity claim, the tort was made out because the presence of knotweed on NR's land was a sufficiently serious interference with the claimants' right of quiet enjoyment/amenity value of their properties to constitute an actionable nuisance. The recorder found that a landowner in the claimants' position would suffer a loss of enjoyment. He considered that the diminution in value of the properties, combined with the fact that any owner would have to live with the concerns and adverse consequences of a devalued property, is properly characterised as an aspect of the amenity of the land protected by the tort of private nuisance.

17   Before the Court of Appeal there was an appeal by NR and a respondent's notice by the claimants. The appeal was to challenge the second basis of the claim.

18   The leading judgment in the Court of Appeal was given by Etherton MR. It starts with a number of general principles (paragraphs 38-45). The section repays reading in full and in this brief summary I am not intending to say anything different.

19   The first principle identified is that private nuisance is a violation of real property rights, which means either interference with the legal rights of an owner or interference with the amenity of the land, that is to say the right to use and enjoy it.

20   The second is that although nuisance is sometimes broken down into different categories, these are merely examples and rigid categorisation may not easily accommodate new social conditions or may undermine proper analysis of factual situations which have aspects of more than one category but do not fall squarely into any one of them.

21   In dealing with this second principle Etherton MR had identified that in *Hunter v Canary Wharf Ltd* [1997] A.C. 655 Lord Lloyd had said that nuisances are of three kinds, encroachment, direct physical injury to land and interference with quiet enjoyment. And of course the Recorder's judgment in *Williams* itself was an example of an approach based on treating an encroachment type of claim differently from a claim based on interference with quiet enjoyment.

22   The third principle was that the frequently stated proposition, based on the old forms of action, that damage is always an essential requirement of the tort of nuisance had to be treated with considerable caution. The proposition was not entirely correct and moreover the concept of damage in this context is a highly elastic one. In a case of nuisance from encroachment by an artificial object, the better view may actually be that damage is formally required but damage is always presumed. It is also well established that, in the case of nuisance through interference with the amenity of the claimant's land, physical damage is not necessary to complete the cause of action. As Etherton MR put it:

> "43 … To paraphrase Lord Lloyd's observations in *Hunter* at 696C, in relation to his third category, loss of amenity, such as results from noise, smoke, smell or dust or other emanations, may not cause any diminution in the market value of the land, such as may directly follow from, and reflect, loss caused by tangible physical damage to the land, but damages may nevertheless be awarded for loss of the land's intangible amenity value. *[…]* What is relevant is the objective effect on the amenity value of the land itself, and it is that effect which satisfies any requirement there may be to show damage. Provided, by reference to all the circumstances of the case and the character of the locality, and according to the objective standards of the average person, the interference with amenity is sufficiently serious, there will be an actionable private nuisance."

23   The fourth principle is that nuisance may be caused by an inaction or omission, and that an occupier will be liable for continuing nuisance if with knowledge or presumed knowledge of the existence of the nuisance they fail to take reasonable steps to bring it to an end when there is ample time to do so. Similarly an occupier will also be liable for failing to act to remove a hazard on their land which they were aware of, and where there was a foreseeable risk it would damage their neighbour's land and it goes on to do so.

24   The fifth and final point is the broad unifying principle of reasonableness between neighbours (citing *Delaware Mansions Ltd v Westminster City Council* [2002] 1 A.C. 321 at para 29, 34).

25   Turning to the appeal itself, which was the challenge to the Recorder's decision in the claimant's favour on the second basis, i.e. the quiet enjoyment/loss of amenity claim, the Court of Appeal decided that appeal was well founded. No tort was made out on the second basis because the presence of knotweed on NR's land does not become an actionable nuisance simply because it diminishes the value of the claimants' land (paragraph 46). In rejecting this way of putting the case Etherton MR said the following:

> "48. The purpose of the tort of nuisance is not to protect the value of property as an investment or a financial asset. Its purpose is to protect the owner of land (or a person entitled to exclusive possession) in their use and enjoyment of the land as such as a facet of the right of ownership or right to exclusive possession. The decision of the Recorder in the present case extends the tort of nuisance to a claim for pure economic loss. Counsel for the claimants did not identify any case in which a similar decision was reached or, more generally, where the amenity of a property has been held, for the purposes of actionable private nuisance, to include the right to realise or otherwise deploy the value of the property in the financial interests of the owner. Contrary to the view of the Recorder, that would not be an incremental development of the common law by way of analogy but a radical reformulation of the purpose and scope of the tort."

26   The first sentence here is the passage quoted by the Circuit Judge in the present proceedings in paragraph 19 of his judgment, quoted above. In the same paragraph 19 the reference to economic damage is I think a reflection of the reference to pure economic loss here.

27   After this, in paragraphs 49 – 51, the *Williams* judgment deals with other authorities found not to be germane.

28   The Court of Appeal then turned to consider the respondent's notice relating to the Recorder's rejection of the first basis, i.e. the claim based on knotweed which had encroached onto the claimant's land. The Recorder was found to have erred in requiring there to be physical damage to the property. In essence the Court of Appeal decided that the (non-trivial) presence of knotweed on the claimant's land is an immediate burden. It interferes with amenity/quiet enjoyment. In so far as damage is needed to complete the tort, it is provided by the diminished ability of the claimant to use and enjoy their property. The relevant passages are paragraphs 55-56 of Etherton MR's judgment as follows:

> 55. Japanese knotweed was rightly described by the Recorder (at [5]) as a pernicious weed. It does not only carry the risk of future physical damage to buildings, structures and installations on the land. Its presence, and indeed the mere presence of its rhizomes, imposes an immediate burden on the owner of the land in terms of an increased difficulty in the ability to develop, and in the cost of developing, the land, should the owner wish to do so. As the RICS paper observed, any improvement or alteration of the property requiring the removal of contaminated soil would require disposal of the

soil either on site or, more likely, off site by special, and probably expensive, procedures. For all those reasons, Japanese knotweed and its rhizomes can fairly be described, in the sense of the decided cases, as a "natural hazard". They affect the owner's ability fully to use and enjoy the land. They are a classic example of an interference with the amenity value of the land.

56. The Recorder found that: (1) NR had actual knowledge of the presence of Japanese knotweed on its land behind the claimants' respective bungalows in 2013; (2) NR was, or ought to have been, aware of the risk of damage and loss of amenity to adjoining properties caused by the close proximity of knotweed no later than some time in 2012 with the publication of the EA code of practice and the RICS paper; and (3) NR failed reasonably to prevent the interference with the claimants' enjoyment of their properties. That is sufficient, on the well-established principles I have outlined earlier, to give rise to a cause of action in nuisance: *Goldman v Hargrave*; *Leakey v National Trust For Places of Historic Interest or Natural Beauty*. If, and insofar as, damage is required to complete that cause of action, it is constituted by the diminished ability of the claimants to use and enjoy the amenity of their properties.

29   The judgment went on in paragraphs 57 to 74 to address other related cases. There is no need to examine that section in detail. I will only highlight four aspects.

30   First, paragraph 59 notes that in *Hunter*, the fact a lawfully built building on the defendant's land interferes with the reception of television signals on the claimant's land does not amount to actionable private nuisance. Moreover paragraph 60 of *Williams* also notes that in *Hunter* in the Court of Appeal, Pill LJ had found that there was only material interference with amenity when there was a physical change which renders an article less useful or less valuable (excessive dust getting into a carpet).

31   Second and similarly to the first aspect, in paragraph 61, referring to *Blue Circle Industries v Ministry of Defence* [1999] Ch. 289, Etherton MR noted that Aldous LJ there said that damage occurred if there was some alteration in the physical characteristics of the land which rendered it less useful or less valuable. In that case the land was unsaleable until contaminated soil had been removed and so a cause of action arose because the amenity or utility of the land was impaired until the contamination was removed.

32   Third, paragraphs 63 and 64 address statements made in *Jan De Nul v Axa Royale Belge* [2002] EWCA Civ 209. Paragraph 64 concludes with an important reference to the economic interests of the claimant in a nuisance case, as follows:

64. Again, I cannot see anything in those statements which is inconsistent with a finding of liability in the present case on the basis of interference with the utility and amenity of the claimants' properties from the presence of the Japanese knotweed rhizomes. On the contrary, consistently with the elastic concept of damage in this area of the law and with a finding of liability in the present case, Schiemann LJ said (at [77]):

'The underlying policy of the law is to protect a claimant against what Markesinis and Deakin in their book on *Tort Law* (4th ed, 1999) describe at p.422 as 'unreasonable interference with the claimant's interest.' Phrases such as 'physical damage to land' are portmanteau phrases which embrace the concept of land being affected and this resulting in damage to the economic interests of another.'

33   Fourth and finally Etherton MR compared knotweed and its rhizomes to the branches of roots and trees, citing a number of cases include *Delaware* in which physical damage had been identified. At paragraphs 69 and 73 he said;

> "69. In that case [*Delaware*], however, physical damage to the buildings had actually occurred. It was not necessary to analyse the situation, and nor was the situation in fact analysed, on the basis of loss of amenity value prior to the physical damage of the buildings. Furthermore, unlike Japanese knotweed and its rhizomes, the branches and roots of a tree are not in themselves a hazard.
> [...]
> 73. In short, there is no reason why the legal position concerning nuisance caused by the encroachment of the branches or roots of trees should undermine the right of the claimants in the present case to claim damages for nuisance by reason of the encroachment of Japanese knotweed and its rhizomes from NR's land."

34   The concluding paragraph in this section of the Court of Appeal's judgment is paragraph 75. It deals with the submission that the manner in which the claimant's case on nuisance was being put on appeal was not open to them. The germane part of the paragraph is as follows:

> "75. [...] I see no reason why the claimants should not be able to argue and succeed before us on the ground of an unlawful interference with their enjoyment of the amenity of their properties due to the impairment of their right to use and enjoy those properties. They have not relied upon any evidence that was not before the Recorder, and the characteristics and damaging nature of Japanese knotweed have always been at the very heart of this litigation."

35   Thus the claimant's claim in nuisance succeeded and they were awarded all the damages which the Recorder had awarded below. Of course those included damages for diminution in value. Any lingering doubt that the Court of Appeal might have accidentally overlooked that point is dispelled by the final point in the appeal. The respondent had a second ground of appeal which related specifically to the calculation of the sum claimed for the residual diminution in value. The ground was rejected in paragraph 76–82. These passages include an express reference to these damages as "residual diminution in value" (para 76) and describe them in terms as "recoverable damages" in paragraph 82.

36   I have gone through *Williams* in some detail and with longer citations from a judgment than would normally be necessary. However it is necessary in this case because while I can see how it is that the judges below may have understood *Williams* in the way they did, I believe I have shown above that it cannot be summarised in the way the judges did below, particularly the Circuit Judge at paragraph 19 of his judgment.

37   In the section of *Williams* which refers to the purpose of the tort of nuisance and to economic loss (paragraphs 46-48), the key word is "simply" in paragraph 46.

This part of the judgment is about the elements necessary to complete the tort of nuisance. The *ratio* of *Williams* here is that there is no actionable nuisance caused by knotweed on a defendant's land simply because it diminishes the market value of the claimant's land. The reason why not is a policy reason which characterises such a claim as one of "pure economic loss". That phrase does not mean that in a case in which the elements of the tort of nuisance are satisfied, the claimant cannot recover for damage to their economic interests (paragraph 64 of *Williams* says the opposite). What the phrase is referring to is the mechanism by which the harm or loss has been caused. As Clerk & Lindsell puts it at paragraph 1-44:

> "'Pure Economic Loss' is the term used to describe an economic loss to the claimant which does not result from any physical damage to or interference with his person or tangible property."

38   In a case in which the knotweed is on the defendant's land, even if it is close to the boundary and at risk of invading the claimant's land, *Williams* holds that the reduction in market value of the claimant's land which this causes does not result from physical damage nor from physical interference with the claimant's property and therefore does not amount to a nuisance. Putting a small gloss on the opening words in paragraph 48 of *Williams*, I would say that the purpose of the tort of nuisance is not *simply* to protect the value of property. After all *Williams* itself later recognises that if the value of the claimant's property is diminished as a result of an interference with the claimant's quiet enjoyment or amenity, due to physical encroachment of knotweed from the defendant's land into the claimant's land, damages including diminution in value of the property will be available. Putting it another way, the reasoning in paragraph 48 of *Williams*, which the judges below relied on, is nothing to do with recoverability of damages in a case in which the tort of nuisance is complete.

39   Subject to one further point I would therefore allow the claimant's appeal and turn to the respondent's notice. The reasoning at the end of paragraph 19 of the Circuit Judge's judgment is flawed because once it is accepted that there was damage leading to a loss (the diminution in value) which was consequential on the nuisance, there is no authority that consequential damage to the claimant's economic interests is irrecoverable.

40   The further point is a submission by the respondent that even if this analysis of *Williams* is right in general terms, *Williams* is not authority which goes as far as saying that any encroachment of knotweed into the claimant's land amounts to material interference with quiet enjoyment or amenity and thereby to actionable nuisance. In oral submissions it was said that what is necessary to complete the tort is "encroachment plus". In other words the materiality aspect of the required interference demands an examination of the impact of the encroaching knotweed. This submission is based on paragraph 55 of *Williams* (cited above). Counsel drew attention to the second sentence which refers to knotweed constituting a future risk to structures, and to the third and fourth sentences which are focussed on an increased difficulty in developing the land if the owner wished to do so. The submission is that at least one of these two features has to be present (or something like them) in order for knotweed on the claimant's land to be an actionable interference with amenity. The point is that in the present case on the evidence no risk to structures was identified, and there was a specific finding that there is no prospect of developing the property.

41   I would agree that a trivial or de minimis encroachment of knotweed would not be actionable on this basis, but that is not what this argument is about. There was no finding in the present case that the knotweed in the claimant's land was merely trivial. The submission is that proving a non-trivial encroachment of knotweed into land is not enough, and that to establish nuisance the claimant also has to prove that the knotweed is also a risk to structures on the land, or that there is a prospect of improving or altering the property which the knotweed interferes with, or something similar.

42   I reject this submission. As I read paragraph 55, the two points – future risk and increased difficulty in development – are given simply as examples of interference with amenity in order to illustrate why knotweed can fairly be called a "pernicious weed" and a "natural hazard". Reading *Williams* as a whole, the point being made is a distinction between "pure economic loss", i.e. loss without physical damage or physical interference which is not actionable, and cases in which there is physical change to the claimant's property as a result of the presence there of knotweed rhizomes. Once that natural hazard is present in the claimant's land (to a non-trivial extent), the claimant's quiet enjoyment or use of it, or putting it another way the land's amenity value, has been diminished. For the purposes of the elements of the tort of nuisance that amounts to damage (paragraph 56 last sentence) and it is the result of a physical interference. If consequential residual diminution in value can be proved, damages on that basis can be recovered. They are not pure economic loss because of the physical manner in which they have been caused.

43   I would uphold the appellant's sole ground of appeal.

The respondent's notice causation point

44   Turning to the respondent's notice, I will deal with the causation argument first. The submission is that the residual diminution in value, which is the reduction in value left even after knotweed has been properly treated, cannot have been caused by the nuisance because the knotweed encroachment had already happened before the breach of duty. I have mentioned already the manner in which the District Judge rejected this point. The Circuit Judge addressed the issue in a slightly different way. Paragraph 16 of that judgment (and see also paragraph 22) approaches the issue as an exception to the "but for" test for causation drawing analogy with trespass as a tort of strict liability. However, as the respondent pointed out, rightly in my judgment, the duty in nuisance which arises in this case depends on actual or presumed knowledge on the part of the defendant of knotweed on its land and the risk it represents. It is not a tort of strict liability.

45   We were provided with a copy of *Delaware* in the authorities bundle although not for the purpose of causation. Nevertheless I believe it is instructive. In *Delaware* tree roots encroaching under a property had caused desiccation of ground, leading to cracking. The tree was on land owned by the highway authority. However this had all happened in 1989 and the property was sold to new owners in 1990. The new owners did not take an assignment of any cause of action. The new owners undertook £½ million of underpinning work and sued the highway authority. The claim failed at trial on the basis that the judge found that the damage had occurred during the previous ownership and the claimant had failed to prove that any remedial work had been necessitated by any new damage caused after they became owners. The Court of Appeal allowed the appeal and that was upheld in the House of Lords.

46   Lord Cooke gave the leading judgment. The extracts relevant for present purposes
        are these:

> "29 [...] I think that the answer to the issue falls to be found by applying the
> concepts of reasonableness between neighbours (real or figurative) and
> reasonable foreseeability which underlie much modern tort law and, more
> particularly, the law of nuisance. [...]
> [...]
> 31 In both the second *Wagon Mound* case and *Goldman v Hargrave* the
> judgments, which repay full rereading, are directed to what a reasonable person
> in the shoes of the defendant would have done. The label nuisance or
> negligence is treated as of no real significance. In this field, I think, the concern
> of the common law lies in working out the fair and just content and incidents
> of a neighbour's duty rather than affixing a label and inferring the extent of
> the duty from it.
> [...]
> 33 Approaching the present case in the light of those governing concepts and
> the judge's findings, I think that there was a continuing nuisance during [*the
> claimant's*] ownership until at least the completion of the underpinning and
> the piling in July 1992. It matters not that further cracking of the superstructure
> may not have occurred after March 1990. The encroachment of the roots was
> causing continuing damage to the land by dehydrating the soil and inhibiting
> rehydration. Damage consisting of impairment of the load-bearing qualities
> of residential land is, in my view, itself a nuisance. This is consistent with the
> opinions of Talbot J in the *Masters v Brent LBC* [1978] Q.B. 841 and the
> Court of Appeal in the instant case, although neither Talbot J nor Pill LJ
> analysed specifically what they regarded as a continuing nuisance. Cracking
> in the building was consequential. Having regard to the proximity of the plane
> tree to Delaware Mansions, a real risk of damage to the land and the
> foundations was foreseeable on the part of [*the defendant*], as in effect the
> judge found. It is arguable that the cost of repairs to the cracking could have
> been recovered as soon as it became manifest. That point need not be decided,
> although I am disposed to think that a reasonable landowner would notify the
> controlling local authority or neighbour as soon as tree root damage was
> suspected. It is agreed that if the plane tree had been removed, the need to
> underpin would have been avoided and the total cost of repair to the building
> would have been only £14,000. On the other hand the judge has found that,
> once the council declined to remove the tree, the underpinning and piling
> costs were reasonably incurred, despite the council's trench.
> [at 35-37 Lord Cooke considered authorities from Australia and the USA]
> 38 In the end, in my opinion, the law can be summed up in the proposition
> that, where there is a continuing nuisance of which the defendant knew or
> ought to have known, reasonable remedial expenditure may be recovered by
> the owner who has had to incur it. [...] "

47   Although the District Judge did not name the *Delaware* case itself, I believe this
        is essentially the logic which he applied in finding for the claimant on the issue of
        causation. The fact the encroachment was historic was no answer when there was
        a continuing breach of duty as a result of persisting encroachment.

48   Although there is attractive simplicity about the respondent's point on causation, I believe it is wrong. Viewed at 2018, after five years of breach of duty on the part of the respondent failing to treat the knotweed on its own land adequately, the knotweed was still encroaching on the claimant's land and any treatment by the appellant would have been futile unless and until the respondent complied with its duty as a good neighbour and dealt with its own knotweed. This is not an exception to the "but for" test. The harm to the quiet enjoyment and amenity suffered by the appellant persists in 2018 precisely because the nuisance is continuing one. The harm then has been caused by the breach of duty.

49   The respondent made a rhetorical point here and below about what would have happened if the period of breach had only been one month. The short answer is that is not this case. Moreover it is worth pointing out that in principle the breach was not found to occur the moment the respondent was aware of the problem. The District Judge explained in paragraph 30 that 2013 was after what he called a "generous amount of time" for consideration of the problem (the 2012 RICS report) and after implementation of a process he found to be "insufficient". No doubt if the respondent had acted properly within one month of being on notice, there would be no breach of duty.

50   I would therefore dismiss this ground of the respondent's notice.

The respondent's notice point on quality of evidence

51   Turning to the second ground of the respondent's notice, the respondent criticises the quality of the evidence given in support of the claim for £4,900 residual diminution in value. This figure was part of the evidence given by the claimant's expert Mr Raine. No evidence to the contrary was called by the respondent. Although the District Judge did at paragraph 32 of his judgment helpfully address aspects of the damages claimed, in case his conclusion that no damages were recoverable was wrong, as it turns out the one head he did not quantify was this one.

52   The claimant's expert Mr Raine was subject to some criticism by the District Judge in that paragraph 32. That included a general observation that the valuation was of limited use, albeit that it was then qualified by reference to a separate aspect of the valuation (neighbour cooperation) which has now been dropped. However I do not read paragraph 32 as a conclusion that Mr Raine's evidence was so poor that it could not be relied on at all. Therefore before this court there is evidence in support of the figure of £4,900 and this court can in these circumstances decide the quantum for itself. To remit this aspect of the claim in these circumstances would be a counsel of despair. This court has the power on an appeal to decide this issue since it has all the powers of the lower court (CPR Part 52 r52.20(1)) and it would plainly be in accordance with the overriding objective for us to do so. We canvassed this option at the oral hearing and neither side objected.

53   The respondent submitted that there were three other flaws in the evidence. First the right time to assess the damages was at the point of the breach (2013 or 2018) but the figure given was the expert's opinion at the date of his report (February 2020), second in this case the actual interference with amenity, even if it is actionable, is very minor for the reasons already addressed above, and third if, as the respondent contended was the appellant's case, the degree of residual diminution in value would itself reduce over time,then the sum should also be reduced because

of passage of time. There was no challenge to the theory of the first point but I do not believe on the facts of this case it justifies a change from the figure stated by the expert as at Feb 2020. The second point does not support a change either since, as the District Judge noted in paragraph 32, the expert was aware that there was no prospect of development and no visible knotweed in the garden. The problem with the third point is that there is no evidence about timescale. If the respondent wanted to advance this as a basis for materially reducing the figure claimed, it was incumbent on the respondent to provide that evidence at trial. There is none. I do note that in *Williams* itself, paragraph 12 refers to knotweed insurance policies, one with a minimum 10 year period and another with a 5 year minimum.

54   Finally I refer to the judgment of Buckley J in *Dennis v Ministry of Defence* [2003] EWHC 793 (QB); [2003] Env. L.R. 34 which counsel for the respondent handed up. In that case the nuisance in question was noise disturbance caused by Harrier jump jets operating at the RAF Wittering airbase which was near the claimant's property. The claim in nuisance succeeded as a claim for interference with the claimant's enjoyment of their property. Damages were awarded under three heads, past and future loss of amenity, past and future loss of use and loss of capital value. In other words the third head is a diminution in value of the property itself. The claimant had accepted that he did not wish to sell (and realise the capital loss) and had no intention of selling before 2012 when the evidence was that the nuisance was going to come to an end because the use of Harriers at RAF Wittering was to cease. Buckley J decided that a sum of about 5 to 10% of the figure given for the actual diminution should be awarded to take account that although he did not wish to sell, there was nevertheless a 5 to 10% chance that the claimant might be forced to sell before 2012. The figure for the diminution in value was £4 million and so the judge awarded £300,000 on that ground.

55   The facts of *Dennis* are a long way from the present case. Nevertheless what happened in that case illustrates another avenue which the respondent could have explored at trial, to examine how likely Mr Davies was to realise the capital loss in the period the diminution persisted. However while I accept the principle that an approach of this kind could be taken, it would have needed some evidence, and there is none.

56   In my judgment taking all these points into account £4,900 would be a fair figure for the residual diminution in value in this case.

Conclusion

57   I would allow the appeal and dismiss the grounds of the respondent's notice.

LORD JUSTICE SNOWDEN:

58   I agree.

LORD JUSTICE BAKER

59   I also agree.

JP v MINISTRE DE LA TRANSITION ÉCOLOGIQUE

European Court of Justice (Grand Chamber)

(C-61/21)

K. Lenaerts, President, L. Bay Larsen, Vice-President, A. Arabadjiev, A. Prechal, E. Regan and L.S. Rossi, Presidents of Chambers, M. Ilešič, J.-C. Bonichot, N. Piçarra, I. Jarukaitis, A. Kumin, N. Jääskinen, N. Wahl, J. Passer (Rapporteur) and O. Spineanu-Matei, Judges: J. Kokott, AG: 22 December 2022

EU:C:2022:1015; [2023] Env. L.R. 22

Air pollution; Air quality; Conditions; Emission limit values; EU law; State liability

H1   *EU law—State liability—air quality—Directive 2008/50 on Ambient Air Quality and preceding provisions—exceedance of limit values—individual suffering damage attributed to resulting pollution—whether relevant provisions intended to confer rights capable of entitling individuals to compensation under principle of State liability for loss and damage as result of breaches—conditions for any such entitlement*

H2   A request for a preliminary ruling was made in proceedings between an individual and the French Minister for Ecological Transition and Prime Minister. The proceedings concerned applications seeking annulment of an implied decision to refuse to take the necessary measures to address the individual's health problems linked to air pollution and compensation for the various heads of damage attributed to that pollution. Compensation was sought for damage arising from the deterioration of ambient air quality alleged to be the result of infringement of the air quality limit values in Directive 2008/50. The questions referred asked, essentially, whether:

(1) Articles 13(1) and 23(1) of Directive 2008/50 and preceding provisions were intended to confer rights on individuals capable of entitling them to compensation from a Member State under the principle of State liability for loss and damage caused to individuals as a result of breaches; and

(2) If so, what conditions was that entitlement subject to, in particular the date on which such failure was to be assessed?

H3   **Held:**

H4   (1) The relevant provisions were not intended to confer such rights on individuals. The Court had repeatedly held that individuals had a right to compensation where three conditions were met: (i) the rule of EU law infringed had to be intended to confer rights on them; (ii) the infringement of that rule had to be sufficiently serious; and (iii) there had to be a direct causal link between that infringement and the loss or damage sustained by those individuals. According to well-established case law those rights arose not only where they were expressly granted by provisions of EU law, but also by reason of positive or negative obligations which those provisions imposed in a clearly defined manner, whether on individuals, on the Member States or on the EU institutions. In the present case, Directive 2008/50 and preceding provisions imposed an obligation on Member States to ensure that the levels of specified pollutants did not exceed specified limit values and, where those limit values were exceeded, an obligation to provide for appropriate measures to remedy those exceedances, inter alia by means of air quality plans. The provisions concerned did not contain any express conferral of rights on individuals in that respect. Nor could such rights regarding Member State's liability for loss and damage caused by breach of the relevant obligations be inferred. It followed that the first of the three conditions, which were cumulative, was not satisfied.

H5   (2) That finding was not altered by the fact that individuals could require national authorities to adopt the measures required where a Member State had failed to comply with the limit values set out, including through court actions. Those rights stemmed, in particular, from the principle of effectiveness of EU law; effectiveness to which affected individuals were entitled to contribute by bringing administrative or judicial proceedings based on their own particular situation. That did not mean that the obligations resulting from Directive 2008/50 arts 13(1) and 23(1) and the analogous provisions of the earlier directives were intended to confer individual rights on interested persons, for the purpose of the first of the three conditions referred to.

H6   (3) Those conclusions did not mean that a Member State could not incur liability under less strict conditions on the basis of national law, nor did it prevent, where appropriate, a failure to fulfil the obligations from being taken into account in that regard as a factor which may be relevant for the purposes of establishing the liability of public authorities on a basis other than EU law. Nor did they preclude the courts of the Member State concerned from issuing orders to ensure that that State complied with the obligations arising under arts 13(1) and 23(1).

H7   (4) In view of the answer to the first question, there was no need to answer the second question

H8 **Cases referred to:**
Aannamaersbedrijf PK Kraaijveld BV v Gedeputeerde Staten van Zuid-Holland (C-72/95) EU:C:1996:404; [1997] 3 C.M.L.R. 1; [1997] Env. L.R. 265
Adeneler v Ellinikos Organismos Galaktos (ELOG) (C-212/04) EU:C:2006:443; [2006] 3 C.M.L.R. 30; [2006] I.R.L.R. 716
Balgarska Narodna Banka (C-501/18) EU:C:2021:249
Berlington Hungary Tanacsado es Szolgaltato kft v Hungary (C-98/14) EU:C:2015:386; [2015] 3 C.M.L.R. 45
BK v Slovenia (Ministry of Defence) (C-742/19) EU:C:2021:597; [2022] 1 C.M.L.R. 19
Blanco Perez v Consejeria de Salud y Servicios Sanitarios (C-570/07) EU:C:2010:300; [2010] 3 C.M.L.R. 37; [2011] C.E.C. 175
Brasserie du Pecheur SA v Germany (C-46/93) EU:C:1996:79; [1996] Q.B. 404; [1996] 2 W.L.R. 506

Fuss v Stadt Halle (C-429/09) EU:C:2010:717; [2011] 2 C.M.L.R. 13; [2011] I.R.L.R. 176

Hochtief Solutions AG Magyarorszagi Fioktelepe v Fovarosi Torvenyszek (C-620/17) EU:C:2019:630; [2020] 1 W.L.R. 1665

Hogan v Minister for Social and Family Affairs (C-398/11) EU:C:2013:272; [2013] 3 C.M.L.R. 27; [2013] Pens. L.R. 185

Janecek v Freistaat Bayern (C-237/07) EU:C:2008:447; [2009] Env. L.R. 12

Kantarev (C-571/16) EU:C:2018:807

Kone AG v OBB-Infrastruktur AG (C-557/12) EU:C:2014:1317; [2014] 5 C.M.L.R. 5; [2015] C.E.C. 539

Leth v Austria (C-420/11) EU:C:2013:166; [2013] P.T.S.R. 805; [2013] Env. L.R. 26

Link Logistik N&N (C-384/17) EU:C:2018:810

Manfredi v Lloyd Adriatico Assicurazioni SpA (C-295/04) EU:C:2006:461; [2007] Bus. L.R. 188; [2007] R.T.R. 7

NV Algemene Transport-en Expeditie Onderneming van Gend en Loos v Nederlandse Administratie der Belastingen (26/62) EU:C:1963:1; [1963] C.M.L.R. 105

Officier van Justitie v De Peijper (104/75) EU:C:1976:67; [1976] 2 C.M.L.R. 271

Pantuso (C-616/16) and (C-617/16) EU:C:2018:32

Paul v Germany (C-222/02) EU:C:2004:606; [2006] 2 C.M.L.R. 62

Popławski (C-573/17) EU:C:2019:530

Presidenza del Consiglio dei Ministri (C-129/19) EU:C:2020:566

Pubblico Ministero v Ratti (148/78) EU:C:1979:110; [1980] 1 C.M.L.R. 96

Proceedings Brought by Wasserleitungsverband Nordliches Burgenland (C-197/18) EU:C:2019:824; [2020] 1 C.M.L.R. 39; [2020] Env. L.R. 24

R. (on the application of ClientEarth) v Secretary of State for the Environment, Food and Rural Affairs (C-404/13) EU:C:2014:2382; [2015] 1 C.M.L.R. 55; [2015] Env. L.R. 17

R. (on the application of Wells) v Secretary of State for Transport, Local Government and the Regions (C-201/02) EU:C:2004:12; [2004] 1 C.M.L.R. 31; [2004] Env. L.R. 27

Robins v Secretary of State for Work and Pensions (C-278/05) EU:C:2007:56; [2007] 2 C.M.L.R. 13; [2007] I.C.R. 779

Rosengren v Riksaklagaren (C-170/04) EU:C:2007:313; [2007] 3 C.M.L.R. 10; [2008] C.E.C. 153

Safa Nicu Sepahan Co v Council of the European Union (C-45/15 P) EU:C:2017:402; [2018] 1 C.M.L.R. 4

Sdruzhenie "Za Zemyata—dostap do pravosadie" (C-375/21) EU:C:2023:173

Specht v Land Berlin (C-501/12)–(C-506/12), (C-540/12) and (C-541/12) EU:C:2014:2005; [2015] 1 C.M.L.R. 7; [2014] I.C.R. 966

Stadt Wiener Neustadt v Niederosterreichische Landesregierung (C-348/15) EU:C:2016:882; [2017] 2 C.M.L.R. 11; [2017] Env. L.R. 20

Stichting Cartel Compensation v Koninklijke Luchtvaart Maatschappij NV (C-819/19) EU:C:2021:904; [2022] 5 C.M.L.R. 2

Test Claimants in the FII Group Litigation v Inland Revenue Commissioners (C-446/04) EU:C:2006:774; [2012] 2 A.C. 436; [2012] 2 W.L.R. 1240

Thelen Technopark Berlin GmbH v MN (C-261/20) EU:C:2022:33; [2022] 2 C.M.L.R. 24; [2022] C.E.C. 1185

Tomášová (C-168/15) EU:C:2016:602
van den Berg v Council and Commission (C-164/01) EU:C:2004:665
Volvo and DAF Trucks (C-267/20) EU:C:2022:494

H9 **Legislation referred to:**
TEU art.3
TFEU arts 191 and 267
EU Charter of Fundamental Rights arts 2, 3 and 37
Directive 80/779 arts 1, 3 and 7 and Annex I
Directive 85/203 arts 1, 3 and 7 and Annex I
Directive 96/62 arts 1, 2, 4, 7, 8, 11 and 13 and Annex IV
Directive 1999/30 arts 1, 4, 5, 9 and 12 and Annexes II, III and VI
Directive 2008/50 arts 1, 2, 13, 14, 22, 23, 31, 33 and 34 and Annexes III, XI, XIII, XIV and XV
Directive 2011/92 (EIA)

H10 *L. Gimalac*, avocat, appeared on behalf of JP.
T. Stéhelin and *W. Zemamta*, acting as Agents, appeared on behalf of the French Government.
M. Browne, *M. Lane* and *J. Quaney*, acting as Agents, appeared on behalf of Ireland.
G. Palmieri, acting as Agent and *G. Palatiello*, avvocato dello Stato, appeared on behalf of the Italian Government.
B. Majczyna and *D. Krawczyk*, acting as Agents, appeared on behalf of the Polish Government.
A. Hanje, acting as Agent, appeared on behalf of the Netherlands Government.
M. Noll-Ehlers and *F. Thiran*, acting as Agents, appeared on behalf of the European Commission.

OPINION[1]

I. Introduction

AG1   The ambitious limit values for ambient air quality under Directive 2008/50[2] are not (yet?) sufficiently observed in many places.[3] Important decisions in this area are, however, expected in 2022. At the political level, the European Commission is planning proposals to revise the current rules.[4] At the same time, various cases in which the Court can clarify important issues concerning the enforcement of the legislation are currently pending. In addition to one request for a preliminary ruling

---

[1] Original language: German.
[2] Directive 2008/50/EC of the European Parliament and of the Council of 21 May 2008 on ambient air quality and cleaner air for Europe ([2008] OJ L152/1), as amended by Commission Directive (EU) 2015/1480 of 28 August 2015 ([2015] OJ L226/4) (Directive 2008/50).
[3] In addition to the judgments concerning the applicant's place of residence, namely judgments of 24 October 2019, *Commission v France (Exceedance of limit values for nitrogen dioxide)* (C-636/18) EU:C:2019:900, and of 28 April 2022, *Commission v France (Limit values—PM10)* (C-286/21) EU:C:2022:319, see, for example, judgments of 5 April 2017, *Commission v Bulgaria* (C-488/15) EU:C:2017:267; of 30 April 2020, *Commission v Romania (Exceedance of the limit values for PM10)* (C-638/18) EU:C:2020:334; of 10 November 2020, *Commission v Italy (Limit values—PM10)* (C-644/18) EU:C:2020:895; of 3 February 2021, *Commission v Hungary (Limit values—PM10)* (C-637/18) EU:C:2021:92; and of 3 June 2021, *Commission v Germany (Limit values—NO2)* (C-635/18) EU:C:2021:437.
[4] *https://ec.europa.eu/info/law/better-regulation/have-your-say/initiatives/12677-Air-quality-revision-of-EU-rules_en*, visited on 25 February 2022.

concerning the relevance of Directive 2008/50 to the authorisation of projects[5] and another concerning the first penalty payment proceedings to enforce a judgment finding that a Member State infringed that directive,[6] the present case raises the question as to whether individuals are able to demand compensation for damage to health resulting from an infringement of the limit values.

AG2   At the heart of this case is the first requirement of non-contractual liability of Member States for infringement of EU law, namely the question as to whether the provisions of Directive 2008/50 establish rights for individuals. In addition, it is necessary to examine the conditions under which a possible infringement of Directive 2008/50 is sufficiently serious, and the proof of a direct causal link between the infringement and the damage, in order to provide the referring court with guidance as to the relevant point in time for the assessment of the infringement.

II. Legal framework

AG3   For the period relevant to the main proceedings, the rules on air quality were initially laid down in Directives 96/62[7] and 1999/30,[8] which were replaced by Directive 2008/50 with effect from 11 June 2010.

A. Directive 96/62

AG4   According to the first indent of Article 1 of Directive 96/62, the aim of that directive was to define the basic principles of a common strategy to 'define and establish objectives for ambient air quality in the Community designed to avoid, prevent or reduce harmful effects on human health and the environment as a whole'. This is also apparent from the second recital.

AG5   Article 2(5) of Directive 96/62 defined the term 'limit value' as 'a level fixed on the basis of scientific knowledge, with the aim of avoiding, preventing or reducing harmful effects on human health and/or the environment as a whole, to be attained within a given period and not to be exceeded once attained'.

AG6   Article 7 of Directive 96/62 contained the general requirements for the improvement of ambient air quality:

> '1. Member States shall take the necessary measures to ensure compliance with the limit values.
>
> 2. Measures taken in order to achieve the aims of this Directive shall:
>   (a) take into account an integrated approach to the protection of air, water and soil;
>   (b) not contravene Community legislation on the protection of safety and health of workers at work;
>   (c) have no significant negative effects on the environment in the other Member States.
>
> 3. Member States shall draw up action plans indicating the measures to be taken in the short term where there is a risk of the limit values and/or alert thresholds being exceeded, in order to reduce that risk and to limit

---

[5] Case *Sdruzhenie 'Za Zemyata—dostap do pravosadie'* (C-375/21) ([2021] OJ C401/2).
[6] Case *Commission v Bulgaria* (C-174/21) ([2021] OJ C206/18).
[7] Council Directive 96/62/EC of 27 September 1996 on ambient air quality assessment and management ([1996] OJ L296/55).
[8] Council Directive 1999/30/EC of 22 April 1999 relating to limit values for sulphur dioxide, nitrogen dioxide and oxides of nitrogen, particulate matter and lead in ambient air ([1999] OJ L163/41).

the duration of such an occurrence. Such plans may, depending on the individual case, provide for measures to control and, where necessary, suspend activities, including motor-vehicle traffic, which contribute to the limit values being exceeded.'

AG7 Article 8 of the directive concerned zones where levels are higher than the limit value:

'1. Member States shall draw up a list of zones and agglomerations in which the levels of one or more pollutants are higher than the limit value plus the margin of tolerance.
Where no margin of tolerance has been fixed for a specific pollutant, zones and agglomerations in which the level of that pollutant exceeds the limit value shall be treated in the same way as the zones and agglomerations referred to in the first subparagraph, and paragraphs 3, 4 and 5 shall apply to them.
...

3. In the zones and agglomerations referred to in paragraph 1, Member States shall take measures to ensure that a plan or programme is prepared or implemented for attaining the limit value within the specific time limit.
The said plan or programme, which must be made available to the public, shall incorporate at least the information listed in Annex IV.

4. In the zones and agglomerations referred to in paragraph 1, where the level of more than one pollutant is higher than the limit values, Member States shall provide an integrated plan covering all the pollutants concerned.
...'

AG8 In accordance with the twelfth recital of Directive 96/62, that provision also served to protect health and the environment as a whole.

AG9 Article 11(1)(a)(iii) of Directive 96/62 specifies a time limit for sending plans under Article 8:

'In the zones referred to in Article 8(1) [Member States] shall:
...
(iii) send to the Commission the plans or programmes referred to in Article 8(3) no later than two years after the end of the year during which the levels were observed'.

AG10 Annex IV to Directive 96/62 provided that the plans or programmes for attaining the limit values were to contain, in particular, information on the causes of pollution and time projections for the improvement in ambient air quality resulting from the measures taken:

'1. Localization of excess pollution
– region
– city (map)
– measuring station (map, geographical coordinates).

2. General information
– type of zone (city, industrial or rural area)

   – estimate of the polluted area (km²) and of the population
     exposed to the pollution
   – useful climatic data
   – relevant data on topography
   – sufficient information on the type of targets requiring protection
     in the zone.
   …

4. Nature and assessment of pollution
   – concentrations observed over previous years (before the
     implementation of the improvement measures)
   – concentrations measured since the beginning of the project
   – techniques used for the assessment.
5. Origin of pollution
   – list of the main emission sources responsible for pollution (map)
   – total quantity of emissions from these sources (tonnes/year)
   – information on pollution imported from other regions.
6. Analysis of the situation
   – details of those factors responsible for the excess (transport,
     including cross-border transport, formation)
   – details of possible measures for improvement of air quality.
7. Details of those measures or projects for improvement which existed
   prior to the entry into force of this Directive i.e.
   – local, regional, national, international measures
   – observed effects of these measures.
8. Details of those measures or projects adopted with a view to reducing
   pollution following the entry into force of this Directive
   – listing and description of all the measures set out in the project
   – timetable for implementation
   – estimate of the improvement of air quality planned and of the
     expected time required to attain these objectives.
9. Details of the measures or projects planned or being researched for
   the long term.
   …,'

B. Directive 1999/30

AG11   Directive 1999/30 laid down the limit values and alert thresholds for sulphur
dioxide, nitrogen dioxide and oxides of nitrogen, particulate matter and lead in
ambient air required for the application of Directive 96/62. Article 1 of Directive
1999/30 confirms that the objective of that legislation was to avoid, prevent or
reduce harmful effects on human health and the environment as a whole.

AG12   For nitrogen dioxide (NO2), the limit values for the protection of human health
as laid down in Article 4 of and Section I of Annex II to Directive 1999/30 applied
from 1 January 2010. First, the one-hour limit value of 200 µg/m³ may not be
exceeded more than 18 times in any calendar year. Second, the annual limit value
was set at 40 µg/m³.

AG13   For particulate matter (PM10), however, the limit values for the protection of
human health as laid down in Article 5 and Annex III, Section I, Stage 1, of
Directive 1999/30 applied already from 1 January 2005. The 24-hour limit value

for the protection of human health of 50 μg/m³ of PM10 may not be exceeded more than 35 times in any calendar year. The annual limit value was set at 40 μg/m³ of PM10.

C. Directive 2008/50

AG14   Recitals 1 and 2 of Directive 2008/50 describe the overarching objectives of that directive:

> '(1) The Sixth Community Environment Action Programme … establishes the need to reduce pollution to levels which minimise harmful effects on human health, paying particular attention to sensitive populations, and the environment as a whole, to improve the monitoring and assessment of air quality including the deposition of pollutants and to provide information to the public.
>
> (2) In order to protect human health and the environment as a whole, it is particularly important to combat emissions of pollutants at source and to identify and implement the most effective emission reduction measures at local, national and Community level. Therefore, emissions of harmful air pollutants should be avoided, prevented or reduced and appropriate objectives set for ambient air quality taking into account relevant World Health Organisation standards, guidelines and programmes.'

AG15   Article 1(1) of Directive 2008/50 sets out its essential objective:

> 'This Directive lays down measures aimed at the following:
> 1. defining and establishing objectives for ambient air quality designed to avoid, prevent or reduce harmful effects on human health and the environment as a whole.'

AG16   Article 2(5) of Directive 2008/50 defines the term 'limit value' as a 'level fixed on the basis of scientific knowledge, with the aim of avoiding, preventing or reducing harmful effects on human health and/or the environment as a whole, to be attained within a given period and not to be exceeded once attained'.

AG17   Article 13(1) of Directive 2008/50 lays down an obligation to comply with various limit values:

> 'Member States shall ensure that, throughout their zones and agglomerations, levels of sulphur dioxide, PM10, lead, and carbon monoxide in ambient air do not exceed the limit values laid down in Annex XI.
> In respect of nitrogen dioxide and benzene, the limit values specified in Annex XI may not be exceeded from the dates specified therein.
> Compliance with these requirements shall be assessed in accordance with Annex III.
> …'

AG18   The limit values for nitrogen dioxide and for particulate matter (PM10) in Annex XI to Directive 2008/50, which are relevant in the present case, correspond to the limit values in Directive 1999/30.

AG19   Article 22 of Directive 2008/50 allows the deadline for conformity to be postponed under certain conditions:

'1. Where, in a given zone or agglomeration, conformity with the limit values for nitrogen dioxide or benzene cannot be achieved by the deadlines specified in Annex XI, a Member State may postpone those deadlines by a maximum of five years for that particular zone or agglomeration, on condition that an air quality plan is established in accordance with Article 23 for the zone or agglomeration to which the postponement would apply; such air quality plan shall be supplemented by the information listed in Section B of Annex XV related to the pollutants concerned and shall demonstrate how conformity will be achieved with the limit values before the new deadline.

2. Where, in a given zone or agglomeration, conformity with the limit values for PM10 as specified in Annex XI cannot be achieved because of site-specific dispersion characteristics, adverse climatic conditions or transboundary contributions, a Member State shall be exempt from the obligation to apply those limit values until 11 June 2011 provided that the conditions laid down in paragraph 1 are fulfilled and that the Member State shows that all appropriate measures have been taken at national, regional and local level to meet the deadlines.

…

4. Member States shall notify the Commission where, in their view, paragraphs 1 or 2 are applicable, and shall communicate the air quality plan referred to in paragraph 1 including all relevant information necessary for the Commission to assess whether or not the relevant conditions are satisfied. In its assessment, the Commission shall take into account estimated effects on ambient air quality in the Member States, at present and in the future, of measures that have been taken by the Member States as well as estimated effects on ambient air quality of current Community measures and planned Community measures to be proposed by the Commission.

Where the Commission has raised no objections within nine months of receipt of that notification, the relevant conditions for the application of paragraphs 1 or 2 shall be deemed to be satisfied.

If objections are raised, the Commission may require Member States to adjust or provide new air quality plans.'

AG20   According to the Commission,[9] for the Paris agglomeration, the area at issue in the present case, the French Republic did send notifications with a view to postponing the deadlines for PM10 and nitrogen dioxide, but the Commission raised objections in each case.[10]

AG21   Article 23(1) of Directive 2008/50 provides that where limit values are exceeded in given zones or agglomerations, air quality plans must be established in order to achieve those values:

'Where, in given zones or agglomerations, the levels of pollutants in ambient air exceed any limit value or target value, plus any relevant margin of tolerance

[9] Air Quality—Time extensions (*https://ec.europa.eu/environment/air/quality/time_extensions.htm*, visited on 21 February 2022).
[10] See, in particular, recitals 21, 25 and 32 of Decision COM(2009) 5244 final of 2 July 2009, recitals 10, 14 to 16, 19 and 30 of Decision COM(2010) 9168 final of 17 December 2010, both concerning PM10, and Article 1 of Decision COM(2013) 920 final of 22 February 2013, concerning nitrogen dioxide.

in each case, Member States shall ensure that air quality plans are established for those zones and agglomerations in order to achieve the related limit value or target value specified in Annexes XI and XIV.

In the event of exceedances of those limit values for which the attainment deadline is already expired, the air quality plans shall set out appropriate measures, so that the exceedance period can be kept as short as possible. …

Those air quality plans shall incorporate at least the information listed in Section A of Annex XV … Those plans shall be communicated to the Commission without delay, but no later than two years after the end of the year the first exceedance was observed.

…'

AG22   The requirements laid down in Section A of Annex XV to Directive 2008/50 correspond, in essence, to those laid down in Annex IV to Directive 96/62.

III. Facts and request for a preliminary ruling

AG23   The request for a preliminary ruling is based on the fact that the limit values for ambient air quality have been exceeded in the Paris agglomeration. In 2019, for example, the Court found that the limit values for nitrogen dioxide had been exceeded since the point at which they had to be complied with, in 2010.[11] Moreover, it recently decided that the limit values for PM10 from 2005 to 2019 were also not complied with.[12] The Conseil d'État (Council of State, France) has also established continuing exceedance of the limit values for Paris for nitrogen dioxide into 2020, as well as exceedance of the limit values for PM10 for the years up to 2018 and for 2019.[13]

AG24   The applicant in the main proceedings requests that the Prefect of the Département du Val-d'Oise, which is an area of the Paris agglomeration, take measures to comply with the limit values under Directive 2008/50. In addition, he seeks compensation for the various heads of damages which he attributes to air pollution, assessed at EUR 21 million. He submits that he has been suffering from the health problems since 2003 and they have become even worse over time.

AG25   In support of his claim for compensation, the applicant submits, in particular, that he has suffered damage to his health as a result of the deterioration of the ambient air in the Paris agglomeration, where he lives. He considers that that deterioration is the result of a breach by the French authorities of their obligations under Directive 2008/50. Therefore, he puts the State's liability in issue in order to obtain compensation for the alleged damage to his health.

AG26   The action having been dismissed by the Tribunal administratif de Cergy-Pontoise (Administrative Court, Cergy-Pontoise, France), an appeal is now pending before the Cour administrative d'appel de Versailles (Administrative Court of Appeal, Versailles, France). The latter court states that the decision on the claim for compensation requires clarification of the scope of Article 13(1) and Article 23(1) of Directive 2008/50. According to that court, the question is whether individuals are entitled to compensation for damage to their health in the event of a sufficiently

---

[11] Judgment of 24 October 2019, *Commission v France (Exceedance of limit values for nitrogen dioxide)* (C-636/18) EU:C:2019:900.

[12] Judgment of 28 April 2022, *Commission v France (Limit values—PM10)* (C-286/21) EU:C:2022:319.

[13] Judgment of the Conseil d'État (Council of State) of 4 August 2021, Association les Amis de la Terre France et autres (428409, FR:CECHR:2021:428409.20210804, AG 4 and 5).

serious breach by an EU Member State of the obligations arising from those provisions.

AG27   The Cour administrative d'appel de Versailles (Administrative Court of Appeal, Versailles) therefore refers the following questions to the Court:

> '(1) Must the applicable rules of EU law resulting from the provisions of Article 13(1) … and of Article 23(1) … of Directive [2008/50] be interpreted as entitling individuals, in the event of a sufficiently serious breach by an EU Member State of the obligations resulting from those rules, to claim compensation from the Member State concerned for damage to their health in cases where there is a direct and certain causal link with the deterioration in air quality?
>
> (2) On the assumption that the provisions referred to above may indeed give rise to such an entitlement to compensation for damage to health, to what conditions is that entitlement subject, in particular with regard to the date on which the existence of the failure attributable to the Member State concerned must be assessed?'

AG28   The applicant in the main proceedings, the French Republic, Ireland the Italian Republic, the Republic of Poland and the Commission submitted written observations. The French Republic, Ireland, the Kingdom of the Netherlands, the Republic of Poland and the Commission attended the hearing held on 15 March 2022.

IV. Legal assessment

AG29   In connection with the enforcement of EU legislation on the protection of ambient air quality, the Court has already recalled the principle of State liability for loss or damage caused to individuals as a result of breaches of EU law for which the State can be held responsible.[14] The present request for a preliminary ruling is now intended to clarify the extent to which an infringement of the limit values for the protection of ambient air quality under EU law can in fact give rise to entitlement to compensation.

AG30   According to settled case-law, the full effectiveness of EU rules would be impaired and the protection of the rights which they grant would be weakened if individuals were unable to obtain reparation when their rights are infringed by a breach of EU law for which a Member State can be held responsible.[15]

AG31   Accordingly, individuals who have suffered damage have a right to compensation if three conditions are met, namely that the rule of EU law infringed is intended to confer rights on them, that the infringement of that rule is sufficiently serious and that there is a direct causal link between that infringement and the damage suffered by those individuals.[16]

AG32   The first question referred proceeds on the basis that there is a sufficiently serious infringement and a direct causal link. It seeks to ascertain whether the ambient air

---

[14] Judgment of 19 December 2019, *Deutsche Umwelthilfe* (C-752/18) EU:C:2019:1114, paragraphs 54 and 55.
[15] Judgments of 19 November 1991, *Francovich* (C-6/90) and (C-9/90) EU:C:1991:428, paragraph 33; of 14 March 2013, *Leth* (C-420/11) EU:C:2013:166, paragraph 40; of 24 June 2019, *Popławski* (C-573/17) EU:C:2019:530, paragraph 56; and of 19 December 2019, *Deutsche Umwelthilfe* (C-752/18) EU:C:2019:1114, paragraph 54.
[16] Judgments of 5 March 1996, *Brasserie du pêcheur and Factortame* (C-46/93) and (C-48/93) EU:C:1996:79, paragraph 51; of 24 March 2009, *Danske Slagterier* (C-445/06) EU:C:2009:178, paragraph 20; and of 10 December 2020, *Euromin Holdings (Cyprus)* (C-735/19) EU:C:2020:1014, paragraph 79.

quality requirements under Directive 2008/50 confer rights on individuals, that is to say, whether an infringement of those requirements can give rise to entitlement to compensation at all (see section A). If that is the case, the second question seeks clarification as to the conditions to which that entitlement is subject, in particular with regard to the date on which the existence of the failure attributable to the Member State concerned must be assessed. To that end, it will then be necessary to examine the conditions under which a serious infringement and a direct causal link must be established (see section B).

A. First question – whether the rules on ambient air quality confer rights

AG33   Entitlement to compensation for an infringement of EU law presupposes, first, that the rule of EU law infringed must be intended to confer rights on individuals.[17]

AG34   It is true that, in connection with the establishment of entitlement to compensation, it does not matter whether the rule in question is directly applicable.[18] Nevertheless, direct applicability provides a significant indication that rights are to be conferred,[19] because, in that case, the content of the right conferred can be identified, which is a condition of entitlement to compensation.[20]

AG35   Therefore, it must first be examined whether the rules on limit values and on measures to improve ambient air quality are sufficiently clear to be able to identify the content of potential rights. It can then be assessed whether those rules are intended to confer rights on individuals.

1. Clarity of the content of the rules of Directives 96/62 and 1999/30

AG36   Although the request for a preliminary ruling relates only to Directive 2008/50, the main proceedings concern harm suffered by the applicant since 2003. Between that point in time and the expiry of the deadline for transposing Directive 2008/50, 11 June 2010, Directives 96/62 and 1999/30 initially regulated ambient air quality in relation to the pollutants referred to in the request for a preliminary ruling, PM10 (particulate matter) and nitrogen dioxide.

(a) Limit values

AG37   According to Article 7(1) of Directive 96/62, Member States are to take the necessary measures to ensure compliance with the limit values. The limit values for nitrogen dioxide resulted from Article 4 of Directive 1999/30, read in conjunction with Annex II thereto, and applied from 1 January 2010.

AG38   The limit values for PM10 were laid down in Article 5 of Directive 1999/30, read in conjunction with Annex III, Section I, Stage 1, and applied from 1 January 2005.

---

[17] Judgments of 19 November 1991, *Francovich* (C-6/90) and (C-9/90) EU:C:1991:428, paragraph 40; of 5 March 1996, *Brasserie du pêcheur and Factortame* (C-46/93) and (C-48/93) EU:C:1996:79, paragraph 51; of 14 March 2013, *Leth* (C-420/11) EU:C:2013:166, paragraph 41; and of 16 July 2020, *Presidenza del Consiglio dei Ministri* (C-129/19) EU:C:2020:566, paragraph 34.

[18] Judgments of 5 March 1996, *Brasserie du pêcheur and Factortame* (C-46/93) and (C-48/93) EU:C:1996:79, paragraphs 21 and 22, and of 10 December 2020, *Euromin Holdings (Cyprus)* (C-735/19) EU:C:2020:1014, paragraph 81.

[19] See judgments of 24 March 2009, *Danske Slagterier* (C-445/06) EU:C:2009:178, paragraphs 22 to 26; of 25 November 2010, *Fuss* (C-429/09) EU:C:2010:717, paragraphs 49 and 50; and of 25 March 2021, *Balgarska Narodna Banka* (C-501/18) EU:C:2021:249, paragraphs 63 and 86.

[20] Judgments of 19 November 1991, *Francovich* (C-6/90) and (C-9/90) EU:C:1991:428, paragraph 40; of 4 July 2006, *Adeneler* (C-212/04) EU:C:2006:443, paragraph 112; and of 24 January 2018, *Pantuso* (C-616/16) and (C-617/16) EU:C:2018:32, paragraph 49.

AG39   The abovementioned limit values and dates were later incorporated unchanged into Annex XI to Directive 2008/50.

AG40   Therefore, the obligation to comply with the limit values has existed since the point in time specified in each case and is clear and unconditional, on the basis of the wording of the relevant provisions.[21]

(b) Improvement of ambient air quality

AG41   In addition, Directive 96/62 already contained rules on the improvement of ambient air quality for the period both before and after the expiry of the time limits for the application of the limit values.

(i) Before the limit values became mandatory

AG42   An initial obligation to improve ambient air quality already existed before the limit values became mandatory in 2005 and 2010, respectively. Member States were required to take measures at that stage to ensure that the limit values would be complied with at the latest at the moment they became mandatory.

AG43   The details of that obligation followed from Article 8 of Directive 96/62. First, in accordance with Article 8(1), Member States were required to identify the zones and agglomerations in which the levels of one or more pollutants were higher than the limit value plus the margin of tolerance, likewise specified in Directive 1999/30. In accordance with Article 8(3) of Directive 96/62, in the zones and agglomerations thus identified, Member States were required to prepare or implement plans or programmes in order to attain the limit value within the specific time limit, that is to say, by the time it became mandatory.

AG44   In that respect, the margin of tolerance referred to a certain percentage of the respective limit values, which was linearly reduced to 0% between the point at which the limit values were set and the time of their application. The margin of tolerance therefore became ever smaller as the time of application of the limit values approached. The margin of tolerance disappeared completely when the associated limit value became applicable.

AG45   That obligation presumably already related to many zones and agglomerations in which the limit values were later exceeded upon the expiry of the time limit for their application, that is to say, in 2005 or 2010.[22]

AG46   Those plans or programmes had to comply with the requirements of Annex IV to Directive 96/62, which were largely identical to those in Section A of Annex XV to Directive 2008/50. Those requirements are not purely formal in nature, as the information in question documents the origin of the pollution (points 5 and 6), an analysis of possible measures for improvement of air quality (point 6), and the measures adopted and implemented (points 7 to 9), including a timetable and an estimate of the improvement in air quality to be achieved (point 8). The assessment as to whether the plan or programme is capable of bringing about compliance with the limit values upon the expiry of the time limits for their application logically requires that information.

---

[21] See judgments of 10 May 2011, *Commission v Sweden* (C-479/10) EU:C:2011:287; of 15 November 2012, *Commission v Portugal* (C-34/11) EU:C:2012:712; and of 19 December 2012, *Commission v Italy* (C-68/11) EU:C:2012:815.

[22] Accordingly, the 2003 annual report (questionnaire) for France (*https://cdr.eionet.europa.eu/fr/eu/annualair /envqwuzxq/*, visited on 24 February 2022) shows that the annual limit value, plus margin of tolerance, for nitrogen dioxide (Table 8b, line 14) and the daily limit value, plus margin of tolerance, for PM10 (Table 8c, line 14) were exceeded in the Paris agglomeration.

AG47   It should also be noted that the first subparagraph of Article 23(1) of Directive 2008/50 creates a similar obligation for fine particulate matter of PM2.5 size, whose limit values had to be complied with only after the transposition deadline of that directive.

(ii) After the expiry of the time limits for the application of the limit values

AG48   Furthermore, Article 7(3) of Directive 96/62 provided that Member States were to draw up action plans indicating the measures to be taken in the short term where there was a risk of the limit values and/or alert thresholds being exceeded, in order to reduce that risk and to limit the duration of such an occurrence.

AG49   On the basis of the wording of Articles 7 and 8 of Directive 96/62, no provision was made for the possibility of the limit values being exceeded. Prior to the point at which they became applicable, Article 8 required Member States to take the necessary measures to ensure that they were complied with by the time they took effect. For the time after that point, Article 7(3) required Member States to counter merely the *risk* of exceedance. The definition of the term 'limit value' in Article 2(5) of Directive 96/62 confirmed this, because, according to that definition, a limit value had to be attained within a given period and could not be exceeded once attained.

AG50   Nevertheless, in the judgment in *Janecek*, the Court ruled that the Member States were not obliged to take measures to ensure that those limit values and/or alert thresholds are never exceeded. On the contrary, it concluded from the broad logic of Directive 96/62 – which sought an integrated reduction of pollution – that it was for the Member States to take measures capable of reducing to a minimum the risk of the limit values and/or alert thresholds being exceeded and the duration of such an occurrence, taking into account all the material circumstances and opposing interests. In so doing, Member States were required to ensure a balance with the various opposing public and private interests. The limits on that discretion were subject to judicial review.[23]

AG51   The logic of that judgment can be followed in so far as it was already known at that time that the limit values for PM10 were exceeded in many Member States and that compliance with them would require considerable efforts. The Commission expected a similar situation with regard to the limit values for nitrogen dioxide, which became applicable in 2010.[24] The expectation that the limit values would not be exceeded, as expressed in the text of Directive 96/62, had therefore proven to be unrealistic. Moreover, shortly before the judgment in *Janecek*, that realisation had led to the adoption of Directive 2008/50, which is examined just below.

AG52   Furthermore, the Court has rightly emphasised the need to balance the conflicting interests when drawing up action plans. Although the legislature had already anticipated that balancing exercise when setting the limit values, EU law cannot require Member States to take measures to comply with the limit values where the disadvantages of those measures outweigh the improvement in the protection of health and the environment resulting from the enforcement of the limit values.[25]

AG53   However, the statements in the judgment in *Janecek* are confined to the obligation to draw up action plans under Article 7(3) of Directive 96/62. Only those plans

---

[23] Judgment of 25 July 2008, *Janecek* (C-237/07) EU:C:2008:447; 'the judgment in *Janecek*'; paragraphs 44 to 46.
[24] Communication from the Commission on notifications of postponements of attainment deadlines and exemptions from the obligation to apply certain limit values pursuant to Article 22 of Directive 2008/50/EC on ambient air quality and cleaner air for Europe (COM(2008) 403 final, p. 2).
[25] See my Opinion in *Commission v Bulgaria* (C-488/15) EU:C:2016:862, AG 95–98.

did not have to be designed to rule out any exceedance of the limit values. The obligation to comply with the limit values was already independent of that under Directives 96/62 and 1999/30.[26] As in the case of other infringements of EU law,[27] Member states could justify exceedances of the limit values only by means of concrete evidence of insurmountable difficulties or *force majeure*.[28]

(c) Interim conclusion

AG54   It must therefore be stated that Articles 7 and 8 of Directive 96/62, read in conjunction with the limit values for nitrogen dioxide and PM10 under Directive 1999/30, established a clear and unconditional obligation to comply with the limit values, which existed since 1 January 2005 in respect of PM10 and since 1 January 2010 in respect of nitrogen dioxide. However, under Article 7(3) of Directive 96/62, the Member States were required only to take measures to reduce the duration of the exceedance to a minimum on the basis of a balance between the conflicting interests. That second obligation is sufficiently clear only with regard to a breach of the limits of the discretion existing in that respect.

2. Clarity of the content of the rules of Directive 2008/50

AG55   Furthermore, it is necessary to assess the clarity of the content of the provisions of Directive 2008/50, which replaced Directives 96/62 and 1999/30 in 2008 with effect from 11 June 2010.

(a) Limit values

AG56   In accordance with the first sentence of Article 13(1) of Directive 2008/50, Member States are required to ensure that, throughout their zones and agglomerations, levels of various pollutants in ambient air, in particular PM10, do not exceed the limit values laid down in Annex XI. Moreover, in accordance with the second sentence of Article 13(1), in respect of nitrogen dioxide and benzene, the limit values specified in Annex XI may not be exceeded from the dates specified therein.

AG57   The different wording of the two sentences does not call into question the clarity of the obligation to comply with the limit values. That difference in wording can be explained by the fact that the limit values for the pollutants referred to in the first sentence of Article 13(1) of Directive 2008/50 had already applied since 2005, as is apparent from Annex XI, whereas the directive did not enter into force until 2008. By contrast, the limit values for nitrogen dioxide and benzene did not become mandatory until 2010, that is to say, after the directive entered into force.

AG58   Therefore, Member States must ensure that, throughout their zones and agglomerations, the levels of the pollutants covered by Article 13(1) of Directive 2008/50 do not exceed the limit values laid down in Annex XI.[29] Under point 1 of

---

[26] See judgments of 10 May 2011, *Commission v Sweden* (C-479/10) EU:C:2011:287; of 15 November 2012, *Commission v Portugal* (C-34/11) EU:C:2012:712; and of 19 December 2012, *Commission v Italy* (C-68/11) EU:C:2012:815.

[27] Judgments of 11 July 1985, *Commission v Italy* (C-101/84) EU:C:1985:330, paragraph 16; of 9 December 1997, *Commission v France* (C-265/95) EU:C:1997:595, paragraphs 55 and 56; and of 13 December 2001, *Commission v France* (C-1/00) EU:C:2001:687, paragraph 131.

[28] Judgment of 19 December 2012, *Commission v Italy* (C-68/11) EU:C:2012:815, paragraphs 64 and 65.

[29] Judgment of 26 June 2019, *Craeynest* (C-723/17) EU:C:2019:533, paragraph 48. See also, in that regard, the judgments cited below in footnote 32.

Section A of Annex III to Directive 2008/50, only certain places where people do not normally stay without protection do not need to be assessed in that respect.[30]

AG59   Therefore, viewed in isolation, Article 13(1) of and Annex XI to Directive 2008/50 appear to be sufficiently precise.[31] This is also demonstrated by the fact that the Court has repeatedly found that Member States have infringed that provision.[32]

(b) Air quality plans under Article 23 of Directive 2008/50

AG60   The obligation to comply with the limit values under Article 13(1) of Directive 2008/50 is accompanied by the obligation to improve air quality under Article 23(1).

AG61   In accordance with that provision, for zones or agglomerations in which the levels of pollutants in ambient air exceed any limit value or target value, plus any relevant margin of tolerance in each case, Member States are to ensure that air quality plans are established in order to achieve the limit value or target value specified in Annexes XI and XIV to Directive 2008/50. In the event of the exceedance of those limit values for which the attainment deadline is already expired, the air quality plans are to set out appropriate measures, so that the exceedance period can be kept as short as possible. Those air quality plans are to incorporate at least the information listed in Section A of Annex XV.

AG62   Article 23 of Directive 2008/50 therefore creates a direct link between exceedance of the limit values for PM10 which are provided for in Article 13(1) of that directive, in conjunction with Annex XI thereto, and the obligation to establish air quality plans.[33]

AG63   The Member States which are party to the proceedings therefore take the view that Directive 2008/50 does not require that any exceedance of the limit values be prevented, but only creates the obligation to establish air quality plans in Article 23(1). The Republic of Poland even argues that, in the light of Article 23(1), the obligation to comply with the limit values is not unconditional.

AG64   That position appears to be supported by the judgment in *Janecek*, already cited above, in which the Court held, in connection with Article 7(3) of Directive 96/62, that Member States are not required to prevent any exceedance of the limit values.[34] Moreover, similarly to the previous legislation, air quality plans under Article 23 of Directive 2008/50 may be adopted only on the basis of the balance between the aim of minimising the risk of pollution and the various opposing public and private interests.[35]

---

[30] See my Opinion in *Craeynest* (C-723/17) EU:C:2019:168, AG78.

[31] See judgments of 5 April 1979, *Ratti* (148/78) EU:C:1979:110, paragraph 23, and of 4 October 2018, *Link Logistik N&N* (C-384/17) EU:C:2018:810, paragraph 49.

[32] Judgments of 5 April 2017, *Commission v Bulgaria* (C-488/15) EU:C:2017:267; of 22 February 2018, *Commission v Poland* (C-336/16) EU:C:2018:94; of 24 October 2019, *Commission v France (Exceedance of limit values for nitrogen dioxide)* (C-636/18) EU:C:2019:900; of 30 April 2020, *Commission v Romania (Exceedance of the limit values for PM10)* (C-638/18) EU:C:2020:334; of 10 November 2020, *Commission v Italy (Limit values—PM10)* (C-644/18) EU:C:2020:895; of 3 February 2021, *Commission v Hungary (Limit values—PM10)* Commission; of 4 March 2021, *Commission v United Kingdom (Limit values—NO2)* (C-664/18) EU:C:2021:171; of 3 June 2021, *Commission v Germany (Limit values—NO2)* (C-635/18) EU:C:2021:437; and of 28 April 2022, *Commission v France (Limit values—PM10)* Commission.

[33] Judgments of 5 April 2017, *Commission v Bulgaria* (C-488/15) EU:C:2017:267, paragraph 83; of 24 October 2019, *Commission v France (Exceedance of limit values for nitrogen dioxide)* (C-636/18) EU:C:2019:900, paragraph 78; and of 10 November 2020, *Commission v Italy (Limit values—PM10)* (C-644/18) EU:C:2020:895, paragraph 133.

[34] Judgment of 25 July 2008, *Janecek* (C-237/07) EU:C:2008:447, paragraph 44.

[35] Judgments of 5 April 2017, *Commission v Bulgaria* (C-488/15) EU:C:2017:267, paragraphs 105 and 106; of 24 October 2019, *Commission v France (Exceedance of limit values for nitrogen dioxide)* (C-636/18) EU:C:2019:900,

AG65   However, whether measures to improve ambient air quality are sufficient to justify an infringement of the limit values was already questionable in connection with Directives 96/62 and 1999/30.[36] Furthermore, in relation to Directive 2008/50, the Court has now repeatedly rejected the view that a Member State has entirely satisfied its obligations under Article 13(1) merely because it has established an air quality plan.[37]

AG66   According to a recent judgment of the Grand Chamber, such an interpretation would leave the achievement of the objective of protection of human health, referred to in Article 1(1) of Directive 2008/50, to the sole discretion of the Member States, which is contrary to the intentions of the EU legislature. The Court derives that from, in particular, the definition of the concept of 'limit value' in Article 2(5), requiring that compliance therewith be guaranteed within a given period and subsequently maintained.[38]

AG67   Furthermore, compared with Directive 96/62, Directive 2008/50 clarified the obligation to comply with limit values by means of a provision that would be undermined if, in addition, merely establishing air quality plans were already sufficient to justify an exceedance.[39] Article 22 of Directive 2008/50 allows the deadlines for compliance with the limit values to be postponed by a maximum of five years for nitrogen dioxide or benzene and a maximum of six years for PM10. The postponement of a deadline requires, in particular, that Member States establish air quality plans to ensure compliance with that postponed deadline. Air quality plans under Article 23(1), on the other hand, are not subject to that deadline.

(c) Interim conclusion

AG68   Article 13(1) of Directive 2008/50 therefore establishes a precisely defined, directly effective obligation on the part of the Member States to prevent exceedance of the limit values for the air pollutants covered.

AG69   In addition, Article 23(1) of Directive 2008/50 imposes a clear *independent* obligation to establish air quality plans, which is triggered by the infringement of limit values.[40]

AG70   It is true that the Republic of Poland takes the view that Article 23(1) of Directive 2008/50 is not sufficiently precise with regard to the content of the air quality plans. According to the Republic of Poland, that provision does not set a fixed time limit for bringing an end to the exceedance, but only requires that the period of non-compliance be kept as short as possible. Furthermore, submits the Republic of Poland, the establishment of the measures requires a balancing of the opposing interests, as also emphasised by the French Republic and Ireland.

AG71   However, in response to that, it must be stated that it is true that the discretion associated with the balancing of interests may be relevant to the question as to

---

paragraph 79; and of 10 November 2020, *Commission v Italy (Limit values—PM10)* (C-644/18) EU:C:2020:895, paragraph 134.
[36] See AG53 above.
[37] Judgments of 19 November 2014, *ClientEarth* (C-404/13) EU:C:2014:2382, paragraph 42; of 5 April 2017, *Commission v Bulgaria* (C-488/15) EU:C:2017:267, paragraph 70; and of 10 November 2020, *Commission v Italy (Limit values—PM10)* (C-644/18) EU:C:2020:895, paragraphs 78 to 81.
[38] Judgment of 10 November 2020, *Commission v Italy (Limit values—PM10)* (C-644/18) EU:C:2020:895, paragraph 80.
[39] Judgments of 19 November 2014, *ClientEarth* (C-404/13) EU:C:2014:2382, paragraphs 43 to 47, and of 10 November 2020, *Commission v Italy (Limit values—PM10)* (C-644/18) EU:C:2020:895, paragraph 81.
[40] Judgments of 25 July 2008, *Janecek* (C-237/07) EU:C:2008:447, paragraph 35, and of 19 November 2014, *ClientEarth* (C-404/13) EU:C:2014:2382, paragraph 53.

whether an infringement is serious,[41] and may also play a role in the assessment of causality.[42] However, it is not a decisive factor in determining whether the provision in question is sufficiently precise to confer rights on individuals. Rather, it is sufficient that compliance with the limits on the exercise of that discretion may be relied upon by individuals before the national courts.[43]

3. Purpose of the limit values and the obligation to improve ambient air quality

AG72   Whether the limit values and the obligation to improve ambient air quality under Directives 96/62, 1999/30 and 2008/50 are intended to confer rights on those who suffer damage to their health as a result of air pollution depends not only on the identifiability of potential rights but, above all, on the objectives of that legislation.[44]

AG73   In accordance with the second recital of Directive 96/62, recital 2 of Directive 2008/50 and Article 1(1) of both directives, those directives aim to avoid, prevent or reduce harmful effects on human health.[45] The rules on ambient air quality laid down in those directives thus put into concrete terms the EU's obligations concerning environmental protection and the protection of public health, which stem, inter alia, from Article 3(3) TEU and Article 191(1) and (2) TFEU. According to those provisions, Union policy on the environment is to aim at a high level of protection, taking into account the diversity of situations in the various regions, and is to be based, inter alia, on the precautionary principle and on the principle that preventive action should be taken.[46] That obligation of protection also follows from Articles 2, 3 and 37 of the Charter of Fundamental Rights of the European Union.[47]

AG74   The fact that the limit values for, in particular, PM10 and nitrogen dioxide serve to protect human health already follows from their designation as limit values for the protection of human health in Annexes II and III to Directive 1999/30 and in Article 13 of and Annex XI to Directive 2008/50. The definition of the concept of 'limit value' in Article 2(5) of both Directive 96/62 and Directive 2008/50, which was emphasised by the applicant, also provides that a limit value is fixed with the aim of avoiding, preventing or reducing harmful effects on human health and/or the environment as a whole.

AG75   Since the respective obligations to improve ambient air quality are triggered by exceedance of those limit values, those obligations are also indisputably aimed at protecting health.

AG76   As the Commission rightly underlines, the Court, on the basis of that premiss of protection, has already held with regard to the older directives on the protection of ambient air quality that individuals must be in a position to rely on the mandatory

---

[41] Judgments of 25 January 2007, *Robins* (C-278/05) EU:C:2007:56, paragraph 72; of 25 April 2013, *Hogan* (C-398/11) EU:C:2013:272, paragraphs 50 to 52; and, specifically in relation to Directive 2008/50, my Opinion in *Commission v Bulgaria* (C-488/15) EU:C:2016:862, AG76. See also AG106 et seq. below.

[42] See in this respect below AG126 et seq.

[43] Judgments of 25 July 2008, *Janecek* (C-237/07) EU:C:2008:447, paragraph 46, and of 5 April 2017, *Commission v Bulgaria* (C-488/15) EU:C:2017:267, paragraph 105. See also judgments of 24 October 1996, *Kraaijeveld* (C-72/95) EU:C:1996:404, paragraph 59; of 26 June 2019, *Craeynest* (C-723/17) EU:C:2019:533, paragraphs 34 and 45; and of 3 October 2019, *Wasserleitungsverband Nördliches Burgenland* (C-197/18) EU:C:2019:824, paragraphs 31 and 72.

[44] Judgments of 8 October 1996, *Dillenkofer* (C-178/94), (C-179/94) and (C-188/94)–(C-190/94) EU:C:1996:375, paragraph 33 et seq.; of 4 October 2018, *Kantarev* (C-571/16) EU:C:2018:807, paragraph 102; and of 10 December 2020, *Euromin Holdings (Cyprus)* (C-735/19) EU:C:2020:1014, paragraphs 88 and 89.

[45] See judgment of 26 June 2019, *Craeynest* (C-723/17) EU:C:2019:533, paragraph 67.

[46] Judgment of 26 June 2019, *Craeynest* (C-723/17) EU:C:2019:533, paragraph 33.

[47] See my Opinion in *Craeynest* (C-723/17) EU:C:2019:168, AG53.

rules of those directives as *rights*.[48] Building on that, it made it possible to invoke Directives 96/62 and 2008/50[49] and has also referred to the judicial protection of *rights* in that connection.[50]

AG77 Although the Republic of Poland and Ireland take the view that the objective of health protection is intended to relate solely to the protection of the general public, that view is not convincing. Particularly the interest in health is highly personal and thus individual in nature and forms the basis of the case-law outlined just above.

AG78 The situation could be different for rules of environmental law, which serve primarily to protect animals, plants and habitats and benefit humans only indirectly. In that respect, one might think of the critical levels for the protection of vegetation under Article 14 of and Annex XIII to Directive 2008/50. However, whether those provisions are intended to confer rights on individuals need not be decided in the present case.

AG79 Contrary to the view taken by Ireland, the polluter-pays principle also does not militate against recognising State liability for damage caused to health as a result of infringement of rules on ambient air quality.

AG80 It is true that the polluter-pays principle is a principle of Union policy on the environment referred to in Article 191(2) TFEU and must therefore also be observed when interpreting rules on ambient air quality. It is also true that, according to that principle, it is the air polluters who should primarily bear the costs, which is expressed even more clearly in other language versions than in the German '*Verursacherprinzip*', with for example the English version using the wording 'that the polluter should pay' or the French version the wording '*principe du pollueur-payeur*'.

AG81 However, that principle cannot release Member States from their own responsibility if they allow, or fail to prevent, air pollution in breach of EU law. Moreover, the fact that the rules on ambient air quality impose that responsibility on Member States is justified because ambient air pollution generally results from various sources, with the result that the Member States must decide the extent to which certain polluters must reduce their emissions.

4. The judgment in Paul and Others

AG82 The importance of those considerations regarding the purpose of the rules on ambient air quality becomes particularly clear when compared with the judgment of 12 October 2004, *Paul* (C-222/02) EU:C:2004:606. That is the only judgment in which the Court has rejected a claim for compensation on the grounds that the rules in question were *not* intended to confer rights on individuals.

AG83 The judgment concerned banking supervision obligations applicable at the time, which also served to protect depositors.[51] Those rules have distinct parallels with

---

[48] Judgments of 30 May 1991, *Commission v Germany* (C-361/88) EU:C:1991:224, paragraph 16, and of 30 May 1991, *Commission v Germany* (C-59/89) EU:C:1991:225, paragraph 19. See also judgment of 17 October 1991, *Commission v Germany* (C-58/89) EU:C:1991:391, paragraph 14.

[49] Judgments of 25 July 2008, *Janecek* (C-237/07) EU:C:2008:447, paragraphs 37 and 38; of 19 November 2014, *ClientEarth* (C-404/13) EU:C:2014:2382, paragraph 54; of 26 June 2019, *Craeynest* (C-723/17) EU:C:2019:533, paragraphs 53 and 54; and of 19 December 2019, *Deutsche Umwelthilfe* (C-752/18) EU:C:2019:1114, paragraph 38.

[50] Judgments of 19 November 2014, *ClientEarth* (C-404/13) EU:C:2014:2382, paragraph 52; of 26 June 2019, *Craeynest* (C-723/17) EU:C:2019:533, paragraphs 31 and 54; and of 19 December 2019, *Deutsche Umwelthilfe* (C-752/18) EU:C:2019:1114, paragraphs 33, 39 and 54.

[51] See judgment of 12 October 2004, *Paul* (C-222/02) EU:C:2004:606, paragraph 38.

the protection of ambient air quality. Both tasks – banking supervision and the protection of ambient air quality – are characterised by a high degree of complexity,[52] and rights of individuals are not expressly mentioned,[53] as emphasised by the French Republic in the present case.

AG84   However, the banking supervision rules applicable at the time differed from the protection of ambient air quality in significant respects. Those differences are not due exclusively to the different subject matter of the respective rules.

AG85   This is because the deposit-guarantee scheme[54] provided a special protection scheme for depositors, which militated against conferring more extensive rights to compensation on the depositors.[55] By contrast, no such specific scheme is apparent with regard to damage to health due to air pollution.

AG86   Above all, however, the main purpose of the banking supervision rules in force at that time was to secure the mutual recognition of authorisations and of prudential supervision systems. This made it possible to grant a single licence recognised throughout the European Union and to apply the principle of home Member State prudential supervision.[56] The banking supervision rules were therefore intended, in accordance with their legal basis, to achieve the freedom of establishment of banks through the harmonisation of the national requirements. State liability in favour of depositors, which was not provided for or was even excluded under national law, was not necessary for that.[57]

AG87   By contrast, the rules on the protection of ambient air quality were based on the EU's environmental competence and therefore, in accordance with Article 191 TFEU, necessarily aim at a high level of protection with regard to human health. It is precisely that protection that is the main purpose, whereas objectives relating to the internal market play a marginal and indirect role at best.

5. No rule on financial claims

AG88   However, the French Republic's objection can also be understood to mean that entitlement to compensation requires the infringement of a rule that provides for rights of individuals to payments or economic benefits. The rules on ambient air quality do not do so.

AG89   In fact, previous decisions establishing State liability for infringements of EU law have often related to the safeguarding of financial claims, such as the safeguarding of wages and old-age pensions in the event of the employer's insolvency[58] or the claims of package travellers in the event of the bankruptcy of the travel undertaking,[59] deposit protection[60] and the protection of investors against

---

[52] See judgment of 12 October 2004, *Paul* (C-222/02) EU:C:2004:606, paragraph 44.
[53] See judgment of 12 October 2004, *Paul* (C-222/02) EU:C:2004:606, paragraph 41.
[54] Directive 94/19/EC of the European Parliament and of the Council of 30 May 1994 on deposit-guarantee schemes ([1994] OJ L135/5).
[55] Judgment of 12 October 2004, *Paul* (C-222/02) EU:C:2004:606, paragraph 45.
[56] Judgment of 12 October 2004, *Paul* (C-222/02) EU:C:2004:606, paragraph 42.
[57] Judgment of 12 October 2004, *Paul* (C-222/02) EU:C:2004:606, paragraph 43.
[58] Judgments of 19 November 1991, *Francovich* (C-6/90) and (C-9/90) EU:C:1991:428; of 25 January 2007, *Robins* (C-278/05) EU:C:2007:56; and of 25 April 2013, *Hogan* (C-398/11) EU:C:2013:272, paragraphs 50 to 52.
[59] Judgment of 8 October 1996, *Dillenkofer* (C-178/94, (C-179/94) and (C-188/94)–(C-190/94) EU:C:1996:375, paragraph 33 et seq.
[60] Judgments of 4 October 2018, *Kantarev* (C-571/16) EU:C:2018:807, and of 25 March 2021, *Balgarska Narodna Banka* (C-501/18) EU:C:2021:249.

excessive prices in the event of takeovers,[61] or the entitlement to compensation of victims of crime.[62]

AG90   The Court's statements according to which an infringement of the rule in question directly affects the legal situation ('*situation juridique*') of the injured party appear to follow along the same lines.[63] That situation related to legally protected asset-related interests in connection with guaranteed deposits and the protection of investors.

AG91   By contrast, the failure of a Member State to ensure compliance with the limit values would not be described as a change in the legal situation of those who experience adverse health effects as a result of that failure. Rather, that failure infringes a legal interest which is much more important than the abovementioned asset-related interests. This is because everyone has the right to respect for his or her physical and mental integrity, which is laid down in Article 3 of the Charter of Fundamental Rights and is ranked in first position in relation to the other legal interests.[64]

AG92   However, even irrespective of the impact on the legal situations of injured parties, it must be emphasised that the case-law on State liability is not based on the protection of financial interests of the persons concerned, but is intended to ensure the full effectiveness of EU law by protecting the rights that it confers on individuals.[65] Therefore, the principle of State liability for loss or damage caused to individuals as a result of breaches of EU law for which the State can be held responsible is inherent in the system of the treaties on which the European Union is based.[66]

AG93   In line with that objective, the Court has also recognised that the purpose of the EIA Directive[67] is to confer rights on individuals,[68] although claims for compensation are generally likely to fail in the absence of a direct causal link.[69]

AG94   Moreover, adverse effects on health are also associated with financial losses, for example treatment costs or loss of earnings. Accordingly, in its proposal for Directive 2008/50, the Commission emphasised not only the health consequences of air pollution, but also the estimated financial damage of EUR 189 to 609 thousand million per annum as at 2020.[70] Such damage, at the least, is covered by the protective purpose of the rules on the protection of ambient air quality.

---

[61] Judgment of 10 December 2020, *Euromin Holdings (Cyprus)* (C-735/19) EU:C:2020:1014.

[62] Judgment of 16 July 2020, *Presidenza del Consiglio dei Ministri* (C-129/19) EU:C:2020:566.

[63] Judgments of 4 October 2018, *Kantarev* (C-571/16) EU:C:2018:807, paragraph 103, and of 10 December 2020, *Euromin Holdings (Cyprus)* (C-735/19) EU:C:2020:1014, paragraph 90.

[64] See, to that effect, judgments of 20 May 1976, *De Peijper* (104/75) EU:C:1976:67, paragraph 15; of 5 June 2007, *Rosengren* (C-170/04) EU:C:2007:313, paragraph 39; of 1 June 2010, *Blanco Pérez and Chao Gómez* (C-570/07) and (C-571/07) EU:C:2010:300, paragraph 44; and of 25 November 2021, *Delfarma* (C-488/20) EU:C:2021:956, paragraph 37.

[65] Judgments of 19 November 1991, *Francovich* (C-6/90) and (C-9/90) EU:C:1991:428, paragraphs 31 to 33; of 5 March 1996, *Brasserie du pêcheur and Factortame* (C-46/93) and (C-48/93) EU:C:1996:79, paragraph 20; and of 19 December 2019, *Deutsche Umwelthilfe* (C-752/18) EU:C:2019:1114, paragraph 54.

[66] Judgments of 19 November 1991, *Francovich* (C-6/90) and (C-9/90) EU:C:1991:428, paragraph 35; of 5 March 1996, *Brasserie du pêcheur and Factortame* (C-46/93) and (C-48/93) EU:C:1996:79, paragraph 31; of 14 March 2013, *Leth* (C-420/11) EU:C:2013:166, paragraph 40; of 28 July 2016, *Tomášová* (C-168/15) EU:C:2016:602, paragraph 18; and of 19 December 2019, *Deutsche Umwelthilfe* (C-752/18) EU:C:2019:1114, paragraph 54.

[67] Now Directive 2011/92/EU of the European Parliament and of the Council of 13 December 2011 on the assessment of the effects of certain public and private projects on the environment ([2012] OJ L26/1).

[68] Judgment of 14 March 2013, *Leth* (C-420/11) EU:C:2013:166, paragraphs 32 and 36. See also judgments of 7 January 2004, *Wells* (C-201/02) EU:C:2004:12, paragraph 66, and of 17 November 2016, *Stadt Wiener Neustadt* (C-348/15) EU:C:2016:882, paragraph 45.

[69] Judgment of 14 March 2013, *Leth* (C-420/11) EU:C:2013:166, paragraphs 45 to 47, but see also my Opinion in *Leth* (C-420/11) EU:C:2012:701, AG 50–55.

[70] Proposal for a Directive of the European Parliament and of the Council on ambient air quality and cleaner air for Europe (COM(2005) 447 final, p. 2).

6. Group of beneficiaries

AG95   That notwithstanding, did the EU really intend to confer on a scarcely delimitable group of persons potentially affected a right to a certain quality of ambient air, infringement of which could give rise to entitlement to compensation?

AG96   The Court has since found, in 12 infringement cases, that 10 Member States failed to meet ambient air quality standards.[71] The nine most recent judgments even found a systematic and persistent infringement of the standards. Seven cases, concerning inter alia three other Member States, are currently still pending.[72] Air quality standards have also been the subject of disputes before national courts in – at the least – Belgium,[73] Germany,[74] France[75] and the United Kingdom.[76]

AG97   Therefore, Member States would have to expect a large number of claims for compensation for infringements of air quality standards if those standards were to confer such rights. Quite apart from the ensuing financial risks, disputes concerning such claims could place a considerable burden on the courts of the Member States.

AG98   However, those considerations do not militate against the recognition of rights that can establish entitlement to compensation, because the large number of persons potentially affected shows, above all, the importance of adequate air quality.

AG99   The expense associated with claims for compensation is also not manifestly disproportionate to the weight of that problem. The limit values for ambient air quality do not relate to minor nuisances, but rather to significant adverse effects on health that can go as far as premature death.[77]

AG100   At the same time, the group of persons actually affected is not so large as to cover almost every inhabitant of the Member States affected, whereby the residents would have to compensate each other through taxes, so to speak. Exceedance of the limit values burdens, above all, certain groups who live or work in particularly polluted areas.[78] Those groups often consist of people of low socio-economic status,[79] who are particularly reliant on judicial protection.

AG101   For that reason also,[80] it is incorrect to assume, together with Ireland and the Republic of Poland, that the rules on ambient air quality serve exclusively to protect the general public. Although ambient air quality must be protected in general, the

---

[71] Judgments of 10 May 2011, *Commission v Sweden* (C-479/10) EU:C:2011:287; of 15 November 2012, *Commission v Portugal* (C-34/11) EU:C:2012:712; of 19 December 2012, *Commission v Italy* (C-68/11) EU:C:2012:815; of 5 April 2017, *Commission v Bulgaria* (C-488/15) EU:C:2017:267; of 22 February 2018, *Commission v Poland* (C-336/16) EU:C:2018:94; of 24 October 2019, *Commission v France (Exceedance of limit values for nitrogen dioxide)* (C-636/18) EU:C:2019:900; of 30 April 2020, *Commission v Romania (Exceedance of the limit values for PM10)* (C-638/18) EU:C:2020:334; of 10 November 2020, *Commission v Italy (Limit values—PM10)* (C-644/18) EU:C:2020:895; of 3 February 2021, *Commission v Hungary (Limit values—PM10)* (C-637/18) EU:C:2021:92; of 4 March 2021, *Commission v United Kingdom (Limit values—NO2)* (C-664/18) EU:C:2021:171; of 3 June 2021, *Commission v Germany (Limit values—NO2)* (C-635/18) EU:C:2021:437; and of 28 April 2022, *Commission v France (Limit values—PM10)* (C-286/21) EU:C:2022:319.
[72] Cases *Commission v Italy (nitrogen dioxide)* (C-573/19); *Commission v Bulgaria (nitrogen dioxide)* (C-730/19); *Commission v Spain (nitrogen dioxide)* (C-125/20); *Commission v Greece (PM10)* (C-70/21); *Commission v Slovakia (PM10)* (C-342/21); *Commission v Greece (nitrogen dioxide)* (C-633/21); *Commission v Portugal (nitrogen dioxide)* (C-220/22).
[73] Judgment of 26 June 2019, *Craeynest* (C-723/17) EU:C:2019:533.
[74] Judgments of 25 July 2008, *Janecek* (C-237/07) EU:C:2008:447, and of 19 December 2019, *Deutsche Umwelthilfe* (C-752/18) EU:C:2019:1114.
[75] Judgment of the Conseil d'État (Council of State) of 4 August 2021, Association les Amis de la Terre France et autres (428409, FR:CECHR:2021:428409.20210804).
[76] Judgment of 19 November 2014, *ClientEarth* (C-404/13) EU:C:2014:2382.
[77] European Environment Agency, Unequal exposure and unequal impacts: Social vulnerability to air pollution, noise and extreme temperatures in Europe, EEA Report No 22/2018, pp. 19 and 21.
[78] See also AG131 et seq. below.
[79] European Environment Agency, Unequal exposure and unequal impacts: Social vulnerability to air pollution, noise and extreme temperatures in Europe, EEA Report No 22/2018, pp. 19-22.
[80] See, moreover, AG 77 and 78 above.

specific problems arise in specific places and affect specific, identifiable groups of people. Therefore, only persons who are directly concerned by an exceedance of the limit values or the risk of an exceedance can rely on Article 23(1) of Directive 2008/50.[81]

AG102   In line with the considerations set out just above, the Court, in connection with the enforcement of rules on ambient air quality, has already alluded to the possibility of entitlement to compensation under EU law.[82]

7. Answer to the first question

AG103   In summary, the limit values for pollutants in ambient air and the obligations to improve ambient air quality under Articles 7 and 8 of Directive 96/62, in conjunction with Directive 1999/30, and under Articles 13 and 23 of Directive 2008/50 are intended to confer rights on individuals.

B. Second question – further requirements for entitlement to compensation

AG104   The second question seeks to ascertain the conditions to which entitlement to compensation for damage to health is subject. Of particular interest to the referring court in that respect is the date on which the existence of the breach of the rules on the protection of air quality must be assessed.

AG105   In that connection, the other two conditions of entitlement to compensation must be recalled: the breach must be sufficiently serious (see section 1) and there must be a direct causal link between that breach and the damage (see section 2).[83]

1. Sufficiently serious infringement

AG106   In order to determine whether a sufficiently serious infringement of EU law has occurred, the national court before which a claim for compensation has been brought must take account of all the factors which characterise the situation brought before it. Those factors include the clarity and precision of the rule infringed, the measure of discretion left by that rule to the authorities, whether the infringement or the damage caused was intentional or involuntary, whether any error of law was excusable or inexcusable, and the fact that the position taken by an EU institution may have contributed towards the adoption or maintenance of national measures or practices contrary to EU law.[84]

AG107   It also follows from the case-law that a breach of EU law will clearly be sufficiently serious if it has persisted despite a judgment finding the breach in question to be established, or despite a preliminary ruling or settled case-law of

---

[81] See judgments of 25 July 2008, *Janecek* (C-237/07) EU:C:2008:447, paragraph 39; of 19 November 2014, *ClientEarth* (C-404/13) EU:C:2014:2382, paragraph 56; and of 26 June 2019, *Craeynest* (C-723/17) EU:C:2019:533, paragraph 56; see also, fundamentally, my Opinion in *Wasserleitungsverband Nördliches Burgenland* (C-197/18) EU:C:2019:274, AG41 et seq.

[82] Judgment of 19 December 2019, *Deutsche Umwelthilfe* (C-752/18) EU:C:2019:1114, paragraphs 54 and 55.

[83] Judgments of 5 March 1996, *Brasserie du pêcheur and Factortame* (C-46/93) and (C-48/93) EU:C:1996:79, paragraph 51; of 14 March 2013, *Leth* (C-420/11) EU:C:2013:166, paragraph 41; and of 16 July 2020, *Presidenza del Consiglio dei Ministri* (C-129/19) EU:C:2020:566, paragraph 34.

[84] Judgments of 5 March 1996, *Brasserie du pêcheur and Factortame* (C-46/93) and (C-48/93) EU:C:1996:79, paragraph 56, and of 29 July 2019, *Hochtief Solutions Magyarországi Fióktelepe* (C-620/17) EU:C:2019:630, paragraph 42.

the Court on the matter from which it is clear that the conduct in question constituted a breach.[85]

(a) Exceedance of the limit values as a serious infringement

AG108   The obligation to comply with the limit values for PM10 (since 2005) and nitrogen dioxide (since 2010) – which arose initially from Article 7(1) of Directive 96/62 and Article 4, in conjunction with Annex II, and Article 5, in conjunction with Annex III, Section I, Stage 1, of Directive 1999/30 and, as of 11 June 2010, from Article 13(1) of and Annex XI to Directive 2008/50 – is unambiguous and leaves no discretion to the Member States. It might be inferred from that that such an infringement was serious by its very nature.

AG109   However, in the judgment in *Janecek*, concerning Directives 96/62 and 1999/30, the Court ruled that the Member States were not obliged to take measures to ensure that those limit values and/or alert thresholds are never exceeded.[86] Although the subsequent judgments concerning those directives suggest that exceedance of the limit values nevertheless constitutes an independent infringement of EU law,[87] Directive 2008/50 was already applicable at that time. Therefore, exceedance of the limit values during the period in which Directives 96/62 and 1999/30 were applicable alone could not be regarded as a serious infringement of EU law.

AG110   Nevertheless, the judgment in *Janecek* confirms the likewise clear and unconditional obligation to draw up action plans under Article 7(3) of Directive 96/62.[88] That obligation is closely linked to the exceedance of the limit values, as such exceedance does not occur or is at least minimised if the Member State has taken sufficient measures to reduce air pollution – whether before or during the period in which the limit values are applicable.

AG111   That connection is also clearly expressed in Directive 2008/50, because the obligation to draw up air quality plans under Article 23 is triggered by exceedance of the limit values under Article 13 and Annex XI.

AG112   I infer that, both under the previously applicable directives and under Directive 2008/50, an exceedance of the limit values for ambient air quality without a corresponding plan to remedy the exceedance constitutes a serious infringement of EU law which may establish entitlement to compensation.

(b) Quality of the plans

AG113   Contrary to the view taken by the Republic of Poland, however, the mere existence of a plan is not sufficient to exclude a serious infringement. Rather, as the Italian Republic submits, in order to exclude a serious infringement of the limit values, a plan must not have any manifest deficiencies.

AG114   In that respect, it is first necessary to determine whether the competent authorities respected the requirements in Section A of Annex XV to Directive 2008/50 or Annex IV to Directive 96/62. Only if a plan is linked to the information provided for therein can it be assessed whether it is at all capable of bringing an end to the exceedance, or by when the exceedance is to be brought to an end.[89]

---

[85] Judgments of 5 March 1996, *Brasserie du pêcheur and Factortame* (C-46/93) and (C-48/93) EU:C:1996:79, paragraph 57; of 12 December 2006, *Test Claimants in the FII Group Litigation* (C-446/04) EU:C:2006:774, paragraph 214; of 30 May 2017, *Safa Nicu Sepahan v Council* (C-45/15 P) EU:C:2017:402, paragraph 31; and of 18 January 2022, *Thelen Technopark Berlin* (C-261/20) EU:C:2022:33, paragraph 47.

[86] Judgment of 25 July 2008, *Janecek* (C-237/07) EU:C:2008:447, paragraph 44.

[87] See AG53 above.

[88] Judgment of 25 July 2008, *Janecek* (C-237/07) EU:C:2008:447, paragraphs 35, 39 and 41. See also judgment of 19 November 2014, *ClientEarth* (C-404/13) EU:C:2014:2382, paragraphs 53 and 56.

[89] See AG46 above.

AG115   However, even if all formal requirements have been complied with, an infringement of the limit values may be sufficiently serious if the plan manifestly does not meet the substantive requirements because the competent bodies have breached the limits of their discretion.[90] Such deficiencies may reside, in particular, in the fact that the expected duration of the exceedance is clearly not 'as short as possible' or in the fact that the remedies are demonstrably inappropriate. It is also conceivable that the plans might be based on obviously incorrectly positioned sampling points[91] or grossly incorrect modelling techniques, with the result that the actual extent to which the limit values are exceeded is not taken into account.

AG116   It is for the national courts to examine those requirements in the main proceedings. In so doing, they should take into account that the Commission, when considering deadline extensions under Article 22 of Directive 2008/50, has already rejected the plans submitted by the French Republic for, inter alia, the Paris agglomeration.[92] Moreover, the Court has already held that, between 11 June 2010 and 16 April 2017, the French Republic manifestly failed to adopt, in a timely manner, appropriate measures, inter alia for that agglomeration, to ensure that the period of exceedance of the limit values for nitrogen dioxide[93] and PM10[94] can be kept as short as possible.

(c) Relevant period

AG117   The connection between a serious infringement of the limit values and the plan to eliminate the exceedance requires that periods of time to be taken into account in the assessment of the claim for compensation must be determined in the light of that plan. This is because any period during which a limit value has been exceeded without a sufficient plan is a period during which the Member State concerned has seriously infringed the air quality rules.

AG118   As regards the case in the main proceedings, that is to say, the Paris agglomeration, in the absence of a relevant postponement of the deadline in accordance with Article 22 of Directive 2008/50, the date of application of the respective limit values results from Annex XI, which corresponds to the previously applicable Directive 1999/30 in that respect. Thus, the limit values for PM10 have been applicable since 1 January 2005 and those for nitrogen dioxide since 1 January 2010.

AG119   By contrast, the obligation to draw up air quality plans under Article 23 of Directive 2008/50 did not come into being until the transposition deadline expired on 11 June 2010.

AG120   According to the third subparagraph of Article 23(1) of Directive 2008/50, those plans are to be communicated to the Commission without delay, but no later than two years after the end of the year the first exceedance was observed. Various Member States which are party to the proceedings infer from this that the obligation

---

[90] See judgments of 25 July 2008, *Janecek* (C-237/07) EU:C:2008:447, paragraph 46, and of 5 April 2017, *Commission v Bulgaria* (C-488/15) EU:C:2017:267, paragraph 105. See also judgments of 24 October 1996, *Kraaijeveld* (C-72/95) EU:C:1996:404, paragraph 59; of 26 June 2019, *Craeynest* (C-723/17) EU:C:2019:533, paragraphs 34 and 45; and of 3 October 2019, *Wasserleitungsverband Nördliches Burgenland* (C-197/18) EU:C:2019:824, paragraphs 31 and 72.
[91] See judgment of 26 June 2019, *Craeynest* (C-723/17) EU:C:2019:533, paragraphs 43 to 45.
[92] See AG20 above.
[93] Judgment of 24 October 2019, *Commission v France (Exceedance of limit values for nitrogen dioxide)* (C-636/18) EU:C:2019:900, paragraph 89.
[94] Judgment of 28 April 2022, *Commission v France (Limit values—PM10)* (C-286/21) EU:C:2022:319, paragraph 77.

to draw up air quality plans did not become effective until that additional period had expired.

AG121   That view may be correct as regards exceedances of the limit values or target values plus any relevant margin of tolerance that occurred for the first time after the deadline for transposing Directive 2008/50 had expired.

AG122   By contrast, exceedances that already existed upon the expiry of the transposition deadline were subject to the previously applicable obligations under Article 7(3) and Article 8 of Directive 96/62, in conjunction with the limit values and margins of tolerance in Directive 1999/30. Those provisions established an obligation which is comparable to Article 23 of Directive 2008/50, but is even more extensive from a temporal point of view.[95] It already applied in the period prior to the application of the limit values, as soon as those values plus the associated margins of tolerance had been exceeded.

AG123   Article 11(1)(a)(iii) of Directive 96/62 also provided a time limit of two years for the submission of those plans. However, those plans had to ensure that the limit values were respected on the date on which they became applicable and therefore already effective at that date.

AG124   Consequently, Member States were already required to have drawn up the respective necessary plans if limit values were exceeded before the deadline for transposing Directive 2008/50. It appears as though that is the situation in the case in the main proceedings, as the French Republic had unsuccessfully applied to the Commission for postponements of the deadlines for PM10 and nitrogen dioxide for the Paris agglomeration,[96] and therefore assumed that the limit values had been exceeded. However, that would have to be reviewed by the national court.

(d) Interim conclusion

AG125   A serious infringement of the rules on the protection of ambient air quality as regards PM10 or nitrogen dioxide laid down in Articles 7 and 8 of Directive 96/62, Directive 1999/30 and Articles 13 and 23 of Directive 2008/50 in the event of an exceedance of the limit values at the end of the time limit for their implementation covers all periods in which the respective applicable limit values were exceeded without there having been an air quality improvement plan which satisfied the requirements of Annex IV to Directive 96/62 or Section A of Annex XV to Directive 2008/50 and which also did not contain any manifest defects in other respects.

2. Direct causal link

AG126   The actual difficulties in enforcing claims for compensation lie in proving a direct causal link between the serious infringement of air quality rules and concrete damage to health.

AG127   The obligation for injured individuals to establish to the requisite legal standard the extent of the damage suffered as a result of a breach of EU law constitutes, in principle, a condition for the State's liability for such damage.[97]

AG128   It is for the national courts to determine the exact standard of proof. They must ascertain whether the loss and damage claimed flows sufficiently directly from the

---

[95] See above, AG42 et seq.
[96] See AG20 above.
[97] Judgment of 25 March 2021, *Balgarska Narodna Banka* (C-501/18) EU:C:2021:249, paragraph 122.

breach of EU law by the Member State;[98] in so doing, however, they must observe the principles of equivalence and effectiveness.[99] The Court may, in order to give the national court a useful answer, provide it with all the guidance that it deems necessary.[100]

AG129   An act or – in the case of inadequate measures to improve ambient air quality – omission is the cause of damage only where such damage can be attributed directly to such an act. The requisite causal link does not exist where the damage would also have occurred in the absence of the relevant act or omission.[101]

AG130   It is true that the limit values for PM10 and nitrogen dioxide are based on the assumption of significant damage, in particular premature deaths, due to air pollution.[102] However, that does not prove that the suffering of certain people is due to exceedances of the limit values and to deficient air quality plans. This is because such suffering can also be caused by other factors, such as predisposition or personal behaviour, such as smoking. Since the World Health Organisation now recommends stricter limit values,[103] it also cannot be ruled out that the air is sufficiently polluted to cause such illnesses despite compliance with Directive 2008/50.

AG131   Therefore, in order to prove a direct causal link, the injured party must *first* prove that he or she has stayed, for a sufficiently long period of time, in an environment in which limit values for ambient air quality under EU law have been seriously infringed. The duration of that period is a medical question that requires a scientific answer.

AG132   Such a stay should in any event be able to result in particular from the workplace or the home, but also from other places where the person concerned has frequently stayed for a relatively long period of time.

AG133   However, it is not sufficient to have stayed in an agglomeration or zone in which the limit values were exceeded at one or more sampling points. This is because certain sampling points are to be established in such a way that they provide information on the pollution of the most polluted locations.[104] Therefore, even in such agglomerations or zones, there will be many places where the air is less polluted and meets the standards of EU law.

AG134   Therefore, the injured party must specifically prove that the limit values were exceeded at the claimed place where he or she stayed and during the claimed periods. However, if there was no sampling point at the place in question, it must be possible to determine the extent of pollution using modelling techniques, because

---

[98] Judgments of 5 March 1996, *Brasserie du pêcheur and Factortame* (C-46/93) and (C-48/93) EU:C:1996:79, paragraph 65; of 20 October 2011, *Danfoss and Sauer-Danfoss* (C-94/10) EU:C:2011:674, paragraph 34; and of 19 June 2014, *Specht* (C-501/12)–(C-506/12), (C-540/12) and (C-541/12) EU:C:2014:2005, paragraph 106.

[99] Judgment of 20 October 2011, *Danfoss and Sauer-Danfoss* (C-94/10) EU:C:2011:674, paragraph 36; and, to that effect, judgments of 13 July 2006, *Manfredi* (C-295/04)–(C-298/04) EU:C:2006:461, paragraph 64; and of 5 June 2014, *Kone* (C-557/12) EU:C:2014:1317, paragraph 24.

[100] Judgment of 20 October 2011, *Danfoss and Sauer-Danfoss* (C-94/10) EU:C:2011:674, paragraph 35.

[101] To that effect, judgment of 28 October 2004, *van den Berg v Council and Commission* (C-164/01 P) EU:C:2004:665, paragraph 57.

[102] Commission Proposal of 21 September 2005 for a Directive of the European Parliament and of the Council on ambient air quality and cleaner air for Europe (COM(2005) 447 final, p. 2). See my Opinions in *Commission v Bulgaria* (C-488/15) EU:C:2016:862, AG 2 and 3, and in *Craeynest* (C-723/17) EU:C:2019:168, AG53.

[103] WHO global air quality guidelines: particulate matter (PM2.5 and PM10), ozone, nitrogen dioxide, sulfur dioxide and carbon monoxide. Executive summary, Geneva: World Health Organisation; 2021.

[104] See judgment of 26 June 2019, *Craeynest* (C-723/17) EU:C:2019:533, paragraph 43, concerning the first indent of point 1(a) of Section B of Annex III to Directive 2008/50. Point (a)(i) of Section I of Annex VI to Directive 1999/30 already contained the same requirements.

Member States are also able to make use of that tool.[105] Accordingly, the European Environment Agency takes the view that the portion of the urban population living within 100 metres of major roads is exposed to excessive levels of pollutants if the limit values are exceeded in the agglomeration concerned.[106]

AG135   *Second*, anyone seeking compensation for air pollution must prove the existence of damage that can be linked to the relevant air pollution in the first place.

AG136   And *third*, the injured party must prove a direct causal link between the abovementioned stay at a place where a limit value for ambient air quality was seriously infringed and the damage claimed.

AG137   This will generally require medical reports, which will certainly also have to take into account the scientific basis on which the limit values were set and the recommendations of the World Health Organisation, which are even stricter in some cases.

AG138   It would be conceivable for that burden of proof to be reduced by way of a rebuttable presumption that a typical type of damage to health is attributable to a sufficiently long stay in an environment in which a limit value has been exceeded. Accordingly, in the case of apparently much more serious air pollution, the ECtHR has derived a presumption of harm from an exceedance of limit values and other strong indications.[107] In order to bring about such a reduction of the burden of proof, the injured party could invoke the principle of effectiveness where the full standard of proof, beyond any reasonable doubt, would make it excessively difficult to obtain compensation.

AG139   However, I do not consider it appropriate for the Court to decide in the present case whether such a presumption arises from EU law and, in particular, the rules on ambient air quality. Neither the request for a preliminary ruling nor the parties to the proceedings have raised that question. However, the acceptance of such a presumption would require an intensive discussion of the scientific basis for establishing a causal link between air pollution and damage to health.

AG140   In addition, some of the parties emphasise that the applicant complained of adverse effects to his health as early as in 2003, that is to say, before the limit value for PM10 became applicable. However, that does not rule out the possibility that he has suffered additional damage resulting from air pollution – whether because his condition has worsened or because healing has been prevented or delayed. An infringement of the limit values would be expected to have such effects in any case, because air pollution often amplifies the effects of existing health problems.[108] That question is also of a scientific nature and must be examined by the national court in each individual case.

AG141   Lastly, it is important to note that even if a direct link between a serious infringement of the limit values and damage to health were proven, the matter would not end there. Rather, the Member State may exonerate itself by proving

---

[105] See judgment of 26 June 2019, *Craeynest* (C-723/17) EU:C:2019:533, paragraph 62, Article 6 of Directive 96/62, Article 7(4) of Directive 1999/30 and Articles 6, 7 and 10 and recitals 6 and 14 of Directive 2008/50.

[106] European Environment Agency, Exceedance of air quality standards in Europe, *https://www.eea.europa.eu/ims /exceedance-of-air-quality-standards*, visited on 1 March 2022. According to that publication, in 2019, 10% of the urban population in the EU and the United Kingdom was exposed to excessive levels of PM10 and 3% to nitrogen dioxide.

[107] Judgment of the ECtHR of 9 June 2005, *Fadeyeva v Russia* (55723/00, CE:ECHR:2005:0609JUD005572300, §§ 87 and 88).

[108] European Environment Agency, Unequal exposure and unequal impacts: Social vulnerability to air pollution, noise and extreme temperatures in Europe, EEA Report No 22/2018, pp. 19-21.

that such exceedances would also have occurred if it had adopted in good time air quality plans that met the requirements of the directive.

3. Answer to the second question

AG142   In summary, entitlement to compensation for adverse effects to health resulting from an established exceedance of the limit values for PM10 or nitrogen dioxide in the ambient air following the end of the relevant time limit laid down in Articles 7 and 8 of Directive 96/62, in conjunction with Directive 1999/30, or Article 13 of Directive 2008/50 requires that the injured party proves a direct link between that adverse effect and his or her stay at a place where the respective applicable limit values were exceeded without there having been an air quality improvement plan which satisfied the requirements of Annex IV to Directive 96/62 or Section A of Annex XV to Directive 2008/50 and which also did not contain any manifest defects in other respects.

V. Conclusion

AG143   I therefore propose that the Court give the following answer to the request for a preliminary ruling:

(1) The limit values for pollutants in ambient air and the obligations to improve ambient air quality under Articles 7 and 8 of Council Directive 96/62/EC of 27 September 1996 on ambient air quality assessment and management, in conjunction with Council Directive 1999/30/EC of 22 April 1999 relating to limit values for sulphur dioxide, nitrogen dioxide and oxides of nitrogen, particulate matter and lead in ambient air, and under Articles 13 and 23 of Directive 2008/50/EC of the European Parliament and of the Council of 21 May 2008 on ambient air quality and cleaner air for Europe are intended to confer rights on individuals.

(2) Entitlement to compensation for adverse effects to health resulting from an established exceedance of the limit values for PM10 or nitrogen dioxide in the ambient air following the end of the relevant time limit laid down in Articles 7 and 8 of Directive 96/62, in conjunction with Directive 1999/30, or Article 13 of Directive 2008/50 requires that the injured party proves a direct link between that adverse effect and his or her stay at a place where the respective applicable limit values were exceeded without there having been an air quality improvement plan which satisfied the requirements of Annex IV to Directive 96/62 or Section A of Annex XV to Directive 2008/50 and which also did not contain any manifest defects in other respects.

JUDGMENT[109]

1   This request for a preliminary ruling concerns the interpretation of Article 13(1) and Article 23(1) of Directive 2008/50/EC of the European Parliament and of the Council of 21 May 2008 on ambient air quality and cleaner air for Europe (OJ 2008 L 152, p. 1).

---

[109] Language of the case: French.

2   The request has been made in proceedings between JP, on the one hand, and the
Ministre de la Transition écologique (Minister for Ecological Transition, France)
and the Premier ministre (Prime Minister, France), on the other, concerning JP's
applications seeking, inter alia, first, annulment of the implied decision of the
Prefect of Val-d'Oise (France) to refuse to take the necessary measures to address
his health problems linked to air pollution and, second, compensation from the
French Republic for the various heads of damage which JP attributes to that
pollution.

Legal context

European Union law

Directive 80/779/EEC

3   Article 3 of Council Directive 80/779/EEC of 15 July 1980 on air quality limit
values and guide values for sulphur dioxide and suspended particulates (OJ 1980
L 229, p. 30) provided:

> '1. Member States shall take appropriate measures to ensure that as from
>   1 April 1983 the concentrations of sulphur dioxide and suspended
>   particulates in the atmosphere are not greater than the limit values
>   given in Annex I, without prejudice to the following provisions.
> 2.   Where a Member State considers that there is a likelihood that, despite
>   the measures taken, the concentrations of sulphur dioxide and
>   suspended particulates in the atmosphere might, after 1 April 1983,
>   exceed in certain zones the limit values given in Annex I, it shall inform
>   the Commission [of the European Communities] thereof before 1
>   October 1982.
>   It shall at the same time forward to the Commission plans for the
>   progressive improvement of the quality of the air in those zones. These
>   plans, drawn up on the basis of relevant information on the nature,
>   origin and evolution of the pollution, shall describe in particular the
>   measures taken or to be taken and the procedures implemented or to
>   be implemented by the Member State concerned. These measures and
>   procedures must bring the concentrations of sulphur dioxide and
>   suspended particulates in the atmosphere within these zones to values
>   below or equal to the limit values given in Annex I as soon as possible
>   and by 1 April 1993 at the latest.'

4   Under Article 7(1) and (2) of that directive:

> '1. Following the entry into force of this Directive, Member States shall
>   inform the Commission, not later than six months after the end (31
>   March) of the annual reference period, of instances in which the limit
>   values laid down in Annex I have been exceeded and of the
>   concentrations recorded.
> 2.   They shall also notify the Commission, not later than one year after
>   the end of the annual reference period, of the reasons for such instances
>   and of the measures they have taken to avoid their recurrence.'

5   Annex I to that directive, entitled 'Limit values for sulphur dioxide and suspended particulates', provided in Table B:

'Limit values for suspended particulates (as measured by the black-smoke method (^{1})) expressed in ug/m^3 [micrograms per cubic metre]

Reference period	Limit value for suspended particulates
Year	80 (median of daily mean values taken throughout the year)
Winter (1 October to 31 March)	130 (median of daily mean values taken throughout the winter)
Year (made up of units of measuring periods of 24 hours)	250 (^{2}) (98 percentile of all daily mean values taken throughout the year)
(^{1}) The results of the measurements of black smoke taken by the OECD method have been converted into gravimetric units as described by the OECD (see Annex III). (^{2}) Member States must take all appropriate steps to ensure that this value is not exceeded for more than three consecutive days. Moreover, Member States must endeavour to prevent and to reduce any such instances in which this value has been exceeded.'	

Directive 85/203/EEC

6   Article 3 of Council Directive 85/203/EEC of 7 March 1985 on air quality standards for nitrogen dioxide (OJ 1985 L 87, p. 1) provided:

> '1. Member States shall take the necessary measures to ensure that as from 1 July 1987 the concentrations of nitrogen dioxide in the atmosphere measured in accordance with Annex III are not greater than the limit value given in Annex I.
>
> 2. However, when in particular circumstances the nitrogen dioxide concentrations in the atmosphere in certain zones are likely, despite the measures taken, to exceed the limit value in Annex I after 1 July 1987, the Member State concerned shall inform the Commission thereof before 1 July 1987.
>
> It shall forward plans for the gradual improvement of the quality of the air in these zones to the Commission as soon as possible. These plans, drawn up on the basis of relevant information on the nature, origin and development of this pollution, shall describe, in particular, the measures taken or to be taken and the procedures implemented or to be implemented by the Member State concerned. These measures and procedures must aim at reducing the nitrogen dioxide concentrations in the atmosphere within these zones to values not exceeding the limit value given in Annex I as rapidly as possible and by 1 January 1994 at the latest.'

7   Under Article 7(1) and (2) of that directive:

'1. From 1 July 1987 Member States shall inform the Commission, not later than six months after the end (31 December) of the annual reference period, of instances in which the limit value laid down in Annex I has been exceeded and of the concentrations recorded.

2. Member States shall also notify the Commission, not later than one year after the end of the annual reference period, of the reasons for such instances and of the measures they have taken to deal with them.'

8   Annex I to that directive, entitled 'Limit value for nitrogen dioxide', provided:

'(The value limit shall be expressed in μg/m^3. The volume must be standardised at the following conditions of temperature and pressure: 293 °K [Kelvin] and 101.3 kPa [kilopascal])

Reference period ([1])	Limit value for nitrogen dioxide
Year	200
	98th percentile calculated from the mean values per hour or per period of less than an hour recorded throughout the year ([2])

([1]) The annual reference period begins on 1 January in any given calendar year and ends on 31 December.
([2]) To ensure that the validity of the calculation of the 98th percentile is recognised, 75% of the possible values must be available and, as far as possible, distributed uniformly throughout the year in question for that particular measurement site. In cases where the values measured on certain sites are not available over a period exceeding 10 days, the calculated percentile must mention this fact. The calculation of the 98th percentile on the basis of the values recorded throughout the year is to be carried out as follows: the 98th percentile must be calculated from the values actually measured. The measured values should be rounded off to the nearest μg/ m^3. All the values are to be listed in increasing order for each site: $X1 \leq X2 \leq X3 \leq \ldots\ldots \leq Xk \leq \ldots\ldots \leq XN\text{-}1 \leq XN$ The 98th percentile is the value of the component of rank k where k is calculated from the following formula: $k = (q \times N)$ where q is equal to 0.98 for the 98th percentile and to 0.50 for the 50th percentile, N being the number of values actually measured. The value of $(q \times N)$ should be rounded off to the nearest whole number. Where measuring equipment does not yet allow the production of discrete values but provides only classes of values higher than 1 μg/m^3, the Member State concerned may, for the calculation of the percentile, use an interpolation, provided that the interpolation formula is accepted by the Commission and that the classes of values are not higher than 10 μg/m^3. This temporary waiver is only valid for equipment currently installed for a time span not exceeding the life of the equipment and in any case limited to 10 years from the application of this Directive.'

Directive 96/62/EC

9   Article 4 of Council Directive 96/62/EC of 27 September 1996 on ambient air quality assessment and management (OJ 1996 L 296, p. 55), entitled 'Setting of the limit values and alert thresholds for ambient air', provided in paragraphs 1 and 5:

'1. … the Commission shall submit to the Council [of the European Union] proposals for the setting of limit values and, as appropriate, alert thresholds …

…

5. In accordance with the Treaty, the Council shall adopt the legislation provided for in paragraph 1 …'

10   Article 7 of that directive, entitled 'Improvement of ambient air quality – General requirements', provided:

'1. Member States shall take the necessary measures to ensure compliance with the limit values.
2. Measures taken in order to achieve the aims of this Directive shall:
    (a) take into account an integrated approach to the protection of air, water and soil;
    (b) not contravene Community legislation on the protection of safety and health of workers at work;
    (c) have no significant negative effects on the environment in the other Member States.
3. Member States shall draw up action plans indicating the measures to be taken in the short term where there is a risk of the limit values and/or alert thresholds being exceeded, in order to reduce that risk and to limit the duration of such an occurrence. Such plans may, depending on the individual case, provide for measures to control and, where necessary, suspend activities, including motor-vehicle traffic, which contribute to the limit values being exceeded.'

11   Under Article 8 of that directive, entitled 'Measures applicable in zones where levels are higher than the limit value':

'1. Member States shall draw up a list of zones and agglomerations in which the levels of one or more pollutants are higher than the limit value plus the margin of tolerance.
    Where no margin of tolerance has been fixed for a specific pollutant, zones and agglomerations in which the level of that pollutant exceeds the limit value shall be treated in the same way as the zones and agglomerations referred to in the first subparagraph, and paragraphs 3, 4 and 5 shall apply to them.
2. Member States shall draw up a list of zones and agglomerations in which the levels of one or more pollutants are between the limit value and the limit value plus the margin of tolerance.
3. In the zones and agglomerations referred to in paragraph 1, Member States shall take measures to ensure that a plan or programme is prepared or implemented for attaining the limit value within the specific time limit.
    The said plan or programme, which must be made available to the public, shall incorporate at least the information listed in Annex IV.
4. In the zones and agglomerations referred to in paragraph 1, where the level of more than one pollutant is higher than the limit values, Member States shall provide an integrated plan covering all the pollutants concerned.
5. The Commission shall regularly check the implementation of the plans or programmes submitted under paragraph 3 by examining their progress and the trends in air pollution.

6. When the level of a pollutant exceeds, or is likely to exceed, the limit value plus the margin of tolerance or, as the case may be, the alert threshold following significant pollution originating in another Member State, the Member States concerned shall consult with one another with a view to finding a solution. The Commission may be present at such consultations.'

12   Article 13(1) of that directive provided:

'Member States shall bring into force the laws, regulations and administrative provisions necessary to comply with this Directive not later than 18 months after it comes into force with regard to the provisions relating to Articles 1 to 4 and 12 and Annexes I, II, III and IV, and at the latest on the date on which the provisions referred to in Article 4(5) apply, with regard to the provisions relating to the other Articles.
…'

Directive 1999/30/EC

13   Article 4 of Council Directive 1999/30/EC of 22 April 1999 relating to limit values for sulphur dioxide, nitrogen dioxide and oxides of nitrogen, particulate matter and lead in ambient air (OJ 1999 L 163, p. 41), entitled 'Nitrogen dioxide and oxides of nitrogen', provided in paragraph 1:

'Member States shall take the measures necessary to ensure that concentrations of nitrogen dioxide and, where applicable, of oxides of nitrogen, in ambient air, as assessed in accordance with Article 7, do not exceed the limit values laid down in Section I of Annex II as from the dates specified therein.
The margins of tolerance laid down in Section I of Annex II shall apply in accordance with Article 8 of Directive 96/62/EC.'

14   Article 5 of Directive 1999/30, entitled 'Particulate matter', provided in paragraph 1:

'Member States shall take the measures necessary to ensure that concentrations of PM10 in ambient air, as assessed in accordance with Article 7, do not exceed the limit values laid down in Section I of Annex III as from the dates specified therein.
The margins of tolerance laid down in Section I of Annex III shall apply in accordance with Article 8 of Directive 96/62/EC.'

15   Article 9 of Directive 1999/30, entitled 'Repeals and transitional arrangements', provided:

'1. [Directive 80/779] shall be repealed with effect from 19 July 2001 except that Articles 1, 2(1), 3(1), 9, 15 and 16 of [Directive 80/779] and Annexes I, IIIb and IV thereto shall be repealed with effect from 1 January 2005.
…

3. [Directive 85/203] shall be repealed with effect from 19 July 2001 except that Articles 1(1), first indent, and (2), 2, first indent, 3(1), 5, 9, 15 and 16 of [Directive 85/203] and Annex I thereto shall be repealed with effect from 1 January 2010.

…'

16   Article 12(1) of Directive 1999/30, entitled 'Implementation', was worded as follows:

'The Member States shall bring into force the laws, regulations and administrative provisions necessary to comply with this Directive by 19 July 2001. They shall forthwith inform the Commission thereof.

…'

17   Annex II to that directive, entitled 'Limit values for nitrogen dioxide (NO2) and oxides of nitrogen (NOx) and the alert threshold for nitrogen dioxide', provided:

'**I. Limit values for nitrogen dioxide and oxides of nitrogen**

Limit values must be expressed in $\mu g/m^3$. The volume must be standardised at a temperature of 293 °K and a pressure of 101.3 kPa.

	Averaging period	Limit value	Margin of tolerance	Date by which limit value is to be met
1. Hourly limit value for the protection of human health	1 hour	200 $\mu g/m^3$NO2, not to be exceeded more than 18 times a calendar year	50% on the entry into force of this Directive, reducing on 1 January 2001 and every 12 months thereafter by equal annual percentages to reach 0% by 1 January 2010	1 January 2010
2. Annual limit value for the protection of human health	Calendar year	40 $\mu g/m^3$NO2	50% on the entry into force of this Directive, reducing on 1 January 2001 and every 12 months thereafter by equal annual percentages to reach 0% by 1 January 2010	1 January 2010
3. Annual limit value for the protection of vegetation	Calendar year	30 $\mu g/m^3$NOx	None	19 July 2001

…'

18   Annex III to that directive, entitled 'Limit values for particulate matter (PM10)', provided:

'	Averaging period	Limit value	Margin of tolerance	Date by which limit value is to be met
STAGE 1				
1. 24-hour limit value for the protection of human health	24 hours	50 µg/m^{3}PM10, not to be exceeded more than 35 times a calendar year	50% on the entry into force of this Directive, reducing on 1 January 2001 and every 12 months thereafter by equal annual percentages to reach 0% by 1 January 2005	1 January 2005
2. Annual limit value for the protection of human health	Calendar year	40 µg/m^{3}PM10	20% on the entry into force of this Directive, reducing on 1 January 2001 and every 12 months thereafter by equal annual percentages to reach 0% by 1 January 2005	1 January 2005
STAGE 2 (^{1})				
1. 24-hour limit value for the protection of human health	24 hours	50 µg/m^{3}PM10, not to be exceeded more than 7 times a calendar year	To be derived from data and to be equivalent to the Stage 1 limit value	1 January 2010
2. Annual limit value for the protection of human health	Calendar year	20 µg/m^{3}PM10	50% on 1 January 2005 reducing every 12 months thereafter by equal annual percentages to reach 0% by 1 January 2010	1 January 2010
(^{1}) Indicative limit values to be reviewed in the light of further information on health and environmental effects, technical feasibility and experience in the application of Stage 1 limit values in the Member States.'				

Directive 2008/50

19　Recital 2 of Directive 2008/50 states:

'In order to protect human health and the environment as a whole, it is particularly important to combat emissions of pollutants at source and to identify and implement the most effective emission reduction measures at local, national and Community level. Therefore, emissions of harmful air pollutants should be avoided, prevented or reduced and appropriate objectives set for ambient air quality taking into account relevant World Health Organisation standards, guidelines and programmes.'

20   Article 1 of Directive 2008/50, entitled 'Subject matter', provides in paragraphs 1 to 3:

> 'This Directive lays down measures aimed at the following:
>   1. defining and establishing objectives for ambient air quality designed to avoid, prevent or reduce harmful effects on human health and the environment as a whole;
>   2. assessing the ambient air quality in Member States on the basis of common methods and criteria;
>   3. obtaining information on ambient air quality in order to help combat air pollution and nuisance and to monitor long-term trends and improvements resulting from national and Community measures.'

21   Article 2 of that directive, entitled 'Definitions', provides in paragraphs 5, 7, 8, 16 to 18 and 24:

> 'For the purposes of this Directive:
>   …
>   5. "limit value" shall mean a level fixed on the basis of scientific knowledge, with the aim of avoiding, preventing or reducing harmful effects on human health and/or the environment as a whole, to be attained within a given period and not to be exceeded once attained;
>   …
>   7. "margin of tolerance" shall mean the percentage of the limit value by which that value may be exceeded subject to the conditions laid down in this Directive;
>   8. "air quality plans" shall mean plans that set out measures in order to attain the limit values or target values;
>   …
>   16. "zone" shall mean part of the territory of a Member State, as delimited by that Member State for the purposes of air quality assessment and management;
>   17. "agglomeration" shall mean a zone that is a conurbation with a population in excess of 250 000 inhabitants or, where the population is 250 000 inhabitants or less, with a given population density per km2 to be established by the Member States;
>   18. "PM10" shall mean particulate matter which passes through a size-selective inlet as defined in the reference method for the sampling and measurement of PM10, EN 12341, with a 50% efficiency cut-off at 10 μm aerodynamic diameter;
>   …
>   24. "oxides of nitrogen" shall mean the sum of the volume mixing ratio (ppbv) of nitrogen monoxide (nitric oxide) and nitrogen dioxide expressed in units of mass concentration of nitrogen dioxide ($\mu g/m^3$).'

22   Article 13 of Directive 2008/50, entitled 'Limit values and alert thresholds for the protection of human health', provides in paragraph 1:

> 'Member States shall ensure that, throughout their zones and agglomerations, levels of sulphur dioxide, PM10, lead, and carbon monoxide in ambient air do not exceed the limit values laid down in Annex XI.

In respect of nitrogen dioxide and benzene, the limit values specified in Annex XI may not be exceeded from the dates specified therein.

Compliance with these requirements shall be assessed in accordance with Annex III.

The margins of tolerance laid down in Annex XI shall apply in accordance with Article 22(3) and Article 23(1).'

23   Article 23 of that directive, entitled 'Air quality plans', states in paragraph 1:

'Where, in given zones or agglomerations, the levels of pollutants in ambient air exceed any limit value or target value, plus any relevant margin of tolerance in each case, Member States shall ensure that air quality plans are established for those zones and agglomerations in order to achieve the related limit value or target value specified in Annexes XI and XIV.

In the event of exceedances of those limit values for which the attainment deadline is already expired, the air quality plans shall set out appropriate measures, so that the exceedance period can be kept as short as possible. The air quality plans may additionally include specific measures aiming at the protection of sensitive population groups, including children.

Those air quality plans shall incorporate at least the information listed in Section A of Annex XV and may include measures pursuant to Article 24. Those plans shall be communicated to the Commission without delay, but no later than two years after the end of the year the first exceedance was observed. Where air quality plans must be prepared or implemented in respect of several pollutants, Member States shall, where appropriate, prepare and implement integrated air quality plans covering all pollutants concerned.'

24   Article 31 of that directive, entitled 'Repeal and transitional provisions', provides in paragraph 1:

'Directives 96/62/EC, 1999/30/EC, ... shall be repealed as from 11 June 2010, without prejudice to the obligations on the Member States relating to time limits for transposition or application of those Directives.

...'

25   Article 33 of Directive 2008/50, entitled 'Transposition', provides in paragraph 1:

'Member States shall bring into force the laws, regulations and administrative provisions necessary to comply with this Directive before 11 June 2010. They shall forthwith communicate to the Commission the text of those measures.

...'

26   Article 34 of that directive, entitled 'Entry into force', is worded as follows:

'This Directive shall enter into force on the day of its publication in the *Official Journal of the European Union*.'

27   In accordance with Annex XI to that directive, entitled 'Limit values for the protection of human health':

'...

B. Limit values

Averaging Period	Limit value	Margin of tolerance	Date by which limit value is to be met
...			
Nitrogen dioxide			
One hour	200 $\mu g/m^3$, not to be exceeded more than 18 times a calendar year	50% on 19 July 1999, decreasing on 1 January 2001 and every 12 months thereafter by equal annual percentages to reach 0% by 1 January 2010	1 January 2010
Calendar year	40 $\mu g/m^3$	50% on 19 July 1999, decreasing on 1 January 2001 and every 12 months thereafter by equal annual percentages to reach 0% by 1 January 2010	1 January 2010
...			
PM10			
One day	50 $\mu g/m^3$, not to be exceeded more than 35 times a calendar year	50%	— (1)
Calendar year	40 $\mu g/m^3$	20%	— (1)
(^{1}) Already in force since 1 January 2005 ...'			

The dispute in the main proceedings and the questions referred for a preliminary ruling

28   JP applied to the tribunal administratif de Cergy-Pontoise (Administrative Court, Cergy-Pontoise, France) seeking, inter alia, first, annulment of the implied decision of the Prefect of Val-d'Oise (France), which is part of the agglomeration of Paris (France), refusing to take the necessary measures to address his health problems linked to air pollution in that agglomeration, problems which began in 2003, and, second, compensation from the French Republic for the various heads of damage which he claims to have suffered on account of that pollution, assessed at EUR 21 million.

29   JP seeks compensation, in particular, for damage arising from the deterioration of his state of health, which he argues was caused by the deterioration of the ambient air quality in the Paris agglomeration, where he lives. He considers that the deterioration of the ambient air quality was the result of a breach by the French authorities of their obligations under Directive 2008/50.

30   By judgment of 12 December 2017, the tribunal administratif de Cergy-Pontoise (Administrative Court, Cergy-Pontoise) rejected JP's claims in their entirety on the ground, in essence, that Articles 13 and 23 of Directive 2008/50 do not confer any right on individuals to obtain compensation for any damage suffered as a result of the deterioration of air quality.

31   By application of 25 April 2018, JP brought an appeal against that judgment before the cour administrative d'appel de Versailles (Administrative Court of Appeal, Versailles, France).

32   The Minister for Ecological Transition contends that the appeal should be dismissed.

33   In those circumstances, the cour administrative d'appel de Versailles (Administrative Court of Appeal, Versailles) decided to stay the proceedings and to refer the following questions to the Court of Justice for a preliminary ruling:

> '(1) Must the applicable rules of EU law resulting from the provisions of Article 13(1) … and of Article 23(1) … of Directive [2008/50] be interpreted as entitling individuals, in the event of a sufficiently serious breach by an EU Member State of the obligations resulting from those rules, to claim compensation from the Member State concerned for damage to their health in cases where there is a direct and certain causal link with the deterioration in air quality?
>
> (2) On the assumption that the provisions referred to above may indeed give rise to such an entitlement to compensation for damage to health, to what conditions is that entitlement subject, in particular with regard to the date on which the existence of the failure attributable to the Member State concerned must be assessed?'

Consideration of the questions referred

The first question

34   According to settled case-law, in the procedure laid down by Article 267 TFEU providing for cooperation between national courts and the Court of Justice, it is for the latter to provide the national court with an answer which will be of use to it and enable it to decide the case before it. To that end, the Court should, where necessary, reformulate the questions referred to it. The Court may also find it necessary to consider provisions of EU law which the national court has not referred to in its questions (judgment of 15 July 2021, *Ministrstvo za obrambo* (C-742/19) EU:C:2021:597, paragraph 31). The fact that a national court has, formally speaking, worded a question referred for a preliminary ruling with reference to certain provisions of EU law does not prevent the Court from providing the national court with all the points of interpretation which may be of assistance in adjudicating on the case pending before it, whether or not that court has referred to them in its questions. In that regard, it is for the Court to extract from all the information provided by the national court, in particular from the grounds of the decision referring the questions, the points of EU law which require interpretation, having regard to the subject matter of the dispute (judgment of 22 June 2022, *Volvo and DAF Trucks* (C-267/20) EU:C:2022:494, paragraph 28).

35   In the present case, it follows from the reply provided by the national court to the Court's request for information that the applicant in the main proceedings seeks compensation for damage allegedly caused to him by exceedances of the NO2 and PM10 concentration limit values set in Annex XI to Directive 2008/50, which have adversely affected his state of health since 2003.

36   It should be noted that, under Article 33(1) and Article 34 of Directive 2008/50, that directive entered into force on the day of its publication in the *Official Journal of the European Union*, namely 11 June 2008, and required Member States to bring into force the laws, regulations and administrative provisions necessary to comply with that directive before 11 June 2010. Furthermore, it follows from Annex XI to that directive that the dates by which the limit values had to be met were 1 January 2005 for PM10 and 1 January 2010 for NO2.

37   In accordance with Article 31(1) of Directive 2008/50, that directive replaced Directives 96/62 and 1999/30, among others, with effect from 11 June 2010.

38   Directive 96/62 entered into force on 21 November 1996. That directive laid down, in Article 7 and, in accordance with Article 13(1) thereof, read in conjunction with Article 12(1) of Directive 1999/30, with effect from 19 July 2001, requirements similar to those flowing from Article 13(1) and Article 23(1) of Directive 2008/50. However, Directive 96/62 did not set limit values for the concentration of pollutants in ambient air. Under Article 4(5) of that directive, those limit values were set by Directive 1999/30. The dates by which the limit values laid down in Annexes II and III to Directive 1999/30 had to be met, in accordance with Article 4(1) and Article 5(1) thereof, were 1 January 2005 for PM10 and 1 January 2010 for NO2.

39   Before those dates, as is clear from Article 9(1) and (3) of Directive 1999/30, the applicable limit values were, subject to the requirements flowing from Article 8(3) and (4) of Directive 96/62, those specified in Annex I, Table B, to Directive 80/779 for PM10 and in Annex I to Directive 85/203 for NO2, annexes to which Article 3 of the latter two directives referred.

40   Furthermore, since, according to the information provided by the national court, the applicant in the main proceedings seeks compensation for damage allegedly caused by exceedances of the NO2 and PM10 concentration limit values, damage 'which began in 2003', it cannot be ruled out that Article 7 of Directives 80/779 and 85/203, which were repealed, as is also apparent from Article 9(1) and (3) of Directive 1999/30, with effect from 19 July 2001, may also be relevant for the resolution of the dispute in the main proceedings.

41   In view of the period to which the national court thus referred in the information supplied, it is therefore necessary to take into account not only the relevant provisions of Directive 2008/50, but also those of Directives 96/62, 1999/30, 80/779 and 85/203.

42   Consequently, in the light of the case-law mentioned in paragraph 34 above, it must be considered that, by its first question, the national court seeks to ascertain whether Article 13(1) and Article 23(1) of Directive 2008/50, Articles 7 and 8 of Directive 96/62, Article 4(1) and Article 5(1) of Directive 1999/30 and Articles 3 and 7 of Directives 80/779 and 85/203 must be interpreted as meaning that they are intended to confer rights on individuals capable of entitling them to compensation from a Member State under the principle of State liability for loss and damage caused to individuals as a result of breaches of EU law attributable to that Member State.

43   In that regard, it is clear from the Court's settled case-law that the principle of State liability for loss and damage caused to individuals as a result of breaches of EU law for which the State can be held responsible is inherent in the system of the treaties on which the European Union is based (judgment of 18 January 2022, *Thelen Technopark Berlin* (C-261/20) EU:C:2022:33, paragraph 42 and the case-law cited). That principle applies to any case in which a Member State infringes EU

law, whichever public authority is responsible for the breach (judgment of 19 December 2019, *Deutsche Umwelthilfe* (C-752/18) EU:C:2019:1114, paragraph 55 and the case-law cited).

44   As regards the conditions for establishing such liability, the Court has repeatedly held that individuals who have been harmed have a right to compensation where three conditions are met: the rule of EU law infringed must be intended to confer rights on them; the infringement of that rule must be sufficiently serious; and there must be a direct causal link between that infringement and the loss or damage sustained by those individuals (judgment of 28 June 2022, *Commission v Spain (Breach of EU law by the legislature)* (C-278/20) EU:C:2022:503, paragraph 31 and the case-law cited).

45   It follows that only a breach of a rule of EU law which is intended to confer rights on individuals is, in accordance with the first of the three conditions mentioned above, capable of giving rise to State liability.

46   According to well-established case-law those rights arise not only where they are expressly granted by provisions of EU law, but also by reason of positive or negative obligations which those provisions impose in a clearly defined manner, whether on individuals, on the Member States or on the EU institutions (see, to that effect, judgments of 5 February 1963, *van Gend & Loos* (26/62) EU:C:1963:1, p. 12; of 19 November 1991, *Francovich* (C-6/90) and (C-9/90) EU:C:1991:428, paragraph 31; of 20 September 2001, *Courage and Crehan* (C-453/99) EU:C:2001:465, paragraph 19; and of 11 November 2021, *Stichting Cartel Compensation and Equilib Netherlands* (C-819/19) EU:C:2021:904, paragraph 47).

47   The breach of such positive or negative obligations by a Member State is liable to hinder the exercise by the individuals concerned of the rights implicitly conferred on them under the provisions of EU law in question, rights they are deemed to be able to invoke at national level, and thus to alter the legal situation which those provisions seek to establish for those individuals (see, to that effect, judgments of 4 October 2018, *Kantarev* (C-571/16) EU:C:2018:807, paragraphs 103 and 104, and of 10 December 2020, *Euromin Holdings (Cyprus)* (C-735/19) EU:C:2020:1014, paragraph 90). That is the reason why the full effectiveness of those rules of EU law and the protection of the rights which they are intended to confer require that individuals have the possibility of obtaining redress (see, to that effect, judgment of 19 November 1991, *Francovich* (C-6/90) and (C-9/90) EU:C:1991:428, paragraphs 33 and 34) irrespective of whether the provisions in question have direct effect, since direct effect is neither necessary (see, to that effect, judgment of 5 March 1996, *Brasserie du pêcheur and Factortame* (C-46/93) and (C-48/93) EU:C:1996:79, paragraphs 18 to 22) nor sufficient in itself (see, to that effect, judgment of 11 June 2015, *Berlington Hungary* (C-98/14) EU:C:2015:386, paragraphs 108 and 109) for the first of the three conditions referred to in paragraph 44 above to be satisfied.

48   In the present case, Directives 2008/50, 96/62, 1999/30, 80/779 and 85/203 impose on Member States, in essence, first, an obligation to ensure that the levels of, inter alia, PM10 and NO2 do not exceed, in their respective territories and with effect from certain dates, the limit values set by those directives and, second, where those limit values are nonetheless exceeded, an obligation to provide for appropriate measures to remedy those exceedances, inter alia by means of air quality plans.

49   As regards the first obligation, it should be noted that the limit values state the exact concentration, expressed in μg/m³ and taking into account, where relevant, the margins of tolerance of the pollutant concerned in ambient air, which Member States must avoid exceeding throughout their zones and agglomerations.

50   As regards the second obligation, the Court has held, in the case of Directive 2008/50, that it follows from Article 23(1) of that directive that, while Member States have a degree of discretion in deciding which measures to adopt, those measures must, in any event, ensure that the period during which the limit values for the pollutant concerned are exceeded is kept as short as possible (judgment of 10 November 2020, *Commission v Italy (Limit values—PM10)* (C-644/18) EU:C:2020:895, paragraph 136).

51   Furthermore, it is true that the Court has found that Article 7(3) of Directive 96/62, which lays down a similar obligation to that contained in Article 23(1) of Directive 2008/50, does not impose an obligation on Member States to take measures to ensure that those limit values are never exceeded, but only to take measures capable of reducing to a minimum the risk of the limit values being exceeded and the duration of such an occurrence, taking into account all the material circumstances and opposing interests. However, the Court has also pointed out that that provision included limits on the exercise of that discretion, which may be relied upon before the national courts, relating to the adequacy of the measures which must be included in the action plan with the aim of reducing the risk of the limit values being exceeded and the duration of such an occurrence, taking into account the balance which must be maintained between that objective and the various opposing public and private interests (see, to that effect, judgment of 25 July 2008, *Janecek* (C-237/07) EU:C:2008:447, paragraphs 44 to 46).

52   The same interpretation must be given, in essence, with respect to the obligations arising under Article 8(3) and (4) of Directive 96/62.

53   As for Article 7 of Directives 80/779 and 85/203, it should be noted that, in the event of exceedance of the limit values, that article required Member States to take measures to 'avoid their recurrence' and 'to deal with them', respectively.

54   It is true that it follows that Article 13(1) and Article 23(1) of Directive 2008/50, like the analogous provisions of Directives 96/62, 1999/30, 80/779 and 85/203, lay down fairly clear and precise obligations as to the result to be achieved by Member States.

55   However, those obligations pursue, as is apparent from Article 1 of the directives mentioned in the previous paragraph, as well as, in particular, recital 2 of Directive 2008/50, a general objective of protecting human health and the environment as a whole.

56   Thus, besides the fact that the provisions concerned of Directive 2008/50 and the directives which preceded it do not contain any express conferral of rights on individuals in that respect, it cannot be inferred from the obligations laid down in those provisions, with the general objective referred to above, that individuals or categories of individuals are, in the present case, implicitly granted, by reason of those obligations, rights the breach of which would be capable of giving rise to a Member State's liability for loss and damage caused to individuals.

57   It follows from all the foregoing that the first of the three conditions referred to in paragraph 44 above, which are cumulative, is not satisfied.

58   That being so, the fact that, where a Member State has not ensured compliance with the limit values set out in Article 13(1) of Directive 2008/50 and the analogous

provisions of the earlier directives, the individuals concerned must be able to require the national authorities, if necessary by bringing an action before the courts having jurisdiction, to adopt the measures required under those directives (see, to that effect, judgments of 19 November 2014, *ClientEarth* (C-404/13) EU:C:2014:2382, paragraph 56 and the case-law cited, and of 19 December 2019, *Deutsche Umwelthilfe* (C-752/18) EU:C:2019:1114 paragraph 56) is not capable of altering that finding.

59   In that regard, it should be borne in mind that, as regards Article 7(3) of Directive 96/62, the Court has found that the natural or legal persons directly concerned by a risk that the limit values or alert thresholds may be exceeded must be in a position to require the competent authorities to draw up an action plan where such a risk exists, if necessary by bringing an action before the courts having jurisdiction (judgment of 25 July 2008, *Janecek* (C-237/07) EU:C:2008:447, paragraph 39).

60   Similarly, as regards the second subparagraph of Article 23(1) of Directive 2008/50, the Court has held that the natural or legal persons directly concerned by the limit values being exceeded after 1 January 2010 must be in a position to require the competent authorities, if necessary by bringing an action before the courts having jurisdiction, to draw up an air quality plan which complies with that provision, where a Member State has failed to secure compliance with the requirements of the second subparagraph of Article 13(1) of that directive and has not applied for a postponement of the deadline as provided for by Article 22 thereof (judgment of 19 November 2014, *ClientEarth* (C-404/13) EU:C:2014:2382, paragraph 56).

61   In accordance with the matters set out in paragraphs 52 and 53 above, that interpretation applies equally as regards the effective implementation of Article 7 of Directives 80/779 and 85/203 and Article 8(3) and (4) of Directive 96/62.

62   However, the right thus recognised by the Court in its case-law, stemming in particular from the principle of effectiveness of EU law, effectiveness to which affected individuals are entitled to contribute by bringing administrative or judicial proceedings based on their own particular situation, does not mean that the obligations resulting from Article 13(1) and Article 23(1) of Directive 2008/50 and the analogous provisions of the earlier directives were intended to confer individual rights on interested persons, for the purpose of the first of the three conditions referred to in paragraph 44 above, and that the breach of those obligations is, in consequence, capable of altering a legal situation which those provisions sought to establish for those persons.

63   It should be added that the conclusion set out in paragraph 57 above does not mean that a Member State cannot incur liability under less strict conditions on the basis of national law (judgment of 28 June 2022, *Commission v Spain (Breach of EU law by the legislature)* (C-278/20) EU:C:2022:503, paragraph 32 and the case-law cited), nor does it prevent, where appropriate, a failure to fulfil the obligations resulting from Article 13(1) and Article 23(1) of Directive 2008/50 or the other provisions of EU law referred to in paragraph 42 above from being taken into account in that regard as a factor which may be relevant for the purposes of establishing the liability of public authorities on a basis other than EU law.

64   That conclusion also does not preclude the courts of the Member State concerned from issuing injunctions together with periodic penalties to ensure that that State complies with the obligations arising under Article 13(1) and Article 23(1) of Directive 2008/50 and the analogous provisions of the earlier directives, such as

the injunctions coupled with periodic penalties issued in several recent judgments of the Conseil d'État (Council of State, France).

65   For all the foregoing reasons, the answer to the first question submitted for a preliminary ruling is that Articles 3 and 7 of Directive 80/779, Articles 3 and 7 of Directive 85/203, Articles 7 and 8 of Directive 96/62, Article 4(1) and Article 5(1) of Directive 1999/30 and Article 13(1) and Article 23(1) of Directive 2008/50 must be interpreted as meaning that they are not intended to confer rights on individuals capable of entitling them to compensation from a Member State under the principle of State liability for loss and damage caused to individuals as a result of breaches of EU law attributable to that Member State.

The second question

66   In view of the answer to the first question, there is no need to answer the second question.

Costs

67   Since these proceedings are, for the parties to the main proceedings, a step in the action pending before the national court, the decision on costs is a matter for that court. Costs incurred in submitting observations to the Court, other than the costs of those parties, are not recoverable.

On those grounds, the Court (Grand Chamber) hereby rules:

> Articles 3 and 7 of Council Directive 80/779/EEC of 15 July 1980 on air quality limit values and guide values for sulphur dioxide and suspended particulates, Articles 3 and 7 of Council Directive 85/203/EEC of 7 March 1985 on air quality standards for nitrogen dioxide, Articles 7 and 8 of Council Directive 96/62/EC of 27 September 1996 on ambient air quality assessment and management, Article 4(1) and Article 5(1) of Council Directive 1999/30/EC of 22 April 1999 relating to limit values for sulphur dioxide, nitrogen dioxide and oxides of nitrogen, particulate matter and lead in ambient air, and Article 13(1) and Article 23(1) of Directive 2008/50/EC of the European Parliament and of the Council of 21 May 2008 on ambient air quality and cleaner air for Europe, must be interpreted as meaning that they are not intended to confer rights on individuals capable of entitling them to compensation from a Member State under the principle of State liability for loss and damage caused to individuals as a result of breaches of EU law attributable to that Member State.

BRIAN LEIGHTON (GARAGES) LTD v ALLIANZ INSURANCE PLC

COURT OF APPEAL (CIVIL DIVISION)

Males, Popplewell and Nugee LJJ: 11 January 2023

[2023] EWCA Civ 8; [2023] Env. L.R. 23

☞ Causation; Contamination; Damage to property; Exclusion clauses; Insurance policies; Interpretation; Pollution

H1 *Insurance—exclusion from policy cover—'proximate cause'—fuel leak at petrol station resulting in contamination of forecourt and building and business interruption through shutdown for health and safety—leak caused by pressure of an object on pipe—whether High Court incorrect to find that damage "caused by pollution or contamination" so as to be excluded from cover—whether judge erred in treating pollution or contamination as cause of damage—whether cause the sharp object movement rupturing pipe*

H2   The appellant (B) was the operator of a garage business trading and repairing vehicles and operating a 24 hour filling station. The respondent (A) was its insurer under a Motor Trade Policy covering various risks under 15 sections. B brought a claim for material damage and business interruption arising out of a fuel leak which resulted in the garage being shut down for health and safety reasons which A declined. The leak occurred from a section of pipe connecting one of the underground fuel tanks to six of the forecourt fuel pumps. It was caused by the pressure of an object such as a sharp stone on the pipe, under pressure and movement from the weight of the concrete slab under the forecourt. Within a matter of days the leak contaminated the forecourt and building. The contamination was such that parts of the premises were at immediate risk of catching fire or exploding, and the business had to be closed. The Policy provided:

"Exclusions to Section 1
The General Exclusions of this Policy apply to this Section and in addition it does not cover:

…

9. Pollution or Contamination
Damage caused by pollution or contamination, but We will pay for Damage to the Property Insured not otherwise excluded, caused by:
    a pollution or contamination which itself results from a Specified Event
    b any Specified Event which itself results from pollution or contamination."

H3   It was common ground that no Specified Event occurred.

H4   In determining various issues in a summary judgment application, the High Court found that damage to the forecourt and building was damage "caused by pollution or contamination" so as to be excluded from cover under Exclusion 9. On appeal, B argued that although the damage for which the claim was made, the effect of the fuel on the forecourt and building, could properly be characterised as pollution or contamination, the judge had erred in treating pollution or contamination as the cause of the damage, which was the inquiry required by the words "caused by" in Exclusion 9. Instead, the cause was the sharp object movement which ruptured the pipe.

H5   **Held,** in allowing the appeal:

H6   (1) Three matters should be emphasised: (i) the relevant commercial context was that of a policy for a small or medium-sized enterprise whose business included the obvious risk of leakage of fuel from pipes, tanks and apparatus against which the operator would naturally desire cover; (ii) there was no room for any presumption that Exclusion 9 was to be narrowly construed or construed against the insurer; and (iii) it was a general principle of insurance law that the insurer was liable, and only liable, for losses proximately caused by a peril covered by the policy. On that third matter, the proximate cause of the loss was not the last cause of the loss, but that which was proximate in efficiency, being the dominant, effective or efficient cause. Where there were concurrent proximate causes, one an insured peril and the other excluded, the exclusion prevailed. That was subject to an important qualification in that this presumed intention of the contracting parties was capable of being displaced if, on its proper interpretation, the policy provided for some other connection between loss and the occurrence of an insured or excepted peril.

H7   (2) In the present case, the chain of causation leading to the damage included the process of pollution or contamination but that was not its proximate cause. The proximate cause of the damage was the puncturing of the pipe by the stone or sharp object. It was critical to the outcome, therefore, whether the exclusion was concerned with pollution or contamination as a proximate cause or merely as an intermediate process in the chain of causation. Exclusion 9 consisted of exclusionary wording, followed by a write-back of cover in the rest of the Exclusion in the sense of providing for cover in circumstances where it would otherwise be excluded by the exclusionary wording. That followed from the word "but"; and from the fact that the structure of cover was for all risks not excluded, so that where it was intended that there should be cover there was no need for any wording granting such cover unless it addressed circumstances which would otherwise be excluded. If the exclusionary wording were taken on its own, it would be tolerably clear that it was concerned with pollution and contamination as a proximate cause. That followed from the presumption arising from the general law of insurance that clauses concerned with defining the scope of insured or excepted perils were concerned with damage proximately caused by those perils. It was reinforced in the present case by the use of the simple expression "caused by" which had historically and uniformly been interpreted in this context as importing the concept of proximate cause. It was further reinforced by the contrast with two other policy terms where wider language was used in connection with pollution and contamination. For these reasons, the presumption that the exclusionary wording was concerned only with proximate causes was a strong one. It was reasonable to attribute this presumed intention to these parties. The write-back wording did not displace that presumption because it was capable of being given meaning consistently with it. Whilst A's construction of Exclusion 9 was one which the parties might perfectly sensibly have chosen as their bargain, it faced the insuperable difficulty that it did not give effect to the language used, which gave rise to the presumption that they intended the exclusion to apply to pollution or contamination as a proximate cause, a presumption which was not displaced by the wording of the write-back or any other wording in the policy.

H8   (3) Males LJ (dissenting): The opening words of Exclusion 9 were not limited to damage proximately caused by pollution or contamination. As a matter of ordinary language, it made perfect sense to say that the damage was "caused by pollution or contamination". Although the pollution and contamination was not the proximate cause of the damage as that term would be used by an insurance lawyer or broker, it was the pollution and contamination which resulted from the penetration of the fuel pipe which caused the damage to the property and meant that the business had to be shut down. For those reasons, the terms of Exclusion 9 did sufficiently demonstrate an intention to displace the general rule that causation language must be taken to refer to the proximate cause of damage, and that the damage in the present case was caused by pollution or contamination within the meaning of the Exclusion.

H9   **Cases referred to:**

Burts & Harvey Ltd v Vulcan Boiler and General Insurance Co Ltd (No. 1) [1966] 1 Lloyd's Rep. 161; 116 N.L.J. 639 QBD

Coxe v Employers Liability Association Corp Ltd [1916] 2 K.B. 629 KBD

Financial Conduct Authority v Arch Insurance (UK) Ltd [2021] UKSC 1; [2021] A.C. 649; [2021] 2 W.L.R. 123

Impact Funding Solutions Ltd v Barrington Support Services Ltd (formerly Lawyers At Work Ltd) [2016] UKSC 57; [2017] A.C. 73; [2016] 3 W.L.R. 1422

Leeds Beckett University (formerly Leeds Metropolitan University) v Travelers Insurance Co Ltd [2017] EWHC 558 (TCC); [2017] Bus. L.R. 2022

Legg v Sterte Garage Ltd [2016] EWCA Civ 97; [2016] 2 Costs L.O. 167; [2016] Env. L.R. D2

Leyland Shipping Co Ltd v Norwich Union Fire Insurance Society Ltd [1918] A.C. 350 HL

Lloyds TSB General Insurance Holdings Ltd v Lloyds Bank Group Insurance Co Ltd [2001] EWCA Civ 1643; [2002] C.L.C. 287; [2001] Pens. L.R. 325

Lloyds TSB General Insurance Holdings Ltd v Lloyds Bank Group Insurance Co Ltd [2003] UKHL 48; [2004] 1 C.L.C. 116; [2003] Pens. L.R. 315

Manchikalapati v Zurich Insurance Plc (t/a Zurich Building Guarantee and Zurich Municipal) [2019] EWCA Civ 2163; [2020] B.L.R. 1; 187 Con. L.R. 62

Navigators Insurance Co Ltd v Atlasnavios-Navegacao Lda (formerly Bnavios-Navegacao Lda) [2018] UKSC 26; [2019] A.C. 136; [2018] 2 W.L.R. 1671

Wayne Tank & Pump Co Ltd v Employers Liability Assurance Corp Ltd [1974] Q.B. 57; [1973] 3 W.L.R. 483; [1973] 2 Lloyd's Rep. 237 CA (Civ Div)

Yorkshire Dale Steamship Co Ltd v Minister of War Transport [1942] A.C. 691; (1942) 73 Ll. L. Rep. 1; 1942 A.M.C. 1000 HL

H10 **Legislation referred to:**
Marine Insurance Act 1906 s.55
Senior Courts Act 1981 s.51

H11   *N. Davidson KC* (instructed by Adie Pepperdine Ltd) appeared on behalf of the
appellant.
J. Evans-Tovey (instructed by Clyde & Co Claims LLP) appeared on behalf of the
respondent.

JUDGMENT

LORD JUSTICE POPPLEWELL:

Introduction

1   This is an appeal by Brian Leighton (Garages) Ltd ('BLG') against a decision
of Ms Clare Ambrose, sitting as a deputy judge of the High Court ('the Judge').
Until June 2014 BLG ran a garage business in Goole, East Yorkshire, trading and
repairing vehicles and operating a 24 hour petrol filling station. The Respondent
('Allianz') was its insurer under a Motor Trade Policy ('the Policy') covering
various risks under 15 sections. BLG has brought a claim under Section 1 (material
damage) and Section 8 (business interruption) arising out of a fuel leak in early
June 2014, which resulted in the garage being shut down for health and safety
reasons. Allianz has declined liability.

2   The Judge was determining various issues in a summary judgment application
brought by Allianz. The decision under appeal was that damage to the forecourt
and shop building was damage "caused by pollution or contamination" so as to be
excluded from cover under Exclusion 9 of the Policy.

The facts

3   Because the issue arose in a summary judgment application by Allianz, and by
reason of the procedural history, the issue of the construction and application of
Exclusion 9 fell to be decided on the basis of facts which were disputed by Allianz
but were to be assumed to be true for the purposes of the application. Those assumed
facts are as follows.

4   A leak occurred from a section of pipe connecting one of the underground fuel
tanks to six of the forecourt fuel pumps. It was caused by the pressure of an object
such as a sharp stone on the pipe, under pressure and movement from the weight
of the concrete slab under the forecourt. The fuel leak started shortly before 4 June
2014 and within a matter of days contaminated the forecourt, yard, paved area and
forecourt pad and ducting ('the forecourt') and the lower parts of the floors, walls
and skirtings of the adjacent shop building ('the building'). The contamination
reached the electrical conduits connecting the pumps to the building. The
contamination was such that by 9 June 2014 those parts of the premises were at
immediate risk of catching fire or exploding, and the business had to be closed.
Allianz did not agree to indemnify BLG and it could not afford to effect the
necessary repairs itself, with the result that the business never reopened and was
ultimately sold.

The Policy

5   The Policy was a renewal for 12 months at 31 December 2013 of cover which Allianz had provided to BLG for a number of years on its "Headlight Motor Trade Policy Wording". Section 1 covers Material Damage, Damage being defined as "accidental loss, destruction or damage to Property Insured". It is common ground that the forecourt and building were Property Insured.

6   Section 1 is structured in five parts. The first part sets out definitions which are to apply to the Section, in addition to "Policy definitions" set out immediately before the Section which are applicable to all sections of the Policy. The second part comprises unnumbered sections addressing "Cover". The third part comprises 26 numbered "Extensions". The fourth part contains 15 numbered "Exclusions". The fifth part contains 5 "Conditions".

7   The first clause in the second part under the heading Cover provides:

> **"Indemnity**
> We will pay You for damage to Property Insured at The Premises shown in the Schedule by any cause not excluded occurring during the Period of Insurance…"

8   In the third part, Extension 26 provides:

> **"Trace and Access**
> In the event of Damage in consequence of escape of water or fuel oil from any tank, apparatus or pipe, or leakage of fuel from any fixed oil heating installation, We will pay costs necessarily and reasonably incurred by You in locating the source of such Damage, and in the subsequent making good of Damage caused as a consequence of locating such source, up to an amount of £10,000 any one claim."

9   In the fourth part, Exclusion 9 provides:

> **"Exclusions to Section 1**
> The General Exclusions of this Policy apply to this Section and in addition it does not cover:
> ……
> **9. Pollution or Contamination**
> Damage caused by pollution or contamination, but We will pay for Damage to the Property Insured not otherwise excluded, caused by:
>   a pollution or contamination which itself results from a Specified Event
>   b any Specified Event which itself results from pollution or contamination."

10   Specified Events are defined in definition 9 in the first part of the section as follows:

> **"9. Specified Events**
> Fire, lightning, explosion, aircraft or other aerial devices or articles dropped from them, riot, civil commotion, strikers, locked-out workers, persons taking part in labour disturbances, malicious persons other than thieves, earthquake, storm, flood, escape of water from any tank apparatus or pipe or impact by any road vehicle or animal."

11   It is common ground that no Specified Event occurred in this case.

12   The indemnity clause in Section 8 covers gross profit lost for business interruption which is a consequence of damage insured under Sections 1, 2 and 3.

The Judgment

13   BLG argued before the Judge that the point was not suitable for summary determination and/or that the way in which it had been raised and argued by Allianz was procedurally unfair. It further argued that the effect of the leak may have been pollution or contamination, but that was merely to define the damage; the cause of the damage was the sharp object which punctured the pipe; and further that Exclusion 9 only applied to environmental pollution of groundwater and subsoils. Allianz argued that the damage was clearly caused by pollution and contamination by the fuel, and relied on *Legg v Sterte Garage* [2016] EWCA Civ 97; [2016] Lloyd's Rep. I.R. 390.

14   The Judge recorded at paras [24] and [47] that the material damage for which BLG was claiming an indemnity (in the respect relevant to the issue under appeal) was the immediate contamination of the forecourt and building, making them susceptible to the immediate risk of fire and explosion. She recorded BLG's expert evidence as to the cause of the rupture of the pipe, and Allianz's willingness for its summary judgment application to proceed on the basis that the cause was accepted notwithstanding that the evidence was disputed. She rejected BLG's overarching submission that none of the issues which arose were suitable for summary determination.

15   When addressing the issue whether the cause of the damage (other than the damage to the leaking pipeline itself) was within Exclusion 9, she first concluded that the point was appropriate for summary determination, being a short point of construction on assumed facts which did not require any further factual investigation or expert evidence, and that there was no unfair prejudice to BLG in the way it had been raised or argued.

16   Paragraphs 57 to 63 contain her essential reasoning for concluding that the damage was within the exclusion, and can be summarised as follows.

17   Allianz's argument that the damage was caused by pollution and contamination better reflected the ordinary meaning of the clause and its likely scope within a policy covering a garage, since it was unlikely that any exclusion only applied to subsoils and groundwater rather than the property insured. Allianz's construction was also more consistent with the express terms of the carve out in Exclusion 9 and the Track and Trace Extension 26. The wording of Exclusion 9, by reference to the Specified Events, acknowledged that the damage caused by pollution or contamination would be caused by something else including, for example, fire, floods or leak of water from a pipe, but on its express terms the policy would not cover escape of fuel from a pipe. There was no support in the wording or context of the Policy for BLG's argument that the exclusion applied only to environmental contamination of subsoils and groundwaters, which was unworkable since BLG was unable to identify what "the environment" would mean. Although pollution is often associated with harmful substances being released into the natural environment, contamination is more commonly used outside that context and on its ordinary meaning would certainly cover leakage of harmful substances being absorbed within the fabric of a shop or forecourt. On its ordinary meaning pollution

would cover leakage of oil from a pipe into something else, whether a beach, river, garage forecourt or shop, and that would extend to the mechanism by which the leak took place (including a pipe failing and leaking oil) rather than solely the condition of being polluted or saturated.

18   BLG's arguments were also inconsistent with the decision in *Legg v Sterte Garage*, in particular paragraph 28 of the judgment of David Richards LJ, which was consistent with Allianz's argument.

The skeleton arguments on appeal

19   Mr Davidson KC, who did not appear below, started from the proposition that the damage for which the claim was made, namely the effect of the fuel on the forecourt and shop, could properly be characterised as pollution or contamination, which were nouns aptly used to describe such damage. However, the fundamental error of the Judge was in treating pollution or contamination as the cause of the damage, which was the inquiry required by the words "caused by" in Exclusion 9. The cause was the sharp object movement which ruptured the pipe. He relied on *Leeds Beckett University v Travelers Insurance Company Ltd* [2017] EWHC 558 (TCC); [2017] Lloyd's Rep. I.R. 417 as illustrating the distinction between contamination being present and contamination being the cause of the damage. Mr Davidson also sought to rely on the wording of a subsequent trade policy issued by Allianz as drawing a clear distinction between damage "consisting of..." and damage "caused by...". He further relied upon the decision of Lawton J in *Burts and Harvey Ltd v Vulcan Boiler and General Insurance Co Ltd* [1996] 1 Lloyd's Rep. 161, approved and applied by this court in *Manchikalapati v Zurich Insurance Plc* [2019] EWCA Civ 2163; [2020] Lloyd's Rep. I.R.. at [180]-[182], and a decision of the Superior Court of Pennsylvania in *Raybestos-Manhattan Inc v Industrial Risk Insurers* (1981) 289 Pa. Super. 479, 433 A.2d 906, as illustrative, in analogous factual circumstances, of the proximate cause of damage being identified as the occurrence which caused the leak to occur. Moreover, if there were any ambiguity in the meaning of Exclusion 9, it should be resolved against Allianz by application of the *contra proferentem* principle and/or the approach articulated by Lords Hamblen and Leggatt JJSC at [77] of *Financial Conduct Authority v Arch Insurance (UK) Ltd* [2021] UKSC 1; [2021] A.C. 649 that:

> "In the case of an insurance policy of the present kind, sold principally to SMEs, the person to whom the document should be taken to be addressed is not a pedantic lawyer who will subject the entire policy wording to a minute textual analysis (cf *Jumbo King Ltd v Faithful Properties Ltd* (1999) 2 HKCFAR 279, para 59). It is an ordinary policyholder who, on entering into the contract, is taken to have read through the policy conscientiously in order to understand what cover they were getting."

20   On behalf of Allianz, Mr Evans-Tovey submitted that the Judge had not conflated damage with the cause of damage. The damage comprised the shop and forecourt being "polluted" or "contaminated" by fuel, but the words "pollution" and "contamination" are apt to describe the process by which such damage is caused. The Judge correctly identified that the process by which the damage to the shop and forecourt occurred in this case was by contamination and pollution, which was what caused it. The argument for BLG therefore presents a false dichotomy between

what the damage consists of and what causes it. That the words pollution or contamination in Exclusion 9 refer to a process is supported by (1) the Shorter Oxford English Dictionary ('OED') definition of their meanings; (2) the clause referring to damage being "caused by" those words; and (3) the part of Exclusion 9 which writes back cover in respect of Specified Events, which also makes clear that contamination or pollution is excluded (if not written back) if it forms any part of the chain of causation giving rise to the damage, whether immediate, intermediate or remote.

21   All this is clear from the wording of the Policy and its context. In any event, there is no room for the *contra proferentem* principle because Exclusion 9 is to be read with the Indemnity clause as simply defining the scope of cover. Reliance by BLG on the subsequent Allianz policy wording is impermissible, and anyway irrelevant. *Legg v Sterte Garage* supports this approach, and none of the other authorities upon which BLG relies cast doubt on it.

The oral argument on appeal

22   The argument became more focused in the course of the hearing. It became common ground that the loss was (on the assumed facts) caused by a process of contamination or pollution as part of the causative chain, but that the proximate cause of the loss was the sharp object rupturing the pipe, which was not itself pollution or contamination. Mr Davidson submitted that the exclusion applied only where pollution or contamination was the proximate cause of the damage. Since it was not, the Exclusion had no effect on the claim for the damage to the forecourt and shop. Mr Evans-Tovey submitted that the expression "caused by" connotes something looser than proximate cause, and applies if the words it governs are part of the chain of causation whether more immediate or more remote than the proximate cause. On this interpretation the effect of the exclusionary wording is to exclude cover for damage where the contamination or pollution forms any part of the process in the chain of causation, and the write-back in clauses a. and b. confers cover where a Specified Event plays any part in the chain of causation whether more remotely or more immediately than the pollution or contamination. Although the exclusionary wording would exclude all cases involving leakage of fuel, there was nevertheless substantial cover written back by reason of clauses a. and b., such that the effect of the Exclusion as a whole was akin to providing cover, in the event of fuel leaks, for the Specified Events as the defined perils. In the current case there was a process of contamination and pollution which engaged the exclusion, and no occurrence of a Specified Event to write back cover.

Discussion

23   The principles applicable to the construction of contractual documents have been the subject of an abundance of recent high authority, and are too well known to need extensive exposition here. In *FCA v Arch* Lords Hamblen and Leggatt JJSC said at [47]:

> "The core principle is that an insurance policy, like any other contract, must be interpreted objectively by asking what a reasonable person, with all the

background knowledge which would reasonably have been available to the parties when they entered into the contract, would have understood the language of the contract to mean."

24   I would, however, emphasise three matters which are of particular relevance to the present dispute.

25   First, the relevant commercial context is that this was a policy for a small or medium sized enterprise whose business included a petrol filling station. The risk of leakage of fuel from pipes, tanks and apparatus is amongst the most obvious risks arising from such an operation, and one against which the operator of the business would naturally desire cover. Mr Evans-Tovey relied on Extension 26 for the purpose of establishing that the parties would have had in mind fuel leaks as a likely hazard. In my view that is obvious without needing to refer to Extension 26.

26   Secondly, there is no room for any presumption that Special Exclusion 9 is to be narrowly construed or construed against the insurer. The scope of cover in Section 1 is defined by the Indemnity in the second part of the Section as being "any cause not excluded", followed in the fourth part by "Exclusions to Section 1", in which Exclusion 9 is to be found. Those exclusions are part of the definition of the scope of cover, not some exemptions from liability for cover which would otherwise exist. This is reinforced in the case of Exclusion 9 itself by the fact that it includes provisions conferring or preserving cover, in relation to Specified Events, as a write-back to the scope of cover excluded in the opening words. There is therefore no room for the application of the relevant aspect of the *contra proferentem* principle, which applies to a clause exempting a party from a liability which would otherwise arise by operation of law or under a contractual term which defines the benefit which it appears it was the purpose of the contract to provide. If authority were needed for such an approach, it is to be found in the judgments of Lord Hodge JSC at [5]-[7] and Lord Toulson JSC at [35] in *Impact Funding Solutions Ltd v Barrington Services Ltd* [2016] UKSC 57; [2017] A.C. 73.

27   Thirdly, it is a general principle of insurance law, codified in s. 55 of the Marine Insurance Act 1906 but equally applicable to non-marine insurance, that the insurer is liable, and only liable, for losses proximately caused by a peril covered by the policy. Because of its historical origins, the expression proximate cause is apt to mislead. The proximate cause of the loss is not the last cause of the loss, but that which is proximate in efficiency, being the dominant, effective or efficient cause: *Leyland Shipping Co v Norwich Union Fire Insurance Society* [1918] A.C. 350, *Yorkshire Dale Steamship Co v Minister of War Transport* [1942] A.C. 691, *FCA v Arch* at [163]-[170]. There may be more than one proximate cause of a loss. Where there are concurrent proximate causes, one an insured peril and the other excluded, the exclusion prevails: *Wayne Tank and Pump Co Ltd v Employers Liability Assurance Corpn Ltd* [1974] Q.B. 57 at pp. 67B-F, 69B-D, 74E-75D; *Atlasnavios-Navega LDA v Navigators Insurance Co Ltd* [2018] UKSC 26; [2019] A.C. 136 at [49], *FCA v Arch* at [174].

28   It is a commonplace in human experience, and therefore insurance claims, that a loss may result from a combination of causes, either operating independently of one another, or, often, in a chain where each would not have arisen but for that preceding it in the chain. Of these causes, the search is for the, or a, proximate cause and it is generally irrelevant if a cause is either more remote in the chain than the proximate cause, or more immediate.

29   This is subject to an important qualification. The requirement of proximate causation is based on the presumed intention of the contracting parties; it is a presumption capable of being displaced if, on its proper interpretation, the policy provides for some other connection between loss and the occurrence of an insured or excepted peril. This is reflected by the words in s. 55 of the Marine Insurance Act "unless the policy otherwise provides". The parties may expressly provide that losses which result from causes which are more immediate or more remote than the proximate cause are to be included or excluded. Typically this is done by a clause referring to losses caused "directly or indirectly" by the insured or excepted peril. So in *Coxe v Employers Liability Assurance Corporation Ltd* [1916] 2 K.B. 629, a soldier was insured against death accidentally caused by violence due to accidental and visible means. The policy excepted losses "directly or indirectly caused by, arising from or traceable to war." During the First World War the soldier was killed by a train whilst walking alongside the railway to visit guards and sentries posted along the line. Scrutton J upheld the finding of the arbitrator that his death was indirectly caused by war because his military duties consequent upon the war put him in special danger. In doing so he held that the proximate cause principle is to be applied in all cases if possible unless the language dictates otherwise; but that the word "indirectly" did so in that case because there could be no such thing as an indirect proximate cause.

30   In *FCA v Arch* it was expressed in this way at [163]:

> "The requirement of "proximate" causation is based on the presumed intention of the contracting parties....But it is a presumption capable of being displaced if, on its proper interpretation, the policy provides for some other connection between the loss and the occurrence of an insured peril."

31   Against this background I turn to the wording of Exclusion 9.

32   The OED definition of pollution includes: "the action of polluting", "the condition of being polluted" and "a thing that pollutes". The definition of contamination includes "the action of making impure or polluting", "something which contaminates" and "an impurity". Each is therefore capable of describing three separate things, namely (1) the damage to property; (2) the process by which such damage is caused; and (3) the state of affairs or occurrence which gives rise to that process.

33   It is common ground that the words are not used in the first sense, namely as a description of the damage. The Exclusion is concerned with the cause of that damage. Whether they are used in the second sense or third sense is a question which itself turns upon whether the clause is concerned with proximate causes. If it is, it will generally only be contamination or pollution as a state of affairs or occurrence which will be engaged, not the process of contamination or pollution which forms part of that chain by which it leads to the damage.

34   In this case the chain of causation leading to the damage included the process of pollution or contamination, but that was not its proximate cause. The proximate cause of the damage was the puncturing of the pipe by the stone or sharp object (on the assumed facts). It is critical to the outcome, therefore, whether the exclusion is concerned with pollution or contamination as a proximate cause or merely as an intermediate process in the chain of causation.

35   Exclusion 9 consists of an exclusion in the first six words ("[this Policy...does not cover] Damage caused by pollution or contamination") which I will call the

exclusionary wording, followed by a write-back of cover in the rest of the Exclusion, which I will call the write-back wording. It is a write-back in the sense of providing for cover in circumstances where it would otherwise be excluded by the exclusionary wording. This follows from the word "but"; and from the fact that the structure of cover is for all risks not excluded, so that where it is intended that there should be cover there is no need for any wording granting such cover unless it addresses circumstances which would otherwise be excluded.

36   If the exclusionary wording were taken on its own, it would be tolerably clear that it was concerned with pollution and contamination as a proximate cause. This follows from the presumption arising from the general law of insurance that clauses concerned with defining the scope of insured or excepted perils are concerned with damage proximately caused by those perils. It is reinforced in this case by the use of the simple expression "caused by" which has historically and uniformly been interpreted in this context as importing the concept of proximate cause.

37   It is further reinforced in this case by the contrast with two other policy terms where wider language is used in connection with pollution and contamination. Section 2 of the Policy covers third party liability risks for death, personal injury or damage arising from use of the insured vehicles. Exclusion 7 to that Section excludes liability for:

> "death, injury, loss or damage *directly or indirectly caused by* pollution or contamination unless the pollution or contamination is directly caused by a sudden identifiable unintended and unexpected incident which occurs in its entirety at a specific time and place during the Period of Insurance."(my emphasis)

38   Section 3 covers third party liability in respect of the use of self-drive rental vehicles in similar terms to that for insured vehicles in Section 2 and has an Exclusion 8 in the same terms as Exclusion 7 in Section 2.

39   Some caution must be exercised in relying on this contrasting wording. Normally it is a legitimate canon of construction that where the parties have chosen different language in relation to related subject matter in different parts of their contract, it suggests that they intended different meanings. However the Policy Wording in this case contemplates that it can be used by assureds selecting cover under some but not all of the Sections. The meaning of Exclusion 9 in Section 1 must be the same for an assured who has not selected cover under Sections 2 and 3 as for one, like BLG, who has. Nevertheless the contrasting wording in the Exclusions in Sections 2 and 3 shows that the drafter had well in mind the distinction between "caused by" meaning proximately caused, and "directly or indirectly caused by" connoting a looser connection between the Damage and pollution or contamination, a distinction which is well established by judicial authority.

40   For these reasons I would regard the presumption that the exclusionary wording is concerned only with proximate causes to be a strong one. It is reasonable to attribute this presumed intention to these parties. Assureds such as BLG have brokers who can advise them, and brokers are to be taken to be familiar with the basic insurance principle of proximate causation, and language which reflects it or, by contrast, modifies it. Both assured and broker have access to legal advice which would involve no pedantry in advising on the presumptions involved in the use of such language. This is part of "the background knowledge which would reasonably have been available to the parties". I do not take what was said in [77]

of *FCA v Arch* as suggesting that the reasonable person in an SME's shoes should not be taken to be familiar with the basic principles of insurance law and the meaning which has been put on phrases used in insurance contracts by consistent judicial authority. Many policies of insurance in many fields contain terms of art which have acquired their meaning by consistent use and judicial interpretation, which it is the duty of brokers to understand and, if necessary, advise on.

41   It is trite that Exclusion 9 is to be read as a whole, but I would not regard that strong presumptive meaning of the exclusionary words as displaced unless the wording of the write-back cannot be reconciled with it. The reasonable reader of the clause would expect the scope of the exclusion to be determined by the language employed to express the exclusion, namely that in the exclusionary words, rather than by what follows. If it is to be displaced in what follows, it can only be on the basis that what follows is inconsistent with the presumption.

42   The write-back wording does not, to my mind, displace this presumption because it is capable of being given meaning consistently with it. The write-back wording is also introduced by the words "caused by" which govern the written back circumstances set out in clauses a. and b. Again the natural presumption is that they connote proximate cause for the reasons already given in relation to the exclusionary wording, and for internal consistency within the clause: where parties use the same language within the same clause the presumption is that they mean the same in each case.

43   Clause a. writes back cover where pollution or contamination is the proximate cause but a Specified Event is a more remote cause in the chain of causation. Clause b. cannot be construed as writing back cover where pollution or contamination is a more remote, non-proximate, cause of a Specified Event as the proximate cause, because that would not be a write-back: the pollution or contamination would not be excluded by the exclusionary words unless it was, on this construction, the proximate cause. However content can be given to clause b. as covering the possibility of two concurrent proximate causes. In such a case the exclusionary wording would bite and prevail under the *Wayne Tank* principle which I have identified were it not for the write-back in clause b.

44   Instances in reported cases of concurrent proximate causes are not common, but are not as rare as might at first be supposed. MacGillivray on Insurance law 15th Ed. goes as far as to say at 19-005 that it "often happens that the insured's loss is attributable to at least two proximate causes acting concurrently". The *Atlasnavios* case is a recent example, in which smugglers affixing cocaine to a ship, and consequent detention by the port authorities upon its discovery, were treated as concurrent proximate causes. Lord Mance DPSC said at [43] in that case that while the general aim in insurance law is to identify a single real, effective or proximate cause of any loss, the correct analysis is in some cases that there are two concurrent causes and this is particularly so where an exceptions clause takes certain perils out of the prima facie cover. Another recent example, and a striking one, is *FCA v Arch*, in which it was held that each and every case of Covid-19 in the United Kingdom, approaching or even exceeding a million in number, was to be treated as a concurrent proximate cause of the national response to the pandemic; and that it was not necessary for such a proximate cause to satisfy a but for test of causation. It is not, therefore, fanciful to suppose that the drafter of Exclusion 9 had concurrent proximate causes in mind, consistently with the language used elsewhere in the Exclusion.

45   This construction involves giving the words "results from" a meaning which is not necessarily that of proximate cause, but I see no difficulty in doing so. Although the expression has been interpreted as connoting proximate cause when applied to the link between insured/excepted perils and damage (*Lloyds TSB General Insurance Holdings Ltd v Lloyds Bank Group Insurance Co Ltd* [2001] EWCA Civ 1643; [2002] Lloyd's Rep. I.R. 113 at [42] (CA), [2003] UKHL 48; [2003] Lloyd's Rep IR 623 at [45] (HL)), there is no reason to do so where, as here, it is being applied to a causative relationship between insured/excepted perils in a chain. Mr Evans-Tovey argued, initially at least, that the words "results from" did connote proximate cause, but this was, in my view, untenable on his construction of the clause. It would involve inconsistent meanings for "pollution or contamination": it has to treat pollution or contamination in b. not merely as part of a process, as he contends it means in the exclusionary words, but as something which gives rise to the process. The further difficulty with such submission from his point of view is that it would suggest that "caused by" in the introductory words of the write-back connote proximate cause: if the Specified Event must be the proximate cause of the (process of) contamination or pollution which causes the damage (clause a.), it is difficult to see how it will not be the proximate cause of the damage itself.

46   Mr Evans-Tovey relied on the omission of any reference to fuel leak escape in the list of Specified Events, suggesting that it was a careful and deliberate omission in the light of the contrast with the inclusion of water escape, and as thereby indicating that the parties did not intend to cover damage resulting from fuel leaks. There are a number of reasons why I cannot accept this submission. First there is a logical flaw in relying on the list of Specified Events to aid construction of the exclusionary words in Exclusion 9. The Specified Events are only engaged by the write-back wording, and the write-back wording only arises if the exclusionary wording bites. The fact that the write-back only applies to some perils tells one nothing about the scope of the exclusion before the write-back becomes operative (or not). There is no blanket write-back for all damage involving fuel leaks, but that does not mean they are all excluded in the first place, so as to need writing back, if there is to be cover. Secondly, Exclusion 9 falls to be construed by reference to all potential forms of contamination or pollution, not merely fuel leaks. Thirdly, and in any event, the definition of Specified Events contains a miscellaneous list of events (or in the mystifying case of "aircraft", an object) some of which may be the cause or the result of fuel leaks (e.g. fire and explosion). It is not the case that the consequences of fuel leaks are all excluded from Specified Events and therefore not within the write-back. As Mr Evans-Tovey accepted, if on the assumed facts of this case the escaped fuel had caught fire or exploded, there would have been cover even on his case. He suggested that this would be because the fire or explosion would be the proximate cause but that is not so; there would be cover, on his construction of the clause, because it would be written back by clause a.

47   Mr Evans-Tovey argued that BLG's construction involved treating the write-back wording as an extension of cover rather than a write-back, which was therefore inconsistent with the word "but" and the fact that the structure of the policy is one of all risks other than excepted perils and therefore an extension would be superfluous. However this is not the effect of the construction which I have suggested is the correct one. Both clauses a. and b. bite in circumstances where cover would otherwise be excluded by the exclusionary words because in each

case they are engaged where, but only where, pollution or contamination is a proximate cause.

48   It may be objected that BLG's construction gives a narrow scope to the exception, and an even narrower scope to the write-back. Circumstances in which pollution or contamination would be a proximate cause of material damage to BLG's business, or that of any other assured likely to take out cover on the terms of this "Motor Trade" Policy, will not be common. Mr Davidson suggested as an example red dust which sometimes occurs from windborne sand in the atmosphere emanating from foreign deserts. Others which come to mind are chemical pollutants/contaminants from historical use of the land or neighbouring land, for example for waste or mining, where the historical source of the problem renders it impossible to investigate or ascertain whether there was any fault, and if so what, in the pollutants/contaminants seeping into the ground. No doubt there are others, but I would accept that they are unlikely to be common. However, the fact that BLG's interpretation gives a narrow scope to the Exclusion is not, to my mind, a reason for rejecting it. This is a policy covering all risks of material damage unless excluded, and it is not inherently surprising in such a policy that an exception should have a narrow scope of application. Moreover, as I have observed, the risk of leakage of fuel from pipes, tanks and apparatus, is amongst the most obvious risks arising from a business like that of BLG, and one against which the operator of the business would naturally desire cover. A narrow interpretation of the exclusion is consistent with such desire.

49   Mr Evans-Tovey also argued that if BLG were correct in its construction, there would be cover for the pollution or contamination of the forecourt by the gradual effect of the daily occurrence of motorists carelessly allowing fuel to spill from the nozzle whilst filling their vehicles. I do not know whether the frequency of such occurrences and the composition of forecourts makes it realistic to posit material damage from such a cause. But assuming that they do, I do not find it self-evident that the parties cannot have intended that there should be cover in such circumstances, in what is in structure an all risks policy with defined exceptions.

50   The cases to which we were referred do not address or shed light on the issue of construction which arises in this case. In *Legg v Sterte Garages* a claim was made against liability insurers for Sterte's costs of defending proceedings brought by neighbours claiming loss from fuel leaking from Sterte's garage premises. The claim succeeded both on the basis that the judge had correctly exercised his discretion under s. 51 of the Senior Courts Act 1981 to render the insurers liable for the costs as non-parties to the proceedings; and that the terms of the liability insurance provided coverage for such costs. There was no claim against the insurers for liability for the damage itself. That was because the policy excluded liability "arising from pollution and contamination" .... "other than caused by a sudden identifiable unintended and unexpected incident which occurs in its entirety at a specific time and place during the period of insurance." There had been such an incident resulting in a spill of 300 litres of diesel from an above ground tank in August 1997. Proceedings were only commenced by the claimants against Sterte in November 2008, which gave rise to a limitation defence in respect of the spill incident which had occurred well before November 2002, by which time the diesel had finished migrating to the claimants' land. The claimants' expert introduced the possibility of a different cause of the contamination/pollution, namely gradual and long term leaks from underground storage tanks and/or associated pipework.

In referring to this evidence as part of the history of proceedings David Richards LJ, giving the leading judgment, said at [28]:

> "This raised, for the first time, as a possible cause of the damage to the claimants' land, long-term leaks from underground storage tanks or associated pipework on Sterte's property. Damage resulting from such leakage would fall outside the public liability cover for pollution damage in section E of the policy."

51   Mr Evans-Tovey relies on the paragraph as demonstrating that the damage in question in that case fell within the pollution and contamination exception and that the same reasoning applies in this case. However the dictum is of no assistance in the present case. The policy wording was different, using the epithet "arising from", in respect of which there are conflicting authorities as to whether it connotes proximate cause. In that case the court was not concerned with the liability of Sterte to the claimants for the damage itself because it formed no part of the claim against insurers, which was limited to costs. David Richards LJ made the passing reference to such liability in paragraph 28 but without having to address either whether the pollution or contamination were the proximate cause, or whether that mattered for the purposes of the exclusion clause. Moreover the case was concerned with liability insurance where the cause of the loss was determined not by the cause of the material damage but by the cause of the liability, which arose in negligence, nuisance and the rule in *Rylands v Fletcher*, which were the causes of action asserted by the claimants against Sterte. Liability under those causes of action is not determined by the insurance concept of proximate cause.

52   Mr Davidson sought to derive support from the decision of Coulson J in *Leeds Beckett University v Travelers*, in which a policy covering material damage contained at exclusion 5 a pollution/contamination exclusion in similar, although not identical, terms to Exclusion 9. Coulson J found, in an obiter section of his judgment at [262]-[266], that the exclusion was not engaged by the escape of water containing ochreous and ferruginous material. This was because although there was evidence of such material in the observed damage to the blockwork to the buildings which had led to the damage, it had played no part in the causation of the damage, which had occurred by the inevitable and non-accidental effect of a separate underground watercourse. Coulson J held that contamination or pollution from the mineshafts did not satisfy a but for test of causation. Mr Davidson argued that by addressing the question, Coulson J must have assumed that, had the contamination been causative, it would have engaged the exception in exclusion 5. However there is no suggestion that there was any argument as to the construction or scope of the exclusion, and in particular whether it was engaged if the contamination were a cause, or only if it were the proximate cause. Coulson J did not have to consider such questions or make any assumptions about them in order to reject the application of the exclusion on the grounds that the escape of water from the mineshafts played no causative part in the damage.

53   In conclusion, therefore, whilst I would readily accept that Allianz's construction of Exclusion 9 is one which the parties might perfectly sensibly have chosen as their bargain, it faces the insuperable difficulty that it does not give effect to the language they have used, which gives rise to the presumption that they intended the exclusion to apply to pollution or contamination as a proximate cause, a

presumption which is not displaced by the wording of the write-back or any other wording in the policy.

Conclusion

54   For these reasons I would allow the appeal.

LORD JUSTICE NUGEE:

55   I have had the great advantage of reading in draft not only the judgment of Lord Justice Popplewell above but that of Lord Justice Males below. Each of them is well reasoned but they reach different conclusions. Faced with persuasive but divergent judgments written by eminent judges with long experience of construing insurance policies, I have not found it easy to settle on a conclusion. For much of the time I have been inclined to the same view as that of Lord Justice Males. But I am ultimately persuaded that Lord Justice Popplewell's is the better view and that the appeal should be allowed for the reasons he gives.

56   Since we are concerned with the construction of one particular policy, I do not intend to give my reasons at any length but will shortly state why I have come to this view.

57   I too agree with the various points set out by Lord Justice Males at [65] below. And I agree that the essential question, as he says at [68] below, is whether Exclusion 9 as a whole would demonstrate to the reasonable reader to whom it is addressed an intention to displace the general rule. I am inclined to think that he is also justified in saying (in the same paragraph) that it is going too far to say that the presumption in favour of reading the opening words as referring to damage proximately caused by pollution or contamination can *only* be displaced if the write-back provisions are inconsistent, and cannot be reconciled, with that meaning, and that the intention to displace the general rule may be demonstrated, even if it is possible to give some meaning to the write-back provisions which does not render them redundant. In *FCA v Arch*, the way in which Lords Hamblen and Leggatt JJSC expressed it (at [163]) was that "The requirement of "proximate" causation is based on the presumed intention of the contracting parties … But it is a presumption capable of being displaced if, on its proper interpretation, the policy provides for some other connection between loss and the occurrence of an insured peril." That seems to me to allow for the general rule to be displaced whenever it appears on the proper interpretation of the policy to be what the parties intended.

58   The question however is whether paragraphs [a] and [b] do require such an interpretation here. I accept that they have to be read with the list of Specified Events, as almost the only role of this list is to provide content to these paragraphs in Exclusion 9. (We were told after the hearing that it does have one other role which is in connection with General Exclusion 9A which excludes damage caused by a computer failing to recognise a date correctly, with a write-back for damage which results from a Specified Event, but I do not find this of any assistance to the present question). Most of the Specified Events are by their very nature likely to be relevant only to paragraph [a] rather than [b]: one can envisage for example lightning or earthquake resulting in pollution or contamination (for example if a fuel tank was damaged), but it is not really possible to imagine a case where lightning or earthquake results from pollution or contamination. The same is no doubt true of such miscellaneous events as articles dropped from aircraft, riot, civil

commotion, and malicious persons other than thieves. Indeed the only Specified Events which one might think of as potentially likely to result from pollution or contamination are perhaps fire and explosion.

59   In these circumstances I find it helpful to consider the question of construction by imagining a particular case. Suppose there were an earthquake which damaged a sewage pipe in the vicinity which then contaminated the petrol station. Lord Justice Males says that in such a case the earthquake would be the proximate cause, and that there is overall very limited scope to the write-back provisions (see [69] below). I agree that the earthquake would be at least a proximate cause. But I think it possible that the resulting spill of sewage into the petrol station could also be regarded as *a* proximate cause of the resulting pollution damage, or at any rate that this might be thought to be an argument that the insurer might otherwise seek to deploy and hence deny cover (under the *Wayne Tank* principle). Seen in this light the effect of paragraph [a] is to ensure that even if the escape of sewage might be capable of being characterised as a proximate cause, it does not matter. There is still cover provided that the escape of sewage itself results from a Specified Event, in this case an earthquake. That seems to me to make perfectly good sense. The reasonable reader of the policy (being conscientious but not pedantic) would on this view understand that provided that the pollution or contamination itself resulted from a Specified Event, one would not even need to ask the question whether the pollution or contamination was a proximate cause. There would still be cover even if it were.

60   Once one sees paragraph [a] in this light, paragraph [b] also to my mind makes sense. In practical terms most Specified Events, as already said, are most unlikely to result from pollution or contamination, the only real contenders being fire or explosion. If there were an escape of fuel which caused a fire which burned down the petrol station, I think the reasonable reader would expect the fire to be regarded as a proximate cause of the resulting damage. What paragraph [b] does in such a case is prevent the argument being run that because the fire was caused by an escape of fuel, that was pollution or contamination that was itself a proximate cause of the damage and hence that cover was denied by Exclusion 9. Again it makes it unnecessary to ask the question whether the pollution was also a proximate cause of the damage, because there would be cover even if it were.

61   Since practical content can in this way be given to paragraphs [a] and [b] without having to rewrite the meaning of "caused by" to include non-proximate causes, I have come to the view that on the true interpretation of Exclusion 9 there is insufficient to displace the presumption that "Damage caused by pollution or contamination" refers only to the case of proximate causation.

62   I add as a footnote that although I agree that provisions in other sections of the policy, being optional, are not to be taken into account on the question of construction of Exclusion 9, we were referred by Mr Davidson in a post-hearing submission to the fact that General Exclusion 9A (the computer date recognition exclusion) does itself use the expression "directly or indirectly caused by". This provision as I understand it does apply to the relevant section of the policy and might be thought to provide support for the view I have preferred on the basis that it shows that the drafter knew how to extend causation to non-proximate causation when required. But we have heard no opposing submissions on the point and it is unnecessary to place any reliance on it.

63   For the reasons I have sought to express I therefore agree with Lord Justice Popplewell that the appeal should be allowed.

LORD JUSTICE MALES:

64   I agree with much of Lord Justice Popplewell's judgment, including his approach to the issue of construction arising in this case, but (with respect and some hesitation) I have reached a different conclusion on the particular wording of Exclusion 9.

65   Thus I agree that:

(1)   The policy is to be interpreted objectively, as it would reasonably be understood by an ordinary policyholder, in this case the owner of a petrol garage, albeit with the benefit of advice from a broker familiar with basic principles of insurance law.

(2)   One such principle is that an insurer is only liable for loss proximately caused by a peril covered by the policy, from which it follows that policy language such as "caused by" must generally be taken to refer to the proximate (or efficient) cause of the loss.

(3)   However, that principle is based on the presumed intention of the contracting parties, and is therefore subject to contrary agreement.

(4)   On the facts assumed for the purpose of this appeal, the proximate or efficient cause of the damage to property in this case was the penetration of the fuel pipe by a sharp object under pressure from the weight of the concrete slab under the forecourt.

(5)   Accordingly the critical issue for decision is whether the opening words of Exclusion 9 (the exclusion of "Damage caused by pollution or contamination") refer only to the proximate cause of the damage; if so, the appeal must be allowed; if not, it must be dismissed.

(6)   That question must be answered without any presumption that Exclusion 9 is an exemption clause which requires to be narrowly construed (rather, it defines the scope of the cover), but giving proper weight to the general rule that causation language in an insurance policy refers to the proximate cause.

(7)   Cases such as *Legg v Sterte Garage Ltd* [2016] EWCA Civ 97; [2016] Lloyd's Rep. I.R. 390 and *Leeds Beckett University v Travelers Insurance Company Ltd* [2017] EWHC 558 (TCC); [2017] Lloyd's Rep. I.R. 417 provide no real assistance in answering the critical issue.

(8)   Exclusion 9 consists of two parts, the exclusion of damage caused by pollution or contamination, followed by the write-back of cover in the two cases dealt with in paragraphs (a) and (b), which it is necessary to construe as a whole.

66   My reasons for concluding that the opening words of Exclusion 9 are not limited to damage proximately caused by pollution or contamination are as follows.

67   First, it is necessary to construe Exclusion 9 as a whole, including the "write-back" provisions, in order to arrive at the meaning of the opening exclusion of cover. While I agree that, if the opening exclusion were taken on its own, it would be clear that the exclusion was of damage proximately caused by pollution or contamination (cf. [36] above), that is because there would then be nothing to displace the general rule. But the exclusionary wording does not stand on its own.

It must be considered together with the write-back of cover which immediately follows, so that Exclusion 9 is considered as a whole.

68   Second, considering the Exclusion as a whole, it is going too far in my view to say that the presumption in favour of reading the opening words as referring to damage proximately caused by pollution or contamination can *only* be displaced if the write-back provisions are inconsistent, and cannot be reconciled, with that meaning (cf. [41] above). Rather, the question is whether Exclusion 9 as a whole would demonstrate to the reasonable reader to whom it is addressed an intention to displace the general rule. That intention may be demonstrated, even if it is possible to give some meaning to the write-back provisions which does not render them redundant.

69   On that point, in agreement with Lord Justice Popplewell at [42] and [43], I would accept that some meaning can be given to the write-back provisions even if the opening exclusion of "Damage caused by pollution or contamination" is to be read as referring only to damage proximately so caused. On that reading, paragraph (a) writes back cover for damage proximately caused by pollution or contamination when that pollution or contamination results from (i.e. is caused by) a Specified Event which is not itself a proximate cause of the damage. But the nature of the Specified Events is such that this is only rarely likely to apply. For the most part the Specified Event would itself be the proximate cause of the damage in question. Paragraph (b) then writes back cover for damage caused by pollution or contamination, but only when both the pollution or contamination and the Specified Event are proximate causes of the damage. However, while this may be a possible reading of Exclusion 9, it affords very limited scope to the write-back provisions and does not seem to me to be a probable reading, or (in other words) to be what would reasonably be understood by the policyholder to whom the clause is addressed.

70   While I recognise the force of the point (at [46]) as a matter of logic that the list of Specified Events cannot aid construction of the exclusionary wording in Exclusion 9, because the write-back provisions are only engaged if the exclusionary wording applies, language is not always used (even in insurance policies) with full logical rigour. In my judgment the ordinary reader of the policy would be assisted in interpreting the exclusionary wording by the write-back provisions, including the list of Specified Events, and would draw three important conclusions from them. The first is that "escape of water from any tank apparatus or pipe" is covered as a Specified Event, but that escape of fuel (which I agree is an obvious risk for the owner of a petrol garage) is not. That suggests a deliberate contrast. Second, fire and explosion are also covered. These are the obvious harmful consequences which may result from an escape of fuel, about which a policyholder would rightly be concerned. Accordingly the fact that damage caused by pollution or contamination is excluded is less significant commercially than would otherwise be the case. The third conclusion to be drawn from the write-back provisions is that, when they apply, it does not matter whether damage is caused by pollution or contamination which itself results from a Specified Event (paragraph (a)) or the Specified Event is the result of pollution or contamination (paragraph (b)). This suggests, to my mind, that the write-back provisions are *not* concerned with the proximate cause of the damage. Rather, their purpose is to ensure that, where there is a Specified Event which either causes or is caused by pollution or contamination,

there will be cover regardless of whether the Specified Event or the pollution/contamination is the proximate cause of the damage.

71   This third conclusion suggests in turn that the words "caused by" in the write-back provisions ("We will pay for Damage to the Property Insured not otherwise excluded, caused by: ...") do not (or do not necessarily) mean "proximately caused by". If that is so, the principle that where parties use the same language within the same clause, it is presumed that they mean the same thing in each case (cf. [42] above), would suggest that the same applies to the use of the words "caused by" in the opening exclusionary wording.

72   Third, in my view the meaning of Exclusion 9 has to be derived from the terms of Section 1 of the policy, without regard to the language of other clauses contained in other Sections of the policy. That is because an insured is entitled to select cover under some but not all of the Sections. As Lord Justice Popplewell points out at [39], the meaning of Exclusion 9 must be the same for an insured who has not selected cover under Sections 2 and 3 as for one, like the claimant in this case, who has. The reasonable policyholder who has selected cover under Section 1 but not Sections 2 or 3, and who is seeking to understand the cover which he has purchased, could not be expected to scrutinise Sections 2 or 3 in search of contrasting wording which might or might not throw light on the meaning of clauses contained in Section 1. Accordingly I do not accept that any reliance can be placed on the use of the term "directly or indirectly caused by pollution or contamination" in Exclusion 7 of Section 2 and Exclusion 8 of Section 3 (cf. [37] and [38] above). I acknowledge that there may be a point to be made that the words "directly or indirectly caused by" are also used in General Exclusion 9A, as Lord Justice Nugee points out at [62] above. However, this was not a point made at the hearing. I think it fair, therefore, to place no reliance on it.

73   Finally, while I have so far been considering the meaning of Exclusion 9 by reference to textual analysis of the particular language used, without (I hope) trespassing too far into the world of the "pedantic lawyer" deprecated by the Supreme Court in *FCA v Arch* at [77], it is striking that it was only in this court, and even then only in oral submissions, that the argument clearly emerged that "Damage caused by pollution or contamination" meant damage proximately so caused. Until then BLG's case was that the only cause of the damage was the penetration of the pipe; that the damage *consisted of* but was not *caused by* pollution or contamination; and that the exclusion of pollution and contamination referred only to environmental contamination of sub soils and groundwaters. It does not appear to have occurred to BLG, or to its legal team or the judge (whom I would count as non-pedantic lawyers), to contend that the exclusion was limited to a situation where pollution or contamination was the proximate cause of the damage. Standing back from the detail, to my mind that is powerful confirmation that the judge's construction accorded with the natural meaning of Exclusion 9 as that would be objectively understood by an ordinary policyholder, suitably advised by a broker or lawyer familiar with basic principles of insurance law.

74   There can in my view be no doubt that, as a matter of ordinary language, it makes perfect sense to say that the damage in this case was "caused by pollution or contamination". Although the pollution and contamination was not the proximate cause of the damage as that term would be used by an insurance lawyer or broker, it was the pollution and contamination which resulted from the penetration of the

fuel pipe which caused the damage to the property and meant that the business had to be shut down.

75   For these reasons, I would hold that the terms of Exclusion 9 do sufficiently demonstrate an intention to displace the general rule that causation language must be taken to refer to the proximate cause of damage, and that the damage in this case was caused by pollution or contamination within the meaning of the Exclusion. I would therefore dismiss the appeal. However, as my Lords take a different view, the appeal will be allowed.

MANCHESTER SHIP CANAL CO LTD v SECRETARY OF STATE FOR ENVIRONMENT, FOOD AND RURAL AFFAIRS

KING'S BENCH DIVISION (ADMINISTRATIVE COURT)

Thornton J, DBE: 19 December 2022

[2022] EWHC 3282 (Admin); [2023] Env. L.R. 24

(LT) Compulsory purchase orders; Discharge; Necessity; Peaceful enjoyment of possessions; Proportionality; Public interest; Sewage effluent; Sewerage undertakers; Water quality

H1   *Water pollution—Water Industry Act 1991—Human Rights—Compulsory Purchase Order under s.155 authorising discharge of water, soil and effluent from sewers into canal—challenge under Acquisition of Land Act 1981 s.23—need for Order arising from public sewerage obligations—right of discharge granted without specific statutory protection for landowner via ss.117, 183 and Sch.12 of 1991 Act—whether conclusion that correct test for inclusion of provisions was whether they were 'necessary' a misdirection as to proper legal and procedural context— whether determination that purposes of CPO sufficiently justified interference with rights under art.1/Protocol 1 to ECHR unlawful*

H2   The claimant (M) was the owner, statutory undertaker and navigation authority for a canal and sought to challenge the decision of the Secretary of State (S) to confirm the United Utilities Water Ltd (Eccles Wastewater Treatment Works) Compulsory Purchase Order 2016 (CPO). The CPO authorised the sewerage undertaker (U) to compulsorily discharge water, soil and effluent from its sewers into the canal. The challenge was brought pursuant to the Acquisition of Land Act 1981 s.23, which provided that a person aggrieved by a compulsory purchase order could apply to the court to question the validity of the order on the ground that there was no power to make it or a relevant requirement had not been complied with. The need for the CPO arose because of the need for U to meet its public sewerage obligations. U operated a Wastewater Treatment Works (WTW) which discharged treated wastewater into a tributary of the canal. That tributary also received the outflow from a combined sewer outfall at the inlet of the WTW. U proposed to discharge treated wastewater and storm overflows directly into the canal via a new outfall, rather than into the tributary, in order to satisfy regulatory standards set by the Environment Agency (EA) for the tributary. U had a statutory right to lay its pipes across land without the need for landowner consent pursuant to the Water Industry Act 1991 s.159 but the new right to discharge into the canal had to be acquired by agreement or by compulsory acquisition under s.155. At the public inquiry, M withdrew its initial principled objection, accepting that there was a "compelling public interest" for U to discharge into its canal. Instead, it challenged the width of the order, describing it as "an unfettered private law right for [U] to discharge effluent in perpetuity in the Canal". M said that the right of discharge was the only one nationwide without specific statutory protection for the landowner; because the vast majority of discharges were implicitly authorised by the 1991 Act, subject to protection for the landowner via ss.117, 183 and Sch.12 of the Act. At the public inquiry, M sought, unsuccessfully, to include those provisions within the terms of the CPO. In broad terms, the provisions provided that; U was not authorised to use the outfall in breach of any environmental regulation or so as to "affect prejudicially the purity and quality of the water" or so as to "injuriously affect" the receiving water, U could not create a nuisance, the landowner's consent was required for certain works, and full compensation for "damage" sustained by a person by reason of the exercise of U's powers was payable.

H3   The Inspector recommended that the order be confirmed without the inclusion of the protective provisions and S agreed. The grounds for the claim were S and/or the Inspector (1) misdirected themselves as to the proper legal and procedural context in which to evaluate and determine the inclusion of the protective provisions sought by M by concluding that the correct test was whether they were necessary; and (2) erred in law in their determination that the purposes for which the CPO was made sufficiently justified the interference with M's rights under art.1 of the First Protocol to the European Convention on Human Rights.

H4   **Held,** in dismissing the claim:

H5   (1) The Inspector reached an assessment that inclusion of the protective provisions sought was unnecessary. That was not because he treated necessity as a legal test but was a judgment reached in the public interest, based on a lengthy examination of the evidence. His main reasons for considering the proviso to be unnecessary were because the discharge would be regulated by EA; the public inquiry had provided an opportunity for an independent scrutiny of the potential interference with M's rights; the discharge provisions did not apply to a right granted under s.155; the water quality evidence demonstrated that the scheme would have a net beneficial effect on the water quality of the canal and compensation was payable. The Inspector's decision disclosed no error of law. Given the nature of the legal provisions sought, there was an obvious rationale to the Inspector taking account of the availability of a detailed and precise environmental regulatory regime, backed up by criminal sanctions and overseen by a specialist regulator, as well as the water quality evidence which demonstrated that the scheme would have a net beneficial impact on the canal. The procedure for the grant of a CPO, in particular the public inquiry, provided an appropriate forum in which to assess any necessary protection for a landowner whose land was subject to a compulsory use. There was a material distinction between an implied right of discharge and the express grant of a right under s.155. The Inspector's decision was not reached on the basis that M had failed to satisfy any particular burden of proof but because he found the case advanced by U to be "convincing". None of the considerations referred to were immaterial and it was not alleged that the overall exercise of the discretion was irrational or the reasoning deficient. The Inspector exercised the discretion available to him and formed his view, taking into account arguments and evidence put forward by both parties, as he was required to do so by the inquiry process.

H6   (2) With regard to the art.1 Protocol 1 ground, it could be said that the balance struck by the statutory regime was to provide a procedure under s.155, whereby landowners could seek appropriate protection from any interference via independent scrutiny of their interests, alongside the wider public interest. Whether the CPO struck a fair balance was inherently more suited for decision by the inquiry process, with further protection of judicial review, than private law litigation involving only the parties to the litigation and without any obvious role for the wider public interest. Accordingly, the terms of the CPO struck a fair balance.

H7   **Cases referred to:**

Allen v Gulf Oil Refining Ltd [1981] A.C. 1001; [1981] 2 W.L.R. 188; [1981] J.P.L. 353 HL

Bank Mellat v HM Treasury [2013] UKSC 38; [2014] A.C. 700; [2013] Lloyd's Rep. F.C. 557 SC

Bank Mellat v HM Treasury [2013] UKSC 39; [2014] A.C. 700; [2013] 3 W.L.R. 179

Barker Mill Estates Trustees v Test Valley BC [2016] EWHC 3028 (Admin); [2017] P.T.S.R. 408; [2017] J.P.L. 417

James v United Kingdom (A/98) (1986) 8 E.H.R.R. 123 ECtHR

Lough v First Secretary of State [2004] EWCA Civ 905; [2004] 1 W.L.R. 2557; [2005] 1 P. & C.R. 5

Marcic v Thames Water Utilities Ltd [2003] UKHL 66; [2004] 2 A.C. 42; [2004] Env. L.R. 25

Margate Town Centre Regeneration Co Ltd v Secretary of State for Communities and Local Government [2013] EWCA Civ 1178

Manchester Ship Canal Co Ltd v United Utilities Water Ltd [2022] EWCA Civ 852; [2023] Ch. 1; [2022] 3 W.L.R. 1193

Manchester Ship Canal Co Ltd v United Utilities Water Plc [2014] UKSC 40; [2014] 1 W.L.R. 2576; [2014] 3 E.G.L.R. 81

Pascoe v First Secretary of State [2006] EWHC 2356 (Admin); [2007] 1 W.L.R. 885; [2007] J.P.L. 607

R. (on the application of Begum) v Denbigh High School Governors [2006] UKHL 15; [2007] 1 A.C. 100; [2006] 2 W.L.R. 719

R. (on the application of Clays Lane Housing Cooperative Ltd) v Housing Corp [2004] EWCA Civ 1658; [2005] 1 W.L.R. 2229; [2005] H.L.R. 15

R. (on the application of Dolan) v Secretary of State for Health and Social Care [2020] EWCA Civ 1605; [2021] 1 W.L.R. 2326; (2021) 177 B.M.L.R. 35

R. (on the application of Friends of Antique Cultural Treasures Ltd) v Secretary of State for the Environment, Food and Rural Affairs [2020] EWCA Civ 649; [2020] 1 W.L.R. 3876; [2021] Env. L.R. 3

R. (on the application of Samaroo) v Secretary of State for the Home Department [2001] EWCA Civ 1139; [2001] U.K.H.R.R. 1150; [2002] I.N.L.R. 55

R. (on the application of TD) v Secretary of State for Work and Pensions [2020] EWCA Civ 618

R. v Secretary of State for Transport Ex p. De Rothschild (1989) 57 P. & C.R. 330; [1989] 06 E.G. 123; [1988] R.V.R. 200 CA (Civ Div)

Sporrong & Lonnroth v Sweden (A/52) (1983) 5 E.H.R.R. 35 ECHR

H8 **Legislation referred to:**
    ECHR art.1 Protocol 1
    Compulsory Purchase Act 1965 s.7
    Acquisition of Land Act 1981 ss.16 and 23 and Sch.3
    Water Industry Act 1991 ss.18, 22, 23, 94, 117, 154, 155, 159, 183 and 186 and
    Sch.12
    Environmental Permitting (England and Wales) Regulations 2016 (SI 2016/1154)
    regs 12 and 38 and Sch.5

H9 *C. Morgan* and *N. Ostrowski* (instructed by BDB Pitmans LLP) appeared on behalf
    of the claimant.
    G. Williams (instructed by the Government Legal Department) appeared on behalf
    of the first defendant.
    J. Strachan KC and *J. Darby* (instructed by Pinsent Masons) appeared on behalf
    of the second defendant.

JUDGMENT

THE HON. MRS JUSTICE THORNTON:

Introduction

1   The Manchester Ship Canal Company ("MSCC"), the owner, statutory undertaker
and navigation authority for the Manchester Ship Canal, challenges the decision
of the Secretary of State to confirm the United Utilities Water Limited (Eccles
Wastewater Treatment Works) Compulsory Purchase Order 2016 ("CPO"). The
CPO authorises the sewerage undertaker for the North West of England, United
Utilities ("UU"), to compulsorily discharge water, soil and effluent from its sewers
into the Manchester Ship Canal. The challenge is brought pursuant to section 23
Acquisition of Land Act 1981, which provides that a person aggrieved by a
compulsory purchase order can apply to the court to question the validity of the
order on the ground that there was no power to make it, or a relevant requirement
has not been complied with.

2   The need for the CPO arises because UU is responsible for the public sewerage
system in the North West of England which serves circa 7 million customers and
200,000 businesses. To meet its sewerage obligations, UU operates a Wastewater
Treatment Works at Eccles, which currently discharges treated wastewater into
Salteye Brook, a tributary of the Manchester Ship Canal. The brook also receives
the outflow from a combined sewer outfall at the inlet of the treatment works. In
order to satisfy regulatory standards, set by the Environment Agency for the brook,
and having considered various alternative options, UU proposes to discharge treated
wastewater and storm overflows directly into the Canal via a new outfall, rather
than into the brook. A gravity outfall pipe, approximately 1.16km long will be
constructed, to carry the final effluent from its treatment works to the new outfall,
which will sit within the canal bank.

3   Whilst UU has a statutory right, pursuant to section 159 of the Water Industry
Act ("WIA"), to lay its pipes across land without the need for landowner consent,
the new right to discharge into the Canal must be acquired either by agreement,
or, failing that, by compulsory acquisition under section 155 WIA.

4   Having failed to secure MSCC's agreement to the scheme, UU proceeded by way of compulsory purchase order which led to the convening of a public local inquiry by the Secretary of State, conducted by an Inspector, to consider objections to the CPO, primarily those of MSCC. The inquiry sat for 29 days.

5   For the majority of the inquiry, MSCC advanced an 'in-principle' objection to the Order; that is to say, its case was that the Order should not be confirmed at all. Shortly before the close of the inquiry, MSCC withdrew its principled objection. Accordingly, by the close of the inquiry, and to date, MSCC accepts that there is a 'compelling public interest' for UU to discharge into its Canal. However, before the Inspector, MSCC challenged the width of the order, describing it as 'an unfettered private law right for UU to discharge effluent in perpetuity in the Canal'.

6   At the end of the inquiry, the Inspector produced a 235 page report concluding that there was a compelling case in the public interest for authorising UU to discharge effluent into the Canal. The Secretary of State agreed and confirmed the CPO by decision letter dated 14 October 2021.

7   The Court was told that the CPO is the first made pursuant to section 155 of the WIA, so as to provide an express grant of authority to discharge water, soil and effluent for the benefit of a sewerage undertaker. MSCC says that the right of discharge into its Canal is the only one nationwide without specific statutory protection for the landowner. This is because the vast majority of discharges are implicitly authorised by the 1991 Act, subject to protection for the landowner via sections 117, 183 and Schedule 12 of the Act. It is these provisions that MSCC sought, unsuccessfully, at the public inquiry to include within the terms of the CPO. The Inspector recommended that the order be confirmed without the inclusion of the protective provisions (report dated 20 February 2020) and the Secretary of State agreed (decision letter dated 3 December 2020).

8   The grounds of challenge are as follows:

1. The Secretary of State and/or the Inspector misdirected themselves as to the proper legal and procedural context in which to evaluate and determine the inclusion of the protective provisions sought by MSCC, by concluding that the correct test was whether they were necessary.

2. The Secretary of State and/or the Inspector erred in law in their determination that the purposes for which the Order was made sufficiently justified the interference with MSCC's rights under Article 1 of the First Protocol to the European Convention on Human Rights. There were no countervailing considerations advanced by UU to those relied upon by MSCC and a fair balance required the inclusion of the protective provisions.

9   Except where expressly stated or apparent, references in the judgment below to the Inspector are to be read as also referring to the Secretary of State who agreed with the recommendation of the Inspector.

Background

The terms of the CPO

10   As confirmed, relevant extracts from the CPO provide that UU is authorised

> '...under section 155(1) and section 155(2)(a) of the Water Industry Act 1991 ...to purchase compulsorily the land and the new rights over land, each

described in paragraph 2 .... for the purposes of and in connection with the carrying out of its functions as a sewerage undertaker namely to lay and use a new pipeline for the benefit of the acquiring authority's undertaking generally and its land at Eccles Wastewater Treatment Works, for the discharge of water and effluent to the Manchester Ship Canal......'

11   The right under scrutiny is set out in a schedule, in relation to land referred to as Plots 6D, 6E and 6H, as follows:

'The right... to discharge water, soil and effluent from the sewers and outfall and groundwater into the Manchester Ship Canal...'

The protective provisions sought by MSCC

12   MSCC proposed protective provisions to be inserted into the terms of the CPO by way of an amendment to terms of the CPO, as follows:

'.... the rights hereby granted shall be subject to the provisions of Schedule 1 in order to protect the statutory undertaking of the Manchester Ship Canal Company Limited (MSCCL).'

13   Schedule 1 provides in material part:

'3. Any right to discharge "water soil and effluent" under this Order shall be subject to the following provisions of the Water Industry Act 1991 (or any re-enactment, replacement or amendment of those provisions), which shall apply as conditions to which the right to discharge is subject in the like manner as if the right arose impliedly under section 116 of the Water Industry Act 1991:
   a. Section 117(5)(a) and (b)
   b. Section 117(6)
   c. Section 186(1), (3), (6) and (7)
   d. Schedule 12 paragraph 4
   (the 'discharge proviso').'

14   Before the Inspector, MSCC referred to the collection of provisions as the 'discharge proviso'.

The legal framework

Compulsory purchase

15   Section 155 of the WIA provides as follows:

'155.—*Compulsory purchase.*
(1) *A relevant undertaker may be authorised by the Secretary of State to purchase compulsorily any land anywhere in England and Wales which is required by the undertaker for the purposes of, or in connection with, the carrying out of its functions.*
(2) *The power of the Secretary of State under subsection (1) above shall include power—*
   (a) *to authorise the acquisition of interests in and rights over land by the creation of new interests and rights.'*

16   Section 154(4) WIA provides that the statutory procedure set out in the Acquisition of Land Act 1981 applies to a CPO under section 155. This includes a test of serious detriment for acquisition of a right over a statutory undertaker's land (paragraph 3 in Part II of Schedule 3 to the 1981 Act).

17   Government guidance on compulsory purchase provides as follows at paragraphs 12 and 13:

> '**12 *How does an acquiring authority justify a compulsory purchase order?***
> *There are certain fundamental principles that a confirming minister should consider when deciding whether or not to confirm a compulsory purchase order*
>
> ......
>
> *A compulsory purchase order should only be made where there is a compelling case in the public interest.*
> *An acquiring authority should be sure that the purposes for which the compulsory purchase order is made justify interfering with the human rights of those with an interest in the land affected. Particular consideration should be given to the provisions of Article 1 of the First Protocol to the European Convention on Human Rights*
>
> ......
>
> **13. *How will the confirming minister consider the acquiring authority's justification for a compulsory purchase order?***
> *The minister confirming the order has to be able to take a balanced view between the intentions of the acquiring authority and the concerns of those with an interest in the land that it is proposing to acquire compulsorily and the wider public interest. The more comprehensive the justification which the acquiring authority can present, the stronger its case is likely to be.*'

18   Once a CPO is confirmed, the Secretary of State's decision to do so is open to challenge in the courts on limited grounds, analogous to those of a judicial review. The principles of review of a compulsory purchase order were laid down by Elias LJ in *Margate Town Centre Regeneration Ltd v Secretary of State for Communities and Local Government* [2013] EWCA Civ 1178:

> '**17. *The applicable law is not in dispute and so I will summarise the relevant principles briefly.***
> a) *A CPO should only be made where there is a compelling case in the public interest. An acquiring authority should be sure that the purposes for which it is making a CPO sufficiently justify interfering with the human rights of those with an interest in the land affected.*
> b) *A consequence of principle (a) is that "the draconian nature of the order will itself render it more vulnerable to successful challenge on Wednesbury/ Ashbridge grounds unless sufficient reasons are adduced affirmatively to justify it on the merits."*
> c) *The grounds of challenge under section 23 do not entitle the court to revisit the merits of the decision, only to see whether there is any legal or procedural error in the confirmation.*

d) *When deciding whether or not to confirm an order, the Secretary of State must have regard to all material considerations and must not take into account immaterial considerations. But it is for the court to decide what are material considerations.*

e) *The reasons for a decision must be intelligible and adequate. In determining whether those criteria are satisfied the decision letter must be read fairly as a whole, as if by a well-informed reader.*

f) *The Court should interfere only if the decision leaves a "genuine as opposed to a forensic doubt" as to what has been decided and why.*

g) *Where a decision maker has erred in law the decision should be quashed unless the court is satisfied that the decision maker would necessarily have made the same decision had the error not been made.'*

The legal provisions which formed the discharge proviso sought by MSCC before the Inspector

19   At the inquiry, MSCC proposed that UU's right of discharge be subject to sections 117(5), (6), 186(1)(3), (6) and (7) and Schedule 12 paragraph 4 of the WIA. These provisions provide as follows:

20   Section 117(5) and (6) WIA provides:

> '(5) *Nothing in sections 102 to 109 above or in sections 111 to 116 above shall be construed as authorising a sewerage undertaker to construct or use any public or other sewer, or any drain or outfall –*
>
> > a. *in contravention of any applicable provision of the Water Resources Act 1991 or the Environmental Permitting (England and Wales) Regulations 2016 (5.1. 2016/1154); or*
> >
> > b. *for the purpose of conveying foul water into any natural or artificial stream, watercourse, canal, pond or lake, without the water having been so treated as not to affect prejudicially the purity and quality of the water in the stream, watercourse, canal, pond or lake.*
>
> > (6) *A sewerage undertaker shall so carry out its functions under sections 102 to 105, 112, 115 and 116 above as not to create a nuisance.'*

21   Section 186(1)(3)(6) and (7) WIA provides as follows:

> **'186 —Protective provisions in respect of flood defence works and watercourses etc.**
>
> (1) *Nothing in this Act shall confer power on any person to do anything, except with the consent of the person who so uses them, which interferes—*
>
> > a. *with any sluices, floodgates, groynes, sea defences or other works used by any person for draining, preserving or improving any land under any local statutory provision; or*
> >
> > b. *with any such works used by any person for irrigating any land.*
>
> …
>
> (3) *Nothing in the relevant sewerage provisions shall authorise a sewerage undertaker injuriously to affect—(a) any reservoir, canal, watercourse, river or stream, or any feeder thereof; or (b) the supply, quality or fall of water contained in, or in any feeder of, any reservoir, canal, watercourse, river or*

stream, without the consent of any person who would, apart from this Act, have been entitled by law to prevent, or be relieved against, the injurious affection of, or of the supply, quality or fall of water contained in, that reservoir, canal, watercourse, river, stream or feeder.

…

(6) A consent for the purposes of subsection (1) above may be given subject to reasonable conditions but shall not be unreasonably withheld.

(7)

> *Any dispute—*
>   a. *as to whether anything done or proposed to be done interferes or will interfere as mentioned in subsection (1) above;*
>   b. *as to whether any consent for the purposes of this section is being unreasonably withheld;*
>   c. *as to whether any condition subject to which any such consent has been given was reasonable; or*
>   d. *as to whether the supply, quality or fall of water in any reservoir, canal, watercourse, river, stream or feeder is injuriously affected by the exercise of powers under the relevant sewerage provisions, shall be referred (in the case of a dispute falling within paragraph (d) above, at the option of the party complaining) to the arbitration of a single arbitrator to be appointed by agreement between the parties or, in default of agreement, by the President of the Institution of Civil Engineers."*

22   Schedule 12 paragraph (4) provides as follows:

> '(1) *Subject to the following provisions of this paragraph, a sewerage undertaker shall make full compensation to any person who has sustained damage by reason of the exercise by the undertaker, in relation to a matter as to which that person has not himself been in default, of any of its powers under the relevant sewerage provisions.*
>
> (2) *Subject to sub-paragraph (3) below, any dispute arising under this paragraph as to the fact of damage, or as to the amount of compensation, shall be referred to the arbitration of a single arbitrator appointed by agreement between the parties to the dispute or, in default of agreement, by the Authority.*
>
> (3) *If the compensation claimed under this paragraph in any case does not exceed £5,000, all questions as to the fact of damage, liability to pay compensation and the amount of compensation may, be referred to the Authority for determination under section 30A of this Act by either party.*
>
> …
>
> (5) *No person shall be entitled by virtue of this paragraph to claim compensation on the ground that a sewerage undertaker has, in the exercise of its powers under the relevant sewerage provisions, declared any sewer, lateral drain or sewage disposal works, whether belonging to that person or not, to be vested in the undertaker.'*

23   It was common ground that 'relevant sewerage provisions' does not extend to section 155 of the WIA (see section 219).

The Inspector's report

24   The Inspector's report sets out a detailed summary of the cases of UU and MSCC (pages 4-179). At the start of his summary of UU's case, the Inspector states that *'the case set out below is an edited summary of the Acquiring Authority's closing submissions… The text below omits matters such as…compensation, which would be a matter for the Upper Tribunal.'* (§15).

25   The summary of each party's case is followed by a shorter section on the Inspector's conclusions, which cross refers to relevant aspects of the case of each party. The Inspector directs himself that the statutory authority for the acquisition is section 155 WIA and addresses the test set out in the CPO guidance as follows (the numbers in square brackets refer to relevant paragraphs of the Inspector's summary of the case for each party):

> '848   …*Much of the advice within the CPO guidance refers to land acquisition under s.226(1)(a) of the Town and Country Planning Act 1990. While this Order is made under s.155 of the 1991 Act, the CPO guidance is nonetheless relevant to the compulsory acquisition of land and rights within the Order. Paragraph 2 of the CPO Guidance states that:*
>
> > a. *An Acquiring Authority should use CPO powers where it is expedient to do so, but a CPO should only be made where there is a compelling case in the public interest;*
> > b. *An Acquiring Authority will be expected to demonstrate that they have taken reasonable steps to acquire all of the land and rights included in the Order by agreement.*
> > c. *Acquiring authorities and authorising authorities should be sure that the purposes for which the compulsory purchase order is made justify interfering with the human rights of those with an interest in the land affected. [437, 438]*
>
> 849. *Paragraph 12 of the CPO Guidance restates points a) and c) as being fundamental principles that an Acquiring Authority should address to justify a CPO. Guidance in paragraph 13 confirms the need for it to be shown that sufficient resources would be available to deliver the scheme. [439, 440]'*

26   The Inspector also notes the test of serious detriment for the acquisition of a right over a statutory undertaker's land before saying

> *'However, before addressing these fundamental matters, I shall deal with the detailed terms of the Order that remain in dispute between the two remaining parties…'*(§853).

27   He addresses various matters in dispute as to the terms of the order before turning to the protective provisions under scrutiny before the Court, which he addresses as follows:

> **'*Dispute over the Discharge Proviso***
> 908. *MSCCL have proposed the inclusion of a discharge proviso… In doing so, MSCCL notes that the justification for the discharge proviso is independent from the evidence that had been heard during the Inquiry as the protections*

it seeks to provide are already a matter of general law. However, the evidence to the Inquiry includes the Acquiring Authority's case, which is the basis of its view that the discharge proviso is not required. [409-411, 738]

909. *The Acquiring Authority is unambiguous that it is the right to discharge that resulted in the need for this Inquiry as other matters could have been addressed through the powers provided under s.159 of the 1991 Act. The company is also clear in its view that MSCCL's proposed discharge proviso is an unnecessary addition to the Order, not least as any discharge would be regulated. Water quality in the Canal and other watercourses that feed into it, such as Salteye Brook, are regulated by the Environment Agency. Also, the Acquiring Authority has dealt with the meaning of s.186 of the 1991 Act, including its application as set out in s.186(1). Consequently, the discharge proviso's reference to s.186 of the 1991 Act would seek to duplicate the regulation that already applies to these watercourses and would do to the proposed outfall. And in any event, and as set out in the detailed legal view provided at paragraph 415 of this report, it has not been shown that s.186 is applicable to the Order Scheme. [48, 72, 74, 102, 137-140, 298, 299, 406-408, 411- 413, 415, 434, 547, 550, 737, 738, 740-777, 815, 824]*

910. *Turning to the discharge proviso's reference to s.117(5) and (6) of the 1991 Act. The Acquiring Authority notes: this Inquiry to have provided the independent scrutiny sought of the potential interference with private rights resulting from acquisition under s.155; that s.117 is intended to be applied to rights exercisable through other sections of the 1991 Act, rather than s.155 which is the subject of this Inquiry; the relevance of environmental permitting as set out above; that as a result of these, constraining a private right would be unnecessary; and, the proviso would be unreasonable and unnecessary as the water quality evidence that sought to support it has been abandoned. I find the Acquiring Authority's arguments on this matter to be convincing. [408, 413, 414, 737, 738, 740-777]*

911. *The Acquiring Authority has also addressed the proposed inclusion of reference to Schedule 12(4) of the 1991 Act in the discharge proviso and noted MSCCL's previous query regarding Schedule 12's relevance for its protection. It is clear from paragraph 1 of Schedule 12, that Schedule 12 protections do not apply to s.155 of the 1991 Act and were not intended to be used as MSCCL propose in its Schedule 1 to the Order (MP/INQ/71.1). As noted above, discharges from the new outfall would be regulated by the Environment Agency and be the subject of an environmental permit. In addition, compensation would be payable for any damage sustained from the Order Scheme. Accordingly, paragraph 3 should be deleted from Schedule 1 of MSCCL's proposed protective provisions. [416-421, 743-760]'*

28   The Inspector then turns to consider the justification for the order. He notes that the starting point for justification is the test in section 155(1) WIA, namely, that the order is required by the undertaker for the purposes of, or in connection with, the carrying out of its functions. He observes that the Inquiry heard extensive evidence from UU regarding the background to the Order Scheme and the regulatory environment that has shaped UU's decision making (912). He goes on to set out the relevant evidence as follows:

'914. *The Acquiring Authority is the statutory water and sewerage undertaker for the North West of England and is obliged to drain its areas and to meet regulatory requirements for its discharge. The Order Scheme is part of the ongoing investment to improve quality of water courses in the catchment, including Salteye Brook. It was the EA's preferred option to divert the Eccles WwTW's final effluent discharges from Salteye Brook to the Canal to improve the water quality in Salteye Brook. The Order Scheme would achieve this through a gravity system that reduces the need for pumping. [17, 25, 30, 44, 47, 73-83, 101, 104, 105, 116-118, 145, 164, 173-193, 422, 423, 427, 431]*

915. *Environmental regulation of the Acquiring Authority's operations is closely aligned with the economic regulation of the company. This has provided the Acquiring Authority with clear objectives for improving the drainage of its areas. The works that are needed to meet those objectives are planned within the context of the company's five-year AMP cycle. Requests to change the 28 February 2015 date for meeting the EA's regulatory objectives have been turned down, and the missed regulatory delivery date is a matter that highlights the Order Scheme is required. [74, 102, 104-108, 120-122]*

......

918. *Alternative options have been considered by the Acquiring Authority, and suggested during the Inquiry. None have been shown to be preferable to the Order Scheme for the meeting of current regulatory requirements. There is no remaining objection in relation to alternatives. [115, 116-120, 140-144, 150, 432, 433, 824]'*

29   His conclusion on the requirement for the proposed scheme is as follows:

'924. *The Order Scheme is required to enable the delivery of the Full Scheme and the public interest (and environmental) benefits that would be realised by completing the Full Scheme. In doing so, the Order Scheme would provide necessary infrastructure that would enable regulatory objectives for Eccles WwTW to be met. [422, 423, 427, 430, 461-463]*

...

926. *The evidence, and the testing of it during the Inquiry, demonstrated that: there is a clear regulatory (and environmental) requirement for the Order Scheme; it is the most appropriate option for meeting that need; ....*

927. *Consequently the Order Scheme and the lands within it, subject to amendments detailed in the Annex below, meet the requirement test in s.155(1) of the 1991 Act.'*

30   He applies, by analogy, the CPO guidance on acquisition of land by local authorities for planning purposes relevant to justification, (paragraphs 104 – 106 of the guidance), and concludes that the purpose of the CPO fits within the adopted planning framework; there are no impediments to implementation; the purpose for which UU is proposing to acquire the land could not be achieved by any other means and the project is financially viable.

31   He then turns to consider the public interest as follows:

'Compelling case in the public interest

938. *Paragraph 2 of the CPO Guidance confirms that an Acquiring Authority should use CPO powers where it is expedient to do so, but a CPO should only be made where there is a compelling case in the public interest. While MSCCL has raised concerns on two matters, which are dealt with above, no objector now disputes the need for the Order or the compelling case in the public interest for it to be confirmed. [24, 424, 437-439, 441, 523]*

939. *Paragraph 106 of the CPO Guidance confirms the factors the Secretary of State will take into account in decisions on whether to confirm a CPO to include the extent to which the proposed purpose will contribute to the achievement of the promotion or improvement of the economic, social or environmental wellbeing of the area. These matters were addressed by the Acquiring Authority's evidence in this case and are summarised in my conclusions on 'Requirement' above. [425- 429]*

940. *As set out above, alternatives to the Order Scheme have been explored, both in terms of: the method by which regulatory and environmental objectives would be met; and for the option chosen, the broad design principles for what is now proposed. [432, 433, 445-455]*

941. *The Inquiry heard extensive evidence regarding: the operation of the Eccles WwTW; the steps taken to improve the quality of water courses in the catchment that includes the Canal and Salteye Brook; and, how the Order Scheme would contribute to the economic, social and environmental well-being of the area. The Order Scheme would provide the improvements in water quality sought for Salteye Brook, and while the new outfall would discharge directly into the Canal, it would nonetheless have an overall beneficial effect on the Canal and the environment around it. [33, 47, 117-120, 124, 456-463, 824]*

942. *In addition to the environmental improvements in relation to water quality, the proposed option would be a better use of resources that would result in economic benefits for both the undertaker and its customers. The astute and convincing fiscal argument for the chosen option, along with the resulting efficient use of resources, would result in social benefits from economic efficiency, and that would be expected to be reflected in reduced bills to the Acquiring Authority's customers. Social benefit would also be derived from a reduction in the level of flood risk to properties on Peel Green Road that connect to the sewer network upstream of Eccles WwTW. [30, 114, 151, 152, 164, 168, 171, 433, 452, 824]*

943. *Given the Acquiring Authority's statutory function, and the regulatory requirements it seeks to meet through the Order Scheme, a compelling case in the public interest has been clearly made for confirmation of the Order. [16-19, 25, 29, 30, 75-83, 422-436, 480, 495, 824].'*

32   His report concludes by addressing human rights:

'Human Rights

944. *Paragraph 2 of the CPO Guidance confirms that when making or confirming an order "...acquiring authorities and authorising authorities should be sure that the purposes for which the compulsory purchase order is made justify interfering with the human rights of those with an interest in the land affected...".*

945. The Acquiring Authority draws attention to benefits that would result from the Order Scheme, including: addressing the need to improve the water quality of Salteye Brook; provision of upgraded sewerage infrastructure next to a regionally significant site; and benefits for the locality, which would include flood risk in the Peel Green Road area. Further details on the Order Scheme's social, economic and environmental benefits are set out above. Also, compensation would be available to those entitled to it.

946. The evidence, along with exchanges during the Inquiry and submissions to it, demonstrate that the Acquiring Authority has considered realistic alternative approaches that were discounted for various reasons and eventually led to selection of the option that is the Order Scheme. In regard to the European Convention on Human Rights and the Human Rights Act 1998, it is apparent that the benefits of the Order Scheme, which would be gained through the purposes for which the compulsory purchase order is made, would justify any interference in interests otherwise protected by Convention rights. [Section 13 of the SoR CD/CPO/3, 474-477]'

The Secretary of State's decision

33   In a "minded to" letter, dated 3 December 2020, the Secretary of State said:

'...the Secretary of State agrees that the requirement for the discharge proviso is unnecessary because [—] the discharge will be regulated by the Environment Agency. In addition, compensation is payable for any damages sustained by the order scheme.'

34   Turning to human rights, the letter stated:

'13. The Secretary of State has carefully considered whether the purposes for which the compulsory purchase order was made sufficiently justify interfering with the human rights of the objectors under section 12(2A) of the Acquisition of Land Act 1981 and he is satisfied that such interference is justified. In particular he has considered the provisions of Article 1 of the First Protocol to, the European Convention on Human Rights. In this respect the Secretary of State is satisfied that in confirming the compulsory purchase order a fair balance would be struck between the public interest and interests of the objectors.'

35   By decision letter dated 14 October 2021, it was said:

'The Secretary of State has carefully considered whether the purposes for which the compulsory purchase order was made sufficiently justify interfering with the human rights of the objectors under section 12(2A) of the Acquisition of Land Act 1981 and he is satisfied that such interference is justified. In particular he has considered the provisions of Article 1 of the First Protocol to, the European Convention on Human Rights. In this respect the Secretary of State is satisfied that in confirming the compulsory purchase order a fair balance would be struck between the public interest and interests of the objectors.'(§8)

Ground 1 Erroneous application of a test of necessity

36   MSCC's overarching case on Ground 1 is that the Inspector erroneously applied a test of necessity in deciding not to include the discharge proviso within the terms of the CPO. More particularly, MSCC alleges seven specific errors in the decision making, as follows:

1. The Inspector treated the issue as being one as to which MSCC bore a persuasive burden whereas, the issue having been raised, the correct approach in law was to impose upon UU as the Acquiring Authority the burden of demonstrating why it needed an unlimited right uncircumscribed by the discharge proviso.

2. The Inspector accordingly disregarded as irrelevant the fact that UU did not advance any positive argument in favour of the grant of a wider right and confined its submissions to criticism of MSCC's case, which did not include any suggestion that the inclusion of the discharge proviso would in any respect undermine the purposes and objective of the scheme underlying the Order.

3. The Inspector construed the protections afforded by the discharge proviso as being equivalent to and no greater than the protection afforded by the regulation of the discharge by the Environment Agency (and accordingly unnecessary since they would add nothing to that method of control), despite the fact that in the 1991 Act Parliament had expressly imposed equivalent provisos upon all similar discharges made pursuant to implied statutory power, notwithstanding that all such discharges would likewise be regulated by the Environment Agency.

4. The Inspector treated the compensation provisions of the compulsory purchase code as being apt and sufficient to compensate MSCC for the injuries and losses whose actionability the discharge proviso would have expressly preserved, whereas the compulsory purchase code is not intended to provide, and does not provide, a substitute for private law remedies for intermittent future injury caused by the exercise of any right granted.

5. The Inspector treated as a material counter-argument to the inclusion of the discharge proviso, the fact that the 1991 Act did not apply the statutory provisos to the operation of section 155, whereby the Secretary of State was empowered in general terms to authorise the compulsory purchase of land by inter alia sewerage undertakers;

6. The Inspector treated the scrutiny of the scheme afforded by the compulsory purchase code, and in particular the process of the Inquiry, as rendering the protections afforded by the discharge proviso unnecessary or otiose.

7. The Inspector treated as a material counter-argument to the inclusion of the discharge proviso the fact that on the evidence the discharge as currently proposed would not be deleterious to water quality in the Canal.

Discussion of Ground 1

The discharge proviso sought by MSCC before the Inspector

37   Before the Inspector, MSCC sought the inclusion of sections 117 (5)(a) and (b); 117(6); 186(1), (3), (6) and (7) and Schedule 12 paragraph, 4 WIA in the terms of

the CPO. The provisions were presented, in effect, as a package of measures. MSCC did not order the provisions in any sort of hierarchy or suggest alternative approaches. Taken together, in broad terms, they provide that the sewerage undertaker is not authorised to use the outfall in breach of any environmental regulation or so as to 'affect prejudicially the purity and quality of the water' or so as to 'injuriously affect' the receiving water. The sewerage undertaker must not create a nuisance. The landowner's consent is required for certain works. Full compensation for 'damage' sustained by a person by reason of the exercise of the undertaker's powers is payable. I have not been pointed to any discussion before the Inspector as to the practicalities of how the provisions, which may be said to form their own complex interlocking scheme of regulation, would operate, alongside the grant of authority to UU to discharge 'water, soil and effluent from the sewers and outfall and groundwater into Manchester Ship Canal'. There do not appear to have been any detailed discussions or negotiations between the parties as to the machinery of the provisions, as might have been expected given the terms of the CPO were the only outstanding issue by the end of the inquiry. As examples; there appears to be the potential for conflict between the grant of a right to UU to discharge effluent into the Canal and section 117(5)(b) which provides that an undertaker is not authorised to convey 'foul water' without treatment. It is not clear how the broad concepts of 'injuriously to affect' or 'prejudicially to affect' would be interpreted. It is not clear whether, in the event of an alleged 'injurious affection' of the canal, the proviso would enable MSCC to seek an interim injunction, to shut down UU's operations pending resolution of the dispute between the parties.

MSCC's case before the Inspector

38   In closing submissions to the inquiry, MSCC made its case in relation to the inclusion of the provisions as follows. Its case was said to be 'independent' of the evidence before the inquiry, including the water quality evidence as to the impacts of the proposed scheme. It was said to rest on parity with the application of the provisions to pre-1991 implied rights of discharge under the Act (it was common ground that the provisions apply to an implied right to discharge). Without the proviso, it was said, UU's discharge to the Canal would be the only one nationwide not to include protective provisions for the benefit of the landowner. The right to discharge would be expressed in the widest possible terms. MSCC drew a contrast, in this regard, with the position in the absence of a CPO where use of a new outfall would require the consent of the owner of the receiving watercourse and the need for consent would itself enable the owner to '*...to regulate carefully the parameters of the outfall and the discharges from it, by reference to the location and dimensions of the outfall and the flows, total volumes and constituency of the discharges through it.*' The lack of parity with an implied right to discharge was said to present an anomaly that could not be justified in the public interest. A similar reference to public interest considerations appears at §236 of the submissions. UU had not justified why it needed such a broad unlimited right to discharge or why there is a compelling case in the public interest for such a right. There was no good reason why the more restricted right proposed by MSCC was not sufficient and it was for UU to demonstrate a compelling case in the public interest for the full extent of the right it sought.

39   MSCC further submitted that the additional layer of statutory protection offered by section 117(5)(b) is to be regarded as separate from and additional to the controls set out in the environmental permitting regime. The drafting of section 117(5) makes clear that the protection afforded by sub-paragraph (b) is in addition to the protection afforded by sub-paragraph (a). The arguments in relation to section 117(6) were said to be essentially the same.

40   It was said that if the terms of the order were given literal effect:

> '...it is an entirely unfettered private law right for UUWL to discharge, in perpetuity, whatever it sees fit into the Canal, including (by way of example) unlimited quantities of entirely untreated raw sewage. No limitation on that right is proposed on the face of the draft Order, either in terms of what may be discharged, the frequency and volume of discharge, or its effects on the Canal. Indeed there is nothing expressed on the face of the order to prevent UUWL in the future from enlarging without limit the outfall and the pipework serving it'(§235 closing submissions).

41   As regards the ability of a landowner to take action to enforce the protection provided, the following was said:

> **'Issues as to enforcement of statutory protections**
> 253. Arguments as to whether or not the owner of a receiving watercourse would or would not themselves be able to take legal action to enforce certain of these statutory protections (the subject of separate legal dispute between the parties) are irrelevant for present purposes. If there are disputes about those matters they are for another day and another forum. Parliament has created the protections and considered them to be appropriate in the public interest regardless of who would ultimately prove to be the person or body able to enforce them. The answer to that question does not detract from their appropriateness for implied rights to discharge and equally it does not detract from their appropriateness in relation to rights to discharge acquired by compulsion.'

An unfettered private law right for UU to discharge effluent in perpetuity

42   MSCC's characterisation of the right granted by the CPO as "an unfettered private law right for UU to discharge effluent in perpetuity into the Canal" ignores the statutory context in which the right was granted; the process by which it was granted and the economic and environmental regulation of UU. In turn, these factors provide necessary context to assess the Inspector's decision and the alleged errors in his decision-making.

43   It is apparent from the relevant paragraphs of the Inspector's report that his reasons for considering the proviso to be unnecessary include: that the discharge will be regulated by the Environment Agency; the public inquiry had provided an opportunity for an independent scrutiny of the potential interference with MSCC's rights; the legal provisions within the discharge proviso do not apply to a right granted under section 155 WIA; the water quality evidence demonstrated a beneficial impact on the water quality of the Canal and compensation would be payable for any damage sustained (§908-911).

The statutory context underpinning the provision of sewerage services

44   Sewage disposal and drainage have been the subject of statutory regulation for 500 years. The current legislation comprises the Water Industry Act 1991 and was analysed by the House of Lords in *Marcic v Thames Water* [2003] UKHL 66 at §11 onwards.

45   UU carries on its business as a sewerage undertaker within the statutory framework of the WIA, which lays down the powers and duties of sewerage undertakers. In particular, section 94 of the Act sets out the principal general duty on every sewerage undertaker to ensure its area is properly drained, by providing an appropriate system of sewers:

> '(1) *It shall be the duty of every sewerage undertaker—*
>> (i) *to provide, improve and extend such a system of public sewers (whether inside its area or elsewhere) and so to cleanse and maintain those sewers as to ensure that that area is and continues to be effectually drained...'*

46   An undertaker's duty under s94 is enforceable by the Water Service Regulation Authority (Ofwat), the regulator of the water and sewerage industry, through the imposition of enforcement orders pursuant to section 18 of the WIA. A company is required to comply with an enforcement order (section 18(5)). A contravention of a statutory requirement to which section 18 applies does not necessarily result in an enforcement order. As an example, the sewerage undertaker may put matters right pursuant to an undertaking, or Ofwat may conclude that other considerations, to which the regulator is obliged to have regard, militate against the making of an order. Where contravention of a statutory requirement is enforceable under section 18, section 18(8) limits the availability of other remedies:

> '(8) *Where any act or omission constitutes a contravention of ... a statutory or other requirement enforceable under this section, the only remedies for that contravention, apart from those available by virtue of this section, shall be those for which express provision is made by or under any enactment and those that are available in respect of that act or omission otherwise than by virtue of its constituting such a contravention.'*

47   Pursuant to section 22 WIA, a company's obligation to comply with an enforcement order is 'a duty owed to any person who may be affected by a contravention of the order'. A breach of this duty causing loss or damage to the person to whom the duty is owed is actionable at the suit of that person. In any ensuing court proceedings, the company has a 'due diligence' defence. An enforcement order is also enforceable by civil proceedings brought by the Director for an injunction or other appropriate relief.

Compulsory purchase under section 155 WIA

48   Sewerage undertakers are provided with various powers under the 1991 Act to enable them to fulfil their statutory functions. These include the power to lay and maintain pipes under private land under section 159 and, of particular relevance for present purposes, the power of compulsory purchase under section 155 WIA.

The latter power extends, not just to the acquisition of land, but also to the creation of new interests and rights.

49   A compulsory purchase order should only be made where there is a 'compelling case in the public interest' (Compulsory Purchase Order Guidance paragraph 12 and *Margate Town Centre Regeneration Ltd v Secretary of State for Communities and Local Government* [2013] EWCA Civ 1178 at (§17)). By the end of the inquiry, MSCC did not dispute that there was a compelling case in the public interest for the Order. The Inspector and Secretary of State concluded to the same effect.

50   Section 155(4) WIA applies the procedure for compulsory purchase set down in the Acquisition of Land Act 1981 to an order under section 155 WIA. When an order is made, notice is given to owners and occupiers who have a specified timescale in which to object. If objections are received a public inquiry will be held at which any objector may be heard. The acquiring authority must make good its case in support of the acquisition by fully detailed evidence which can be challenged by the landowner. It is at this stage that the merits of the proposed acquisition are examined and assessed. A Ministerial decision to give authority for the compulsory acquisition will generally be based on the facts found and recorded in the report produced by the Inspector following the inquiry.

51   The nature of the public inquiry into a CPO was explored by the Court of Appeal in *R. v Secretary of State for Transport Ex p. De Rothschild* (1989) 57 P. & C.R. 330. The Secretary of State's decision to confirm a CPO is not a hearing simply between the parties. In the event of objections, it follows a public inquiry at which the acquiring authority and the objectors are present and put forward their cases. There is also an unseen party who is vitally interested and is not represented. It is the public at large. It is the duty of the Secretary of State to have regard to the public interest. In making his decision, there are a multitude of different and competing factors which the Secretary of State has to take into account and into the balance of the decision making. All the facts and arguments are investigated and ultimately the decision maker performs a balancing exercise, balancing factors against each other which are not all compatible; and cannot be the subject of direct comparison. These principles are reflected in the Government's CPO guidance, cited by the Inspector in his report, which provides that the minister confirming the order has to be able to take a balanced view between the intentions of the acquiring authority and the concerns of those with an interest in the land that it is proposing to acquire compulsorily and the wider public interest (paragraph 13 of the CPO Guidance).

Economic regulation of UU

52   Economic regulation of UU is provided by Ofwat. The role of Ofwat is set out in the WIA and includes; protecting the interests of customers and promoting competition; ensuring water companies can finance their statutory functions; and securing long term resilience of companies' water and wastewater systems so that they are able, in the long term, to meet customers' expectations of the service.

Environmental regulation of UU

53   Environmental regulation of UU is of particular relevance to the issues raised by the challenge. It is principally provided by the Environment Agency, which participates in the process of regulation by Ofwat, but also sets relevant

environmental restrictions on UU's activities. The Agency is responsible for implementing, monitoring and enforcing the Environmental Permitting (England and Wales) Regulations 2016 (S.I. 2016/1154). The reason UU has found it necessary to seek the right to discharge into the Canal is because its discharges into Salteye Brook are not meeting the requisite environmental standards set by the Agency. Going forwards, UU will be required to obtain an environmental permit in respect of any discharge from the new pipe and outfall into the Canal. Under the 2016 Regulations:

> '12.   (1) *A person must not, except under and to the extent authorised by an environmental permit*
> > (a) *operate a regulated facility, or*
> > (b) *cause or knowingly permit a water discharge activity or groundwater activity.' (Regulation 12)*

54   The terms of an environmental permit are determined by the Environment Agency pursuant to Schedule 5 of the Regulations and may cover the quality and volume of the discharged effluent and the circumstances in which it is permitted to occur. The permit will enable ongoing supervision and control of the discharge of effluent into the Canal. In the event of any failure to comply with the permit there are a range of enforcement measures, including revocation of permits and prosecution. Any entry or discharge of poisonous, noxious or polluting matter or of sewage or trade effluent to waters is a criminal offence unless done under and in accordance with an environmental permit (Regulations 12 and 38).

Parity of landowner protection: implied and express right to discharge (Errors 3 and 5)

55   Before the Inspector MSCC's case for inclusion of the proviso was based, in large part, on a point of general principle, namely that it should have parity of protection with the protection available to a landowner under an implied right to discharge under the WIA, which is the basis for the existing discharge into Salteye Brook. This principle underlies Errors 3 and 5.

56   Under the WIA, there is, however, a material distinction between an express and implied right to discharge effluent. As was common ground, the various provisions of the WIA which comprises the discharge proviso, do not apply to the grant of a right pursuant to section 155 WIA. Parliament has therefore seen fit to exclude them.

57   An explanation for the distinction is provided by the Supreme Court in *Manchester Ship Canal Ltd v United Utilities Water Plc* [2014] UKSC 40, a case in which MSCC sought damages for trespass in respect of UU's discharges from its outfalls into its canals. UU applied for summary judgment on the basis that on privatisation of the water industry it inherited a pre-existing implied statutory power to discharge into private watercourses without the owner's consent. The Supreme Court held that a general right to discharge into private watercourses could not be implied in the WIA 1991 but the Act implicitly authorised the continued use of existing sewers since otherwise it would be impossible for undertakers to lawfully perform their functions. In his judgment Lord Sumption explained the rationale for the distinction and made specific reference to the position where, as in the

present case, the undertaker, proposes to bring an outfall into use for the first time after December 1991:

> '17 ... *A sewerage undertaker bringing an outfall into use for the first time after 1 December 1991 can reasonably be expected to have obtained any necessary consents to discharge onto private property in advance of laying the pipes, either by negotiation or by compulsory purchase in the course of the planning or the works. But if the outfall was already in use at that date, it cannot do this. The pipes will already have been laid. The location of their outfalls will have been determined.....'*

The importance of the inquiry process (Error 6)

58   As alluded to by Lord Sumption in his analysis above, the process by which an Order under section 155 is obtained enables a case by case assessment of the appropriate protection for a landowner. This takes place either by consensual negotiation or by way of public inquiry. The latter provides a landowner whose interests will be affected by the order with the opportunity to raise objections which are independently scrutinised by an Inspector. The Inspector balances the interests of the landowner in question against the intentions of the acquiring authority, the concerns of other objectors (if any) and the wider public interest.

59   The Inspector was alive to the role of the inquiry, as is apparent from his reference to '*this Inquiry to have provided the independent scrutiny sought of the potential interference with private rights resulting from acquisition under s.155; that s.117 is intended to be applied to rights exercisable through other sections of the 1991 Act, rather than s.155 which is the subject of this Inquiry;'* (§909). There is therefore no error of law in him treating the scrutiny of the scheme afforded by the inquiry process as significant (Error 6).

The significance of environmental regulation (Error 3)

60   MSCC seeks to criticise the Inspector for construing the protection afforded by the proviso as equivalent to the regulation of the discharge by the Environment Agency (Error 3). This criticism seeks to downplay the precise and detailed system of control provided by the environmental regulation of UU's activities (see above).

61   Moreover, in closing submissions, to the Inspector, MSCC highlighted the position without a CPO in place, where the owner of a receiving watercourse could, it was said, '...<u>regulate carefully</u> *the parameters of the outfall and the discharges from it, by reference to the location and dimensions of the outfall and the flows, total volumes and constituency of the discharges through it*'. (underlining is Court's emphasis). The implication of the submission appears to be that MSCC ought to exercise some form of supervisory control over UU activities. This would be to subject UU to two 'regulators'- regulation by the Environment Agency, operating a detailed and precise regulatory regime and regulation by MSCC operating via statutory provisions expressed in loose terms with next to no machinery for their effect and operation. Given the litigious history between MSCC and UU, the result could produce uncertainty for UU which has a statutory duty under the WIA to provide a public sewerage system in the North West of England. Accordingly, there is no error in the Inspector placing weight on the Environment Agency

regulating the discharge, over and above the 'regulation' afforded by the discharge proviso.

The relevance of the water quality impact of the scheme (Error 7)

62   I am not persuaded of any error of law in the Inspector treating as material the evidence that the discharge will not be deleterious to water quality in the Canal (Error 7). There is an obvious rationale for the Inspector to take account of the evidence given the provisions sought by MSCC are directed in large part to the impact on the receiving water. The inquiry looked in detail at the water quality evidence before MSCC withdrew its objection to the evidence. In this respect the Inspector was doing no more than considering the evidence and balancing the relevant factors (*R. v Secretary of State for Transport Ex p. De Rothschild* (1989) 57 P. & C.R. 330 and paragraph 13 of the Guidance). The ground is, in essence, a repeat of MSCC's case before the Inspector that the discharge proviso should be considered independently of the evidence. Given the water quality evidence supports a conclusion that the proviso is not needed, there may be said to be some force in UU's submission that MSCC is simply seeking to exclude unfavourable evidence from consideration.

Compensation (Error 4)

63   Before the Inspector MSCC sought the inclusion of Schedule 12, paragraph 4 WIA, which provides, in relevant part, that a sewerage undertaker shall make full compensation to any person who has sustained damage by reason of the exercise by the undertaker of any of its powers under the relevant sewerage provisions.

64   Schedule 12, paragraph 4 WIA does not apply to the grant of a right under section 155 WIA and the only point made by MSCC in relation to the issue in its closing submissions was as follows:

> '*As with the other statutory provisions identified above, there is no proper public interest rationale for leaving MSCCL in a worse position than it is at present, simply because the right is acquired by compulsion (§252 closing submissions).*'

65   Accordingly, before the Inspector the point being made was a repeat of MSCC's broader case, considered above, that it should have parity of protection as between rights implicitly and explicitly authorised under the WIA. However, as pleaded, error 4 is that the Inspector treated the compensation provisions of the compulsory purchase code as being apt and sufficient to compensate MSCC for the injuries and losses whose actionability the discharge proviso would have expressly preserved, whereas the compulsory purchase code is not intended to provide, and does not provide, a substitute for private law remedies for intermittent future injury caused by the exercise of any right granted. It is apparent from a review of the MSCC's closing submissions that nothing was said as to the compulsory purchase code being inadequate. The absence of submissions is also apparent from the fact the Inspector expressly excluded compensation from his summary of UU's case, on the basis it was a matter for the Lands Tribunal.

66   Accordingly, error 4 seeks to criticise the Inspector and Secretary of State for not dealing with a case that was not put to them. They cannot be criticised for

taking matters on the basis they did, namely that compensation would be available for damage sustained by the order scheme.

Persuasive burden erroneously imposed on MSCC and failure of UU to justify the grant of the wider right (Errors 1 and 2)

67   I am not persuaded that the Inspector treated inclusion of the discharge proviso as an issue on which MSCC bore a persuasive burden (Error 1). His consideration of the proviso was an integral part of his wider decision making and followed, in this respect, his rejection of MSCC's proposition that he should consider the proviso independently from the evidence (§908). His report begins with a detailed summary of the cases of UU and MSCC, which runs to approximately 180 pages. His conclusions are expressed succinctly, by means of cross references to the relevant paragraphs from the parties' case, on which his conclusions are based.

68   He begins his conclusions by directing himself on the legal framework, as to which there is no challenge, namely that the statutory authority for the acquisition is section 155 WIA. A CPO should only be made where there is a compelling case in the public interest. The purposes for which the compulsory purchase order is made must justify interfering with the human rights of those with an interest in the land affected. As a statutory undertaker, MSCC's land can only be taken if it can be done without serious detriment to the company (section 16(2) Acquisition of Land Act). The Inspector then states:

> 'However, before addressing these fundamental matters, I shall deal with the detailed terms of the Order that remain in dispute between the two remaining parties...'.

69   He addresses the inclusion of the discharge proviso at §908-911, concluding that the proviso is not necessary before turning to consider the requirement for the CPO and the compelling case in the public interest for the order.

70   There is nothing in the language of §908-911 to suggest the Inspector is applying any burden of proof. It is apparent from the paragraphs in question, particularly the cross referencing, that the Inspector has formed his view by taking into account the arguments and evidence put forward by both parties and by weighing up the competing factors. This is the task he was required to perform ((*R. v Secretary of State for Transport Ex p. De Rothschild* (1989) 57 P. & C.R. 330), as reflected in paragraph 13 of the CPO guidance to which he directed himself to). His decision was reached on the basis that he found the case advanced by UU to be 'convincing' (the Inspector's own words).

71   MSCC submits that the Inspector failed to take into account that UU did not advance any positive argument in favour of the grant of a wider right and confined its submissions to criticism of MSCC's case (Error 2). This rests on an artificially narrow assessment of paragraphs 908-911. The Inspector's analysis is based on all the evidence before him, having specifically rejected MSCC's suggestion that the proviso be considered independently from the evidence. It is apparent, therefore, that UU's justification was extensively explored over 29 days of public inquiry and set out in the Report. It included evidence which demonstrated a beneficial impact on water quality in circumstances where the discharge proviso is directed in large part to the quality of the receiving water. Having assessed the evidence and arguments the Inspector concluded that that discharge proviso was unnecessary.

Drawing the strands together

72   Drawing the strands together: the Inspector reaches an assessment that inclusion of the protective provisions sought by MSCC in the CPO is unnecessary. This is not because he treats necessity as a legal test, as MSCC contends under Ground 1. It is a judgment reached in the public interest, based on a lengthy examination of the evidence, over twenty nine days of the inquiry, where MSCC was represented and put its case fully (as the only remaining objector). His main reasons for considering the proviso to be unnecessary are because the discharge will be regulated by the Environment Agency; the public inquiry had provided an opportunity for an independent scrutiny of the potential interference with MSCC's rights; the discharge provisions do not apply to a right granted under section 155 WIA; the water quality evidence demonstrates that the scheme will have a net beneficial effect on the water quality of the Canal and compensation is payable.

73   The Inspector's decision discloses no error of law. Given the nature of the legal provisions sought by MSCC, there is an obvious rationale to the Inspector taking account of the availability of a detailed and precise environmental regulatory regime, backed up by criminal sanctions and overseen by a specialist regulator, as well as the water quality evidence which demonstrates the scheme will have a net beneficial impact on the Canal. The procedure for the grant of a CPO, in particular the public inquiry, provides an appropriate forum in which to assess any necessary protection for a landowner whose land is subject to a compulsory use. There is a material distinction, in this regard, between an implied right of discharge and the express grant of a right under (*Manchester Ship Canal Co Ltd v United Utilities Water Plc* [2014] UKSC 40). It is apparent from a reading of the relevant paragraphs of the Inspector's report that his decision was not reached on the basis that MSCC had failed to satisfy any particular burden of proof but was because he found the case advanced by UU to be, in his words, 'convincing'. None of the matters referred to at paragraphs 908 – 911 are immaterial and it is not alleged that the overall exercise of the discretion is irrational or that the reasoning is deficient. The Inspector exercised the discretion available to him and formed his view, taking into account arguments and evidence put forward by both parties, as he was required to do so by the inquiry process (*R. v Secretary of State for Transport p. De Rothschild* (1989) 57 P. & C.R. 330).

Raising new points on appeal

74   Before the Court, MSCC developed its case in in ways that were not put to the Inspector (or the Secretary of State).

The scope of the discharge proviso

75   Before the Inspector MSCC sought to include sections 117(5)(a) and (b); 117(6); 186(1)(3), (6) and Schedule 12 para 4 of the WIA to the terms of the order. Before the Court, the company confined the scope of its challenge to sections 117(5) and 186(3) WIA (Counsel for MSCC said during submissions that the company was 'neutral' on the inclusion of section 117(6) WIA).

Private law remedies

76   The Inspector was specifically told that arguments as to whether or not the owner of a receiving watercourse would be able to take legal action to enforce the statutory protections were the subject of a separate legal dispute between the parties and were irrelevant for present purposes. Any disputes about these matters were said to be 'for another day and another forum' (closing submissions at §253). Before the Court, Counsel for MSCC sought to downplay the submission but it appears in MSCC's closing submissions and it is difficult to see how it can be read in any other way than a disavowal of the relevance of private law remedies to the issues before the inquiry.

77   The reference in the closing submission to a 'separate legal dispute' is assumed to be a reference to the ongoing litigation between MSCC and UU concerning the availability of private law remedies in nuisance and trespass in the event of discharges which lack authorisation (by virtue of the provisions of section 117(5) and section 186(3)). The first instance decision (*Manchester Ship Canal Co Ltd v United Utilities Water Ltd* [2021] 1 W.L.R. 5871 (Fancourt J)) had been handed down by the time the company issued its grounds for judicial review in this case and is referred to in the grounds for judicial review. The grounds explain that Fancourt J held that the tortious remedies were ousted by section 18 WIA and related provisions of the Act and there that was an extant appeal before the Court of Appeal. By the time of the hearing in this case, the Court of Appeal had handed down its judgment (*Manchester Ship Canal Co Ltd v United Utilities Water Ltd* [2022] 3 W.L.R. 1193), a decision I return to below.

78   Before the Court, MSCC's case for inclusion of sections 117(5) and 186(3) included the consequent availability of private law remedies to the company in the event of future problems. The effect of the provisions was said to be to deny a sewerage undertaker any authority, in particular a defence of statutory authority, to make polluting discharges (MSCC Grounds). Regulation by the Environment Agency was said to be a form of public law protection which provides no remedy to those affected by breaches of permit. Private law causes of action in trespass or nuisance were said to constitute the only fully effective remedy for injurious discharges. It was said that, absent the discharge proviso, such claims would be met with a version of the defence of "consent" arising from the unfettered terms of the statutory grant of the right of discharge by exercise of compulsory powers (MSCC's skeleton argument). Reliance was placed on the expression of the doctrine of statutory authority in *Allen v Gulf Oil Refining Ltd* [1981] A.C. 1001 ('*We are here in the well chartered field of statutory authority. It is now well settled that where Parliament by express direction or by necessary implication has authorised the construction and use of an undertaking or works that carries with it an authority to do what is authorised with immunity from any action based on nuisance. The right of action is taken away*' [1011] Lord Wilberforce).

79   MSCC continued to refine its case further during the hearing, narrowing its focus to the value of the discharge proviso being to protect MSCC's right to bring a claim based on negligence or deliberate wrongdoing by UU in breach of its environmental permit. Without the proviso, it was said that UU would have a defence of statutory authority to a claim which could otherwise be pursued by MSCC. In his reply, Counsel for MSCC produced, for the first time, a copy of the order of Fancourt J

in the first instance proceedings in *Manchester Ship Canal Co Ltd v United Utilities Water Ltd*. The order provides as follows at paragraph 2:

> '*Upon the true construction of the Water Industry Act 1991, where a discharge into the Canal from sewers vested in United Utilities contravenes ss.117(5) and/or 186(3) of the Water Industry Act 1991, the Canal Company may not bring an action in trespass or nuisance against United Utilities in respect of such discharge absent an allegation of negligence or deliberate wrongdoing ....*'(underlying is the Court's emphasis)

80   In the circumstances, I permitted all parties to submit written submissions on the point after the hearing. MSCC put its case in writing as follows:

> '*The matter was addressed in closing in the light of questions from the court as to how practical effect was to be given to the provisos and their use of the general terms of "foul water" and "injurious affection" to define limitations upon statutory authority. It is sufficient on the facts of this case to say that the concession made at the Inquiry represents an acknowledgment that the proposed discharges, if properly permitted by the Environment Agency and made in compliance with the terms of such permit, would not be harmful to water quality in the canal. In this respect (and this respect alone) the point made by UU concerning the rigorous examination of the issue at the Inquiry has relevance and force. Thus on the facts of this case, it is inherently unlikely that discharges made in compliance with an environmental permit (and thus not contravening a proviso in the form of section 117(5)(a)) could be stigmatised as nevertheless contravening a provision in the form of section 117(5)(b) or section 117(6) or section 186(3).*
>
> *It is however inherently likely that a discharge in exceedance of permit limits might also contravene the provisos in sections 117(5)(b), 117(6) and 186(3). It is in those circumstances that MSCCL asserts that there can be no good reason why such discharges should be permitted (as they prima facie would be) by the terms of the grant in its unfettered form. If such discharges were being made pursuant to the statutory implied right then they would lack statutory authority. The defence of statutory authority would thus not be available to claims in nuisance or trespass. If the discharges were made in circumstances of operational negligence or deliberate misconduct then nor could the principle in Marcic be invoked to oust such claims and to require instead that complaint to Ofwat under section 18 of the Water Industry Act 1991. There would be no possibility of a defence of consent. Private law claims in trespass and nuisance could proceed by way of litigation in the High Court. That possibility cannot properly be stigmatised as an unwarranted "inhibition" on the activities of the undertakers. It is a proper limitation on their powers which is inherent in the statutory scheme. The Supreme Court went to great pains in 2014 to ensure that such was the case.*
>
> ......
>
> *The paradigm example is that due to operational negligence in the management of the treatment works, there is a catastrophic failure of treatment and a discharge of undiluted, untreated sewage through the new outfall into the canal, with resulting pollution and injurious affection. Another example would involve premature spilling of the overflows, resulting in a discharge*

of (somewhat) diluted untreated sewage. Such circumstances would ordinarily (including in the case of the existing discharges into Salteye Brook) constitute the torts of trespass and nuisance and private law claims would not be "Marciced" since the element of negligence or deliberate misconduct would be present. Such discharges do occur and frequently come before the criminal courts for trial and sentence see e.g. the sentencing remarks of Johnson J in Environment Agency v Southern Water Services Ltd 9 July 2021, unreported. If the grant in the Order remains as confirmed, then, as identified above, the defence of consent is prima facie available. There would be nothing in the terms of the Order to preclude such discharges so long as they satisfy the description of "water, soil or effluent".'

Adequacy of compensation

81   In relation to the adequacy of compensation, the following was said in MSCC's grounds for appeal:

'53 ...*The modified form of section 7 of the Compulsory Purchase Act 1965 which is applicable .... is apt to provide compensation for what might be termed "chronic injurious affections" arising from the permanent and/or inevitable effects of the creation and routine exercise of a new right over land, but manifestly inapt to do so in the case of "acute" loss or damage arising from a serious pollution discharge occurring on some future occasion at some distance in the future. That is not its purpose. Nor does it provide any remedy by way of injunction in such circumstances.'*

82   In written submissions produced after the hearing, MSCC made the following points:

'*MSCCL repeats its contention, fully developed in oral submissions, that it is no purpose of a statutory compensation scheme, including that operative here, to anticipate future tortious claims that might arise out of the wrongful use of acquired land or the wrongful exercise of a right acquired over land. That is not a criticism of the Compensation Code, merely an accurate statement of its limited purpose, which is to compensate on a once and for all basis for the then current value of land taken or the then current diminution in value of retained land as a resulting of the scheme underlying the exercise of compulsory purchase powers*'

'*If the grant remains as in the Order, then any discharge of "water, soil and effluent" is prima facie lawful and within the scope of the right acquired. To that extent, it might indeed be reflected in the assessment of compensation immediately following acquisition by some sophisticated method of discounting valuation process seeking to identify and quantify the diminution in current market value of the canal including by reference to the possibility of injury at some future date. That only has to be stated for its failure to meet the needs of the present situation to be apparent. The discounting would plainly be significant and the resulting valuation would inevitably be on a very "broad brush" basis. Since it would be attempting to value a chance, it would be bound to be "wrong", in the sense that it will not accurately represent the situation if no injurious breach in fact ever occurs, nor the situation if such*' *a breach does occur. The actual consequences of a breach will not be the subject of full compensation. Compensation which is discounted to reflect a chance (as opposed to reflecting, say, simply early receipt of a future payment) is not full compensation if that chance comes up. It is simply no part of the role of the Upper Tribunal to speculate upon such eventualities.*

Such a rough and ready approach is neither satisfactory nor inevitable. Compare and contrast the position if the grant is limited in scope by the discharge proviso. Then only discharges that do not contravene the limits of the proviso will be within its terms. The effect of the right to make those upon the value of the canal will be determined under the Compensation Code. The consequences of the making of future discharges which fall foul of the discharge proviso will instead be the subject of tortious proceedings where available (as discussed above) seeking damages.'

83   In its written representations submitted after the hearing, UU explained that MSCC's evidence in relation to compensation was provided at the inquiry by a witness, Mr Rhodes, who did not cover the points now made before the Court about the adequacy of the compensation regime (a point disputed by MSCC). It was, however, common ground that Mr Rhodes was not called to give evidence. UU further explained that its evidence at the inquiry in relation to the statutory compensation scheme was presented by Mr Smith, who was subject to detailed cross examination, during which the points taken before the Court were not canvassed. UU explained that there was no mention of any of the points now advanced, either in MSCC's closing submissions or in a note provided in response to UU's closing submissions, despite the fact that the latter addressed the adequacy and availability of compensation.

84   In *Barker Mill Estates Trustees v Test Valley BC* [2016] EWHC 3028 (Admin), in the context of an application for statutory review of a development plan the Court said as follows:

'77 *In an application for statutory review of a planning decision there is no absolute bar on the raising of a point which was not taken before the inspector or decision-maker. But it is necessary to examine the nature of the new point sought to be raised in the context of the process which was followed up to the decision challenged to see whether the claimant should be allowed to argue it. For example, one factor which weighs strongly against allowing a new point to be argued in the High Court is that if it had been raised in the earlier inquiry or appeal process, it would have been necessary for further evidence to be produced and/or additional factual findings or judgments to be made by the inspector, or alternatively participants would have had the opportunity to adduce evidence or make submissions (or the inspector might have called for more information...'(Holgate J)*

85   In my view, the proposition above also applies to the compulsory purchase context. A CPO can only be confirmed by the Secretary of State on the basis of a compelling public interest and there can often be multi party interests in play at a CPO inquiry. As explained above the public inquiry process provides the appropriate mechanism for an examination of the appropriate protection for a landowner. The interests in play in the present case extend beyond the parties to the Court proceedings. There were other objectors at the start of the public inquiry into the

order under scrutiny. There are wider public interests in the proper performance of UU's sewerage functions under the WIA and in the water quality issues that led to the Environment Agency requiring an alternative sewerage solution for Salteye Brook.

86   Had the case now advanced by MSCC been put before the Inspector, it would, in my judgment, have been necessary for further evidence to be produced to consider UU's regulatory performance including; the history of its regulatory performance; previous pollution episodes; the scope of the environmental permit; and the monitoring provisions in the permit. Mr Rhodes and Mr Smith could have given evidence on whether/how MSCC could be compensated for the risks of damage to MSCC's land interests as a result of the right granted and if/how the compensation regime could deal with future uncertainty of damage. The Inspector could then have made any necessary additional factual findings or judgments to feed into his assessment as to inclusion of the discharge proviso in the terms of the compulsory purchase order. As an example, had the evidence demonstrated a history of poor regulatory compliance by UU then it may have become necessary for the Inspector to consider greater protection for MSCC, itself a statutory undertaker and navigation authority for the Canal.

87   Turning to the refinement of MSCC's case during the hearing. The Court has repeatedly emphasised the need for procedural rigour in judicial review. The following statement is taken from the decision of the Court of Appeal in *Dolan v Secretary Of State For Health And Social Care* [2020] EWCA Civ 1605:

> '116 *In a number of recent cases this Court has noted that there is "increasing concern about the need for appropriate procedural rigour in judicial review cases": seeRegina (Spahiu) v Secretary of State for the Home Department: Practice Note* [2018] EWCA Civ 2604; [2019] 1 W.L.R. 1297, *at para. 2, where earlier authorities are set out (Coulson LJ). The present case leads us to repeat that concern.*
> 117. *Procedural rigour is important not for its own sake. It is important in order for justice to be done. It is important that there must be fairness to all concerned, including the wider public as well as the parties. It is important that everyone should know where they stand, so that, for example, the defendant can properly prepare evidence in a timely fashion.*'

88   Whilst I permitted all parties the opportunity to make submissions in writing after the hearing to deal with MSCC's refined case, the outcome has been a limited opportunity to explore the complexities raised by the case, in particular in relation to the availability of compensation; the assessment of the interference with the company's property rights and the availability of the defence of statutory authority in negligence claims (see further below the discussion in Ground 2).

89   A challenge under section 23 of the Acquisition of Land Act does not entitle a disappointed party to attempt a second go at its case and the Court must be astute to prevent any attempt to do so. The role of the Court is to consider whether there is any legal or procedural error in the confirmation (*Margate Town Centre Regeneration Ltd v Secretary of State for Communities and Local Government* [2013] EWCA Civ 1178).

90   For the reasons set out above, the Inspector, and Secretary of State, cannot be criticised for not dealing with a case that was not put to them and I decline to do

so. I am satisfied that there is no error of law in their assessment of the matters put before them.

91   Ground 1 fails.

Ground 2 Article 1 Protocol 1

MSCC's case

92   Ground 2 is that the Secretary of State and/or the Inspector erred in law in their consideration of MSCC's right to peaceful enjoyment of its possessions (Article 1 Protocol 1 ECHR).

93   MSCC submits that the requisite fair balance to justify the interference with the peaceful enjoyment of its property requires the inclusion of the discharge proviso and the Inspector failed to identify any reasons why the balance would be disturbed by its inclusion. The Inspector failed to consider whether a less intrusive measure could have been used (i.e. the CPO with discharge proviso), as required by *Bank Mellat v HM Treasury* [2013] UKSC 38. The margin of appreciation is highly context and fact specific. In the particular context of the compulsory purchase at issue in the present case the Court should not afford the Inspector a particularly wide margin of appreciation, if any. The Court should emulate the rigorous and detailed assessment of alternative approaches adopted by the first instance judge (and approved by the Court of Appeal) in *R. (Friends of Antique Cultural Treasures Ltd) v Secretary of State for the Environment, Food and Rural Affairs* [2020] EWCA Civ 649; [2020] 1 W.L.R. 3876 at [79] - [80]. Moreover, compensation is not available to MSCC for discharges by United Utilities in breach of any environmental permit.

Legal framework

94   Article 1 Protocol 1 (A1P1) reads as follows:

> '1. *Every natural or legal person is entitled to the peaceful enjoyment of his possessions. No one shall be deprived of his possessions except in the public interest and subject to the conditions provided for by law and by the general principles of international law.*
> *The preceding provisions shall not, however, in any way impair the right of a State to enforce such laws as it deems necessary to control the use of property in accordance with the general interest or to secure the payment of taxes or other contributions or penalties.'*

95   A1P1 is, in substance, a guarantee of the right to property. It comprises three distinct, but interconnected rules. The first is a general principle that every natural or legal person is entitled to the peaceful enjoyment of his possessions (first sentence of the first paragraph). The second is that there should be no deprivation of possessions except in the public interest and by lawful means (second sentence of the first paragraph). The third is an explicit recognition that states are entitled to control the use of property in accordance with the general interest (second paragraph). The second and third rules are concerned with particular instances of interference with the right to peaceful enjoyment of property and should therefore be construed in the light of the general principle enunciated in the first rule

(*Sporrong and Lonnroth v Sweden* Sporrong and Lönnroth v Sweden (1983) 5 E.H.R.R. 35, § 61 and *James v United Kingdom* (1986) 8 E.H.R.R. 123, § 37).

96   Accordingly, assessment of whether there has been a violation of A1P1 involves consideration of whether a "possession" exists, whether there has been an interference with the possession, and, if so, the nature of the interference. More broadly, to establish whether an interference amounts to a violation of the right to the peaceful enjoyment of possessions:

> 'The court must determine whether a fair balance was struck between the demands of the general interest of the community and the requirements of the protection of the individual's fundamental rights. The search for this balance is inherent in the whole of the Convention and is also reflected in the structure of article 1.
> (*Sporrong and Lonnroth v Sweden* (1983) 5 E.H.R.R. 35 at [69]).'

97   The parties were agreed that, in the present case, there is a possession (MSCC's ownership of the Canal) and the CPO constitutes an interference with the possession, (by means of a control on use given MSCC's land is not taken but UU is permitted to discharge into its canal).

98   If, as in the present case, an interference has been established, it is necessary to consider whether the interference constitutes a violation of the A1P1 right. It must be shown that the interference complies with the principle of lawfulness and pursues a legitimate aim. By virtue of my analysis under Ground 1, I have concluded that the CPO was granted by lawful means. The parties were agreed that the CPO pursues a legitimate aim (provision of sewerage services and environmental improvement).

99   The final question, and the one at large in the proceedings, is whether the interference with MSCC's property is proportionate.

100   The parties were agreed that Lord Sumption's analysis in *Bank Mellat v HM Treasury* [2013] UKSC 38 and [2013] UKSC 39 provides a structured framework for the assessment of proportionality, as follows:

> '20 ...the question [of proportionality] depends on an exacting analysis of the factual case advanced in defence of the measure, in order to determine:
>   i) whether its objective is sufficiently important to justify the limitation of a fundamental right;
>   ii) whether it is rationally connected to the objective;
> iii) whether a less intrusive measure could have been used; and
>   iv) whether, having regard to these matters and to the severity of the consequences, a fair balance has been struck between the rights of the individual and the interests of the community.'

101   The parties were at odds as to whether, in the compulsory purchase context, proposition iii) applies, namely whether it is necessary for the CPO to amount to the least intrusive measure in order for the interference to be proportionate. In this respect the relevance of the discharge proviso, and the rights said to be preserved by them, goes not to the degree of interference caused by the Order itself but rather to whether there is a less intrusive measure that could have been used without compromising the achievement of the objectives of the Order, and how that feeds into the fair balance assessment. There was also a dispute as to the appropriate margin of judgment to be afforded by the Court to the Inspector.

The assessment of proportionality in the context of a CPO

102   Proportionality in the context of a compulsory transfer of land was addressed
by the Court of Appeal in *R. (Clays Lane Housing Cooperative Ltd) v The Housing
Corp* [2004] EWCA Civ 1658, a case relied on by Counsel for the Secretary of
State. The regulatory body for registered social landlords came to a determination
that there was a compelling case in the public interest for requiring the claimant
housing association to transfer its land to another registered social landlord
following mismanagement by the claimant. The claimant contended that the first
instance judge failed to apply a sufficiently rigorous test of proportionality in
considering its A1P1 rights. In his judgment, Kay LJ observed that the presumption
against the removal of property rights means that a compulsory purchase order
must be '*sufficiently justified by the Secretary of State*' and went on to observe
that:

'*Even before the Human Rights Act 1998, the courts of this country were alert
to the need to scrutinise compulsory purchase orders with rigour'(§12).*

103   He characterised the decision making as:

'*although not in every respect the same as a planning decision, it approximated
to what Keene LJ was describing inLough v First Secretary of State* [2004]
1 W.L.R. 2557; *namely "a situation where the essential conflict is between
two or more groups of private interests".'(§25)*

104   He concluded as follows:

'*I conclude that the appropriate test of proportionality requires a balancing
exercise and a decision which is justified on the basis of a compelling case
in the public interest and as being reasonably necessary but not obligatorily
the least intrusive of Convention rights. That accords with Strasbourg and
domestic authority. It is also consistent with sensible and practical
decision-making in the public interest in this context. If "strict necessity"
were to compel the "least intrusive" alternative, decisions which were
distinctly second best or worse when tested against the performance of a
regulator's statutory functions would become mandatory. A decision which
was fraught with adverse consequences, would have to prevail because it was,
perhaps quite marginally, the least intrusive. Whilst one can readily see why
that should be so in some Convention contexts, it would be a recipe for poor
public administration in the context of cases such as Lough and the present
case.'(§25)*

105   The case of *Lough v First Secretary of State*, referred to by the Court in *Clays
Lane*, concerned a challenge to the grant of planning permission. There the Court
of Appeal characterised the decision making as involving competing private interests
between landowners and also a public interest in beneficial land use; observing
that: "*The concept of proportionality is inherent in the approach to decision making
in planning law...[49]*".

106   In both *Lough* and *Clays Lane*, the Court of Appeal distinguished cases involving
a direct interference with an individual's rights by a state body (as in *Samaroo v
Secretary of State for the Home Department* [2001] U.K.H.R.R. 1150) with the
planning context where the essential conflict is between two or more groups of

private interests in the context of a wider community interest. The question whether the objective of the measure under scrutiny can be achieved by means that do not interfere as much with a person's rights under the Convention was said not to be wholly appropriate to decision making in the planning context in not taking account of the right of a landowner to make use of his land, a right which is, however, to be weighed against the rights of others affected by the use of land and of the community in general (Pill LJ in *Lough* at §49).

107   In the first instance decision of *Pascoe v First Secretary of State* [2007] 1 W.L.R. 885, a challenge to a CPO, Forbes J followed the approach in *Clays Lane*, in accepting that a measure can be proportionate even if it is not the least intrusive means possible. He also accepted the proposition that the decision maker ought to be afforded a wide margin of appreciation in the assessment of the proportionality of a measure and that the policy requirement that a CPO will not be confirmed unless there is a compelling case in the public interest fairly reflects the necessary element of balance required in the application of A1P1. In addition, he observed that:

> '... there is no requirement to set out in a formulaic way the extent to which rights are interfered with. The inspector's report and the Secretary of State's decision letter should be read as a whole in order to determine whether the necessary balancing exercise has been properly carried out.' (§66)

108   Counsel for MSCC sought to distinguish *Clays Lane* on its facts, on the basis it concerned a housing regulator requiring a transfer of land, which is not a conventional CPO. I do not see, however, that the distinction is material. The test applied by the housing regulator was the same – a compelling public interest. Moreover, I bear in mind that the approach of the Court of Appeal in *Clays Lane* and *Lough* is consistent with the nature of the public inquiry into a CPO as explored by the Court of Appeal in *R. v Secretary of State for Transport Ex p. De Rothschild* (1989) 57 P. & C.R. 330. Counsel also sought to distinguish between the acquisition of land (on a once and for all basis) and the acquisition of a right of discharge where the extent of future interference will vary. In my view the point goes to the evidential context for assessing the interference rather than to a principle of general distinction.

109   Counsel for MSCC further submitted that *Clays Lane* and *Pascoe* predated *Bank Mellat* which sets down a requirement for the measure to be the least intrusive. I am not however persuaded that there is any tension between *Bank Mellat* and the approach in the compulsory purchase context (*Clays Lane* and *Pascoe*).

110   *Bank Mellat* was not a planning case. It was concerned with the imposition of sanctions on an Iranian Bank. The focus was, as here, on the question of the least intrusive measure. Lord Sumption acknowledged the overlap between the four propositions in the proportionality framework:

> 'the four requirements are logically separate, but in practice they inevitably overlap because the same facts are likely to be relevant to more than one of them. Before us, the only issue about them concerned (iii), since it was suggested that a measure would be disproportionate if any more limited measure was capable of achieving the objective. For my part, I agree with the view expressed in this case by Maurice Kay LJ that this debate is sterile in the normal case where the effectiveness of the measure and the degree of

interference are not absolute values but questions of degree, inversely related to each other. The question is whether a less intrusive measure could have been used without unacceptably compromising the objective.'

111   In his assessment, Lord Reed referred to the development of the more structured approach to proportionality adopted by the common law. He explained the attraction of this approach as a heuristic tool: *'by breaking down an assessment of proportionality into distinct elements it can clarify different aspects of such an assessment and make value judgements more explicit'* (§72 and §74). As to the wider principle, he observed that a search for fair balance between the demands of the general interest of the community and the requirements of the protection of the individual's fundamental rights is inherent in the whole of the Convention and that '...*an assessment of proportionality inevitably involves a value judgment at the stage at which a balance has to be struck between the importance of the objective pursued and* <u>the value of the right intruded upon</u>' (§74) (underlining is Court's emphasis).

112   I take from the analysis of Lord Sumption and Lord Reed (above) that the structured framework for the assessment of proportionality should not be allowed to obscure the application of the underlying principle of fair balance, as is apparent from the expression of the fourth principle in *Bank Mellat* ("*whether, having regard to these matters and to the severity of the consequences, a fair balance has been struck between the rights of the individual and the interests of the community)*". The factors identified in the proportionality framework will "*inevitably*" overlap. The effectiveness of the measure and the degree of interference are not absolute values, but questions of degree inversely related to each other (*Bank Mellat*). The fact that an alternative proposal may give rise to a different or lesser effect of compulsory purchase is to be taken into account in the balancing exercise, but it does not, of itself, erode the public interest test in the submitted scheme (*Clays Lane* at §25).

The role of the Court

113   The role of the Court was, largely, common ground between the parties. Under the Human Rights Act the question of justification for an interference with a Convention right is a substantive question and not merely a process question. The Court must go beyond the task traditionally adopted to judicial review in a domestic setting. There is no shift to a merits review, but the intensity of review is greater than that appropriate to domestic judicial review. Proportionality must be judged objectively by the Court. What matters is whether the ultimate decision taken is, or is not, objectively justified. Unlike in domestic public law cases, it will not necessarily be fatal if a decision-maker has failed to take into account an issue under the European Convention on Human Rights. It is the compatibility of the outcome of the process with Convention rights which has to be assessed by the Court, not the process by which that outcome was reached. That said, it is also well established that the fact that an issue has been considered by a decision maker is relevant to the question which the Court has to determine. It may affect the weight which the Court should give to the views of the decision maker when coming to its own assessment of justification (*R. (Begum) v Headteacher, Governors of Denbigh High School* [2006] UKHL 15 and *R. (on the application of TD) v Secretary of State for Work and Pensions* [2020] EWCA Civ 618 (§52-53).

114   The decision-maker has a margin of judgment which is highly fact and context specific. A wide margin of judgment may be appropriate in a compulsory purchase context, but not necessarily. It will depend on the particular context. However, it is not for the court to take over the role of the decision-maker. In the particular context of assessing a less intrusive measure 'a judge would be unimaginative indeed if he could not come up with something a little less drastic or a little less restrictive in almost any situation especially if he is unaware of the relevant practicalities and indifferent to considerations of cost'. (Lord Reed in *Bank Mellat* at §74. See also Lord Sumption at [21])

Application of the legal framework to the facts

115   Counsel for MSCC submitted that the human rights assessment by the Inspector and Secretary of State was cursory. However, there is no requirement to set out in a formulaic way the extent to which rights are interfered with (*Pascoe* at §66). The Inspector's assessment of human rights at §944-946 of the Report is be viewed as a concluding expression of the matters of fact and judgment set out in the report as a whole. The same can be said for the Secretary of State's assessment.

116   The CPO interferes with MSCC's ownership of the Canal. The provision of sewerage services and the environmental improvement of Salteye Brook is sufficiently important to justify a limitation on MSCC's right of ownership. The right for UU to discharge effluent into the Canal is rationally connected to the provision of sewerage services.

117   Before the Inspector MSCC proposed a less intrusive measure namely the order with discharge proviso. The Inspector came to a judgment that the protection was unnecessary for reasons that I do not consider to be tainted by legal error. He did so on the basis of the case put to him by MSCC (which focussed, largely, on a point of principle and in the language of public interest). Before the Inspector MSCC made clear that its case for inclusion of the proviso was <u>not</u> based on its right to be able to bring a private law claim against UU.

118   For the reasons explained at paragraphs 37 and 68 above, I have a concern that the protection sought by MSCC could undermine the objective of the CPO. It is a concern that I sought to explore during the hearing with Counsel for MSCC. Before the Inspector, MSCC sought the inclusion of sections 117 (5)(a) and (b); 117(6); 186(1), (3), (6) and (7) and Schedule 12 paragraph, 4 WIA in the terms of the CPO. Taken together, they may be said to form their own complex interlocking scheme of regulation to sit alongside the grant of authority to UU to discharge effluent into the Canal as part of the terms of the Order. This would appear to give rise to the potential for a conflict, on the face of the order, between UU's right to discharge effluent with the removal of authority for the company to discharge 'foul water', without treatment (Section 117(5)(b)). It is not clear how the broad concepts of 'injuriously to affect' or 'prejudicially to affect' would be interpreted. It is not clear whether, in the event of an alleged 'injurious affect' on the canal, the proviso would enable MSCC to seek an interim injunction, to shut down the statutory undertaker's operations, pending resolution of the dispute between the parties. In closing submissions to the inquiry, MSCC appeared to posit a role for itself as a second regulator of UU's operations. This presents an unfortunate scenario in which UU's operations are supervised by two 'regulators' – the Environment Agency, operating a detailed and precise regulatory regime and MSCC operating via statutory

provisions expressed in loose terms with next to no machinery for their effect and operation. Such an outcome would produce too much uncertainty for UU in seeking to discharge its statutory duty to provide sewerage services. There may be an impact on the wider public interest in the proper performance of UU's sewerage functions, given the history of litigation between these two statutory undertakers. In the words of the Court of Appeal in *Clays Lane*, it could amount to a recipe for poor public administration.

119   Stepping back then (as I am required to do by proposition iv) in *Bank Mellat* I turn to consider the question of a fair balance.

120   By the end of the inquiry it was common ground that there was a compelling public interest in the compulsory purchase order. The Inspector reached the same view in his decision:

> '924. *The Order Scheme is required to enable the delivery of the Full Scheme and the public interest (and environmental) benefits that would be realised by completing the Full Scheme. In doing so, the Order Scheme would provide necessary infrastructure that would enable regulatory objectives for Eccles WwTW to be met.*
>
> ......
>
> 926. *The evidence, and the testing of it during the Inquiry, demonstrated that: there is a clear regulatory (and environmental) requirement for the Order Scheme; it is the most appropriate option for meeting that need;*
>
> ......
>
> 940. *As set out above, alternatives to the Order Scheme have been explored, both in terms of: the method by which regulatory and environmental objectives would be met; and for the option chosen, the broad design principles for what is now proposed.*
>
> 941. *The Inquiry heard extensive evidence regarding: the operation of the Eccles WwTW; the steps taken to improve the quality of water courses in the catchment that includes the Canal and Salteye Brook; and, how the Order Scheme would contribute to the economic, social and environmental well-being of the area. The Order Scheme would provide the improvements in water quality sought for Salteye Brook, and while the new outfall would discharge directly into the Canal, it would nonetheless have an overall beneficial effect on the Canal and the environment around it.*
>
> 942. *In addition to the environmental improvements in relation to water quality, the proposed option would be a better use of resources that would result in economic benefits for both the undertaker and its customers. The astute and convincing fiscal argument for the chosen option, along with the resulting efficient use of resources, would result in social benefits from economic efficiency, and that would be expected to be reflected in reduced bills to the Acquiring Authority's customers. Social benefit would also be derived from a reduction in the level of flood risk to properties on Peel Green Road that connect to the sewer network upstream of Eccles WwTW.*
>
> 943. *Given the Acquiring Authority's statutory function, and the regulatory requirements it seeks to meet through the Order Scheme, a compelling case in the public interest has been clearly made for confirmation of the Order. [16-19, 25, 29, 30, 75-83, 422-436, 480, 495, 824].'*

121   I afford the Inspector a considerable margin of judgment in his assessment in
this regard. He had overseen the inquiry and heard the evidence over 29 days of a
public inquiry. I was not taken to the evidence, which was a matter of common
ground.

122   Turning to the severity of the consequences for MSCC. MSCC accepts that the
order with the discharge proviso amounts to a fair balance, but submits that the
order without the discharge proviso amounts to a disproportionate interference
with its property right.

123   However, the evidence in relation to the interference generated by the order
without the discharge proviso, as compared with the proviso, remains theoretical.
The impacts of the scheme underlying the Order on water quality and quantity was
the subject of detailed evidence at the public inquiry, which demonstrated a benefit
to the water quality of the Canal. It was common ground that the Environment
Agency will supervise the discharge. Discharge standards will be set and monitored.
The regulatory framework under which the Environment Agency operates was
common ground. It is a detailed regulatory regime, backed up by criminal sanctions
and overseen by a specialist regulator. MSCC has not produced any evidence of
poor regulatory compliance by UU or inadequate regulation of UU by the
Environment Agency to indicate a need for the discharge proviso. On the evidence
before him, the Inspector did not consider the proviso to be necessary.

124   Before the Court, MSCC advanced a case that the value of the discharge proviso
comprises the private law protection (in nuisance and negligence) provided by
sections 117(5) and 183(6) WIA in the event of future polluting incidents.

125   However: so far as a claim in nuisance is concerned, the difficulty with MSCC's
case is the decision in *Marcic v Thames Water Utilities Ltd* [2003] UKHL 66 and,
more recently and specifically, in the decision in *Manchester Ship Canal Company
Ltd v United Utilities Water Ltd* [2022] EWCA Civ 852. The latter was handed
down after pleadings were filed in this case and before the hearing. On behalf of
MSCC, I was informed after the hearing that the Supreme Court has granted
permission to appeal. However, for present purposes, I am bound by both decisions.
Their effect is that MSCC does not have a private law claim in nuisance against
UU in respect of discharges from outfalls in breach of the foul water provisos,
identified by the Court as discharges in breach of section 117(5) and section 186(3)
WIA, such as to affect prejudicially or injuriously affect the purity or quality of
the water in the canal (these are the provisions relied upon by MSCC before this
Court). In his judgment Nugee LJ said as follows:

> '64 .... *I do not see why it is any less inconsistent to allow MSCC to sue
> UU for trespass (or nuisance) for operating a sewerage system that
> discharges untreated sewage into the canal in breach of the foul water
> provisos than it was to allow Mr Marcic to sue Thames for nuisance
> for operating a sewerage system that flooded his garden with untreated
> sewage.*
>
> 73. ... *Marcic shows that in certain cases the existence of a private law
> right to sue a sewerage undertaker in tort is inconsistent with the
> statutory scheme and such a right must be regarded as impliedly
> ousted.'*

126   On this basis, Nugee LJ arrived at the view that the role of the provisos is
diminished, leaving their practical effect unclear (§87).

127   So far as a claim in negligence is concerned; there was limited opportunity to explore the issue with the parties at the hearing because the point was developed primarily in reply and in written submissions after the hearing. However, the answer to this complaint appears to be that no defence of statutory authority arises where the powers in question been carelessly exercised:

> 'it is now well settled that where Parliament by express direction or by necessary implication has authorised the construction and use of an undertaking or works that carries with it an authority to do what is authorised with immunity from any action based on nuisance... To this there is made the qualification or condition that the statutory powers are exercised without "negligence" that word here being used in special sense to require the undertaker, as a condition of obtaining immunity from action to carry out the work and conduct the operation with all reasonable regard and care for the interests of other persons.'

Allen v Gulf Oil [1981] A.C. 1001 Lord Wilberforce at [1011]. Underlining is the Court's emphasis.

128   If so, MSCC can bring a claim at common law, in the event of any negligence or deliberate misconduct by UU, with, or without, the discharge proviso.

129   On the analysis above therefore, I have come to the view that there may be said to be limited value in the protection provided by the discharge proviso. The interference is, evidentially, theoretical. The tortious remedy of a nuisance claim is ousted. The tortious remedy of a negligence claim remains available.

130   MSCC sought to advance a case that compensation for the interference with its property is inadequate. I accept that the availability of compensation for interference with a person's A1P1 rights is, and has long been held to be, highly relevant to proportionality. Generally, a right to compensation is a necessary part of ensuring the deprivation or control of use of property is proportionate:

> '76 Mr Maurici's fourth key point was that other than in exceptional circumstances, compensation is required in cases involving the deprivation of property. However, he submitted, correctly, in my view, that the Strasbourg case law shows a marked reluctance to entertain allegations that the quantum of compensation is inadequate, unless the method for its calculation is manifestly without any reasonable foundation.' (Pascoe at paragraph 76).

131   MSCC's case that compensation is inadequate for the interference with its property right was not developed at the inquiry despite the availability of witnesses with considerable experience in compensation. Valuation is a complex exercise. MSCC's grounds and skeleton argument did not provide me with any detail as to the framework and operation of the compensation code. Accordingly, in the words of the Court in *Pascoe*) I am 'reluctant to entertain allegations' that the compensation code is inadequate.

132   In his oral submissions, in response to my queries, Counsel for the Secretary of State provided a general explanation that, pursuant to S.7 of the Compulsory Purchase Act 1965 (as modified by the Water Industry Act 1991) compensation is payable for the diminution in the value of MSCC's land as a result of the acquisition of UU's right to discharge. On reference to the Lands Tribunal, MSCC can make its case in relation to the terms on which the order was granted (i.e. where the right is not constrained by the discharge proviso). Any award will seek to put

MSCC in the same position so far as money can do so as it was in in the absence of the grant of the right. MSCC will be compensated with reference to, and on the strength of, its evidence as to that depreciation in reality. The method of valuation is not a matter of law but of valuation judgment. Risk is an element of the valuation exercise. The compensation regime is well versed in dealing with future uncertainty, even on a 'once and for all' basis, where the assessment of valuation is fixed at the valuation date and albeit in practice that valuation issues may be complex. If the extent of the effect of the restriction imposed by the CPO on MSCC's land interests depends on future events then the assessment of risk will reflect the terms of the right granted, and evidence as to the risk. How risk influences the valuation depends upon the valuation method used. Whatever valuation method is used it will necessarily involve a consideration of MSCC's land interests in the absence of the order compared to its land interests with the Order, as at the Valuation Date. The valuation will reflect that the right granted confers the right to discharge water, soils and effluent into the Canal. I did not understand Counsel for MSCC to dispute this general explanation.

133   As developed, MSCC's argument on compensation appeared to be that the compensation code provides compensation for when things go right but not when they go wrong. It is the common law and the availability of damages that provides compensation for when things go wrong as where the conditions of an environmental permit are breached and loss/damage is caused at some point in the future. Without having heard detailed argument on the point, I am inclined to accept as arguable, MSCC's contention as to the difficulty in using the compensation code to arrive at a capital figure which is supposed to express in present value terms the effect on the value of the land of not being able to bring a common law claim for damages in the future. It does not appear easy to arrive at an estimate of how likely a breach of a permit would be, how serious the breach or how much loss, or how far into the future. The complexity of this issue highlights why it would have been essential for this point to be taken at the inquiry. The fact remains however that the point was not taken and the issue is, on present facts, theoretical, for the reasons explained above. Similarly, on present caselaw, the issue does not arise because a common law claim in nuisance is ousted (*Marcic v Thames Water Utilities Ltd* [2003] UKHL 66 and *Manchester Ship Canal Company Ltd v United Utilities Water Ltd* [2022] EWCA Civ 852) and a common law claim for negligence remains open to MSCC (*Allen v Gulf Oil* [1981] A.C. 1001 Lord Wilberforce at [1011]).

134   Further, I note that in *Marcic*, in the context of the flooding of a garden with sewage, the House of Lords concluded that a human rights claim was ill founded because of the presence of the statutory scheme. The balance struck by the statutory scheme between the interest of customers of the sewage company whose properties suffer damage with the conflicting interests of the remaining customers in the event that more sewers (necessitating higher bills) had to be built to alleviate the flooding, is to impose a general drainage obligation on a sewerage undertaker but to entrust enforcement of this obligation to an independent regulator who has regard to all the different interests involved (Lord Nicholls at §42). The Court concluded in this respect that the question whether the system adopted by a sewerage undertaker is fair was a matter inherently more suited for decision by the industry regulator than by a court and the statutory scheme provided a remedy.

135   Applying this analysis to the present context, it may be said that the balance struck by the statutory regime is to provide a procedure under section 155 WIA,

whereby landowners can seek appropriate protection from any interference, via independent scrutiny of their interests, alongside the wider public interest. Applying the language of *Marcic*, it may be concluded that whether the CPO strikes a fair balance is inherently more suited for decision by the inquiry process (with further protection of judicial review) than private law litigation involving only the parties to the litigation and without any obvious role for the wider public interest.

136   Accordingly, on the case advanced before by MSCC, for the reasons set out above, I remain satisfied that the terms of the Order strike a fair balance.

137   Ground 2 fails.

Conclusion

138   For the reasons set out above the claim is dismissed.

R. (ON THE APPLICATION OF ASHCHURCH RURAL PARISH COUNCIL) v TEWKESBURY BC

Court of Appeal (Civil Division)

Andrews, Elisabeth Laing and Warby LJJ: 7 February 2023

[2023] EWCA Civ 101; [2023] Env. L.R. 25

⚖ Bridges; Development plans; Environmental impact assessments; Material considerations; Planning permission; Residential development; Screening opinions

H1   *Town & Country Planning—judicial review—environmental assessment—Town and Country Planning (Environmental Impact Assessment) Regulations 2017—bridge project related to proposed Garden Town development—whether judge erred in findings as to whether Officer's Report advising Committee to take into account public benefits of development facilitated by bridge but omit concomitant harms was irrational—whether erred in application of the principle in 'R. (on the application of Samuel Smith Old Brewery) v North Yorkshire CC'—whether erred in consideration of correct legal test and scope of 'project' under "project" Town and Country Planning (Environmental Impact Assessment) Regulations 2017*

H2   The appellant (A) appealed against dismissal of its claim for judicial review of the grant of permission by the respondent (T) for a road bridge over a mainline railway. The grounds of appeal were that the judge erred in: (1) his interpretation of the Officer's Report, which was said to have been irrational in advising the Planning Committee to take into account the public benefits of the development facilitated by the bridge but to leave out of account the concomitant harms; (2) his application of the principle in *R. (on the application of Samuel Smith Old Brewery) v North Yorkshire CC*; and (3) his consideration of whether the Committee unlawfully considered that the "project" for the purposes of the Town and Country Planning (Environmental Impact Assessment) Regulations 2017 was the subject-matter of the planning application; the bridge looked at in isolation. On the third ground, A submitted that the judge failed to address the argument that the Committee applied the incorrect legal test and erred in finding that the development of the bridge and its supporting infrastructure for which permission was sought and granted was a single project for the purpose of the EIA Regulations, given that the bridge had no purpose of its own but was to be built solely to serve future development. The sole purpose of the bridge was to help to facilitate the proposed Tewkesbury Garden Town based on a Masterplan. The planning application for the bridge was brought forward as a result of a successful bid for grant funding from the Government. The overall project was split into the bridge and a wider one including link roads and housing development. A Screening Report concluded that the bridge was Sch.2 development but, in isolation, would not be likely to have significant effects on the environment.

H3   **Held,** in allowing the appeal:

H4   (1) It was common ground and clear from the Officer's Report that no account was taken of any adverse impact that any development in accordance with the Masterplan would have. Indeed, the Committee was told that the assessment of harm was to be confined to the bridge structure. Yet the Report stated that "substantial public benefits" identified as the housing and associated infrastructure that would be delivered under the Masterplan would outweigh identified harms. A had submitted that the Committee acted irrationally by taking into account the benefits of the wider development that the bridge would facilitate, but not considering the harms, because the benefits could not be realised without the harms. The judge had rejected that submission on the basis that on an appropriately benevolent reading of the Officer's Report, the benefits that were being considered were not the benefits of any future development enabled by the bridge but, rather, the benefits of granting permission for the construction of the bridge *at that time*, instead of waiting for proposals for the wider development to be brought forward. In so finding, the judge had misinterpreted the Officer's Report. The question of timing was undoubtedly one matter addressed, but the public benefits to which the Planning Officer referred were not confined to the benefits of allowing the bridge to be built in advance of the rest of Phase 1 of the Masterplan. On a fair reading of the Officer's Report, the Planning Officer did place substantial weight on the contingent benefits that, in his assessment, would accrue from the development in Phase 1, and he invited the Committee to do the same. His overall approach was to invite the Committee to attribute substantial or significant weight to the prospective benefits of the wider development whilst directing them that they must leave out of account entirely any possible harms. Whilst it was open to the decision maker to treat the prospective benefits of the wider development as material factors, it was irrational to do so without taking account of any adverse impact that the envisaged development might have, to the extent that it was possible to do so.

H5   (2) The judge had also erred in considering that the principle in *Samuel Smith* was applicable, because that principle arose when the decision-maker had itself determined whether a factor was material or not and thereby exercised an unfettered discretion to leave something out of consideration. That was not what happened in the present case. The effect of the instruction given in the Officer's Report that the harms had to be left out of account was the skewed approach complained of in Ground 1; the decision maker could not rationally treat the benefits of the development facilitated by the bridge as material without also treating the harms of the development as material. The direction by the Planning Officer could equally be characterised as a misdirection in law. Therefore, Ground 2 also succeeded.

H6   (3) The identification of the "project" was based on a fact-specific inquiry. That meant other cases, decided on different facts, were only relevant to the limited extent that they indicated the type of factors which might assist in determining whether or not the proposed development was an integral part of a wider project. The question whether an application was part of a larger project could still be answered if planning permission had not been sought for the larger project or the details of the larger project had not been finalised. Insofar as the author of the Screening Opinion decided that the "project" had to be confined to the bridge because "any future contemplated development could not be [robustly] assessed at the time of the screening decision", they fell into error by conflating two separate inquiries; "what is the project?" and "what are the environmental impacts of that project?". The difficulty of carrying out any assessment of the impacts of a larger project which was lacking in detail, was a matter which was separate from and irrelevant to the question whether the application under consideration formed an integral part of that larger project. The developer's lack of nefarious intent in accelerating one aspect of a development in advance of the rest was irrelevant; the question was whether, on an objective analysis of the facts, the "project" for the purpose of the EIA Regulations would be too narrowly confined if the screening authority looked at the subject of the application in isolation, with the upshot that the environmental impact of the wider project would be looked at piecemeal instead of as a whole. In deciding not to carry out an EIA Assessment, T had not considered, as it was legally obliged to, whether the bridge application was an integral part of a larger project. There was strong support for the case that it was, though ultimately that would be a matter for T's planning judgment when it came to consider the matter afresh, approaching the issue in a legally correct manner. There could be no Phase 1 development without the bridge and the bridge served no purpose in the absence of the Phase 1 development. None of that information appeared to have been taken into consideration when determining the identity of the "project" for screening purposes. The judge never addressed those objections and that was enough to allow the appeal on the first aspect of Ground 3.

H7   (4) The judge erred in finding that the bridge had lawfully been considered a single "project" for the purpose of the EIA Regulations. That was not a rationality challenge to that conclusion but a challenge to the way in which it had been arrived at. None of the justifications provided by the judge for his conclusion that there was no error of law in the Screening Report withstood scrutiny. If and insofar as T justified treating the bridge as a stand-alone "project" by reference to; the difficulty of assessing the environmental impacts of the wider project, the fact that the Masterplan had no formal planning status, or the fact that EIA assessments would be carried out in future as and when Phase 1, or other aspects of it, become the subject of planning applications, it fell into error.

H8   (5) The appeal would be allowed on all three Grounds, the decision quashed and the matters remitted the matters to the respondent for reconsideration.

H9 **Cases referred to:**
Bowen-West v Secretary of State for Communities and Local Government [2012] EWCA Civ 321; [2012] Env. L.R. 22; [2012] J.P.L. 1128
Derbyshire Dales DC v Secretary of State for Communities and Local Government [2009] EWHC 1729 (Admin); [2010] 1 P. & C.R. 19; [2010] J.P.L. 341
Ecologistas en Accion-CODA v Ayuntamiento de Madrid (C-142/07) EU:C:2008:445; [2009] P.T.S.R. 458; [2009] Env. L.R. D4
Mansell v Tonbridge and Malling BC [2017] EWCA Civ 1314; [2019] P.T.S.R. 1452; [2018] J.P.L. 176
R. (on the application of Bateman) v South Cambridgeshire DC [2011] EWCA Civ 157; [2011] N.P.C. 22
R. (on the application of Burridge) v Breckland DC [2013] EWCA Civ 228; [2013] J.P.L. 1308; [2013] 18 E.G. 102 (C.S.)
R. (on the application of Champion) v North Norfolk DC [2015] UKSC 52; [2015] 1 W.L.R. 3710; [2016] Env. L.R. 5

R. (on the application of Finch) v Surrey CC [2022] EWCA Civ 187; [2022] P.T.S.R. 958; [2022] Env. L.R. 27

R. (on the application of Friends of the Earth Ltd) v Heathrow Airport Ltd [2020] UKSC 52; [2021] P.T.S.R. 190; [2021] J.P.L. 905

R. (on the application of Larkfleet Ltd) v South Kesteven DC [2015] EWCA Civ 887; [2016] Env. L.R. 4; [2015] P.T.S.R. D50

R. (on the application of Samuel Smith Old Brewery) v North Yorkshire CC [2020] UKSC 3; [2020] P.T.S.R. 221; [2020] 2 P. & C.R. 8

R. (on the application of Wingfield) v Canterbury CC [2019] EWHC 1975 (Admin); [2020] J.P.L. 154

R. v Rochdale MBC Ex p. Milne (No.2) [2001] Env. L.R. 22; (2001) 81 P. & C.R. 27; [2001] J.P.L. 470

H10 **Legislation referred to:**
Directive 2011/92 (EIA) art.1
Town and Country Planning (Environmental Impact Assessment) Regulations 2017 (SI 2017/571) regs 2 and 3 and Sch. 2

H11 *P. Brown KC* and *L. Glenister* (instructed by Richard Buxton Solicitors) appeared on behalf of the appellant.
J. Pereira KC and *H. Waller* (instructed by One Legal) appeared on behalf of the respondent.

JUDGMENT

LADY JUSTICE ANDREWS:

INTRODUCTION

1   This is an appeal against the decision of Lane J [2022] EWHC 16 (Admin) ("the Judge") dismissing the claim by the Appellant ("ARPC") for judicial review of the decision of the Respondent's ("TBC") Planning Committee on 22 April 2021 to grant planning permission for:

> "Development of a road bridge over the Bristol to Birmingham mainline railway north of Ashchurch, Tewkesbury. The proposal includes temporary haul roads for construction vehicles, site compounds, security fencing, surface water drainage channels and attenuation points."

The development was referred to in the application as "Ashchurch Bridge over Rail" or "ABoR" but I shall refer to it simply as "the bridge".

2   ARPC has raised three grounds of appeal, although, as will become apparent, there is a degree of overlap between Grounds 1 and 2. These both relate to the Planning Officer's Report to the Planning Committee which informed its decision ("the OR"). Ground 1 is that the Judge erred in his interpretation of the OR, which on ARPC's case advised the Planning Committee to take into account the public benefits of the development facilitated by the bridge but directed them to leave out of account the concomitant harms. Ground 2 is that the Judge fell into error in his

application of the principle in *R. (Samuel Smith Old Brewery) v North Yorkshire CC* [2020] UKSC 3; [2020] P.T.S.R. 221 ("*Samuel Smith*").

3   Ground 3 is that the Judge erred in his consideration of whether TBC unlawfully considered that the "project" for the purposes of the Town and Country Planning (Environmental Impact Assessment) Regulations 2017 ("the EIA Regulations") was the subject-matter of the planning application, i.e. the bridge, looked at in isolation. It is contended that the Judge (1) failed to address ARPC's argument that TBC applied the incorrect legal test and (2) erred in finding that the development of the bridge and its supporting infrastructure for which permission was sought and granted was a single project for the purpose of the EIA Regulations, given that the bridge had no purpose of its own but was to be built solely to serve future development.

4   The Court was greatly assisted by the able and succinct submissions of counsel, Paul Brown KC and Leon Glenister on behalf of ARPC, and James Pereira KC and Horatio Waller on behalf of TBC.

5   For the reasons set out in this judgment, I would allow the appeal on all three grounds, quash the decision of the Planning Committee, and remit the application for reconsideration.

BACKGROUND

6   In March 2019, Tewkesbury and its surrounding area was awarded Garden Town status for a potential development of up to 10,195 new homes, around 100 ha of employment land, and related infrastructure. This was based on the Tewkesbury Area Draft Concept Masterplan Report ("the Masterplan"), which sets out potential largescale development over an area described as the "North Ashchurch Development Area". TBC is the "lead authority" for the Garden Town.

7   The Masterplan is not a development plan document, but it provides a foundation for the formulation of such a plan in due course. The proposals for the Garden Town are not, as yet, supported by any allocation or policies in the Joint Core Strategy ("JCS") adopted in 2017 by TBC and two other local planning authorities, Gloucester City Council and Cheltenham Borough Council, working in partnership.

8   By the time the JCS was adopted, Tewkesbury Borough had an identified shortfall of 2,455 dwellings measured against the housing needs identified in the JCS. The challenge of meeting that shortfall was exacerbated by the decision of the Ministry of Defence ("MOD") to retain for operational purposes the whole of a site which had been expected to be released for development and to deliver most of the requisite housing.

9   Although in 2017 TBC considered it had identified sufficient sites to deliver housing in the short to medium term, it regarded it as critical to address the shortfall over the period of the JCS (to 2031). The three JCS authorities intended to do so in a strategic and plan-led way. They therefore decided to undertake a review of Tewkesbury's housing supply immediately after the adoption of the JCS. The aim of the review was to identify and allocate sites that would deliver housing and employment growth.

10   The Masterplan was drawn up in January 2018 to inform the JCS review. It provides a spatial growth strategy in order to meet the shortfall in the JCS requirements to 2031 and beyond. However, at the time that planning permission was granted for the bridge, the JCS review was not expected to be completed and

submitted until the Spring of 2023, and no action would be taken on it until, at the earliest, later that year.

11   The Masterplan contemplates that the development of the Garden Town would be delivered in phases. Phase 1 concerns an area to the north of MOD Ashchurch which straddles the Bristol to Birmingham railway line, though the largest part of that area is to the east of the railway line ("the Phase 1 area"). The Phase 1 area is bounded to the north by a brook known as Carrant Brook, and to the south by existing development on the edge of the town. Phase 1 envisages that by 2031 around 3,180 new homes would be built in that area, as well as the delivery of 46 ha of new employment land, a local centre with retail services, a new primary school and a new Green Infrastructure corridor. The Masterplan states that: "Road transport upgrades would be required to deliver this growth in capacity terms."

12   In the section of the Masterplan entitled "phasing principles" it is explained that the Masterplan concentrates on developing land to the eastern side of the railway tracks first, with the aim of creating a compact community with walkable neighbourhoods that eliminate fragmentation. However, in order to achieve any of the identified objectives it would be necessary to build a new link road across the railway line to which existing roads would be connected, thereby relieving pressure on the A46 corridor. This in turn required the construction of a new railway bridge.

13   The Masterplan expressly recognises that delivery of the northern development plots for Phase 1 development relies on "the provision of a northern link over the main rail line, overcoming severance and completing the link between existing local roads". It identifies the bridge as one of the "short-term enabling interventions". The bridge is therefore an essential prerequisite to the delivery of *any* housing development in the Phase 1 area. It is common ground that the sole purpose of its construction is to facilitate such development.

14   The construction of the bridge was described in the Planning Statement submitted in support of the application for planning permission as:

>   "Critical to the success of the overall development plan in the area to unlock parcels of land to the east of the railway through improving east-west access".

15   In the normal course of events, one might have expected any application for planning permission to be made only after the JCS review and the adoption of a local plan, and for TBC to seek permission for the Phase 1 development of which the bridge would form an integral part, including the link road and any other vital transport infrastructure. Instead, the application was made, and granted, for the bridge alone.

16   Mr Brown told the Court that the bridge is known locally as "the bridge to nowhere," because after it has been constructed, the temporary haul roads will be removed and there will be no connecting roads on either side, just a bridge in the middle of a field, which will be fenced off. Without a functioning highway unlocking the land within the Phase 1 area on the eastern side of the railway, the bridge will serve no useful purpose.

17   This unusual state of affairs has arisen because TBC wished to avail itself of funding from the Government which was only available for a limited period. In July 2017, the Government launched a £2.3 billion Housing Infrastructure Fund ("HIF") in order to support housing delivery through the funding of vital physical infrastructure, such as roads and bridges, with the opportunity to facilitate the

development of some 100,000 homes in England. The fund was split into two key areas, namely, forward funding (for larger schemes up to £250 million) and marginal funding (for schemes up to £10 million). The deadline for applications was September 2017.

18   TBC made a marginal funding bid for just over £8.1 million to deliver the bridge on the basis that this, in turn, would facilitate the development strategy of the wider Ashchurch area. In February 2018, TBC was informed that its bid had been successful. TBC subsequently entered into discussions with Homes England regarding the terms of the funding agreement. The Deputy Chief Executive of TBC, in a Report to the Executive Committee recommending approval of the proposed terms, said that the funding would "unlock a number of sites and forms an early phase of the development strategy to realise the Garden Town".

19   TBC approved the funding conditions and authorised entry into a formal agreement with Homes England on the proposed terms at its meeting on 19 June 2019. The funding agreement subsequently entered into between TBC and Homes England included a requirement that the funds be drawn down by 31 March 2022 (though that deadline has since been extended because of this litigation).

20   Given that the express purpose of the HIF was to support the delivery of housing, Homes England understandably required TBC to make a commitment to deliver the housing which the vital physical infrastructure to be built with the assistance of the funding would facilitate. The Homes England documentation split the project into the "main project" (comprising the bridge) and a "wider project" which included the link road and the housing development unlocked by the funding, detailed as 826 residential units. Homes England accepted that delivery of the "wider project" was outside the control of the "main project". It therefore agreed to accept a "best endeavours" obligation from TBC in respect of the development unlocked by the funding. TBC agreed with Homes England that it would use its best endeavours to build 826 residential units and commence the construction of those units in 2021, with the wider project being completed by 31 March 2030.

21   It follows, therefore, that at the time when the application for planning permission for the bridge was considered, there was a clear expectation that the bridge would serve at least 826 houses, to be built within the Phase 1 area on the eastern side of the railway track, and the road infrastructure, including the link road over the bridge, would need to cater for at least that number.

22   Prior to making the application for planning permission, TBC commissioned an Environmental Impact Assessment Screening Report, for the purpose of determining whether an Environmental Impact Assessment ("EIA") was required. The Screening Report was produced in May 2020. The Judge quotes relevant extracts at paras 17 to 26 and para 33 of his judgment. The Screening Report noted that the bridge would not be used until future development came forward to make it operational. It recorded that the current proposals identified that the development area was anticipated to provide 826 new houses. Nevertheless it treated the bridge as a stand-alone "project", to be considered independently from any environmental assessment of the highway and residential elements of the development that it was envisaged the bridge would facilitate. It noted that an assessment of those elements would be carried out in future, as and when it was envisaged that any development under Phase 1 of the Masterplan would be implemented.

23   The Screening Report recognised that the bridge was Schedule 2 development under the EIA Regulations, but concluded that, looked at in isolation, it was not

likely to have significant effects on the environment. It was therefore unnecessary to carry out an EIA. TBC issued its Screening Opinion to that effect, adopting the conclusions of the Screening Report, on 22 June 2020.

24   A Transport Assessment was also commissioned by TBC. This was produced on 11 September 2020. It specifically confined itself to consideration of the bridge proposal, focusing primarily on the transport impacts of its construction. However, "for information", it also considered:

> "the potential impacts of an associated link road that would connect Hardwick Bank Road with the B4079 via the ABoR and the development of 826 residential dwellings that could achieve access via the ABoR and associated link road. It is important to note that the associated link road and 826 residential dwellings will be supported by separate future planning applications that will include further assessments."

25   The authors of the Transport Assessment indicated the approximate alignment of the link road, which closely mirrored the intended location of the haul road. They were also able to model the likely traffic flows on that link road and surrounding road network from the link road and anticipated residential development.

26   A Heritage Assessment, which was also produced on 11 September 2020, identified "the Scheme" as "just the construction of the bridge," and considered the potential impacts of what the authors termed the "construction phase" and the "operational phase" of the Scheme (as so defined). It identified the closest listed buildings to the site as two Grade 2 listed buildings, Northway Mill and Northway Mill House, 90m to the north of the site of the bridge. The impact on them was assessed from a purely visual perspective, and the conclusion was reached that the bridge would cause a minor adverse impact on the setting of those heritage assets. Because the assessment was confined to the impact of the bridge alone, it did not take into account the impact on those assets or their setting that the link road over the bridge might have. Looking at the geographical layout on the plan, irrespective of its precise configuration, any link road would have to run to the west of the railway line and below the brook, and, as Mr Brown pointed out, it would necessarily be closer to the heritage assets than the bridge itself.

27   On 22 September 2020 TBC, as developer, sought planning permission for the bridge. They did not seek permission for the roads which would inevitably serve as a connection to the existing highway network, nor for any development arising from Phase 1 of the Masterplan, including the 826 homes to which TBC had committed. This was made clear in the Planning Statement.

28   The OR is dated 16 March 2021. It is a detailed report which runs to 43 pages, excluding the appended plans. The Judge quotes extensively from the OR in paras 28 to 48 of his judgment. I shall consider the content in more detail when addressing Grounds 1 and 2. Suffice it to say, at this juncture, that it identifies the main issues to be considered as:

> "the principle of the proposed development and phasing, design and visual impact including landscape impact and impact on AONB, highway matters, flood risk, impact on amenity, impact on ecology and trees, and impact on heritage assets."

It then goes on to address each of those issues before reaching a conclusion and making a positive recommendation.

29   The "Overall Balance and Recommendation" was expressed in these terms:

> "It is concluded that the benefits of the proposal, *including* the benefits of progressing the proposal at the current time, outweigh the identified harm. It is also concluded that the application is generally in accordance with development plan policy.
> It is therefore recommended that the application is permitted."[Emphasis added].

30   At the meeting of the Planning Committee on 16 March 2021 there was an oral presentation by TBC's Development Manager. This largely repeated and reinforced what was said in the OR. The Minutes record that among the things he said were that:

> "whilst clearly the bridge was intended to serve a particular function in the future, at this stage it was not certain what level of development it would serve, although Phase 1 of the masterplan would deliver over 3,000 homes…"

> "Impacts related to the wider Garden Town proposals would be considered in any future planning applications for that development."

> "… issues related to the wider development that the bridge was intended to serve were for another day."

> "There were significant benefits arising from this development in enabling the delivery of the Masterplan and Garden Communities programme and ensuring that the necessary infrastructure was in place to achieve well planned development and that the delivery timescale of the Masterplan was maintained. There were also benefits arising through job creation during the construction."

(Later, in the course of the discussions following his presentation):

> "Future development and the impacts of it were not relevant currently and could not be considered as part of the application before the Committee today."

31   After extensive debate, the application was "permitted in accordance with the officer recommendation" by ten votes to seven, with one abstention.

GROUNDS 1 AND 2

32   A Planning Officer's Report serves two main purposes: providing information to the decision maker (in this case, TBC's Planning Committee), and making a recommendation as to how they should deal with the planning application. It must not be construed as if it were a statute, but approached from the perspective of how it would be understood by those for whose benefit it is prepared, and read with what Lindblom LJ described as "reasonable benevolence": *Mansell v Tonbridge and Malling BC* [2017] EWCA Civ 1314; [2019] P.T.S.R. 1452 at [42](2). The Planning Officer is likely to express personal opinions, for example, as to the weight to be attributed to various factors for or against the proposal, but the decision maker is not bound to agree with those views. They are free to accept or reject the recommendation made; but if they accept it, without expressing any further reasons, they will be taken to have adopted the reasoning in the OR.

33   Subject to any matter which they are legally obliged to take into account, materiality (i.e. relevance) is something for the decision-maker alone to determine. If something is capable of being regarded as relevant to the decision on a planning application, but the planning authority does not take it into account, their decision can only be challenged on an irrationality basis, i.e. on the basis that that factor was "so obviously material" that no reasonable decision-maker could have failed to consider it. That principle is established by a long line of authority including *Samuel Smith*, in which at [30] Lord Carnwath JSC adopted verbatim a passage from his earlier judgment in *Derbyshire Dales DC v Secretary of State for Communities and Local Government* [2009] EWHC 1729 (Admin); [2010] 1 P. & C.R. 19. See also the helpful exposition of the principle by Lord Hodge and Lord Sales JJSC in *R. (Friends of the Earth) v Heathrow Airport Ltd* [2020] UKSC 52; [2021] P.T.S.R. 190 at [116]-[121].

34   Ground 1 is founded upon a rationality challenge to the approach adopted in the OR which, on ARPC's case, treated certain identified benefits as material, but left out of consideration the concomitant harms.

35   It is common ground, and indeed is clear from the OR, that no account was taken of any adverse impact that any development in accordance with Phase 1 of the Masterplan would have (not even the impact of the construction of the link road across the bridge, or of the minimum development in fulfilment of TBC's "best endeavours" commitment to Housing England to build 826 homes).

36   Indeed, the Committee was told in no uncertain terms that the assessment of harm was to be confined to the bridge structure. For example, in a section headed "Access and Highway Issues" the OR stated as follows:

> "Significant concerns have been raised by the local community both in relation to traffic impacts during the construction period *and those related to potential future development in the area*, enabled by the proposed bridge. Whilst concerns in relation to the latter are understandable, as set out above, *those matters are not material to this application, the assessment of which relates solely to the construction of the bridge structure and related haul roads/compounds etc."* [Emphasis added].

37   Later, the OR said:

> "In terms of the operational phase of the development, the proposed scheme is to construct the ABoR and leave it in place but it *does not include the future highway that would utilise the bridge as part of the future development of the area, nor the associated planned housing to come forward.* Therefore at this stage of the ABoR scheme, *there are no operational effects to assess* in respect of noise, vibration and emissions. The effects of the operational phase of the development would therefore be considered when future applications come forward enabling the operational phase." [Emphasis added].

38   When dealing with heritage issues, the OR stated that:

> "It is acknowledged that the impact of the bridge is not likely to be in isolation. The bridge *is part of the garden town initiative which would result in additional* within the setting of the listed buildings *development on the land. However, at present, the application should be judged on its own merits."*

[Emphasis added. The rather clumsy syntax in the penultimate sentence is in the original text and was corrected by the Judge in para 41 of his judgment to "additional development on the land within the setting of the listed buildings"].

39   Yet only two paragraphs later, the OR stated that:

"It is the case that *there would be public benefits arising from this proposal,which is the first phase of the Garden Communities programme whichwould deliver housing and associated infrastructure.* It is also considered that there is *a clear and convincing justification for the proposed bridge to facilitate the Garden Communities programme…* officers consider that *the substantial public benefits arising from the proposal outlined above* would outweigh the identified harms [i.e. harms to the setting of heritage assets of high significance caused by the impact of the bridge alone] in this instance and that there is *a clear and convincing justification for the proposal."[Emphasis added].*

The "substantial public benefits" identified in that passage are the housing and associated infrastructure that would be delivered under Phase 1.

40   In the "Conclusion and Recommendation" section, under the heading "Benefits", the OR states that:

"Whilst it is recognised of course that the [Masterplan] is an evidence base document which carries very little weight in the decision making process, the application proposals are a first stage Short Term Enabling Intervention within [the Masterplan] and Garden Communities programme. *There are significant benefits arising from this development in enabling the delivery [of] the [Masterplan] and Garden Communities programme* and ensuring that necessary infrastructure is in place to achieve well planned development. The application site itself spans across land parcels 14 and 15 which are identified to have an indicative capacity for 2005 homes within [the Masterplan] *which would make a significant contribution to housing land supply. The HIF Funding financial modelling obligation is for the delivery of 826 new houses."[Emphasis added].*

41   This section of the OR then goes on to address the benefits of progressing the application proposals at the present time, which it characterises as "substantial". It states that this would:

"ensure the delivery timescale of [the Masterplan] is maintained seeking to achieve the aspirations and timelines of [the Masterplan] in the context of achieving the JCS and JCS Review Strategic Objectives and to meet the HIF funding deadline…"

42   Before the Judge, ARPC submitted that the Committee acted irrationally by taking into account the benefits of the wider development that the bridge would facilitate, but not considering the harms, because the benefits could not be realised without the harms.

43   The Judge (rightly) did not take issue with the proposition that if that is what the Committee did, it would have acted unlawfully. He rejected APRC's submission on the basis that on an appropriately benevolent reading of the OR, the benefits that were being considered were **not** the benefits of any future development that the bridge was enabling, but rather, the benefits of granting permission for the

construction of the bridge *at that time*, instead of waiting for proposals for the wider development to be brought forward.

44   In my judgment, in so finding, the Judge misinterpreted the OR. The question of timing was undoubtedly one matter which the OR addressed, but the public benefits to which the Planning Officer referred were not confined to the benefits of allowing the bridge to be built in advance of the rest of Phase 1.

45   The principle of the development was addressed in a section of the OR which preceded the "phasing" section, and which was devoted to the Masterplan. The level of detail in that section goes well beyond anything that would be needed to explain why it was important to keep the Masterplan on track. After correctly stating that the Masterplan is not a development plan document and that "as a planning document it carries very little weight" the OR elevated its importance by describing it as "part of the plan-led approach" and identifying a number of benefits that were integral to it. The OR explained how an area to the north of Ashchurch, which includes the application site, is highlighted as Phase 1, to be delivered by 2031 according with the timeline of the JCS requirement to deliver the shortfall of jobs and homes identified. It stated that:

> "The application site itself spans across land parcels 14 and 15 which are identified to have an indicative capacity for 2055 homes within the Masterplan."

46   There is then a description of the Transport Strategy included in the Masterplan, and it was noted that the Masterplan identifies that there is no transport solution yet for the quantum of development in Phase 1. In this context the bridge across the railway, and the road over it, were treated as part of an integrated means of delivering Phase 1:

> "However, the [Masterplan] identifies that a northern link (Northern Access Road link) is needed, crossing over mainline rail, joining up existing roads...."

47   This section of the OR went on to state that to deliver the Masterplan, the Transport Strategy identifies Short-Term, Medium-Term and Long-Term Enabling Interventions. The Northern Access Road is identified as:

> "a Short Term Enabling Intervention which is required for the delivery of the northern development plots which rely on the provision of a northern link over the rail line, overcoming severance and completing the link between existing local roads."

48   As the Planning Officer clearly recognised, and as is further demonstrated by the following section of the OR dealing with phasing, the bridge was an integral component of Phase 1 of the Masterplan and had no function other than to facilitate development in the Phase 1 area. At the start of that section, the OR identifies delivery of a new garden community as "*a* complex long-term *project*" (singular, emphasis added). There is then an explanation of why the planning application for the construction of the bridge was being made at that particular time, and why it was being made in advance of other associated infrastructure or land use developments notwithstanding that the bridge, on its own, served no purpose.

49   The Planning Officer identified the two reasons as being:

"due to a spending deadline associated with HIF Funding. It is necessary for the HIF Funding to be spent by the end of 2022 and the submission documents indicate that the construction period would be circa 12 months.

The applicant also advises that the ABoR is being advanced prior to the formalisation of site allocations within planning policy documents in recognition of the considerable lead in time and constraints associated with working on railway assets....

The application is therefore being progressed at the current time to deliver the Short-Term Enabling Intervention timescales of the Masterplan and to meet the HIF funding deadline."

Thus the OR made it clear that the bridge was never intended to be a stand-alone development. It was perceived to be necessary to give an explanation for splitting it out from the rest of the project of which it formed an integral part.

50   The Planning Officer concluded that section of the OR as follows:

"Therefore the principle of progressing with the ABoR application *at the current time*, is a matter of planning balance. There are substantial benefits of seeking to achieve the aspirations and timelines of the [Masterplan] in the context of achieving the JCS and SCS Review Strategic Objectives, and ensuring that necessary infrastructure is [in] place to achieve well planned development. This weighs in favour of the principle of *progressing the application at the current time*. However, weighing against the principle of *progressing with the application at the current time* is that the [Masterplan] is an evidence base document which carries very little weight in the decision-making process." [Emphasis added].

51   The Judge said, at para 74, that two related benefits were identified, namely "to ensure the delivery timescale of the [Masterplan] is maintained... and to meet the HIF funding deadline."

"In other words, constructing the bridge now would keep the aspirations of the defendant and the other local authorities for the Garden Town alive and on track"

52   He identified that the OR also made the point that construction of a bridge over a railway would take a considerable time, because it could only take place during periods when the railway was not in use, and that it was therefore sensible to bring forward the bridge proposal at the present time. The Judge said at para 79 that:

"this approach did not involve an assumption that any part of the Phase 1 development 826 homes will come to pass. Rather the point being made was that, if any such development were to be brought forward, the bridge would enable that development to take place in a timely manner. It went to the benefit of keeping the Masterplan on track, in that, should Phase 1 development be approved, the construction of the bridge would not be a delaying factor in seeing that development carried out."

53   That analysis, with respect to the Judge, fails to grapple with the point that there would be no benefit in keeping the Masterplan "on track," nor in hiving off and accelerating the delivery of part of a wider project, unless it was envisaged that

the wider project was in principle desirable and that Phase 1 would be, or was at least very likely to be, carried out - in other words, that there *would* be a link road over the bridge and a housing development of at least 826 new homes in the "unlocked" area - since that was the sole justification for building the bridge in the first place. If that did not materialise, the bridge would serve no purpose, and in addition, as identified in the OR, it would cause some harm to the setting of two Grade II listed buildings.

54   It is noteworthy that when addressing the pros and cons of dealing with the application for the bridge, no account is taken in the OR of the prospect that the wider development envisaged by the Masterplan would not be permitted, leaving a useless bridge standing in the middle of a field. That point is only mentioned in the OR in the context of summarising the objections to the application. In the passages containing the advice and recommendations, there is an inherent underlying assumption that if the bridge is built, the road over it will be built in due course, and that some development will take place in the Phase 1 area. That is understandable, given that the time-limited funding from Homes England which was the impetus behind the timing of the application was linked by contractual condition to the development of at least 826 new homes. So too were the milestones agreed by TBC.

55   It is important in this context to maintain the distinction between two related, but separate concepts: whether in principle this bridge should be built, and whether it should be built *now*. The Planning Officer, and the Committee, had to deal with both (as the OR expressly identified at the start of section 8) and, contrary to the Judge's findings, that is what they did. Read as a whole, the public benefits identified in the OR were **not** confined to the benefits of granting the application at the current time so as to allow potential future development to be planned and delivered in a timely way, or, as Mr Pereira put it in his oral argument, keeping the planning options open. They included the benefits to be achieved by constructing the bridge at all.

56   This is clear from the first paragraph of the conclusions and recommendations. The public benefits identified there include "enabling the delivery" of the Masterplan itself, and "ensuring the necessary infrastructure is in place" [to achieve this], as well as "seeking to achieve the aspirations and timelines of" the Masterplan. They are not confined to ensuring that the delivery timescale of the Masterplan is maintained and that the HIF funding is achieved. Meeting the HIF funding deadline was just another of the identified benefits. The short-term job creation during the construction phase, a further identified benefit, was plainly a makeweight, which by itself would not have outweighed the identified harm to the heritage assets acknowledged in the OR, let alone the (unacknowledged) harm of building what could become a white elephant.

57   For the Planning Officer, the benefit which plainly tipped the balance in favour of granting the application was enabling the delivery of Phase 1 of the Masterplan, which could not happen unless there was a bridge over the railway line at that location. But even if the identified benefits *had* been confined to preserving the viability of the Masterplan, they cannot be artificially divorced from the public benefits of Phase 1 of the development envisaged in the Masterplan. As Mr Brown submitted, there is no inherent value in the timetable for delivery of the Garden Town on its own; the public interest lies in the substantive development for which the timetable sets the milestones.

58   The distinction drawn by the Judge between (i) the benefits of a form of development and (ii) the benefits of enabling or facilitating such development, is a fine one. There is a distinction between the two concepts, but they are inextricably linked. One can only attribute significant value to the latter if one attributes significant value to the former. Put very simply, one cannot rationally conclude that it is beneficial to facilitate or enable a development to be carried out in future (especially when the means of facilitation serves no useful purpose in itself) without forming the view that the putative development is in principle desirable. That in turn involves considering, even at a very high level, whether the benefits of the envisaged development outweigh the harms it is likely to cause.

59   This proposition can be tested by assuming that the development which the bridge unlocked was something that might be seen as objectionable – such as, for example, the development of agricultural land for industrial activity such as an abattoir or a tannery, which would lead to many heavy lorries using the access road. One could only reach the conclusion that the benefits of keeping the prospect of that development alive (and on track in accordance with an envisaged timescale) by building the bridge, outweighed the potential harms of building a bridge that would serve no purpose without the link road or envisaged development, if one considered and weighed up the benefits and detriments of building a tannery or abattoir in that location and concluded that on balance it would be beneficial.

60   Mr Pereira raised the objection that at the time of the OR and the Committee's decision there was not, as yet, any specific housing proposal on the table for the development within Phase 1, and (because there was as yet no local plan, even in draft form) no specific sites had been identified for the delivery of the housing that was the subject of the "best endeavours" commitment. He also contended that it would not be possible to assess the impacts on traffic from any road over the bridge servicing the proposed development without knowing more details about the proposed road development.

61   However, as the Transport Assessment indicated, there would be some inescapable impact from the minimum development of 826 homes envisaged at the time, and it was possible, through modelling, to assess what that impact might be. There would be no need to know the precise layout of the link road, although it would be possible to make educated assumptions about the route it would take (bearing in mind the existing geographical constraints, which are obvious from the plans).

62   As for the location of the 826 homes within the Phase 1 area, it was unnecessary to know this with any precision to work out the likely impact on traffic flows of servicing that number of additional houses. The authors of the Transport Assessment had already done this exercise "for information". The various potential sites for the Phase 1 development were identified in the Masterplan; all of them would need to use the envisaged link road over the bridge. The Planning Officer had drawn specific attention in the OR to Parcels 14 and 15, within which the site of the bridge falls, as being likely candidates for the location of more than twice the number of houses within Phase 1 than the 826 which TBC was committed to use its best endeavours to build within the timescales in the agreement with Homes England. Parcel 15, which is the larger of the two, falls on the eastern side of the railway, the part of the Phase 1 area which the Masterplan envisaged would be developed first.

63   It is clear from reading the OR as a whole that its author worked on the premise
that the construction of a bridge facilitating Phase 1 of the Masterplan was a good
thing, because achieving Phase 1 (including enabling TBC to honour its commitment
to Housing England to start building 826 houses in that area by 2021) was a
desirable objective. The OR rightly recognised that the public benefit to be gained
by building the bridge was something different from the benefit(s) flowing from
building it now. The Judge was wrong to conclude otherwise.

64   On a fair reading of the OR, the Planning Officer did place substantial weight
on the contingent benefits that, in his assessment, would accrue from the
development in Phase 1, and he invited the Committee to do the same. His overall
approach was to invite the Committee to attribute substantial or significant weight
to the prospective benefits of the wider development whilst directing them that
they must leave out of account entirely any possible harms. Whilst it was open to
the decision maker to treat the prospective benefits of the wider development as
material factors, and it is understandable why they did, it was irrational to do so
without taking account of any adverse impact that the envisaged development
might have, to the extent that it was possible to do so, (which it was, albeit at a
high level). The two go hand in hand; you cannot have one without the other.
Ground 1 is therefore made out.

65   Ground 2 does not strictly arise in the light of my conclusion on Ground 1. I can
therefore express my views on Ground 2 more succinctly.

66   There is a distinction between, on the one hand, the situation in which a Planning
Officer expresses a view or gives advice with which the decision maker is free to
disagree; and, on the other hand, the situation in which the Planning Officer
misdirects the decision maker. The distinction between the two does not turn simply
on the language or expressions used in an OR, but rather, upon the substance of
the message being conveyed to the reasonable reader.

67   In this particular case, I am satisfied on an appropriately benevolent reading of
the OR as a whole that the Planning Officer in substance directed the members of
the Planning Committee that they could not or must not take account of the harms
of the proposed development that the bridge would facilitate. That went beyond
mere advice or the expression of a personal view about relevance. Those harms
were at least *potentially* relevant: materiality was a matter for the Committee to
determine, and they were being told that they must not consider something to be
material which they might otherwise have regarded as material.

68   The fact that the members of the Committee may have regarded the harms as
material is borne out by the fact that, as the Minutes of the Planning Committee
meeting reveal, some Councillors raised the issues of traffic on the link road, and
the 826 new homes, only to be advised by the Development Manager that "these
impacts *were not relevant* currently and *could not be considered* as part of the
application before committee today." That advice must have been based upon the
Development Manager's understanding of the OR. His advice served only to
confirm the impression of a legal direction which that document naturally conveyed.

69   The Judge erred in considering that the principle in *Samuel Smith* was applicable,
because that principle arises when the decision-maker has itself determined whether
a factor is material or not, and thereby exercised an unfettered discretion to leave
something out of consideration. That was not what happened here. The effect of
the instruction given in the OR that the harms had to be left out of account was the
skewed approach complained of in Ground 1; the decision maker could not

rationally treat the benefits of the development facilitated by the bridge as material without also treating the harms of the development as material. The direction by the Planning Officer could equally be characterised as a misdirection in law. Therefore, Ground 2 succeeds.

GROUND 3

70   This was the Ground of appeal which understandably occupied the most time in oral argument. The legal framework is uncontentious and can be summarised as follows.

71   Regulation 3 of the EIA Regulations provides that:

> "The relevant planning authority… must not grant planning permission or subsequent consent for EIA development unless an EIA has been carried out in respect of that development."

72   "EIA Development" is defined in regulation 2 as:

> "development which is…
> (b) Schedule 2 development likely to have significant effects on the environment by virtue of factors such as its nature, size or location.""

The bridge was correctly identified in the OR as a Schedule 2 development.

73   These provisions implement article 1(1) of the Environmental Impact Assessment Directive 2011/92/EU ("the EIA Directive"). The Directive requires the effects of the "project" to be assessed; the reference in the EIA regulations to the assessment of the effects of the "proposed development" is intended to give effect to this: *R. (Larkfleet) v South Kesteven DC* [2015] EWCA Civ 887; [2016] Env. L.R. 4 ("*Larkfleet*"). As a general principle, if an EIA is required it should be carried out as early as possible.

74   "Project" is defined in art 1 of the Directive as "the execution of construction works or of other installations or schemes" and "other interventions in the natural surroundings and landscapes". The term has to be understood "broadly, and realistically." The decision-making authority should consider "the degree of connection… between the development and its putative effects" and whether a particular consequence is "truly an effect": see *R. (Finch) v Surrey CC* [2022] EWCA Civ 187; [2022] P.T.S.R. 958 especially at [15](4), [33], [42] and [60].

75   "Likely" in this context means "possible", in the sense of "something more than a bare possibility, though any serious possibility would suffice": *R. (Bateman) v South Cambridgeshire DC* [2011] EWCA Civ 157, ("*Bateman*") at [15]-[21]; *Bowen-West v Secretary of State for Communities and Local Government* [2012] EWCA Civ 321; [2012] Env. L.R. 22 at [28].

76   Regulation 5 contains general provisions relating to screening: the Judge quoted relevant aspects in his judgment at para 94. The requirement in Article 5(2) to provide "information on the site, design and size of the project" is a flexible one, which enables the planning authority to provide more or less information on those factors depending on the nature and characteristics of the project to be assessed. In *R. v Rochdale MBC Ex p. Milne* [2001] Env. L.R. 22, ("*Rochdale*") Sullivan J (as he then was) said at [H7] and [H8]:

"If a particular kind of project was, by its very nature, not fixed at the outset, but was expected to evolve over a number of years … there was no reason why a "description of the project" for the purposes of the Directive should not recognise that reality.…

The Directive sought to ensure that as much knowledge as could reasonably be obtained, given the nature of the project, about its likely significant effect on the environment was available to the decision taker. It is not intended to prevent the development of some projects because, by their very nature, "full knowledge" was not available at the outset."

77   As Moore-Bick LJ pointed out in *Bateman* at [20], a screening opinion is designed to identify those cases in which the development (i.e. the project) is likely to have significant effects on the environment. That assessment is necessarily based on less than complete information. It is not intended to involve a detailed assessment of factors relevant to the grant of planning permission, nor a full assessment of any identifiable environmental effects.

78   The identity of the "project" for these purposes is not necessarily circumscribed by the ambit of the specific application for planning permission which is under consideration. The objectives of the Directive and the Regulations cannot be circumvented (deliberately or otherwise) by dividing what is in reality a single project into separate parts and treating each of them as a "project" – a process referred to in shorthand as "salami-slicing": see e.g. the observations of the CJEU in *Ecologistas en Accion-CODA v Ayuntamento de Madrid* (C-142/07) EU:C:2008:445; [2009] Env. L.R. D4 at [48] (adopting the approach taken in para [51] of the Advocate-General's opinion).

79   In *Larkfleet*, it was held that a proposed urban extension development and a link road were not a single project because despite the connections between them, there was a "strong planning imperative" for the construction of the link road as part of a town by-pass, which had nothing to do with the proposed development of the residential site. By contrast, in *Burridge v Breckland DC* [2013] EWCA Civ 228, ("*Burridge*") the Court of Appeal held that a planning application for a biomass renewable energy plant and a planning application for a combined heat and power plant linked to it by an underground gas pipe were a "single project," on the basis that they were "functionally interdependent and [could] only be regarded as an "integral part" of the same development."

80   It follows that the identification of the "project" is based on a fact-specific inquiry. That means other cases, decided on different facts, are only relevant to the limited extent that they indicate the type of factors which might assist in determining whether or not the proposed development is an integral part of a wider project.

81   Lang J, in her judgment in *R. (Wingfield) v Canterbury City Council* [2019] EWHC 1975 (Admin); [2020] J.P.L. 154, ("*Wingfield*") stated at [63] that the question as to what constitutes the "project" is a matter of judgment for the competent planning authority, subject to challenge on grounds of *Wednesbury* rationality or other public law error. At [64] she set out a non-exhaustive list of potentially relevant criteria, which serves as a useful aide-memoire. These include whether the sites are owned or promoted by the same person, functional interdependence, and stand-alone projects. In relation to the last of these factors she said:

"where a development is justified on its own merits and would be pursued independently of another development, this may indicate that it constitutes a single individual project that is not an integral part of a more substantial scheme".

The reverse may also be true, and that reflects the position in this case.

82   Mr Brown contended that the Judge did not address ARPC's assertion that the wrong legal test was applied by TBC in the screening assessment, and that in any event he erred in finding that TBC lawfully considered the bridge was a single "project" for the purpose of the EIA Regulations. As to the first of these submissions, it is right that the Judge makes no mention in his judgment of ARPC's submission that the wrong legal test was applied by TBC (or, perhaps more accurately, that the correct legal approach was not adopted). He moved straight into consideration of whether there was a public law error in the Screening Report (at paras 119 and following). There is no mention in his analysis of an alleged failure by TBC to consider whether the bridge was an integral part of a wider project.

83   Mr Pereira's answer to this was that there is not a "legal test" as such, because, as Lang J held in *Wingfield*, the identification of the project is a matter of planning judgment for the decision maker. Whilst it is true that the identification of the project is a matter of planning judgment, an important aspect of ARPC's substantive complaint in the lower court, reiterated by Mr Brown in this appeal, was that nowhere in the Screening Report (nor the OR, nor the Minutes of the meeting) is there any indication that the question whether the bridge formed an integral part of a wider project for the purposes of the EIA Regulations was even considered by TBC, and therefore the relevant planning judgment was never exercised.

84   There is no reference in the Screening Report to *Larkfleet* or *Burridge*, nor to the factors identified in *Wingfield*. The author did not address the question whether the bridge and the highway that was envisaged to run across it were "functionally interdependent"; nor the question whether building a non-functioning bridge in the middle of a field was justified on its own merits, as a stand-alone project, without regard to the development it facilitated; nor the question whether the application for permission would have been pursued in the absence of the proposed development of Phase 1 of the Masterplan.

85   The author of the Screening Opinion and the Screening Report provided a witness statement, but although that says that he was satisfied that the "project" in this case comprised the bridge only, he does not explain why, or identify what considerations led him to that conclusion. The nearest one gets to an explanation is in the passages in the Screening Report that perceive difficulties in carrying out a "robust" assessment of the environmental impacts of the wider Phase 1 development which had, as yet, no formal planning status. It could be inferred that these difficulties and/or the fact that the Masterplan had, as yet, no formal planning status were treated as a justification for concentrating on the bridge alone, leaving the environmental impacts of the link road and of the minimum of 826 houses to be built in the Phase 1 area to be considered on a future occasion as and when a planning application was made in respect of them.

86   Mr Pereira accepted that the Screening Opinion made it clear that the screening which had been carried out related to the bridge alone. He submitted that the Screening Report was not defective because it did consider whether the wider

impacts of the development could be assessed, and concluded for valid reasons that they could not. He referred to a passage in the Summary and Conclusions of the Screening Report which said:

> "it is noted that the ABoR is essentially advance works for anticipated future growth to the north of Ashchurch, providing a crossing point over the railway that could, in the future, be connected into the highway network to provide additional network capacity. However the planning policy context for the growth of this part of Tewkesbury is not yet fixed within adopted policy documents and no planning applications have been submitted to date in respect of sites directly to the north or east of the proposed ABoR site (specifically the North Ashchurch Development Area). Consequently, the preparation of a robust assessment of cumulative effects of the ABoR in light of a future baseline scenario incorporating growth in the North Ashchurch Development Area is not possible and any attempt to prepare such a document would arguably be premature – the developments would fall outwith the usual definition of reasonably foreseeable future projects on the basis of their lack of formal planning status."

87   Mr Pereira also submitted that there can be no question of "salami-slicing" in a situation where there is, as yet, no defined wider project for which planning permission has been sought or even contemplated, equating to the salami. The putative development under Phase 1 of the Masterplan was far too nebulous to be regarded in that way. There was no more than a draft concept masterplan which needed to go through a lengthy legal process before any permission would be granted for any part of that development.

88   I reject the proposition that in a case in which the specific development for which permission has been sought clearly forms an integral part of an envisaged wider future development, without which the original development would never take place, there can only be a single "project" for the purposes of the Directive and the Regulations if the contemplated wider development has reached the stage where an application has been made or could be made for planning permission. That proposition appears to me to be antithetic to the approach taken in *Rochdale* and inherently illogical. The question "is this application part of a larger project?" can still be answered even if planning permission has not yet been sought for the larger project or the details of the larger project have not been finalised.

89   Taken to its logical conclusion, Mr Pereira's argument about what constitutes a "salami" in this context would leave it open to a developer to conceal his plans for a far larger development from the planning authority and only bring them forward in piecemeal sections, thereby defeating the purpose of the EIA Regulations. This is not such a case, but the example illustrates the flaws in Mr Pereira's argument.

90   Insofar as the author of the Screening Opinion, and the Development Manager, decided that the "project" must be confined to the bridge because "any future contemplated development could not be [robustly] assessed at the time of the screening decision", they fell into error by conflating two separate inquiries, namely, "what is the project?" and "what are the environmental impacts of that project?" The difficulty of carrying out any assessment of the impacts of a larger project which is lacking in detail, is a matter which is separate from and irrelevant to the

question whether the application under consideration forms an integral part of that larger project.

91   In any event TBC did not conclude that it was impossible to carry out any assessment and, as the Transport Assessment demonstrated, it *was* possible to provide some high-level estimate of the likely effects on traffic on the basis of the link road and the minimum of 826 homes that TBC had promised to use its best endeavours to deliver as part of Phase 1 in order to secure the funding to build the bridge.

92   The Phase 1 project may not be easy to define in detail because it is at a relatively early stage, which explains why the Screening Report refers to a "lack of definition". That may affect the way in which the overall assessment of whether there is a significant impact on the environment is carried out – it would necessarily be based on less concrete information than an assessment at a later stage of the planning process would be. However, in my judgment it cannot affect the answer to the initial question at the screening stage, "is this application part of a larger project"? If and to the extent that TBC treated it as if it did, they fell into error.

93   The fact that the Planning Practice Guidance addresses the potential relevance of "other existing or approved developments" and tells local planning authorities that they should always have regard to the possible cumulative effects arising from any existing or approved development, should not be taken as restricting consideration of the impact of larger projects to "existing or approved" developments.

94   I accept that there was no evidence of any deliberate attempt by TBC to "salami-slice" in the present case. There were cogent justifications provided for hiving off and accelerating the application for the bridge, which had nothing to do with a wish to avoid the impacts of a full EIA assessment. But it does not follow from the fact that the application for the bridge was hived off in that way that its relationship to Phase 1 of the Masterplan, which provided the sole underlying justification for its existence, could be lawfully ignored when deciding on the identity of the "project".

95   The developer's lack of nefarious intent in accelerating one aspect of a development in advance of the rest is irrelevant; the question is whether, on an objective analysis of the facts, the "project" for the purpose of the EIA Regulations would be too narrowly confined if the screening authority looked at the subject of the application in isolation, with the upshot that the environmental impact of the wider project would be looked at piecemeal instead of as a whole.

96   I accept Mr Brown's submission that in deciding not to carry out an EIA Assessment, TBC did not consider, as it was legally obliged to, whether the bridge application was an integral part of a larger project. The evidence that TBC ought to have taken into consideration provides strong support for ARPC's case that it was, though ultimately that will be a matter for the planning judgment of TBC when they come to consider the matter afresh, approaching the issue in a legally correct manner.

97   The Screening Report described the bridge as "essentially enabling works for future development of sites proposed for new residential and community development within [the Masterplan]". Consistently with the explanation given by the Planning Officer in the OR, it said that the bridge was "being advanced prior to the formalisation of site allocations within planning documents in recognition of the considerable lead in time and constraints associated with working on railway

assets." As I have already observed, the necessary implication is that it would otherwise have been advanced at the same time (as is confirmed by the OR itself, see paras 48 and 49 above).

98   The bridge serves no purpose other than to unlock the sites to the east of the railway line for development, and is of no use at all without a functioning highway running across it. As Mr Brown submitted, there would be no rational justification for building a non-functional bridge over the railway line in that location, particularly if it would harm the setting of Grade 2 listed buildings, unless it was intended to serve at least the minimum of 826 new homes within the Phase 1 development which the HIF funding was designed to facilitate. In short, there could be no Phase 1 development without the bridge, and the bridge served no purpose in the absence of the Phase 1 development, including the functioning link road which would run across it. None of this information appears to have been taken into consideration by TBC when determining the identity of the "project" for screening purposes.

99   The Judge never addressed those objections, which are well-founded, and that is enough to allow this appeal on the first aspect of ARPC's case on Ground 3.

100   I also accept Mr Brown's further submission that in any event the Judge erred in finding that TBC lawfully considered the bridge was a single "project" for the purpose of the EIA Regulations. This is not a rationality challenge to that conclusion, but a challenge to the way in which TBC arrived at it. However, Mr Brown did submit that if the author of the Screening Report had addressed the right question, it is hard to see how he could have reached any conclusion other than that the bridge was integral to other development, at the very least as regards the roads serving it. I have already indicated that there is powerful support for that conclusion in the evidence, but as Mr Pereira stressed in the course of his oral submissions, it is not the function of this Court to usurp the planning judgment of the relevant authority. At most, it can indicate to TBC how it should have gone about the identification of the "project" and what factors are and are not relevant to that assessment.

101   Regrettably, none of the justifications provided by the Judge for his conclusion that there was no error of law in the Screening Report withstand scrutiny. In para 119, he appears to have regarded it as conclusive of the question whether Phase 1 was a "project" for the purposes of the 2017 Regulations that the application was simply for the bridge and not for the totality of the relevant development. Insofar as he did so, he erred in law. That would be true in any "salami-slicing" case, which necessarily concerns a situation in which the application is confined to one aspect of a larger development. Moreover, in para 120, he appeared to consider that the lack of any intention to "salami-slice" was conclusive of the question whether considering the bridge in isolation would be tantamount to "salami-slicing". As explained above, it is not relevant, let alone conclusive.

102   The Judge also appeared to consider that because the EIA Regulations would apply in future when Phase 1 is brought forward for application, or when the Masterplan is given formal planning status, they cannot apply now. That is not a test set out in the case law and, indeed, appears to me to be contrary to the decision of the Supreme Court in *R. (Champion) v North Norfolk DC* [2015] UKSC 52; [2015] 1 W.L.R. 3710. In that case it was held that a legally defective opinion not to require an EIA at an appropriate stage cannot be cured by carrying out an EIA at a later stage (nor even by carrying out an equivalent assessment outside the

Regulations at the correct stage). As that case makes clear, it is entirely possible for there to be a series of EIA assessments over time, as the details of a project are fleshed out.

103   The Judge appeared to accept at para 121 that the bridge, if constructed, may be taken into account in determining applications resulting from Phase 1 of the Masterplan when assessing whether "significant effects are likely as a consequence of a proposed development" but gave no cogent explanation for why the reverse is not true. Insofar as he was relying on the Planning Practice Guidance, the approval of the bridge is not a matter which makes all the difference to whether that structure is or is not to be regarded as an integral part of a more substantial project.

104   In conclusion on Ground 3, I am satisfied that TBC did not take a legally correct approach to the decision whether an EIA assessment was required. They never asked themselves the right questions. If and insofar as they justified treating the bridge as a stand-alone "project" by reference to (a) the difficulty of assessing the environmental impacts of the wider project (b) the fact that the Masterplan has no formal planning status or (c) the fact that EIA assessments will be carried out in future as and when Phase 1, or other aspects of it, become the subject of planning applications, they fell into error.

CONCLUSION

105   For those reasons, I would allow the appeal on all three Grounds, quash the decisions and remit the matters to TBC for reconsideration. I should make it clear, however, that nothing in this judgment is intended to influence the outcome of the future decisions that TBC will need to take as to whether to grant permission for the bridge alone, and as to whether the environmental impacts of the "project" (once it has been lawfully identified) are likely to be substantial so as to trigger a requirement for an EIA.

LADY JUSTICE ELISABETH LAING:

106   I agree.

LORD JUSTICE WARBY:

107   I also agree.

R. (ON THE APPLICATION OF FRIENDS OF THE EARTH LTD) v SECRETARY OF STATE FOR INTERNATIONAL TRADE/UK EXPORT FINANCE (UKEF)

COURT OF APPEAL (CIVIL DIVISION)

Sir Geoffrey Vos MR, Bean LJ and Sir Keith Lindblom: 13 January 2023

[2023] EWCA Civ 14; [2023] Env. L.R. 26

⊕ Dualism; Environmental policy; Export credits; Fossil fuel energy; Greenhouse gas emissions; Irrationality; Judicial review; Liquefied natural gas; Margin of appreciation; Mitigation of climate change; Treaties

H1 *Climate Change—International law—Paris Agreement—export credits—funding fossil fuel project in Mozambique—greenhouse gas emissions—whether funding project aligned with the UK's obligations in the Paris Climate Change Agreement— unincorporated Treaty—interpretation of obligations under Treaty—whether decision-makers could be challenged if adopting a 'tenable' view of obligations under an unincorporated Treaty—margin of appreciation—mitigation of climate change obligations*

H2   UKEF was an export credit agency whose mission was to ensure that no viable UK export failed for lack of finance or insurance from the private sector. A project considered for investment by UKEP comprised the development of offshore deep-water gas production facilities 50 kilometres from the coast of Northern Mozambique which was connected to an onshore gas receiving and liquefaction facility (the Project). The investment decision was said to be one of the largest single financing packages ever offered by UKEF to a foreign fossil fuel project.

H3   In making the investment decision, UKEF decided that climate change impacts and consideration of the 2015 Paris Climate Change Agreement (the Paris Agreement) should be taken into account alongside other factors. Consequently, UKEF prepared a climate change report which noted that gas was a transition fuel that was likely to displace higher polluting fossil fuels and result in a net decrease in emissions, but that it was not possible to accurately quantify the indirect emissions from fossil fuels (Scope 3 emissions). UKEF took the view that support for the project was in accordance with its obligations under the Paris Agreement.

H4   The claimant/appellant (FoE) was a campaigning organisation and challenged the decision by way of judicial review, arguing that the defendant/first respondent (SSIT) and the second defendant/respondent (CE) had acted unlawfully in approving UKEF's investment in relation to the Project. The Divisional Court refused the application finding that the view that the project was in accordance with the Paris Agreement was tenable. FoE appealed. The main issues in the appeal were:

(1) Whether SSIT and CE had erred in law in concluding UKEF funding of overseas fossil fuel project was in accordance with the UK's obligations under the unincorporated Paris Agreement.
(2) Whether SSIT's view that the Project was in accordance with the Paris Agreement was merely 'tenable' rather than substantively 'correct'.
(3) Whether the failure to quantify the Project's Scope 3 emissions was irrational.

H5   **Held,** in dismissing the appeal:

H6   (1) Article 3 to the Paris Agreement made it clear that the specific obligations on state parties to the Agreement were to be undertaken with a view to achieving the stated purposes of the Paris Agreement set out in art.2. The actions which parties were to undertake were not merely aims and aspirations. Article 2(1)(a) included a temperature goal, which was a clear objective of the Paris Agreement to which all parties had committed. The Paris Agreement was pre-eminently an international agreement negotiated to deal with a global problem. It was not helpful to seek to derive hard-edged obligations that one might more commonly expect to find in a commercial agreement to be interpreted under domestic law.

H7   (2) The question of whether investing in the project was aligned with the UK's international obligations under the Paris Agreement was justiciable, but the SSIT and CE were not compelled by domestic law to take account of the UK's obligations under an unincorporated treaty. They had chosen to do so, but the Agreement was only one of a range of factors to which they decided to have regard. It was not for the courts to allocate weight as between competing factors. If it was tenable for UKEF to reach the view that funding the project was aligned with the UK's obligations under the Agreement, a court could not and should not hold that it had made an error of law. UKEF's view was indeed a tenable one, bearing in mind the huge complexities explained in its climate change report on the project.

H8   (3) There was no domestic law requirement for the respondents to be certain that the decision complied with the UK's obligations under the Paris Agreement. It could not have been irrational for SSIT and CE to decide to provide finance for the project. SSIT and CE had been advised that the project could, in some scenarios, align with the obligations under the Paris Agreement. That was at least a tenable view when it was taken. It was known and understood by UKEF that Scope 3 emissions from the project would significantly exceed Scope 1 and 2 emissions, but it was not clear to what extent the project would contribute to fossil fuel transition. If liquefied natural gas entirely displaced coal and oil, it could lead to an overall net reduction in emissions. The precise outcome could not be predicted.

H9   (4) Subject to a challenge on the grounds of irrationality, it was for the decision-maker, not the court, to decide upon the manner and intensity of any inquiry to be undertaken to quantify possible Scope 3 Emissions. There was a wider margin of appreciation in decision-making involving the application of scientific knowledge or expertise. Quantification of Scope 3 emissions would not answer the far more difficult question of whether, and to what extent, gas from the project would replace more polluting fossil fuels and over what timescale. UKEF's decision was well within the substantial margin of appreciation allowed to decision-makers.

H10 **Cases referred to:**

Associated Provincial Picture Houses Ltd v Wednesbury Corp [1948] 1 K.B. 223; (1947) 63 T.L.R. 623; (1948) 112 J.P. 55 CA

Benkharbouche v Secretary of State for Foreign and Commonwealth Affairs [2017] UKSC 62; [2019] A.C. 777; [2017] I.C.R. 1327

Bumper Development Corp v Commissioner of Police of the Metropolis [1991] 1 W.L.R. 1362; (1991) 135 S.J. 382 CA (Civ Div)

Czech Republic v European Media Ventures SA [2007] EWHC 2851 (Comm); [2008] 1 Lloyd's Rep. 186; [2007] 2 C.L.C. 908

Deep Vein Thrombosis and Air Travel Group Litigation, Re [2005] UKHL 72; [2006] 1 A.C. 495; [2005] 3 W.L.R. 1320

Ecuador v Occidental Exploration & Production Co [2005] EWCA Civ 1116; [2006] Q.B. 432; [2006] 2 W.L.R. 70

Edwards (Inspector of Taxes) v Bairstow [1956] A.C. 14; [1955] 3 W.L.R. 410; 48 R. & I.T. 534 HL

FS Cairo (Nile Plaza) LLC v Lady Brownlie [2021] UKSC 45; [2022] A.C. 995; [2021] 3 W.L.R. 1011

GPF GP Sarl v Poland [2018] EWHC 409 (Comm); [2018] Bus. L.R. 1203; [2018] 1 Lloyd's Rep. 410

Heathrow Airport Ltd v HM Treasury [2021] EWCA Civ 783; [2021] S.T.C. 1203; [2021] B.V.C. 16

IBA Health Ltd v Office of Fair Trading [2004] EWCA Civ 142; [2005] E.C.C. 1; [2004] I.C.R. 1364

JH Rayner (Mincing Lane) Ltd v Department of Trade and Industry [1990] 2 A.C. 418; [1989] 3 W.L.R. 969; (1990) 87(4) L.S.G. 68 HL

Kennedy v Information Commissioner [2014] UKSC 20; [2015] A.C. 455; [2014] 2 W.L.R. 808

Kuwait Airways Corp v Iraqi Airways Co (No.6) [2002] UKHL 19; [2002] 2 A.C. 883; [2002] 2 W.L.R. 1353

Mohammed v Secretary of State for Defence [2017] UKSC 2; [2017] A.C. 821; [2017] 2 W.L.R. 327

Norris v United States [2010] UKSC 9; [2010] 2 A.C. 487; [2010] 2 W.L.R. 572

R. (on the application of Abbasi) v Secretary of State for Foreign and Commonwealth Affairs [2002] EWCA Civ 1598; [2003] U.K.H.R.R. 76; (2002) 99(47) L.S.G. 29

R. (on the application of Adan (Lul Omar)) v Secretary of State for the Home Department [2001] 2 A.C. 477; [2001] 2 W.L.R. 143; (2001) 98(4) L.S.G. 49 HL

R. (on the application of Barclay) v Secretary of State for Justice [2009] UKSC 9; [2010] 1 A.C. 464; [2009] 3 W.L.R. 1270

R. (on the application of Campaign for Nuclear Disarmament) v Prime Minister [2002] EWHC 2777 (Admin); [2003] A.C.D. 36

R. (on the application of Corner House Research) v Director of the Serious Fraud Office [2008] UKHL 60; [2009] 1 A.C. 756; [2008] 3 W.L.R. 568

R. (on the application of Elliott-Smith) v Secretary of State for Business, Energy and Industrial Strategy [2021] EWHC 1633 (Admin); [2021] P.T.S.R. 1795; [2022] Env. L.R. 5

R. (on the application of Friends of the Earth Ltd) v Heathrow Airport Ltd [2020] UKSC 52; [2021] P.T.S.R. 190; [2021] J.P.L. 905

R. (on the application of ICO Satellite Ltd) v Office of Communications [2010] EWHC 2010 (Admin)

R. (on the application of Khatun) v Newham LBC [2004] EWCA Civ 55; [2005] Q.B. 37; [2004] H.L.R. 29

R. (on the application of Mott) v Environment Agency [2018] UKSC 10; [2018] 1 W.L.R. 1022; [2018] Env. L.R. 20

R. (on the application of Privacy International) v Investigatory Powers Tribunal [2017] EWHC 114 (Admin)

R. (on the application of SC) v Secretary of State for Work and Pensions [2021] UKSC 26; [2022] A.C. 223; [2021] 3 W.L.R. 428

R. v DPP Ex p. Kebeline [2000] 2 A.C. 326; [1999] 3 W.L.R. 972; [2000] 1 Cr. App. R. 275 HL

R. v Secretary of State for the Home Department Ex p. Launder (No.2) [1997] 1 W.L.R. 839; (1997) 94(24) L.S.G. 33; (1997) 147 N.L.J. 793 HL

Reyes v Al-Malki [2017] UKSC 61; [2019] A.C. 735; [2017] 3 W.L.R. 923

Secretary of State for Education and Science v Tameside MBC [1977] A.C. 1014; [1976] 3 W.L.R. 641; (1976) 120 S.J. 735 HL

Ukraine v Law Debenture Trust Corp Plc [2018] EWCA Civ 2026; [2019] Q.B. 1121; [2018] 2 C.L.C. 627

H11 **Legislation referred to:**
Vienna Convention on the Law of Treaties 1969
ECHR art.6
Export and Investment Guarantees Act 1991 s.1
Human Rights Act 1998

H12 *J. Simor KC, Z. Douglas KC, K. Cook* and *G. Sarathy*, instructed by Leigh Day, appeared on behalf of the claimant.
J. Eadie KC, R. Honey KC, H. Higgins and *C. Fegan*, instructed by the Government Legal Department, appeared on behalf of the defendant.
A. Heppinstall KC and *F. Foster*, instructed by Latham & Watkins, appeared on behalf of the interested parties.

JUDGMENT

SIR GEOFFREY VOS MR:

Introduction

1   The main issue in this appeal is whether the UK Government acted unlawfully in approving UKEF's $1.15 billion investment in a liquified natural gas project in Mozambique (the project). The Divisional Court (Stuart-Smith LJ and Thornton J) could not agree on the outcome, and the application by Friends of the Earth for judicial review of the Government's decision (the decision) was dismissed. Both judges gave substantive judgments, and none of the facts that they recited in their judgments has been contested before us. The argument has, however, assumed a rather different focus in this court.

2   We recognise at the outset that the 197 state parties to the Paris Agreement of 12 December 2015 (the Paris Agreement) said that climate change represented an urgent and potentially irreversible threat to human societies and the planet and "thus require[d] the widest possible cooperation by all countries, and their participation in an effective and appropriate international response, with a view to accelerating the reduction of global greenhouse gas emissions". Notwithstanding that stark statement of the position, this case concerns an application for judicial review of UK Government decision-making and is to be determined, as the parties agree, on the basis of accepted and familiar principles of public law. Nothing we say in this judgment should be construed as supporting or opposing any political view of the issues. Our task is only to establish whether the decision is vitiated by an error of law.

The essential facts

3   The Divisional Court set out the facts on which both sides relied at [1]-[93] and [248]-[270]. Reference should be made to those paragraphs. In this section, we set out only those matters that are essential to understanding our decision. We have recorded the most relevant terms of the Paris Agreement in the annex to this judgment. Reference should be made to the entirety of the Paris Agreement for a full understanding of its provisions.

4   Friends of the Earth is a not-for-profit organisation that undertakes campaigning and other work in furtherance of environmental protection objectives. UKEF is an export credit agency whose mission is to ensure that no viable UK export fails for lack of finance or insurance from the private sector.

5   The project comprises the development of offshore deep-water gas production facilities 50 kilometres from the coast of Northern Mozambique connected to an onshore gas receiving and liquefaction facility. It is to be operated by TotalEnergies E&P Mozambique Area 1 Limitada (Total) and funded via MOZ LNG1 Financing Company Limited. The decision is said to be one of the largest single financing packages ever offered by UKEF to a foreign fossil fuel project. It formed part of a larger package worth in the region of $14.4 billion provided by other countries' export credit agencies, including the USA ($3.75 billion), Japan ($5 billion), South Africa (up to $0.96 billion), Italy (up to $0.95 billion), the Netherlands ($0.75 billion) and Thailand ($0.15 billion) (the figures changed but are given as at mid-2019). Various commercial lenders, including the African Development Bank, and regional banks from Southern Africa also supported the project. UKEF's support was conditional on Total procuring UK goods and services and is expected to create approximately 2,000 UK jobs.

6   We were told that Mozambique is one of the least developed and poorest countries in the world and is extremely vulnerable to climate change impacts.

7   We will now enumerate in chronological order the main events upon which the challenge to the decision was based.

8   In June 2019, the House of Commons Environmental Audit Committee reported on the scale and impact of UKEF's support for overseas fossil fuel projects including the project. It concluded that calculating Scope 3 emissions (all indirect emissions from the fossil fuels extracted by a project not included in Scope 1 (direct emissions) and Scope 2 (indirect emissions from the generation of purchased electricity)) was essential for an understanding of the full emissions impact of a project. It

recommended that the Greenhouse Gas Protocol provided an appropriate methodology.

9   In July 2019, the UK Government issued its Green Finance Strategy saying that it would ensure that any investment support for fossil fuels affecting emissions was in line with the Paris Agreement. The respondents say that this passage was expressly limited to official development assistance (ODA), and did not relate to export finance provided by UKEF, which is not a form of ODA.

10   In March 2020, consultants Wood Mackenzie produced a report entitled *Mozambique LNG—Carbon Emission Benchmarking*, saying that they were unable to model the project's emissions impact with any degree of certainty, but that there was particular scope for the gas produced to displace coal in power generation in China, India and Indonesia to "potentially reduce emissions". Wood Mackenzie said that they could not provide a definitive assessment of the emission reduction associated with the project.

11   On 29 May 2020, UKEF's final climate change report on the project (the CCR) concluded after a detailed analysis that "[g]as from the [project] is ... considered by the Government of Mozambique to be an important contributor to the energy transition of Mozambique in line with its NDC [nationally determined contribution] and its Paris Agreement commitments" and that "[t]his aligns with the UK Government's commitment to support developing countries to respond to the challenges and opportunities of climate change as part of its own Paris Agreement obligations". The CCR concluded that the project's Scope 3 emissions would significantly exceed its Scope 1 and Scope 2 emissions.

12   On 1 June 2020, Mr Louis Taylor, Chief Executive of UKEF (Mr Taylor), briefed the Secretary of State for International Trade (SSIT) recommending support for the project. He suggested that the SSIT read the CCR and said at [37] that "UKEF has a requirement to consider Climate Change risks as part of its consideration of support for the Project".

13   On 10 and 12 June 2020, the SSIT and the Chancellor of the Exchequer (CHX) provided their respective consents for the project. The Secretary of State for Business, Energy and Industrial Strategy and the Secretary of State for Foreign and Commonwealth Affairs opposed the project on environmental grounds.

14   On 18 June 2020, Mr Taylor briefed the Prime Minister saying that different Ministers and Departments held opposing views on the project, but that the requisite approvals from the CHX and the SSIT had been received, and that there were material legal risks to a decision either way. The briefing noted that gas was a transition fuel that was likely to displace higher polluting fossil fuels like coal and oil, and result in a net decrease in emissions in countries where that was the case. It was not possible to assess accurately the Scope 3 emissions. Friends of the Earth submitted that these latter points were wrong.

15   On 26 June 2020, the Prime Minister's private secretary indicated that the Prime Minister had reviewed the details of UKEF support for the project and was content for it to proceed. By a separate email, the Prime Minister's office asked the Department for International Development and the Department for Business, Energy and Industrial Strategy to provide advice on how a facility could be created for carbon capture, utilisation and storage to offset the emissions generated through the project.

16   On 30 June 2020, Mr Taylor was given a "very rough" estimate of 805.75 Mt (megatonnes) of carbon dioxide (CO_2) for the Scope 3 emissions over the life of

the project. Mr Taylor approved the underwriting minute for the project on 30 June 2020 and cleared the necessary legal documents on 1 July 2020. He gave these approvals in the exercise of his delegated power under section 1 of the Export and Investment Guarantees Act 1991. In that way, the UK Government made the decision to invest in the project without commissioning any detailed quantitative analysis of the Scope 3 emissions.

17   On 1 July 2020, the Commonwealth Development Corporation (the CDC-now called British International Investment), whose shares are wholly owned by the UK Government, issued its climate change strategy document. The CDC said that: "[c]rucially, we will not make new investments … in fossil fuel sub-sectors that we have classified as misaligned with the Paris Agreement", including standalone upstream gas exploration and production. The respondents submitted that this related only to ODA, not UKEF, investments and demonstrated that different policies applied to different parts of Government.

18   On 12 December 2020, the Prime Minister announced to the Climate Ambition Summit that the UK would end direct government support for the fossil fuel energy sector overseas, including natural gas projects, with very limited exceptions. That was said to be a significant change in policy to be implemented before COP26 (the 26th UN Climate Change Conference), which was to be held in Glasgow in November 2021.

19   In March 2021, the UK Government issued its *Guidance: Aligning UK international support for the clean energy transition*, which set out the detail of the new policy. The guidance said that the UK Government would "no longer provide new direct financial or promotional support for the fossil fuel energy sector overseas" other than in limited circumstances. It was expressed to apply to both ODA and UKEF support.

The main arguments of the parties

20   Friends of the Earth's grounds of appeal were that: (i) the respondents were required to adopt a view of the Paris Agreement that was more than merely tenable (the tenability issue), (ii) there was no rational basis on which the respondents could conclude that the decision was compatible with the whole of the Paris Agreement and article 2(1)(c) in particular (the rationality challenge), and (iii) the respondents failed in their duty of enquiry under *Secretary of State for Education and Science v Metropolitan Borough of Tameside* [1977] A.C. 1014 at 1065 (*Tameside*) to obtain a quantification of the project's Scope 3 emissions, and their view that the CCR was sufficient was irrational (the *Tameside* challenge). It may be noted at the outset that Friends of the Earth did not contend that the decision was irrational on the basis that it would, if it had been made some 6 months later, have contravened the Government's then climate change policy.

21   The first two issues, which were central to the appeal, resolved into the questions of (i) whether it was an error of law for the respondents to have concluded that the decision was aligned with the UK's obligations under the Paris Agreement, (ii) whether, once the respondents had decided to finance the project on the basis that such funding was in accordance with the UK's obligations under the Paris Agreement, it could ask the court to assess that question on the basis only of whether the respondents' view was or was not a tenable, rather than the correct, one, and

(iii) whether this court should determine the proper construction of article 2(1)(c) and, if so, what that construction was.

22   Friends of the Earth contended that, on the true construction of the Paris Agreement, by the application of the rules of interpretation contained in the Vienna Convention on the Law of Treaties (1969) (VCLT), such funding was not in accordance with the UK's obligations. The respondents had accepted throughout that they had indeed concluded that their decision was aligned with the UK's obligations under the Paris Agreement, not merely that there was a tenable view that it was so aligned. Friends of the Earth pointed to [1] of the respondents' skeleton, which said:

> In taking [the decision], as part of its due diligence, UKEF decided to have regard to the extent to which that Decision would be consistent with the UK's international law obligations under the Paris Agreement ... UKEF judged that [the decision] was consistent with those obligations ... UKEF concluded that, whilst the Project will have a significant climate change impact by increasing global [greenhouse gas emissions] emissions, [liquified natural gas] can act as a 'transition fuel' by displacing the use of more polluting fuels such as coal and oil and the Project will have transformational economic benefits for the Mozambican economy and has the "*potential to lift millions of Mozambicans out of poverty*". UKEF rightly considered that the [Paris Agreement] imposes no prohibition on developed countries assisting developing countries in such circumstances.

23   Friends of the Earth submitted that the court was bound by the House of Lords' decisions in *R. v Secretary of State for the Home Department Ex p. Launder* [1997] 1 W.L.R. 839 at pages 866-8 (*Launder*), and *R. v DPP Ex p. Kebilene* [2000] 2 A.C. 326 at pages 341-2, 367 and 375-6 (*Kebilene*). Lord Hope had explained at page 867 in Launder that:

> If the applicant is to have an effective remedy against a decision which is flawed because the decision-maker has misdirected himself on the Convention which he himself says he took into account, it must surely be right to examine the substance of the argument. The ordinary principles of judicial review permit this approach because it was to the rationality and legality of the decisions, and not to some independent remedy, that Mr. Vaughan directed his argument.

24   That view was supported, argued Friends of the Earth, by Lord Sumption in *Benkharbouche v Secretary of State for Foreign and Commonwealth Affairs* [2017] UKSC 62; [2019] A.C. 777 (*Benkharbouche*), who had said this at [35]:

> But I decline to treat these examples as pointing to a more general rule that the English courts should not determine points of customary international law but only the "tenability" of some particular view about them. If it is necessary to decide a point of international law in order to resolve a justiciable issue and there is an ascertainable answer, then the court is bound to supply that answer.

25   Since the respondents had accepted that the international law question of whether funding the project was consistent with the UK's obligations under the Paris

Agreement was justiciable, Friends of the Earth submitted that the court could not re-introduce justiciability factors and the tenability approach by the back door.

26   In response, the respondents submitted that Friends of the Earth were confusing treaties that had been incorporated into English law with unincorporated treaties that had not. The approach of Friends of the Earth breached the fundamental principle of dualism. Dualism meant that only treaties that had a legislative foothold in domestic law gave rise to legally enforceable rights. Unincorporated treaties did not. (See *J H Rayner (Mincing Lane) Ltd v Department of Trade and Industry* [1990] 2 A.C. 418 at pages 499-501 (often referred to as the *Tin Council* case), *R. (Miller) v Secretary of State for Exiting the European Union* [2017] UKSC 5; [2018] A.C. 61 at [55] (often referred to as *Miller* (1)), and *R. (SC) v Secretary of State for Work and Pensions* [2021] UKSC 26; [2022] A.C. 223 at [74]-[91] (SC)).

27   The respondents submitted that Benkharbouche did not apply to this case because it concerned article 6 of the European Convention of Human Rights (ECHR), which was a provision of international law that had been incorporated into domestic law through domestic legislation (the Human Rights Act 1998). They contended that Launder and Kebilene were explained by Lord Bingham (with whom Lords Hoffmann, Rodger and Brown agreed) in *R. (Corner House Research) v Serious Fraud Office* [2008] UKHL 60; [2009] 1 A.C. 756 (Corner House) at [44]:

> … reliance was placed in particular on [Launder] and [Kebilene]. Both cases concerned decision-makers claiming to act consistently with the [ECHR] at a time when it had not been given effect in domestic law. The courts accepted the propriety of reviewing the compatibility with the [ECHR] of the decisions in question. But there was in the first case no issue between the parties about the interpretation of the relevant articles of the [ECHR], and in the second there was a body of [ECHR] jurisprudence on which the courts could draw in seeking to resolve the issue before it. Whether, in the event that there had been a live dispute on the meaning of an unincorporated provision on which there was no judicial authority, the courts would or should have undertaken the task of interpretation from scratch must be at least questionable. It would moreover be unfortunate if decision-makers were to be deterred from seeking to give effect to what they understand to be the international obligations of the United Kingdom by fear that their decisions might be held to be vitiated by an incorrect understanding.

28   Lord Brown at [65] in Corner House echoed what Lord Bingham had said at [44] and added that "[f]or a national court itself to assume the role of determining such a question (with whatever damaging consequences that may have for the state in its own attempts to influence the emerging consensus) would be a remarkable thing, not to be countenanced save for compelling reasons".

29   The respondents argued that there was no jurisprudence as to the precise legal meaning of the Paris Agreement. Questions as to the interpretation of an unincorporated treaty were for the executive to determine. For those reasons, Lord Brown had been right in Corner House to suggest that, in such a case, the decision-makers could not be challenged if they adopted a tenable view as to a point of unincorporated international law. The respondents endorsed [66]-[68] of Lord Brown's speech in Corner House (with which Lord Rodger agreed), in which he had approved parts of an article entitled *International Law in Domestic Courts: The Developing Framework* 124 L.Q.R. 388 (July 2008) by Philip Sales QC and

Joanne Clement (the Sales article). In particular, the Sales article said at pages
405-6 that:

> If the rule of law in Launder is treated as unlimited it will lead to very extensive
> direct application of treaties and international law in the domestic courts,
> thereby for practical purposes undermining the basic constitutional principle
> about non-enforceability of unincorporated treaties. One solution might be
> for the domestic courts, in recognition of the limits of their competence …
> either to decline to rule or to allow the executive a form of margin of
> appreciation on the legal question, and to examine only whether a tenable
> view has been adopted on the point of international law (rather than ruling on
> it themselves, as if it were a hard-edged point of domestic law) … Adoption
> of a 'tenable view' approach would be a way … to allow space to the executive
> to seek to press for legal interpretations on the international plane to favour
> the United Kingdom's national interest, while also providing a degree of
> judicial control to ensure that the positions adopted are not beyond what is
> reasonable.

30   The respondents commended Lord Brown's conclusion that, in that case, he had
no doubt that the "tenable view" approach was the furthest the court should go in
examining the point of international law. They pointed to Lord Reed's clear
statement in SC at [84] to the effect that there was "no basis in the case law of the
European court, as taken into account under the Human Rights Act, for any
departure from the rule that our domestic courts cannot determine whether this
country has violated its obligations under unincorporated international treaties".

31   The competing positions of the parties as to the meaning of the Paris Agreement
centred on whether article 2(1)(c) imposed positive obligations on the parties. That
article provided that the Paris Agreement aimed to "strengthen the global response
to the threat of climate change, in the context of sustainable development and
efforts to eradicate poverty, including by: … (c) making finance flows consistent
with a pathway towards low greenhouse gas emissions and climate-resilient
development".

32   The interested parties focussed their submissions on the inequality between
developed countries and the least developed countries, of which Mozambique was
a prime example. They argued that the project would be economically transformative
for Mozambique, and that Friends of the Earth's attack would deny those benefits
to its population. Export finance from developed nations would help increase
Mozambique's gross domestic product by a projected $67.1 billion. These resources
would allow Mozambique to alleviate poverty, improve food security, invest in
green energy and to become climate change resilient. The Paris Agreement itself
invoked the equitable principle that least developed countries should be permitted
to address their high levels of poverty and low economic growth by exploiting
their natural resources so that their emissions peaked later than those of the
developed world. All that was in the context, argued the interested parties, that the
impacts of climate change had overwhelmingly been caused by the developed
nations.

The Divisional Court's decision

33   On the central questions that we have described above, Stuart-Smith LJ adopted the tenable view approach at [106]-[124]. He held at [230]-[231] that he would not "attempt … to give a definitive interpretation of the provisions of the Paris Agreement … or their legal effect", but that UKEF's view that the project was in overall alignment with Mozambique's stated climate policies was tenable. At [241], he held that UKEF had been entitled to form the view that its support for the project was in accordance with the UK's obligations under the Paris Agreement. Thornton J agreed with the tenability analysis at [262]-[270], but disagreed with Stuart-Smith LJ's construction of the Paris Agreement.

34   Stuart-Smith LJ concluded at [122] that the stated aims of the Paris Agreement were in tension "if not in frank opposition to one another". He held at [231] that the Paris Agreement should be approached "on the basis that it [did] not give rise to hard-edged free-standing obligations" but was "a composite package of aims and aspirations" that were "in tension or frankly irreconcilable". Thornton J's view of the meaning of the Paris Agreement was that it did give the UK hard-edged obligations. She said at [268] that "in order for UKEF to demonstrate compliance with Article 2(1)(c), it had to demonstrate that funding the project [was] consistent with a pathway towards limiting global warming to well below 2°C and pursuing efforts to 1.5°C", although the broad wording of article 2(1)(c) afforded UKEF discretion as to how it demonstrated compliance.

35   Thornton J's central holding, however, was at [331] to the effect that UKEF had "failed to discharge its duty of inquiry in relation to the calculation of Scope 3 emissions" and that "[i]ts judgment that a high level qualitative review of the impact was sufficient was unreasonable". Stuart-Smith LJ reached the opposite conclusion on the *Tameside* challenge at [214]-[224], especially [219].

36   After judgment had been reserved, the Divisional Court informed the parties that the two judges could not agree and offered them a re-hearing before a three-judge court. That offer was declined, and the parties agreed that the application should be dismissed, with the Divisional Court being requested instead to grant permission to appeal on the three grounds we have mentioned. Permission was granted accordingly.

Our conclusions in outline

37   Against that background, we have decided that this appeal must be dismissed. In broad terms, we agree with the respondents and the Divisional Court as to the tenability point and with the respondents as to the rationality and *Tameside* challenges. We do not, however, agree completely with either member of the Divisional Court as to the correct approach to the Paris Agreement.

38   It seems to us that, whilst the authorities to which we have already referred differ as to whether or not a domestic court ought to be reaching firm conclusions as to the proper construction of an unincorporated treaty, it is important first to understand the basic structure of the Paris Agreement. That is particularly important here where the two judges below reached clearly contrasting conclusions on the point. Our conclusion is that the specific obligations on state parties to the Paris Agreement are primarily to be found in articles 4, 7, 9, 10, 11 and 13, as article 3 indicates, and that the provisions of article 2, as article 3 also makes clear, represent the

purposes of the Paris Agreement. The specific obligations are to be undertaken with a view to achieving those stated purposes.

39   Once it is understood that article 2 reflects the purposes of the Paris Agreement, the other questions before the court fall into focus. The purposes in article 2 including "holding the increase in the global average temperature" and "making finance flows consistent with a pathway towards low greenhouse gas emissions" are to be achieved, for example, through the setting of nationally determined contributions (article 4), and through developed countries providing financial resources to assist developing countries (article 9). It is against that background that the questions we have set out at [20] and [21] above need to be resolved.

40   Our conclusions on the tenability issue and the rationality challenge are as follows:

  i)   The Paris Agreement is pre-eminently an unincorporated international treaty that does not give rise to domestic legal obligations.
  ii) The question of whether funding the project was aligned with the UK's international obligations under the Paris Agreement is accepted to be justiciable.
  iii) The Paris Agreement was, however, only one of a range of factors to which the respondents decided to have regard in reaching the decision.
  iv) The question of whether it was an error of law for the respondents to have concluded that funding the project was aligned with the UK's obligations under the Paris Agreement must be judged by considering whether the decision-makers adopted a tenable view of that question.
  v)   In other words, provided it was tenable for UKEF to reach the view that funding the project was aligned with the UK's obligations under the Paris Agreement, the court could not and should not hold that it had made an error of law.
  vi) UKEF's view was indeed a tenable one, bearing in mind the huge complexities explained in the CCR.
  vii) This conclusion may look as if it is reintroducing justiciability considerations through the back door, but it is actually an application of the constitutional law principle of dualism: the court cannot and should not second guess the executive's decision-making in the international law arena where there is no domestic legal precedent or guidance. The standard for judicial review may be, and is in this case, less intense where the issue is one that is not properly within the province of the domestic court (see, for example, Lord Mance at [53] in *Kennedy v Charity Commission* [2014] UKSC 20; [2015] A.C. 455).
  viii) These views are not affected by the fact that the respondents said they had formed a definitive view that their approval decision was compliant with the UK's obligations under the Paris Agreement, rather than simply saying there was a tenable view that it was compliant.

41   In relation to the *Tameside* challenge, we have concluded that it too cannot succeed. The Scope 3 emissions were always fully understood to be significantly larger than the Scope 1 and 2 emissions, even if no precise quantification was available until the Prime Minister raised the matter. It is true that the estimate of Scope 3 emissions given to the SSIT was much smaller than the estimate later given to the Prime Minister, but it is not possible to say that it was irrational to

take the funding decision without quantifying the Scope 3 emissions. It was known at the time that the project would go ahead with or without finance from UKEF. The absolute level of Scope 3 emissions did not answer the nuanced question of whether approval of the financing would or would not align with the UK's obligations under the Paris Agreement. The obligations in question were, anyway, not absolute requirements to restrict the increase in global average temperatures, and to make finance flows consistent with a pathway towards low greenhouse gas emissions and climate-resilient development. These were some of the purposes of the Paris Agreement.

42   We will now proceed to deal with the issues in detail as follows (a) the Paris Agreement, (b) the tenability issue, (c) the rationality challenge, and (d) the *Tameside* challenge.

The Paris Agreement

43   As we said at [38]-[39], the structure of the Paris Agreement is important. Article 3 specifically provides that parties are to undertake ambitious efforts "as defined in Articles 4, 7, 9, 10, 11 and 13" with a view to achieving the purpose set out in article 2. We have set out the most relevant parts of those articles in the annex. They provide, in broad summary, for:

  i) Each party to prepare, communicate and maintain successive nationally determined contributions that it intends to achieve;
  ii) The establishment of a global goal on enhancing adaptive capacity, strengthening resilience and reducing vulnerability to climate change;
  iii) Developed countries to provide financial resources to assist developing countries and to take the lead in mobilising climate finance;
  iv) The establishment of a technology framework;
  v) Parties to cooperate to enhance the capacity of developing countries to implement the Paris Agreement, and
  vi) The establishment of an enhanced transparency framework to support developing countries in implementation.

44   These actions do not seem to us to be merely aims and aspirations as Stuart-Smith LJ thought. All these actions are to be taken (a) with the aim of strengthening the global response to the threat of climate change, (b) in the context of sustainable development and efforts to eradicate poverty, and (c) for purposes including "[h]olding the increase in the global average temperature to well below 2°C above pre-industrial levels" and "making finance flows consistent with a pathway towards low greenhouse gas emissions."

45   It is worth mentioning at this stage that, in our view, Friends of the Earth was correct to say that the temperature goal in article 2(1)(a) was a clear objective of the Paris Agreement to which all parties committed.

46   We do not make these points about the structure and contents of the Paris Agreement by way of construction of its precise meaning, but in order to clarify what it appears, from its wording, to be intending to achieve. We do not find it helpful either to point to conflicts in the wording, nor to seek to derive from its text hard-edged obligations that one might more commonly expect to find in a commercial agreement to be interpreted under domestic law. The Paris Agreement is pre-eminently an international agreement negotiated, as we have said, by some

197 states to deal with a global problem. As Lord Sumption pointed out at [12] in *Al-Malki v Reyes* [2017] UKSC 61; [2019] A.C. 735, multilateral treaties are the result of an intensely deliberative process in which the language is minutely debated. The text is the only thing that all the many state parties can be said to have agreed: "A domestic court should not therefore depart from the natural meaning of [in that case, the Vienna Convention on Diplomatic Relations] unless the departure plainly reflects the intentions of the other participating states, so that it can be assumed to be equally acceptable to them". These characteristics apply equally to the Paris Agreement, and are important when one comes to consider the tenability issue.

47   It is also helpful to keep in mind in this context what the Supreme Court said in *R. (Friends of the Earth Ltd) v Heathrow Airport Ltd* [2020] UKSC 52; [2021] P.T.S.R. 190 at [71]:

> Notwithstanding the common objectives set out in articles 2 and 4(1), the Paris Agreement did not impose an obligation on any state to adopt a binding domestic target to ensure that those objectives were met. The specific legal obligation imposed in that regard was to meet any [nationally determined contribution] applicable to the state in question.

The tenability issue

48   Friends of the Earth placed reliance under this heading on the mandatory nature of article 31(1) of the VCLT which provides that: "[a] treaty shall be interpreted in good faith in accordance with the ordinary meaning to be given to the terms of the treaty in their context and in the light of its object and purpose". The tenability approach advocated by the respondents was the antithesis of interpretation, was contrary to the principle of effectiveness and was inconsistent with a binding line of authorities starting with Launder. This was not a Corner House case because there was no evidence that the respondents would have reached the same decision if they had not thought that the project was compliant with the Paris Agreement. Friends of the Earth submitted that, once a question under a treaty is justiciable, the court must determine it.

49   Whilst compelling in one sense, this line of argument ignores constitutional norms and seeks to turn a series of exceptions into the general rule. Lloyd-Jones J (as he then was) put the point well in *R. (ICO Satellite Ltd) v Office of Communications* [2010] EWHC 2010 (Admin) when he said at [92] that "… Launder and Kebilene were treated in Corner House as exceptions to the general rule (Lord Brown at [65]) and justified as cases in which there was no live dispute over the provisions of international law in issue or where there was a body of [ECHR] jurisprudence on which the national court could draw in deciding the issue before it (Lord Bingham at [44] and Lord Brown at [66])."

50   The reasons why the decision in this case is to be judged by the "tenability" standard, rather than the "correctness" test, can be summarised briefly as follows:

i) We accept the respondents' submissions summarised at [26]-[30] above and reiterate our conclusions summarised at [40] above.

ii) The respondents in this case chose, but were not compelled by domestic law, to take into account the UK's obligations under an unincorporated treaty that formed no part of it.

iii) There is a lack of clear guidance as to how unincorporated treaties like the Paris Agreement should be construed as a matter of domestic law. The approach mandated by the VCLT does not remedy the absence of parameters that, for example, existed in the case of the ECHR in Launder, but do not exist here.

iv) The Paris Agreement, therefore, was one of a range of factors to which the respondents decided to have regard in reaching the decision. It is not for the courts to allocate weight as between competing factors. Moreover, to make it necessary for the domestic courts definitively to construe unincorporated treaties every time the executive decided to have regard to them in making decisions would be problematic and unworkable for the reasons explained in Corner House.

v) The fact that the respondents said they had concluded that their decision was compliant with the UK's obligations under the Paris Agreement does not affect this conclusion. It must be open to the executive to say that it wants to comply with an unincorporated treaty, even though there may be different views as to what precisely it means. It must also be able to say, without successful challenge, that it thinks on balance and in good faith that a particular decision is compliant, even if it later changes its policy or is shown to have been wrong in the view that it took.

The rationality challenge

51   Friends of the Earth submitted that the respondents made an error of law in concluding that the decision to finance the project aligned with the UK's obligations under the Paris Agreement. Mr Taylor said that UKEF's analysis of and conclusions on whether the project was consistent with the Paris Agreement were set out in the CCR.

52   Those conclusions were contained in three places in the CCR (emphasis added):

i) First, the CCR said that gas from the project was "considered by the Government of Mozambique to be an important contributor to the energy transition of Mozambique in line with its NDC and its Paris Agreement commitments. **This aligns with the UK Government's commitment to support developing countries to respond to the challenges and opportunities of climate change as part of its own Paris Agreement obligations**".

ii) Secondly, the CCR contained this summary: "It cannot be stated with certainty whether or not the Project will contribute to fossil fuel transition due to the flexibility of the [supply purchase arrangements] and not knowing with any confidence how and where the Project's LNG volumes will be used. This uncertainty is an unavoidable consequence of the Project's off-taking arrangements and could not be resolved with further analysis or due diligence. For this Project, the end-uses are highly likely to be in multiple countries, so the impact of the Scope 3 emissions will contribute to the [greenhouse gas] emissions (and possibly the NDCs) of a range of countries and be spread across them. **Where the Project replaces and/or displaces coal or oil, the Project can be viewed as a transition fuel as it** provides lower carbon energy. **Where the Project displaces lower carbon fuels or potential use of renewable energy however, it cannot**".

iii) Thirdly, the CCR concluded: "**On balance**, taking the three posited scenarios, it appears more likely than not that, over its operational life, **the gas from the Project will at least replace some and/or displace some more polluting fuels, with a consequence of some net reduction in emissions**".

53   Friends of the Earth contended that science was the starting point. *The Special Report on 1.5 degrees* by the Intergovernmental Panel on Climate Change (IPCC) was crucial, because it included the various possible pathways to low emissions mandated by article 2(1)(c). Mr Taylor had confirmed in his evidence at [102.2] that UKEF had expressly considered whether the decision was consistent with a pathway towards low greenhouse gas emissions and had concluded that it was.

54   The case advanced by Friends of the Earth was not that the decision was irrational because it did not accord with UK Government policy as reflected in the CDC report or the new policy of December 2020 and March 2021 (see [17]-[19] above). It was irrational because, as a matter of law, as the Government itself later acknowledged in these policies, financing the project did not align with the UK's obligations under the Paris Agreement.

55   In our judgment, this argument breaks down for a number of reasons that can now be shortly expressed.

i)   Whilst it was known and understood by UKEF that Scope 3 emissions from the project would significantly exceed its Scope 1 and 2 emissions, it was not clear to what extent the project would contribute to fossil fuel transition. If the liquified natural gas entirely displaced coal and oil, it would lead to an overall net reduction in emissions. If it displaced lower carbon fuels, it would lead to an overall net increase in emissions. This uncertainty and the reports and materials obtained by the respondents made clear that the precise outcome could not be predicted.

ii)   In that situation, the respondents had to make the decision taking into account all relevant and material factors including the UK's obligations under the Paris Agreement. There was no domestic law requirement for them to be certain that the decision complied with those obligations, even if they did in fact eventually form the view that it did.

iii) Friends of the Earth's argument that the respondents had, in effect, to show that their decision was compliant, as a matter of law, with the UK's obligations under an unincorporated international agreement like the Paris Agreement points strongly, in our judgment, to the appropriateness of the tenability test in these circumstances. The compliance question is hugely complex as the CCR demonstrates. It is beset by uncertainties as to future events that were not and, in many cases, could not be known. It would be unworkable and impracticable if the Government could only make such a decision if it were able to demonstrate that its view of the factual and legal position was correct. In fact, the decision-makers knew that there were possible legal challenges whatever it decided.

iv)   In our judgment, the correct standard by which such decisions must be judged is one of tenability. The question under this heading is only whether the respondents' view that the decision aligned with the UK's obligations under the Paris Agreement was a tenable one when it was taken – not with the benefit of hindsight.

v) In our judgment also, and because of the complexity we have mentioned, the respondents' view was indeed tenable. It was supported by the initial Wood Mackenzie report and by the CCR. In essence, however, the argument to the contrary could only succeed if Thornton J at [262]-[268] and Friends of the Earth's submissions as to the proper meaning of the Paris Agreement were correct. In our view, they are not.

vi) To reach this conclusion, we do not believe that it is necessary to take any firm view as to the precise nature of the UK's obligations under the Paris Agreement. It is necessary only to be clear about what the Paris Agreement did not oblige the UK to do. As we have already said, article 2(1)(c) does not create an obligation on the UK to demonstrate that its overseas funding was consistent with a pathway towards limiting global warming to well below 2°C and pursuing efforts to 1.5°C. Article 2(1)(c) demonstrably contains the aims and purposes of the Paris Agreement, including "holding the increase in the global average temperature" and "making finance flows consistent with a pathway towards low greenhouse gas emissions."

56   In short, it cannot possibly have been irrational for the respondents to decide to provide finance for the project, when they were being advised that the project could, in some scenarios, align with the UK's obligations under the Paris Agreement. That was at least a tenable view.

The Tameside challenge

57   The *Tameside* principle is well established and uncontroversial. As Lord Diplock said in *Tameside* at page 1065: "[T]he question for the court is, did the Secretary of State ask himself the right question and take reasonable steps to acquaint himself with the relevant information to enable him to answer it correctly?". Subject to an irrationality challenge, it is for the decision-maker, and not for the court, to decide upon the manner and intensity of the inquiry to be undertaken (*R. (Khatun) v Newham LBC* [2004] EWCA Civ 55; [2005] Q.B. 37, at [35]). There is a wider margin of appreciation in decision-making involving the application of scientific knowledge or expertise (*R. (Mott) v Environment Agency* [2016] EWCA Civ 564; [2016] 1 W.L.R. 4338, at [68]-[82], upheld by the Supreme Court at [2018] UKSC 10; [2018] 1 W.L.R. 1022).

58   Friends of the Earth relied on six factual propositions: (i) the Environmental Audit Committee had said in June 2019 that quantification of Scope 3 emissions was essential, (ii) Scope 3 emissions dwarfed both Scope 1 and 2 emissions, (iii) Wood Mackenzie had been requested to assess Scope 3 emissions, but had said they could not do so, (iv) there was significant internal criticism of UKEF's failure to quantify the Scope 3 emissions, (v) UKEF also failed to consider the totality of the emissions against the world's remaining available carbon budgets having regard to the relevant timescales for their use, and (vi) when the Prime Minister requested a quantification, one was provided within 24 hours. These and other criticisms are explained in detail in [278]-[329] of Thornton J's judgment.

59   In our judgment, however, the flaw in Thornton J's approach appears from [335] of her judgment where she says that the failure to quantify the Scope 3 emissions and the other flaws in the CCR meant "that there was no rational basis by which

to demonstrate that funding for [the project was] consistent with" article 2(1)(c) and a pathway to low greenhouse gas emissions. Article 2(1)(c), as already explained, is an aim and a purpose of the Paris Agreement, not an obligation of the UK Government, with which compliance or consistency must be demonstrated.

60   Moreover, UKEF was entitled, in the context of its decision, to decide to "consider Climate Change risks as part of its consideration of support for [the project]" (see [12] above), without being required to assess those risks mathematically. Mr Taylor's evidence explained the wide range of considerations that UKEF took into account in making its decision.

61   As we have already said, the project was going ahead whether or not UKEF contributed to its financing. The decision was, therefore, not one that could have reduced or avoided the project's Scope 3 emissions.

62   The ultimate question for the court is whether it can be said to have been irrational for UKEF to have taken the funding decision without quantifying the Scope 3 emissions and supplementing the CCR report. Quantification of the Scope 3 emissions did not answer the far more difficult question considered in both the CCR and the Wood Mackenzie report, which was whether, and to what extent, gas from the project would replace more polluting fossil fuels and over what timescale. It was, as we have already said, well understood that Scope 3 emissions would far exceed Scope 1 and 2 emissions.

63   We conclude that UKEF's decisions as to the quantification of the Scope 3 emissions and the adequacy of the CCR were well within the substantial margin of appreciation allowed to the decision-makers. The decision to fund the project was not irrational, even bearing in mind that an estimate of the Scope 3 emissions proved to be obtainable in a short timescale when the Prime Minister, in effect, asked for it. Any estimate is by its nature uncertain. A failure to make such an estimate as part of a multifaceted decision-making process does not itself render the decision irrational.

Conclusion

64   For the reasons we have given, we dismiss Friends of the Earth's appeal.

R. (ON THE APPLICATION OF WILD JUSTICE) v WATER SERVICES REGULATION AUTHORITY

COURT OF APPEAL (CIVIL DIVISION)

Bean LJ: 17 January 2023

[2023] EWCA Civ 28; [2023] Env. L.R. 27

Breach of statutory duty; Enforcement; Judicial review; OFWAT; Rivers; Sewage; Sewage effluent

H1   *Water quality—water and sewerage undertakers—OFWAT—enforcement duties—Water Industry Act s.94—adequate provision for sewage disposal—whether OFWAT failed to discharge duty under s.94—Urban Waste Water Treatment Regulations 1994 reg.4—prevention of leaks—limiting pollution from storm overflows—Water Industry Act 1991 s.27(2)—OFWAT's duty to obtain information as to compliance with 1994 Regulations—whether OFWAT passive or failed in duty to obtain information on compliance—whether OFWAT failed in duty to exercise functions to ensure compliance with 1994 Regulations—whether unlawfully relied on information from Environment Agency regarding compliance with 1994 Regulations*

H2   The claimant (WJ), was a not for profit company set up with various purposes connected to wildlife and nature conservation in the UK. The defendant (OFWAT) was the economic regulator (amongst other regulators) of the water and sewerage industry in England and Wales. In April 2022, WJ sent a letter under the pre-action protocol for judicial review to OFWAT referring to a perceived lack of action (including monitoring and enforcement) in relation to the planned and unplanned discharge of untreated sewage into rivers and other water bodies. OFWAT responded by letter, setting out its current approach to monitoring and enforcement and arguing that bringing a claim for judicial review would be premature and that WJ's concerns would be better considered in a forthcoming consultation.

H3   WJ issued a claim for judicial review in May 2022, arguing that OFWAT had:

(1) failed to properly discharge its duty under s.94 of the Water Industry Act 1991 (the 1991 Act) to ensure that water companies make adequate provision for sewage disposal;

(2) failed to properly discharge its duty under reg.4 of the Urban Waste Water Treatment Regulations 1994 (the 1994 Regulations), to ensure that sewerage systems satisfied certain requirements such as preventing leaks and limiting pollution from storm overflows;

(3) unlawfully taken a passive stance and failed in its duty under s.27(2) of the 1991 Act to take steps to obtain information relating to water companies' compliance with their duties under reg.4 of the 1994 Regulations;

(4) failed in its duty under s.2(2A) of the 1991 Act to exercise its functions in a way that secured that water companies' duties under reg.4 were properly carried out;

(5) acted unlawfully in relying on data from the Environment Agency (EA) regarding water companies' compliance with reg.4 of the 1994 Regulations, because the EA had different statutory duties that arose under reg.6 of the 1994 Regulations.

H4   In the High Court, the application for permission was refused. WJ appealed.

H5   **Held,** in dismissing the application for permission:

H6   (1) There was no arguable case of unlawful action or inaction. OFWAT had not taken a passive stance but had gathered information, issued requests to water companies for compliance data, and commenced enforcement proceedings.

H7   (2) The distinction between s.94 of the 1991 Act and reg.4 of the 1994 Regulations was artificial as s.94 incorporated the requirements of reg.4. The duty under s.94 of the 1991 Act imposed obligations which OFWAT could enforce under its statutory powers set out in the 1991 Act. This included the substantive content of regs 4 and 5 of the 1994 Regulations. OFWAT's enforcement powers under s.94(3) of the 1991 Act also applied to the requirements imposed on water companies by reg.4(2) and 4(4) of the 1994 Regulations.

H8   (3) It was plain and obvious that the data collected by the EA, and by the OFWAT enforcement action and the subsequent s.203 notices, remained relevant to the obligations of water companies under the 1994 Regulations.

H9   **No further cases were referred to in the judgment**

H10   **Legislation referred to:**
Water Industry Act 1991 ss.2(1)(2A), 18, 27(2), 94(1) and 203
The Urban Waste Water Treatment (England and Wales) Regulations 1994 (SI 1994/2841) regs 4(1)(2)(4), 5 and 6
Environmental Information Regulations 2004 (SI 2004/3391)

H11   *D. Wolfe KC* and *E. Foubister*, instructed by Leigh Day appeared on behalf of the appellant.
H. Mussa KC and *N. Simonsen*, instructed by Gowling WLG, appeared on behalf of the respondent.

JUDGMENT

LORD JUSTICE BEAN:

1   This is an application for permission to appeal from a decision of Bourne J at an oral hearing refusing permission to apply for judicial review.

2   The Claimant is a not-for-profit company set up to advocate on behalf of wildlife to further nature conservation in the UK, to encourage public participation in nature conservation issues and to ensure that UK laws, policies and practices protect wildlife. No issue has been taken as to its standing to bring this claim. The Defendant, commonly known as "OFWAT", is the economic regulator and one of several environmental regulators of the water and sewerage industry in England and Wales.

3   By this proposed challenge the Claimant contends that OFWAT is not properly carrying out its environmental regulatory duties in relation to the planned and unplanned discharge of untreated sewage into rivers and other water bodies by water and sewerage undertakers.

4   Section 2 of the Water Industry Act 1991 provides:

> "(1) This section shall have effect for imposing duties on the Secretary of State and on the Authority [ie OFWAT] as to when and how they should exercise and perform the powers and duties conferred or imposed on the Secretary of State or the Authority by virtue of any of the relevant provisions.
>
> …
>
> (2A) The Secretary of State or, as the case may be, the Authority shall exercise and perform the powers and duties mentioned in subsection (1) above in the manner which he or it considers is best calculated–
>
> > …
>
> > (b) to secure that the functions of a water undertaker and of a sewerage undertaker are properly carried out as respects every area of England and Wales;
>
> …."

5   Section 94(1) of the 1991 Act imposes a duty:

> "(a) to provide, improve and extend such a system of public sewers (whether inside its area or elsewhere) and so to cleanse and maintain those sewers and any lateral drains which belong to or vest in the undertaker as to ensure that that area is and continues to be effectually drained; and
>
> (b) to make provision for the emptying of those sewers and such further provision (whether inside its area or elsewhere) as is necessary from time to time for effectually dealing, by means of sewage disposal works or otherwise, with the contents of those sewers."

6   Section 18 of the 1991 Act empowers the Secretary of State and OFWAT to make enforcement orders to secure compliance by water companies with statutory and other requirements including those referred to above. Section 94(3) provides that the section 94(1) duty is enforceable under section 18 by the Secretary of State, or by OFWAT in accordance with a general authorisation given by the Secretary of State. Such authorisation has been given.

7   The Urban Waste Water Treatment Directive, which sets standards for the treatment of sewage across the EU, was implemented through the Urban Waste Water Treatment (England and Wales) Regulations 1994 ("the 1994 Regulations"). The 1994 Regulations remain in force as retained EU law.

8   Regulation 4(2) of the 1994 Regulations requires sewerage undertakers to ensure the provision of collecting systems, i.e. sewers, which satisfy the requirements of schedule 2, in certain places or in certain circumstances. Paragraph 2 of schedule 2 to the 1994 Regulations provides:

> "The design, construction and maintenance of collecting systems shall be undertaken in accordance with the best technical knowledge not entailing excessive costs, notably regarding–

> (a) volume and characteristics of urban waste water;
> (b) prevention of leaks;
> (c) limitation of pollution of receiving waters due to storm water overflows."

9   Regulation 4(4) imposes a duty to ensure that urban waste water entering collecting systems is, before discharge, treated in accordance with regulation 5, which imposes certain requirements on the treatment of urban waste water, and that:

> "a. plants built in order to comply with that regulation are designed (account being taken of seasonal variations of the load), constructed, operated and maintained to ensure sufficient performance under all normal local climatic conditions;
> b. treated waste water and sludge arising from waste water treatment are reused whenever appropriate; and
> c. disposal routes for treated waste water and sludge minimise the adverse effects on the environment."

10   Regulation 4(1) provides:

> "(1) This regulation supplements the duty imposed on every sewerage undertaker by section 94 of the Water Industry Act 1991 (general duty to provide sewerage system) and any contravention of the requirements of this regulation shall be treated for the purposes of that Act as a breach of that duty."

11   The Claimant accuses the Defendant of failing to police the specific requirements arising under regulation 4. The claim is not directed at enforcement of the other, more general requirements under section 94.

12   Section 27(2) further imposes a duty on OFWAT, so far as appears practicable from time to time, to collect information with respect to the carrying on by companies of the functions of water and sewerage undertakers and of the carrying on by licensees of the activities authorised by their licences. The Claimant also contends that OFWAT is failing to perform that duty, in so far as it concerns the water companies' obligations under regulation 4, to whom I will refer collectively as "water companies". The present scale and the effect of such discharges have recently received considerable press and public attention.

13   On 4 February 2022, the Claimant made a request to OFWAT for information under the Environmental Information Regulations 2004 ("the EIR request"). The information requested included an explanation of OFWAT's function in monitoring and enforcing compliance with the obligations of water companies under Section 94(1) of the 1991 Act and regulation 4 of the 1994 Regulations. On the same date it also addressed targeted requests to DEFRA, the Environment Agency ("the EA") and all of the water companies in England.

14   OFWAT responded to the EIR request on 3 March 2022. Among other things, the response stated that, when monitoring and enforcing compliance with section 94(1) and regulation 4, OFWAT uses (1) information on compliance by companies with environmental permits and (2) information obtained from companies in the course of (a) setting regulatory price controls, under which companies explain what funding they need in relation to their assets to meet their legal obligations and (b)

annual monitoring of performance commitments given in the price control process. It also referred to a current OFWAT investigation of non-compliance by the English water companies with permit conditions and the possibility that this would lead to enforcement action by OFWAT for breach of duties under section 94. It did not provide any internal documents discussing OFWAT's enforcement strategy.

15   On 9 March 2022, OFWAT commenced enforcement processes against five water companies, serving statutory notices which referred to breaches of duty under section 94. OFWAT's case is that these included breaches of regulations 4(4) and 5 of the 1994 Regulations.

16   On 19 April 2022, the Claimant sent a letter to OFWAT under the judicial review pre-action protocol ("the PAP letter"), referring to a "lack of action (including monitoring and enforcement action) in relation to the planned and unplanned discharge of untreated sewage into rivers and other water bodies" and alleged that "OFWAT is unlawfully taking an entirely passive stance... including taking no steps to obtain information relating to compliance".

17   OFWAT responded to the PAP letter on 17 May 2022. It explained the related functions of OFWAT and the EA in relation to waste water treatment works. It set out OFWAT's current general approach to monitoring and enforcement in relation to the obligations of companies under section 94 and regulations 4 and 5 and denied that OFWAT was taking no steps to obtain information in relation to compliance. It also asserted that no useful purpose would be served by commencing a claim because (1) OFWAT was in fact currently investigating all of the water companies and (2) OFWAT was also developing the manner in which wastewater monitoring and compliance assessment takes place. It suggested that if the Claimant had specific points to make as to how monitoring and enforcement could be improved, it should raise those separately rather than bringing a claim, for example in the forthcoming consultation on its draft methodology for setting price controls for the next price control period.

18   The OFWAT response set out in great detail the monitoring activities which OFWAT carried out. These were stated to include the collection of information pursuant to annual monitoring of performance commitments given by companies during price reviews by OFWAT. As part of the annual performance reporting process each company is required to include information on specific performance commitments related to the companies' obligations under the 1994 Regulations. The letter argued that "although annual performance reporting against these performance commitments does not involve the submission or collection of site-specific data as such, it does provide OFWAT with relevant data to ascertain whether there is a potentially material problem with a company's performance which would warrant more specific intervention or data requests." The letter referred to the use of such data in OFWAT's investigation into Thames Water's leakage performance.

19   The letter also referred to the fact that OFWAT obtains data from the EA and Natural Resources Wales. Companies are also required to self-report any material non-compliance with obligations. It annexed a copy of a circular from the interim chief executive of OFWAT on 18 November 2021 to the chief executive of each water company. That circular referred to OFWAT's "significant concerns about the possible scale and extent of companies' non-compliance with the Flow to Full Treatment ("FFT") conditions set out in the environmental permits for their waste water treatment works in England." These concerns were stated to be based on

ongoing analysis by the EA of flow data as well as information which companies themselves had shared with OFWAT. The letter stated:-

> "It is for the Environment Agency and Natural Resources Wales to consider how they enforce compliance with individual environmental permits, including in relation to FFT and storm overflow conditions. OFWAT will be keeping abreast of that and any new information that becomes available, to inform the next steps we may need to take using our own regulatory tools. That includes but is not limited to enforcement action.
>
> If we find that use of our enforcement tools is necessary, we will apply the principles set out in our published approach to enforcement, including taking appropriate action to secure compliance, and being proportionate and targeted in focusing our intervention on areas of greatest detriment. We expect companies to come forward if they consider a breach of their obligation(s) is occurring and to take action to remedy the damage that breach has caused. Failure to do so would be considered in our approach to any enforcement.
>
> Alongside further information and steps that may come from the Environment Agency and Natural Resources Wales in due course, I want to hear urgently and directly from companies on this issue. Your response will inform what we do next. Therefore, I expect you to respond to the requests for information set out in Annex 1 and 2 of this letter as soon as possible."

20   The request for information set out in Annex 1 to the circular required the addressee company to provide details of the extent of any potential non-compliance with FFT permit conditions of which it was aware and the key root causes of potential non-compliance with those conditions.

21   Having referred to the circular of 18 November 2021, OFWAT's letter of 17 May 2022 went on to state that in March 2022 OFWAT had sent a notice to five companies pursuant to section 203 of the 1991 Act requesting further site specific information for enforcement purposes. The potential contraventions highlighted in each of these notices included the duty under section 94(1)(b) of the 1991 Act to make provision for dealing effectually by means of sewage disposal works or otherwise with the contents of the sewers in its sewerage system and including but not limited to breaches of regulations 4(4) and 5 of the UWWT Regulations. Each of the section 203 notices was said to set out further detailed site-specific questions. The letter also referred to a published decision of OFWAT in respect of its investigation into Southern Water.

22   The claim was issued on 30 May 2022. The challenge is stated to be against "the Defendant's failure to discharge its obligations under section 94 of the Water Industry Act 1991, as articulated in its Environmental Information Regulations 2004 response of 3 March 2022 and its pre-action protocol response letter of 17 May 2022".

23   The permission application in the Administrative Court was first considered in the usual way on the papers by Ellenbogen J. She referred it to an oral hearing. That hearing, which I am told occupied half a day, took place on 27 September 2022 before Bourne J. In a reserved judgment handed down on 18 October 2022 he refused permission for judicial review.

24   Ground 1 of the claim accused the Defendant of unlawfully taking a passive stance in relation to enforcement of the 1994 Regulations including taking no steps to obtain information relating to compliance with them from undertakers with

specific obligations in relation to their sewage treatment works. As Bourne J observed:

> "The accusation of a failure to act is put in a general or generic way, the Claimant has not identified any specific action which the Defendant should have taken and has failed to take. Rather it alleges a general failure to act and relies on an asserted lack of evidence of any such action."

25   Bourne J continued at paragraphs 50-55 of his judgment:-

> "50. It is …… clear that OFWAT's letter to water companies of 18 November 2021 (which included a requirement to state the causes of non-compliance with FFT permit conditions – which logically could include issues arising from the design, construction or maintenance of treatment plants) related at least in part to compliance with regulation 4 and not merely with the generality of section 94. So does the enforcement action against five water companies which began before the PAP letter was sent (and therefore before this claim was issued) and the action against a sixth which has begun since.
>
> 51. That is very important, because the Claimant's case is put in such sweeping terms. What is alleged is the taking of an entirely passive stance and an entire failure to obtain information.
>
> 52. In light of these investigation and enforcement steps which have occurred and are continuing, it is simply not arguable that the Defendant has not turned its mind to compliance with its statutory duties or that it is guilty of an entire failure to perform those duties.
>
> 53. None of this means that OFWAT has necessarily discharged its investigation and enforcement duties in a sufficient or satisfactory way. This claim does not allege any specific, individual failure to do so (despite some more specific criticism in the supporting witness statements) but is expressed in general terms. This Court may not be well placed to assess, and has not been asked to assess, the merits or demerits of the specific action which OFWAT is taking. Instead, the claim is based on a lack of connection with the regulation 4 obligations but, as I have said, there is plainly a connection with those obligations.
>
> 54. Moreover, there is no proper basis on which this Court should go behind OFWAT's assertion that, rather than being purely passive, it gathers information in several ways and uses that information for enforcement purposes, as is demonstrated by the current enforcement action. The Claimant has not shown that each of those types of information (which are listed in the summary grounds) is irrelevant to the potential enforcement of the regulation 4 obligations.
>
> 55. For these reasons there is no real prospect that the Administrative Court at a substantive hearing will find that OFWAT is simply not performing its monitoring and enforcement obligations in respect of water companies' section 94 duties."

26   When the application for permission to appeal came before me on the papers I directed that it was to be considered at an oral hearing.

27   In his oral submissions Mr Wolfe KC drew a distinction between the powers and duties of the EA on the one hand and OFWAT on the other. I asked what

remedy would be available to a member of the public or a group of individuals who alleged that the water company in their area was performing its duties so lamentably that a local river had become effectively an open sewer. Mr Wolfe responded that the EA could say that the company was in breach of its permit conditions, whereas OFWAT could say it was a breach of the company's obligations under section 94 and regulations 4 and 5.

28   Mr Wolfe said that "if OFWAT had satisfied themselves that the EA had imposed conditions on each permit which would effectively enforce regulations 4 and 5, we would have no complaint". He accepted that OFWAT has a discretion as to how it performs its statutory duties, but argued that the Authority has failed to show that it even addressed its mind to the enforcement of the obligations imposed by regulations 4 and 5 as opposed to the more general duty under section 94.

29   I accept the submissions of Mr Mussa KC for the Respondent that it is artificial to draw a distinction between duties under section 94 of the 1991 Act and those under regulations 4 and 5 of the 1994 Regulations. Section 94 of the parent Act is the section imposing obligations which OFWAT can enforce under its statutory powers set out in the Act. The duty under section 94 includes within it the substantive content of regulations 4 and 5. OFWAT's enforcement powers under section 94(3) also apply to the requirements imposed on water companies by regulation 4(2) and 4(4) (which also include the requirement to comply with regulation 5).

30   Part of Mr Wolfe's complaint is that OFWAT had been asked to make detailed disclosure of documents (even on a sample basis so as to avoid imposing a disproportionate burden) to demonstrate that it has actively addressed its collective mind to the requirements of the 1994 Regulations, but had declined to give such disclosure. When Bourne J said at paragraph 54 that "there is no proper basis on which this court should go behind OFWAT's assertion that, rather than being purely passive, it gathers information in several ways and uses that information for enforcement purposes" he was not, in my view, stating as a general proposition that a mere assertion by a defendant is enough to defeat a judicial review claim. Rather, he was saying that the detailed information given in OFWAT's letter of 17 May 2022 (which runs to 13 closely argued pages) is a sufficient response to the broad general allegation made by the Claimant.

31   I also do not accept that it is arguable that, even before the issue of section 203 notices to five companies and enforcement proceedings against a sixth, OFWAT's attitude was "merely passive". Such a contention overlooks, among other things, what seems to me to be a very significant feature of the regulatory regime, namely that OFWAT extracts performance commitments from the regulated companies in the course of its price reviews.

32   In short, I agree with all that Bourne J said about Ground 1.

33   Turning to Grounds 2 and 3 of the original claim: Ground 2 alleged that, in breach of section 27(2) of the 1991 Act, OFWAT has unlawfully failed to collect information in relation to the performance of the obligations under the 1994 Regulations. The statement of facts and grounds argued that "the Defendant does not appear to have even considered or decided how this duty will be exercised" in respect of the 1994 Regulations. It continues "It is not for the Claimant to specify what is required." The judge described this claim as "being, if anything put in even more general terms" than Ground 1. Similarly Ground 3 of the original claim alleged that in breach of section (2)(2A) of the 1991 Act, OFWAT has unlawfully

failed to discharge its functions so as best to secure that the obligations of water companies under the 1994 Regulations are properly carried out. Again, the allegation is of a wholesale failure rather than merely taking a passive stance. But again I agree with Bourne J, who dealt with this briskly as follows:-

> "Neither of grounds 2 and 3 is arguable. OFWAT has collected information and has taken enforcement action. However well or badly it has done those things it is not arguable that it has simply failed to do them."

34   The final ground for seeking permission for judicial review below was that insofar as OFWAT approached data passed on by the EA on the basis that such data discharged the separate obligations imposed by OFWAT under regulation 4 of the 1994 Regulations it acted unlawfully since the EA's obligations are different and arise under regulation 6. This seems to me extraordinarily technical. Like the judge, I consider it plain and obvious that the data collected by the EA, and by the OFWAT enforcement action set in train by its circular of November 2021 and the subsequent section 203 notices, were and remain relevant to the obligations of water companies under the 1994 Regulations.

35   In the result I agree with the judge that no arguable case of unlawful action or inaction on the part of OFWAT has been shown. I do not consider that an appeal from his decision would have any real prospect of success or that there is any other compelling reason for such an appeal to proceed.

36   I therefore refuse permission to appeal.

37   Although I allowed Mr Mussa to make brief oral submissions, I consider that save in exceptional circumstances a Respondent who attends such a hearing should do so at its own expense; and Mr Mussa accepted that if permission to appeal were to be refused it should be with no order as to costs. I am grateful to counsel on both sides for their considerable assistance.

R. (ON THE APPLICATION OF BRISTOL AIRPORT ACTION NETWORK CO-ORDINATING COMMITTEE) v SECRETARY OF STATE FOR LEVELLING UP, HOUSING AND COMMUNITIES

KING'S BENCH DIVISION (ADMINISTRATIVE COURT)

Lane J: 31 January 2023

[2023] EWHC 171 (Admin); [2023] Env. L.R. 28

⚖ Airports; Carbon budgets; Climate change; Development; Environmental impact assessments; Greenhouse gas emissions; Habitats; Material considerations; National Planning Policy Framework; Planning permission; Planning policy; Special Areas of Conservation

H1 *Climate Change—air pollution—greenhouse gas emissions—environmental impact assessment—nature conservation—airports—planning permission for expansion of local airport—potential increase in greenhouse gas emissions—relevance of development plan policies on climate change—Climate Change Act 2008—National Planning Framework para.188—relevance of local carbon budget—whether Secretary of State under duty to comply with local carbon budgets—adequacy of Environmental Statement—whether assessment of non-CO$_2$ emissions from aircraft required in Environmental Statement—replacement bat habitats—Conservation of Habitats and Species Regulations 2017 reg.63—whether ameliorative measures were 'mitigation' or 'compensation' measures*

H2 The first interested party, Bristol Airport Ltd (BAL), applied to North Somerset Council (NSC) for planning permission to expand the airport's capacity by two million passengers per year. NSC refused permission and BAL appealed to the Secretary of State under s.78 TCPA 1990. An inquiry was held over nine weeks from July-October 2021 before a Panel of three inspectors (the Panel). The Panel allowed BAL's appeal in February 2022. The claimant (BANCC), a network of environmental groups and local residents, had appeared at the inquiry and argued the appeal should be dismissed due to the airport expansion's serious effects on climate change. The claimant's expert evidence focused on the increase in greenhouse gas (GHG) emissions, especially CO$_2$, that would result from additional flights. It was agreed that the expansion would increase GHG, especially CO$_2$.

H3 The Panel found that:

(a) the relevant development plan policy CS1 on addressing climate change and carbon reduction, and policy CS23, which required Bristol Airport development to demonstrate satisfactory resolution of environmental issues, did not directly address aviation emissions;

(b) Another relevant policy document, *Beyond the Horizon—the Future of UK Aviation: Making Best Use of Existing Runways* (MBU) provided that increased carbon emissions should be dealt with at the national, rather than local level;

(c) Given the extent of scientific uncertainty in assessing non-CO_2 emissions; no policy as to how they should be dealt with; and BAL's intention to consider non-CO_2 emissions further in its Carbon and Climate Change Action Plan (CCCAP); it would be unreasonable to weigh that matter in the balance against the proposal.

H4   The Panel did not take into account the extent of the impact on the local authority's carbon budget in determining the significance of the proposal's climate change impact. The Panel concluded that aviation emissions resulting from the proposal were not so significant that they would have a material impact on the government's ability to meet its climate change target and carbon budgets and allowed the appeal.

H5   In challenging the Panel's decision, the claimant argued:

(1) The Panel misinterpreted development plan policies CS1 and CS23 by finding they did not directly address aviation emissions. Properly interpreted, the broad wording clearly encompassed aviation emissions. The Panel was also mistaken in deciding that the MBU document was not a matter for local decision-makers.

(2) The Panel was wrong to decide that the National Planning Framework para. 188, did not oblige the Secretary of State to comply with a legal duty to meet the relevant carbon budgets under the Climate Change Act 2008 (CCA). The CCA was not a "pollution control regime" within the meaning of the NPPF.

(3) The Panel failed to take into account the evidence on impact of emissions on North Somerset Council's local carbon budget and ignored applicable guidance on using local budgets to assess significance. This was an error of law or inadequately reasoned.

(4) The Panel erred in law in not requiring BAL's environmental statement to assess non-CO_2 emissions from aircraft, for which an emissions multiplier should have been applied. The Panel wrongly relied on BAL's future Climate Change Action Plan regarding non-CO_2 emissions.

(5) The Panel erred in treating replacement bat habitat as lawful 'mitigation' which complied with the Conservation of Habitats and Species Regulations 2017 reg.63, rather than 'compensation' which would fall under reg.64. This incorrectly assumed that any land lost as a result of the proposals was outside a nearby Special Area of Conservation (SAC) which avoided the need for a negative appropriate assessment and a decision that the project should be only permitted due to "imperative reasons of overriding public interest".

H6   **Held,** in refusing the application:

H7   (1) On a fair reading, the Panel did not misinterpret development plan policies CS1 and CS23 or fail to give adequate reasons regarding their application to aviation emissions. Policy CS1's broad wording allowed scope for judgment as to how they addressed aviation emissions, and the decision maker had a discretion to determine how such emissions were to be addressed, in any particular case.

H8   (2) The Panel had not misinterpreted MBU. The Panel had considered the carbon emissions from all sources in some detail, including from aviation. They did so appropriately by reference to whether the predicted aviation emissions from the proposal would have a material impact on the government's ability to meet its climate change targets and budgets. MBU had to be read in its entirety in order to understand what was meant by "environmental impacts" and considering "each case on its merits". It was apparent from the text of the MBU that one "important environmental element" which "should be considered at a national level" was the issue of "aviation carbon".

H9   (3) The CCA comprised a national emissions control regime regarding GHG emissions from aircraft. It was not irrational for the Panel to apply the assumption in NPPF para.188 in that context. The Panel gave adequate consideration to whether the assumption was rebutted on the evidence.

H10   (4) The Panel was entitled to give no weight to evidence on the local carbon budget, which had no basis in law or policy. This involved no error of law or inadequate reasoning. The Panel had engaged with BAANC's approach that the increased emissions would consume the local carbon budget, but had given it no weight. In doing so, the Panel had not acted irrationally. The fact that there was no policy basis for local carbon budgets was significant, given that the decision-making process was concerned with matters of policy.

H11   (5) The Panel made no error of law in finding BAL's environmental statement adequate, given the scientific uncertainty over non-CO_2 aviation emissions. Leaving non-CO_2 aircraft emissions to be dealt with when the science enabled them to be brought into account for the purposes of the CCA, was a decision that was open to those preparing the environmental statement, and one that the local authority and the Panel were entitled to accept. For the Panel to have attempted directly to address the non-CO_2 effects of aircraft emissions would have been highly anomalous. Therefore, even if they might have acted lawfully if they had embarked on such an exercise, it was not irrational for them to conclude that they would not do so. The Panel's reliance on the Climate Change Action Plan was therefore lawful and rational.

H12   (6) The Panel made no error of law regarding the replacement bat habitat. The Panel relied upon uncontested evidence from BAL and therefore did not reach its decision on the basis that the land to be lost was outside the SAC. As a result any measures taken by BAL would necessarily be 'mitigation' rather than 'compensation' and the Panel was entitled to rely on that unchallenged evidence that it constituted lawful mitigation avoiding harm to the SAC.

H13 **Cases referred to:**

Associated Provincial Picture Houses Ltd v Wednesbury Corp [1948] 1 K.B. 223; (1947) 63 T.L.R. 623; (1948) 112 J.P. 55 CA

Barker Mill Estates Trustees v Test Valley BC [2016] EWHC 3028 (Admin); [2017] P.T.S.R. 408; [2017] J.P.L. 417

Bloor Homes East Midlands Ltd v Secretary of State for Communities and Local Government [2014] EWHC 754 (Admin); [2017] P.T.S.R. 1283

Briels v Minister van Infrastructuur en Milieu (C-521/12) EU:C:2014:330; [2014] P.T.S.R. 1120

ClientEarth v Secretary of State for the Environment, Food and Rural Affairs [2016] EWHC 2740 (Admin); [2017] P.T.S.R. 203; [2016] A.C.D. 137

Dover DC v Campaign to Protect Rural England (Kent) [2017] UKSC 79; [2018] 1 W.L.R. 108; [2018] Env. L.R. 17

East Staffordshire BC v Secretary of State for Communities and Local Government [2017] EWCA Civ 893; [2018] P.T.S.R. 88; [2018] 1 P. & C.R. 4

European Commission v Germany (C-137/14) EU:C:2015:683

European Commission v Germany (C-142/16) EU:C:2017:301

Gateshead MBC v Secretary of State for the Environment [1995] Env. L.R. 37; (1996) 71 P. & C.R. 350; [1995] J.P.L. 432 CA (Civ Div)

Gladman Developments Ltd v Canterbury City Council [2019] EWCA Civ 669; [2019] P.T.S.R. 1714; [2019] J.P.L. 1085

Gladman Developments Ltd v Secretary of State for Communities and Local Government [2017] EWHC 2768 (Admin); [2018] P.T.S.R. 616; [2018] Env. L.R. 15

Gladman Developments Ltd v Secretary of State for Communities and Local Government [2019] EWCA Civ 1543; [2020] P.T.S.R. 128; [2020] Env. L.R. 15

Grace v An Bord Pleanala (C-164/17) EU:C:2018:593; [2019] P.T.S.R. 266; [2018] Env. L.R. 37

Horada v Secretary of State for Communities and Local Government [2016] EWCA Civ 169; [2016] P.T.S.R. 1271

Malkins Nominees v Societe Finance [2002] EWHC 1221 (Ch)

Mansell v Tonbridge and Malling BC [2017] EWCA Civ 1314; [2019] P.T.S.R. 1452; [2018] J.P.L. 176

R. (on the application of An Taisce (National Trust For Ireland)) v Secretary of State for Energy and Climate Change [2013] EWHC 4161 (Admin)

R. (on the application of An Taisce (National Trust For Ireland)) v Secretary of State for Energy and Climate Change [2014] EWCA Civ 1111; [2015] P.T.S.R. 189; [2018] J.P.L. 176

R. (on the application of Cherkley Campaign Ltd) v Mole Valley DC [2014] EWCA Civ 567; [2014] 2 E.G.L.R. 98; [2014] P.T.S.R. D14

R. (on the application of Finch) v Surrey CC [2022] EWCA Civ 187; [2022] P.T.S.R. 958; [2022] Env. L.R. 27

R. (on the application of Friends of the Earth Ltd) v Heathrow Airport Ltd [2020] UKSC 52; [2021] P.T.S.R. 190; [2021] J.P.L. 905

R. (on the application of Friends of the Earth Ltd) v Secretary of State for International Trade/UK Export Finance (UKEF) [2023] EWCA Civ 14; [2023] 1 W.L.R. 2011

R. (on the application of Goesa Ltd) v Eastleigh BC [2022] EWHC 1221 (Admin); [2022] P.T.S.R. 1473; [2022] J.P.L. 1309

R. (on the application of Keir) v Natural England [2021] EWHC 1059 (Admin); [2022] Env. L.R. 3

R. (on the application of Khatun) v Newham LBC [2004] EWCA Civ 55; [2005] Q.B. 37; [2004] 3 W.L.R. 417

R. (on the application of Mott) v Environment Agency [2016] EWCA Civ 564; [2016] 1 W.L.R. 4338; [2017] Env. L.R. 1

R. (on the application of Plan B Earth) v Secretary of State for Transport [2020] EWCA Civ 214; [2020] P.T.S.R. 1446; [2020] J.P.L. 1005

R. (on the application of Squire) v Shropshire Council [2019] EWCA Civ 888; [2020] 1 C.M.L.R. 2; [2019] Env. L.R. 36

R. v Derbyshire CC Ex p. Woods [1998] Env. L.R. 277; [1997] J.P.L. 958 CA (Civ Div)

Royal Society for the Protection of Birds v Secretary of State for Communities and Local Government [2014] EWHC 1523 (Admin); [2014] Env. L.R. 30

Secretary of State for Communities and Local Government v Hopkins Homes Ltd [2017] UKSC 37; [2017] 1 W.L.R. 1865; [2017] P.T.S.R. 623

Seddon Properties Ltd v Secretary of State for the Environment (1981) 42 P. & C.R. 26; [1978] J.P.L. 835 QBD

Simplex GE (Holdings) Ltd v Secretary of State for the Environment [2017] P.T.S.R. 1041; (1989) 57 P. & C.R. 306; [1988] J.P.L. 809 CA (Civ Div)

Smyth v Secretary of State for Communities and Local Government [2015] EWCA Civ 174; [2015] P.T.S.R. 1417; [2016] Env. L.R. 7

South Buckinghamshire DC v Porter [2004] UKHL 33; [2004] 1 W.L.R. 1953; [2005] 1 P. & C.R. 6

St Modwen Developments Ltd v Secretary of State for Communities and Local Government [2017] EWCA Civ 1643; [2018] P.T.S.R. 746; [2018] J.P.L. 398

Tesco Stores Ltd v Dundee City Council [2012] UKSC 13; [2012] P.T.S.R. 983; 2012 S.C. (U.K.S.C.) 278

Tesco Stores Ltd v Secretary of State for the Environment [1995] 1 W.L.R. 759; 93 L.G.R. 403; (1995) 70 P. & C.R. 184 HL

H14   **Legislation referred to:**
Senior Courts Act 1981 s.31
Civil Aviation Act 1982
Environmental Protection Act 1990
Town and Country Planning Act 1990 ss.78, 228 and 288
Directive 92/43 (Habitats) art.6(3)(4)
Planning and Compulsory Purchase Act 2004 s.38
Climate Change Act 2008 ss.1, 4, 5, 8, 10, 30, 32, 35 and 44
Directive 2008/50 (Ambient Air Quality)
Directive 2011/92 (Environmental Impact Assessment)
Air Quality Standards Regulations 2010 (SI 2010/1001)
Town and Country Planning (Environmental Impact Assessment) Regulations 2017 (SI 2017/571) regs 2, 3, 4, 18 and Schs 1, 2 and 4
Conservation of Habitats and Species Regulations 2017 (SI 2017/1012) regs 63 and 64
Greenhouse Gas Emissions Trading Scheme Order 2020 (SI 2020/1265) arts 23, 28, 34, 44, Schs 1 and 2
Air Navigation (Carbon Offsetting and Reduction Scheme for International Aviation) Order 2021 (SI 2021/534)
Carbon Budget Order 2021 (SI 2021/750)

H15   *E. Dehon KC*, instructed by Leigh Day, appeared on behalf of the claimant.
M. Westmoreland Smith and *C. Streeten*, instructed by the Government Legal Department, appeared on behalf of the defendant.

M. Humphries KC and *D. Noble*, instructed by Womble Bond Dickinson (UK) LLP, appeared on behalf of the first interested party.

The second interested party was not represented and did not appear.

JUDGMENT

MR JUSTICE LANE:

1   Climate change, with its consequences for human and other life on this planet, is generally regarded as a matter of very great importance. In the same month in which this appeal was heard in Bristol, world leaders and other policy makers gathered in Sharm El-Sheik, Egypt for COP27, in order to discuss this matter. There is an international consensus on the need to achieve substantial reductions in CO_2 emissions. The Intergovernmental Panel on Climate Change 2021 was widely reported as being a "Code Red for Humanity", such is the present level of concern.

A. Background

2   This appeal is about the proposed expansion of Bristol Airport. The first interested party, Bristol Airport Ltd ("BAL"), applied to North Somerset Council ("NSC") for outline planning permission and the amendment of four existing planning conditions, which together would enable the capacity of Bristol Airport to rise by 2 million passengers per year, an increase of about 20 per cent on current numbers.

3   NSC refused the application in February 2020 and BAL appealed against that refusal to the defendant under section 78 of the Town and Country Planning Act 1990 ("the 1990 Act"). The appeal was heard by a Panel of three inspectors ("the Panel"), over a period of some nine weeks, between July and October 2021. On 2 February 2022, the Panel allowed BAL's appeal.

4   The claimant is a network of groups comprised of members of various environmental organisations in the south-west region of England, as well as residents from local communities affected by the proposed expansion of Bristol Airport.

5   The claimant appeared at the inquiry. The broad thrust of the claimant's case was that BAL's appeal should be dismissed because the expansion of Bristol Airport would have a serious and unacceptable effect on climate change. The claimant led evidence from Professor Kevin Anderson, who holds a joint Professorship in energy and climate change in the School of Engineering at the University of Manchester, as well as other appointments; Mr Finlay Asher, an aerospace engineer formerly employed by Rolls-Royce, with expertise on new aircraft technology and sustainable aviation fuels; and Mr Sam Hunter-Jones, a solicitor practising as an in-house lawyer at ClientEarth.

6   On 9 May 2022, Lang J granted the claimant permission to apply for planning statutory review on each of six grounds. The first five of those grounds can be grouped under the broad heading of challenges to the Panel's decision in respect of emissions of greenhouse gases from aircraft (predominantly, but not exclusively, in the form of CO_2). The sixth ground concerns the effect of the Airport's expansion upon a special area of conservation in which horseshoe bats roost and breed.

7   So far as climate change is concerned, the general question underlying Grounds 1 to 5 is whether and to what extent aviation emissions should play a role in deciding whether permission should be granted under the 1990 Act.

B. An Overview of the Panel's Decision Letter

8   The following is an overview of the relevant parts of the Panel's decision letter ("DL"). It will be necessary to examine passages of the DL in more detail, when dealing with the claimant's grounds of challenge.

9   At DL33, the Panel referenced section 38(6) of the Planning and Compulsory Purchase Act 2004. This requires planning applications to be determined in accordance with the development plan unless material considerations indicate otherwise. The development plan in the present case includes the North Somerset Core Strategy, adopted in January 2017 ("CS"). At DL37, the Panel noted that, *inter alia*, CS1 was concerned with addressing climate change and reducing greenhouse gas ("GHG") emissions. CS1 was described as stating, amongst other matters, that NSC is committed to reducing carbon emissions and tackling climate change, mitigating further impacts and supporting adaptation. One of the principles guiding development is that it should demonstrate a commitment to reducing carbon emissions.

10   Beginning at DL45, the Panel addressed the National Planning Policy Framework ("NPPF"). For present purposes, we are concerned with paragraph 188 of the NPPF. At DL62, the Panel described paragraph 188 as requiring the focus of a decision to be on whether a proposed development is an acceptable land use, rather than focusing on the control of emissions, which are the subject of separate pollution control regimes. Paragraph 188 states that it should be assumed that such other regimes will operate effectively.

11   Beginning at DL65, the Panel addressed National Aviation Policy, beginning with the Aviation Policy Framework (March 2013) ("APF"), which sets out the government's high-level objectives and policy for aviation. A key priority of the APF is to make better use of existing runway capacity at all UK airports. The APF recognises, however, that development of airports can have negative as well as positive local impacts "including on noise levels". As a result, proposals for expansion should be judged on their individual merits.

12   At DL68, the Panel referred to a document entitled "Beyond the Horizon - the Future of UK Aviation: Making Best - Use of Existing Runways" (June 2018) ("MBU"). The Panel described the MBU as recognising "the importance of aviation growth while acknowledging the need to tackle environmental impacts" and as providing "that increased carbon emissions be dealt with at the national level" (DL70).

13   DL 78 to 82 are headed "Climate change policy". Here, the Panel made reference to the Paris Agreement, which is an unincorporated treaty on climate change within the United Nations Framework Convention on Climate Change. The Paris Agreement set a long-term temperature goal of limiting global warming to well below 2 degrees above pre-industrial levels. It remains the foundation for much subsequent legislation and guidance. It is worth mentioning here that the legal nature of the Paris Agreement has been examined by the Supreme Court in *R. (Friends of the Earth Ltd) v Heathrow Airport Ltd* [2020] UKSC 52 ("*Friends of the Earth*") and, very recently, by the Court of Appeal in *R. (Friends of the Earth*

Ltd) v Secretary of State for International Trade/Export Finance [2023] EWCA Civ 14.

14   At DL80, the Panel noted that the Paris Agreement was reflected in the United Kingdom by the Climate Change Act 2008 ("CCA"). At DL81, the Panel referenced two government documents published in July 2021. These were "Decarbonizing Transport: A Better, Greener Britain" and the "Jet Zero Consultation". The latter was a consultation document "but the main messages are not dissimilar, and they both emphasise the need for very significant action to be taken". At DL 82, the Panel noted that COP26 was held in Glasgow in the autumn 2021, following which the "Glasgow Climate Pact" was adopted (November 2021).

15   At DL103, the first of the "main issues" debated in the inquiry was described by the Panel as follows:-

> "The impact of the proposed development on GHG emissions and the ability of the UK to meet its climate change obligations."

16   The section of the DL entitled "Climate Change" runs from DL143 to 216. It will be necessary to address a good many of these paragraphs in more detail, in dealing with grounds 1 – 5. The Panel observed that there was no dispute between the parties about the importance of climate change – "at the local, national and international levels". There was also agreement that there would be an increase in GHG, especially CO_2, if the appeal scheme went ahead, compared with the position if it did not. Under those circumstances "the climate change position would be worse" (DL146).

17   At DL147, the Panel was categoric that "the contribution of the appeal scheme to climate change related to CO_2 admissions is an important material consideration".

18   At DL149, the Panel recorded there being "no substantial dissent" from the formulation of the key question, which was whether emissions from the proposal would be so significant that they would materially affect the ability of the UK to meet its carbon budgets and the target of net zero GHG emissions by 2050. The Panel considered that the "mathematics of the increase" was almost entirely agreed.

19   At DL150, the Panel said it was "common ground that an international response is necessary", with individual nations determining their own contributions. At DL151, the Panel considered that the main difference between BAL and NSC (and other parties) was about "the way in which the issue of the emissions from this proposal should be addressed". BAL relied on national action to address aviation carbon limits, whereas the other parties looked to airport capacity limits, including the restriction of individual airport expansion, such as that envisaged at Bristol Airport.

20   The DL then turned to the development plan and the NPPF in respect of the climate change issue. It described NSC's Policy CS1 as the key development plan policy, concluding there was "every reason to conclude that the policy does not directly address aviation omissions". Policy CS23, which relates specifically to Bristol Airport, "takes one little further than policy CS1".

21   DL153 to 155 addressed the NPPF. DL156-162 concern the CCA and carbon budgets, about which considerably more needs to be said later in this judgment. Carbon budgets are ways in which the Secretary of State seeks to comply with his duties under the CCA.

22   In DL160, the Panel recognised that, in order to achieve the target of the sixth carbon budget, and of any previous budgets, any increased emissions in one sector arising from the proposals will necessitate reductions elsewhere. In this regard, the Panel detected a difference between BAL and the other parties to the inquiry as to the current position in relation to future carbon budgets.

23   In DL161, the Panel recognised that the government "is not on track to meet the 4th and 5th carbon budgets – with significant reductions needed in relatively short periods." The Panel, however, considered "the suggestion that the Government is off track at this time means little in relation to budget periods which have not yet started".

24   DL162 reads:

> "162. There are three important points to make in relation to the carbon budgets and the way in which they operate. Firstly, although the approach to Net Zero and the carbon budget is a material consideration, the CCA places an obligation on the SoS, not local decision makers, to prepare policies and proposals with a view to meeting the carbon budgets. Secondly, as advised in the NPPF, there is an assumption that controls which are in place will work. Finally, and consequent on the previous points, NSC's position that grant of permission in this case would breach the CCA and be unlawful is not accepted. That does not mean that these matters are not material considerations, but the CCA duty rests elsewhere."

25   Beginning at DL163, the Panel examined carbon "offsetting schemes". I shall describe these further in due course. There are two such trading schemes. The first is the UK Emissions Trading Scheme ("UK ETS"). In the UK, this replaced the former EU Emissions Trading Scheme ("EU ETS"). The second trading scheme is CORSIA. This was adopted by the International Civil Aviation Organisation in 2016. Both offsetting schemes are time-limited, being scheduled to stop "well short of 2050" (DL168).

26   At DL183, the Panel said there had been no disagreement between BAL and NSC concerning the methodology and calculation of the CO_2 effects of the Airport's expansion proposal. For that reason, the numerical position was not considered in any depth. BAL's position was that the increase would not amount to a significant effect, as described in the Environmental Statement and its Addendum. The proposal's opponents, however, argued that the effect would consume the local carbon budget of NSC between 2028 and 2032. The Panel, at DL188, was unpersuaded that the arguments surrounding the local carbon budget were of significance. The Panel then said:-

> "189. Overall, it remains the case that the extent to which this decision, related to a local scheme, would increase the amount of GHG emissions is a material consideration. The issue is how such increases, of whatever magnitude, should be addressed."

27   Beginning at DL190, the Panel examined the cumulative impact of the Airport's expansion. It observed that the position of NSC and other objectors (including the claimant) was that the impact of all airport development should be assessed before permission was granted in the present case. No such national assessment was, however, before the Panel. In the absence of any national assessment, the implication of the approach of the objectors would be that the appeal should be

dismissed. But, even in the absence of a national assessment, the Panel concluded that the approach of the objectors was not supported by policy. There was no requirement to conduct a cumulative assessment of GHG emissions on the global climate and, in any event, it would not be feasible to do so (DL194, 195).

28   At DL204 to 207, the Panel set out its approach to the issue of non-CO_2 emissions. The Panel concluded that there was considerable uncertainty in assessing these emissions and no policy as to how they should be dealt with. Given the extent of scientific uncertainty, and the intention of BAL to consider non-CO_2 emissions further in its Carbon and Climate Change Action Plan, ("CCCAP") the Panel concluded that it would be "unreasonable to weigh this matter in the balance against the proposal" (DL207).

29   The draft CCCAP was discussed by the Panel at DL208 to 210. Noting that the production of a final version of the CCCAP would be the subject of a planning condition, and that the CCCAP's current status was "as a draft", the Panel concluded that "it has very limited weight" (DL210).

30   DL211 to 216 contain the Panel's conclusions on climate change. At DL211, the Panel reiterated there was "no doubt that climate change is a very serious issue facing this country and the world". Nor was there any doubt that BAL's proposal would increase CO_2 emissions from aircraft.

31   At DL212, the Panel recorded the "in principle support at the national level for the increased use of runways and other existing facilities", albeit subject to addressing environmental issues. The development plan reflected the need to reduce carbon emissions and tackle climate change. The key point of difference between the parties at the inquiry was over how this was to be achieved.

32   DL213 said that, whilst an increase in CO_2 emissions in one location will have consequences elsewhere and make the Secretary of State's duty under the CCA more difficult, the comparative magnitude of the increase from the proposal was limited and it had to be assumed the Secretary of State will comply with his legal duty under the CCA. There were several options and future approaches to assist in the attainment of the target, albeit there were problems and uncertainties associated with some approaches. On the other hand, there was no national policy that seeks to limit airport expansion.

33   The conclusion of the Panel was that the aviation emissions would not be so significant as to have a material impact on the government's ability to meet its climate change target and budgets. "Overall, this matter [climate change] must be regarded as neutral in the planning balance" (DL214 to 216).

34   Biodiversity was addressed by the Panel, beginning at DL481. The Panel noted that the proposed development would result in a loss of 3.7 HA of agricultural land in order to allow the expansion of an Airport car park, and a small area (0.16HA) of woodland edge in order for improvement works to the A38 road to be delivered.

35   At DL482, the Panel noted that these two areas were outside of, but relatively close to, the North Somerset and Mendip Bats SAC. The SAC had been designated because of the presence of lesser and greater horseshoe bats. The two areas provided foraging land for the bats and were therefore functionally linked to the SAC.

36   At DL488, the Panel observed that BAL's proposal was to provide land as replacement habitat in exchange for the functionally-linked land, "thereby avoiding any impact on the SAC itself". The Panel considered that this would be a "protective mitigation measure" which would "ensure that the project does not adversely affect

the integrity of the SAC". The replacement land "would be provided in advance of any works being carried out that would affect existing foraging land."

37   At DL490, the Panel observed that the Parish Council Airport Association ("PCAA") raised the legal status of the proposed replacement land. The issue was whether the replacement foraging habitat would be "mitigation" or "compensation". At DL490, the Panel noted that the only expert ecological evidence, presented by BAL, was that the proposed replacement foraging land met the test for "mitigation", and that this position had been agreed by NSC officers and Natural England. There was "no contrary expert evidence."

38   The argument put by PCAA was that the replacement land was intended to replace "significant" bat habitat which would be destroyed by the proposal. Accordingly, the replacement land had to be viewed as "compensation" rather than "mitigation". This meant that planning permission could not be granted, compatibly with the relevant legislation concerning SACs (DL491).

39   At DL492, the Panel concluded that there would not, in fact, be any adverse effect on the integrity of the SAC.

C. The Climate Change Act 2008 and Legislation Made Under It

40   As will already be apparent, the CCA and the legislation made under it feature heavily in the DL. It is therefore necessary at this stage to describe these in some detail.

41   The Long Title of the CCA explains that one of its purposes is to set a target for the year 2050 for the reduction of targeted greenhouse gas emissions. The Act also provides for a system of carbon budgeting, establishing a Committee on Climate Change ("CCC"); and conferring paths to establish trading schemes for the purpose of limiting greenhouse gas emissions. Further purposes of the CCA include providing financial incentives to produce less domestic waste and making provision about charging for single use carrier bags.

42   When the CCA came into force, it placed a duty on the Secretary of State to ensure that the "net UK carbon account" for the year 2050 was at least 80% lower than the 1990 baseline: section 1. This target was, however, amended in June 2019 to be at least 100% below the baseline (the "net zero" target). This is a balanced figure and does not mean absolute zero emissions. The "net zero" target was substituted in 2019, following the Paris Agreement.

43   Section 4 of the CCA imposes a duty on the Secretary of State to set carbon budgets for each succeeding period of five years, beginning with 2008-2012. The Secretary of State must ensure that the net carbon account for a budgeting period does not exceed the carbon budget. Section 5 specifies the level of carbon budgets, whilst section 8 requires the Secretary of State to set the carbon budget for a budgetary period by order. The carbon budget for a period must be set with a view to meeting the target in section 1 and the requirements in section 5.

44   Each five yearly carbon budget is to be set 12 years in advance as a series of interim targets. The carbon budgets must be set to achieve the 2050 carbon target.

45   Section 30 of the CCA provides that emissions from international aviation do not count as emissions from sources within the UK. Section 10, however, requires that, in setting carbon budgets, the Secretary of State shall take into account the estimated amount of reportable emissions from international aviation and international shipping for the budgetary period or periods in question. The

"estimated amount" of such reportable emissions means the aggregates of the amounts relating to emissions of targeted greenhouse gases from international aviation that the Secretary of State is required to report for that period in accordance with international carbon reporting practice: section 10(3).

46   Section 32 of the CCA establishes the CCC in order to advise the government on matters relating to climate change. This includes the carbon target and carbon budgets, as well as international aviation: section 35. The CCC's role is advisory. It is the Secretary of State who continues to make policy in this area.

47   Six carbon budgets have been adopted so far under the CCA. The fifth, set in 2016, runs from 2028 to 2032. Emissions from international aviation were not formally included within the first to fifth carbon budgets. Instead, these emissions were taken into account, pursuant to section 10, by setting the budgets at a level which allowed headroom for them. The budgets were, in other words, set lower by the amount of this headroom. The figure allowed for aviation emissions is known as the "planning assumption". This is explained in the Aviation Policy Framework 2013.

48   The Sixth Carbon Budget was announced in April 2021. It covers the period from 2033 to 2037. The government also announced a new target to reduce emissions by 78 per cent, compared with 1990 levels, to be achieved by 2035.

49   The Sixth Carbon Budget will, for the first time, formally include emissions from international aviation within the budget figure. The change does not, however, alter the fact that aviation emissions have hitherto been accounted for in the carbon budgets in the way described above. The decision formally to include international aviation in the Sixth Carbon Budget Order 2021 follows the recommendation of the CCC in its Sixth Carbon Budget Report on Aviation in December 2020.

50   I turn now to the trading schemes under Part 3 of the CCA. From 2005, the UK participated in the EU ETS. Since 2012, this has included the aviation sector. Following the UK's withdrawal from the EU, the UK ETS replaced the UK's participation in the EU ETS, with effect from 1 January 2021.

51   The UK ETS was established through the Greenhouse Gas Emissions Trading Scheme Order 2020, made under section 44 of the CCA. Schedule 2 to that Act requires any trading scheme to specify the period to which it relates. Accordingly, the 2020 Order relates to the period up to 2030. The total of "given allocations" for all participants in the UK ETS, including airlines, is approximately 60% of the total number within the UK ETS. The remaining 40% is available for purchase by any participants in the scheme.

52   The UK ETS relates not solely to aviation but to the entire UK traded sector. Under the UK ETS, the cap on allowances each year has been initially set at five per cent below the UK's expected notional share of the EU ETS cap, with year on year reductions in the cap specified up to 2030.

53   Article 23 of the 2020 Order permits allowances to be traded, except where prohibited by other legislation. Article 28 prescribes the mechanism for aviation "monitoring plans". Under these, an "aircraft operator" monitors emissions and reports to government. Article 34 provides for the surrender of allowances against emissions and establishes a system of penalties in the following year for operators that exceed their allocated allowances. Enforcement provisions are contained in article 44. These take the form of enforcement notices.

54   The scope of the UK ETS is set out in Schedule 1 to the Order; namely, flights to and from the UK (including Gibraltar) and the EEA. BAL says that this includes 88-90 per cent of flights in and out of Bristol Airport.

55   As stated in the Explanatory Memorandum to the 2020 Order, the government intends to consult on an appropriate trajectory for the UK ETS cap, following the CCC's Sixth Carbon Budget Report. The aim is to align the cap with the net zero trajectory by January 2023.

D. The Air Navigation (Carbon Offsetting and Reduction Scheme for International Aviation) Order 2021: CORSIA

56   The Air Navigation (Carbon Offsetting and Reduction Scheme for International Aviation) Order 2021 came into force on 26 May 2021. The Order is made under powers conferred by the Civil Aviation Act 1982. The Order notifies the International Civil Aviation Organisation of the UK's participation in "CORSIA", which is the Carbon Offsetting and Reduction Scheme for International Aviation. The monitoring, reporting and verification requirements of UK ETS, EU ETS and CORSIA are consistent, in that one tonne of CO_2 is accounted for in the same way under all three schemes.

57   CORSIA has three phases: a pilot scheme from 2021 to 2023, a first phase from 2024 to 2026 and a second phase from 2027 to 2035. The pilot and first phases are voluntary, albeit that the UK intends to participate in them. The second phase is intended to include the majority of countries based on the proportion of aircraft movements. From 2025, CORSIA facilitates the reporting and offsetting of the emissions of aeroplane operators.

58   The intention is for CORSIA to apply to those emissions not covered by the UK ETS. It will enable airline operators to purchase carbon credits from the carbon market to offset emissions. The apparently preferred option for the relationship between the UK ETS and CORSIA is a hybrid scheme, under which aeroplane operators can claim a reduction in their UK ETS obligations equivalent to their CORSIA obligations on flights from the UK and EEA States. In effect, each CORSIA carbon credit will be matched by the removal of one UK ETS allowance. The CCC considers that this approach will work but requires consideration of how to avoid the lower price of CORSIA carbon credits distorting the value of UK ETS allowances. The present intention is for a statutory instrument to come into force, which would either amend the existing CORSIA Order or replace it.

E. The Claimant's Grounds of Challenge

59   The claimant advances six grounds of challenge to the Panel's decision, pursuant to the grant of permission by Lang J.

60   Ground 1 contends that the Panel erred in law in its interpretation of development plan policies CS1 and CS23; alternatively, that the Panel failed to give adequate reasons for its interpretation of those policies. Ground 2 states that the Panel erred in law in its interpretation of the MBU; alternatively, that it failed to give adequate reasons for its interpretation. Ground 3 argues that the Panel erred in law in finding that it was required to "assume" that the Secretary of State would comply with his legal duty under the CCA. This ground concerns the correct interpretation of paragraph 188 of the NPPF. Ground 4 asserts that the Panel erred in law in discounting the impact of the expansion of Bristol Airport in relation to the local

carbon budget for NSC. Ground 5 concerns an alleged error of law in the Panel's conclusion that the impact of non-CO_2 emissions from aircraft could be excluded from the EIA prepared by BAL and should not weigh in the balance against the proposed airport expansion; alternatively, that there was a failure to give adequate reasons for the Panel's decision. Ground 6 concerns what is said to be an error on the part of the Panel in determining that replacement habitat for the greater and lesser horseshoe bats amounted to "mitigation" rather than "compensation", contrary to the law regarding SACs; alternatively, that the Panel failed to give adequate reasons for its decision on this matter.

Ground 1

61   Policy CS1 is entitled "Addressing Climate Change and Carbon Reduction". It provides that NSC is committed to reducing carbon emissions and tackling climate change, mitigating further impacts and supporting adaptation to its effects. In order to support this, CS1 sets out eleven principles to "guide development". Under these principles, development should demonstrate a commitment to reducing carbon emissions, including reducing energy demand through good design. Developers are encouraged to incorporate site-wide renewable energy solutions. Opportunities should be maximised for all new homes to contribute to tackling climate change. A network of multi-functional green infrastructure will be planned for and delivered through new development. Bio-diversity across North Somerset will be protected and enhanced. There should be emphasis on the re-use of previously developed land and existing buildings in preference to the loss of greenfield sites.

62   Under the heading "Background" there is the following:-

> "3.7 Tackling climate change is a key priority for the planning system and in particular implementing the national carbon reduction strategy of an 80% reduction in carbon dioxide emissions by 2050. Given the scale of development allocated to North Somerset there are significant opportunities and indeed a responsibility to deliver action on the ground which should be led by a strong policy framework. In terms of the Core Strategy this action is primarily aiming to reduce carbon emissions and to places for the likely impacts of climate change. The Core Strategy approach
> The Core Strategy approach
> 3.8 Policy CS1 sets out a broad policy framework drawing together various themes where development can address climate change issues. Many of the specific themes are dealt with elsewhere in the Core Strategy including green infrastructure (Policy CS9) and sustainable construction and design (Policy CS2), but are included in this more general policy as a means of co-ordinating action to address climate change. Primarily the Core Strategy seeks to address climate change by:
>   • Reducing unsustainable carbon emissions,
>   • Making all buildings more sustainable,
>   • Encouraging sustainable transport patterns, and
>   • Planning for a sustainable distribution of land uses
>
> …
>
> 3.17 The scope of this policy translates to the variety of interests responsible for delivering action on climate change and meeting the strategic objectives and realising the visions set out in this strategy and the need to co-ordinate

action, towards comprehensive place-making. Developers and other bodies with development interests should work closely with local communities, specialist groups and the council in order to bring development forward that meets the challenges climate change brings."

63   Policy CS23 is entitled "Bristol Airport". It provides that proposals for the development of Bristol Airport will be required to demonstrate the satisfactory resolution of environmental issues, including the impact of growth on surrounding communities and surface access infrastructure. It is stated that this policy contributes towards achieving Priority Objective 3. That objective concerns growth in North Somerset.

64   The background to CS23 states, amongst other things, that:-

> "3.294 As well as taking account of the wide range of environmental issues including climate change, the Core Strategy emphasises the importance of assessing the local impacts, particularly in relation to surrounding communities and surface access issues."

65   The claimant's case before the Panel at the inquiry was that the impact of the expansion of Bristol Airport on climate change was relevant to determining whether the proposals complied with policies CS1 and CS23, as well as being capable of amounting to a standalone material consideration and being relevant to weight. As I have mentioned, section 38(6) of the 2004 Act requires a determination of planning permission to be made in accordance with the development plan, unless material considerations indicate otherwise. In its closing submissions to the inquiry, the claimant argued that the appeal proposal failed to accord with the development plan "because BAL cannot demonstrate satisfactory resolution of the impact associated with the increased greenhouse gas emissions (both CO_2 and non-CO_2) caused by the appeal proposal."

66   BAL's case was that CS1 was "of primary relevance to carbon emissions from airports, buildings, ground operations and surface access, which are matters of local policy concern". BAL did not submit that the impact of aviation emissions was excluded from CS1.

67   The Panel addressed the development plan in relation to climate change at DL152. This reads:-

> "152. Policy CS1 is the key development plan policy related to this issue and emphasises the reduction of carbon emissions and the need to tackle climate change. BAL's position is that this is of primary relevance to ground based carbon emissions. However, this is largely based on their position that climate change is a matter to be dealt with at the national level. Neither the policy nor the justification makes that distinction but, as will be discussed below, there is every reason to conclude that the policy does not directly address aviation emissions. CS policy CS23 does not provide unqualified support for growth of BA, but it takes one little further than policy CS1."

68   The claimant contends that the only place at which the Panel returned to discuss CS1 and CS23 was at DL216, where the Panel stated that "the two development plan policies summarised above are not considered to directly address aviation emissions".

69   The claimant says that, from what little reasoning it gave, the Panel appears to have taken the view that, despite the broad wording of Policy CS1, and the broad wording of the policy justification which followed it, aviation emissions are not included within the policy requirement that "development should demonstrate a commitment to reducing carbon emissions", or, indeed within any of Policy CS1's other requirements. It also appears, the claimant says, that the Panel took the view that the impact of the proposals on aviation emissions was not relevant under Policy CS23 to the requirement that BAL "demonstrate the satisfactory resolution of environmental issues", as required under that policy.

70   The claimant submits that the Panel's interpretation of Policy CS1 and Policy CS23 is incorrect as a matter of law. Interpreted objectively, in accordance with the language used in the policies and in their proper context, they both encompass the impact of aviation emissions. This is supported by the reasoned justifications for the policies.

71   For the claimant, Ms Dehon KC acknowledged the distinction drawn in the case law between the interpretation of a planning policy, which is a matter for the court, and the application of that policy, which is for the relevant decision-maker, in the exercise of their judgment, with the court's function in that regard being one of intervention only on public law grounds.

72   At paragraph 19 of *Tesco Stores Ltd v Dundee CC* [2012] UKSC 13, Lord Reed explained that policy statements are not to be construed as if they were statutory or contractual provisions. Development plans are broad statements of policy, many of which may be mutually irreconcilable. This means that, in a particular case, one such policy must give way to another. Furthermore, many of the provisions of development plans are framed in language whose application to a given set of facts requires the exercise of judgment. Such matters fall within the jurisdiction of planning authorities, subject only to challenge on the grounds of irrationality or perversity.

73   However, as Lord Reed emphasised, "planning authorities do not live in the world of Humpty Dumpty: they cannot make the development plan mean whatever they would like it to mean." As was pointed out in *R. v Derbyshire CC Ex p. Woods* [1997] J.P.L. 958, a decision-maker cannot attach a meaning to the words of a policy which those words are not properly capable of bearing.

74   With these authorities in mind, Ms Dehon submitted that, in relation to Ground 1, the Panel misinterpreted the words of Policies CS1 and CS23. In making that submission, Ms Dehon said the claimant was not resorting to "excessive legalism" which, as Lindblom LJ held at paragraph 50 of *East Staffordshire BC v the Secretary of State for Communities and Local Government* [2018] 1 P. & C.R. 4, has no place in the planning system; in proceedings before the Planning Court; or in subsequent appeals. Courts should always resist over-complication of concepts that are basically simple. Nevertheless, "the decision-maker must understand relevant national and local policy correctly and apply it lawfully to the particular facts and circumstances of the case in hand, in accordance with the requirements of the statutory scheme" (paragraph 50).

75   Ms Dehon further submitted that, in the language of paragraph 7 of Lindblom LJ's judgment in *St Modwen Developments Ltd v Secretary of State for Communities and Local Government* [2018] P.T.S.R. 746, the claimant's criticisms of the DL did not amount to "hypercritical scrutiny that this court has always rejected"; nor that the claimant's analysis required the DL to "be laboriously dissected in an effort

to find fault". Ms Dehon said that the defendant and BAL could not invoke the supporting text of the policies, in effect to rob those policies of what was their true meaning, based on their actual language. In this regard, she relied upon the judgment of Richards LJ in *R. (Cherkley Campaign Ltd) v Mole Valley DC* [2014] P.T.S.R. D14. Richards LJ held that the supporting text of a policy was relevant to the interpretation of the policy to which it related but was not itself a policy or part of a policy. Nevertheless, that supporting text could not trump the policy. Thus, a proposed development which accorded with the policies in the local plan could not be said to lack conformity with that plan because it failed to satisfy an additional criterion, which was referred to only in the supporting text.

76   In Policy CS1(1), Ms Dehon emphasised the fact that reducing energy demand through good design etc was only a non-exhaustive example of the general requirement for development to "demonstrate a commitment to reducing carbon emissions". Paragraph 3.7 of the background to policy CS1 was, likewise, in broad terms, referring to the need to tackle climate change as a "key priority for the planning system" and stating that the need to deliver "action on the ground" was primarily "to reduce carbon emissions and to prepare places for the likely impacts of climate change."

77   In similar vein, policy CS23, which specifically concerns Bristol Airport, states that proposals for the development of the Airport need to demonstrate "the satisfactory resolution of environmental issues". The use of the word "including" before the phrase "the impact of growth on surrounding communities and surface access infrastructure" showed that this was merely an example of environmental issues. Properly read, the phrase "environmental issues" includes emissions from aircraft. Ms Dehon also drew attention to paragraph 3.294 under the heading "the core strategy approach", which emphasises the importance of assessing local impacts "as well as taking account of the wide range of environment issues including climate change".

78   Ms Dehon said that, at the inquiry, none of the parties suggested to the Panel that Policies CS1 and CS23 did not apply to aviation emissions. BAL spoke about the primary relevance of the two policies being concerned with ground emissions, such as from buildings.

79   Ms Dehon emphasised the claimant's submission that the words "as will be discussed below" in DL152 can, at best, refer only to DL216. There, in its concluding paragraph about Climate Change, the Panel concluded that "aviation emissions are not so significant that they would have a material impact on the government's ability to meet its climate change targets and budgets" and that "the two development plan policies summarised above are not considered to directly address aviation emissions". This meant that overall, the issue of emissions "must be regarded as neutral in the planning balance."

80   According to the claimant, the defendant is unable to contend that policies CS1 and CS23 cannot encompass aviation emissions on the ground that BAL has no control over them. In *R. (Finch) v Surrey CC* [2022] P.T.S.R. 958, the majority of the Court of Appeal held that, in considering whether a particular impact on the environment was a "likely significant effect" of proposed development for the purposes of Council Directive 2011/92/EU and the Town and Country Planning (Environmental Impact Assessment) Regulations 2017 ("the 2017 Regulations"), the real question was not the meaning of "the project" or "the proposed development" in the case concerned, but the ascertainment of the "effects" of the

proposed development and the degree of connection needed to link that development with its putative effects. There was, accordingly, no merit in seeking to invoke the absence of control over aviation emissions in interpreting policies CS1 and CS23.

Ground 1: discussion

81   It is clear that Policy CS1 is broad enough to include the issue of aircraft emissions. I did not understand Mr Westmoreland Smith or Mr Humphries KC to contend otherwise. That said, none of the eleven principles contained in policy CS1 has anything specific to say about aviation emissions. This contrasts with what those principles say about other matters, such as maximising opportunities for new homes to contribute to tackling climate change, requiring developments of ten or more dwellings to demonstrate a commitment to maximising the use of sustainable transport solutions, particularly in Weston Super Mare; and reducing, re-using and recycling waste with particular emphasis on waste minimisation on development sites.

82   I accept what Ms Dehon says about paragraphs 3.7 and 3.8 of the background to Policy CS1, as regards the generality of some of the wording concerning climate change and reducing greenhouse gases. The fact remains, however, that no attempt is made in Policy CS1 or Policy CS23 to articulate the way in which aviation emissions might be addressed by NSC as planning authority. This is significant, given the obvious fact that aviation emissions, which can occur at any point in an aircraft's journey to and from Bristol Airport, are of a different character from, for example, carbon emissions that can be addressed by reducing energy demand through good design of buildings in the area of NSC.

83   It is also noteworthy that NSC has not sought to challenge the way in which the Panel dealt with that council's policies CS1 and CS23.

84   As is evident from my summary of the relevant parts of the DL, the Panel had regard to the way in which aviation emissions are addressed in the CCA, including the systems of carbon budgets. At DL149, the Panel recorded there being no substantial dissent from the formulation of the key question under the heading "Climate Change"; namely, whether the emissions from the BAL proposal would be so significant that they would materially affect the ability of the UK to meet its carbon budgets and the target of net zero GHG emissions by 2050.

85   The claimant contends that the Panel was, here, merely discussing whether aviation emissions fell to be treated as a material consideration in the purely general sense; and that this should be contrasted with what the claimant argues is the discrete section 38(6) issue of whether the proposed development was in accordance with the development plan. It would, however, be very odd if the Panel considered that the emissions issue fell be treated in the way described in DL149 only in this general sense, with the inevitable inference that the Panel considered the issue fell to be treated in some different (and unspecified) way for the purpose of assessing compliance or otherwise with Policy CS1 and Policy CS23. Reading the DL with the degree of benevolence demanded by the case law, one simply cannot draw such a conclusion.

86   I have set out DL152 above. DL152 shows that the Panel was concerned to determine how Policy CS1 and Policy CS23 bore on aircraft emissions. The Panel disagreed with BAL's submission that Policy CS1 was of "primary relevance to ground based carbon emissions". The Panel was clear that neither that policy nor

the justification for it made such a distinction. Nevertheless, the CCA and its system of carbon budgets were relevant to explain the key question in respect of the development plan; namely, how that plan should apply to aviation emissions occasioned by the implementation of BAL's proposals for the expansion of Bristol Airport.

87   We are, here, firmly in the territory identified by Lord Reed in the first part of paragraph 19 of *Tesco*, rather than sitting on Humpty Dumpty's wall. Although Policy CS1 is capable of including aircraft emissions, the decision-maker is entitled to exercise their judgment in order to determine <u>how</u> such emissions are, in a particular case, to be dealt with under the policy.

88   This point was made by the Panel itself at DL212 where, as part of its conclusions on climate change, the Panel said that the "development plan reflects the need to reduce carbon emissions and tackle climate change – but the key point of difference is <u>how</u> this is to be achieved" (my emphasis).

89   I do not accept Ms Dehon's submission that the words "as will be discussed below" in DL152 are referable only to DL216, where the Panel said "that the two development plan policies summarised above are not considered to directly address aviation emissions." If that were the case, then I agree the Panel's explanation would have been circular. It is, however, plain that the quoted words in DL152 include the Panel's description and analysis of the CCA, carbon budgets, UK ETS and CORSIA, which begin at DL156 and which are specifically referred to in the last sentence of DL155.

90   Ms Dehon contends that, if the words "as will be discussed below" in DL152 do include those paragraphs, then they must also include DL153 to 155, in which the Panel discussed the significance of the NPPF. Ms Dehon says that this must mean the Panel impermissibly used the NPPF in order to interpret Policy CS1 and Policy CS23.

91   In fact, the NPPF applies to planning policies as well as to development control decisions, providing guidance to local planning authorities on the formulation of development plan policies. That said, there is no doubt as to what the Panel was about, in saying what it did. It was observing that the NPPF acknowledges that, where other systems of control exist, it is to be assumed that those systems or regimes will operate effectively: DL154.

92   On any fair and proper reading of DL143 to 216, all of which fall under the Panel's general heading of *"Climate Change"*, the Panel did not err in law, as alleged in Ground 1. As I have found, it did not find that Policy CS1 and Policy CS23 had no purchase upon the issue of aviation emissions arising from the proposal. That is not a proper reading of the Panel's conclusion that those policies did not "directly" address such emissions.

93   At DL216, the Panel found that "aviation emissions are not so significant that they would have a material impact on the government's ability to meet its climate change target and budgets". That was the test articulated in DL149, as to which there was "no substantial dissent". Aviation emissions fell to be addressed for the purposes of the policies "indirectly", in that these emissions become relevant for the purposes of the development plan if, and only if, they are likely to be such as to have a material impact on the Secretary of State's ability to meet his obligations under the CCA, including by means of carbon budgets. Since the Panel found this was not the position, and given that ground-based emissions could be addressed in the way described in DL216, this meant that granting permission for the

development would not be contrary to the development plan. It also meant that aviation emissions were not otherwise a material consideration pointing to a dismissal of BAL's appeal.

94   I do not consider that, in the alternative, the Panel failed to give adequate reasons. Those reasons are contained in the paragraphs which follow DL152.

95   Ground 1 accordingly fails.

Ground 2

96   Ground 2 involves the Panel's approach to MBU. The claimant says that the Panel erred in its interpretation of MBU; alternatively, that it failed to give legally adequate reasons for that interpretation.

97   The claimant puts the first part of Ground 2 in two ways. It is said that the Panel ignored a material consideration in not considering the claimant's interpretation of MBU, as advanced at the inquiry. Further or in the alternative, the claimant says it is unclear whether, at DL70, in saying MBU "provides that increased carbon emissions be dealt with at the national level", the Panel was assuming that it could treat the admitted increase in CO_2 emissions from aircraft as a result of the proposal as not significant and thus neutral in the planning balance. If so, the claimant submits the Panel erred in law.

98   MBU followed a call for evidence, contained in the Aviation Strategy and the responses to it. Under the heading, "Implications for the UK's Carbon Commitments", 1.14 to 1.21 describe the carbon traded scenario and the carbon cap scenario. Under the first, UK aviation emissions could continue to grow provided that compensatory reductions are made elsewhere in the global economy. The carbon cap scenario was developed to explore the case for expansion even in the future where aviation emissions were limited to the CCC's planning assumption of 37.5Mt of CO_2 in 2050. 1.17 and 1.18 deal with the use of single-engine taxiing at UK airports and renewable fuels policy. 1.20 states that other measures are likely to be available and may turn out to be more cost effective or have greater abatement potential. 1.21 concludes that on balance it is likely that these or other measures would be available to meet the planning assumption under this policy.

99   Paragraph 1.8 of MBU identifies the main issues raised as including the need for environmental matters such as noise, air quality and carbon to be fully addressed as part of any airport proposals. Under the heading "Role of Local Planning" there is the following:-

> "1.9 Most of the concerns raised can be addressed through our existing policies as set out in the 2013 Aviation Policy Framework, or through more recent policy updates such as the new UK Airspace Policy or National Air Quality Plan. For the majority of environmental concerns, the government expects these to be taken into account as part of existing local planning application processes. It is right that decisions on the elements which impact local individuals such as noise and air quality should be considered through the appropriate planning process and CAA airspace change process."

100   Under the heading "Role of National Policy", MBU states:-

"1.11 There are, however, some important environmental elements which should be considered at a national level. The government recognises that airports making the best use of their existing runways could lead to increased air traffic which could increase carbon emissions.

1.12 We shall be using the Aviation Strategy to progress our wider policy towards tackling aviation carbon. However, to ensure that our policy is compatible with the UK's climate change commitments we have used the DfT aviation model to look at the impact of allowing all airports to make best use of their existing runway capacity. We have tested this scenario against our published no expansion scenario and the Heathrow Airport North West Runway scheme (LHR NWR) option, under the central demand case.

1.13 The forecasts are performed using the DfT UK aviation model which has been extensively quality assured and peer reviewed and is considered fit for purpose and robust for producing forecasts of this nature. Tables 1-3 show the expected figures in passenger numbers, air traffic movements, and carbon at a national level for 2016, 2030, 2040, and 2050."

101   Under the heading "Local Environmental Impacts", 1.22 says that the government recognises the impact on communities living near airports and understands their concerns over local environmental issues. It is said to be important that communities surrounding those airports share in the economic benefits and that adverse impacts such as noise are mitigated where possible.

102   1.23 says that for the majority of local environmental concerns, the government expects these to be taken into account as part of existing local planning application processes.

103   In 1.26 there is the following:-

"1.26 … As part of any planning application airports will need to demonstrate how they will mitigate against local environmental issues, taking account of relevant national policies, including any new environmental policies emerging from the Aviation Strategy. This policy statement does not prejudge the decision of those authorities who will be required to give proper consideration to such applications. It instead leaves it up to local, rather than national government, to consider each case on its merits."

104   The concluding paragraph, 1.29, as follows:-

"1.29 **Therefore the government is supportive of airports beyond Heathrow making best use of their existing runways. However, we recognise that the development of airports can have negative as well as positive local impacts, including on noise levels. We therefore consider that any proposal should be judged by the relevant planning authority, taking careful account of all relevant considerations, particularly economic and environmental impacts and proposed mitigation. This policy statement does not prejudge the decision of those authorities who will be required to give proper consideration to such applications. It instead leaves it up to local, rather than national government, to consider each case on its merits."** (original emphasis)

105   The DL discusses MBU under the heading "National Aviation Policy". DL69 sets out in full paragraph 1.29, which the Panel described as "the key section".

106   As I have already mentioned, at DL70 the Panel stated that MBU, under the heading "Role of National Policy", provides that "increased carbon emissions be dealt with at the national level". DL71 recorded that the government reaffirmed its position on MBU on two occasions during the inquiry, confirming that MBU remains the most up-to-date policy on planning for airport development.

107   DL72 noted that NSC and others argued that MBU should be afforded limited or no weight as it pre-dates the government's adoption of the 2050 net zero target and the sixth carbon budget in June 2021. The Panel considered those were material considerations. However, "MBU itself recognises there is uncertainty over climate change policy and over international measures, and notes that therefore matters might change after its publication".

108   At DL73, it was recorded that the status of MBU was debated in some detail at the inquiry. The Panel concluded that there was nothing from government to suggest that MBU should be given reduced weight. At DL74, the Panel said that, although many might disagree with the direction of current government aviation policy, it was not the role of the Panel to question the merits or otherwise of that.

109   DL75 reads as follows:-

> "75. There was also an argument put forward that MBU would only come into effect once the planning balance had been established. In effect, it would weigh for or against a proposal only once the overall conclusion has been reached. However, this approach to national policy was not supported by evidence of examples of this methodology being adopted elsewhere, and it does not appear logical."

Ground 2: discussion

110   The claimant says that its approach to MBU was different from that of NSC at the inquiry. The claimant submitted to the Panel that although MBU and APF were the most up-to-date policies concerning the government's approach to airport capacity, they did not contain an unconditional mandate for expansion. At paragraph 8 of its written closing submissions, the claimant said that, in order to determine whether MBU and APF supported or counted against the proposed development, it was necessary to consider:-

> "the prior question of whether the general support for making best use of runways is reduced or removed because of environmental impacts of these specific applications. If so, the MBU and APF will weigh in the planning balance against the grant of planning permission. If, however, the environmental impacts of making best use of an airport runway are acceptable, the MBU and APF will lend support to the grant of permission in the overall planning balance."

111   The claimant contends that the Panel did not address the claimant's case in this regard. Thus, it either ignored a material consideration or failed to give adequate and intelligible reasons for rejecting the claimant's interpretation.

112   I do not consider there is merit in this submission. As set out above, DL75 did address the argument - which must be that of the claimant – that MBU would only

come into effect once the planning balance had been established. The Panel gave a reason for rejecting this; namely that the approach was not supported by evidence of examples of the methodology being adopted elsewhere, and that it did not appear logical. There is no justification for saying that this finding was not open to the Panel.

113   The claimant also submits that the Panel did not take account of the part of its closing submissions which argued that 1.29 of MBU required account to be taken of all relevant considerations, particularly environmental impacts. The claimant said this should be interpreted to include climate impacts assessed in the light of the UK's current climate change obligations. The Panel was thus told that it should take into account the introduction of the net zero target, the sixth carbon budget and its inclusion of international aviation, as well as the fact that the UK is off-track to meet the fourth and fifth carbon budgets, in deciding whether the airport expansion benefited from MBU's policy support.

114   So far as this criticism is concerned, I agree with Mr Humphries that it is readily apparent from the DL that the Panel considered in detail the carbon emissions from <u>all</u> sources. These included carbon emissions from aviation. It did so, as I have explained, by reference to whether the predicted aviation emissions from the proposal would have a material impact on the government's ability to meet its climate change targets and budgets.

115   That this was an appropriate approach is apparent from the judgment of Holgate J in *R. (Goesa Ltd) v Eastleigh Borough Council and Southampton International Airport Ltd* [2002] EWHC 1221 (Admin). At paragraph 122, Holgate J held that "acceptability is for the judgment of the decision maker" and that "there is nothing unlawful in the decision maker using benchmarks he considers to be appropriate in order to help arrive at a judgment on those issues. The statutory carbon budgets are one example...". At paragraph 123, Holgate J concluded that, given current policy and law, "it is permissible for a planning authority to look at the scale of GHG emissions relative to a national target and to reach a judgment, which may inevitably be of a generalised nature, about the likelihood of the proposal harming the achievement of that target".

116   The claimant argues the Panel misinterpreted MBU by taking it to mean that the admitted increase in CO_2 emissions was not a matter for local decision-making. As I have already said, there is nothing in the DL to suggest that, even if the Panel was wrong in its interpretation of MBU, it treated the increase in aviation emissions occasioned by the proposals as, for that reason, insignificant. On the contrary, as I have explained, the Panel had regard to the increase in emissions in determining the question (which it recorded as being agreed) of whether those emissions would materially affect the ability of the Secretary of State to comply with his obligations under the CCA etc.

117   Ms Dehon nevertheless contends that 1.29 of MBU requires planning decision makers to take into account all "environmental impacts", rather than leaving these to be addressed at the national level. Thus, even if the claimant's other arguments fail, the existence of MBU meant that the Panel erred in looking at aviation emissions from the proposal through the lens of the national system created by and under the CCA. She particularly relies on the closing words of 1.29, which say that it is for "local rather than national government, to consider each case on its merits".

118   I do not accept this submission. Although 1.29 is printed in bold type and is manifestly intended as a summation of the preceding paragraphs, MBU needs to be read in its entirety in order to understand what is meant by "environmental impacts" and considering "each case on its merits". It is apparent from 1.12 and 1.13 that one "important environmental element" which "should be considered at a national level" is the issue of "aviation carbon". It is in that important light that 1.29 falls to be read.

119   Accordingly, what the Panel said at DL70 was correct, as a matter of the interpretation of MBU.

120   The second part of Ground 2 asserts a failure by the Panel to give adequate reasons. I do not consider that the claimant has identified any unlawful failure by the Panel to give reasons for its approach to MBU. The case made by the claimant was addressed in the DL, either specifically (as at DL70 and 75) or in the wider context of the significance of increased aviation emissions in the planning process, in the light of the Secretary of State's responsibilities under the CCA.

121   Ground 2 accordingly fails.

Ground 3

122   Ground 3 involves paragraph 188 of the NPPF. This paragraph occurs in the part of the Framework headed "Ground conditions and pollution". Paragraph 188 reads as follows: -

> "The focus of planning policies and decisions should be on whether proposed development is an acceptable use of land, rather than the control of processes or emissions (where these are subject to separate pollution control regimes). Planning decisions should assume that these regimes will operate effectively. Equally, where a planning decision has been made on a particular development, the planning issues should not be revisited through the permitting regimes operated by pollution control authorities."

123   At DL62, the Panel summarised paragraph 188 of the NPPF as follows:-

> "62. At paragraph 188, the NPPF states that the focus of decisions should be on whether a proposed development is an acceptable land use, rather than focusing on the control of emissions which are the subject of separate pollution control regimes. It is stated that it should be assumed that such other regimes will operate effectively."

124   At DL146, the Panel recorded all parties as agreeing that there would be an increase in GHG, especially CO_2, if the appeal scheme were to go ahead, when compared with the position if it did not. The Panel noted that under these circumstances "the climate change position would be worsened".

125   I have already set out DL162. It is, however, convenient at this point to do so again, along with the immediately preceding paragraph, as well as highlighting the sentence in DL162, relating to the NPPF, to which the claimant's Ground 3 relates:-

> "161. The evidence suggests that the Government is not on track to meet the 4th and 5th carbon budgets – with significant reductions needed in relatively short periods. This largely uncontested position is shown in the CCC report. However, we are not yet in the period of either budget and the suggestion that

the Government is off track at this time means little in relation to the budget periods which have not yet started. However, no party has suggested that complacency is indicated or that the 4th and 5th budgets can be ignored.

162. There are three important points to make in relation to the carbon budgets and the way in which they operate. Firstly, although the approach to Net Zero and the carbon budget is a material consideration, the CCA places an obligation on the SoS, not local decision makers, to prepare policies and proposals with a view to meeting the carbon budgets. **Secondly, as advised in the NPPF, there is an assumption that controls which are in place will work.** Finally, and consequent on the previous points, NSC's position that grant of permission in this case would breach the CCA and be unlawful is not accepted. That does not mean that these matters are not material considerations, but the CCA duty rests elsewhere."

126   At DL213, the Panel said:-

"213. It is self-evident that any increase in CO_2 emissions in one location will have consequences elsewhere and that this could make the duty of the SoS under the CCA more difficult. But in this case the comparative magnitude of the increase is limited and it has to be assumed that the SoS will comply with the legal duty under the CCA."

127   Ground 3 advances two criticisms of the Panel's decision concerning paragraph 188 of the NPPF. The first is that the Panel erred in law in treating the CCA and the various duties placed on the Secretary of State under it as a "separate pollution control regime", within the scope of that paragraph. The second criticism is that, even if that part of the challenge were to fail, the Panel still erred in treating the assumption in paragraph 188 as irrebuttable.

128   In support of its first head of challenge, the claimant relies upon *Gladman Developments Ltd v Secretary of State for Communities and Local Government* [2019] EWCA Civ 1543. *Gladman* concerned an appeal against the refusal of planning permission for a residential development. Following an inquiry, an inspector dismissed the appeal on grounds which included the impact of the development on air quality. The inspector took into account the fact that the government's air quality plan made in December 2015 had been quashed because it failed to comply with Article 23 (1) of Directive 2008/50/EC on Ambient Air Quality and Cleaner Air for Europe, and with the domestic Regulations which implemented the Directive. The inspector found it would be unsafe to rely on vehicle emissions falling between the years 2015 and 2020, to the extent assumed in the models relied on by the claimant, and that, despite proposed mitigation measures, the proposals would have an adverse effect on air quality.

129   The claimant applied under section 288 of the 1990 Act to quash the inspector's decision. It did so, amongst other grounds, on the basis that the inspector should have proceeded on the assumption that the government would comply with the law, rather than assuming breaches of the Directive and Regulations would continue; and that the inspector had failed to give effect to the principle in paragraph 122 of the NPPF (now paragraph 188) that the planning system presumed other schemes of regulatory control were legally effective.

130   At first instance, the High Court refused the claimant's application. The Court of Appeal dismissed the claimant's appeal against that decision. In giving the Court of Appeal's judgment, Lindblom LJ said:-

> "43. Supperstone J. also rejected the submission, which Mr Kimblin sought to base on government policy in paragraph 122 of the NPPF, that the inspector failed to apply the principle that the planning system assumes other schemes of regulatory control will operate effectively. This policy, in his view, was directed at a situation where there is a parallel system of control, such as that operated by H.M.'s Inspectorate of Pollution (see *Gateshead MBC v Secretary of State for the Environment* [1995] Env. L.R. 37), or the "licensing or permitting regime for nuclear power stations" (see *R. (on the application of An Taisce) v Secretary of State for Energy and Climate Change* [2013] EWHC 4161 (Admin)), the essential principle being that the planning system should not duplicate those other regulatory controls, but should generally assume they will operate effectively. As the judge saw it, the Air Quality Directive was "not a parallel consenting regime to which paragraph 122 is directed". There was "no separate licensing or permitting decision that will address the specific air quality impacts of [Gladman's] proposed development" (paragraph 39 of the judgment).
>
> 44. Again, I agree with the judge. If it were right to regard the regime for the protection of human health and the environment against the adverse effects of air pollutants, under the Air Quality Directive and the 2010 regulations, as a regime to which the policy in paragraph 122 of the NPPF related, I do not think the inspector failed to assume it would "operate effectively". He manifestly had regard to it. And he did not doubt that, with the added urgency imparted by Garnham J.'s decision in *ClientEarth (No.2)*, the United Kingdom would discharge its responsibility under the Air Quality Directive to comply with the relevant limit values. But this broad assumption did not negate the conclusions he reached, in the light of the evidence before him, on the likely effects of the proposed development on local air quality in Newington and Rainham.
>
> 45. In my view, however, Supperstone J. was right to conclude that the policy in paragraph 122 was not engaged here. The policy was directed to situations where some proposed process or operation liable to cause pollution is subject to control under another regulatory regime. As the judge recognized, its purpose was to avoid needless duplication between two schemes of statutory control. It was concerned with "the control of processes or emissions … where these are subject to approval under pollution control regimes" and with "permitting regimes operated by pollution control authorities" (my emphasis). Such regulatory regimes would include those to which the judge referred, and also, for example, the regime for the issuing of environmental permits under the Environmental Protection Act 1990, which operates in parallel to the land use planning system.
>
> 46. As Mr Moules and Dr Bowes submitted, the Air Quality Directive and the 2010 regulations are not a licensing or permitting regime of that kind. The Air Quality Directive is "programmatic in nature". It imposes obligations on the state to comply with the relevant limit values within the shortest possible time, and by the means chosen to achieve compliance. In the United Kingdom

the approach adopted by the Government is to promulgate an air quality plan for the relevant zones or agglomerations. Paragraph 122 of the NPPF, properly understood, did not contemplate any assumption being made about that process. It does not require a planning decision-maker to assume that the Government will have acted expeditiously to take the action required to discharge its own responsibilities under the legislative scheme for air quality. 47. Government planning policy did engage with air quality, explicitly, in paragraph 124 of the NPPF. The policy in that paragraph was not qualified or expanded by the policy in paragraph 122. It was directed both to planning policies – which were expected to "sustain compliance with and contribute towards EU limit values or national objectives for pollutants ..." – and to individual planning decisions – which were expected to "ensure that any new development in Air Quality Management Areas is consistent with the local Air Quality Action Plan". But there was no requirement to assume the Government would have complied with the Air Quality Directive by the time the development was carried out.

48. It follows in my view that the NPPF did not compel the inspector to assume that the requirements of the Air Quality Directive would have been complied with soon enough, and in such a way, as to make the effects of the proposed development on air quality acceptable. He was not obliged by any such policy to disregard the Government's failure to comply with the Air Quality Directive, as found by the court in *ClientEarth (No.2)*, or to assume that it would comply within any given time. In submissions both before us and in the court below, effectively on behalf of the Government, this was accepted by Mr Moules."

131   The claimant submits that, just as with the air quality regime considered in Gladman, the CCA is "programmatic in nature", imposing obligations on the State to comply with relevant limit values. In Gladman, these were air quality plans. In what the claimant says is the same vein, the CCA imposes obligations on the Secretary of State to comply with relevant emission limits, set in the carbon budgets, by the time specified in those budgets, via the policy means chosen by the Secretary of State. Properly understood, Ms Dehon submits that paragraph 188 of the NPPF does not require a planning decision-maker to assume that the Secretary of State will have acted within the time span of the carbon budgets to take the action required in order to discharge his responsibilities under the legislative scheme for climate.

132   Ms Dehon contends that the claimant is not questioning the application by the Panel of paragraph 188. Rather, it is a question of law as to whether the CCA is included within the type of "pollution control regime" referred to in that paragraph.

133   The second part of the claimant's case under Ground 3, is that, even if I do not accept the first part, the Panel assumed that the assumption in paragraph 188 is irrebuttable. Not only is such an assumption legally wrong; there was, in fact, evidence which the claimant says rebutted the assumption.

134   The claimant says that DL161 and DL162 do not "run together" and that DL161 does not, even on its most benign reading, expressly engage with rebutting the assumption. It does not mention the assumption at all. No connection is made in the DL between this paragraph and any of the paragraphs in which the assumption is applied. Ms Dehon submits it was implausible that the Panel, in saying what it did at DL161, accepted the argument put by BAL in paragraph 546 of its closing submissions, which was that "being off track now in relation to a budget period

that [has] not even started and in respect of which further legal and policy matters can be taken is, in reality, meaningless".

135   In any event, DL161 fails to take into account or to explain the Panel's reasoning in relation to other relevant evidence that was before them; namely, the time it takes for policy to be developed and have a practical effect, meaning that it would be very difficult to get "on track" within the five year budget period when the government is presently so far off track; the physics of how carbon emissions work, particularly the length of time they persist in the atmosphere; and the fact that the emissions caused by the Airport's expansion would occur during the fourth and fifth carbon budget periods.

136   The claimant points out that Mr Melling, BAL's own witness, accepted that the United Kingdom is not on track to meet the fourth and fifth carbon budgets.

137   In her oral submissions to me, Ms Dehon said there was no illogicality in (i) the claimant's acceptance that the UK ETS was a pollution control regime falling within paragraph 188 of the NPPF and (ii) the claimant's stance that the Secretary of State's direct obligations under the CCA are not part of such a regime but, rather, fall to be excluded, on the authority of *Gladman*. Contrary to the defendant's case, the judgment in *Gladman* did not turn on whether air quality control was a "local" as opposed to a "national" issue. This can be seen from paragraph 46 of the judgment of Lindblom LJ.

Ground 3: discussion

138   I agree with the claimant that the mere fact the Panel accurately summarised paragraph 188 of the NPPF does not mean it must have correctly construed the meaning of that paragraph. Nevertheless, I do not consider that *Gladman* enables the claimant to make good the first part of its challenge under Ground 3.

139   The relationship between local and national decision-making in the area of air quality is significantly different from the position with regard to greenhouse gas emissions from aircraft. Such emissions are controlled at the national level, pursuant to the CCA. In contrast, air quality issues have a significant and discrete local element. As Mr Humphries points out, paragraph 186 of the NPPF states that decision-makers:-

> "should sustain and contribute towards compliance with relevant limit values or national objectives for pollutants, taking into account the presence of Air Quality Management Areas and Clean Air Zones, and the cumulative impacts from individual sites in local areas ... Planning decisions should ensure that any new development in Air Quality Management Areas and Clean Air Zones is consistent with the local air quality action plan."

140   A similar point is also to be seen at paragraph 47 of the judgment in *Gladman*. In marked contrast, the way in which the Secretary of State seeks to discharge his duty under CCA in the case of greenhouse gas emissions from aircraft involves the setting at a national level of carbon budgets and the use of both national and (through CORSIA) international trading schemes. All this is apparent from the above analysis of the CCA and the delegated legislation made under it, including the Greenhouse Gas Emissions Trading Scheme Order 2020. The application of the assumption in paragraph 188 of the NPPF in respect of emissions from aircraft

would therefore not cut across any other requirements of the NPPF or other national planning policy.

141 Whilst it is the case that the CCA deals with a range of matters, including restricting the use of single use plastic bags, the fact remains that the overall responsibilities of the Secretary of State under the CCA in respect of emissions from aircraft needs, for this purpose, to be examined in its entirety, starting with section 1. It is artificial to contend, as the claimant does, that the UK ETS falls for this purpose to be considered in isolation. Some 88-90% of all flights to and from Bristol Airport are covered by the UK ETS. The CORSIA system is relevant to non-UK/EEA flights (see above).

142 The UK ETS system therefore cannot be separated for this purpose from the CCA, in the way the claimant contends. There is, accordingly, indeed an illogicality in the claimant's stance on this issue, from which the claimant cannot escape.

143 Furthermore, the consequence of accepting the claimant's first submission in respect of paragraph 188 of the NPPF would not merely be to duplicate the system of controlling aircraft emissions, put in place by the CCA. It would lead local planning decision-makers into an area of national policy, with which they are not directly concerned. This takes us back to Ground 1, where the Panel was, I have found, entitled to conclude that the relevant local planning policies did not directly address aviation emissions. Again, it is necessary to refer to what the Panel said at DL149; namely, that there was no substantial dissent at the inquiry from the formulation of the key question being whether the emissions from the proposal would be so significant that they would materially affect the ability of the UK to meet its carbon budgets and the target at net zero GHG emissions by 2050. The Panel was entitled to take that approach in determining the relationship between local development control and the progressive restriction of aviation emissions by the CCA etc.

144 At this point, it is instructive to look again at DL162. The highlighted sentence referring to paragraph 188 is not the primary reason why the Panel found as it did. The primary reason was that the CCA places an obligation on the Secretary of State, not local decision makers, to prepare policies and proposals with a view to meeting the carbon budgets. Reading the DL fairly, the Panel's reference to paragraph 188 of the NPPF was not an essential part of the Panel's reasoning. On the contrary, the Panel's essential reasoning does not depend on that sentence. Accordingly, to treat the existence of the sentence as undermining the Panel's careful articulation of the relationship between emissions from aircraft and the development control decision would be wholly wrong.

145 For these reasons, the first part of the challenge under Ground 3 fails. I therefore turn to consider whether the Panel wrongly interpreted paragraph 188 of the NPPF as containing an irrebuttable assumption.

146 There was no disagreement by BAL at the inquiry that the paragraph 188 assumption can be rebutted. This is apparent from paragraph 533 of BAL's written closing submissions: "Of course a policy presumption may be rebutted". At paragraph 19 of Appendix 1 to those submissions, BAL reiterated that "this assumption could, logically, be 'rebutted'".

147 BAL's position was that no proper basis had been identified by the claimant and NSC for doing so.

148 Against this background, I find there is no basis for contending that the Panel, in the relevant paragraphs of the DL set out above, somehow assumed that the

NPPF paragraph 188 assumption was irrebuttable. The claimant's submission that DL161 and 162 have to be read in isolation from each other goes directly against the Higher Courts' judgments explaining how planning decision letters are to be construed. The Panel's DL was written primarily to explain to the parties that had taken part in the inquiry why the Panel had decided matters as it did. There is no basis to assume that the Panel took a view which was contrary to what was common ground at the inquiry.

149   At this point, the claimant's challenge under Ground 3 becomes a "reasons" challenge. Ms Dehon says that, given the Panel accepted the cogency of the evidence before it (including from one of BAL's expert witnesses), which was that the proposal would make the meeting of the Secretary of State's obligations under the CCA more difficult, the Panel failed to explain why, on the basis that the assumption was rebuttable, it had come to the conclusion that the assumption was not rebutted.

150   I am unpersuaded by this residual element of Ground 3. I remind myself again that decision letters are not to be construed as if they were legislative instruments. Rather, they should be examined in the round. That is particularly important in the present case where, as will be apparent, the relevant issues were closely interrelated. It is plain that DL161 and 162 fall to be read together. In DL161, the Panel specifically engaged with the fact that the evidence shows the government is not on track to meet the fourth and fifth carbon budgets, with significant reductions needed in relatively short periods. Importantly, however, the Panel found that "we are not yet in the period of either budget and the suggestion that the government is off track at this time means little in relation to budget periods which have not yet started". Read in context, that is a legally sufficient engagement with the issue.

151   Furthermore, at DL163 to 170 the Panel engaged expressly with the alleged shortcomings of the UK ETS and CORSIA. At DL169, the Panel considered that neither the objectors nor BAL were "entirely correct" as to what should be drawn from these shortcomings; and that there was "currently an offsetting gap beginning in the next decade and, this cannot be ignored". However, the Panel went on to say that "given the international and national context it is not unreasonable to assume that something will come forward to fill the space." The Panel concluded that it remained to be seen whether there would be a refreshment of UK ETS/CORSIA or whether other available measures would be deployed. There is nothing unreasoned or irrational in the Panel's conclusions on that issue. Likewise, there is nothing unreasoned or irrational in DL170, where the Panel reiterated that "UK ETS/CORSIA are only two of the measures available to address aviation carbon emissions in the light of the legal duty to ensure that carbon budgets are not breached".

152   Ground 3 accordingly fails.

Ground 4

153   Ground 4 alleges an error of law by the Panel in discounting the impact of the expansion of Bristol Airport in relation to the local carbon budget for NSC. The Panel decided not to take into account the extent of the impact on NSC's carbon budget in determining the significance of the climate change impact of the proposal and, in so doing, the claimant says the Panel ignored the Institute of Environmental Management and Assessment ("IEMA") Guidance for assessing greenhouse gas

emissions in environmental impact assessments. Alternatively, the claimant argues that the Panel did not give an adequate or intelligible explanation for its conclusions.

154   The IEMA Guidance provides that the significance of a project's carbon impact can be determined by comparing the project's carbon budget with "global, national, sectoral, regional, or local" carbon budgets "as available". It suggests that a "sense of scale" of the project's carbon footprint can be provided by "contextualising" that footprint against certain of those budgets.

155   Professor Anderson explained at the inquiry that carbon budgets have been calculated for every local authority in Britain. He set out the budget for NSC. Using BAL's forecast of the CO_2 emissions resulting from the Airport's expansion, Professor Anderson calculated the emissions from it which could reasonably be allocated to the NSC area. He then determined the extent of the impact of those admissions on the local carbon budget.

156   The claimant submits that Professor Anderson's conclusion was stark; namely, that NSC's share of Bristol Airport's aviation emissions will consume the local authority's entire carbon budget in the five years from the start of 2028. By 2040, a single year of NSC's share of aviation emissions from Bristol Airport will consume the entire carbon budget intended for the five years 2038-2042. Professor Anderson's view was that this was a far more appropriate comparison of the significance of aviation emissions, than comparing them with the national total.

157   The claimant points out that BAL's climate expert, Dr Ösund-Ireland, did not take any issue with the methodology of Professor Anderson and accepted that, based on the IEMA guidance, it was "one relevant approach which could be applied". The claimant says that, when compared to the local carbon budget, the impact of the expansion is profound, overwhelming the local carbon budget.

158   The Panel addressed the CO_2 impact of the proposal at DL183 to 189. The Panel recorded BAL's evidence that the impact of the expansion would represent around 0.22 - 0.28% of the 37.5Mt CO_2/annum of the planning assumption related to the fourth and fifth carbon budgets; and between 0.29 - 0.34% of the CCC "balanced pathway" assumption. The increase would, accordingly, "not amount to a significant effect as described in the ES/ESA [viz. BAL's environmental assessment and its Addendum]."

159   At DL188, the Panel said:-

"… In contrast, the approach of opponents is that the increased emissions would consume the local carbon budget of NSC between 2028 and 2032. However limited detail of this approach was provided, and it was not suggested that local carbon budgets have any basis in law or policy. In addition, it is argued that any increase in emissions would limit the Government's room for manoeuvre in relation to the Net Zero target."

160   The claimant says it appears from this that the Panel discounted, or at any rate did not take into consideration, the extent of the impact on the local carbon budget in determining the significance of the climate change impact of the proposal. The Panel accordingly failed to take into account a material consideration; alternatively, it failed to give adequate reasons for its conclusion.

161   The claimant argues that the reasons given by the Panel ignore (a) the detailed evidence given by Professor Anderson; (b) the fact that BAL did not challenge his methodology or calculation; and (c) the IEMA Guidance, which is directly relevant

and applicable guidance, that refers explicitly to the use of local carbon budgets in assessing the significance of impact of a project.

162   Ms Dehon says it is not an answer to Ground 4 to assert that there is no legal or policy basis which requires the local carbon budget to be taken into account. That is not the correct test in deciding whether the Panel's approach on this matter was lawful. Much, if not most, of the detailed professional guidance on best practice in undertaking an environmental impact assessment is neither statutory nor based on policy. The fact remains that the only practitioner guidance concerning the assessment of greenhouse gas emissions and evaluating their significance is that produced by IEMA. It advises comparison against local budgets, where they are available. The IEMA Guidance was plainly material to determining, as required by the 2017 Regulations, what constituted "the information reasonably required for reaching a reasoned conclusion on the significant effects of the development on the environment, taking into account current knowledge and methods of assessment" (regulation 18(4)(b)).

163   In *R. (Goesa) v Eastleigh BC Southampton International Airport Ltd* [2022] J.P.L. 1309, Holgate J held it was well-established that whether an effect is significant and whether any assessment of significant effects is adequate are both matters of judgment for the decision-maker, in that case the local planning authority: paragraph 100. Such judgments are only open to challenge applying the conventional *Wednesbury* standard. Furthermore, at paragraph 102, Holgate J held that "the court should allow a substantial margin of appreciation to judgments based upon scientific, technical or predictive assessments by those with appropriate expertise."

164   The environmental statement produced by Southampton International Airport Ltd in Goesa relied upon guidance from IEMA that, given ongoing research on how to measure significance in the approach of treating or GHG emissions as potentially significant "it is down to the practitioner's professional judgment on how best to contextualise a project's GHG impact": paragraph 105. Ms Dehon submits that *Goesa* affirms the relevance of the IEMA Guidance, albeit that compliance with that Guidance is not determinative of the lawfulness of the assessment. This emerges from paragraph 120 of the judgment.

Ground 4: discussion

165   The passages relied upon by the claimant in the IEMA Guidance occur in the following paragraph under the heading "Targets based on scientific projections":-

> "There is currently little evidence of these science-based targets being used in the UK's development consent system, or related EIA process to assess a project's significance. However, this quantitative approach provides a good indicator of significance and could be used in EIA to calculate a project's carbon budget. This budget can then be compared against an existing budget (global, national, sectoral, regional, or local - as available), to identify the percentage impact the project will contribute to climate change. Consequently, the greater the project's carbon budget, the greater its significance."

166   The Guidance then identifies a number of different methods which can be used to allocate a project's carbon budget, including grandfathering, carbon space, contraction and convergence, blended sharing and common but differentiated

convergence. The Guidance says that due to inconsistencies between different methods and their assumptions for assessment, "there is not one single agreed method by which to assess a project's carbon budget". Therefore, the Guidance recommends that a review of these methods should be undertaken, to identify which one can best represent a project's potential carbon footprint.

167   In *Friends of the Earth*, the Supreme Court reiterated that, in determining whether a public authority has failed to take into account a relevant consideration, three categories of consideration can be identified. They are (i) considerations clearly identified by statute as ones to which regard must be had; (ii) considerations so identified as ones to which regard must not be had; and (iii) considerations to which the decision-maker may have regard if, in their judgment and discretion, they think it is right to do so.

168   The test of whether a consideration falling within the third category is "so obviously material" that it must be taken into account is the *Wednesbury* irrationality test: paragraph 119 of *Friends of the Earth*. The third category of consideration can be subdivided into two. The first sub-category is where the decision-maker does not avert at all to a particular consideration falling within the third category. In such a case, unless the consideration is obviously material according to *Wednesbury* principles, the decision is not affected by any unlawfulness. The Supreme Court held that there "is no obligation on a decision maker to work through every consideration which might conceivably be regarded as potentially relevant to the decision they have to take and positively decide to discount it in the exercise of their discretion": paragraph 120.

169   At paragraph 121, the Supreme Court described the second sub-category. This is where a decision-maker turns their mind to a particular consideration falling within the third category but decides to give the consideration no weight. The question here is, again, whether the decision-maker acts rationally in so deciding: paragraph 121.

170   It is quite apparent from DL188 that the Panel engaged with the approach of the claimant and others that the increased emissions would consume the local carbon budget of NSC. We are, therefore, concerned with the second sub-category of the third category of consideration, as described by the Supreme Court in *Friends of the Earth*. As it is apparent that the Panel gave the matter no weight, the claimant has to show public law illegality in an area where the courts are traditionally careful not to adopt a stance which may result in the court wrongly substituting its own view of weight for the view taken by the primary decision-maker.

171   Applying these principles, I am in no doubt that the Panel did not act irrationally in giving the issue of local carbon budgets no weight, on the ground that such budgets have no basis either in law or in policy. They plainly have no basis in law. Contrary to Ms Dehon's submission, the fact that they have no basis in policy is significant, given that, in the planning field, we are concerned with decision-making which is intensely concerned with matters of policy.

172   The fact that Professor Anderson's evidence on this issue was not contradicted by BAL's climate expert did not, therefore, mean the Panel had no alternative but to ascribe weight to what Professor Anderson had said about local carbon budgets.

173   BAL makes the point that its EIA had focused on aircraft emissions in the national context. As the IEMA Guidance indicates, this is one of the ways of assessing the impact of a project. Indeed, in the present context, looking at the effect of the

Airport's expansion proposal in the national context was manifestly appropriate, for the reasons I have already given.

174   I accordingly find the Panel was entitled to ascribe no weight to the evidence about the local carbon budget.

175   Finally on Ground 4, I do not accept that the Panel failed to give a legally adequate explanation for its stance. The Panel's rationale for placing no weight on the impact on local carbon budgets emerges clearly from the DL, as just described.

176   Ground 4 accordingly fails.

Ground 5

177   Ground 5 is concerned with the impact of non-CO_2 emissions from aircraft. The claimant submits that the impact of non-CO_2 emissions was a matter of critical importance to determining the impact of the Airport's expansion on climate change. The claimant says that this impact was not lawfully addressed in BAL's environmental statement, as required by the 2017 Regulations. The Panel therefore erred in finding that BAL's environmental statement was lawful.

178   The claimant says that non-CO_2 emissions had to be taken directly into account by the Panel in determining whether consent should be given to BAL. The Panel could not rely, in this regard, on BAL's Carbon and Climate Change Action Plan ("CCCAP") as a justification for not treating the effects of non-CO_2 emissions as weighing in the balance against the proposal. This is particularly so because, elsewhere in the DL, the Panel concluded that the CCCAP had only very limited weight.

179   The claimant also contends that the Panel failed to apply the precautionary principle which, had it been invoked, would in any event have required the Panel directly to consider non-CO_2 emissions.

180   Underlying these submissions is the claimant's contention that, despite any scientific doubts about the contribution made by non-CO_2 emissions to climate change, a relevant "multiplier" for assessing the potential effects from non-CO_2 emissions has nevertheless emerged. Had it been applied, this multiplier would have almost doubled the assessment of greenhouse gas emissions from aviation, resulting from the proposal, and so would have had a material effect on the Panel's assessment of whether that increase would make the Secretary of State's compliance with his duties under the CCA materially harder.

181   Finally, in the alternative, the claimant submits that the Panel failed to give legally adequate reasons for its stance on non-CO_2 emissions.

182   The Panel found as follows:-

> "Failure to Assess non-CO_2 Emissions
>
> 204. Along with CO_2 emissions, non-CO_2 effects have the potential to bring about climate change. These effects, such as contrails and cirrus clouds, appear (as far as is known) to be short term in duration. However, there is considerable uncertainty as to their effect and longevity.
>
> 205. As recognised by the CCC there is considerable uncertainty in assessing these emissions, and the ESA recognised this point and did not seek to quantify their effect. It has been suggested that a multiplier might take account of non-CO_2 effects but this has yet to emerge and there is no policy as to how they should be dealt with.

206. The criticism of BAL's position is the allegation that non-CO_2 effects have been ignored and that it is unreasonable to ignore the effects due to measurement issues.

207. However, the draft Carbon and Climate Change Action Plan (CCCAP) (below) provides that such emissions should not be ignored in future selection of GHG reduction measures. Given the extent of scientific uncertainty, and given the intention of the CCCAP to consider the effects further, it would be unreasonable to weigh this matter in the balance against the proposal."

183   DL208-210 then described the CCCAP. As I have earlier mentioned, the CCCAP was a draft. It envisaged BAL's operations and activities becoming carbon net zero by 2030 and becoming net zero as a whole, including aviation, by 2050. The draft CCCAP was published in May 2021. It set out a range of targets related to emissions from all sources. It would include a package of deliverable measures at agreed intervals. The submission of a CCCAP to NSC would be the subject of a condition, which would also require the CCCAP to be independently audited and reviewed. It should also reflect any changes arising from any updated emissions targets and national policy changes. The Panel noted that NSC and others were "concerned, understandably, about the nature and level of enforceable commitments related to CO_2 emissions reduction in the final document."

184   DL210 says:-

"210. The CCCAP indicated the direction of travel of BA in this respect. It is necessary that the production of a final version will be the subject of a condition but, at the moment as a draft, it has very limited weight."

185   Regulation 3 of the 2017 Regulations provides that the relevant planning authority, the Secretary of State or an inspector must not grant planning permission for EIA development unless an EIA has been carried out in respect of that development. Regulation 2 defines "EIA development" as development which is either Schedule 1 development; or Schedule 2 development likely to have significant effects on the environment by virtue of factors such as its nature, size or location. The Schedules in question are those contained in the 2017 Regulations. It is common ground that BAL's proposals constitute EIA development.

186   Regulation 4 describes the environmental impact assessment process. It involves, inter alia, the preparation of an environmental statement. The EIA must identify, describe and assess, in an appropriate manner, in light of each individual case, the direct and indirect significant effects of the proposed development on, amongst other things, "climate": regulation 4 (2)(c).

187   Regulation 18 explains what an environmental statement must include. One of the overarching, minimum requirements is "a description of the likely significant effects of the proposed development on the environment": regulation 18 (3)(b). Regulation 18(4)(b) states that an environmental statement must:-

"include the information reasonably required for reaching a reasoned conclusion on the significant effects of the development on the environment, taking into account current knowledge and methods of assessment;".

188   Schedule 4 contains further provisions regarding information for inclusion in environmental statements. Paragraph 5 requires a description of the likely significant effects arising from:-

"(f) the impact of the project on climate (for example the nature and magnitude of greenhouse gas emissions) and the vulnerability of the project to climate change;".

189   Paragraph 6 requires a "description of the forecasting methods or evidence, used to identify and assess the significant effects on the environment, including details of difficulties (for example technical deficiencies or lack of knowledge) encountered compiling the required information and the main uncertainties involved".

190   I have mentioned the claimant's reliance on the emergence of a multiplier for non-CO_2 emissions. In August 2019, the Department for Business, Energy & Industrial Strategy ("BEIS") published the government's "Greenhouse Gas Conversion Factors for Company Reporting - Methodology Paper for Emission Factors, Final Report". The BEIS document provides the methodological approach and key data sources for the assumptions used to define the emissions factors provided in the 2019 Government Greenhouse Gas Conversion Factors for Company Reporting, expanding upon the information provided in the data tables of that report. Paragraph 1.8 states that the document is not intended to provide guidance on the practicalities of reporting for organisations but rather to provide an overview with key information, so that the basis of the factors provided can be better understood and assessed.

191   Later in the document we find the following:-

""non-CO_2 impacts and Radiative Forcing"

8.36. The emission factors provided in the 2019 GHG Conversion Factors section "Business Travel – air" and "Freighting goods" refer to aviation's direct CO_2, CH4 and N_2O emissions only. There is currently uncertainty over the other non-CO_2 climate change effects of aviation (including water vapour, contrails, NOx, etc.) which have been indicatively accounted for by applying a multiplier in some cases.

8.37. Currently there is no suitable climate metric to express the relationship between emissions and climate warming effects from aviation, but this is an active area of research. Nonetheless, it is clear that aviation imposes other effects on the climate which are greater than that implied from simply considering its CO_2 emissions alone.

8.38. The application of a "multiplier" to take account of non-CO_2 effects is a possible way of illustratively taking account of the full climate impact of aviation. A multiplier is not a straight forward instrument. In particular, it implies that other emissions and effects are directly linked to production of CO_2, which is not the case. Nor does it reflect accurately the different relative contribution of emissions to climate change over time, or reflect the potential trade-offs between the warming and cooling effects of different emissions. **On the other hand, consideration of the** non-CO_2 **climate change effects of aviation can be important in some cases, and there is currently no better way of taking these effects into account. A multiplier of 1.9 is recommended as a central estimate, based on the best available scientific evidence, as summarised in**

8.39. Table 46 and the GWP100 figure…from the ATTICA research presented in Table 47 below…

8.40. It is important to note that **the value of this 1.9 multiplier is subject to significant uncertainty** and should only be applied to the CO_2 component of direct emissions…" (original emphases).

192   A BEIS "Updated Energy and Emissions Projections 2019" document (October 2020) contains a paper by D.S. Lee and others titled "The contribution of global aviation to anthropogenic climate forcing for 2000 to 2018". The paper states that "Historically, estimating aviation non-CO_2 effects has been particularly challenging" and that, although understanding aviation's impacts on the climate system has improved, it "remains incomplete". The paper aims to present "a best estimate and uncertainty (sic) based on the results from global climate models employing process-based contrail cirrus parameterizations".

193   Under the heading "7. Aviation CO_2 vs non-CO_2 forcings", the paper notes that aviation non-CO_2 forcings are not covered by the former Kyoto Protocol and that it is "unclear whether future developments of the Paris Agreement… will include short-lived indirect greenhouse gases like N03 and CO_2, aerosol-cloud effects or other aviation non-CO_2 effects". Although aviation is not mentioned explicitly in the text of the Paris Agreement, nevertheless total global greenhouse-gas emissions need to be reduced rapidly to achieve a balance between anthropogenic emissions by sources and removals by sinks of greenhouse gases in the second-half of this century.

194   Later under the same heading, the paper says the fact that aviation's non-CO_2 forcings are not included in global climate policy has resulted in studies as to whether they could be incorporated into existing policies, such as the European Emissions Trading Scheme, using an appropriate overall emissions "multiplier". It is said, however, that "scientific uncertainty has so far precluded this". As an alternative, proposals have been made to reduce aviation's non-CO_2 forcings by avoiding contrail formation by re-routing aircraft or optimising flight times to avoid the more positive (warming) fractional forcings (e.g. by avoiding night flights).

195   At DL205, the Panel said it had been recognised by the CCC that there is considerable uncertainty in assessing non-CO_2 emissions from aircraft. The source for this is a letter dated 24 September 2019 from the CCC to the Secretary of State for Transport. In the Annex to the letter, there is the following:-

"Aviation and shipping both emit very small amounts of regulated non-CO_2 greenhouse gases (methane and nitrous oxide) but also have additional warming and cooling effects that are not included in the basket of gases covered by the Paris Agreement and the Climate Change Act …

- **Aviation produces a range of different pollutants that affect the climate in different ways. The most significant effect is from creation of contrails and high clouds, although the impact of these are short-lived as these clouds are high in the atmosphere. Measuring these effects on an annual basis is challenging, given their short term nature and dependence on localised conditions. Overall, non-CO_2 effects from aviation warm the climate and approximately double the historic warming effect of CO_2 alone.**

…

In both aviation and shipping these non-CO_2 effects are mainly short-lived, meaning that if they were to stop, their effects on the climate would rapidly disappear.

The appropriate approach to policy at this stage is not to include these effects within the net-zero target, but to improve scientific understanding (e.g. for annual reporting) and develop options to markedly reduce them over the coming decades that are not at the expense of GHG emissions.

In aviation, policies are already in place to limit some non-CO_2 effects due to their impact on air quality…While addressing non-CO_2 effects is important, this does not change the need to reduce CO_2 emissions which are the dominant factor contributing to IAS' impact on the climate.

We will continue to monitor progress to reduce the non-CO_2 effects of IAS in our annual progress reports to Parliament and in our advice on setting carbon budgets."

196   At the inquiry, Professor Anderson accepted the CCC had advised that non-CO_2 effects "should not be accounted for in the UK's carbon budgets, because it is challenging to aggregate their effects accurately". Having referred to the BEIS Journey Emissions Comparison Methodology, Professor Anderson said that "there is as yet no consistent methodology for applying emissions 'multipliers' for the non-CO_2 emissions from other sectors" and that "if we are to compare 'like with like' a multiplier for aviation alone is theoretically imbalanced".

197   Professor Anderson and Mr Asher referred the Panel to the precautionary principle. They considered that BAL's failure to apply the BEIS multiplier to calculate the full climate impact of the proposed development breached that principle.

198   In its closing submissions at the inquiry, the claimant argued that the environmental information before the Panel was flawed because it omitted any assessment of the non-CO_2 impacts of aviation at altitude. The claimant also submitted that the warming effect of the non-CO_2 emissions was relevant to the question of whether the expansion of the Airport would materially affect the United Kingdom's ability to meet its climate change obligations.

Ground 5: discussion

199   Referring to DL204-207, Ms Dehon submitted that the Panel did not mention the BEIS 1.9 multiplier or any of the evidence that recommended it as a way of taking account of the full climate change impact of aviation. Nor did the Panel record what she said was a concession by BAL's expert witness, that the multiplier could have been used to calculate the climate impact of the proposal. Ms Dehon says this is an error of law, in that the Panel ignored a material consideration.

200   In my view, it is quite obvious, in the light of the evidence before and submissions made to the Panel, that the reference in DL205 to a multiplier is to the BEIS 1.9 multiplier. No other specific multiplier had been relied upon at the inquiry.

201   Ms Dehon says that, in any event, even if the BEIS multiplier was the one referenced in that paragraph of the DL, then, contrary to the Panel's conclusion, that multiplier had plainly "emerged". It was in both the 2019 and 2020 BEIS documents, which were before the Panel. There was, furthermore, no justification

for requiring any separate policy obligation before non-CO_2 emissions fell to be taken into account by the Panel.

202   I do not accept these submissions. However much the claimant may seek to invoke the BEIS 1.9 multiplier, there is very far from being any scientific consensus that it is a relevant tool in determining non-CO_2 emissions from aviation, other than in the context of company reporting. Professor Anderson's evidence to the Panel was to that effect.

203   The CCC's attitude to non-CO_2 emissions is, plainly, of high relevance, given that the CCC is concerned with the discharge of the Secretary of State's obligations under the CCA. As I have already explained, the Panel properly concluded that the relevance of aviation emissions to the Panel's decision was whether the implementation of BAL's proposals for expansion "would materially affect the ability of the United Kingdom to meet its carbon budgets and the target of net-zero GHG emissions by 2050": DL149.

204   Given the CCC's view that non-CO_2 effects should not be included within the net-zero target, it is difficult to see how the Panel could make use of the BEIS 1.9 multiplier in order to answer that central question. In any event, the issue for this court is whether the Panel was entitled, in the exercise of its planning judgment, to refuse to make use of the multiplier. Plainly, it was.

205   Ms Dehon criticises the defendant's justification of the last phrase in DL205, concerning there being no policy as to how non-CO_2 aviation emissions are to be dealt with. The defendant says that there is no statutory duty to have regard to such non-CO_2 effects and no policy which identifies them as mandatory. Ms Dehon describes this approach as utterly wrong.

206   DL205 needs, however, to be read in its entirety. If the whole issue of non-CO_2 emissions had not been subject to uncertainty as regards assessing their effects, and if the CCC had regarded them as currently being relevant to the Secretary of State's CCA obligations, then it might have been problematic for the Panel to disregard all of that, purely because there was no specific policy requiring the Panel to use the multiplier. That, however, was not the position. Everything pointed in the opposite direction. The Panel was entitled, for the reasons it gave, to conclude, as a matter of its judgment, that it was not appropriate to apply the multiplier.

207   Concise though they are, DL204 and 205 contain adequate reasons for the Panel's decision. Although Ms Dehon did not take the point, the words "these effects" in DL204 need to be read as "some of these effects", since the evidence before the Panel indicated that some non-CO_2 effects are longer term. That was, I consider, recognised by the Panel in the last sentence of DL204.

208   I need now to turn to the related issue of BAL's environmental statement. As I have recorded, the claimant contends that the statement is not compliant with the 2017 Regulations, in failing to deal with non-CO_2 emissions.

209   It is now well-established that a planning authority's or inspector's conclusion that an environmental statement is compliant with the 2017 Regulations is a matter of planning judgment, challengeable only on a *Wednesbury* basis. At paragraph 137 of *R. (Plan B Earth) v Secretary of State for Transport* [2020] P.T.S.R. 1446, Lindblom LJ held that "it is not the Court's task to adjudicate on the content of an environment statement... unless there is some patent defect in the assessment, which has not been put right in the making of the decision". Ms Dehon submits

that there is such a "patent defect" in the present case, indistinguishable from that found in *R. (Squire) v Shropshire Council* [2019] Env. L.R. 36.

210   *Squire* was a challenge to the grant of permission for a poultry-rearing facility in the countryside. At paragraphs 65 to 69 of the Court of Appeal's judgment, Lindblom LJ held that the environmental statement prepared in connection with the project was unlawful. The statement did not specify the third party land on which manure from the chickens was going to be spread. Although it dealt with odour likely to emanate from the poultry buildings themselves, the environmental statement did not set out any parallel assessment or indeed any meaningful assessment of the effects of odour and dust from the storage and spreading of chicken manure, either on the land of the farmer who was the proposed developer or on that of any other farmer. It did not seek to anticipate the content of any future manure management plan, including the fields to which it would relate. It could not be inferred from the environmental statement that its authors had concluded that the proposed storage and spreading of manure was not a potential source of pollution, including odour and dust, which ought to be addressed in determining the application for planning permission. Finally, the future manure management plan was not a substitute for the assessment lacking in the environment statement. Not only was the manure management plan yet to come into existence, even when it did, it was only going to relate to the storage and spreading of manure on the land of the farmer seeking to build the facility, not to the substantial qualities that were going to have to be disposed of elsewhere.

211   All of this meant that "the environmental statement was deficient in its lack of a proper assessment of the environmental impacts of the storage and spreading of manure as an indirect effect of the proposed development": paragraph 69. Accordingly, it was not compliant with the requirements of the 2017 Regulations.

212   With these cases in mind, I return to the relevant paragraphs of the DL. At DL206, the Panel noted criticism of the position of BAL, which was said to have ignored non-CO_2 effects in its environmental statement.

213   In fact, BAL's environmental statement did deal with non-CO_2 emissions. In the environmental statement Addendum of November 2020, paragraphs 10.6.20 to 10.6.25 specifically addressed "consideration of non-CO_2 aviation emissions". The Addendum noted that (as the Panel subsequently accepted) non-CO_2 effects are associated with much greater uncertainty, compared with CO_2 emissions from aviation sources.

214   The Addendum opined that the state of scientific knowledge of non-CO_2 effects is too uncertain for accurate measurement at this stage. Accordingly, non-CO_2 effects for aviation "are not currently included in any domestic or international legislation or emission targets, including the Paris Agreement". Accordingly, whilst it was acknowledged that non-CO_2 effects may well have a climate impact, these had not been considered in the environmental assessment (10.6.25).

215   As can be seen from the 2017 Regulations, referenced earlier, the legislation specifically acknowledges there may be limits on "current knowledge and methods of assessment" (regulation 18)(4)(b)) and that forecasting methods or evidence should include "details of difficulties (for example technical deficiencies or lack of knowledge) encountered compiling the required information and the main uncertainties involved" (Schedule 4, paragraph 6).

216   I find that the Addendum to the environmental statement adopted an approach which discloses no "patent defect" that the Panel unlawfully failed to recognise. On the contrary, the Addendum articulated an approach to the issue of the non-CO_2 effects of aviation which commended itself to the Panel. For the reasons I have given earlier, the Panel's overall approach in that regard has not been shown to be legally flawed.

217   Importantly, at DL207, the Panel noted that BAL's draft CCCAP provides that non-CO_2 emissions should not be ignored in future selection of GHG reduction measures. In the light of that, together with the extent of scientific uncertainty, the Panel concluded that "it would be unreasonable to weigh this matter in the balance against the proposal".

218   The claimant submits that the Panel's reliance on the CCCAP is unlawful, for the same reason that the Court of Appeal (per Lindblom LJ) found reliance on a future manure management plan to be unlawful in Squire.

219   I find that *Squire* does not assist the claimant. The effects of the development as a result of odour and dust from the storage and spreading of manure were not subject to any scientific uncertainty. This contrasts with the position regarding non-CO_2 emissions where, as I have explained, there currently exist uncertainties in assessing effects, such that they do not at present feature in the CCC's assessment of what should be included within the net-zero target for the CCA. Accordingly, in Squire, requiring the issue to be dealt with by a future manure management plan was simply not open to the environmental statement. The management plan was, furthermore, only going to be of partial assistance, even when it emerged. In short, leaving matters to the future was, in Squire, not an option.

220   By contrast, leaving non-CO_2 aircraft emissions to be dealt with when the science enables them to be brought into account for the purposes of the CCA was a decision that was entirely open to those preparing the environmental statement. It was a decision that both NSC (which did not object to the environmental statement on this ground) and the Panel were entitled to accept.

221   That is not, however, the end of the claimant's challenge to the Panel's reliance on the CCCAP. The claimant argues that such reliance was, in effect, irrational, given that, in DL207, the Panel placed weight on the "intention of the CCCAP to consider the effects [of non-CO_2 emissions] further"; whereas at DL210, the Panel concluded that the CCCAP fell to be given "only very limited weight."

222   The claimant's argument is superficially attractive but dissolves upon analysis. The CCCAP fell to be given very limited weight in relation to its overarching aim of making BAL's own operations and activities net-zero by 2030 and by 2050, including aviation. In this regard, the CCCAP's draft status was significant. It had not yet been incorporated into a planning condition. In other words, at the relevant time, its overarching aims did not carry significant weight in favour of the grant of planning permission for the proposals.

223   On the separate issue of non-CO_2 emissions, given the current scientific position, the Panel was, by contrast, entitled to place weight on the fact that the CCCAP would, in effect, track and react to the way in which such emissions may (or, more likely, will) in the future be regarded by the CCC and thus, by the Secretary of State in setting targets under the CCA, and otherwise.

224   The penultimate aspect of the claimant's challenge under Ground 5 concerns the Panel's alleged failure to have regard to the precautionary principle. It is the

case that there is no reference to the precautionary principle in the DL. The claimant's position is that, even if the Panel may have been justified in not having direct regard to non-CO_2 emissions for the reasons it gave, the existence of the multiplier, and what was said about it by BEIS and the claimant's expert witness, were such as to require the Panel to deploy it in pursuance of the precautionary principle.

225   The answer to this aspect of Ground 5 is to be found in the Supreme Court judgment in *Friends of the Earth*.

226   One of the issues addressed by the Supreme Court in *Friends of the Earth* was that of non-CO_2 emissions. The Court agreed with the Divisional Court it was not reasonably arguable that the Secretary of State acted irrationally in not addressing the effect of the non-CO_2 emissions in the Airports NPS.

227   The Supreme Court said:-

> "164. The Court of Appeal (para 258) upheld FoE's challenge stating the precautionary principle and common sense suggested that scientific uncertainty was not a reason for not taking something into account at all, even if it could not be precisely quantified at this stage. The Court did not hold in terms that the Secretary of State had acted irrationally in this regard but said (para 261) that, since it was remitting the ANPS to the Secretary of State for reconsideration, the question of non-CO_2 emissions and the effect of post-2050 emissions would need to be taken into account as part of that exercise.
>
> 165. We respectfully disagree with that approach. The precautionary principle adds nothing to the argument in this context and we construe the judgment as equating the principle with common sense. But a court's view of common sense is not the same as a finding of irrationality, which is the only relevant basis on which FoE seeks to impugn the designation in its section 10 challenges. In any event we are satisfied that the Secretary of State's decision to address only CO_2 emissions in the ANPS was not irrational.
>
> 166. In summary, we agree with the Divisional Court that it is not reasonably arguable that the Secretary of State acted irrationally in not addressing the effect of the non-CO_2 emissions in the ANPS for six reasons. First, his decision reflected the uncertainty over the climate change effects of non-CO_2 emissions and the absence of an agreed metric which could inform policy. Secondly, it was consistent with the advice which he had received from the CCC. Thirdly, it was taken in the context of the Government's inchoate response to the Paris Agreement. Fourthly, the decision was taken in the context in which his department was developing as part of that response its Aviation Strategy, which would seek to address non-CO_2 emissions. Fifthly, the designation of the ANPS was only the first stage in a process by which permission could be given for the NWR Scheme to proceed and the Secretary of State had powers at the DCO stage to address those emissions. Sixthly, it is clear from both the AoS and the ANPS itself that the applicant for a DCO would have to address the environmental rules and policies which were current when its application would be determined."

228   The precautionary principle is capable of being invoked where the nature of the decision-making leaves space for it. In the present case, as in *Friends of the Earth*, the decision-making process was about how to address at the present time an issue

(non-CO_2 emissions), about which there is currently scientific uncertainty. In both cases, the decision was to leave that matter for further consideration, within the overall development consent process.

229   It was in this context that the Supreme Court held that the "precautionary principle adds nothing to the argument". In fact, to have recourse to the precautionary principle in such a situation would subvert the decision-making process, by requiring consideration here and now of the very issue which the decision-making process has rationally concluded should be dealt with later.

230   Ms Dehon submitted that, unlike *Friends of the Earth* - where the Secretary of State had powers under the Development Consent Order (DCO), whereby he could later address non-CO_2 emissions, according to whatever environmental rules and policies would be in force when the DCO application was determined - there is no comparable future consenting process in the present case. The Panel has granted outline planning permission for the Airport's expansion.

231   There are, of course, differences between the decision-making regimes addressed by the Supreme Court in *Friends of the Earth* and the present case. Nevertheless, the fact of the matter is that, of the six reasons given by the Supreme Court in paragraph 166 for agreeing with the Divisional Court that the Secretary of State did not act irrationally in not addressing the effect of non-CO_2 emissions in the ANPS, only two involve the fact that the Secretary of State has powers to address those emissions at the DCO stage. In the present case, for the Panel to have attempted directly to address the non-CO_2 effects of aircraft emissions, in considering the appropriateness of the expansion of a regional airport, would have been highly anomalous. Therefore, even if the Panel <u>might</u> have acted lawfully if it had embarked on such an exercise, it was clearly not irrational for the Panel to conclude that it would not do so.

232   It is important to recognise that the CCCAP will be secured by way of a planning condition, requiring BAL to "reflect any changes arising from any updated emissions targets and national policy changes" (DL209). Thus, the issue of non-CO_2 emissions will not be left hanging.

233   Accordingly, as in *Friends of the Earth*, properly understood, there was no "space" in the present case for the operation of the precautionary principle.

234   The final aspect of Ground 5 is the contention that the Panel failed to give legally adequate reasons for its conclusions on non-CO_2 emissions. It will, however, be apparent from the foregoing analysis that it has been perfectly possible to discern the Panel's reasoning in this regard.

235   Ground 5 accordingly fails.

Ground 6

236   As I have already mentioned, Ground 6 is about horseshoe bats. The proposal would result in the loss of 3.7ha of agricultural land in order to allow for the expansion of a car park, together with 0.16ha of woodland, in order for the A38 road improvement works to be delivered. These two areas lie outside, but relatively close to, the North Somerset and Mendip Bats Special Area of Conservation ("the SAC"). The SAC was designated because of the presence there of lesser and greater horseshoe bats.

237   The two areas which would be lost to the development provide foraging land for the horseshoe bats. The areas are, therefore, functionally linked to the SAC.

238   The conservation area objectives for the SAC include the need for the integrity of that site to be maintained or restored as appropriate, in relation to the habitats of qualifying species (in this case, the horseshoe bats). The conservation objectives accordingly seek to ensure that habitats for the bats are maintained. This applies to habitat used by the bats, when foraging outside the SAC. The agricultural land to be taken is, in particular, considered to provide foraging habitat needed to maintain the favourable conservation status of the SAC.

239   The above description comes from DL481-484. Beginning at paragraph 485, the Panel described the adoption by NSC in 2018 of the North Somerset and Mendip Bats Special Area of Conversation Guidance on Development: SPD (Supplementary Planning Documents). Amongst other things, the SPD set up a Bat Consultation Zone. Where existing habitats or features of value to bats cannot be retained as part of the development proposals, the SPD requires the provision of replacement habitat.

240   In connection with the proposal, NSC officers carried out an appropriate assessment, informed by the information provided by BAL. The Panel noted at DL487 that this matter "did not form a reason for refusal" and that "No party opposed to the overall proposal has presented contrary evidence". The only evidence of relevance was "the undisputed Technical Note presented by BAL."

241   The DL continues as follows:-

> "488. The proposal is to provide land as replacement habitat in exchange for the functionally linked land in bands B and C, thereby avoiding any impact on the SAC itself. This would be a protective mitigation measure which is part of the proposal, intended to avoid or reduce any adverse effects so as to ensure that the project does not adversely affect the integrity of the SAC. This replacement land, which would be controlled by conditions, would be provided in advance of any works being carried out that would affect existing foraging land."

242   At DL489, the Panel concluded that it was sufficiently certain that "the replacement land would make an effective contribution to avoiding harm, guaranteeing beyond reasonable doubt that the project would not adversely affect the integrity of the SAC". The Panel then continued as follows:-

> "490. Before concluding on this matter, the legal status of the proposed replacement land was raised, most particularly by [the Parish Council Airport Association] (notwithstanding the fact that they did not put forward any evidence on biodiversity). The issue is whether the proposed replacement foraging habitat is "mitigation" or "compensation". The only expert ecological evidence, that presented by BAL, is that the proposed replacement foraging land meets the test for "mitigation". This was also the position agreed by NSC officers and Natural England. There is no contrary expert evidence.
>
> 491. The argument put by PCAA is that the replacement foraging land is not "mitigation" but "compensation". This is on the basis that it is not intended to avoid or limit harm to an acceptable level, but is intended to replace "significant" bat habitat, which would be destroyed by the proposal. If that were the case it was argued that planning permission could not be granted. However, the case law cited by PCAA related to proposals within European sites - which were therefore directly affected by development. The measures

proposed in those sites would replace directly lost habitat and were "compensation". This is in contrast with the measures currently proposed which are "mitigation" aimed at reducing or eliminating the effect of the proposal.

492. Overall, the impact on the functionally linked habitat is small in comparison to the overall availability of the functional habitat (as shown in the [Supplementary Planning Documents]) and the proposed mitigation would at least counter the impact. The Panel has considered the potential for likely significant effects on the qualifying features of the SAC. Taking account of the potential for adverse effects on integrity and mitigation proposed, it can be concluded that there would be no adverse effect on the integrity of the SAC."

243   SACs are the product of Directive 92/43/EEC (21 May 1992). Article 6(3) of the Directive requires any plan or project "not directly connected with or necessary to the management of the site but likely to have a significant effect thereon…[to] be subject to appropriate assessment of its implications for the site in view of the site's conservation objectives". The Directive is given domestic effect by the Conservation of Habitats and Species Regulations 2017.

244   Regulation 63 provides, so far as relevant:-

> "(1) A competent authority before deciding to undertake, or give any consent, permission or other authorization for, a plan or project which—
>
> > (a) is likely to have a significant effect on a European or a European offshore marine site (either alone or in combination with other plans or projects), and
> >
> > (b) is not directly connected with or necessary to the management of that site,
> > must make an appropriate assessment of the implications of the plan or project for that site in view of that site's conservation objectives.
>
> (2) A person applying for any such consent, permission or other authorisation must provide such information as the competent authority may reasonably require for the purposes of the assessment or to enable it to determine whether an appropriate assessment is required.
> …
> (5) In the light of the conclusions of the assessment, and subject to regulation 64, the competent authority may agree to the plan or project only after having ascertained that it will not adversely affect the integrity of the European site or the European offshore marine site (as the case may be)."

245   Regulation 64 deals with considerations of overriding public interest:—

> "(1) if the competent authority is satisfied that, there being no alternative solutions, the plan or project must be carried out for imperative reasons of overriding public interest (which, subject to paragraph (2), may be of a social or economic nature), it may agree to the plan or project notwithstanding a negative assessment of the implications for the European site or the European offshore marine site (as the case may be).

> (2) Where the site concerned hosts a priority natural habitat type or a priority species, the reasons referred to in paragraph (1) must be either—
>> (a) reasons relating to human health, public safety or beneficial consequences of primary importance to the environment; or
>> (b) any other reasons which the competent authority, having due regard to the opinion of the appropriate authority, considers to be imperative reasons of overriding public interest."

246   The claimant submits that the Panel erred in finding that BAL's provision of replacement land for the bats was "mitigation", which accordingly complied with Article 6(3) and regulation 63. Instead, the claimant says that the Panel should have treated the replacement land as "compensation". This meant there should have been a negative assessment and thus consideration would have focused on whether there was an absence of alternative solutions; in the absence of which the project could be agreed only "for imperative reasons of overriding public interest".

247   There is, the claimant says, a distinction between "mitigation measures", which fall within Article 6(3) and regulation 63, and "compensation measures" which fall within Article 6(4) and regulation 64.

248   This distinction was addressed by the Court of Appeal in *Smyth v SSCLG* [2015] P.T.S.R.1417. *Smyth* concerned a housing development outside an SPA and an SAC. The development included a grassland area of public open space in order to absorb recreational use by residents of the development and so alleviate adverse impacts on the SPA and the SAC.

249   The Court of Appeal held that if a preventative safeguarding measure "eliminates or reduces the harmful effects", so that "those harmful effects either never arise or never arise to a significant degree", then that is directly relevant to the question which arises at the Article 6(3)/regulation 63 stage and may be properly taken into account at that stage (Sales LJ at paragraph 66). On the other hand, where measures are proposed which would not prevent the harm from occurring but which would (once harm had occurred) provide some form of offsetting compensation, then:-

> "it cannot be said that those offsetting measures prevent harm from occurring so as to meet the preventative and precautionary objectives of Article 6(3). In such a situation the competent authority is asked to allow harm to a protected site to occur, on the basis that this harm will be counterbalanced and offset by other measures to enhance the environment elsewhere. However, in such a case, the competent authority "will have to be satisfied that such harm can be justified under Article 6(4), taking account of the offsetting compensation measures at the stage of analysis under Article 6 (4) … Such measures would not be capable of bearing on the application of the tests under article 6(3) and so could not be relevant at the Article 6(3) stage"" (paragraph 68).

250   In *RSPB v SSCLG* [2014] Env. L.R. 30, Ouseley J held, at paragraph 27, that the fact that functionally linked land was not within a protected site did not mean the effect which a deterioration could have on the protected site is to be ignored. The indirect effect was still protected. The fact that the functionally linked land, although not carrying a particular legal status, is linked to the protected site meant that "the indirectly adverse effects on a protected site, produced by effects on

[functionally linked land] are scrutinised in the same legal framework just as the direct effect of acts carried out on the protected site itself" (paragraph 27).

251   The claimant argues that the *RSPB* case, which was not before the Panel, effectively determines the disagreement in favour of the PCAA. It is, the claimant says, absolutely clear that "the same legal framework" is used to scrutinise functionally linked land outside the boundary of the SAC, as is used to scrutinise acts carried out on the protected site itself. This meant the Panel erred in law in deciding that the replacement land was mitigation for the reason that it was outside the SAC. This issue cannot be resolved in favour of the defendant by categorising the issue as one of the *application* of the relevant law. Rather, the issue is about the applicable legal principles.

Ground 6: discussion

252   Mr Humphries points out that *Smyth* was before the Panel and that BAL quoted directly from it as authority for the legal definition of mitigation and compensation measures. It was, in fact, this legal definition that was applied by BAL's ecologist in carrying out the ecological assessment presented in the environmental statement (Appendix B, Ecology Technical Note). At paragraph 1.1.21 of this note, it was stated that the replacement habitat land was to replace land outside the SAC (albeit functionally linked land) "thereby avoiding any impact on the SAC itself". Accordingly, since there would be no impact, "the project does not adversely affect the integrity of the SAC". Paragraph 1.1.22 emphasised that the replacement land would make an effective contribution to avoiding harm "guaranteeing beyond all reasonable doubt that the project would not adversely affect the integrity of the SAC". The "success of the measure will be established prior to the taking of any action that has the potential to give rise to an adverse impact". There would, therefore, be "no adverse impact" in respect of "the SAC or the bats for which it is designated, and there is no impact on the integrity of the site".

253   The claimant says that at DL491, the Panel misunderstood the relevant law when it said that "the case law cited by PCAA related to proposals within European sites - which were therefore directly affected by development. The measures proposed in those cases would replace directly lost habitat and were compensation". I agree with the defendant and BAL that, reading the relevant paragraphs as a whole, neither this statement in DL491 or anything else in the DL discloses that the Panel misunderstood the relevant law or misapplied it. The Panel's emphasis upon the uncontested ecological evidence from BAL, which I have just mentioned, puts it beyond doubt that the Panel did not reach its decision on the basis that the land to be lost as a result of the proposals was outside the SAC, with a result that any ameliorative measure to be taken by BAL would necessarily be "mitigation" as opposed to "compensation". Rather, the Panel reached its decision by reference to the uncontested evidence, which was that the replacement land would be provided in advance, so as to avoid any impact on the SAC. Since there would be no "deterioration", the *RSPB* case is therefore of no assistance to the claimant.

254   Once again, the claimant argues in the alternative that the Panel gave legally insufficient reasons. As can be seen, the Panel's reasons, are however, present, on any fair reading of the DL.

255   Ground 6 accordingly fails.

F. Section 31(2A) of the Senior Courts Act 1981

256   Since I have found that all grounds fail to disclose any material error of law on the part of the Panel, it is unnecessary to address section 31(2A) of the Senior Courts Act 1981.

G. Conclusion

257   This judicial review is dismissed.

258   By way of postscript, I should make clear that nothing in this judgment is to be taken as contradicting what is said in its opening paragraph, regarding the significance of climate change and GHGs. As will by now be apparent, the main issue in this case is not whether emissions from any additional aircraft using Bristol Airport should be ignored. Plainly, they should not. Rather, it is about how and by whom those emissions should be addressed.

R. (ON THE APPLICATION OF TOGETHER AGAINST SIZEWELL C LTD) v SECRETARY OF STATE FOR ENERGY SECURITY AND NET ZERO

KING'S BENCH DIVISION (ADMINISTRATIVE COURT)

Holgate J: 22 June 2023

[2023] EWHC 1526 (Admin); [2023] Env. L.R. 29

Construction projects; Development consent; Environmental impact; Nuclear power; Water supply

H1 *Nuclear power—development consent—environmental impact assessment—water supply—whether water supply part of "project" for purposes of Environmental Assessment—Habitats Regulations assessment—whether failure to assess water supply impacts before granting consent was unlawful—whether water supply separate "project" for purposes of Environmental Assessment—whether obligation to assess theoretical supply options*

H2 The claimant (TASC) was set up by a local community group as a special purpose vehicle to oppose the development of the Sizewell C nuclear power station (the development). TASC sought to challenge the Defendant's (SSENZ) decision to grant development consent for the Sizewell C nuclear power station to the Interested Party (SZC). At the relevant examination stage, no permanent potable water supply solution for the development had been identified, as this depended on a separate statutory process undertaken by the local water company (NWL) as part of the preparation and publication of the relevant Water Resources Management Plan (WRMP).

H3 The Panel at the examination stage reported that because there was no assured supply of potable water identified, the cumulative effects of the development could not be assessed for the purposes of both the environmental impact assessment and the 'appropriate assessment' required under the Conservation of Habitats and Species Regulations 2017 (reg.63(1)) (the Habitats Regulations). Consequently, the Panel could not recommend approval without additional information on the provision of a permanent water supply. Subject to this issue, the Panel considered that the benefits of the proposal strongly outweighed the adverse impacts. The panel also advised that an assessment of the cumulative impacts of the water supply should be undertaken before granting consent. In considering the Panel's report and recommendations, SSENZ requested further information from (amongst others) SZC, the Environment Agency (EA) and Natural England (NE). The Secretary of State disagreed with the Panel's recommendations and granted consent on the basis the impacts would be properly assessed under the WRMP process.

H4 TASC sought to challenge SSENZ's decision, arguing that SSENZ had:

(1) failed to assess the environmental impacts of the permanent water supply as part of the "project" contrary to reg.63(1) of the Habitats Regulations. Alternatively, SSENZ had failed to assess the cumulative environmental impacts of the development along with the solution for the potable water supply.

(2) failed to supply adequate reasons for disagreeing with NE's advice that the permanent water supply should be considered to be a fundamental component of the 'operation of the project' and its effects.

(3) failed to consider 'alternative solutions' to the development before concluding that there were imperative reasons of overriding public interest justifying the environmental harm it would cause, as required by reg.64(1) of the Habitats Regulations.

(4) unlawfully taken into account an irrelevant consideration—in that it was supported by no evidence—namely the contribution the development might make to reducing greenhouse gas emissions by 78% from 1990 levels by 2035.

(5) acted irrationally in concluding that the development site would be clear of nuclear material by 2140 and/or failed to supply adequate reasons for rejecting TASC's arguments on this issue.

(6) erred in law in concluding that the development's greenhouse gas emissions would not have a significant effect on the UK's ability to meet its climate change obligations.

H5   **Held,** in dismissing the claim:

H6   (1) The question of what a 'project' was in any particular case, was a matter of judgment for the decision maker. That decision could only be challenged on *Wednesbury* principles. SSENZ was entitled to conclude that the permanent potable water supply for the development was a separate "project" from the power station itself. This was based on various factors including; the water supply and power station were not on adjacent land, but separated by over 1km; the two 'projects' had separate promoters; there was no functional interdependence—the water company responsible for the water supply had a duty to plan water supply for the whole region, not just the development; and the water supply would be subject to a separate statutory process to approve the water company's WRMP.

H7   (2) Although development consent had been granted in the knowledge that the development was dependent on the future provision of a water supply, (a) it was not dependent on the provision of any particular form of supply and that was currently unknown; and (b) the cumulative environmental impact would have to be assessed properly in an integrated environmental assessment following the WRMP process.

H8   (3) When considering the context of the whole decision letter, SSENZ had adequately explained why he disagreed with NE's views were the water supply was an integral part of the project. NE's views were not so much advice as assertions without detailed reasoning or supporting evidence.

H9   (4) In considering the application of reg.64(1) of the Habitats Regulations, SSENZ had considered the Panel's assessment and the need for nuclear power was seen as an integral part of the strategy for tackling climate change by achieving the net zero target. In the same vein, SSENZ had accepted the Panel's rejection of TASC's arguments that alternative solutions should be considered and that the approach taken by SZC was too narrow. TASC's arguments depended upon an illegitimate attempt to rewrite policy aims by pretending that a central policy objective was at a higher level of abstraction, without any regard to diversity of energy sources and security of supply.

H10   (5) SSENZ had sufficient material before him to entitle him to reach the conclusion on the contribution the development might make to reducing greenhouse gas emissions by 2035. It was impossible to say that his judgment on such an evaluative subject was irrational. On that basis, there was no legal reason why SSENZ could not take into account the contribution which the development was expected to make to reducing the shortfall in electricity generation or to the target for reducing GHGs.

H11   (6) SSENZ's reasoning on the issue of whether the site would be clear of nuclear material by 2140 could not be treated as irrational or legally inadequate. When reading the decision letter as a whole, it was plain that SSENZ relied, as he was entitled to do, upon the normal assumption that relevant regulatory regimes would be operated properly.

H12   (7) In determining whether emission of GHGs from the development would not have a significant impact upon the UK's ability to meet climate change obligations, the SSENZ had relied upon the Panel's conclusions. There was ample material to support the Panel's conclusions and accordingly SSENZ's decision letter was not unreasonable following *Wednesbury* principles. SSENZ was not required to undertake a personal quantitiatve assessment by delving into the Environmental Statement or the Life Cycle Assessment for the development. The summary provided in the Panel's Report and in the draft decision letter, both of which were provided to the SSENZ, were as, a matter of law, perfectly adequate.

H13 **Cases referred to:**

Bowen-West v Secretary of State for Communities and Local Government [2012] EWCA Civ 321; [2012] Env. L.R. 22; [2012] J.P.L. 1128

East Quayside 12 LLP v Newcastle upon Tyne City Council [2023] EWCA Civ 359

Jones v Mordue [2015] EWCA Civ 1243; [2016] 1 W.L.R. 2682; [2016] 1 P. & C.R. 12

Pearce v Secretary of State Business, Energy and Industrial Strategy [2021] EWHC 326 (Admin); [2022] Env. L.R. 4; [2021] J.P.L. 1229

Preston New Road Action Group v Secretary of State for Communities and Local Government [2018] EWCA Civ 9; [2018] Env. L.R. 18; [2018] J.P.L. 807

R. (on the application of Akester) v Department for the Environment, Food and Rural Affairs [2010] EWHC 232 (Admin); [2010] Env. L.R. 33; [2010] A.C.D. 44

R. (on the application of Ashchurch Rural Parish Council) v Tewkesbury BC [2023] EWCA Civ 101; [2023] Env. L.R. 25; [2023] J.P.L. 1099

R. (on the application of Champion) v North Norfolk DC [2015] UKSC 52; [2015] 1 W.L.R. 3710; [2016] Env. L.R. 5

R (on the application of ClientEarth) v Secretary of State for Business, Energy and Industrial Strategy [2021] EWCA Civ 43; [2021] P.T.S.R. 1400; [2021] J.P.L. 1107

R. (on the application of Friends of the Earth Ltd) v Heathrow Airport Ltd [2020] UKSC 52; [2021] P.T.S.R. 190; [2021] J.P.L. 905

R. (on the application of Goesa Ltd) v Eastleigh BC [2022] EWHC 1221 (Admin); [2022] P.T.S.R. 1473; [2022] J.P.L. 1309

R. (on the application of Khan) v Sutton LBC [2014] EWHC 3663 (Admin)

R. (on the application of Larkfleet Ltd) v South Kesteven DC [2015] EWCA Civ 887; [2016] Env. L.R. 4; [2015] P.T.S.R. D50

R. (on the application of Littlewood) v Bassetlaw DC [2008] EWHC 1812 (Admin); [2009] Env. L.R. 21; [2009] J.P.L. 478

R. (on the application of Mott) v Environment Agency [2016] EWCA Civ 564; [2016] 1 W.L.R. 4338; [2017] Env. L.R. 1

R. (on the application of National Association of Health Stores) v Secretary of State for Health [2005] EWCA Civ 154

R. (on the application of Newsmith Stainless Ltd) v Secretary of State for Environment, Transport and the Regions [2001] EWHC Admin 74; [2017] P.T.S.R. 1126

R. (on the application of Plan B Earth) v Secretary of State Transport [2020] EWCA Civ 214; [2020] P.T.S.R. 1446; [2020] J.P.L. 1005

R. (on the application of Spurrier) v Secretary of State Transport [2019] EWHC 1070 (Admin); [2020] P.T.S.R. 240; [2019] J.P.L. 1163

R (on the application of Swire) v Canterbury City Council [2022] EWHC 390 (Admin); [2022] J.P.L. 1026

R. (on the application of Wingfield) v Canterbury City Council [2019] EWHC 1975 (Admin); [2020] J.P.L. 154

R. (on the application of Wyatt) v Fareham BC [2022] EWCA Civ 983; [2023] Env. L.R. 14; [2022] J.P.L. 1509

R. (on the application of Rights: Community: Action) v Secretary of State for Housing, Communities and Local Government [2020] EWHC 3073 (Admin); [2021] P.T.S.R. 553; [2021] Env. L.R. 21

R. (on the application of Transport Action Network Ltd) v Secretary of State Transport [2021] EWHC 2095 (Admin); [2022] P.T.S.R. 31; [2021] A.C.D. 105

R. v Rochdale MBC Ex p. Milne (No.2) [2001] Env. L.R. 22; (2001) 81 P. & C.R. 27; [2001] J.P.L. 229 (Note) QBD

R. (on the application of Association of Independent Meat Suppliers) v Food Standards Agency [2019] UKSC 36; [2019] P.T.S.R. 1443

R. (on the application of Burridge) v Breckland DC [2013] EWCA Civ 228; [2013] J.P.L. 1308; [2013] 18 E.G. 102 (C.S.)

R. (on the application of Finch) v Surrey CC [2022] EWCA Civ 187; [2022] P.T.S.R. 958; [2022] Env. L.R. 27

R. (on the application of Forest of Dean (Friends of the Earth)) v Forest of Dean DC [2015] EWCA Civ 683; [2015] P.T.S.R. 1460; [2016] Env. L.R. 3

R. (on the application of Friends of the Earth Ltd) v Secretary of State for Business, Energy and Industrial Strategy [2022] EWHC 1841 (Admin); [2023] 1 W.L.R. 225; [2022] H.R.L.R. 18

R. (on the application of Law Society) v Lord Chancellor [2018] EWHC 2094 (Admin); [2019] 1 W.L.R. 1649; [2018] 5 Costs L.R. 937

R. v Swale BC Ex p. Royal Society for the Protection of Birds (1990) 2 Admin. L.R. 790; [1991] 1 P.L.R. 6; [1991] J.P.L 39 QBD

Save Britain's Heritage v Number 1 Poultry Ltd [1991] W.L.R. 153; (1991) 3 Admin. L.R. 437; (1991) 62 P. & C.R. 105 HL

Smyth v Secretary of State for Communities and Local Government [2015] EWCA Civ 174; [2015] P.T.S.R. 1417; [2016] Env. L.R. 7

H14 **Legislation referred to:**
Nuclear Installations Act 1965 ss.1 and 3
Directive 92/43 (Habitats)
Senior Courts Act 1981 s.31
Water Industry Act 1991 ss.18, 37A, 55 and 56
Environmental Assessment of Plans and Programmes Regulations 2004 (SI 2004/1633)
Directive 2009/147 (Wild Birds)
Water Resources Management Plan Regulations 2007 (SI 2007/727)
Climate Change Act 2008 s.11
Planning Act 2008 ss.5, 6, 104, 105, 106, 114, 118 and 120
Infrastructure Planning (Environmental Impact Assessment) Regulations 2017 (SI 2017/572) regs 4, 5, 14, 20 and 21
Conservation of Habitats and Species Regulations 2017 (SI 2017/1012) regs 62, 63, 64 and 84
Carbon Budget Order 2021 (SI 2021/750)
Sizewell C (Nuclear Generating Station) Order 2022 (SI 2022/853) Sch.19 Pt 6
CPR r.23.12

H15 *D. Wolfe KC, A. Bowes* and *R. Parekh*, instructed by Leigh Day Solicitors, appeared on behalf of the claimant.
J. Strachan KC and *R. Grogan*, instructed by Government Legal Department, appeared on behalf of the defendant.
H. Phillpot KC and *H. Flanagan*, instructed by Herbert Smith Freehills, appeared on behalf of the interested party.

JUDGMENT

MR JUSTICE HOLGATE:

Introduction

1   The claimant seeks to challenge by judicial review under s.118(1) of the Planning Act 2008 ("the 2008 Act") the decision dated 20 July 2022 made under s.114 of that Act to make the Sizewell C (Nuclear Generating Station) Order 2022 (SI 2022 No. 853) ("the Order") under s.114 of that Act. That decision was made by, and the proceedings were brought against, the Secretary of State for Business, Energy and Industrial Strategy. However, with effect from 3 May 2023 the relevant functions have been transferred to the Secretary of State for Energy Security and Net Zero and he has therefore been substituted as the defendant.

2   The Order grants development consent for the construction, operation, maintenance and decommissioning of a nuclear power station comprising two UK European Pressurised Reactors, each with a net electrical output of 1,670 MW, and a total capacity of 3,340 MW.

3   The claimant, Together Against Sizewell C Limited ("TASC"), is a private company. It was set up on 8 July 2022 by members of a local community group as a special purpose vehicle for the bringing of this claim and to receive public donations to that end. TASC was established in 2013 to oppose the project. It has had about 280 supporters. The group responded to pre-application consultations and participated in the statutory Examination of the draft order. It made written representations on a range of subjects and oral representations at "issue-specific hearings" ("ISHs") held during the Examination.

4   The Order granted development consent to the interested party, NNB Generation Company (SZC) Limited ("SZC").

5   The application for consent was made on 27 May 2020. The defendant appointed a panel of five inspectors ("the Panel") to conduct the Examination of the application under Chapter 4 of Part 6 of the 2008 Act. The Examination took place between April and October 2021.

6   At the time of the Examination, SZC was unable to identify a permanent supply of potable water for the project, because this was to be decided as part of the preparation and publication by Northumbrian Water Limited ("NWL") of a Water Resources Management Plan pursuant to s.37A of the Water Industry Act 1991 ("the 1991 Act") for Essex and Suffolk over the period 2025 to 2050 (referred to as WRMP24).

7   SZC produced a Water Supply Strategy Report in September 2021 which identified the amounts of potable water required during the construction, commissioning and operational phases of Sizewell C. When the station is operating the peak demand will be up to 2,800 m^3/day. This is an entirely separate issue from the cooling water needed in connection with electricity generation, which is obtained directly from the sea.

8   The Panel's Report ("PR") was submitted to the defendant on 25 February 2022. In its assessment of the benefits of the project as part of the overall planning balance the Panel relied upon the contribution of the power station to low-carbon energy production. It would meet the aim of Government policy to achieve delivery of major energy infrastructure including new nuclear electricity generation. They considered that "there is clearly an urgent need for development of the type proposed" and gave "very substantial weight" to the contribution that the scheme would make to meeting that need (PR 7.5.4).

9   Because the project is likely to have a significant effect on "European sites", an "appropriate assessment" was required to be carried out under reg.63(1) of the Conservation of Habitats and Species Regulations 2017 (SI 2017 No. 101 2) ("the Habitats Regulations"). The Panel concluded that an adverse effect on the integrity of the marsh harrier feature of the Minsmere-Walberswick SPA resulting from noise and visual disturbance during the construction phase could not be excluded (PR 6.4.598). Under reg.64 the Panel advised that there were no "alternative solutions" to the proposed development (PR 6.6.12) and the defendant could conclude that the project must be carried out for "imperative reasons of overriding public interest" ("the IROPI test"). The public interest reasons included the continuing growth in the demand for electricity, the retirement of existing generation capacity, the shortfall in generation of 95GW by 2035, the scale of the need for nuclear new build, the UK's commitment to the net zero target for 2050, the continuity and reliability of supply delivered by nuclear energy as part of a diverse energy mix and the urgent need for new nuclear power stations (PR 6.7.4 and

6.7.9). The Panel also identified some additional areas where the information before them was insufficient for the purposes of the Habitats Regulations, but those matters do not give rise to any legal challenge.

10   However, there remained the outstanding issue about a permanent supply of potable water. The power station could not be licensed by the Office for Nuclear Regulation ("ONR") under the Nuclear Installation Act 1965 ("the 1965 Act") and could not be operated without such a supply. The Panel said that because an assured supply of potable water had not been identified, the cumulative environmental effects of the proposed development and that supply could not be assessed (PR 7.5.7) They stated that they could not recommend approval of the application without additional information and assurance on the provision of a permanent water supply. They regarded this "as an important matter of such magnitude that it should not be left unresolved to a future date" (PR 7.5.8). Subject to the permanent water supply issue, the Panel considered that the benefits of the proposal strongly outweighed the adverse impacts. But in view of that unresolved issue as at the close of the Examination, the Panel considered that the case for the grant of development consent had not yet been made out (PR 7.5.9 and 10.3.1)

11   On 18 March 2022 the defendant requested further information from SZC, the Environment Agency ("EA"), Natural England ("NE") and the ONR. The defendant referred to a letter from NWL's Solicitors of 23 February 2022 advising that the company was unable to meet the project's long-term demand for water supply from existing resources and that a number of demand management and supply side options were being appraised. The defendant asked SZC to explain the progress being made to secure a permanent solution so that he could reach a reasoned conclusion on the cumulative environmental effects of different permanent water supply solutions (see DL 4.29).

12   SZC responded to that request on 8 April 2022. In summary, they relied firstly upon the duty of NWL under the 1991 Act to identify through WRMP24 new water resources to meet the demand forecast for its region, including Sizewell C. NWL would carry out an integrated environmental assessment of the Plan, including strategic environmental assessment ("SEA") under The Environmental Assessment of Plans and Programmes Regulations 2004 (SI 2004 No.1633) and a Habitats Regulations Assessment ("HRA"). These assessments would be completed before Sizewell could receive the new supply (DL 4.32). SZC submitted that the long-term planning of water supply was subject to the separate requirements of the 1991 Act and could not yet be identified for the power station (and other developments). Indeed, it could change again during the lifetime of the power station as the water undertaker manages its resources in response to inter alia changing demand. In accordance with national policy, the decision under the 2008 Act should be taken on the assumption that other statutory regimes will be properly applied (DL 4.33). SZC submitted that there was insufficient information on the permanent solutions that might come forward for any meaningful assessment to be made at that stage.

13   Secondly, SZC said that in the unlikely event of NWL being unable to provide a permanent supply for the power station, SZC could develop a permanent desalination plant. SZC considered that such a plant would be unlikely to generate any new or materially different significant environmental effects (DL 4.30 and 4.66).

14   On 25 April 2022 the defendant invited comments from interested parties on the responses he had received. TASC replied on 23 May 2022. They raised

objections to a permanent desalination plant but offered no comments on the WRMP route. TASC maintained their position that the lack of a guaranteed water supply meant that not all significant environmental effects were being assessed at the development consent stage.

15   The defendant's decision letter was issued on 20 July 2022. The briefing to the Secretary of State for his consideration of SZC's application included the Panel's Report of some 1500 pages, the final HRA for Sizewell C and the draft decision letter, which itself ran to nearly 190 pages.

16   The defendant addressed the potable water supply issue at some length in DL 4.43 to 4.69 (reproduced in the Annex to this judgment). He was satisfied with the tankering arrangements and the temporary desalination plant proposed for the construction period and the assessment of their impacts (DL 4.43). Those conclusions are not challenged in these proceedings.

17   The defendant concluded that the proposed development and NWL's WRMP24 are separate "projects" (DL 4.49). On that basis there was no requirement for an assessment to be made of the permanent water supply solution as a part of the power station project. He then went on to consider the Panel's view that the cumulative impacts of that water supply should nonetheless be considered at the development consent stage for the power station. The defendant concluded firstly, that a long-term water supply for Sizewell C is viable. Secondly, any proposal for the supply of water by NWL will be properly assessed under the WRMP24 process and other relevant regulatory regimes. Thirdly, no further information was required on that subject for the application for development consent to be determined (DL 4.67). Disagreeing with the Panel, the defendant did not consider the present uncertainty over the permanent water supply strategy to be a barrier to granting development consent for the project (DL 4.68).

18   The remainder of this judgment is set out under the following headings:

Heading	Paragraph Number
Grounds of challenge	19-23
Statutory framework	24-49
The Planning Act 2008	24-34
Water Industry Act 1991	35-40
The Nuclear Installations Act 1956	41
The Conservation of Habitats and Species Regulations 2017	42-45
The Infrastructure Planning (Environmental Impact Assessment) Regulations 2017	46-49
Ground 1	50-93
A summary of the claimant's submissions	50-53
NWL's position on water supply	54-64
The decision letter	65-68
Discussion	69-93
Ground 2	94-105
Discussion	97-105

Heading	Paragraph Number
Ground 3	106–114
Ground 4	115–132
Discussion	120–132
Ground 5	133–152
Discussion	137–152
Ground 6	153–177
Discussion	157–177
Ground 7	178–187
Discussion	180–187
Conclusions	188–191
Annex – paragraphs 4.43 – 4.69 of the Secretary of State's decision letter	

The grounds of challenge

19   In summary the claimant seeks to advance the following grounds of challenge:

Ground 1: Contrary to reg.63(1) of the Habitats Regulations the defendant failed to assess the environmental impacts of the "project" (including the necessary permanent potable water supply solution).

Ground 2: In the alternative, contrary to reg.63(1), the defendant failed to assess cumulatively the environmental impacts of the power station together with those of the permanent potable water supply solution.

Ground 3: The defendant failed to supply lawfully adequate reasons for departing from the advice of NE that the permanent water supply should be considered to be a fundamental component of the "operation of the project" and its effects at this stage.

Ground 4: Contrary to reg.64(1) of the Habitats Regulations, the defendant also failed lawfully to consider "alternative solutions" to the power station before concluding that there were imperative reasons of overriding public interest justifying the environmental harm it would cause.

Ground 5: The defendant took into account a legally irrelevant consideration (because it was supported by no evidence), namely the contribution the power station might make to reducing greenhouse gas ("GHG") emissions by 78% from 1990 levels by 2035.

Ground 6: The defendant also acted irrationally in concluding that the power station site would be clear of nuclear material by 2140 and/or failed to supply adequate reasons for rejecting the claimant's case on that point.

Ground 7: The defendant also erred in law in concluding that the power station's operational GHG emissions would not have a significant effect on the UK's ability to meet its climate change obligations.

20   On 19 October 2022 Kerr J refused the claimant permission to apply for judicial review on the papers.

21   On the same day the claimant filed an application to amend its statement of facts and grounds to add a new ground 8. The claimant then renewed its application for permission on grounds 1 to 7.

22   On 14 December 2022 I refused permission for the claimant to add ground 8. Having regard to the parties' submissions, I also ordered that the renewed application for permission should be adjourned to a rolled-up hearing. On 10 January 2023 the claimant withdrew its renewed application for permission to argue ground 8.

23   Projects such as Sizewell C may attract both strong opposition and strong support. It is therefore necessary to reiterate what was said by the Divisional Court in *R. (Rights: Community: Action) v Secretary of State for Housing, Communities and Local Government* [2021] P.T.S.R. 553 at [6]:

> "6. It is important to emphasise at the outset what this case is and is not about. Judicial review is the means of ensuring that public bodies act within the limits of their legal powers and in accordance with the relevant procedures and legal principles governing the exercise of their decision-making functions. The role of the court in judicial review is concerned with resolving questions of law. The court is not responsible for making political, social, or economic choices. Those decisions, and those choices, are ones that Parliament has entrusted to ministers and other public bodies. The choices may be matters of legitimate public debate, but they are not matters for the court to determine. The court is only concerned with the legal issues raised by the claimant as to whether the defendant has acted unlawfully. The claimant contends that the changes made by the SIs are radical and have been the subject of controversy. But it is not the role of the court to assess the underlying merits of the proposals. Similarly, criticism has been made of the way in which, or the speed with which, these changes were made. Again, these are not matters for the court to determine save and in so far as they involve questions concerning whether or not the appropriate legal procedures for making the changes were followed."

Statutory framework

The Planning Act 2008

24   The 2008 Act provides a dedicated regime for applications to be made for the grant of development consent orders for "nationally significant infrastructure projects" ("NSIPs"). The framework of the Act has been set out in a number of authorities and need not be repeated in detail here. I refer in particular to the decision of the Supreme Court in *R. (Friends of the Earth Ltd) v Secretary of State for Transport* [2021] P.T.S.R. 190 at [19] to [37].

25   One of Parliament's aims was to make the application of development control to NSIPs more efficient and to reduce delays in decision-making. Issues such as the need for different types of infrastructure and the policy of the Government on such development was to be settled in advance by National Policy Statements ("NPSs"). A draft version of a NPS is subject to SEA, HRA, consultation, public involvement and Parliamentary scrutiny before being designated by the relevant Minister by statutory instrument under s.5 of the 2008 Act.

26   Under s.104(2), when determining an application for development consent, the
Secretary of State must have regard to any NPS which "has effect" in relation to
development of the description to which that application relates (a "relevant NPS").
Under s.104(3) he must determine the application in accordance with that relevant
NPS, save to the extent that one or more of the exceptions in s.104(4) to (8) applies.
Section 105 applies in relation to an application for an order granting development
consent if s.104 does not apply. Section 105(2) provides that in deciding the
application the Secretary of State must have regard to *inter alia* any matters which
he considers are both important and relevant to his decision. Section 106 enables
the Secretary of State to disregard any representation (including evidence) which
he considers *inter alia* relates to the merits of policy set out in a NPS. Section 106
applies whether an application is subject to s.104 or to s.105.

27   In the present case there were two relevant NPSs, the Overarching National
Policy Statement for Energy (EN-1) and the National Policy Statement for Nuclear
Power Generation (EN-6). Both documents were "designated" by the defendant
in July 2011.

28   Paragraphs 3.1.1 to 3.1.4 of EN-1 set out the approach for deciding applications
for development consent. The UK needs all the types of energy infrastructure
covered by the NPS, which include nuclear power, in order to achieve energy
security and reduce GHGs dramatically. Applications should be determined on the
basis that the need for these types of infrastructure has been demonstrated in the
NPS. There is an urgent need for new nuclear power generation which will play
an increasingly important role (para 3.5.1). It is Government policy that new nuclear
power should be able to contribute as much as possible to the UK's need for new
capacity (para. 3.5.2). New nuclear power stations will help to ensure a diverse
mix of technology and fuel sources, increasing the resilience of the UK's energy
system (para. 3.5.3). New nuclear power forms one of the three key elements of
the Government's strategy for moving towards a decarbonised, diverse electricity
sector by 2050 (para. 3.5.5). Given the urgent need for low carbon forms of
electricity, it is important that new nuclear power stations are constructed and
operational as soon as possible "and significantly earlier than 2025." Accordingly,
the sites identified in Part 4 of EN-6 were those considered to be capable of
deployment by the end of 2025 (paras 3.5.9 and 3.5.10).

29   EN-6 contains similar policy statements (paras. 2.2.1 and 2.2.2). In Part 4 of
EN-6 Sizewell was identified as a potentially suitable site for a new nuclear power
station along with Hinkley Point and six other sites.

30   On 7 December 2017 the Government issued a Written Ministerial Statement
announcing a consultation document on designating in a NPS potentially suitable
sites for nuclear power stations expected to be deployed after 2025 and before the
end of 2035. The Government stated that EN-6 only has effect for the purposes of
s.104 of the 2008 Act in relation to a project expected to be deployed before the
end of 2025, that is when a station first begins to feed electricity into the national
grid. The statement says that s.105 of the 2008 Act applies to EN-6 in so far as
s.104 does not. For projects due to be deployed beyond 2025 the Government
continues to give its strong in principle support to proposals for those sites listed
in EN-6. Both EN-1 and EN-6 contain information, assessments and statements
which continue to be important for projects being deployed after 2025.

31   The Panel considered that the application for Sizewell C should be assessed
under s.105 and that EN-1 and EN-6 were important considerations. There have

been no relevant changes in circumstances reducing the weight to be given to those policies. The acceptability of the proposal in terms of planning policy should be assessed primarily against the nuclear-specific policies in the NPSs. The defendant agreed with the Panel (DL 4.4 and 4.5).

32   The defendant also agreed with the Panel's assessment of the need for nuclear power projects, to which he attached substantial weight. Thus, there is an urgent need for new nuclear energy generating infrastructure of the kind proposed at Sizewell. The contribution that the development would make to the delivery of low carbon energy would assist in the decarbonisation of the UK economy in line with the UK's obligations under the Paris Agreement (DL 4.5 to DL 4.11).

33   The main consequence of s.105 of the 2008 Act applying to the determination of SZC's application was that the presumption in s.104(3) did not apply. Thus, the defendant did not have to decide the application in accordance with the NPS unless one or more of the exceptions in s.104(4) to (8) applied. Nevertheless, it is relevant to note that where s.104 is engaged, the balancing exercise described in s.104(7) may not be used to circumvent s.106(1)(b), which has the effect of preventing challenges to the merits of policy in a NPS in an Examination or before the Secretary of State. So, for example, changes of circumstance after the designation of a NPS are to be addressed instead through the process under s.6 for a formal review of a NPS (*R. (ClientEarth) v Secretary of State for Business, Energy and Industrial Strategy* [2021] P.T.S.R. 1400 at [105]; *R. (Spurrier) v Secretary of State for Transport* [2020] P.T.S.R. 240 at [106] to [110]).

34   There is no dispute that the NPSs were material considerations for the defendant to take into account under s.105 when determining SZC's application. Section 106 applies to a determination by the Secretary of State under s.105 just as it does to a decision under s.104. Accordingly, the provisions in the 2008 Act preventing challenges to the merits of policy in a NPS were applicable. Although a review of EN-6 under s.6 of the 2008 Act is being carried out, the defendant has decided not to exercise the power in s.11 to suspend either EN-1 or EN-6 pending the completion of that review.

Water Industry Act 1991

35   Section 37(1) lays down a general duty on every water undertaker in the following terms:

> "(1) It shall be the duty of every water undertaker to develop and maintain an efficient and economical system of water supply within its area and to ensure that all such arrangements have been made—
>
> > (a) for providing supplies of water to premises in that area and for making such supplies available to persons who demand them; and
> >
> > (b) for maintaining, improving and extending the water undertaker's water mains and other pipes,
>
> as are necessary for securing that the undertaker is and continues to be able to meet its obligations under this Part."

This primary duty is enforceable by the Secretary of State or OFWAT under s.18 of the 1991 Act.

36   Water undertakers are legally obliged to plan to meet demand within their area through a Water Resource Management Plan. Section 37A provides so far as material:

> "(1) It shall be the duty of each water undertaker to prepare, publish and maintain a water resources management plan.
>
> (2) A water resources management plan is a plan for how the water undertaker will manage and develop water resources so as to be able, and continue to be able, to meet its obligations under this Part.
>
> (3) A water resources management plan shall address in particular—
>
>   (a) the water undertaker's estimate of the quantities of water required to meet those obligations;
>
>   (b) the measures which the water undertaker intends to take or continue for the purpose set out in subsection (2) above (also taking into account for that purpose the introduction of water into the undertaker's supply system by or on behalf of water supply licensees);
>
>   (c) the likely sequence and timing for implementing those measures; and
>
>   (d) such other matters as the Secretary of State may specify in directions (and see also section 37AA).
>
> (4) The procedure for preparing and publishing a water resources management plan (including a revised plan) is set out in section 37B below.
>
> (5) Before each anniversary of the date when its plan (or revised plan) was last published, the water undertaker shall —
>
>   (a) review its plan; and
>
>   (b) send a statement of the conclusions of its review to the Secretary of State.
>
> (6) The water undertaker shall prepare and publish a revised plan in each of the following cases—
>
>   (a) following conclusion of its annual review, if the review indicated a material change of circumstances;
>
>   (b) if directed to do so by the Secretary of State;
>
>   (c) in any event, not later than the end of the period of five years beginning with the date when the plan (or revised plan) was last published,
>
>   and shall follow the procedure in section 37B below (whether or not the revised plan prepared by the undertaker includes any proposed alterations to the previous plan).
>
> (7) ...."

37   Under s.37AA(8) before preparing its WRMP the water undertaker must consult *inter alia* the EA, OFWAT and the Secretary of State.

38   Section 37B lays down the procedure for the preparation and publication of a WRMP. The undertaker is obliged to publish a draft of the plan so that representations may be made on its proposals to the Secretary of State (s.37B(3)). The WRMP must be sent to *inter alia* OFWAT, the EA, NE and Historic England so that they too may make representations (see reg.2 of The Water Resources Management Plan Regulations 2007 (SI 2007 No.727)). The undertaker may then

comment on those representations (s.37B(4)). The Secretary of State may cause a public inquiry or hearing to be held to consider any issues arising (s.37B(5) and reg.5 of the 2007 Regulations). The Secretary of State has the power to direct that the WRMP must differ from the draft sent to him and the undertaker must then comply with that direction (s.37B(7)). The undertaker must publish the final version of the plan (s.37B(9)).

39   The duties of a water undertaker under s.37A and s.37B are enforceable by the Secretary of State under s.18.

40   Where the owner or occupier of premises in the area of a water undertaker requests a supply of water for non-domestic purposes it is the undertaker's duty, in accordance with terms and conditions determined under s.56, to take steps to provide that supply. Those terms and conditions are to be determined by agreement between the parties or, in default, by OFWAT according to what appears to it to be reasonable. Section 55(3) qualifies the duty under s.55:

> "A water undertaker shall not be required by virtue of this section to provide a new supply to any premises, or to take any steps to enable it to provide such a supply, if the provision of that supply or the taking of those steps would—
>
> (a) require the undertaker, in order to meet all its existing obligations to supply water for domestic or other purposes, together with its probable future obligations to supply buildings and parts of buildings with water for domestic purposes, to incur unreasonable expenditure in carrying out works; or
>
> (b) otherwise put at risk the ability of the undertaker to meet any of the existing or probable future obligations mentioned in paragraph (a) above."

Any dispute arising under s.55(3) is determined by OFWAT (s.56(2))

The Nuclear Installations Act 1965

41   The use of a site for the installation and operation of a nuclear reactor is prohibited unless authorised by a nuclear site licence by the "appropriate national authority", the ONR (ss. 1 and 3). When granting a licence the ONR must attach such conditions as it considers necessary or desirable in the interests of safety and may also attach conditions to the licence at any time (s.4(1)). Conditions may be attached providing for *inter alia* the design, construction, operation, siting or modification of any plant or other installation on the site (s.4(3)(b)).

The Conservation of Habitats and Species Regulations 2017

42   The defendant is a "competent authority" for the purposes of the Habitats Regulations. Regulations 63 and 64 apply in relation to the making of an order granting development consent under the 2008 Act (regs. 62(1) and 84(1)).

43   In so far as is material, reg.63 provides:

> "(1) A competent authority, before deciding to undertake, or give any consent, permission or other authorisation for, a plan or project which—
>
> (a) is likely to have a significant effect on a European site or a European offshore marine site (either alone or in combination with other plans or projects), and

(b) is not directly connected with or necessary to the management of that site,

must make an appropriate assessment of the implications of the plan or project for that site in view of that site's conservation objectives.

(2) A person applying for any such consent, permission or other authorisation must provide such information as the competent authority may reasonably require for the purposes of the assessment or to enable it to determine whether an appropriate assessment is required.

(3) The competent authority must for the purposes of the assessment consult the appropriate nature conservation body and have regard to any representations made by that body within such reasonable time as the authority specifies.

(4) It must also, if it considers it appropriate, take the opinion of the general public, and if it does so, it must take such steps for that purpose as it considers appropriate.

(5) In the light of the conclusions of the assessment, and subject to regulation 64, the competent authority may agree to the plan or project only after having ascertained that it will not adversely affect the integrity of the European site or the European offshore marine site (as the case may be).

(6) In considering whether a plan or project will adversely affect the integrity of the site, the competent authority must have regard to the manner in which it is proposed to be carried out or to any conditions or restrictions subject to which it proposes that the consent, permission or other authorisation should be given.
…"

The "appropriate nature conservation" body in this case was NE (reg.5(1)).

44   Regulation 64(1) provides:

"(1) If the competent authority is satisfied that, there being no alternative solutions, the plan or project must be carried out for imperative reasons of overriding public interest (which, subject to paragraph (2), may be of a social or economic nature), it may agree to the plan or project notwithstanding a negative assessment of the implications for the European site or the European offshore marine site (as the case may be)."

It is not suggested that reg.64(2) was engaged in this case.

45   In relation to the application of regs.63 and 64 to the development consent procedure, reg.84(2) provides:

"(2) Where those provisions apply, the competent authority may, if it considers that any adverse effects of the plan or project on the integrity of a European site or a European offshore marine site would be avoided if the order granting development consent included requirements under section 120 of the Planning Act 2008 (what may be included in order granting development consent), make an order subject to those requirements."

The Infrastructure Planning (Environmental Impact Assessment) Regulations 2017

46   Regulation 4 of the Infrastructure Planning (Environmental Impact Assessment Regulations 2017 (SI 2017 No. 572) ("the EIA Regulations") prohibits the Secretary of State from making an order granting development consent for "EIA development" under the 2008 Act unless EIA has been carried out (reg.4). Sizewell C constituted EIA development. By reg.5 "EIA" is a process consisting of the preparation of an "environmental statement" ("ES"), the carrying out of consultation under the EIA Regulations and compliance by the defendant with reg.21. Regulation 21 required the defendant when deciding whether to make the development consent order, to examine the environmental information and, taking that into account, to reach a reasoned conclusion on the significant effects of the development on the environment to integrate that conclusion into the decision on whether to grant the order, and to consider whether it was appropriate to impose monitoring measures. Environmental information "means the ES and the representations made by statutory consultees and other persons about the environmental effects of the development" (reg.3(1)).

47   Regulation 5(2) and (3) of the EIA Regulations provides:

> "(2)   The EIA must identify, describe and assess in an appropriate manner, in light of each individual case, the direct and indirect significant effects of the proposed development on the following factors—
>
> > (a)   population and human health;
> >
> > (b)   biodiversity, with particular attention to species and habitats protected under Directive 92/43/EEC and Directive 2009/147/EC;
> >
> > (c)   land, soil, water, air and climate;
> >
> > (d)   material assets, cultural heritage and the landscape;
> >
> > (e)   the interaction between the factors referred to in sub-paragraphs (a) to (d).
>
> (3)   The effects referred to in paragraph (2) on the factors set out in that paragraph must include the operational effects of the proposed development, where the proposed development will have operational effects."

48   Regulation 14 prescribes the contents of an ES. It must include a description of "the likely significant effects of the proposed development on the environment" (reg.14(2)(b)). By reg.14(2)(f) the ES must contain any additional information specified in sched. 4 relevant to "the specific characteristics of the particular development or type of development and to the environmental features likely to be significantly affected". Paragraph 5 of sched. 4 refers to:

> "A description of the likely significant effects of the development on the environment resulting from, *inter alia*—
>
> …
>
> > (e)   the cumulation of effects with other existing and/or approved projects, taking into account any existing environmental problems relating to areas of particular environmental importance likely to be affected or the use of natural resources;
> >
> > …"

49   Regulation 14(3) provides (so far as is relevant):

> "The environmental statement referred to in paragraph (1) must—
>   (a) ...
>   (b) include the information reasonably required for reaching a reasoned conclusion on the significant effects of the development on the environment, taking into account current knowledge and methods of assessment; and
>   (c) ..."

Ground 1

A summary of the claimant's submissions

50   The claimant submits that in breach of reg.63 of the Habitats Regulations the defendant failed to make an appropriate assessment of the implications of the "project" for European sites because he wrongly excluded from that project the permanent potable water supply solution without which the project is incomplete and cannot function. As at the date of the decision to make the order, that solution would potentially give rise to further impacts on protected areas which have not been assessed and could not be ruled out.

51   The permanent potable water supply was a fundamental component of the operation of the power station according to NE (para. 2.1.2. of representations in October 2021). The defendant agreed with the ONR that in order to satisfy the conditions of any nuclear site licence for the project, SZC will have to put in place a reliable supply of water before any nuclear safety related activities can take place that are dependent on such a supply.

52   The nuclear power station is functionally interdependent with the permanent water supply solution (*R. (Wingfield) v Canterbury City Council* [2020] J.P.L 154 at [64]).

53   The reasons advanced by the defendant as to why the permanent water supply did not form part of the power station project are irrelevant. The claimant relies in particular upon *R. (Ashchurch Parish Council) v Tewksbury BC* [2023] EWCA Civ 101.

NWL's position on water supply

54   SZC's Water Supply Strategy Report (September 2021) summarised NWL's position as at that stage. The local "water resource zone" Blyth WRZ would be unable to supply water to meet the needs of the power station. NWL had identified the possibility of a connection being made to the Northern/Central WRZ which might have sufficient capacity in the River Waveney, subject to completion of NWL's part of the Water Industry National Environment Programme ("WINEP") study led by the EA. This would require the construction of a new transfer main from Barsham Water Treatment Works to Saxmundham, a distance of 28km, and other water network enhancements. The proposed transfer main would connect into the local Blyth distribution network at Saxmundham Water Tower and at other locations. "These local connections have the potential to provide significant legacy benefit by increasing capacity and resilience of the distribution network" (para 3.2.3 and DL 4.53). The main would benefit consumers in the local area and not

simply Sizewell. There were issues affecting the availability of a sustainable supply across the whole of the East of England, which, if confirmed, would require a strategic response by NWL so that it could discharge its duties under the 1991 Act. Accordingly, longer term plans would need to be put in place by NWL "to serve the region and its committed growth."

55   In the decision letter the defendant noted that the transfer main from Barsham to Saxmundham did not form part of SZC's application for development consent (DL 4.59). But SZC had been able to provide information on the environmental impact of that pipeline and concluded that this would not give rise to any new or different significant cumulative impacts (DL 4.65). The defendant agreed (DL 4.51 to 4.52).

56   On 14 September 2021 the Panel held Issue Specific Hearing 11 ("ISH 11"), which covered water supply issues (DL 4.18). SZC provided a written note on issues arising out of that hearing, including the legal framework for WRMPs and the legal obligations of NWL.

57   On 5 October 2021 the Panel held ISH 15. A statement of common ground was agreed between NWL and SZC on 8 October 2021. In that statement NWL said that it would confirm whether it would be able to meet Sizewell C's long-term needs from the Northern/Central WRZ following completion of the WINEP modelling. If it could not, then NWL would have to develop new supply schemes through WRMP24, but that would not meet Sizewell C's long-term needs until the late 2020s at the earliest. The parties agreed 2032 as the backstop date for this long-term supply to be fully available.

58   NWL was represented by counsel at ISH 15 and agreed with SZC's position at the hearing. SZC pointed out that the Water Resources Planning Guidelines state that water undertakers must ensure that their planned property and population forecasts and resulting supply "must not constrain planned growth". Accordingly, even if NWL could not at that stage identify a water supply for Sizewell C, it was obliged to do so. NWL confirmed that that was the case.

59   After the Examination had closed on 14 October 2021, NWL's solicitors wrote to the defendant on 23 February 2022 to provide an update on the permanent supply of potable water. They said that the WINEP modelling showed that NWL would "not be able to supply all forecast household and non-household demand, including the Project's long-term demand, from existing water resources". "NWL will therefore need to identify new water resources to meet the forecast demand". NWL had included SZC's demand figures from 2032 in its WRMP24 demand forecast for the Suffolk supply area.

60   NWL stated that in addition to demand management options (e.g. reduction in leakage from networks and compulsory metering of households), it was appraising options which included:

    (i) Imports from Anglian water (subject to exporting water from the Essex WRZ);

    (ii) Nitrate removal at Barsham water treatment works to reduce raw sewage outages;

    (iii) Effluent re-use and desalination;

    (iv) Winter reservoirs post-2035.

The options in the WRMP24, due for submission to Defra by October 2022, would depend on the final WINEP modelling of abstraction in the River Waveney.

61   NWL reiterated its commitment to providing a long-term supply for Sizewell C, although it was unlikely to be available before the late 2020s at the earliest. This was dependent on finalising and funding new supply schemes to meet future demands in Suffolk, including the power station.

62   On 8 April 2022 SZC provided its response to the defendant's request dated 18 March 2022 for further information. The document summarised the submissions and information already supplied and stated that there was no difference between the positions of SZC and NWL. SZC summarised the range of options being considered by NWL, which included water transfer. It emphasised that WRMP24 would be subject to SEA and HRA. NWL had said that after submitting its plan for consultation it would work with SZC to negotiate an agreement under s.55 of the 1991 Act. Paragraphs 2.1.16 and 2.1.17 read as follows:

> "2.1.16 It is because the long-term planning of water supply is the subject of separate statutory provisions and processes that the identification of the source of Sizewell's long-term supply cannot be known at this stage. Indeed, the source may well change during the lifetime of the power station as the undertaker develops and manages its water resources in response to changing demand and other considerations. For the same reasons, and because on the evidence the source of supply is unlikely to be a constraint to the construction and operation of the new power station, the source does not need to be known for the purposes of the DCO.
>
> 2.1.17 NPS EN-1 is clear that that the DCO decision maker should work on the assumption that other regimes and regulatory processes will be properly applied and enforced so that decisions on DCO applications should complement but not seek to duplicate other processes (NPS EN-1 paragraph 4.10.3). That same principle is clear from paragraph 188 of the NPPF, i.e. planning decisions should assume that regimes will operate effectively."

SZC stated that it had put in place plans for a temporary desalination unit which would cover the project's water requirements up to the commissioning of unit 1 of the power station. That would give NWL 10 years to plan for and deliver a permanent water supply.

63   TASC sent to the defendant representations in response by letters dated 8 April 2022 and 23 May 2022. The first made criticisms of the proposal for a temporary desalination plant and said nothing about WRMP24. The second objected to a possible location for a permanent desalination plant and again said nothing about WRMP24. They made a general point to the effect that SZC had failed to assess impacts on receptors in relation to a permanent water supply solution, relying on the views of NE.

64   On 16 June 2022 SZC responded to the defendant's request for further information about any progress made with NWL. They said that NWL had confirmed that draft WRMP24 would make full provision for the long-term demand from Sizewell C and that, subject to the necessary approvals from Defra and OFWAT, it is likely to be possible to deliver the necessary infrastructure. NWL and SZC had agreed to begin negotiations under the 1991 Act in October 2022 for funding the design and delivery of infrastructure specific to Sizewell C, so as to be ready to sign an agreement once NWL's Business Plan had been approved by

OFWAT, most likely in early 2024. SZC said that there was no reason to think that a new water supply scheme for a "critical NSIP" would not be approved in the 2024 Price Review and every reason to expect that NWL, using reasonable endeavours, would be able to deliver the necessary infrastructure for the permanent water supply connection before the end of construction of Sizewell C (see also DL 4.42).

The decision letter

65   This material on NWL's position regarding a permanent water supply was well summarised in the defendant's decision letter at DL 4.12 to 4.42. At DL 4.44 the defendant considered that the options identified by NWL were potentially viable solutions, as was the "fall back" of SZC providing a permanent desalination plant. He concluded that if development consent were to be granted for the power station, there was a "reasonable level of certainty" that a permanent solution could be found before the commissioning of the first reactor. Plainly in arriving at that conclusion the defendant would have taken into account his further conclusions about the need for environmental impacts to be assessed and considered. The defendant's confidence that a permanent solution would be provided before operation of the power station was a matter for his judgment.

66   The defendant also noted that if, and only if, the WRMP process fails to provide a solution, SZC will have to consider providing its own permanent desalination plant (DL 4.60). He noted the objections which had been raised to this possible option and said that a detailed assessment of the impacts would be required if it were to be pursued. The defendant had not asked for an assessment at this stage because (a) this option did not form part of the proposed development and (b) SZC's position was that it was unlikely to be required (DL 4.61).

67   The defendant dealt with environmental assessment in relation to a mains link to Barsham water treatment works, the WRMP process and the possible fallback of a permanent desalination scheme between DL 4.43 to DL 4.69 in some detail. That section needs to be read as a whole.

68   Part 6 of Sched.19 to the Order contains provisions for the protection of NWL. Paragraph 70 states that subject to either condition 1 or condition 2 being satisfied, and subject to the terms of any agreement made under s.55 or determination made by OFWAT under s.56 of the 1991 Act, NWL will use its reasonable endeavours to supply Sizewell C with the quantities of water required for its operational phase as soon as reasonably practicable. Condition 1 is that the EA confirms the new annual licensed quantities which may be abstracted from the River Waveney and NWL confirms to SZC that there is a sufficient resource in the Northern/Central WRZ to meet forecast demand from its existing and future customers, including demand for Sizewell C (paras.71 to 72). Condition 2 is satisfied if there are new supply schemes in WRMP24, the Secretary of State for Environment, Food and Rural Affairs approves the publication of the final version of WRMP24 and OFWAT approves "the required supply schemes" from the approved WRMP24 in its Final Determination for the 2024 Price Review (paras. 73 to 75).

Discussion

69   Neither the Habitats Regulations nor the EIA Regulations define a "project". It is common ground in this case that principles in the case law on the EIA Regulations

are applicable when considering the scope of a project under the Habitats Regulations.

70   The question of what is the project in any particular case is a matter of judgment for the decision-maker, here the Secretary of State. That judgment may only be challenged in this court on *Wednesbury* principles (*Bowen-West v Secretary of State for Communities and Local Government* [2012] Env. L.R. 22 at [39] to [42]; *Smyth v Secretary of State for Communities and Local Government* [2015] P.T.S.R. 1417; *Wingfield* at [63] and *Ashchurch* at [81], [83], [100] and [105].) In the present case the issue is whether the defendant took into account a consideration which was legally irrelevant and, if not, whether his judgment was otherwise irrational. The threshold for irrationality in the making of such a judgment is a difficult obstacle to surmount (see e.g. *Newsmith Stainless Ltd v Secretary of State for the Environment, Transport and the Regions* [2017] P.T.S.R. 1126).

71   The courts have been astute to detect "salami-slicing", that is the device of splitting a project into smaller components that fall below the threshold for "EIA development" so as to avoid the requirement to carry out EIA altogether (*R. v Swale BC Ex p. RSPB* [1991] 1 P.L.R. 6 at [16]; *Preston New Road Action Group v Secretary of State for Communities and Local Government* [2018] Env. L.R 18 at [69]).

72   In *R. (Larkfleet Ltd) v South Kesteven DC* [2016] Env. L.R. 4 stated at [36] that it is clear from the legislation that the mere fact that two sets of proposed works have a cumulative effect on the environment does not make them a single project. Instead, they may constitute two projects but with cumulative effects which need to be assessed. The court went on to discuss a second type of salami-slicing ([37]-[38]). It acknowledged that the scrutiny of cumulative effects between two projects may involve less information than if the two sets of works are treated together as one project. Accordingly, a planning authority should be astute to ensure that a developer has not sliced up what is in reality one project in order to try to make it easier to obtain planning permission for the first part of the project and thereby gain a foot in the door in relation to the remainder. But the Directives and jurisprudence of the European Court of Justice recognise that it is legitimate for different development proposals to be brought forward at different times, even though they may have a degree of interaction, if they are different "projects". The Directives apply in such a way as to ensure appropriate scrutiny to protect the environment, whilst avoiding undue delay in the operation of the planning control system. Undue delay would be likely if all the environmental effects of every related set of works had to be definitively examined before any of those works could be allowed to proceed. Where two or more linked sets of works are in contemplation, which are properly to be regarded as distinct "projects", the objective of environmental protection is sufficiently secured under the Directives by consideration of their cumulative effects, so far as that is reasonably possible, when permission for the first project is sought, combined with the requirement for subsequent scrutiny under the Directives for the second and each subsequent project.

73   In *Wingfield* at [64] Lang J indicated some factors which *may* be taken into account in determining the extent of a project:

> "64. Relevant factors may include:

i) Common ownership – where two sites are owned or promoted by the same person, this may indicate that they constitute a single project (*Larkfleet* at [60])

ii) Simultaneous determinations – where two applications are considered and determined by the same committee on the same day and subject to reports which cross refer to one another, this may indicate that they constitute a single project (*Burridge* at [41] and [79]);

iii) Functional interdependence – where one part of a development could not function without another, this may indicate that they constitute a single project (*Burridge* at [32], [42] and [78]);

iv) Stand-alone projects – where a development is justified on its own merits and would be pursued independently of another development, this may indicate that it constitutes a single individual project that is not an integral part of a more substantial scheme (*Bowen-West* at [24 – 25])"

The judge made it clear that these factors were not exhaustive. The weight to be given to them will depend upon the circumstances of each case and is a matter for the decision maker.

74   Interdependence would normally mean that *each* part of the development is dependent on the other, as, for example, in *Burridge v Breckland DC* [2013] J.P.L. 1308 at [32] and [42].

75   At DL 4.46 the defendant referred to para 5.15.6 of EN-1 which requires the decision-maker to take into account the interaction of a proposed project with WRMPs (DL 4.46). He had regard to SZC's analysis of the obligations of NWL under the 1991 Act to prepare WRMP24 and to supply water (e.g. DL 4.47, 4.49 to 4.50, 4.55 to 4.60, 4.64 to 4.65 and 4.67). He accepted the key components of that analysis.

76   The defendant's conclusions included the following:

(i) SZC's preferred solution was a link to Barsham *provided by NWL*. SZC's cumulative assessment stated that the pipeline would follow existing roads and boundaries wherever possible. Cut and fill would progress quickly and would impact upon a single receptor for a small number of days at most. Given the footprint and locations of the works ecological impacts "would be minimal and avoidable or mitigable". There would be no significant cumulative effects. The defendant agreed. (DL 4.50 to DL 4.52 and 4.58);

(ii) If NWL's solution for the permanent supply of potable water should require a change to that pipeline connection, that would be subject to its own environmental assessment, including HRA. This would be for NWL to assess (DL 4.56 and 4.58);

(iii) WRMP24 will need to identify new water resources to meet long-term demand in Suffolk, both household and non-household demand. Those new supplies are not limited to meeting the demand for Sizewell C (DL 4.55);

(iv) Sizewell C and the WRMP24 process for identifying new water sources are separate or standalone projects, given that NWL has a duty to undertake WRMP24 regardless of whether Sizewell C proceeds. These two projects have separate "ownership" and "are subject to distinct and asynchronous determination processes". The WRMP process is carried out by NWL and is not something that SZC can dictate (DL 4.49 and 4.60);

(v) Assessment of potential environmental impacts associated with the permanent water supply to be provided by NWL could not be carried out because of the stage reached in the WRMP24 process and the fact that the preferred solution was unknown (DL 4.50 and 4.59);

(vi) Any pipeline or connection needed for the solution adopted by NWL will be the subject of a separate application by that company. That infrastructure does not form part of the current application (DL 4.57 and 4.59);

(vii) The defendant was satisfied with the control that will be exercised by the ONR through the conditions of the nuclear site licence, which will require a reliable supply of potable water to be in place before any nuclear safety-related activities can take place. The cumulative or in-combination environmental effects will be assessed under NWL's WRMP24 process, including a HRA, before operation can commence (DL 4.64);

(viii) The provision of a permanent water supply is not an integral part of the Sizewell C proposal (DL 4.65).

77   Plainly this is not a case where the promoter of a project has sliced up the development in order to make it easier to obtain consent for the first part of a larger project. Sizewell C was initially promoted on the basis that NWL would meet its obligations under the 1991 Act by providing a permanent water supply at Barsham and a transfer main to Saxmundham. Accordingly, the provision of that infrastructure by NWL was not included in SZC's application for development consent. The present uncertainty about what form the long term supply will take only emerged subsequently. In the circumstances, it is inappropriate for the claimant to say that SZC has caused uncertainty by "keeping its options open". SZC has had to react to the changing circumstances of the WINEP modelling and NWL's evolving response to that assessment. SZC has made it plain that it wishes to rely upon the solution that NWL says it will be able to deliver through the WRMP24 process and not upon permanent desalination on-site. On the other hand the defendant's decision recognises that in the unlikely event of NWL being unable to provide a solution, SZC would seek to provide a desalination plant (DL 4.66).

78   In summary, the claimant submits that the defendant took into account the following irrelevant considerations:

(i) The current uncertainty as to the final source of the water supply was irrelevant. The lack of definition of that supply cannot "of itself" provide the answer to the question whether that supply forms part of the project;

(ii) The infrastructure for the potable water supply did not form part of the application for development consent;

(iii) The potable water supply would be subject to a separate and asynchronous decision process;

(iv) Separate ownership.

79   The claimant seeks to base these criticisms upon *Ashchurch*. That case concerned the grant of planning permission for a bridge over a railway line. This is sometimes referred to as "the bridge to nowhere", because when viewed in isolation it served no purpose. It did not connect to any existing road or development. It was a bridge in the middle of a field. It would only begin to be used if and when housebuilders obtained planning permission for and developed a link road and housing site. The claim for judicial review had to succeed in any event because the officer's report

wrongly directed the defendant's planning committee that they could take into account the benefits which would arise from the housing development anticipated but not any of the harm that that development would cause. The benefits of the additional development could not be realised without the concomitant harms. So the decision involved a failure to take into account an obviously material consideration and was irrational (grounds 1 and 2 at [32] to [69]).

80   The claimant relies upon the later part of the judgment of Andrews LJ which dealt with ground 3 at [70] to [104] and the defendant's decision that the bridge should be treated as a single project for the purposes of the EIA Directive. She held that the identification of a project is a fact-specific matter. Consequently, other cases, decided on different facts, are only relevant to the limited extent that they indicate the type of factors which might assist in determining whether a proposed development forms an integral part of a wider project.

81   Andrews LJ referred to the principle under the EIA Regulations that where EIA is required, it should generally be carried out as early as possible. As Lang J said in her second judgment in *Wingfield* [2019] EWHC 1974 (Admin) at [72]-[77] there is no objective in the Habitats Directive (92/43/EEC) requiring appropriate assessment at the earliest possible stage. Instead, the Directive focuses on the end result of avoiding damage to a European site. In the case of a "multi-stage consent" (or a multi-consent) it may be a subsequent rather than the first consent which authorises the implementation of the project (see also *No Adastral New Town Ltd v Suffolk Coastal DC* [2015] Env. L.R. 28 and *R. (Swire) v Canterbury City Council* [2022] J.P.L. 1026 at [94] to [95]).

82   The central flaw in the Council's decision in *Ashchurch* was its failure even to consider whether the bridge formed an integral part of a wider project for the purposes of the EIA Regulations ([82] to [84] and [96]). The court rejected the notion that in a case where the specific development for which permission is sought clearly forms an integral part of an envisaged wider future scheme, without which that development would never take place, there *can only* be a single project if the wider scheme has reached the stage where it could be the subject of an application for planning permission ([88] and see also [101]).

83   The Court then stated that the mere "difficulty" of carrying out any assessment of the impacts of a larger future project which is lacking in detail, is irrelevant to the question whether the application under consideration forms an integral part of that larger project ([90]). *Ashchurch* was a case where it was possible to carry out some assessment of the future scheme. It was not a case where that was impossible ([91] to [92]).

84   At [102] and [104] Andrews LJ held that the fact that the EIA Regulations would require EIA to be carried out on the future wider scheme could not be conclusive on the issue of whether the earlier phase, the bridge, should be treated as a standalone project. But the Court did not suggest that this factor was altogether irrelevant and therefore must be disregarded. For example, it could be relevant to an assessment of whether the procedure being followed would have the effect of avoiding the requirements of the legislation, as in a salami-slicing case.

85   In the present case, unlike *Ashchurch*, the defendant considered whether the provision of a permanent water supply formed an integral part of the Sizewell C development and concluded that it did not. In reaching that conclusion the defendant did not take into account any irrelevant considerations.

86   The defendant did not rely upon the mere "difficulty" of carrying out an assessment of the water supply solution or the mere lack of detail on any option. Rather, WRMP24 had yet to be published in draft. NWL's solution to the water supply issue for Suffolk was unknown and would remain so until that process was completed. There was no option to assess. In any event, the defendant did not treat this factor as conclusive. Instead, it was one of a number of matters to which he had regard in the exercise of his judgment.

87   The defendant was entitled to take into account the fact that the permanent water supply had not formed part of the application for development consent and would be dealt with under a subsequent, separate process and subject to an integrated environmental assessment. He did not treat those matters as conclusive. His approach was lawful in accordance with *Wingfield* at [64] and *Ashchurch*.

88   I understand that "separate ownership" in DL 4.49, read in context, to be a reference to the separate responsibilities of SZC, for Sizewell C, and NWL, for WRMP24 and the supply of water. As the defendant noted, NWL is under a statutory duty to prepare and publish WRMP24 and SZC has no control over that process. Undoubtedly this was a relevant factor which the defendant was entitled to take into account.

89   The claimant alleges that there is functional interdependence between the Sizewell C scheme and the provision of a permanent water supply. This argument relies upon the assertion that "the need for the permanent potable water supply arose from the power station development." The implication would appear to be that there would be no such need in the absence of that development and so there is interdependence. This was not an argument which appears to have been pursued before the Panel during the Examination or subsequently before the Secretary of State. The claimant has not identified any evidence to support its assertion. Rather NWL stated that they would need to make additional water supplies available to meet the forecast demand and not just the demand from Sizewell C. The defendant had regard to NWL's obligation to undertake WRMP24 so as to be able to meet its duties under the 1991 Act. Beyond that the defendant took into account the requirement for the permanent water supply to be available before Sizewell C can operate under a nuclear site licence.

90   I have already summarised the considerations to which the defendant had regard in deciding that the provision by NWL of additional water sources for Suffolk is not part of the Sizewell C project. There is no basis upon which the defendant's evaluative judgment can be said to be irrational.

91   The claimant's argument has much wider implications. The need for the supply of utilities such as water is common to many, if not all, forms of development. A utility company's need to make additional provision so as to be able to supply existing and new customers in the future does not mean that that provision (or its method of delivery) is to be treated as forming part of each new development which will depend upon that supply. The consequence would be that where a new supply has yet to be identified by the relevant utility company, decisions on those development projects would have to be delayed until the company is able to define and decide upon a proposal. That approach would lead to sclerosis in the planning system which it is the objective of the legislation and case law to avoid (*R. (Forest of Dean (Friends of the Earth)) v Forest of Dean DC* [2015] P.T.S.R. 1460 at [18]).

92   Lastly, in his reply Mr. Wolfe chose to focus more on the complaint that a permanent desalination plant was not treated as forming part of the Sizewell C

project. He submits that SZC could have put forward a design for assessment. He claims that the absence of that information and an assessment was unlawful by virtue of *Ashchurch* at [90] and [92]. I disagree. In *Ashchurch* the bridge was only going to be constructed in order to serve the wider development in the Masterplan area. As Andrews LJ said, although it was a matter for the local authority to address on a redetermination, it was difficult to see how the bridge could not be treated as an integral part of the wider project ([100]). The unassessed wider project was a real proposal. But there is no obligation to assess a hypothetical scheme (*Preston New Road* at [75]). Here SZC considered that a permanent desalination plant was unlikely to be necessary and was not currently proposing that option. The defendant's decision that such a desalination plant was not an integral part of the Sizewell C project cannot be faulted.

93　　For all these reasons ground 1 must be rejected.

Ground 2

94　　On the assumption that the defendant was entitled to treat Sizewell C and the provision of a permanent water supply as separate projects, the claimant argues that the defendant acted in breach of reg.63 of the Habitats Regulations by failing to assess the cumulative impacts of both. The defendant relies upon the Panel's conclusion that even if the water supply did not form part of the project, nevertheless those cumulative effects should be assessed at the development consent stage (PR 5.11.284 to 5.11.287 and 7.5.7).

95　　The claimant accepts that the adequacy of the information in an assessment is a matter for the judgment of the competent authority, the defendant, subject to a legal challenge on *Wednesbury* principles, whether under the Habitats Regulations or the EIA Regulations (*R. (Champion) v North Norfolk DC* [2015] 1 W.L.R. 3710 at [41]; *Wingfield* at [97]; *R. (Friends of the Earth Ltd) v Secretary of State for Transport* [2021] P.T.S.R. 190 at [142] to [148]). The claimant submits that the defendant exercised his judgment irrationally and in breach of the principle stated in *Ashchurch* at [90] and [92] (see above). It is also suggested that the approach taken by the defendant is inconsistent with the decision in *R. v Rochdale MBC Ex p. Milne* [2001] Env. L.R. 22 (referred to by Andrews LJ in Ashchurch at [76] and [88]).

96　　In this case the grant of development consent depended upon the IROPI test being satisfied. Mr. Wolfe submits that if assessment of the cumulative effects of power station and water supply are left to a subsequent decision, the IROPI test cannot be applied properly at that stage. By that he means that it cannot be applied in the same way as if the cumulative impacts were being assessed before the decision on whether to grant the development consent order was made. He suggests that the prior grant of the Order under the 2008 Act will make it easier for the public interest in Sizewell C going ahead to override cumulative harm or, indeed, that that would "automatically" be the outcome.

Discussion

97　　It is well-established that a decision-maker may rationally reach the conclusion that the consideration of cumulative impacts from a subsequent development which is inchoate may be deferred to a later consent stage (e.g. *R. (Littlewood) v Bassetlaw DC* [2009] Env. L.R. 21; *Larkfleet* at [37]-[38]; Forest of Dean at [13] to [18]; *R.*

(Khan) v Sutton LBC [2014] EWHC 3663 (Admin) at [121] – [134] approved in Preston New Road at [67] and *R. (Finch) v Surrey CC* [2022] P.T.S.R. 958 at [15 (4)]).

98   In the present case the defendant referred to the possibility that new sources of water might enable a connection to be made by NWL providing a tunnel to Barsham. He accepted the assessment that that option would not give rise to additional cumulative impacts (e.g. DL 4.52). Beyond that, he decided that the new sources of water and any consequential need for a different connection were simply unknown and could not be assessed at the development consent stage. He agreed that they would instead be appropriately assessed under the WRMP process. Those judgments cannot be faulted as irrational.

99   Ground 2 is predicated upon ground 1 having failed. In other words the provision of the permanent water supply does not form part of the Sizewell C project for the purposes of the decision under challenge. On that basis the claimant's suggestion that the insufficiency of detail could have been addressed by the defendant assessing a "*Rochdale* envelope" is misconceived. *Rochdale* was concerned with the grant of outline planning permission for a project which *included* uncertain components. In any event, the claimant did not develop this submission so as to show how an "envelope" could even be defined (and then assessed) covering possible options for additional water supplies and the connections that could be necessary, all of which would be outside the development site at Sizewell C. The suggestion was wholly unrealistic.

100   The defendant's conclusion that an assessment of the permanent water supply could not be carried out does not conflict with *Ashchurch* at [90] and [92]. Those paragraphs were concerned with whether subsequent works formed part of the current project (i.e. ground 1 of this challenge). They do not detract from the principles in the case law referred to in [97] above.

101   Mr. Wolfe made a faint attempt to rely upon the decision in *Pearce v Secretary of State for Business, Energy and Industrial Strategy* [2022] Env. L.R. 4 as requiring cumulative impacts of the permanent water supply to be assessed in the decision on whether to make the Order. The decision in Pearce turned on its own special facts (see e.g. [118] to [119]). The circumstances of the present case are completely different. Furthermore, in Pearce the promoter had been able to produce a cumulative impact assessment and the reasons given by the decision-maker for deferring consideration of that material were legally flawed. Here options for providing a permanent water supply were unknown at the time of the decision.

102   I do not think there is any merit in Mr. Wolfe's IROPI point. If a future assessment should show that the water supply option chosen would adversely affect the integrity of a European site, whether by itself or in combination with Sizewell C, IROPI would have to be applied according to the language of the Habitats Regulations and the relevant principles in the case law. It would not be appropriate to take into account the overall *benefits* of Sizewell C without also taking into account the overall *harms* of that project. The court has not been shown any authority in which deferral of the consideration of the cumulative impacts to a subsequent consent stage has caused the application of the IROPI test to be distorted or biased or watered down in some way. I note that in *Forest of Dean* Sales LJ (as he then was) stated at [19] that the earlier grants of planning permission for the original project in that case created no presumption and added no force to the contention that planning permission should subsequently be granted for the spine

road that connected the two sites. The earlier permissions had not been granted on the footing that the development of those two sites was dependent upon the spine road.

103   True enough, in this case Sizewell C cannot be operated without a permanent water supply. But although the development consent has been granted in the knowledge that the power station is dependent on the future provision of a water supply, (a) it is not dependent on the provision of any particular form of supply and that is currently unknown and (b) the cumulative impact will have to be assessed properly in accordance with the legislation without any bias or distortion. The benefits of Sizewell C could not be taken into account in that future IROPI assessment without also taking into account the disbenefits. I understood Mr. Strachan KC for the defendant and Mr. Phillpot KC for SZC to adopt this analysis. They both submitted that the defendant's decision has not allowed SZC to have a "foot in the door."

104   I also note that, according to the evidence before the defendant, NWL and SZC expect a s.55 agreement to be signed in early 2024 following the WRMP process in which the integrated environment assessment will have been carried out. It is also expected that the water supply scheme will be approved in the 2024 Price Review. Paragraph 75 of sched.19 to the Order under the 2008 Act has been drafted on that basis (see [68] above).

105   Accordingly, ground 2 must be rejected.

Ground 3

106   NE is the "nature conservation body" for the purposes of the Habitats Regulations. In this case it performed the role of providing specialist advice within its remit to the defendant as the competent authority. There is no dispute that the defendant is entitled to disagree with NE. But the claimant complains that when the defendant did so in the present case he failed to comply with the line of authority which indicates that the decision-maker is expected to give significant weight to the views of an expert body such as NE and to give "cogent reasons" for disagreeing with their views (see e.g. *R. (Akester) v Department for Environment, Food and Rural Affairs* [2010] Env. L.R. 33 at [112] and *R. (Wyatt) v Fareham BC* [2023] Env. L.R. 14 at [9 (4)]).

107   But it is important to note two additional points. First, this issue arises in the context of s.116 of the 2008 Act by which the defendant is obliged to prepare a statement of his reasons for deciding to make an order granting development consent. Even when disagreeing with the expert views of a body such a NE, the relevant standard to apply in assessing the adequacy of the reasons given is that set out in *Save Britain's Heritage v Number 1 Poultry Ltd* [1991] 1 W.L.R. 153 and *South Bucks District Council v Porter (No.2)* [2004] 1 W.L.R. 257 (see Sales LJ in *Mordue v Secretary of State for Communities and Local Government* [2016] 1 W.L.R. 2682 at [26] and Sir Keith Lindblom SPT in *East Quayside 12 LLP v Newcastle upon Tyne City Council* [2023] EWCA Civ 359 at [51], drawing also a parallel with *R. (Mott) v Environment Agency* [2016] 1 W.L.R. 4338 at [69] to [77]).

108   Second, the basis for the deference given to the decision of an expert body such as NE in proceedings to review their own decisions was explained more fully by Beatson LJ in Mott at [69] to [77]. He also stated at [64] that the court may insist

upon being provided with a sufficiently clear and full explanation of the reasons for that decision as a *quid pro quo* for that deference. In my judgement similar considerations apply where a decision-maker is expected to show deference to the advice of an expert body. The level of reasoning which the law expects of a decision-maker disagreeing with the view of an expert body may depend upon whether that view is an unreasoned statement or assertion, or a conclusion which is supported by an explanation and/or evidence. It may also depend upon the nature of the subject-matter. Some advice may not call for reasoning and/or supporting evidence, other advice may do.

109   The views of NE shown to the court were sent in a submission dated 12 October 2021. They provided comments to the defendant on a Report by the Panel on the implications of the proposed development for European protected sites and species which had been submitted to the defendant. The claimant has not relied upon any other document from NE. In paragraphs 2.1.1. and 2.1.2. NE said:

> "2.1.1. It is Natural England's advice that pushing any Habitats Regulations Assessment (HRA) conclusions for integral and inextricably linked elements of the project down the line into other consenting regimes beyond the Development Consent Order (DCO) raises the likelihood that cumulative and 'in combination' impacts in these regards may get missed/ downplayed, and we wish to draw the Examining Authority's attention to this point.
>
> 2.1.2. For example, the current Water Supply Strategy proposes a mains pipeline to the site from the central/ northern Suffolk Water Resource Zone (WRZ). The environmental impacts of this pipeline have not yet been fully assessed through the HRA process. Neither have the interim solutions of a desalination plant as proposed through Change 19 [PD-050] (not considered within the RIES) and tankered water supply. Currently, the Applicant's position is 'no likely significant effects (LSE)' to any European sites from water use as stated in [REP7 -073] and summarised in paragraph 3.2.55 of the REIS. Clearly, such works could lead to a LSE on those European sites already scoped into the HRA or European sites further afield through the pipeline works, abstraction of this magnitude and other associated works to facilitate it. The water supply is a fundamental component of the eventual operation of the project, and the potential impacts of its construction should be clearly assessed in accordance with sections 4.2 and 5.15 of National Policy Statement EN-1 (NPS EN-1), sections 3.7 and 3.9 of NPS EN-6 and paragraph 3.3.9 of the Planning Inspectorate's Scoping Opinion for the Proposed Sizewell C Nuclear Development (July 2019) [APP-169]…"

110   In essence NE said no more than:

(i)   The water supply is a fundamental component of the eventual operation of the project and potential impacts of its construction should be assessed with Sizewell C;

(ii) Pushing any HRA for integral and inextricably linked elements of the project down the line into other consenting regimes beyond the development consent order raises the likelihood that cumulative and in combination impacts may be missed or downplayed.

In relation to NE's comments on the pipeline connection to Barsham and the temporary desalination plant, the defendant has explained why he is satisfied with the assessment of the impacts from those elements. There is no legal challenge to that part of his decision.

111   The two bare points set out in [110] above were not so much advice as assertions without any reasoning or supporting evidence. There was no explanation as to why the water supply should be considered part of, or integral to, the project, nor any application of considerations of the kind indicated in *Wingfield*. Why should relevant impacts be altogether missed in a subsequent assessment, any more than if assessed as part of the power station project? The same statutory regime will be applicable and NE will scrutinise the environmental information provided by NWL. Why should those impacts be downplayed without any consultee noticing, or downplayed by the decision-maker? It should not be forgotten that the water supply solution is to address a regional issue. On any view, it will be a project in its own right and the normal standards of assessment will apply to the proposal as a whole, including any connection to Saxmundham. Why should any cumulative impact of NWL's proposal not take into account cumulative impacts with Sizewell C? None of these points were addressed by NE to justify their apparent concerns.

112   I also note that, notwithstanding the national importance of the proposed project, SZC found it necessary to complain about the "unfairness" of NE having failed to attend Examination hearings to which they had been specifically invited, so that their views could be clarified and tested, in the same way as those of experts relied upon by SZC and other participants (see para. 1.3.1 of SZC's written summary of oral submissions made at ISH 15 held on 5 October 2021).

113   NE's views were summarised by the Panel in PR 5.11.284. No complaint is made about the adequacy of that summary, nor could there be. To the limited extent that NE expressed any views on this subject, they were before the defendant.

114   In my judgment the defendant did adequately explain in DL 4.65 why he disagreed with the bare assertions of NE, all the more so when that paragraph is read properly in the context of the other parts of the decision letter dealing with the same subject. The present case illustrates the inappropriateness of relying upon statements in the *Akester* line of authority as a mantra, rather than looking properly at the materials in any given case in context. Ground 3 should never have been raised by the claimant.

Ground 4

115   The defendant concluded that the project would have an adverse effect upon the integrity of the breeding marsh harrier feature of the Minsmere – Walberswick SPA arising from noise and disturbance during the construction phase (DL 5.20). Accordingly, under reg.64(1) of the Habitats Regulations the defendant had to be satisfied that there were no "alternative solutions" to the project. At DL 5.33 he did so conclude, in agreement with the Panel.

116   The claimant made representations in the Examination that there were alternative means of achieving the objective of generating electricity compatibly with the Climate Change Act 2008 which do not involve the use of nuclear power. It submits that the defendant failed to comply with the requirement in reg.64(1) to consider

alternative solutions by failing to consider how that objective could be met without relying upon new nuclear power. In so far as nuclear power is considered to have particular benefits, those matters ought to have been assessed as part of a wider consideration of alternative methods of generating electricity and their respective benefits. The defendant acted unlawfully by basing his conclusion on too narrow a policy objective, namely to provide additional nuclear power. However, if the defendant was legally entitled to adopt that approach, the claimant does not contend that he failed to assess "alternative solutions" lawfully.

117   The claimant submits that the decision-maker must consider alternative solutions which fulfil the "core policy objectives" or the "central policy objective", these being legal terms of art. They are not simply factual descriptions of a decision-maker's policy position. They fall to be identified not by the "mere election of the decision-maker", but with reference to the purpose of reg.64(1) and case law. The central policy objective should not be drawn so narrowly as to curtail the ability of the Habitats Regulations to inhibit unnecessarily harmful development in favour of less harmful alternatives. Furthermore, the phrase "alternative solutions" means that the "central policy objective" must comprise, or closely relate to, a problem "capable of solutions".

118   The claimant submits that the policy goal of providing nuclear power is "artificially limiting", to the extent that it "cannot logically be characterised as 'central'". The claimant says that, by contrast, the provision of comparatively clean energy does qualify as a central policy objective because that goes to the heart of what is sought to be achieved. Relying on its submission that the "solutions" referred to in the Habitats Regulations correspond to problems, the claimant asserts that a lack of nuclear energy is not a problem. Instead, a lack of clean energy is a problem capable of a range of alternative solutions, and so it is the provision of clean energy which qualifies as a central policy objective.

119   Lastly, the claimant suggests that the defendant erred in law by treating NPS EN-6 as determinative in deciding what were the appropriate policy objectives and alternative solutions.

Discussion

120   That last point can be rejected immediately. There is no basis for suggesting that the defendant in his decision treated the NPSs, or either of them, as conclusive on the issue of what could be considered to be relevant objectives or alternative solutions. Plainly, they were treated as "important" considerations (see e.g. DL 4.9), about which no complaint could possibly be made.

121   NPS EN-1 and EN-6 treat the need for nuclear power generation as having been demonstrated as part of the national strategy for achieving the net zero target in 2050 and ensuring diversity of supply and energy security. The Government's Energy White Paper, "Powering our Net Zero Future" (published in December 2020), announced a review of the suite of the energy NPSs but confirmed that they would not be suspended under s.11 of the 2008 Act in the meantime (DL 4.9). The White Paper includes as a "key commitment" the aim to bring at least one large-scale nuclear project to the point of Final Investment Decision by the end of the current Parliament (pp.16 and 48). The British Energy Security Supply Strategy (April 2022) states that the Government's aim is that by 2050 up to 25% of the electricity consumed in Great Britain will be generated by nuclear power, a

deployment of up to 24GW (see p.197 of the defendant's HRA and DL 4.656 and 8.10).

122   The Panel accepted SZC's case that there is an urgent need for new nuclear energy generating infrastructure of the kind proposed for Sizewell C, the proposed development responds directly to that need and would make a significant contribution to low-carbon electricity generation. Furthermore, that need case accords with Government policy (see e.g. PR 5.19.1 to 5.19.18, 5.19.90 to 5.19.110, 5.19.129 to 5.19.138, 5.19.261 to 5.19.266, 6.6.4 to 6.6.5, 6.7.4, 6.7.8, 7.2.1. to 7.2.4, 7.5.4, 7.5.9 and 10.2.19).

123   The defendant's conclusions on need in the HRA and in his decision letter were based upon the Panel's assessment (see e.g. HRA at pp.189 to 190 and 196 to 201 and DL 4.1 to 4.11, 4.242, 7.1 to 7.4 and 7.13 to 7.15). The need for new nuclear power was seen as an integral part of the strategy for tackling climate change by achieving the net zero target.

124   In the same vein, the Panel rejected submissions by the claimant and others that alternative technologies should be considered and that the approach taken by SZC was too narrow (see e.g. PR 5.4.106 to 5.4.108 and 6.6). The defendant accepted those conclusions (DL 4.133 and 4.148 to 4.152 and 4.155).

125   The claimant seeks to base its approach to the identification of objectives and alternative solutions upon the judgments of the Divisional Court and the Court of Appeal in the legal challenge to the "Airports National Policy Statement" designated in June 2018 (*Spurrier* and *R. (Plan B Earth) v Secretary of State for Transport* [2020] P.T.S.R. 1446).[1] But they lend no support to the claimant's case.

126   The Court of Appeal held that the standard of review in relation to both art.6(3) and art.6(4) of the Habitats Directive, and therefore reg.64 of the Habitats Regulations, is the *Wednesbury* standard ([77] to [79]). Subject to those principles, it is a matter for the decision-maker to determine the relevant objectives which need to be met and which alternative solutions would or would not meet that need.

127   At [92] and [93] the Court of Appeal addressed the problem of when objectives are defined in an unlawfully narrow manner. It endorsed the approach of the Divisional Court that an option that does not meet the core objectives of a policy statement is not an alternative solution for the purposes of reg.64(1). Such objectives must be both "genuine and critical", in the sense that a development which failed to meet those objectives would have no policy support. But it would clearly be insufficient to exclude an option simply because, in the decision-maker's view, it would meet those policy objectives to a lesser degree than the proposed or preferred option. The extent to which an option meets those policy objectives is different from an option failing to meet them at all. The judgments of the Divisional Court and the Court of Appeal provide no support for any of the additional glosses which the claimant now seeks to place on reg.64.

128   In *Plan B Earth* the objectives of the NPS under challenge were to increase airport capacity in the south east *and* to maintain the international "hub status" of the UK. The NPS rejected the option of a second runway at Gatwick as an "alternative solution" to a north west runway at Heathrow because expansion at Gatwick would not enhance, rather it would threaten, the UK's hub status ([64] to [65]). The Court of Appeal held that the Secretary of State had been legally entitled to reach that conclusion ([87] to [93]). The "hub objective" had been one of the

---

[1] I mention for completeness that this issue was not before the Supreme Court.

"central", or "essential", or "genuine and critical", objectives of the policy. That objective had not been constructed with deliberate and unlawful narrowness so as to exclude other options improperly.

129   The objectives of EN-1 and EN-6 include the generation of clean energy but the central or essential objectives of those policies is not limited to that aim. They also include diversity of methods of generation and security of supply. The Government sees new nuclear power as an essential component of those objectives, just as wind and solar power. That has remained the Government's policy in its recent statements (see also [28] to [32] above). Accordingly, there can be no legal challenge to the approach taken by the Panel and by the defendant which excluded alternative technologies as alternative solutions. In the light of the Court of Appeal's decision in Plan B Earth the legal position is crystal clear.

130   The claimant's argument depends upon an illegitimate attempt to rewrite the Government's policy aims by pretending that the central policy objective is at a higher level of abstraction, namely to produce clean energy, without any regard to diversity of energy sources and security of supply. But it is not the role of a claimant, or of the court, to rewrite Government policy, or to airbrush objectives of that policy which are plainly of "central" or "core" or "essential" importance.

131   The absurdity of the claimant's argument was well-demonstrated by Mr. Strachan KC and by Mr. Phillpot KC for the defendant and SZC respectively. The implication of ground 4 would be that a decision-maker dealing with a proposal for a solar farm or wind turbine array, obliged to comply with reg.64(1), would have to consider as alternative solutions nuclear power and, as the case may be, wind power or solar power options, But in my judgment there is nothing artificial or unlawfully limiting about a Government policy which identifies as core objectives the need to provide a mix of new electricity generation technologies, comprising solar, wind and nuclear power. Indeed, in para. 9.1.1 of the HRA the defendant noted a decision of the CJEU that the objective of ensuring security of supply may constitute IROPI.

132   For these reasons, ground 4 must be rejected. In my order providing for a rolled up hearing, I directed the claimant to review the legal merits of its various grounds, taking as an example its failure to address (a) the content of the Government's policy on nuclear power as part of a mix of energy sources and (b) the decision in Plan B Earth. The claimant should have abandoned ground 4, but chose instead, in effect, to try to continue its challenge to the merits of Government policy through the means of judicial review. The use of the court's process in that way is wholly inappropriate.

Ground 5

133   The claimant submits that when the defendant carried out his IROPI assessment he took into account a legally irrelevant consideration and/or one which was "unevidenced", namely that the project would contribute to achieving the objective of reducing GHG emissions by 78% by 2035 from the UK's 1990 baseline (para. 74 of skeleton).

134   I interpose to make one point straight away. The claimant's two propositions cannot both be correct. Either a consideration is irrelevant or it is not. If it is, then it does not matter whether any evidence was before the decision-maker on the point. Not surprisingly, it turns out that the claimant does not really contend that this consideration is incapable of being relevant. Instead, the complaint is that the

defendant drew a conclusion which was unsupported, or "insufficiently" supported, by evidence (skeleton paras. 76 and 80 to 81).

135   The claimant points out that, according to SZC's Construction Method Statement, it is expected that the first of the two reactors would be operational at the end of 2033 and the second by mid-2034. But that depends upon a number of assumptions, including the provision of a permanent potable water supply before the power station can be operated. The claimant submits that there was no evidence that that water supply would be implemented before 2035. It is said that SZC's expectation does not take into account uncertainty and delay in resolving that issue (paras. 75 to 76 of skeleton). The claimant complains about the absence of a timeline for the provision of the water supply and of evidence as to the degree of contribution Sizewell C would make to "the 2035 target". These are said to have been "obviously material considerations", applying the irrationality test laid down by the Supreme Court in the *Friends of the Earth* case. But ultimately, the criticism that the contribution to reducing GHG emissions by 2035 was not estimated comes down to an allegation that the timescale for determining and providing a permanent potable water solution was unclear (para. 85 of skeleton).

136   The claimant also submits that the defendant could not maintain that there was insufficient information about the eventual water supply to assess its environmental impacts (under ground 2) and at the same time rely upon the environmental benefits of Sizewell C where its operation is dependent upon that supply.

Discussion

137   A reduction in GHG emissions by 78% by 2035 relates to the Sixth Carbon Budget ("CB6") which was set under the Climate Change Act 2008 by the Carbon Budget Order 2021 (SI 2021 No. 750). It requires the UK's net carbon account not to exceed 965 Mt CO2e over the period 2033-2037 (see *R. (Friends of the Earth Ltd) v Secretary of State for Business, Energy and Industrial Strategy* [2023] 1 W.L.R. 225 at [2] to [12]). This is said to equate to a reduction in GHG emissions from the 1990 baseline by 78% by 2035.

138   Initially the claimant's argument was a little difficult to follow because the main sources upon which it relied in the Statement of Facts and Ground and its skeleton do not address the 78% target. Instead, it referred to the IROPI case for Sizewell C, which was based upon the national importance and urgent need for new nuclear power generation, including:

    (i) The continuing growth in the UK's electricity demand, the retirement of existing electricity capacity and "a generation shortfall of 95GW by 2035."
    (ii) The UK's commitment to reducing GHG emissions to net zero by 2050 (page 195 of the defendant's HRA and see also paras. 8.1, 8.3.4 and 8.3.5).

Similarly, the HRA rejected alternatives which would involve a significant delay to the construction programme, because Sizewell C would not contribute to addressing the shortfall in generation capacity of 95GW in 2035.

139   Likewise, the Panel had referred in its Report to the 95GW shortfall in 2035 and the contribution which Sizewell C could make (PR 6.6.4 and 6.7.4). But Mr Bowes showed how that issue was linked to the CB6 target, relying upon PR 5.19.137. That explained that in a report by the Climate Change Committee making recommendations for the sixth carbon budget, the "Balanced Net Zero Pathway",

which they treated as a central scenario, assumed that it would be necessary for the power sector to reach zero emissions by 2035, or to decarbonise completely.

140   The defendant and SZC sought to argue that the focus of the decision letter was on the net zero target for 2050 rather than any 2035 target along the way. But I do not agree. The Panel's conclusions took into account the contribution that Sizewell C could make to meeting a shortfall in generating capacity by 2035 and not simply the net zero target for 2050. Although one part of the decision letter referred in broad terms to the contribution of Sizewell C to limiting climate change in accordance with the objectives of the Paris Agreement (DL 5.35), other parts rely upon the Panel's Report at PR 7.5.4 (i.e. DL 7.3). PR 7.5.4 was based in turn upon the detailed assessment in PR 5.19. That section of the Report relied upon the urgent need for new nuclear power to contribute to electricity generation by 2035 (see e.g. PR 5.19.78, 5.19.136 to 5.19.137 and 5.19.163).

141   Furthermore, the defendant's decision also took into account his HRA. In that document he decided that the IROPI test was satisfied, basing himself upon the policy context for the project, its benefits as presented by SZC and the UK's commitment to decarbonising the electricity sector by 2035 (pp.195-6). In his overall conclusion on IROPI the defendant also relied upon section 6.7 of the Panel's Report which, as we have seen, was based upon section 5.19 of that document. Accordingly, it cannot be said that the project's claimed contribution to addressing the shortfall in 2035 in electricity generation did not materially influence the defendant's decision on the application of the Habitats Regulations as well as his decision to grant development consent. That leaves the gravamen of the claimant's complaint, namely the claimed lack of evidential support for the Secretary of State's view that the project would make such a contribution by 2035.

142   I have previously summarised under ground 1 much of the material before the Examination and the defendant on the steps which NWL and SZC stated would be followed in relation to WRMP24 so that NWL will comply with its duties under ss. 37, 37A and 37B.

143   In a statement of common ground between NWL and SZC dated 8 October 2021, NWL acknowledged that 2032 had been identified by SZC in discussion as "the backstop date" for the permanent water supply to be "fully available". The Panel referred to this date in its Report (PR 5.11.283).

144   In its letter to the defendant dated 23 February 2022 NWL confirmed that the water demand figures for the operational phase of Sizewell C had been included in WRMP24 from 2032 and that new schemes would be required in that Plan to meet all the forecast demand in the Suffolk supply area, including that of the project. NWL reiterated its commitment to providing the supply required for Sizewell C. That would be reliant upon the finalisation of new supply schemes and their identification in WRMP24, the completion of a s.55 agreement under the 1991 Act and "the costs approval process". The defendant was informed that the draft WRMP would be submitted to Defra by October 2022.

145   The position of both NWL and SZC was that after the submission of the draft WRMP for statutory consultation, they would work together from October 2022 to negotiate an agreement under s.55, which would include funding for the design and delivery of any infrastructure specific to Sizewell C.

146   SZC pointed out that the WRMP24 would be subject to a fully integrated environmental appraisal, including SEA and, where necessary, HRA. That would involve consultation with *inter alia* NE. The final version of the plan would have

to be compliant with the Habitats Regulations and by definition that would have to precede the installation of a permanent water supply. I also note that the defendant has already stated in his decision letter that he is satisfied with the assessment of the Barsham transfer pipeline if that connection should be chosen.

147   The provision of a *temporary* supply by SZC (which has been assessed in the process under the 2008 Act and is not itself the subject of legal challenge) gives NWL 10 years within which to provide a permanent solution. In addition, SZC indicated (in para. 2.2.5 of its response dated 8 April 2022) that, subject to detailed assessment, the lifespan of the temporary desalination plant could be extended for a short period after the end of the construction phase, if necessary.

148   Subsequently, SZC informed the defendant that an agreement with NWL under s.55 and/or s.56 of the 1991 Act would be likely to be ready to be signed once NWL's Business Plan had been approved by OFWAT most likely in 2024. There was no reason to suppose that a new water supply scheme for a critical NSIP would not be approved in the 2024 Price Review.

149   This material was carefully summarised in the decision letter (DL 4.12 to 4.42). The weight to be given to it was a matter for the defendant. He concluded that there was a reasonable level of certainty that a permanent water supply solution can be found before the first reactor is commissioned (DL 4.44). He was satisfied on the basis of the information supplied on the WRMP process under the 1991 Act that "there is a requisite degree of confidence that a long-term solution is deliverable" (DL 4.64).

150   In my judgment the material before the defendant was legally adequate to entitle him to reach those conclusions. It is impossible to say that his judgment on such an evaluative subject looking into the future was irrational. Once that position is reached, there is no legal reason why the defendant could not take into account the contribution which Sizewell C is expected to make to reducing the shortfall in electricity generation in 2035 (or to the target for reducing GHGs).

151   Lastly, there is no internal contradiction in the decision letter between the approach taken by the defendant to the assessment of cumulative effects arising from the permanent water supply for Sizewell C and his reliance upon environmental benefits which are dependent upon the provision of that supply. As to the former, the defendant decided that there was no option under the WRMP24 process which could be assessed at the stage when the decision letter was issued. As to the latter, the defendant was sufficiently confident that a solution would be found through the WRMP24 process (after having been subject to environmental assessment) and then completed before the operation of the power station is expected to begin in 2033. It is therefore apparent from the decision letter that there is no inconsistency in the defendant's reasoning or lack of coherence. The two conclusions are self-evidently compatible.

152   For all these reasons, ground 5 must be rejected.

Ground 6

153   The claimant submits that the defendant acted irrationally in concluding that the Sizewell C site would be clear of nuclear material by 2140 and/or failed to give legally adequate reasons for rejecting the claimant's case on this subject. Inadequacy of reasoning depends upon the claimant showing a lacuna in the decision raising

a substantial doubt as to whether it was tainted by a public law error (see *Save* and *South Bucks*).

154   The Panel noted that it is a requirement of Government policy that spent fuel be stored on a new nuclear site such as Sizewell C until a UK Geological Disposal Facility ("GDF") becomes available (PR 5.20.57 and 5.20.97). NPS EN-6 states that the key factors in determining the duration of on-site storage are the availability of a GDF and the time needed for spent fuel to cool sufficiently for disposal in a GDF (PR 5.20.96.).

155   The claimant submits that the defendant was aware of an estimate provided by SZC that a GDF would not be available to accept spent fuel from a new build project until 2145. Furthermore, during the Examination the claimant had relied upon information provided by the ONR in relation to Hinkley Point C which, according to the claimant, suggested that spent fuel would need to be kept at the Sizewell C site until about 2165.

156   The claimant submits that it was irrational for the defendant to proceed on the basis that spent fuel would be removed from the site by 2140. The modelling of future sea levels, storm events and the adequacy of the coastal defences only ran to 2140. It was irrational for the defendant not to engage with the risk of the site being flooded from the sea while spent fuel remains on site after 2140 and before the site is decontaminated.

Discussion

157   It is well-established that an enhanced margin of appreciation is to be afforded to a decision-maker relying on scientific, technical and predictive assessments (*Mott* at [69] to [78]). Plainly that principle is engaged when dealing with the evaluation of predictions far into the future about such matters as the effects of climate change on sea levels, the availability of a GDF and the life span and decommissioning of a project such as Sizewell C. It is also clear that a decision-maker deciding whether to grant development consent for such a project does so in the context of a range of statutory regimes which address changes in circumstance (and predictions) as they occur during the remainder of this century and well into the next. Those regimes are obviously material considerations.

158   SZC stated in the Examination that for the purposes of the EIA of the project it is assumed that the operation of the power station will end in the 2090s and by 2140 the interim spent fuel store will have been decommissioned (PR 5.20.19 to 5.20.20). Under its nuclear site licence SZC is required to demonstrate that the on-site facilities for interim storage of spent fuel can be designed, operated and decommissioned in a safe manner that ensures any risks to *inter alia* the environment are suitably and sufficiently controlled, including risks from flooding (PR 5.20.55). At PR 5.20.104 the Panel noted that Suffolk County Council and East Suffolk Council had raised no concerns regarding radioactive waste and said that that was to be expected because ONR would regulate on-site radioactive waste management and the EA would regulate gaseous and aqueous emissions.

159   The Panel summarised objections to the modelling work made by the claimant (e.g. at PR 5.20.59).

160   The Panel referred to the Government's firm policy commitment to the GDF for the long-term storage of high-level radioactive waste, in order to meet the UK's international obligations (PR 5.20.123 to 5.20.125). SZC's assumptions regarding

on-site storage of spent fuel had been based upon there being a GDF available for transfer in the long term. The Panel considered that to be a reasonable assumption (PR 5.20.130), although it acknowledged that there was a degree of uncertainty in relation to the timing of the GDF (PR 5.20.131). The Panel reached the judgment that there was sufficient evidence to be able to conclude that the policy tests for the handling of the waste were met, taking into account SZC's statement that spent fuel would be removed from Sizewell C by 2140 (PR 5.20.133 to 5.20 134). They said that this issue should not weigh against the making of the Order (PR 7.4.195 to 7.4.202).

161   On 7 August 2020 the ONR had provided information in an email which responded to questions sent to them by the claimant on 15 June 2020. Those questions covered a range of issues. One question asked ONR whether, in the light of a comment made by the Nuclear Decommissioning Agency (NDA), the spent fuel from Sizewell C would not be accepted at the GDF until about 140 years from the end of operations, and so would have to remain on site for about 200 years from start up. ONR responded that they did not have information on this subject in relation to Sizewell C. But for Hinkley Point C their understanding was that:

(i)   The cooling period was dependent upon the burn-up rate assumed for the fuel used in a reactor. The NDA had used a maximum peak burn-up rate and had not taken into account a number of aspects of the strategy for Hinkley Point C. The average burn-up for spent fuel at that power station would be lower than the NDA had assumed and would therefore have a lower heat output;

(ii)   The thermal output of a dry disposal canister containing four spent fuel assemblies is dependent upon a mixing strategy which combines high and low burn-up fuel assemblies within a single cannister;

(iii) An analysis had shown that a storage period of 55-60 years after the end of operation would be needed to meet the assumed GDF thermal limits for disposal for all fuel assemblies, using the strategy for Hinkley Point C;

(iv)   Accordingly, on the assumption that generation at Hinkley Point C begins in 2025 and ends in 2085, that fuel would be sufficiently cool to transfer to the GDF in 2140-2145. Assuming that it takes just over 9 years to remove fuel to the GDF, all fuel would be transferred from Hinkley Point C by between 2150 and 2155, which would determine the end of use of the fuel stores at that site.

The ONR also stated that the "assumed availability date for the GDF" to accept fuel from new reactors is around 2130, which is earlier than the date relied upon by the claimant taken from a document produced by SZC (see [155] above).

162   The ONR's response also stated that if there were to be a subsequent acceleration in the effects of climate change, so that the impacts were greater or more rapid than currently predicted, that would involve timescales of several decades, so that monitoring would be able to inform decisions under the conditions of the nuclear site licence on the protective measures required. "Managed adaptive options", such as an increase in the height of a coastal defence, with trigger points, would ensure that the site remains safe under the terms of the nuclear site licence.

163   In its representations to the Panel dated 24 September 2021 the claimant relied upon the email from the ONR and submitted that, assuming Sizewell C begins

operation in 2035 and ceases to operate in 2095, a 60-year cooling period would end in 2155 and the removal of spent fuel off site would take until 2165.

164   In its representations to the Panel in September 2021 after ISH 11, SZC stated that the Fourth Addendum to the Environmental Statement for the project assumed that Sizewell C would cease to operate in the 2090s, the fuel store will have been decommissioned by "the 2140s" and 2190 was "the theoretical maximum site lifetime". An EIA for decommissioning would be required in the years leading up to the end of electricity generation (paras. 1.11.1 to 1.11.2 on p.14).

165   An Addendum to the Flood Risk Assessment for the main development site, produced by SZC in January 2021, had increased the height of the proposed "hard coastal defence feature" to 14.6m above Ordnance Datum. Updated modelling was said to show that this would be sufficient to protect the site against events up to 2190 under reasonably foreseeable climate change scenarios. More extreme events are to be dealt with in SZC's safety case which will be assessed by the ONR (para. 1.36 of the Flood Risk Assessment and the Panel's Report at PR 5.8.91).

166   The issues concerning the adequacy of coastal defence proposals and long-term flood risks impact not only on-site radiological waste management but also a number of other subjects. The issues were considered by the Panel in some detail in a number of sections of their report, such as sections 5.7, 5.8 and 5.20. The Panel's Report has an interlocking structure and needs to be read as whole. The Panel was well aware of the objections on this point raised by the claimant and by other participants, such as Professor Blowers. The Report provided a good summary of the material submitted, including that provided by SZC (e.g. PR 5.7.35 to 5.7.40, 5.8.252 and 5.8.259 to 5.8.260, 5.8.276, 5.8.295 to 5.8.296, 5.20.6, 5.20.18 to 5.20.20, 5.20.59 and 5.20.98). In several places in its Report the Panel expressed satisfaction with *inter alia* the "adaptive design" for the proposed coastal defences, the monitoring of future sea levels through the Coastal Processes Monitoring and Mitigation Plan ("CPMMP") and future modifications of the design through the controls exercisable by the ONR and EA (e.g. 5.8.97, 5.8.99, 5.8.231, 5.8.239, 5.8.259 to 5.8.260, 5.8.299, 5.8.315 to 5.8.320, 5.20.98 to 5.20.102). At PR 5.8.313 the Panel noted that the design parameters of the sea defences would be secured by Requirement 19 of the development consent.

167   Participants continued to make representations after the close of the Examination. For example, a Mr. Parker returned to the subject of the lifetime and adequacy of the sea defences at Sizewell C. The EA and ONR provided a joint response dated 7 June 2022 which was forwarded to the defendant. At DL 4.366 the Secretary of State relied upon this response which he had summarised at DL 4.365:

"4.365 The Secretary of State notes the post-Examination representations submitted by IPs related to flood risk, including Mr Bill Parker who raised concerns regarding the protection from flooding during operation, decommissioning and the residual time spent fuel is stored on site. The Secretary of State notes the EA's letter to Mr Bill Parker of 7 June 2022 which confirmed that the FRA extended to 2190, and that for the Reasonably Foreseeable actual risk up to 2190, there would be no inundation of the main platform or SSSI crossing from overtopping of the HCDF or the remaining lower northern and southern sand dunes/shingle defences in all events up to the 0.1% annual probability flood events in 2019. The EA's letter also included a subsection titled 'ONR' response, confirming that during the operation of a nuclear licenced site, it is a regulatory expectation for the licensee to periodically review the validity of the safety case for all facilities on site against external hazards, to ensure the site remains protected, including the dry fuel store and taking updated climate change projections into account for coastal flood hazard."

The ONR specifically said that the design of the sea defences had been based upon the period running up to 2140, but if the life-time of the station extended beyond that year, SZC would need to demonstrate that the sea defences will continue to protect the site adequately, and if not provide additional protection.

168   In DL 4.250 the defendant agreed with the conclusions of the Panel summarised in DL 4.244 to DL 4.248. In DL 4.295 he expressed satisfaction with the modelling of sea level rises to 2140 for reasonably foreseeable events, including up to the 1 in 10,000 year event and in DL 4.246 with the adaptive design to provide a feasible means of increasing the crest height of the Hard Coastal Defence Feature to cope with a "credible maximum sea level rise". The defendant also relied upon further work carried out by SZC and the EA after the close of the Examination which had resolved all of the Agency's outstanding concerns at that stage. The defendant was also satisfied that matters such as the monitoring of climate change and adaptive measures would be adequately addressed by the ONR through the nuclear site licensing regime (DL 4.235 to DL 4.241, 4.247 and 4.250).

169   The defendant returned to these issues at DL 4.279 which summarised the Panel's views as follows:

"4.279 The ExA considers [ER 5.8.232 et seq.] the adequacy of the proposed climate change adaptation measures and the resilience of the Proposed Development to ongoing and potential future coastal change during its operational life and any decommissioning period including the scope for the HCDF to undergo design adaptation to maintain nuclear safety against predicted sea level rises. The Sizewell Coastal Defences Design Report [REP8-096] provides a design description of the HCDF Adaptive Design at section 3.11 and is designed to protect the Proposed Development from a 1 in 10,000 year storm event with reasonably foreseeable ("RF") climate change effects up to the end of its design life in 2140. The ExA consider that the Applicant recognises that, given the inherently uncertain nature of climate change, the RF climate change scenario may be exceeded. ONR and EA guidance requires that the sea defence be capable of adaptation to a credible maximum sea level rise [ER 5.8.252]. The sea defences have therefore been designed to allow for future adaptation to accommodate the credible maximum scenario, should it develop. The Adaptive Design would provide a simple means of increasing the crest height of the HCDF to reach a crest level of 16.4m OD [ER 5.8.252]. The implementation of measures to enact the Adaptive Design would be driven by progressively observed effects of climate change, specifically mean sea level rise. The MDS FRA [AS-018] confirms that the impacts of climate change on sea level rise would be monitored and assessed at set intervals to determine the trajectory of the projections, and consider whether there is any change from either the current considered projections or the climate change guidance as applied in the application [ER 5.8.253]. A number of issues were raised by IPs in relation to Adaptive design and its implementation [ER 5.8.254 et seq.]. Having considered the submissions and responses from the Applicant [ER 5.8.252 et seq.] the ExA takes the view that as indicated in relation to the SMP, and having regard to the details and explanation provided by the Applicant, that the HCDF, including the Adapted Design, would be positioned as landward as possible. In addition, the requirement 19 in the Order would provide a means whereby the design details of various aspects of the HCDF would require ESC approval in consultation with the MMO and the EA before commencement of that work. The ExA considers that this would provide an appropriate safeguard at detailed design stage in relation to matters relating to layout, scale and external appearance of the HCDF, and its integration with other marine infrastructure [ER 5.8.256]."

The defendant agreed (DL 4.293) (and see also DL 4.280, 4.284, 4.285 and DL 4.290).

170   DL 4.261 referred to the Fourth Addendum to the Environmental Statement (see [164] above) and additional modelling work carried out during the Examination. DL 4.266 referred to the suitability of the CPMMP to provide controls in the future for coastal defence. Certain extreme events are to be left to regulation by the ONR (DL 4.267).

171   The decision letter began to deal with radiological issues at DL 4.583 and in that context it returned to the subject of climate change, sea levels and the safe storage of fuel rods. The defendant summarised the views of the Panel at DL 4.589 to DL 4.597. At DL 4.598 the defendant agreed with the Panel's conclusions and referred to the further information on coastal defence modelling and the requirement for a nuclear site licence.

172   The claimant relied upon DL 4.590 which states:

"The issues of coastal defences, and the impact of climate change on the modelling for the safety of those defences, were considered by the ExA in section 5.8 and section 5.7 of the ExA Report respectively. The ExA considers [ER 5.20.101] that the coastal defences have been designed so they can be modified if it is necessary to do so, with the monitoring of the sea levels secured through the CPMMP, and this is further reinforced by the obligations required by the NSL regime regulated by the ONR and the permits regulated by the EA. The ExA is persuaded [ER 5.20.102] that the Applicant's conclusions are predicated on the basis that the site will be clear of nuclear material by 2140, the period which has been modelled for coastal defences, and under these circumstances the ExA consider the tests set out in paragraph 2.11.5 of NPS EN-6 would be met."

The claimant places a good deal of emphasis on the last sentence, and also upon DL 4.245. These paragraphs refer to an assumption that spent fuel will be removed from Sizewell C by 2140, which is also the year to which the modelling for predicted extreme sea levels runs.

173   The claimant complained that the defendant failed to give reasons addressing its reliance upon the ONR's email dated 7 August 2020. In my judgment he was under no legal obligation to do so. The limitations of that material produced in 2020 were obvious on the face of the document itself, without there being any need for the Panel or the defendant to spell that out by simply repeating them. The comments by the ONR related to the Hinkley Point C project in the absence of

information on Sizewell C. They were not of any real significance. Naturally the Panel and the defendant would focus on later material produced in 2022 which specifically related to the Sizewell C project (see e.g. [167] above). An application for a nuclear site licence for that scheme had yet to be submitted. SZC said to the Examination that the fuel store would be decommissioned by the 2140s, that is not necessarily by 2140 (DL 4.252). Although the ONR had estimated in 2020 that the GDF would be available by 2130, the claimant relies upon an alternative prediction, 2145, emanating from SZC. The Panel stated that it was reasonable to assume that storage would be available in a GDF in the long term, but added, not surprisingly, that there is a degree of uncertainty (PR 5.20.131), referring no doubt to timing.

174   It is obvious that the issue of how far into the next century spent fuel will need to remain at Sizewell C is subject to uncertainty. But that is not the only uncertainty about the future. The ONR, EA, SZC and others have addressed the possibility that climate change may cause sea levels to increase more quickly. Estimates about the availability of facilities and projections are having to be made an unusually long way into the future. On any fair reading of the Panel's Report and the decision letter, that uncertainty was recognised. I agree with counsel for the defendant and for SZC that what matters is how that subject was addressed.

175   The claimant's ground 6 is a classic example of a failure to read the decision letter fairly and as a whole. It is plain that in DL 4.590 the defendant also relied upon the adaptive nature of the design for the coastal defences, the monitoring of sea levels through the CPMMP and the controls which will be applied by the ONR and the EA through their respective regulatory regimes. That paragraph has to be read in the context of the many passages in the Panel's Report and in the decision letter where those matters were explained and relied upon. The suggestion by the claimant's counsel that the defendant did not rely upon those matters when addressing the future adequacy of coastal defences in relation to the storage of spent fuel is wholly untenable. The point was made clear in relation to the ONR and the nuclear site licence, for example in DL 4.365. The defendant relied, as he was entitled to do, upon the normal assumption that those other regulatory regimes will be operated properly. The defendant's reasoning cannot be treated as irrational or legally inadequate.

176   In addition, Requirement 19 of the development consent requires details of coastal defence features to be submitted and approved by the local planning authority, before construction of those works may commence, which must include a monitoring and adaptive sea defence plan that sets out periodic monitoring proposals and the trigger point for when the crest height of the sea defence would need to be increased to 16.9m above Ordnance Datum.

177   Accordingly, ground 6 must be rejected. In reaching that conclusion, I have not found it necessary to consider the application of s.31(2A) or (3C) and (3D) of the Senior Court Act 1981.

Ground 7

178   This ground is concerned with GHG emissions from the operation of Sizewell C. The claimant refers to DL 4.248 and DL 4.250 in which the defendant agreed with the Panel that "emissions of the magnitude demonstrated would not have a significant effect on the UK's ability to meet its carbon budget commitments or the ability of the Government to meet the UK's obligations under the Paris

Agreement". The claimant then says that that conclusion is inconsistent with this part of DL 8.9:

> "Operational emissions will be addressed in a managed, economy-wide manner, to ensure consistency with carbon budgets, net zero and our international climate commitments. The Secretary of State does not, therefore need to assess individual applications for planning consent against operational carbon emissions and their contribution to carbon budgets, net zero and our international climate commitments."

179　　The claimant submits firstly, that DL 8.9 should be read as meaning that the defendant has made no assessment of the contribution of *operational* GHG emissions to the carbon budgets and secondly, there was no evidential basis upon which he could conclude in DL 4.248 and DL 4.250 that operational emissions from Sizewell C would not have a significant effect on the UK's ability to meet its climate change obligations (skeleton paras. 106 to 110).

Discussion

180　　DL 8.9 appears in section 8 of the decision letter which is entitled "Other Matters". Under that heading DL 8.8 to DL 8.9 refer to the Climate Change Act 2008 and the Net Zero Target in broad terms. The context for the part of DL 8.9 which the claimant quotes is set by the opening two sentences to which it did not refer. Thus, the context is the continuing significance of the NPSs and the need for nuclear generation of the kind represented by Sizewell C in accordance with those policy statements.

181　　EN-1 states that carbon emissions from a new nuclear power station are likely to be much less than from a fossil fuelled plant (para. 3.5.5.). New nuclear power forms one of the three key elements of the Government's strategy for moving towards a decarbonised, diverse electricity sector by 2050, along with *inter alia* renewable electricity generation (para. 3.5.6 and see also para 3.5.10). I agree with the defendant and SZC that the part of DL 8.9 which the claimant seeks to criticise is entirely consistent with para 5.2.2 of EN-1 which states:

> "5.2.2. CO_2 emissions are a significant adverse impact from some types of energy infrastructure which cannot be totally avoided (even with full deployment of CCS technology). However, given the characteristics of these and other technologies, as noted in Part 3 of this NPS, and the range of non-planning policies aimed at decarbonising electricity generation such as EU ETS (see Section 2.2 above), Government has determined that CO_2 emissions are not reasons to prohibit the consenting of projects which use these technologies or to impose more restrictions on them in the planning policy framework than are set out in the energy NPSs (e.g. the CCR and, for coal, CCS requirements). Any ES on air emissions will include an assessment of CO_2 emissions, but the policies set out in Section 2, including the EU ETS, apply to these emissions. The IPC does not, therefore need to assess individual applications in terms of carbon emissions against carbon budgets and this section does not address CO_2 emissions or any Emissions Performance Standard that may apply to plant."

182   Section 4 of the decision letter is entitled "Matters considered by the ExA [the Panel] during the Examination." DL 4.232 to DL 4.250 dealt with climate change and resilience. Within that part DL 4.242 to DL 4.243 addressed GHG emissions and the carbon footprint. DL 4.244 to DL 4.250 summarised the Panel's overall conclusions on various climate change issues and stated that the defendant agreed with the Panel on those matters.

183   DL 4.242 and DL 4.248 referred back to the parts of the Panel's Report which summarised the quantitative analysis before the Examination, the responses of other parties to that material, and the Panel's conclusions at PR 5.7.56 to PR 5.7.100. That summary covered the quantitative analysis in the ES and in the subsequent Life Cycle Analysis carried out for SZC.

184   At PR 5.7.90 the Panel concluded:

> "The ExA concludes that the ES [APP-342], as updated by [AS-181, REP2-110], and [REP10-152], demonstrates that construction emissions from the Proposed Development would be less than 1% of the UK Government's carbon budget for the relevant period, and would not be significant in accordance with the criteria as described in Chapter 26 [APP-342]. The ExA is therefore content that those emissions would not materially affect the ability of the Government to meet the UK's obligations under the Paris Agreement. Similarly, the gross emissions associated with the operational phase have been found to be less than 1% of relevant periods in which they arise. The ExA also recognises the support provided by national policy for low carbon power generation projects such as the Proposed Development, and that the importance for the UK's carbon budgets should also be considered from the perspective of the carbon emissions that would otherwise be produced by other sources, if they were not generating. The national policy support for such low carbon generation projects has been considered in detail in section 5.19 of this Report."

That conclusion was then carried forward to PR 5.7.100. It is also relevant to note the reference here to the policy support for new nuclear power generation because of the contribution it makes to reducing GHGs that would otherwise be produced from other sources (as opposed to the "gross" emissions from a nuclear power station taken in isolation).

185   The defendant's decision letter accepted both PR 5.7.90 and PR 5.7.100. There was therefore ample quantitative material to support the conclusions of the Panel and, in turn, the Secretary of State. Mr. Wolfe KC relies once again upon a dictum in *R. (Association of Independent Meat Suppliers) v Food Standards Agency* [2019] P.T.S.R. 1443 at [8]. But for the reasons set out in *R. (Goesa Ltd) v Eastleigh BC* [2022] P.T.S.R. 1473 at [19] that passage does not alter the well-known *Wednesbury* principles applied by the Courts (see also *R. (Law Society) v Lord Chancellor* [2019] 1 W.L.R. 1649 at 98]).

186   The claimant then complains that there is no evidence that the defendant personally considered the quantitative assessment carried out for SZC, whether in the ES or the Life Cycle Assessment. This is yet another attempt to rely upon part of the judgment of Sedley LJ in *R. (National Association of Health Stores) v Secretary of State for Health* [2005] EWCA Civ 154 without reading the relevant passages as a whole. The High Court has analysed the principles in *R. (Transport Action Network Ltd) v Secretary of State for Transport* [2022] P.T.S.R. 31 at [60] to [73] and *R. (Save Stonehenge World Heritage Site Ltd) v Secretary of State for*

Transport [2020] P.T.S.R. 74 at [62] to [66] and [178]. A Minister is entitled to rely upon a summary prepared by his officials of the material which his department has received. The issue is therefore the narrower one of whether there are any grounds for criticising the legal adequacy of that summary in the context of ministerial decision-making. In my judgment the Secretary of State was not required himself to delve into the ES or the Life Cycle Assessment in the way the claimant suggests. The summary provided in the Panel's Report and in the draft decision letter, both of which were provided to the defendant for him to consider, were as, a matter of law, perfectly adequate.

187   Ground 7 is utterly hopeless and must be rejected.

Conclusions

188   The court is faced with a similar situation to that which arose in the Heathrow litigation where, having heard full submissions in a rolled-up hearing (in that case dealing with five different claims), it had to decide whether permission to apply for judicial review should be granted on each ground (*Spurrier* at [667]). In the present case as in *Spurrier*, the mere fact that the court has had to consider in a rolled-up hearing, and in a judgment, a substantial amount of material and legal submissions, does not mean that the grounds raised pass the threshold for arguability.

189   I consider that each of grounds 3 to 7 is totally without merit (CPR 23.12). Accordingly, permission must be refused in relation to those grounds.

190   In relation to grounds 1 and 2 I conclude that both are unarguable and permission should be refused.

191   The application for permission to apply for judicial review is dismissed.

C G FRY AND SON LTD v SECRETARY OF STATE FOR LEVELLING UP HOUSING AND COMMUNITIES

KING'S BENCH DIVISION (ADMINISTRATIVE COURT)

Sir Ross Cranston (sitting as a High Court Judge): 30 June 2023

[2023] EWHC 1622 (Admin); [2023] Env. L.R. 30

Assessment; Brexit; Drainage and sewerage management plans; Habitats; Planning conditions; Planning permission; Ramsar sites; Residential development; Retained EU legislation; Somerset; Water pollution

H1 *Nature conservation—appropriate assessment—planning permission—application to discharge conditions—multi-stage consent—Conservation of Habitats and Species Regulations 2017—Habitats Directive 92/43—Ramsar sites—nutrient neutrality—phosphate loading—housing development—whether appropriate assessment required when considering application to discharge planning conditions*

H2 The claimant (CGF) obtained outline planning permission in 2015 from the Second Defendant (SC) for a phased, 650 home mixed-use development in Somerset, subject to conditions including a condition relating to a site-wide drainage strategy. In 2020, following completion of Phases 1 and 2, CGF obtained reserved matters approval for 190 homes in Phase 3, subject to pre-commencement conditions on matters including tree protection zones and surface water drainage. In 2021, CGF, sought to discharge those pre-commencement conditions. SC refused the application, on the basis that an appropriate assessment (AA) was needed concerning phosphate loading impacts on the nearby Somerset Levels and Moors Ramsar wetland site. On appeal, a Planning Inspector determined that an AA was required under the Conservation of Habitats and Species Regulations 2017 reg.63 (the 2017 Regulations), before final consent to implement the project.

H3 CGF sought to challenge the Planning Inspector's decision, arguing that an AA was only required at the planning permission stage; that the specific conditions related to matters that were incapable of being affected by phosphate loading impacts on the relevant Ramsar sits; and that any AA should be limited to the scope of the particular conditions.

H4 **Held,** in refusing the application:

H5 (1) Article 6(3) of Directive 92/43 (Habitats Directive) required a project should not be agreed until an AA had been undertaken. Under the European Union (Withdrawal) Act 2018 s.4(2)(b) that requirement continued to have affect in UK law following Brexit as the requirement had been accepted as previous rulings of the European Court of Justice proceedings prior to Brexit. A planning consent was part of agreeing a project when it was necessary to implement a development. In the current case, the discharge of pre-commencement conditions was a necessary step in the implementation of the development. An AA had not been undertaken and the inspector had determined that the conditions could not be discharged in the absence of an AA. This conclusion was consistent with art.6(3).

H6 (2) The 2017 Regulations demanded a purposive interpretation so that the appropriate assessment provisions of reg.63 applied to a subsequent consent stage including reserved matters applications and the discharge of conditions. A broad and purposive interpretation flowed from a strict precautionary approach taken by the European Court of Justice in applying the AA provisions of the Habitats Directive. This enabled reg.70 of the 2017 Regulations to be read in light of reg.63, so that a competent authority must conduct an AA before any consent, permission or other authorisation was given for a project. In a multi-stage consent process, there was no agreement until reserved matters were granted or conditions discharged. Previous case law suggested that an AA could apply at the reserved matters or discharge of conditions stage even if there had been a grant of outline planning permission where the subsequent approval was the implementing decision.

H7 (3) Regulation 63 required an AA to consider the implications of the whole project, not the implications of the part of the project to which the consent related. The subject matter of the AA was what would be permitted by the consent, so that where the decision was the final stage in granting consent for a development, the whole development fell to be assessed.

H8 **Cases referred to:**

Aberdeen City and Shire Strategic Development Planning Authority v Elsick Development Co Ltd [2017] UKSC 66; [2017] P.T.S.R. 1413; [2018] 1 P. & C.R. 14

Commission of the European Communities v United Kingdom (C-508/03) EU:C:2006:287; [2006] 3 W.L.R. 492; [2007] Env. L.R. 1

Cooperatie Mobilisation for the Environment UA v College van Gedeputeerde (C-293/17) EU:C:2018:882; [2019] Env. L.R. 27

Dansk Industri (DI) v Rasmussen's Estate (C-441/14) EU:C:2016:278; [2016] 3 C.M.L.R. 27; [2016] Pens. L.R. 299

Friends of the Irish Environment Ltd v An Bord Pleanala (C-254/19) EU:C:2020:680; [2021] Env. L.R. 16

Harris v Environment Agency [2022] EWHC 2264 (Admin); [2022] P.T.S.R. 1751; [2023] Env. L.R. 10

Holohan v An Bord Pleanala (C-461/17) EU:C:2018:883; [2019] P.T.S.R. 1054; [2019] Env. L.R. 16

Inter-Environnement Wallonie ASBL v Conseil des Ministres (C-411/17) EU:C:2019:622; [2020] Env. L.R. 9

Landelijke Vereniging tot Behoud van de Waddenzee v Staatssecretaris van Landbouw, Natuurbeheer en Visserij (C-127/02) EU:C:2004:482; [2005] 2 C.M.L.R. 31; [2005] Env. L.R. 14

People Over Wind v Coillte Teoranta (C-323/17) EU:C:2018:244; [2018] P.T.S.R. 1668; [2018] Env. L.R. 31

Proberun Ltd v Secretary of State for the Environment (1991) 61 P. & C.R. 77; [1990] 3 P.L.R. 79; [1991] J.P.L. 159 CA (Civ Div)

R. (on the application of Barker) v Bromley LBC [2006] UKHL 52; [2007] 1 A.C. 470; [2007] Env. L.R. 20

R. (on the application of Fulford Parish Council) v York City Council [2019]
EWCA Civ 1359; [2020] P.T.S.R. 152; [2020] 1 P. & C.R. 3
R. (on the application of Harvey) v Mendip DC [2017] EWCA Civ 1784; [2018]
J.P.L. 419
R. (on the application of Noble Organisation Ltd) v Thanet DC [2005] EWCA Civ
782; [2006] Env. L.R. 8; [2006] 1 P. & C.R. 13
R. (on the application of Swire) v Canterbury City Council [2022] EWHC 390
(Admin); [2022] J.P.L. 1026
R. (on the application of Wingfield) v Canterbury City Council [2019] EWHC 1974
(Admin)
R. (on the application of Wingfield) v Canterbury City Council [2020] EWCA Civ
1588; [2021] 1 W.L.R. 2863; [2021] J.P.L. 885
R. (on the application of Wyatt) v Fareham BC [2022] EWCA Civ 983; [2023]
Env. L.R. 14; [2022] J.P.L. 1509

H9 **Legislation referred to:**
European Communities Act 1972 s.2
Wildlife and Countryside Act 1981 (c.69)
Town and Country Planning Act 1990 ss.97, 107 and 288
Directive 92/43 (Habitats) art.6(2)(3)
Conservation (Natural Habitats, & c.) Regulations 1994 (SI 1994/2716)
Directive 2011/92 (Environmental Impact Assessment)
Conservation of Habitats and Species Regulations 2017 (SI 2017/1012) regs 3A,
8, 9, 62(1), 63(1)(5)(7), 64, 70(1)–(3) and 86(1)
European Union (Withdrawal) Act 2018 ss.2(1), 4(2), 5(2), 6(3)(7), 9(3) and Sch.1

H10 *C. Banner KC* and *A. Bowes*, instructed by Clarke Willmott LLP, appeared on
behalf of the claimant.
R. Moules and *N. Grant*, instructed by the Government Legal Department, appeared
on behalf of the first defendant.
L. Wilcox, instructed by Somerset Council, In-house Solicitor, appeared on behalf
of the second defendant.

JUDGMENT

SIR ROSS CRANSTON:

Introduction

1   This case concerns potential adverse effects on the Somerset Levels and Moors
Ramsar Site from the claimant's proposed housing-led development on land east
of Wellington, Somerset.

2   The claim arises in the context of the issue of nutrient neutrality. In broad terms,
this issue relates to the phosphate loading of protected water habitats, leading to
eutrophication. This is caused by reasons including agricultural practices and
under-investment in water infrastructure. There is a risk of the problem being
exacerbated by water generated by new developments which contain phosphates,
principally from foul water. The Home Builders Federation states that, due to the

unavailability of mitigation options, this issue is holding up the building of no fewer than 44,000 homes in England which already have planning permission.

3   In the present case the Somerset Council ("the Council"), and then on appeal the Secretary of State's Inspector, refused to discharge certain conditions attached to the planning permission which the Council (or at least its predecessor) had earlier granted the claimant developer. That was because there had not been an appropriate assessment under the Habitats Regulations 2017 (the Conservation of Habitats and Species Regulations 2017, SI 2017/1012, as amended). Consequently, certain pre-commencement conditions have not been discharged, and phase 3 of the development has not been able to proceed.

4   The claimant therefore launched this claim for statutory review under section 288 of Town and Country Planning Act 1990 ("the 1990 Act"), challenging the Inspector's decision. As a matter of law the challenge raises issues about the scope and application following the UK's withdrawal from the European Union of the Habitats Regulations 2017 and the Habitats Directive on which it was based. It is on legal grounds that the case was argued and must be decided. It is for others to resolve the significant public policy issues underlying this claim, raised by the Home Builders Federation and the Ministerial Statement, both outlined later in the judgment.

Background

Planning permission

5   In December 2015 the Council granted outline planning permission for a mixed-use development of up to 650 houses, community and commercial uses, a primary school and associated infrastructure. Planning permission was subject to several conditions including condition 4 (requiring the submission of a site-wide surface water drainage strategy) and condition 7 (requiring the submission of a foul water drainage scheme). Condition 4 was discharged about a year later.

6   Pursuant to the planning permission the development was to take place in eight phases. Phases 1 and 2 were commenced under separate reserved matters approvals. In June 2020, the claimant obtained reserved matters approval for phase 3, relating to 190 dwellings, which was subject to a number of conditions including: (1) condition 3: tree protection measures (a pre-commencement condition); (2) condition 4: surface water drainage (a pre-commencement condition); (3) condition 5: a construction environment management plan (a pre-commencement condition); (4) condition 6: external works (a pre-construction condition); (5) condition 7: cycle and footpath network connection details (a pre-occupation condition); and (6) condition 10: materials (pre-construction of any development above damp proof course level).

Natural England advice note, 2020

7   In August 2020 Natural England published their advice note to Somerset's local authorities (including the Council's predecessors) on development in relation to the Somerset Levels and Moors Ramsar Site ("the Natural England advice note"). The advice note referred to the judgment of the Court of Justice of the European Union in Case *Cooperatie Mobilisation for the Environment and Vereniging Leefmilieu v College van gedeputeerde staten Van Limberg* (C-293/17) and

(C-294/17) [2019] Env. L.R. 27 (the *"Dutch Nitrogen case"*). In the wake of that case, the advice note read, greater scrutiny was required of plans and projects that will result in increased nutrient loads which may have an effect on Special Protection Areas ("SPAs"), Special Areas of Conservation ("SACs"), and sites designated under the Ramsar Convention. SPAs and SACs are sites designated under the Habitats Regulations 2017. Ramsar sites are not but, as a matter of national planning policy in the National Planning Policy Framework ("NPPF"), they are afforded the same protection as if they were.

8   While Natural England was satisfied that the effects of additional nutrients on the Somerset Levels and Moors SPA could be screened out and so not require appropriate assessment under the Habitats Regulations 2017, the Somerset Levels and Moors Ramsar site had been designated for different natural features:

> "…the interest features of the Somerset Levels and Moors Ramsar Site are considered unfavourable, or at risk, from the effects of eutrophication caused by excessive phosphates. Further, although improvements to the Sewage Treatment Works, along with more minor measures to tackle agricultural pollution have been secured, these will not reduce phosphate levels sufficiently to restore the condition of the Ramsar Site features. The scope for permitting further development that would add additional phosphate either directly or indirectly to the site, and thus erode the improvements secured, is necessarily limited."

9   Accordingly, Natural England advised that competent authorities (which included the Council) should undertake an appropriate assessment under the Habitats Regulations 2017 of the implications of a plan or project, and only grant consent to the extent that the assessment allows the competent authorities to ascertain the development "will not have an adverse effect on the integrity of the site". As to the development types affected, the advice note stated in relation to additional residential units and commercial development:

> "Additional residential units within the catchment are likely add phosphate to the designated site via the waste water treatment effluent, thus contributing to the existing unfavourable condition and further preventing the site in achieving its conservation objectives. Natural England therefore advises that your authority carry out an appropriate assessment of planning applications that will result in a net increase in population served by a wastewater system, including new homes, student and tourist accommodation."

Inspector's decision

10   In June 2021 the claimant sought discharge of conditions 3, 4, 5, 6, 7 and 10 of the reserved matters approval. These conditions required the submission and approval of specific matters that did not go to the principle of the development. The Council withheld approval on the basis that an appropriate assessment under the Habitats Regulations 2017 was required before the conditions could be discharged.

11   In April 2022 the claimant appealed to the Secretary of State and an Inspector was appointed. Before the Inspector the claimant contended that no appropriate assessment under the Habitat's Regulations 2017 was required at the stage of

discharge of conditions on reserved matters or, if it was, it should be confined to the scope of what was for consideration in relation to the discharge of the conditions in question.

12   The Council resisted the appeal on the basis that, in line with the Natural England advice note, it was necessary for an appropriate assessment to be undertaken to determine the effect of additional nutrients on the Somerset Levels and Moors Ramsar site. It also submitted a shadow appropriate assessment, dated July 2022. This stated that the proposed development might have a negative effect on the qualifying features of the Ramsar site through the increase in nutrients, especially phosphorous. No mitigation was proposed so it could not be concluded that the project would not adversely affect the integrity of the Ramsar site.

13   The Inspector dismissed the claimant's appeal. He determined that it was legitimate to apply paragraph 181 of the NPPF to give the Ramsar site the same protection in all respects as a European site under the Habitats Regulations 2017. That was because the discharge of the conditions would be an authorising act, as part of the wider consent process, that would allow the realisation of potential effects on the Ramsar site which the Natural England advice note sought to manage. Considering the overarching nature of paragraph 181, this applied regardless of the specific subject matter of the conditions themselves: DL24-26. The Inspector considered that the grant of outline planning permission and reserved matters approval did not have an effect on the scope of any necessary appropriate assessment; the validity of the planning permission was not in question: DL41.

14   The inspector then determined that the requirement for an appropriate assessment in the Habitats Regulations 2017 applied to the discharge of conditions stage. He rejected the claimant's argument that inclusion of specific provisions relating to the grant of planning permission, including outline planning permission, at regulation 70 of the Habitats Regulations 2017, did not diminish the applicability of regulation 63, which was simply a sweep up provision: DL44. Even adopting the claimant's approach that the permission in relation to "consent, permission or other authorisation" in regulation 63 is the planning permission referred to in regulation 70, the concept of "other authorisation" was a broad one. The claimant's approach would create loopholes counter to a purposive approach to the Habitats Regulations 2017: DL45-47.

15   As the competent authority, the Inspector said, he was unable to carry out the necessary appropriate assessment to agree the conditions: DL71. He said that he had considered the other relevant planning considerations, in particular the impact on housing delivery: DL72, 74. However, the unfulfilled requirement for an appropriate assessment was an issue of material significance: DL77. In other words he conducted the balancing exercise and concluded that in this case the delay in housing delivery was outweighed by the need to protect the Ramsar site.

Secretary of State statement, July 2022

16   In July 2022 the Secretary of State for Environment Food and Rural Affairs issued a Written Ministerial Statement about tackling nutrient pollution and improving water quality. Part of that was to impose a statutory duty on water and sewerage companies to upgrade wastewater treatment works to the highest technically achievable limits by 2030 in nutrient neutrality areas. The impact of

new housing was a small proportion of overall nutrient pollution, the statement said, but mitigation requirements had a significant impact on overall house building.

17   The statement added that the government understood the concerns that some local planning authorities had around the impact of nutrient neutrality on their ability to demonstrate they have a sufficient and deliverable housing land supply. While it would be disappointing to developers whose sites were affected, the statement added, the government's position was that:

> "The Habitats Regulations Assessment provisions apply to any consent, permission, or other authorisation, this may include post-permission approvals, reserved matters or discharges of conditions. It may be that Habitats Regulation Assessment is required in situations including but not limited to where the environmental circumstances have materially changed as a matter of fact and degree (including where nutrient load or the conservation status of habitat site is now unfavourable) so that development that previously was lawfully screened out at the permission stage cannot now be screened out…"

Statement by Home Builders Federation, April 2023

18   James Stevens, Director for Cities at the Home Builders Federation, prepared a statement for the court about the claimant's development. He explains how, following Natural England's advice note, the issue of nutrient neutrality has become a serious obstacle for house building in England. It was delaying an estimated 120,000 homes across the 27 catchments currently affected in England, with some 40 percent having already secured (as in this case) outline or full planning permission.

19   Mr Stevens states that the availability of nature-based solutions, the government's favoured mitigation, is extremely sparse. Three of the four Somerset local authorities were opposed to market schemes (buying credits), even if available. Solutions were unlikely to release many of the 18, 234 homes delayed in Somerset. SME house building companies were especially exposed to the issue of nutrient neutrality on their developments.

Legal Framework

Habitats Directive, article 6(3)

20   The Habitats Regulations 2017 transpose the requirements of Council Directive 92/43/EEC of 21st May 1992 on the Conservation of Natural Habitats and of Wild Flora and Fauna (the "Habitats Directive"). The directive was first implemented in UK law by the Conservation (Natural Habitats, & c.) Regulations 1994, SI 1994/2716.

21   Articles 6(2) and 6(3) of the Habitats Directive provide:

> "2. Member States shall take appropriate steps to avoid, in the special areas of conservation, the deterioration of natural habitats and the habitats of species as well as disturbance of the species …
>
> 3. Any plan or project not directly connected with or necessary to the management of the site but likely to have a significant effect thereon, either individually or in combination with other plans or projects, shall

be subject to appropriate assessment of its implications for the site in view of the site's conservation objectives. In the light of the conclusions of the assessment of the implications for the site and subject to the provisions of paragraph 4 [overriding public interest cases], the competent national authorities shall agree to the plan or project only after having ascertained that it will not adversely affect the integrity of the site concerned and, if appropriate, after having obtained the opinion of the general public."

22   The European jurisprudence establishes, first, as with any EU Directive, these provisions could be relied upon directly in the English courts when the UK was a member of the EU to trump domestic law (including the 1990 Act). An EU Directive could also be relied upon directly where it was claimed that the wording of the Habitats Regulations 2017 was too narrow or fell short of achieving all that it required.

23   Secondly, the CJEU adopted a strict precautionary approach to the assessment provisions of the Habitats Directive, so that "competent national authorities are to authorise an activity on the protected site only if they have made certain that it will not adversely affect the integrity of that site": Case *Holohan v An Bord Pleanala* (C-461/17) [2019] P.T.S.R. 1054, [33]. As Sir Keith Lindblom SPT explained in *R. (on the application of Wyatt) v Fareham BC* [2022] EWCA Civ 983, article 6(3) embodies the precautionary principle "and makes it possible effectively to prevent adverse effects on the integrity of protected sites as a result of the plans or projects being considered", citing paragraph 58 of Case *Landelijke Vereniging tot Behoud van de Waddenzee v Staatssecretaris Van Landbouw, Natuurbeheer en Visserij* (C-127/02) [2005] 2 C.M.L.R. 31 ("*Waddenzee*"): [9(6)].

24   Thirdly, as the CJEU held in the Dutch Nitrogen Case, the appropriate assessment required in the first sentence of article 6(3) not only has to identify "all the aspects of the plan or project which can, either individually or in combination with other plans or projects, affect the conservation objectives of that site", [95], but it also "cannot have lacunae and must contain complete, precise and definitive findings and conclusions capable of removing all reasonable scientific doubt as to the effects of the plans or the projects proposed on the protected site concerned..." [98].

25   Fourthly, the concept of "agree[ing]" in the second sentence of article 6(3) has a broad import so that plans or projects should only be allowed to proceed if the adverse effects have been considered. That follows from CJEU decisions holding that the definition of "development consent" in article 1(2)(c) of the EIA Directive (Directive 2011/92/EU on the assessment of the effects of certain public and private projects on the environment) is relevant to the meaning of the expression "agree" in article 6(3) of the Habitats Directive: Case *Friends of the Irish Environment Ltd v An Bord Pleanala* (C-254/19) [2021] Env. L.R. 16, [42] and *Inter-Environnement Wallonie ASBL v Conseil des Ministres* (C-411/17) [2020] Env. L.R. 9, [142]-[143]. Although these decisions were based on particular facts, there is no suggestion that the CJEU was limiting the general statement of principle which they enunciate.

EU law and the Withdrawal Act 2018

26   In repealing the European Communities Act 1972, the European Union (Withdrawal) Act 2018 ("the Withdrawal Act 2018") provided in general terms

for the application of the same rules and laws on the day after Brexit as on the day before.

27   Section 2(1) provides that, subject to section 5 and schedule 1, EU-derived domestic legislation, as it had effect in domestic law immediately before the implementation period ("IP") completion day (31 December 2020), continues to have effect in domestic law on and after that day. The Habitats Regulations 2017 fall under section 2(1).

28   Section 4 of the Withdrawal Act 2018 provides:

> 4.   (1) Any rights, powers, liabilities, obligations, restrictions, remedies and procedures which, immediately before IP completion day—
>
>> (a) are recognised and available in domestic law by virtue of section 2(1) of the European Communities Act 1972, and
>> (b) are enforced, allowed and followed accordingly,
>> continue on and after IP completion day to be recognised and available in domestic law (and to be enforced, allowed and followed accordingly).
>
> (2) Subsection (1) does not apply to any rights, powers, liabilities, obligations, restrictions, remedies or procedures so far as they…
>
>> (b) arise under an EU directive… and are not of a kind recognised by the European Court or any court or tribunal in the United Kingdom in a case decided before IP completion day (whether or not as an essential part of the decision in the case).

29   Section 5(2) provides for the principle of the supremacy of EU law to continue to apply on or after IP completion day so far as relevant to the interpretation, disapplication or quashing of any enactment or rule of law passed or made before. The continued application of EU principles in interpreting retained domestic and EU case law is addressed in section 6(3). Section 6(7) defines retained general principles of EU law as "the general principles of EU law, as they have effect in EU law immediately before IP completion day", subject to the provisions set out in that section. In combination sections 6(3) and 6(7) in relation to retained case law preserve the effect of the pre-Brexit case-law of the CJEU in relation to the interpretation of EU law.

Habitats Regulations 2017

30   The Habitats Regulations 2017 continue in English law under section 2(1) of the Withdrawal Act 2018 as EU-derived domestic legislation.

31   The Habitats Regulations 2017 provide that the Habitats Directive is to be construed for the purposes of the regulations as if references to a Member State included a reference to the United Kingdom: reg 3A. The regulations concern the effect on a European site, which as defined in regulation 8 does not include a Ramsar site.

32   Regulation 9(1) provides that the Secretary of State, the nature conservation bodies and a competent authority in relation to the marine area must exercise their functions which are relevant to nature conservation, including marine conservation, so as to secure compliance with the requirements of the directives (the Habitats

Directive and the new Wild Birds Directive). As regards competent authorities, regulation 9(3) provides:

9(3) "Without prejudice to the preceding provisions, a competent authority, in exercising any of its functions, must have regard to the requirements of the Directives so far as they may be affected by the exercise of those functions."

33   In *Harris v Environment Agency* [2022] EWHC 2264 (Admin) Johnson J held that given its context "have regard to" in section 9(3) meant that the competent authority had to discharge those requirements or be in a position to justify departure from them [87].

34   Part 6 of the Regulations, "Assessments of plans and projects", contains in chapter 1 general provisions. Regulation 62(1) refers to the application of the provisions of chapter 1. It provides that the requirements of the assessment provisions in regulation 63 and 64 apply:

"(a) subject to and in accordance with the provisions of Chapters 2 to 7, in relation to the matters specified in those provisions; and
 (b) subject to regulation 63(7)(c), in relation to all other plans and projects not relating to matters specified in Chapters 2 to 9."

35   Regulation 63 is concerned with the assessment, inter alia, of the implications for European sites. As far as relevant it reads:

63(1) "A competent authority, before deciding to undertake, or give any consent, permission or other authorisation for, a plan or project which—

(a) is likely to have a significant effect on a European site…

(5) In the light of the conclusions of the assessment, and subject to regulation 64, the competent authority may agree to the plan or project only after having ascertained that it will not adversely affect the integrity of the European site…

(6) In considering whether a plan or project will adversely affect the integrity of the site, the competent authority must have regard to the manner in which it is proposed to be carried out or to any conditions or restrictions subject to which it proposes that the consent, permission or other authorisation should be given."

36   Parts 2 to 7 of part 6 of the regulations, referred to in regulation 62(1), cover a range of matters - planning permission (part 2), highways and roads (part 3), electricity (part 4), pipelines (part 5), transport and work (part 6), and environmental controls (part 7).

37   Part 2 of the regulations begins with regulation 70. That regulation makes provision for assessment prior to the grant of planning permission:

70(1) The assessment provisions apply in relation to—

(a) granting planning permission on an application under Part 3 of the TCPA 1990 (control over development); …
(c) granting planning permission, or upholding a decision of the local planning authority to grant planning permission (whether or not subject to the same conditions and limitations as those imposed by the local planning authority), on determining an appeal under section

78 of that Act (right to appeal against planning decisions) in respect of such an application…

38   By regulation 70(2), where the assessment provisions apply the competent authority may grant conditional permission if it considers that the conditions would avoid any adverse effects on a European site. Regulation 70(3) adds that where the assessment provisions apply, outline planning permission must not be granted unless the competent authority is satisfied that no development likely adversely to affect the integrity of a European site could be carried out under the permission, whether before or after obtaining approval of any reserved matters.

39   The import of regulation 63 of the Habitats Regulations 2017 was considered in *R. (on the application of Wingfield) v Canterbury City Council* [2019] EWHC 1974 (Admin). There a local resident challenged the local planning authority's decision to grant approval for reserved matters relating to a mixed-use development. Outline planning permission had been granted without a habitats assessment. There were mitigation measures in the environmental statement which included a "Report to inform a Habitats Regulations Assessment". After the permission had been granted, the CJEU held in *People Over Wind v Coillte Teoranta* (C-323/17) [2018] P.T.S.R. 1668 that mitigation measures were not to be taken into account at the screening stage. In light of that decision the local authority decided to carry out an appropriate assessment under regulation 63, which the developer supported. It was satisfactory so the local authority granted approval of the reserved matters. Lang J held that an appropriate assessment under regulation 63 could be carried out at the reserved matters stage, drawing on cases relating to environment impact assessments (EIA). These established that where the need for an EIA assessment had been overlooked at the outline planning stage it should be carried out at the reserved matters stage.

40   *R. (on the application of Barker) v Bromley LBC* [2006] UKHL 52 was one of these EIA cases. There the Town and Country Planning (Environmental Impact Assessment) Regulations 1988 referred only to decisions to grant planning permission, but Lord Hope held that the case for assessment might become apparent at the reserved matters stage or where further consideration was necessary due to a material change of circumstances: [5]. By failing to provide for these situations, the House of Lords held, the EIA Regulations 1988 failed to implement fully the Environmental Impact Assessment (EIA) Directive 2011/92/EU because the relevant development consent might be regarded as multi-staged. Lord Hope said that the competent authority may be obliged in some circumstances to carry out an EIA even after outline planning permission has been granted, because:

> "24   …it is not possible to eliminate entirely the possibility that it will not become apparent until a later stage in the multi-stage consent process that the project is likely to have significant effects on the environment. In that event account will have to be taken of all the aspects of the project which have not yet been assessed or which have been identified for the first time as requiring an assessment. This may be because the need for an EIA was overlooked at the outline stage…"

41   Lang J applied the principle in Barker that it might be said that the need for an appropriate assessment under the Habitats Directive was "overlooked" at outline permission stage in the case before her because of the change in the law brought

about by the CJEU judgment in People Over Wind: [70]. Thus, she held, the Council could lawfully conduct an appropriate assessment at the reserved matters stage: [71]. After quoting article 6(3) of the Habitats Directive, she added:

> "74　…The relevant date is 'the date of adoption of the decision authorising implementation of the project': see *Commission v Germany* [2017] EUECJ (C-142/16) at [42]. In a 'multi-stage consent', there is no 'agreement to the … project' until reserved matters consent has been granted; indeed the CJEU described the reserved matters approval as 'the implementing decision' in *Wells* at [52] and *Commission v UK* [2006] Q.B. 764 at [101], [104]. By regulations 63(1) and 63(5), reserved matters consent cannot be granted unless it has been established that the integrity of the European site will not be adversely affected. So an [habitats assessment] was required."

42　In *R. (Swire) v Canterbury City Council* [2022] EWHC 390 (Admin), one ground of challenge was that the local authority's decision to approve the masterplan under condition 8 of the outline planning permission was unlawful because there was a failure to comply with requirements for environmental impact and habitat assessments. Holgate J held that the ground failed because it was not irrational for the planning officer to conclude that sufficient information on environmental impact and habitats assessments had been provided in respect of condition 8. In the course of his reasoning, Holgate J said this:

> "94. In *R. (Wingfield) v Canterbury City Council* [2019] EWHC 1974 (Admin) it was held at [72]-[77] that for the purposes of the Habitats Regulations, there is no decision authorising the implementation of the project in the case of a multi-stage consent until reserved matters are approved. Reserved matters approval is the 'implementing decision'. Unlike the EIA Regulations, there is no legislative objective requiring HRA to be carried out at the earliest possible stage. Accordingly, HRA may lawfully be completed at the reserved matters stage, even if not carried out prior to the grant of outline permission. The various attempts by the claimant in Wingfield to challenge the decision by Lang J were rejected by the Court of Appeal (as recorded in [2021] 1 W.L.R. 2863)."

NPPF, paragraph 181 and Ramsar sites

43　Ramsar sites are notified to local planning authorities under section 37A of the Wildlife and Countryside Act 1981, pursuant to the UK's obligations under the Convention on Wetlands of International Importance especially as Waterfowl Habitat. They are not covered by the Habitats Regulations 2017.

44　Paragraph 181 of the NPPF states:

> "181.　The following shall be given the same protection as habitats sites: (a) Potential Special Protection Areas and possible Special Areas of Conservation; (b) Listed or proposed Ramsar sites; and (c) Sites identified, or required, as compensatory measures for adverse effects on habitats, potential Special Protection Areas, possible Special Areas of Conservation, and listed or proposed Ramsar sites."

Grounds of Challenge

45   The claimant's case in general terms is that the effect of additional phosphate loading resulting from its proposed development was not a material consideration to the determination of the conditions at issue in the case. It was legally irrelevant because it fell outside the specific parameters of what the outline planning permission and the reserved matters approval had left over for consideration under these conditions. The material for the discharge of these conditions was satisfactory, and the only thing preventing their discharge was whether an appropriate assessment of the impact of phase 3 of the development on the Ramsar site from additional phosphate loading was required. There was no nexus between the conditions in relation to phosphates, even with the condition relating to waste water. Nor, on the claimant's case, does the combination the Habitats Regulations 2017 and paragraph 181 of NPPF change that. The Inspector was wrong in his analysis and conclusions.

Ground 1: Inspector misconstrued Habitats Regulations 2017

46   In broad terms ground 1 is firstly, that the Inspector wrongly construed the Habitats Regulations 2017 and should not have applied regulation 63, as he did, to the discharge of conditions on a reserved matters approval. Mr Banner KC contended that regulation 70 was the relevant provision, and it is confined to planning (including outline planning) permission. The grant of approval of reserved matters (as in this case) is not a planning permission: *R. (Fulford Parish Council) v City of York Council* [2019] EWCA Civ 2109, [22], per Lewison LJ. Secondly, Mr Banner submitted, there is no legal basis to produce a result contrary to the plain interpretation of the regulations. EU law could not be used to produce a *contra legem* interpretation (citing Case *Dansk Industri (DI), acting on behalf of Ajos A/S v Estate of Karsten Eigil Rasmussen,* (C-441/14) [2016] 3 C.M.L.R. 27, [AG68], [32]). Domestic law had no purchase on this aspect of the case.

47   In my view Mr Banner is correct that on the face of it the assessment provisions of regulation are confined in their application to the planning permission stage and do not extend to the discharge of conditions. The regulations are explicit on the application of regulation 63. Under regulation 62(1)(a), regulation 63 is "subject to and in accordance with the provisions of Chapters 2 to 7", and that language means that regulation 63 is subject to and in accordance with part 2, which includes regulation 70(1). The words of regulation 70(1) confine its remit to planning permission, which as a result of regulation 70(3) includes outline planning permission. On its face regulation 70 does not encompass reserved matters or the discharge of conditions as in this case. The language of regulation 62(1)(b) - "all other plans and projects" – does not take the matter further. The claimant's development is a "planning project" - a chapter 2 planning project under 62(1)(a) - but it is the same project as it was at the time planning permission was granted, not an "other project" as in regulation 62(1)(b).

48   While on a strict reading of the Habitats Regulations 2017 the assessment provisions of regulation 63 do not cover the discharge of conditions, in my view they do apply as a result of firstly, article 6(3) of the Habitats Directive, secondly, a purposive interpretation of their provisions and thirdly, case law binding on me.

Habitats Directive, article 6(3)

49   As we saw, article 6(3) of the Habitats Directive requires that an appropriate assessment should be undertaken before a project is agreed to. In *Harris v Environment Agency* [2022] EWHC 2264 (Admin) Johnson J applied section 4 of the Withdrawal Act 2018 and held that the Environment Agency had breached article 6(2) of the Habitats Directive by limiting its investigation into the impact of water abstraction licences to only three SSSIs in a special area of conservation (SAC) on the Norfolk Broads. Johnson J held that article 6(2) continued to have direct effect in domestic law because its obligations had been recognised in cases decided prior to Brexit such as Waddenzee: [90], [94].

50   Mr Banner contended that the Habitats Directive had no status in the UK legal system, except through regulation 9(3) of the Habitats Regulations 2017. The provisions of the European Union (Withdrawal) Act 2018 do not take the argument any further, he submitted, because there is no CJEU pre-existing case law which interprets the Habitats Directive as imposing a requirement to conduct an appropriate assessment at subsequent stages, such as the discharge of conditions on a reserved matters approval. He submitted that Harris concerned whether the claimed obligation under article 6(2) had been recognised by the court before Brexit, and it had. By contrast there is no CJEU or domestic case preceding exit day which supports the view that article 6(3) of the Habitats Directive can be relied upon to impose a requirement for an appropriate assessment at the discharge of conditions stage. Unlike Harris section 4(2)(b) of the Withdrawal Act 2018 is not engaged in this case given the absence of relevant pre-exit case-law.

51   In my view article 6(3) of the Habitats Directive continues to have effect in domestic law as a result of section 4(2)(b). Johnson J explained in Harris that the requirements of article 6(3) were accepted as binding by the CJEU in Waddenzee: [90]. Articles 6(2) and 6(3) of the Habitats Directive are closely related, so as to be "of a kind" with one another for the purposes of section 4: [91]. The demands of section 4(2)(b) are therefore met. The section is explicit that the recognition in the case law does not have to be by way of the *ratio* of a case "(whether or not as an essential part of the decision in the case)".

52   Consequently, the requirements of article 6(3) of the Habitats Directive remain part of UK law. That article requires that the competent authorities should not agree a project until an appropriate assessment has been undertaken and it shows that it will not adversely affect the integrity of a site. A planning consent is part of agreeing a project when it is necessary to implement a development. In this case the discharge of pre-commencement conditions was a necessary step in the implementation of the development. An appropriate assessment had not been undertaken up to that point, so consequently the Inspector determined that he could not discharge the conditions prior to one being undertaken. His conclusion was consistent with article 6(3) of the Habitats Directive.

Purposive interpretation

53   Secondly, the Habitats Regulations 2017 demand a purposive interpretation so that the appropriate assessment provisions of regulation 63 apply to a subsequent consent stage including reserved matters applications and the discharge of conditions. A broad and purposive interpretation of the regulations flows from the strict precautionary approach which the CJEU has adopted to the assessment

provisions of the Habitats Directive, as explained in the passage quoted earlier from Sir Keith Lindblom SPT's judgment in *R. (on the application of Wyatt) v Fareham BC* [2022] EWCA Civ 983. The CJEU has adopted the purposive approach in other cases as well such as Case *People Over Wind v Coillte Teoranta* (C-323/17) [2018] Env. L.R. 31, [37]. As Lang J observed in the Wingfield case [2019] EWHC 1974 (Admin), "the HRA regime is focused on ensuring the avoidance of harm to the integrity of protected sites": [72].

54   Mr Banner accepted that the precautionary principle is well-established in EU law and applies to the interpretation of the Habitats Directive. However, he submitted that regulation 70(3) of the Habitats Regulations 2017 already embraces the precautionary principle by requiring an assessment at the outline stage to consider the effect on any European site "whether before or after obtaining approval of any reserved matters." Regulation 70(3) answers the assertion that his construction would open up a lacuna in the scheme of habitats assessment. Mr Banner contended that the issue is about the timing not the scope of an appropriate assessment. On his case the scheme of habitats protection in the UK context is for the front-loading of the appropriate assessment, in other words at the permission or outline permission stage. That ensures that habitats considerations are considered at the earliest possible point.

55   Adopting Mr Banner's submissions would open up a lacuna in habitats assessment leading to the possibility that, as here, development would proceed without an assessment being undertaken - the possibility when negative environmental effects were only ascertained only after the first stage in a multi-stage consent process. On Mr Banner's case, although no appropriate assessment had been undertaken, it was now too late for that to occur. In this regard I accept the Secretary of State's submission that the argument for an habitats assessment at the subsequent consent stage is stronger in the context of the Habitats Regulations 2017 than in the EIA context because they impose a prohibition on granting consent unless an appropriate assessment is made, as opposed to the EIA Directive which merely lays down an environmental assessment procedure without prescribing outcomes.

56   A purposive interpretation of the Habitats Regulations 2017 enables regulation 70 to be read in light of ("in accordance with") regulation 63, so that a competent authority must conduct an appropriate assessment before, as regulation 63(1) provides, any consent, permission or other authorisation is given for a project. In a multi-stage consent, consent amounts to taking the implementing decision, as Lang J put it in *R. (Wingfield) v Canterbury City Council* [2019] EWHC 1974 (Admin). In that case and in *R. (Swire) v Canterbury City Council* [2022] EWHC 390 (Admin) it was said that there is no agreement until reserved matters are granted: [74] and [94] respectively, quoted earlier in the judgment. I accept the submission of the Secretary of State that the same applies to the discharge of conditions, in circumstances where commencing development in breach of them results in that development not being development authorised by that permission.

57   Mr Banner cited *R. (Fulford Parish Council) v City of York Council* [2019] EWCA Civ 1359 to the effect that reserved matters approval is not a planning permission, and that would include the discharge of a condition on a reserved matters approval. However, a close reading of Lewison LJ's judgment reveals that his conclusion in this regard was the product of the statutory context. I accept the Secretary of State's submission that regulation 70(3) can be read as requiring an

assessment at that stage in circumstances where it might otherwise be argued that it is too early in the scheme's development for an appropriate assessment to take place. It is in that respect an extending provision, not a restrictive one. Crucially, it is silent as to what should happen at the reserved matters or condition discharge stage and does not prohibit an appropriate assessment at those points.

The caselaw

58   Mr Banner submitted that there was no caselaw directly in point about refusing to discharge conditions on a planning permission in the absence of a negative appropriate assessment. *R. (Barker) v Bromley LBC* [2006] UKHL 52 was an EIA Case, on a differently worded text than in the Habitats Directive and with a differently structured approval process. *R. (Wingfield) v Canterbury City Council* [2019] EWHC 1974 (Admin) involved a different situation, where following the CJEU case the local authority voluntarily undertook an appropriate assessment under the Habitats Regulations 2017, supported by the developer, in association with the grant of reserved matters. Even if Lang J had decided that an appropriate assessment was legally required at the reserved matters stage that was *obiter*. Nothing was said about a requirement to subject conditions attached to a reserved matters approval to an appropriate assessment. As for *R. (Swire) v Canterbury City Council* [2022] EWHC 390 (Admin), Mr Banner contended that Holgate J was not considering whether it was a legal requirement of the Habitats Regulations 2017 to subject further approvals, after the grant of planning permission, to an appropriate assessment, as was clear from paragraph [94] of his judgment.

59   In my view Wingfield and Swire are authority for the proposition that an appropriate assessment can apply at the reserved matters or discharge of condition stage even if there has been a grant of outline planning permission where the subsequent approval is the implementing decision. There is support, as Lang J found in Wingfield, in the case law concerning the EIA multi-stage consenting procedure such as Barker. There, as we saw, Lord Hope recognised that a material change in circumstances could require an assessment at the reserved matters stage. It will be recalled that in Friends of the Irish Environment Ltd the CJEU stated that the meaning of "development consent" was relevant to defining the equivalent term "agree" in the Habitats Directive. All this is retained case law under the Withdrawal Act 2018 concerning the interpretation of the Habitats Directive and the Habitats Regulations 2017. That the facts in Wingfield and Swire were different is no basis for undermining the principle they established. The common law system would not survive if this were the case, since there will always be a variation, even if slight, in the facts of later cases. That does not preclude the continued application of principle.

Validity of planning permission

60   Mr Banner invoked regulation 86(1) of the Habitats Regulations 2017, which states that that part 6, chapter 2 (with exceptions which are not relevant) is to be construed as one with the 1990 Act. Mr Banner contended that since in this case planning permission had been granted under the 1990 Act the principle of development could not be disturbed by later events, as the Inspector had wrongly decided. There were, he submitted, a variety of rules in support. In discharging conditions, for example, matters falling for consideration at an earlier stage cannot

be revisited: *R. (Harvey) v Mendip DC* [2017] EWCA Civ 1784, [41], per Sales LJ (with whom McFarlane LJ agreed).

61   Mr Banner also invoked the principle that, in approving the details required by a condition, the decision-taker must not misuse their functions to achieve indirectly - and without paying compensation - what would amount to a revocation or modification of a permission already given: *Medina Borough Council v Proberun Ltd* (1991) 61 P. & C.R. 77, 85, per Glidewell LJ. *R. (Noble Organisation Ltd) v Thanet DC* [2005] EWCA Civ 782 underlined the point in upholding outline planning permission at the reserved matters stage when (it was said) it had been granted in breach of the EIA Regulations. Therefore in this case the valid permission had to be given all the force in law of a regulation 70 compliant permission. If that position was to be altered, Mr Banner referred to the provisions enabling planning permission to be revoked, but only on payment of compensation: 1990 Act, ss.97, 107 (1).

62   There are difficulties with these submissions. First and foremost, if there is a conflict between the obligations imposed on the one hand under the Habitats Directive and Habitats Regulations 2017, and on the other the rights recognised under the 1990 Act these have to be reconciled in accordance with established principle. Prior to the UK's exit from the EU, the Habitats Directive and Habitats Regulations 2017 had supremacy over domestic planning law through the European Communities Act. As we have seen, the Withdrawal Act 2018 continues this position. The 2017 Regulations and Habitats Directive are given effect by sections 2 and 4, and the principle of supremacy still applies by virtue of section 5(2).

63   In any event, there is no issue of the continued validity of the claimant's planning permission. Refusal of consent for the discharge of conditions does not invalidate the permission granted. Proberun (1991) 61 P. & C.R. 77 concerned local planning authorities not misusing their powers when determining reserved matters applications (or applications to discharge conditions) not with situations where there is a specific statutory direction not to grant consent until the assessment provisions are satisfied. Noble [2005] EWCA Civ 782 was a challenge to a planning permission. The position here is different: the claimant obtained outline planning permission subject to the law which at the time provided (on a correct interpretation) that until there was an appropriate assessment, implementing consent would not be granted.

Conclusion

64   The upshot is that the Habitats Directive and Habitats Regulations 2017 mandate that an appropriate assessment be undertaken before a project is consented. That is irrespective of whatever stage the process has reached according to UK planning law. The basal fact in this case is that neither at the permission, reserved matters, or conditions discharge stage has there has been an appropriate assessment. Application of the Habitats Directive and a purposive approach to the interpretation of the Habitats Regulations 2017 require the application of the assessment provisions to the discharge of conditions. The strict precautionary approach required would be undermined if they were limited to the initial - the permission - stage of a multi-stage process.

Ground 2: NPPF, paragraph 181

65   For the claimant Mr Banner contended that paragraph 181 of the NPPF did not enable the Inspector to take into account considerations which were legally irrelevant to those conditions. Phosphate generation was outside the scope of the considerations capable of being relevant to the discharge of the conditions in question relating as they do, as we saw earlier, to tree protection, a construction environmental management plan, estate roads and furniture layout, cycle and footway connections, materials on external surfaces and surface (not foul) water. Material planning considerations in this context are the material considerations defined by each condition itself, not general material considerations like phosphate loading. Mr Banner submitted that policy – in this case in the form of paragraph 181 of the NPPF – could not change that position to make legally relevant what otherwise would be irrelevant, namely, the requirement for a negative appropriate assessment of the wider development. In this regard Mr Banner invoked *Aberdeen City and Shire Development Planning Authority v Elsick Development Co Ltd* [2017] UKSC 66.

66   In Elsick a planning authority's supplementary planning guidance provided that new developments should make a financial contribution via a planning obligation towards improvements to the local highway network. That was irrespective of the impact to which the development would give rise. Giving the judgment of the Supreme Court, Lord Hodge held that it was unlawful to make the grant of planning permission dependent upon paying money towards infrastructure unconnected to the development: [42]-[43]. Planning permission cannot be bought or sold: [44]. Inclusion in the development plan could not make such contributions a material consideration if they were otherwise legally irrelevant. "[T]he policy seeking to impose such an obligation is an irrelevant consideration when the planning authority considers the application for planning permission": [51].

67   In my view the situation in this case is not the situation in Elsick. The impacts on the Somerset Levels and Moors Ramsar Site and paragraph 181 of the NPPF cannot be said to be irrelevant considerations in this development. The issue is the read-across of the Habitats Regulations 2017 to Ramsar sites as provided by the NPPF in circumstances where the Council's shadow appropriate assessment shows that if the project if permitted it will cause harm to the Ramsar site. As Mr Wilcox for the Council submitted, to understand the scope of the discharge of conditions it is necessary to consider the legal consequences, and in this case one of these would be that a development with a potential impact on a Ramsar site protected by national policy would be authorised by the planning system. That creates the nexus to the NPPF's policy on the protection of Ramsar sites. It is open to the Secretary of State to introduce such a consideration as a matter of national planning policy.

Ground 3: scope of regulation 63

68   Mr Banner submitted that even if regulation 63 applies to the discharge of conditions, it ought to be interpreted in such a way that the scope of the appropriate assessment reflects the scope of the conditions being considered. Thus, for example, in the context of an application to discharge a condition relating to root protection zones for trees, an appropriate assessment would concern any effects on site integrity arising from the range of choices the decision-maker has in relation to root

protection zones, given the permission granted (and any conditions already discharged). The appropriate assessment would not consider the effects of the scheme as a whole on the habitat in question.

69   Regulation 63 requires an appropriate assessment to consider the implications of the project, not the implications of the part of the project to which the consent relates. In this regard regulation 63 is consistent (unsurprisingly) with the Habitats Directive, which the CJEU has held requires a full assessment of a project which has not been assessed: Case *Friends of the Irish Environment* (C-254/19). (In my view it does not undermine the principle of that decision that a fresh consent was involved.) This reading is supported by other case law. Thus in *Barker* [2006] UKHL 52 the House of Lords recognised that it was the environmental effects of the development which were to be assessed, not the effects of the reserved matters. And to return to Wingfield it was the integrity of the site as a whole which was of concern, so that reserved matters approval could not be given when it was that which authorised implementation of the development. As Mr Wilcox for the Council put it, the thing which is to be the subject of the appropriate assessment is the thing which will be permitted by the authorisation, so that where the decision is the final stage in granting authorisation for a development, it is the development which is to be assessed.

Conclusion

70   For the reasons given the claimant's case is dismissed.

R. (ON THE APPLICATION OF LLANDAFF NORTH RESIDENTS' ASSOCIATION) v CARDIFF CITY COUNCIL

King's Bench Division (Planning Court)

HH Judge Jarman KC (sitting as a Judge of the High Court): 10 July 2023

[2023] EWHC 1731 (Admin); [2023] Env. L.R. 31

⏎ Environmental impact assessments; Planning permission; Residential development; Sewage

H1   *Environmental impact assessment—whether planning authority erred in law in its approach to proposed pumping station and discharge of planning condition relating to strategic foul drainage masterplan—whether pumping station part of same "project" as large residential development—whether failure to consider integral part of pumping station project namely surface water removal scheme—whether officers' reports materially misleading*

H2   The claimant residents' association (LNRA) challenged two decisions of the defendant planning authority (CC). The first was the grant of planning permission to the first interested party (DC) for a pumping station to serve a mixed-use development with a minimum of 5000 homes on land in Cardiff (the housing development). The second challenge was against the discharge of a planning condition requiring a strategic foul drainage masterplan informed by hydraulic modelling which was attached to the grant of outline permission to the second interested party (RH) for the housing development itself. The pumping station was needed to serve the housing development, but DC said it would also serve other existing and potential developments in the surrounding area. The site for the pumping station was around 1km from the site for the housing development. DC had requested the discharge of the planning condition.

H3   In challenging both decisions, LNRA argued:

H4   On the first claim in relation to the grant of planning permission for the housing development:

> (1)   CC had failed to take into account that there was functional interdependence between the housing development and DC's application for the pumping station and wrongly took into account that the pumping station would serve other developments in the area. The pumping station and housing development should have been treated as one "project" for the purposes of the Environmental Impact Assessment as they were functionally interdependent.

(2) CC had failed to consider an integral part of DC's proposal, namely a scheme to remove surface water from its network thus increasing its capacity for foul sewerage. So considered, the scheme as a whole would amount to Sch.2 development under the Town and Country Planning (Environmental Impact Assessment) (Wales) Regulations 2017 (the 2017 Regulations) requiring an environmental statement (ES).

(3) The officers' reports on the pumping station application were materially misleading by omitting key details about construction impacts and effects on rugby pitches.

H5   On the second claim in relation to the discharge of the planning condition:

(4) CC had not considered a material consideration namely the need to obtain a further hydraulic model for the revised scheme which was different from that dealt with in the Model submitted with the original scheme.

(5) CC had failed to consider the need for an Environmental Statement to include reasonable alternatives or the environmental impact of off-site works and the main reason for the choosing the selected option.

H6   **Held,** in dismissing the claim and finding that the high threshold to establish irrationality had not been met in relation to any of the grounds of challenge:

H7   (1) CC was entitled to conclude that the two proposed developments were not part of the same "project" for EIA purposes based on factors including whether they were on adjacent sites, undertaken by the same entity, and functionally interdependent. The fact that the pumping station was needed for the housing development did not mean that it would not also serve other existing and potential developments in the area, and CC was entitled to have regard to those matters.

H8   (2) There was no obligation on CC to expressly consider DC's surface water removal scheme as part of the pumping station project when determining whether the 2017 Regulations applied. The level of detail to consider was a matter for judgment for the officer.

H9   (3) The officers' reports were not materially misleading regarding construction impacts of the pumping station or effects on rugby pitches. Applying the relevant principles, the reports were not significantly defective, and any flaws were inconsequential. The level of detail was a matter for the officer's judgment, and it was not irrational to approach the matter in this way.

H10   (4) CC's approach to the discharge of the planning condition relating to the foul drainage masterplan was not irrational, given that the condition was requested by DC to avoid overloading, and DC did not object to the discharge. The fact the ultimate drainage solution differed from that originally envisaged did not mean the masterplan was not informed by the prior hydraulic modelling assessment.

H11   **Cases referred to:**
Barratt Homes Ltd v Dwr Cymru Cyfyngedig (Welsh Water) [2009] UKSC 13; [2010] P.T.S.R. 651; [2010] Env. L.R. 14
E v Secretary of State for the Home Department [2004] EWCA Civ 49; [2004] Q.B. 1044; [2004] 2 W.L.R. 1351
Lambeth LBC v Secretary of State for Housing, Communities and Local Government [2019] UKSC 33; [2019] 1 W.L.R. 4317; [2019] 2 P. & C.R. 18
Manchester Ship Canal Co Ltd v United Utilities Water Ltd [2022] EWCA Civ 852; [2023] Ch. 1; [2023] Env. L.R. 13

Mansell v Tonbridge and Malling BC [2017] EWCA Civ 1314; [2019] P.T.S.R. 1452; [2018] J.P.L. 176

R. (on the application of Ashchurch Rural Parish Council) v Tewkesbury BC [2023] EWCA Civ 101; [2023] Env. L.R. 25; [2023] J.P.L. 1099

R. (on the application of Burridge) v Breckland DC [2013] EWCA Civ 228; [2013] J.P.L. 1308; [2013] 18 E.G. 102 (C.S.)

R. (on the application of Friends of the Earth Ltd) v Heathrow Airport Ltd [2020] UKSC 52; [2021] P.T.S.R. 190; [2021] J.P.L. 905

R. (on the application of Larkfleet Ltd) v South Kesteven DC [2015] EWCA Civ 887; [2016] Env. L.R. 4; [2015] P.T.S.R. D50

R. (on the application of Newsmith Stainless Ltd) v Secretary of State for the Environment, Transport and the Regions [2001] EWHC Admin 74; [2017] P.T.S.R. 1126

R. (on the application of Sahota) v Herefordshire Council [2022] EWCA Civ 1640; [2023] Env. L.R. 20; [2023] J.P.L. 808

R. (on the application of Together against Sizewell C Ltd) v Secretary of State for Energy Security and Net Zero [2023] EWHC 1526 (Admin)

R. (on the application of Wingfield) v Canterbury City Council [2019] EWHC 1975 (Admin); [2020] J.P.L. 154

R. v Mendip DC Ex p. Fabre [2017] P.T.S.R. 1112; (2000) 80 P. & C.R. 500; [2000] J.P.L. 810 QBD

Trump International Golf Club Scotland Ltd v Scottish Ministers [2015] UKSC 74; [2016] 1 W.L.R. 85; [2016] J.P.L. 555

H12 **Legislation referred to:**

Water Industry Act 1991 ss.94, 98, 99, 101, 158, 159 and 168–171
Town and Country Planning (General Permitted Development) Order 1995 (SI 1995/418) art.3(1)(10) and Sch.2
Directive 2011/92 (Environmental Impact Assessment)
Town and Country Planning (Environmental Impact Assessment) (Wales) Regulations 2017 (SI 2017/567) regs 2(1), 6, 9, 17(3) and Sch.2
European Union (Withdrawal) Act 2018 s.6(3)

H13   *I. Buono*, instructed by Leigh Day, appeared on behalf of the claimant.
R. Williams and *Dr A. Williams* instructed by Cardiff Council Legal Services, appeared on behalf of the defendant.
R. Kimblin KC, instructed by Hugh James, appeared on behalf of the first interested party.
N. Pindham, instructed by Burges Salmon LLP, appeared on behalf of the second to fourth interested parties.

JUDGMENT

HH JUDGE JARMAN KC:

Introduction

1   In January 2016 the defendant, as local planning authority (the authority), adopted the Cardiff Local Development Plan 2006-2026. One of its strategic policies, KP2(C), provided for an allocation of a large area of land to the northwest of Cardiff for mixed use development with a minimum of 5000 homes. There had been a lengthy period of preparation and consultation in respect of that policy prior to its adoption, including with the first interested party (Dŵr Cymru), as statutory undertaker with the responsibility of providing a sewerage system under the Water Industry Act 1991 (the 1991 Act). In 2014, the second interested party (the developer) applied for planning permission to build just under 6000 homes on an area of the land so allocated known as Plasdŵr. The application was accompanied by an environmental statement (ES) which stated that Dŵr Cymru had confirmed that the significant volume of foul sewage which would be generated by the proposal could be accommodated on its network, but a hydraulic modelling assessment (HMA) would be needed before the extent of infrastructure improvements and storm water removal from the network could be finalised. Outline permission was granted on the application in March 2017, condition 24 of which required a HMA to be approved.

2   Dŵr Cymru in November 2021 submitted an application to build a pumping station to serve the developer's proposal. This would comprise a pumping station at the north end of a large open space called Hailey Park to the east of, and on the banks of, the River Taff. The site of the pumping station is about 1km away from the site of the developer's proposed development. Also included in the application is a valve kiosk on the other side of the river. What is not included is a pipe under the river to connect the two, as Dŵr Cymru proposes to use permitted rights to construct it. The authority granted that application in September 2022.

3   At the same time, the authority granted an application made by the developer to discharge condition 24 after a HMA had been obtained. Two applications were made, because of re-design, and each was granted by the authority, the latest one in September 2022.

4   The claimant is an association of residents of Llandaff North, which adjoins Hailey Park to the east. With permission granted by Steyn J, it challenges both decisions of the authority to grant planning permission for the pumping station and to discharge condition 24.

5   In respect of the former, there are four grounds of challenge which may be summarised thus:

    i) The authority failed to take into account that there is functional interdependence between the Plasdŵr development and Dŵr Cymru's application and wrongly took into account that the pumping station will serve other developments in the area;

    ii) The authority failed to consider an integral part of Dŵr Cymru's proposal, namely a scheme to remove surface water from its network thus increasing its capacity for foul sewerage. So considered, the scheme as a whole would amount to Schedule 2 development under the Town and Country Planning

(Environmental Impact Assessment) (Wales) Regulations 2017 (the EIA Regulations) requiring an environmental statement (ES);

iii) The officer's report in respect of the application failed to set out crucial details of the construction works and their impacts;

iv) That report also failed to set out impacts on rugby pitches in Hailey Park.

6   The grounds in respect of the discharge of condition 24 are:

i) The authority did not take into account a material consideration namely the need to obtain a further HMA for the scheme now proposed, which differs from that dealt with in the submitted HMA;

ii) The authority failed to consider the need for an ES to include a description of the reasonable alternatives and the main reasons for the option chosen;

iii) The authority failed to consider the environmental effects of various offsite works which were part of such effects of the developer's proposal.

7   Before me, the authority was represented by Ms Buono, the defendant by Mr Williams and Dr Williams, and Dŵr Cymru by Mr Kimblin KC. The remaining parties, the developer and the landowners, were represented by Ms Pindham. Each made focussed submissions in writing and orally. The parties agreed a list of issues, a chronology, and a list of legal principles. Not only was this helpful but it assisted the fulfilment of the overriding objective in that although the hearing was listed for two days, submissions were completed in one. This may be seen as a model of how such cases should be presented, and I am grateful to all concerned.

Statutory framework

8   The agreed legal principles may be summarised as follows.

9   Schedule 2 of the EIA Regulations relates to development likely to have significant effects on the environment by virtue of factors such as its nature, size, or location. These include urban development, other than housing, of over 1 hectare, and housing development of over 150 houses.

10   Regulation 2(1) provides that EIA is the process of preparing an ES, consultation, publication, and notification, examining the environmental information, and reaching a reasoned conclusion of the significant effects of the proposed development on the environment. It also provides that a screening opinion means a written opinion as to whether development is EIA development. Regulation 6 provides that a proposed developer may request such an opinion from the relevant planning authority, and the request must be accompanied by a description of the development and its likely significant effects. Regulation 9 deals with subsequent applications where environmental information has already been provided. Regulation 17(3) requires an environmental statement to include a description of the reasonable alternatives studied by the applicant and an indication of the main reasons for the option chosen.

11   Article 2(1) of EU Directive 2011/92/EU (the Directive) requires EU Member States to adopt all necessary measures to ensure that projects likely to have a significant effect on the environment are made subject to an assessment of their effects, before consent is given. "Project" is defined in article 1 as "the execution of construction works or other installations or schemes" and "other interventions in the natural surroundings and landscape".

12   The EIA Regulations use the term "development" rather than "project". Nothing turns on that difference in this case. They remain in force notwithstanding the withdrawal of the UK from the European Union. Their meaning and effect should continue to be determined in accordance with retained EU and domestic case law, as well as retained general principles of EU law, under section 6(3)(a) of the EU (Withdrawal) Act 2018.

The 1991 Act

13   Turning now to examine the duties and powers of Dŵr Cymru under the 1991 Act in more detail, section 94 imposes a general duty to provide a sewerage system. The owner or occupier of premises may requisition the provision of a public sewer for domestic purposes under section 98, and the undertaker may charge for such a provision under section 99. Section 101 provides a right to connect sewers and drains to the public sewer, on notice. Undertakers may lay pipes in streets and on other land and may enter land for works purposes, to survey, for sewerage purposes and other purposes under sections 158 and 159 and 168-171. "Pipe" is widely defined to include "accessories".

Legal principles

Projects

14   In *R. (Ashchurch Rural Parish Council) v Tewkesbury BC* [2023] EWCA Civ 101, Andrews LJ, giving the lead judgment, said at [74] that the term "project" should be interpreted "broadly, and realistically". At [80], she added that the identification of the project is based on a fact-specific inquiry.

15   What constitutes the project is a matter of judgment for the planning authority, subject to challenge on grounds of rationality or other public law error. Lang J in *R. (Wingfield) v Canterbury City Council* [2019] EWHC 1975 (Admin) at [64] after a review of the authorities, identified four criteria against which that judgment may be made: (i) whether two sites are owned or promoted by the same person; (ii) simultaneous determination; (iii) functional interdependence; and (iv) stand-alone projects. These were cited with approval in Ashchurch at [81] as "a non-exhaustive list of potentially relevant criteria, which serves as a useful aide-memoir".

16   These criteria were recently considered by Holgate J in *R. (Together against Sizewell C Ltd) v SSESNZ* [2023] EWHC 1526 (Admin). At [73-4], he said:

> "The weight to be given to them will depend upon the circumstances of each case and is a matter for the decision maker.
> Interdependence would normally mean that *each* part of the development is dependent on the other, as, for example, in *Burridge v Breckland DC* [2013] J.P.L. 1308 at [32] and [42]."

17   At [70], Holgate J pointed out that an irrationality challenge presents a high threshold:

> "The threshold for irrationality in the making of such a judgment is a difficult obstacle to surmount (see e.g. *Newsmith Stainless Ltd v Secretary of State for the Environment, Transport and the Regions* [2017] P.T.S.R. 1126)."

18   Although two sets of proposed works may have a cumulative effect on the environment, this does not make them a single project for these purposes. Two potential projects but with cumulative effects may need to be assessed, see *R. (Larkfleet Ltd) v South Kesteven DC* [2015] EWCA Civ 887, Sales LJ (as he then was) at [36]. At [38] he continued:

> "The EIA Directive is intended to operate in a way which ensures that there is appropriate EIA scrutiny to protect the environment whilst avoiding undue delay in the operation of the planning control system which would be likely to follow if one were to say that all the environmental effects of every related set of works should be definitively examined before any of those sets of works could be allowed to proceed (and the disproportionate interference with the rights of landowners and developers and the public interest in allowing development to take place in appropriate cases which that would involve). Where two or more proposed linked sets of works are in contemplation, which are properly to be regarded as distinct "projects", the objective of environmental protection is sufficiently secured under the scheme of the Directive by consideration of their cumulative effects, so far as that is reasonably possible, in the EIA scrutiny applicable when permission for the first project…is sought, combined with the requirement for subsequent EIA scrutiny under the Directive for the second and each subsequent project. The adequacy and appropriateness of environmental protection by these means under the EIA Directive are further underwritten by the fact that alternatives will have been assessed at the strategic level through scrutiny of relevant development plans…"

19   However, the device of splitting a project into smaller components that fall below the EIA thresholds in an attempt to avoid the requirement to carry out an environmental assessment (colloquially known as salami slicing) is not permissible. The failure to take account of the cumulative effect of several projects must not mean that they all escape the obligation to carry out an assessment when, taken together, they are likely to have significant effects on the environment, see Wingfield at [51-52].

20   At [72] in *Sizewell*, Holgate J said:

> "But the Directives and jurisprudence of the European Court of Justice recognise that it is legitimate for different development proposals to be brought forward at different times, even though they may have a degree of interaction, if they are different "projects". The Directives apply in such a way as to ensure appropriate scrutiny to protect the environment, whilst avoiding undue delay in the operation of the planning control system. Undue delay would be likely if all the environmental effects of every related set of works had to be definitively examined before any of those works could be allowed to proceed. Where two or more linked sets of works are in contemplation, which are properly to be regarded as distinct "projects", the objective of environmental protection is sufficiently secured under the Directives by consideration of their cumulative effects, so far as that is reasonably possible, when permission for the first project is sought, combined with the requirement for subsequent scrutiny under the Directives for the second and each subsequent project."

Statutory undertakers

21   The problem of granting planning permission for substantial residential development to connect with a sewage network which was not adequate to bear the additional load, was dealt with by the Supreme Court in *Barratt Homes Ltd v Dwr Cymru Cyf* [2009] UKSC 13. The narrow point in that case was whether a sewerage undertaker has a right to select the point of connection or to refuse a developer the right to connect with a public sewer because of dissatisfaction with the proposed point of connection. The court concluded that it did not. Lord Phillips, giving the lead judgment of the majority, addressed the wider problem at [45], referring also to the regulator of the industry, OFWAT:

> "If conditions of planning permission are to provide the answer to the problem of the connection of private sewers to public sewers which are not adequate to bear the additional load, it would seem essential that there should be input to planning decisions from both the relevant sewerage undertaker and OFWAT."

22   At [58], he observed that it was desirable that the statutory undertaker and OFWAT should be consulted as part of the planning process. Consequently, sewage undertakers became further involved in the planning process and amendments were made to the 1991 Act. The Secretary of State for Wales made the Town and Country Planning (General Permitted Development) Order 1995. By Article 3(1), planning permission is granted for the classes of development which are described in Schedule 2. In Part 16 of Schedule 2 development undertaken by undertakers is permitted under Class A(a) for all the development authorised under the 1991 Act which is not above ground level. Article 3(10) provides that planning permission is not granted by Article 3(1) and Schedule 2 Part 16 unless the local planning authority has adopted a screening opinion (or equivalent ministerial direction) under the EIA Regulations.

23   In *Marcic v Thames Water Utilities Ltd* [2003] UKHL 66, the House of Lords held that there is no duty at common law for undertakers to provide adequate sewers so as to avoid flooding by overloading. Lord Hoffmann said at [70]:

> "The 1991 Act makes it even clearer than the earlier legislation that Parliament did not intend the fairness of priorities to be decided by a judge. It intended the decision to rest with the Director, subject only to judicial review. It would subvert the scheme of the 1991 Act if the courts were to impose upon the sewerage undertakers, on a case by case basis, a system of priorities which is different from that which the Director considers appropriate."

24   That principle was applied in *Manchester Ship Canal v United Utilities Water Ltd* [2022] EWCA Civ 852. Nugee LJ, giving the lead judgment, held that to hold that statutory undertaker liable for trespass or nuisance for unauthorised discharges into the canal would be inconsistent with the statutory scheme applicable to it as sewerage undertaker. In the present case there is some disagreement between the parties on how this principle is to be applied.

The court's approach to planning decisions

25   The next set of principles relate to considerations which were material to the decisions of the authority under challenge. Such considerations fall into three broad

categories. The first comprises those identified by statute as considerations to which regard must be had. The second are those identified by the statute as considerations to which regard must not be had. The third are those to which the decision-maker may have regard as a matter of judgment, see *R. (Friends of the Earth Ltd) v Heathrow Airport Ltd* [2020] UKSC 52. The test whether a consideration falling within the third category is so obviously material that it must be taken into account is the *Wednesbury* irrationality test. Lord Hodge and Lord Sales, giving the lead judgment, said at [120]:

> "It is possible to subdivide the third category of consideration into two types of case. First, a decision-maker may not advert at all to a particular consideration falling within that category. In such a case, unless the consideration is obviously material according to the *Wednesbury* irrationality test, the decision is not affected by any unlawfulness... There is no obligation on a decision-maker to work through every consideration which might conceivably be regarded as potentially relevant to the decision they have to take and positively decide to discount it in the exercise of their discretion."

26   Next is the law relating to conditions attached to planning permissions. These are not to be read like statutes but as by a reasonable reader, see *Trump International Golf Club Scotland Ltd v Scottish Ministers* [2015] UKSC 74 at [36] and *Lambeth LBC v Secretary of State* [2019] UKSC 33 at [19].

27   The principles relating to the proper approach of the court to a report compiled by planning officers for a planning authority as part of the latter's decision-making process are summarised by Lindblom LJ, giving the lead judgment, in *Mansell v Tonbridge & Malling BC* [2017] EWCA Civ 1314 at [42] as follows:

> "The principles are not complicated. Planning officers' reports to committee are not be read with undue rigour, but with reasonable benevolence, and bearing in mind that they are written for councillors with local knowledge...Unless there is evidence to suggest otherwise, it may reasonably be assumed that, if the members followed the officer's recommendation, they did so on the basis of the advice that he or she gave... The question for the court will always be whether, on a fair reading of the report as a whole, the officer has materially misled the members on a matter bearing upon their decision, and the error has gone uncorrected before the decision was made. Minor or inconsequential errors may be excused. It is only if the advice in the officer's report is such as to misdirect the members in a material way — so that, but for the flawed advice it was given, the committee's decision would or might have been different — that the court will be able to conclude that the decision itself was rendered unlawful by that advice.
> Where the line is drawn between an officer's advice that is significantly or seriously misleading — misleading in a material way — and advice that is misleading but not significantly so will always depend on the context and circumstances in which the advice was given, and on the possible consequence of it. There will be cases in which a planning officer has inadvertently led a committee astray by making some significant error of fact... or has plainly misdirected the members as to the meaning of a relevant policy...There will be others where the officer has simply failed to deal with a matter on which the committee ought to receive explicit advice if the local planning authority

is to be seen to have performed its decision-making duties in accordance with the law…But unless there is some distinct and material defect in the officer's advice, the court will not interfere."

28   Such a report is not required to consider the various issues in exhaustive detail. Part of a planning officer's expert function "must be to make an assessment of how much information needs to be included… in order to avoid burdening a busy committee with excessive and unnecessary detail", see Sullivan J in *R. v Mendip DC Ex p. Fabre* (2000) 80 P. & C.R. 500, at 509, cited with approval in by Singh LJ in *R. (Sahota) v Herefordshire Council* [2022] EWCA Civ 1640 at [23]. That a report could have explored issues in greater detail does not necessarily mean it has materially misled the committee.

29   The circumstances in which a decision may be amenable to judicial review based on a mistake of fact were examined by Carnwath LJ (as he then was) in *E v SSHD* [2004] EWCA Civ 49. At [66] he said:

> "…First, there must have been a mistake as to an existing fact, including a mistake as to the availability of evidence on a particular matter. Secondly, the fact or evidence must have been 'established', in the sense that it was uncontentious and objectively verifiable. Thirdly, the appellant (or his advisers) must not have been responsible for the mistake. Fourthly, the mistake must have played a material (not necessarily decisive) part in the Tribunal's reasoning."

The pumping station

30   I now turn to apply those principles to the facts of this case and deal with the background to the planning permission for the pumping station in a little more detail. The application was accompanied by a planning statement by Dŵr Cymru's consultants, Arup, which stated that the need for the proposed development "derives from" the grant of planning permission for 6000 homes at Plasdŵr. Arup submitted a screening request in relation to the sewage scheme which was being provided for that development, recognising that it was "effectively part of" that development on the basis that it would provide that additional capacity needed "to serve the increase in the local population size." Arup considered the proposed development to be listed as Schedule 2 development and identified several potential impacts, including to protected sites of international significance such as those located on the Severn Estuary, but did not consider the impacts to be significant.

31   The authority issued a negative screening opinion on the basis that the sewage scheme and the residential development are stand-alone projects, and gave several reasons. The two schemes would not be located on adjacent land. The former was being undertaken by Dŵr Cymru and the latter by the developer. The former was being undertaken not only to serve the latter but also other existing and potential developments in the area so that there was a functional relationship between the two but no functional interdependence. The former was considered to be the project for EIA purposes and did not exceed the thresholds set out in Schedule 2. Accordingly, the authority did not consider whether any potential impacts would be significant. A separate screening opinion was issued in respect of the pumping station, which mirrored that in respect of the sewage scheme.

32   The authority's planning officer issued a report on the application for planning permission in respect of the pumping station in September 2022, and included the following, referring to Dŵr Cymru by its English name, Welsh Water:

> "Detailed consideration has also been given as to whether the 'Sewer Reinforcement Scheme' forms part of the same project as the strategic mixed-use development of Plasdŵr. However, it was concluded that there are a number of factors that militate strongly against the scheme being an extension to the mixed-use scheme including that the proposal is:
> - being constructed on/under land which is not directly connected or adjacent to the mixed-use scheme and, in reality, is an expansion of the existing public sewerage network and, therefore, they are effectively stand-alone projects;
> - being undertaken by Welsh Water, a statutory undertaker, not the developer of the mixed-use scheme and on land within separate ownership;
> - being undertaken not to serve only the foul needs of the mixed-use scheme, but also of existing (and potential future) developments in the area, therefore, whilst there is a functional relationship there is no functional interdependence.
>
> 3.13 In light of the above, Members should note that a revised Screening Opinion has been adopted for the current application, which mirrors the Opinion for the overall infrastructure works (i.e. is not considered under 11(c) and is concluded to - not amount to EIA development)."

Ground 1-interdependence

33   Ms Buono submits that this reasoning is wrong and that there is functional interdependence between the Plasdŵr development and the pumping station as the two are dependent on one another, however else the pumping station might have been funded. The fact that it may serve other developments in the area is immaterial. The authority should have had regard to Arup's description of the wider sewage scheme as part of the Plasdŵr development because it is required to serve the latter. This is not mentioned in the report.

34   In my judgment, as the other parties submit, the officer was entitled to deal with this issue in this way and the authority was entitled to rely upon it. The fact that the pumping station is needed for the Plasdŵr development does not mean that it will not also serve other existing and potential developments in the area, and the officer and the authority were entitled to have regard to those matters. The high threshold of irrationality in this approach has not been surmounted.

Ground 2-surface water removal

35   The next ground is that the authority left out of account an integral part of the project, the surface water removal scheme. The removal of such water from the sewage network was identified by Arup as needed as a result of lack of capacity at the Hailey Park connection point. Had this been taken into account, then it may together with the pumping station proposal amount to Schedule 2 development by, for example, exceeding the one hectare threshold.

36   However, the officer was aware of this issue because the discharge application was considered on the same day and the report for that application referred to the application in respect of the pumping station. It was noted that Dŵr Cymru would be responsible for surface water removal and that the Plasdŵr development could not be fully occupied until such works had been completed. There are many options for removal as part of the management and improvement of a large urban network. In my judgment there was no obligation on the officer or the authority to work through such options.

Ground 3-construction

37   The officer's report did not set out details of the construction works for the pumping station, their duration, or impacts. These are likely to include noise, air pollution, visual intrusion, and diversion in the setting of a public park. The report referred to the construction and environmental management plan, and one of the proposed conditions was that the development should be undertaken in accordance with such a plan. The officer said this at [9.7.1]:

> "Some disruption and inconvenience is likely to result from demolition and construction works, however, given the scale and nature of the works being undertaken in accordance with the submitted CEMP. It should be noted that the contents of the CEMP are wide ranging and separate legislation, including control in respect of health and safety and over noise and other sources of pollution, are relevant in respect of some matters."

38   The level of detail was a matter for the officer's judgment, and it was not irrational to approach the matter in this way. In my judgment the report is not materially misleading.

Ground 4 - the rugby pitches

39   Finally, it is contended that the report made no mention of the fact that one of the two rugby pitches at the north end of Hailey Park where the pumping station is to be situated, will be partly taken out of use for the duration of the works, and on completion one of the pitches would need to be reconfigured. The officer's report stated that the loss of land caused by the development would not negatively impact the adjacent areas of informal and formal recreational space. The local rugby club did not object. The report referred to the fact that the authority's park officer who is responsible for the management of Hailey Park had no objections, having considered the impact on the pitches and associated changing rooms.

40   Policy C4 of the local plan refers to the loss of open space, which in my judgment clearly contemplates such loss which is permanent. Again, the level of detail was a matter of judgment for the officer. There is no irrationality and nothing materially misleading.

The discharge of condition 24

41   I turn now to consider the grounds in relation to the discharge of condition 24. The condition provides:

"STRATEGIC FOUL DRAINAGE MASTERPLAN

No reserved matter application shall be approved by the Local Planning Authority until a strategic foul drainage masterplan for the whole outline permission site, accompanied by a foul drainage catchment plan and informed by a Hydraulic Modelling Assessment (HMA), have been submitted to and approved in writing by the Local Planning Authority. The submitted strategic foul drainage masterplan shall include details of the following:

a) suitable points of connection for each foul drainage catchment to connect to the existing public sewerage system

b) how each development phase within each drainage catchment will be effectively drained to the existing public sewerage system and demonstrate how each phase will accommodate and include a provision for foul drainage flows for all subsequent phases

c) any improvement or reinforcement works required to the public sewerage system in order to accommodate the development

d) an implementation programme, which shall take into consideration the phasing schedule and plan approved under condition 17 (PHASING).

Thereafter, any subsequent Reserved Matter application shall accord with the approved details or any modification as may be approved through subsequent discharge of condition applications. No building shall be occupied on any reserved matters site until the works, identified by the Hydraulic Modelling Assessments and through part C of this condition, have been completed on the public sewerage system serving that reserved matters site.

Reason: To prevent hydraulic overloading of the public sewerage system, protect the health and safety of existing residents, ensure no pollution of or detriment to the environment and to ensure the site can be effectively drained."

Ground 1 - HMA

42   Thus, the foul drainage masterplan was required by condition 24 to be informed by a HMA and to include details of any improvement or reinforcement works required to the sewage network to accommodate the development. The submitted HMA did neither because the scheme now pursued was developed subsequently. The ES referred to a HMA to determine the extent of infrastructure reinforcement and/or storm water removal measurers. The ES also identified a moderate adverse environmental impact in respect of offsite works, which may be reduced to negligible, but that depended on implementation of mitigation measures as identified by a HMA. The officer's report to committee on the discharge application does not refer to the latter point but says that the lack of significant environmental effects is evidenced through the screening opinions, whereas all that these opinions do is consider the applicability of the quantitative thresholds in Schedule 2. The failure to conclude that there was functional interdependence is another criticism of this officer's report.

43   I have already determined the latter point. In response to the remainder, the other parties make various nuanced points. The crucial one, in my judgment, is that it was Dŵr Cymru who requested condition 24 to be imposed. It is clear from the reason given for the condition that its purpose was to attempt to address the sort of problem referred to in *Barratt Homes*, namely overloading the network. The officer's report on the discharge application sets out the response of Dŵr Cymru,

which supported the discharge. The response made clear that the developer had been engaging with Dŵr Cymru to produce solutions and a point of connection had been agreed. Dŵr Cymru made clear that until the works to deliver the connection to the sewage network at the identified point have been completed and surface water has been removed, no communication of flows from the majority of the Plasdŵr development will be permitted to discharge to the network. In my judgment, the fact that the solution ultimately identified in the masterplan was not one of the notional solutions canvassed in the HMA does not mean that the masterplan was not informed by the HMA. The masterplan also identified mitigation measures, including connection to a point of adequacy. In my judgment it was not irrational for the authority to discharge condition 24 in these circumstances and there was nothing materially misleading about the officer's report.

Ground 2 - alternatives

44   Much of the same reasoning applies to the second and third grounds, that the authority failed to consider alternatives or off-site works including surface water removal. It is not in dispute that the discharge application was a subsequent application within the meaning of regulation 9(1) of the EIA Regulations, so the issue was whether the authority had adequate environmental information already before it to assess the significant effect of the development within the meaning of regulation 9(2). The officer's report concluded that it had, and so the requirement in regulation 17(3) for the ES to describe reasonable alternatives was not engaged in the discharge application.

Ground 3 - off site works

45   In terms of off-site works and surface water removal, the officer's report recognised that these are the responsibility of Dŵr Cymru as statutory undertaker and, as indicated above, Dŵr Cymru and the developer agreed that the majority of the Plasdŵr development will not be connected to the network until the works for the agreed connection and surface water removal have been undertaken.

46   In my judgment, there was nothing irrational about this approach.

Conclusions

47   Accordingly, notwithstanding the focussed submissions of Ms Buono, the claim must fail. Counsel helpfully indicated that any consequential matters which cannot be agreed can be dealt with on the basis of written submissions. A draft order, agreed as far as possible, and any such submissions, should be filed within 14 days of this judgment being handed down.